OXFORD STUDIES IN EUROPEAN LAW

Series Editors

PAUL CRAIG

Professor of English Law at St John's College, Oxford

GRÁINNE DE BÚRCA

Professor of Law at New York University School of Law

The Constitutional Foundations of European Contract Law

A Comparative Analysis

OXFORD STUDIES IN EUROPEAN LAW

Series Editors

Paul Craig, Professor of English Law at St John's College, Oxford and
Gráinne de Búrca, Professor of Law at New York University School of Law

The aim of this series is to publish important and original research on EU law. The focus is on scholarly monographs, with a particular emphasis on those which are interdisciplinary in nature. Edited collections of essays will also be included where they are appropriate. The series is wide in scope and aims to cover studies of particular areas of substantive and of institutional law, historical works, theoretical studies, and analyses of current debates, as well as questions of perennial interest such as the relationship between national and EU law and the novel forms of governance emerging in and beyond Europe. The fact that many of the works are interdisciplinary will make the series of interest to all those concerned with the governance and operation of the EU.

OTHER TITLES IN THIS SERIES

The Constitutional Foundations of European Contract Law
A Comparative Analysis
Kathleen Gutman

The Criminalization of European Cartel Enforcement
Theoretical, Legal, and Practical Challenges
Peter Whelan

Fundamental Rights in Europe
Challenges and Transformations in Comparative Perspective
Federico Fabbrini

The Principle of Loyalty in EU Law
Marcus Klamert

Constitutional Pluralism in the EU
Klemen Jaklic

EU Consumer Law and Human Rights
Iris Benöhr

The Principle of Mutual Recognition in EU Law
Christine Janssens

The Coherence of EU Free Movement Law
Constitutional Responsibility and the Court of Justice
Niamh Nic Shuibhne

European Law and New Health Technologies
Edited by Mark Flear, Anne-Maree Farrell, Tamara Hervey, and Thérèse Murphy

European Agencies
Law and Practices of Accountability
Madalina Busuioc

The Legal Effect of EU Agreements
Mario Mendez

The Foundations of European Union Competition Law
The Objective and Principles of Article 102
Renato Nazzini

The Emergence of EU Contract Law
Exploring Europeanization
Lucinda Miller

Participation in EU Rule-making
A Rights-Based Approach
Joana Mendes

Regulating Cartels in Europe
Second Edition
Christopher Harding and Julian Joshua

Religion and the Public Order of the European Union
Ronan McCrea

Governing Social Inclusion
Europeanization through Policy Coordination
Kenneth A Armstrong

Judicial Control in the European Union
Reforming Jurisdiction in the Intergovernmental Pillars
Alicia Hinarejos

EU Counter-Terrorist Policies and Fundamental Rights
The Case of Individual Sanctions
Christina Eckes

The Constitutional Foundations of European Contract Law

A Comparative Analysis

KATHLEEN GUTMAN

OXFORD
UNIVERSITY PRESS

OXFORD
UNIVERSITY PRESS

Great Clarendon Street, Oxford, OX2 6DP,
United Kingdom

Oxford University Press is a department of the University of Oxford.
It furthers the University's objective of excellence in research, scholarship,
and education by publishing worldwide. Oxford is a registered trade mark of
Oxford University Press in the UK and in certain other countries

First Edition published in 2014

Impression: 1

Published in the United States of America by Oxford University Press
198 Madison Avenue, New York, NY 10016, United States of America

British Library Cataloguing in Publication Data
Data available

Library of Congress Control Number: 2014951369

ISBN 978–0–19–969830–1

Printed and bound by
CPI Group (UK) Ltd, Croydon, CR0 4YY

This book is dedicated to the memory of my mother and father,
Donna and Stanley Gutman

Foreword

Kathleen Gutman's book, which is based on her PhD thesis, is an impressive piece of academic work. As her PhD supervisor, I was a first-hand witness of her openness towards different ideas and critical comments, her perseverance in constructing a convincing argument, and the enormous amount of research and analytical thinking that she put into it.

This book contains a detailed and cohesive assessment of the constitutional foundations of European contract law. It is not, however, limited to examining the vertical allocation of powers between the EU and its Member States in the field of contract law. As she herself explains, the exercise of powers at EU level 'is not the only element in the debate about European contract law, but it is an important one that permeates the others'. Accordingly, the book also looks at alternative and complementary routes to the adoption of instruments that aim to achieve a degree of convergence between the contract laws of the Member States. This shows that the development of European contract law has not only a 'top-down' dimension in accordance with the EU constitutional principles of conferral, subsidiarity and proportionality, but may also be the result of a 'bottom-up' approach.

In addition, the book is enriched by Kathleen Gutman's expertise in US law. As a secondary research focus, the book embarks on a very interesting comparative study with regard to the constitutional dimensions of contract law on both sides of the Atlantic. Throughout her meticulous analysis, the author draws important lessons from the US experience on issues such as the federalization of contract law, federal common law, the uniform law process and the Uniform Commercial Code.

Like all great classics, this book is divided into three parts. Part I defines the context in which the debate about European contract law should, in the author's view, take place. At the outset, she brings to the reader's attention the fact that there are no universal definitions of key concepts such as 'contract law' and 'private law'. Accordingly, by defining those key concepts, the author stresses the importance of semantic clarification as the pre-condition for a productive discussion. Next, she moves on to examine the EU legislative instruments that constitute the 'hard core' of the EU contract law *acquis*, and the way in which the ECJ has interpreted them. Written with an audience unfamiliar with the American contract law framework in mind, this Part of the book also comprises a concise account of the way in which the constitutional dimensions of contract law have developed in the US.

In Part II, the book sets out, in a chronological order, the main events that have given rise to the debate about European contract law. It looks, for example, at the influence of the Commission's three seminal Communications on European contract law, as well as at the reasons that triggered the adoption of the Consumer Rights Directive. This part of the book seeks to determine, in particular, whether the constitutionality of European contract law has ever been considered, either implicitly or explicitly, at European level.

Once the contours of the debate about European contract law have been drawn, Part III begins by examining whether the EU has power to act in the field of contract law. To that end, the author explores whether and, if so, to what extent Articles 81, 114, 115, 169, 352 TFEU may operate as appropriate legal bases for the adoption of a European contract law instrument. In so doing, she examines the problems connected with the principles of subsidiarity and proportionality that the EU legislator may encounter. The absence of legislative competence at EU level does not, however, put an end to the Europeanization of contract law. For example, by looking at the US experience, the strengths and weaknesses of softer policy-making techniques, such as the Open Method Coordination (OMC), are also examined.

Finally, the concluding chapter of the book supports the contention that Article 114 TFEU and, as the case may be, Article 352 TFEU constitute a proper legal basis for the adoption of a European contract law instrument. Whilst Articles 81, 115, and 169 TFEU may not secure compliance with the principle of conferral, they have, nonetheless, an indirect role in highlighting the viability of the EU's internal market competence under Article 114 TFEU. As to the OMC, she notes that, because of its limitations, it may only serve as a complementary route for pursuing the European contract law project.

Written in a clear and entertaining style, this book succeeds in providing a solid analytical basis for future debates about European contract law. It is a thoughtful and rigorous study that addresses a challenging set of questions for lawyers, scholars and students in both Europe and the US. Overall, the book written by Kathleen Gutman is an excellent contribution to the literature on European Union law and I warmly congratulate her.

Prof. Dr. Koen Lenaerts
Vice-President of the Court of Justice of the European Union

Series Editors' Preface

The European Union has adopted a range of measures in the field of private and contract law, and a debate on the desirability and feasibility of harmonizing European contract law has been active for some years now. Kathleen Gutman's book makes an informative and important contribution to this debate by focusing not just on the movement to unify or harmonize European private law, but specifically on the question of the legal and constitutional basis for EU contract law.

Noting that the political and legal debate on the unification of European private law has proceeded apace with surprisingly little attention being given to the underlying question of the nature and scope of the EU's competence to take action in this field, the author sets out to remedy that deficit in this book. The chapters in the first part of the book address both abstract and concrete aspects of the topic, from a survey of different models of approximation of contract law, to an examination of some of the major pieces of EU contract legislation such as the Doorstep Selling Directive, the Consumer Credit Directive, the Commercial Agents Directive and the Unfair Contract Terms Directive, and to an analysis of the approach of the EU Court of Justice.

These EU-focused chapters are followed by an interesting and instructive comparison with the experience of the United States in which contract law has been treated as remaining largely within the purview of states, with federal intervention coming largely in the form of restatements, uniform and model laws, and the Uniform Commercial Code. Analysing the various instruments and approaches adopted in the US context, the author warns against any easy assumption about the success of the US approach to the question of a uniform American contract law or its applicability to the EU context, and points to the range of tensions and debates which continue in the United States today.

In the second part of the book, Gutman presents the evolution of the debate which has taken place in Europe since the earliest days of European integration on the feasibility and desirability of harmonizing private law, and surveys the various academic and institutional contributions to this debate. She traces the debate across the decades, leading to the emergence of the Common Frame of Reference and numerous initiatives which followed it, and giving particular attention to the influential interventions of the Commission in the debate.

The final chapters of the book are devoted to an examination of what Gutman calls the constitutionality of the adoption of EU measures in the field of contract law – including their possible legal basis in provisions of the Treaties dealing with the internal market, consumer law and civil justice – as well as their compliance with principles of subsidiarity, proportionality and sincere cooperation. She concludes by arguing that the EU enjoys sufficient competence to adopt an appropriate European contract law instrument under the internal market provisions of the Treaty, perhaps in conjunction with the residual powers clause, and alongside various alternative and complementary routes such as the Open Method of Coordination.

This is a very clearly written, meticulous, and comprehensive work on an important subject of considerable contemporary interest in EU and private law. It should be of considerable interest to scholars and students of European integration and to contract and private lawyers alike.

Gráinne de Búrca
Paul Craig

Acknowledgments

This book is based on my doctoral thesis defended at the University of Leuven in 2010. Unknowingly, what started out as a glance at an issue of the *European Review of Private Law* became both an academic and personal passion. One could even say that this subject found me, instead of the other way around. It combined my interests in various fields of European Union law, such as constitutional, private, and procedural law, and their counterparts in American law. It also captured my penchant for delving into subjects that had not yet been fully explored in either the European or the American settings. Yet, there were some trade-offs in undertaking this work, and truthfully, at times, it resembled something akin to the 'Myth of Sisyphus', where the more I attempted to go forward, the more I became mired in a sea of further unknowns, innumerable complexities, and of course considerable controversy. Thankfully, there were several persons who helped me along the way to bring this book to completion.

First and foremost, to my promoter, Professor Dr Koen Lenaerts, under whom I worked as a doctoral assistant and a post-doctoral fellow at the Institute for European Law of the University of Leuven, words cannot do justice to the ways in which he has given me invaluable guidance and helped me to grow in my academic career generally. I would also like to thank the other members of my doctoral jury, Professor Dr Wouter Devroe for his never-ending encouragement, as well as Professor Dr Jules Stuyck, Professor Dr Verica Trstenjak, and Professor Stephen Weatherill, all of whom prompted me to rethink and fine-tune my analysis of various points.

Secondly, there are several members of the Law Faculty of the University of Leuven, including Professor Dr Geert De Baere, Professor Dr Sophie Stijns, Professor Dr Geert Van Calster, Professor Dr Walter van Gerven, and Professor Dr Piet Van Nuffel, who inspired me along the way. And in the United States, a special note of appreciation goes to Professor Stephen Wallenstein for his support since my days as a law school student at the Duke University School of Law.

Thirdly, there are various persons and institutions without which the research for this book would not have been possible. I would like to thank the staff of the Law Library of the University of Leuven, particularly Jorinde Sercu who went beyond the call of duty to process my interlibrary loan requests and locate various publications on my behalf. I would also like to thank the Historical Archives of the European Commission, Claude Kappella of the European Economic and Social Committee Document Registry, and, most importantly, the European Parliament Document Registry for locating numerous documents that were pivotal to my research. I am further indebted to Pierre Schmitt for his translation of certain materials, and to Frans Van de Ven and Robin Schouten for their help with the logistics of relocating my research materials overseas.

Turning to the United States, I would like to express my utmost appreciation to Rodney A Ross of the Center for Legislative Archives. His invaluable assistance in locating various Congressional bills and responding to my numerous questions helped to make this book what it is, and, in fact, these materials proved to be one of the most eye-opening and exciting parts of my research. I would also like to thank the staff of the Law Libraries of Harvard University, New York University (NYU), and especially the University of California at Berkeley (Boalt) for allowing me access to their facilities and helping me to locate publications that would have been difficult to find elsewhere.

Fourthly, I owe a debt of gratitude to all those persons at Oxford University Press who helped to bring this book to print. In particular, this includes my editor Natasha Flemming for her patience and understanding throughout the process.

Finally, on a personal note, I feel grateful to say that I have four sets of 'families' whose support has been invaluable. My first 'family' is the Institute for European Law of the University of Leuven, which in addition to the above comprises Viviane Verbist, the Administrator of the Institute, and my colleagues, past and present—Angelina, Janek, Jos, Karl, Kristien, Marlies, Nana, Nathan, Pieter-Augustijn, Roel, Tim, Timothy, Tina, Tinne, Vanessa, and Vincent. My second 'extended family' from the second floor of the Valk and neighbouring buildings includes Hanne, Katrien, Sanderijn, Charline, Pierre, Thalia, Iasson, Govert, Bart, Dimitri, Jed, Thomas, Valérie, and so many more. My third 'family' consists of my friends in Belgium and the United States, especially Marianick and Patrick, Yolande and Carl, Vanessa and Bruno, Elke and Stefan, Glory, Lex, Alice, and TGS. Finally, there is my real 'family', including my best friend and soul sister Paula, my partner in life Luis, and my surrogate sister and aunt, Julie and Carol, respectively. And to my late mother and father, Donna and Stanley Gutman, who did not live to see this book in print, thank you for making my dreams possible and giving me the courage to follow them.

Admittedly, with the completion of this book—which generally reflects the state of the activities and law as of 1 June 2013—the all-consuming debate about European contract law and European private law continues to progress. Given the fast-paced nature of this debate, it is surely a challenge to complete any work in this area that will not be superseded by events soon after, or even before, publication. Nevertheless, if this book can play some part in helping to facilitate the 'constitutional conversation' about European contract (and private) law in the European Union and the 'comparative conversation' with the United States, then that is more than I could have hoped for.

KRG

Contents

Abbreviations xxi
Table of Cases xxvii
Table of Legal Instruments and Other Documents xxxiii

Introduction 1
Setting of the Problem 1
Objective and Structure 4
Scope and Potential Challenges 6

I. CONTEXT

1. The Constitutional Framing of European Contract Law 13
1.1 Introduction 13
1.2 Terminology 13
1.2.1 Constitutionality and the 'constitutional' designation 14
1.2.2 European contract law and its relationship to European private law 17
1.2.2.1 The meaning(s) of European contract law 17
1.2.2.2 The meaning(s) of European private law and similar variants 21
1.2.2.3 Comparative leaps to the US 24
1.2.3 Approximation and related processes 25
1.2.3.1 Approximation, harmonization, and unification 27
1.2.3.2 Harmonization models 31
1.2.3.3 Coordination 36
1.2.3.4 Codification 37
1.2.3.5 Europeanization (and formerly Communitarization) 39
1.2.3.6 Convergence 40
1.2.3.7 Comparative leaps to the US 40
1.3 The Scope of EU Contract Law and Its 'Hard Core' 41
1.3.1 The Doorstep Selling Directive (85/577/EEC), repealed by the Consumer Rights Directive (2011/83/EU) 44
1.3.2 The Commercial Agents Directive (86/653/EEC) 45
1.3.3 The Consumer Credit Directive (87/102/EEC), repealed by the new Consumer Credit Directive (2008/48/EC) 46
1.3.4 The Package Travel Directive (90/314/EEC) 48
1.3.5 The Unfair Contract Terms Directive (93/13/EEC) 49
1.3.6 The Timeshare Directive (94/47/EC), repealed by the new Timeshare Directive (2008/122/EC) 51
1.3.7 The Distance Selling Directive (97/7/EC), repealed by the Consumer Rights Directive (2011/83/EU) 53
1.3.8 The Consumer Sales Directive (1999/44/EC) 54

1.3.9 The Late Payment Directive (2000/35/EC), repealed by the new Late Payment Directive (2011/7/EU) 55
1.4 Perennial Themes 56
1.4.1 Union competence and the roles played by Articles 114 and 115 TFEU 56
1.4.2 The relationship between consumer and general contract law 59
1.4.3 The Union legislature's piecemeal approach 60
1.5 Conclusions 61

2. The Role of the Court of Justice in European Contract Law 62
2.1 Introduction 62
2.2 The Court of Justice's Interpretative Role 63
2.2.1 The relationship between certain directives within EU contract law 63
2.2.2 The relationship between EU contract law and the national contract law regimes 69
2.3 The Court of Justice's Lawmaking Role 76
2.3.1 The definition of European 'federal common law' and its 'hard core' 77
2.3.2 Illustrations of European 'federal common law' in contract law 78
2.4 Recourse to Comparative European Contract Law Materials by the Advocates General 84
2.4.1 Illustrations: *Quelle, Ilsinger*, and *Messner* 85
2.4.2 Potential implications for the Court's role in European contract law 89
2.5 Conclusions 92

3. The American Contract Law Framework 93
3.1 Introduction 93
3.2 American 'Federal Common Law' 94
3.2.1 General overview 94
3.2.2 Origins of American 'federal common law' 95
3.2.2.1 *Swift v Tyson* 95
3.2.2.2 *Erie Railroad Co. v Tompkins* 97
3.2.3 Tensions underlying American 'federal common law' in contract law 101
3.3 The NCCUSL and the Uniform Law Process 103
3.3.1 General overview 103
3.3.1.1 The meaning of uniform laws 104
3.3.1.2 The distinction between uniform laws and model laws 105
3.3.1.3 The NCCUSL and the American federal system 106
3.3.2 Origins of the NCCUSL 107
3.3.3 Tensions underlying the uniform law process 114
3.3.3.1 State-by-state enactment 114
3.3.3.2 State variation 114
3.3.3.3 The need for revision 115

3.4 The ALI and the Restatement Project 115
3.4.1 General overview 115
3.4.1.1 The work of the ALI 116
3.4.1.2 The Restatement project 117
3.4.1.3 The meaning of a Restatement 117
3.4.2 Origins of the ALI and the Restatement project 119
3.4.3 Tensions underlying the Restatement project 121
3.4.3.1 Restating the law 'as it is' versus 'as it ought to be' 122
3.4.3.2 The Restatements and codification 123
3.4.3.3 The impact of the Restatements 123
3.5 The UCC 124
3.5.1 General overview 124
3.5.1.1 Structure 125
3.5.1.2 Functional approach 125
3.5.1.3 The meaning of the 'Uniform Commercial Code' 125
3.5.2 Origins of the UCC 127
3.5.2.1 From the Uniform Sales Act to the Williston-ABA Federal Sales Act 127
3.5.2.2 The Merchants' Association Federal Sales Act 130
3.5.2.3 From the Federal Sales Act to the UCC 131
3.5.2.4 The UCC takes shape: Federal and state versions 133
3.5.3 Tensions underlying the UCC 135
3.5.3.1 The UCC and interstate/intrastate uniformity 135
3.5.3.2 The UCC and federalization 136
3.5.3.3 The UCC and consumer protection 138
3.6 Conclusions 141

II. DEBATE

4. **The Debate Begins** 147
4.1 Introduction 147
4.2 Academic Projects 148
4.2.1 The Commission on European Contract Law 149
4.2.2 The Study Group on a European Civil Code 152
4.2.3 The Network of Excellence 153
4.3 The Early European Parliament Resolutions 156
4.3.1 The 1989 Resolution 156
4.3.2 The Commission's response to 'Problems of harmonizing civil law' 163
4.3.3 The 1994 Resolution 165
4.3.4 The 1999 Working Paper 168
4.3.5 The 2000 Resolution 170
4.4 The European Council Meeting at Tampere 172
4.4.1 Events leading to Tampere and the Vienna Action Plan 172
4.4.2 The Tampere Conclusions 175
4.5 Conclusions 178

5. The Debate Solidifies 180

5.1 Introduction 180
5.2 The 2001 Communication 180
5.3 The 2003 Action Plan 186
5.3.1 Responses to the 2001 Communication 187
5.3.1.1 The European Parliament's 2001 Resolution 187
5.3.1.2 The Council's 2001 Report 192
5.3.1.3 The EESC's 2002 Opinion 194
5.3.1.4 Stakeholder responses to the 2001 Communication 196
5.3.2 Content of the 2003 Action Plan 199
5.4 The 2004 Communication 204
5.4.1 Responses to the 2003 Action Plan 205
5.4.1.1 The European Parliament's 2003 Resolution 205
5.4.1.2 The Council's 2003 Resolution 206
5.4.1.3 The European Central Bank's 2003 Letter 207
5.4.1.4 Stakeholder responses to the 2003 Action Plan 208
5.4.2 Content of the 2004 Communication 210
5.4.3 Aftermath of the 2004 Communication 216
5.4.3.1 The Hague Programme 216
5.4.3.2 The EESC's Opinion on European insurance contract law 218
5.5 Conclusions 219

6. The Debate Continues 221

6.1 Introduction 221
6.2 The Path to the CFR 221
6.2.1 The 2005 Progress Report 221
6.2.1.1 The Council's 2005 Conclusions 224
6.2.1.2 The European Parliament's 2006 Resolutions 224
6.2.1.3 The Commission's 2006 Note to the Council 227
6.2.2 The 2007 Progress Report 228
6.2.3 The publication of the Draft Common Frame of Reference 229
6.2.4 Ongoing reflection about the CFR by the Union institutions 232
6.2.4.1 The European Parliament's 2007 Resolution 232
6.2.4.2 The European Parliament's 2008 Resolution 233
6.2.4.3 The Council's 2008 Report on four fundamental aspects of the CFR 234
6.2.4.4 The Council's 2008 and 2009 Reports on further aspects of the CFR 238
6.3 The Review of the Consumer *Acquis* and the Path to the Consumer Rights Directive 240
6.3.1 The EC Consumer Law Compendium 240
6.3.2 The 2007 Green Paper 242
6.3.2.1 Responses to the 2007 Green Paper 245
6.3.2.2 The EESC's 2007 Opinion 245
6.3.2.3 The European Parliament's 2007 Resolution 246
6.3.2.4 Stakeholder responses to the 2007 Green Paper 247
6.3.3 The Consumer Rights Directive 248

6.4 The Path to the Proposed CESL and Beyond 252
6.4.1 The Stockholm Programme 252
6.4.2 The 2010 Green Paper 253
6.4.2.1 Responses to the 2010 Green Paper 257
6.4.2.2 The EESC's 2011 Opinion 258
6.4.2.3 The European Parliament's 2011 Resolution 258
6.4.2.4 Stakeholder responses to the 2010 Green Paper 260
6.4.3 The Expert Group and the 2011 Feasibility Study 261
6.4.4 The Proposal for a Regulation on a Common European Sales Law 264
6.4.4.1 Opinions of the national parliaments 268
6.4.4.2 Responses of the Union institutions and bodies 269
6.4.5 Ongoing reflection about specific types of contracts 271
6.5 Conclusions 272

III. CONSTITUTIONALITY

7. The Constitutional Parameters of European Contract Law 277
7.1 Introduction 277
7.2 Reasons for the Neglect of Constitutionality at the European Level 277
7.3 The Overarching Treaty Framework 280
7.4 The Principles of Conferral, Subsidiarity, Proportionality, and Sincere Cooperation 282
7.4.1 General overview 282
7.4.2 The principle of conferral 285
7.4.2.1 The definition of the principle of conferral 285
7.4.2.2 The legal basis requirement 287
7.4.2.3 The Lisbon Treaty 291
7.4.3 The principle of subsidiarity 294
7.4.3.1 The definition(s) of the principle of subsidiarity 294
7.4.3.2 The distinction between material and procedural subsidiarity 297
7.4.3.3 The Lisbon Treaty 303
7.4.4 The principle of proportionality 305
7.4.4.1 The definition(s) of the principle of proportionality 305
7.4.4.2 Proportionality inside and outside subsidiarity 306
7.4.4.3 The Lisbon Treaty 308
7.4.5 The principle of sincere cooperation 310
7.4.5.1 The definition of the principle of sincere cooperation 310
7.4.5.2 The role(s) of the principle of sincere cooperation in European contract law 310
7.4.5.3 The Lisbon Treaty 311
7.5 Conclusions 311

8. European Contract Law and the Internal Market 313
8.1 Introduction 313

8.2 The Relationship between Articles 114 and 115 TFEU 313
8.2.1 Overview of approximation in the Treaties and the three-level hierarchy 313
8.2.2 Text of Articles 114 and 115 TFEU compared and the order of preference 316
8.2.3 Lingering ambiguities concerning Articles 114 and 115 TFEU 319
8.2.3.1 The 'internal market' versus the 'common market' 320
8.2.3.2 'Object' versus 'directly affect' 322
8.2.3.3 Establishment 'and' versus 'or' functioning 323
8.3 The Scope of Article 114 TFEU 324
8.3.1 The 'object' and 'approximation' prongs of the case law 324
8.3.2 The limits of Union competence under Article 114 TFEU 325
8.3.2.1 The 'object' prong: *Tobacco Advertising I* and its evolving 'refinement' 327
8.3.2.2 Parameters of obstacles to trade: Distinguishing obstacles *sensu lato* and obstacles *sensu stricto* 338
8.3.2.3 Parameters of existing (and future?) appreciable distortions of competition 345
8.3.3 The exercise of Union competence under Article 114 TFEU 350
8.3.3.1 The 'object' prong 350
8.3.3.2 The 'approximation' prong 353
8.3.3.3 Implications for European contract law 357
8.3.4 Comparative reflection with the US 358
8.4 The Relationship between Articles 114 and 352 TFEU 360
8.4.1 The roles played by Article 352 TFEU vis-à-vis Article 114 TFEU 360
8.4.2 A contract law instrument modifying national contract law 361
8.4.3 An optional instrument of contract law 365
8.4.3.1 The *European Cooperative Society* case and related jurisprudence 365
8.4.3.2 Dimensions of a European optional instrument of contract law 369
8.5 Conclusions 377

9. European Contract Law and Consumer Protection 378
9.1 Introduction 378
9.2 The Template for the Analysis of Article 169 TFEU 380
9.2.1 The Treaties: The emergence and development of Article 169 TFEU 380
9.2.1.1 The former Treaty framework 381
9.2.1.2 The present Treaty framework 388
9.2.2 The case law: The indirect role of Article 169 TFEU 390
9.2.3 Usage: Theory versus practice and proposals for change 398
9.2.3.1 Theory 398
9.2.3.2 Practice 403
9.2.3.3 Proposals for change 406

9.3 The Scope of Article 169 TFEU 409
9.3.1 The limits of Union competence under Article 169(2)(b) TFEU 410
9.3.2 The exercise of Union competence under Article 169(2)(b) TFEU 413
9.4 The Relationship between Articles 169, 114, and 352 TFEU in European Contract Law 415
9.4.1 European consumer contract law and ties that bind: Consumer protection and the internal market 415
9.4.2 Comparative reflection with the US 419
9.5 Conclusions 420

10. European Contract Law and Judicial Cooperation in Civil Matters 421
10.1 Introduction 421
10.2 Article 81 TFEU as a Potential Legal Basis in European Contract Law 423
10.2.1 The former Treaty framework 423
10.2.2 The present Treaty framework 427
10.2.3 Missed opportunity for European contract law? 436
10.3 The Relationship between Articles 81, 114, and 352 TFEU in European Contract Law 437
10.3.1 Union measures adopted under Article 81 TFEU (ex Article 65 EC) 439
10.3.2 The limits of Union competence under Article 81 TFEU and the linkage to Article 114 TFEU 444
10.3.3 The exercise of Union competence under Article 81 TFEU and the linkage to Articles 114 and 352 TFEU 447
10.4 Conclusions 448

11. Alternative and Complementary Routes in European Contract Law 450
11.1 Introduction 450
11.2 Enhanced Cooperation 451
11.2.1 The virtues and vices of enhanced cooperation 451
11.2.2 Can enhanced cooperation be authorized? 454
11.2.2.1 The existence of Union competence: A 'boomerang' to constitutionality 457
11.2.2.2 The internal market-related conditions: Linkage to Articles 114 and 352 TFEU 459
11.2.2.3 Enhanced cooperation as a last resort: Linkage to the principle of sincere cooperation 462
11.2.3 Should enhanced cooperation be used? 463
11.3 An Intergovernmental Treaty 465
11.3.1 Distinguishing levels and approaches 465
11.3.2 An intergovernmental treaty under public international law 466
11.3.2.1 Historical relic of days past in the debate about European private law? 466
11.3.2.2 Problems associated with an intergovernmental treaty 468
11.3.3 An ad hoc convention method 469

11.4 'Softer' Models: The OMC, American Techniques, and the CFR 471
11.4.1 The OMC 471
11.4.2 American techniques 474
11.4.3 The CFR 477
11.5 Conclusions 479

Conclusion 481

The Constitutionality of European Contract Law *In Toto* 481
The Future Path of European Contract Law 483

Index 485

Abbreviations

AALS	Association of American Law Schools
ABA	American Bar Association
ABAJ	American Bar Association Journal
ABLJ	American Business Law Journal
ADR	Alternative Dispute Resolution
AFSJ	Area of Freedom, Security and Justice
AG	Advocate General
AJCL	American Journal of Comparative Law
AJIL	American Journal of International Law
AJLH	American Journal of Legal History
Ala L Rev	Alabama Law Review
ALI	American Law Institute
Am Bankr LJ	American Bankruptcy Law Journal
APSR	American Political Science Review
BEUC	Bureau Européen des Unions de Consommateurs (European Consumers' Organization)
BCICL Rev	Boston College International and Comparative Law Review
BIICL	British Institute of International and Comparative Law
B2B	Business-to-business
B2C	Business-to-consumer
Buff L Rev	Buffalo Law Review
Bus Law	Business Lawyer
Cal L Rev	California Law Review
CAP	Common Agricultural Policy
Case WRL Rev	Case Western Reserve Law Review
CCBE	Council of Bars and Law Societies of Europe/Conseil des barreaux européens
CCPA	Consumer Credit Protection Act
CDC	Centre de droit de la consommation
CDE	Cahiers de droit européen
CECL	Commission on European Contract Law
CESL	Common European Sales Law
CFR	Common Frame of Reference
CFSP	Common Foreign and Security Policy
CISG	United Nations Convention on Contracts for the International Sale of Goods
CJEL	Columbia Journal of European Law
CLJ	Cambridge Law Journal
CLP	Current Legal Problems
Col L Rev	Columbia Law Review
Comm LJ	Commercial Law Journal
Cons LJ	Consumer Law Journal
Const Comm	Constitutional Comment
Cons Fin LQ Rep	Consumer Finance Law Quarterly Report
CML Rev	Common Market Law Review
CoR	Committee of the Regions
Croatian YELP	Croatian Yearbook of European Law and Policy
CSECL	Centre for the Study of European Contract Law
CST	EU Civil Service Tribunal

CYELS	Cambridge Yearbook of European Legal Studies
DC	District of Columbia
DCFR	Draft Common Frame of Reference
DCT	Draft Constitutional Treaty
DG	Directorate General
Del J Corp L	Delaware Journal of Corporate Law
DJCIL	Duke Journal of Comparative and International Law
Duquesne BLJ	Duquesne Business Law Journal
EAEC	European Atomic Energy Community
EBLR	European Business Law Review
EC	European Community or (after Article number) Treaty establishing the European Community before the entry into force of the Lisbon Treaty
ECB	European Central Bank
ECCG	European Consumer Consultative Group
ECHR	European Convention for the Protection of Human Rights and Fundamental Freedoms
ECJ	European Court of Justice
ECL	European Contract Law
ECLG	European Consumer Law Group
E Const L Rev	European Constitutional Law Review
ECR	European Court Reports
ECSC	European Coal and Steel Community
Edin L Rev	Edinburgh Law Review
EEC	European Economic Community or (after Article number) Treaty establishing the European Economic Community
EESC	European Economic and Social Committee
EGC	General Court
EHLASS	European Home and Leisure Accidents Surveillance System
EIPA	European Institute of Public Administration
EIPR	European Intellectual Property Review
EJL & Econ	European Journal of Law and Economics
EJLR	European Journal of Legal Reform
ELF	The European Legal Forum
ELI	European Law Institute
ELJ	European Law Journal
Elon L Rev	Elon Law Review
ELR	European Law Review
Emory LJ	Emory Law Journal
EMU	Economic and Monetary Union
ENISA	European Network and Information Security Agency
EPL	European Public Law
ERA	Academy of European Law
ERCL	European Review of Contract Law
ERPL	European Review of Private Law
EU	European Union or (after Article number) Treaty on European Union before the entry into force of the Lisbon Treaty
EUVR	Zeitschrift für Europäisches Unternehmens- und Verbraucherrecht/Journal of European Consumer and Market Law
Fordham ILJ	Fordham International Law Journal
Fordham L Rev	Fordham Law Review
FTC	Federal Trade Commission
FTT	Financial Transaction Tax

GLJ	German Law Journal
GPO	United States Government Printing Office
GPR	Zeitschrift für Gemeinschaftsprivatrecht/European Community Private Law Review/Revue de droit privé communautaire
Hamline L Rev	Hamline Law Review
Hanse L Rev	Hanse Law Review
Harv ILJ	Harvard International Law Journal
Harv L Rev	Harvard Law Review
Harv L & Pol'y Rev	Harvard Law and Policy Review
Hastings LJ	Hastings Law Journal
Hofstra L Rev	Hofstra Law Review
ICLQ	International and Comparative Law Quarterly
IEE	Institut d'etudes européenne
IGC	Intergovernmental Conference
Ind L Rev	Indiana Law Review
Intl Rev L & Econ	International Review of Law and Economics
Iowa L Rev	Iowa Law Review
JCL	Journal of Comparative Law
JCMS	Journal of Common Market Studies
JCP	Journal of Consumer Policy
JDI	Journal du droit international
JHA	Justice and Home Affairs
JI	Juridica International
J Mar L & Comm	Journal of Maritime Law and Commerce
JPIL	Journal of Private International Law
J Soc Comp Legis	Journal of the Society of Comparative Legislation
KCLJ	The King's College Law Journal
La L Rev	Louisiana Law Review
L & Contemp Probs	Law and Contemporary Problems
L & Hist Rev	Law and History Review
L & Soc Inquiry	Law and Social Inquiry
Lewis & Clark L Rev	Lewis and Clark Law Review
LIEI	Legal Issues of Economic Integration
Loy L Rev	Loyola Law Review
Loy LAL Rev	Loyola of Los Angeles Law Review
LQ Rev	Law Quarterly Review
Mercer L Rev	Mercer Law Review
MEP	Member of the European Parliament
METRO	Maastricht University Institute for Transnational Legal Research/Maastrichts Europees Instituut voor Transnationaal Rechtswetenschappelijk Onderzoek
Mich L Rev	Michigan Law Review
Minn L Rev	Minnesota Law Review
MJ	Maastricht Journal of European and Comparative Law
MLR	Modern Law Review
MMWA	Magnuson-Moss Warranty Act
NCCUSL	National Conference of Commissioners on Uniform State Laws
NCL Rev	North Carolina Law Review
NIL	Negotiable Instruments Law
Notre Dame L Rev	Notre Dame Law Review
NTIR	Nederlands Tijdschrift voor Internationaal Recht/Netherlands International Law Review
Nw UL Rev	Northwestern University Law Review

NY	New York
NYLF	New York Law Forum
NYSBJ	New York State Bar Journal
NYULQR	New York University Law Quarterly Review
NYUL Rev	New York University Law Review
Ohio St LJ	Ohio State Law Journal
OJ	Official Journal of the European Union
OJLS	Oxford Journal of Legal Studies
Okla L Rev	Oklahoma Law Review
OMC	Open Method of Coordination
Pace IL Rev	Pace International Law Review
Pace L Rev	Pace Law Review
PEB	Permanent Editorial Board
PECL	Principles of European Contract Law
PEICL	Principles of European Insurance Contract Law
PEL	Principles of European Law
Penn St IL Rev	Pennsylvania State International Law Review
Pepp L Rev	Pepperdine Law Review
PJCCM	Police and Judicial Cooperation in Criminal Matters
Rabels Z	Rabels Zeitschrift für ausländisches und internationales Privatrecht/ The Rabel Journal of Comparative and International Private Law (Rabels Z)
RAE	Revue des affaires européennes/Law & European Affairs
RCDIP	Revue critique de droit international privé/French publication on Private International Law
RDUE	Revue du droit de l'Union Européenne
REDC	Revue européenne de droit de la consummation/European Journal of Consumer Law
RIDC	Revue internationale de droit comparé
RTDC	Revue trimestrielle de droit civil
RTDE	Revue trimestrielle de droit européen
Rutgers-Cam LJ	Rutgers Camden Law Journal
San Diego L Rev	San Diego Law Review
SCE	Société coopérative européenne/Statute for a European Cooperative Society
SEA	Single European Act
S Ill ULJ	Southern Illinois University Law Journal
SME	Small and Medium-sized Enterprise
SPE	European Private Company
Stan L Rev	Stanford Law Review
St John's L Rev	St John's Law Review
St Louis ULJ	St Louis University Law Journal
Sw JIL	Southwestern Journal of International Law
TED	Tenders Electronic Daily
Temp L Rev	Temple Law Review
TEU	Treaty on European Union after the entry into force of the Lisbon Treaty
Tex L Rev	Texas Law Review
TFEU	Treaty on the Functioning of the European Union
TFL Rev	Tilburg Foreign Law Review
The Harv Rev	The Harvard Review
Tul Eur & Civ LF	Tulane European and Civil Law Forum
Tul L Rev	Tulane Law Review

UCC	Uniform Commercial Code
UCCC	Uniform Consumer Credit Code
UC Davis L Rev	UC Davis Law Review
U Chi L Rev	University of Chicago Law Review
UCITA	Uniform Computer Information Transactions Act
U Colo L Rev	University of Colorado Law Review
U Ill L F	University of Illinois Law Form
U Kan L Rev	University of Kansas Law Review
ULC	Uniform Law Commission
UK	United Kingdom
U Miami L Rev	University of Miami Law Review
UN	United Nations
UNIDROIT	Institut international pour l'unification du droit privé/ International Institute for the Unification of Private Law
Unif L Rev	Uniform Law Review/Revue du droit uniforme
U Pa JIL	University of Pennsylvania Journal of International Law
U Pa L Rev	University of Pennsylvania Law Review
US	United States
Utah L Rev	Utah Law Review
Utrecht L Rev	Utrecht Law Review
TILEC	Tilburg Law and Economics Center
Va L Rev	Virginia Law Review
Vand L Rev	Vanderbilt Law Review
Vill L Rev	Villanova Law Review
Vt L Rev	Vermont Law Review
Wash ULQ	Washington University Law Quarterly
Willamette JIL & Disp Resol	Willamette Journal of International Law and Dispute Resolution
Wm & Mary L Rev	William & Mary Law Review
YJIL	Yale Journal of International Law
YLJ	Yale Law Journal
YEL	Yearbook of European Law
YPIL	Yearbook of Private International Law
Z Eu P	Zeitschrift für Europäisches Privatrecht/Journal of European Private Law

Abbreviations

Table of Cases

COURT OF JUSTICE

Accession by the Communities to the Convention for the Protection of Human Rights and Fundamental Freedoms (Opinion 2/94) [1996] ECR I-1759 . . . . 362, 363
AGM-COS.MET (Case C-470/03) [2007] ECR I-2749 33
Agreement establishing the World Trade Organization (Opinion 1/94) [1994] ECR I-5267 . . . . 29, 365
Alliance for Natural Health and Others (Joined Cases C-154/04 and C-155/04) [2005] ECR I-6451 . . . . 323, 333, 334, 340, 351, 352
Alsthom Atlantique (Case C-339/89) [1991] ECR I-107 341
Arnold André (Case C-434/02) [2004] ECR I-11825 . . . . 323, 332, 351, 352
Asbeek Brusse and de Man Garabito (Case C-488/11), Judgment of 30 May 2013, not reported 70
Asturcom Telecomunicaciones (Case C-40/08) [2009] ECR I-9579 70
Aziz (Case C-415/11), Judgment of 14 March 2013, not reported 70, 74, 75

Banco Español de Crédito (Case C-618/10), Judgment of 14 June 2012, not reported 70, 80
Banif Plus Bank (Case C-472/11), Judgment of 21 Feb 2013, not reported 70
Bejan (Case C-102/10) [2010] ECR I-139*, Summ pub. 394
Benincasa (Case C-269/95) [1997] ECR I-3767. 394
Berliner (Case C-208/98) [2000] ECR I-1741 . . . . .65, 67, 68, 69
Bonn Fleisch (Case C-1/06) [2007] ECR I-5609 85
British American Tobacco (Investments) and Imperial Tobacco ('*BAT*') (Case C-491/01) [2002] ECR I-11453 . . . . . 324, 329, 331, 332, 335, 337, 339, 345, 351, 352

C (Case C-435/06) [2007] ECR I-10141 . . . . 426, 438
Caffaro (Case C-265/07) [2008] ECR I-7085. . . . . .35, 444
Caja de Ahorros y Monte de Piedad de Madrid (Case C-484/08) [2010] ECR I-4785 . . . . . 35, 74
Clinique La Ramée and Winterthur Europe Assurance (Case C-397/02) [2004] ECR I-7947 80
CMC Motorradcenter (Case C-93/92) [1993] ECR I-5009 341
Cofidis (Case C-473/00) [2002] ECR I-10875 70
Color Drack (Case C-386/05) [2007] ECR I-3699 29
Commerzbank Frankfurt (Case C-24/93), withdrawn 66
Commission v Belgium (Case C-312/03) [2004] ECR I-1975 85
Commission v Council ('*Titanium Dioxide*') (Case C-300/89) [1991] ECR I-2867 . . . . 288, 290, 291, 321, 322, 327, 329, 346, 348, 364
Commission v Council (Case C-271/94) [2004] ECR I-4829 .315
Commission v Council ('*CIS*') (Case C-209/97) [1999] ECR I-8067 323
Commission v Council (Case C-338/01) [2004] ECR I-4829 . . . . 315, 318
Commission v Council (Case C-94/03) [2006] ECR I-1 288
Commission v Council (Case C-533/03) [2006] ECR I-1025 .315
Commission v Council (Case C-370/07) [2009] ECR I-8917 . . . . 287, 289
Commission v European Parliament and Council (Case C-178/03) [2006] ECR I-107. . . . 288, 289
Commission v European Parliament and Council (Case C-411/06) [2009] ECR I-7585 289
Commission v France (Case C-52/00) [2002] ECR I-3827 . . . . 394, 395
Commission v France (Case C-311/03), Judgment of 1 July 2004, not reported 85
Commission v France (Case C-177/04) [2006] ECR I-2461 395
Commission v Germany (Case C-539/09) [2011] ECR I-11235 298
Commission v Greece (Case C-154/00) [2002] ECR I-3879 . . . . 394, 395
Commission v Italy (Case C-91/79) [1980] ECR 1099. 329
Commission v Italy (Case C-193/80) [1981] ECR 3019 340

Commission v Italy (Case C-372/99) [2002] ECR I-819. 70
Commission v Italy (Case C-110/05) [2009] ECR I-519 341
Commission v Italy (Case C-275/07) [2009] ECR I-2005 . . . . 85, 91
Commission v Luxembourg (Case C-310/03) [2004] ECR I-1969 85
Commission v Netherlands (Case C-144/99) [2001] ECR I-3541 69
Commission v Slovakia (Case C-264/09) [2011] ECR I-8065 85
Commission v Spain (Case C-70/03) [2004] ECR I-7999 70
Commission v Sweden (Case C-478/99) [2002] ECR I-4147 70
Commission v Systran and Systran Luxembourg (Case C-103/11 P), Judgment of 18 April 2013, not reported. 80, 85
Commission and Others v Kadi (Joined Cases C-584/10 P, Case C-593/10 P, and Case C-595/10 P), Judgment of 18 July 2013, not reported 362
Constructora Principado (Case C-226/12), Judgment of 16 Jan 2014, not reported 75
Content Services (Case C-49/11), Judgment of 5 July 2012, not reported 53
Crailsheimer Volksbank (Case C-229/04) [2005] ECR I-9273 . . . . 81, 82, 83

Danske Slagterier (Case C-445/06) [2009] ECR I-2119. . . . . 33, 85
Derouin (Case C-103/06) [2008] ECR I-1853 30
Dietzinger (Case C-45/96) [1998] ECR I-1199 . . . . .65, 66, 67, 68, 69
Di Pinto (Case C-361/89) [1991] ECR I-1189. 35
Draft Agreement on the European and Community Patents Court (Opinion 1/09) [2011] ECR I-1137 453

E. Friz (Case C-215/08) [2010] ECR I-2947 . . . . 80, 82, 85
El Corte Inglés (Case C-192/94) [1996] ECR I-1281 . . . . .390, 391, 392, 397, 415
Engler (Case C-27/02) [2005] ECR I-481. 85
European Parliament v Council (Case C-271/94) [1996] ECR I-1689. 315
European Parliament v Council (Case C-259/95) [1997] ECR I-5303 . . . . 393, 405
European Parliament v Council ('*European Cooperative Society*') (Case C-436/03) [2006] ECR I-3733 . . . . 268, 269, 325, 365–9, 367, 482
European Parliament v Council (Case C-155/07) [2008] ECR I-8103. . . . . .288, 289, 315
European Parliament v Council ('*International Fund for Ireland*') (Case C-166/07) [2009] ECR I-7135 . . . . .289, 290, 291, 364, 365, 419
European Parliament v Council ('*Legal Basis for Restrictive Measures*') (Case C-130/10), Judgment of 19 July 2012, not reported. 288, 291

Falco Privatstiftung and Rabitsch (Case C-533/07) [2009] ECR I-3327 85
Freiburger Kommunalbauten (Case C-237/02) [2004] ECR I-3403. . . . . .71, 72, 73, 74, 75, 76, 92

Gaston Schul Douane Expediteur (Case 15/81) [1982] ECR 1409 321
Gebr Weber and Putz (Joined Cases C-65/09 and C-85/09) [2011] ECR I-5257 86
Germanwings (Case C-413/11), Order of 18 April 2013, not reported 17
Germany v Council ('*Product Safety*') (Case C-359/92) [1994] ECR I-3681 353
Germany v European Parliament and Council ('*Deposit Guarantees*') (Case C-233/94) [1997] ECR I-2405 . . . . 392, 393, 397, 412
Germany v European Parliament and Council ('*Tobacco Advertising I*') (Case C-376/98) [2000] ECR I-8419 . . . . . 170, 184, 188, 190, 316, 325, 326, 327–38, 339, 345, 347, 348, 349, 350, 351, 358, 359, 361, 396, 460, 469
Germany v European Parliament and Council (Case C-406/01) [2002] ECR I-4561 332
Germany v European Parliament and Council ('*Tobacco Advertising II*') (Case C-380/03) [2006] ECR I-11573 . . . . 3, 306, 323, 329, 334, 335, 336, 337, 340, 341, 344, 345, 347, 348, 352, 359, 396, 469
GIL Insurance and Others (Case C-30801) [2004] ECR I-4777. 316
Gintec International Import-Export (Case C-374/05) [2007] ECR I-9517. . . . . .33, 396
González Sánchez (Case C-183/00) [2002] ECR I-3901 . . . . 394, 395
Gourmet International Products (Case C-405/98) [2001] ECR I-1795 . . . . 335, 340
Grisoli (Case C-315/08) [2011] ECR I-139*, Summ pub 394

Grunkin and Paul (Case C-353/06) [2008] ECR I-7639 435
Gysbrechts and Saturel Inter (Case C-205/07) [2008] ECR I-9947 341

Hamilton (Case C-412/06) [2008] ECR I-2383 . . . . 80, 81, 82, 83, 84, 89, 90, 92
Hansen (Case C-326/88) [1990] ECR I-2911 33
Heine (Case C-511/08) [2010] ECR I-3047. . . . . 35, 88
Heininger (Case C-481/99) [2001] ECR I-9945 . . . . 81, 82, 83
Holcim (Deutschland) v Commission (Case C-282/05 P) [2007] ECR I-2941 85

Ideal-Standard (Case C-9/93) [1994] ECR I-2789 365
Idryma Typou (Case C-81/09) [2010] ECR I-10161 30
Ilsinger (Case C-180/06) [2009] ECR I-3961 . . . . 80, 85, 86, 87, 89, 90
Imperial Tobacco and Others (Case C-74/99) [2000] ECR I-8599. . . . . .328, 350, 351
Inuit Tapiriit Kanatami and Others v European Parliament and Council
(Case C-398/13 P), pending. 323, 338, 353
Invitel (Case C-472/10), Judgment of 26 April 2012, not reported 70
Ireland v European Parliament and Council (Case C-301/06) [2009] ECR I-593 323

Jersey Produce Marketing Organisation (Case C-293/02) [2005] ECR I-9543 321
Jörös (Case C-397/11), Judgment of 30 May 2013, not reported 70

Kadi and Al Barakaat International Foundation v Council and Commission
(Joined Cases C-402/05 P and C-415/05 P) [2008] ECR I-6351 . . . . 289, 360, 362
Keck and Mithouard (Joined Cases C-267/91 and C-268/91) [1993]
ECR I-6097. . . . . 332, 335, 340, 341
Klein and Others (Case C-73/04) [2005] ECR I-8667 65

Laserdisken (Case C-479/04) [2006] ECR I-8089 394
Laval un Partneri (Case C-341/05) [2007] ECR I-11767 36
Leitner (Case C-168/100) [2002] ECR I-2631 . . . . 78–9, 81, 83, 84, 92, 181, 199, 337, 346, 347, 348, 349
Lindqvist (Case C-101/01) [2003] ECR I-12971 . . . . 336, 352
Luxembourg v European Parliament and Council (Case C-176/09) [2011] ECR I-3727 . . . 299, 306

McB. (Case C-400/10 PPU) [2010] ECR I-8965 438
Marcinová (Case C-30/12), Order of the President of 4 Oct 2012, not reported 394
Marques Almeida (Case C-300/10), Judgment of 23 Oct 2012, not reported 85
Martín Martín (Case C-227/08) [2009] ECR I-11939 . . . . 70, 82, 85, 394
Masdar (UK) v Commission (Case C-47/07 P) [2008] ECR I-9761 91
Mediaprint Zeitungs-und Zeitschriftenverlag (Case C-540/08) [2010] ECR I-10909 . . . 33, 85, 404
Messner (Case C-489/07) [2009] ECR I-7315 . . . . .85, 88, 89, 90
Monsanto Agricoltura Italia (Case C-236/01) [2003] ECR I-8105. 393
Mostazo Claro (Case C-168/05) [2006] ECR I-10421 . . . . 70, 72, 75

Nelson and Others (Joined Cases C-581/10 and C-629/10), Judgment of 23 Oct 2012,
not reported. 306
Netherlands v European Parliament and Council (*'Biotechnology'*) (Case C-377/98)
[2001] ECR I-7079 . . . . 330, 331, 337, 340, 341, 345, 351, 365, 366
New Lugano Convention (Opinion 1/03) [2006] ECR I-1145 444

Océano Grupo and Salvat Editores (Joined Cases C-240/98 to C-244/98)
[2000] ECR I-4941 . . . . .70, 71, 72, 73
Österreichischer Rundfunk and Others (Joined Cases C-465/00, C-138/01, and
C-139/01) [2003] ECR I-4989 336
Owusu (Case C-281/02) [2005] ECR I-1383 . . . . .29, 444

Pannon GSM (Case C-243/08) [2009] ECR I-4713 . . . . .70, 73, 74
Pereničová (Case C-453/10), Judgment of 15 March 2012, not reported 33, 35, 72, 80

Piageme (Case C-85/94) [1995] ECR I-2955 393
Plus Warenhandelgesellschaft (Case C-304/08) [2010] ECR I-217. 33
Pohotovosť (Case C-76/10) [2010] ECR I-11557 . . . . 70, 72
Polydor and Others (Case 270/80) [1982] ECR 329 321
Pringle (Case C-370/12), judgment of 27 Nov 2012, not reported 467
Pupino (Case C-105/03) [2005] ECR I-5285 310

Quelle (Case C-404/06) [2008] ECR I-2685 . . . . .35, 80, 85, 86, 88, 89

Rampion and Godard (Case C- 429/05) [2007] ECR I-8017 70
Rechberger and Others (Case C-140/97) [1999] ECR I-3499 394
Roda Golf and Beach Resort (Case C-14/08) [2009] ECR I-5439 438

SC Volksbank România (Case C-602/10), Judgment of 12 July 2012, not reported 47
Salgado González (Case C-282/11), Judgment of 21 Feb 2013, not reported 36
Schulte (Case C-350/03) [2005] ECR I-9215 . . . . 81, 82, 83
Société Thermale d'Eugénie-les-Bains (Case C-277/05) [2007] ECR I-6415 83
Spain v Council (Case C-350/92) [1995] ECR I-1985 . . . 29, 319, 320, 327, 329, 346, 348, 361, 365
Spain v Council (Case C-147/13), pending 454
Spain and Italy v Council (Joined Cases C-274/11 and C-295/11), Judgment of 16 April 2013, not reported 314, 369, 453, 459, 461, 462
Spain v European Parliament and Council (Case C-146/13), pending 454
Swedish Match (Case C-210/03) [2004] ECR I-11893 . . . . .323, 332, 333, 351, 352

Tacconi (Case C-334/00) [2002] ECR I-7357. 85
Travel Vac (Case C-423/97) [1999] ECR I-2195 . . . . 64–5, 92, 181, 199

UK v Council ('*Working Time*') (Case C-84/94) [1996] ECR I-5755 315
UK v Council (Case C-209/13), pending 454
UK v European Parliament and Council ('*Smoke Flavourings*') (Case C-66/04) [2005] ECR I-10553. . . . . 325, 353, 354, 355, 356, 357, 358, 366, 373
UK v European Parliament and Council ('*ENISA*') (Case C-217/04) [2006] ECR I-3771 . . . . 325, 353, 354, 355, 356, 357, 358, 366, 368, 373, 375

van der Weerd and Others (Joined Cases C-222/05 to C-225/05) [2007] ECR I-4233 70
van Hilten-van der Heijden (Case C-513/03) [2006] ECR I-1957. 30
VB Pénzügyi Lízing (Case C-137/08) [2010] ECR I-10847 . . . . .70, 73, 74
Vodafone and Others (Case C-58/08) [2010] ECR I-4999. . . . . . . 299, 306, 323, 325, 336, 337, 338, 340, 346, 351, 352, 353, 396
VTB-VAB (Joined Cases C-261/07 and C-299/07) [2009] ECR I-2949 33

GENERAL COURT

Inuit Tapiriit Kanatami and Others v European Parliament and Council (Case T-18/10 R) [2010] ECR II-75*, Summ pub 323
Inuit Tapiriit Kanatami and Others v European Parliament and Council (Case T-526/10), Judgment of 25 April 2013, not reported 323, 338, 353
Italy v Commission (Case T-53/08) [2010] ECR II-3187. 84

Masdar (UK) v Commission (Case T-333/03) [2006] ECR II-4377 91

Pelle and Konrad v Council and Commission (Joined Cases T-8/95 and T-9/95) [2007] ECR II-4117. 91
Poland v Commission (Case T-370/11), Judgment of 7 March 2013, not reported. 306

Salamander and Others v European Parliament and Council (Joined Cases T-172/98 and T-175 to T-177/98) [2000] ECR II-2487 328

NATIONAL COURTS

Germany

Bundesverfassungsgericht, judgment of 30 June 2009, 2 BvE 2/08, 2 BvE 5/08, 2 BvR 1010/08, 2 BvR 1022/08, 2 BvR 1259/08, and 2 BvR 182/09. 286

USA

Alderman v United States, 131 S Ct 700 (2011) 359
Atherton v FDIC, 519 US 213 (1997) 102

Bank of America National Trust and Savings Association v Parnell, 352 US 29 (1956) 102

Clearfield Trust Co. v United States, 318 US 363 (1943) 101, 102, 103
Commercial National Bank of New Orleans v Canal-Louisiana Bank and Trust Co., 239 US 520 (1915) 113

Empire Healthchoice Assurance, Inc. v McVeigh, 547 US 677 (2006). 102, 103
Erie Railroad Co. v Tompkins, 304 US 64 (1938) 95, 97–101, 131

Gonzales v Raich, 545 US 1 (2005) 359

Hinderlider v La Plata River and Cherry Creek Ditch Co., 304 US 92 (1938) 99

National Federation of Independent Business v Sebelius, 132 S Ct 2566 (2012). 359

O'Melveny & Myers v FDIC, 512 US 79 (1994) 102

Perez v United States, 402 US 146 (1971) 140

Sosa v Alvarez-Machain, 542 US 692 . . . . *.99, 101*
Swift v Tyson, 41 US (16 Pet) 1 (1842) 95, 96, 97, 98, 100, 101, 103, 108, 109, 142

Texas Industries, Inc. v Radcliff Materials, Inc., 451 US 630 (1981) 101
Tompkins v Erie Railroad Co., 92 F2d 49 (2d Cir 1938) 98

United States v Danks, 221 F3d 1037 (8th Cir 1999) 359
United States v Kimbell Foods, Inc., 440 US 715 (1979) 102
United States v Lopez, 514 US 548 (1995) 358, 359
United States v Morrison, 529 US 598 (2000) 358
United States v Standard Oil Co., 332 US 301 (1947) 102

Table of Legal Instruments and Other Documents

EU DOCUMENTS

Treaties, Protocols, and Declarations

1951 European Coal and Economic Steel Community Treaty (ECSC Treaty) 147
1957 European Atomic Energy Community Treaty (EAEC Treaty) 147
European Economic Community Treaty (EEC Treaty) 147, 284, 321, 382, 386, 398
Title I 28
Art 2 . . . . 321, 322, 383
Art 3 . . . . 321, 322
Art 3(h) 28, 159
Art 99 28
Art 100 . . . . 28, 44, 46, 166, 317, 319, 322, 394
Art 112(1) 28
Art 117 28
Art 220 423
Art 235 . . . . 159, 319
European Community Treaty, as applicable until the entry into force of the Lisbon Treaty (EC Treaty) (as amended) 6, 7, 147, 162, 300, 307, 320, 384, 440
Title IV 172, 173, 193, 423, 424, 425, 430, 435
Title VI 28
Title XIV 381
Art 2 . . . . 291, 314
Art 3 . . . . 291, 292, 314, 381, 386
Art 3(1)(c) 314
Art 3(1)(g) 314
Art 3(1)(h) 28, 159, 314
Art 3(1)(j) 386
Art 3(1)(l) 386
Art 3(1)(p) 386
Art 3(1)(q) 386
Art 3(1)(t) 381, 384, 399
Art 5 . . . . 284, 291, 304, 309
Art 5(2) 303, 304
Art 5(3) 309
Art 10 . . . . 284, 310, 311
Art 11 . . . . 452, 454
Art 11a 452, 454
Art 14 . . . . 55, 314, 317, 318, 320, 322, 324
Art 14(1) 314
Art 14(2) 314, 455, 456
Art 15 314
Art 26 . . . . 314, 319
Art 28 . . . . 340, 341, 401
Art 29 341
Art 42 290
Art 47 316
Art 47(2) 290, 314, 328, 334, 355
Art 49 314
Art 55 . . . . 316, 328, 334, 355
Art 57 . . . . 392, 416
Art 57(2) 328, 392, 393
Art 60 289
Art 61 444
Art 61(c) 425, 437
Art 65 . . . . 169, 172, 174, 187, 188, 191, 215, 235, 237, 293, 401, 421, 423–49, 447, 448, 449, 461, 467
Art 65(1) 432, 434
Art 65(a) 187, 426
Art 65(b) 426, 445
Art 65(c) 172, 174, 175, 176, 421, 432, 445
Art 66 328
Art 67 . . . . 424, 425, 437
Art 67(5) 424
Art 68 424
Art 80 314
Art 93 . . . . 28, 314
Art 94 . . . . 28, 46, 100, 169, 288, 291, 300, 315, 317, 318, 319, 320, 322, 323, 327, 365, 394, 395
Art 95 . . . . 28, 47, 51, 52, 53, 55, 169, 170, 184, 186, 188, 189, 191, 198, 204, 215, 219, 226, 242, 248, 288, 300, 302, 303, 314, 315, 316, 317, 318, 319, 320, 321, 322, 323, 327, 328, 330, 331, 332, 333, 334, 338, 347, 350, 354, 355, 363, 365, 366, 378, 380, 387, 390, 394, 395, 396, 402, 403, 407, 408, 416, 422, 424, 428, 429, 445, 446, 460, 469
Art 95(1) 290, 317, 318, 319, 446
Art 95(2) 317
Art 95(3) 384, 396
Art 96 315
Art 97 315
Art 100 391
Art 132(1) 28

Art 133 . . . . 288, 331, 332
Art 133(4) 288
Art 136 28
Art 151(5) 290
Art 152 . . . . 328, 361, 396, 401
Art 152(4)(b) 416
Art 152(4)(c) 328
Art 153 . . . . 198, 226, 288, 378, 380, 381, 387, 388, 389, 390, 393, 394, 395, 396, 401, 402, 403, 406, 407, 408, 409, 411
Art 153(1) 381, 387
Art 153(2) 381, 387, 389, 390, 406, 407
Art 153(3) 381, 387, 388, 396, 401, 407
Art 153(3)(b) 401, 404, 406
Art 153(4) 381, 387, 390, 396, 404, 406
Art 153(5) 381, 388, 394, 407, 411
Art 157(3) 405
Art 159 . . . . 289, 290, 364
Art 168(5) 328
Art 175 288
Art 175(1) 289, 290, 416
Art 189 392
Art 228 395
Art 230 409
Art 235 . . . . 362, 405
Art 251 . . . . 289, 317, 396, 424
Art 293 . . . . 164, 169, 423, 466
Art 301 289
Art 308 . . . . 169, 170, 184, 215, 289, 290, 291, 319, 320, 327, 354, 356, 360, 361, 362, 363, 364, 366, 367, 405, 422

Protocols annexed to the EC Treaty (as amended)
Protocol (No 30) on the principles of subsidiarity and proportionality (1997) 297, 298, 317
point 5 . . . . 301, 302
points 6–7 . . . . 298, 307, 309
point 8 311
point 9 299

1986 Single European Act (SEA) 28, 48, 158, 161, 284, 316, 321, 322, 380, 384, 386
Art 8a 320
Art 100a 28, 29, 48, 51, 53, 160, 166, 290, 317, 319, 321, 322, 328, 330, 380, 385, 391, 392, 393, 407, 408, 469
Art 100a(1) 29, 317
Art 100a(3) 384, 392
Art 100a(4)–(5) 28
Art 118a(3) 386
Art 130r(4) 300
Art 130s 290
Art 130t 386

Declarations annexed to the Single European Act
Declaration on Article 100a of the EEC Treaty 29, 317

1992 Maastricht Treaty
Title IV EU 423
Art K.1 423
Art K.1(6) 423
Art K.3 423
Art K.3(2)(c) 423
Art 3(i) EC 386
Art 3(k) 386
Art 3(o) 386
Art 3(p) 386
Art 3(s) 384, 399
Art 3b 284
Art 126(1) 386
Art 126(4) 386
Art 128(1) 386
Art 128(5) 386
Art 129(1) 386
Art 129(1)(b) 392
Art 129(4) 386
Art 129a 380, 385, 386, 393, 397, 399, 400, 401, 403, 404, 407, 415
Art 129a(1) 385
Art 129a(1)(b) 407, 408
Art 129a(2) 385, 404, 405
Art 129a(3) 385, 407

Treaty on European Union, as applicable until the entry into force of the Lisbon Treaty (EU Treaty) (as amended)
Recital 11 424
Title VI 424
Art 2 . . . . 424, 425, 433
Arts 27a–27e 452
Art 27c 452
Art 34(2)(d) 466
Arts 40–41 452
Art 40a 452
Art 43 454
Arts 43–45 454
Art 43(a) 454, 455, 462
Art 43(b) 454
Art 43(c) 455
Art 43(d) 455
Art 43(e) 455
Art 43(f) 455
Art 43(g) 454
Art 43(h) 454
Art 43(i) 454
Art 43(j) 454
Art 44 455

Art 44(1) .455
Art 44(2) .455
1997 Amsterdam Treaty. 172, 173, 174, 297, 386, 387, 392, 397, 401, 402, 424, 451, 455, 466
Art B EU 424
Art 43(1)(a). 454
Art 43(1)(b) 454
Art 43(1)(d) 455
Art 11(1)(b). 455
Art 11(1)(c). 455
Art 11(1)(d). 455
Art 11(1)(e). 455
2000 Charter of Fundamental Rights of the European Union (as amended). 18, 389
Art 38. 389
2001 Nice Treaty 280, 387, 424, 451, 455, 456, 459
Declarations annexed to the Nice Treaty
Declaration (No 23) on the future of the Union. 280
2003 Draft Constitutional Treaty 281, 397, 431
Pt III, Title III, Ch III 389
Pt III, Title III, Ch 14. 431
Pt III, Title III, Ch V 389
Art 3(2) 431
Art 13(2) 389
Art 16. 389
Art 17. 363
Art 32. . . . . .389, 432
Art 43. 456
Art 43(2) 462
Art III-5 389
Art III-132(3). 389
Art III-132 389
Art III-132(2)(b). 389
Art III-170 . . . . .431, 432
Art III-170(1) 431
Art III-170(2). 432
Art III-170(3). 432
Arts III-322–329 456
2004 Draft Constitutional Treaty 7, 16, 279, 281, 282, 304, 309, 312, 325, 363, 380–1, 388, 389, 410, 425, 431, 433
Pt III, Title III, Ch III 389
Pt III, Title III, Ch IV 431
Pt III, Title III, Ch V 389
Art I-3(2) .431
Art I-12(5) 389
Art I-14(2) 389
Art I-17 389
Art I-18 363
Art I-33 433
Art I-44 456
Art I-44(2). 462
Art II-38. 389
Art III-172 . . . . .324, 389
Art III-176 369
Art III-235 389
Art III-235(2)(a). 389
Art III-269 . . . . 432, 433
Art III-269(1) 432
Art III-269(2). 432, 433
Art III-269(3). 432
Arts III-416–423 456
2007 Lisbon Treaty. . . 3, 6, 7, 28, 39, 147, 164, 178, 268, 280, 281, 282, 285, 287, 290, 291, 296, 297, 300, 301, 303–5, 308–10, 311, 312, 317, 363, 380, 381, 384, 388, 389, 397, 410, 422, 425, 427, 433, 435, 436, 445, 446, 452, 454, 456
Protocols annexed to the Lisbon Treaty
Protocol (No 1) amending the Protocols annexed to the EU Treaty, to the EC Treaty and/or to the EAEC Treaty. 298
point 9(g). 298
Declarations annexed to the Lisbon Treaty
Declaration (No 1) concerning the Charter of Fundamental Rights of the European Union 389
2012 Treaty on European Union, as amended by the Lisbon Treaty (TEU) (consolidated version) 6, 7, 48, 57, 162, 172, 280, 281, 300, 385, 386, 397, 399, 400, 403, 408, 423, 452
Recital 12. . . . . 424, 433
Title I. 284
Title III 452
Title IV 452
Title VI 172, 173
Art 2. 286
Art 3. 291
Art 3(2) 433
Art 3(3) 314, 424, 433
Art 3(6) 292
Art 4(1). 291
Art 4(2) 167
Art 4(3) 15, 284, 310, 311, 351, 462, 468
Art 5. 284
Art 5(1). 304
Art 5(2) 15, 285, 291, 308
Art 5(3) 15, 167, 295, 296, 297, 298, 300, 301, 302, 304, 306, 308, 364, 413, 415, 469
Art 5(4). 15, 297, 303, 305, 306, 308, 309
Art 6(1). 389
Art 6(2) 19, 363
Art 12(b) 304
Art 13(1). .178
Art 13(2) 285, 310, 311

Art 19(1) . . . 62
Art 20 . . . 452, 456
Art 20(1) . . . 457
Art 20(2) . . . 457, 462
Art 20(4) . . . 457

Treaty on the Functioning of the European Union (TFEU) (consolidated version) . . . 7, 36, 281, 452
Pt 3 . . . 390
Title V . . . 172, 433
Title VII . . . 28, 316
Art 1(1) . . . 292
Art 2 . . . 292
Art 2(1) . . . 292
Art 2(2) . . . 292
Art 2(5) . . . 292
Art 2(6) . . . 292
Art 3 . . . 292
Arts 3–6 . . . 28, 159, 292, 314
Art 4(1) . . . 292
Art 4(2) . . . 389
Art 4(2)(a) . . . 292
Art 4(2)(f) . . . 292
Art 4(2)(j) . . . 292
Art 4(3) . . . 284
Art 6 . . . 292, 389
Art 12 . . . 390, 397, 406, 419
Art 26 . . . 55, 314, 320, 324
Art 26(1) . . . 314, 324
Art 26(2) . . . 314, 456
Art 34 . . . 340, 341, 401
Arts 34-36 . . . 33, 325, 339
Art 35 . . . 341
Art 48 . . . 290
Art 53 . . . 37, 57, 290, 316, 416
Art 53(2) . . . 328, 334, 355, 392
Art 62 . . . 37, 316, 328, 355
Art 66 . . . 334
Art 67(4) . . . 438
Art 75 . . . 291
Art 81 . . . 2, 3, 4, 5, 9, 148, 169, 172, 179, 187, 188, 191, 215, 235, 237, 258, 273, 282, 291, 293, 295, 302, 368, 401, 410, 421, 422, 423–49, 453, 461, 467, 481, 482, 483, 4845
Art 81(1) . . . 433, 434
Art 81(2) . . . 421, 433, 438
Art 81(2)(a) . . . 438
Art 81(2)(c) . . . 438
Art 81(2)(e) . . . 438
Art 81(2)(f) . . . 172, 175
Art 81(3) . . . 434, 438
Art 113 . . . 28, 453
Art 114 . . . 2, 3, 4, 5, 9, 27, 28, 29, 30, 34, 37, 43, 47, 49, 51, 52, 53, 55, 56, 57, 58, 59, 79, 84, 160, 166, 169, 179, 184, 186, 188, 189, 191, 198, 204, 215, 219, 220, 226, 242, 248, 250, 251, 258, 259, 261, 265, 266, 267, 269, 270, 273, 279, 282, 283, 288, 290, 291, 293, 297, 300, 302, 303, 308, 312, 313, 315, 316, 318, 319, 321–76, 378, 379, 380, 381, 390, 392, 395, 396, 402, 403, 409, 410, 413, 415, 416, 417, 418, 419, 420, 422, 424, 428, 436, 437, 439, 458445, 446, 447, 448, 449, 458, 459, 460, 461, 462, 469, 479, 481, 482, 483, 484
Art 114(1) . . . 28, 269, 290, 315, 318, 319, 325, 354, 356, 368, 375, 416, 446
Art 114(2) . . . 318
Art 114(3) . . . 266, 333, 384, 396, 397, 418
Art 114(4) . . . 28, 36
Art 114(4)–(9) . . . 35
Art 114(5) . . . 28, 36
Art 114(5)–(9) . . . 59
Art 114(8) . . . 28
Art 114(10) . . . 28, 35
Art 115 . . . 2, 3, 4, 5, 9, 27, 28, 29, 44, 46, 47, 56, 57, 58, 59, 84, 166, 169, 179, 288, 291, 293, 295, 313, 315, 316, 317, 318, 319, 320, 322, 323, 324, 327, 329, 340, 360, 361, 365, 391, 394, 428, 460, 481, 482, 483, 484
Art 116 . . . 315
Art 117 . . . 315
Art 118 . . . 315, 369, 372, 374, 453, 482
Art 121 . . . 36
Art 151 . . . 28
Art 167(5) . . . 290
Art 168 . . . 328, 333, 396, 401
Art 168(4) . . . 405
Art 168(4)(b) . . . 416
Art 168(5) . . . 328, 333
Art 169 . . . 2, 3, 4, 5, 9, 42, 49, 57, 59, 198, 226, 250, 251, 259, 273, 287, 288, 291, 293, 295, 378, 379, 380–420, 481, 482, 484
Art 169(1) . . . 406, 409, 410, 412
Art 169(2) . . . 396, 397, 398, 409, 411, 416, 417
Art 169(2)(a) . . . 390
Art 169(2)(b) . . . 379, 397, 404, 406, 410, 411, 412, 413, 414, 417, 418, 419
Art 169(3) . . . 390, 404, 405, 406
Art 169(4) . . . 390, 394, 411, 413
Art 171(2) . . . 36
Art 173(2) . . . 36
Art 173(3) . . . 405
Art 175 . . . 289
Art 192 . . . 288, 290, 416

Art 192(1) 289, 290, 416
Art 207 . . . . 288, 331, 332
Art 215(2) 291
Art 252 90
Art 256(3) 62
Art 260 395
Art 263 409
Art 288 . . . . 29, 307, 375, 392
Art 326 . . . . 457, 459
Arts 326–334 452
Art 329 452
Art 331 452
Art 333 452
Art 352 . . . . 2, 3, 4, 5, 9, 169, 179, 184, 215, 219, 259, 268, 269, 282, 289, 290, 291, 293, 302, 308, 313, 315, 316, 319, 327, 354, 356, 358, 360–76, 378, 379, 380, 405, 410, 419, 422, 436, 437, 439, 448, 449, 458, 459, 461, 462, 479, 481, 482, 483, 484
Art 352(1) 316, 363
Art 352(2) 364
Art 352(3) 361
Art 352(4) 363

Protocols annexed to the TEU and the TFEU
Protocol (No 2) on the application of the principles of subsidiarity and proportionality 297, 298, 307, 309, 311
Art 1 298
Arts 2–5 298
Art 5 . . . . 301, 306
Arts 6–7 304
Art 7(2)–(3) 268
Art 8 304
Art 9 299
Protocol (No 25) on the exercise of shared competence 292

EU Legal Acts

Regulations

1971 Reg 1408/71 on the application of social security schemes to employed persons and their families moving within the Community [1971] OJ L149/2, OJ Spec Ed 1971 II, p 416 36
1992 Reg 1768/92 concerning the creation of a supplementary protection certificate for medicinal products [1992] OJ L182/1 320
2000 Reg 1346/2000 on insolvency proceedings [2000] OJ L160/1 . . . . 438, 467
2001 Reg 44/2001 on jurisdiction and the recognition and enforcement of judgments in civil and commercial matters [2001] OJ L12/1 . . . . 86, 87, 438
Reg 1206/2001 on cooperation between the courts of the Member States in the taking of evidence in civil or commercial matters [2001] OJ L174/1 438
Reg 2157/2001 on the Statute for a European Company (SE) [2001] OJ L294/1 184
2002 Reg 743/2002 establishing a general Community framework of activities to facilitate the implementation of judicial cooperation in civil matters [2002] OJ L115/1 176
Art 2(1)(d) 176
2003 Reg 1435/2003 on the Statute for a European Cooperative Society (SCE) [2003] OJ L207/1 . . . . . 366, 367
Recitals 3-5 366
Recital 12 366
Recital 13 366
Recital 20 366
Art 9 367
Reg 2065/2003 on smoke flavourings used or intended for use in or on foods [2003] OJ L309/1 . . . 353, 354
Recital 11 354
Recital 14 354
Art 1(2) 354
Art 4(2) 354
Art 8 354
Reg 2201/2003 concerning jurisdiction and the recognition and enforcement of judgments in matrimonial matters and the matters of parental responsibility, repealing Reg 1347/2000 [2003] OJ L338/1 . . . . . . 438, 467
2004 Reg 460/2004 establishing the European Network and Information Security Agency [2004] OJ L77/1 . . . 355
Recital 3 355
Recitals 4–9 355
Recital 10 355
Arts 1–3 355
Reg 805/2004 creating a European Enforcement Order for uncontested claims [2004] OJ L143/15 438
2006 Reg 842/2006 on certain fluorinated greenhouse gases [2006] OJ L161/1 416
Arts 7–9 416
Reg 1896/2006 creating a European order for payment procedure [2006] OJ L399/1 442
Recital 8 442
Recital 10 442
Art 1 442
Art 2(1) 442

Reg 1968/2006 concerning Community financial contributions to the International Fund for Ireland (2007 to 2010) [2006] OJ L409/86 289

2007 Reg 717/2007 on roaming on public mobile telephone networks within the Community and amending Dir 2002/21/EC [2007] OJ L171/32 . . . 336
- Recitals 4-9 336
- Recital 12 336
- Recital 16 336
- Recitals 17–18 336
- Art 1 336

Reg 861/2007 establishing a European Small Claims Procedure [2007] OJ L199/1 444
- Recitals 7–8 444
- Arts 1–2 444

Reg 864/2007 on the law applicable to non-contractual obligations (Rome II) [2007] OJ L199/40 438

Reg 1393/2007 on the service in the Member States of judicial and extrajudicial documents in civil or commercial matters (service of documents) and repealing Reg 1348/2000 [2007] OJ L324/79 438

2008 Reg 593/2008/EC on the law applicable to contractual obligations (Rome I) [2008] OJ L177/6 . . . . 18, 254, 266, 342, 438

2010 Reg 1259/2010 implementing enhanced cooperation in the area of the law applicable to divorce and legal separation [2010] OJ L343/10 . . . . . 438, 453, 461

2012 Reg 650/2012 concerning matters of succession [2012] OJ L201/107 438

Reg 1215/2012 on jurisdiction and the recognition and enforcement of judgments in civil and commercial matters [2012] OJ L351/1 . . . . 86, 438

Reg 1257/2012 implementing enhanced cooperation in the area of the creation of unitary patent protection [2012] OJ L361/1 453

Reg 1260/2012 implementing enhanced cooperation in the area of the creation of unitary patent protection with regard to the applicable translation arrangements [2012] OJ L361/89 453

2014 Reg 254/2014 on a multiannual consumer programme for the years 2014-20 and repealing Dec 1926/2006/EC [2014] OJ L84/42 398

Reg 282/2014 on the establishment of a third Programme for the Union's action in the field of health (2014-2020) and repealing Dec 1350/2007/EC [2014] OJ L86/1 405

Directives

1985 Dir 85/374/EEC on the approximation of the laws, regulations and administrative provisions of the Member States concerning liability for defective products [1985] OJ L210/29 . . . . 42, 80, 157, 188, 394, 395

Dir 85/577/EEC to protect the consumer in respect of contracts negotiated away from business premises [1985] OJ L372/31 . . . 42, 44–5, 53, 58, 63, 64, 65, 66, 67, 68, 69, 70, 81, 82, 157, 181, 183, 188, 190, 199, 223, 241, 242, 248, 249, 383
- Recitals 1–2 44
- Recital 5 44
- Recital 6 45
- Art 1 44
- Art 1(1) 66
- Art 1(3) 82
- Art 1(4) 82
- Art 2 45
- Art 3 45
- Art 3(1) 45
- Art 3(2)(a) 64
- Art 3(3) 45
- Art 4 . . . . 45, 82, 83
- Art 5 . . . . 44, 82
- Art 5(1) 45, 82
- Art 5(2) 44, 83
- Art 7 45
- Art 8 45

1986 Dir 86/653/EEC on the coordination of the laws of the Member States relating to self-employed commercial agents [1985] OJ L382/17 . . . 42, 45, 57, 181, 199
- Ch IV 46
- Recital 2 45
- Recital 3 45
- Recital 5 45
- Art 1 45
- Art 1(2) 46
- Arts 3–5 46
- Art 3(1) 46
- Art 4(1) 46
- Arts 6–12 46

Art 7 . . . 46
Arts 13–16 . . . 46
Art 17 . . . 46
1987 Dir 87/102/EEC for the approximation of the laws, regulations and administrative provisions of the Member States concerning consumer credit [1987] OJ L42/48 . . . 42, 47, 63, 65, 67, 68, 69, 190, 383, 390, 400
Recital 1 . . . 46
Recital 2 . . . 46
Recital 4 . . . 46
Recital 7 . . . 46
Art 1(2)(c) . . . 68
Art 1a . . . 46
Arts 4-6 . . . 46
Art 7 . . . 46, 47
Art 8 . . . 46
Art 9 . . . 46
Art 15 . . . 47
Annex I . . . 47
1990 Dir 90/88/EEC amending Dir 87/102/EEC [1990] OJ L61/14 . . . 46
Dir 90/314/EEC on package travel, package holidays and package tours [1990] OJ L158/59 . . . 42, 48–9, 80, 81, 181, 190, 199, 241, 242, 346, 400
Recital 1 . . . 347
Recital 2 . . . 48, 346
Recital 3 . . . 48, 346
Recital 5 . . . 347
Recital 8 . . . 48
Art 1 . . . 48
Art 3 . . . 48
Art 4 . . . 48
Art 5 . . . 48, 76, 79
Art 5(2) . . . 78, 79
Art 7 . . . 48
Art 8 . . . 48
Annex . . . 48
1993 Dir 93/13/EEC on unfair terms in consumer contracts [1993] OJ L95/29 . . . 42, 49–50, 54, 60, 63, 69, 70, 71, 72, 73, 74, 168, 190, 199, 223, 241, 242, 248, 249, 250, 383, 395, 400
Recital 5 . . . 50
Recital 6 . . . 50
Recital 7 . . . 50
Recital 12 . . . 50
Art 3(1) . . . 50, 74
Art 3(2) . . . 50
Art 3(3) . . . 74
Art 4 . . . 74
Art 5 . . . 50
Art 6 . . . 50
Art 7 . . . 50
Art 8 . . . 50
1994 Dir 94/19/EC on deposit-guarantee schemes [1994] OJ L135/5 . . . 392
Dir 94/47/EC on the protection of purchasers in respect of certain aspects of contracts relating to the purchase of the right to use immovable properties on a timeshare basis [1994] OJ L280/83 . . . 42, 51–2, 63, 64, 65, 181, 183, 190, 241, 242, 400
Recital 1 . . . 51
Recital 3 . . . 51
Recitals 8–9 . . . 51
Recital 14 . . . 51
Art 1 . . . 51
Art 2 . . . 51
Art 3 . . . 51
Art 4 . . . 51
Arts 5–8 . . . 51
Art 11 . . . 51
1997 Dir 97/7/EC on the protection of consumers in respect of distance contracts [1999] OJ L144/19 . . . 43, 53–4, 88, 89, 183, 188, 190, 223, 241, 242, 249, 400
Recital 3 . . . 53
Recital 4 . . . 53
Recital 18 . . . 54
Art 1 . . . 53
Art 2(1) . . . 53
Art 3 . . . 53
Art 4(2) . . . 53
Art 6 . . . 53, 88
Art 6(1) . . . 53
Arts 7–9 . . . 53
Art 11 . . . 53
Art 11(3)(c) . . . 54
Art 14 . . . 53
1998 Dir 98/6/EC on consumer protection in the indication of the prices of products offered to consumers [1998] OJ L 80/27 . . . 42, 241, 404, 407
Recital 1 . . . 404
Recital 2 . . . 404
Recital 12 . . . 404
Art 1 . . . 404
Art 10 . . . 404
Dir 98/7/EC amending Dir 87/108/EEC [1998] OJ L101/17 . . . 46
Dir 98/27/EC on injunctions for the protection of consumers [1998] OJ L166/51 . . . 42, 241

Dir 98/44/EC on the legal protection of biotechnological inventions [1998] OJ L213/13 330

1999 Dir 99/44/EC on certain aspects of the sale of consumer goods and associated guarantees [1999] OJ L171/12. . . . 43, 54, 57, 60, 85, 168, 188, 190, 223, 241, 242, 248, 249, 250, 383
- Recitals 1–2 54
- Recital 3. 54
- Recital 5. 54
- Recital 6. 54
- Recitals 62–63 54
- Arts 2–6. 54
- Art 3. 86
- Art 3(2) 86
- Art 3(3) 86
- Art 8(1). 54
- Art 8(2) 54
- Art 33. 54

Dir 99/93/EC on a Community framework for electronic signatures [2000] OJ L13/12 41
- Recital 4. 43

2000 Dir 2000/31/EC on certain legal aspects of information society services, in particular electronic commerce, in the Internal Market [2000] OJ L178/1 . . . . .41, 188
- Recital 5. 43
- Recital 7. 43

Dir 2000/35/EC on combating late payment in commercial transactions [2000] OJ L200/35. . . . . . .43, 55–6, 183, 190
- Recital 5. 55
- Recital 9. 55
- Recital 10. .55
- Recital 13. .55
- Recital 19. .55
- Recital 21. 56
- Recital 22. .55
- Art 1. 55
- Art 2(1). 55
- Art 2(3) 55
- Art 3. 55
- Art 4. . . . . .55, 56
- Art 5. 55
- Art 6(2) 55

2001 Dir 2001/37/EC on the approximation of the laws, regulations and administrative provisions of the Member States concerning the manufacture, presentation and sale of tobacco products [2001] OJ L194/26. . . . . .331, 332, 345, 351
- Art 8. . . . . .332, 333

Dir 2001/83/EC on the Community code relating to medicinal products for human use [2001] OJ L311/67. 395

2002 Dir 2002/46/EC on the approximation of the laws of the Member States relating to food supplements [2002] OJ L183/51 . . . . 333, 334
- Art 3. . . . . .333, 334, 335
- Art 4. . . . . .334, 335
- Art 4(1). 333
- Art 15(b). .333

Dir 2002/65/EC concerning the distance marketing of consumer financial services and amending Dirs 90/619/EEC, 97/7/EC, and 98/27/EC [2002] OJ L271/16 42
- Recitals 1–5 43
- Recital 12. 43

2003 Dir 2003/8/EC to improve access to justice in cross-border disputes by establishing minimum common rules relating to legal aid for such disputes [2003] OJ L26/41 . . . . 434, 439
- Recital 9. 439
- Art 1. 439

Dir 2003/33/EC on the approximation of the laws, regulations and administrative provisions of the Member States relating to the advertising and sponsorship of tobacco products [2003] OJ L152/16 334–6
- Arts 3–4. . . . . 334–6, 352

2004 Dir 2004/80/EC relating to compensation to crime victims [2004] OJ L261/15 165

2005 Dir 2005/29/EC concerning unfair business-to-consumer commercial practices in the internal market and amending Dirs 84/450/EC, 97/7/EC, 98/27/EC, and 2002/65/EC and Reg 2006/2004 [2005] OJ L149/22. . . .42
- Recital 4. 43
- Recital 13. 43

2006 Dir 2006/66/EC on batteries and accumulators and waste batteries and accumulators and repealing Dir 91/157/EEC [2006] OJ L266/1. 416
- Art 4. 416
- Art 6. 416
- Art 21. 416

Dir 2006/123/EC on services in the internal market [2006] OJ L373/36 . . . . .34, 36, 41
- Recital 7. 34

2007 Dir 2007/64/EC on payment services in the internal market amending Dirs 97/7/EC, 2002/65/EC, 2005/60/EC, and 2006/48/EC and repealing Dir 97/5/EC [2007] OJ L319/1 . . . . 42, 43

2008 Dir 2008/48/EC on credit agreements for consumers and repealing Dir 87/102/EEC [2008] OJ L133/66 . . . . 42, 46, 47, 65, 70
- Recital 4 47
- Recital 5 47
- Recital 7 47
- Recital 8 47
- Recital 9 47
- Recital 9–11 47
- Recital 22 47
- Recital 30 47
- Arts 1–2 47
- Art 3(c) 68
- Art 14 48
- Art 15 48
- Art 16 48
- Art 22(1) 47

Dir 2008/52/EC on certain aspects of mediation in civil and commercial matters [2008] OJ C136/3 . . . . 435, 438
- Recital 8 440
- Arts 1–2 440

Dir 2008/112/EC amending Dirs 76/768/EEC, 88/378/EEC, 1999/13/EC, 2000/53/EC, 2002/96/ EC, and 2004/42/ EC in order to adapt them to Reg 1272/2008 on classification, labelling and packaging of substances and mixtures [2008] OJ L345/68 416

Dir 2008/122/EC on the protection of consumers in respect of certain aspects of timeshare, long-term holiday product, resale and exchange contracts [2009] OJ L33/10 . . . . 42, 51, 52
- Recital 1 52
- Recital 2 52
- Recital 3 52
- Recital 4 52
- Art 1(1) 52
- Art 1(2) 52
- Art 2(1)(a)–(d) 52
- Arts 4–5 52
- Arts 6–11 52
- Arts 13–15 52
- Art 18 52
- Annexes I-V 52
- Annex VI 52

2009 Dir 2009/22/EC on injunctions for the protection of consumers [2009] OJ L110/30 42

Dir 2009/28/EC on the promotion of the use of energy from renewable sources and amending and subsequently repealing Dirs 2001/177/EC and 2003/30/ EC [2009] OJ L140/16 416

2011 Dir 2011/7/EU on combating late payment in commercial transactions [2011] OJ L48/1 . . . . 43, 55, 56
- Recital 28 56
- Art 7 56
- Art 13 56

Dir 2011/83/EU on consumer rights, amending Dirs 93/13/EEC and 1999/44/EC and repealing Dirs 85/577/EEC and 97/7/EC [2011] OJ L304/64 . . . 1, 4, 7, 34, 42, 43, 44, 53, 54, 63, 223, 239, 240, 248–51, 254
- Recital 2 . . . . 249, 250
- Recital 4 251
- Recital 6 250
- Recital 7 . . . . 250, 251
- Recital 8 251
- Recital 9 250
- Recitals 13–16 250
- Recital 14 251
- Recital 21 249
- Recital 28 250
- Recital 62 250
- Recital 63 250
- Art 1 . . . . 250, 251
- Art 2(8) 249
- Art 3(4) 250
- Art 4 . . . . 34, 250
- Art 5 251
- Art 5(3)–(4) 250
- Art 6(7)–(8) 250
- Art 7(4) 250
- Art 8(6) 250
- Art 9(3) 250
- Art 18(4) 250, 251
- Art 29 250
- Art 30 250
- Art 31 . . . . 44, 53, 249
- Art 32 50
- Arts 32–33 250
- Annex I 250
- Annex II 249

Decisions

1994 Dec 3092/94/EC introducing a Community system of information on home and leisure accidents [1994] OJ L331/1 . . . 404, 405, 406, 407

Recital 3 405
Art 1(1)–(2) 405
1999 Dec 276/1999/EC adopting a multiannual Community action plan on promoting safer use of the Internet by combating illegal and harmful content on global networks [1999] OJ L33/1 . . . . 405, 406
Recital 4 405
Art 3 405
Dec 372/1999/EC adopting a programme of Community action on injury prevention in the framework for action in the field of public health (1999 to 2003) [1999] OJ L46/1 405
2003 Dec 1151/2003/EC amending Dec 276/1999/EC adopting a multinational Community action plan on promoting safer use of the Internet by combating illegal and harmful content on global networks [2003] OJ L162/1 406
2005 Dec 854/2005/EC establishing a multiannual Community programme on promoting safer use of the Internet and new online technologies [2005] OJ L149/1 406
2007 Dec 1149/2007/EC establishing for the period 2007-2013 the Specific Programme 'Civil Justice' as part of the General Programme 'Fundamental Rights and Justice' [2007] OJ L257/16 176
Art 2(1)(b) 176
Art 3(a)(iii) 176
2008 Dec 1351/2008/EC establishing a multiannual Community programme on protecting children using the Internet and other communication technologies [2008] OJ L348/118 406
2009 Dec 568/2009/EC amending Dec 2001/470/EC establishing a European Judicial Network in civil and commercial matters [2009] OJ L168/35 . . . . .435, 438
2010 Dec 2010/233/EU setting up the Expert Group on a Common Frame of Reference in the area of European contract law [2010] OJ L105/109 . . . . .261, 262
Recital 7 262
Recital 8 261
Recital 9 262
Art 2 261
Art 4(1)–(4) 262
Art 5(1) 262
Art 5(2) 261
Dec 2010/309/EU amending Dec 2007/721/EC as regards indemnities paid to members of scientific committees and experts in the field of consumer safety, public health and the environment [2010] OJ L138/24 398
Dec 2010/405/EU authorising enhanced cooperation in the area of the law applicable to divorce and legal separation [2010] OJ L189/12 453
2011 Dec 2011/167/EU authorising enhanced cooperation in the area of the creation of unitary patent protection [2011] OJ L76/53 453
Dec No 2011/283/EU on the conclusion of a Protocol to the Partnership and Cooperation Agreement establishing a partnership between the European Communities and their Member States, of the one part, and the Republic of Moldova, of the other part, on a Framework Agreement between the European Union and the Republic of Moldova on the general principles for the participation of the Republic of Moldova in Union programmes [2011] OJ L131/1 398
2012 Dec 2012/714/ EU confirming the participation of Lithuania in enhanced cooperation in the area of the law applicable to divorce and legal separation [2012] OJ L323/18 453
2013 Dec 2013/52/EU authorising enhanced cooperation in the area of financial transaction tax [2013] OJ L22/11 .453
Dec on setting up the Commission Expert Group on a European Insurance Contract Law [2013] OJ C16/6 271
Recital 5 271
Recital 7 271
Art 1 271
Art 2 271
Dec on setting up the Commission expert group on cloud computing contracts [2013] OJ C174/6 272
Recital 6 272
Art 2 272

Recommendations

Recommendation 92/295/EEC on codes of practice for the protection of consumers in respect of contracts negotiated at a distance [1992] OJ L156/21 54

Proposals

1989 Proposal for a Council Dir on the advertising of tobacco products in the press and by means of bills and posters, COM (89) 163 final/2, 7.4.1989 328

1990 Amended proposal for a Council Dir on the authorized advertising of tobacco products in the press and by means of bills and posters, COM (90) 147 final, 19.4.1990 328

1997 Proposal for a Council Dec adopting a multiannual Community action plan on promoting safe use of the Internet, COM (97) 582 final, 27.11.1997 . . . 405

1998 Amended proposal for a European Parliament and Council Dec adopting a multiannual Community action plan on promoting safer use of the Internet [1998] OJ C324/6. . . . 406

2002 Proposal for a Council Dir to improve access to justice in cross-border disputes by establishing minimum common rules relating to legal aid and other financial aspects of civil proceedings, COM (2002) 13 final, 18.1.2002. 439

2004 Proposal for a Reg of the European Parliament and of the Council creating a European order for payment procedure, COM (2004) 173 final/3, 25.5.2004 . . . . 441, 442

Proposal for a Dir of the European Parliament and of the Council on certain aspects of mediation in civil and commercial matters, COM (2004) 718 final, 22.10.2004 . . . . 439, 440

2005 Proposal for a Reg of the European Parliament and of the Council establishing a European Small Claims Procedure, COM (2005) 87 final, 15.3.2005 . . . . 442, 443, 444

Proposal for a Dec of the European Parliament and of the Council establishing a Programme of Community action in the field of Health and Consumer Protection 2007–2013, COM (2005) 15 final, 6.4.2005 403

Amended proposal for a new Consumer Credit Dir, COM (2005) 483 final/2, 23.11.2005 47

Proposal for the 'Rome I' Reg on the law applicable to contractual obligations, COM (2005) 650 final, 15.12.2005. 223

2006 Amended proposal for a Dec of the European Parliament and of the Council establishing a Programme of Community action in the field of consumer policy (2007–2013), COM (2006) 235 final, 24.5.2006. 403

2008 Proposal for a Dir of the European Parliament and of the Council on consumer rights, COM (2008) 614 final, 8.10.2008 . . . . 33, 34, 248, 249, 250, 251

- Recital 5. 249
- Recital 6. .251
- Recital 7. .251
- Recital 8. 249
- Art 4. . . . . 34, 249

2009 Proposal for a Dir of the European Parliament and of the Council on combating late payment in commercial transactions (Recast)—Implementing the Small Business Act, COM (2009) 126 final, 8.4.2009 56

2010 Proposal for a Council Dec authorising enhanced cooperation in the area of the law applicable to divorce and legal separation, COM (2010) 104 final/2, 30.3.2010. . .457, 463

Proposal for a Council Dec authorising enhanced cooperation in the area of the creation of unitary patent protection, COM (2010) 790 final, 14.12.2010. . . . . 457, 461, 463

2011 Proposal for a Reg of the European Parliament and of the Council on a Common European Sales Law, COM (2011) 635 final, 11.10.2011 . . . . .1, 4, 7, 9, 14, 26, 35, 60, 221, 264–72, 283, 299, 304, 313, 317, 325, 342, 344, 348, 350, 357, 358, 370, 372, 373, 374, 375, 376, 377, 403, 417, 418, 419, 448, 464, 467, 471, 473, 477, 478, 479, 481, 483, 484

- Recitals 1-8 266
- Recital 7. 265
- Recital 9. 266
- Recitals 10-12. 266
- Recital 26. 264
- Recital 27. 264
- Recital 28. 264

Recital 35 264
Art 1 266
Art 15(2) 264
Annex 264
2012 Proposal for a Council Dec authorising enhanced cooperation in the area of financial transaction tax, COM (2012) 631 final/ 2, 25.10.2012 . . . . 457, 461, 463
2013 Proposal for a Council Dir implementing enhanced cooperation in the area of financial transaction tax, COM (2013) 71 final, 14.2.2013 453
Proposal for a Dir of the European Parliament and of the Council on package travel and assisted travel arrangements, amending Reg 2006/2004, Dir 2011/83/EU and repealing Dir 90/314 EEC, COM (2013) 512 final, 9.7.2013 . . . . 48, 49, 81
Recital 1 49
Recital 3 49
Recital 6 49
Recital 41 49
Art 1 49
Annex I 49

Texts of the EU Institutions and Bodies

Communications, Green Papers, and Reports

1985 Commission Communication, A New Impetus for Consumer Protection Policy, COM (85) 314 final, 27.6.1985 383
point 2 382
point 18 384
1990 Commission Communication, Three-Year Action Plan of Consumer Policy in the EEC 1990–1992, COM (90) 98 final, 3.5.1990 . . . . . . 383, 384, 398, 399
point B 398
point 4(i) 398
point 4(ii) 399
point 4(iii) 399
point 18 384
point 29 384
points 29-31 384
point 35 384
point 37 384
1992 Commission Communication, The principle of subsidiarity, SEC(92) 1990 final, 27.10.1992 301
Annex
pt II 300
pt IV 305
1993 Commission Communication, Second Three-Year Action Plan on Consumer Policy 1993–1995— Placing the single market at the service of European consumers, COM (93) 378 final, 28.7.1993 . . . . 399, 400
point 10 . . . . 399, 400
point 11 400
point 12 400
point 14 400
points 24–43 400
1995 Commission Communication, Priorities for Consumer Policy 1996–1998, COM (95) 519 final, 31.10.1995 . . . 400
points 1–2 400
point 3 400
point 4 400
1997 Commission Communication, Action Plan on promoting safe use of the Internet, COM (97) 582 final, 27.11.1997 405
1998 Commission Communication, Consumer Policy Action Plan 1999–2001, COM (1998) 696 final, 1.12.1998 401
point 2 401
2000 Green Paper, Legal aid in civil matters: The problems confronting the cross-border litigant, COM (2000) 51 final, 9.2.2000 439
Commission Communication, Scoreboard to Review Progress on the Creation of an Area of 'Freedom, Security and Justice' in the European Union, COM (2000) 167 final/2, 13.4.2000 177–178
point 3.3 178
Commission Communication, Biannual Update of the Scoreboard to Review Progress on the Creation of an Area of 'Freedom, Security and Justice' in the European Union (Second Half of 2000), COM (2000) 782 final, 30.11.2000 178
point 3.3 178
2001 Commission Communication, E-commerce and Financial Services, COM (2001) 66 final, 7.2.2001 184
point 3 184
Commission Communication, Biannual Update of the Scoreboard to Review Progress on the Creation of an Area of 'Freedom, Security and Justice' in the European Union (First Half of 2001), COM (2001) 278 final, 23.5.2001 177
point 3.3 177

Commission Communication on European Contract Law, COM (2001) 398 final, 11.7.2001 . . . . 1, 65, 172, 180–186, 187, 189, 194, 195, 201, 202, 204, 209, 218, 220, 254, 279
Executive Summary
para 3 184
para 4 183
point 3 171
point 5 184
points 10–11 180
point 13 180
point 14 181
point 15 181
points 17–22 181
point 23 181
point 24 184
points 26–33 181
points 35 65
points 35–40 181
point 41 . . . . 21, 181, 182
points 41–42 185
points 42–43 185
points 42–45 185
point 43 185
point 44 185
point 45 185
point 46 182
points 46–47 181
point 48 182
point 49 182
point 50 182
point 51 182
point 52 182
point 53 . . . . 182, 183
point 55 183
point 56 183
points 58–59 299
point 60 183
point 61 183
point 63 184
point 64 184
point 65 184
point 66 184
point 67 184
point 69 184
point 70 181
point 72 184
point 73 180
section 4.4 21
Annex I 181, 183
Annex II 18, 181, 183, 468
Annex III 181, 183
Green Paper on EU Consumer Protection, COM (2001) 531 final, 2.10.2001 402
point 3.4 186
Commission Communication, Biannual Update of the Scoreboard to Review Progress on the Creation of an Area of 'Freedom, Security and Justice' in the European Union (Second Half of 2001), COM (2001) 628 final, 30.10.2001 178
point 3.3 178
2002 Commission Communication, Consumer Policy Strategy 2002-2006, COM (2002) 208 final, 7.5.2002 . . . . 402, 403
point 2.1 403
points 3.1.2.2-3.1.2.3 . . . . 186, 402
point 3.2.3.3 . . . . 176, 186
Commission Communication, Biannual Update of the Scoreboard to Review Progress on the Creation of an Area of 'Freedom, Security and Justice' in the European Union (First Half of 2002), COM (2002) 261 final, 30.5.2002 178
point 3.3 178
Commission Follow-up Communication to the Green Paper on EU Consumer Protection, COM (2002) 289 final, 11.6.2002 . . . 186
point 27 186
Commission Communication, Biannual Update of the Scoreboard to Review Progress on the Creation of an Area of 'Freedom, Security and Justice' in the European Union (Second Half of 2002), COM (2002) 738 final, 16.12.2002 . . . 178
point 3.3 178
Green Paper on a European order for payment procedure and on measures to simplify and speed up small claims litigation, COM (2002) 746 final, 20.12.2002 440
2003 Commission Communication, Updating and simplifying the Community acquis, COM (2003) 71 final, 11.2.2003 299
Commission Communication, A more coherent European Contract Law—An Action Plan, COM (2003) 68 final, 12.2.2003 . . . . . 1, 21, 84, 177, 180, 186–204, 205, 207, 208, 210, 211, 217, 218, 220, 221, 223, 254, 279, 281, 342, 343, 349
point 1 . . . . 180, 196
point 3 186
point 4 187
points 4–11 187

points 4.1–4.3 201
point 4.3. 21
point 7 201
point 15 .199
points 16–24 199
points 20–21 84
points 26–33 199
point 27 200
points 28–30 200
point 32 200
points 34–35 199
point 35 200
points 36–38 199
points 37–38 200
points 39–40 . . . . .199, 200
points 41–50 199
points 43–46 200
point 46 349
point 47 200
point 48 200
point 49 . . . . 200, 349
point 50 200
point 52 . . . . .199, 200, 204, 299
points 53–54 201
point 54 203
points 56–58 201
point 59 201
point 62 . . . . 202, 203
point 63 202
point 64 202
point 66 202
point 67 202
points 69–72 201
points 70–71 299
point 73 201
point 76 201
point 77 201
point 78 . . . . .201, 211
point 80 201
points 82–85 202
points 86–87 203
point 87 203
point 88 203
points 90–91 203
point 92 . . . . 203, 204
point 93 203
point 95 203
point 98 . . . . .186, 203
point 99 186
Annex. 186, 187, 196, 205, 208, 209
point 2 192
point 2.1. 193
point 2.2. . . . . 190, 191
point 3.1.1 197
point 3.1.2 197
point 3.1.3 197
point 3.1.4 197
point 3.1.5 197
point 4.1.1 197
point 4.1.2 197
point 4.1.3 197
point 4.1.4 197
point 4.1.5 197
point 4.2.1 197
point 4.2.2 197
point 4.2.3 197
point 4.2.4 197
point 4.2.5 197
point 4.3.1 198
point 4.3.2 198
point 4.3.4 198
point 4.3.5 198
point 4.4.1 198
point 4.4.2 198
point 4.4.3 198
point 4.4.4 198
point 4.4.5 199
point 4.5.1 196
point 4.5.2 196
point 4.5.4 . . . . 197, 199
Commission Communication, Biannual Update of the Scoreboard to Review Progress on the Creation of an Area of 'Freedom, Security and Justice' in the European Union (First Half of 2003), COM (2003) 291 final, 22.5.2003 178
point 3.3. .178
Commission Communication, Biannual Update of the Scoreboard to Review Progress on the Creation of an Area of 'Freedom, Security and Justice' in the European Union (Second Half of 2003), COM (2003) 812 final, 30.12.2003 178
point 3.3. .178
2004 Commission Communication, Area of Freedom, Security and Justice: Assessment of the Tampere programme and future orientations, COM (2004) 401 final, 2.6.2004. . . . . 178, 216, 443
point 2.7. . . . . 178, 216, 443
Commission Communication, European Contract Law and the revision of the *acquis*: the way forward, COM (2004) 651 final, 11.10.2004 . . .1, 21, 91, 180, 194, 204-216, 217, 218, 220, 221, 222, 223, 224, 227, 278, 279, 299, 369, 370, 477
point 2.1. . . . . 210, 211

point 2.1.1 . . . . 211, 212
point 2.1.2 212
point 2.1.3 212
point 2.2.2 210
point 2.2.3 210
point 2.2.3.1. 211
point 2.2.3.2 211
point 2.2.3.3 211
point 2.3. . . . . 21, 210, 214, 215
point 3.1. .210
point 3.1.1 212
point 3.1.2 212
point 3.1.3 . . . . 212, 214
point 3.2. .210
point 3.2.1 212
point 3.2.2 212
point 3.2.3 212
point 3.2.4 212
Annex I 210, 214
Annex II. 210, 214
points 1-6. 215
2005 Commission Communication, Healthier, safer, more confident citizens: a Health and Consumer Protection Strategy, COM (2005) 15 final, 6.4.2005. 403
point 1.2. 403
Commission Communication, The Hague Programme: Ten Priorities for the next five years—The Partnership for European renewal in the field of Freedom, Security and Justice, COM (2005) 184 final, 10.5.2005. 218
point 2.3. .218
Annex. 218
First Annual Progress Report on European Contract Law and the Acquis Review, COM (2005) 456 final, 23.9.2005. . . .21, 216, 221-223, 224, 227, 228, 240, 272, 279, 477
point 1 221
point 2 222
point 2.1. 222
point 2.2.2 222
point 2.3. 222
point 2.6. 222
point 2.6.1 222
point 2.6.2 222
point 2.6.3 222
point 3 222
point 3.1. 223
points 3.2.1–3.2.4 223
point 3.3. 223
point 4.1. 223
point 4.2. 223
2006 Commission Communication on the implementation of Dir 1998/6/EC, COM (2006) 325 final, 21.6.2006 . . . . .404, 411
Commission Communication concerning the common position of the Council on the adoption of a Regulation of the European Parliament and of the Council creating a European order for payment procedure, COM (2006) 374 final, 4.7.2006. . . . 442
point 3.1. 442
2007 Green Paper on the Review of the Consumer Acquis, COM (2006) 744 final, 8.2.2007 . . . . . 223, 242–248
point 1 242
point 2.1. 243
point 3 . . . . 34, 242
point 3.2. 243
point 3.3. 243
point 4 243
point 4.1. . . . . 243, 244
point 4.2. . . . . 243, 244
point 4.3. 243
point 4.4. 244
point 4.5. 244
point 4.6. . . . . 243, 244
Annex I 243, 245
points 1-3. 245
point 4.3. 245
point 4.5. 245
point 4.9. 245
point 5.3. 245
point 5.4. 245
point 5.6. 245
point 6 245
Commission Communication, EU Consumer Policy Strategy 2007–2013—Empowering consumers enhancing their welfare, effectively protecting them, COM (2007) 99 final, 13.3.2007. . . . 403
Second Progress Report on the Common Frame of Reference, COM (2007) 447 final, 25.7.2007. . . . .228–229, 234, 272, 273, 279, 477
point 1 228
point 2 228
point 3.1. 228
point 3.2. 228
point 3.3. 228
point 4 228
point 5.2. 228
point 5.2.2 228
point 6 . . . . 228, 229

Commission Communication, Commission Legislative and Work Programme for 2008, COM (2007) 640 final, 23.10.2007. 248
Annex I 248
Annex II. 248
2008 Commission Communication concerning the common position of the Council on the adoption of a Directive of the European Parliament and of the Council on certain aspects of mediation in civil and commercial matters, COM (2008) 131 final, 7.3.2008 440
2009 Commission Communication, An area of freedom, security and justice serving the citizen, COM (2009) 262 final, 10.6.2009 252
point 1 252
point 3.4.2 252
Commission Communication, Justice, Freedom and Security in Europe since 2005: An Evaluation of the Hague Programme and Action Plan, COM (2009) 263 final, 10.6.2009 252
Commission Communication on the enforcement of the consumer acquis, COM (2009) 330 final, 2.7.2009 402
point 2.3. 402
2010 Commission Communication, EUROPE 2020—A strategy for smart, sustainable and inclusive growth COM (2010) final, 3.3.2010. 254
point 3.1. 254
Commission Communication, Delivering an area of freedom, security and justice for Europe's citizens—Action Plan Implementing the Stockholm Programme, COM (2010) 171 final, 20.4.2010. 253
point 4 253
Annex. 253
Green Paper on policy options for progress towards a European Contract Law for consumers and businesses, COM (2010) 348 final, 1.7.2010 . . . . . . 20–1, 38, 253–261, 262, 263, 269, 271, 272, 273, 279, 297, 342, 343, 348, 357, 363, 370, 448, 471, 475, 476, 479
point 1 254
point 2 254
point 4 . . . . .21, 255
point 4.1 (Option 1) 255
point 4.1 (Option 2) 255
point 4.1 (Option 3) 256
point 4.1 (Option 4) 21, 255, 256
point 4.1 (Option 5) 256
point 4.1 (Option 6) 256
point 4.1 (Option 7) 256
point 4.2.1 257
point 4.2.2 257
point 4.3. .257
point 4.3.1 257
point 4.3.2 257
point 4.3.3 257
point 4.3.4 257
point 5 254
section 3 254
section 3.1 254
section 3.2 255
Commission Communication, A Digital Agenda for Europe, COM (2010) 245 final/2, 26.8.2010 254
point 2.1.3 254
2011 Commission Communication, A Common European Sales Law to Facilitate Cross-Border Transactions in the Single Market, COM (2011) 636 final, 11.10.2011 . . . . .180, 263, 264
point 1 266
point 1.2. 263
point 2.1. . . . . .21, 264
point 2.2. 267
point 2.4. 264
point 3 267
2012 Commission Communication, A European Consumer Agenda—Boosting confidence and growth, COM (2012) 225 final, 22.5.2012. 403
Commission Communication, Unleashing the Potential of Cloud Computing in Europe, COM (2012) 529 final, 27.9.2012 . . . 272
point 1 272
point 3.4. 272

Opinions

1991 EESC Opinion on 'Consumer Protection and Completion of the Internal Market' [1991] OJ C339/16 408
point 1.2.2 408
1993 EESC Opinion on 'The Consumer and the Internal Market' [1993] OJ C19/22 408
point 2.1. 408

1996 CoR Opinion on the Third Three-Year Action Plan [1996] OJ C337/49 401
point 1.1.2 401
EESC Opinion on the 'Single Market and Consumer Protection: opportunities and obstacles' [1996] OJ C39/55 408
point 1.1.1 408
points 2.1.2.1-2.1.2.2 408
points 6.1.2.1–6.1.2.2 408
point 6.2.3 408
EESC Opinion on the Third Three-Year Action Plan [1996] OJ C295/64 401
point 1.3 401
point 1.6 401
1999 EESC Opinion on the 'Consumer policy action plan 1999–2001' [1999] OJ C209/1 . . . . .378, 402
point 2.2 402
point 2.4 378
2000 CoR Opinion on the Fourth Three-Year Action Plan [2000] OJ C57/74 . . . 402
point 3.4 402
point 3.6 402
point 5.3 402
point 5.7 402
2002 EESC Opinion on the 2001 Communication [2002] OJ C241/1 194–196
point 1 195
point 1.12 195
points 1.7–1.10 195
points 1.7-1.8 195
point 2.1.2 195
point 2.1.3 195
point 2.1.4 195
point 2.2.1.1 195
points 2.3–2.5 195
points 3–7 196
points 3.10–3.11 196
point 3.5 .195
points 3.6 195
points 3.7–3.8 195
2003 EESC Opinion on the Green Paper on a European order for payment procedure and on measures to simplify and speed up small claims litigation [2003] OJ C220/5 440
point 2 440
2005 EESC Opinion on 'Consumer policy post-enlargement' [2005] OJ C221/153 408
points 6.3–6.4 408
point 6.4 408
EESC Opinion on 'The European Insurance Contract' [2005] OJ C157/1 218–19
point 1.3 218
point 1.4 219
points 2.3-2.4 218
point 4 218
point 4.2 218
point 6.1 219
point 6.4 219
point 6.4.4 219
point 6.5 219
point 6.5.2.1 219
point 6.5.2.6 219
point 6.6 219
point 8.4 219
point 8.6 219
point 8.8 219
2006 CoR Opinion on the Communication, Healthier, safer, more confident citizens: a Health and Consumer Protection Strategy/Proposal for a Dec of the European Parliament and of the Council establishing a Programme of Community action in the field of Health and Consumer Protection 2007–2013 [2006] OJ C192/8 403
point 1.10 403
EESC Opinion on the 'Legal framework for consumer policy' [2006] OJ C185/71 408–409
points 1.3–1.5 408
point 1.7 408
point 2.1.1 408
point 4.6.5 408
point 6 . . . . 408, 409
EESC Opinion on the Proposal for a Dec of the European Parliament and of the Council establishing a Programme of Community action in the field of Health and Consumer Protection 2007-2013 [2006] OJ C88/1 403
point 3.1.1 403
EESC Opinion on the Proposal for a Reg of the European Parliament and of the Council establishing a European Small Claims Procedure [2006] OJ C88/1 444
point 4.4 444
EESC Opinion on the Proposal for the 'Rome I' Reg [2006] OJ C318/56 371
point 3.2.3 371

2007 EESC Opinion on the 2007 Green Paper [2007] OJ C256/27 . . . 245–246
point 1.7 . . . 246
point 4.4 . . . 246
point 5.3 . . . 246
2009 CoR Opinion on the Proposal for a Dir of the European Parliament and of the Council on consumer rights [2009] OJ C200/76 . . . 249
points 7–9 . . . 251
European Data Protection Supervisor Opinion on the Communication, An area of freedom, security and justice serving the citizen [2009] OJ C276/8 . . . 252
EESC Opinion on the Proposal for a Dir of the European Parliament and of the Council on consumer rights [2009] OJ C317/54 . . . 249
points 4.4–4.5 . . . 249
EESC Opinion on 'The proactive law approach: a further step towards better regulation at EU level' [2009] OJ C175/26 . . . 371
point 6.1.2.7 . . . 371
2010 CoR Opinion on the Communication, An area of freedom, security and justice serving the citizen [2010] OJ C79/37 . . . 252
EESC Opinion on the Communication, An area of freedom, security and justice serving the citizen [2010] OJ C128/80 . . . 252
point 4.2.4.1 . . . 252
2011 EESC Opinion on the Communication on the enforcement of the consumer acquis [2011] OJ C18/100 . . . 402
point 4.2 . . . 402
EESC Opinion on the 2010 Green Paper [2011] OJ C84/1 . . . 258
point 1.1 . . . 258
point 1.2 . . . 258
point 1.3 . . . 258
point 1.6 . . . 258
point 4.10 . . . 258
point 4.12 . . . 258
point 4.5 . . . 258
EESC Opinion on the proposals relating to matrimonial property regimes and the property consequences of registered partnerships [2011] OJ C376/87 . . . 371
point 1.4 . . . 371
point 2.1.2 . . . 371
EESC Opinion on 'The 28th regime—an alternative allowing less lawmaking at Community level' [2011] OJ C21/26 . . . 370, 371
point 3.1 . . . 375
points 3.3.1–3.3.4 . . . 371
point 3.3.3 . . . 374
point 3.5.3 . . . 371, 375
point 3.6.3 . . . 371, 375
point 4.1.1 . . . 374
2012 EESC Opinion on the CESL Proposal and Communication [2012] OJ C181/75 . . . 269–270
points 1.1–1.2 . . . 269
point 1.2 . . . 270
point 1.3 . . . 270
point 1.5 . . . 269
point 4.2 . . . 270
point 5.4.1 . . . 270
point 1.6 . . . 270
point 1.7 . . . 269
point 5.3 . . . 269
point 4.3 . . . 270
point 4.5 . . . 269
point 4.8 . . . 270

Resolutions

1975 Council Resolution of 14 April 1975 on a preliminary programme of the EEC for a consumer protection and information policy [1975] OJ C92/1 . . . 382
Recitals 1–3 . . . 383
1981 Council Resolution of 19 May 1981 on a second programme of the EEC for a consumer protection and information policy [1981] OJ C133/1 . . . 383
point 8(1) . . . 383
point 10 . . . 383
1986 Council Resolution of 23 June 1986 concerning the future orientation of the policy of the EEC for the protection and promotion of consumer interests [1986] OJ C167/1 . . . 384
1989 European Parliament Resolution of 26 May 1989 on action to bring into line the private law of the Member States [1989] OJ C158/400 . . . 156, 161, 162, 163, 165, 167, 225, 313, 469
Recital A . . . 161
Recital B . . . 161
Recital C . . . 161
Recital E . . . 161
Recital F . . . 161
Recital G . . . 161

Recital I 161
Recital J 161
point 1 161
point 2 161
point 3 161
point 4 161
1990 European Parliament Resolution of 12 July 1990 on the principle of subsidiarity [1990] OJ C231/163 ....162, 163
point 7 162
European Parliament Resolution of 21 Nov 1990 on the principle of subsidiarity [1990] OJ C324/167 162
1992 European Parliament Resolution of 11 March 1992 on the consumer protection and public health requirements to be taken into account in the completion of the internal market [1992] OJ C94/217 399
Recital A. 399
Council Resolution of 13 July 1992 on future priorities for the development of consumer protection policy [1992] OJ C186/1 399
point 1 399
point 2 399
1994 European Parliament Resolution of 6 May 1994 on the harmonization of certain sectors of the private law of the Member States [1994] OJ C205/518...............163, 165, 167, 168, 225
Recitals B–C 165
Recitals D. 165
points 1–2 165
point 4 165
1997 European Parliament Resolution of 20 Feb 1997 on the Third Three-Year Action Plan [1997] OJ C85/133 401
point 4 401
1999 Council Resolution of 19 Jan 1999 on the Consumer Dimension of the Information Society [1999] OJ C23/1 400
European Parliament Resolution of 13 April 1999 on the draft action plan of the Council and Commission on how best to implement the provisions of the Treaty of Amsterdam on an area of freedom, security and justice [1999] OJ C219/61...........174
point 21 174
point 23 174
European Parliament Resolution of 4 May 1999 on the Fourth Three-Year Action Plan [1999] OJ C279/84............... 402
point 10 402
Council Resolution of 28 June 1999 on Community consumer policy 1999 to 2001 [1999] OJ C206/1 402
point 6 402
2000 European Parliament Resolution of 16 March 2000 on the Commission's annual legislative programme for 2000 [2000] OJ C377/323 .... 170–1, 187
2001 European Parliament Resolution of 15 November 2001 on the approximation of the civil and commercial law of the Member States [2002] OJ C140E/538...... 187–191, 192, 225
Recital A. 189
Recital C 187, 189
Recital D 187, 191
Recitals E–I 189, 191
Recital J 189, 191
point 1 .... 187, 190
points 1–4 189
point 6 .... 189, 191
point 8 .... 189, 191
point 9 189
point 10 .... 190, 191
point 11 190
point 12 190
point 13 189
point 14 190
point 14(a) 190
point 14(c) 190
point 14(e)–(g)...............190
point 14(h)...................190
point 14(i)–(j)................190
point 15 190
point 16 190
point 17 .... 187, 191
point 18 191
points 20–21 191
point 28 171
2003 European Parliament Resolution of 13 March 2003 on the Communication on Consumer Policy Strategy 2002–2006 [2003] OJ C61E/401.................. 403
point 15 403
point 16 403
European Parliament Resolution of 2 September 2003 on the 2003 Action Plan [2004] OJ C76E/95..... 205–6, 207, 225

Recitals A–B. 205
point 4 206
point 6 206
points 8–9 205
point 11 206
point 12 205
point 14 206
point 15 206
point 16 206
Council Resolution of 22 Sept 2003 on 'A More Coherent European Contract Law' [2003] OJ C246/1 206–7
point II.1 206
point II.2 207
point III.1. 206
point III.2 206
point IV.1. 207
point IV.2. 207
point IV.3. 207
point V. 206
2004 European Parliament Resolution of 12 Feb 2004 on the prospects for approximating civil procedural law in the European Union [2004] OJ C97E/643 176
2006 European Parliament Resolution of 23 March 2006 on European contract law and revision of the *acquis*: the way forward [2006] OJ C292E/109. . . . . 224–6, 227
Recital A. 224, 226
Recital B. 225, 226
Recital C 226
Recitals C–D 225
Recital F. 225
Recital G 225
point 1 225
point 2 225
points 3–11 225
points 4–6 225
points 8–9 225
point 10 225
point 12 225
point 14 226
points 15–28 226
point 18 226
point 19 226
point 20 226
points 21–22 226
point 23 226
European Parliament Resolution of 7 Sept 2006 on European contract law [2006] OJ C305E/247. 226–7
Recital A. 227
points 1–2 227
points 3–4 227
point 5 227
2007 European Parliament Resolution of 4 Sept 2007 on institutional and legal implications of the use of 'soft law' instruments 232
Recital W. 232
point 13 232
European Parliament Resolution of 6 Sept 2007 on the 2007 Green Paper [2008] OJ C187E/231. . . 246–7
Recitals A–B. 246
Recital E. 246
Recitals G–H. 246
point 5 246
point 8 246
point 10 . . . . 243, 246
point 14 246
point 15 246
point 19 246
point 29 246
point 41 246
European Parliament Resolution of 12 Dec 2007 on European contract law. 232–3
Recitals A–D 232
Recital E. 232
Recital F. 232
points 2–7 232
points 7–8 233
point 9 233
2008 European Parliament Resolution of 3 Sept 2008 on the common frame of reference for European contract law [2009] OJ C295E/31 233–4
Recital A. 233
Recital C 233
point 1 233
point 2 233
point 4 233
point 5 . . . . .32, 233
point 8 233
point 10 233
points 11–12. 234
point 12 234
point 13 233
2009 European Parliament Resolution of 25 Nov 2009 on the Commission Communication, An area of freedom, security and justice serving the citizen—Stockholm Programme. 252
points 99–101 252
2010 European Parliament Resolution of 9 March 2010 on consumer protection [2010] OJ C349E/1 402
point 40 402
European Parliament Resolution of 20 May 2010 on delivering a single market to consumers and citizens [2011] OJ C161E/84 418

European Parliament Resolution of 23 Nov 2010 on civil law, commercial law, family law and private international law aspects of the Action Plan Implementing the Stockholm Programme [2012] OJ C99E/19 253
Recital G .253
point 16 253
2011 European Parliament Resolution of 6 April 2011 on a Single Market for Europeans [2012] OJ C296E/59 418
European Parliament Resolution of 8 June 2011 on the 2010 Green Paper [2012] OJ C380E/59 . . . . .21, 258–9
Recital A 21, 258
Recitals B, E, H, J, L, M, Q 258
Recitals D, I, K, O, P 258
Recitals G, N 258
Recital T .259
point 1 . . . . .21, 258
point 3 . . . . .21, 258
point 5 259
points 7–8 259
point 9 259
point 11 259
point 13 259
point 14 259
point 19 259
point 20 259
points 23–25 259
point 25 259
point 26 259
point 28 259
point 30 259
points 31–36 259
point 41 259
2014 European Parliament Legislative Resolution of 26 Feb 2014 on the CESL Proposal 270

Presidency Conclusions and Programmes

1992 Presidency Conclusions, Edinburgh European Council, 11–12 Dec 1992 . . . . .284, 302, 305, 307
Annex I
point I(1)-(2) 284
point 2(i) 286
point 2(iii) 296
point II(ii) 302
point iv 307
point v 307
point vi 307
1998 Presidency Conclusions, Cardiff European Council, 14–15 June 1998 173
Presidency Conclusions, Vienna European Council, 11–12 Dec 1998 173
1999 Council and Commission Action Plan on How Best to Implement the Provisions of the Treaty of Amsterdam on an Area of Freedom Security and Justice [1999] OJ C19/1 173–175
points 6–8 173
points 9–14 173
point 15 173
point 16 173
point 39 . . . . 173, 174, 175, 176
point 40 174
point 41 174
point 41(d) 174
point 41(f) 174
Presidency Conclusions, Tampere European Council, 15–16 Oct 1999 . . . . 1, 175-8, 192, 421, 437
first para .175
second para 175
point 5 175
point 28 175
points 29–32 175
point 33 175
points 35–36 175
point 38 175
point 39 . . . . 175, 176, 177, 179, 192, 217, 421
2000 Presidency Conclusions, Lisbon European Council, 23–24 March 2000 216
2001 Presidency Conclusions, Laeken European Council, 14–15 Dec 2001 . . . . 6, 187, 280
Annex I: Laeken Declaration on the Future of the European Union 6, 280, 281, 363
Annex IV .187
2004 Presidency Conclusions, Brussels European Council, 4–5 Nov 2004 . . .217
Annex I ('The Hague Programme: Strengthening Freedom, Security and Justice in the European Union') 217–8, 235, 252, 253, 422, 437
point 3.4.4 . . . . 217, 218
2005 Council and Commission Action Plan implementing the Hague Programme on strengthening freedom, security and justice in the European Union [2005] OJ C198/1 . . .218
2007 Presidency Conclusions, Brussels European Council, 21–22 June 2007 252
point 39 252

2008 Presidency Conclusions, Brussels European Council, 19–20 June 2008 252
point 20 252
2009 Presidency Conclusions, Brussels European Council, 10–11 Dec 2009 252
The Stockholm Programme—An open and secure Europe serving and protecting citizens. 252–3, 254, 422, 437
point 3.4. .252
point 3.4.4 253

European Convention Documents

Working Groups

Final Report of Working Group V on Complementary Competencies (CONV 375/1/02REV1) 309, 388
Commission Note on 'Delimitation of powers: a matter of scale of intervention', Working Group V on Complementary Competencies, Working Document 4 . . . .293, 309
Mandate of the Working Group on Complementary Competencies (CONV 75/02) 388
Summary of meeting on 7 Oct 2002 (CONV 347/02) 388
Final Report of Working Group IX on Simplification (CONV 424/02) .467, 473
Final Report of Working Group X on Freedom, Security and Justice (CONV 426/02) 427, 431
Exposé of A Borrás, Working Group X Working Document 08 427
Mandate of Working Group X 'Freedom, Security and Justice' (CONV 258/02) 427
Note on the plenary meeting—Brussels, 6–7 June 2002 (CONV 97/02) 427
Summary of meeting on 16 Sept 2002 (CONV 274/02) 427
Summary of proposed amendments regarding the area of freedom, security and justice (CONV 644/1/03REV1). 427
Final Report of Working Group XI on Social Europe (COV 516/1/03 REV1) 472, 473

Other Documents

Contribution of M Barnier and A Vitorino on the 'Community method' (CONV 231/02 CONTRIB 80) 467
Contribution of A Duff, 'Do we really need enhanced cooperation?' (CONV 759/03 CONTRIB 336) 458
Contribution of J Meyer (CONV 447/02 CONTRIB 164) 429
Contribution of E Teufel and W Senff, 'German Bundesrat Resolution 430
Having Regard to the Themes of the Convention on the future of the European Union'
Praesidium Document on enhanced cooperation (CONV 723/03). 462
Proposals by the CDU and CSU for a European Constitutional Treaty (CONV 616/03) 428
Proposed amendments concerning enhanced cooperation: draft Articles for Part One (CONV 779/03) 456
Proposed amendments concerning enhanced cooperation: draft Articles for Part Three (CONV 791/03) 456
Suggestion for amendment of Art 14a(neu) by J Fischer 428–429
Suggestion for amendment of Art 14bis by E Teufel 430
Suggestion for amendment of Art 32b(2) (Enhanced cooperation) by M Frendo. 462
Suggestion for amendment of Art III-127 by L Hjelm-Wallén, S-O Petersson, and S Lekberg 388–389

INTERNATIONAL CONVENTIONS

Conventions Concluded Among EU Member States

1968 Brussels Convention on jurisdiction and the enforcement of judgments in civil and commercial matters 164, 423, 467
1980 Rome Convention on the law applicable to contractual obligations. 164, 181, 189, 467

Other International Conventions

1950 European Convention for the Protection of Human Rights and Fundamental Freedoms . . . 19, 39, 40, 362
1980 United Nations Convention on Contracts for the International Sale of Goods. 18, 151, 181, 259, 468

NATIONAL DOCUMENTS

UK

Bills of Exchange Act 112
Sale of Goods Act. 113

USA
Constitution 9, 14, 94, 98, 100, 111, 128, 138, 139, 142, 286, 296, 419
Art I, s 8, cl 3 . . . . 9, 100, 358–360, 419
Art I, s 8, cl 14 9
Art II, s 2, cl 2. 137
Art III, s 2, cl 2. 95
Art VI, cl 2. 100–101
Tenth Amendment. 286, 291
Consumer Credit Protection Act 139, 140
15 USC s 1666 140
15 USC s 1667c 140
15 USC s 1667e 140
15 USC s 1675 140
15 USC s 1692n 140
15 USC s 1692o 140
15 USC s 2304 141
18 USC s 891 140
Federal Trade Commission Door to Door Sales Rule 141
16 CFR s 429.1. .141
16 CFR s 429.2. .141
Judiciary Act 1789 s 34 (Rules of Decision Act) 95, 96
Magnuson-Moss Warranty-Federal Trade Commission Improvement Act 141
Patient Protection and Affordable Care Act. 359
Uniform Bills of Lading Act. 113, 114, 115
Uniform Chattel Mortgage Act 113
Uniform Commercial Code. 3, 5, 10, 24, 40, 41, 93, 104, 105, 114, 115, 124–41, 142, 151, 157, 198, 233, 450, 471, 474, 475, 476, 481, 483
Art 1. . . . . .125, 126
s 1-103(a)(1)-(2) 126
s 1-103(a)(3) 126
Art 2. . . . . .125, 139
Art 2A 125, 139
Art 3. . . . . .125, 139
Art 4. . . . . .125, 139
Art 4A 125, 139
Art 5. 125
Art 6. 125
Art 7. 125
Art 8. 125
Art 9. . . . . .125, 139
Art 10. 125
Art 11. 125
Uniform Conditional Sales Act 113, 114
Uniform Consumer Credit Code. 139, 140
Uniform Negotiable Instruments Act. 112, 113, 114
Uniform Sales Act 113, 114, 115, 128, 130, 131
Uniform Stock Transfer Act. 113
Uniform Trust Receipts Act. 113, 114
Uniform Warehouse Receipts Act. 113, 114, 115

Introduction

Setting of the Problem

At present, European contract law embodies one of the most far-reaching and controversial debates in the European Union (EU). As the story is commonly told, with the work of several prominent academic projects, certain European Parliament resolutions, and the European Council meeting at Tampere serving as catalysts, the Commission promulgated the 2001 Communication on European contract law[1], which placed this subject on the EU's political agenda. This Communication has been followed by a steady stream of documents issued by the Commission, as well as other Union institutions and bodies, which continue to refine the EU's role in European contract law.[2] Recent activities emanating from these documents—such as the Draft Common Frame of Reference (DCFR),[3] the Consumer Rights Directive,[4] and the proposal for a Regulation on a Common European Sales Law (proposed CESL)[5]—have only served to intensify the discussion of the future path of contract law at the European level. Nevertheless, detailed examination of the constitutional dimensions of European contract law, or its so-called constitutionality, continues to lag behind. In effect, the debate about European contract law has proceeded in somewhat of a 'backwards' fashion: while the plans and the activities envisaged for 'the way forward'[6] for European contract law progress, in-depth assessment of the EU's competence in this context remains largely unattended to, instead of the other way around.

This is certainly not to say that there has been no attention paid to the constitutional dimensions of European contract law or European private law generally.[7] In fact, over a decade ago, in 1997, an international conference was convened at Scheveningen in the Netherlands, at the bequest of the then Dutch Presidency of the Council, during which the morning session was devoted to the question of whether there was a proper legal basis for a European civil code.[8] Likewise, both before and after this conference,

[1] Commission Communication on European Contract Law, COM (2001) 398 final, 11.7.2001 (2001 Communication).

[2] See generally Part Two.

[3] C von Bar and E Clive (eds), *Principles, Definitions and Model Rules of European Private Law—Draft Common Frame of Reference (DCFR)*, full edn (Sellier, 2009/Oxford Univ Press, 2010). See Chapter 6, § 6.2.3.

[4] Dir 2011/83/EU of the European Parliament and of the Council of 25 Oct 2011 on consumer rights, amending Council Dir 93/13/EEC and Dir 99/44/EC of the European Parliament and of the Council and repealing Council Dir 85/577/EEC and Dir 97/7/EC of the European Parliament and of the Council, [2011] OJ L304/64 (Consumer Rights Directive).

[5] Proposal for a Regulation of the European Parliament and of the Council on a Common European Sales Law, COM (2011) 635 final, 11.10.2011 (proposed CESL). See Chapter 6, § 6.4.4.

[6] This is taken from the title of the Commission Communication, European Contract Law and the revision of the *acquis*: the way forward, COM (2004) 651 final, 11.10.2004.

[7] For discussion of the relationship between European contract law and European private law, see Chapter 1, § 1.2.2.

[8] For a record of the conference papers, see (1997) 5 *ERPL* 455. See also 'Editorial: European Private Law between Utopia and Early Reality' (1997) 4 *MJ* 1.

the extent of the EU's competence in contract law and other fields of private law has attracted a range of opinions from scholars in publications too numerous to mention, perhaps explaining the remark by one commentator that '[m]uch ink has already been poured on the question of legal competence for [Union] measures in this field'.[9] Still, significant problems exist in the treatment of this subject. In particular, three stand out.

First, many crucial questions concerning the limits and exercise of Union competence in European contract law have yet to be fully addressed. It is usually the case that certain Treaty provisions are singled out for analysis, the most prominent candidates being Articles 114, 115, 169, 81, and 352 TFEU. However, some of these provisions, such as Articles 169 and 81 TFEU concerning the Union's competence in consumer protection and judicial cooperation in civil matters, respectively, are often discarded without cognizance of the extent to which they are interwoven in the constitutional assessment of European contract law. For other provisions, the *limits* of Union competence are read restrictively without engagement with the evolution of the relevant case law, as illustrated by the controversy concerning Article 114 TFEU. Moreover, only exceptionally does one find detailed discussion of the *linkages* between these Treaty provisions, whether it is confronting the residual scope of Article 115 TFEU vis-à-vis Article 114 TFEU, the symbiotic relationship between Articles 114 and 169 TFEU, the boundary line between Articles 114 and 352 TFEU, or the extent to which some of these provisions may be used together. As a related point, over the years, various alternative or complementary routes to Union action in contract law have been contemplated in the debate, such as enhanced cooperation, an intergovernmental treaty, and the Open Method of Coordination (OMC), without much detailed inquiry as to their constitutionality and suitability in relation to European contract law.

For that matter, much of the focus has been placed on the *existence* of Union competence, ie the legal basis requirement, and not so much on the *exercise* of Union competence, in terms of the roles played by the principles of subsidiarity, proportionality, and sincere cooperation in this context. Certainly, the principles of subsidiarity and proportionality readily appear in the discourse, often as arguments opposing far-reaching Union action in contract law (and other fields of private law). Yet, generally speaking, there is not much deep investigation as to the operation of these two principles, as well as the principle of sincere cooperation, in connection with the aforementioned Treaty provisions or the alternative and complementary routes to Union action put forward in the debate. Surely, this is one area in which there may never be unanimous agreement, and for certain issues, it is only with recent case law that answers have started to emerge. Be that as it may, until matters concerning the existence and exercise of Union competence are thoroughly explored, the debate about the constitutionality of European contract law continues to be as elusive as ever.

Secondly, there is no standardized semantic and legal framework governing the constitutional assessment of European contract law, which makes delving into this topic something of a Herculean task. Semantically, there are no universal definitions for the prevalent terms used in the debate about European contract law. Instead, many terms are used in different ways or have the potential to inject particular nuances and biases into the discussion, which makes even talking about the constitutional dimensions of European contract law extremely difficult. Legally, there is no template upon which to frame the analysis of the relevant Treaty provisions or alternative and complementary

[9] S Swann, 'Elective European Contract Law. A Possible Response to the Action Plan' in M Meli and MR Maugeri (eds), *L'Armonizzazione Del Diritto Privato Europeo—Il Piano D'Azione 2003* (Giuffrè Editore, 2004) 23, 40.

routes to Union action mooted in the debate. Each of the Treaty provisions under discussion—Articles 114, 115, 169, 81, and 352 TFEU—underpins a distinct chronology in the Treaty framework and enlivens its own set of controversies, which to a great extent have not yet been explicitly answered in the case law or by the changes brought about by the Lisbon Treaty.[10] Likewise, several alternative and complementary routes to a European contract law instrument are situated within broader topics that generate a complex and controversial debate of their own apart from that concerning European contract law, as illustrated by the discussion of enhanced cooperation vis-à-vis 'flexibility' and 'differentiation' in the EU or the OMC vis-à-vis the so-called 'new modes of governance'. Most importantly, the 'institutional record' of constitutionality in the documents disseminated by the Union institutions in this setting is largely unexplored, with the result that it remains unclear to what extent the discussion of Union competence has played a role in the developments underpinning European contract law (and European private law generally) at the European level.

Thirdly, despite the fact that references to the United States (US) have steadily crept into the debate about European contract law,[11] in-depth comparative reflection with the EU in this context is sorely lacking. Generally, such references have either been used in a positive sense as a source for potential models for use in the debate about European contract law—usually involving Restatements, uniform and model laws, and the Uniform Commercial Code (UCC)—or in a negative sense, as part of arguments against far-reaching action in contract law and other fields of private law at the European level by pointing to the American 'internal market' in which private law is regulated for the most part at the state level without the need for any federal contract or commercial law code. Yet, there does not seem to be much realization of the numerous attempts to unify areas of state contract law at the federal level and the extent to which these attempts have coloured the American contract law landscape through to the present day. In addition, in seeking to transplant American techniques to the EU, there does not seem to be much appreciation of the problems resulting from their use in the US and of the dangers, let alone terminological confusion, associated with their application to European contract law.

These problems are surely not the only ones plaguing the constitutional assessment of European contract law, but they have potentially devastating consequences for the developments taking place in this setting. They leave the legality of present and future European contract law initiatives uncertain. They affect the identification of the most appropriate solutions to the problems that the debate about European contract law is supposed to solve. They may also lead to misperceptions about the scope of Union competence and the viability of supposed alternatives to Union action in contract law, which have the potential to put the debate about European contract law on the wrong path. As will be seen, matters relating to the EU's constitutional competence have already started to play a part in steering the course of the activities envisaged for European contract law and the decisions taken at the European level. Union competence is therefore not the only element in the debate about European contract law, but it is an important one that permeates the others.

[10] See, eg, L Miller, 'European contract law after Lisbon' in D Ashiagbor et al (eds), *The European Union After the Treaty of Lisbon* (Cambridge Univ Press, 2012) 227.

[11] This includes scholarly literature and institutional documents issued in the debate, as discussed in Part Two. Although this book does not discount that there are various differences between the EU and the US in this setting, references to the US have become a part of the debate itself, which indicates the need for such comparative reflection.

Objective and Structure

In view of the foregoing problems, the objective of this book is to provide a cohesive assessment of the constitutional dimensions of European contract law by examining the scope of certain prominent Treaty provisions in the debate, namely Articles 114, 115, 169, 81, and 352 TFEU, which potentially confer competence on the Union to adopt a comprehensive instrument of substantive contract law, on the one hand, and the viability of certain alternative and complementary routes to the adoption of such an instrument contemplated in the debate, on the other. This will be done with a *primary focus* placed on the analysis of the limits of, and the linkages between, these Treaty provisions and their interplay with the principles of subsidiarity, proportionality, and sincere cooperation, as well as a *secondary focus* as to how comparative analysis with the US may contribute to the constitutional assessment of European contract law, with the overarching aim that this book may be of practical value to lawmakers, practitioners, and scholars in connection with the initiatives envisaged in the debate about European contract law for the foreseeable future.

In line with this objective, this book is divided into three interlocking parts. Part One comprises three chapters (Chapters 1–3), which concern the *context* for the debate about European contract law in the EU and comparative reflection with the US. Chapter 1 sets forth the constitutional framing of European contract law, with a view to clarifying the meanings of the various terms used in the debate and elucidating a specific set of Union contract law measures—referred to as the 'hard core' of the EU contract law *acquis*—which underpin certain perennial themes relating to the role and competence wielded by the Union legislature in the field of contract law. Chapter 2 explores the three distinct roles played by the Court of Justice in European contract law, which include the Court's interpretation of these Union contract law measures, the Court's formulation of Union judge-made rules of contract law, and the increasing recourse by the Advocates General to comparative European contract law materials. Chapter 3 turns to the US and focuses on four major strands of the American contract law framework—American 'federal common law', uniform and model laws, Restatements, and the UCC—to facilitate understanding of their meaning, the problems associated with their usage, and the extent to which attempts to approximate contract law at the federal level were part of their emergence and development.

Part Two concerns the *debate* about European contract law. It encompasses three chapters (Chapters 4–6), which are roughly divided according to the chronological sequence of events through which this debate has evolved at the European level. Chapter 4 details the beginnings of the debate through the work of certain academic projects, the European Parliament's early resolutions, and the European Council meeting in Tampere. Chapter 5 evaluates the Commission's three seminal Communications on European contract law and the responses from the other Union institutions and stakeholder groups. Chapter 6 outlines the present path of the debate about European contract law, with particular regard to activities relating to the CFR, the Consumer Rights Directive, and the proposed CESL.

Part Three contains five chapters (Chapters 7–11), which concern the *constitutionality* of European contract law. Chapter 7 provides an overview of the constitutional parameters governing Union competence in contract law in order to evaluate several reasons advanced to explain the neglect of detailed discussion of constitutionality at the European level, to delineate the overarching Treaty framework, and to elucidate the roles played by the principles of subsidiarity, proportionality, and sincere cooperation in this setting. Chapter 8 examines the scope of Union competence under Articles 114, 115, and 352 TFEU for the adoption of a European contract law instrument, optional or otherwise, to achieve the Union's internal market objectives. Chapter 9 explores the scope of Union competence under Article 169 TFEU in the field of consumer protection and the linkage with Articles 114 and 352 TFEU as far as the adoption of a European contract law instrument including consumer contract law, in all or in part, is concerned. Chapter 10 analyses the scope of Union competence under Article 81 TFEU concerning judicial cooperation in civil matters and the linkage with Articles 114 and 352 TFEU in connection with the adoption of a European contract law instrument. Chapter 11 investigates the viability of several alternative and complementary routes to the adoption of a European contract law instrument contemplated in the debate, which include enhanced cooperation, an intergovernmental treaty, and certain so-called 'softer' models comprising the OMC, certain American techniques (Restatements, uniform and model laws, and the UCC), and the CFR. This is followed by the general conclusions of this book.

Together, these three parts comprise the constitutional foundations of European contract law. Part One lays the 'grounding' for the discussion of the debate about European contract law and the contract law framework in the US, both semantically in terms of the terminology used in each setting and legally in terms of providing the template for understanding the approach taken to matters of contract law in the European and American legal orders. Part Two illuminates the 'institutional record' of constitutionality in the various documents issued by the Union institutions and bodies and thus contains the 'meat' for understanding the ways in which Articles 114, 115, 169, 81, and 352 TFEU, along with certain potential alternative and complementary routes, have, explicitly and implicitly, come into play. Building on these layers, Part Three provides detailed study of the extent to which the aforementioned Treaty provisions may constitute proper legal bases for the adoption of a European contract law instrument and the extent to which certain alternative and complementary routes to such an instrument may be resorted to.

Following from this three-part structure, however, there are certain caveats placed on the analysis. First, as a general matter, the presentation of the material is not always linear and sometimes jumps back and forth in time. This is in part the result of the way in which the debate about European contract law has developed at the European level. This is also to some extent the outcome of the three-part structure of this book, in the sense that issues covered in one chapter become relevant later on, after other chapters have been presented. In the present author's view, this cannot be avoided on account of the need to place certain chapters in the relevant parts in order to construct a sound framework for the discussion. Moreover, with regard to the US, it should not be missed that until this book, the extent to which attempts to approximate areas of private law, including contract law, at the federal level had largely been concealed amidst historical documents and scattered literature over the years, which meant that the true picture was relatively unknown even to American audiences. In order to provide a cohesive record of such attempts, it is necessary to discuss the emergence and development of certain components comprising the American contract law framework in substantial detail. Finally, as already mentioned, Part Two aims to set forth very much for the first time a detailed account of the 'institutional record' of constitutionality at the European level, which until now was mostly hidden beneath the various documents issued in the debate. This explains why, in relevant chapters, the discussion may be considered descriptive at times. The presentation of the Union institutions' engagement with constitutionality is done with a view to laying the groundwork for the analysis of the relevant Treaty provisions that follows.

Scope and Potential Challenges

Given the importance of the constitutionality of European contract law, it may be wondered why this subject has not yet occupied a premier place in the debate. The answer to this question alludes to three main challenges posed by this subject, which in turn draw out the scope and limitations of this book. At least in part, these challenges may also help to explain why issues surrounding the constitutionality of European contract law have been bypassed in the literature and why the Union institutions have been reluctant to delve deeply into this subject so far.[12]

First, there is *the evolving nature of the debate about European contract law and the overarching Treaty framework*. The constitutional assessment of European contract law has been situated within two ever-changing constellations. On the one hand, the debate about European contract law is essentially a 'moving target', since its momentum and the constitutional issues underlying it are constantly morphing over time. As aptly described by one jurist:

> Anyone taking it up with the intention or hope of keeping up with the pace of legal policy development and remaining on top of the current stage of academic debate is letting themselves in for a race in which he will inevitably feel like the unfortunate hare which, despite all its efforts, kept on arriving too late: something else will have changed or articles whose relevance has to be assessed first will have appeared.[13]

As a result, this debate does not follow one single path, but instead meanders down several roads, all the while raising unprecedented constitutional issues in its wake and whose endpoint has not yet been determined. The research into the constitutionality of European contract law therefore suffers from the limitation that it does not have the benefit of hindsight and instead is captured by the ongoing activities taking place in European contract law as they occur.

On the other hand, the overarching Treaty framework in which the constitutional inquiry is situated has also evolved considerably during the years in which the debate about European contract law has unfolded at the European level. Over the past decade, the former Treaty framework comprising the EU and EC Treaties[14] has been the subject of major institutional reform. As set into motion by the Laeken Declaration,[15]

[12] See Chapter 7, § 7.2.

[13] C Joerges, *On the Legitimacy of Europeanising Private Law: Considerations on a Law of Justi(ce)-fication (Justum Facere) for the EU Multi-level System* (METRO, 2003) 1–2 (reprinted in A Hartkamp et al (eds), *Towards a European Civil Code*, 3rd rev and expanded edn (Kluwer/Ars Aequi Libri, 2004) 159). Though referring to European private law generally, such remarks may be considered to apply equally to European contract law. For similar remarks of frustration, see, eg, T Wilhelmsson, 'The Ethical Pluralism of Late Modern Europe and Codification of European Contract Law' in J Smits (ed), *The Need for a European Contract Law—Empirical and Legal Perspectives* (Europa, 2005) 121, 123.

[14] Consolidated versions of the Treaty on European Union (EU Treaty), [2006] OJ C321E/5, and the Treaty establishing the European Community (EC Treaty), [2006] OJ C321E/37. To avoid confusion, the provisions of the former EU Treaty are denoted by EU, whereas those of the EU Treaty as amended by the Lisbon Treaty are denoted by TEU.

[15] Presidency Conclusions, Laeken European Council, 14–15 Dec 2001, Annex I: Laeken Declaration on the Future of the European Union, [2001] 12 EU Bulletin, point I.27 (Laeken Declaration).

the work of the European Convention paved the way for the failed Draft Treaty establishing a Constitution for Europe (Draft Constitutional Treaty[16]) and ultimately the Lisbon Treaty,[17] which amended the EU Treaty (TEU) and the EC Treaty, renamed the Treaty on the Functioning of the European Union (TFEU). Consequently, the discussion of the Union's competence in European contract law has had to straddle these institutional developments, and with the entry into force of the Lisbon Treaty on 1 December 2009, has had to contend with the replacement of the relevant provisions of the EU and EC Treaties cited in the debate (as well as the references to the European Community, now superseded by the Union) and the changes brought about by the Lisbon Treaty in relation to these provisions and the constitutional framework of the EU generally.[18]

Together, these points have significant implications for the scope of this book. Despite the fact that the TEU and the TFEU now constitute the governing Treaty framework, this book includes discussion of the relevant provisions of the former EU and EC Treaties, the work of the European Convention, and the failed Draft Constitutional Treaty, since they have left an indelible imprint on the constitutionality of European contract law.[19]

Moreover, although the debate about European contract law is likely to continue for the foreseeable future, activities at the European level have reached a crucial culmination stage with the proposed CESL, which alongside the adoption of the Consumer Rights Directive and the completion of the DCFR constitute an important basis from which to evaluate the EU's competence in this setting. The fact that the proposed CESL and the final or political version of the CFR have not yet been adopted and that further initiatives may still be in the pipeline is not fatal to the analysis because it works within the frame of the debate as it has developed thus far and is not contingent on the political choices to be made. In line with its overarching aim, this book seeks to provide the constitutional groundwork for the initiatives envisaged for European contract law so as to be of practical value when the definitive choices are made. As already noted, matters relating to Union competence have started to have an impact on the course of the activities contemplated at the European level, with the result that laying such groundwork would appear to be of the utmost importance, especially under circumstances in which these initiatives and potentially others are undergoing discussion and formulation at the European level. This explains why the analysis is framed broadly to cover the adoption of a comprehensive instrument encompassing contract law rules relating to commercial and consumer transactions in a general sense, whether optional or otherwise, thereby including but not necessarily being limited to the proposed CESL, as well as several potential alternative or complementary routes to such an instrument.[20]

[16] Draft Treaty establishing a Constitution for Europe, [2004] OJ C310/1. There was a previous version of this Treaty promulgated in 2003. See Chapter 7, § 7.3.

[17] Treaty of Lisbon amending the Treaty on European Union and the Treaty establishing the European Community, [2007] OJ C306/1; consolidated versions of the Treaty on European Union (TEU), [2012] OJ C326/13, and the Treaty on the Functioning of the European Union (TFEU), [2012] OJ C326/47.

[18] Where the discussion pertains to matters that took place before the entry into force of the Lisbon Treaty, reference is made to the EU or Union in place of or alongside that of the former EC or Community, as well as to the numbering of the relevant Treaty provisions under the former and present Treaty frameworks. For brevity's sake, quoted passages referring to the former Community or EC Treaty may be replaced by the Union or TFEU in brackets.

[19] See Chapter 7, § 7.3.

[20] For further discussion of the concept of a 'comprehensive' instrument of contract law, see Chapter 1, § 1.2.2.1.

Thus, apart from the field of consumer contract law, which is an inherent feature of the debate itself, this book excludes detailed consideration of the constitutionality of possible Union instruments concerning specific types of contracts, such as insurance contracts, which manifest special considerations and individualized treatment in the debate. This is so even though the discussion of insurance contracts intersects to some extent with the constitutional assessment of European contract law with particular regard to optional instruments and thus cannot be left out altogether.

Secondly, there is the *breadth of the debate about European contract law and the constitutional inquiry*. As already alluded to, the literature on European contract law is massive and has become something of a 'cottage industry' in itself.[21] Taking account of the increasing array of books and journals in several Union languages, this makes for superhuman efforts to keep track of all of the commentary bearing on the constitutionality of European contract law. Furthermore, the debate is considerably broader than the label 'European contract law' would seem to indicate. As will be seen in the coming chapters, the debate about European contract law emanated from, and still remains entangled with, a larger debate about European private law and a so-called 'European civil code'.[22] As a result, the constitutional assessment of European contract law inevitably bumps up against questions concerning the Union's competence to take far-reaching action in other areas of private law beyond contract law. Through this linkage, such assessment may also become intertwined within a broad array of political, economic, cultural, and social arguments relating to the role to be played by a comprehensive European private or contract law instrument,[23] for example, whether it is to make the internal market function better or whether it represents deeper social, cultural, or political values.[24] This makes it quite easy for everything to blur together, and as a result, the objectives underlying the debate about European contract law (and European private law generally) can become linked to the discussion of Union competence. This may explain, for instance, why the potential impact of European contract law for Union citizenship and European 'social justice' have become subsumed within the discussion of legal basis,[25] or why, given the implications heralded by European contract law for the future course of comparative legal research and education, some scholars have contemplated the Treaty provisions on research and development as potential legal bases for Union action in this setting.[26]

[21] As with European private law generally: see, eg, JM Smits, 'European private law and the comparative method' in C Twigg-Flesner (ed), *The Cambridge Companion to European Union Private Law* (Cambridge Univ Press, 2010) 33.

[22] See Chapter 1, § 1.2.3.4.

[23] For a summary of the various arguments, see, eg, D Mazeaud, 'Faut-il avoir peur d'un droit européen des contrats?' in *De tous horizons: Mélanges Xavier Blanc-Jouvan* (Société de législation comparée, 2005) 309; S Weatherill, 'Why Object to the Harmonization of Private Law by the EC?' (2004) 12 *ERPL* 633.

[24] See T Wilhelmsson, 'The Legal, the Cultural, and the Political—Conclusions from Different Perspectives on Harmonisation of European Contract Law' (2002) 13 *EBLR* 541.

[25] See, eg, MW Hesselink, 'European Contract Law: A Matter of Consumer Protection, Citizenship, or Justice?' (2007) 15 *ERPL* 323 (reprinted in S Grundmann (ed), *Constitutional Values and European Contract Law* (Kluwer, 2008) 241); L Moccia, 'Du "marché" à la "citoyenneté": à la recherche d'un droit privé européen durable et de sa base juridique' (2004) *RIDC* 291; and more recently, L Moccia, 'European Law: From "Market" to "Citizenship"' in L Moccia (ed), *The Making of European Private Law: Why, How, What, Who* (Sellier, 2013) 47; S Nadaud, *Codifier le droit civil européen* (Larcier, 2008) 223–225.

[26] See, eg, J Ziller, 'The Legitimacy of the Codification of Contract Law in View of the Allocation of Competences between the European Union and its Member States' in MW Hesselink (ed), *The Politics of a European Civil Code* (Kluwer, 2006) 89, 112–113 (rejecting such provisions).

It is not disputed that the various political, economic, social, and cultural arguments have an important role in the debate, and it cannot be foreclosed that other Treaty provisions may eventually become relevant in relation to the constitutional dimensions of European contract law. Nonetheless, the scope of this book is primarily limited to the analysis of the extent of the Union's (internal[27]) competence under Articles 114, 115, 169, 81, and 352 TFEU.[28] This is because, as illustrated in Part Two, these five Treaty provisions have been the predominant focus of the institutional documents and scholarly literature on European contract law thus far. For the same reason, although the extent to which other fields of private law will be included in the initiatives envisaged at the European level remains to be seen, the scope of this book is limited to the field of contract law in line with the way in which the debate has unfolded at the European level, although it should not be discounted that this book may be of value to the discourse on Union competence in other fields of private law. In addition, given the growing volume of literature on European contract and private law, this book does not claim to be exhaustive. It is based on a broad, representative selection of scholarly literature, institutional documents, Treaty materials, and case law of the Union courts that is considered most relevant for a cohesive assessment of the constitutional foundations of European contract law.

Finally, there is the *wide expanse for comparative reflection between the EU and the US* in connection with the debate about European contract law. Inside the constitutional inquiry, the determination of the extent of the Union's competence under the abovementioned Treaty provisions inevitably invites inquiry into comparable provisions of the US Constitution, such as the Interstate Commerce Clause[29] in relation to Article 114 TFEU or the Necessary and Proper Clause[30] in relation to Article 352 TFEU, both of which command an extensive body of literature and jurisprudence of the US Supreme Court. Outside the constitutional inquiry, there are several subjects related to the debate about European contract law that lend themselves to fruitful reflection with the US.[31] So far, these subjects generally appear to fall into three baskets or categories. First, there are matters related to the *institutional framework* needed to support the ongoing activities in European contract law (and European private law generally), for example, the creation of the European Law Institute (ELI), which beckons analogy to the American Law Institute (ALI),[32] or the reform of the EU judicial architecture,

[27] As part of the evolving discourse on European contract and private law, attention has been placed on external aspects of the Union's competence in this setting, the detailed discussion of which also exceeds the scope of this book. See, eg, J Wouters, 'Private Law, Global Governance and the European Union' in ALM Keirse and MBM Loos (eds), *Alternative Ways to Ius Commune—The Europeanisation of Private Law* (Intersentia, 2012) 21, 32.

[28] To a lesser extent, there is also discussion of provisions related thereto, eg, the free movement provisions in connection with Art 114 TFEU: see Chapter 8, § 8.3.2.2.

[29] US Constitution, Art I, § 8, cl 3 (providing in relevant part that Congress 'shall have Power . . . [t]o regulate commerce . . . among the several States').

[30] US Constitution, Art I, § 8, cl 14 (providing that Congress 'shall have Power . . . [t]o make all Laws which shall be necessary and proper for carrying into Execution the foregoing Powers, and all other Powers vested by this Constitution in the Government of the United States, or in any Department or Officer thereof').

[31] Within the European setting, these issues are often related to the 'legitimacy' of Union action in European contract law and European private law generally. See further Chapter 1, § 1.2.1.

[32] The European Law Institute (ELI) was founded on 1 June 2011 at the Inaugural Congress held in Paris: see in particular the presentation given there by Professor George Bermann, providing salient reflections on the functioning of the two organizations (on file with author). See also eg, L Liebman, 'The American Law Institute: a model for the new Europe?' in F Cafaggi and H Muir-Watt (eds), *Making European Private Law: Governance Design* (Edward Elgar, 2008) 209; CU Schmid, 'Legitimacy Conditions for a European Civil Code' (2001) 8 *MJ* 277, 291–294. Although previously removed from the EU's agenda (see Chapter 5, § 5.3.1.1), the creation of the ELI was revisited in recent

which has included mention of the American system of federal courts.[33] Secondly, the *substance* of the contract law rules formulated by academic projects associated with European contract law or in instruments to be adopted at the European level, as in the case of the proposed CESL, may merit discussion of the approach taken in the US in relevant instruments, such as the UCC. Thirdly, issues and concerns related to the *process* by which rules of contract law and other fields of private law are formulated, especially in terms of the role played by these academic projects and the participation of various interested parties in the debate about European contract and private law, may direct attention to the American scholarship on the decision-making processes of the so-called 'private legislatures' of the ALI and the National Conference of Commissioners on Uniform State Laws.[34]

The detailed discussion of these subjects would not only make this book considerably longer in length, but also would be likely to take the constitutional inquiry off-track. Therefore, the scope of this book is limited to those aspects drawn from the American setting that, in the present author's view, make a salient contribution to the constitutional assessment of European contract law. This means that all such provisions of the US constitutional framework comparable to those relevant to the debate about European contract law cannot be treated in depth. This also means that this book must exclude discussion of the abovementioned topics falling outside the confines of constitutional inquiry; yet, as will be seen, they are interrelated to some extent with the discussion of the debate about European contract law and the American contract law framework, with the result that this book may at least provide a 'launching pad' for further development in the literature.

In sum, given all of the problems and challenges underlying the constitutional foundations of European contract law, it may be asked why anyone would want to undertake such an endeavour. In response, for far too long, this subject has been stunted in various ways, whether by way of assumptions about the scope of Union competence and the operation of the principles of subsidiarity and proportionality, the lack of recognition of the extent to which the discussion of Union competence has crept into the debate at the European level from the very beginning, and the fallacy of the American contract law experience. The time has come to change this path and to place more focus on the 'constitutional conversation' about European contract law and the 'comparative conversation' with the US. It is therefore hoped that this book may help to bring the constitutional dimensions of European contract law to the forefront and to provide a firm foundation upon which the complex issues and the perennial tensions miring this area can be constructively discussed and appropriate solutions can be found.

years. It is a private organization with its secretariat in Vienna, and one of its first activities following the opening ceremony on 17 Nov 2011 concerned the proposed CESL: see F Jacobs, 'The European Law Institute' (2012) 18 *ELJ* 175; Written Question E-008069/2012 by A Fox, 'Common European Sales Law', available at <http://www.europarl.europa.eu/>; for the ELI's activities, see its website, <http://www.europeanlawinstitute.eu/>.

[33] See, eg, J Basedow, 'The Court of Justice and Private Law: Vacillations, General Principles and the Architecture of the European Judiciary' (2010) 18 *ERPL* 443, 469–472; Schmid, n 32, 288 and citations therein.

[34] See Chapter 3, § 3.5.3.3.

PART ONE

CONTEXT

1

The Constitutional Framing of European Contract Law

1.1 Introduction

In order to examine the constitutional dimensions of European contract law, it is important to have a firm grasp of the terminology employed in the debate and the particular set of Union measures adopted in this field. To begin with, there are no universal definitions for most of this terminology, and in fact, the discourse on European contract law is mired to a large extent in terms that may inadvertently inject certain nuances or biases into the discussion. Additional difficulties are posed by comparative reflection with the US, since some terms found in the American context have no equivalent to those used in the European setting or embody subtleties of the American legal framework. Moreover, several measures within the EU contract law *acquis* are at the root of what prompted the debate about European contract law in the first place and of the envisaged initiatives contemplated therein.

It is therefore the aim of this chapter to clarify the prevalent terminology used in the European and American settings and to elucidate these Union contract law measures in order to have a constructive discussion of the constitutionality of European contract law and a clear understanding of the backdrop to the debate, both of which feed into each other. First, the terminology associated with the constitutionality of European contract law is explored, with a view to establishing functional definitions for the chapters to come. Secondly, the scope of EU contract law is examined, with focus placed on a special set of Union contract law measures that lie at the heart of the debate about European contract law. Thirdly, certain perennial themes underlying these measures are highlighted in order to set the scene for the launching of this debate and to underscore several aspects related to the Union's competence that continue to permeate the constitutionality of European contract law through to the present day. Together, these three interrelated elements comprise the constitutional framing of European contract law: they are the basis for the constitutional assessment of European contract law and the prelude for what is to come.

1.2 Terminology

The terms associated with the constitutionality of European contract law generally fall into three main categories. First, there is 'constitutionality' itself and related terms carrying the 'constitutional' moniker. Secondly, there is 'European contract law', which is inextricably intertwined with 'European private law' and similar variants, such as 'European civil law' and 'European patrimonial law'. Thirdly, there are the various processes by which European contract law (and European private law generally) come about, which implicate the well-known 'trinity of terms'[1]—approximation,

[1] D Vignes, 'The Harmonization of National Legislation and the EEC' (1990) 15 *ELR* 358, 361.

harmonization, and coordination—among many others. On the whole, there are terminological problems associated with all three categories. As mentioned above, there is no general agreement on the definitions of most terms used in the debate about European contract law. Some are used in different ways by the Union institutions and scholars, thereby making it difficult to establish common ground, much less to find or to maintain formal boundary lines between them. Others have splintered into distinct subsets, which embody their own particular meanings. As an apt illustration, the title of this book could at face value be interpreted in a number of ways depending upon one's view of the 'European contract law' and the 'constitutional' containers. Furthermore, much of the sensitivity underlying the constitutionality of European contract law leads back to the terms used. Many terms have become so 'politically loaded' that it is virtually impossible to find neutral words to discuss the ongoing activities in this field or to escape the implied connotations of terms that have become entrenched in the discourse. Complicating matters further is that each of these categories illuminates differences between the EU and the US.

It is often overlooked that these terminological problems have a direct impact on the constitutional assessment of European contract law. This is because, as fleshed out below, depending upon which terms are used, this may misdirect or prejudge the discussion of Union competence in this setting. Moreover, there is not as yet any convenient, overarching way in which to frame this subject without bumping up against the limitations of some of these terms. This explains the penchant for generic references to the Union's 'far-reaching' or 'comprehensive' action in contract law, since to specify terms such as approximation or harmonization may be interpreted to exclude the prospect of an optional instrument existing alongside the pre-existing national laws, even if the proposal for a Regulation on a Common European Sales Law (proposed CESL)[2] begs renewed inquiry into this matter.[3] As a result, it is argued here that terminology is everything in European contract law, particularly when exploring its constitutional dimensions. It provides the template for engaging, as much as possible, in an objective 'constitutional conversation' about European contract law and a 'comparative conversation' with the US in this regard. Thus, each of the three categories is analysed in turn, so that a working set of terms can be fixed for the discussion. Along the way, certain 'comparative leaps' to the US will be made to spotlight differences in approach and to explain certain terms indigenous to the American setting.

1.2.1 Constitutionality and the 'constitutional' designation

The term *constitutionality* and the '*constitutional*' designation used in conjunction with words such as foundations, assessment, dimensions, etc are used here to denote the determination of the extent of the Union's competence to adopt a comprehensive instrument of contract law and the extent to which certain alternative and complementary routes to such an instrument may be resorted to in accordance with primary Union law, namely the Treaties. Specifically, they encompass inquiry into both the existence and exercise of Union competence in contract law.[4] The existence of Union competence

[2] Proposal for a Regulation of the European Parliament and of the Council on a Common European Sales Law, COM (2011) 636 final, 11.10.2011.

[3] See further § 1.2.3.

[4] In the US, reference is typically made to the 'powers' granted to the Federal Government in line with the wording of the US Constitution, whereas in the EU, reference is often made to the 'competences' conferred on the Union, even though one finds both terms in the Treaties. Technically speaking, it has long been recognized that there is a distinction between the terms 'competences' and 'powers'

implicates the principle of conferral enshrined in Article 5(2) TEU, which mandates that the Union may only take action in accordance with the competences conferred upon it, either explicitly or implicitly, pursuant to one or more legal bases under the Treaties. Provided that sufficient Union competence exists, the exercise of such Union competence is regulated by the principles of subsidiarity, proportionality, and sincere cooperation as defined in Articles 5(3), 5(4), and 4(3) TEU, respectively. This may seem basic to most readers well versed in EU law, and in principle, this category of terms does not appear to present much of a problem. After all, in the commentary, references to constitutionality as a shorthand for the inquiry into the EU's competence in contract law (or other fields of private law) abound without much controversy or need for explanation or justification.[5] Still, certain complications arise.

First, looking below the surface, the meaning, operation, and relationship between the principles of conferral, subsidiarity, proportionality, and sincere cooperation governing Union competence under the Treaties (as well as the allowance for certain alternative routes put forward in the debate) is far more complex than may appear. And while constitutionality and the 'constitutional' designation are not as such problematic in the US, the American constitutional framework is markedly different from that of the EU, especially when it comes to these four principles. Accordingly, detailed discussion of these principles is saved for Chapter 7, where they can be given cohesive treatment within the context of outlining the constitutional parameters of European contract law.

Secondly, constitutionality and related terms bearing the 'constitutional' designation could conceivably encompass issues relating, in one way or another, to the 'legitimacy' of Union action in European contract law. Generally speaking, legitimacy is a famously elastic concept capable of many expressions.[6] Yet, at least in European contract law, it is often depicted through the distinction between 'formal legitimacy' and 'social legitimacy': formal legitimacy is commonly used to signify the importance of adhering to the formal limits of Union competence under the Treaties,[7] whereas social legitimacy is largely viewed as placing emphasis on aspects linked to the social acceptance of the initiatives envisaged for European contract law at the European level.[8] For example, social legitimacy has been used to underscore the important role of democratic processes in connection with the preparation and adoption of a European contract

in the EU setting. See, eg, R Schütze, 'The European Community's Federal Order of Competences—A Retrospective Analysis' in M Dougan and S Currie (eds), *50 Years of the European Treaties—Looking Back and Thinking Forward* (Hart, 2009) 63 fn 3. In practice, however, these two terms are used interchangeably: see, eg, G de Búrca and B de Witte, 'The Delimitation of Powers Between the EU and its Member States' in A Arnull and D Wincott (eds), *Accountability and Legitimacy in the European Union* (Oxford Univ Press, 2002) 201, 203 fn 3; A von Bogdandy and J Bast, 'The Federal Order of Competences' in A von Bogdandy and J Bast (eds), *Principles of European Constitutional Law*, 2nd rev edn (Hart/Verlag CH Beck, 2010) 275, 278. Despite the variation in the Treaties, the term 'competence' will generally be resorted to in connection with the EU.

[5] See, eg, E Hondius, 'Towards a European Civil Code' in A Hartkamp et al (eds), *Towards a European Civil Code*, 4th rev and expanded edn (Kluwer/Ars Aequi Libri, 2011) 3, 4–5; L Miller, *The Emergence of EU Contract Law: Exploring Europeanization* (Oxford Univ Press, 2011) 63. Compare, eg, L Niglia, 'Of Constitutionality and Private Consumer Law in Europe' (2012) 1 *EUVR* 223.

[6] For a general account, see, eg, *Accountability and Legitimacy in the European Union*, n 4; A Estella, *The EU Principle of Subsidiarity and Its Critique* (Oxford Univ Press, 2002) 37–73.

[7] Also referred to as 'constitutional legitimacy': see Miller, n 5, 54–55.

[8] See S Weatherill, 'Competence and Legitimacy' in C Barnard and O Odudu (eds), *The Outer Limits of European Union Law* (Hart, 2009) 17.

law instrument,[9] as in the case of the involvement and participation of the European Parliament, national parliaments, and European civil society,[10] or issues related to the institutional and judicial framework needed to support such an instrument and to orchestrate the interactions of the various actors involved.[11] There is no question of the latter notion's importance or of the way in which these two expressions of legitimacy build upon each other in relation to European contract law, but these broader aspects of legitimacy (and relevant comparisons with the American setting[12]) fall outside the scope of the analysis. As defined here, constitutionality and other terms related to the constitutional inquiry into Union competence may essentially be considered a distinct subset or component of legitimacy in the context of European contract law.

Finally, this category is inevitably drawn into the web of other terms carrying the 'constitutional' appellation, such as constitutionalism, constitutionalization, and of course constitution itself. As regards European contract law (and European private law generally), these terms have started to assume their own meaning and discourse. In particular, the interplay between contract law and fundamental rights is the subject of a growing volume of literature often viewed through the lens of the 'constitutionalization' of European contract or private law.[13] Such literature may also relate to the discussion of 'social justice' in this context,[14] as well as other aspects concerning the interaction between European contract or private law and the 'constitutional' realm.[15] While these aspects are certainly exciting from a research standpoint, they exceed the scope of the analysis as well. When it comes to the EU generally, these other terms may provoke considerable controversy. Indeed, it may be interesting to ponder whether the need to address them would have arisen with quite as much fervour today had it not been for the failed Draft Treaty establishing a 'Constitution' for Europe (Draft Constitutional Treaty),[16] which catapulted centre stage issues relating to the fixture of the 'constitutional' label on the European project. Yet, starting long before the Draft Constitutional Treaty, there was already a quite burgeoning scholarship on these terms in the EU setting,[17] and even with the demise of that Treaty, tensions remain as

[9] For this reason, it has also been referred to as 'democratic legitimacy': see, eg, JM Smits, 'Democracy and (European) private law: a functional approach' in M Faure and A van der Walt (eds), *Globalization and Private Law: The Way Forward* (Edward Elgar, 2010) 15.

[10] See, eg, W van Gerven, 'About Rules and Principles, Codification and Legislation, Harmonization and Convergence, and Education in the Area of Contract Law' in A Arnull et al (eds), *Continuity and Change in EU Law—Essays in Honour of Sir Francis Jacobs* (Oxford Univ Press, 2008) 400, 404; J Ziller, 'The Legitimacy of the Codification of Contract Law in View of the Allocation of Competences between the European Union and its Member States' in MW Hesselink (ed), *The Politics of a European Civil Code* (Kluwer, 2006) 89, 102–103.

[11] See, eg, CU Schmid, 'Legitimacy Conditions for a European Civil Code' (2001) 8 *MJ* 277.

[12] See Introduction.

[13] For a brief selection, see, eg, S Grundmann (ed), *Constitutional Values and European Contract Law* (Kluwer, 2008); 'Special Issue on the European Constitutionalization of Private Law' (2004) 12 *ERPL* No 5.

[14] See, eg, Study Group on Social Justice In European Private Law, 'Social Justice in European Contract Law: a Manifesto' (2004) 10 *ELJ* 653; H-W Micklitz (ed), *The Many Concepts of Social Justice in European Private Law* (Edward Elgar, 2011); A Somma (ed), *The Politics of the Draft Common Frame of Reference* (Kluwer, 2009).

[15] See, eg, L Niglia (ed), *Pluralism and European Private Law* (Hart, 2013); C Mak, 'Europe-building through private law. Lessons from constitutional theory' (2012) 8 *ERCL* 326.

[16] See Chapter 7, § 7.3.

[17] For a brief selection, see, eg, M Claes, *The National Courts' Mandate in the European Constitution* (Hart, 2006) 402–408; M Wind and JHH Weiler (eds), *Constitutionalism Beyond the State* (Cambridge Univ Press, 2003); *Principles of European Constitutional Law*, n 4.

regards the application of 'constitutional' terminology to the EU. This begs the question whether other words, such as legality, could presumably fit just as well and should be used instead.

In response, constitutionality and related terms bearing the 'constitutional' designation have been chosen because they are beneficial for embodying certain quintessentially 'constitutional' aspects of the debate about European contract law. Despite the foregoing tensions, there does not seem to be much disagreement among commentators as to the application of the constitutional descriptor to matters concerning the division of competence in the EU setting, both vertically between the Union and the Member States and horizontally between the Union institutions themselves.[18] The vertical division of competences between the Union and the Member States is commonly associated with the term 'federalism' in the US,[19] whereas the horizontal division of competences among the Union institutions is generally encapsulated by the term 'institutional balance' in the EU, as opposed to the 'separation of powers' in the US.[20] As will be seen in the coming chapters, these matters cast a long shadow over the discussion of Union competence in European contract law, as well as that of federal competence in American contract law. Consequently, constitutionality and the other terms bearing the 'constitutional' designation are, arguably, better-targeted descriptors than other, somewhat more generic terms and enable parallels to be drawn with the US in this regard.

1.2.2 European contract law and its relationship to European private law

As already alluded to, European contract law is by no means a simple term, but instead a multilayered topic. This may explain why in the steady stream of Commission Communications on European contract law, an explicit definition of this term has not yet been given. In turn, the meaning of European contract law is tied to that of European private law and related terms, as well as those used in the American setting. Each is explored in turn.

1.2.2.1 The meaning(s) of European contract law

At first glance, it could be thought that taking apart its various components—'European', 'contract', and 'law'—could be helpful for defining European contract law. With further reflection, however, this does not appear to advance the ball much, and in fact, demonstrates that the conception of European contract law itself embodies elements that have propelled the debate about this topic forward at the European level.

[18] See, eg, K Lenaerts, 'The Basic Constitutional Charter of a Community Based on the Rule of Law' in MP Maduro and L Azoulai (eds), *The Past and the Future of EU Law: Revisiting the Classics on the 50th Anniversary of the Rome Treaty* (Hart, 2010) 295, 298–301.

[19] For comparative reflection on the notion of 'federalism' in the EU and US, see, eg, Geert De Baere and Kathleen Gutman, 'Federalism and International Relations in the EU and the US: A Comparative Outlook' in E Cloots et al (eds), *Federalism in the European Union* (Hart, 2012) 131 and citations therein.

[20] This is not to say that 'separation of powers' has no place in the EU (see, eg, Case C-413/11 (Order of 18 April 2013) *Germanwings*, not reported), but given its roots in the classical functions of a nation state, it assumes particular nuances framed by the term 'institutional balance': see further K Lenaerts and P Van Nuffel, (R Bray and N Cambien (eds)), *European Union Law*, 3rd edn (Sweet & Maxwell, 2011) § 15-007–§ 15-013.

The 'European' container is not strictly limited to the EU, but rather must be seen in the three dimensions of the international, European, and national spheres, which makes it difficult to locate its precise boundaries, particularly in the EU setting. It also remains controversial to what extent there is, or can be, a common 'European' conception of contract.[21] As noted by commentators, this implicates a glaring paradox underlying European contract law: on the one hand, there is a mass of comparative work aimed at the distillation of common contract rules shared by the Member States, but on the other hand, the entire debate is centred around the very lack of commonality among national contract laws so as to bolster the need for further action at the European level.[22] In addition, European contract law covers a variety of sources transcending the classical conception of 'law' adopted by way of the prescribed decision-making procedures of a particular entity, such as international and European principles, model laws, and customary practices.

Nevertheless, as ventilated from the scholarly literature and institutional documents, European contract law may be considered an umbrella term that can be viewed in three interrelated ways: (1) a *wide view* taking into account the various international, European, and national instruments; (2) a *narrow view* focused on the EU contract law *acquis*; and (3) a *future view* towards the adoption of a European contract law instrument.[23] Each of these views helps to pinpoint terms utilized in the discussion.

The *wide view* envelops several sources of European contract law emanating from the international, European, and national levels, which include:

(1) *international conventions and other instruments* adopted under the rubric of public and private international bodies,[24] such as the 1980 United Nations Convention on Contracts for the International Sale of Goods (CISG);[25]

(2) *primary and secondary Union law*, such as relevant provisions of the Treaties, the Charter of Fundamental Rights of the European Union (Charter), and a wide variety of Union measures adopted pursuant to such Treaty provisions that may be considered to fall within or otherwise touch on the field of contract law, whether as a matter of substantive law or private international law (eg, the 'Rome I' Regulation on the law applicable to contractual obligations[26]);

[21] See, eg, B Pozzo, 'Multilingualism, Legal Terminology and the Problems of Harmonising European Private Law' in B Pozzo and V Jacometti (eds), *Multilingualism and the Harmonization of European Law* (Kluwer, 2006) 3, 8; Netherlands Delegation, 'Common Frame of Reference for European Contract Law', DOC 13697/08 ADD 3, dated 7 Oct 2008, point (b), at 2. The issue may be considered to transcend the field of contract law: see C Joerges, 'The Challenges of Europeanization in the Realm of Private Law: A Plea for a New Legal Discipline' (2004) 14 *DJCIL* 149, 159.

[22] See, eg, MW Hesselink and GJP de Vries, *Principles of European Contract Law* (Kluwer, 2001) 22; N Roos, 'NICE Dreams and Realities of European Private Law' in M Van Hoecke (ed), *Epistemology and Methodology of Comparative Law* (Hart, 2004) 197, 220.

[23] See, eg, S Grundmann, 'General Standards and Principles, *Clauses Générales*, and *Generalklauseln* in European Contract Law—A Survey' in S Grundmann and D Mazeaud (eds), *General Clauses and Standards in European Contract Law—Comparative Law, EC Law and Contract Law Codification* (Kluwer, 2006) 1, 4–6 (framing the matter as 'a Multi-Level' European contract law).

[24] See, eg, Commission Communication on European Contract Law, COM (2001) 398 final, 11.7.2001 (2001 Communication), Annex II ('List of International Instruments Relating to Substantial Contract Law Issues'); and more recently, R Goode et al, *Transnational Commercial Law: International Instruments and Commentary*, 2nd edn (Oxford Univ Press, 2012).

[25] 11 April 1980, 1489 UNTS 3. It is presently in force in most, though not all, Member States; at the time of writing, the exceptions are Ireland, Malta, Portugal, and the UK. See <http://www.uncitral.org/>.

[26] Reg (EC) No 593/2008 of the European Parliament and of the Council of 17 June 2008 on the law applicable to contractual obligations (Rome I), [2008] OJ L177/6. It applies to all Member States

(3) *European (extra-EU) conventions and other instruments* adopted outside the EU but linked thereto, such as the European Convention for the Protection of Human Rights and Fundamental Freedoms (ECHR)[27] adopted under the auspices of the Council of Europe to which all Member States are (and in the near future the EU will be[28]) parties;

(4) *national laws and other instruments* emanating from the Member States (and possibly third States), such as legislative and executive measures or case law;

(5) the *lex mercatoria* denoting various national and international customary practices and instruments pertaining to international commercial contracts and other aspects of international commercial dealings;[29] and

(6) *comparative contract law materials*, which are often referred to under the label of 'ius commune' (common law of Europe) because they embody efforts to a large extent to formulate common rules and principles underpinning the laws of the Member States (and possibly third States) and range from the works of individual jurists (such as books or treatises)[30] to those emanating from a wide array of academic projects,[31] such as the Principles of European Contract Law (PECL)[32] and the UNIDROIT Principles of International Commercial Contracts.[33]

Noticeably, part of what makes European contract law so difficult to grasp is that there are no neat dividing lines between these categories. European contract law rests on interlocking international, European, and national layers that blur and feed into each other. For instance, the existing corpus of Union contract law measures is itself grounded in shared rules and principles of the national contract laws. In turn, such laws feed into the comparative contract law materials that form its own discrete category at the same time that they are informed by the various measures taken at both the European and international levels. The PECL is an apt illustration because it seems to fall squarely into most of the categories: as a set of common contract law principles of the Member States, it constitutes a key element of comparative legal materials and claims to be part and parcel of other components—advocated for use by the national authorities, considered to fall within the *lex mercatoria*, proposed as the applicable law under private international law, and envisaged to constitute the basis for a comprehensive instrument to be adopted at the European level.[34] Moreover, each individual category listed above is itself open-ended, thereby encompassing a broad spectrum of instruments that makes the boundaries of European contract law even more malleable. For instance, what is generally referred to as the

but Denmark. See further, eg, F Ferrari and S Leible (eds), *Rome I Regulation: The law applicable to contractual obligations in Europe* (Sellier, 2009 and Suppl forthcoming 2014).

[27] 4 Nov 1950, 213 UNTS 222. [28] See Art 6(2) TEU.

[29] See generally KP Berger, *The Creeping Codification of the New Lex Mercatoria*, 2nd edn (Kluwer, 2010); J Dalhuisen, 1 *Dalhuisen on Transnational, Comparative, Commercial and Trade Law* (Hart, 2010); R Goode et al, *Transnational Commercial Law: Text, Cases, and Materials* (Oxford Univ Press, 2007) 3–56. For further discussion in the context of European contract law, see, eg, Miller, n 5, ch 5; AM López Rodríguez, *Lex Mercatoria and Harmonization of Contract Law in the EU* (DJØF, 2003).

[30] Eg, famously, H. Kötz, (T Weir trans), 1 *European Contract Law* (Clarendon, 1997).

[31] The various academic projects are generally discussed in Chapter 4, § 4.2. For discussion of these materials in the case law of the Court of Justice, see Chapter 2, § 2.4.

[32] See Chapter 4, § 4.2.1.

[33] *Unidroit Principles of International Commercial Contracts 2010* (Unidroit, 2010), available at <http://www.unidroit.org/> (providing link to extensive bibliography).

[34] See Chapter 4, § 4.2.1.

(new) *lex mercatoria* is not considered to represent a coherent and consistent category, but rather a more loose set of customs, practices, and other norms concerning international commercial contracts.[35]

Despite these complexities, the term *European contract law* is employed here with the wide view in mind. This is because most of the components play their own role in the constitutional assessment, whether arguing for or against the need for a European contract law instrument, helping to delineate its shape, or providing an alternative to such an instrument. Thus, while at first sight the title of this book may seem a little vague, arguably, there is no better substitute for the analysis undertaken therein. To call this book the constitutional foundations of 'EU contract law', for example, could imply the exclusion of components, such as comparative contract law materials produced by academic projects, which bear directly on the debate and the constitutional assessment of European contract law. Even so, commentators often focus on the EU contract law *acquis*,[36] which leads to the next point.

In the second, *narrow view*, European contract law is often used interchangeably with the term 'EU contract law' (formerly 'EC contract law' before the entry into force of the Lisbon Treaty) in order to hone in on the relevant Union *acquis* in the field.[37] There is an important link between the definition of EU contract law and its scope, since the broader it is defined, the greater its expanse over various areas of Union law (formerly Community law and even pre-Lisbon EU law).[38] In principle, EU contract law encompasses a plethora of Union measures spanning the gamut of fields, such as competition law, non-discrimination law, labour and employment law, public procurement law, intellectual property law, data protection, and so-called 'travel law',[39] not to mention the Union's activities related to the internal market.[40] In practice, however, EU contract law is typically used to spotlight a specific subset of Union measures as discussed in the next section.[41] For now, it should be recognized that the term *EU contract law* will be used to denote the various Union measures adopted so far in the field of contract law taken as a whole.

The third, *future view* of European contract law is often identified by reference to 'a' or 'the' European contract law[42] in order to signify the progression towards the

[35] See, eg, FW Grosheide, 'Legal Borrowing and Drafting International Commercial Contracts' in FW Grosheide and E Hondius (eds), *International Contract Law—Articles on Various Aspects of Transnational Contract Law* (Intersentia, 2004) 221, 225–226. There is considerable controversy underlying the nature and status of the (new) *lex mercatoria*: see, eg, Berger, n 29, ch 2.

[36] See, eg, R Schulze, 'Consumer Law and European Contract Law' in G Howells et al (eds), *The Yearbook of Consumer Law 2007* (Ashgate, 2007) 153, 154–158.

[37] See, eg, Miller, n 5, particularly ch 2; C Quigley, 1 *European Community Contract Law* (Kluwer, 1997); S Grundmann, 'The Structure of European Contract Law' (2001) 9 *ERPL* 505, 508; K Riesenhuber, 'System and Principles of EC Contract Law' (2005) 1 *ERCL* 297.

[38] See Riesenhuber, n 37, 300–301.

[39] See, eg, J Karsten, 'Travel law' in C Twigg-Flesner (ed), *The Cambridge Companion to European Union Private Law* (Cambridge Univ Press, 2010) 201.

[40] See, eg, C Twigg-Flesner, *The Europeanisation of Contract Law* (Routledge-Cavendish, 2008) 52–53; S Vogenauer and S Weatherill, 'The European Community's Competence to Pursue the Harmonization of Contract Law—an Empirical Contribution to the Debate' in S Vogenauer and S Weatherill (eds), *The Harmonization of European Contract Law: Implications for European Private Laws, Business and Legal Practice* (Hart, 2006) 105, 106. See also 2001 Communication, n 24, Annex I ('Important Community *Acquis* in the Area of Private Law').

[41] See § 1.3.

[42] See, eg, D Busch, *Indirect Representation in European Contract Law* (Kluwer, 2005) 1; Editorial (2005) 1 *ERCL* 1; R Schulze and J Stuyck (eds), *Towards a European Contract Law* (Sellier, 2011); J Smits (ed), *The Need for a European Contract Law: Empirical and Legal Perspectives* (Europa, 2005); S Weatherill, *EU Consumer Law and Policy*, 2nd edn (Edward Elgar, 2005) 159. As regards institutional documents, see,eg, the title of the 2010 Green Paper on policy options for progress towards 'a'

adoption of a European contract law instrument at the European level. It is thus akin to various descriptors for such an instrument, such as a European contract law act or code. To avoid confusion with European contract law generally and potential nuances associated with the word 'code' discussed later,[43] the term *European contract law instrument* is used here to denote the enactment of a comprehensive instrument of substantive contract law at the European level. Admittedly, the reference to a 'comprehensive' contract law instrument is not exact. It is chosen to correspond to the way in which such an instrument has been framed in the debate so far, in terms of denoting a systematic instrument encompassing contract law rules relating to commercial and consumer transactions in a general sense.[44]

Taking things a step further, the Union institutions have started referring to the 'European contract law initiative'[45] or the 'European contract law project'[46] as a way to frame the ongoing activities taking place in European contract law at the European level. Both are beneficial because they are means by which to encapsulate on a more neutral and overarching basis such activities without implying any normative judgment as to what that end point should be or what form it should take, although one wonders whether the word 'initiative' may infer some sort of legislative action.[47] To forestall this, the term *European contract law project* will be used to denote the ongoing course of events and activities emanating from the debate about European contract law at the European level.

1.2.2.2 *The meaning(s) of European private law and similar variants*

As already mentioned, the focus on European contract law inevitably brings European private law and similar variants into play. This is perhaps not all that surprising, since contract law is generally viewed as a distinct subset of private law, and hence as a scientific matter, they are linked. Thus, one could say that European contract law has sprouted up like a seed from the mother plant along with other distinct fields of private law, with the result that European private law has too become an umbrella term encompassing an increasing variety of offshoots (eg, European tort law, European property law, European family law, etc), making it a challenge to find many fields of private law that do not command their own growing discourse. But, important to the constitutional

European Contract Law for consumers and businesses, COM (2010) 348 final, 1.7.2010 (2010 Green Paper), discussed further in Chapter 6, § 6.4.2.

[43] See § 1.2.3.4.

[44] See, eg, 2001 Communication, n 24, point 41 and section 4.4; Commission Communication, A more coherent European Contract Law—An Action Plan, COM (2003) 68 final, 12.2.2003 (2003 Action Plan), point 4.3; Commission Communication, European Contract Law and the revision of the *acquis*: the way forward, COM (2004) 651 final, 11.10.2004 (2004 Communication), point 2.3; 2010 Green Paper, n 42, points 4, 4.1 (Option 4), second para. As regards the proposed CESL, see also Commission Communication, A Common European Sales Law to Facilitate Cross-Border Transactions in the Single Market, COM (2011) 636 final, 11.10.2011, point 2.1, second and eighth paras.

[45] See, eg, First Annual Progress Report on European Contract Law and the Acquis Review, COM (2005) 456 final, 23.9.2005 (2005 Progress Report), point 1; European Parliament Resolution of 8 June 2011 on policy options for progress towards a European Contract Law for consumers and businesses, [2012] OJ C380E/59 (2011 Resolution), recital A.

[46] See, eg, 2005 Progress Report, n 45, point 3; 2011 Resolution, n 45, point 1.

[47] Some commentators read further nuances between the two: see, eg, B Flodgren, 'The European Contract Law Project—Reflections on the Lawmaking Process' in M Johansson et al (eds), *Liber Amicorum in Honour of Sven Norberg: A European for all seasons* (Bruylant, 2006) 219, 220.

assessment, the relationship between European contract law and European private law emanates from the debate itself.

As illustrated in Part Two, the debate about European contract law started out within a larger debate about the approximation of the private laws of the Member States, which to a large extent has persisted through to the present day despite the 'European contract law' label. In view of the academic projects and attention devoted to it at the European level, European contract law has, and continues to be, the motor for Union developments and activities overall, but the line between it and the overarching momentum of European private law has never completely been severed. This explains why it is terminologically difficult to discuss the debate about European contract law without mentioning European private law, or why institutional documents in the debate may frame the matter as European contract law, but implicate to varying degrees other fields of private law as well. In other words, the debate plays 'fast and loose' with the label European contract law, and sitting in the background are ambiguities that creep into the 'constitutional conversation' of European contract law, such as whether Union inroads into national contract law are the pathway to more far-reaching action covering other fields of private law at the European level. The bottom line is that the term European contract law often implicitly reads or beckons European private law, and the debate itself has not yet resolved the linkage or the tensions between the two.

In any case, much of the difficulty in parsing out the definition of European contract law also exists for European private law,[48] perhaps even more so because it is seen on a much broader scale and has given way to overarching political and institutional issues related to, inter alia, the European multilevel framework, new modes of governance, and the dynamics of private and public regulation.[49] Like European contract law, no express definition of European private law can be found so far in the various documents disseminated by the Union institutions in the debate, but as distilled from such documents and the relevant literature, European private law may also be viewed in the following three ways from which similar terms can be fixed: (1) the *wider view* comprising various international and European (extra-EU) instruments, primary and secondary Union law, national laws of the Member States (and possibly third States), the *lex mercatoria*, and comparative private law materials comprising the 'ius commune' aspects of the legal systems of the Member States,[50] which will be referred to as *European private law*; (2) a *narrower view* focusing on the Union *acquis* in private law, ie *EU private law* (formerly EC private law);[51] and (3) a *future view* looking towards the emergence of 'the

[48] See, eg, K Boele-Woelki and RH van Ooik, 'The Communitarization of Private International Law' in *International Contract Law*, n 35, 343, 347; Miller, n 5, 5 fn 16; J Smits and P Letto-Vanamo, 'Introduction' in J Smits and P Letto-Vanamo (eds), *Coherence and Fragmentation in European Private Law* (Sellier, 2012) 1.

[49] For a brief selection, see, eg, F Cafaggi (ed), *The Institutional Framework of European Private Law* (Oxford Univ Press, 2006); F Cafaggi and H Muir-Watt (eds), *Making European Private Law: Governance Design* (Edward Elgar, 2008); K Garcia, *Le droit civil européen* (Larcier, 2008).

[50] See, eg, G Alpa, 'European Private Law: Results, Projects and Hopes' (2003) 14 *EBLR* 379, 379–385 (reprinted in G Alpa, *Markets and Comparative Law* (BIICL, 2010) 164–168); Boele-Woelki and van Ooik, n 48, 351–353; S. Whittaker, 'The Interpretation of Concepts in European Private Law' in K Boele-Woelki and W Grosheide (eds), *The Future of European Contract Law—Essays in honour of Ewoud Hondius* (Kluwer, 2007) 333.

[51] See, eg, M Kenny, 'The 2004 Communication on European Contract Law: those magnificent men in their unifying machines' (2005) 30 *ELR* 724; C Twigg-Flesner, 'Introduction: key features of European Union private law' in *The Cambridge Companion to European Union Private Law*, n 39, 1, 1–3 (with further discussion of this distinction in the book review by L Niglia (2011) 36 *ELR* 760). See also Written Question E-4389/2007 by G Papstamkos, 'European private law', available at <http://www.europarl.europa.eu/>.

new European private law'[52] or 'a' European private law,[53] which embodies the debate about the adoption of a *European private law instrument*, a comprehensive instrument adopted at the European level encompassing various fields of private law, often framed as a 'European civil code'.

Leaving the word 'code' aside for the moment, this in turn warrants inquiry into the distinction between 'private law' and other spheres, especially 'civil law', 'commercial law', and 'patrimonial law', with which European private law is generally associated. Starting with *private law*, as a formal matter, this term is considered to denote the fields of law governing relationships between individuals, as opposed to public law, which in principle covers fields of law governing relationships emanating from the state or government, even though the boundary line between the two is porous and various relationships involving public or state entities may fall on the private law side of the line.[54] As a practical matter, private law is usually employed to denote the fields of contract, tort, property, family, and succession law.[55] It is often used interchangeably with *civil law*, particularly in the debate about European contract law by both scholars and the Union institutions,[56] and may envelop subject matters falling within the rubric of *commercial law*.[57] However, the term civil law is problematic because it may evoke, intentionally or not, the distinction between the Member States having civil or continental, as opposed to common law, legal systems, and thus, depending upon the way it is interpreted, it may not be altogether representative of the national legal traditions.[58] Likewise, the Member States take different approaches to the organization of the branches of civil and commercial law, with some segregating them into separate codes.[59] Therefore, the use of the term *private law* will generally be preferred, so as to avoid confusion over the varying civil and commercial law categories in the Member States and prevent injecting any sort of bias into the discussion, even if references to civil law and to some extent commercial law have become commonplace in the debate and thus to some degree are unavoidable.

Finally, *patrimonial law* is an important subset of private law as far as the debate about European contract law is concerned. European patrimonial law is largely equated

[52] See, eg, MW Hesselink, *The New European Private Law: Essays on the Future of Private Law in Europe* (Kluwer, 2002) 7–8.

[53] See, eg, J Smits, (N Kornet trans), *The Making of European Private Law—Towards a Ius Commune Europaeum as a Mixed Legal System* (Intersentia, 2002) § 2–§ 3.

[54] See, eg, G Alpa, 'European Community Resolutions and the Codification of "Private Law"' (2000) 8 *ERPL* 321, 324. As a result, the boundary line between 'private' and 'public' law has been considered thin (see, eg, M Freedland and J-B Auby (eds), *The Public Law/Private Law Divide—Une entente assez cordiale?* (Hart, 2006)), ill-defined (see, eg, F Cafaggi, 'Introduction' in *The Institutional Framework of European Private Law*, n 49, 1, 2), or ill-fitting (see, eg, Miller, n 5, 15–20).

[55] See, eg, Alpa, 'European Private Law', n 50, 380; Hondius, n 5, 7 (also mentioning restitution and trust law); M Reimann and D Halberstam, 'Unification of Private Law in Federal Systems' in R Brownsword et al (eds), *The Foundations of European Private Law* (Hart, 2011) 363, 374 (referring to these fields as the 'classic core' of private law).

[56] Compare, eg, Hondius, n 5, 7, with E Hondius, 'Towards a European Civil Code' in AS Hartkamp et al (eds), *Towards a European Civil Code*, 3rd rev and expanded edn (Kluwer/Ars Aequi Libri, 2004) 3, 6. As regards the Union institutions, the recourse to one or the other without explanation is a common practice in documents circulated in the debate. See Part Two.

[57] See, eg, Alpa, 'European Private Law', n 50, 380.

[58] See N MacCormick, *Institutions of Law—An Essay in Legal Theory* (Oxford Univ Press, 2007) 225. Eg, this may arise in relation to the Court's references to the general principles of 'civil law' as opposed to 'private law' in the case law: see Chapter 2.

[59] See Alpa, n 54, 324–325. For an early but still valuable source on this point, see D Tallon, 'Civil Law and Commercial Law' in K Zweigert (chief ed), VIII *International Encyclopedia of Comparative Law* (Mohr/Martinus Nijhoff, 1983).

with the work of the Study Group on a European Civil Code, one of the academic projects involved in the debate, and comprises the law of contractual obligations (including general contract law and special contract law governing particular types of contracts), the law of non-contractual obligations (ie tort law, unjust enrichment, and the law of benevolent intervention in another's affairs or *negotiorum gestio*), and certain areas of movable property law, but excludes areas such as family, succession, and real (or immovable) property law.[60] Thus, within the debate, sometimes what is referred to as European private law (or a European civil code) is really meant to denote the more specific subset of European patrimonial law.[61]

1.2.2.3 Comparative leaps to the US

In the US, the term private law is not as widespread as in the EU, and often the emphasis is put on the particular field concerned, such as contracts or torts. Yet, the private law container is not unknown, and this difference in approach has certainly not halted the 'comparative conversation' between the EU and the US in this regard.[62] Nonetheless, in the American setting, there are certain nuances in approach as regards the distinction between contract and commercial law. References to commercial law and the distinct fields within it (such as negotiable instruments, the sale of goods, and secured transactions) abound, particularly in the discussion of certain American mechanisms relevant to the analysis, such as uniform laws and the Uniform Commercial Code (UCC).[63] The field of commercial law includes aspects of contract law, but is not exclusively directed at that particular field of law. This explains why this book often frames the matter as contract law and other fields of commercial law. Moreover, given its coverage of areas related to contract law, such as movable property law, commercial law as the comparative reference point to the debate about European contract law may risk inciting tensions similar to those underlying the relationship between European contract law and European private law in the sense of implying a wider ambit for Union action beyond the confines of contract law. Admittedly, the analogies between commercial law in the US and contract law in the EU are not exact. Still, on the whole, the references to commercial law in the documents and literature in the American setting are mainly concerned with aspects of contract law and other fields of state private law governing commercial and consumer transactions, which bear a remarkable likeness to the debate about European contract law. This is so even though, as with the debate about European contract law, areas of private law outside the confines of commercial law do come into play in the discussion. Accordingly, while contract law and other fields of commercial law will be a common reference point in the American context, the term *American contract law framework* is chosen as a suitable term that dovetails nicely with the European setting.

[60] See its website, <http://www.sgecc.net/>. For further discussion, see Chapter 4, § 4.2.2.

[61] This is illustrated by the DCFR: its title (*Principles, Definitions and Model Rules of European Private Law*) espouses European private law, but it essentially comprises areas of European patrimonial law: see Chapter 6, § 6.2.3.

[62] See, eg, D Caruso, 'The Missing View of the Cathedral: The Private Law Paradigm of European Legal Integration' (1997) 3 *ELJ* 3, 5 fn 4; FH Miller, 'The Uniform Law Process for the Development of Private State Law in the United States: A Model For Other Systems?' (2006) 60 *Cons Fin LQ Rep* 4, 5; M Reimann, 'American Private Law and European Legal Unification—Can the United States be a Model?' (1996) 3 *MJ* 217, 219.

[63] See Chapter 3.

1.2.3 Approximation and related processes

It is certainly no understatement to say that much ink has been spilled over the intricacies of what is meant by approximation, harmonization, and unification.[64] Additional terms, old and new, have made their way into the discussion, such as coordination, codification, Europeanization, and convergence. Still others have given birth to further subsets, as in the case of the various harmonization models or techniques, eg, full, complete, total, maximum, minimum, and so on. These terms are certainly not the only ones to have crept into the discussion of European contract law (and European private law generally).[65] Yet, this group of terms and sub-terms represents those that most commonly appear in the discourse surrounding the constitutionality of European contract law at present.

What is shared by all of these terms is that they generally refer to processes, the objective of which is to eliminate differences, to varying degrees, between national laws with a view to bringing such laws closer together largely by way of 'positive' action of some sort. Beyond this generality, however, problems of terminological clarity and consistency arise. First, as highlighted by the debate about European contract law, the formal distinction between many of these terms has eroded in practice, and several others have splintered to the point that two or three meanings are hidden within a single term. For instance, one could think it helpful to frame these processes in terms of a sliding scale ranging from 'bottom up' means of organic, voluntary, or spontaneous movement bringing national laws closer together to 'top down' means orchestrated through an institutionalized process. Yet, characteristic of the debate about European contract law, the 'top down' and 'bottom up' approaches are not mutually exclusive, but instead interrelated. This is evidenced by several academic projects involved with European contract law, which can be situated within the 'bottom up' approach of producing comparative law materials on contract law, but at the same time advocate the use of such materials for the promulgation of a contract law instrument at the European level.[66] And within the 'top down' spectrum itself, there are numerous difficulties in attempting to pinpoint such processes to a single location given the evolution in their various meanings.

Secondly, further complications arise in the particular environment in which these terms are used. Many of these terms are specifically associated with the Treaty framework governing the EU and thus are prevalent in the discussion of the Union's activities in relation to national contract (and private) law, but this is not always the case. Some extend to the national, European, and international spheres in the broader sense, which in turn gives way to further nuances. Others assume particular connotations when transplanted to the US on account of the federal framework and the creation of certain mechanisms at the state level that have no exact counterpart in the EU.

[64] As noted by one scholar: 'The discussion of the difference between unification and harmonization has lost the lively character it had in the late 1960s and the early 1970s'. PJ Slot, 'Harmonization' (1996) 21 *ELR* 378, 389 fn 6. Anyone who has perused the literature (mostly in French) from that era would likely agree. Similar remarks may be made regarding these terms and others as the years went on. See, eg, C Jamin and D Mazeaud (eds), *L'harmonization du droit des contrats en Europe* (Economica, 2001); F. Osman, 'Codification/unification/harmonization du droit en Europe: un rêve en passe de devenir réalité?' in F Osman (ed), *Towards a European Consumer Code* (Bruylant, 1998) 12.

[65] See, eg, E Stein, 'Assimilation of National Laws as a Function of European Integration' (1964) 58 *AJIL* 1.

[66] See Chapter 4, § 4.2.

Lastly, by focusing on processes that aim to bring national laws closer together in some shape or form by way of 'positive' action, this may exclude other types of processes or instruments contemplated in the debate about European contract law. In particular, *mutual recognition*, as emanating from the case law of the Court of Justice, is generally considered to denote the principle that one Member State must admit the free circulation of goods or services that have been lawfully produced or marketed in another Member State, so long as overriding requirements of public interest established in the case law do not justify the more restrictive rule.[67] Thus, mutual recognition veers on the side of the 'negative' approach taken by the Court in eliminating barriers to trade caused by a particular national law in the well-known dichotomy of 'positive' and 'negative' integration, although it may pertain to the adoption of 'positive' Union measures as well. This explains why it may be framed as a separate or hybrid category straddling the two types of integration.[68] In any event, reference to mutual recognition does arise on occasion in the debate,[69] but it has not yet garnered a prominent role in the initiatives envisaged at the European level.[70] Furthermore, it is with some irony that one of the key forms of Union action in the debate about European contract law, that of one or more *optional instruments*, may be considered, depending upon the eye of the beholder, to evade these confines. This is because as the debate developed, such an instrument has been portrayed to exist alongside the national contract laws as opposed to modifying their content. Yet, the dividing line between optional instruments and approximation is not altogether clear,[71] as illustrated by the proposed CESL.[72] Suffice it to say for now, the interface of this form of Union action with approximation bolsters the need to understand the meaning of this term and other related processes.

In light of the foregoing remarks, it should be clear that for the purposes of this discussion, the terms within this category will be situated within the EU, with particular regard to the debate about European contract law. The analysis begins with approximation, harmonization, and unification because they are three of the most prevalent terms in the debate and constitute the reference point for the other terms examined in the sections that follow. As will be seen, none of these terms is perfect. Each involves its own particular trade-off, and it is probably impossible to find one term that pleases

67 For a brief selection, see, eg, KA Armstrong, 'Mutual Recognition' in C Barnard and J Scott (eds), *The Law of the Single European Market: Unpacking the Premises* (Hart, 2002) 225; C Barnard, *The Substantive Law of the EU: The Four Freedoms*, 3rd edn (Oxford Univ Press, 2010) 624–626. As regards the distinction between mutual recognition and the country of origin (or home state control) principle, see M Radeideh, *Fair Trading in EC Law: Information and Consumer Choice in the Internal Market* (Europa, 2005) 103–104; Written Question E-3441/2004 by D Wallis, 'The "country of origin" principle', available at n 51.

68 See, eg, AA Gkoutzinis, *Internet Banking and the Law in Europe: Regulation, Financial Integration and Electronic Commerce* (Cambridge Univ Press, 2006) 87; F Padoa Schioppa (ed), *The Principle of Mutual Recognition in the European Integration Process* (Palgrave Macmillan, 2005); J Pelkmans, *European Integration: Methods and Economic Analysis*, 3rd edn (Pearson, 2006).

69 Eg, in the context of the Commission's plans for the review of the consumer *acquis*: see Chapter 6, § 6.3.

70 For possible reasons for its limited utility in the debate, see, eg, J Drexl, 'Continuing Contract Law Harmonization under the White Paper of 1985?—Between Minimum Harmonization, Mutual Recognition, Conflict of Laws, and Uniform Law' in S Grundmann and J Stuyck (eds), *An Academic Green Paper on European Contract Law* (Kluwer, 2002) 103, 112.

71 Interestingly, one scholar referred to the concept of the optional instrument as '*unification additionnelle*', as opposed to '*unification substitutive*', which replaces national law with uniform rules: J Basedow, 'Rapport de synthèse: Quel droit privé pour l'Europe?' in J-S Bergé and M-L Niboyet (eds), *La réception du droit communautaire en droit privé des États membres* (Bruylant, 2003) 234, 234–235.

72 See Chapter 6, § 6.4.4.

all, let alone fits all uses. Yet, it is this core set of terms that underlies the constitutional assessment of European contract law, and as such, functional definitions must be found.

1.2.3.1 Approximation, harmonization, and unification

Approximation, harmonization, and unification are three of the most difficult terms to define and distinguish clearly inside and outside the debate about European contract law. There are no standard definitions for these terms, and they require wading through an inordinate amount of literature espousing differing views. Nonetheless, as distilled from the literature and the Treaty framework, it is submitted that even though approximation and harmonization may in principle be used to mean the same thing, these two terms embody different nuances and that approximation may be viewed as an overarching term encompassing harmonization and unification.

To begin, approximation and harmonization are explicitly mentioned in various provisions of the Treaties, but unfortunately, no explicit definitions are given. In contrast, unification has never appeared in the text of the Treaties as such,[73] which would seem to beg the question whether it can be used at all within the EU legal framework, not to mention why it is grouped together with approximation and harmonization. In the steady stream of literature and institutional documents on European contract law, many scholars, as well as the Union institutions, often consider approximation and harmonization to be synonymous and use the two interchangeably, whereas unification is commonly treated as a specific subset representing a more intensified version of these processes. This being so, certain commentators have highlighted a slight nuance between the two. For example, one jurist opined that harmonization's emphasis is more on 'purpose', whereas approximation's emphasis is more on 'result': 'While harmonization refers to legislation that is intended to do away with disparities, approximation refers to the result to be achieved, i.e., that legal systems come closer to each other. The latter, "result", need not necessarily be the fruit of a deliberate effort to harmonize, as it can also be the consequence of incremental development of the law through case law.'[74] Framed in this way, harmonization sounds more like 'doing it' in the sense of harmonizing aspects of national laws, whether minimally or exhaustively, whereas approximation signifies 'working towards it' as in setting the stage for a process that is still largely to take place thereafter, whether it is all at once, in stages, etc.[75] This seems to mark out approximation as an overarching process within which harmonization takes place.[76] There is further evidence to support this reading from the Treaty framework.

Both approximation and harmonization are explicitly tied to the Union's competence to approximate national laws under Articles 114 and 115 TFEU. While detailed discussion of these provisions must be saved for a later chapter,[77] the use of these terms

[73] See, eg, C Esplugues, 'Use of Separate Conventions Between Member States in the Context of the European Community Itself' in J Usher (ed), *The State of the European Union: Structure, Enlargement and Economic Union* (Longman, 2000) 151, 153. But compare Vignes, n 1, 360.

[74] W van Gerven, 'Bringing (Private) Laws Closer to Each Other at the European Level' in *The Institutional Framework of European Private Law*, n 49, 37, 47.

[75] Multi-stage approximation is further discussed in Chapter 8, § 8.3.3.2.

[76] See, eg, Osman, n 64, 15; P-E Partsch, *Le droit international privé européen: De Rome à Nice* (Larcier, 2003) 30–31. See also 2385th Council meeting—Justice, Home Affairs and Civil Protection—Brussels, 16 Nov 2001, DOC 13758/01, para 5 ('the search for greater approximation between Member States' substantive laws, whether by harmonization or unification').

[77] See Chapter 8.

in this context provides important clues for unearthing the ambiguous relationship between approximation, harmonization, and unification. Since the original EEC Treaty, approximation has been given pride of place as the heading of a specific chapter (and eventually title) of what is now the TFEU concerning the 'Approximation of Laws'.[78] This special section originally included, among others, Article 115 TFEU and eventually Article 114 TFEU, both of which employ this term. Article 115 TFEU (ex Article 94 EC, originally Article 100 EEC) authorizes the adoption of directives for the 'approximation' (eg, *rapprochement, aanpassing, Angleichung, ravvicinamento*, and *aproximación* in other language versions) of national laws 'as directly affect the establishment or functioning of the internal [formerly common] market'.[79] This is not to say that harmonization (or a derivation of it) was completely absent from the EEC Treaty, but already its usage in certain provisions seemed to embody a slightly different feel, in terms of emphasis placed on action taken by the Member State level, as compared to approximation, even if, admittedly, this was not always the case.[80]

Some years later, when Article 114 TFEU (ex Article 95 EC, originally Article 100a EEC) was introduced into the Treaty framework by way of the Single European Act, harmonization appeared alongside approximation in different paragraphs of this provision. The first paragraph of Article 114 TFEU sets forth the general outlines of this provision for the adoption of 'measures for the approximation' of national laws 'which have as their object the establishment and functioning of the internal market', whereas in subsequent paragraphs of Article 114 TFEU concerning special procedures permitting, under certain circumstances, national measures that derogate from a particular Union measure adopted thereunder, references to singular and pluralized versions of a harmonization measure (eg, *mesure d'harmonization, harmonisatiemaatregel, Harmonisierungsmaßnahme, misura di armonizzazione*, and *medida de armonización* in other language versions) are used.[81] With the Maastricht Treaty and subsequent amendments to the Treaties, references to the term harmonization increased in connection with other provisions.[82] Yet, the place of approximation as a distinct heading in the Treaties and in Articles 114(1) and 115 TFEU has never been altered through to the present day.

Accordingly, the text of the Treaties may, arguably, be read to indicate a subtle distinction between approximation, harmonization, and unification. As illustrated by Articles 114 and 115 TFEU, approximation covers both the use of directives, with

[78] Originally, this was placed at the forefront of the EEC Treaty in Title I 'Common Rules', which encompassed Ch 3 on 'Approximation of Laws'. Later, this became Title VI of the former EC Treaty on 'Common Rules on Competition, Taxation and Approximation of Laws', within which Ch 3 on 'Approximation of Laws' was placed. This has been preserved with the entry into force of the Lisbon Treaty, which merely modifies the numbering of the relevant title, now Title VII of the TFEU.

[79] Under the former Treaty framework, this corresponded to one of the Community's activities enshrined in Art 3(1)(h) EC (ex Art 3(h) EEC) concerning the 'approximation of the laws of the Member States to the extent required for the functioning of the common market'. With the entry into force of the Lisbon Treaty, this language was deleted and replaced in substance by Arts 3–6 TFEU. Table of equivalences, [2012] OJ C326/363.

[80] See, eg, ex Art 112(1) EEC (later ex Art 132(1), first para, EC; now repealed by the Lisbon Treaty); ex Art 117 EEC (later ex Art 136 EC; now Art 151 TFEU); but compare ex Art 99 EEC (later ex Art 93 EC; now Art 113 TFEU).

[81] See Art 114(4), (5), (8), (10) TFEU. Originally, under the SEA, see ex Art 100a(4)–(5) EEC.

[82] This was particularly the case in relation to various, so-called 'flanking' provisions of the Treaties, many of which were introduced for the first time with explicit clauses precluding harmonization (eg, culture, education, and public health) or supplemented by additional clauses mentioning harmonization measures (eg, environmental protection) in the Treaties. See further Chapter 9, § 9.2.1.

which harmonization is generally equated, and regulations, which are typically associated with unification.[83] Article 115 TFEU dictates that approximation can proceed only by way of directives and thus encompasses harmonization, not unification.[84] Directives are in principle devised to provide leeway to the Member States to translate the objectives concerned into the language of the national legal systems.[85] The link between directives and harmonization explains why harmonization is equated with the (Member) State level in the EU (as well as in the US), since it signifies 'the process by which state law on a given matter comes to resemble the laws of other states . . . while nevertheless retaining its identity as state law'.[86] In fact, particularly in the early years of the debate, under circumstances where harmonization was used in the more general sense on a par with approximation, care was taken to distinguish this conception of harmonization from its meaning *sensu stricto* related to directives.[87] In view of the Union's intervention in contract law by means of a well-known set of directives discussed further below, this may explain in part why harmonization is commonly resorted to in the discourse on European contract law.

Alongside the link between harmonization and directives, there is that between unification and regulations. In contrast to directives, regulations set down directly applicable binding legal rules as a matter of Union law.[88] Unification thereby represents a more intensified version of harmonization, since it brings about the promulgation of one uniform law at the Union, as opposed to the Member State, level. By stipulating the use of 'measures', Article 114 TFEU dictates that approximation may proceed by way of, inter alia, regulations or directives, thereby encompassing in principle both unification and harmonization.[89] This helps to explain why scholars do not deny the role to be played by unification, especially in the debate about European contract law, even if not mentioned explicitly in the Treaties. This also explains judgments of the Court of Justice and Opinions of the Advocates General assimilating the use of regulations with unification[90] and distinguishing unification from harmonization.[91]

[83] See, eg, van Gerven, n 74, 46; M Fallon and S Francq, 'Vers un droit proprement communautaire des conflits de lois ou de juridiction' in O De Schutter and P Nihoul (eds), *Une Constitution pour l'Europe: Réflexions sur les transformations de droit de l'Union européenne* (Larcier, 2004) 239, 265. The association of directives with harmonization and that of regulations with unification is not subject to universal agreement, however, and may depend on one's views concerning, inter alia, the practical versus theoretical effects of directives or whether approximation is synonymous with harmonization. See, eg, K Boele-Woelki, *Unifying and Harmonizing Substantive Law and the Role of Conflict of Laws* (Recueil des Cours 340 (2009), Hague Academy of International Law/Martinus Nijhoff, 2010) 275; EJ Lohse, 'The meaning of harmonisation in the context of European Union law—a process in need of definition' in M Andenas and CB Andersen (eds), *Theory and Practice of Harmonisation* (Edward Elgar, 2011) 282.

[84] van Gerven, n 74, 46.

[85] See Art 288, third para, TFEU.

[86] GA Bermann, 'Harmonization and Regulatory Federalism' in I Pernice (ed), 1 *Harmonization of Legislation in Federal Systems* (Nomos, 1996) 37, 38–39. See already FG Jacobs and KL Karst, 'The "Federal" Legal Order: The U.S.A. and Europe Compared—A Juridical Perspective' in M Cappelletti et al (eds), *1 Integration Through Law: Europe and the American Federal Experience* (Walter de Gruyter, 1986) 167, 242–243.

[87] See Chapter 4, § 4.3.

[88] See Art 288, second para, TFEU.

[89] This is so notwithstanding that the Declaration on Art 100a EEC (now Art 114 TFEU) annexed to the SEA ascribes a preference for directives under the following circumstances: 'In its proposals pursuant to Article 100a(1) the Commission shall give precedence to the use of the instrument of a directive if harmonization involves the amendment of legislative provisions in one or more Member States.' Declaration on Art 100a of the EEC Treaty, [1987] OJ L169/24.

[90] See, eg, Case C-386/05 *Color Drack* [2007] ECR I-3699, para 24; Opinion of AG Léger in Case C-281/02 *Owusu* [2005] ECR I-1383, point 203 (albeit linking approximation with directives and hence assimilating it to harmonization).

[91] See, eg, Opinion 1/94 *Agreement establishing the World Trade Organization* [1994] ECR I-5267, para 100; Case C-350/92 *Spain v Council* [1995] ECR I-1985, para 19; Opinion of AG Léger in

Indeed, unification by itself generates its own set of problems. Given its link to the proliferation of one uniform set of Union rules, unification is invariably associated with 'uniformity'.[92] This is so even though scholars are quick to point out that unification and uniformity are not necessarily the same thing, since depending upon the way uniformity is framed, it invites the distinction between how such law appears 'on the books' and how it is applied 'in practice'.[93] For example, as often repeated in the debate, a European contract law instrument unifying the laws of the Member States in theory may still lack uniformity in practice depending upon the way that it is applied and interpreted by national courts and other national authorities.

On a more general note, this should not be taken to mean that harmonization and unification are limited to those two Union instruments, directives and regulations, respectively. Likewise, notwithstanding the emphasis placed on legislative action, these terms have also been applied in connection with the workings of the other Union institutions besides the Union legislature, such as those performing judicial or executive functions.[94] The bottom line is that the choice between unification and harmonization is not neutral. As one scholar remarked, 'talking about "harmonization" of law transmits a signal of tolerance for diversity that is absent in the notion of "unification"'.[95] In the EU, the association of regulations with unification implies that action is to be taken at the central or Union level. As such, unification embodies tensions that harmonization does not.

In view of the foregoing remarks, *harmonization* will be used in this discussion to denote the process of eliminating differences in national laws through the adoption of an instrument that emanates from EU institutional processes, but maintains the character of Member State law, that is to say, it has the identity of a national norm. For example, this would encompass the Union legislature's foray into contract law by means of the various directives within the EU contract law *acquis*. By comparison, *unification* will be used to signify the process leading to the adoption of an instrument applicable throughout the Member States, which emanates from EU institutional processes and which embodies the character of Union (or international) law, that is to say, it has the identity of a Union or international norm. Thus, it could envelop the adoption of a European contract law instrument (whether binding or non-binding, optional, or otherwise) or other instruments, such as conventions, which depending upon the

Case C-513/03 *van Hilten-van der Heijden* [2006] ECR I-1957, point 76; Opinion of AG Mengozzi in Case C-103/06 *Derouin* [2008] ECR I-1853, point 27. With particular regard to Art 114 TFEU, see also Opinion of AG Trstenjak in Case C-81/09 *Idryma Typou* [2010] ECR I-10161, point 43.

[92] This is so, even if unification has splintered off into nuanced variations such as 'uniformization', which seems to veer towards harmonization. See U Drobnig, 'Unification of National Law and the Uniformisation of the Rules of Private International Law' in P Bourel et al, *The Influence of the European Communities upon Private International Law of the Member States* (Larcier, 1981) 1, 2; A Jeammaud, 'Unification, uniformisation, harmonization: de quoi s'agit-il?' in *Towards a European Consumer Code*, n 64, 35, 47.

[93] See, eg, C Baasch-Andersen, 'Defining Uniformity in Law' (2007) 12 *Unif L Rev* 5. This has relevance in the American context as regards the 'uniform law process': see Chapter 3, § 3.3.

[94] See van Gerven, n 74, 47, 65.

[95] U Mattei, 'Hard Minimal Code Now—A Critique of "Softness" and a Plea for Responsibility in the European Debate over Codification' in *An Academic Green Paper on European Contract Law*, n 70, 215, 223. See also, eg, A Klip, 'European Integration and Harmonization and Criminal Law' in D Curtin et al, *European Integration and Law: Four Contributions on the Interplay between European Integration and European and National Law to celebrate the 25th Anniversary of Maastricht University's Faculty of Law* (Intersentia, 2006) 109, 110; M van Hoecke, 'The Harmonization of Private Law in Europe: Some Misunderstandings' in M van Hoecke and F Ost (eds), *The Harmonization of European Private Law* (Hart, 2000) 1, 2–3.

Member States concerned may or may not necessitate certain implementing measures to become part of a particular national legal order, but nevertheless retain the form and character of the instrument concerned.

Approximation will be used here as the container term for the institutionalized process at the European level encompassing harmonization and unification in the general sense. While harmonization has been used in the same way, this will not be done here in order to avoid confusion between the two terms in terms of having to clarify harmonization's general meaning from its more specific meaning associated with the use of directives. This also proves to be a convenient, overarching way to describe the activities (legislative, judicial, or otherwise) surrounding European contract law at the European level without being hemmed in by either harmonization or unification. For example, as will be seen in the next chapter, approximation aptly describes the role played by the Court of Justice in European contract law, given its interpretation of directives within the EU contract law *acquis*, thereby involving harmonization, as well as its formulation of judge-made rules of Union law, which falls on the unification side of the line.[96] Admittedly, the definitions advocated here, especially that of approximation, go against the grain of much of the standard practice of scholars and the Union institutions, both of which have grown accustomed to using approximation and harmonization interchangeably or preferring the use of the latter term in the context of the debate about European contract law (and European private law generally).[97] Nevertheless, these definitions may finally help to draw markers between these three terms and to highlight their nuances, which is important not only for clarity's sake, but also because they are the gateway through which the other terms are viewed.

1.2.3.2 Harmonization models

With the definition of harmonization in place, this leads to the discussion of the various types of techniques or models subsumed within harmonization. In this regard, one often finds the standard 'laundry list' of harmonization models used at the European level, which includes total, full, maximum, exhaustive, complete, minimum, optional, partial, and alternative harmonization, alongside the continuing introduction of new terms.[98] In principle, the definitions are clear enough, but in practice, there seems to be some ambiguity surrounding some of these models and even blurring between them. With some irony, one could say that these models are themselves in need of some harmonization, and in fact, it is particularly in light of the Commission's professed shift from minimum to maximum harmonization as part of its review of the consumer

[96] See Chapter 2.

[97] That said, they appeal to some scholars: see, eg, ALM Keirse, 'European impact on contract law—A perspective on the interlinked contributions of legal scholars, legislators and courts to the Europeanization of contract law' (2011) 7 *Utrecht L Rev* 34, 37.

[98] Eg, the term 'reflexive harmonization' has emerged in the literature, although not as yet in the context of the debate about European contract law: see Barnard, n 67, 642 and citations therein; the term 'horizontal harmonization' has been coined by one commentator to denote the harmonization of national laws on a broad scale beyond specific sectors as in the case of 'vertical harmonization': see Radeideh, n 67, 98; and the term 'half harmonization' has been used to distinguish aspects that should be subject to full versus minimum harmonization: see N Reich, 'The Social, Political and Cultural Dimension of EU Private Law' in R Schulze and H Schulte-Nölke (eds), *European Private Law—Current Status and Perspectives* (Sellier, 2011) 57, 81.

acquis within the European contract law project that renewed attention has been placed on this topic.[99]

Generally, it may be said that there is a sliding scale of harmonization models, which predicates the extent to which residual leeway is left for Member State action. On the side of strong Union action without much leeway for the Member States is *total harmonization*, also referred to as *maximum* or *full harmonization*.[100] This model generally occurs in situations where a Union norm replaces the national provisions in the relevant area and thus no derogations are allowed, save for what is provided in the Union harmonization measure itself (eg, safeguard clauses or derogations provided therein). This means that Member States cannot supplement, or lay down different rules diverging from, those provided for in the Union harmonization measure itself. Importantly, these terms may become entangled with issues surrounding the scope and degree of harmonization. On the one hand, total harmonization has been used to point to the *scope* of harmonization, ie the coverage of the relevant field by the Union harmonization measure concerned. Hence the association of total harmonization with *exhaustive harmonization*[101] or *complete harmonization* in the sense that the Union measure regulates the area 'completely' or 'occupies the field', with the result that national laws are ousted or pre-empted in the relevant field.[102] In contrast, *partial harmonization* has been used in this context to denote the fact that the Union harmonization measure is only 'partial', meaning that it only covers certain issues, leaving the rest to the

[99] For a brief selection, see, eg, H-W Micklitz, 'The Targeted Full Harmonization Approach: Looking Behind the Curtain' in G Howells and R Schulze (eds), *Modernising and Harmonising Consumer Contract Law* (Sellier, 2009) 47; S Weatherill, 'Maximum or Minimum Harmonization: What Kind of "Europe" Do We Want?' in *The Future of European Contract Law*, n 50, 133; and more recently, S Weatherill, 'Maximum versus Minimum Harmonization: Choosing between Unity and Diversity in the Search for the Soul of the Internal Market' in NN Shuibhne and LW Gormley (eds), *From Single Market to Economic Union: Essays in Memory of John A Usher* (Oxford Univ Press, 2012) 175. With regard to the Consumer Rights Directive, see further Chapter 6, § 6.3.3. Beyond the consumer sphere, see, eg, W Devroe, 'Limits of Differentiation in European Economic Law: *Ne Bis In Idem* and Minimum versus Maximum Harmonization' (2009) 16 *MJ* 141.

[100] See, eg, A Johnston and H Unberath, 'European private law by directives: approach and challenges' in *The Cambridge Companion to European Union Private Law*, n 39, 85, 88; J Stuyck et al, 'Confidence through fairness? The new Directive on unfair business-to-consumer commercial practices in the internal market' (2006) 43 *CML Rev* 107, 115 fn 43.

[101] See, eg, M Dougan, *National Remedies Before the Court of Justice: Issues of Harmonization and Differentiation* (Hart, 2004) 128–131; E Vos, 'Differentiation, Harmonization and Governance' in B de Witte et al (eds), *The Many Faces of Differentiation in EU Law* (Intersentia, 2001) 145, 148–149; S Weatherill, 'Beyond Preemption? Shared Competence and Constitutional Change in the European Community' in D O'Keeffe and PM Twomey (eds), *Legal Issues of the Maastricht Treaty* (Wiley Chancery Law, 1994) 13, 17–18. Compare SA de Vries, *Tensions within the Internal Market: The Functioning of the Internal Market and the Development of Horizontal and Flanking Policies* (Europa, 2006) 250–251.

[102] Some scholars find exhaustive or complete harmonization to be more of a 'theoretical' possibility on the grounds that it is rarely the case that the Union occupies the field completely. See, eg, Radeideh, n 67, 97 fn 55. Yet, this seems to depend on the eye of the beholder in terms of delineating the area concerned and the relevant measures that have been adopted therein. Also, to be clear, the concept of pre-emption is not limited to so-called 'occupation of the field'. See further, eg, ED Cross, 'Pre-emption of Member State Law in the European Economic Community: A Framework For Analysis' (1992) 29 *CML Rev* 447; LW Gormley, 'Free Movement of Goods and Pre-emption of State Power' in A Arnull et al (eds), *A Constitutional Order of States? Essays in EU Law in Honour of Alan Dashwood* (Hart, 2011) 365; R. Schütze, 'Supremacy Without Pre-emption? The Very Slowly Emergent Doctrine of Community Pre-emption' (2006) 43 *CML Rev* 1023; M Waelbroeck, 'The Emergent Doctrine of Community Pre-emption–Consent and Re-delegation' in T Sandalow and E Stein (eds), *II Courts and Free Markets: Perspectives from the United States and Europe* (Clarendon, 1982) 549.

Member States.[103] The determination of the scope, exhaustive or not, of the Union harmonization measure has crucial implications for assessing the compatibility of diverging national rules either on the basis of the measure concerned or on the basis of the free movement rules, namely Articles 34–36 TFEU concerning the free movement of goods.[104] On the other hand, total harmonization has been used to denote the *level* or *degree* of harmonization and thus is equated with *full* or *maximum* harmonization in the sense that, as already mentioned, the Union measure lays down the common standard to be followed within the regulatory space covered—ie the floor and ceiling of regulatory protection—with the result that Member States cannot go any further downwards or upwards as compared to minimum harmonization discussed below in the latter case.[105]

Admittedly, it is not always clear in what way commentators and even the Court of Justice are using these terms,[106] and care should be taken not to confuse the scope of harmonization (the area covered by the Union rules) with the degree of harmonization (the type of harmonization model chosen within the space covered by those Union rules).[107] Practically speaking, however, it is sometimes difficult to separate the two. This is illustrated by the interplay between *full harmonization* and *full targeted harmonization*. As noted earlier, full harmonization is generally considered to mean the same thing as maximum harmonization in terms of denoting the degree of harmonization concerned.[108] In the context of the Commission's plans for revising the EU consumer *acquis* by way of the proposal for a Directive on consumer rights,[109] the term

[103] See, eg, Radeideh, n 67, 97; R Schütze, *From Dual to Cooperative Federalism: The Changing Structure of European Law* (Oxford Univ Press, 2009) 195; Vos, n 101. See also Case C-453/10 (Judgment of 15 March 2012), *Pereničová*, not reported, para 34 and citations therein.

[104] Under the case law, the determination that a Union harmonization measure exhaustively covers the area concerned dictates that such a measure constitutes the relevant framework for assessing the national rules at issue, whereas if this is not the case, the relevant framework is constituted by the general provisions of the Treaties, namely Arts 34–36 TFEU. Recent case law has presented some interesting nuances in this regard. Compare, eg, Case C-445/06 *Danske Slagterier* [2009] ECR I-2119, paras 23–26, with Case C-470/03 *AGM-COS.MET* [2007] ECR I-2749, paras 50–54. See also Opinion of AG Trstenjak in Joined Cases C-261/07 and C-299/07 *VTB-VAB* [2009] ECR I-2949, point 99; the Court did not get to this issue: see para 67.

[105] See, eg, Radeideh, n 67, 99–101; V Mak, 'Review of the Consumer Acquis: Towards Maximum Harmonization?' (2009) 17 *ERPL* 55, 58–59.

[106] See, eg, Chapter 9, § 9.2.2. So far, the term 'maximum harmonization' appears less frequently in the Court's judgments as compared to the AG Opinions: see, eg, Opinion of AG van Gerven in Case C-326/88 *Hansen* [1990] ECR I-2911, point 10; Opinion of AG Ruiz-Jarabo Colomer in C-374/05 *Gintec International Import-Export* [2007] ECR I-9517, caption A, points 22, 29, 31, 33, 41, 47, 81.

[107] See further, eg, MW Hesselink, 'Towards a Sharp Distinction between B2B and B2C? On Consumer, Commercial and General Contract Law after the Consumer Rights Directive' (2010) 18 *ERPL* 57, 78–81; Schütze, n 103, 194–197; Slot, n 64, 388–389; de Vries, n 101, 253.

[108] Though as noted by one commentator, it may be a little confusing, since the word 'full' would seem to be aimed at the scope, as opposed to the degree, of harmonization concerned. See Radeideh, n 67, 100 fn 75. It may be wondered whether the translation of these terms in different language versions, eg, 'full harmonization' in English is translated as 'harmonisation complète' in French (the Court's working language) may add to the confusion as to whether full harmonization is being used to indicate the scope or degree of harmonization concerned. Compare, eg, Case C-540/08 *Mediaprint* [2010] ECR I-10909, paras 27, 30, with Opinion of AG Trstenjak, heading 3(a)(i) ('Full and maximum harmonisation of national rules as a regulatory objective') and points 33, 61, 63; see also Opinion of AG Trstenjak in Joined Cases C-261/07 and C-299/07 *VTB-VAB* [2009] ECR I-2949, heading 3(a)(i) and points 74, 76, 85; Opinion of AG Trstenjak in Case C-304/08 *Plus Warenhandelsgesellschaft* [2010] ECR I-217, heading 3(a)(i) and points 37, 69, 71.

[109] Proposal for a Directive of the European Parliament and of the Council on consumer rights, COM (2008) 614 final, 8.10.2008 (Proposal).

full targeted harmonization is used alongside that of full harmonization.[110] In this proposal, the Commission defines full targeted harmonization as harmonization 'targeted at those issues raising substantial barriers to trade for business and/or deterring consumers from buying cross-border'.[111] This implies full harmonization on a more limited scale, ie laying down a common Union standard not across the board but just for certain specific areas, thus relating to the scope of the proposed Directive. At the same time, however, this term is situated within the discussion of the shift from minimum harmonization (employed for the measures that were envisaged to be replaced by the proposed Directive) to maximum harmonization, thereby implicating the degree of harmonization involved.[112] Reading between the lines, full targeted harmonization appears to be a politically preferable term to take into account Member State sensitivities concerning further Union inroads into what used to be space for Member State action, either in terms of the shift from minimum to maximum harmonization or to areas subject to Union standards that were not previously covered.[113] In any event, it remains to be seen whether full targeted harmonization will be used on a more general scale, and noticeably, only the term full harmonization appears in the text of the proposal[114] and the Consumer Rights Directive itself[115] in reference to the level of harmonization envisaged. Therefore, despite some ambiguities in connection with full harmonization, for the purposes of this discussion, the terms *maximum* and *full harmonization* will be used to denote the degree of harmonization concerned, which is in line with the treatment of such terms in most literature and institutional documents in European contract law.

Continuing along the spectrum, there are the intermediary models of alternative, partial, and optional harmonization. *Alternative harmonization* is a harmonization model that permits the Member States to choose between certain alternatives provided in the Union harmonization measure concerned in order to achieve the objectives pursued.[116] In addition to its usage in connection with the scope of harmonization discussed earlier, *partial harmonization* may be employed to denote the harmonization model in which harmonized rules are set down only for cross-border, not domestic, transactions.[117] Taking it one step further, *optional harmonization* has been defined as the model of harmonization in which national operators are provided with the 'option' of following the Union harmonized standard or the relevant national standard in the context of domestic transactions, whereas for cross-border transactions, such operators must abide by the harmonized rules.[118]

110 This is not the first time that such phrasing appeared, eg, reference is made to 'targeted harmonization' in the seventh recital of the Services Directive (n 162).

111 Proposal, n 109, point 2, at 4. See also Green Paper on the Review of the Consumer Acquis, COM (2006) 744 final, 8.2.2007, point 3, first indent.

112 The proposed shift from minimum to maximum harmonization was one of the most controversial elements of the Proposal and was scaled down in the Directive as adopted: see Chapter 6, § 6.3.3.

113 See, eg, S Weatherill, 'The Consumer Rights Directive: How and Why a Quest for "Coherence" Has (Largely) Failed' (2012) 49 *CML Rev* 1279, 1287.

114 See Proposal, n 109, Art 4.

115 Dir 2011/83/EU of the European Parliament and of the Council of 25 Oct 2011 on consumer rights, amending Council Dir 93/13/EEC and Dir 1999/44/EC of the European Parliament and of the Council and repealing Council Dir 85/577/EEC and Dir 97/7/EC of the European Parliament and of the Council, [2011] OJ L304/64 (Consumer Rights Directive), fifth, seventh recitals; Art 4.

116 Slot, n 64, 387.

117 See Slot, n 64, 384.

118 See, eg, Barnard, n 67, 631–632; D Curtin, 'Emerging Institutional Parameters and Organised Difference in the European Union' in *The Many Faces of Differentiation in EU Law*, n 101, 347, 361–362; Schütze, n 103, 197–198; Slot, n 64, 383–384.

Two points of clarification are in order when it comes to optional harmonization. First, to some ears, optional harmonization may imply some sort of harmonization process on a more voluntary basis, say where the Member States are given the option to decide whether or not to adhere to the particular Union rules. However, this has not been the way this term has been used in the literature and institutional practice so far. Secondly, optional harmonization should not be conflated with the adoption of an optional instrument as far as the debate on European contract law is concerned. As noted above, questions persist as regards whether an optional instrument may be considered to approximate national contract laws, especially in light of the proposed CESL.[119] Yet, at least so far, such an instrument is envisaged to constitute an additional set of contract rules alongside the pre-existing national contract laws, as opposed to modifying them with a Union harmonized standard in the case of optional harmonization.[120] As matters stand at present, these three models have not garnered much attention in the debate about European contract law, which explains why the spotlight is largely placed on minimum harmonization.

Finally, at the other end of the spectrum is *minimum harmonization*, one of the most well-known harmonization models and, until recently, an ingrained feature of the EU consumer contract law *acquis*.[121] *Minimum harmonization* means that a common, minimum standard is set down in a particular Union harmonization measure, but that the Member States can provide for more stringent rules within the area covered by the measure.[122] The idea is that the Union harmonization measure provides the 'floor' of protection, but the Member States may go further upwards to the 'ceiling' of the Treaties (namely the free movement rules) in this regard.[123] Minimum harmonization is therefore concerned with the degree of harmonization involved.[124] To be clear, minimum harmonization means that the Member States can go further in providing a more protective or stringent standard, but they cannot go below the Union minimum standard.[125] Sometimes the minimum harmonization clause in the measure concerned is explicit in terms of the more stringent protection to be provided by the Member States.[126] Moreover, minimum harmonization is different from the special derogation procedure laid down in Article 114 TFEU.[127] Unlike minimum harmonization, opting

[119] See Chapter 6, § 6.4.4. [120] See Chapter 8, § 8.4.3.2.

[121] See M Dougan, 'Minimum Harmonization and the Internal Market' (2000) 37 *CML Rev* 853; P Rott, 'Minimum Harmonization for the Completion of the Internal Market? The Example of Consumer Sales Law' (2003) 40 *CML Rev* 1107; J Stuyck, 'Patterns of Justice in the European Constitutional Charter: Minimum Harmonization in the Field of Consumer Law' in L Krämer et al (eds), *Law and Diffuse Interests in the European Legal Order—Liber amicorum Norbert Reich* (Nomos, 1997) 279. [122] See, eg, Dougan, n 121; Rott, n 121; Stuyck, n 121.

[123] A remark attributed to Professor Stephen Weatherill: see, eg, S Weatherill, *Law and Integration in the European Union* (Clarendon, 1995) 153.

[124] See, eg, Case C-361/89 *Di Pinto* [1991] ECR I-1189, paras 21–22.

[125] See, eg, Opinion of AG Trstenjak in Case C-404/06 *Quelle* [2008] ECR I-2685, point 52; Opinion of AG Trstenjak in Case C-484/08 *Caja de Ahorros y Monte de Piedad de Madrid* [2010] ECR I-4785, points 52, 86; Opinion of AG Mengozzi in Case C-511/08 *Heinrich Heine* [2010] ECR I-3047, points 62–63; Opinion of AG Trstenjak in Case C-453/10 (Judgment of 15 March 2012) *Pereničová*, not reported, points 71–72.

[126] Eg, Opinion of AG Trstenjak in Case C-265/07 *Caffaro* [2008] ECR I-7085, point 41.

[127] Art 114(10) TFEU concerns the possibility of a safeguard clause on a temporary basis, as opposed to Art 114(4)–(9) TFEU, which concern the possibility of maintaining or introducing measures derogating from the Union measure on a general, not merely provisional, basis. See further N De Sadeleer, 'Procedures for Derogations from the Principle of Approximation of Laws under Article 95 EC' (2003) 40 *CML Rev* 889; I Maletić, 'Theory and practice of harmonisation in the European internal market' in *Theory and Practice of Harmonisation*, n 83, 314.

out by way of this procedure is subject to much more strict control by the Commission on a case-by-case basis, meaning that it is not given to all Member States collectively, but instead is granted to a particular Member State on an individual basis, provided that the Member State concerned satisfies all of the requisite conditions for either maintaining (Article 114(4) TFEU) or introducing (Article 114(5) TFEU) more stringent or otherwise derogating national rules. In short, while it could appear as such, minimum harmonization is not an 'oxymoron' in terms,[128] but rather an ingenious way to achieve the Union's internal market objectives while giving the Member States a certain amount of leeway (in accordance with Union law) to provide for a more stringent standard of protection in certain areas, including consumer protection. It is for this reason that it has played an important role in the development of EU contract law, and by the same token, the shift away from minimum harmonization has provoked considerable controversy as part of the debate.

1.2.3.3 Coordination

Like approximation and harmonization, coordination is a process that has appeared in the Treaty framework since the original EEC Treaty and is equally chameleonic. Coordination may be used to denote a number of different forms, which can largely be subsumed within the two-fold distinction between mandatory or binding coordination, on the one hand, and certain, so-called 'softer' forms of coordination, on the other.[129]

Mandatory or binding coordination refers to the process by which Union law leaves intact the separate national legal systems but makes their coordination mandatory, such that it determines the applicable national law in cross-border settings.[130] This can be considered the formal definition of coordination (coordination *sensu stricto*). On the face of the various provisions in which this form of coordination appears in the Treaties, coordination *sensu stricto* can in principle be considered 'one stop short' of harmonization, let alone unification, because even though EU law is imposing a binding solution, it does not require the elimination of differences among the national laws so that they resemble each other in a similar substantive sense so as to facilitate the tasks to be achieved in the relevant policy field. This form of coordination has therefore been considered to evoke a 'lighter touch' on the part of the EU because it has a lesser impact on the legal orders of the Member States.[131] This explains why coordination invariably appears in the context of sensitive policy sectors, such as that concerning economic policy,[132] for which approximation may be considered as going too far. That

[128] S Weatherill, 'Minimum Harmonization as Oxymoron? The case of consumer law' in H-W Micklitz (ed), *Verbraucherrecht in Deutschland—Stand und Perspektiven* (Nomos, 2005) 15.

[129] See TK Hervey and JV McHale, *Health Law and the European Union* (Cambridge Univ Press, 2004) 59–62.

[130] Classic examples are Union measures requiring the mandatory coordination of national social security systems, such as Council Reg (EEC) No 1408/71 of 14 June 1971 on the application of social security schemes to employed persons and their families moving within the Community, [1971] OJ L149/2, OJ Spec Ed 1971 II, p 416 (see, eg, Case C-282/11 (Judgment of 21 Feb 2013) *Salgado González*, not reported, para 35); or Dir 96/71/EC of the European Parliament and of the Council of 16 Dec 1996 concerning the posting of workers in the framework of the provision of services, [1997] OJ L18/1 (see, eg, Case C-341/05 *Laval un Partneri* [2007] ECR I-11767, paras 59–60).

[131] This may be further evidenced by the use of 'coordination' in the Treaties as a process directed by not only the Union institutions, but also the Member States among themselves, in liaison with the Commission, in certain policy fields. See Arts 171(2) and 173(2) TFEU.

[132] See, eg, Art 121 TFEU.

being said, coordination may become blurred with harmonization in certain cases.[133] Article 53 TFEU is a notable example in this regard, since this provision concerning the right of establishment (and by cross-reference, Article 62 TFEU on the free movement of services) prescribes the 'coordination' of national laws, but it is often used alongside Article 114 TFEU whose harmonizing objectives take precedence, as illustrated by the *Tobacco Advertising I* case law.[134]

'Softer' forms of coordination have been used to denote processes that transcend approximation in some shape or form,[135] especially by virtue of the association with the Open Method of Coordination (OMC) as part of the so-called 'new modes of governance' in the EU. Although difficult to generalize, the OMC is based on looser coordination practices, such as guidelines, exchange of best practices, benchmarking, and action plans, among the Member States, and diverges from the standard Union (formerly Community) method, which may explain why it has been posited in the debate about European contract law.[136] To avoid confusion, coordination will be used in its strict sense for this discussion.

1.2.3.4 Codification

In the EU, the term codification may take several forms. For instance, it has a specific meaning in the context of the EU 'better regulation' programme, in which it signifies the bringing together of all amendments to a given Union measure adopted at different times into one instrument.[137] Yet, in the debate about European contract law (and European private law generally), codification is commonly used in connection with the adoption of a comprehensive instrument encompassing various fields of private law at the European level.[138] It can therefore be viewed as a widescale form of approximation.[139] As explained by one scholar:

> Codification is therefore 'comprehensive' in two regards: first, in that it is conceived and structured as a whole which implies that it normally includes, or is intended to include, more than one chapter of *in casu* private law; and secondly, in that it takes a global view aiming to regulate matters in general, for reasons of legal certainty and consistency, which does not preclude rules focusing on the protection of specific interests from being incorporated in the larger whole. In consequence, to unify the general part of contract and certain specific types of contract only, is *not* codification in the proper sense of the word whilst unifying large parts of the 'patrimonial' law . . . would deserve that denomination.[140]

In line with these remarks, the use of codification in conjunction with contract law through reference to a 'European contract code' may either be considered ill-fitting or else may imply that it is merely the prelude of more to come. To complicate matters

[133] See, eg, Jeammaud, n 92, 46. [134] See Chapter 8, § 8.3.2.1.

[135] See, eg, K Lilleholt, 'European Private Law: Unification, Harmonisation or Coordination' in *The Foundations of European Private Law*, n 55, 353. [136] See Chapter 11, § 11.4.1.

[137] See <http://ec.europa.eu/smart-regulation/better_regulation/key_docs_en.htm>.

[138] Surely codification may be used in other senses. See, eg, N Jansen, *The Making of Legal Authority: Non-legislative Codifications in Historical and Comparative Perspective* (Oxford Univ Press, 2010).

[139] For detailed discussion of the characteristics and functions of codification as situated against the backdrop of the national experience, see, eg, J Basedow, 'Transjurisdictional Codification' (2009) 83 *Tul L Rev* 973; JM Smits, *Private Law 2.0: On the Role of Private Actors in a Post-National Society* (Eleven International, 2011) 13–16; R Zimmerman, 'Codification' (2012) 8 *ERCL* 367.

[140] W van Gerven, 'Codifying European private law? Yes, if . . .!' (2002) 27 *ELR* 156, 161.

further, codification within the context of European contract law does not necessarily have to mean a code that replaces national law, since references to various designs of 'optional codes' supplementing national laws abound.[141]

Be that as it may, the term European contract code has become a steady fixture in the discourse. Since the very beginning, the debate about European contract law has been encapsulated within the discussion of a 'European civil code' or similar derivation,[142] and despite recent protestations to the contrary by the Commission[143] Union institutions and scholars still continue to refer to such an instrument.[144] In all fairness, the references to a European contract code and a European civil code are a convenient shorthand for the adoption of a comprehensive Union contract or private law instrument, respectively, without having to go through all the histrionics of explaining what is comprehensive, far-reaching, or the like. And with particular regard to a European civil code, it may assume broader, holistic dimensions, as illustrated by its association with the building of a European civil society.[145]

Yet, the drawbacks associated with the use of the terms European contract code and European civil code are heavy because they are likely to inject sensitivities implicating the EU's encroachment on the competences of the Member States. These terms are even more potentially damaging because they threaten to misalign, even silence, the 'constitutional conversation' about European contract law. Most scholars, even those who argue that the EU has sufficient competence to adopt a European contract law instrument, admit that it does not have sufficient competence to adopt a comprehensive instrument covering vast areas of civil (or private) law as often signified by a European civil code.[146] Thus, under circumstances where the two terms are intertwined or blurred in the discussion, this essentially provides an 'easy way out' of the constitutionality of European contract law since it leads to generalizations, mostly of a negative nature, about Union competence, which may preclude a more in-depth assessment of such competence in contract law. Accordingly, while it is not disputed that the terms European contract code and European civil code have utility, they carry considerable 'political baggage' in the 'constitutional conversation' about European contract law. This explains why codification and its variants will not generally be relied upon in the analysis, save where reference is made to them in the relevant institutional documents and scholarly literature. As noted earlier, in their place, the term *European contract law instrument* will be employed to denote in a

[141] See, eg, *An Academic Green Paper on European Contract Law*, n 70, particularly pt IV. Compare A Chamboredon, 'The Debate on a European Civil Code: For an "Open Texture"' in *The Harmonization of European Private Law*, n 95, 63.

[142] Eg, a 'European Code of Private Law' cited in the European Parliament's early resolutions: see Chapter 4, § 4.3.

[143] See Chapters 5–6.

[144] As for the Union institutions, see, eg, the reference to a 'European civil code' as one of the options in the Commission's 2010 Green Paper: Chapter 6, § 6.4.2; see also Opinion of AG Trstenjak in Case C-404/06 *Quelle* [2008] ECR I-2685, point 51 fn 37; A. Fuchs, 'European contract law: the way forward' (2011) 12 *ERA Forum* 1, 3 (noting the remarks of Commissioner Viviane Reding, declaring that the CFR is 'the embryo for a European civil code'). As for the scholarly literature, see, eg, M Andenas et al (eds), *Liber Amicorum Guido Alpa—Private Law Beyond the National Systems* (BIICL, 2008); *Making European Private Law*, n 49; N Jansen and L Rademacher, 'European Civil Code' in JM Smits (ed), *Elgar Encyclopedia of Comparative Law, Second Edition* (Edward Elgar, 2012) 299; Twigg-Flesner, n 51, 14–18.

[145] See H Collins, *The European Civil Code: The Way Forward* (Cambridge Univ Press, 2008); and more recently, H Collins, 'Why Europe Needs a Civil Code' (2013) 21 *ERPL* 907.

[146] See, eg, Basedow, n 139, 980–981. This is so at least in the abstract, since the term 'European civil code' may be viewed in varying ways, eg, it may be affiliated with European patrimonial law: see § 1.2.2.2.

general sense the adoption of a comprehensive substantive contract law instrument at the European level without provoking anxieties and misunderstandings underlying the word 'code'.

1.2.3.5 Europeanization (and formerly Communitarization)

Depending upon the way that they are employed, Europeanization and Communitarization (before the entry into force of the Lisbon Treaty) may embody aspects of approximation, harmonization, and unification. By virtue of their roots to 'Europeanize' or 'Communitarize', these two terms have been used to denote the intervention of the EU (or the former Community in the case of the latter) in a particular domain, including private or contract law.[147] In this way, they may be considered general container terms for the harmonization and unification of national laws on a par with approximation.[148] They also need not be limited to the sphere of legislative action at the European level; for instance, Europeanization has been used to denote the prospect of the Court of Justice's fashioning 'Europeanized' concepts of contract law in its judgments.[149]

However, Europeanization has been defined more broadly so as to go beyond the EU sphere, for example, in reference to national laws being approximated not only by virtue of Union law, but also other factors, such as the ECHR and the influence of comparative law.[150] In particular, scholars link Europeanization with the emergence of the new 'ius commune' and the growing together of national legal systems in various ways outside institutionalized processes emanating from the European level.[151] In past years, Communitarization (also spelled Communautarization) was therefore the more specific term honing in on what was then Community (now Union) action, whereas Europeanization encompasses a spectrum of activities that could conceivably extend beyond such action.

With the entry into force of the Lisbon Treaty, Communitarization is not likely to be used much longer on account of its linkage to the former European 'Community', at least as regards the description of the EU's present day activities. This may have the

[147] See, eg, P Nebbia, 'Law as Tradition and the Europeanization of Contract Law: A Case Study' (2004) 23 *YEL* 363; Twigg-Flesner, n 40, 38; R Zimmermann, 'Comparative Law and the Europeanization of Private Law' in M Reimann and R Zimmermann (eds), *The Oxford Handbook of Comparative Law* (Oxford Univ Press, 2006) 539.

[148] See, eg, O Lando, 'Guest Editorial: European Contract Law After the Year 2000' (1998) 35 *CML Rev* 821, 821. See also Miller, n 5, 2–14 (outlining three different perspectives of this term including, but not limited to, harmonization).

[149] See Chapter 2.

[150] W van Gerven, 'Bridging the Gap Between Community and National Laws: Towards a Principle of Homogeneity in the Field of Legal Remedies' (1995) 32 *CML Rev* 679, 698 fn 62 (1995). See further M Reimann, 'Comparative Law and Private International Law' in *The Oxford Handbook of Comparative Law*, n 147, 1363, 1389; S Weatherill, 'Prospects for the Development of European Private Law through "Europeanisation" in the European Court—The Case of the Directive on Unfair Terms in Consumer Contracts' (1995) 3 *ERPL* 307, 308 fn 3.

[151] Compare, eg, 'Special Issue on Interactive Private Law Adjudication in the European Multi-level System—Analytical Explorations and Normative Challenges' (2000) 8 *ERPL* No 1, particularly s III; A Albors-Llorens, 'Consumer Law, Competition Law and the Europeanization of Private Law' in *The Institutional Framework of European Private Law*, n 49, 245, 247–249; Hesselink, n 52, 8; R Michaels and N Jansen, 'Private Law Beyond the State? Europeanization, Globalization, Privatization' (2006) 54 *AJCL* 843, 861–864; R Zimmermann, 'Roman Law and the Harmonization of Private Law in Europe' in *Towards a European Civil Code*, n 5, 27, 31–32 (referring to the 'Re-Europeanization' of private law through case law and legal scholarship).

result that Europeanization may be more widely used, or other terms may be coined to take its place (eg, Unionization, albeit somewhat awkward). This does not change the fact that Europeanization remains a somewhat imprecise term in terms of delineating its expanse beyond the EU setting. Also, Europeanization (as with Communitarization pre-Lisbon or synonymous terms post-Lisbon) has the potential to inject a subtle negative bias regarding the EU's inroads into national contract law and thus may invoke sensitivities regarding the impact and extent of the EU's action in this field and others.[152] For these reasons, although these terms arise in the discourse, they will not be relied upon here.

1.2.3.6 Convergence

Convergence may be considered among the widest of the terms mentioned here because it encompasses institutionalized processes emanating from the EU and in the broader European sense (eg, the ECHR framework), as well as more organic processes. As described by one scholar, 'convergence is a generic name comprising both approximation of laws through an institutionalized (legislative or judicial) process and the growing together of legal systems as a result of voluntary action, or even spontaneous behaviour, on the part of legislatures, regulators or courts'.[153] Accordingly, convergence is a wonderful umbrella term encompassing various sorts of processes bringing national (contract) laws closer together without necessarily being tied to any sort of EU institutionalized action. At the same time, convergence may cause uncertainty in the sense of failing to delineate on just what side—approximation and/or more voluntary forms of action—the emphasis is placed. These ambiguities should be kept in mind, since they have filtered into the debate about European contract law.[154] This explains why convergence will not be resorted to, save for the institutional documents and literature in which it appears.

1.2.3.7 Comparative leaps to the US

Not surprisingly, some of the abovementioned terms that stem from the Treaty framework or otherwise embody a distinctive European flavour are not used much in the US as far as the discourse on the American contract law framework is concerned. That said, several prevalent terms in the debate about European contract law, particularly approximation, harmonization, unification, and codification, find parallels with the American setting. As documented in a coming chapter, the term codification has attracted its share of debate stemming from its association with the 'Uniform Commercial Code'.[155] Moreover, one of the mainstays of the American contract law framework is the adoption of uniform laws at the state level.[156] This explains why such laws have been classified under the rubric of harmonization by scholars.[157]

[152] Hence the emergence of the term 'non-Europeanization' as a negative counterexample: see, eg, L Niglia, 'The Non-Europeanisation of Private Law' (2001) 9 *ERPL* 575.

[153] van Gerven, n 74, 60–61, 65. This author's use of this term relates to his advocacy of an 'Open Method of Convergence' modelled after the OMC: see Chapter 11, § 11.4.1. For a similar position, see H-W Micklitz, 'Monistic Ideology versus Pluralistic Reality: Towards a Normative Design for European Private Law' in *Pluralism and European Private Law*, n 15, 29, 49.

[154] Eg, with regard to the Tampere Conclusions, see Chapter 4, § 4.4.2.

[155] See Chapter 3, § 3.5.1.3.

[156] See Chapter 3, § 3.3.

[157] See Bermann, n 86, 38–39.

There is one term, however, which typically arises in the American setting: *federalization*. This term may be equated with unification as defined earlier, since it denotes a process of bringing state laws closer together by taking action at the federal level covering a particular area or field and thus bringing it within the ambit of federal competence, ie federalizing it.[158] It is commonly associated with the adoption of federal legislation by Congress, as illustrated by its usage in relation to the prospect of a federal UCC or the adoption of federal measures covering certain areas of contract and commercial law in the US.[159] Presumably it may also apply to the actions taken by the executive and judicial branches at the federal level in this regard. Federalization is therefore extremely useful because by a single word it imparts federal action over one or more fields of state (private) law.

Federalization has started to make its way into the discourse on European contract law and European private law, among others.[160] In principle, there seems to be no reason why it could not be applied to the European setting as an overarching term akin to approximation in the sense of denoting action taken at the Union level comparable to the federal level in the US. In practice, however, given the sensitivities concerning the application of the 'federal' label to the EU, this may require putting in place the necessary caveats to make clear that its usage does not imply that the EU is being equated with the federal structure of a nation state, such as the US. To avoid this, federalization will be used mainly in the discussion of the American contract law framework, whereas terms such as approximation, harmonization, and unification fare just as well on either side of the Atlantic and will be used in connection with both the EU and US settings.

1.3 The Scope of EU Contract Law and Its 'Hard Core'

As mentioned earlier, EU contract law encompasses a plethora of Union measures adopted in a wide variety of policy fields, but it has become something of a standard practice in the discourse on European contract law over the years to focus on a certain collection of Union measures rooted in the achievement of the Union's internal market objectives and concerned for the most part (though not exclusively) with consumer contract law on the grounds that Union measures in other policy fields, such as competition law, intellectual property law, or labour and employment law, are based on special considerations.[161] As for what makes up this collection, the exact number typically varies. This can be attributed to several factors, such as the constant stream of new Union measures, especially those adopted during the time period in which the debate about European contract law was getting underway at the European level and thereafter,[162]

[158] Bermann, n 86, 39. [159] See Chapter 3, § 3.5.

[160] See, eg, J Lookofsky, 'Desparately [sic] Seeking Subsidiarity: Danish Private Law in the Scandinavian, European, and Global Context' (2008) 19 *DJCIL* 161, 166; R Van den Bergh, 'Subsidiarity as an Economic Demarcation Principle and the Emergence of European Private Law' (1998) 5 *MJ* 129, 130 fn 7. Outside this context, see, eg, T Tridimas, 'EU Financial Regulation: Federalization, Crisis Management, and Law Reform' in P Craig and G de Búrca (eds), *The Evolution of EU Law*, 2nd edn (Oxford Univ Press, 2011) 783.

[161] See, eg, Riesenhuber, n 37, 300–301; Vogenauer and Weatherill, n 40, 106–107.

[162] Eg, Dir 1999/93/EC of the European Parliament and of the Council of 13 Dec 1999 on a Community framework for electronic signatures, [2000] OJ L13/12 (Directive on electronic signatures); Dir 2000/31/EC of the European Parliament and of the Council of 8 June 2000 on certain legal aspects of information society services, in particular electronic commerce, in the Internal Market, [2000] OJ L178/1 (E-commerce Directive); Dir 2006/123/EC of the European Parliament and of the Council of 12 Dec 2006 on services in the internal market, [2006] OJ L 376/36 (Services Directive).

or differing opinion among commentators as to the impact, or not, of particular Union measures on contract law.[163] Moreover, some commentators consider measures within specific fields that embody complex legal frameworks unto themselves, such as insurance contract law[164] and financial services law,[165] while others point to measures that play an important role in the development of European private law generally, even if not, strictly speaking, dealing with contract law.[166]

In all likelihood, there may never be unanimous agreement on the number of relevant Union measures in this area. Nevertheless, there is a special set of Union measures within EU contract law that is a solid fixture in the lists of scholars and Union institutions alike in the debate about European contract law.[167] This set of nine directives may be called the 'hard core' of the EU contract law *acquis* and is listed chronologically as follows:

(1) The Doorstep Selling Directive (85/577/EEC), repealed by the Consumer Rights Directive (2011/83/EU);
(2) The Commercial Agents Directive (86/653/EEC);
(3) The Consumer Credit Directive (87/102/EEC), repealed by the new Consumer Credit Directive (2008/48/EC);
(4) The Package Travel Directive (90/314/EEC);
(5) The Unfair Contract Terms Directive (93/13/EEC);
(6) The Timeshare Directive (94/47/EC), repealed by the new Timeshare Directive (2008/122/EC);

[163] Eg, sometimes commentators include measures situated within EU consumer law overall, such as Dir 2005/29/EC of the European Parliament and of the Council of 11 May 2005 concerning unfair business-to-consumer commercial practices in the internal market and amending Council Dir 84/450/EC, Dirs 97/7/EC, 98/27/EC, and 2002/65/EC and Reg (EC) No 2006/2004, [2005] OJ L149/22 (Unfair Commercial Practices Directive); Dir 98/6/EC of the European Parliament and of the Council of 16 Feb 1998 on consumer protection in the indication of the prices of products offered to consumers, [1998] OJ L80/27 (Price Indication Directive); and Dir 98/27/EC of the European Parliament and of the Council of 19 May 1998 on injunctions for the protection of consumers' interests, [1998] OJ L166/51, codified as Dir 2009/22/EC, [2009] OJ L110/30 (Injunctions Directive). The latter two are part of the Commission's review of the consumer *acquis* discussed in Chapter 6; the Price Indication Directive is one of the rare measures based on what is now Art 169 TFEU: see further Chapter 9, § 9.2.3.2.

[164] See Chapter 5, § 5.4.3.2.

[165] Eg, Dir 2002/65/EC of the European Parliament and of the Council of 23 Sept 2002 concerning the distance marketing of consumer financial services and amending Council Dir 90/619/EEC and Dirs 97/7/EC and 98/27/EC, [2002] OJ L271/16. It was later amended by Dir 2007/64/EC of the European Parliament and of the Council of 13 Nov 2007 on payment services in the internal market amending Dirs 97/7/EC, 2002/65/EC, 2005/60/EC, and 2006/48/EC and repealing Dir 97/5/EC, [2007] OJ L319/1 (Payment Services Directive).

[166] Eg, Council Dir 85/374/EEC of 25 July 1985 on the approximation of the laws, regulations and administrative provisions of the Member States concerning liability for defective products, [1985] OJ L210/29 (Product Liability Directive). Relevant case law on this measure bears on the assessment of Art 169 TFEU: see Chapter 9, § 9.2.2.

[167] As for scholars, see, eg, A Hartkamp, *European Law and National Private Law: Effect of EU Law and European Human Rights Law on Legal Relationships between Individuals* (Kluwer, 2012) Annex I; O Radley-Gardner et al, *Fundamental Texts on European Private Law* (Hart, 2003) pt 1; Twigg-Flesner, n 40, 54–63; S Weatherill, 'European Private Law and the Constitutional Dimension' in *The Institutional Framework of European Private Law*, n 49, 79, 81–82. As for the Union institutions, see, eg, 2001 Communication, n 24, point 8 fns10–11, Annex I ('Important Community *Acquis* in the Area of Private Law'). See also Commission's response to Written Question E-4389/2007, n 51 (referring to the consumer contract law *acquis* as the 'core' of European private law).

(7) The Distance Selling Directive (97/7/EC), repealed by the Consumer Rights Directive (2011/83/EU);
(8) The Consumer Sales Directive (1999/44/EC); and
(9) The Late Payment Directive (2000/35/EC), repealed by the new Late Payment Directive (2011/7/EU).

The choice to focus on these nine directives and to refer to them as the 'hard core' of the EU contract law *acquis* warrants clarification. In recent years, the discourse on European contract law (as well as European private law generally) seems to be moving away to some extent from the emphasis on consumer contract law and highlighting the role that other areas of EU contract law can play in helping to outline commonalities and coherent features of this field as a whole.[168] As a result, this raises important scientific questions, especially in the context of the constitutional assessment of European contract law, as to whether too much emphasis is being placed on consumer contract law and whether the discourse should be focused on other kinds of Union measures, such as those that have had a substantial impact on national contract law and in which the Union's competence to adopt them has been less controversial.[169]

In response, it is not disputed that other kinds of Union measures are relevant, to varying degrees, in unearthing the scope of EU contract law generally and the Union's competence in contract law in particular. For instance, within the field of competition law, it may be wondered whether block exemption regulations have a greater impact on the approximation of contract law than all of the well-known consumer contract law directives put together, and in fact, given the lack of literature on such matters, this is an area that calls out for further research.[170] It is also not disputed that the legal bases and rationale put forward to substantiate the adoption of various other Union measures may be relevant to the constitutional assessment of European contract law, as illustrated by certain measures within the fields of commercial practices,[171] e-commerce,[172] and financial services,[173] which contain salient arguments concerning barriers to trade and the 'consumer confidence' rationale in connection with Article 114 TFEU.

To be clear, these directives are carved out as the 'hard core' of EU contract law because of their integral role in the debate about European contract law and the constitutional issues underlying it. The 'hard core' provides the platform for the debate

[168] Eg, as regards financial services, see S Grundmann and YM Atamer (eds), *Financial Services, Financial Crisis and General European Contract Law: Failure and Challenges of Contracting* (Kluwer, 2011); for other areas, see, eg, H-W Micklitz and F Cafaggi, 'Introduction' in H-W Micklitz and F Cafaggi (eds), *European Private Law After the Common Frame of Reference* (Edward Elgar, 2010) viii; R Schulze, 'Contours of European Private Law' in R Schulze and H Schulte-Nölke (eds), *European Private Law—Current Status and Perspectives* (Sellier, 2011) 3.

[169] See, eg, H-W Micklitz, 'The Visible Hand of European Regulatory Private Law—The Transformation of European Private Law from Autonomy to Functionalism in Competition and Regulation' (2009) 28 *YEL* 3, 7, 20–29; Schulze, n 168, 17–24. This point dovetails with scholarly critique of the DCFR: see, eg, Micklitz and Cafaggi, n 168, xvi–xxv (as part of the 'plea for a second generation of research' in European private law); R. Schulze, 'The Academic Draft of the CFR and the EC Contract Law' in R Schulze (ed), *Common Frame of Reference and Existing EC Contract Law*, 2nd rev edn (Sellier, 2009) 3, 20, 23.

[170] See, eg, Micklitz and Cafaggi, n 168, xxi.

[171] Eg, Unfair Commercial Practices Directive, n 163, fourth, thirteenth recitals.

[172] Eg, E-commerce Directive, n 162, fifth, seventh recitals; Directive on electronic signatures, n 162, fourth recital.

[173] Eg, Dir 2002/65/EC, n 165, first–fifth, twelfth recitals. It was later amended by the Payment Services Directive, n 165, which in turn underpins issues relating to the treatment of B2C and B2B matters in the same measure.

and the solutions broached at the European level as a result. The fact that many of these directives have been amended or replaced by subsequent measures as part of the activities taking place at the European level is indicative of this. The 'hard core' also underpins certain perennial themes relating to the Union legislature's competence in contract law, which have become interwoven into the constitutional fabric of European contract law through to the present day. Moreover, as will be seen in the next chapter, it provides the basis upon which to evaluate the Court of Justice's role in European contract law. As such, while the debate about European contract law may progress for years and even decades to come, arguably, the discourse will continue to pay tribute to the 'hard core' of the EU contract law *acquis*, since it is essentially built into the constitutional foundations of European contract law.

On the whole, these directives are familiar to those well versed in the debate about European contract law and have generated comprehensive study already, which will not be repeated here.[174] Rather, the aim is to provide a brief description of these directives in the order listed above in order to spotlight certain salient points bearing on the constitutionality of European contract law, which will then be evaluated in the section that follows. The choice to examine them in chronological order, as opposed to making a systematic distinction between those that regulate consumer contracts and those that do not, is merely intended to capture the evolution in approach as regards the Union's competence in this area.

1.3.1 The Doorstep Selling Directive (85/577/EEC), repealed by the Consumer Rights Directive (2011/83/EU)

Council Directive 85/577/EEC to protect the consumer in respect of contracts negotiated away from business premises (Doorstep Selling Directive)[175] was one of the earliest measures to be adopted in the EU contract law *acquis*, but has been repealed by the Consumer Rights Directive.[176] It was adopted under what is now Article 115 TFEU (ex Article 94 EC, then Article 100 EEC). This was based on the fact that such contracts and engagements were the subject of legislation which differed from one Member State to another, and as 'any disparity between such legislation may directly affect the functioning of the common [now internal] market', it was necessary to approximate the national laws in this area.[177] It applied to both cross-border and domestic transactions, ie those concluded by consumers and traders in different Member States and within the same Member State, respectively.

Stripped to its essence, the Directive sought to do two things. First, it provided the consumer with the right to cancel certain contracts for the supply of goods and services that were concluded in the context of a 'doorstep selling' situation[178] within a period of at least seven days.[179] This would have the effect of releasing the consumer from any obligations under the contract.[180] Secondly, it required the trader to provide the

[174] In addition to numerous books, the Consumer Law Compendium contains detailed inquiry of most of these directives: see Chapter 6, § 6.3.1.

[175] Council Dir 85/577/EC of 20 Dec 1985 to protect the consumer in respect of contracts negotiated away from business premises, [1985] OJ L372/31 (Doorstep Selling Directive).

[176] Consumer Rights Directive, n 115, Art 31.

[177] Doorstep Selling Directive, n 175, first–second recitals.

[178] Doorstep Selling Directive, n 175, Art 1.

[179] Doorstep Selling Directive, n 175, fifth recital; Art 5.

[180] Doorstep Selling Directive, n 175, Art 5(2).

consumer with written notice of this right at a particular time depending upon certain circumstances related to the 'doorstep selling' context.[181] This right was not subject to uniform wording, being called the right of cancellation and the right of renunciation,[182] and the word 'contract' itself was not defined.[183] Noticeably, it stipulated that some issues depended on the national contract rules, eg, the sending of the notice of the consumer's exercise of the right of cancellation and the legal effects of such cancellation were governed by national law.[184] Moreover, the Member States were given discretion to choose whether certain aspects fell within its scope of application, eg, whether it would apply only to contracts that exceeded a certain amount,[185] or not apply to certain contracts where the consumer had requested the visit of the trader.[186] It included a minimum harmonization clause,[187] and made clear that the Member States' freedom to prohibit, either totally or partially, the conclusion of doorstep selling contracts in the interests of consumers must not be affected.[188]

1.3.2 The Commercial Agents Directive (86/653/EEC)

Council Directive 86/653/EEC on the coordination of the laws of the Member States relating to self-employed commercial agents (Commercial Agents Directive)[189] was adopted under what is now Article 115 TFEU (ex Article 94 EC, then Article 100 EEC) and Article 53(1) TFEU (ex Article 47(2) EC, then Article 57(2) EEC) concerning the right of establishment. It is one of the earliest directives in the EU contract law *acquis* falling outside the consumer contract sphere. At first glance, as evidenced by its title (and one of its legal bases), the Directive seems to be directed at the 'coordination' of the laws of the Member States. Yet, with a closer look at the Preamble and its substantive provisions, the Directive generally aims to harmonize the laws of the Member States relating to commercial agents.[190] As indicated in the Preamble, 'the differences in national laws concerning commercial representation substantially affect the conditions of competition and the carrying-on of that activity within the Community [now Union] and are detrimental both to the protection available to commercial agents vis-à-vis their principals and to the security of commercial transactions'.[191] Moreover, 'those differences are such as to *inhibit* substantially the conclusion and the operation of commercial representation contracts where principals and commercial agents are established in different Member States'.[192] This necessitated the 'approximation of the legal systems of the Member States to the extent required for the proper functioning of the common [now internal] market'.[193]

[181] Doorstep Selling Directive, n 175, Art 4.
[182] Doorstep Selling Directive, n 175, fourth recital; Arts 4, 7.
[183] Doorstep Selling Directive, n 175, Arts 2–3.
[184] Doorstep Selling Directive, n 175, Arts 5(1), 7.
[185] Doorstep Selling Directive, n 175, Art 3(1).
[186] Doorstep Selling Directive, n 175, Art 3(3).
[187] Doorstep Selling Directive, n 175, Art 8.
[188] Doorstep Selling Directive, n 175, sixth recital.
[189] Council Dir 86/653/EEC of 18 Dec 1986 on the coordination of the laws of the Member States relating to self-employed commercial agents, [1986] OJ L382/17 (Commercial Agents Directive).
[190] Commercial Agents Directive, n 189, third, fifth recitals; Art 1. Approximation is used only once: see text accompanying n193.
[191] Commercial Agents Directive, n 189, second recital.
[192] Commercial Agents Directive, n 189, second recital (emphasis added).
[193] Commercial Agents Directive, n 189, third recital.

The Directive is divided into several parts, setting forth common rules concerning the rights and obligations of commercial agents and principals,[194] the commercial agent's remuneration,[195] and the conclusion and termination of agency contracts.[196] It contains an elaborate definition of 'commercial agent',[197] but as far as the relations between such agents and principals are concerned, provisions such as the duty to act 'in good faith'[198] and what is meant by an 'agency contract' are not defined.[199] No limitation is carved out as regards its coverage of only cross-border relations; the Directive applies to both cross-border and domestic situations. There is no minimum harmonization clause, although it gives the Member States certain alternatives in a few provisions.[200]

1.3.3 The Consumer Credit Directive (87/102/EEC), repealed by the new Consumer Credit Directive (2008/48/EC)

Council Directive 87/102/EEC for the approximation of the laws, regulations and administrative provisions of the Member States concerning consumer credit (Consumer Credit Directive)[201] was based on what is now Article 115 TFEU (ex Article 94 EC, then Article 100 EEC). As explained in the Preamble, this was because 'wide differences exist in the laws of the Member States in the field of consumer credit', and those differences 'can lead to distortions of competition between grantors of credit in the common [now internal] market' and 'have an influence on the free movement of goods and services obtainable by consumers on credit and thus directly affect the functioning of the common market'.[202] Those differences also resulted in 'unequal consumer protection in the field of consumer credit from one Member State to another'.[203] It was applicable to consumer credit agreements concluded in the context of cross-border and domestic transactions.

Generally, the Directive laid down a set of common rules concerning pre-contractual and contractual information[204] and particular issues connected with consumer credit agreements, such as repossession of goods,[205] early repayment by the consumer,[206] and assignment.[207] The calculation of the annual percentage rate of interest[208] was a particular point of contention, which ultimately led to two amendments of the Directive within which to put a single formula in place.[209] It contained a minimum

[194] See Commercial Agents Directive, n 189, Arts 3–5.
[195] See Commercial Agents Directive, n 189, Arts 6–12.
[196] See Commercial Agents Directive, n 189, Arts 13–16.
[197] See Commercial Agents Directive, n 189, Art 1(2).
[198] Commercial Agents Directive, n 189, Arts 3(1), 4(1).
[199] See, eg, Commercial Agents Directive, n 189, ch IV.
[200] See Commercial Agents Directive, n 189, Arts 7, 17.
[201] Council Dir 87/102/EEC of 22 Dec 1986 for the approximation of the laws, regulations and administrative provisions of the Member States concerning consumer credit, [1987] OJ L42/48 (Consumer Credit Directive).
[202] Consumer Credit Directive, n 201, first, second, fourth recitals.
[203] Consumer Credit Directive, n 201, seventh recital.
[204] Consumer Credit Directive, n 201, Arts 4, 6.
[205] Consumer Credit Directive, n 201, Art 7.
[206] Consumer Credit Directive, n 201, Art 8.
[207] Consumer Credit Directive, n 201, Art 9.
[208] Consumer Credit Directive, n 201, Art 1a.
[209] Council Dir 90/88/EEC of 22 Feb 1990 amending Council Dir 87/102/EEC, [1990] OJ L61/14; Dir 98/7/EC of the European Parliament and of the Council of 16 Feb 1998 amending Council Dir 87/102/EEC, [1998] OJ L101/17.

harmonization clause.[210] It also left open certain choices for the Member States, such as the provision for a cooling-off period allowing the consumer to cancel the credit agreement.[211] In situations involving credit granted for the acquisition of goods, it was left to the Member States to establish the conditions under which goods may be repossessed with the stipulation that this should not entail any unjustified enrichment,[212] though that concept was not defined.

In 2008, the Union legislature adopted Directive 2008/48/EC on credit agreements for consumers (new Consumer Credit Directive), which repealed the previous Directive.[213] This Directive is based on what is now Article 114 TFEU (ex Article 95 EC), not Article 115 TFEU like its predecessor. The impetus for its adoption stemmed from two sources: first, the evolution in the types of credit instruments on the market that warranted the revision and the extension of the scope of the previous Directive;[214] and secondly, the impact of the existing differences among the laws of the Member States on the internal market, which 'in some cases leads to distortions of competition among creditors in the [Union] and creates obstacles to the internal market where Member States have adopted different mandatory provisions more stringent than those provided for in Directive 87/102/EEC'.[215] As a result, the new Directive seeks 'to facilitate the emergence of a well-functioning internal market in consumer credit' by providing for a harmonized Union framework 'in a number of core areas'.[216] It also aims to provide a 'sufficient degree of consumer protection to ensure *consumer confidence*' so as to stimulate the free movement of credit in the EU.[217]

On this basis, the new Directive replaces the scheme of minimum harmonization under the previous Directive with that of full harmonization to ensure that consumers 'enjoy a high and equivalent level of protection of their interests and to create a genuine internal market'.[218] This shift constitutes one of the controversial aspects of the Directive,[219] which may explain the lengthy recitals making clear the extent to which the Member States are free to retain or introduce legislation on matters outside its scope.[220] It also does not regulate contract law issues related to the validity of credit agreements, which fall within the ambit of the national legal regimes.[221] Indeed, as before, it harmonizes only 'certain aspects' of national law concerning consumer credit agreements[222] and is applicable to consumer credit agreements concluded in cross-border and domestic settings. It is longer than its predecessor and contains

[210] Consumer Credit Directive, n 201, Art 15.

[211] See Consumer Credit Directive, n 201, Annex I.

[212] Consumer Credit Directive, n 201, Art 7.

[213] Dir 2008/48/EC of the European Parliament and of the Council of 23 April 2008 on credit agreements for consumers and repealing Council Dir 87/102/EEC, [2008] OJ L133/66; *corrigenda*, [2009] OJ L207/14, [2010] OJ L199/40, [2011] OJ L234/46 (new Consumer Credit Directive).

[214] New Consumer Credit Directive, n 213, fifth recital.

[215] New Consumer Credit Directive, n 213, fourth recital.

[216] New Consumer Credit Directive, n 213, seventh recital.

[217] New Consumer Credit Directive, n 213, eighth recital (emphasis added).

[218] New Consumer Credit Directive, n 213, ninth recital; see also Art 22(1). See, in this regard, Case C-602/10 (Judgment of 12 July 2012) *SC Volksbank România*, not reported, paras 38–39.

[219] See, eg, European Parliament Second Report on the proposal for a new Consumer Credit Directive, A5-0224/2004, dated 2 April 2004, Explanatory Statement, 84; European Economic and Social Committee Opinion on the proposal for a new Consumer Credit Directive, [2003] OJ C234/1, points 2.4.2–2.4.3, 2.4.7, 4.11–4.12; compare, eg, Amended proposal for a new Consumer Credit Directive, COM (2005) 483 final/2, 23.11.2005, Explanatory Memorandum, point 5.11.

[220] New Consumer Credit Directive, n 213, ninth–eleventh, twenty-second recitals.

[221] New Consumer Credit Directive, n 213, thirtieth recital.

[222] New Consumer Credit Directive, n 213, Arts 1–2.

augmented sections concerning such matters as pre-contractual and contractual information and the consumer's right of withdrawal from a consumer credit agreement.[223]

1.3.4 The Package Travel Directive (90/314/EEC)

Council Directive 90/314/EEC on package travel, package holidays and package tours (Package Travel Directive)[224] is based on what is now Article 114 TFEU (ex Article 95 EC, then Article 100a EEC).[225] As indicated in the Preamble, 'national practices in this field are markedly different, which gives rise to obstacles to the freedom to provide services in respect of packages and distortions of competition amongst operators established in different Member States'.[226] As such, the establishment of common rules on package travel would 'contribute to the elimination of those obstacles and thereby to the achievement of a common market in services'.[227] Additionally, 'disparities in the rules protecting consumers in different Member States are a *disincentive* to consumers in one Member State from buying packages in another Member State'.[228] The aim of the Directive is therefore to approximate the laws of the Member States relating to packages sold and offered for sale in the EU territory.[229] It is applicable to both cross-border and domestic transactions. It establishes a set of common rules relating to package travel contracts largely dealing with pre-contractual and contractual information, the form and elements of such contracts, and a right of withdrawal.[230] In particular, it contains provisions concerning damages stemming from the failure to perform or the improper performance of the contract,[231] though no explicit definition of that concept is provided. Furthermore, it is not strictly limited to the contractual sphere, and includes rules on matters such as the advertising and presentation of package travel materials[232] and the provision of security on the part of the package travel organizer and/or retailer.[233] It also includes a minimum harmonization clause.[234]

Recently, the Commission issued a proposal for a new Package Travel Directive,[235] which was prompted by the need to revise the old Directive to make it more suitable

[223] Among the noticeable changes, it introduces a provision giving the consumer the right to withdraw from the consumer credit agreement generally within a period of fourteen days and the right to repay early at any time: see new Consumer Credit Directive, n 213, Arts 14, 16. It also contains revised provisions on linked credit agreements: see Art 15. The notion of linked contracts figures in the Court's case law on this Directive: see Chapter 2, § 2.3.2.

[224] Council Dir 90/314/EEC of 13 June 1990 on package travel, package holidays and package tours, [1990] OJ L158/59 (Package Travel Directive).

[225] Under the SEA, ex Art 100a EEC had prescribed the cooperation procedure. This was changed to the co-decision procedure under the Maastricht Treaty. This explains why the directives adopted under ex Art 100a EEC before the entry into force of the Maastricht Treaty (ie 1 Nov 1993) were adopted by the Council alone, as compared to those adopted by the European Parliament and the Council together thereafter.

[226] Package Travel Directive, n 224, second recital.

[227] Package Travel Directive, n 224, third recital.

[228] Package Travel Directive, n 224, eighth recital (emphasis added).

[229] Package Travel Directive, n 224, Art 1.

[230] Package Travel Directive, n 224, Art 4. There is also an Annex containing a list of various elements to be included in the contract if relevant to the particular package.

[231] Package Travel Directive, n 224, Art 5.

[232] Package Travel Directive, n 224, Art 3.

[233] Package Travel Directive, n 224, Art 7.

[234] Package Travel Directive, n 224, Art 8.

[235] Proposal for a Directive of the European Parliament and of the Council on package travel and assisted travel arrangements, amending Reg (EC) No 2006/2004, Dir 2011/83/EU and repealing Council Dir 90/314/EEC, COM (2013) 512 final, 9.7.2013 (Proposal). For related documents and

for the internal market, to remove ambiguities, and to close legislative gaps.[236] It, too, would be based on Article 114 TFEU, with the overarching aim to enhance the functioning of the internal market and to achieve a high level of consumer protection by approximating 'certain aspects' of the laws of the Member States in respect of contracts on package travel and assisted travel arrangements concluded between travellers and traders,[237] and its Preamble contains an explicit reference to Article 169 TFEU to underscore that the Union is to contribute to the attainment of a high level of consumer protection through measures adopted under Article 114 TFEU.[238] It would introduce various changes to the existing legal framework, as detailed in the Explanatory Memorandum.[239] Of particular note, as part of its internal market justification, it is claimed that disparities in national laws are a '*disincentive*' for travellers in one Member State from buying packages and assisted travel arrangements in another Member State, as well as for organizers and retailers in one Member State from selling such services in another Member State.[240] Moreover, emphasis is placed on the obstacles to cross-border trade resulting from significant divergences among the laws of the Member States that still remain on account of the minimum harmonization clause and the broad discretion given to the Member States under the old Directive.[241] As a result, this clause would be deleted,[242] but as noted by the Commission, the proposed Directive would give Member States the possibility to impose stricter rules in certain areas.[243] Above all, this measure, like the old Directive, would cover 'only certain aspects' of packages and other combinations of travel services and thus would not interfere with general national contract law.[244] Likewise, it would apply to cross-border and domestic transactions.

1.3.5 The Unfair Contract Terms Directive (93/13/EEC)

Council Directive 93/13/EEC on unfair terms in consumer contracts (Unfair Contract Terms Directive)[245] is based on what is now Article 114 TFEU (ex Article 95 EC, then Article 100a EEC). Its purpose is to approximate the laws of the Member States relating to unfair terms in contracts concluded between sellers or suppliers, on the one hand, and consumers, on the other.[246] As indicated in the Preamble, the laws of the Member States relating to contract terms between traders of goods and services and consumers 'show many disparities, with the result that the national markets for the sale of goods and services to consumers differ from each other and that distortions of competition may arise amongst the sellers and suppliers, notably when they sell and supply in other Member States'.[247] It is further claimed that 'consumers do not know the rules of law which, in Member States other than their own, govern contracts for the sale of goods

activities, see the Commission's website on DG Justice through the link to 'consumer and marketing law', <http://ec.europa.eu/justice/consumer-marketing/index_en.htm>.

236 Proposal, n 235, first recital; Explanatory Memorandum, points 1.1–1.2.
237 Proposal, n 235, Art 1; Explanatory Memorandum, points 1.3, 3.1–3.2.
238 Proposal, n 235, third recital.
239 For a summary, see Proposal, n 235, Explanatory Memorandum, point 4.
240 Proposal, n 235, sixth recital (emphasis added).
241 Proposal, n 235, fourth recital; Explanatory Memorandum, point 1.1, fifth para; point 1.2.2.
242 Proposal, n 235, Annex I.
243 Proposal, n 235, Explanatory Memorandum, point 3.4.
244 Proposal, n 235, recital 41; Art 1; Explanatory Memorandum, point 3.4.
245 Council Dir 93/13/EEC of 5 April 1993 on unfair terms in consumer contracts, [1993] OJ L95/29 (Unfair Contract Terms Directive).
246 Unfair Contract Terms Directive, n 245, Art 1(1).
247 Unfair Contract Terms Directive, n 245, second recital.

or services' and 'this lack of awareness *may deter them* from direct transactions for the purchase of goods or services in another Member State'.[248] As a result, 'in order to facilitate the establishment of the internal market and to safeguard the citizen in his role as consumer when acquiring goods and services under contracts which are governed by the laws of the Member States other than his own, it is essential to remove unfair terms from those contracts'.[249] The Directive covers cross-border and domestic transactions, since such rules will help sellers and suppliers 'in their task of selling goods and supplying services, both at home and throughout the internal market'.[250]

On the whole, the Directive sets forth rules that apply across the board to all consumer contracts and thus constitutes a paradigm shift from previous directives that had merely set forth rules on information disclosure and the formation of consumer contracts.[251] Nevertheless, its scope is limited in certain ways. In particular, it covers only contractual terms that have not been individually negotiated, ie where the term concerned is 'drafted in advance and the consumer had not been able to influence the substance of the term, particularly in the context of a pre-formulated standard contract'.[252] Yet, in accordance with the minimum harmonization clause provided therein, the Member States have the option of affording consumers a higher level of protection through more stringent national provisions.[253] This aspect of the Directive was amended by the Consumer Rights Directive so as to allow the Commission to monitor the specific provisions adopted by the Member States in certain areas.[254]

The heart of the Directive concerns the assessment of the unfairness of terms used in consumer contracts. It involves a three-part scheme. There is the so-called 'general clause' of Article 3(1) defining in a general way the factors rendering a particular term 'unfair'.[255] This provision states that a term is unfair 'if, contrary to the requirement of good faith, it causes a significant imbalance in the parties' rights and obligations arising under the contract, to the detriment of the consumer'.[256] Yet, good faith is not defined.[257] This general clause is backed up by Article 4, providing further guidance as to the assessment, and an accompanying Annex setting forth an indicative, non-exhaustive (so-called 'grey') list of the types of clauses that may be regarded as unfair. The Directive contains related rules concerning the effects of terms deemed unfair and the form of such terms in written contracts,[258] as well as provisions concerning the enforcement of unfair terms.[259]

248 Unfair Contract Terms Directive, n 245, fifth recital (emphasis added).

249 Unfair Contract Terms Directive, n 245, sixth recital.

250 Unfair Contract Terms Directive, n 245, seventh recital.

251 See, eg, U Bernitz, 'The Commission's Communications and Standard Contract Terms' in *The Harmonisation of European Contract Law*, n 40, 185; Weatherill, n 42, 115. Not surprisingly, there is a mountain of literature devoted to it. For a brief selection, see, eg, H Collins (ed), *Standard Contract Terms in Europe: A Basis for and a Challenge to European Contract Law* (Kluwer, 2008); P Nebbia, *Unfair Contract Terms in European Law: A Study in Comparative and EC Law* (Hart, 2007); L Niglia, *The Transformation of Contract in Europe* (Kluwer, 2003); 'Special Issue on The Impact of European Integration on Private Law: The Case of the Directive on Unfair Terms in Consumer Contracts' (1995) 3 *ERPL* No 2; 'Special Issue on the Unfair Contract Terms Directive' (1997) 5 *ERPL* No 2.

252 Unfair Contract Terms Directive, n 245, Art 3(2).

253 Unfair Contract Terms Directive, n 245, twelfth recital; Art 8.

254 Consumer Rights Directive, n 115, sixty-second–sixty-third recitals; Art 32.

255 J Stuyck, Case note (2001) 38 *CML Rev* 719, 721. See generally *General Clauses and Standards in European Contract Law*, n 23.

256 Unfair Contract Terms Directive, n 245, Art 3(1). While the notion of 'good faith' is not further elaborated therein, some glimpses could be seen in the sixteenth recital.

257 The notion of 'good faith' in this Directive (as well as European contract law generally) prompted a massive commentary unto itself. See generally R Zimmerman and S Whittaker (eds), *Good Faith in European Contract Law* (Cambridge Univ Press, 2000).

258 Unfair Contract Terms Directive, n 245, Arts 5, 6.

259 Unfair Contract Terms Directive, n 245, Art 7.

1.3.6 The Timeshare Directive (94/47/EC), repealed by the new Timeshare Directive (2008/122/EC)

Directive 94/47/EC on the protection of purchasers in respect of certain aspects of contracts relating to the purchase of the right to use immovable properties on a timeshare basis (Timeshare Directive)[260] was based on what is now Article 114 TFEU (ex Article 95 EC, then Article 100a EEC). The justification for its adoption stemmed from the fact that 'disparities between national legislations [sic] on contracts relating to the purchase of the right to use one or more immovable properties on a timeshare basis are likely to create barriers to the proper operation of the internal market and distortions of competition and lead to the compartmentalization of national markets'.[261] It applied to both cross-border and domestic transactions.

Notably, the Directive covered 'certain minimal items' in order to provide effective protection for purchasers (akin to consumers) in this field.[262] As explained in the Preamble, 'the legal nature of the rights which are the subject of the contracts covered by this Directive varies considerably from one Member State to another' and for this reason, 'references should therefore be made in summary form to those variations, giving a sufficiently broad definition of such contracts, without thereby implying harmonization within the Community [now Union] of the legal nature of the rights in question'.[263] In other words, the Directive was 'not designed to regulate the extent to which contracts for the use of one or more immovable properties on a timeshare basis may be concluded in Member States or the legal basis of such contracts'.[264] In fact, the limited scope of the Directive was one of its most glaring features. Not only was this apparent in its title referencing its coverage of 'certain aspects' of timeshare contracts, but also quite uniquely, Article 1 made clear that the Directive only covered those aspects of timeshare contracts relating to 'information on the constituent parts of a contract and the arrangements for the communication of that information', on the one hand, and 'the procedures and arrangements for cancellation and withdrawal', on the other.[265] The Member States remained competent for all other matters, such as the determination of the legal nature of the rights that were the subject of the contracts covered by the Directive.[266] There was also a minimum harmonization clause allowing the Member States to maintain or enact more favourable provisions for protecting purchasers in the field concerned.[267]

In 2009, the Union legislature adopted Directive 2008/122/EC on the protection of consumers in respect of certain aspects of timeshare, long-term holiday product,

[260] Dir 94/47/EC of the European Parliament and of the Council of 26 Oct 1994 on the protection of purchasers in respect of certain aspects of contracts relating to the purchase of the right to use immovable properties on a timeshare basis, [1994] OJ L280/83 (Timeshare Directive).

[261] Timeshare Directive, n 260, first recital.

[262] Timeshare Directive, n 260, eighth–ninth recitals. Under Art 2, fourth indent, a purchaser was akin to a consumer. References to consumers were also sprinkled through the Directive in synonymous fashion: see, eg, Timeshare Directive, n 260, fourteenth recital.

[263] Timeshare Directive, n 260, third recital. This was exemplified by the tortured definition of 'contract' set forth in Art 2, first indent.

[264] Timeshare Directive, n 260, fourth recital.

[265] Timeshare Directive, n 260, Art 1, first para. As for rules regarding information duties, see Timeshare Directive, n 260, Arts 3–4. There was also an Annex setting forth a minimum list of items to be included in timeshare contracts pursuant to Art 4. As for rules regarding the purchaser's cancellation and withdrawal, see Timeshare Directive, n 260, Arts 5–8.

[266] Timeshare Directive, n 260, Art 1, second para.

[267] Timeshare Directive, n 260, Art 11.

resale and exchange contracts (new Timeshare Directive),[268] which repealed the previous Directive.[269] It is also based on what is now Article 114 TFEU (then Article 95 EC) and is essentially a 'beefed up' version of its predecessor. As explained in the Preamble, there were various regulatory gaps left open by the previous Directive in terms of its lack of coverage of new holiday products and certain transactions related to timeshare, and even the subjects that were covered were in need of updating and clarifying, particularly in order to prevent the development of holiday products aimed at circumventing the Directive.[270] These gaps 'create appreciable distortions of competition and cause serious problems for consumers, thereby hindering the smooth functioning of the internal market' and warranting a new, up-to-date directive.[271] As such, the aim of this Directive is to contribute to the proper functioning of the internal market and to achieve a high level of consumer protection by approximating the laws of the Member States in respect of certain aspects of the marketing, sale, and resale of timeshares and long-term holiday products.[272] As with the previous Directive, it is applicable to cross-border and domestic transactions between traders and consumers.[273] Yet, in the interests of enhancing legal certainty and fully achieving the benefits of the internal market for consumers and businesses, the new Directive fully harmonizes the laws of the Member States.[274] That said, it attempts to 'soften the blow' of this shift from minimum to full harmonization by stating, inter alia, that the requirement of full harmonization is without prejudice to a host of national rules falling outside its scope, such as general contract law remedies and the determination of the legal rights that are the subject of the contracts covered by the Directive.[275]

As far as its content is concerned, the new Timeshare Directive contains a battery of more detailed rules on various aspects that far surpasses the previous Directive, such as pre-contractual information[276] and the right of withdrawal,[277] even setting out in several annexes standard information for the various types of contracts concerned and a standard withdrawal form for facilitating the right of withdrawal.[278] The enforcement mechanisms are also considerably enhanced.[279] Yet, as its title indicates, it still covers only 'certain aspects' of these various types of timeshare products, and glaringly, in the updated definitions of timeshare contracts and related products, the concept of 'consideration' is left undefined.[280]

[268] Dir 2008/122/EC of the European Parliament and of the Council of 14 Jan 2009 on the protection of consumers in respect of certain aspects of timeshare, long-term holiday product, resale and exchange contracts, [2009] OJ L33/10 (new Timeshare Directive).

[269] New Timeshare Directive, n 268, Art 18.

[270] New Timeshare Directive, n 268, first recital.

[271] New Timeshare Directive, n 268, second recital.

[272] New Timeshare Directive, n 268, Art 1(1).

[273] New Timeshare Directive, n 268, Art 1(2).

[274] New Timeshare Directive, n 268, third recital. Surprisingly, there is not a specific provision in the Directive itself (called 'full harmonization' or some variant) setting forth the applicable harmonization model.

[275] New Timeshare Directive, n 268, third–fourth recitals; Art 1(2), particularly (a), (d).

[276] See new Timeshare Directive, n 268, Arts 4–5.

[277] See new Timeshare Directive, n 268, Arts 6–11.

[278] See new Timeshare Directive, n 268, Annexes I–V. The final Annex VI contains a correlation table.

[279] See new Timeshare Directive, n 268, Arts 13–15.

[280] See new Timeshare Directive, n 268, Art 2(1)(a)–(d).

1.3.7 The Distance Selling Directive (97/7/EC), repealed by the Consumer Rights Directive (2011/83/EU)

Directive 97/7/EC on the protection of consumers in respect of distance contracts (Distance Selling Directive)[281] was based on what is now Article 114 TFEU (ex Article 95 EC, then Article 100a EEC), and like the Doorstep Selling Directive, is repealed by the Consumer Rights Directive.[282] As explained in the Preamble, it was 'essential to the smooth operation of the internal market for consumers to be able to have dealings with a business outside their country, even if it has a subsidiary in the consumer's country of residence',[283] but 'some Member States have already taken different or diverging measures to protect consumers in respect of distance selling, which has had a detrimental effect on competition between businesses in the internal market'.[284] It established a minimum set of common rules concerning the regulation of distance contracts between consumers and suppliers in the EU.[285] It covered both cross-border and domestic transactions.[286]

Much of the Directive was taken up with rules concerning information disclosure and the consumer's right of withdrawal. It set forth the information that must be provided to the consumer prior to the conclusion of the contract and the manner in which it must be given, 'with due regard to the principles of good faith in commercial transactions', though such principles were not explicitly elaborated.[287] It also contained various rules on the consumer's right to withdraw from the contract.[288] The consumer was given a period of at least seven working days in which to exercise the right of withdrawal under Article 6(1), which was accompanied by a Statement issued by the European Parliament and the Council noting their intention to examine the possibility of harmonizing the method of calculating the cooling-off period under the then existing Community consumer protection legislation.[289] There were additional rules protecting consumers in relation to the performance of the contract, payment by credit card, and inertia selling,[290] as well as its enforcement.[291] Notably, it contained a minimum harmonization clause, which explicitly allowed, with due regard to the Treaties, the introduction of a ban in the general interest as regards the marketing of certain goods and services, particularly medicinal products, by means of distance contracts.[292] Its novelty lay in the fact that alongside the minimum set of rules, the Directive was

[281] Dir 97/7/EC of the European Parliament and of the Council of 20 May 1997 on the protection of consumers in respect of distance contracts, [1997] OJ L144/19, as amended by Dir 2002/65/EC (n 165), Dir 2005/29/EC (n 163), and Dir 2007/64/EC (n 165) (Distance Selling Directive).

[282] Consumer Rights Directive, n 115, Art 31.

[283] Distance Selling Directive, n 281, third recital.

[284] Distance Selling Directive, n 281, fourth recital.

[285] Distance Selling Directive, n 281, Art 1. For the definition of distance contracts, see Art 2(1). Under Art 3, certain contracts such as those relating to financial services were excluded. Dir 2002/65/EC, n 165, filled the gap in this regard.

[286] Distance Selling Directive, n 281, Art 1.

[287] Distance Selling Directive, n 281, Art 4(2).

[288] Distance Selling Directive, n 281, Art 6. See, in this regard, Case C-49/11 (Judgment of 5 July 2012) *Content Services*, not reported.

[289] See Distance Selling Directive, n 281, 'Statement by the Council and the Parliament re Article 6(1)'.

[290] See Distance Selling Directive, n 281, Arts 7–9.

[291] See Distance Selling Directive, n 281, Art 11.

[292] See Distance Selling Directive, n 281, Art 14.

envisaged to be supplemented where appropriate by voluntary arrangements of the traders concerned.[293]

1.3.8 The Consumer Sales Directive (1999/44/EC)

Directive 1999/44/EC on certain aspects of the sale of consumer goods and associated guarantees (Consumer Sales Directive)[294] is based on what is now Article 114 TFEU (then Article 95 EC). Starting off with a reference to what is now Article 169 TFEU (then Article 153 EC) in its first recital, the Preamble underlines that 'consumers resident in one Member State should be free to purchase goods in the territory of another Member State on the basis of a uniform minimum set of fair rules governing the sale of consumer goods'.[295] Yet, the laws of the Member States concerning the sale of consumer goods are 'somewhat disparate, with the result that national consumer goods markets differ from one another and that competition between sellers may be distorted'.[296] Consequently, 'the creation of a common set of minimum rules of consumer law, valid no matter where goods are purchased within the Community [now Union], will strengthen *consumer confidence* and enable consumers to make the most of the internal market'.[297] While seeking to improve the cross-border sale of consumer goods, this Directive covers both cross-border and domestic transactions.

Since the 'main difficulties' encountered by consumers concerned the non-conformity of goods with the contract, the Directive sets forth rules in that respect, 'without however impinging on provisions and principles of national law relating to contractual and non-contractual liability'.[298] This explains its title referring to 'certain aspects' of the sale of consumer goods and associated guarantees in the internal market. Generally, it contains various rules relating to the conformity of goods under the contract, the rights and remedies of the consumer against the seller for lack of conformity, and guarantees.[299] Yet, it stipulates that the rights under the Directive do not prejudice other rights which the consumer may invoke under national rules governing contractual or non-contractual liability.[300] It also includes a minimum harmonization clause.[301] Like the Unfair Contract Terms Directive, it was amended by the Consumer Rights Directive, which inserted an additional provision requiring the Member States to inform the Commission of more stringent rules adopted on the basis of this clause.[302]

[293] See Distance Selling Directive, n 281, eighteenth recital; Arts 11(3)(c), 16. This was in line with Commission Recommendation 92/295/EEC of 7 April 1992 on codes of practice for the protection of consumers in respect of contracts negotiated at a distance, [1992] OJ L156/21.

[294] Dir 1999/44/EC of the European Parliament and of the Council of 25 May 1999 on certain aspects of the sale of consumer goods and associated guarantees, [1999] OJ L171/12 (Consumer Sales Directive). See generally S Grundmann and MC Bianca (eds), *EU Sales Directive: Commentary* (Intersentia, 2002); 'Special Double Issue on the Implementation of the Directive on the Sale of Consumer Goods and Associated Guarantees' (2001) 9 *ERPL* Nos 2–3; S Grundmann, 'Consumer Law, Commercial Law, Private Law: How can the Sales Directive and the Sales Convention be so Similar?' (2003) 14 *EBLR* 237; D Staudenmayer, 'The Directive on the Sale of Consumer Goods and Associated Guarantees—a Milestone in European Consumer and Private Law' (2000) 8 *ERPL* 547.

[295] Consumer Sales Directive, n 294, first–second recitals.

[296] Consumer Sales Directive, n 294, third recital.

[297] Consumer Sales Directive, n 294, fifth recital (emphasis added).

[298] Consumer Sales Directive, n 294, sixth recital.

[299] Consumer Sales Directive, n 294, Arts 2–6.

[300] Consumer Sales Directive, n 294, Art 8(1).

[301] Consumer Sales Directive, n 294, Art 8(2).

[302] Consumer Rights Directive, n 115, sixty-second–sixty-third recitals; Art 33.

1.3.9 The Late Payment Directive (2000/35/EC), repealed by the new Late Payment Directive (2011/7/EU)

Directive 2000/35/EC on combating late payment in commercial transactions (Late Payment Directive)[303] was adopted under what is now Article 114 TFEU (then Article 95 EC). It concerned commercial transactions between traders, as opposed to those involving consumers, as well as between traders and public authorities.[304] As indicated in the Preamble, there were mounting problems in the internal market caused by late payments by debtors.[305] Late payment is defined as 'a breach of contract which has been made financially attractive to debtors in most Member States by low interest rates on late payments and/or slow procedures for redress'.[306] The differences in the payment rules and practices of the Member States were considered an obstacle to the proper functioning of the internal market[307], which had 'the effect of considerably limiting commercial transactions between the Member States' and thus contravened Article 26 TFEU (ex Article 14 EC), whereby 'entrepreneurs should be able to trade throughout the internal market under conditions which ensure that transborder operations do not entail *greater risks* than domestic sales'.[308] Moreover, '[d]istortions of competition would ensue if substantially different rules applied to domestic and transborder operations'.[309] As a result, the Directive established rules applicable to all payments made as remuneration for commercial transactions,[310] covering cross-border and domestic transactions. In doing so, it claimed not to affect national provisions 'relating to the way contracts are concluded or regulating the validity of contractual terms which are unfair to the debtor'.[311] It also contained a minimum harmonization clause, which allowed the Member States to maintain or introduce national legislation that was more favourable to the creditor.[312]

Content-wise, the Directive was of a limited nature, focusing on the interest in the case of late payments,[313] recovery procedures for unchallenged claims,[314] and retention of title.[315] As regards the recovery procedures, this was to ensure that they would be completed in a short time, but the provisions did 'not require the Member States to adopt a specific procedure or to amend their existing national legislation in a specific way'.[316] For the retention of title provision, this, too, did not intend to disturb the national legal regimes. As defined in the Directive, retention of title denoted a contractual agreement allowing the seller to retain title in the debtor's goods until the price was paid in full.[317] The idea was to ensure that where a retention of title clause had been agreed between a creditor and a buyer, the creditor was put in the position to exercise the clause throughout the EU, but this depended upon whether

[303] Dir 2000/35/EC of the European Parliament and of the Council of 29 June 2000 on combating late payment in commercial transactions, [2000] OJ L200/35 (Late Payment Directive).
[304] Late Payment Directive, n 303, thirteenth, twenty-second recitals; Art 2(1).
[305] Late Payment Directive, n 303, seventh recital.
[306] Late Payment Directive, n 303, sixteenth recital.
[307] Late Payment Directive, n 303, ninth recital.
[308] Late Payment Directive, n 303, tenth recital (emphasis added).
[309] Late Payment Directive, n 303, tenth recital.
[310] Late Payment Directive, n 303, Art 1.
[311] Late Payment Directive, n 303, nineteenth recital.
[312] Late Payment Directive, n 303, Art 6(2).
[313] Late Payment Directive, n 303, Art 3.
[314] Late Payment Directive, n 303, Art 5.
[315] Late Payment Directive, n 303, Art 4.
[316] Late Payment Directive, n 303, fifth recital.
[317] See Late Payment Directive, n 303, Art 2(3).

the clause was valid under the applicable national provisions designated by private international law.[318]

In 2011, the Union legislature adopted Directive 2011/7/EU on combating late payment in commercial transactions (new Late Payment Directive),[319] which repealed the previous Directive.[320] Many of the main elements of the previous Directive remain unchanged, including its legal basis and justifications for recourse to Article 114 TFEU, its scope, the retention of title, and the recovery procedure for unchallenged claims. The new Directive is generally geared at introducing additional tools to reduce the number of late payments in commercial transactions, to shorten payment periods for public administrations, and to reinforce the incentives for public authorities to pay on time.[321] The proposal to revise this Directive was situated within the context of certain Union policy programmes concerned with improving the position of small and medium-sized enterprises (SMEs) in the internal market and problems caused by the economic crisis.[322] Although not mentioned much in the commentary so far, this Directive is one of the first measures that explicitly refers to the Draft Common Frame of Reference in the Preamble (albeit not in the text of the Directive itself) as regards its aim to prohibit abuse of freedom of contract to the disadvantage of the creditor.[323]

1.4 Perennial Themes

Through these broad brushstrokes, three perennial themes bearing on the constitutionality of European contract law can be gleaned from the 'hard core' of the EU contract law *acquis*. The first relates to matters concerning Union competence and the roles played by Articles 114 and 115 TFEU. The second concerns the relationship between consumer contract law and general contract law. The third implicates the problems generated by the piecemeal nature of the 'hard core' at the European and national levels. Each is evaluated in turn.

1.4.1 Union competence and the roles played by Articles 114 and 115 TFEU

One of the most predominant themes underlying the 'hard core' relates to the use of the Union's competences under Articles 114 and 115 TFEU concerning the approximation of national laws for the purposes of the internal market. While the vast majority of the foregoing directives embody objectives related to consumer protection as well, it has generally been these Treaty provisions, mainly Article 114 TFEU, which have served as

[318] See Late Payment Directive, n 303, twenty-first recital; Art 4. This approach was criticized by scholars: see, eg, E-M Kieninger, *Security Rights in Movable Property in European Private Law* (Cambridge Univ Press, 2004).

[319] Dir 2011/7/EU of the European Parliament and of the Council of 16 Feb 2011 on combating late payment in commercial transactions, [2011] OJ L48/1 (new Late Payment Directive).

[320] New Late Payment Directive, n 319, Art 13.

[321] Proposal for a Directive of the European Parliament and of the Council on combating late payment in commercial transactions (Recast)—Implementing the Small Business Act, COM (2009) 126 final, 8.4.2009, point 1, at 4; point 5, at 8 (as well as improving the list of essential terms 'in order to put an end to divergent interpretations').

[322] See Proposal, n 321, point 1. For detailed discussion, see, eg, IR Alfonso, 'Une nouvelle legislation européenne en matière de lutte contre les retards de paiement' (2011) *RDUE* 223.

[323] See new Late Payment Directive, n 319, twenty-eighth recital; but compare Art 7.

the legal bases for these directives.[324] Even after the introduction of Article 169 TFEU by way of the Maastricht Treaty, which preceded the timeframe in which many of these directives were adopted (and as illustrated by the Consumer Sales Directive was cited in the text itself), this did not affect the Union legislature's steady reliance on what is now Article 114 TFEU. The use of the Union's internal market competences coloured the EU contract law *acquis* with particular characteristics, and in doing so, highlights several interrelated issues concerning the interplay between the Union's internal market and consumer policy objectives, the extent of its competence under Articles 114 and 115 TFEU, and the potential role of Article 169 TFEU.

First, while most of the directives rest upon the Union's *dual objectives rooted in the internal market and consumer protection*, the use of Articles 114 and 115 TFEU demonstrates the place of consumer protection objectives inside, as opposed to outside, the Union's internal market programme. In fact, as examined in greater detail in a coming chapter, it was the symbiotic relationship between the protection of consumers' economic interests and the internal market programme as part of the development of Union consumer policy which led to the adoption of several directives within the 'hard core'.[325] This relationship has come to be symbolized by the 'Janus face' of EU consumer contract law, one side geared at protecting consumers and the other side aimed at furthering the establishment and functioning of the internal market.[326] Nevertheless, as recognized by commentators, it is the 'market making' of Article 114 TFEU that underpins the various directives.[327] This has led to tensions underlying EU contract law in terms of building a truly integrated market, on the one hand, and ensuring a high level of consumer protection, on the other. As such, the perennial question to find the right balance between the two underlies some of the sensitivity for resorting to Article 114 TFEU in relation to the adoption of a consumer contract law instrument in the debate about European contract law. This also raises provocative questions about the severance of Union consumer contract law measures from the internal market programme by virtue of recourse to Article 169 TFEU as opposed to Article 114 TFEU.

Secondly, the 'hard core' highlights issues relating to the *scope of the Union's competence under Articles 114 and 115 TFEU* and the Union legislature's justifications for relying on these provisions. In the first place, hardly anything has been made of the fact that all of the foregoing directives cover not only cross-border transactions, but also domestic ones. Given the ensuing debate about the scope of Article 114 TFEU, these measures demonstrate its extension to domestic transactions very early on. In the second place, the justifications underpinning some of these directives are significant, which is borne out by their chronological progression. As illustrated by the early directives, much of the language attesting to the particular measure's elimination of obstacles to trade and/or distortions of competition is framed in hypothetical or subjective terms without

324 The exception is the Commercial Agents Directive, n 189, based on what are now Arts 53 and 114 TFEU, which is still rooted in the EU's internal market policy.

325 See Chapter 9, § 9.2.3.

326 A remark attributed to Professor Norbert Reich: see, eg, T Wilhelmsson, 'The Abuse of the "Confident Consumer" as a Justification for EC Consumer Law' (2004) 27 *JCP* 317, 319 and citations therein.

327 See, eg, G Howells and T Wilhelmsson, 'EC consumer law: has it come of age?' (2003) 28 *ELR* 370; S Weatherill, 'Constitutional Issues—How Much is Best Left Unsaid?' in *The Harmonisation of European Contract Law*, n 40, 89; CU Schmid, 'The Instrumentalist Conception of the Acquis Communautaire in Consumer Law and its Implications on a European Contract Law Code' (2005) 1 *ERCL* 211. This prompted specific terms within which to frame EU contract law: see, eg, H-W Micklitz, 'The Concept of Competitive Contract Law' (2005) 23 *Penn St IL Rev* 549; N Reich, 'European Consumer Law and its Relationship to Private Law' (1995) 3 *ERPL* 285, 289.

much substantiation. While the Doorstep Selling Directive is often held up as a quintessential example in this regard,[328] others embody similarly tenuous reasoning. It is somewhat understandable that the earlier directives would be framed in 'looser' terms, as compared to the more recent directives that evidence alignment with the case law on Article 114 TFEU, eg, citing 'appreciable' distortions of competition.[329] Even so, the rationale for these directives has generally remained rooted in the likelihood of obstacles to trade and distortions of competition caused by disparities in national contract laws. This is so even for some of the early directives that were adopted before the case law on Article 114 TFEU proclaimed as much. Importantly, while some directives are concerned with differences in national mandatory or protective standards, many are framed more generally on grounds that such differences in consumer and commercial contract laws inhibit or deter cross-border transactions from taking place and cause detrimental effects on competition between businesses in the internal market. As such, these directives permeate the inquiry into the scope of Article 114 TFEU, especially as regards the assessment of the parameters of obstacles to trade and appreciable distortions of competition that this provision is charged to eliminate.

Alongside these arguments often comes some variation of the so-called '*consumer confidence*' rationale, which appears in a number of the directives within the 'hard core', among others. As illustrated by these directives, the idea behind this rationale seems to be that disparities between national rules cause consumers to abstain from engaging in cross-border transactions, and therefore, by harmonizing national contract laws so as to set down a set of common European rules in the relevant area, the measure concerned gives consumers the confidence to engage in such transactions, thereby enhancing the free movement of goods and services in the internal market.[330] At present, it remains controversial in academic circles, and as yet unsettled by the Court of Justice, how far arguments relating to consumer confidence may be used to justify measures based on Article 114 TFEU.[331] That being said, these directives demonstrate that so far where such arguments have been used they have appeared alongside justifications rooted in the elimination of obstacles to trade and distortions of competition caused by disparities in national laws, not in place of them.

Finally, past reliance on Articles 114 and 115 TFEU was not without political compromise in the form of *minimum harmonization*. As seen earlier, minimum harmonization clauses are found in most of the original measures within the 'hard core', whereas the recent revisions of several of these directives profess a shift to full or maximum harmonization, thereby removing the assumption that minimum harmonization is an automatic feature of the EU (consumer) contract law *acquis*. The Commission's arguments used to justify such a shift is the subject of increasing commentary from scholars, much of it critical at least as regards the shift across the board as opposed to a case-by-case basis where the need for maximum harmonization can be shown.[332] This discussion is linked to the Union's competence in this area. Recourse to the special

[328] See, eg, Weatherill, n 327, 91; 'Editorial Comments: Union competences in the field of contract law: Some questions—no answers' (2011) 48 *CML Rev* 653, 657–658.

[329] See further Chapter 8.

[330] See further Niglia, n 152.

[331] Compare, eg, F Cafaggi, 'The making of European private law: governance design' in *Making European Private Law*, n 49, 289, 293–294 and citations therein; Nebbia, n 251, 19–21; S Weatherill, 'Reflections on the EC's Competence to Develop a "European Contract Law"' (2005) 13 *ERPL* 405, 416–417; Wilhelmsson, n 326. The 'confidence' rationale may extend beyond the consumer sphere to denote issues relating to business or investor confidence. See, eg, S Weatherill, 'The Constitutional Competence of the EU to Deliver Social Justice' (2006) 2 *ERCL* 131, 141.

[332] See, eg, Micklitz, n 99; Weatherill, n 99.

procedure of Article 114(4)–(9) TFEU on grounds of consumer protection is foreclosed, which has placed renewed attention on Article 169 TFEU as a 'safe haven' for preserving recourse to minimum harmonization. The matter has also raised questions in the literature as to whether the case law on Article 114 TFEU emanating from the first *Tobacco Advertising* judgment dictated such a shift, although at present this largely seems to have been decided in the negative.[333] As a result, the dichotomy between minimum and maximum harmonization enlivens the controversy surrounding the scope of Article 114 TFEU and its relationship to Article 169 TFEU.

In sum, the roles played by Articles 114 and 115 TFEU in the context of the 'hard core' of EU contract law illuminate key constitutional issues, which surprisingly have so far not been tested. Despite the uncertainties related to the 'consumer confidence' rationale, the 'loose' justification for Articles 114 and 115 TFEU on occasion, and questions concerning the possible recourse to Article 169 TFEU in place of Article 114 TFEU, the Union legislature's competence to adopt any of the foregoing measures has yet to be challenged before the Union courts, either directly by way of an action for annulment or indirectly by way of a preliminary ruling on the validity of Union law or an objection of illegality. Indeed, there is a growing body of case law concerning the Court's interpretation of these directives, but as regards the matter of legal basis, there has not been one case so far over the course of the past three decades.[334] The result is that the use of the Union's competences in connection with the 'hard core' draws attention to various issues percolating below the surface of European contract law, which brings the need to confront its constitutional dimensions around full circle.

1.4.2 The relationship between consumer and general contract law

As demonstrated by the 'hard core', consumer contract law commands a prominent place within the EU contract law *acquis*. Notwithstanding the controversy concerning the scope of EU contract law beyond this area, it may at least be said that the EU contract law *acquis* is substantially grounded in rules concerning transactions between consumers and traders, referred to as business-to-consumer (B2C) transactions, as compared to rules concerning commercial transactions between traders, referred to as business-to-business (B2B) transactions. This has injected various issues relating to the relationship between consumer contract law and general contract law into the debate about European contract law and the constitutionality of the initiatives envisaged in this area. On the one hand, it was the consumer element that served as the inroad into contract law (and even private law generally to some extent) at the European level.[335] This is illustrated by the fact that the categories of consumer contract law and European contract law are blurred, one often serving as a subset for the other.[336] On the other

[333] See, eg, M Dougan, 'Vive La Différence? Exploring the Legal Framework for Reflexive Harmonisation Within the Single European Market' in RA Miller and PC Zumbansen (eds), *I Annual of German and European Law* (Berghahn, 2003) 113, 151–161; PJ Oliver (S Enchelmaier et al (contributing eds)), *Oliver on Free Movement of Goods in the European Union*, 5th edn (Hart, 2010) § 13.95; but see M Dougan, 'Minimum Harmonization after *Tobacco Advertising* and *Laval Un Partneri*' in M Bulterman et al (eds), *Views of European Law from the Mountain—Liber Amicorum Piet Jan Slot* (Kluwer, 2009) 3.

[334] For a lament and possible solution in this regard, see 'Editorial Comments', n 328, 655, 659.

[335] See, eg, Miller, n 5, 45. See also more generally E Hondius, 'The Innovative Nature of Consumer Law' (2012) 35 *JCP* 165, 168.

[336] See, eg, H-W Micklitz, 'An Expanded and Systematized Community Consumer Law as Alternative or Complement?' (2002) 13 *EBLR* 583; Weatherill, n 42, 149.

hand, consumer contract law has been viewed as feeding into general rules of contract law, as illustrated by scholars who prefer to view EU contract law beyond its consumer underpinnings,[337] for example, as constituting a European 'market law'[338] or 'business law', even if it is one based on a high level of consumer protection.[339] As a result, the question of segregation or integration of consumer contract law vis-à-vis general contract law looms large in the debate about European contract law.[340] As will be seen, the ongoing activities taking place in the European contract law project continue to be mired in this relationship, whether it is the plans for the revision of consumer *acquis* or the treatment of such issues in the Common Frame of Reference and potentially one or more optional instruments of contract law, such as the proposed CESL.[341] This has an impact on the constitutional assessment of European contract law, particularly in terms of the controversy surrounding the extent of the Union's competence to adopt a systematic instrument covering commercial or B2B transactions apart from the consumer contract law field.

1.4.3 The Union legislature's piecemeal approach

Finally, whether concerning consumer or commercial transactions, these directives for the most part regulate significant, albeit discrete, topics. Even if the Unfair Contract Terms Directive and Consumer Sales Directive may be deemed to go quite far in their application to the substance of consumer contracts, a notable feature of the directives within the 'hard core' is that they are limited in nature in terms of the 'certain aspects' addressed and hence embody an 'interstitial' quality situated against the broader backdrop of the contract law regimes of the Member States. In other words, they signify a piecemeal approach taken by the Union legislature in EU contract law, which was not conceived to blanket the field, but instead to deal only with a specific set of issues relating to certain types of contracts, marketing techniques, contractual settings, etc when the particular need arose.

As further illustrated by these directives, however, there were significant problems with this approach at the European and national levels. At the European level, problems stemmed from, among other things, the Union legislature's failure to provide definitions for key terms and numerous gaps and inconsistencies in the various directives, and at the national level, these directives introduced unknown or inconsistent terminology and imposed additional legal layers, which wreaked havoc with the coherence of the national legal systems in various ways.[342] As one scholar summed it up, the Union's

[337] This has been greatly prompted by the Unfair Contract Terms and Consumer Sales Directives, which have 'generated a readiness to consider the shape of contract law beyond the consumer sphere': Vogenauer and Weatherill, n 40, 106. See also Schmid, n 327, 212. But compare, eg, P Remy-Corlay, 'The Law of Sales: Acquis and Improved Acquis in European Contract Law' (2003) 4 *ERA Forum* 39.

[338] S Grundman, 'The Future of Contract Law' (2011) 7 *ERCL* 490, 519. See also B Lurger, 'The Future of European Contract Law between Freedom of Contract, Social Justice, and Market Rationality' (2005) 1 *ERCL* 442, 457 and citations therein.

[339] Riesenhuber, n 37, 305–306.

[340] Compare, eg, the contributions in S Grundmann and M Schauer (eds), *The Architecture of European Codes and Contract Law* (Kluwer, 2006), particularly pt III; G Howells, 'The Scope of European Consumer Law' (2005) 1 *ERCL* 360; Lurger, n 338, 454–462; U Mattei, *The European Codification Process: Cut and Paste* (Kluwer, 2003) 129–159; Schulze, n 36.

[341] See, eg, D Staudenmayer, 'The Place of Consumer Contract Law Within the Process on European Contract Law' (2004) 27 *JCP* 269.

[342] The commentary on this point is pervasive. In the words of one scholar: 'Up until 1998 . . . I couldn't find a single reference which would not have condemned European Contract

'functionally selective approach . . . led to an incomprehensible permeation of national systems with islands of [Union] law that grow ever larger, causing numerous fragmentations, unforeseen constraints to harmonization and contradictions'.[343] These problems combined to produce something of a 'countermovement'[344] against EU contract law and to draw attention to the possible need for a more systematic response to matters of contract law at the European level. In this way, the 'hard core' helped to set the scene for a fundamental re-evaluation of the EU's role in contract law and for ways to address the problems plaguing the EU contract law *acquis* at the European and national levels.

1.5 Conclusions

In view of the foregoing discussion, at the base of European contract law lies the *raison d'être* for the debate and for the various solutions contemplated as a result. For this reason, the nuances underlying the terminology used in the debate had to be teased out, so as to facilitate a constructive discussion of the constitutional assessment of European contract law from the European and American perspectives. By the same token, the 'hard core' of the EU contract law *acquis* provides the contours for the Union legislature's role in European contract law and certain perennial themes that pervade the debate. In much the same way, the 'hard core' helps to illuminate the Court of Justice's role in European contract law, which leads to the next chapter.

Law as fragmentary, pointillistic and inconsistent': S Grundmann, 'Plan of Action for a Coherent European Contract Law—Observations' in A Fuchs, 'A Common Frame of Reference—How should it be filled?' (2003) 4 *ERA Forum* 99, 125. For a brief selection of scholarly criticism and some imaginative characterizations in this regard, see, eg, W-H Roth, 'Transposing "Pointillist" EC Guidelines into Systematic National Codes—Problems and Consequences' (2002) 10 *ERPL* 761; T Wilhelmsson, 'Private Law in the EU: Harmonised or Fragmented Harmonisation' (2002) 10 *ERPL* 77 ('jack-in-the-box effects of EC law').

343 Schmid, n 11, 286. See further, eg, W van Gerven, 'Comparative Law in a Texture of Communitarisation of National Laws and Europeanisation of Community Law' in D O'Keeffe (ed), 1 *Judicial Review in European Union Law—Liber Amicorum Lord Slynn of Hadley* (Kluwer, 2000) 433, 433–40 (underscoring the 'dark side' of harmonization generally).

344 J Basedow, 'Codification of Private Law in the European Union: the making of a Hybrid' (2001) 9 *ERPL* 35, 38–39. See also Mattei, n 340, 109 (calling it an 'academic jihad against Brussels bureaucrats').

2

The Role of the Court of Justice in European Contract Law

2.1 Introduction

In tandem with the role of the Union legislature in the development of the EU contract law *acquis*, increasing attention has been placed on the role of the Union courts in European contract law (as well as European private law generally). By and large, such attention centres on the Court of Justice (Court), as opposed to the General Court (EGC) and the EU Civil Service Tribunal (CST), which are also part of the institution of the Court of Justice of the European Union.[1] This may be explained by the fact that the majority of cases concerning the EU contract law *acquis*, particularly the 'hard core', have come before the Court pursuant to its exclusive jurisdiction (at least for the present time[2]) over preliminary rulings and infringement actions.[3] Consequently, the literature is replete with a wide variety of opinions as to the extent to which it can play the role of a 'private law court'[4] in furthering the approximation of private law, including contract law, and smoothing out the deficiencies in the Union *acquis*.[5]

This chapter offers a broader perspective. It highlights that there are in fact three key roles played by the Union courts in European contract law (as well as European private law generally), with focus placed on the Court of Justice (including the Advocates General) for the purposes of this discussion.[6] First, there is the Court's *interpretative*

[1] See Art 19(1), first para, TEU. This book refers to the Court of Justice to denote the highest court of this institution.

[2] The possibility of conferring jurisdiction on the EGC 'in specific areas' is envisaged under Art 256(3) TFEU; however, to date, this has not come about. See K Lenaerts, I Maselis, and K Gutman (JT Nowak (ed)), *EU Procedural Law* (Oxford Univ Press, 2014) ch 2.

[3] See, eg, V Trstenjak, 'The "Instruments" for Implementing European Private Law—The Influence of the ECJ Case Law on the Development and Formation of European Private Law' in L Moccia (ed), *The Making of European Private Law: Why, How, What, Who* (Sellier, 2013) 77, 77–78.

[4] CU Schmid, 'The ECJ as a Constitutional and a Private Law Court: A Methodological Comparison' (2006) *ZERP-Diskussionspapier* 4/2006, available at <http://www.zerp.uni-bremen.de/index.pl>.

[5] For a selection, see, eg, J Basedow, 'The Court of Justice and Private Law: Vacillations, General Principles and the Architecture of the European Judiciary' (2010) 18 *ERPL* 443; P Rott, 'What is the Role of the ECJ in EC Private Law?—A Comment on the ECJ judgments in *Océano Grupo, Freiburger Kommunalbauten, Leitner* and *Veedfald*' (2005) 1 *Hanse L Rev* 6; Schmid, n 4; J Stuyck, 'The European Court of Justice as a motor of private law' in C Twigg-Flesner (ed), *The Cambridge Companion to European Union Private Law* (Cambridge Univ Press, 2010) 101; H Unberath and A Johnston, 'Law at, to or from the Centre? The European Court of Justice and the Harmonization of Private Law in the European Union' in F Cafaggi (ed), *The Institutional Framework of European Private Law* (Oxford Univ Press, 2006) 149; W van Gerven, 'The ECJ Case-law as a Means of Unification of Private Law?' in AS Hartkamp et al (eds), *Towards a European Civil Code*, 3rd rev and expanded edn (Kluwer/Ars Aequi Libri, 2004) 101; S Weatherill, 'Interpretation of the Directives: The Role of the Court' in AS Hartkamp et al (eds), *Towards a European Civil Code*, 4th rev and expanded edn (Kluwer/Ars Aequi Libri, 2011) 185.

[6] It is not foreclosed that the EGC and the CST may play a role in European contract law, whether in the interpretative or lawmaking contexts as discussed below (or in the context of a case lodged

role by virtue of its interpretation of various measures falling within the Union contract law *acquis*. Secondly, while perhaps not as widely recognized, there is the Court's *lawmaking role* by virtue of its formulation of Union judge-made rules of law falling under the rubric of what is called European 'federal common law'. Thirdly, there is the recourse made to *comparative European contract law materials* in the Opinions of the Advocates General, which although not yet undertaken by the Court still has potential implications for its role in European contract law. These three aspects are analysed in turn in the following sections.

Importantly, these three roles are not airtight, but very much interrelated. As seen below, certain cases falling within the Court's interpretative role also highlight instances of the Court's lawmaking role, and the Advocate Generals' recourse to comparative European contract law materials is situated within both. Moreover, it should be underlined that the analysis presented here is by no means exhaustive or comprehensive. Several topics that may be considered in connection with the Court's contribution to the development of European contract law (or other fields of private law), such as those relating to the Court's case law on the fundamental freedoms, the 'direct effect' of directives in relationships between private parties, or its elaboration of rules on the liability of the Union, Member States, and individuals for breach of EU law, are not dealt with.[7] Yet, the perspective offered by this chapter may be of added value in delving further into those topics.

2.2 The Court of Justice's Interpretative Role

Notwithstanding the rising volume of cases concerning the Court's interpretation of directives falling within the 'hard core' of the EU contract law *acquis*, there are two sets of cases that are highly relevant for evaluating the Court's interpretative role in European contract law. Indeed, most of the discourse on the Court's role in this setting mentions this jurisprudence in one way or another. The first set of cases concerns the Court's interpretation of the (old) Doorstep Selling, Timeshare, and Consumer Credit Directives, which highlights the relationship between certain directives within EU contract law. The second set of cases concerns the Court's interpretation of the Unfair Contract Terms Directive, which provides a window into the relationship between EU contract law and the national contract law regimes.

2.2.1 The relationship between certain directives within EU contract law

As discussed in Chapter 1, the (old) Doorstep Selling Directive established a set of common rules for consumer contracts involving the sale of goods and services concluded in the 'doorstep selling' context, the heart of which concerned the consumer's right of cancellation that would release the consumer from any obligations under the contract.[8] Through the preliminary ruling procedure, the Court has been confronted

before the EGC involving a challenge to the legality of a Union contract law measure if ever such a case would be brought).

[7] See, eg, Stuyck, n 5; Unberath and Johnston, n 5; Weatherill, n 5.

[8] Council Dir 85/577/EEC of 20 Dec 1985 to protect the consumer in respect of contracts negotiated away from business premises, [1985] OJ L372/31. It is repealed by the Consumer Rights Directive: see Chapter 1, § 1.3.1.

with complex questions concerning the application of this Directive to various types of contracts, which essentially find the parties in the national proceedings 'fighting for their right' of cancellation as provided in the Directive. At the same time, several of these cases have required the Court to confront head-on the relationship between various directives within the EU contract law *acquis*.

Travel Vac[9] concerned the potential overlap between the (old) Doorstep Selling and Timeshare Directives.[10] Specifically, the case raised the issue of the potential applicability of the Doorstep Selling Directive to a timeshare contract that would have fallen within the scope of the Timeshare Directive but for the fact that it was concluded before the date that the latter Directive had to be transposed by the Member States.[11] Thus, the consumer's right of cancellation hinged on the Doorstep Selling Directive, thereby presenting the Court with questions as to whether a timeshare contract fell within the scope of this Directive and in turn, what in fact constituted a timeshare contract. Under Article 3(2)(a), 'contracts for the construction, sale and rental of immovable property or contracts concerning other rights relating to immovable property' were excluded from its scope, which begged the question whether the timeshare contract at issue fell within this provision.

All of the parties in the national proceedings, as well as the Spanish Government and the Commission, had differing opinions on the concept of a timeshare contract and whether it fell within the scope of the Directive.[12] In his Opinion, Advocate General Alber drew attention to the differences between the two Directives: the Timeshare Directive intended to protect a consumer who purchased rights to use immovable properties on a timeshare basis, whereas the Doorstep Selling Directive afforded protection to a consumer 'not primarily because he purchases certain goods but because of the way in which the goods are purchased or the contract concluded'.[13] He also underlined that they laid down different time periods in which the consumer could renounce the contract.[14] Importantly, neither Directive expressly stated whether it applied to contracts covered by the other.[15] This brought him to the concept of a timeshare contract. He noted that a so-called 'timeshare contract' was not a contract whose features could be clearly defined and that the interpretation and form of such a contract differed widely among the Member States.[16] As a result, the relevant features of the timeshare contract at issue had to be examined in order to determine whether it fell within the scope of the Directive, regardless of whether it was described as a 'timeshare contract' in the national proceedings.[17] In line with the objectives of the Doorstep Selling Directive, the Advocate General found that contracts mainly concerning rights other than those relating to immovable property fell within its scope,[18] and therefore, for the contract at hand, it had to be determined whether 'the real property rights are of limited significance, both in terms of their content and having regard to the whole contract'.[19]

[9] Case C-423/97 *Travel Vac* [1999] ECR I-2195.

[10] Dir 94/47/EC of the European Parliament and of the Council of 26 Oct 1994 on the protection of purchasers in respect of certain aspects of contracts relating to the purchase of the right to use immovable properties on a timeshare basis, [1994] OJ L280/83. It is repealed by the new Timeshare Directive: see Chapter 1, § 1.3.6.

[11] Opinion of AG Alber in Case C-423/97 *Travel Vac*, point 7.

[12] See Case C-423/97 *Travel Vac*, paras 18–21.

[13] Opinion of AG Alber in Case C-423/97 *Travel Vac*, point 21.

[14] Opinion of AG Alber in Case C-423/97 *Travel Vac*, point 25.

[15] Opinion of AG Alber in Case C-423/97 *Travel Vac*, point 26.

[16] Opinion of AG Alber in Case C-423/97 *Travel Vac*, points 27, 29, 33.

[17] Opinion of AG Alber in Case C-423/97 *Travel Vac*, points 27–28.

[18] Opinion of AG Alber in Case C-423/97 *Travel Vac*, point 31.

[19] Opinion of AG Alber in Case C-423/97 *Travel Vac*, point 35.

He answered this question in the affirmative, since the major part of the contract comprised services and other contractual obligations.[20]

The Court followed suit, but its judgment was startlingly short. Rather than delving into the concepts of a timeshare contract and immovable property, the Court implicitly adopted much of the Advocate General's reasoning on the issue. It held that neither Directive ruled out the application of the other, and 'since a contract like that at issue in the main proceedings does not only concern the right to use a time-share apartment, but also concerns the provision of separate services of a value higher than that of the right to use the property', that contract was not excluded by the Doorstep Selling Directive.[21] Yet, the Court's ruling left several lingering issues in its wake. First, as the transposition period for one of the Directives had not yet expired at the time of this case, the Court's judgment did not address the situation where both the Doorstep Selling and Timeshare Directives would be applicable.[22] Indeed, Advocate General Alber's remarks about the inconsistencies between these Directives raised questions as to how to reconcile them under such circumstances. For this reason, this case stood as a figurehead for criticism of the incoherent nature of the EU contract law *acquis* in Commission documents disseminated in the debate about European contract law.[23] Moreover, *Travel Vac* made apparent the continuing divergences in the treatment of timeshare contracts among the laws of the Member States. The fact that the Timeshare Directive did not elaborate the concept of a timeshare contract was revealing. To recall, this Directive had expressly disavowed the harmonization of the national timeshare contract regimes.[24] As stressed in the Advocate General's Opinion, this meant that no general rules could be laid down on the concept of a timeshare contract. That said, the Court's elaboration, albeit sparse, of the nature of a timeshare contract for the purposes of determining whether it was a contract related to immovable property did not go unnoticed[25] and filtered into cases concerning the interpretation of other Union instruments.[26]

Around the same time period, *Dietzinger*[27] and *Berliner*[28] presented the Court with a parallel situation involving the nature of a guarantee contract for the purposes of interpreting the (old) Doorstep Selling and Consumer Credit Directives.[29] *Dietzinger* concerned the relationship between a credit agreement involving a commercial loan given by a German bank to a business run by Mr Dietzinger's father, on the one hand, and a guarantee contract (also called a contract of suretyship[30]) concluded by

[20] Opinion of AG Alber in Case C-423/97 *Travel Vac*, points 30, 36.

[21] Case C-423/97 *Travel Vac*, paras 23, 25–26.

[22] See H Schulte-Nölke et al (eds), *EC Consumer Law Compendium—Comparative Analysis* (Version of Feb 2008), available at <http://ec.europa.eu/consumers/rights/docs/consumer_law_compendium_comparative_analysis_en_final.pdf> (Consumer Law Compendium), 207. See further Chapter 6, § 6.3.1.

[23] See, eg, Commission Communication on European Contract Law, COM (2001) 398 final, 11.7.2001 (2001 Communication), point 35.

[24] See Chapter 1, § 1.3.6. See also Opinion of AG Geelhoed in Case C-73/04 *Klein and Others* [2005] ECR I-8667, points 20–21.

[25] See E Ioratti, Case note (2001) 9 *ERPL* 441, 444.

[26] See, eg, Case C-73/04 *Klein* [2005] ECR I-8667, paras 21–22.

[27] Case C-45/96 *Dietzinger* [1998] ECR I-1199.

[28] Case C-208/98 *Berliner* [2000] ECR I-1741.

[29] Council Dir 87/102/EEC of 22 Dec 1986 for the approximation of the laws, regulations and administrative provisions of the Member States concerning consumer credit, [1987] OJ L42/48. It is repealed by the new Consumer Credit Directive: see Chapter 1, § 1.3.3.

[30] A guarantee may also be called contract of suretyship: see Opinion of AG Jacobs in Case C-45/96 *Dietzinger* [1998] ECR I-1199, point 13. The terminology itself begged for further elaboration and common understanding among the contract laws of the Member States: see also n 181.

Mr Dietzinger with that bank at his parents' home securing his parents' obligations under that loan, on the other.[31] Thereafter, Mr Dietzinger attempted to cancel the guarantee contract on the grounds that he was not informed of his right of cancellation under the Doorstep Selling Directive. By way of a request for a preliminary ruling from a German court, the Court was faced with the question whether a guarantee contract fell within the scope of this Directive.[32]

Noticeably, the very concept of 'contract' was not defined anywhere in the Doorstep Selling Directive.[33] Thus, the question whether a guarantee contract was a contract for the supply of goods or services concluded between a consumer and a trader in the 'doorstep selling' context could not be answered by the text of the Directive. All four Member States (Germany, Belgium, France, and Finland) involved in the proceedings argued that a guarantee contract fell outside the Directive, since a guarantee contract was considered to be a unilateral undertaking on the part of the guarantor, as opposed to a bilateral contract involving mutual and reciprocal obligations on the part of both parties, which was required by the Directive.[34] In their view, the protection of guarantors was 'a matter for national law alone'.[35] By comparison, Mr Dietzinger and the Commission advocated a broad reading of the Directive to include guarantee contracts on the grounds that '[l]ike a purchaser, a guarantor undertakes to perform obligations and is even more in need of protection since he receives no consideration in exchange for his commitment'.[36]

In its judgment, the Court held that a guarantee contract could in principle fall within the scope of the Directive. It based its holding on several points, which forced it to elaborate the notion of a guarantee contract.[37] A guarantee contract was considered the provision of a service, as it was 'merely ancillary to the principal contract, of which in practice it is usually a precondition'.[38] Moreover, 'nothing in the wording of the [D]irective requires that the person concluding the contract under which goods and services are to be supplied be the person to whom they are supplied', meaning that the unilateral nature of the guarantee contract did not oust it from the Directive's scope.[39] There was also a 'close link' between a credit agreement and a guarantee contract and the fact that 'the person guaranteeing repayment of a debt may either assume joint and several liability for payment of the debt or be the guarantor of its repayment'.[40] However, the Court limited its holding according to the status of the parties involved. The Directive covered 'only a guarantee ancillary to a contract whereby, in the context of "doorstep selling", a consumer assumes obligations towards a trader with a view to

[31] There had been a previous case, Case C-24/93 *Commerzbank Frankfurt*, involving a similar factual scenario, but it was withdrawn before the Court was able to rule. See Commission Report on the operation of Dir 87/102/EEC, COM (95) 117, 11.5.1995, point 344.

[32] Case C-45/96 *Dietzinger*, para 11.

[33] Opinion of AG Jacobs in Case C-45/96 *Dietzinger*, point 11.

[34] Case C-45/96 *Dietzinger*, paras 14–15; compare Opinion of AG Jacobs, point 14. As noted therein, these Member States attempted to frame this argument in terms of the lack of 'consideration'. While perhaps not too much should be read into this, it is remarkable that four Member States largely emanating from the civil law tradition utilized a concept ingrained in the common law definition of a contract. They also attempted to support their argument with the English version of Art 1(1) of the Directive that embodied a more limited scope than the French version with which most other language versions were aligned: see Opinion of AG Jacobs in Case C-45/96 *Dietzinger*, point 17. This meant that these Member States were attempting to rely on a language version of the Directive other than their own.

[35] Case C-45/96 *Dietzinger*, para 16.

[36] Case C-45/96 *Dietzinger*, para 12.

[37] For detailed discussion, see N Ramforth, 'The limits of European Union consumer contract law' (1999) 24 *ELR* 410.

[38] Case C-45/96 *Dietzinger*, para 18.

[39] Case C-45/96 *Dietzinger*, para 19.

[40] Case C-45/96 *Dietzinger*, para 20.

obtaining goods or services from him'.[41] Since the Directive was designed to protect only consumers, a guarantee contract fell within its scope only where 'the guarantor has entered into a commitment for a purpose which can be regarded as unconnected with his trade or profession'.[42] As the present case involved a guarantee contract securing the performance of a credit agreement by a third party acting in a commercial capacity (as was the case with Mr Dietzinger's parents), that contract fell outside the scope of the Directive.[43]

Dietzinger received mixed opinions from scholars, some criticizing the lack of protection given to the party concerned,[44] and others praising the Court for not unduly expanding the limits of the Directive.[45] Overall, this judgment exposed a 'protection gap' in the scope of the Doorstep Selling Directive as regards guarantees for business loans that were not covered, as opposed to guarantees for consumer loans that were, which was singled out as something to be remedied in the revision of this Directive several years later.[46] This case also exposed inconsistencies in the language versions regarding the treatment of contracts falling within the scope of the Doorstep Selling Directive, whereby certain kinds of guarantee contracts fell easily within its scope according to some language versions, but not others.[47]

Thereafter, *Berliner*[48] presented the Court with a startlingly similar question to *Dietzinger*, this time in connection with the (old) Consumer Credit Directive. The case involved a loan contract granted by a commercial undertaking, Berliner, to a third party, Mr Diesterbeck, which was secured by a guarantee contract entered into by Mr Siepert.[49] Pursuant to the German legislation implementing the Directive, both Mr Diesterbeck and Mr Siepert were considered consumers.[50] Mr Siepert had not been informed of his right of cancellation and thereafter sought to exercise this right in reliance on the Directive. Like the Doorstep Selling Directive, the Consumer Credit Directive did not contain an explicit provision either including or excluding guarantee contracts from its scope. Therefore, the key issue was whether a guarantee contract may be deemed a consumer credit agreement under the Consumer Credit Directive.[51] In essence, the Court was being asked whether the Consumer Credit Directive should be interpreted in the same way as the Doorstep Selling Directive.[52]

Not surprisingly, many of the parties' arguments resembled those made in *Dietzinger*. In particular, the same three Member States (Germany, Belgium, and Finland) submitted that the Consumer Credit Directive did not apply to guarantee

41 Case C-45/96 *Dietzinger*, para 22.

42 Case C-45/96 *Dietzinger*, para 22.

43 Case C-45/96 *Dietzinger*, para 23. The AG reached the same result, but by a different route rooted in the nature of the guarantee contract at issue, as opposed to the status of the party concerned: Opinion of AG Jacobs in Case C-45/96 *Dietzinger*, points 38–42.

44 But as regards its impact beyond Mr Dietzinger, see P Rott, 'Renationalisation of direct selling—the impact of the new Consumer Rights Directive on financial services' (2012) 13 *ERA Forum* 35, 37–38.

45 See M Schillig, 'The Interpretation of European Private Law in the light of Market Freedoms and EU Fundamental Rights' (2008) 15 *MJ* 285, 309 fn 151.

46 See Consumer Law Compendium, n 22, 184.

47 See Consumer Law Compendium, n 22, 184.

48 Case C-208/98 *Berliner* [2000] ECR I-1741.

49 Case C-208/98 *Berliner*, para 9.

50 The German implementing legislation provided a wider definition of consumer than that set forth in the Directive, with the result that Berliner's arguments that the case was inadmissible were quickly dealt with by the AG and not even addressed by the Court. See Opinion of AG Léger in Case C-208/98 *Berliner*, points 9, 26–27.

51 Case C-208/98 *Berliner*, para 12.

52 Opinion of AG Léger in Case C-208/98 *Berliner*, point 31.

contracts because they were not credit agreements, ie bilateral contracts, but instead unilateral undertakings guaranteeing the repayment of credit.[53] France switched sides, however, joining Spain, the Commission, and Mr Siepert in arguing that due to the 'close link' between the guarantee contract and the credit agreement, the former could be covered by the Directive.[54] The Commission added that it was 'an unintentional oversight' that the Directive was silent on the matter.[55]

The Court held that the Consumer Credit Directive did not apply to a guarantee contract where both the guarantor and borrower were acting as consumers.[56] Leaving aside Advocate General Léger's slightly caustic remark concerning the Court's dubious reasoning on certain points in *Dietzinger*,[57] the Court's judgment was largely a condensed version of the Advocate General's Opinion. Both approached the matter from the classical modes of interpretation, looking to the text, scheme, and purpose of the Directive. This made the Advocate General's more strenuous engagement with contract law concepts stand out. First, as regards *the text* of the Directive, the Court quickly disposed of the matter by reiterating the definition of credit agreement in the Consumer Credit Directive and stating that it was 'common ground that a contract of guarantee is not a credit agreement' as defined in that Directive.[58] In contrast, the Advocate General delved into the notion of a guarantee contract so as to distinguish the two:

> A guarantee constitutes a personal security. More precisely, what is concerned is an agreement by which a person makes a commitment to the creditor, in the form of a guarantee, to discharge the obligation of the principal debtor should the latter have failed to do so himself. Therefore a guarantee represents neither 'a loan', nor 'a deferred payment', nor 'other similar financial accommodation' within the meaning of the Directive. Furthermore, in so far as the guarantee commitment does not entail any *quid pro quo* on the part of the creditor or the principal debtor, the guarantee also constitutes a unilateral contract.[59]

In his view, the Consumer Credit Directive contained a series of provisions that indicated that its scope was strictly limited to bilateral contracts.[60] As such, the *Dietzinger* judgment, in which the unilateral nature of a guarantee contract did not preclude its applicability to the Doorstep Selling Directive, could not be transposed to the present case.[61]

Secondly, as far as *the scheme* of the Directive was concerned, both the Court's and the Advocate General's reasoning were grounded in legislative intent. For the Court, although the Annex to the Directive mentioned the existence of a security in the credit agreement, it could not be inferred in the absence of an explicit provision that the Directive also governed the legal situation created by the guarantee contract.[62] Likewise, the Advocate General noted that the Directive contained various references

[53] Case C-208/98 *Berliner*, para 13.
[54] Case C-208/98 *Berliner*, para 15.
[55] Case C-208/98 *Berliner*, para 15.
[56] Case C-208/98 *Berliner*, para 27.
[57] See Opinion of AG Léger in Case C-208/98 *Berliner*, point 65.
[58] Case C-208/98 *Berliner*, para 18. Under Art 1(2)(c) of the (old) Consumer Credit Directive, a 'credit agreement' was defined as 'an agreement whereby a creditor grants or promises to grant to a consumer a credit in the form of a deferred payment, a loan or other similar financial accommodation'. This was generally retained in Art 3(c) of the new Consumer Credit Directive, save for additional language excluding agreements for the provision of goods or services on a continuing basis where the consumer pays in installments.
[59] Opinion of AG Léger in Case C-208/98 *Berliner*, points 36–37.
[60] Opinion of AG Léger in Case C-208/98 *Berliner*, point 39.
[61] Opinion of AG Léger in Case C-208/98 *Berliner*, points 38, 40.
[62] Case C-208/98 *Berliner*, para 19.

to real securities and personal securities, which demonstrated that the Union legislature was aware of the fact that credit agreements were frequently subject to the condition that the consumer obtain a guarantee, but the fact that the Directive did not contain any provisions on the status or the treatment of guarantees meant that the legislature intended to exclude guarantee contracts.[63]

Finally, as regards *the purpose* of the Directive, the Court again focused on legislative intent. The fact that the Directive recognized a guarantee as part of the credit agreement from the borrower's perspective but stayed silent as to the legal implications demonstrated the legislature's intention to exclude guarantee contracts from its scope.[64] This led the Court to contrast the two Directives: for the Doorstep Selling Directive, the sole restriction that it placed on the types of contracts falling within its scope was that they must concern the supply of goods or services, provided that the purposes pursued by the consumer can be regarded as outside his trade or profession,[65] whereas the Consumer Credit Directive was almost entirely concerned with the information given to the principal debtor, not with safeguarding the guarantor, and thus was not designed to apply to guarantee contracts.[66] The Court hastened to add that the scope of the Consumer Credit Directive could not extend to guarantee contracts 'solely on the ground that such agreements are ancillary to the principal agreement whose performance they underwrite', since there was no support for such an interpretation in the wording, scheme, and purpose of the Directive.[67] The Advocate General reached similar conclusions, finding that the Consumer Credit Directive was focused on protecting the recipients of credit, not guarantors, and although guarantors may be in a 'weak position' comparable to that of the borrower in a credit agreement, protection for borrowers under the Directive was of a different nature than that for guarantors.[68] As a result, taking *Dietzinger* and *Berliner* together, a guarantee contract that would have fallen within the scope of the Doorstep Selling Directive did not fall within the scope of the Consumer Credit Directive. Framed another way, the two cases brought to the fore the different nature of directives within the *acquis*, that is to say, those pertaining to certain types of contracts and others pertaining to selling methods, whose interpretation would lead to different outcomes.

2.2.2 The relationship between EU contract law and the national contract law regimes

The second set of cases concerns the Court's interpretation of the Unfair Contract Terms Directive.[69] To recall from the previous chapter, the Unfair Contract Terms Directive is one of the most far-reaching directives in the EU contract law *acquis*.[70] By setting forth a set of common rules concerning the regulation of unfair terms in consumer contracts, it has had a significant impact on the national contract law regimes.[71] The heart

[63] Opinion of AG Léger in Case C-208/98 *Berliner*, points 46–48.
[64] Case C-208/98 *Berliner*, para 22. See also para 23.
[65] Case C-208/98 *Berliner*, para 24.
[66] Case C-208/98 *Berliner*, para 25.
[67] Case C-208/98 *Berliner*, para 26.
[68] Opinion of AG Léger in Case C-208/98 *Berliner*, points 57–68.
[69] Council Dir 93/13/EEC of 5 April 1993 on unfair terms in consumer contracts, [1993] OJ L95/29.
[70] See Chapter 1, § 1.3.5.
[71] In this respect, it may not be coincidental that the Unfair Contract Terms Directive brought about several infringement actions against certain Member States for their varied means of transposing it, some (but not all) of which were successful. See, eg, Case C-144/99 *Commission v Netherlands*

of the Directive concerns the assessment of the unfairness of particular terms in consumer contracts, thereby including certain concepts that are unknown or defined differently in the Member States, such as 'good faith', which appears as part of the scheme for determining whether a particular term is unfair. In the aftermath of implementing this Directive, the extent of divergences between the Member States as to the evaluation of unfair terms was widely discussed in the commentary.[72] Consequently, the case law on the interpretation of this Directive was watched with bated breath, particularly as to the extent to which the Court would formulate uniform notions of unfairness and good faith, which would bring clarity and uniformity to this area.

On the whole, a considerable portion of the Court's case law on this Directive has been concerned with the duty placed on national courts to examine of their own motion whether a particular term in a consumer contract is unfair in accordance with its provisions. Accordingly, there is a growing number of rulings dealing with this issue[73] and related procedural matters,[74] which are largely situated within the interplay between so-called 'national procedural autonomy' and the Union principles of equivalence and effectiveness.[75] At the same time, however, several of these same cases, as well as others, have directly confronted the Court with questions concerning the extent of its role in the assessment of unfair terms pursuant to this Directive and in doing so provide reflection on the relationship between this Directive and the national contract law regimes.

The five joined cases known as *Océano Grupo*[76] constituted the Court's first opportunity to interpret provisions of the Unfair Contract Terms Directive.[77] The cases stemmed from standard form contracts concluded between various consumers resident

[2001] ECR I-3541; Case C-372/99 *Commission v Italy* [2002] ECR I-819; Case C-478/99 *Commission v Sweden* [2002] ECR I-4147; Case C-70/03 *Commission v Spain* [2004] ECR I-7999.

[72] See, eg, F Cafaggi, 'The making of European private law: governance design' in F Cafaggi and H Muir-Watt (eds), *Making European Private Law: Governance Design* (Edward Elgar, 2008) 289, 311–313 and citations therein.

[73] See, eg, Joined Cases C-240/98 to C-244/98 *Océano Grupo and Salvat Editores* [2000] ECR I-4941; Case C-473/00 *Cofidis* [2002] ECR I-10875; Case C-168/05 *Mostaza Claro* [2006] ECR I-10421; Case C-243/08 *Pannon GSM* [2009] ECR I-4713, paras 19–35; Case C-40/08 *Asturcom Telecomunicaciones* [2009] ECR I-9579; Case C-137/08 *VB Pénzügyi Lízing* [2010] ECR I-10847, paras 45–56; Case C-76/10 (Order of 16 Nov 2010) *Pohotovost'* [2010] ECR I-11557, paras 36–54; Case C-472/10 (Judgment of 26 April 2012) *Invitel*, not reported, paras 32–44; Case C-618/10 (Judgment of 14 June 2012) *Banco Español de Crédito*, not reported, paras 38–57; Case C-397/11 (Judgment of 30 May 2013) *Jőrös*, not reported; Case C-488/11 (Judgment of 30 May 2013) *Asbeek Brusse and de Man Garabito*, not reported, paras 35–53. The Court has transposed its rulings in this regard to other EU contract law measures: as regards the Consumer Credit Directive, see, eg, Case C-429/05 *Rampion and Godard* [2007] ECR I-8017, paras 60–69; Case C-76/10 (Order of 16 Nov 2010) *Pohotovost'* [2010] ECR I-11557, paras 64–77; as regards the Doorstep Selling Directive, see, eg, Case C-227/08 *Martín Martín* [2009] ECR I-11939; compare Opinion of AG Trstenjak, points 62–92. See also Joined Cases C-222/05 to 225/05 *van der Weerd and Others* [2007] ECR I-4233, para 40.

[74] See, eg, Case C-472/11 (Judgment of 21 Feb 2013) *Banif Plus Bank*, not reported, paras 17–36; Case C-415/11 (Judgment of 14 March 2013) *Aziz*, not reported, paras 43–64.

[75] For further discussion, see, eg, Lenaerts, Maselis, and Gutman, n 2, ch 4; AÓ Caoimh, 'Issues of EU Law Raised by National Courts of their Own Motion' in P Cardonnel et al (eds), *Constitutionalising the EU Judicial System—Essays in Honour of Pernilla Lindh* (Hart, 2012) 123; V Trstenjak, 'Procedural Aspects of European Consumer Protection Law and the Case Law of the CJEU' (2013) 21 *ERPL* 451. In particular, the Court's recent decisions in *Pannon* and *Asturcom Telecomunicaciones* (n 73) have been a focal point in the commentary: see, eg, the case notes by J Stuyck (2010) 47 *CML Rev* 879; and M Ebers (2010) 18 *ERPL* 823.

[76] Joined Cases C-240/98 to C-244/98 *Océano Grupo and Salvat Editores* [2000] ECR I-4941.

[77] Opinion of AG Saggio in Joined Cases C-240/98 to C-244/98 *Océano Grupo and Salvat Editores*, point 1. This is to distinguish the infringement actions brought by the Commission against certain Member States before and after this case: see n 71.

throughout Spain and two Spanish companies concerning the sale of home encyclopedias. The contracts contained a clause stipulating that the courts in Barcelona, where the companies had their principal place of business, would have exclusive jurisdiction in the event of a dispute arising out of such contracts.[78] In the context of litigation brought against these consumers by the companies for unpaid amounts due under the contract, one such Barcelona court submitted a request to the Court for a preliminary ruling as to whether the Directive required it to examine the unfairness of a term of its own motion, which would have the result that it could decline jurisdiction in the case.[79]

In its judgment, the Court considered that the term at issue satisfied all of the criteria enabling it to be classified as unfair under the Directive.[80] It explained that a term of this kind obliged the consumer to travel far from home for the purposes of litigation, and especially for cases involving small amounts of money, the resulting costs could cause the consumer to forego any legal remedy or defence, thereby recognizing that it fell squarely within the category of terms listed in the Annex to the Directive that have the effect of excluding or hindering the consumer's right to take legal action.[81] In addition, such a term made it easier for the company to deal with litigation and enter an appearance in such matters.[82] The Court concluded that where a jurisdiction clause like the one at issue is included in a consumer contract, it must be regarded as unfair for the purposes of the Directive.[83]

Some years later, in *Freiburger*,[84] the Court refined its approach taken in *Océano Grupo*. This case concerned the alleged unfairness of a particular term in a consumer contract between a German couple, Mr and Mrs Hofstetter, and Freiburger, a German construction company, for the sale of a parking space in a multi-story car park.[85] The term stipulated that the total purchase price for the parking space would be due upon the delivery of a bank guarantee by the contractor, and in the event of late payment of this amount, the purchaser would be required to pay default interest.[86] The bank guarantee was duly delivered to the Hofstetters, but they refused to pay the purchase price until after they had accepted the parking space free of defects.[87] As a result, Freiburger brought an action to enforce the contract,[88] leading to a reference by a German court as to whether such a clause was unfair under the Directive.[89]

Advocate General Geelhoed issued a short but biting Opinion, stressing the limits of the Court's 'interpretational function' in relation to the assessment of potentially unfair terms under the Directive:

> [T]here are reasons for setting strict limits to this interpretational task, given that the Directive allows the Member States a wide margin of discretion in deciding what terms they consider unfair within their respective national legal spheres. To construe this interpretational task

[78] Joined Cases C-240/98 to C-244/98 *Océano Grupo and Salvat Editores*, para 16.
[79] Joined Cases C-240/98 to C-244/98 *Océano Grupo and Salvat Editores*, paras 18–19.
[80] Joined Cases C-240/98 to C-244/98 *Océano Grupo and Salvat Editores*, para 21.
[81] Joined Cases C-240/98 to C-244/98 *Océano Grupo and Salvat Editores*, para 22. Para 1(q) of the Annex refers to '[t]erms which have the object or effect of: . . . excluding or hindering the consumer's right to take legal action or exercise any other legal remedy, particularly by requiring the consumer to take disputes exclusively to arbitration not covered by legal provisions . . .'.
[82] Joined Cases C-240/98 to C-244/98 *Océano Grupo and Salvat Editores*, para 23.
[83] Joined Cases C-240/98 to C-244/98 *Océano Grupo and Salvat Editores*, para 24.
[84] Case C-237/02 *Freiburger Kommunalbauten* [2004] ECR I-3403.
[85] Case C-237/02 *Freiburger Kommunalbauten*, para 9.
[86] Case C-237/02 *Freiburger Kommunalbauten*, paras 10–11.
[87] Case C-237/02 *Freiburger Kommunalbauten*, para 12.
[88] Case C-237/02 *Freiburger Kommunalbauten*, para 13.
[89] Case C-237/02 *Freiburger Kommunalbauten*, para 14.

broadly would significantly affect this discretion, which . . . was expressly *not* the intention of the [Union] legislature. In short, it is primarily for the national court to decide whether a clause which is the subject of proceedings before it is to be treated as being unfair.[90]

He also stressed that there was no need for the Court to ensure the uniform application of Union law under these circumstances: 'The terms in question are relevant only in private-law relations which are to a significant extent still governed by national law, under which the same type of terms may even have different legal effects in different national legal systems.'[91] His remarks seem to have infiltrated the Court's judgment to some extent.

The Court ruled that as to the question whether a particular term is, or is not, unfair, the Directive requires that the answer should be reached taking into account the nature of the goods or services for which the contract is concluded and by referring to, at the time of conclusion of the contract, all the circumstances attending the conclusion of the contract.[92] It then added: '*It should be pointed out in that respect that the consequences of the term under the law applicable to the contract must also be taken into account. This requires that consideration be given to the national law.*'[93] The above quoted language in paragraph 21 of the judgment was the Court's creation; it did not appear in the text of the Directive itself.[94] On this basis, citing the Advocate General's Opinion, the Court underlined that it was only able to interpret the general criteria used by the Union legislature to define the concept of unfair terms, and that it could not rule on the application of those general criteria to a particular term, 'which must be considered in the light of the particular circumstances of the case in question'.[95] It also distinguished its previous ruling in *Océano Grupo* as follows:

[T]hat assessment was reached in relation to a term which was solely to the benefit of the seller and contained no benefit in return for the consumer. Whatever the nature of the contract, it thereby undermined the effectiveness of the legal protection of the rights which the Directive affords to the consumer. It was thus possible to hold that the term was unfair without having to consider all the circumstances in which the contract was concluded and without having to assess the advantages and disadvantages that that term would have under the national law applicable to the contract.[96]

In contrast, that did not apply to the term involved in the present case.[97] The Court concluded that it was left to the national court to decide whether the term was unfair in accordance with the Directive.[98]

In subsequent decisions, the Court has continued to underscore its holding in *Freiburger*.[99] For instance, in *Mostaza Claro*,[100] the Court prefaced its judgment with a reference to the case, so as to reiterate that it was for the national court alone to decide

[90] Opinion of AG Geelhoed in Case C-237/02 *Freiburger Kommunalbauten*, points 2–4 (emphasis added). See further points 17–21, 26–29.

[91] Opinion of AG Geelhoed in Case C-237/02 *Freiburger Kommunalbauten*, point 30.

[92] Case C-237/02 *Freiburger Kommunalbauten*, para 21.

[93] Case C-237/02 *Freiburger Kommunalbauten*, para 21 (emphasis added).

[94] See L Niglia, 'The "Rules" Dilemma–The Court of Justice and the Regulation of Standard Form Contracts in Europe' (2006) 13 *CJEL* 125, 142.

[95] Case C-237/02 *Freiburger Kommunalbauten*, para 22.

[96] Case C-237/02 *Freiburger Kommunalbauten*, para 23.

[97] Case C-237/02 *Freiburger Kommunalbauten*, para 24.

[98] Case C-237/02 *Freiburger Kommunalbauten*, para 25.

[99] See, eg, Case C-76/10 (Order of 16 Nov 2010) *Pohotovost'* [2010] ECR I-11557, paras 59–60; Case C-453/10 (Judgment of 15 March 2012) *Pereničová and Perenič*, not reported, para 44; Opinion of AG Trstenjak in Case C-453/10 *Pereničová and Perenič*, point 69.

[100] Case C-168/05 *Mostaza Claro* [2006] ECR I-10421.

whether a particular term was unfair under the Directive.[101] Advocate General Tizzano went a bit further in his Opinion, not just underlining the significance of *Freiburger*, but also declaring that *Océano Grupo* constitutes 'a precedent that is most exceptional and is therefore not generally applicable, since in the majority of cases, it will not be clear whether a term is unfair and therefore will be for the national courts to decide'.[102]

Furthermore, *Pannon*[103] presented an opportunity for the Court to confirm its approach in a case that bore a remarkable resemblance to *Océano Grupo*, involving a term in a standard form contract for mobile telephone services that required the consumer to accept the jurisdiction where the trader had its principal place of business for any dispute arising under the contract.[104] Among the questions referred, the Hungarian court sought guidance from the Court on the factors that it must consider in assessing the unfairness of a particular term under the Directive.[105]

The Court disposed of this issue in eight paragraphs.[106] After reiterating its previous decisions in *Freiburger* and *Océano Grupo*,[107] the Court pulled the two together by declaring that while it was true that in exercising its preliminary ruling jurisdiction in the latter case, it interpreted the general criteria used by the legislature in order to define the concept of unfair terms, in accordance with the former case, it could not rule on the application of those general criteria to specific terms, which must be considered in the light of the particular circumstances of the national proceedings.[108] Thus, it was for the national court to assess whether a contractual term may be regarded as unfair within the meaning of the Directive.[109] Yet, in doing so, the national court must take into account that a term like the one in the present case may be considered to be unfair.[110]

Notably, although the Court cited its previous findings in *Freiburger*, it made no explicit reference to the language of paragraph 21.[111] It is not clear whether this omission was intentional,[112] but on balance, it seems to be more the result of the particular circumstances of the case concerned. Given *Pannon*'s similarity to *Océano Grupo*, where the Court had declared the particular term unfair, this was a case in which taking account of the consequences of the term under the relevant national law was not going to loom that large. As such, the Court's judgment in *Pannon* staked out a middle ground. Although the Court was careful not to overstep its bounds as elaborated in *Freiburger*, it essentially sought to 'nudge' the national court towards the outcome in *Océano Grupo* so as to give it a 'helping hand' in the assessment of the term at issue in the main proceedings. In short, *Pannon* was a nice blending of the two cases. Yet, it was not the end of the matter.

VB Pénzügyi Lízing[113] squarely confronted the Court with the division of tasks between it and the national courts in relation to the assessment of unfair terms.[114]

[101] Case C-168/05 *Mostaza Claro*, paras 22–23.
[102] Opinion of AG Tizzano in Case C-168/05 *Mostaza Claro*, points 30, 32.
[103] Case C-243/08 *Pannon GSM* [2009] ECR I-4713.
[104] Case C-243/08 *Pannon GSM*, para 12.
[105] Case C-243/08 *Pannon GSM*, para 36.
[106] Case C-243/08 *Pannon GSM*, paras 37–44.
[107] See Case C-243/08 *Pannon GSM*, paras 37–41.
[108] Case C-243/08 *Pannon GSM*, para 42.
[109] Case C-243/08 *Pannon GSM*, para 43.
[110] Case C-243/08 *Pannon GSM*, para 44.
[111] See n 93 and accompanying text.
[112] The fact that the Court delivered its judgment without an AG Opinion, as is provided under Art 20, fifth para, of the Statute of the Court of Justice of the European Union for cases raising 'no new points of law', suggests that it was not using this case to signal a major departure from its approach to the assessment of unfair terms.
[113] Case C-137/08 *VB Pénzügyi Lízing* [2010] ECR I-10847.
[114] Case C-137/08 *VB Pénzügyi Lízing*, para 36. The case had initially been joined to *Pannon* (see Order of the President of the Court dated 4 Aug 2008 in Case C-137/08 and Case C-243/08, not reported), but was disjoined (see Order of the President of the Court dated 14 Oct 2008 in

In its judgment, the Court addressed this issue in eight paragraphs.[115] It began with its 'standard formula' that Articles 3(1) and 4 of the Directive, taken as a whole, define the general criteria permitting the assessment as to whether the contractual terms subject to the Directive are unfair, thereby including an indirect citation to several paragraphs (including paragraph 21) of *Freiburger*.[116] It then reiterated its previous ruling in *Pannon*, which led it to conclude that its jurisdiction extends to the interpretation of the concept of 'unfair term' used in Article 3(1) and the Annex of the Directive and to the criteria that the national court may or must apply when examining a particular term, 'bearing in mind that is for that court to determine, in light of those criteria, whether a particular contractual term is actually unfair in the circumstances of the case'.[117] In contrast to the Court's guarded approach, Advocate General Trstenjak considered this issue in more detail,[118] stressing among other things the Court's task to elaborate what constitutes unfairness and to give specific expression to the abstract criteria for classifying a particular term as unfair and hence 'to establish a profile for reviewing the unfairness of terms at the level of [Union] law'.[119]

Recently, in *Aziz*,[120] the Court has taken a step in that direction. By way of a reference from a Spanish court, the Court was asked to clarify the concept of 'unfair term' in light of Articles 3(1) and (3) of the Directive and the Annex thereto.[121] In its ruling, the Court began by running through previous case law, underlining that its jurisdiction extends to the interpretation of the concept of 'unfair term' used in Article 3(1) and the Annex and to the criteria applied by the national court when examining contractual terms pursuant to the Directive, but that it is for the national court to determine, in light of those criteria, whether a particular term is actually unfair in the circumstances of the case and hence that the Court is limited to providing guidance to the referring court, which that court must take into account in order to assess whether the term at issue is unfair.[122]

It then noted that, in referring to the concepts of good faith and significant imbalance in the parties' rights and obligations arising under the contract to the detriment of the consumer, Article 3(1) of the Directive merely defines in a general way the factors that render a non-individually negotiated term unfair.[123] This led the Court to elaborate these concepts, supported by relevant points of Advocate General Kokott's Opinion, which took particular account of the backdrop of the relevant national law. In order to ascertain whether a term causes a 'significant imbalance' in the parties' rights and obligations, 'it must in particular be considered what rules of national law would apply in the absence of an agreement by the parties in that regard', since this kind of comparative analysis 'will enable the national court to evaluate whether and, as the case may be, to what extent the contract places the consumer in a legal situation less

Case C-137/08 and Case C-243/08, not reported). It was then stayed pending delivery of *Pannon*, with the result that the referring court rescinded two questions (the third concerned the preliminary ruling procedure: see Case C-137/08 *VB Pénzügyi Lízing*, paras 26–35) and added three questions: see Case C-137/08 *VB Pénzügyi Lízing*, paras 21–25.

[115] Case C-137/08 *VB Pénzügyi Lízing*, paras 37–44.

[116] See Case C-137/08 *VB Pénzügyi Lízing*, para 40 (citing Case C-484/08 *Caja de Ahorros y Monte de Piedad de Madrid* [2010] ECR I-4785, para 33 'and the case-law cited', which in turn referred to, inter alia, Case C-237/02 *Freiburger Kommunalbauten*, paras 18, 19, and 21).

[117] Case C-137/08 *VB Pénzügyi Lízing*, paras 41–44.

[118] See Opinion of AG Trstenak in Case C-137/08 *VB Pénzügyi Lízing*, points 85–101.

[119] Opinion of AG Trstenak in Case C-137/08 *VB Pénzügyi Lízing*, point 99.

[120] Case C-415/11 (Judgment of 14 March 2013) *Aziz*, not reported.

[121] Case C-415/11 *Aziz*, para 65.

[122] Case C-415/11 *Aziz*, para 66.

[123] Case C-415/11 *Aziz*, para 67.

favourable than that provided for by the national law in force'; an assessment should also be carried out of the legal situation of that consumer having regard to the means at his disposal under national legislation to prevent the continued use of unfair terms.[124] Moreover, with respect to the situation in which such an imbalance arises 'contrary to the requirement of good faith', the national court must assess 'whether the seller or supplier, dealing fairly and equitably with the consumer, could reasonably assume that the consumer would have agreed to such a term in individual contract negotiations'.[125] In this regard, the Court repeated its previous rulings on the scheme of unfairness under the Directive, including the language of paragraph 21 of *Freiburger*.[126] The Court concluded with guidance for the national court in respect of the particular terms at issue in the main proceedings.[127]

While the Court's approach continues to evolve in light of the onslaught of references from the national courts,[128] its jurisprudence on the Unfair Contract Terms Directive has by and large produced something of a let-down in the literature as far as the Court's role in furthering the harmonization of national contract law set in play by this Directive was concerned. *Freiburger* was a particular source of disappointment, especially in light of the Court's emphasis on national law in paragraph 21, which was considered to further, not foreclose, the divergent approaches of the Member States in relation to the assessment of unfair terms and thus to preclude the development of harmonized concepts.[129] *Mostaza Claro* also attracted similar remarks.[130] Certainly, the Court's approach has its defenders, in terms of embodying the intent to remain within the limits of its competences laid down in the Treaties.[131] Nevertheless, the result of *Freiburger* and its progeny to date is that the assessment of the unfairness of the relevant terms under the Directive will continue to be situated within the context of the particular national system where such assessment takes place.

Yet, one wonders whether this line of criticism of the Court's case law misses the larger point. Early on, in its 2000 Report on the implementation of the Unfair Contract Terms Directive, the Commission recognized the close relationship between the control of unfair terms and the national contract law regimes, much of which was not harmonized by the Directive and raised a number of problems, which provoked the question of the need for a more comprehensive approximation of national contract law and other fields of private law.[132] To recall, the scheme set forth in the Directive already puts considerable emphasis on the unfairness assessment taking place against the background of national contract law.[133] Thus, with or without the Court's 'overindulgence'

[124] Case C-415/11 *Aziz*, para 68.
[125] Case C-415/11 *Aziz*, para 69.
[126] Case C-415/11 *Aziz*, para 71.
[127] Case C-415/11 *Aziz*, paras 72–75.
[128] See, eg, Case C-226/12 (Judgment of 16 Jan 2014) *Constructora Principado*, not reported.
[129] See, eg, Basedow, n 5, 455–458; MW Hesselink, Case note (2006) 2 *ERCL* 366, 373–375; M Schillig, 'Inequality of Bargaining Power versus Market for Lemons: Legal Paradigm Change and the Court of Justice's Jurisprudence on Directive 93/13 on Unfair Contract Terms' (2008) 33 *ELR* 336, 354–356; S Whittaker, 'On the Development of European Standard Contract Terms' in H Collins (ed), *Standard Contract Terms in Europe: A Basis for and a Challenge to European Contract Law* (Kluwer, 2008) 141, 161. For broader insight into the Court's approach, see Niglia, n 94, 142–144.
[130] See, eg, MBM Loos, Case note (2007) 3 *ERCL* 439, 445; compare N Reich, 'More clarity after "*Claro*"?' (2007) 3 *ERCL* 41.
[131] See, eg, W-H Roth, Case note (2011) 7 *ERCL* 425, 435–437; J Stuyck, Case note (2001) 38 *CML Rev* 719, 729 fn 36.
[132] Commission Report on the implementation of Council Dir 93/13/EEC, COM (2000) 248 final, 27.4.2000, 31.
[133] See emphasis placed on this point as part of the background for understanding *Freiburger* itself in H Unberath and A Johnston, 'The Double-Headed Approach of the ECJ Concerning Consumer Protection' (2007) 44 *CML Rev* 1237, 1265–1267.

in *Freiburger* in emphasizing national law, its jurisprudence on this Directive cannot make up for the legislature's limited approach or overcome the continuing divergences among the national contract law regimes, which have been displayed through the steady stream of cases presented to it.

Taken together, the two sets of cases discussed above demonstrate that the Court's interpretative role takes a 'backseat' to that of the Union legislature in terms of what has, or has not, been achieved in the decision-making process. These cases expose inconsistencies and lacunae in the various directives within EU contract law, on the one hand, and the ongoing divergences between the national contract laws, on the other, both of which the Court itself is unable to remedy. Thus, while an important feature (and criticism) of the Court's interpretative role has been its unwillingness to interpret the various directives by analogy and thus to stay close to the text of the particular directive concerned at the expense of providing a more coherent framework,[134] the foregoing cases find the Court walking a 'fine line' of adjudicating the cases before it while being careful not to encroach on the competences of the Union legislature and of the Member States in terms of discerning what areas that the legislature intended, or not, to place within the scope of the directive concerned and *a fortiori* what areas remain outside for the Member States. Accordingly, the Court's interpretative role invites reflection on the need for a more systematic legislative response to the problems of the EU contract law *acquis*.

2.3 The Court of Justice's Lawmaking Role

Alongside its interpretation of various provisions of EU contract law stands another way in which the Court of Justice contributes to the development of European contract law. This is the Court's lawmaking role by virtue of its formulation of Union judge-made rules of contract law falling under the rubric of what is called European 'federal common law'. Although references to judicial lawmaking by the Court of Justice have crept into the literature over the years, it has only been recently that European 'federal common law' has started to garner detailed attention in the literature.[135] Not surprisingly, this subject commands particular sensitivity in the European setting, especially in Member States where it is considered that the judicial task does not in principle include making law at all, but instead, is strictly confined to interpretation. Moreover, the reference to European 'federal common law' should not be read as implying that the EU embodies a 'federal' construct or a 'common law' system akin to the US where the doctrine of American 'federal common law' originated.

European 'federal common law' denotes a special term of art modelled after the American setting because of its particular embodiment of the formulation of judge-made rules of law at the European level. Indeed, as with American 'federal common law',[136]

[134] This has also been referred to as 'cross-directive' interpretation: see, eg, V Mak, 'Harmonisation through "Directive-Related" and "Cross-Directive" Interpretation: The Role of the ECJ in the Development of European Consumer Law' (2008) TICOM Working Paper No 2008/8, 27; van Gerven, n 5, 117. See also D Staudenmayer, 'The Commission's Communication on European Contract Law and the Future Prospects' (2002) 51 *ICLQ* 673, 679.

[135] See K Lenaerts and K Gutman, '"Federal Common Law" in the European Union: A Comparative Perspective from the United States' (2006) 54 *AJCL* 1. It may be framed in other ways: see, eg, K Riesenhuber, 'Interpretation and Judicial Development of EU Private Law—The Example of the *Sturgeon* Case' (2010) 6 *ERCL* 384.

[136] See Chapter 3, § 3.2.

European 'federal common law' is equally entangled in the debate about the approximation of contract law and other fields of private law. Generally speaking, the analysis of the emergence and development of European 'federal common law' is an extensive undertaking, much like that of American 'federal common law', which far exceeds the scope of this book.[137] This discussion concentrates on two key aspects that provide the template for evaluating the Court's lawmaking role in European contract law: first, the definition of European 'federal common law' and its so-called 'hard core'; and secondly, certain illustrations of European 'federal common law' in the field of contract law.

2.3.1 The definition of European 'federal common law' and its 'hard core'

European 'federal common law' is defined here as Union concepts, principles, and rules of decision formulated by the Court of Justice that are not clearly suggested from the face of a provision of primary or secondary Union law.[138] Three important points follow from this definition. First, this definition is a functional one. It essentially envisions European 'federal common law' as 'gap-filling *sensu lato*', meaning that it transcends the mere filling in of missing terms and concepts in a Union measure and embodies the notion of filling all gaps that may be considered to preclude the achievement of the objectives of the Union legal order.[139] Thus, it extends to the formulation of rules, as in the case of contract law, and even broader principles, such as the principle of State liability essential to the Union legal order.

Secondly, the distinction between judicial interpretation and judicial lawmaking is difficult to discern in relation to European 'federal common law'. This may be explained by the fact that the Court's lawmaking role often takes place within the context of its preliminary ruling jurisdiction. Accordingly, judicial interpretation and judicial lawmaking are very much interrelated in the European setting, since it is often through the Court's interpretation of a provision of Union law that the need for judicial lawmaking arises.[140] This is especially relevant for the field of contract law, in which the Court has been confronted with the prospect of formulating European 'federal common law' through its interpretation of various Union contract law measures as discussed below.

Thirdly, this definition brings to light the so-called 'hard core' of European 'federal common law', which arises in particular in connection with matters of private law, including contract law.[141] This denotes the fact that European 'federal common law' includes judge-made rules fashioned by the Court of Justice for which the Union has not yet been conferred legislative competence, either explicitly or implicitly, under the Treaties. To explain, in the process of deciding a case, the Court is confronted with a term, concept, or rule derived from the Treaties or a particular Union measure—eg, what is a 'contract' or what is 'damage'—for which the Union legislature has *not* yet been attributed competence under the Treaties; yet, in order to make the objectives and choices under the relevant Treaty provision or duly-adopted Union measure work for the fields in which the Union legislature *has* been given competence to act, say as regards the internal market, the Court is nonetheless faced with making European

[137] See Lenaerts and Gutman, n 135.
[138] Lenaerts and Gutman, n 135, 7.
[139] Lenaerts and Gutman, n 135, 7.
[140] Lenaerts and Gutman, n 135, 8–9.
[141] Lenaerts and Gutman, n 135, 7.

'federal common law'.[142] Illustrations of the 'hard core' of European 'federal common law' may be found in the field of contract law.

2.3.2 Illustrations of European 'federal common law' in contract law

Leitner[143] is one of the most well-known examples of European 'federal common law' because it intensified criticism about the Court's lawmaking role in contract law. The case involved a reference for a preliminary ruling from an Austrian court concerning the interpretation of Article 5 of the Package Travel Directive,[144] which set down certain rules concerning the liability of the package organizer and/or retailer for 'damage resulting for the consumer from the failure to perform or the improper performance of the contract'.[145] Specifically, the fourth paragraph of Article 5(2) provides in relevant part: 'In the matter of damage other than personal injury resulting from the non-performance or improper performance of the services involved in the package, the Member States may allow compensation to be limited under the contract'.[146] However, the term 'damage' was not defined in the Directive.

Thereafter, a dispute arose in the Austrian courts between Ms Leitner and TUI Deutschland, a package travel organizer, arising out of a two-week package club holiday booked by her parents through an Austrian travel agent.[147] Ms Leitner contracted salmonella poisoning from the food served by the club responsible for her package holiday eight days after her arrival, which caused her to be violently ill and require her parents' care for the remaining six days of the vacation.[148] Ms Leitner brought an action for damages against TUI Deutschland, claiming recovery for material damage (ie physical pain and suffering caused by the food poisoning) and for non-material damage to compensate her for the loss of the enjoyment of her package holiday.[149] The first instance court awarded Ms Leitner compensation for her material damage, but dismissed her claim for non-material damage.[150] She appealed the case to an Austrian court, which requested a preliminary ruling from the Court of Justice as to whether the Directive covered non-material damage.[151] As part of its request, the national court underscored the differences between Austrian contract law, which did not provide for such compensation, and the contract law regimes of other Member States, such as Germany, which did, thereby contemplating that this may preclude the achievement of the Directive's objectives of eliminating obstacles to trade in the internal market and ensuring a uniform level of consumer protection in the EU.[152]

The case provoked serious disagreement among the parties involved. Three out of the four Member States that submitted written observations (Austria, France, and Finland) argued, along with TUI Deutschland, that the existence of a right to compensation for

[142] Lenaerts and Gutman, n 135, 7–8.
[143] Case C-168/00 *Leitner* [2002] ECR I-2631.
[144] Council Dir 90/314/EEC of 13 June 1990 on package travel, package holidays and package tours, [1990] OJ L158/59. It may be repealed by a new measure in the near future: see Chapter 1, § 1.3.4.
[145] Package Travel Directive, n 144, Art 5(2), first para.
[146] Package Travel Directive, n 144, Art 5(2), fourth para.
[147] Case C-168/00 *Leitner*, paras 7–9.
[148] Case C-168/00 *Leitner*, para 8; Opinion of AG Tizzano in Case C-168/00 *Leitner*, point 12.
[149] Case C-168/00 *Leitner*, para 10.
[150] Case C-168/00 *Leitner*, para 10.
[151] Case C-168/00 *Leitner*, para 13.
[152] Case C-168/00 *Leitner*, para 12; Opinion of AG Tizzano in Case C-168/00 *Leitner*, point 16.

non-material damage could not be found in the absence of an express reference thereto in the Package Travel Directive.[153] Since the Directive prescribed minimum harmonization, all that could be inferred from Article 5 was that the Member States have the right to provide for such compensation in their national legislation.[154] In contrast, Belgium and the Commission advocated a wide interpretation of 'damage' that would in principle include non-material damage.[155] The Commission expressly noted that 'liability for non-material damage was recognized in most Member States, over and above compensation for physical pain and suffering traditionally provided for in all legal systems, although the extent of that liability and the conditions under which it is incurred vary in detail'.[156]

In a short judgment of six paragraphs, the Court held that Article 5(2) of the Directive includes the right to compensation for non-material damage.[157] It based its finding on the purpose and text of the Directive. Following from the second and third recitals, the purpose of the Directive is to eliminate disparities between national laws and practices concerning package holidays, which were liable to give rise to distortions of competition between operators in different Member States.[158] Thus, 'the existence in some Member States but not in others of an obligation to provide compensation for non-material damage would cause significant distortions of competition'.[159] As regards the text of the Directive, the Court reasoned that although Article 5 referred to the concept of 'damage' in a general way, the fact that the fourth paragraph of Article 5(2) provides that the Member States may, in the matter of 'damage other than personal injury', allow compensation to be limited under the contract meant that the Directive implicitly recognizes the existence of a right to compensation for damage other than personal injury, including non-material damage.[160] As a result, the Court's judgment signified a Union concept of 'damage' that essentially conferred on consumers the right to compensation for non-material damage for the non-performance or improper performance of the services constituting a package holiday under the Directive.[161]

The Court's judgment in *Leitner* should be read against Advocate General Tizzano's Opinion, which provided additional arguments supporting a wide view of damage on the basis of the Directive. As part of his rationale,[162] the Advocate General elaborated a broad definition of 'material damage' that included non-material damage within its scope: 'material damage is damage to the person, in other words both physical and psychological damage, in the sense of the psychological stress suffered as a result of physical damage (*pretium doloris, Schmerzengeld*)'.[163] Though in doing so, he prefaced this with acknowledgment of 'the caution required in a matter which, even at the terminological level, is marked by a notable inconsistency between—and even within—different legal authorities'.[164] In fact, his Opinion in *Leitner* is one of the few Opinions to date that

[153] Case C-168/00 *Leitner*, para 16.

[154] Opinion of AG Tizzano in Case C-168/00 *Leitner*, point 19.

[155] Case C-168/00 *Leitner*, paras 17–18.

[156] Case C-168/00 *Leitner*, para 18.

[157] Case C-168/00 *Leitner*, paras 19–24.

[158] Case C-168/00 *Leitner*, para 20.

[159] Case C-168/00 *Leitner*, para 21. This language figures into the analysis of Art 114 TFEU: see Chapter 8, § 8.3.2.3.

[160] Case C-168/00 *Leitner*, para 23.

[161] Case C-168/00 *Leitner*, para 24. Although at the time, there was no express provision in Austrian law entitling Ms Leitner to non-material damage, the national court was under the obligation to interpret national law in conformity with the Directive: see Case C-168/00 *Leitner*, paras 10–11; Opinion of AG Tizzano in Case C-168/00 *Leitner*, point 46.

[162] See Opinion of AG Tizzano in Case C-168/00 *Leitner*, points 37–44.

[163] Opinion of AG Tizzano in Case C-168/00 *Leitner*, point 30.

[164] Opinion of AG Tizzano in Case C-168/00 *Leitner*, point 30.

explicitly referred to one of the Commission's Communications on European contract law[165] in the context of highlighting the Member States' divergent approaches to the concept of 'damage', which, in his view, bolstered the 'demand for the [Union] to intervene in this field in response to the discrepancies, if not the flagrant inequalities, resulting from what has been referred to as real assessment chaos'.[166] He also compared the Package Travel Directive to the Product Liability Directive,[167] spurred by arguments of the Austrian and French Governments to read the two Directives synonymously by virtue of the fact that the latter Directive had explicitly left it to the Member States to regulate aspects of civil liability in relation to non-material damage caused by defective products.[168] This led the Advocate General to note the various differences between the two Directives, concluding that no analogies could be drawn in this regard, since they were adopted at different times, regulated different types of liability, and their different wording was 'anything but accidental'.[169]

The Court's judgment in *Leitner* was the subject of mixed opinion by scholars. Among others, one commentator argued that the competence to 'fill in the blanks' in directives lay with the Member States, not the Court of Justice.[170] By comparison, others pointed out that the judgment was in line with most Member States' contract law regimes,[171] and that it could 'turn out to be an important signpost for the future development of European contract law'.[172] It is rarely mentioned in the commentary that the differences between national laws regarding non-material damage had in fact been raised in the decision-making process concerning the Package Travel Directive, but were not dealt with in the final text, thereby prompting calls for the need to harmonize this matter at the European level.[173] Accordingly, the case is apt to inflame fears of the Court's perceived encroachment on the competences of the Union legislature and of the Member States in terms of what had, or had not, been set down in the measure concerned.[174] Even so, the Court's approach in *Leitner* can, arguably, be defended. In light of the failure of the legislature to provide a definition of 'damage' in the Package

165 There is an increasing number of AG Opinions referring to the Commission's Communications and subsequent documents concerning the European contract law project. See, eg, Opinion of AG Léger in Case C-397/02 *Clinique La Ramée and Winterthur Europe Assurance* [2004] ECR I-7947, point 34 fn 27; Opinion of AG Poiares Maduro in Case C-412/06 *Hamilton* [2008] ECR I-2383, point 24 fn 9; Opinion of AG Trstenjak in Case C-404/06 *Quelle* [2008] ECR I-2685, point 53 fn 42; Opinion of AG Trstenjak in Case C-180/06 *Ilsinger* [2009] ECR I-3961, point 66 fns 79–80; Opinion of AG Trstenjak in Case C-215/08 *E. Friz* [2010] ECR I-2947, points 61 fn 56, 65 fn 58; Opinion of AG Trstenjak in Case C-453/10 (Judgment of 15 March 2012) *Pereničová and Perenič*, not reported, point 88 fn 40; Opinion of AG Trstenjak in Case C-618/10 (Judgment of 14 June 2012) *Banco Español de Crédito*, not reported, point 4 fn 10; Opinion of AG Cruz Villalón in Case C-103/11 P (Judgment of 18 April 2013) *Commission v Systran and Systran Luxembourg*, not reported, point 72 fn 24. To some extent, such references coincide with those made to comparative European contract (or private) law materials: see § 2.4.

166 Opinion of AG Tizzano in Case C-168/00 *Leitner*, point 33 fn 14; see also point 30 fn 13.

167 Council Dir 85/374/EEC of 25 July 1985 on the approximation of the laws, regulations and administrative provisions of the Member States concerning liability for defective products, [1985] OJ L210/29.

168 Opinion of AG Tizzano in Case C-168/00 *Leitner*, point 34.

169 Opinion of AG Tizzano in Case C-168/00 *Leitner*, points 34–35.

170 W-H Roth, Case note (2003) 40 *CML Rev* 937, 948–949; but compare the later case note by the same author, n 131, 432–433. See also, eg, Unberath and Johnston, n 133, 1276–1277.

171 MBM Loos et al, Case notes (2003) 11 *ERPL* 91, 94.

172 MBM Loos, Dutch case note (2003) 11 *ERPL* 94.

173 See Written Question No 73 by M Papayannakis (H-1338/90), dated 23 Jan 1991, 'Harmonization of legislation governing compensation for non-material damage', Debates of the EP (English edn), No 3–398/223.

174 See, eg, Weatherill, n 5, 190–191.

Travel Directive, it fell upon the Court to elaborate this concept in line with its mandate under the Treaties to assist the national court in the adjudication of the case at hand and to secure the uniform application of Union law, which given the variation among the national laws in the particular area of contract law, as highlighted by the Advocate General and the national court, was in some peril.[175]

Hamilton[176] provides a comparable illustration of the Court's lawmaking role in contract law. It followed in the footsteps of the Court's previous rulings in *Heininger*,[177] *Schulte*,[178] and *Crailsheimer Volksbank*[179] concerning the (old) Doorstep Selling Directive.[180] Those rulings concerned a set of interrelated transactions involving a contract for the purchase of immovable property, on the one hand, and a secured credit agreement financing the purchase of the property, on the other, within the German legal setting.[181] In brief, the issue in *Heininger*[182] was whether the Doorstep Selling Directive applied to a secured credit agreement despite the explicit exclusion of contracts for the sale of immovable property from its scope, which the Court held that it did.[183] One of its most well-known aspects[184] was the Court's ruling that the consumer's right of cancellation under the Directive did not start until notice of that right had been given to the consumer, with the result that German legislation imposing a one-year limitation period on the right of cancellation from the conclusion of the contract was precluded by the Directive.[185]

[175] Incidentally, as with European 'federal common law' generally (see n 135), the Court's formulation of 'damage' in *Leitner* is in principle subject to 'legislative override', but to date, this has not occurred. In fact, it has been just the opposite. In the Commission's recent proposal, there is a provision that would codify the Court's ruling: see Proposal for a Directive of the European Parliament and of the Council on package travel and assisted travel arrangements, amending Reg (EC) No 2006/2004, Dir 2011/83/EU and repealing Council Dir 90/314/EEC, COM (2013) 512 final, 9.7.2013, point 4.4 (Art 12(2)).

[176] Case C-412/06 *Hamilton* [2008] ECR I-2383.

[177] Case C-481/99 *Heininger* [2001] ECR I-9945.

[178] Case C-350/03 *Schulte* [2005] ECR I-9215.

[179] Case C-229/04 *Crailsheimer Volksbank* [2005] ECR I-9273.

[180] For further discussion, see, eg, G-P Calliess, 'The Limits of Eclecticism in Consumer Law: National Struggles and the Hope for a coherent European Contract Law. A Comment on the ECJ's and the FCJ's "*Heininger*" decisions' (2002) 3 *GLJ* No 8; Johnston and Unberath, n 5, 173–178; P Rott, Case note in G Howells et al (eds), *The Yearbook of Consumer Law 2007* (Ashgate, 2007) 403; E Terryn, Case note (2007) 44 *CML Rev* 501.

[181] The nuances in the terminology used to denote the type of agreement concerned called attention to the need for common contract terminology in the EU. In these three cases, there was a loan agreement concluded between certain consumers and a German financial institution in order to finance the purchase of immovable property. The loan given by the German institution was secured by means of a charge on the property concerned (*Grundschuld*), explaining why such an agreement was referred to by the Court as a secured credit agreement (see Case C-350/03 *Schulte*, para 11; Opinion of AG Léger in Case C-229/04 *Crailsheimer Volksbank*, point 2), as well as a mortgage loan agreement (*Realkreditvertrag*) (see Case C-481/99 *Heininger*, para 16; Opinion of AG Léger in Case C-481/99 *Heininger*, points 3 fn 4, 5 fn 7).

[182] Case C-481/99 *Heininger* [2001] ECR I-9945.

[183] Case C-481/99 *Heininger*, paras 35, 40. This prompted the Court to elaborate the concept of a secured credit agreement: see Case C-481/99 *Heininger*, para 33; compare Opinion of AG Léger, points 31–32.

[184] Perhaps another notable aspect is that after the Court delivered its ruling in *Heininger*, the national court found that there was no 'doorstep selling' situation: see, eg, P Rott, 'The *Quelle* Case and the Potential of and Limitations to Interpretation in the Light of the Relevant Directive' (2008) 16 *ERPL* 1119, 1127–1128 fn 41.

[185] Case C-481/99 *Heininger*, paras 45–48. Although minor variations occur, this part of the holding largely figures in later descriptions of the case. See, eg, Case C-350/03 *Schulte*, paras 10–13; Case C-229/04 *Crailsheimer Volksbank*, paras 11–14. Incidentally, the right of cancellation led the Court to contemplate the relationship between the Doorstep Selling and Consumer Credit Directives, again underscoring differences between the two: see Case C-481/99 *Heininger*, paras 36–39.

A few years later, the issues raised in *Heininger* were revisited in the companion cases of *Schulte*[186] (delivered by the Grand Chamber) and *Crailsheimer Volksbank*[187] (delivered by the Second Chamber) decided on the same day.[188] The two cases revolved around three interrelated issues. The first issue concerned the effects of the cancellation of the secured credit agreement on the contract for the purchase of immovable property, ie whether the purchase contract could 'piggyback' on the secured credit agreement so as to fall within the scope of the Doorstep Selling Directive and thus evade the exclusion of contracts for the sale of immovable property. The Court held that it could not.[189] The second issue concerned the effects of the cancellation of the secured credit agreement, the question being whether German legislation requiring consumers to repay the amount of the loan immediately and with interest deterred them from exercising their right of cancellation and was therefore precluded by the Directive. The Court held that it was not.[190] The third issue pertained to the effects of the German bank's failure to inform the consumer of the right of cancellation of the secured credit agreement.[191] Recognizing that this had resulted in financial risks for the consumers in the national proceedings,[192] the Court looked to the third paragraph of Article 4 of the Directive,[193] declaring that the Member States are required to ensure that their legislation protects consumers who had been unable to avoid exposure to such risks by adopting measures allowing them 'to avoid bearing the consequences of the materialisation of those risks'.[194]

This paved the way for *Hamilton*.[195] At issue was whether German legislation providing that the consumer's right of cancellation expired one month after both parties had fully performed their obligations under the contract was precluded by the Doorstep Selling Directive.[196] The Court held that the German legislation was an 'appropriate consumer protection measure' within the third paragraph of Article 4 of the Directive.[197] In doing so, it examined various provisions of the Directive, which included Article 5 governing the exercise of the right of cancellation. Under Article 5(1), which provided in relevant part that '[t]he consumer shall have the right to renounce

[186] Case C-350/03 *Schulte* [2005] ECR I-9215.

[187] Case C-229/04 *Crailsheimer Volksbank* [2005] ECR I-9273.

[188] The *Schulte* composition may be explained by the broad range of issues that the Court was called upon to clarify in the wake of *Heininger*. See Opinion of AG Léger in Case C-350/03 *Schulte*, point 3. *Crailsheimer Volksbank* concerned a subset of similar questions, which explained the Court's treatment of these issues in summary fashion. As such, reference is made to the *Schulte* case.

[189] Case C-350/03 *Schulte*, paras 75–81.

[190] Case C-350/03 *Schulte*, paras 86, 89, 93. As part of its reasoning in this regard, the Court stressed that under Art 5(2), the giving of notice of cancellation has the effect of releasing the consumer from any obligations under the cancelled contract and such cancellation entails for the consumer and lender 'the restoration of the status quo ante' (para 88). This aspect of the Court's ruling was recently revisited in Case C-215/08 *E. Friz* [2010] ECR I-2947, paras 35–50; compare Opinion of AG Trstenjak, points 41–89.

[191] This was probably the most novel aspect of the judgment, since it had not been addressed in the AG Opinion and did not constitute a specific question posed by the referring court.

[192] Case C-350/03 *Schulte*, paras 97–99.

[193] This provision states in relevant part: 'It [written notice of the right of cancellation] shall be given to the consumer: . . . in the case of Article 1(3) and 1(4), when the offer is made by the consumer. Member States shall ensure that their national legislation lays down appropriate consumer protection measures in cases where the information referred to in this Article is not supplied.'

[194] Case C-350/03 *Schulte*, para 101. The Court then pointed to the obligation placed on national courts to interpret national law in conformity with the Directive: Case C-350/03 *Schulte*, para 102. See further Case C-227/08 *Martín Martín* [2009] ECR I-11939, paras 31–34.

[195] Case C-412/06 *Hamilton* [2008] ECR I-2383.

[196] Case C-412/06 *Hamilton*, paras 10, 11, 19–20.

[197] Case C-412/06 *Hamilton*, para 45.

the effects of his undertaking', it interpreted 'undertaking' as meaning that the right of cancellation can be exercised 'as long as the consumer is not bound, at the time that the right is exercised, by any undertaking under the cancelled contract'.[198] The Court then explained: 'That logic flows from one of the *general principles of civil law*, namely that the full performance of a contract results, as a general rule, from discharge of the mutual obligations under the contract or from termination of that contract'.[199] Then, looking to Article 5(2) of the Directive, which provided that exercising the right of cancellation released the consumer from 'any obligations under the cancelled contract', the Court inferred that the reference to 'obligation' presupposed that the consumer has exercised his right of cancellation in relation to a contract that was in the process of being performed, whereas after the full performance of the contract, there was no further obligation.[200] This allowed the Court to distinguish the present case from its previous rulings in *Heininger, Schulte*, and *Crailsheimer Volksbank*, which concerned credit agreements that had not been fully performed.[201]

The Court's reference to the 'general principles of civil law' in *Hamilton* should be read alongside Advocate General Poiares Maduro's Opinion, which fleshed out this issue in greater detail. The Advocate General considered that there were good arguments to find that a Member State was entitled, in the exercise of the discretion accorded under the third paragraph of Article 4 of the Directive, to fix a time limit during which the right of cancellation may be validly exercised.[202] He considered that the placing of such a time limit was 'a principle common to the laws of the Member States',[203] which he supported with reference to comparative European contract law materials disseminated by several academic projects.[204] He also surmised that this principle 'might well ultimately appear at [Union] level in the context of the creation of a common frame of reference for European contract law', citing certain Commission documents on the subject.[205] On that basis, he argued that 'the existence of a general principle of limitation should therefore be recognised, while leaving the Member States the necessary discretion to implement it in their respective legal systems'.[206] He bolstered this argument with a comparison of a few other directives within the EU contract law *acquis*, which in his view suggested the existence of a principle common to the laws of the Member States and also found at the European level on the fixing of such a time limit.[207] Noticeably, the Court did not cite any comparative European contract law materials or examine other directives within the EU contract law *acquis* as the Advocate General had done. Nevertheless, *Hamilton* heralded the Court's recognition of 'general principles of civil law' on which the Court elaborated rules of contract law.[208]

In sum, *Leitner* and *Hamilton* illuminate several themes underpinning the Court's lawmaking role in European contract law, some of which are similar to the Court's interpretative role in this setting. First, these cases constitute salient examples of the 'hard core' of European 'federal common law' and the tensions that it engenders. In

[198] Case C-412/06 *Hamilton*, para 42.
[199] Case C-412/06 *Hamilton*, para 42 (emphasis added).
[200] Case C-412/06 *Hamilton*, para 43. [201] Case C-412/06 *Hamilton*, paras 46–47.
[202] Opinion of AG Poiares Maduro in Case C-412/06 *Hamilton*, points 23–24.
[203] Opinion of AG Poiares Maduro in Case C-412/06 *Hamilton*, point 24.
[204] Opinion of AG Poiares Maduro in Case C-412/06 *Hamilton*, point 24 fn 8.
[205] Opinion of AG Poiares Maduro in Case C-412/06 *Hamilton*, point 24 fn 9.
[206] Opinion of AG Poiares Maduro in Case C-412/06 *Hamilton*, point 24.
[207] Opinion of AG Poiares Maduro in Case C-412/06 *Hamilton*, points 29–31.
[208] Notably, the Court may formulate rules of contract law on the basis of so-called 'general principles of civil law' in cases involving Union instruments outside the EU contract law *acquis*: see, eg, Case C-277/05 *Société thermale d'Eugénie-les-Bains* [2007] ECR I-6415, para 24.

both cases, the Court was faced with the formulation of judge-made rules of contract law, which in principle the Union legislature has not yet been given explicit or implicit competence under the Treaties, in the context of deciding a case concerning a duly-adopted EU contract law measure, which the Union legislature has been given the requisite competence to adopt under the Treaties. In other words, the Union legislature's competence to adopt the directives concerned (pursuant to its internal market competences of what are now Articles 114 and 115 TFEU) was not in dispute. As a consequence, these cases find the Court formulating European 'federal common law' so as to enable such measures to work in the relevant field. Yet, in doing so, the Court's lawmaking role is nevertheless feared to trespass on the competences of the Union legislature and of the Member States in terms of what has not (yet) been decided upon in the decision-making process and hence in principle left to the Member States in the area concerned. In this way, the Court's lawmaking role augments the controversy surrounding the limits of both judicial and legislative competence in the field of contract law, which strikes at the heart of the debate about European contract law.

Furthermore, it is not coincidental that in both *Leitner* and *Hamilton*, the Opinions of the Advocates General referred to, among other things, the Commission's Communications on European contract law and other activities taking place as part of the debate. Indeed, the very nature of European 'federal common law' brings to the fore differing approaches to matters of contract law among the Member States, as illustrated by *Leitner*, and the need to situate the EU contract law rules against the background of the overarching national contract law regimes, as illustrated by *Hamilton*, which in turn directs attention to the need for a more comprehensive and cohesive response at the European level. *Leitner* is especially noteworthy, since it appeared in the Commission's 2003 Action Plan on European contract law in order to illustrate the inconsistencies in the treatment of the concept of 'damage' among the various directives and the threat of fragmentation of national contract law legislation as a result of the Court's interpretation of 'damage' solely in light of the Directive concerned.[209] Accordingly, the Court's lawmaking role is symptomatic of the deficiencies in the EU contract law *acquis* and hence part of the overall momentum concerning the need for further approximation of contract law in the debate.

2.4 Recourse to Comparative European Contract Law Materials by the Advocates General

At present, there has been increasing recourse made to comparative materials formulated by various academic projects on European contract law and other fields of European private law[210] in the Opinions of the Advocates General.[211] For example,

[209] See Commission Communication, A more coherent European Contract Law—An Action Plan, COM (2003) 68 final, 12.2.2003 (2003 Action Plan), points 20–21.

[210] Admittedly, the reference here to comparative European contract (or private) law materials may be imprecise. It is meant to spotlight the composite works of academic projects in European contract law and other fields of European private law, as opposed to other types of materials, such as the individual works of scholars, whether or not members of such projects, which may also appear in the AG Opinions. Both aspects fall within the wide view of European contract law: see Chapter 1, § 1.2.2.1.

[211] Such materials may also appear as part of the parties' arguments in a particular case. See, eg, Case T-53/08 *Italy v Commission* [2010] ECR II-3187, paras 87–96. See further K Gutman, 'The Evolution of the Action for Damages Against the European Union and Its Place in the System of Judicial Protection' (2011) 48 *CML Rev* 695, 748.

references to the Principles of European Tort Law formulated by the Study Group on a European Civil Code (Study Group) and by the European Group on Tort Law were cited by one Advocate General as part of the analysis of an unjust enrichment claim brought against the Union.[212] With particular regard to European contract law, there is a growing number of references to materials, such as the UNIDROIT Principles of International Commercial Contracts,[213] the Principles of Law series disseminated by the Study Group,[214] and the Principles of European Contract Law (PECL) authored by the Commission on European Contract Law.[215] Moreover, in view of the activities taking place in the European contract law project, there are references to the Draft Common Frame of Reference (DCFR),[216] which sometimes appear in conjunction with those to the PECL,[217] in such Opinions. Some salient illustrations of the ways in which comparative European contract law materials are used by the Advocates General are provided below, followed by the assessment of the potential implications for the Court's role in European contract law.

2.4.1 Illustrations: *Quelle*, *Ilsinger*, and *Messner*

Advocate General Trstenjak's Opinion in *Quelle*[218] concerned the use of the PECL in connection with the interpretation of the Consumer Sales Directive.[219] This case was the first time that the Court of Justice was asked to interpret the Consumer Sales Directive in the context of the preliminary ruling procedure.[220] At issue was whether the Directive precluded a German rule providing that, in cases involving the

[212] Opinion of AG Mengozzi in Case C-282/05 P *Holcim (Deutschland) v Commission*, [2007] ECR I-2941, point 115 fn 58. See also Opinion of AG Jacobs in Case C-27/02 *Engler* [2005] ECR I-481, point 58 fn 22 (referring to, inter alia, the Ius Commune Casebook for the Common Law of Europe on Tort Law).

[213] See, eg, Opinion of AG Geelhoed in Case C-334/00 *Tacconi* [2002] ECR I-7357, points 55, 59 fn 45.

[214] See, eg, Opinion of AG Trstenjak in Case C-533/07 *Falco Privatstiftung and Rabitsch* [2009] ECR I-3327, point 66 fn 66. As regards this academic project, see further Chapter 4, § 4.2.2.

[215] See, eg, Opinion of AG Trstenjak in Case C-1/06 *Bonn Fleisch* [2007] ECR I-5609, points 68, 70 fns 31–32; Opinion of AG Trstenjak in Case C-404/06 *Quelle* [2008] ECR I-2685, point 44 fn 28; Opinion of AG Jääskinen in Case C-264/09 *Commission v Slovakia* [2011] ECR I-8065, point 37. As regards the PECL, see further Chapter 4, § 4.2.1.

[216] See, eg, Opinion of AG Trstenjak in Case C-445/06 *Danske Slagterier* [2009] ECR I-2119, point 94 fn 57; Opinion of AG Trstenjak in Case C-227/08 *Martín Martín* [2009] ECR I-11939, point 51 fns 40–44; Opinion of AG Trstenjak in Case C-215/08 *E. Friz* [2010] ECR I-2947, points 69 fn 62, 74 fn 65, 81 fn 72; Opinion of AG Trstenjak in Case C-540/08 *Mediaprint Zeitungs- und Zeitschriftenverlag* [2010] ECR I-10909, point 33 fn 7; Opinion of AG Trstenjak in Case C-300/10 (Judgment of 23 Oct 2012) *Marques Almeida*, not reported, point 71 fn 66. As regards the DCFR, see further Chapter 6, § 6.2.3.

[217] See, eg, Opinion of AG Trstenjak in Case C-275/07 *Commission v Italy* [2009] ECR I-2005, point 90 fns 48–49; Opinion of AG Trstenjak in Case C-180/06 *Ilsinger* [2009] ECR I-3961, points 49, 51–52; Opinion of AG Trstenjak in Case C-489/07 *Messner* [2009] ECR I-7315, point 85; Opinion of AG Cruz Villalón in Case C-103/11 P (Judgment of 18 April 2013) *Commission v Systran and Systran Luxembourg*, not reported, point 72 fn 24.

[218] Opinion of AG Trstenjak in Case C-404/06 *Quelle* [2008] ECR I-2685.

[219] Dir 1999/44/EC of the European Parliament and of the Council of 25 May 1999 on certain aspects of the sale of consumer goods and associated guarantees, [1999] OJ L171/12. See Chapter 1, § 1.3.8.

[220] Opinion of AG Trstenjak in Case C-404/06 *Quelle*, point 1. There had already been several successful infringement actions brought against certain Member States for their failure to implement the Directive. See, eg, Case C-310/03 *Commission v Luxembourg* [2004] ECR I-1969; Case C-312/03 *Commission v Belgium* [2004] ECR I-1975; Case C-311/03 (Judgment of 1 July 2004) *Commission v France*, not reported.

replacement of defective goods, the seller can charge the consumer for use of those goods.[221] In her Opinion, the Advocate General explained that the issue boiled down to the expression 'free of charge' in Article 3 of the Directive.[222] She approached the matter from the classic modes of interpretation, looking to the text, context, and purpose of the Directive.[223] Her reference to the PECL came within the discussion of the text of the Directive. Article 3(2) of the Directive gives the consumer the right 'to have the goods brought into conformity free of charge' either by repair or replacement.[224] As between repair and replacement, she stressed that the consumer must choose what is both possible and proportionate, thereby citing two provisions of the PECL to support her point.[225] She concluded that based on the normal meaning of the expression 'free of charge', the German rule was precluded by the Directive.[226] Although this already indicated the answer to the referring court's question, she considered that the context and purpose of the Directive strengthened this conclusion.[227] As such, the Advocate General's reliance on the PECL was helpful for bolstering her assessment of the matter at issue and providing the context for the interpretation of the Directive concerned.

In its judgment, the Court followed the Advocate General's approach by looking to the text, context, and purpose of the Directive and held that the German rule was precluded by the Directive.[228] It emphasized that the text and *travaux préparatoires* indicated that the Union legislature intended to make 'free of charge' an essential element of the protection afforded to consumers under the Directive, and this meant that the seller could not make any financial claim in connection with bringing the defective goods in conformity.[229] Yet, the Court did not refer to the PECL in its judgment.

Thereafter, Advocate General Trstenjak's Opinion in *Ilsinger*[230] invoked references to the PECL and the DCFR in the context of interpreting the 'Brussels I' Regulation.[231] By way of a reference for a preliminary ruling from an Austrian court, one of the questions in the case concerned whether, for the purposes of the national court's jurisdiction, the consumer's claim should be deemed a right related to a contract under circumstances where the entitlement of the prize was not made conditional on the

[221] Opinion of AG Trstenjak in Case C-404/06 *Quelle*, point 24.
[222] Opinion of AG Trstenjak in Case C-404/06 *Quelle*, point 42.
[223] Opinion of AG Trstenjak in Case C-404/06 *Quelle*, points 60–65.
[224] Opinion of AG Trstenjak in Case C-404/06 *Quelle*, point 44.
[225] Opinion of AG Trstenjak in Case C-404/06 *Quelle*, point 44 fn 28 (also referring to a selection of literature on the subject).
[226] Opinion of AG Trstenjak in Case C-404/06 *Quelle*, point 44. See further points 45–49.
[227] As part of her analysis, the AG emphasized that the aim of the Directive was to strengthen consumer protection and then added in a footnote: 'Improvement of the functioning of the internal market is also to remain the principal aim of consumer policy in the future. . . . It is likely that the provisions of Directive 1999/44 will be adopted in the draft of the *European Civil Code* in which the importance of consumer protection will be given expression very clearly'. Opinion of AG Trstenjak in Case C-404/06 *Quelle*, point 51 fn 37 (emphasis added).
[228] Case C-404/06 *Quelle*, paras 33–36, 43.
[229] Case C-404/06 *Quelle*, paras 33–34. The Court has ruled on further issues related to the scheme of remedies for lack of conformity set forth in Arts 3(2) and 3(3) of the Directive: see, eg, Joined Cases C-65/09 and C-85/09 *Gebr. Weber and Putz* [2011] ECR I-5257. For detailed discussion, see, eg, A Johnston and H Unberath, Case note (2012) 49 *CML Rev* 793.
[230] Opinion of AG Trstenjak in Case C-180/06 *Ilsinger* [2009] ECR I-3961.
[231] Council Reg (EC) No 44/2001 of 22 Dec 2000 on jurisdiction and the recognition and enforcement of judgments in civil and commercial matters [2001] OJ L12/1, recast by Reg (EU) No 1215/2012 of the European Parliament and of the Council of 12 Dec 2012 on jurisdiction and the recognition and enforcement of judgments in civil and commercial matters [2012] OJ L351/1 ('Brussels I' Regulation).

ordering of any goods.[232] This brought into play the issue of what was considered the conclusion of a consumer contract for the purposes of interpreting certain provisions of the Regulation.

The Advocate General began by recognizing that the Regulation did not define when a consumer contract was concluded and that there were no Union rules determinative of the matter.[233] Nevertheless, she surmised that it was possible to deduce when and under what conditions a contract is concluded from various sources, which included comparative European contract law materials.[234] She referred to relevant provisions of the DCFR, which in her view 'may in the future be the starting point for a uniform system of European private law', and those of the PECL, so as to find that a contract was concluded on the basis of the concordance of intentions between the parties.[235] This was further supported by literature on European contract law and a comparative survey of the laws of several Member States.[236] She also cited certain provisions of the DCFR, alongside the relevant literature and the laws of certain Member States, in connection with the related question regarding the classification of the type of contract at issue.[237] Yet, when it came to the legal classification of prize notifications, she noted that the laws of the Member States took divergent approaches.[238] Consequently, she concluded that it was for the national court to determine whether a contract had been concluded in the main proceedings by taking into account, among other things, whether the conditions of offer and acceptance were satisfied, thereby giving rise to a concordance of intentions.[239]

In its judgment, the Court reached conclusions similar to those of the Advocate General, but the references to the DCFR and the PECL (as well as the literature and comparative analysis of national laws cited by the Advocate General) were absent. It considered that the relevant provision of the 'Brussels I' Regulation required the conclusion of a consumer contract, which conceivably meant that one of the parties merely indicates its acceptance without assuming any legal obligation to the other party to the contract.[240] However, it continued, 'it is necessary, for a contract to exist within the meaning of that provision, that the latter party should assume such a legal obligation by submitting a firm offer which is sufficiently clear and precise with regard to its object and scope as to give rise to a link of a contractual nature as referred to by that provision'.[241] This is satisfied only where, in the context of a prize notification such as that at issue, there has been a legal commitment contracted by the mail-order company, that is to say, that company must have expressed clearly its intention to be bound by such a commitment, if it is accepted by the other party, by declaring itself to be unconditionally willing to pay the prize at issue to consumers who so request.[242] It was for the national court to determine whether that requirement was fulfilled in the main proceedings.[243]

[232] Opinion of AG Trstenjak in Case C-180/06 *Ilsinger*, points 30–37. For detailed discussion, see, eg, EB Crawford, Case note (2009) *REDC* 861.
[233] Opinion of AG Trstenjak in Case C-180/06 *Ilsinger*, point 44.
[234] Opinion of AG Trstenjak in Case C-180/06 *Ilsinger*, point 45.
[235] Opinion of AG Trstenjak in Case C-180/06 *Ilsinger*, point 49 fn 49; see also points 51–52.
[236] Opinion of AG Trstenjak in Case C-180/06 *Ilsinger*, point 50.
[237] Opinion of AG Trstenjak in Case C-180/06 *Ilsinger*, point 53 fns 61–62.
[238] Opinion of AG Trstenjak in Case C-180/06 *Ilsinger*, points 54–57.
[239] Opinion of AG Trstenjak in Case C-180/06 *Ilsinger*, points 59–63, 69–70.
[240] Case C-180/06 *Ilsinger*, paras 53–54.
[241] Case C-180/06 *Ilsinger*, para 54.
[242] Case C-180/06 *Ilsinger*, para 55.
[243] Case C-180/06 *Ilsinger*, para 55.

Advocate General Trstenjak's Opinion in *Messner*[244] provides an apt comparison. The circumstances at issue in *Messner* bore some similarity to *Quelle*,[245] this time involving a reference for a preliminary ruling from a German court on the interpretation of the (old) Distance Selling Directive.[246] The main issue presented by this case concerned whether German legislation entitling the seller, in the context of the repayment of the purchase price of the goods sold, to deduct from that price compensation for the consumer's use of such goods was precluded by Article 6 of the Directive concerning the right of withdrawal.[247] In the main proceedings, a consumer, Ms Messner, purchased a second-hand laptop computer from a company engaged in an internet mail-order business. Later, the computer display became defective, but the seller refused to repair the defect free of charge, so she sought to withdraw from the contract and get her money back. The 'rub' in the case was that despite the lapse of about eight months, the consumer's withdrawal took place within the period laid down to that end, since the consumer had not received effective notice of such right from the seller, and thus placed the consumer within the terms of the German legislation stipulating that in such circumstances the consumer must pay compensation for the benefits obtained by the consumer from the use of the goods concerned, which was higher than the purchase price paid by the consumer for the computer in the first place.[248]

In her Opinion, Advocate General Trstenjak approached the matter from the standpoint of the text, scheme, and purpose of the Directive. The text of the Directive did not produce a clear answer, since there was no explicit definition of the concept of costs or charges within the meaning of Article 6's stipulation that the only charge that could be imposed on the consumer as a result of the exercise of his right of withdrawal was 'the direct cost of returning the goods'.[249] As regards the scheme and purpose of the Directive, in her view, compensation of the kind provided under German law would impair or undermine the Directive's aim, especially since this could deter the consumer from exercising his right of withdrawal.[250] She supported this finding with detailed analysis of the distribution of risk between the seller and the consumer underlying the Directive.[251] In this regard, she mentioned 'in passing' that certain comparative European contract law materials (as well as the Commission's then proposal for a Consumer Rights Directive) took a different approach.[252] In particular, she cited relevant provisions of the Acquis Principles of Existing EC Contract Law and the DCFR, which expressly require the consumer to pay compensation in the case of normal use of the goods.[253] She then remarked:

> It should be noted that these works and legislative proposals are based on a different concept of compensation for use than the exclusion relating to the bearing of costs under Directive 97/7. Apart from the fact that in my view they lead to complex problems of distinguishing between inspection or testing and use, which are detrimental to legal certainty and can ultimately mean

244 Opinion of AG Trstenjak in Case C-489/07 *Messner* [2009] ECR I-7315.

245 See Opinion of AG Trstenjak in Case C-489/07 *Messner*, points 38, 40, 42 (distinguishing the present proceedings). See also Case C-511/08 *Heinrich Heine* [2010] ECR I-3047.

246 Dir 97/7/EC of the European Parliament and of the Council of 20 May 1997 on the protection of consumers in respect of distance contracts, [1997] OJ L144/19. It is repealed by the Consumer Rights Directive: see Chapter 1, § 1.3.7.

247 Case C-489/07 *Messner* [2009] ECR I-7315, paras 4, 17.

248 Case C-489/07 *Messner*, paras 10–16.

249 Opinion of AG Trstenjak in Case C-489/07 *Messner*, points 68–70.

250 Opinion of AG Trstenjak in Case C-489/07 *Messner*, points 76–77.

251 Opinion of AG Trstenjak in Case C-489/07 *Messner*, points 80–84.

252 Opinion of AG Trstenjak in Case C-489/07 *Messner*, point 85.

253 Opinion of AG Trstenjak in Case C-489/07 *Messner*, point 85 fns 79, 82.

that purchasing by distance selling is less attractive to consumers, they are *merely proposals and cannot assist in the interpretation of the directive in force.*[254]

She ultimately concluded that a provision of national law, as in the case of the German legislation, was precluded by the Directive.[255]

In its judgment, the Court reached a similar, though slightly different, conclusion. On the one hand, as the Advocate General had done, the Court found that a provision of national law that provides in general that, in the case of withdrawal by a consumer within the withdrawal period, a seller may claim compensation for the value of the use of the consumer goods acquired under a distance contract is precluded by the Directive.[256] On the other hand, however, the Directive does not preclude, in principle, a provision of national law that requires a consumer to pay fair compensation 'in the case where he has made use of the goods acquired under a distance contract in a manner incompatible with the *principles of civil law, such as those of good faith or unjust enrichment*'.[257] The Court cautioned that this is on condition that the purpose of the Directive and, in particular, the functionality and efficacy of the right of withdrawal are not adversely affected, as in the case where, for example, the amount of compensation were to appear disproportionate in relation to the purchase price of the goods concerned or the provision of national law were to put on the consumer the onus of proving that he did not use those goods during the period for withdrawal in a manner going beyond what was necessary to allow him to make effective use of his right of withdrawal.[258] Despite the Court's explicit reference to 'principles of civil law', there was no mention of any comparative European contract law materials, such as those cited in the Advocate General's Opinion.

2.4.2 Potential implications for the Court's role in European contract law

As evidenced by the steady stream of Advocate General Opinions to date, references to comparative European contract law materials generally serve as an 'interpretative aid', not as a direct source of authority that dictates the result in a particular case. For example, as shown by *Quelle* and *Ilsinger*, they may assist the Advocate General in an 'informative sense' by providing further context or background to a particular matter or gaining a perspective on ambiguous matters for which there is no direct answer or source on point. As further illustrated by *Quelle* and *Hamilton*, they may also play a 'confirmatory' role by supporting or strengthening the Advocate General's particular interpretation of a certain matter. Or, as demonstrated by *Messner*, such materials may be of use in a more 'contrasting' fashion in terms of highlighting a particular approach that need not be followed in the case at hand. Above all, as stressed by Advocate General Trstenjak in *Messner*, comparative European contract law materials are 'merely proposals' and do not control the interpretation of binding Union rules.[259]

Along these lines, the use of comparative materials on European contract law (and European private law generally) may be considered part and parcel of the Advocate

[254] Opinion of AG Trstenjak in Case C-489/07 *Messner*, point 85 (emphasis added).
[255] Opinion of AG Trstenjak in Case C-489/07 *Messner*, points 99, 111.
[256] Case C-489/07 *Messner*, para 29.
[257] Case C-489/07 *Messner*, para 26 (emphasis added).
[258] Case C-489/07 *Messner*, para 27. This was left for the national court to determine: see paras 28–29.
[259] See n 254 and accompanying text.

General's overarching duty enshrined in Article 252 TFEU of assisting the Court of Justice by bringing to its attention all possibly relevant issues for the purposes of adjudicating the case before it. These materials are therefore on a par with the other kinds of legal sources that regularly appear in the Opinions of Advocates General, which in fact seems to be the way Advocate General Trstenjak framed the matter at a conference on the CFR.[260] Indeed, as illustrated by the examples above, such materials may be cited in conjunction with an array of scholarly literature and a comparative summary of the laws of the Member States in a particular area. Thus, such materials could be viewed within the overall context of the Court of Justice's comparative method of interpretation.[261] This may explain why this subject has not yet generated much detailed discussion in the commentary so far.

Yet, there seems to be more to it than that. The use of these comparative materials raises issues that bear directly upon the Court's interpretative and lawmaking roles in connection with European contract law. Importantly, the intended nature of these materials as common rules and principles shared by the Member States could prove a useful tool for the Court of Justice in discerning commonalities among the laws of the Member States and thus may go some way in contributing to the judicial approximation of national contract law (and other areas of national private law) at the European level. In view of cases such as *Hamilton* and *Messner*, such materials may conceivably constitute a concrete source of so-called 'general principles of civil law',[262] which could be used by the Court to bring national contract laws closer together in the process of interpreting relevant provisions of Union law and formulating judge-made rules within the rubric of European 'federal common law'. Indeed, as shown by *Ilsinger*, this has as much relevance for Union measures concerning substantive contract law as for those in other fields of Union law, such as EU private international law instruments, touching on matters of contract law.

That being said, certain problems arise. First, since the various comparative European contract materials have been formulated by academic projects of a private or non-governmental nature,[263] they do not have (yet) any binding authority as a matter of EU law and have not (yet) been adopted by the Union institutions within the confines of the EU decision-making process. This may serve to undercut their potential recourse by the Court of Justice.[264] In fact, this may be one of the reasons to explain the

[260] Presentation of AG Trstenjak at ERA Conference, 'The Draft Common Frame of Reference', Trier, 6–7 March 2008 (on file with author). See also V Trstenjak, 'Die Auslegung privatrechtlicher Richtlinien durch den EuGH: Ein Rechtsprechungsbericht unter Berücksichtigung des Common Frame of Reference' (2007) *Z Eu P* 145.

[261] See, eg, K Lenaerts, 'Interlocking Legal Orders in the European Union and Comparative Law' (2003) 52 *ICLQ* 873; G Schermers and DF Waelbroeck, *Judicial Protection in the European Union*, 6th edn (Kluwer, 2001) § 46–§ 52.

[262] For varying opinions on the subject, see, eg, Basedow, n 5, 460–469; MW Hesselink, 'A Toolbox for European Judges' (2011) 17 *ELJ* 441, 449–451; K Purnhagen, 'Principles of European Private or Civil Law? A Reminder of the Symbiotic Relationship between the ECJ and the DCFR in a Pluralistic European Private Law' (2012) 18 *ELJ* 844; V Trstenjak, 'European Consumer Protection Law: *Curia Semper Dabit Remedium*?' (2011) 48 *CML Rev* 95, 114–118; S Weatherill, 'The "principles of civil law" as a basis for interpreting the legislative *acquis*' (2010) 6 *ERCL* 74, 79–80. The Court's references to 'general principles of civil law' are entangled to some extent with the broader discussion of general principles of EU law: see, eg, W Devroe, 'Impact van door het Europees Hof van Justitie ontwikkelde algemen beginselen op privaatrechtelijke verhoudingen' in AS Hartkamp et al (eds), 1 *De invloed van het Europese recht op het Nederlandse privaatrecht* (Kluwer, 2007) 133; MW Hesselink, 'The General Principles of Civil Law: Their Nature, Roles and Legitimacy' in D Leczykiewicz and S Weatherill (eds), *The Involvement of EU Law in Private Relationships* (Hart, 2013) 131.

[263] This is so although certain projects have received funding from the Union institutions. See Chapter 4, § 4.2.

[264] See in that regard S Weatherill, 'The Consumer Rights Directive: How and Why a Quest for "Coherence" Has (Largely) Failed' (2012) 49 *CML Rev* 1279, 1304.

glaring difference in the treatment of such materials in the Opinions of the Advocates General, as compared to the Court's judgments. So far, neither the Court of Justice nor the General Court (not to mention the EU Civil Service Tribunal) have referred to comparative European contract (or private) law materials in their decisions, although a few rulings of the General Court could be interpreted as leaving the door slightly open in this regard.[265] Furthermore, as demonstrated by the foregoing discussion, some of the most controversial cases have been those in which differences exist among national contract laws, as opposed to cases where commonalities among the national contract laws can be found. This strikes at the heart of issues concerning the character and content of these 'comparative' materials, especially the extent to which they can be considered to embody common rules and principles shared by the Member States, as opposed to hiding differences or advocating a change in course, which are controversial themes underpinning the work of the academic projects involved in European contract law and European private law generally.[266]

The references to the DCFR in the Opinions of the Advocates General merit special remarks. As will be seen in coming chapters, it is not entirely clear at the time of writing how the DCFR will be incorporated into the final version of the CFR, much less how the CFR will be used by the Court of Justice.[267] This throws a strong light on important and as yet unanswered questions concerning the formal status of the CFR (ie its legal basis, binding effects, scope, content, and purpose) and its relationship with the DCFR, all of which are percolating in the commentary and the institutional documents as part of the debate about European contract law. The fact that the DCFR incorporates certain comparative European contract law materials, such as the PECL and Principles elaborated by the Acquis Group and the Study Group, albeit with certain amendments, raises further questions in terms of the status of the DCFR and ultimately that of the CFR vis-à-vis the works of these groups taken separately. In this way, the usage of comparative European contract law materials by the Advocates General as much as their non-usage by the Court place further attention on the debate about European contract law. Such materials highlight deficiencies in the relevant Union (contract) measures and the need to find common ground among the national laws, which prompted their reference in the first place. Such materials also direct attention to legislative developments at the European level and heighten questions concerning the status, form, and constitutionality of initiatives contemplated in the debate, as in the case of future decisions to be taken on the CFR.

[265] See, eg, Joined Cases T-8/95 and T-9/95 *Pelle and Konrad v Council and Commission* [2007] ECR II-4117, paras 43, 54, 97; Case T-333/03 *Masdar (UK) v Commission* [2006] ECR II-4377, paras 89–104 (appeal dismissed in Case C-47/07 P *Masdar (UK) v Commission* [2008] ECR I-9761). As regards the Court, in one case, it cited the specific paragraph of the AG Opinion containing reference to, inter alia, the PECL and DCFR, but seemingly only in reference to the first sentence concerning the recognition of a common principle among the laws of the Member States in connection with the consideration of default interest: compare Case C-275/07 *Commission v Italy* [2009] ECR I-2005, para 98, with Opinion of AG Trstenjak, point 90. In other words, so close but yet so far.

[266] See further Chapter 4, § 4.2.

[267] Eg, in its 2004 Communication (Commission Communication, European Contract Law and the revision of the *acquis*: the way forward, COM (2004) 651 final, 11.10.2004), the Commission considered that the CFR would serve as an 'inspiration' for the Court's interpretation of the EU contract law *acquis*: see Chapter 5, § 5.4.2.

2.5 Conclusions

To sum up, three main points emanate from the foregoing discussion of the role played by the Court of Justice in European contract law. First, it is important to recognize the Court of Justice's distinct roles of interpreting the EU contract law *acquis*, formulating European 'federal common law', and, as far as the Advocates General are concerned, utilizing comparative European contract law materials. Until now, the discourse has been primarily focused on the Court's interpretative role. Its formulation of European 'federal common law' dramatically changes this picture. Moreover, with the coming developments of the European contract law project, it remains to be seen how far activities, such as the CFR, may impact both the Court's lawmaking and interpretative roles, as well as the ways in which such materials are used by the Advocates General (and potentially the Court itself).

Secondly, even though the role of the Court of Justice in European contract law is broader than commonly perceived, it remains a limited one.[268] Whether it is interpretation, lawmaking, or recourse to comparative European contract law materials, these roles are of an 'interstitial' or piecemeal character; they are not comprehensive. As such, the Court by itself cannot remedy the problems plaguing the EU contract law *acquis* and the divergences among the laws of the Member States, and if anything, the questions presented to the Court only make them further apparent. The Court's discomfort in deciding various cases, many of which cause it to be drawn further and further into the national contract law regimes and the incoherent maze of Union measures is almost palpable in certain judgments. This may explain in part why several of the Court's judgments discussed earlier are so short in length.[269]

Finally, the common thread running through these distinct roles carried out by the Court of Justice in European contract law is that by exposing the underlying divergences among the national contract laws, as well as the inconsistencies and gaps in the various EU contract law measures, they enliven the discussion as to whether a more systematic approach to matters of contract law at the European level may be necessary. This explains why the discussion of the Court's role in European contract law is part of the context for the debate, not a solution in its own right. As seen in the next chapter, these remarks mirror the role played by the American federal judiciary in relation to the approximation of contract law and other fields of commercial law in the US.

[268] This is a common remark among scholars over the years. See, eg, A Hartkamp, 'Perspectives for the Development of a European Civil Law' in M Bussani and U Mattei (eds), *The Common Core of European Private Law* (Kluwer, 2003) 67, 70; van Gerven, n 5; S Weatherill, 'Prospects for the Development of European Private Law Through "Europeanisation" in the European Court—the Case of Directive on Unfair Terms in Consumer Contracts' (1995) 3 *ERPL* 207; R Zimmermann, 'Comparative Law and the Europeanization of Private Law' in M Reimann and R Zimmermann (eds), *The Oxford Handbook of Comparative Law* (Oxford Univ Press, 2006) 539, 545.

[269] See, eg, Case C-423/97 *Travel Vac* [1999] ECR I-2195 (5 paras); Case C-168/00 *Leitner* [2002] ECR I-2631 (6 paras); Case C-237/02 *Freiburger Kommunalbauten* [2004] ECR I-3403 (7 paras); Case C-412/06 *Hamilton* [2008] ECR I-2383 (13 paras). See also J Basedow, 'The Judge's Role in European Integration' in H-W Micklitz and B De Witte (eds), *The European Court of Justice and the Autonomy of the Member States* (Intersentia, 2012) 65, 77.

3

The American Contract Law Framework

3.1 Introduction

As one prominent American legal scholar remarked several decades ago: 'It is a noteworthy but little noticed fact of our political history how often issues which might have been resolved in favor of nation-wide uniformity have been resolved instead in favor of decentralization'.[1] These remarks have particular salience for American contract law and American private law generally, since for the most part, contract law and other fields of private law are primarily regulated at the state, not federal, level in the US. Especially for European audiences, the bulk of American private law is generally depicted as resting on a sturdy framework of the Uniform Commercial Code (UCC), uniform state laws promulgated by the National Conference of Commissioners on Uniform State Laws (NCCUSL), and Restatements published by the American Law Institute (ALI). Looking below the surface, however, one discovers that many of these components have been subject to long-standing debate and are inextricably intertwined with the prospect of federalization, particularly in relation to contract law and other fields of commercial law. For example, as will be seen, the emergence and development of the NCCUSL and the UCC were mired in proposals to federalize portions of state contract and commercial law, and the doctrine of American 'federal common law', which is entangled with these components, emanated from the federal judiciary's aspirations for a uniform commercial law throughout the country. This is not often appreciated or fully grasped, particularly in the debate about European contract law where analogies to the US are frequently made.

The aim of this chapter is therefore to examine the following four key strands of the American contract law framework: American 'federal common law', the NCCUSL and the uniform law process, the ALI and the Restatement project, and the UCC, with a view to elucidating their meaning, the problems associated with their usage, and the extent to which they are related to the prospect of federalization of contract law. For this reason, this chapter is divided into four main sections, which provide a general overview of each strand, its origins, and certain tensions underlying it. Notwithstanding their presentation, these strands are very much interrelated. Indeed, it is the linkage between them, much like successive layers of sedentary rock, which together form the foundations of the American contract law framework. It also bears emphasis that this examination does not claim to be comprehensive or exhaustive. Each of these strands commands a massive literature in itself, and they are certainly not the only aspects of the American contract law framework that have relevance to the debate about European contract law. For example, the role played by American 'national' legal education and scholarship[2] and the debate about the codification of American law that

[1] HM Hart, Jr, 'The Relations between State and Federal Law' (1954) 54 *Col L Rev* 489, 528.

[2] See, eg, B de Witte and C Forder (eds), *The common law of Europe and the future of legal education* (Kluwer, 1992); MA Eisenberg, 'Why is American Contract Law so Uniform?—National Law in the United States' in H-L Weyers (ed), *Europäisches Vertragsrecht* (Nomos, 1997) 23 (printed with some modification as 'The Unification of Law' in M Bussani and U Mattei (eds), *The Common Core of European Private Law* (Kluwer, 2003) 35). Compare, eg, M Reimann, 'American Private Law

took place during the early to mid-1800s[3] inevitably spring to mind, among other things.[4] Nevertheless, focus is placed on these four strands because they have steadily filtered into institutional documents and scholarly literature on European contract law and provide the basis for comparative reflection between the EU and the US in relation to the constitutional assessment of European contract law.

3.2 American 'Federal Common Law'

3.2.1 General overview

In the simplest of terms, American 'federal common law' denotes the making of federal judge-made law by the American federal courts, comprising the US Supreme Court (Court) and the lower federal courts, as well as state courts.[5] It is the subject of considerable US Supreme Court jurisprudence and scholarly literature going back to the early days of the American Republic.[6] It also embodies remarkable parallels with European 'federal common law', the detailed discussion of which exceeds the scope of this book.[7] Still, American 'federal common law' is highly relevant here on account of its entanglement with the judicial approximation of contract law and the course of its development in this field.

and European Legal Unification—Can the United States be a Model?' (1996) 3 *MJ* 217, 222–224; M Reimann and D Halberstam, 'Top-Down and Bottom-Up? A Look at the Unification of Private Law in Federal Systems' in R Brownsword et al (eds), *The Foundations of European Private Law* (Hart, 2011) 363, 372.

[3] See generally CM Cook, *The American Codification Movement: A Study of Antebellum Legal Reform* (Greenwood Press, 1981); LM Friedman, *The History of American Law*, 3rd edn (Simon & Schuster, 2005); MJ Horwitz, *The Transformation of American Law 1870–1960: The Crisis of Legal Orthodoxy* (Oxford Univ Press, 1992). This debate is symbolized by the battle between David Dudley Field, who formulated several draft codes for NY, and James C Carter, a member of the NY Bar, which is often viewed as America's equivalent to the 'Thibault-Savigny' debate in the European setting. See A Reppy (ed), *David Dudley Field Centenary Essays—Celebrating One Hundred Years of Legal Reform* (New York Univ Press, 1949); M Reimann 'The Historical School Against Codification: Savigny, Carter, and the Defeat of the New York Civil Code' (1989) 37 *AJCL* 95. See also G Weiss, 'The Enchantment of Codification in the Common-Law World' (2000) 25 *YJIL* 435. It should be clarified, however, that this debate was rooted at the state level, meaning that there were no proposals for federal codification, since this was considered impossible in light of the 19th century constitutional theory: G Gilmore, 'Commercial Law in the United States: its codification and other misadventures' in JS Ziegel and WF Foster (eds), *Aspects of Comparative Commercial Law: Sales, Consumer Credit and Secured Transactions* (McGill Univ Press, 1969) 449, 453.

[4] The interstate compact was floated from time to time as a possible mechanism to bring about the unification of US commercial law. See, eg, A Dunham, 'A History of the National Conference of Commissioners on Uniform State Laws' (1965) 30 *L & Contemp Probs* 233, 242–243; PA Freund, 'The Device of an Interstate Compact in relation to the Uniform Commercial Code' in 3 *State of New York Report of the Law Revision Commission for 1955—Study of the Uniform Commercial Code* (Williams Press, 1955) 2109, 2175. Yet, it never rose to much prominence in this regard. An interstate compact is a type of agreement entered into by a group of states, which is authorized by the US Constitution. For detailed discussion, see, eg, DB Hollis, 'Unpacking the Compact Clause' (2010) 88 *Tex L Rev* 741.

[5] See further n 69.

[6] See generally RH Fallon, Jr et al, *Hart and Wechsler's The Federal Courts and the Federal System*, 6th edn (Foundation Press, 2009 and Suppl 2013) ch 7.

[7] See K Lenaerts and K Gutman, '"Federal Common Law" in the European Union: A Comparative Perspective from the United States' (2006) 54 *AJCL* 1.

3.2.2 Origins of American 'federal common law'

The origins of American 'federal common law' are rooted in two landmark cases: *Swift v Tyson*[8] and *Erie Railroad Co. v Tompkins*.[9] To European readers, wrapped up in these two cases are unique attributes of the American legal system and the relationship between the American federal and state courts, which include the use of diversity jurisdiction allowing citizens from different states to adjudicate their cases in the federal, as opposed to the state, courts[10] and the nature of American common law itself, which is rooted in judicial decisions or case law.[11] That said, these two cases not only paved the way for American 'federal common law', but also implicate the American federal judiciary's attempt to unify certain areas of state private law, with the result that their legacy lives on in the ongoing discussion of federal competence in this area.

3.2.2.1 Swift v Tyson

Swift v Tyson[12] was decided by the US Supreme Court in 1842. The opinion was authored by Justice Joseph Story on behalf of a near-unanimous Court.[13] The case involved an issue of state commercial law arising out of certain speculative land transactions that ended up in a New York federal court pursuant to its diversity jurisdiction.[14] Yet, 'the conclusion is inescapable that [Justice Story] and his colleagues had decided to use this ridiculous case as the opportunity for federalizing—or nationalizing—a large part of the common law of the United States'.[15] As framed by the Court, the issue boiled down to whether a doctrine of New York commercial law as promulgated by state court decisions was binding on the Court if it differed from the principles of general commercial law.[16] The Court answered with a resounding no.

At the heart of the opinion was the Court's interpretation of Section 34 of the Judiciary Act of 1789, known as the Rules of Decision Act, which governed the source of law that should be applied by the federal courts in diversity cases. At the time, it provided that 'the *laws of the several states*, except where the constitution, treaties, or statutes of the United States shall otherwise require or provide, shall be regarded as rules of decision in trials at common law in the courts of the United States in cases in which they apply'.[17] In *Swift*, the Court found that 'laws' in the abovementioned passage were generally understood to mean legislative rules and enactments of the state, not state court decisions since such decisions were only evidence of what the laws were, but were not laws themselves.[18] On that basis, it reasoned that the Act

[8] 41 US (16 Pet) 1 (1842).

[9] 304 US 64 (1938).

[10] See US Constitution, Art III, § 2, cl 2. It is presently codified, as amended, at 28 USC § 1332. See further Lenaerts and Gutman, n 7, 20–23 and citations therein.

[11] See L Weinberg, 'Federal common law' (1989) 83 *Nw UL Rev* 805, 834.

[12] 41 US (16 Pet) 1 (1842).

[13] Justice Catron, the sole dissenter, quarrelled with the breadth of the *Swift* opinion as regards matters of commercial law beyond the point of law at issue in the case: *Swift*, 41 US at 23–24.

[14] The plaintiff, Joseph Swift, was a citizen of Maine, whereas the defendant, George W Tysen (his name was misspelled in the heading of the case, but due to its fame, the error persisted) was a citizen of NY. For a detailed account, see T Freyer, *Harmony and Dissonance: The* Swift *and* Erie *Cases in American Federalism* (New York Univ Press, 1981).

[15] G Gilmore, *The Ages of American Law* (Yale Univ Press, 1977) 3.

[16] *Swift*, 41 US at 18.

[17] Judiciary Act of 1789, § 34, 1 Stat at 92 (emphasis added). It is presently codified, as amended, at 28 USC § 1652.

[18] *Swift*, 41 US at 18.

only required the federal courts to follow state court decisions in matters of 'local', not 'general', concern:

In all the various cases, which have hitherto come before us for decision, this [C]ourt have [sic] uniformly supposed, that the true interpretation of the 34th section [of the Judiciary Act of 1789] limited its application to *state laws, strictly local*, that is to say, to the positive statutes of the state, and the construction thereof adopted by the local tribunals, and to rights and titles to things having a permanent locality, such as the rights and titles to real estate, and other matters immovable and intra-territorial in their nature and character. *It never has been supposed by us, that the section did apply, or was designed to apply, to questions of a more general nature, not at all dependent upon local statutes or local usages of a fixed and permanent operation, as, for example, to the construction of ordinary contracts or other written instruments, and especially to questions of general commercial law . . .*[19]

As a result, the Court held that the Rules of Decision Act did 'not extend to contracts and other instruments of a commercial nature, the true interpretation and effect whereof are to be sought, not in the decisions of the local tribunals, but in the general principles and doctrines of commercial jurisprudence', which the federal courts could decide for themselves.[20] It brushed aside the decisions of the New York courts and formulated a broad rule of negotiability regarding bills of exchange, which led to a jury verdict in favour of Mr Swift.[21]

The distinction between 'general' and 'local' matters was of great importance in the *Swift* opinion because it delineated the scope of the federal courts' lawmaking power. Under *Swift*, the federal courts were bound to follow state court decisions, as well as state statutes, in matters of 'local' concern, such as those concerning real (or immovable) property law, which were seen as being confined to a single state. In contrast, as regards 'general' matters, such as contract and commercial law, which were considered to transcend the interests of a single state, the federal courts were not bound by state court decisions and could elaborate their own rules, although (at least initially) they were still bound by state statutes on the subject.[22]

In essence, *Swift v Tyson* embodied the US Supreme Court's aspiration for uniform commercial law throughout the country.[23] The idea was that the state courts would follow the federal courts' pronouncements on 'general' matters, such as contract and commercial law, and divergences among the states on such matters would be eliminated. This aspiration was not predicated on any binding obligation of the state courts to adhere to the federal courts' decisions, but instead on what was hoped to be their persuasive force.[24] Its rationale is somewhat difficult to understand by today's standards and has evoked a number of differing views.[25] Often, explanations point to what has been called the 'declaratory' theory of law, which conceived of the common law as based on principles existing independently of judicial decisions so that the role of the judges was merely to find, declare, and apply those pre-existing principles to the case at

[19] *Swift*, 41 US at 18–19 (emphasis added).

[20] *Swift*, 41 US at 19.

[21] See Freyer, n 14, 16–17.

[22] MA Field, 'Sources of Law: The Scope of Federal Common Law' (1986) 99 *Harv L Rev* 881, 902. There is some dispute on this point. See, eg, CA Heckman, 'The Relationship of *Swift v. Tyson* to the Status of Commercial Law in the Nineteenth Century and the Federal System' (1973) 17 *AJLH* 246; CA Heckman, 'Uniform Commercial Law in the Nineteenth Century: The Decline and Abuse of the *Swift* Doctrine' (1978) 45 *Emory LJ* 45.

[23] It should not be missed that Justice Story authored the *Swift* opinion, since he was associated with federalizing commercial law, as well as admiralty law, in the US. See, eg, Gilmore, n 15, 30–31; MJ Horwitz, *The Transformation of American Law 1780–1860* (Harvard Univ Press, 1977) 250–252.

[24] The word 'hoped' is intentional, since this did not turn out as expected: see n 30 and accompanying text.

[25] See Fallon, Jr et al, n 6, 554–556.

hand.[26] The emphasis on contract and commercial law in *Swift* was also explained by the fact that these fields were rooted in prevailing notions of the *lex mercatoria*, which embodied a set of international commercial laws, customs, and trade practices as part of the general law of nations prevalent at that time.[27] That being said, *Swift* is hard to pin down because the crucial distinction between 'general' and 'local' matters eroded, and it was gradually transformed by the federal courts to encompass many 'local' areas, which went far beyond the ambit of Justice Story's opinion in that case.[28]

Ultimately, the US Supreme Court's aspirations for uniform commercial law were not realized, and the *Swift* doctrine had devastating results. In *Erie Railroad Co. v Tompkins*,[29] discussed below, the Court acknowledged this in the strongest of terms:

> Experience in applying the doctrine of *Swift v. Tyson*, had revealed its defects, political and social; and the benefits expected to flow from the rule did not accrue. Persistence of state courts in their own opinions on questions of common law prevented uniformity; and the impossibility of discovering a satisfactory line of demarcation between the province of general law and that of local law developed a new well of uncertainties. On the other hand, the mischievous results of the doctrine had become apparent . . . *Swift v. Tyson* introduced grave discrimination by non-citizens against citizens. It made rights enjoyed under the unwritten 'general law' vary according to whether enforcement was sought in the state or in the federal court; and the privilege of selecting the court in which the right should be determined was conferred upon the noncitizen. Thus, the doctrine rendered impossible equal protection of the law. In attempting to promote uniformity in the law throughout the United States, the doctrine had prevented uniformity in the administration of the law of the state.[30]

On the whole, there were many factors that contributed to *Swift*'s demise,[31] and the scene was set for its overruling in *Erie*. Yet, no case could wholly eliminate *Swift v Tyson* from the American legal landscape. It will forever represent the attempt to achieve greater uniformity in American private law at the federal level by judicial means. At the same time, it displayed the fallacy of attempting to do so through the federal courts at the expense of the states, something that would not be tried again in the American setting.

3.2.2.2 Erie Railroad Co. v Tompkins

Erie Railroad Co. v Tompkins[32] was decided by the US Supreme Court in 1938. It was a personal injury action brought by a citizen of Pennsylvania, Mr Harry J Tompkins, who had been gravely injured by a passing train of a New York corporation, the Erie Railroad Company.[33] The nature of the case was not without importance, since it implicated one of the local fields of law, that of tort law, which the *Swift* doctrine eventually came to invade.[34] As in *Swift*, the case was brought before a New York federal

[26] See, eg, EA Purcell, Jr, *Brandeis and the Progressive Constitution:* Erie, *the Judicial Power, and the Politics of the Federal Courts in Twentieth-Century America* (Yale Univ Press, 2000) 51.

[27] See further B Clark, '*Erie*'s Constitutional Source' (2007) 95 *Cal L Rev* 1289, 1292; Heckman, *AJLH*, n 22, 248–250.

[28] For detailed discussion, see, eg, Freyer, n 14, 45–100.

[29] 304 US 64 (1938).

[30] *Erie*, 304 US at 74–75 (citations omitted).

[31] See, eg, Field, n 22, 900–902; HJ Friendly, 'In Praise of *Erie*—And of the New Federal Common Law' (1964) 39 *NYUL Rev* 383, 405–407.

[32] 304 US 64 (1938).

[33] *Erie*, 304 US at 69. See further I Younger, 'What Happened in *Erie*' (1978) 56 *Tex L Rev* 1011.

[34] The extension of the *Swift* doctrine to the area of tort law was particularly apparent in the Court's case law concerning railroads and their employees. See, eg, Heckman, *Emory LJ*, n 22, 57–60. See also *Erie*, 304 US at 76 fn 12.

court pursuant to its diversity jurisdiction.[35] The Erie Railroad Company rested on the relevant state (Pennsylvania) court decisions that were in its favour, whereas Mr Tompkins relied on the *Swift* doctrine to argue that the Railroad's liability should be determined by the federal courts as a matter of 'general law'.[36]

The Court's opinion in *Erie* was written by Justice Louis Brandeis.[37] It was divided into four parts, united under the main question as to 'whether the oft-challenged doctrine of *Swift v. Tyson* shall now be disapproved'.[38] The Court answered this question in the affirmative, thereby expressly overruling a case that had built up a substantial body of case law for the past ninety-six years. It explained: 'If only a question of statutory construction were involved, we should not be prepared to abandon a doctrine so widely applied throughout nearly a century. But the unconstitutionality of the course pursued has now been made clear, and compels us to do so.'[39] As indicated by this statement, the Court's judgment in *Erie* rested on both statutory and constitutional grounds, the former by virtue of its reinterpretation of the Rules of Decision Act so as to include state court decisions as 'laws' of the states,[40] and the latter by virtue of its declaration that the *Swift* doctrine was 'an unconstitutional assumption of powers by the Courts of the United States which no lapse of time or respectable array of opinion should make us hesitate to correct'.[41] In short, the *Swift* doctrine was held to have invaded rights reserved to the states under the US Constitution.[42] In one of the most celebrated passages of the case, the Court declared:

> Except in matters governed by the Federal Constitution or by acts of Congress, the law to be applied in any case is the law of the state. And whether the law of the state shall be declared by its Legislature in a statute or by its highest court in a decision is not a matter of federal concern. There is no federal general common law. Congress has no power to declare substantive rules of common law in a state whether they be local in their nature or 'general', be they commercial law or a part of the law of torts. And no clause in the Constitution purports to confer such a power upon the federal courts.[43]

It is no understatement to say that much ink has been spilled over the meaning and import of the abovementioned language, as well as the constitutional rationale of *Erie* generally.[44] Thus, it is paramount to underline three main points concerning the implications of *Erie*'s holding, *Erie*'s prohibition against 'federal general common law', and the scope of federal judicial competence.

First, the implications of *Erie*'s holding went far beyond the instant case. By overruling *Swift*, the Court held that the federal courts could not infer from their diversity jurisdiction the power to formulate independent 'general' rules, but instead must follow the decisions of the state courts, as well as state statutes, on the matter concerned.[45] On this basis, the Court reversed the decision of the lower federal court that had decided the matter pursuant to 'general common law' and remanded the case to be decided in accordance with state (ie Pennsylvania) law, which resulted in judgment in favour of the Erie Railroad Company.[46] Generally, the Court's judgment in *Erie* spawned two

[35] *Erie*, 304 US at 69. [36] *Erie*, 304 US at 70.

[37] Justice Butler, joined by Justice McReynolds, dissented, and Justice Reed concurred in part with the majority opinion. [38] *Erie*, 304 US at 69 (citations omitted).

[39] *Erie*, 304 US at 77–78 (citations omitted). [40] *Erie*, 304 US at 78–79.

[41] *Erie*, 304 US at 79. [42] *Erie*, 304 US at 80. [43] *Erie*, 304 US at 78.

[44] For a brief selection, see, eg, Clark, n 27; Fallon, Jr et al, n 6, 562–564; 'Symposium: Law Without a Lawmaker' (2013) 54 *Wm & Mary L Rev* 655; J Tidmarsh and BJ Murray, 'A Theory of Federal Common Law' (2006) 100 *Nw UL Rev* 585. [45] *Erie*, 304 US at 78–79.

[46] *Erie*, 304 US at 79. See *Tompkins v Erie Railroad Co.*, 92 F2d 49 (2d Cir 1938).

distinct lines in relation to the relevant *substantive law* to be applied by the federal courts depending upon whether the source of such law was state or federal law.[47] On the one hand, when a federal court is faced with substantive issues of state law, whether pursuant to diversity or another jurisdictional basis, it must look to the law of the state in which it is sitting for the controlling rule and cannot assert its independent judgment in the matter.[48] On the other hand, when the federal court is faced with substantive issues of federal law, it is confronted with the possibility of formulating 'federal common law', ie federal judge-made rules of decision, regardless of whether its jurisdiction stems from diversity or otherwise.[49] In other words, *Erie* did not speak to the elimination of 'federal' judge-made rules, but to the elimination of 'general common law', which leads to the next point.

Secondly, *Erie*'s prohibition against 'federal general common law' must not be confused with 'federal common law'. As often noted by American scholars, on the same day that Justice Brandeis delivered the Court's opinion in *Erie*, he also delivered its unanimous opinion in *Hinderlider*,[50] confirming that 'whether the water of an interstate stream must be apportioned between the two States [concerned] is a question of "*federal common law*" upon which neither the statutes nor the decisions of either State can be conclusive'.[51] Perhaps this was deliberate in order to ensure the viability of 'federal common law' in the face of *Erie*, and indeed, the two cases have been seen to go hand-in-hand.[52] In any event, *Erie* struck down the federal courts' ability to formulate their own opinion about issues of state law, but it did not preclude them from formulating substantive rules of authentic 'federal common law'.[53] Accordingly, *Erie* may be equated with clear line-drawing between the two domains of state and federal law because it signified that American law must be in the form of either state or federal law; there could be no third option.[54] This is often associated with the shift from the 'declaratory' theory in *Swift* to the 'positivistic' conception of common law enshrined in *Erie*, in the sense that law must emanate from a 'positive legal source' whether at the state or federal level.[55] Importantly, however, *Erie* said nothing as regards which law—state or federal—applied to which type of issue.[56] This ambiguity carries over to the final point.

Thirdly, *Erie*'s implications for the scope of federal judicial competence are controversial. *Erie's* famous phrase cited earlier—Congress has no power to declare substantive rules of common law applicable *in a state* whether they be local in their nature or 'general', be they commercial law or a part of the law of torts. And no clause of the Constitution purports to confer such a power on the federal courts[57]—is intentionally conjunctive. The language was directed not only at the federal courts, but also at the Federal Government as a whole.[58] By overruling the *Swift* doctrine, the Court in *Erie* sought to preserve, indeed restore, the federal-state balance of powers enshrined in the

[47] This is not to discount the role played by the state courts: see n 69.

[48] Field, n 22, 912 fn 41 and citations therein.

[49] Field, n 22, 912 fn 41 and citations therein.

[50] *Hinderlider v La Plata River and Cherry Creek Ditch Co.*, 304 US 92 (1938).

[51] *Hinderlider*, 304 US at 110 (emphasis added).

[52] See, eg, Purcell, Jr, n 26, 186–191.

[53] LH Tribe, 1 *American Constitutional Law*, 3rd edn (Foundation Press, 2000) 472.

[54] Weinberg, n 11, 820. But see AJ Bellia Jr and BR Clark, 'General Law in Federal Court' (2013) 54 *Wm & Mary L Rev* 655.

[55] For detailed discussion, see, eg, Purcell, Jr, n 26, 181–185. See also *Sosa v Alvarez-Machain*, 542 US 692, 745–746 (2004) (Scalia, J, dissenting).

[56] MA Field, 'The Legitimacy of Federal Common Law' (1992) 12 *Pace L Rev* 303, 306; see also Field, n 22, 983.

[57] *Erie*, 304 US at 78 (emphasis added).

[58] Tribe, n 53, 471.

US Constitution by ensuring that federal law only governed those matters that the US Constitution specifically authorized or delegated to the federal level.[59] It is for this reason that *Erie* was heralded as 'the very essence' of American federalism.[60] However, it remained unclear under *Erie* whether judicial lawmaking extended as far as Congress' competence or whether it was precluded even in areas within Congress' reach.[61] In that regard, the words 'in a state' should be emphasized. While it may have been the case that 'Congress has no power to adopt a code of laws governing *wholly intrastate* matters of contract or tort', this was an entirely different matter from federal legislation over *interstate* matters falling within Congress' powers under the US Constitution.[62] In fact, there is wide agreement among scholars that the factual situation implicated in *Erie*, that of tort duties of railroads operating in interstate commerce, fell within the scope of Congress' competence under the Interstate Commerce Clause.[63] In this sense, the Court's language was considered to underscore that even where there was clear federal legislative power, it did not automatically imply lawmaking power in the federal courts.[64] At the very least, *Erie* indicated that federal courts were not general lawmaking courts that could formulate rules that fell beyond Congress' purview, as had been the case under *Swift*.[65]

Nevertheless, this led to disagreement regarding *Erie*'s implications for the relationship between federal and state competence, especially in matters of private law. On the one hand, *Erie* has been viewed by some as preserving the states' primary role as the 'makers of private law'.[66] On the other hand, *Erie*'s capability of defending areas of state competence from federal encroachment was perceived by others as exaggerated.[67] Indeed, *Erie* overruled the *Swift* doctrine at the same time that it gave birth to the emergence of the so-called 'new' American 'federal common law'.[68] As explained by Judge Henry J Friendly (a former law clerk of Justice Brandeis) in a well-known article, *Erie* 'cleared the way for the truly uniform federal common law on issues of national concern', since unlike 'general common law' formulated under *Swift*, post-*Erie* 'federal common law' formulated by the US Supreme Court was truly federal law and binding on the state and lower federal courts as a matter of the Supremacy Clause of the US Constitution.[69] In this way, *Erie* set into motion the ensuing course of American

[59] See *Erie*, 304 US at 79.

[60] JH Ely, 'The Irrepressible Myth of *Erie*' (1974) 87 *Harv L Rev* 693, 695. Yet, debate continues to flourish as regards *Erie*'s significance on federalism and separation of powers grounds. See, eg, EA Young, 'Preemption and Federal Common Law' (2008) 83 *Notre Dame L Rev* 1639, 1656–1660 and citations therein.

[61] See Field, n 22, 924–927.

[62] A Hill, 'The *Erie* Doctrine and the Constitution' (1958) 53 *Nw UL Rev* 427, 445 (emphasis added).

[63] US Constitution, Art I, § 8, cl 3 (providing that Congress 'shall have Power . . . [t]o regulate commerce . . . among the several States'). See, eg, L Weinberg, 'Back to the Future: The New General Common Law' (2004) 35 *J Mar L & Comm* 523, 524–525; Young, n 60, 1658.

[64] PJ Mishkin, 'The Variousness of "Federal Law": Competence and Discretion in the Choice of National and State Rules For Decision' (1957) 105 *U Pa L Rev* 797, 800 fn 13. See also *Wallis v Pan American Petroleum Corp.*, 384 US 63, 68 (1966).

[65] See *Erie*, 304 US at 72. One scholar even posited that Justice Brandeis had important reasons for ignoring the 'interstate' aspects of the case so as to make clear that lawmaking was to be dictated by the federal legislature, not the federal judiciary. See Purcell, Jr, n 26, 172–177.

[66] GD Brown, 'Federal Common Law and the Role of the Federal Courts in Private Law Adjudication—A (New) *Erie* Problem?' (1992) 12 *Pace L Rev* 229, 251.

[67] Field, n 22, 888, 982.

[68] Friendly, n 31, 405.

[69] Friendly, n 31, 384, 405; accord Field, n 22, 897; TW Merrill, 'The Common Law Powers of the Federal Courts' (1985) 52 *U Chi L Rev* 1, 6; Weinberg, n 11, 838. Although state courts are able to fashion 'federal common law' rules, there is a complex relationship with the Supremacy Clause (US

'federal common law' and signalled the end of judicial attempts to approximate state private law under *Swift*. Yet, it failed to resolve certain tensions concerning the relationship between federal and state competence within American 'federal common law', which are particularly evident in the field of contract law as discussed below.

3.2.3 Tensions underlying American 'federal common law' in contract law

By way of background, perhaps the one point of agreement among scholars about American 'federal common law' is that its definition and scope are fraught with ambiguity. Aside from its general description as federal judge-made rules of law, there is no universal definition of American 'federal common law', and a multitude of variations and nuances abound.[70] As for its scope, the cases 'reveal an extensive federal common law, of many different varieties, with no coherent unifying principle, and whose current boundaries remain uncertain'.[71] Even so, the US Supreme Court has established some important guidelines. In *Texas Industries, Inc. v Radcliff Materials, Inc.*,[72] then Chief Justice Berger elaborated, on behalf of a unanimous Court, the landmark ruling on the subject:

> [T]he Court has recognized the need and authority in some limited areas to formulate what has come to be known as 'federal common law'. These instances are 'few and restricted', and fall into essentially two categories: those in which a federal rule of decision is 'necessary to protect uniquely federal interests', and those in which Congress has given the courts the power to develop substantive law. The vesting of jurisdiction in the federal courts does not in and of itself give rise to authority to formulate federal common law, nor does the existence of congressional authority under Art. I mean that federal courts are free to develop a common law to govern those areas until Congress acts. Rather, absent some congressional authorization to formulate substantive rules of decision, federal common law exists only in *such narrow areas as those concerned with the rights and obligations of the United States*, interstate and international disputes implicating the conflicting rights of States or our relations with foreign nations, and admiralty cases. In those instances, our federal system does not permit the controversy to be resolved under state law, either because the authority and duties of the United States as sovereign are intimately involved or because the interstate or international nature of the controversy makes it inappropriate for state law to control.[73]

By virtue of these 'narrow areas', the Court sought to confine American 'federal common law' to certain specific categories, often referred to as 'enclaves',[74] although as noted by scholars, these enclaves are not exhaustive.[75] As listed above, a core area of American 'federal common law' concerns 'the rights and obligations of the United States', which provides some illustrations of federal lawmaking in contract law and related matters of commercial law, as well as the tensions underlying it.

Starting with the seminal case of *Clearfield Trust*,[76] the US Supreme Court declared that, 'The rights and duties of the United States on commercial paper which it issues

Constitution, Art VI, cl 2) in this regard. See A Bellia Jr, 'State Courts and the Making of Federal Common Law' (2005) 153 *U Pa L Rev* 825.

[70] See, eg, Lenaerts and Gutman, n 7, 33–35.

[71] Field, n 22, 909. [72] 451 US 630 (1981).

[73] *Texas Industries*, 451 US at 640–641 (citations omitted) (emphasis added).

[74] See also, eg, *Sosa v Alvarez-Machain*, 542 US 692, 726, 729 (2004) (referring to 'havens of specialty' and 'limited enclaves').

[75] See, eg, Tribe, n 53, 473–474; Weinberg, n 11, 812.

[76] *Clearfield Trust Co. v United States*, 318 US 363 (1943).

are governed by federal rather than local law', thereby necessitating the formulation of a 'federal common law' rule.[77] The use of state law was ruled out as 'singularly inappropriate', since subjecting the rights and duties of the Federal Government to state law would lead to much uncertainty and diversity in results given the differences between state laws on the subject.[78] Thus, the case affirmed the use of American 'federal common law' in federal contract cases. Even so, *Clearfield Trust*'s preference for a federal rule was criticized as wreaking havoc with intrastate uniformity, since it led to different regimes within a particular state depending upon the type of contract concerned.[79]

In subsequent cases, however, the Court chipped away at the *Clearfield Trust* rule, finding that it was inapplicable to certain private transactions.[80] For example, in *Parnell*,[81] the Court held that a dispute between private parties involving the conversion of certain Government bonds was governed by state, not federal, law and that the rule in *Clearfield Trust* was not controlling because the dispute did 'not touch the rights and duties of the United States'[82] and represented '*too essentially a private transaction* not be dealt with by the local law of Pennsylvania where the transactions took place'.[83] In dissent, Justice Black and Justice Douglas argued that the *Clearfield Trust* rule should apply to all transactions involving commercial paper of the US and highlighted the problems created by the Court's attempt to carve out certain matters for the application of state law: 'Federal law is to govern some portion of the dispute between private parties, while that portion of the dispute which is "essentially of local concern" is to be governed by local law. The uncertainties which inhere in such a dichotomy are obvious. If the rule of *Clearfield* is to be abandoned as to some parties, it should be abandoned as to all and we should start afresh on this problem'.[84]

Thereafter, in *Kimbell*,[85] the Court ruled that the issue of priority of liens stemming from federal lending programmes was controlled by federal, not state, law, pursuant to *Clearfield Trust*.[86] Yet, when it came time to formulate an American 'federal common law' rule, the Court declined to do so, preferring that state law should be incorporated as the federal rule: 'Because the state commercial codes "furnish convenient solutions in no way inconsistent with adequate protection of the federal interest[s]," we decline to override state laws of general applicability on which private creditors base their daily commercial transactions'.[87] As a result, this case was viewed as embodying a preference for state law in commercial cases, one that was considerably fortified in the Court's subsequent opinions in *O'Melveny & Meyers v FDIC*[88] and *Atherton v FDIC*.[89]

More recently, in *Empire Healthchoice Assurance, Inc. v McVeigh*,[90] the Court ruled that the interpretation of a federal health insurance contract was not covered by the *Clearfield Trust* rule.[91] In his dissenting opinion, Justice Breyer, joined by Justices

[77] *Clearfield Trust*, 318 US at 366–367.

[78] *Clearfield Trust*, 318 US at 367. The Court formulated a uniform federal rule to govern the case that was plucked from the 'federal law merchant' developed under *Swift*, which resulted in judgment in favour of the Federal Government. *Clearfield Trust*, 318 US at 369–370.

[79] See Friendly, n 31, 410.

[80] See Lenaerts and Gutman, n 7, 109–118 and citations therein.

[81] *Bank of America National Trust and Savings Association v Parnell*, 352 US 29 (1956).

[82] *Parnell*, 352 US at 33.

[83] *Parnell*, 352 US at 34 (emphasis added).

[84] *Parnell*, 352 US at 34 (Black, J and Douglas, J, dissenting).

[85] *United States v Kimbell Foods, Inc.*, 440 US 715 (1979).

[86] *Kimbell*, 440 US at 726.

[87] *Kimbell*, 440 US at 729 (quoting *United States v Standard Oil Co.*, 332 US 301, 309 (1947)) (citations omitted).

[88] 512 US 79 (1994).

[89] 519 US 213 (1997).

[90] 547 US 677 (2006).

[91] *McVeigh*, 547 US at 690–693.

Kennedy, Souter, and Alito, argued that the case fell squarely within *Clearfield Trust* and its progeny.[92] He cited several reasons pursuant to *Clearfield Trust* to apply 'federal common law' in this context, including the fact that the real party in interest was the US, there was a need for uniformity in relation to the federal programme concerned, and the provisions of the contract were 'just a few scattered islands in a sea of federal contractual provisions', which made it illogical to treat them differently under state law and would in fact lead to state-to-state variation.[93]

In view of the foregoing discussion, American 'federal common law' in matters of contract and commercial law engenders tensions similar to that of European 'federal common law' in contract law. American 'federal common law' presents the ongoing challenge to ensure the application of uniform rules, here relating to federal contractual and commercial transactions, without unduly sacrificing the coherency of state law. For instance, the Court of Justice's elaboration of a concept of 'damage' extending to non-material damage that was only recognized in some, not all, Member States in *Leitner* can be placed side by side with the US Supreme Court's *Clearfield Trust* jurisprudence, which illustrates the overlap between American 'federal common law' of federal contracts and commercial dealings, on the one hand, and private transactions related to such contracts or dealings that are governed by state law, on the other. Together, these cases show the extent to which the interplay between 'federal common law' rules and the surrounding areas of state or Member State law often leads to problems of fragmentation and complexity in the area concerned. Moreover, like European 'federal common law', American 'federal common law' makes divergences among the state contract and commercial laws more apparent, as evidenced by the emphasis placed in *Clearfield Trust* and its progeny on evading the state-by-state variation for resolving contractual transactions involving the US as a party. In this way, as with European 'federal common law', American 'federal common law', from its origins in *Swift* through its development following *Erie*, could not by itself remedy the divergences among state contract laws. Indeed, even before the 'new' brand of American 'federal common law' was underway, attention had already turned to the legislative route at both the federal and state levels.

3.3 The NCCUSL and the Uniform Law Process

3.3.1 General overview

The National Conference of Commissioners on Uniform State Laws (NCCUSL), also known as the Uniform Law Commission (ULC)[94], is linked to the promulgation of uniform laws in the states, which is referred to as the 'uniform law process' or the

[92] *McVeigh*, 547 US at 706–707 (Breyer, J, dissenting).

[93] *McVeigh*, 547 US at 706–712 (Breyer, J, dissenting).

[94] To date, the legal name of this organization is the National Conference of Commissioners on Uniform State Laws (NCCUSL). In 2007, the Executive Committee approved a recommendation to shorten its name for 'branding' purposes and to revise the Constitution accordingly; from that point forward, most communications use the name Uniform Law Commission (ULC), but no change was made to its legal name (email from Katie Robinson, NCCUSL Deputy Legislative Director and Communications Officer, dated 26 July 2013 (on file with author)). Art 1.1 of its Constitution, available at its website, <http://uniformlaws.org/> (NCCUSL Constitution), states: 'This organization shall be known as the "National Conference of Commissioners on Uniform State Laws." The organization may also be known by the name of "Uniform Law Commission."'

'uniform state law movement'. The NCCUSL is a 'private' organization[95] comprised of state commissioners from all fifty states, the District of Columbia, and other US territories,[96] which is separate from the state and federal lawmaking apparatus.[97] The NCCUSL claims a quite distinguished list of members, which include former President Woodrow Wilson and several members of the US Supreme Court, such as former Chief Justice William Rehnquist and Justice Louis Brandeis (author of the *Erie* opinion).[98] Three important points should be clarified at the outset: the meaning of uniform laws, the distinction between uniform laws and model laws, and the link between the NCCUSL and the American federal system.

3.3.1.1 The meaning of uniform laws

The NCCUSL's purpose is 'to promote uniformity in the law among the several [s]tates on subjects as to which uniformity is desirable and practicable'.[99] It does this primarily through the adoption of uniform acts, which are also called uniform (state) laws. Uniform laws are essentially the 'bread and butter' of the NCCUSL's work, or at least what it is generally known for in the US. It also promulgates model laws (or model acts), which basically require a lesser form of uniformity among the states. Leaving the distinction between uniform and model laws aside for the moment, a uniform law is a special term of art to denote an act that is officially adopted by the NCCUSL for passage by the states. The NCCUSL certainly does not have the monopoly in this regard, and uniform (and model) laws have been used by other entities both inside and outside the US.[100]

Nevertheless, as the term is used in the context of the NCCUSL, a uniform law embodies certain characteristics. First, a uniform law is usually of a limited nature, meaning that it does not lay down comprehensive rules over an entire field of (private) law, but is chiefly targeted at specific issues or subjects. For instance, there has never been a general uniform law of contracts, but rather several uniform laws touching upon various aspects relating to contractual transactions. This highlights the distinction between a uniform law and the UCC, which is a more comprehensive form of a uniform law as discussed below.[101] Moreover, the term uniform law is somewhat misleading in the sense that it is not necessarily 'uniform' or a 'law' in terms of a binding legislative enactment. A uniform law has no formal binding status in and of itself. It receives its binding force only through its adoption by the states, thus explaining the reference to uniform 'state' laws.[102] Once a uniform law has gone through the drafting process, it is

[95] As noted on its website (n 94), the NCCUSL is a non-profit, unincorporated association in Chicago, Illinois, and is supported by state appropriations.

[96] At present, Puerto Rico and the US Virgin Islands. To avoid confusion, 'state' in this context denotes the fifty states, the District of Columbia (DC), and related US territories. See NCCUSL Constitution, n 94, Art 9.

[97] Although some state legislators have served as commissioners, most commissioners are practitioners, judges, and professors who serve specific terms and receive no fees for their work; the main requirement is bar membership. See NCCUSL Constitution, n 94, Art 2, s 2.5.

[98] See, eg, RB Long, 'The National Conference of Commissioners on Uniform State Laws' (2007) 79 *NYSBJ* 40.

[99] NCCUSL Constitution, n 94, Art 1.2.

[100] Eg, there are organizations similar to the NCCUSL model outside the US, such as the Canadian Uniform Law Conference. See, eg, D Halberstam and M Reimann, 'Federalism and Legal Unification: Comparing Methods, Results and Explanations Across 20 Systems' (Feb 2010, rev Sept 2011) Univ of Mich Law School Public Law and Legal Theory Working Paper No 186, 15.

[101] See § 3.5.

[102] See RH Heimanson, 'Federalism and the Uniform Law Movement' (1960) 6 *NYLF* 161, 164.

officially adopted by the NCCUSL for recommendation to the various state legislatures with the hope that it will be taken up by the states in its 'official' or at least substantially unamended form, thereby achieving greater uniformity among the respective states in the area concerned. As one jurist famously put it, a uniform law becomes law '*ex proprio vigore*', meaning only if the substance of the act itself (along with the efforts of the commissioners as seen below) influences the respective state legislative authorities to pass it.[103] Yet, there is no binding obligation on the states to do so. It is purely up to each state concerned as to if, when, and how a uniform law should be adopted. This means that a state is free to disregard a uniform law completely or to change it as it sees fit by what are commonly called non-uniform amendments. Depending upon the extent and degree of state variation, this may preclude the envisaged uniformity in the area concerned, which may explain why the term uniform state law has been called an 'oxymoron in terms' on occasion.[104]

3.3.1.2 The distinction between uniform laws and model laws

Over the years, the reference to uniform and model laws has become blurred, with scholars on both sides of the Atlantic using the term model law to refer to uniform laws promulgated by the NCCUSL, as well as to the UCC.[105] This makes it confusing to understand which of the two types of acts is being referred to, especially when scholars are making analogies between the European and American settings. This also discounts the distinction between uniform laws and model laws in the NCCUSL's guidelines, which set forth the criteria for the designation of an act as either a uniform law or a model law.[106]

The difference between a uniform law and a model law boils down to the prospect of uniformity sought by the act and the role to be played by the commissioners. First, an act is designated a uniform law if it is expected to be enacted in a large number of states and the uniformity of the provisions of the act is considered to be a principal objective.[107] In contrast, in the case of a model law, uniformity may be a desirable, though not a principal, objective, and the act can minimize diversity or otherwise achieve its purpose even though it may not be adopted by a significant number of states in its entirety.[108] For example, through the years, the model law category has come to include uniform laws that failed to garner significant adoption in the states.[109] Secondly, the distinction between a uniform law and a model law implicates the duties of the commissioners: in the case of a uniform law, the commissioners are obliged to attempt to secure passage of the act in their state legislatures in 'pure' unamended form, whereas

[103] JJ White, 'Ex Proprio Vigore' (1991) 89 *Mich L Rev* 2096.

[104] LT Gavin, 'Commercial Calamities: An Introduction and Sermon' (2007) 68 *Ohio St LJ* 1, 5.

[105] This can be traced back to early scholarship. See, eg, R David, 'The International Unification of Private Law' in R David (chief ed), II *International Encyclopedia of Comparative Law* (Mohr/Mouton/Oceana, 1971) § 272–§ 274. This continues to filter through the literature, particularly in the debate about European contract law. See, eg, J Basedow, 'Transjurisdictional Codification' (2009) 83 *Tul L Rev* 973, 978; Harry M Flechtner, 'The U.S. Experience with the UCC and the CISG: Some Insights for the Proposed CESL?' in U Magnus (ed), *CISG vs. Regional Sales Law Unification—With a Focus on the New Common European Sales Law* (Sellier, 2012) 5, 9.

[106] NCCUSL, 'Statement of Policy Establishing Criteria and Procedures for Designation and Consideration of Uniform and Model Acts', available at its website, n 94 (NCCUSL Project Criteria).

[107] NCCUSL Project Criteria, n 106, point 2(e)(1).

[108] NCCUSL Project Criteria, n 106, point 2(e)(2).

[109] Dunham, n 4, 247. The Model (ex Uniform) Consumer Credit Code is a good example: see § 3.5.3.3.

in the case of a model law, the commissioners have no such duty other than supplying copies of the act to those interested in their respective state upon request.[110] As such, uniform laws and model laws are not synonymous, at least as far as the uniform law process is concerned.

3.3.1.3 The NCCUSL and the American federal system

One of the most important aspects of the NCCUSL and the uniform law process is their linkage to the American federal system. They are equated with the objective to achieve uniformity among the laws of the various states at the state, as opposed to the federal, level. Recourse to uniform laws may be considered an important 'stronghold' of the states in preserving their competence in the areas concerned.[111] The NCCUSL and the uniform law process therefore represent 'unity out of diversity',[112] that is to say, as a way to let the diversity of the states flourish but at the same time as a means to channel that diversity to ensure uniformity among the states in certain areas where needed. As such, the uniform law process is considered a crucial part of maintaining the delicate balance between federal and state competence in matters of private law.[113]

At the same time, it is important to recognize that from the beginning, the NCCUSL embodied an ambiguous approach to issues of federal competence over such matters. On the one hand, it is often repeated that an important theme underlying the creation of the NCCUSL was that it would strive for uniformity in areas that were considered to fall outside the scope of federal competence.[114] On the other hand, the work of the NCCUSL through voluntary state action was originally conceived as a way to pre-empt federal regulation by making action at the federal level unnecessary.[115] In short, the uniform state law process was born out of fears of federalization.[116] This implies that the boundary between federal and state competence was not so clear-cut. Yet, the NCCUSL apparently did not work out an overarching theory as regards the division of matters that should be dealt with via uniform state legislation and those that were better handled via federal legislation.[117]

At present, with the expansion of federal competence, this has raised important questions about the role of the NCCUSL and the uniform law process in an era where it is commonly recognized that many of the NCCUSL's uniform laws could very well be the subject of federal legislation. Paradoxically, this has been viewed as giving new

110 Dunham, n 4, 247. See also NCCUSL Project Criteria, n 106, point 5; NCCUSL Constitution, n 94, Art 6.

111 Heimanson, n 102, 167.

112 WP Armstrong, Jr, *A Century of Service: A Centennial History of the National Conference of Commissioners on Uniform State Laws* (West, 1991) 14. See also BI Bittker, 'The Dormant Commerce Clause Doctrine, *Swift v. Tyson*, Uniform State Commercial Laws, and Federal Common Law: Ships That Passed in the Night?' (1991) 8 *Const Comm* 87, 94 (calling the NCCUSL 'Task Force E Pluribus Unum').

113 See, eg, AJ Harno, 'Uniform State Laws and the Federal System' (1949) 2 *Okla L Rev* 38; B Overby, 'Our New Commercial Law Federalism' (2003) 76 *Temp L Rev* 297, 314–315; CC Ring, Jr, 'A New Era: Cooperative Federalism-Through the Uniform State Law Process' (2010) 33 *Hamline L Rev* 375.

114 See, eg, Dunham, n 4, 236–237; White, n 103, 2100.

115 See Dunham, n 4, 237; GB Young, 'Uniform State Laws' (1922) 8 *ABAJ* 181.

116 See WA Schnader, 'Why the Commercial Code Should be "Uniform"' (1964) 69 *Comm LJ* 117; EH Taylor, Jr, 'Foreword: Federalism or Uniformity of Commercial Law' (1980) 11 *Rutgers-Cam LJ* 527, 529; EH Taylor, Jr, 'Uniformity of Commercial Law and State-by-State Enactment: A Confluence of Contradictions' (1978) 30 *Hastings LJ* 337, 339.

117 Dunham, n 4, 237. But for recent developments in this regard, see, eg, RA Stein, *Forming a More Perfect Union: A History of the Uniform Law Commission* (LexisNexis, 2013) ch 14.

impetus to the NCCUSL because the uniform law process provides an alternative route apart from federal legislation and thus a 'rallying point for the states against federal encroachment'.[118] The uniform law process is also often viewed as the 'first choice' over federal action because it has advantages of resources and experience at the state level so as to ensure a 'smoother' fit within the state legal environment.[119] That said, in recent decades, the NCCUSL has been confronted with particular challenges and opportunities, which have arisen in response to the interface between the federal, state, and international levels, which offer further reflection on the role played by the NCCUSL in the American federal system.

As regards the federal-state dynamic, it has been acknowledged that the action via the NCCUSL as opposed to action at the federal level is no longer an 'all or nothing' game in which private law is regulated either at the state level or pre-empted completely at the federal level, but instead one involving a complex interrelationship between the two. On various occasions, the Federal Government exhibits willingness to cooperate with the NCCUSL, rather than usurp its function. For example, it has turned to the NCCUSL to prepare uniform acts that complement federal policies or legislation.[120] Congress may also defer to uniform state laws when it enters a particular field, thereby allowing the states to 'opt out' of the relevant federal legislation provided that a similar uniform law is in place, but this is not free from controversy, since it has been viewed as a more subtle form of federal intrusion into state domains.[121]

On the international level, the relationship between the NCCUSL and the Federal Government has also been affected by the increasing number of international conventions concerning areas of state competence, especially private law. While this brief discussion cannot do justice to the issues (constitutional and otherwise) involved, suffice it to say that these developments pose further challenges to the viability of the uniform law process at the same time that it provides the NCCUSL with new opportunities to increase its presence in the international arena.[122] In this way, the link between the NCCUSL and the American federal system means that it will continue to confront various issues related to the interplay between federal and state competence in matters of private law. It was in fact the prospect of federalization that prompted the creation of the NCCUSL in the first place.

3.3.2 Origins of the NCCUSL

The NCCUSL was founded in 1892 under the auspices of the American Bar Association (ABA),[123] amidst discussion of the need for greater uniformity in state law and at what

[118] White, n 103, 2102.

[119] See, eg, FH Miller, 'The Future of Uniform State Legislation in the Private Law Area' (1995) 79 *Minn L Rev* 861.

[120] See, eg, Dunham, n 4, 238–239; FH Miller, 'The Uniform Law Process and Its Global Impact' (2002) 56 *Cons Fin LQ Rep* 136, 137.

[121] See, eg, Overby, n 113.

[122] See, eg, AH Boss, 'The Future of the Uniform Commercial Code Process in an Increasingly International World' (2007) 68 *Ohio St LJ* 349; SB Burbank, 'A Tea Party at the Hague?' (2012) 18 *Sw JIL* 629; WH Henning, 'The Uniform Law Commission and Cooperative Federalism: Implementing Private International Law Conventions Through Uniform State Laws' (2011) 2 *Elon L Rev* 39; PH Pfund, 'Federalism and U.S. Participation in Intergovernmental Efforts to Unify Private Law' (2011) 56 *Vill L Rev* 559.

[123] The ABA is a national organization generally composed of lawyers, law students, and other law-related professionals and serves as a forum for various issues related to the legal profession. See its website, <http://www.americanbar.org/>.

level, state or federal, such action should be taken. To put matters in perspective, the need for uniformity in state commercial law, including contract law, had been the subject of discussion since the founding of the US and hence long before the advent of *Swift v Tyson* in 1842.[124] Against this background, when the ABA was established in 1878, one of its principal objectives was to 'promote the administration of justice and uniformity of legislation throughout the Union'.[125] At its first meeting, a Committee on Commercial Law was set up to make suggestions to strengthen uniformity among the state laws in this area.[126] It was not long until proposals were put before the Committee concerning federal bills unifying certain aspects of contract and commercial law.

At the ABA's annual conference in 1887, this Committee issued a report concerning the need for federal legislation to regulate, inter alia, commercial transactions between the citizens of different states.[127] The report recommended that Congress should adopt, pursuant to its competence under the Interstate Commerce Clause, legislation concerning the regulation of bills of exchange and commercial paper.[128] Although the federal legislation in these areas would only cover interstate matters, it was surmised that the states would enact the same provisions for intrastate transactions, and together, this would unify commercial law throughout the country.[129] In the Appendix to the report, there was a proposal for a Federal bill 'to regulate commerce among the several States, and to codify the law relating to bills of exchange and other commercial paper'.[130] This bill was called the Federal Bills of Exchange Act and included provisions concerning bills of exchange, cheques, promissory notes, and other types of negotiable instruments used in interstate transactions.[131] It had in fact already been introduced, without success, in the 48th Congress on 12 May 1884.[132] Full discussion of this bill and the accompanying report was held over to the ABA's annual conference two years later in 1889.[133] In the meantime, the need for federal legislation regulating commercial transactions continued to be discussed.[134]

[124] Narrative accounts by Professor William Winslow Crosskey spotlight the call made by James Sullivan as early as 1801 for federal legislation unifying the law of contracts. See WW Crosskey, 1 *Politics and the Constitution in the History of the United States* (Univ of Chicago Press, 1953) 36–37.

[125] First Conference and Annual Report of the American Bar Association (ABA Annual Report) 30 (1878). This objective remains. See ABA Constitution and Bylaws—Rules of Procedure House of Delegates 2012–2013, available at its website, n 123, Art 1.2.

[126] ABA Annual Report 26–27 (1878).

[127] Report of the Committee on Commercial Law, ABA Annual Report 332 (1887).

[128] Report of the Committee on Commercial Law, ABA Annual Report 352 (1887).

[129] Report of the Committee on Commercial Law, ABA Annual Report 344 (1887). This was not the first time that an interstate commercial code had been aired. Narrative accounts point to discussion of this topic in 1851 by John William Wallace: see LJ Bugge, 'Commercial Law, Federalism, and the Future' (1992) 17 *Del J Corp L* 11, 19–20.

[130] App to the Report of the Committee on Commercial Law, ABA Annual Report 362 (1887).

[131] App to the Report of the Committee on Commercial Law, ABA Annual Report 364 (1887).

[132] HR 6985, 48th Congress, 1st session (1884). The Committee's report stated that the Federal Bills of Exchange Act had been prepared by a member of the Committee for the American Bankers' Association and introduced in Congress by Representative Luke P Poland from Vermont. Report of the Committee on Commercial Law, ABA Annual Report 353–354 (1887). Looking closely at this bill, it seemed that what Mr Poland submitted was a text of an original bill dated earlier. The first page reads: 'The American Bankers' Association—Uniform Regulations of Commercial Paper—Proposed Act of Congress—C.C. Bonney—1884'; originally, it was dated 1883, but the number 4 was written on the 3. The header of subsequent pages of the bill read 'Bills of Exchange Act 1882', but the 2 was crossed out first by a 3, and then by a 4.

[133] ABA Annual Report 23, 343 (1889).

[134] The next year, John Randolph Tucker submitted a paper titled 'Congressional power over Inter-state Commerce', which reiterated Congress' competence over commercial paper and the need for a uniform system of interstate commercial law in the US. ABA Annual Report 247 (1888).

At the ABA's 1889 annual conference, there was heated debate concerning the federalization of commercial law based on the Committee's previous report and the attached Federal Bills of Exchange Act.[135] As noted by the Committee's chairman, George A Mercer: 'I do not think anybody who reads that report can doubt the power of Congress in the matter. Therefore, the main question is about the propriety of Congress exercising this power.'[136] It was in fact this Federal bill, rather than the report itself, which generated most of the attention as regards the role that should be played by the ABA vis-à-vis the legislative process.[137] The ABA adopted a resolution affirming its approval of the report as it related to commercial transactions, but expressly stating that the ABA did not commit itself to the substance of the Federal bill.[138] Interestingly, an amendment was put forward that would have explicitly affirmed Congress' power to regulate interstate commercial contracts, but it was not approved.[139] In 1890, this led to the introduction in Congress of a proposal for a Federal Bills of Exchange Act, which was based on the Federal bill annexed to the Committee's report.[140] This proposal died in committee.[141] By that time, the tide had already turned to the prospect of state, as opposed to federal, action.

At the ABA's 1890 annual conference, Henry C Tompkins submitted a paper titled 'The Necessity for Uniformity in the Laws Governing Commercial Paper'.[142] Following a diatribe concerning the problems caused by the *Swift* doctrine,[143] he concluded that there was a strong need for uniformity in the law governing commercial paper, but that such uniformity should come by way of state, not federal, action.[144] In his view, the adoption of a commercial code by Congress was only a 'partial remedy' because its competence was strictly limited to interstate transactions.[145] His reasoning in this regard is not altogether clear, but he seemed to argue that there was a substantial volume of intrastate transactions with interstate consequences that Congress was without power to regulate.[146] As a result, he posited that legislation adopted by the states was the answer. Although it would not be possible to get the states to adopt a complete commercial code all at once, procuring uniformity 'by degrees' would be possible by getting the states to adopt statutes unifying particular issues on a gradual basis.[147]

This idea coincided with the ongoing discussion over the past few years in certain states urging the creation of committees composed of state representatives charged with making recommendations as to uniform laws to be adopted by the states.[148] This led to the adoption of a resolution at the ABA's 1889 annual conference for the establishment of a 'Committee on Uniform State Laws' composed of a member of the ABA from each state, which would meet in a convention to consider the various state laws and to make appropriate recommendations.[149] This resolution, presented by WA Collier,

[135] ABA Annual Report 23, 343 (1889).
[136] ABA Annual Report 23 (1889).
[137] ABA Annual Report 23–35 (1889).
[138] ABA Annual Report 29, 35 (1889).
[139] ABA Annual Report 31–32 (1889).
[140] HR 6957, 51st Congress, 1st Session (1890). The bill was introduced by Congressman George Everett Adams from Illinois.
[141] See, eg, Bittker, n 112, 92; R Braucher, 'Federal Enactment of the Uniform Commercial Code' (1951) 16 *L & Contemp Probs* 100, 101; Taylor, Jr, *Hastings LJ*, n 116, 338–339 fn 4.
[142] ABA Annual Report 247 (1890).
[143] ABA Annual Report 249–260 (1890).
[144] ABA Annual Report 260–262 (1890).
[145] ABA Annual Report 262 (1890).
[146] ABA Annual Report 262 (1890).
[147] ABA Annual Report 262–263 (1890).
[148] See Armstrong, Jr, n 112, 16–18.
[149] ABA Annual Report 50–51 (1889). This Committee was initially titled one concerning 'uniform state laws relating to wills, acknowledgments, divorce, etc.' (ABA Annual Report 96 (1889)); however, this gave way to the general reference to 'uniform state laws, etc.' (ABA Annual Report 11, 96 (1890)).

placed particular emphasis on achieving greater uniformity among state laws dealing with marriage and divorce, descent and distribution of property, acknowledgment of deeds, and the execution and probate of wills.[150]

Accordingly, at the ABA's 1890 annual conference, it was this ABA Committee on Uniform State Laws, appointed pursuant to Mr Collier's resolution, to which Mr Tompkins' paper was referred.[151] This Committee submitted a report of its own, calling for a resolution on the passage by each state of an act similar to that which had recently been adopted in New York establishing a board of 'Commissioners for the Promotion of Uniformity of Legislation in the United States'.[152] The idea was for the New York legislation to serve as a model to prompt the other states into action, albeit with certain changes as regards the topics that would be covered.[153] In addition to those topics appearing in the New York legislation, such as marriage and divorce, insolvency, and notarial certificates,[154] three additional topics were added that had appeared in Mr Collier's previous resolution (ie descent and distribution of property, acknowledgement of deeds, and the execution and probate of wills).[155] To be clear, however, by following the model of the New York legislation, this resolution contemplated not a mere committee of the ABA as Mr Collier's resolution had done, but instead the formation of a separate body composed of commissioners on uniform state laws appointed by the various states.[156] This resolution supporting the New York legislation was approved by the ABA on 21 August 1890, and work began on the establishment of the various commissions in the states.[157]

At the next annual conference in 1891, the ABA Committee on Uniform State Laws issued a special report on the establishment of these state commissions on uniform state laws.[158] The report contained discussion of the answers to five main questions that had been asked to each member of the Committee.[159] Apart from the first question concerning the progress on the formation of various commissions, the remaining four questions were targeted at issues regarding the utility of

150 ABA Annual Report 50 (1889).

151 ABA Annual Report 385 (1890).

152 Report of the Committee on Uniform State Laws, Appointed under Mr Collier's Resolution Adopted at Chicago, August 1889, ABA Annual Report 336 (1890).

153 See WA Schnader, Presidential Address 'Fifty Years' in *Handbook of the National Conference of Commissioners on Uniform State Laws* (NCCUSL, 1940) (NCCUSL Handbook) 35, 36; WL Snyder, 'The Problem of Uniform Legislation in the United States', ABA Annual Report 289 (1892).

154 ABA Annual Report 336–337 (1890).

155 ABA Annual Report 337 (1890).

156 See ABA Annual Report 50 (1890).

157 ABA Annual Report 29–37 (1890).

158 Report of the Committee on Uniform State Laws, ABA Annual Report 365 (1891).

159 The five questions are listed as follows:

(1) What steps, if any, have been taken in your state (territory or district) toward the formation of a Commission on Uniformity of Laws?
(2) In what respects, if any, in your judgment, is a greater uniformity of the laws of the various states and territories desirable? (a) Marriage. (b) Divorce. (c) Jurisdiction in Divorce Cases. (d) Residence in same. (e) Descent. (f) Distribution. (g) Wills. (h) Probate. (i) Insolvency. (j) Notarial Certificates. (k) Commercial Paper. (l) Acknowledgment of Deeds.
(3) If greater uniformity is desirable, how far is it practicable?
(4) What special evils or inconveniences, if any, result in your state from the present want of uniformity?
(5) Could these inconveniences be adequately or considerably remedied by other methods?

E.G. (1) By making the *lex fori* conform more nearly to the *lex loci*. (2) By statutory enactments broadening the principle of comity as now recognized by the courts—such as the validation of foreign wills and deeds, if valid where executed. (3) By fuller recognition of extra territorial judicial appointments such as Receivers, Trustees and Executors.

Report of the Committee on Uniform State Laws, ABA Annual Report 365–366 (1891).

the uniform state law process, as opposed to federal action. Remarkably, some of the questions echoed matters voiced in the debate about European contract law, such as the desirability and practicability of achieving greater uniformity in areas of state private law.

In the report, focus was placed on the need for unifying contract and commercial law, as opposed to family and succession law that were expected to meet with resistance in the states.[160] There was also general agreement that the desired uniformity in these areas would be best secured by uniform state laws, not federalization.[161] In this regard, the Committee emphasized that such a systematic movement in the direction of uniformity among the states would preserve, not destroy, state autonomy and that 'the proposed method of voluntary state action *takes from the general government any excuse for absorbing powers now confined to the states*'.[162] It was conceded that proceeding by way of federal action would have the advantage of more complete uniformity and of permanency, but there were 'insuperable difficulties' related to federal action that rendered this route 'really out of the question'.[163] As regards the commercial context, the argument seemed to rest on Congress' apparent lack of federal competence in the relevant areas and the inability to deal with such matters sufficiently on the federal level.[164] The incongruities with the previous assertion of federal competence in interstate transactions and the ABA's support for federal legislation regulating bills of exchange went unaddressed.[165] The report concluded with a motion for a resolution recommending the passage of acts in the various states to set up commissions on uniform state laws.[166] The resolution was adopted by the ABA on 28 August 1891,[167] which led to the birth of the NCCUSL.

The first meeting of what was then called the 'Conference of State Boards of Commissioners for Promoting Uniformity of Law in the United States' was held the following year in Saratoga Springs, New York for three days starting on 24 August 1892, which was considered the founding date of the NCCUSL.[168] Seven states were represented at that first meeting.[169] This was a very small percentage of the then forty-four states of the American Union.[170] Over the years, additional states joined the NCCUSL, which came to include all of the states at that time, as well as most

[160] Report of the Committee on Uniform State Laws, ABA Annual Report 366–367 (1891).

[161] Report of the Committee on Uniform State Laws, ABA Annual Report 366 (1891).

[162] Report of the Committee on Uniform State Laws, ABA Annual Report 370–371 (1891) (emphasis added).

[163] Report of the Committee on Uniform State Laws, ABA Annual Report 373–374 (1891).

[164] Report of the Committee on Uniform State Laws, ABA Annual Report 374 (1891). Most of the emphasis was put on Congress' lack of competence to unify state laws on marriage and divorce, with similar difficulties for national action recognized 'in the other matters in question', which seemingly included commercial matters. The possibility of amending the US Constitution was contemplated in this regard, but the idea was to adopt 'prohibitory amendments' to ensure that the matters concerned would be left to the states. Report of the Committee on Uniform State Laws, ABA Annual Report 374 (1891).

[165] See Bittker, n 112, 92 fn 20.

[166] Report of the Committee on Uniform State Laws, ABA Annual Report 375 (1891).

[167] ABA Annual Report 51–53 (1891).

[168] See, eg, Armstrong, Jr, n 112, 11. The NCCUSL underwent several name changes over the years, but some variant of 'uniform' has remained: see Armstrong, Jr, n 112, 27, 30; see also n 94.

[169] The number of states present at the first NCCUSL conference has been subject to differing accounts, but several authoritative sources report that seven states (Delaware, Georgia, Massachusetts, Michigan, New York, New Jersey, and Pennsylvania) were represented. See, eg, Armstrong, Jr, n 112, 11; Schnader, n 153, 38; Stein, n 117, ch 1.

[170] Leaving aside DC and other US territories, the six remaining states of the fifty that now comprise the US, taking account of their accession dates—Utah (1896); Oklahoma (1907); New Mexico (1912); Arizona (1912); Alaska (1959); and Hawaii (1959)—were admitted in the years following the 1892 conference.

territories, by 1912.[171] The report of the NCCUSL's first meeting demonstrated the importance of the event by equating it to the US Constitutional Convention.[172]

Incidentally, on the same day as the NCCUSL's first meeting, a paper titled 'The Problem of Uniform Legislation in the United States' by William L Snyder was read at the ABA's 1892 annual conference.[173] The paper underscored the importance of securing uniformity by way of voluntary action of the states, not the Federal Government.[174] It set forth a somewhat novel plan for unifying several areas of state private law. As regards state laws in the field of real property law, Mr Snyder advanced the possibility of using 'alternative legislation', namely that of optional uniform laws, which would provide uniform models co-existing alongside the particular forms in use in a particular state.[175] For the fields of family, succession, and real property law, the relevant state laws would be incorporated into a 'uniform statute', which would contain in a systematic fashion the law as it then existed in the states.[176] In contrast, for matters of contract and commercial law, the states would adopt an 'inter-state commercial code'.[177] This would certainly not be the last time that the proposal for a uniform commercial code would be made in the American setting. Yet, the idea of 'alternative' uniform state laws apparently never caught on in the work of the NCCUSL, even though in hindsight, it cast a glance to the use of optional instruments in the debate about European contract law over a century later.

Ironically, despite the fact that the work of the NCCUSL is perhaps best known in the areas concerning commercial transactions, this was not the NCCUSL's only focus. As seen above, the NCCUSL grew out of concerns for uniformity in matters of family, real property, and succession law alongside that of contract and commercial law. The very first acts adopted by the NCCUSL dealt with wills and forms of acknowledgement in relation to conveyances of real property.[178] Still, it was the field of commercial law, including contract law, for which the work of the NCCUSL yielded great success. With the establishment of the NCCUSL, several committees were appointed, which included one on commercial law that was responsible for the promulgation of several important uniform laws in this area. In 1895, a request was put to this committee to prepare a bill relating to commercial paper based on the English Bills of Exchange Act and other relevant sources.[179] This led to the drafting of the Uniform Negotiable Instruments Act (also referred to as the Negotiable Instruments Law or NIL) by John J Crawford of the New York Bar, which was thereafter adopted, with some amendment, by the NCCUSL in 1896.[180] It was heralded as the first major attempt to secure uniformity of state commercial law in America.[181]

[171] 1912 is pegged as the year when the NCCUSL encompassed all of the then forty-eight states, as well as DC, Puerto Rico, Alaska, and Hawaii (the latter two of which joined the NCCUSL in 1912 and 1920, respectively, but did not accede to the American Union until 1959), as well as the Philippines. See Report of the Forty-Fourth Annual Conference of the NCCUSL, ABA Annual Report 692–693 (1921). When the Philippines was granted its independence, it left the NCCUSL. See Schnader, n 116, 118 fn 2. The US Virgin Islands was the last to join the NCCUSL in 1988. See Armstrong, Jr, n 112, App D.

[172] See Armstrong, Jr, n 112, 11.

[173] ABA Annual Report 7, 287–311 (1892).

[174] ABA Annual Report 288 (1892).

[175] ABA Annual Report 293–294 (1892).

[176] ABA Annual Report 289–290 (1892). He set forth a substantive proposal in this regard: see ABA Annual Report 291–307, 309–311 (1892).

[177] ABA Annual Report 289–290, 307–309 (1892).

[178] See Schnader, n 153, 38.

[179] Schnader, n 153, 39–40.

[180] Reprinted in CT Terry, *Uniform State Laws in the United States, fully annotated* (Baker, Voorhis and Co., 1920 and Suppl 1923).

[181] Terry, n 180, 17. See also Schnader, n 153, 42.

The NIL did not stand alone for long. Professor Samuel Williston, a premier authority on American contract law from Harvard Law School, was soon tasked with drafting four additional uniform acts in the commercial law field.[182] Based on his drafts, the Uniform Sales Act and the Uniform Warehouse Receipts Act were adopted by the NCCUSL in 1906; the Uniform Bills of Lading Act and the Uniform Stock Transfer Act came three years later in 1909.[183] These acts were followed by the Uniform Conditional Sales Act in 1918, drafted by Professor George G Bogert of Cornell Law School, and the Uniform Trust Receipts Act in 1933, drafted by Professor Karl N Llewellyn, then at Columbia Law School.[184] This cadre of seven uniform acts are commonly grouped together because they established a set of uniform rules encompassing a substantial portion of commercial transactions in the US, and collectively, they would lay significant groundwork for what would later become several Articles of the UCC.[185]

As seen below, the Uniform Sales Act played a major role in providing the impetus for the UCC itself.[186] Like the NIL, the Uniform Sales Act was also modelled after the relevant English statute, in this case the English Sale of Goods Act of 1893.[187] Its object was to establish a uniform set of rules concerning the sale of goods.[188] It contained a provision that sought to ensure the uniform interpretation of its provisions: 'This act shall be so interpreted and construed, as to effectuate its general purpose to make uniform the laws of those states which enact it'.[189] This type of clause had started to be inserted in various uniform acts in order to counteract differing judicial interpretations.[190] In the words of the US Supreme Court, such a clause was intended to ensure that the content of a uniform act would not merely be regarded as 'an offshoot of local law' and that 'the principle of the Uniform Act should have recognition to the exclusion of any inconsistent doctrine which may have previously obtained in any of the states enacting it'.[191] It thus revealed certain tensions

[182] For the Uniform Warehouse Receipts Act, Professor Williston was aided by Barry Mohun of the DC Bar. See WG Smith and MD Chalmers, 'National Conference of Commissioners on Uniform State Laws in the United States' (1916) 16 *J Soc Comp Legis* 154, 161.

[183] Reprinted in Terry, n 180.

[184] Reprinted in Terry, n 180. Professor Llewellyn also drafted the Uniform Chattel Mortgage Act, which was initially adopted by the NCCUSL in 1926 and approved in amended form in 1927. Presumably it is not included with the rest because of its poor approval rate. See G Gilmore, I *Security Interests In Personal Property* (Little Brown and Co., 1965) § 4.4, at 99.

[185] See, eg, General Comment of National Conference of Commissioners on Uniform State Laws and the American Law Institute (UCC Text General Comment), *Uniform Commercial Code 2013-2014 Edition* (West, 2013); R Braucher, 'The Legislative History of the Uniform Commercial Code' (1958) 58 *Col L Rev* 798, 799; B Stone and KD Adams, *Uniform Commercial Code in a Nutshell*, 8th edn (West, 2012) xi–xii; W Twining, *Karl Llewellyn and the Realist Movement*, 2nd edn, (Cambridge Univ Press, 2012) 273.

[186] See § 3.5.2.

[187] See Armstrong, Jr, n 112, 30.

[188] Terry, n 180, 189.

[189] See Terry, n 180, § 74 ('Interpretation Shall Give Effect to Purpose of Uniformity').

[190] This coincided with the creation, in 1913, of a Committee on Uniformity of Judicial Decisions to combat problems related to differing judicial interpretations of uniform acts. See further JAC Grant, 'The Search for Uniformity of Law' (1938) 32 *APSR* 1082, 1087; C Rey, *La Commission américaine d'uniformité des lois d'Etats* (M Giard, 1927) 122–128. In the NCCUSL/ULC Drafting Rules for Uniform and Model Acts, available at its website, n 94, a 'uniformity of application and construction' provision falls within the standard sections to be included in all uniform (but not model) acts so as to foster uniformity after the act's enactment. Rule 601 provides: 'In applying and construing this uniform act, consideration must be given to the need to promote uniformity of the law with respect to its subject matter among states that enact it.'

[191] *Commercial National Bank of New Orleans v Canal-Louisiana Bank and Trust Co.*, 239 US 520, 528–529 (1915).

underlying the uniform law process as regards the extent to which divergences among the states remained despite the existence of uniform acts.

3.3.3 Tensions underlying the uniform law process

In the ensuing decades, various uniform laws were adopted by the NCCUSL in a wide array of areas for passage by the states.[192] It was not long before certain defects associated with the uniform law process became apparent. In particular, such defects concerned the state-by-state enactment of uniform laws, the degree of state variation, and the need for revision. These defects were strongly voiced in the years leading up to the UCC in order to demonstrate the need for such a Code.[193] Although the NCCUSL attempted to remedy these problems, they are nonetheless inherent in the nature of the uniform law process and are of the utmost significance for assessing the effectiveness of uniform laws in achieving the envisaged uniformity in the area concerned, both then and now.

3.3.3.1 State-by-state enactment

First, there were problems relating to the varying acceptance rate of the uniform laws adopted by the NCCUSL. Many acts in the commercial law field were considered 'success stories', but even in this field, most were not accepted by all states and those that were typically took several decades. For example, from its promulgation in 1896, it took almost thirty years for all states to adopt the Uniform Negotiable Instruments Act and almost forty years for the Uniform Warehouse Receipts Act and the Uniform Stock Transfer Act.[194] Although never adopted by all states, the Uniform Sales Act and Uniform Bills of Lading Act took at least thirty-five years to claim a substantial majority, and both the Uniform Conditional Sales Act and the Uniform Trust Receipts Act more than twenty years to do so.[195] As the work of the NCCUSL progressed, several uniform laws came to be passed in a few, sometimes only one or two, states at most.[196]

3.3.3.2 State variation

Secondly, the extent of variation among the states in relation to the adoption and interpretation of the uniform acts posed significant problems. State variations generally stemmed from legislative and judicial causes: uniform acts were subject to many non-uniform amendments by the state legislatures in the process of their adoption, and the same provision of a uniform act was interpreted differently by the courts in each state. For instance, as regards the Uniform Negotiable Instruments Act, it was noted that there were non-uniform amendments pertaining to more than two-thirds of its sections and conflicts in judicial interpretation of about seventy-five sections.[197] This degree of state variation via legislative and judicial means created additional layers of complexity, thereby hindering the envisaged uniformity among the states.

[192] See generally Armstrong, Jr, n 112.
[193] See, eg, R Braucher, 'The Progress of the Uniform Commercial Code' (1962) 11 *AJCL* 293, 294.
[194] See Braucher, n 185, 799.
[195] See Braucher, n 185, 799.
[196] See Schnader, n 153, 44–48.
[197] Braucher, n 193, 294.

3.3.3.3 *The need for revision*

Finally, there were problems associated with the need to revise the uniform laws. In particular, there were inconsistencies between the various uniform laws themselves that had to be addressed, and some uniform laws became obsolete and thus required replacement or substantial modification. This resulted in a complex array of multiple versions of the same uniform law. For instance, in 1909 and 1922, the NCCUSL promulgated a series of uniform amendments relating to the Uniform Sales Act and its relationship with the Uniform Warehouse Receipts Act and the Uniform Bills of Lading Act, but many states did not enact these amendments, with the result that there were several versions of these uniform acts in force at the same time.[198] The need for revision was especially evident in the case of uniform acts, such as the Uniform Sales Act, which had been drafted early in the history of the NCCUSL and hence with the subsequent expansion of commercial transactions in the US, required extensive amendment.[199] With regard to the commercial field, the need for revision also highlighted the piecemeal nature of the uniform acts in the sense that they only covered certain 'slices' of the commercial 'pie', and as such, their inconsistencies and overlaps made the need for a more coherent legal framework more apparent. This is not to say that uniform laws were completely ineffective. They continue to serve as important means by which to achieve greater uniformity, both directly and indirectly, among state (private) laws in the US.[200] Nevertheless, as a result of these problems, complementary mechanisms came on the scene in the form of the American Law Institute's Restatement project and the UCC.

3.4 The ALI and the Restatement Project

3.4.1 General overview

The American Law Institute (ALI) is a private organization[201] which boasts a prestigious membership of lawyers, judges, and scholars throughout the US and some foreign countries.[202] It was created in 1923 under the auspices of the Association of American Law Schools (AALS).[203] Specifically, it grew out of discussions which took place at several AALS meetings concerning 'the existing dissatisfaction with the law and its administration and a recognition of a growing feeling among the members of the legal profession that the bar owed a duty to the public to improve the administration of justice'.[204] The improvement of the law and the administration of justice are fundamental themes underpinning the ALI's activities,[205] which include, but are not limited

[198] WE McCurdy, 'Uniformity and A Proposed Sales Act' (1940) 26 *Va L Rev* 572, 584.

[199] See § 3.5.2.1. [200] See, eg, Reimann, n 2, 227.

[201] The ALI is a non-profit corporation founded and incorporated under DC law. Its present headquarters are in Philadelphia, Pennsylvania.

[202] See its website, <http://www.ali.org/>, which offers a bibliography of publications on the ALI and its works.

[203] The AALS is a non-profit association founded in 1900 with the purpose to improve the legal profession through legal education. See its website, <http://www.aals.org/>.

[204] GW Wickersham, 'The American Law Institute and the Projected Restatement of the Common Law in America' (1927) 43 *LQ Rev* 449, 449. George W Wickersham not only was involved in the meetings that led to the ALI's creation, but also served as the ALI's first President. See *The American Law Institute Seventy-Fifth Anniversary 1923-1998* (ALI, 1998) 322.

[205] The ALI's Charter (available at its website, n 202) provides in relevant part: 'The particular business and objects of the society [the ALI] are educational, and are to promote the clarification and

to, the Restatements. This calls to mind three important aspects concerning the work of the ALI, the Restatement project, and the meaning of the term Restatement.

3.4.1.1 The work of the ALI

The ALI carries out various types of projects in line with its overarching mandate to improve the law and the administration of justice. They generally fall within three main categories: Restatements, model codes (as well as other statutory proposals), and Principles.[206] Leaving aside the Restatements for the moment, model codes are used somewhat generically to cover both model and uniform codifications, such as the UCC, a joint endeavour of the ALI and the NCCUSL, and the Model Penal Code, which was adopted by the ALI alone, both of which are not law themselves but whose provisions, all or in part, have been adopted or exerted great influence in the states.[207] Compared to the Restatements and model codes, the Principles category is of a more recent vintage, starting in the late 1980s and 1990s, and increasingly concerns subjects of international relevance.[208]

As framed by the ALI, there are differences between model codes and Principles as regards their respective aims in bringing about the envisaged improvements to the law in the area concerned: model codes or statutes and other statutory proposals are addressed mainly to legislative authorities with a view to their enactment, whereas Principles have a somewhat wider ambit, with the aim to provide guidance to legislative, judicial, and other institutional authorities and to recommend reform in the area concerned.[209] There is some overlap between the two, and in practice, it is sometimes difficult to make a clear theoretical distinction between them.[210] Nonetheless, the ALI's work on model codes and Principles signals that the ALI is engaged in projects that are directed in varying degrees at bringing about legislative or statutory change, whether at the state, federal, or international level. In this way, they contrast with the objectives underlying the Restatement project.

simplification of the law and its better adaptation to social needs, to secure the better administration of justice, and to encourage and carry on scholarly and scientific legal work.'

[206] While this is reflected on the ALI's website and in much of the scholarship, some publications also mention a fourth category composed of studies. See GE White, 'From the Second Restatements to the Present' (2013) 16 *Green Bag* 305, 312. For general discussion of the ALI's work within and beyond these categories, see *Seventy-Fifth Anniversary*, n 204.

[207] As regards this and other model codes, see n 202. As regards the UCC, see § 3.5.

[208] See, eg, GA Bermann, 'The American Law Institute Goes Global: The Restatement of International Commercial Arbitration' (2008) 16 *Willamette JIL & Disp Resol* 300; R Hyland, 'American Private Legislatures and the Process Discussion' in AS Hartkamp et al (eds), *Towards a European Civil Code*, 4th rev and expanded edn (Kluwer/Ars Aequi Libri, 2011) 71, 75; M Traynor, 'The First Restatements and the Vision of the American Law Institute, Then and Now' (2007) 32 *S Ill ULJ* 145, 165–170. See also n 202.

[209] See the 'Projects Overview' on the ALI's website, n 202. See also GC Hazard, Jr, *The American Law Institute: What it Is and What it Does* (Centro di studie e ricerche di diritto comparato e straniero, 1994) 4. Compare White, n 206.

[210] These categories are sometimes intertwined in their development. Eg, the Principles of the Law of Software Contracts emerged from failed attempts to amend Art 2 of the UCC, which also led the NCCUSL to promulgate a uniform law (the Uniform Computer Information Transactions Act or UCITA) enacted by only a few states. See further, eg, L Liebman, 'Director's Foreword' in *Principles of the Law of Software Contracts* (ALI, 2010) ix; 'Symposium: The Principles of the Law of Software Contracts: A Phoenix Rising from the Ashes of Article 2B and Ucita' (2010) 84 *Tul L Rev* 1557. On these Principles, see also JJ White et al, 1 *Uniform Commercial Code*, 6th edn, Practitioner Treatise Series (West, 2012) ch 14.

3.4.1.2 *The Restatement project*

Notwithstanding the ALI's other tasks, the Restatements are undoubtedly one of the ALI's signature products. The Restatement project denotes the series of Restatements published by the ALI covering several fields of American law. Restatements are commonly associated with subjects of private law, such as contracts, but they are not limited to such.[211] To date, there have been three series of Restatements.[212] Each Restatement is the result of collective deliberation by the ALI membership under the helm of one or more Reporters who are responsible for drafting the provisions of a Restatement.[213] Depending upon the subject, some Restatements are subdivided into specific topics.[214]

3.4.1.3 *The meaning of a Restatement*

In the American setting, the word Restatement is a term of art generally equated with the ALI. In basic terms, a Restatement denotes a set of rules that aims to synthesize a particular field of American law in clear and simple language.[215] The function of a Restatement is essentially to 'restate' what the law is in the area concerned. As framed by William Draper Lewis, a prominent figure of the ALI, '[t]he best short description of the Restatement is to say that it is an attempt to give orderly expression to the common law' of the US.[216] A Restatement is mostly concerned with the decisions of the courts in the relevant area (ie common law), but it does take account of statutory law.[217]

In the US, a Restatement has certain distinctive characteristics relating to its form and authoritative status. First, regardless of the subject, each Restatement follows a similar format. At present,[218] each Restatement is organized into a series of chapters containing various sections, which in turn generally comprise the following four components: the Black-letter rule, the Comment, one or more Illustrations, and the

211 For a comprehensive list, see n 202.

212 At present, the Restatement Third series is generally consulted, but for certain topics such as contracts, the Restatement Second remains applicable. See *Restatement (Second) of Contracts* (ALI, 1981). Work on the Restatement Fourth series has begun with US foreign relations law: see n 202.

213 Eg, with respect to the First Restatement on contracts, Professor Samuel Williston of Harvard Law School was the Reporter, and Professor Arthur L Corbin of Yale Law School was a Special Reporter for the chapter on remedies. As regards the Second Restatement on contracts, Professor Robert Braucher of Harvard Law School served as Reporter until 1971 when he was appointed to the bench; Professor E Allan Farnsworth of Columbia Law School was the Reporter until its completion. Professor Corbin was a consultant on the Second Restatement until his death. As regards the drafting, revision, and approval process of a Restatement, see n 202.

214 Eg, as regards torts, there are specific volumes on apportionment of liability, liability for physical and emotional harm, and products liability; as regards contracts, there is work underway on a Restatement devoted to consumer contracts. See n 202.

215 See, eg, Hazard, Jr, n 209, 7; WD Lewis, 'History of the American Law Institute and the First Restatement of the Law—"How We Did It"' in *Restatement in the Courts, Permanent Edition 1932-1945* (ALI, 1945) 1, 19.

216 Statement of William Draper Lewis to the ABA, ABA Annual Report 272 (1924). He was the ALI's first Director. See *Seventy-Fifth Anniversary*, n 204, 324. As regards his role in the ALI's creation and development, see citations in n 225.

217 This was assumed from the beginning: see ns 235–236 and accompanying text.

218 The First Restatement series was envisaged to be accompanied by comments, illustrations, and treatises, but the treatise idea was soon dropped and Reporters' Notes were added later. See JP Frank, 'The American Law Institute: 1923–1998' in *Seventy-Fifth Anniversary*, n 204, 3. The progression from the First to the Second Restatement on contracts exemplifies the changes in form in the Restatement project. See H Wechsler, 'Foreword' in *Restatement (Second) of Contracts*, n 212, vii.

Reporter's Note. The Black-letter rule contains the rule of law being expounded.[219] The Comment provides explanation of the rule concerned and cross-references to other provisions of the same or other Restatements. The Illustrations provide examples of the application of the rule. The Reporter's Note, which was added to the Restatements starting with the second series, sets forth the background and context of the rule, a listing of authoritative sources including the relevant citations to case law, statutory enactments, and treatises, and any modifications or new additions as compared to that in the previous series of Restatements. While this information may seem banal, the structure of the Restatement is often used as a point of similarity in relation to the work of several academic projects involved in the debate about European contract law. Secondly, as for its status, a Restatement does not constitute binding law in any US jurisdiction. In principle, a Restatement has only persuasive authority in the sense that the excellence and quality of its draftsmanship influence the courts to follow it.[220] Therefore, a Restatement and a uniform law of the NCCUSL differ fundamentally. Both are non-binding sources, but a uniform law is contemplated to become binding law when adopted by the state legislatures, whereas a Restatement is not envisaged to be incorporated into a legislative enactment.

Although the Restatement project is linked to the work of the ALI, this does not mean that the term Restatement cannot be used outside the US in other jurisdictions, such as the EU.[221] Generically, a Restatement may be used to denote a set of rules or principles purporting to synthesize the law in a particular area. In other words, it does not necessarily lose its efficacy if it is dissociated from the American setting. At the same time, however, there remain certain challenges in doing so. This stems from the fact that in relying on the term Restatement certain assumptions may automatically be made, especially when the use of this term is said to be linked to the ALI and the Restatement project. One assumption is that such rules or principles do in fact exist and can be 'restated' in a clear and coherent form. Another is that the recourse to a Restatement implies the use of non-binding law. Thus, it becomes confusing when a Restatement is used to denote the formulation of rules or principles that are envisaged to become a binding instrument enacted at the European level, as illustrated by certain academic projects involved in the debate about European contract law discussed in the next chapter.[222] This demonstrates that the use of the term Restatement is liable to provoke tensions that are already apparent in the American setting and may 'pop up' in others where the term is employed.[223] Thus, while the term is useful, there should be caution in making the choice. In fact, this argues for a terminological

[219] Many publications refer to principles and rules of law in this regard, but the distinction between the two is often not clarified, which may explain in part why commentators, as well as the ALI, rely on generic language, such as black-letter 'formulations': see, eg, its website, n 202. This issue arises in the context of the so-called 'rules versus standards' debate in respect of the ALI's work generally: see, eg, Traynor, n 208, 162 and citations therein.

[220] However, in certain jurisdictions, such as the US Virgin Islands, the Restatements have been adopted as the controlling authority. See further KD Adams, 'The Folly of Uniformity? Lessons from the Restatement Movement' (2004) 33 *Hofstra L Rev* 423.

[221] In particular, there has been increasing attention devoted to comparative reflection between the ALI's Restatement project (and its other activities to some extent) and the European setting. See, eg, N Jansen, *The Making of Legal Authority—Non-legislative Codifications in Historical and Comparative Perspective* (Oxford Univ Press, 2010); H Schulte-Nölke, '"Restatements" in Europe and the US: Some Comparative Lessons' in *The Foundations of European Private Law*, n 2, 11; W Twining, 'Surface Law' in H Petersen et al (eds), *Paradoxes of European Legal Integration* (Ashgate, 2008) 157, 174–178.

[222] See Chapter 4, § 4.2.

[223] Eg, as regards the DCFR, see N Jansen and R Zimmerman, '"A European Civil Code in All But Name": Discussing the Nature and Purposes of the Draft Common Frame of Reference' (2010) 69

distinction, used here, as regards the notion of Restatement in its *pure* form associated with the ALI, as opposed to a more *functional* sense laying claim to its methodological aspects, which seems to be the way in which the majority of the academic community is utilizing the term so far in the European setting.[224] This also points to the importance of understanding the origins of the Restatement project.

3.4.2 Origins of the ALI and the Restatement project

The ALI was founded in 1923 on the basis of a Report presented by a group of prominent judges, lawyers, and scholars known as 'The Committee on the Establishment of a Permanent Organization for the Improvement of the Law' at a meeting in Washington, DC attended by several hundred leaders of the bench, the bar, and law schools from all over the country.[225] There has been much debate about the intentions of the ALI's founders in terms of the extent to which they aimed to reform American law.[226] Nevertheless, the express reference to the 'improvement of the law' in the title of this Committee was central to the ALI's creation. The Committee's report recommended that the ALI should be established in order to remedy what were considered to be the two 'chief defects' of American law: its uncertainty and its complexity.[227] The law's uncertainty was caused by many factors, including the lack of agreement among lawyers as to the fundamental principles of the common law, the lack of precision in the use of legal terminology, conflicting and badly drawn statutes, and the rising volume of reported decisions.[228] The law's complexity was attributed to its lack of systematic development and to the widespread variation in the law of the different jurisdictions, state and federal, in the US, among other things.[229] On that basis, the Committee recommended the creation of the ALI, with the primary objective 'to enable the legal profession in America to carry out its public obligation to improve the law'.[230] This Report was widely received, and the ALI was born.

The origins of the ALI were joined with that of the Restatements. Alongside its recommendations on the establishment of the ALI, the Committee's Report set forth the need for a 'Restatement of the Law', which was envisaged to remedy the uncertainties and complexities plaguing American law and thus 'will do more to improve the law than any other thing the legal profession can undertake'.[231] The Report suggested that the first task of the ALI should be to produce a Restatement of Law in several areas and

CLJ 98, 100–104. Moreover, reference to the work of the ALI Restatements and certain groups involved with European contract or private law as a private or non-legislative 'codification' (see, eg, Jansen, n 221, 6–7; N Jansen, 'Dogmatising Non-legislative Codifications: Non-legislative Reference Texts in European Legal Discourse' in *The Foundations of European Private Law*, n 2, 31, 32–37) may evoke tensions similar to those underlying the Restatement project on this issue: see § 3.4.3.2.

[224] See, eg, N Jansen and L Rademacher, 'European Civil Code' in JM Smits (ed), *Elgar Encyclopedia of Comparative Law, Second Edition* (Edward Elgar, 2012) 299, 302–304; Schulte-Nölke, n 221, 13–14.

[225] Report of the Committee on the Establishment of a Permanent Organization for the Improvement of the Law Proposing the Establishment of an American Law Institute in *Seventy-Fifth Anniversary*, n 204, 173 (ALI Report). It can also be found in *The American Law Institute Fiftieth Anniversary* (ALI, 1973) 1. There were several events that set the scene for ALI's founding. See generally *Seventy-Fifth Anniversary*, n 204; HF Goodrich and PA Wolkin, *The Story of the American Law Institute* (ALI, 1961); Lewis, n 215.

[226] See, eg, 'Symposium: Did the First Restatement Adopt a Reform Agenda?' (2007) 32 *S Ill ULJ* 1; NEH Hull, 'Restatement and Reform: A New Perspective on the Origins of the American Law Institute' (1990) 8 *L & Hist Rev* 55 (reprinted in *Seventy-Fifth Anniversary*, n 204, 49).

[227] ALI Report, n 225, 184.

[228] ALI Report, n 225, 86–189, 225–233.

[229] ALI Report, n 225, 233–239.

[230] ALI Report, n 225, 210.

[231] ALI Report, n 225, 194.

set forth some general outlines as to how to go about this. In particular, it underlined three points concerning the purpose, authoritativeness, and representativeness of the Restatement project.

First, the *purpose* of a Restatement was not only 'to help make certain much that is now uncertain and to simplify unnecessary complexities, but also to promote those changes which will tend better to adapt the laws to the needs of life'.[232] A Restatement was viewed in terms of three characteristics: analytical, critical, and constructive.[233] It would be 'analytical' in the sense that each topic would be treated analytically, rather than historically, and based on a definite classification of the law as the result of thorough study by a group of qualified persons.[234] It would be 'critical' in the sense that it would be more than a mere collection and comparison of statutes and court decisions or an exposition of existing law as in a treatise or encyclopedia, but instead provide an extensive examination of legal theory, including the reasons and uncertainties related to the law concerned.[235] Lastly, it would be 'constructive' in two senses: first, while necessarily based to a large extent on the two official sources of law, statutes and decisions, it should take account of situations not yet dealt with by the legislatures or discussed by the courts; and secondly, where the law was uncertain or where there were differences in the law of the various jurisdictions, the Restatement would set forth what was believed to be the proper rule of law.[236] This indicated that a Restatement would not merely 're-state' the law, but would also set forth certain changes in the law where necessary. In the Report, there were certain areas where making changes in the law by way of a Restatement was considered inappropriate, eg, those involving matters of general public concern.[237] But for the most part, a Restatement would be focused on changes in the law for the purposes of either simplifying the law where it was unnecessarily complex or adapting it so that it was better able to accomplish its objectives.[238] As a consequence, a Restatement was conceived from the beginning as a 'theoretical hybrid' between a neutral exposition of the law 'as it is' (descriptive approach) and a statement of preference or recommendation as to what the law 'ought to be' (prescriptive or normative approach).[239] It is this dichotomy that lies at the root of certain tensions underlying the Restatement project in the US, as discussed below.

Secondly, as for *authoritativeness*, the Committee's Report emphasized that a Restatement should not take the form of a code, ie it should not be prepared with a view to adoption by the state legislatures or Congress as a binding statutory enactment.[240] This stemmed from fears that to do so would jeopardize the flexibility and the 'fullness of detail' of the common law.[241] In this regard, the Report compared the Restatements with uniform laws of the NCCUSL in the field of commercial law. The lack of flexibility in uniform laws was viewed as a 'distinct gain', since it was more important for the law to be certain and to remedy the divergences among state laws in the areas concerned.[242] In contrast, a Restatement was to be considered a highly persuasive legal authority emanating from a pre-eminent private body, that of the ALI, but it should not have the force of law itself.[243]

232 ALI Report, n 225, 190.
233 ALI Report, n 225, 190.
234 ALI Report, n 225, 191.
235 ALI Report, n 225, 191.
236 ALI Report, n 225, 191–192.
237 ALI Report, n 225, 192.
238 ALI Report, n 225, 193.
239 Twining, n 185, 274.
240 ALI Report, n 225, 201. See also section titled 'Legislative Enactment of the Restatement as a Code of Law Not Desirable': ALI Report, n 225, 197–199.
241 ALI Report, n 225, 198.
242 ALI Report, n 225, 200.
243 ALI Report, n 225, 200.

Finally, the *representativeness* of the ALI was linked to the Restatement project. The Committee's Report considered that an important attribute of the ALI was that it would be a 'representative gathering' of the American legal profession, which included judges, lawyers, and scholars.[244] This was crucial to bestowing the Restatement project with its persuasive authority, since 'any [R]estatement of the law to acquire the authority necessary to enable it to accomplish results of importance, must be undertaken by an organization representative of all branches of the legal profession'.[245] Certainly, much responsibility for the content of the Restatements would be placed on the shoulders of legal scholars, but it was the triumvirate of the bench, bar, and academia that was deemed decisive to the success of the Restatement project.[246]

Though espoused in 1923, the Committee's Report served as an 'amazingly durable blueprint'[247] of the Restatement project for the coming years. On the whole, the Report underlined the importance and distinctiveness of the Restatement project. The Restatements were conceived as a novel mechanism to overcome the failure of the courts and the legislatures as instruments for the simplification and unification of American law.[248] Tellingly, the Report highlighted the defects stemming from the uniform law process.[249] The Restatements therefore embodied an additional route apart from the traditional judicial and legislative means in American (private) law. The Report was also instrumental in highlighting that the ALI's Restatements and the NCCUSL's uniform laws served different but related purposes. In contrast to the NCCUSL and the uniform law process, the Restatements were not concentrated on the adoption of uniform substantive law provisions in the various states, but rather on more scientific aspirations for achieving greater clarification, simplification, and modernization of American law. This is not to say that uniformity was not a goal of the Restatements,[250] but to some extent, concerns for uniformity were overshadowed by these other aspirations, for example, in cases where the 'best' rule chosen for a particular issue did not necessarily coincide with the rule followed by the majority of the states.[251] In this way, the Report foreshadowed certain perennial tensions underlying the Restatement project.

3.4.3 Tensions underlying the Restatement project

It is surely no understatement to say that the ALI and the Restatements have invited their fair share of controversy over the years. Three tensions underlying the Restatement project stand out because they provide salient reflection with the debate about European contract law.

[244] ALI Report, n 225, 206–209. This is further reflected in the classes of membership of the ALI. See Rules of Council, available at its website, n 202, Rule 2.

[245] ALI Report, n 225, 205.

[246] ALI Report, n 225, 205.

[247] Frank, n 218, 11.

[248] See Twining, n 187, 275–276.

[249] See ALI Report, n 225, 193–194, 215–217, 250–251. The *Swift* doctrine appeared in a specific section devoted to factors tending to unify American law, but it was not mentioned by name, and the tenor of much of the discussion seemed to counteract the power of the federal courts over state common law. See ALI Report, n 225, 252–253.

[250] LM Friedman and G Teubner, 'Legal Education and Legal Integration: European Hopes and American Experience' in M Cappelletti et al (eds), *1 Integration Through Law: Europe and the American Federal Experience* (Walter de Gruyter, 1986) 345, 361.

[251] In this regard, scholars have emphasized that the Restatements largely reflect, as opposed to creating, uniformity in the area concerned. See, eg, Eisenberg, n 2; A Rosett, 'Unification, Harmonization, Restatement, Codification and Reform in International Commercial Law' (1992) 40 *AJCL* 683, 693.

3.4.3.1 *Restating the law 'as it is' versus 'as it ought to be'*

As noted above, from their inception in 1923, the Restatements were envisaged not only to provide a clear and concise synthesis of existing law 'as it is', but also to make clear what was believed to be the best solution for the issue concerned or the law 'as it ought to be'. Yet, through the course of their development, the Restatements continued to attract much discussion as to whether or to what extent they should embody a descriptive statement of the law 'as it is', as opposed to a normative statement of the law 'as it ought to be'.[252] For example, the progression from the First to the Second Restatement of Contracts provoked critical remarks regarding the extent to which normative goals had been incorporated into the Restatement project, which led one scholar to argue that the Restatements should be called something else.[253]

In response to this criticism, commentators have stressed that there is a very fine line between restating existing law and modernizing it, and that the two are interrelated.[254] As Professor Herbert Wechsler, then the ALI's Director, explained, the 'as it is' versus the 'as it ought to be' dichotomy was superficial because both were equally part of reaching a decision as to what the law was in a particular area, and as such, part of the role of a Restatement was to bring 'continual refreshment' of the law.[255] On that basis, he framed the approach taken by the Restatements' drafters as follows: 'we should feel obliged in our deliberations to give weight to all of the considerations that the courts, under a proper view of the judicial function, deem it right to weigh in theirs. . . . In judging what was right, a *preponderating balance of authority* would normally be given weight, . . . but it would not be thought to be conclusive.'[256] This standard became an important figurehead in the work of the ALI, symbolizing that the Restatement project seeks to follow the law whenever possible, but would diverge where necessary in line with its aim to improve the law.[257]

Arguably, this tension between the descriptive and normative approach of the Restatement project may never be completely resolved. For example, at the 2007 Annual Conference, the ALI's Director, Professor Lance Liebman, contemplated six important questions for the future of the ALI, one of which concerned the extent to which a rule enunciated in a Restatement could vary from existing law.[258] Nonetheless, it is an important reminder of the tensions that inevitably accompany projects that stand at the boundary line between 'restating' the law and choosing the 'best' rule that should be applied under the circumstances.

[252] See, eg, Adams, n 220, 437–439 and citations therein; Frank, n 218, 10.

[253] WN Keyes, 'The Restatement (Second); Its Misleading Quality and a Proposal for Its Amelioration' (1985) 13 *Pepp L Rev* 13, 25. In fact, this scholar took issue with Professor Ole Lando, Chairman of the Commission on European Contract Law (see Chapter 4, § 4.2.1) because of his assumption that the Restatement project purported to set forth the existing American law: see Keyes, 25 fn 6. Compare the remarks of another scholar in the same issue: JW Wade, 'The Restatement (Second): A Tribute to its Increasingly Advantageous Quality, and an Encouragement to Continue the Trend' (1985) 13 *Pepp L Rev* 59.

[254] See, eg, E Rabel, 'A Draft of an International Law of Sales' (1938) 5 *U Chi L Rev* 543, 563–564 (framing matters as between a 'Scylla and Charybdis').

[255] H Wechsler, 'Restatements and Legal Change: Problems of Policy in the Restatement Work of the American Law Institute' (1968) 13 *St Louis ULJ* 185, 194. He was the ALI's Director from 1963-1984. See *Seventy-Fifth Anniversary*, n 204, 324.

[256] Wechsler, n 255, 190 (emphasis added).

[257] See L Liebman, Report of the Director, *American Law Institute Annual Report 2007*, available at n 202, 2.

[258] Liebman, n 257, 2. The following year, he found that this question could be answered in the affirmative, ie the ALI could 'recommend doctrine that reaches substantially beyond current law'. L Liebman, Report of the Director, *American Law Institute Annual Report 2008*, available at n 202, 3.

3.4.3.2 The Restatements and codification

The connection between the Restatement project and the codification of American law has also been a topic of great debate. This was so, even though as already mentioned the 'framers' of the ALI negated the possibility that the Restatements would take the form of a code, ie a comprehensive legislative enactment adopted at the state or federal level.[259] The debate usually centres around three main positions, which view the Restatement project as a defence of the common law against codification, as a substitute for codification, or as a transition to codification.[260] This matter was no doubt encouraged by the fact that the form and objectives of the Restatements as setting out the law in systematic and generalized fashion resembled those sought by codification.[261]

Although an important part of the Restatement's lineage, this topic has become somewhat academic from the present standpoint. The Restatements were conceived as, and still remain, a non-binding source of law whose *raison d'être* was to stand apart from the relevant lawmaking processes. Indeed, the merit of the Restatement project was largely rooted in *not* being dependent on the state or federal legislative apparatus. As remarked by the ALI's first Director, William Draper Lewis:[262]

> Though the rules are expressed in a form of a Code, except in sporadic instances, there never has been any desire to give them statutory authority. The Restatement is an agency tending to promote the clarification and the unification of the law in a form similar to a Code. But it is not a Code or a statute. It is designed to help preserve not to change the common system of expressing law and adapting it to changing conditions in a changing world.[263]

In this way, while there are similarities between the ALI and codification, there remains an important distance between the two.

3.4.3.3 The impact of the Restatements

The third tension relates to the impact of the Restatements. On the whole, it is difficult to make generalizations in this regard, since some Restatements have been highly effective, whereas others have been followed only as regards particular provisions or have had marginal influence.[264] Over the past decades, the ALI and the Restatement project have garnered substantial controversy on various issues, ranging from the ALI's membership and working methods to the viability of the Restatement project for successfully achieving its aspirations for improving the law.[265] In particular, the Restatements share some of the problems embodied by a code in terms of achieving real clarification

[259] See n 240 and accompanying text.

[260] See KD Adams, 'Blaming The Mirror: The Restatements and the Common Law' (2007) 40 *Ind L Rev* 205, 226–230 and citations therein. See also HF Goodrich, 'Restatement and Codification' in *David Dudley Field Centenary Essays*, n 3, 241; HE Yntema, 'The Jurisprudence of Codification' in *David Dudley Field Centenary Essays*, n 3, 251.

[261] See, eg, Hazard, Jr, n 209, 7; AT von Mehren, 'Some Reflections on Codification and Case Law in the Twenty-First Century' (1998) 31 *UC Davis L Rev* 659, 669; HE Yntema, 'What Should The American Law Institute Do?' (1936) 34 *Mich L Rev* 461, 469.

[262] See n 216. [263] Lewis, n 215, 19.

[264] M Reimann, 'Towards A European Civil Code: Why Continental Jurists Should Consult Their Transatlantic Colleagues' (1999) 73 *Tul L Rev* 1337, 1340.

[265] See generally Adams, n 260. There have been many symposia on these issues: see, eg, 'Symposium on the American Law Institute: Process, Partisanship, and the Restatements of Law' (1998) 26 *Hofstra L Rev* 567; 'From the Trenches and Towers: The Case for an In-Depth Study of the American Law Institute' (1998) 23 *L & Soc Inquiry* 621. See also citations in n 400.

and simplification of the law, since as stressed by one scholar, both are merely 'a premature attempt to reach an ideal toward which judges and scholars are struggling: a time when all the rules are simple, clear and coherently related'.[266]

Even so, it is with comparative reflection between the US and the EU that the impact of the Restatements may be fully appreciated. This is because after so many years, it is easy to take for granted the role played by the Restatements in the American setting. Despite its purported defects, the Restatement project brought about major improvements to American law by providing a common source of legal terminology and by establishing a baseline for sorting out the mass of American common law in some of the most important fields of private law, including contract law.[267] It is when one sets foot in the European setting in which such aspects are only beginning to come about at the European level that the true value of the Restatement project becomes apparent. Nonetheless, the Restatement project did not, and was not intended to, cure the divergences among state laws bearing directly on commercial transactions. It was not long before another mechanism came into view: the UCC.

3.5 The UCC

3.5.1 General overview

The Uniform Commercial Code (UCC or the Code) is a comprehensive uniform law on commercial transactions co-sponsored by the NCCUSL and the ALI. It is not a binding enactment in itself, but embodies certain characteristics of a uniform law discussed above, meaning that it must be adopted by a particular state legislature for it to have binding force within that state. Since it is adopted by each state individually, the UCC is applicable to intrastate transactions within the state concerned, and there are specific provisions to determine which state's law is applicable in interstate (and international) transactions and the parties' power to choose the applicable law.[268] In other words, there is no federal statute incorporating the UCC for the purpose of regulating interstate transactions, although as seen below, the matter was repeatedly contemplated. A general overview of the UCC can be gleaned through its structure, functional approach, and name.

[266] J Gordley, 'European Codes and American Restatements: Some Difficulties' (1981) 81 *Col L Rev* 140, 157.

[267] In this regard, Professor Arthur Corbin's remarks have resonance today:

> It is possible that laymen and members of the Bar may be led to expect too much of the Restatement. They may expect simplicity, where life is itself too complex to permit of simplicity. They may expect finality, when the truth is that no legislature or jurist has the capacity to anticipate or to control the future. They may expect near perfection, as the result of what seems to them a mighty effort of scholars and jurists. These they will not get; and the ensuing judicial development of the law ought soon to disabuse their minds of the error. It may still be hoped, however, that they will get a better systematic statement than they have had before, one that will itself mark some progress in the evolution of law and society.

AL Corbin, 'The Restatement of the Common Law by the American Law Institute' (1929) 15 *Iowa L Rev* 19, 41. For his role in the Restatement project, see n 213.

[268] See UCC § 1–301.

3.5.1.1 *Structure*

The UCC encompasses various subjects falling within the rubric of commercial transactions and replaces several uniform laws that had previously regulated such subjects. It is presently comprised of eleven Articles, of which two of the most well-known are Article 2 on Sales, concerning matters relating to contracts for the sale of goods, and Article 9 on Secured Transactions, regulating the creation and enforcement of security interests in areas of movable property law.[269] Each Article is divided into a certain number of parts, which are in turn subdivided into a number of sections. Each section is accompanied by the official comment, which contains the references to the relevant provisions of any previous uniform acts, purposes of the particular rule, any changes made thereto, and cross-references to other sections of the Code. Although it is up to the particular state whether to enact the official comments in the process of adopting the UCC, they are still considered authoritative statements of the drafter's intention and thus of tremendous guidance to courts, practitioners, and scholars in the interpretation of the Code.[270]

3.5.1.2 *Functional approach*

One of the overarching ideas behind the UCC is that 'commercial transactions' is a single subject with many interrelated parts, and thus, it aims to deal with all of the phases that may arise in the handling of a commercial transaction 'from start to finish'.[271] In short, the UCC embodies a functional approach. It is not separated into distinct fields of private law, but brings together various areas of law relevant for commercial transactions under one umbrella. A notable example is Article 2, which encompasses both the contract law and personal property law phases involved in regulating the sale of goods. This explains why the UCC is often not thought of as the harmonization of distinct fields of private law, such as contract law, in the American mindset—it is truly 'commercial' law. In doing so, however, it makes apparent the linkage between contract law and related fields of private law, which reverberates in the debate about European contract law.

3.5.1.3 *The meaning of the 'Uniform Commercial Code'*

The name 'Uniform Commercial Code' is not without significance, since it may be misinterpreted, particularly when viewed through European eyes. First, the UCC is not '*uniform*' in the sense that the same provisions exist in all fifty states and territories of the US. To date, there is some version of the UCC in force in all states and territories,

[269] There are eleven substantive articles: Art 1 General provisions; Art 2 Sales; Art 2A Leases; Art 3 Negotiable Instruments; Art 4 Bank Deposits and Collections; Art 4A Funds Transfers; Art 5 Letters of Credit; Art 6 Bulk Sales; Art 7 Documents of Title; Art 8 Investment Securities; and Art 9 Secured Transactions. Arts 10 and 11 concern effective dates, repeal of previous statutes, and transitional issues.

[270] See further JJ White and RS Summers, *Uniform Commercial Code*, 5th edn, Hornbook Series (West, 2000) 13–14. The use of the official comments in the interpretation of the Code has not been free from controversy. See, eg, R Hyland and D Patterson, *The Commercial Sales Transaction: An Introduction to the U.C.C.*, 2nd edn (West, 2007) 10. As regards Professor Llewellyn's thoughts on the matter, see, eg, WD Hawkland, 'The Uniform Commercial Code and the Civil Codes' (1995) 56 *La L Rev* 231, 243–244.

[271] UCC Text General Comment, n 185.

except for Louisiana that adopted most, but not all, provisions of the Code.[272] Yet, not all states and territories have the same version. With successive revisions of all or parts of the Code, there is variation among the states as to those that adopt, or not, the official amendments made to the Code over the years, or that enact, or not, non-uniform amendments. In addition, the Code itself strays from absolute uniformity. Certain articles contain 'alternative' provisions that contain two versions of a rule, with the result that some states adopt one version, while other states adopt another.[273] There is also much made of the so-called 'open-textured' nature of the UCC by virtue of articles that contain broad, open-ended phrases, such as 'commercial reasonableness' and 'good faith', which allow for flexibility in its interpretation.[274] The bottom line is that there remains an important caveat attached to the UCC to check the particular state's version of the Code because of potential 'traps' in the form of divergences from the official text.

Secondly, the UCC does not cover in a comprehensive fashion all matters falling within the confines of '*commercial law*' or even all aspects of the fields that are covered.[275] For instance, as regards sales law, it does not generally cover insurance contracts or other types of services contracts, and most issues of contract formation are left to general contract law outside the UCC.[276] Furthermore, it generally covers consumer and commercial transactions, as opposed to being limited to transactions involving merchants, as was done in the European commercial codes.[277] Finally, there is the issue whether or to what extent the UCC may be considered a '*code*', which has been heavily debated in the literature.[278] Without delving deeply into this well-charted territory, suffice it to say that the UCC is a code 'within the American frame of reference'.[279] Among other things, this is because it may be supplemented by law that was enacted before the Code or that is not covered by it.[280] In other words, in contrast to European codifications, the UCC maintains, rather than displaces, pre-existing state law.

Opinions may continue to vary on the uniformity, comprehensiveness, and codificatory nature of the UCC.[281] Nevertheless, each of the UCC's composite words sets it apart as a landmark feature of American contract law. As enshrined in Article 1, one of its purposes is 'to make uniform the law among the various jurisdictions'.[282] Although

272 Eg, Louisiana has not adopted Art 2 on Sales. Aside from the fifty states, several US jurisdictions and territories have adopted the UCC, including DC (enacted by Congress), Puerto Rico, Guam, the Northern Mariana Islands, and the US Virgin Islands.

273 See, eg, Hyland and Patterson, n 270, 8–9.

274 See, eg, Stone and Adams, n 185, xvi–xvii. Compare, eg, Hyland and Patterson, n 270, 11–12.

275 See, eg, JB McDonnell, 'The Code Project Confronts Fundamental Dilemmas' (1993) 26 *Loy L Rev* 683, 683–684.

276 White and Summers, n 270, 7–8.

277 See further § 3.5.3.3.

278 Compare, eg, WD Hawkland, 'Uniform Commercial "Code" Methodology' (1962) 1962 *U Ill LF* 291; S Herman, 'The Fate and the Future of Codification in America' (1996) 40 *AJLH* 407, 427; Weiss, n 2, 520.

279 RM Buxbaum, 'Is the Uniform Commercial Code a Code?' in U Drobnig and M Rehbinder (eds), *Rechtsrealismus, multikulturelle Gesellschaft und Handelsrecht—Karl N. Llewellyn und seine Bedeutung heute* (Duncker and Humblot, 1994) 197, 220.

280 See, eg, G Gilmore, 'Article 9: What It Does for the Past' (1966) 26 *La L Rev* 285, 285–286. That said, as part of the revision of Art 1, efforts were made to clarify what law supplements the UCC: see JJ White and RS Summers, *Uniform Commercial Code*, 6th edn, Hornbook Series (West, 2010) § 1–§ 2.

281 In the Hornbook Series written by Professors James J White and Robert S Summers, there used to be a section in the Introduction devoted to the disagreement between them on these aspects. See White and Summers, n 270, 21–22. This was discontinued in the subsequent edition. In the Practitioner Treatise Series by the same authors, no such section is included.

282 UCC § 1–103(a)(3). Its other purposes are 'to simplify, clarify, and modernize the law governing commercial transactions' and 'to permit the continued expansion of commercial practices through custom, usage, and agreement of the parties'. UCC § 1–103(a)(1)–(2).

the UCC does not envelop every aspect of contract or commercial law, its coverage is still substantial, and while it may remain a 'code' with a uniquely American mindset, its consolidation of a substantial portion of commercial law into a single statutory scheme transcended the problems of selective piecemeal enactment of the previous uniform laws by the states.[283] In any event, this illustrates that many aspects of the UCC cannot be readily assumed, including its adoption at the state level.

3.5.2 Origins of the UCC

Already in 1958, an American jurist remarked: 'The problem of a lawyer who wants to find out something about the Code is not a dearth of literature on the subject. It is rather that discussion has been too plentiful.'[284] Indeed, the literature on the UCC envelops various layers including its theoretical underpinnings linked to the role of Professor Karl Llewellyn,[285] its legislative history,[286] its substance,[287] and the discussion of its continuing relevance.[288] Yet, with respect to the 'inside story' concerning the UCC and federalization, the opposite seems to be true. With the deaths of Professor Llewellyn and William A Schnader, the two primary actors involved with its emergence and development, this has presented difficulties in constructing an authentic record of the Code project.[289] This is especially true with respect to piecing together the origins of the Code amidst successive proposals for federal legislation. As compared to the massive discourse on European contract law, it is remarkable that to the present author's knowledge there does not yet exist any coherent study of this particular aspect of the Code. In effect, rather than leaping fully formed from the drafters' table to the states, as seen below, the UCC emerged out of demands for federal action and continued to be mired in proposals to adopt it at the federal level.

3.5.2.1 From the Uniform Sales Act to the Williston-ABA Federal Sales Act

The impetus for the UCC stemmed in large part from the need to revise the Uniform Sales Act. To recall, that Act was drafted by Professor Samuel Williston and approved by the NCCUSL in 1906 for adoption by the states.[290] By the early 1920s, with the passage of time and changes in commercial developments, it, along with the other uniform acts in the commercial law field, was considered to be outmoded and inadequate in many respects.[291] Moreover, at that time, at least half of the states had not yet enacted it.[292]

[283] See, eg, Hawkland, n 270, 235; RE Scott, 'The Rise and Fall of Article 2' (2002) 62 *La L Rev* 1009, 1031.

[284] Braucher, n 185, 798.

[285] See generally Twining, n 185, particularly chs 11–12 and citations therein.

[286] See, eg, Braucher, n 185; WA Schnader, 'A Short History of the Preparation and the Enactment of the Uniform Commercial Code' (1967) 22 *U Miami L Rev* 1.

[287] See the ALI's bibliography on the UCC available at n 202.

[288] See, eg, 'Symposium: Commercial Calamities' (2007) 68 *Ohio St LJ* 1; 'Symposium: Essays in Honor of William D. Hawkland—Unifying Commercial Law in the 20th Century: Understanding the Impulse and Assessing the Effort' (2002) 62 *La L Rev* 991; 'Symposium: Is the UCC Dead, or Alive and Well?' (1993) 26 *Loy LAL Rev* 535; 'Symposium: Is the UCC Dead, or Alive and Well? Practitioners' Perspectives' (1994) 28 *Loy LAL Rev* 89.

[289] White and Summers, n 270, 4–5.

[290] See ns 183–189 and accompanying text.

[291] See, eg, WA Schnader, 'The New Commercial Code: Modernizing Our Uniform Commercial Acts' (1950) 36 *ABAJ* 179; WA Schnader, 'The Uniform Commercial Code' (1965) 3 *The Harv Rev* 48, 56–57; see also n 329.

[292] See ABA Annual Report 560, 562 (1920); ABA Annual Report 314 (1921).

Problems regarding the achievement of uniformity in matters of commercial law stemming from these uniform acts spurred discussion of the potential federal role in this area, since as long as such acts were not adopted by all, or a substantial number of, states, this invited the prospect of their enactment by Congress in order to achieve the requisite uniformity for interstate transactions.[293]

With this background, in 1921, the ABA Commercial Law Committee submitted for the ABA's consideration a first tentative draft of proposed federal legislation to regulate the sale of goods.[294] The proposal was formally titled a 'Bill relating to sales and contracts to sell in interstate and foreign commerce', referred to as the Federal Sales Act.[295] The general purpose of the Federal Sales Act was 'to unify the law of sales and contracts to sell in commerce among the states and with foreign nations'.[296] It was drafted by Professor Samuel Williston in collaboration with this Committee and based largely on the Uniform Sales Act.[297] This explains why it was referred to as the Williston-ABA Federal Sales Act. Following further revision, a second draft of this Act was issued at the ABA's annual conference in August 1922.[298]

The Williston-ABA Federal Sales Act only covered interstate and foreign transactions involving the sale of goods.[299] The idea was that the law governing interstate and foreign transactions concerning sales and contracts of sale should not differ from that governing similar intrastate transactions regulated by the Uniform Sales Act.[300] Thus, it was not an attempt to displace the states and federalize the entire field, but rather to achieve greater interstate uniformity, which in turn was envisaged to incite the states that had not yet done so to enact the Uniform Sales Act or make the requisite changes in their version of the Uniform Sales Act to coincide with the Federal Sales Act.[301] It was regarded as falling within Congress' competence under the Interstate Commerce Clause. As the ABA Commercial Law Committee's then Chairman, Judge William HH Piatt[302], explained:

> With the federal control of foreign and interstate commerce, it is illogical and inconsistent that there should not long ago have been enacted a Federal Sales Act making the law of sales and contracts to sell in foreign and interstate commerce, a unity throughout the jurisdiction of the U.S.

[293] See McCurdy, n 198, 584–585.

[294] ABA Annual Report 310–311, 314–332 (1921). The submission of the Uniform Sales Act in Congress had been broached at the 1917 NCCUSL Annual Conference: see McCurdy, n 198, 585. However, it is not clear whether this concerned the passage of a statute in relation to DC, which at that time had not yet enacted the Act, or a truly federal enactment in relation to interstate transactions. See NCCUSL Proceedings, ABA Annual Report 689, 695 (1917).

[295] ABA Annual Report 314, 331–332 (1921). While the 'Federal Sales Act' was inscribed in the bill, this proposal garnered several informal names, such as 'the National Sales Act' (ABA Annual Report 52 (1922)), 'the Act for Unity of Sales Law', and 'a United States Sales Contract Law' (ABA Annual Report 52 (1924)).

[296] First Tentative Draft of a Bill Relating to Sales and Contracts to Sell in Interstate and Foreign Commerce § 61, ABA Annual Report 330 (1921).

[297] ABA Annual Report 314 (1921); ABA Annual Report 52, 292 (1922); ABA Annual Report 315 (1929). But see ABA Annual Report 332 (1921).

[298] ABA Annual Report 289, 292, 296–314 (1922).

[299] See ABA Annual Report 296 (1922); ABA Annual Report 314–315 (1921).

[300] ABA Annual Report 314 (1921).

[301] There was a proposal during this period to amend the US Constitution 'so as to put it within the power of Congress by a general act, to regulate the matter of Negotiable Instruments, Warehouse Receipts, Bills of Lading, and other subjects which have hitherto always been regarded as falling strictly within the domain of the legislative power of each state'. President's Address, NCCUSL Forty-Fourth Annual Conference, ABA Annual Report 717 (1921). Nothing came of it, however.

[302] Judge William HH Piatt, from Kansas City, Missouri, served as Chairman from 1922–1925. He was also a longstanding member of the NCCUSL. See Armstrong, Jr, n 112, 204.

Constitution. I am in full sympathy and accord with the idea against increasing federal power and interference with private and local matters, but sales and contracts of sale of chattels, goods, wares and merchandise touches alike every individual from the highest to the lowest within and under the jurisdiction of the [F]ederal [G]overnment and any of the states.[303]

The second draft of the Federal Sales Act was approved by the ABA for submission to Congress.[304]

A few months later, in December 1922, a bill for a Federal Sales Act was introduced in Congress.[305] It was not adopted 'by reason of the shortness of the term'.[306] It was resubmitted to Congress in 1923,[307] 1926,[308] 1928,[309] and 1930.[310] This spanned five consecutive Congressional sessions.[311] Along the way, it received favourable recommendation from commercial organizations.[312] Nevertheless, it was not passed, despite the ABA's unwavering support from 1921 to 1932.[313] Among the reasons to explain its failure were that it was passed over for more pressing matters and that its substantial length proved unwieldy for arousing Congressional interest.[314] In May 1936, a bill for the Federal Sales Act was reintroduced for the sixth time by Walter Chandler, a member of the House of Representatives from Tennessee.[315] Again, it failed. Apparently, this was because it had been introduced too late in the 74th Congressional session to be acted upon, but still, there was hope that it would eventually succeed upon its resubmission at the next session.[316] About eight months later, in January 1937, for the seventh time, the bill was introduced in the 75th Congress by Mr Chandler.[317]

303 ABA Annual Report 328 (1930).

304 ABA Annual Report 52–53, 292 (1922).

305 67th Congress, 4th Session, HR 13523, S 4213 (1922). The House bill was introduced by Ogden L Mills of New York, and the Senate bill was introduced by Thomas Sterling of South Dakota. The bill differed from the previous 1922 draft by a minor amendment: see ABA Annual Report 614 (1936).

306 ABA Annual Report 285 (1923). See also ABA Annual Report 284 (1924).

307 68th Congress, 1st Session, HR 747, S 1006 (1923). The bill was again introduced by Mr Mills in the House and Mr Sterling in the Senate: see n 305.

308 69th Congress, 1st Session, HR 8944, S 2792 (1926). The House bill was again introduced by Mr Mills, but for the Senate bill, Mr Sterling's name was crossed out and what appears to be Richard P Ernst of Kentucky put in its place.

309 70th Congress, 1st Session, HR 13413, S 3033 (1928). The House bill was introduced by George S Graham of Pennsylvania.

310 71st Congress, 2nd Session, HR 10671, S 3033 (1930). The House bill was introduced by Edgar C Ellis of Missouri and the Senate bill by Robert F Wagner of New York.

311 This included the 67th to the 71st Congresses. There was no bill submitted in the 72nd Congress. See ABA Annual Report 405 (1932). There were also no bills submitted in the 73rd and 74th Congresses; there were proposals for a bill 'to regulate sales in interstate commerce' during this period, but they concerned the levying of taxes on sales of tangible personal property, not the Federal Sales Act. See 73rd Congress, 2nd Session, HR 8231 (1934); 74th Congress, 1st Session, HR 3971, S 994 (1935).

312 ABA Annual Report 52, 305 (1924).

313 ABA Annual Report 614–615 (1936). See further ABA Annual Report 52, 284–285 (1923); ABA Annual Report 52, 279, 284–285, 304–306 (1924); ABA Annual Report 354, 362 (1925); ABA Annual Report 385, 387–388 (1926); ABA Annual Report 242, 244–245 (1927); ABA Annual Report 337, 339 (1928); ABA Annual Report 308–309, 315–316 (1929); ABA Annual Report 328 (1930); ABA Annual Report 341–342 (1931); ABA Annual Report 404–405 (1932); ABA Annual Report 159, 161–162, 603, 614–615 (1936).

314 See ABA Annual Report 52 (1924); ABA Annual Report 362 (1925); ABA Annual Report 387–388 (1926); ABA Annual Report 316 (1929); ABA Annual Report 328 (1930); ABA Annual Report 341–342 (1931); ABA Annual Report 405 (1932); ABA Annual Report 615 (1936).

315 74th Congress, 2nd Session, HR 12695 (1936). This proposal sufficed by merely scratching out the previous bill number submitted to the House in the 71st Congress (HR 10671), n 310, and adding a new bill number and Mr Chandler's name in place of Mr Ellis' name.

316 ABA Annual Report 615 (1936).

317 75th Congress, 1st Session, HR 1619 (1937).

3.5.2.2 *The Merchants' Association Federal Sales Act*

In the meantime, in 1936, the Williston-ABA Federal Sales Act was taken up for study by the Merchants' Association of New York, a leading commercial organization.[318] It appointed a Special Committee, composed of lawyers and businessmen with wide experience in interstate and foreign commercial dealings,[319] which was chaired by Hiram Thomas, a prominent member of the New York Bar.[320] In February 1937, this Committee issued a report recommending several amendments to the Williston-ABA Federal Sales Act and the Uniform Sales Act.[321] This report laid the basis for the preparation of a new Merchants' Association Federal Sales Act, which was then submitted by Mr Chandler in July 1937 to take the place of the previous Williston-ABA Federal Sales Act that had been submitted in January 1937.[322] The ABA praised the work of the Merchants' Association and supported the adoption of its new Act.[323] There were considerable differences between that Act, the ABA-Williston Federal Sales Act, and the Uniform Sales Act.[324] The primary focus seemed to be on its content and not so much on its constitutionality: Congress' competence to adopt the Merchants' Association's Act seemed to be readily assumed, or at least discussions were quiet.[325] Ultimately, the Merchants' Association Federal Sales Act died in Congressional committee, but the ABA pressed for its submission in the next session.[326]

In January 1940, the Merchants' Association Federal Sales Act was reintroduced for the second time in the 76th Congress by Representative Herron Pearson of Tennessee.[327] It was the subject of an important round-table discussion held during the AALS' Thirty-Seventh Annual Meeting in December 1939,[328] which formed the basis of a special Symposium issue in the *Virginia Law Review*.[329] The issue encompassed the contributions of several persons involved with the Federal Sales Act, including Hiram Thomas, Professor Samuel Williston, and Professor Karl Llewellyn,[330] and served as a window to certain broader themes.

First, the matter of preserving interstate versus intrastate uniformity divided the contributors. Mr Thomas argued that the Federal Sales Act would induce the states to adopt the Federal statute to govern intrastate transactions, with the result that there would be one single uniform law regarding sales and contracts to sell goods in intrastate, interstate, and foreign commerce.[331] Others, including Professor

[318] H Thomas, 'The Federal Sales Bill as Viewed by the Merchant and the Practitioner' (1940) 26 *Va L Rev* 537, 543.

[319] Thomas, n 318, 543.

[320] See Editorial Board, (1940) 26 *Va L Rev* 687.

[321] *Report of Special Committee on Federal Sales Bill of the Merchants' Association of New York* (18 Feb 1937), available in the Collection of Karl Llewellyn Papers at the Univ of Chicago Law School: Twining, n 185, 277 fn 28. See further Thomas, n 318, 544; ABA Annual Report 610–611 (1937).

[322] 75th Congress, 1st Session, HR 7824 (1937), thereby replacing 75th Congress, 1st Session, HR 1619 (1937).

[323] ABA Annual Report 599, 610–611 (1937).

[324] See further LBB, 'A Federal "Uniform Sales Act"' (1938) 24 *Va L Rev* 793; McCurdy, n 198, 588–635; Thomas, n 318, 544–557.

[325] See, eg, Rabel, n 254, 545 fn 5; Schnader, *The Harv Rev*, n 291, 57–58.

[326] See ABA Annual Report 222–223 (1938).

[327] 76th Congress, 3rd Session, HR 8176 (1940). The bill was introduced on 29 Jan 1940. On 2 Jan 1940, Mr Chandler resigned to serve as the mayor of Memphis, Tennessee, which may explain why he was not the one to introduce the bill during this session.

[328] Handbook of the Proceedings of the Thirty-Seventh Annual Meeting of the AALS 159 (1939).

[329] 'Symposium: The Proposed Federal Sales Act' (1940) 26 *Va L Rev* 537.

[330] See Contributors To March Issue (1940) 26 *Va L Rev* 687–688.

[331] Thomas, n 318, 557. See also McCurdy, n 198, 589–590; Schnader, *The Harv Rev*, n 291, 58.

Williston, countered that because of the significant departures of the Merchants' Association Federal Sales Act from the Uniform Sales Act and the slow progress of states in the uniform law process, the Act would only impair interstate and intrastate transactions further.[332]

Secondly, constitutionality was not given much attention by the participants, with Mr Thomas underlining that Congress' competence to adopt the Federal Sales Act under the Interstate Commerce Clause was 'unquestionable'.[333] Tucked away at the end of the Symposium issue, however, was a specific comment on this subject. [334] The comment concluded that the Act was a valid exercise of Congress' competence under the Interstate Commerce Clause, and emphasized that given the problems with the uniform law process, the Federal Sales Act was the only means by which to unify state laws governing commercial transactions.[335]

Finally, there was ambivalence among the participants with respect to the continued reliance on action taken at the state level. Mr Thomas stressed the need for the Federal Sales Act by pointing out that the uniform law process was plagued by conflicts between the states that had adopted the Uniform Sales Act and those that had not.[336] He also noted that the US Supreme Court's decision in *Erie*, overruling the *Swift* doctrine, perpetuated, instead of ironing out, differences in state commercial laws.[337] Notably, Professor Llewellyn's contribution presented a nuanced position. He recognized that there was a 'vital need' for a Federal Sales Act on account of the problems with the Uniform Sales Act.[338]Yet, he urged that before proceeding further, the NCCUSL should be allowed the opportunity to remodel the Uniform Sales Act.[339] He reasoned that a 'codificatory act' covering a wide expanse of private law should be treated as permanent, not merely ordinary, legislation that 'enters into the commercial structure of the country' and should therefore receive the benefit of the NCCUSL's experience.[340] Although not said as much, Llewellyn's comments hinted at the beginnings of the path towards the UCC.

3.5.2.3 From the Federal Sales Act to the UCC

Since the late 1930s, prompted by efforts of the Merchants' Association to bring forth a Federal Sales Act, Professor Llewellyn had rallied for a broader reform of sales law, and particularly during the years between 1936 and 1940, he made great efforts to bring this about.[341] He eventually joined forces with William Schnader, who as President of the NCCUSL during that time period supported action through the uniform law process.[342] In truth, the complete story regarding the progression from the Federal Sales Act to the UCC and the roles played by Professor Llewellyn and Mr Schnader in this regard may never be fully known. There was a complex series of events involving

[332] See S Williston, 'A Statement By Professor Williston' (1940) 26 *Va L Rev* 637; McCurdy, n 198, 636.

[333] Thomas, n 318, 537.

[334] MC, 'Federal Sales Act: Constitutional Comment' (1940) 26 *Va L Rev* 688.

[335] MC, n 334, 689–690, particularly 690–691 fn 20.

[336] Thomas, n 318, 539.

[337] Thomas, n 318, 539.

[338] K Llewellyn, 'The Needed Federal Sales Act' (1940) 40 *Va L Rev* 558, 558–561.

[339] Llewellyn, n 338, 562.

[340] Llewellyn, n 338, 561–562, 571.

[341] See generally ZB Wiseman, 'The Limits of Vision: Karl Llewellyn and The Merchant Rules' (1987) 100 *Harv L Rev* 465.

[342] Twining, n 185, 278. William Schnader was NCCUSL President from 1939–1942. See Armstrong, Jr, n 112, 148–149. He also served as the ALI's First Vice President from 1947–1968. See *Seventy-Fifth Anniversary*, n 204, 323. See further § 3.5.2.4.

Professor Llewellyn's lobby for passage of the Federal Sales Act in conjunction with his wider aspirations for a comprehensive overhaul of commercial law.[343] In the literature, the most common version seems to be that Professor Llewellyn obtained agreement from the Merchants' Association to put the enactment of the Federal Sales Act on hold pending action by the NCCUSL to revise the Uniform Sales Act.[344] Yet, questions persist as regards the extent to which the Federal Sales Act remained viable as the UCC got underway.[345] It is a testament to the ambiguity surrounding these events that much of the literature remains silent or else merely jumps from the proposals for a Federal Sales Act to the start of preparations for the UCC without much detail in between. It can at least be said that the delays in the enactment of the Federal Sales Act and the action taken by the NCCUSL to revise the Uniform Sales Act led to plans starting in 1940 by Professor Llewellyn and Mr Schnader for the UCC.

At the NCCUSL's annual conference in September 1940, Mr Schnader first publicly unveiled plans for the UCC in his Presidential Address, which looked back at the first 'fifty years' of the NCCUSL and outlined the future course of action.[346] He began by emphasizing the importance of the uniform law process, stating that, 'certainly in matters affecting the conduct of business on a nation-wide scale, efficient state government can be conducted only under uniform state laws'.[347] He then turned to problems associated with uniform laws in the commercial field, which prompted him to ask: 'Could not a great uniform commercial code be prepared, which would bring the commercial law up to date, and which could become the uniform law of our fifty-three jurisdictions, by the passage of only fifty-three acts, instead of many times that number?'[348] Not coincidentally, at the same conference, Professor Llewellyn presented the First Draft and Report on the Revised Uniform Sales Act, which constituted a completely reworked version of the Uniform Sales Act.[349] This prompted the NCCUSL to set up a Committee on the Revised Uniform Sales Act, with instructions to produce a second draft of the Act 'as a chapter in the projected Uniform Commercial Code'.[350]

In 1941, Professor Llewellyn disseminated the Second Draft and Report of the Revised Uniform Sales Act.[351] This document acknowledged the Federal Sales Act but focused on the NCCUSL:

> [W]hile the proposed Federal Act thus serves as an impetus, and an occasion, for reexamination of the Uniform Sales Act, and while its proposed provisions are extremely suggestive and repeatedly embody mercantile rules of first importance, yet the office of the Conference would not be

[343] See Wiseman, n 341, 477–492.

[344] See, eg, Taylor, Jr, *Hastings LJ*, n 116, 340–341; Twining, n 185, 277–280; Wiseman, n 341, 491 fn 116, 525; 'Article 2-Sales' in 1 *State of New York Report of the Law Revision Commission for 1955—Study of the Uniform Commercial Code* (Williams Press, 1955) 335, 348. This is the story that is followed by most of the primary actors in the Code project. As regards William Schnader, see, eg, 'The Case for the Uniform Commercial Code' (1960) 77 *Banking Law Journal* 633. As regards Karl Llewellyn, see, eg, Handbook of the NCCUSL 89 (1940) (quoted in Taylor, Jr, *Hastings LJ*, n 116, 340). As regards Robert Braucher, see, eg, ns 185, 193. It also is unclear to what extent Mr Schnader and the NCCUSL were in favour of the Federal Sales Act or threatened by federalization. See, eg, Scott, n 283, 1030; Twining, n 185, 278.

[345] See, eg, Braucher, n 193, 301; AR Kamp, 'Downtown Code: A History of the Uniform Commercial Code 1949–1954' (2001) 49 *Buff L Rev* 359, 376 fn 54.

[346] Schnader, n 153. [347] Schnader, n 153, 56. [348] Schnader, n 153, 58.

[349] Twining, n 185, 279–280.

[350] *Revised Uniform Sales Act—Second Draft (Text and Comments)* (1941) 4, available in the Collection of Karl Llewellyn Papers at the Univ of Chicago: Twining, n 185, 280 fn 38.

[351] *Revised Uniform Sales Act*, n 350.

performed by any mere approval of the draft before Congress. Such an [Revised Uniform Sales Act] can meet all those pressing needs which have given rise to the Federal Sales Bill.[352]

Indeed, by this time, the Federal Sales Act had been overshadowed by the UCC. In the aftermath of the 1939 AALS round-table discussion, Hiram Thomas and others continued to engage in critical study of the Federal Sales Act.[353] There was a last-ditch effort to reintroduce the Federal Sales Act in Congress in January 1941.[354] Yet, by and large, the tide had turned to the state level. Nevertheless, the fact that the Federal Sales Act was conceived at all and repeatedly submitted to Congress for adoption testified to the problems of achieving uniform commercial law at the state level via the uniform law process.[355] The prospect of federal action would continue to permeate the Code project.

3.5.2.4 The UCC takes shape: Federal and state versions

In the ensuing decade of the 1940s, plans for the UCC solidified. Following initial discussions between the NCCUSL and the ALI about co-sponsoring the sales portion of the Code, in 1941, these two organizations entered into a definitive agreement, which laid down the governing framework for the Code project.[356] Professor Llewellyn was appointed the Chief Reporter, and Ms Soia Mentschikoff was appointed the Associate Chief Reporter.[357] On this basis, Professor Llewellyn appointed various persons to serve as the drafters of the main Articles of the UCC.[358] The drafting of the Code was supervised by an Editorial Board composed of members of the NCCUSL and the ALI.[359] Between the years of 1944 and 1950, much work went into the preparation of the UCC, which culminated in the first official text in September 1951, published as the '1952 Official Text'.[360] Since the Code's subtle introduction in 1940, it had taken a little over ten years to produce the first complete version.

Notably, in what has been called the 'almost forgotten Proposed Final Draft' promulgated in 1950, the UCC had initially contained both state and federal versions.[361] This meant that the UCC was envisaged to be adopted not only at the state level via the uniform law process, but also at the federal level by way of a federal statute applicable to interstate and foreign transactions pursuant to Congress' competence under the Interstate Commerce Clause. In the draft text, the federal version was justified as follows:

Today the number of commercial transactions which pass between the states or which directly or indirectly affect interstate commerce has become so great as to warrant the Congress of the

[352] *Revised Uniform Sales Act*, n 350, 17. But again, it is difficult to discern Professor Llewellyn's position during this period because certain letters in 1942 seemed to indicate his support for Congressional action: see Kamp, n 345, 375 fn 50.

[353] See Wiseman, n 341, 488–489.

[354] 77th Congress, 1st Session, HR 2681 (1941). It was introduced by Representative Herron Pearson of Tennessee. See further ABA Annual Report 156, 232 (1941).

[355] Bittker, n 112, 103.

[356] See Twining, n 185, 280–285.

[357] See Twining, n 185, 283. For a personal account of her role, as well as others, in the Code project, see 'Symposium on Origins and Evolution: Drafters Reflect Upon the Uniform Commercial Code' (1982) 43 *Ohio St LJ* 535.

[358] See Twining, n 185, 284–285. See further UCC Text General Comment, n 185.

[359] See Report No 1 of the Permanent Editorial Board, in *Uniform Commercial Code 2013–2014 Edition*, n 185.

[360] See, eg, White and Summers, n 270, 3.

[361] Bittker, n 112, 104. See UCC § 1–105, Proposed Final Draft (Spring 1950), reprinted in ES Kelly (ed), 10 *UCC Drafts* (F.B. Rothman, 1984) 51.

United States in entering this field by enacting this Code to apply wherever the contract or transaction falls within the permissible jurisdiction of Congress under the commerce clause as that jurisdiction has been defined in the recent decisions of the Supreme Court of the United States construing the words 'affects interstate commerce'.[362]

The federal version received the approval of commentators, including those involved with the uniform law process.

In a definitive article on the federal version of the UCC, Professor Robert Braucher favoured the federal enactment of the Code, although he found the present text unsatisfactory.[363] He proposed certain changes to the text, such as clarifying the scope of federal coverage and adding provisions regarding federal contracts and federal court jurisdiction over cases arising under the federal version of the Code.[364] Still, he considered that federal enactment was 'vital' and should proceed either before or in tandem with state enactment, since this would entice the states to ensure that intrastate transactions were governed by a similar set of rules, thereby providing a catalyst to state enactment of the Code.[365] As regards the constitutionality of the federal version, he dismissed the matter in one sentence, finding that Congress' power was clear and needed no further discussion.[366]

Other commentators reiterated the importance of the federal enactment of the Code.[367] This included William Schnader, who found that coverage of both interstate and intrastate transactions by virtue of the federal and state versions of the UCC 'would constitute one of the greatest achievements in the history of American law'.[368] Federal encroachment on matters of state competence was confronted head-on in one publication, which still has resonance for the American and European settings:

Perhaps a bone should be thrown to those who may bark 'states' rights' at the fearful prospect of a federal commercial code. Without intending to dignify with a reply those whose use of the 'states' rights' slogan is a technique for covertly opposing governmental activity at any level, it might be said to those more earnestly concerned over a federal commercial law that their fears are too late. The United States is in fact a single market; it is the model which we are holding up to Western Europe, rent not only by diversity of laws but political and economic barriers as well. The national market has been with us for over half a century; federal enactment of the Uniform Commercial code is aimed at closing the gap between this fact and the backwardness of 48 or so separate legal marketplaces in which to shop for different laws.[369]

In the end, however, the federal version was dropped in the Spring 1951 draft of the Code with no explanation.[370] Difficulties in getting such a comprehensive act through Congress and enthusiastic endorsement of the Code by the states were cited as possible reasons.[371] From then on, the UCC was confined to the state

[362] Bittker, n 112, 104–105 (quoting UCC Proposed Final Draft (May 1949) 14).

[363] Braucher, n 141, 100. Professor Robert Braucher, then at Harvard Law School, served as a NCCUSL commissioner from 1955–1970 and Vice President from 1967–1970. See Armstrong, Jr, n 112, 152, 199. See also n 213.

[364] Braucher, n 141, 104–113.

[365] Braucher, n 141, 104, 113. Compare S Williston, 'The Law of Sales in the Proposed Uniform Commercial Code' (1950) 63 *Harv L Rev* 561, 562–563.

[366] Braucher, n 141, 102. But see 108.

[367] See, eg, WT Dean, Jr, 'Conflict of Laws under the Uniform Commercial Code: The Case for Federal Enactment' (1953) 6 *Vand L Rev* 479; FE Horack, Jr, 'The Future of Uniform Laws—The Commercial Code' (1948) 9 *Ohio St LJ* 555, 563.

[368] Schnader, *ABAJ*, n 291, 254.

[369] Dean, Jr, n 367, 485.

[370] See Bittker, n 112, 106.

[371] HA Hintze, 'Disparate Judicial Construction of the Uniform Commercial Code—The Need for Federal Legislation' (1969) 1969 *Utah L Rev* 722, 724. Compare Kamp, n 345, 376.

arena, and by the early 1960s, prospects for federal enactment were remote.[372] Even so, this matter would arise again and constitute a major tension underlying the Code project.

3.5.3 Tensions underlying the UCC

Although the UCC has generated a voluminous literature, much of which includes critical analysis of the Code project and its various Articles, three tensions underlying the UCC are singled out here because they touch upon salient issues within the debate about European contract law.

3.5.3.1 The UCC and interstate/intrastate uniformity

As the UCC was adopted at the state, not federal, level along the lines of the uniform law process, this invited problems related to the reliance on state legislatures and variation in the state versions of the Code, which exacerbated the struggle between achieving interstate and intrastate uniformity in commercial transactions. First, as with uniform laws, the UCC was at the mercy of each individual state jurisdiction for enactment. At present, with the adoption of all (or most) of the UCC by the states, this may seem a moot point. In the beginning, however, the adoption of the UCC was not a foregone conclusion. After passage of the Code by the first state, Pennsylvania, in 1953,[373] authorities in New York put a halt to the process by referring the matter to the New York Law Revision Commission for recommendations as to whether the UCC should be adopted in that state.[374] After three years of intensive study, the Commission decided that the Code should not be enacted in New York until further revision had taken place.[375] This led to amendment of the Code and the publication of subsequent official texts, which resulted in the adoption of the UCC by all states, save for Louisiana, by the end of the 1960s.[376] For its part, New York adopted the UCC in 1962, six years after the Commission's decision.[377] The New York events surely did

[372] Braucher, n 193, 301. See also Bittker, n 112, 105–106, particularly 105 fn 69.

[373] As Pennsylvania was William Schnader's home state, many credited him with playing a role in its being the first to adopt the Code and with no variations from the official text. See WA Schnader, 'The Uniform Commercial Code—Today and Tomorrow' (1966) 22 *Bus Law* 229 (Editor's Note). Even so, it already had an exemplary record with the adoption of uniform laws: WA Schnader, 'The New Movement Towards Uniformity in Commercial Law—The Uniform Commercial Code Marches On' (1958) 13 *Bus Law* 646, 649.

[374] 'Report of the Law Revision Commission for 1954' in 1 *State of New York Report of the Law Revision Commission for 1954 and Record of Hearings on the Uniform Commercial Code* (Williams Press, 1954) 7.

[375] 'Report of the Law Revision Commission to the Legislature Relating to the Uniform Commercial Code' in *State of New York Report of the Law Revision Commission for 1956—Report Relating to the Uniform Commercial Code* (Williams Press, 1956) 11, 68. That said, the Commission supported a uniform code of commercial law. Report of the Law Revision Commission, 67–68. In this context, Professors Edwin W Patterson and Rudolf B Schlesinger (one of the 'fathers' of the Common Core project: see Chapter 4, § 4.2) prepared a detailed study on the codification of commercial law, including a comparative view of the UCC, which reads to a large extent like much of the literature on European contract and private law decades later. See 'Problems of Codification of Commercial Law' in 1 *State of New York Report of the Law Revision Commission for 1955—Study of the Uniform Commercial Code* (Williams Press, 1955) 31.

[376] See WA Schnader, 'The Permanent Editorial Board For The Uniform Commercial Code: Can It Accomplish Its Object?' (1965) 3 *ABLJ* 137.

[377] Schnader, n 286, 9.

not prevent the long-term success of the Code. Still, the UCC took several decades to achieve general acceptance in the states.

Moreover, one of the aspirations of the Code was that the states would adopt the official text of the UCC as promulgated by the NCCUSL and the ALI, but in practice, state-by-state variation in the form of non-uniform legislative amendments and divergent judicial interpretations crept into the Code from the beginning. By the early 1960s, of the eighteen states that had already adopted the UCC, most had inserted non-uniform amendments into their version of the Code, leading to the creation of the Permanent Editorial Board (PEB), which was responsible for reviewing all proposed non-uniform amendments and making the necessary revisions to the Code.[378] Still, state variation continued as additional states adopted the Code, which led to a patchwork of state versions depending upon the extent to which each state took up the official amendments to the various Articles.[379] The state variations to the Code and the preference for intrastate uniformity within the individual state constituted a significant barrier to achieving interstate uniformity in commercial matters covered by the UCC, and the prospect of adopting the Code at the federal level was raised again.

3.5.3.2 The UCC and federalization

The advocacy of a federal UCC became prevalent in the early years of the Code project in response to the proliferation of state variations of the Code. To a large extent, this took the form of repeated threats issued by William Schnader to goad the states into line with the official version of the Code. To recall, Mr Schnader was a prominent figure in the Code project[380] and at the time was also serving as the PEB Chairman, which made his statements of great import. The rising volume of non-state uniform amendments—'statutory tinkerers', as he called them[381]—and the slow progress in adoption of the official amendments to the Code prompted him to threaten Congressional adoption of the UCC if the states did not repeal their non-uniform amendments.[382] He found that Congress' competence under the Interstate Commerce Clause easily stretched over interstate transactions, but that a Constitutional amendment would be needed to allow such a federal code to cover intrastate transactions; yet, he considered that if the state laws were not made uniform, it was 'not unlikely' that a movement would be initiated for amending the Constitution in this regard.[383] He also reasoned that no state could afford not to conform its state version to the federal Code.[384] While his threats were well-known, he was not alone in advocating federal action.

Agitation for the adoption of a federal commercial code covering interstate and intrastate commercial transactions began even before the ink was dry on the first official text of the Code. In 1947, a Comment was published in the *Michigan Law Review* devoted to the constitutionality of the federal UCC.[385] It concluded that Congress had

[378] Reports Nos 1 and 2 of the PEB (annexed to *Uniform Commercial Code 2013-2014 Edition*, n 185) attest to the frustration concerning the state non-uniform amendments of the Code.

[379] See n 272 and accompanying text.

[380] See n 342.

[381] Schnader, n 116, 119.

[382] See, eg, Schnader, n 286, 12; Schnader, n 376, 143; Schnader, *The Harv Rev*, n 291, 62. In at least one publication, he set a specific deadline: see Schnader, *Bus Law*, n 373, 232.

[383] Schnader, n 116, 117.

[384] Schnader, *Bus Law*, n 373, 232. See also Schnader, n 376, 143. There were some publications in which it was not clear which scope of application was intended: see Schnader, n 286, 12; Schnader, *The Harv Rev*, n 291, 62.

[385] MN Johnson, 'Comment: Constitutional Law—A Federal Commercial Code—Some Possibilities Under the Constitution' (1947) 45 *Mich L Rev* 1021.

competence to enact a federal commercial code under either the federal treaty-making power[386] or the Interstate Commerce Clause.[387] After the promulgation of the Code, discussion continued. In particular, in Judge Friendly's article on the 'new' American 'federal common law' mentioned earlier, the problems associated with the uniform law process led him to advocate federal enactment of the UCC.[388] Its constitutionality was not a serious problem since 'Congress would simply be enacting a code on a technical subject, approved, after years of discussion, by representatives of the states and of the bar generally, and already adopted by many states'.[389]

As the Code project progressed, the prospect of federal enactment arose in the literature, much of which stemmed from the continuing lack of uniformity.[390] Many publications expressly highlighted Congress' competence over both interstate and intrastate transactions in this context.[391] Yet, there was also a steady stream of publications from scholars opposing federalization, stressing that the uniform law process was preferable to federal action on various grounds.[392] Others took a moderate position, finding that federal incursions into specific areas were necessary, but not across the board.[393]

Admittedly, recent references to the enactment of a federal UCC are sporadic at best. As of 2001, it was remarked that 'the idea of a federal code for commercial law has never quite gone away'.[394] Still, by most present accounts, the prospect of federalization seems to have faded from view without triggering a groundswell for federal action even remotely resembling the debate about European contract law.[395] Mr Schnader's threats went unheeded, and the UCC has remained entrenched at the state level. That said, the interplay between the UCC and federalization shows that the prospect of a federal UCC is a much more persistent theme than is commonly perceived. Furthermore, in constitutional terms, it highlights that it has not been so much the existence of federal competence that has been the stumbling block, but rather the exercise of such

[386] US Constitution, Art II, § 2, cl 2. See further G De Baere and K Gutman, 'Federalism and International Relations in the European Union and the United States: A Comparative Outlook' in E Cloots et al (eds), *Federalism in the European Union* (Hart, 2012) 131, 153–155 and citations therein.

[387] Johnson, n 385, 1023–1032.

[388] Friendly, n 31, 419–421. He did not outright refer to intrastate applicability, but it was assumed in the phrasing. At least this was how it was interpreted by other scholars. See, eg, Bittker, n 112, 107 fn 75.

[389] Friendly, n 31, 420.

[390] See, eg, Hintze, n 371; L Liebman, 'The ALI and the UCC' (2001) 52 *Hastings LJ* 645, 650; CW Mooney, Jr, 'Introduction to the Uniform Commercial Code Annual Survey: Some Observations on the Past, Present, and Future of the U.C.C.' (1986) 41 *Bus Law* 1343; WJ Woodward, Jr, 'Private Legislation in the United States—How the Uniform Commercial Code Becomes Law' (1999) 72 *Temple L Rev* 451.

[391] See, eg, Hintze, n 371, 744–742; Taylor, Jr, *Hastings LJ*, n 116, 362–363; compare Taylor, Jr, *Rutgers-Cam LJ*, n116, 549–550.

[392] See, eg, Bugge, n 129; NB Cohen and BL Zaretsky, 'Drafting Commercial Law for the New Millennium: Will the Current Process Suffice?' (1993) 26 *Loy LAL Rev* 551; FR Kennedy, 'Federalism and the Uniform Commercial Code' (1974) 29 *Bus Law* 1225; FH Miller, 'The Uniform Commercial Code: Will the Experiment Continue?' (1992) 43 *Mercer L Rev* 799; and more recently, WH Henning, 'Amended Article 2: What Went Wrong?' (2009) 11 *Duquesne BLJ* 131, 141.

[393] See, eg, RK Rasmussen, 'The Uneasy Case Against The Uniform Commercial Code' (2002) 62 *La L Rev* 1097. Some scholars have concentrated on certain Code Articles. See, eg, J Camero, 'Level Up: Employing the Commerce Clause to Federalize the Sale of Goods' (2013) 50 *San Diego L Rev* 89; DB Goldstein, 'Federal Versus State Adoption of Article 4A' (1990) 45 *Bus Law* 1513.

[394] D Litowitz, *Perspectives on the Uniform Commercial Code* (Carolina Academic Press, 2001) 91.

[395] See, eg, FS Knippenberg and WJ Woodward, Jr, 'Uniformity and Efficiency in the Uniform Commercial Code: A Partial Research Agenda' (1990) 45 *Bus Law* 2519, 2520–2521; JB McDonnell, 'The Code Project Confronts Fundamental Dilemmas' (1993) 26 *Loy LAL Rev* 683, 686; Rosett, n 253, 694.

competence. Congress' competence to federalize state contract and commercial law is accepted by many jurists as falling within the US Constitution, mainly under the Interstate Commerce Clause.[396] Nevertheless, there is a longstanding pattern of Congressional deference to the states in matters of private law.[397] This means that while in principle Congress is perceived as having sufficient powers to unify various areas of state private law, such as contract law, in practice it generally uses such powers on a more limited basis to deal with specific matters that are considered to warrant federal action. This is particularly apparent in the area of consumer (contract) law, which leads to the next section.

3.5.3.3 The UCC and consumer protection

It is certainly no understatement to say that the relationship between the UCC and consumer protection has been a core tension from the beginning. The debate over the inclusion of certain provisions regulating consumer transactions in the original text of the Code has been called 'one of the most violent in the history of the Code's drafting'.[398] In later years, with the revision of several Articles, controversies over the matter of consumer protection in the Code split the NCCUSL and the ALI,[399] caused resignations of draftsmen and divisiveness among participants, and spurred a vast quantity of literature critically examining the politics and drafting process of the Code project generally.[400] To be clear, the UCC in principle covers consumer and commercial transactions, with some exceptions.[401] From the outset, it was generally perceived that consumer transactions were already too much a part of commercial law to be excluded completely from the Code or to be treated the same as commercial transactions in all instances.[402] The controversy surrounding the treatment of consumer issues in the Code centred on the extent to which special rules would be

[396] See, eg, Halberstam and Reimann, n 2, 46; Heimanson, n 102, 165; Kennedy, n 392, 1229; White, n 103, 2100–2101. This is so notwithstanding certain recent Supreme Court jurisprudence on the Interstate Commerce Clause: see, eg, J Braucher, 'Under the Surrounding Circumstances: Amended Article 2's Redundant (or Worse) Electronic Commerce Provisions' (2007) 68 *Ohio St LJ* 115, 117 fn 10; Camero, n 393, 114–124. See further Chapter 8, § 8.3.4.

[397] See, eg, Hyland, n 208, 77; Overby, n 113, 312; Taylor, Jr, *Rutgers-Cam LJ*, n 116, 527.

[398] Gilmore, n 184, 293.

[399] See, eg, Scott, n 283, 1049–1053; RE Spiedel, 'Revising UCC Article 2: A View from the Trenches' (2001) 52 *Hastings LJ* 607.

[400] One of the most well-known publications in this latter regard is A Schwartz and RE Scott, 'The Political Economy of Private Legislatures' (1995) 143 *U Pa L Rev* 595 (whose tenets have expanded beyond the American setting: see CP Gillette and RE Scott, 'The Political Economy of International Sales Law' (2005) 25 *Intl Rev L & Econ* 446). See also K Patchel, 'Interest Group Politics, Federalism, and the Uniform Laws Process: Some Lessons from the Uniform Commercial Code' (1993) 78 *Minn L Rev* 83; Hyland, n 208. Much of the literature on the Code process is intermingled with critical analysis of the revision of particular Articles. See, eg, Symposium, 'Essays in Honor of William D. Hawkland—Unifying Commercial Law in the 20th Century: Understanding the Impulse and Assessing the Effort' (2002) 62 *La L Rev* 991; 'Symposium on the Revision of Article 9 of the Uniform Commercial Code' (1994) 80 *Va L Rev* 1783; 'Symposium: Perspectives on the Uniform Law Revision Process' (2001) 52 *Hastings LJ* 603. On the relationship between the UCC and consumer protection specifically, see, eg, 'Symposium: Consumer Protection and the Uniform Commercial Code' (1997) 75 *Wash ULQ* iii; 'Symposium: Revised U.C.C. Articles 3 and 4 and New Article 4' (1991) 42 *Ala L Rev* 351; J Braucher, 'Deadlock: Consumer Transactions Under Revised Article 9' (1999) 73 *Am Bankr LJ* 83; ME Budnitz, 'The Revision of U.C.C. Articles 3 and Four: A Process Which Excluded Consumer Protection Requires Federal Action' (1992) 43 *Mercer L Rev* 827.

[401] K Patchel, 'Consumer Transactions and the Code: Some Considerations' (1996) 51 *Bus Law* 1343, 1348–1357.

[402] Patchel, n 401, 1357.

carved out for consumers with respect to certain issues and how far they would go in ensuring sufficient protection.[403]

In the initial drafting of the UCC, an attempt was made to include specific consumer protection provisions, but such provisions were largely eliminated from the final text.[404] In all fairness, emphasis on consumer protection was not in the original drafters' frame of mind, since the US consumer movement started in the 1960s, the decade following the dissemination of the original text of the Code.[405] Thereafter, changes to the UCC brought attention to the appropriate level of protection afforded to consumers. In particular, starting in the 1980s and 1990s, with significant revisions to core Articles, such as Articles 2, 3, 4, and 9, along with the insertion of Articles 2A and 4A, criticism erupted as regards the treatment of consumer matters in the Code, whereby it was often lamented that certain Articles favoured commercial, as opposed to consumer, interests.[406] This is not to say that the UCC has remained transfixed in the 1950s. At present, many Articles include affirmative provisions on consumer matters.[407] Nonetheless, the UCC's limited treatment of consumer issues early on injected the Federal Government into the process.

In the 1960s, Congress began to enact consumer protection legislation that modified or supplemented the rules set out in the UCC. Congress' first major foray was in the area of consumer credit. In 1968, Congress adopted the Consumer Credit Protection Act (CCPA),[408] an umbrella statute encompassing a number of specific federal acts regulating various matters related to consumer credit, such as credit reporting, debt collection, and electronic fund transfers. In the years leading to its passage, there was significant divergence and complexity among state laws regulating consumer credit, since matters were usually scattered across a host of different statutes.[409] With the CCPA, Congress stepped in with the objective to lay down a uniform set of rules in the consumer credit field that would provide a baseline of consumer protection and remedy the substantial divergence among the states in the areas concerned. There are three notable features about the CCPA: its constitutionality, scope, and interplay with the NCCUSL's Uniform Consumer Credit Code.

First, Congress' rationale varied depending upon the particular federal statute, but several titles of the CCPA are rooted in the twofold objective to eliminate divergences among state laws for the purposes of interstate commerce and to ensure an adequate level of consumer protection. For example, as regards the regulation of debt collection practices, existing state laws were deemed insufficient to protect consumers against such practices and even those purely intrastate in nature directly affected interstate commerce.[410] As a result, the CCPA provoked debate as to whether its extension into 'local' matters of state competence went beyond Congress' competence under the US Constitution.[411] Yet, so far, no part of the CCPA has been declared unconstitutional,

[403] Patchel, n 401, 1357. [404] See Kamp, n 345, 368–369.

[405] See, eg, C Edwards, 'Article 2 of the Uniform Commercial Code and Consumer Protection: The Refusal To Experiment' (2004) 78 *St John's L Rev* 663.

[406] See citations regarding the relationship between the UCC and consumer protection in n 400.

[407] For extensive discussion, see, eg, FH Miller and JD Lackey, *The ABCs of the UCC: Related and Supplementary Consumer Law*, 2nd edn (ABA, 2004).

[408] Pub L 90–321, 82 Stat 146 (1968), codified, as amended, at 15 USC § 1601 et seq and 18 USC § 891 et seq.

[409] See C Felsenfeld, 'Uniform, Uniformed and Unitary Laws Regulating Consumer Credit' (1968) 37 *Fordham L Rev* 209, 212–220. [410] 15 USC § 1692.

[411] See, eg, C Felsenfeld, 'Competing State and Federal Roles in Consumer Credit Law' (1950) 45 *NYUL Rev* 487.

even though provisions on extortionate credit transactions were challenged, the argument being that 'loan sharking' was a purely intrastate activity that did not affect interstate commerce.[412] This resulted in the US Supreme Court's judgment in *Perez v United States*,[413] which upheld the relevant portions of the Act under the Interstate Commerce Clause.[414]

Secondly, the CCPA does not replace state law entirely. Many federal statutes housed within the CCPA include provisions making clear that state laws would be displaced only to the extent that they are inconsistent with their provisions, and for several, it is further provided that a state law would not be deemed inconsistent if it sets forth a level of protection greater than that afforded by the federal statute concerned.[415] In other words, the CCPA allows for minimum harmonization. Some federal statutes also exempt credit transactions under the law of a state that imposes requirements that are 'substantially similar' to their provisions.[416] This was deliberate, as the CCPA was intended to dovetail with the Uniform Consumer Credit Code.

Thirdly, the CCPA and the Uniform Consumer Credit Code (UCCC) were adopted within months of each other in 1968.[417] The UCCC was a comprehensive uniform act promulgated by the NCCUSL, which was designed to regulate virtually all aspects of consumer credit, as opposed to the federal CCPA, which was narrower in scope.[418] The UCCC was prepared with the CCPA in mind,[419] since states enacting the UCCC would essentially be given an 'opt out' from the CCPA. Given its comprehensive nature, the UCCC was considered to remove the threat of further federal action in the consumer credit field.[420] In the end, however, it did not succeed. Although it was enacted in a few states and had some influence in others, the UCCC was generally considered a failure and eventually turned into a model law.[421] Thus, the federal overlap on the patchwork of numerous state statutes in the consumer credit field remained. This prompted calls for a comprehensive federal code to address the complexity and lack of uniformity in this area.[422]

Thereafter, Congress proceeded to other areas within the consumer sphere, sometimes directly touching upon aspects covered by the UCC.[423] For example, in 1975,

412 See 18 USC § 891. 413 402 US 146 (1971). 414 *Perez*, 402 US at 157.

415 See, eg, 15 USC § 1666 (credit billing); 15 USC § 1667e (consumer leases); 15 USC § 1692n (debt collection). But for recent developments in this regard, see, eg, RT Wutscher and DL Beam, 'The Dodd-Frank Act's New Federalism' (2011) 66 *Bus Law* 519, 528.

416 See, eg, 15 USC § 1667c (consumer leases); 15 USC § 1675 (garnishment); 15 USC § 1692o (debt collection).

417 The CCPA was passed on 29 May 1968, and the UCCC was approved by the NCCUSL on 30 July 1968. See *Uniform Consumer Credit Code Official Text (With Comments)* (West, 1969). It was amended thereafter: see FH Miller and WD Warren, '1974 Uniform Consumer Credit Code' (1975) 23 *U Kan L Rev* 619.

418 See GR Richter, Jr, 'The Uniform Consumer Credit Code of the National Conference of Commissioners on Uniform State Laws' (1968) 24 *Bus Law* 183. For general discussion, see 'Symposium on the Uniform Consumer Credit Code' (1968) 24 *Bus Law* 183.

419 Felsenfeld, n 411, 503–504. 420 Felsenfeld, n 411, 502.

421 For reasons to explain its lack of success: see, eg, Miller and Lackey, n 407, 83–84; William D Warren, 'Consumer Credit Law: Rates, Costs, and Benefits' (1975) 27 *Stan L Rev* 951, 964–967.

422 See, eg, TD Crandall, 'It is Time for a Comprehensive Federal Consumer Credit Code' (1979) 58 *NCL Rev* 1. Compare, eg, D D'Onfro, 'A New Uniform Code of Consumer Credit' (2011) 5 *Harv L & Pol'y Rev* 44.

423 Among recent developments at the federal level, the Dodd-Frank Wall Street Reform and Consumer Protection Act, enacted in 2010, introduced monumental reforms to the consumer financial protection regime. For an overview, see, eg, K Gutman, 'The Development of Consumer Law in the US: Comparisons with the EU Experience' (2012) 1 *EUVR* 212 and citations therein.

Congress passed the Magnuson-Moss Warranty Act (MMWA).[424] The MMWA establishes certain minimum standards for written warranties on consumer products.[425] It sought to fill the gap in the UCC in terms of providing special rules regarding consumer warranties that had not been needed in the case of purely commercial dealings.[426] Yet, in doing so, it diverges from the UCC in certain respects.[427] Furthermore, federal action is not limited to legislation adopted by Congress. For example, the Federal Trade Commission (FTC) has issued many regulations in the consumer (contract) law field,[428] such as the 'Door to Door Sales Rule',[429] which provides buyers with a three-day cooling-off period for sales of consumer goods in the 'doorstep selling' setting,[430] but does not displace state laws giving the buyer 'substantially the same or greater' rights than that afforded by the FTC Rule.[431]

On the whole, there are various instances in which federal law has displaced portions of the state law, both within and outside the Code, in the field of consumer protection. This has produced a complex array of federal and state law sources in the consumer sphere, which certain scholars have termed 'Swiss cheese' because federal law may partially, but not totally, pre-empt some parts of state law and leave other parts of the same law intact.[432] Basically, the treatment of consumer protection, or the neglect thereof, in the UCC led to a complex overlay of federal consumer law atop the UCC and other state law sources, which as illustrated by the examples above concerning consumer credit, consumer warranties, and 'doorstep selling' immediately calls to mind some of the problems arising in the debate about European contract law.

3.6 Conclusions

Three important observations emerge from the foregoing discussion. The first is that the prospect of federalization is a long-standing fixture of the American contract law framework. As demonstrated by the *Swift* opinion in 1842 and the proposals for a Federal Bills of Exchange Act and a Federal Sales Act, which gave birth to the NCCUSL and the UCC, respectively, one cannot take at face value the fact that contract law has always been considered to be purely a state matter in the US. In fact, given the recurring proposals for a Federal Sales Act spanning two decades and the repeated proposals for a federal UCC, it is remarkable just how close the US came to a federal enactment approximating state contract and commercial law. Consequently, the extent to which the American literature on various mechanisms to achieve uniformity in contract law—whether it is the discussion of the Federal Sales Act, the debate about the need for a UCC, let alone a federal UCC, or the interplay between the UCC and federal consumer protection legislation—echoes the literature on European contract law is astounding.

One may ask whether retracing the path of attempts to federalize portions of contract and commercial law in the US has much importance for the debate about European contract law at a time in which it is generally considered that the days of far-reaching federalization in the American setting have long passed. In response, as seen above, the

[424] Magnuson-Moss Warranty-Federal Trade Commission Improvement Act (MMWA), Pub L 93–637, 88 Stat 2183 (1975), codified, as amended, at 15 USC § 2301 et seq.

[425] 15 USC § 2304.

[426] Miller and Lackey, n 407, 51–52.

[427] Miller and Lackey, n 407, 52.

[428] See the FTC's website, <http://www.ftc.gov/>.

[429] 16 CFR § 429.

[430] 16 CFR § 429.1.

[431] 16 CFR § 429.2.

[432] Miller and Lackey, n 407, 133.

matter of federal competence, whether real or perceived, had an impact on the path of American contract law (as well as other fields of private law). It dictated the choices early on, and it stimulated the creation of the mechanisms that exist today in the American contract law framework. This was so, even though ultimately many of the mechanisms resorted to—uniform laws, Restatements, and the UCC—emerged outside the federal framework and hence were not adopted pursuant to federal competence under the US Constitution. As such, comparative reflection with the US highlights the important role, albeit an indirect one, played by constitutionality and shows that superficial arguments based on the lack of federal engagement with contract law in the US for the purposes of opposing Union competence in contract law in the debate about European contract law do not hold.

The second observation concerns the difficulties and tensions underlying the four strands of the American contract law framework. Each has generated its fair share of controversy, especially as regards its role in bringing greater uniformity and coherency to areas of American private law, including contract law. The failure of *Swift* and the injection of American 'federal common law' in federal contracts, the effectiveness of uniform laws in the face of state variation, the struggle between normative and descriptive aspirations of the Restatements, and the interplay between the UCC and consumer protection, to name just a few examples, illustrate that these strands have not been a complete panacea for eliminating complexity and divergence in American contract law. Accordingly, this analysis cautions against blindly transplanting models from the US into the debate about European contract law without cognizance of their distinctive place and problems in the American setting.

The third observation concerns the linkage between these strands. Uniform laws, Restatements, and the UCC share an important attribute: they constitute unique mechanisms for the approximation of contract law and other fields of private law, which are rooted for the most part in action taken at the state level. Framed another way, they are *sui generis* fixtures of the American contract law framework that, despite being situated outside the formal confines of the federal institutional framework, do much to sustain the balance of power between the federal and state levels. In fact, each strand, including American 'federal common law', has played an important role in adjusting, maintaining, or restoring the equilibrium in this process.

This illuminates certain parallels between the US and the EU in contract law. Both entities continue to grapple with similar matters regarding the tensions between intrastate and interstate uniformity, the interplay between contract law and consumer protection, and how much competence has been given and should be exercised at the federal or Union level to make the system work. Yet, it is striking that the approach to matters of contract law in the European and American settings emerged from different starting points. In the American contract law framework, the *Swift* doctrine, uniform laws, and the UCC were aimed at eliminating divergences among state laws concerning commercial transactions, whereas the debate about European contract law has proceeded largely from the opposite direction, that is to say, from Union measures concerning consumer transactions. As a result, the burden placed on the EU is somewhat heavier in this regard. In the US, for example, the UCC came at a time in which consumer protection had not yet achieved widespread attention and discussion of the economic, social, and political choices and values affecting the substance of the UCC had not yet arisen. It was only in later decades after the Code was up and running that the focus became directed at these issues and the scholarship concerning the balancing of consumer and commercial interests in the Code erupted. In the EU, the debate about European contract law must take into account an array of issues that remained on the sidelines in the American setting for some time, and matters relating to the interplay between commercial transactions and consumer protection and the political and social values underlying the formulation of contract law rules lie at the heart of much of this debate.

Above all, what has been achieved up until now in the American contract law framework has not been absolute uniformity. It is commonly remarked that the US contends with an incredible amount of diversity in matters of private law.[433] Without entering into the discussion about the role played by certain compensatory factors in the American setting, such as those relating to a common language and a common legal culture that may differ from that existing in the EU, the foregoing analysis demonstrates that the four strands of the American contract law framework manifest difficulties in reconciling interstate and intrastate uniformity. Among other things, this is because these strands form part of the 'compromise' or 'bargain' underlying the American federal system that places primary responsibility for matters of private law, including contract law, at the state, not federal, level. The extent to which such a 'compromise' can be made in the EU remains to be explored in the forthcoming chapters.

[433] See, eg, H Kötz, 'Contract Law in Europe and the United States: Legal Unification in the Civil Law and Common Law' (2012) 27 *Tul Eur & Civ LF* 1, 3, 12; Reimann, n 2.

PART TWO

DEBATE

4

The Debate Begins

4.1 Introduction

Technically speaking, one could say that the debate about the approximation of private law in Europe[1] began even before the founding of the European Communities in the 1950s.[2] As early as 1949, an English scholar advocated the adoption of a uniform code of commercial law for a nascent European Community.[3] In 1955, the conception of a 'European civil law' was cited in a publication advocating unification primarily in the commercial fields of private law, at least as a first stage.[4] As the course of European integration progressed, additional scholars contemplated the approximation of private law—including a 'European civil code'[5]—among the Member States.[6] As a formal matter, however, the impetus for the debate about European contract law (and European private law generally) as understood in the discourse today is usually traced back to three interlocking elements beginning in the 1980s: the work of several academic projects, certain early European Parliament resolutions, and the European Council meeting in Tampere. These three elements combined to place the matter of European contract law on the EU's political agenda and paved the way to the promulgation of the Commission's three landmark Communications on European contract law.[7] Admittedly, scholars may bicker as to the impact of some of these elements,

[1] This leaves aside the various regional initiatives for private law unification, eg, the proposed 1929 Franco-Italian Code of Obligations, which was never adopted. See M Rotondi, 'The Proposed Franco-Italian Code of Obligations' (1954) 3 *AJCL* 345. There was also a draft code of obligations prepared by the *Association Henri Capitant* in 1953, which was alluded to in the press release for the conference convened by the French Council Presidency in Oct 2008 titled 'Which European Contract Law for the European Union?', 23–24 Oct 2008 (on file with author).

[2] To recall, the European Coal and Steel Community (ECSC) Treaty was signed in 1951 and entered into force in 1952; it expired on 23 July 2002. The European Economic Community (EEC), later European Community (EC), and European Atomic Energy Community (EAEC) Treaties were signed in 1957 and entered into force in 1958. With the entry into force of the Lisbon Treaty, the former EC and EU were replaced by a new EU, but the EAEC exists as a separate legal entity based on an amended EAEC Treaty (consolidated version, [2012] OJ C327/1). See generally K Lenaerts and P Van Nuffel (N Cambien and R Bray (eds)), *European Union Law*, 3rd edn (Sweet & Maxwell, 2011), chs 1, 4.

[3] FH Lawson, 'Private Law Aspects of Western Union' (1949) 2 *CLP* 226, 236–237.

[4] HK Elbir, 'L'idée d'un droit civil européen' (1955) 6 *Annales de la Faculté de Droit de l'Université de Bordeaux* 71, 84–86.

[5] AG Chloros, 'Principle, Reason and Policy in the Development of European Law' (1968) 17 *ICLQ* 849, 875. This author was a Judge of the Court of Justice from 1981 until his death in 1982.

[6] See, eg, R David, 'The International Unification of Private Law' in R David (chief ed), II *International Encyclopedia of Comparative Law* (Mohr/Mouton/Oceana, 1971) § 180; JG Polach, 'Harmonization of Laws in Western Europe' (1959) 8 *AJCL* 148; G van Hecke, 'Integration economique et unification de droit privé' (1962) 9 *NTIR* 198; E von Caemmerer, 'The Problem of the Unification of Private Law in Europe' (1964) 36 *U Colo L Rev* 307. Incidentally, in Case 12/76 *Tessili* [1976] ECR 1473, para 14, the Court of Justice took note of differences between national contract laws and the absence at that stage of legal development of any unification among the Member States.

[7] In particular, this is the way the Commission's Communications have been presented by Commission officials involved with the European contract law project. See, eg, D Staudenmayer, 'The Commission Communication on European Contract Law and the Future Prospects' (2002) 51

and they may not have been the only stimulus for the debate about European contract law at the European level. Nevertheless, they are repeatedly cited in institutional documents and scholarly literature as crucial features in the lineage of the debate about European contract law.

Importantly, each element in its own way served to drive the momentum of the debate forward at the European level and had a decisive impact on the constitutional dimensions of European contract law. The work of certain academic projects not only provided a fertile ground for Union developments in contract law and other fields, but also filtered into the activities of the Union institutions, including those examining the Union's competence in this setting. The European Parliament's early resolutions advocated the need for far-reaching approximation of private law, with particular emphasis on contract law, and in doing so, made an important, albeit largely unseen, contribution to situating such endeavours within the Union's internal market competences under the Treaties. The European Council's meeting in Tampere ingrained the linkage between European contract law and the Area of Freedom, Security, and Justice, thereby injecting implicit references to the Union's competence concerning judicial cooperation in civil matters under what is now Article 81 TFEU. The aim of this chapter is therefore to examine the beginnings of the debate about European contract law emanating from these three elements, with primary focus placed on exploring their impact on the constitutional assessment of European contract law. Each of these elements is analysed in the respective sections that follow.

4.2 Academic Projects

Generally speaking, there are a large number of academic projects involved with European contract law and other fields of European private law, which encapsulate a diverse range of objectives. Such objectives include the promulgation of Principles of European Contract Law (PECL) by the Commission on European Contract Law or a European contract code by the Academy of European Private Lawyers (*Académie des privatistes européens*),[8] both of which are aimed at the further approximation of national contract law at the European level. By comparison, there are other academic projects that place central focus on comparative research and legal education, as illustrated by the Trento Common Core Project[9] and the Ius Commune Casebook Project for a Common Law of Europe.[10] Indeed, the work of these and other academic groups feeds into the definition of European contract law itself.[11]

It is not the intention here to provide an in-depth analysis of all of the academic projects involved in European contract law, let alone European private law generally.[12]

ICLQ 673, 681–684; D Staudenmayer, 'The Commission Communication on European Contract Law: What Future for European Contract Law?' (2002) 10 *ERPL* 249, 250–252.

[8] Also referred to as the Pavia or Gandolfi Group after its chairman, Professor Giuseppe Gandolfi. See generally <http://www.accademiagiusprivatistieuropei.it/>. See also n 12.

[9] See generally <http://www.common-core.org/>. See also n 12.

[10] See generally <http://www.casebooks.eu/>. See also n 12.

[11] See Chapter 1, § 1.2.2.1.

[12] See, eg, A Fuchs, 'A Common Frame of Reference—How should it be filled?'(2003) 4 *ERA Forum* 99; E Hondius, 'European Private Law—Survey 2000–2002' (2002) 10 *ERPL* 865, 869–876; R Zimmerman, 'Comparative Law and the Europeanization of Private Law' in M Reimann and R Zimmermann (eds), *The Oxford Handbook of Comparative Law* (Oxford Univ Press, 2006) 539. For a somewhat more critical bent as regards certain groups, see L Nottage, 'Convergence, Divergence, and the Middle Way in Unifying or Harmonizing Private Law' in RA Miller and PC Zumbansen

There already exists quite an extensive literature on the subject, and to do so would likely be a book in itself. The analysis presented here is limited to the following: the Commission on European Contract Law, the Study Group on a European Civil Code, and the Network of Excellence encompassing several academic projects involved with the preparation of the Draft Common Frame of Reference (DCFR). As will be seen in this chapter and those to come, this set of academic projects has played a significant role in the debate about European contract law at the European level, and their work has both contributed to and been incorporated into the particular course taken by the Union institutions and the constitutional discourse related thereto.[13] Moreover, the work of some of these projects has been compared to the Restatements promulgated by the American Law Institute (ALI).[14] Thus, they constitute important background for the constitutional assessment of European contract law and comparative reflection with the US.

4.2.1 The Commission on European Contract Law

The Commission on European Contract Law (CECL) is one of the most well-known academic projects involved with European contract law. It is commonly referred to as the Lando Commission after its chairman, Professor Ole Lando, who reportedly started the project in the early 1980s because of his frustration with the inability of private international law rules to remedy the problems caused by the divergences between national contract laws in the EU.[15] It is a private academic organization, even if it did receive financial funding from the Commission for a period of time.[16] It consisted of several professors from each of the then fifteen Member States and certain third States.[17] It is associated with its seminal work, the PECL, which undoubtedly explains why 'the Lando Commission has acquired the greatest repute in this respect'.[18] It has now since disbanded,[19] but its work continues to influence activities taking place in the debate about European contract law, such as the DCFR.[20]

The PECL was published in three volumes. Volume One concerns performance, non-performance, and remedies and was published in 1995.[21] Volume Two is a revised

(eds), I *Annual of German and European Law 2003* (Berghahn, 2004) 166. With respect to the groups within the Network of Excellence, see further § 4.2.3.

[13] Certainly, other academic projects have received attention from the Union institutions. See Chapter 5, § 5.3.1.1.

[14] See Chapter 3, § 3.4.

[15] See O Lando and H Beale (eds), *Principles of European Contract Law Parts I and II (Combined and Revised)* (Kluwer, 2000) xi. The CECL's founding date often varies by a few years in the literature, which may be explained by the fact that the initial meeting of the members of the CECL began in 1980, but the work on the PECL was not undertaken until 1982. See *Principles of European Contract Law Parts I and II*, xi–xii.

[16] *Principles of European Contract Law Parts I and II*, n 15, xv–xvii. See further Written Question No 1865/91 by U Braun-Moser, 'Codification of civil law with a bearing on economic matters in the Community', [1992] OJ C102/94; Written Question H-0558/95 by M Mosiek-Urbahn, 'Payment of appropriations for the Lando Commission', Debates of the EP (English edn) 1995 No 467, p 177.

[17] There were three separate Commissions for each volume of the PECL. See *Principles of European Contract Law Parts I and II*, n 15, xi–xiii; O Lando et al (eds), *Principles of European Contract Law Part III* (Kluwer, 2003) ix–xiii.

[18] G Betlem and E Hondius, 'European Private Law after the Treaty of Amsterdam' (2001) 9 *ERPL* 3, 19.

[19] See *Principles of European Contract Law Part III*, n 17, ix–x.

[20] As regards their usage as part of the DCFR, see Chapter 6, § 6.2.3.

[21] O Lando and H Beale (eds), *Principles of European Contract Law Part I: Performance, Non-Performance and Remedies* (Martinus Nijhoff, 1995).

and completed version of the PECL, combining Volume One with additional subjects concerning general contract law (formation, authority of agents, validity, interpretation, contents, and effects), which was published in 2000.[22] Volume Three, published in 2003, covers not only principles of general contract law, but also subjects going beyond the scope of contract law strictly speaking, such as assignment of claims, set-off, and prescription.[23] In all, the PECL consists of seventeen chapters, each of which comprises a series of articles followed by comments, illustrations, and/or notes indicating the primary sources for each rule and how each rule is treated under the Member States' legal systems.[24]

There are three important aspects concerning the PECL that stand out for the purposes of this discussion: its objectives, drafting, and scope. First, the PECL is envisaged to have short-term and long-term objectives. In the short term, it aims to provide rules for contracting parties, constitute a modern formulation of the *lex mercatoria* for use by arbitrators and others, and embody a model available for legislative, judicial, and other authorities in developing laws whether at the national or international level,[25] whereas in the long term, the PECL is contemplated to lead to the unification of contract law in the EU, which is often framed in the form of a European contract code.[26] Indeed, long before the first volume of the PECL was published, Professor Ole Lando had articulated the need for a comprehensive contract law instrument at the European level.[27] This was to facilitate cross-border trade within the EU and to strengthen the internal market.[28] Whether or not all of its former members may have agreed with this objective, the PECL is intertwined with the prospect of far-reaching Union action in contract law and potentially other fields of private law.[29]

[22] *Principles of European Contract Law Parts I and II*, n 15.

[23] *Principles of European Contract Law Part III*, n 17.

[24] See generally MW Hesselink and GJP de Vries, *Principles of European Contract Law* (Kluwer, 2001). Incidentally, although framed as 'principles', it has been noted that the PECL are in fact 'rules': see, eg, E Clive, 'PECL III-An Overview and Assessment' in A Vaquer (ed), *The Principles of European Contract Law Part III* (Tirant lo blanch, 2005) 15, 17; W van Gerven, 'About Rules and Principles, Codification and Legislation, Harmonization and Convergence, and Education in the Area of Contract Law' in A Arnull et al (eds), *Continuity and Change in EU Law—Essays in Honour of Sir Francis Jacobs* (Oxford Univ Press, 2008) 399, 403.

[25] To be clear, however, the PECL are designed primarily for use in the EU Member States: *Principles of European Contract Law Parts I and II*, n 15, xxv.

[26] *Principles of European Contract Law Parts I and II*, n 15, xxii–xxiv; *Principles of European Contract Law Part III*, n 17, xv–xvi. See further H Beale, 'The Principles of European Contract Law and Harmonisation of the Laws of Contract' in LL Andersen et al (eds), *Festskrift til Ole Lando—Papers dedicated to Ole Lando* (Gadjura, 1997) 21, 25.

[27] See, eg, O Lando, 'European Contract Law' (1983) 31 *AJCL* 653; O Lando, 'Teaching a European Code of Contracts' in B De Witte and C Forder (eds), *The common law of Europe and the future of legal education* (Kluwer, 1992) 223, 227; P Hay et al, 'Conflict of Laws as a Technique for Legal Integration' in M Cappelletti et al (eds), *1 Integration Through Law: Europe and the American Federal Experience* (Walter de Gruyter, 1986) 161, 258. This has continued in more recent publications: see, eg, O Lando, 'A Plea for a Binding Instrument' in J Kleineman (ed), *A Common Frame of Reference for European Contract Law* (Stockholm Centre for Commercial Law, 2011) 91; O Lando, 'Comments and Questions Relating to the European Commission's Proposal for a Regulation on a Common European Sales Law' (2011) 19 *ERPL* 717, 719, 728; O Lando, 'European Private Law: Why, How, What and Who?' in L Moccia (ed), *The Making of European Private Law: Why, How, What, Who* (Sellier, 2013) 1; but compare O Lando, 'Have the PECL Been a Success or a Failure?' (2009) 17 *ERPL* 367.

[28] *Principles of European Contract Law Parts I and II*, n 15, xxi.

[29] See, eg, *Principles of European Contract Law Part III*, n 17, xv; Lando, 'Teaching a European Code of Contracts', n 27, 236; O Lando, 'Why Does Europe Need a Civil Code?' in S Grundmann and J Stuyck (eds), *An Academic Green Paper on European Contract Law* (Kluwer, 2002) 207, 212.

Secondly, with respect to the drafting of the PECL, it is explicitly acknowledged that some provisions of the PECL 'reflect suggestions and ideas which have not yet materialised in the law of any State'.[30] This is because the overarching objective has been to find the 'best solutions' to particular issues, that is to say, '[t]he search has been for the most appropriate rules for the future, not for prevailing trends or for compromises'.[31] Consequently, the PECL is not exclusively grounded in the existing laws of the Member States, and some rules emanate from outside the EU, such as the United Nations Convention on Contracts for the International Sale of Goods (CISG) or US law.[32] The PECL has been referred to as a 'Restatement' of contract law drawing upon the model of the Restatements promulgated by the ALI.[33] This is both in terms of its format and its attempt to 'state' what is common to the contract laws of the Member States.[34] Yet, it has been repeatedly stressed that this analogy is not exact, since the PECL often does not 're-state', but in fact states very much for the first time purportedly common contract law principles of the Member States,[35] and it does so with a view to their approximation at the European level beyond a merely non-binding status.[36]

Thirdly, the scope of the PECL is under- and over-inclusive. On the one hand, as already mentioned, it covers matters beyond the strict confines of contract law. From the first two volumes, the CECL took a 'functional approach' in deciding which topics were to be included in the PECL, and thus, these Principles encompass rules that in some legal systems were considered part of the law of torts or restitution.[37] With the publication of the third volume, the PECL came to comprise matters that relate not only to contractual obligations, but also to 'obligations in general', although the title of 'Principles of European Contract Law' was retained nonetheless.[38] On the other hand, the PECL is confined to general contract law and does not deal with specific types of contract or address consumer contracts.[39] This is not to say that consumer contracts are excluded from its scope, but rather that the PECL did not incorporate special rules in line with those set out in the various measures comprising the EU contract law *acquis*. In other words, the PECL is intended to apply to contracts generally, including

[30] *Principles of European Contract Law Parts I and II*, n 15, xxvi.

[31] *Principles of European Contract Law Part III*, n 17, xvi.

[32] *Principles of European Contract Law Parts I and II*, n 15, xxv–xxvi. See further O Lando, 'Salient Features of the Principles of European Contract Law: A Comparison with the UCC' (2001) 13 *Pace IL Rev* 339.

[33] The PECL were inspired by, inter alia, the American Restatements and the UCC. See, eg, O Lando, 'The Principles of European Contract Law and American Legal Thinking' in JAR Nafziger and SC Symeonides (eds), *Law and Justice in a Multi-State World: Essays in Honour of Arthur T. von Mehren* (Transnational, 2002) 741, 743; Hesselink and de Vries, n 24, 12.

[34] See, eg, H Beale, 'European contract law: the Common Frame of Reference and beyond' in C Twigg-Flesner (ed), *The Cambridge Companion to European Union Private Law* (Cambridge Univ Press, 2010) 116, 118.

[35] *Principles of European Contract Law Parts I and II*, n 15, xxvi. See further, eg, Lando, 'Teaching a European Code of Contracts', n 27, 230; C von Bar, 'Paving the Way Forward with Principles of European Private Law' in *An Academic Green Paper on European Contract Law*, n 29, 137; J Smits, 'The Principles of European Contract Law and the Harmonisation of Private Law in Europe' in *The Principles of European Contract Law Part III*, n 24, 567, 580–583; T Wilhelmsson, 'The Design of an Optional (Re)statement of European Contract Law—Real Life Instead of Dead Concepts' in *An Academic Green Paper on European Contract Law*, n 29, 353, 354.

[36] See, eg, Hesselink and de Vries, n 24, 20, 23, 29 (also pointing out differences in relation to the respective decision-making processes); R Van den Bergh, 'Subsidiarity as an Economic Demarcation Principle and the Emergence of European Private Law' (1998) 5 *MJ* 129, 129 fn 4.

[37] *Principles of European Contract Law Parts I and II*, n 15, xxv.

[38] *Principles of European Contract Law Part III*, n 17, xvi.

[39] *Principles of European Contract Law Parts I and II*, n 15, xxv.

contracts between businesses and consumers (B2C contracts) and contracts between businesses (B2B contracts).[40] This explains in part the emergence of a separate academic project, the Acquis Group, which is devoted to filling this gap as detailed below.

4.2.2 The Study Group on a European Civil Code

As the successor or 'heir apparent' to the Lando Commission,[41] the Study Group on a European Civil Code (Study Group) continued essentially where the CECL left off, with the aim of drafting a set of European principles for other areas of private law, namely that of patrimonial law comprising the general part of contract law and specific types of contracts, as well as the law of extra-contractual obligations and aspects of movable property law.[42] The Study Group was constituted in 1998, when it was envisaged that the CECL would be bringing its work to a close, and has been active since 1999.[43] It was founded under the leadership of Professor Christian von Bar, and 'represents the largest—and in this form unique—network of European experts in the field of private law'.[44] It is a private academic organization divided up into a series of working teams under the general supervision of certain coordinating groups and advisors.[45] Although it includes former members of the CECL,[46] the Study Group encompasses a much larger group of scholars from the Member States, as well as certain third States, across a wider terrain of private law.[47] Its principal aim is to produce a set of principles for European patrimonial law, which are published as the Principles of European Law (PEL) series.[48]

The Study Group's focus on European patrimonial law has been explained by the considerable interdependence between the laws of contract, tort, and movable property, which makes it problematic to single out certain fields but not others.[49] As a consequence, it has been remarked in the literature that the name 'Study Group on a European civil code' is unfortunate. In part, this is because the ambit of the Study Group does not extend to all fields of 'civil law', including family law, immovable property law, and the law of succession. More often, this is because of the conflation between

[40] *Principles of European Contract Law Parts I and II*, n 15, xxv. See further Hesselink and de Vries, n 24, 42–46.

[41] E Hondius, 'Towards a European Civil Code' in A Hartkamp et al (eds), *Towards a European Civil Code*, 4th rev and expanded edn (Kluwer/Ars Aequi Libri, 2011) 3, 13.

[42] von Bar, n 35, 139.

[43] See, eg, C von Bar, 'From Principles to Codification: Prospects for European Private Law' (2002) 8 *CJEL* 379; C von Bar, 'The Study Group on a European Civil Code' in European Parliament DG for Research Working Paper, *The Private Law Systems in the EU: Discrimination on Grounds of Nationality and the Need for a European Civil Code* (Legal Affairs Series, JURI-103 EN), available at <http://www.europarl.europa.eu/> (1999 Working Paper), 133, 135. This may explain why 1999 has been cited as the date of its founding in the literature, including materials authored by the Study Group itself. See, eg, the 'Foreword' authored by C von Bar in various volumes of the PEL series.

[44] C von Bar et al, 'Communication on European Contract Law: Joint Response of the Commission on European Contract Law and the Study Group on a European Civil Code' (2002) 10 *ERPL* 183, 192.

[45] For detailed discussion, see the Study Group's website, <http://www.sgecc.net/>.

[46] von Bar et al, n 44, 189.

[47] The Co-ordinating Group, which is the Study Group's decision-making body, consists of representatives from most Member States. See C von Bar and E Clive (eds), 1 *Principles, Definitions and Model Rules of European Private Law—Draft Common Frame of Reference (DCFR)*, Full edn (Sellier, 2009/Oxford Univ Press, 2010) 25.

[48] For a list of publications and activities, see n 45.

[49] See, eg, von Bar, n 35, 140. For the definition of European patrimonial law, see Chapter 1, § 1.2.2.2.

the work of the Study Group and tensions underlying the term 'European civil code'. Even if the language of codification has been toned down and it has been assimilated to that of a 'Restatement'[50] or set of 'model rules' of European patrimonial law,[51] the work of the Study Group has been envisaged to lay the basis for the approximation of areas of private law at the European level.[52] This is so even if there is no general agreement among the members of the Study Group itself as to what extent this should be the case.[53] In fact, Professor Christian von Bar, the chairman of the Study Group, admitted that despite the Group's nameplate, the term 'European civil code' should be avoided at all costs, since it 'raises emotions and fears which for the time being are impossible to overcome'.[54] Be that as it may, the Study Group's involvement in the European contract law project has to some extent exacerbated sensitivities surrounding the potential adoption of a comprehensive instrument of private (or even contract) law at the European level.[55] At the same time, the Study Group's repeated advocacy in institutional documents of taking a broad view of the national private law systems adds to such tensions in terms of the scope, not just the means, of Union action. These points have particular resonance in the Study Group's role in the CFR project as part of the Network of Excellence.[56]

4.2.3 The Network of Excellence

While detailed discussion of the CFR project must await the next two chapters, it should be understood at the outset that the framework for the participation of certain academic projects in this project was established under the auspices of the Network of Excellence. Starting in May 2005, the Study Group and several other academic projects joined together as the Network of Excellence for the preparation of the draft or academic version of the CFR (DCFR).[57] The Network's preparation of the DCFR was funded by the Commission as part of the former European Community's Sixth Framework Programme for Research and Technological Development (known as FP6).[58] The Network of Excellence was also called the Joint Network on European

[50] See, eg, von Bar, n 35, 137; C von Bar, 'The Draft Common Frame of Reference: Scope and Purpose' in V Sagaert et al (eds), *The Draft Common Frame of Reference: national and comparative perspectives* (Intersentia, 2012) 3.

[51] See, eg, C von Bar, 'Foreword' in E Hondius et al, *Study Group on a European Civil Code—Principles of European Law on Sales* (Sellier/Bruylant/Stæmpfli, 2008) vii.

[52] This is presently stated as part of its aims on its website, n 45.

[53] See, eg, von Bar, 'From Principles to Codification', n 43, 380 (with similar remarks about the CECL); von Bar, 'The Draft Common Frame of Reference', n 50, 3. Eg, certain members of the Study Group are also members of the Study Group on Social Justice in European Private Law, which severely criticized the movement towards further approximation of contract law at European level: see Study Group on Social Justice in European Private Law, 'Social Justice in European Contract Law: a Manifesto' (2004) 10 *ELJ* 653.

[54] C von Bar, 'A Common Frame of Reference for European Private Law—Academic Efforts and Political Realities' (2008) 23 *Tul Eur & Civ LF* 37, 40.

[55] This has led to publications in which certain scholars fervently oppose such codification in connection with the work of the Study Group and its chairman. See, eg, P Legrand, 'Antivonbar' (2006) 1 *JCL* 13; Y Lequete, 'Quelques remarques à propos du projet de code civil européen de M. von Bar' (2002) *Recueil Dalloz* 2202.

[56] See, eg, H Beale, 'The European Commission's Common Frame of Reference Project: a progress report' (2006) 2 *ERCL* 303, 304; Written Question E-5000/07 by P van Buitenen, 'European Civil Code and Study Group on a European Civil Code', available at <http://www.europarl.europa.eu/>.

[57] See further Chapter 5, § 5.4.

[58] See the Joint Network on European Private Law (Co-PECL)'s website, <http://www.copecl.org/>.

Private Law or the Co-PECL, since the aim was to produce the DCFR for European contract law in the form of a set of 'Common Principles of European Contract Law'.[59] Yet, this is somewhat of a misnomer, since the DCFR includes not only common principles but also definitions and model rules concerning contract law and other fields of private law, which largely correspond to the fields of European patrimonial law covered by the Study Group.[60] With the completion of the DCFR, it disbanded in 2009.[61]

The Network of Excellence encompassed the following eight academic projects: (1) the Study Group; (2) the Acquis Group; (3) the Project Group on a Restatement of European Insurance Contract Law (Insurance Group); (4) a group of French academic institutions comprising the *Association Henri Capitant des Amis de la Culture Juridique* (*Association Henri Capitant*); (5) the Trento Common Core Project (Common Core Group); (6) the Research Group on the Economic Assessment of Contract Law Rules (Economic Impact Group) led by the Tilburg Law and Economics Center (TILEC); (7) the Database Group under the helm of the *Institut Charles Dumoulin* of the University of Paris XI Faculty of Law; and (8) the Academy of European Law (ERA) in Trier, Germany.[62] The Study Group and the Acquis Group were charged with the principal drafting of most of the substantive content of the DCFR, save for certain sections devoted to particular subjects: the provisions on insurance contracts were dealt with by the Insurance Group[63] and the work on terminology, guiding principles, and the revision of the PECL was done by the *Association Henri Capitant* as part of its task to analyse the philosophical underpinnings of the suggested rules for the DCFR.[64] The remaining four groups were occupied in various ways with further comparative and evaluative analysis of the DCFR.[65] Accordingly, encased within the Network of Excellence are several groups that embody very different approaches to European contract law. As regards the substantive drafting of the DCFR, aside from the Study Group, the Acquis Group and the Insurance Group have key roles.

The Acquis Group, formally called the European Research Group on Existing EC Private Law, was founded in 2002 and currently comprises scholars from most Member States.[66] Its main founders are Professor Gianmaria Ajani and Professor Hans Schulte-Nölke.[67] As its name indicates, it is focused on the EU private law *acquis* and has placed, at least for now, considerable focus on the field of contract law.[68] Its objective

[59] See n 58. [60] See Chapter 6, § 6.2.3.

[61] A link to one of the Study Group's Working Groups (<http://www.uni-graz.at/bre1www/tom/index.html>) indicates that the Co-PECL's work lasted from May 2005 to May 2009.

[62] See n 58. For full discussion of the role played by these groups within the CFR project, see 'Special Issue on European Contract Law' (2008) 9 *ERA Forum*.

[63] See n 76 and accompanying text.

[64] See B Fauvarque-Cosson and D Mazeaud (eds), *European Contract Law, Materials for a Common Frame of Reference: Terminology, Guiding Principles, Model Rules* (Sellier, 2008).

[65] As regards the work of the Common Core Group, see L Antoniolli and F Fiorentini (eds), *A Factual Assessment of the Draft Common Frame of Reference* (Sellier, 2011); the conclusions are summarized in L Antoniolli et al, 'A Case-Based Assessment of the Draft Common Frame of Reference' (2010) 58 *AJCL* 343. As regards the work of the Economic Impact Group, see P Larouche and F Chirico (eds), *Economic Analysis of the DCFR—The work of the Economic Impact Group within CoPECL* (Sellier, 2010). As the Database Group was charged with the collection and distribution of relevant data for the researchers and eventually the public and the ERA was tasked with organizing conferences involving practitioners, scholars, and researchers, their work did not of itself result in specific publications. [66] See the Acquis Group's website: <http://www.acquis-group.org/>.

[67] As indicated on its website (n 66), Professor Gianmaria Ajani acts as the speaker of the Acquis Group, and Professor Hans Schulte-Nölke acts as the Group's coordinator.

[68] See, eg, G Ajani and H Schulte-Nölke, 'The Principles of the Existing EC Contract Law: A Preliminary Output of the Acquis Group' in Research Group on the Existing EC Private

is to formulate the existing Union *acquis* in the form of a so-called Restatement, which is titled the 'Principles of the Existing EC Contract Law' or the Acquis Principles.[69] As explained by its founders, the Acquis Principles claim similarity with the American Restatements to some extent:

> [T]he Principles have similar aims to the classical restatements of the American Law Institute and the very successful effort to transfer this method to the variety of European national laws. It is an attempt to present and structure the bulky, manifold and rather incoherent patchwork of EC private law in such way that should allow the current state of its development to be made clear, and for relevant legislation and case law to be easily found.[70]

Pursuant to Article 1:101 of the Acquis Principles of EC Contract Law, for example, the Principles are envisaged to serve 'as a source for the drafting, the transposition and the interpretation' of Union law.[71] That said, its work is not without controversy. Among other things, the extent to which general principles can be identified on the basis of a piecemeal set of directives that were not envisaged to operate independently of the national contract law regimes has been the subject of debate.[72] Furthermore, as regards the objectives of the Acquis Principles, they are meant to stand by themselves as well as to feed into the ongoing activities concerning European contract law at the European level, which include the DCFR[73] and legislative initiatives focused specifically on the Union consumer contract law *acquis*.[74] In effect, the Group has one foot in the European contract law project and another in the parallel track of the revision of the EU consumer *acquis*, which have come together in the debate about European contract law as discussed further in the next chapters.

The Project Group on a Restatement of European Insurance Contract Law (Insurance Group) was, as just mentioned, charged with elaborating the insurance contract law provisions of the DCFR,[75] which it also published separately as the Principles of European Insurance Contract Law (PEICL).[76] Apparently, the idea for a

Law (Acquis Group), *Contract I—Pre-contractual Obligations, Conclusions of Contract, Unfair Terms* (Sellier, 2007) ix; R Schulze, 'European Private Law and Existing EC Law' (2005) 13 *ERPL* 3, 7.

69 See *Contract I*, n 68; Research Group on the Existing EC Private Law (Acquis Group), *Contract II—General Provisions, Delivery of Goods, Package Travel and Payment Services* (Sellier, 2009). *Contract III—General Provisions, Delivery of Goods, Package Travel, Payment Services, Consumer Credit and Commercial Agency Contracts* is expected to be published shortly. For a list of its activities, see n 66.

70 Ajani and Schulte-Nölke, n 68, ix. This is inscribed as part of the Principles themselves: see H Schulte-Nölke and C Busch, Commentary for Paragraph (1): Restatement of the Existing EC Contract Law—Acquis Principles of Existing Contract Law § 1:101 in *Contract I*, n 68, 17, 17–18.

71 Acquis Principles of Existing EC Contract Law § 1:101(2).

72 See, eg, N Jansen and R Zimmerman, 'Restating the *Acquis Communautaire*? A Critical Examination of the "Principles of the Existing EC Contract Law"' (2008) 71 *MLR* 505; C Twigg-Flesner, 'The *acquis* principles: an insider's critical reflections on the drafting process' in M Andenas and C Baasch Andersen (eds), *Theory and Practice of Harmonisation* (Edward Elgar, 2011) 474 (also printed in (2011) *GPR* 54); see also C Twigg-Flesner, *The Europeanisation of Contract Law* (Routledge-Cavendish, 2008) 153–155.

73 See H Schulte-Nölke and C Busch, Commentary for Paragraph (2): Purpose of the Acquis Principles—Acquis Principles of Existing Contract Law § 1:101 in *Contract I*, n 68, 19–20. For further discussion of the role of the Acquis Principles in the DCFR, see, eg, R Schulze, 'The Academic Draft of the CFR and the EC Contract Law' in R Schulze (ed), *Common Frame of Reference and Existing EC Contract Law*, 2nd rev edn (Sellier, 2009) 3; R Schulze and T Wilhelmsson, 'From the Draft Common Frame of Reference towards European Contract Law Rules' (2008) 4 *ERCL* 154.

74 See Chapter 6, § 6.3.

75 See H Heiss, 'The Common Frame of Reference (CFR) of European Insurance Contract Law' in *Common Frame of Reference and Existing EC Contract Law*, n 73, 235.

76 J Basedow et al (eds), *Principles of European Insurance Contract Law* (Sellier, 2009). For commentary on the PEICL, see, eg, *Principles of European Insurance Contract Law*, xxxiv–ilvii; H Heiss et al (eds), *Principles of European Insurance Contract Law: A Model Optional Instrument* (Sellier, 2011).

'Restatement of European insurance contract law' originated at an international conference in 1998, and thereafter, the Group was formed under the chairmanship of Professor Fritz Reichert-Facilides; upon his death, Professor Helmut Heiss took up the reins.[77] As indicated by its name, it claims to share a theoretical link to the American Restatements. This seems to indicate that it follows the 'same idea' as that in the US as regards the synthesis of the laws of insurance contracts among the Member States.[78] There is an important difference, however. Unlike the American context, the Insurance Group aims at the drafting of a 'European Insurance Contract Act' at the European level.[79] Indeed, its preparation of the relevant sections of the DCFR was done in the form of an optional instrument that would be capable of being adopted by the Union institutions.[80] Its place in the debate has not only helped to place further attention on the use of optional instruments, but also highlights important issues concerning the need for Union action in the area of insurance contract law and the relationship of this area to more general matters of contract law.[81]

Together, the CECL, the Study Group, and the additional academic projects within the Network of Excellence have become firmly ensconced within the overall momentum surrounding European contract law. As will be seen in the coming chapters, the emphasis placed on the relationship between contract law and related fields of private law, as well as that between contract law and specific subsets, by these groups has become interwoven within the activities of the Union institutions in the debate. The 'functional' linkage between some of these groups and the ALI's Restatement project also percolates through the debate, alongside additional American techniques. Yet, the work of some of these projects already fed into the momentum surrounding European contract law (and European private law generally) generated by several early European Parliament resolutions, to which the discussion now turns.

4.3 The Early European Parliament Resolutions

The European Parliament disseminated three seminal resolutions on the approximation of European private law in 1989, 1994, and 2000. These resolutions are often cited in the discourse surrounding European contract law. However, it is not generally known that underlying these resolutions was considerable discussion of the former Community's (now Union's) competence in this area. Each is evaluated in turn, along with certain related documents.

4.3.1 The 1989 Resolution

On 26 May 1989, the European Parliament adopted a Resolution on action to bring into line the private law of the Member States (1989 Resolution).[82] The events leading to its passage began much earlier in April 1985 when the Parliament tabled a motion for a resolution of the same name by two Greek MEPs, Nikolaos Gazis and

[77] For detailed information and a bibliography of publications, see the Insurance Group's website: <http://www.restatement.info/>.

[78] 'Way of Working and Goals', available on its website, n 77.

[79] 'Way of Working and Goals', n 78.

[80] See, eg, Heiss, n 75.

[81] See further Chapter 5, § 5.4.3.2.

[82] European Parliament Resolution of 26 May 1989 on action to bring into line the private law of the Member States, [1989] OJ C158/400 (1989 Resolution).

Georgios Mavros.[83] This motion for a resolution set the groundwork for the 'drawing up of a common European civil code' by way of comparative legal research and the formation of an 'ad hoc committee' to oversee the process.[84]

This motion was referred to the Parliamentary Committee on Legal Affairs and Citizens' Rights, which prompted Mr Gazis to disseminate a Working Document in January 1986 examining in further detail the need for a uniform system of private law in the EU.[85] The 1986 Working Document was organized around three central questions concerning the need for such a code, whether it was possible, and if so, what method should be followed.[86] As regards the first question, Mr Gazis noted that despite the fact that there had been a number of special subjects on which common rules had been adopted at the European level, 'having separate legislation on specific questions is a different matter from having a uniform system of law covering all subjects'.[87] As regards the second question, the difficulties involved were not deemed insurmountable. For the civil law systems, this was due to three 'optimistic' factors concerning the recent codifications in Italy and Greece and the Lando Commission's work on European contract law.[88] As regards the common law systems, this was considered 'the most difficult' case because it was 'not just a question of different codes but of different legal *systems*'.[89] Yet, he considered that there were still reasons for optimism, 'at least, initially, as far as contract law is concerned', as shown by the codification of large sections of commercial law in England, various international conventions in fields of private law, and the situation in the US 'where the existence of the common law and its truly chaotic development in the various states did not prevent all the American states from adopting a uniform Commercial Code'.[90] In fact, the idea of having a Restatement of the common law of the UK and Ireland, similar to the American Restatements, was floated for use by civil law practitioners on the grounds that it would make it easier for them 'to understand common law and might be a first step towards the codification of the common law', albeit it was for English lawyers to take the initiative in this regard.[91] It was also mentioned that 'a modernized European civil code' would have influence outside the EU for countries with outdated codes or no codes at all.[92]

[83] Mr Gazis was a member of the Committee on Legal Affairs and Citizens' Rights from 1984–1989 (serving as Vice Chairman from 1984–1987). Mr Mavros served as a substitute for the same Committee from 1984–1987. See <http://www.europarl.europa.eu/>. This may explain why after the initial 1985 motion for a resolution, Mr Mavros' name does not appear on successive documents related thereto.

[84] Motion for a resolution (B 2-55/85), attached as Annex I to Report drawn up on behalf of the Committee on Legal Affairs and Citizens' Rights on action to bring into line the private law of the Member States, A 2-0157/89, dated 28 April 1989 (1989 Report).

[85] Working Document on action to bring into line the private law of the Member States, B 2-55/85/rev, dated 9 Jan 1986 (1986 Working Document).

[86] 1986 Working Document, n 85, point 1.

[87] 1986 Working Document, n 85, point 2, second para (citing O Lando, 'European Contract Law' (1983) 31 *AJCL* 653). This comment is interesting when it is considered that at the time that this Working Document was issued (9 Jan 1986), there had been only a few Community (now Union) measures adopted, at least in the core private law *acquis*, eg, the Product Liability and Doorstep Selling Directives. See Chapter 1, § 1.3.

[88] 1986 Working Document, n 85, points 5–8.

[89] 1986 Working Document, n 85, point 9.

[90] 1986 Working Document, n 85, point 12.

[91] 1986 Working Document, n 85, point 11.

[92] 1986 Working Document, n 85, point 13. Such a Code was also considered to strengthen relations with Latin America and would be of 'cultural and political' benefit to Europe even if it was not immediately adopted by all Member States: 1986 Working Document, n 85, points 14–15.

On this basis, Mr Gazis concluded that the private law of the Member States, 'especially as regards the law [of] obligations and contract, and what are known as general principles of civil law',[93] can be unified.[94] He stressed that this endeavour constituted neither 'a theoretical scientific activity' nor 'a new draft international convention to which it would be possible to accede in whole or in part', but instead was aimed at the establishment of 'a uniform body of positive law'.[95] Moreover, he reasoned that even if one or more Member States were not willing to join, unification with less than all the Member States would still be 'a benefit to a United Europe and its transactions'.[96] He proposed that if the reaction of the Member States was positive, an ad hoc committee could be set up, which could organize, together with the Commission, the project as a whole.[97] In closing, he remarked: 'A common system of private law is a vital and indispensable need for second-generation Europe. It is undoubtedly an arduous and time-consuming task. However, this task will have to be started one day. Why not start now?'[98]

This Working Document was considered by the Parliamentary Committee on Legal Affairs and Citizens' Rights at its meetings of 22 and 23 April 1986, when the Committee decided to draw up a Report and appointed Mr Gazis as Rapporteur.[99] Up to this point, there had been no explicit discussion of the EU's competence to engage in this endeavour. Chronology is important here. The initial motion for a resolution and subsequent Working Document were made in April 1985 and January 1986, respectively, and thus before the Single European Act (SEA) was adopted in February 1986 and entered into force on 1 July 1987.[100] In contrast, the Report drawn up by Mr Gazis as Rapporteur on behalf of the Committee was adopted a few years later on 28 April 1989 and contained detailed discussion of this subject.[101] The heart of the Report was the Explanatory Statement authored by Mr Gazis. It was organized into nine separate sections, the first five essentially reflecting the points covered in the previous Working Document with some elaboration.[102] The remaining four sections (Parts VI–IX), along with the Introduction, were new and concerned the legal foundation for the proposal, the type of harmonization to be carried out, the declaration of willingness to participate, and the first steps to be taken, respectively.

In the Introduction, Mr Gazis underlined that the aim of the motion for a resolution was 'to bring about the unification of private law of the Member States', but not all branches of private law at the same time.[103] Rather, specific branches would be progressively chosen, in which contract law and 'so-called general principles of civil law (capacity, conditions, deadlines, prescription and private international law, etc)' were expected to go first.[104] The EU's competence was directly addressed in the section

[93] This category included 'inter alia the rules relating to conditions governing and capacity to enter into legal transactions, and private international law': 1986 Working Document, n 85, point 3.

[94] 1986 Working Document, n 85, point 16.

[95] 1986 Working Document, n 85, point 16.

[96] 1986 Working Document, n 85, point 16.

[97] 1986 Working Document, n 85, point 16.

[98] 1986 Working Document, n 85, point 18.

[99] See 1989 Report, n 84, 3.

[100] Notification relating to the date of entry into force of the SEA, signed at Luxembourg on 17 Feb 1986 and at The Hague on 28 Feb 1986, [1987] OJ L169/29.

[101] There was also a Draft Report on action to bring into line the private law of the Member States, dated 12 Nov 1987 (PE 118.124), the substance of which is generally the same as the 1989 Report, n 84.

[102] Compare 1989 Report, n 84, pts I–V, with 1986 Working Document, n 85, points 1–15.

[103] 1989 Report, n 84, points 1–2.

[104] 1989 Report, n 84, points 1–2. The reference to 'general principles of civil law' was no doubt taken from the 1986 Working Document (n 85).

concerning the legal foundation for the proposal. After a short incursion into the objectives of the Treaty and various provisions concerning the approximation of national laws in areas chiefly of an economic nature,[105] the Report focused on what were then the Community's competences under Articles 100 and 235 EEC (now Articles 115 and 352 TFEU, respectively).[106] This led to the following conclusions:

A uniform legal system to cover private law as a whole or major branches of it is, particularly since the objectives of the European Community were widened, a necessity for which the fragmented and disjointed harmonization of various individual subject-areas can no longer be a substitute. The EC, in a serious and sensitive area like that of the law, can no longer express itself 'with one voice', as required by the Single [European] Act, through twelve different legal systems. There has to be a general legal framework which facilitates trade—and competition—and offers trading partners greater security. The twelve different systems of law which exist at present are tantamount to twelve frontiers which call for constant vigilance and care, as well as additional expenditure, on the part of those involved in international trade if they are to avoid falling into legal traps. The current system in the private law sector as a *whole* has clearly been left lagging slowly behind in comparison with the endeavours made in other sectors, *even though the institutional powers for a broader updating of the law were always there from the outset (in the form of Articles 100 and 235)*.[107]

Mr Gazis then drew attention to the SEA, which was considered to make legal harmonization more urgently needed on account of the creation of the internal market, on the one hand, and simpler to carry out, on the other hand, by virtue of the introduction of Article 100a EEC (now Article 114 TFEU).[108] Article 100a EEC was deemed more wide-ranging than Article 100 EEC (now Article 115 TFEU) because it did not require a 'direct link' to the establishment or the functioning of the common (now internal) market as a precondition; it was not limited to the use of directives; and it stipulated qualified majority, as opposed to unanimous, voting in the Council.[109] On this basis, he proclaimed that 'a complete legal foundation for the attempt to unify private law or branches thereof' could be found on the combined interpretation of the principles set out in the Preambles of the EEC Treaty and the SEA, together with Articles 3(h), 100, 100A, and 235.[110] In present terms, this signified in relevant part the legal bases of Articles 114, 115, and 352 TFEU.[111]

In line with this finding, Mr Gazis set forth certain novel proposals concerning the type of 'harmonization' envisaged and the involvement of the Member States in this regard. In his view, although harmonization could in principle be pursued in different ways, that is to say, by means of directives, regulations, or conventions, here the aim was the unification of private law such that the question of harmonization by way of directives did not arise.[112] Likewise, the idea of drawing up a convention in its traditional form was not considered suitable, since it 'probably cannot constitute the "substantive law" of all the Member States (for instance, because of non-conformity with other legislation or with a different system of law or the Constitution in a certain Member State or States, or even for historical reasons)'.[113] Therefore, given that the aim was to unify the substantive private law of the Member States—since that was 'the only thing

105 1989 Report, n 84, points 16–18. 106 1989 Report, n 84, points 18–19.
107 1989 Report, n 84, point 20 (emphasis added). 108 1989 Report, n 84, point 21.
109 1989 Report, n 84, point 22. 110 1989 Report, n 84, point 23.
111 Ex Art 3(h) EEC, later Art 3(1)(h) EC, specified as one of the Community's activities 'the approximation of the laws of the Member States to the extent required for the functioning of the common market'. With the entry into force of the Lisbon Treaty, this provision was repealed and replaced in substance by Arts 3–6 TFEU. Table of equivalences, [2012] OJ C326/363.
112 1989 Report, n 84, points 25–26. 113 1989 Report, n 84, point 27.

which will fully meet the requirements of a genuinely single market'—this called for a solution whereby the Member States would first have to express their intentions in principle of proceeding with unification and then an attempt would be made to unify the private laws of those Member States that responded positively.[114] This led to his contemplation of a solution containing certain features of a convention and a regulation, but without being either a convention of the 'classical type' to which the Member States were expected to accede with or without reservations or a 'pure' regulation whose provisions were directly binding on all the Member States.[115] This novel solution was considered to fall within the scope of the Community's competence under Article 100a EEC (now Article 114 TFEU) on the view that its broad drafting (referring to 'measures for the approximation') allowed 'complete freedom of manoeuvre as regards both the extent and the form of harmonization carried out'.[116]

As for what would go into the so-called 'convention', this would have to be worked out by those Member States deciding to combine their efforts to draw up a uniform system of private law that supplemented their substantive law currently in force.[117] Yet, in contrast to what usually happens with traditional conventions in which countries are subsequently free to accede, 'an attempt will be made right from the outset to draw up a common system of private law capable of replacing the corresponding provisions in the substantive law of the *specific* Member States which express their willingness to pursue this course of action'.[118] Moreover, as for what would go into the so-called 'regulation', this would have to be sought in the fact that even if the framing of a uniform body of private law was not intended to involve all Member States from the outset or to be mandatorily imposed on all Member States, partial unification of this kind (meaning partial as regards the number of participating Member States but complete as far as the new law to be adopted was concerned) was still of concern to all Member States, since they—including those not involved in the drafting—have an interest in ensuring that unification is carried out, even if it is not global.[119] This was because even partial unification was a measure that has as its object the 'better functioning of the internal market' in accordance with Article 100a EEC (now Article 114 TFEU), which was not to the desired extent, but at any rate to a degree that constituted serious progress in comparison with the situation existing today.[120] Of course, the 'ideal thing' would be for all Member States to acquire a single system of private law, but if that should prove unattainable, the unification of certain branches of private law by a 'relatively substantial number' of Member States would still constitute 'a serious and necessary step towards the completion of the internal market "without frontiers"'.[121]

In the section titled 'Declaration of willingness to participate', Mr Gazis elaborated specific procedures to determine which Member States would participate in the unification project and how to move forward in the process. He broached the subject of the participation of the Member States with the recognition that the proposal was 'such a wide-ranging overthrow of the legal status quo', it was likely to encounter strong opposition especially from lawyers in the Member States.[122] As a first stage, there should be negotiations between the Member State Governments concerned and scholars specializing in the relevant fields, in order to come up with an initial approach, which could be confined in the beginning to '*the law of obligations (or contracts)* which

[114] 1989 Report, n 84, point 28.
[115] 1989 Report, n 84, point 29.
[116] 1989 Report, n 84, point 30.
[117] 1989 Report, n 84, point 29.
[118] 1989 Report, n 84, point 29.
[119] 1989 Report, n 84, point 29.
[120] 1989 Report, n 84, point 29.
[121] 1989 Report, n 84, point 30.
[122] 1989 Report, n 84, point 33.

is the backbone of trade'.[123] To set the project in motion at this stage, a 'representative committee of appropriate experts' could be set up, which would be established by the Commission, following consultation with the Member State Governments.[124] Then, as part of the 'first steps' to be taken, if and when the Member States (all or some of them) decide in principle to go ahead with unification, the Member States in question, in consultation with the Commission, would set up an 'ad hoc committee of lawyers responsible for determining priorities and organizing the whole undertaking (working parties, etc.)'.[125]

The European Parliament's 1989 Resolution followed this Report about a month later.[126] Compared to the detail of the Report, the Resolution was much shorter, amounting to about one page. Yet, many of its points can be understood only by looking at the two together. The Resolution began by taking aim at the Community's (now Union's) piecemeal harmonization of 'many individual aspects of private law but not whole branches of it', which did 'not meet the needs and objectives of the single market without frontiers, particularly as formulated since the entry into force of the Single [European] Act'.[127] Consequently, the Parliament declared that 'the most effective way of carrying out harmonization with a view to meeting the Community's legal requirements in the area of private law is to unify major branches of that law', particularly those which are highly important for the development of the single market, such as contract law.[128] As regards the matter of competence, the Parliament simply proclaimed that 'the Treaty and the Single [European] Act offer a comprehensive legal basis for the objective pursued in this resolution', without mentioning any specific provisions.[129] There was also no reference to the means by which the instrument would be formulated, namely by way of the hybrid convention-regulation method discussed in the Report.

The Parliament concluded the Resolution by making several requests. First, in perhaps its most-cited provision, it asked that 'a start be made on the necessary preparatory work on drawing up a common European Code of Private Law, the Member States, being invited, having deliberated [on] the matter, to state whether they wish to be involved in the planned unification'.[130] Secondly, it envisaged that following discussions among the Member States that agreed in principle to unification, 'a committee of appropriate experts' should be set up to define the priorities and to organize the whole undertaking of unifying private law in those Member States.[131] Finally, in line with the importance of promoting reciprocal understanding of the various systems of private law in the Member States, it requested that aid be given to centres for comparative legal studies in the EU and to codifying endeavours in general and that the necessary financial arrangements be made to carry out this project.[132]

[123] 1989 Report, n 84, point 34 (emphasis added).

[124] 1989 Report, n 84, point 35.

[125] 1989 Report, n 84, point 36. This seemed to correspond to the previous mention of an 'ad hoc committee... to oversee the overall organization and progress of this undertaking' in the initial motion for a resolution, n 84, point 1(e).

[126] To recall, the Report was issued on 28 April 1989 (n 84), and the Resolution was adopted on 26 May 1989 (n 82 and accompanying text).

[127] 1989 Resolution, n 82, recitals A–B.

[128] 1989 Resolution, n 82, recitals C, E.

[129] 1989 Resolution, n 82, recital F.

[130] 1989 Resolution, n 82, recital I; point 1.

[131] 1989 Resolution, n 82, recital J; point 2. This was in contrast to the 1989 Report, which had envisaged two types of committees (first, 'a representative committee of appropriate experts' to set the project in motion; and second, 'an ad hoc committee of lawyers responsible for determining priorities and organizing the whole undertaking': ns 124–125 and accompanying text). Thus, it was not clear to what extent the Parliament's request sought to merge the two committees together or turn one into the other, among other things.

[132] 1989 Resolution, n 82, recital G; points 3–4.

With those bold statements, the 1989 Resolution was heralded as 'a symbolic starting point' for the EU's engagement in the debate about the promulgation of a uniform code of private (and contract) law.[133] It is repeatedly cited in documents concerning European contract law issued by the Union institutions and is a steady fixture in the scholarly literature concerning European contract law and European private law generally. Regrettably, however, the Parliament's explicit engagement with the EU's internal market competences and the unique method of unification proposed, that of the convention-regulation hybrid, remained hidden in the documents accompanying the Resolution.

Notably, the Parliament's assumption of sufficient competence to unify national private law in the 1989 Resolution may have appeared surprising when placed alongside another resolution of the European Parliament issued about a year later, which drew a connection between national private law and the principle of subsidiarity.[134] On 12 July 1990, the Parliament adopted a Resolution on the principle of subsidiarity (1990 Resolution),[135] the first of many leading up to the Intergovernmental Conference on the Maastricht Treaty.[136] This Resolution was generally concerned with the role played by subsidiarity in relation to patrolling the division of competence between the European Community (now Union) and the Member States. Among other things, the Parliament stressed that there were very few areas in which the Community had been given exclusive competence under the EC Treaty, and that most areas of Community competence were areas in which Member States could also act under the rubric of concurrent competences, which were also referred to as shared, parallel, or overlapping competences.[137] The principle of subsidiarity should therefore 'be a guide not just to determine legally the areas in which the Community may act (which has been done in the Treaties) but also, and especially, as a political guide to the extent of Community action in the fields of concurrent competence'.[138] Following this, the Parliament declared that '*far-reaching competences will remain with the Member States in the fields*

[133] M van Hoecke, 'The Harmonisation of Private Law in Europe: Some Misunderstandings' in M van Hoeke and F Ost (eds), *The Harmonisation of European Private Law* (Hart, 2000) 1.

[134] It is perhaps with a tinge of irony that with all of the sensitivities surrounding the objectives of the Study Group, its chairman, Professor Christian von Bar, in his seminal work concerning European tort law is one of the rare scholars who noted the Parliament's 1990 Resolution on the principle of subsidiarity in relation to the EU institutions' engagement with private law. See C von Bar, 1 *The Common European Law of Torts: The Core Areas of Tort Law, its Approximation, and its Accommodation in the Legal System* (Clarendon, 1998) 387. See also E Hondius, 'Towards a European Civil Code. General Introduction' in A Hartkamp et al (eds), *Towards a European Civil Code*, 1st edn (Martinus Nijhoff/Ars Aequi Libri, 1994) 1, 1 fn 3; however, this reference was taken out in subsequent editions: see E Hondius, 'Towards a European Civil Code' in A Hartkamp et al (eds), *Towards a European Civil Code*, 2nd rev and expanded edn (Kluwer/Ars Aequi Libri, 1998) 3, 7 fn 4; E Hondius, 'Towards a European Civil Code' in A Hartkamp et al (eds), *Towards a European Civil Code*, 3rd rev and expanded edn (Kluwer/Ars Aequi Libri, 2004) 3 fn 7; Hondius, 'Towards a European Civil Code', n 41, 4 fn 9. In contrast, this Resolution and the accompanying documents are often cited in the literature on the principle of subsidiarity, but nothing has been said about their linkage to private law. See, eg, J Santer, 'Some Reflections on the Principle of Subsidiarity' in *Subsidiarity: The Challenge of Change—Proceedings of the Jacques Delors Colloquium* (EIPA, 1991) 19, 23–24; DZ Cass, 'The Word that Saves Maastricht? The Principle of Subsidiarity and the Division of Powers Within the European Community' (1992) 29 *CML Rev* 1107, 1121–1125.

[135] European Parliament Resolution of 12 July 1990 on the principle of subsidiarity, [1990] OJ C231/163 (1990 Resolution).

[136] In 1990, the Parliament adopted two resolutions on the principle of subsidiarity, the first of 12 July 1990 cited above and the second of 21 Nov 1990, [1990] OJ C324/167. This should be seen in the light of the Intergovernmental Conference held in Dec 1990, which led to the adoption of the Maastricht Treaty.

[137] 1990 Resolution, n 35, point 7.

[138] 1990 Resolution, n 35, point 7.

of economics, taxation, education, culture, social security, health, family policy, the organization of local government, public transport, infrastructure, police, penal code, *private law*, religion and many other areas'.[139]

At first sight, this statement seemed to contradict the 1989 Resolution supporting the far-reaching approximation of private law at the European level. With a closer look, however, the meaning of this statement in the 1990 Resolution appears to have been more nuanced when read in the light of the Reports accompanying this Resolution, which had been drafted by Valéry Giscard d'Estaing as Rapporteur on behalf of the Parliamentary Committee of Institutional Affairs.[140] In the first Interim Report of 22 June 1990, the above-quoted passage was framed slightly differently: 'far-reaching competences will remain, *for a certain period of time*, with the Member States in the fields of economics, taxation, education and the provisions of public and *private law*'.[141] In the subsequent Interim Report of 4 July 1990, under the heading 'Powers which should not be removed from the Member States', it was explained that in practice, 'the complexity of situations sometimes leads to a certain overlapping of powers which cannot be ignored'.[142] In particular, this was the case with '*[c]ivil law*, the status of individuals and goods, civil procedure', under which 'marital status, *contracts* and the status of minors' were listed as examples.[143]

These Reports suggested that the Member States' competence over private law was not absolute, and this was particularly so with regard to contract law in the second one. Still, the 1990 Resolution made no reference to the 1989 Resolution, and their relationship remains unclear. The two Resolutions were written by two different Parliamentary Committees with different aims, and it is therefore uncertain how much to read the content of one in relation to the other. Be that as it may, the interplay between the 1989 and 1990 Resolutions was never addressed by the Parliament. Five years later, when it issued its second 1994 Resolution on the approximation of private law, no reference was made to the 1990 Resolution, let alone to the principle of subsidiarity. In the events leading up to the 1994 Resolution, however, the EU's competence in private law was given renewed reflection by the Commission.

4.3.2 The Commission's response to 'Problems of harmonizing civil law'

On 6 April 1992, in the interim between the 1989 Resolution and the 1994 Resolution discussed below, a Greek MEP, Filippos Pierros, submitted a written question to the Commission titled 'Problems of harmonizing civil law'.[144] This was not the first time that questions concerning the approximation of civil law had come before the

[139] 1990 Resolution, n 35, point 9 (emphasis added).

[140] There were three Reports in total: (1) the Interim Report on the principle of subsidiarity, A3-163/90, dated 22 June 1990 (June 1990 Interim Report); (2) the Interim Report on the principle of subsidiarity, A3-163/90/Part B, dated 4 July 1990 (July 1990 Interim Report); and (3) the Report on the principle of subsidiarity, A3-0267/90, dated 31 Oct 1990.

[141] June 1990 Interim Report, n 140, point 10 (emphasis added).

[142] July 1990 Interim Report, n 140, point 3, at 9.

[143] July 1990 Interim Report, n 140, point 3, at 10 (emphasis added). 'Justice and organization of the legal system', which included the judicial and legal professions and organization of the courts, and 'Commercial law (except Community competition law)' were also listed. See July 1990 Interim Report, n 140, eighth, tenth indents, at 10.

[144] Written Question No 776/92 by F Pierros, 'Problems of harmonizing civil law', [1993] OJ C32/7.

Commission by way of Parliamentary questions.[145] Yet, it was Commissioner Martin Bangemann's answer to this question that infiltrated the discussion of the Community's (now Union's) competence in matters of private law in the commentary and institutional documents.

Mr Pierros began by pointing out the 'considerable discrepancies between the average length of legal proceedings, legal aid provisions, compensation, legal costs, appeal procedures etc. in the different Member States'.[146] There were different periods of time between taking a matter to court and a court judgment depending upon the country in which the lawyer brought his case, as exemplified by six months in Greece and as much as forty-two months in Italy.[147] There were also differences in the amount of compensation awarded to victims of fatal accidents across the EU.[148] In his view, 'this undermines efforts to achieve a single European market, reduces prospects of fair competition and discriminates against certain European consumers'.[149] This led him to pose the following question: 'What practical measures will the Commission take to achieve a minimum degree of harmonization between the Member States on such sensitive matters of substantive and procedural civil law?'[150]

On 19 October 1992, Commissioner Bangemann provided an answer to this question on behalf of the Commission.[151] The beginning lines are probably the most quoted:

> The Honourable Member is correct in pointing out that discrepancies exist in the Member States as regards substantive and procedural aspects of civil law. *While the Community has no direct power in terms of the EEC Treaty to intervene directly in the matters cited by the Honourable Member,* Article 220 of the Treaty does permit Member States, where necessary, to enter negotiations with each other to make Conventions with a view to securing benefits for their nationals.[152]

He then gave the examples of the Brussels Convention on the recognition and enforcement of judgments and the Rome Convention on the law applicable to contractual obligations, which 'go some way to reduce the differences between the Member States in relation to civil law', and noted that steps were being taken to evaluate whether the Brussels Convention should be extended to other areas of the law.[153]

Thereafter, Commissioner Bangemann's response was cited in the commentary in order to substantiate the Community's (now Union's) lack of sufficient competence to adopt a European code of private law.[154] Looking closely, however, it is doubtful whether his answer can be taken that far.[155] Commissioner Bangemann limited his answer to 'the matters cited' by Mr Pierros, which were, to recall, 'the average length of proceedings, legal aid provisions, compensation, legal costs, appeal procedures, etc.'.

[145] See, eg, Written Question No 1865/91 by U Braun-Moser, 'Codification of civil law with a bearing on economic matters in the Community', [1992] OJ C102/24. With regard to contract law, see n 186 and accompanying text.

[146] Written Question No 776/92, n 144, first para.

[147] Written Question No 776/92, n 144, first para.

[148] Written Question No 776/92, n 144, first para.

[149] Written Question No 776/92, n 144, second para.

[150] Written Question No 776/92, n 144, second para.

[151] Answer given by Mr Bangemann on behalf of the Commission, [1993] OJ C32/8.

[152] Answer, n 151 (emphasis added). As regards Art 220 EC (later Art 293 EC), which has been repealed by the Lisbon Treaty, see further Chapter 10, § 10.2.1.

[153] Answer, n 151.

[154] See, eg, T Wilhelmsson, *Social Contract Law and European Integration* (Dartmouth, 1995) 93 fn 309.

[155] See, eg, E Hondius, 'Consumer Law and Private Law: the Case for Integration' in W Heusel (ed), *New European Contract Law and Consumer Protection: The Concepts Involved in Community Regulations and Their Consequences for Domestic Civil Law* (Bundesanzeiger, 1999) 19, 25.

Thus, the Commissioner's response seemed to have been focused primarily on procedural, as opposed to substantive, civil law matters. The one topic raised in Mr Pierros' written question that could be considered to concern substantive civil law matters pertained to 'compensation' for victims of fatal accidents, in which some inroads have since been made at European level.[156] In any event, it remains ambiguous to what extent Mr Bangemann's answer spoke to the EU's competence to take action in substantive private law, particularly as regards contract law. This may have been furthered by publications authored by Commissioner Bangemann (and other EU officials) in a private capacity expressing a negative opinion on the subject.[157] The bottom line is that while his response no doubt contributed to the discussion of the EU's competence in this setting, even filtering into the Parliament's 1994 Resolution, it was certainly not the last word on the matter.

4.3.3 The 1994 Resolution

On 6 May 1994, the European Parliament adopted a second Resolution on the harmonization of certain sectors of the private law of the Member States (1994 Resolution).[158] As evidenced by reference to 'certain sectors' of private law in its title, there was a subtle change of position in this Resolution as compared to the one in 1989. The 1994 Resolution was short, taking up less than a page.[159] The Parliament began by recalling its previous 1989 Resolution, asking for the necessary preparatory work to be started on a Common European Code of Private law, and criticizing the Commission for not yet undertaking such work.[160] It then declared that the 'progressive harmonization of certain sectors of private law is essential to the completion of the internal market',[161] and made several requests that were similar, though not identical, to those set out in the 1989 Resolution. It asked the Commission to start work 'on the possibility of drawing up a Common European Code of Private Law' and called for the creation of a committee of experts 'to propose priorities for partial harmonization in the short term and more general harmonization in the long term'.[162] Noticeably, it neither defined what it meant by 'certain sectors of private law' nor clarified what fields should be included in such a Code, although again, it put emphasis on contract law, singling out the Lando Commission for which 'support should continue to be given. . . in its work on the harmonization of contract law'.[163]

The subtle differences between the 1989 and 1994 Resolutions may be explained by looking at the Explanatory Statement in the accompanying Report drawn up by a Spanish MEP, Carlos María Bru Puron, as Rapporteur on behalf of the Parliamentary Committee on Legal Affairs and Citizens' Rights.[164] It was divided into two main parts

[156] See, eg, Council Dir 2004/80/EC of 29 April 2004 relating to compensation to crime victims, [2004] OJ L261/15. But see, eg, Written Question No 1036/96 by G Ford, 'Automatic compensation for victims of accidents', [1996] OJ C297/74. As indicated on its website for DG Justice through the link to 'Civil Justice' (within the context of civil and commercial matters), the Commission is currently undertaking work on limitation periods for the victims of traffic accidents: see <http://ec.europa.eu/justice/>.

[157] See, eg, M Bangemann, 'Privatrechtsangleichung in der Europäischen Union' (1994) *Z Eu P* 377; IE Schwartz, 'Perspektiven der Angleichung des Privatrechts in der Europäischen Gemeinschaft' (1994) *Z Eu P* 559.

[158] European Parliament Resolution of 6 May 1994 on the harmonization of certain sectors of the private law of the Member States, [1994] OJ C205/518 (1994 Resolution).

[159] There were nine points in total: four introductory clauses (recitals A–D) and five paras (1–5).

[160] 1994 Resolution, n 158, recitals B–C.

[161] 1994 Resolution, n 158, recital D.

[162] 1994 Resolution, n 158, points 1–2.

[163] 1994 Resolution, n 158, point 4.

[164] The text of the Report was divided into two parts: Part A concerned the motion for a resolution, and Part B contained the Explanatory Statement. The final Report containing Part A was dated 27

concerning, first, general questions connected with the harmonization of private law, and secondly, special areas for harmonization or unification.[165] At the forefront of the first part was the discussion of the former Community's (now Union's) competence. Although he recognized that some harmonization of private law was needed, the question 'whether there is a need for the general harmonization of private law, however, remains open; it does *not* appear to be essential to the smooth operation of the single market'.[166] He also stressed that although there were various Treaty provisions conferring specific competence on the Community to take action in certain areas, which included Articles 100 and 100a EC (now Article 115 and 114 TFEU, respectively) in the realm of 'private economic law', the Community did '*not* have general competence for harmonizing private law as a whole', citing Commissioner Bangemann's response discussed above.[167]

At the same time, however, he underlined that although the harmonization or unification of private law as a whole was not possible at present, 'an approximation of whole sectors appears attainable and adequate'.[168] He proceeded to identify certain appropriate sectors for harmonization, which included 'the law of obligations and contract law'.[169] He envisaged that some basic legal concepts in this area should be harmonized first, using the Lando Commission's work as an initial step in this regard.[170] Then, he pointed to several fundamental principles, which would provide the basis for a 'future code of obligations and private property contracts at Community level'.[171]

Depending upon the matters concerned, the Rapporteur considered the various forms of harmonization or unification that could be availed of, which included reference to certain American techniques.[172] In its general sense, harmonization could be carried out in the form of a convention, regulation, or directive.[173] He surmised that other methods to achieve harmonization could be uniform laws, model laws, and Restatements taken from the American setting, but noted that these methods were not recognized in Community (now Union) law.[174] As for Restatements, the main aim was

April 1994: A3-0329/94/Part A. Part B was supposed to have been published separately, but the final publication of Part B is missing from the European Parliament and Commission archives. Thus, the version of Part B contained in the Draft Report on the harmonization of certain sectors of the private law of the Member States, A3-0000/04/Pt B, dated 7 April 1994 (1994 Report) is relied upon in this discussion.

[165] 1994 Report, n 164, 2, 5. [166] 1994 Report, n 164, point 1.2.1 (emphasis added).

[167] 1994 Report, n 164, point 1.2 (emphasis added). This was prefaced by the words 'As already noted', which appears to be directed at the previous statement following discussion of Commissioner Bangemann's response that 'legal authorities normally consider that the Community has no general power to harmonize private law': see 1994 Report, n 164, point 1.1.

[168] 1994 Report, n 164, point 4.

[169] 1994 Report, n 164, point 6. He also mentioned private international law and certain issues falling within the realm of family law: points 4–5. Moreover, he cited immovable property law, but decided that it was not a priority for the Community: point 7.

[170] 1994 Report, n 164, point 7 (mentioning 'absence of intention', 'privilege', 'property held in trust', and 'reservation of ownership' as examples).

[171] 1994 Report, n 164, point 7 (listing 'respect for an agreement made ("pacta sunt servanda"), adaptation to circumstances ("rebus sic stantibus"), the prevalence of "bona fides", the presumption "juris tantum" as regards forms authenticated by a lawyer, except where there is proof of falsehood, the protection of legal transactions or respect for what appears to be the case, particularly when using data from public record offices (in the case of property, commercial activities, etc.), etc.').

[172] 1994 Report, n 164, point 2.2.

[173] 1994 Report, n 164, point 2.2. The discussion seemed to jump back and forth between harmonization viewed in its general sense and its specific sense equated with directives, which provides further impetus for terminological consistency between approximation, harmonization, and unification: see Chapter 1, § 1.2.3.1.

[174] 1994 Report, n 164, point 2.2. Mutual recognition was also tentatively considered, but ruled out.

'to influence the development of law directly and indirectly to ensure greater uniformity of contract law in the Member States' and was a method identified with the work of the Lando Commission.[175] In Community law, a Restatement was to be regarded as a measure comparable to a recommendation.[176] As for uniform laws and model laws, there was no further elaboration, save for the reference to the Benelux Uniform Law on Trademarks as an example of a uniform law.[177] Thus, it remained ambiguous to what extent the meaning of these terms in the American setting was taken into account. It also remained unclear to what extent the Rapporteur considered a uniform law a viable instrument, since he made further reference to it as a possible means of unification even though, as noted previously, it was not recognized in the Community legal order.[178]

In closing, the Rapporteur concluded: 'The differences are still too great for overall harmonization or unification. In other words, we have not yet reached the stage where we can have a European Code.'[179] Yet, approximation of laws in certain sectors was still advisable and attainable, with the law of contracts and obligations among the most appropriate areas.[180] This seems to explain the emphasis placed on 'certain sectors' of private law in the 1994 Resolution, although they went unnamed in the final text. Nevertheless, the reference to a European Code of Private Law and to the progression towards 'more general harmonization' in the 1994 Resolution sits somewhat uncomfortably with the accompanying Report that disclaimed such broadscale harmonization and singled out contract law and the law of obligations.

Importantly, during the time leading up to the adoption of the 1994 Resolution, the draft motion for the resolution already prompted a response from the Commission on the issue of the EU's competence in matters of private law. The Commission made certain written statements in the form of a 'Projet de Declaration' and a 'Note d'information' as part of its file on the 1994 Resolution, although these documents do not appear to have been officially published.[181] These statements firmly denounced the EU's competence to adopt a European code of private law.

In the 'Projet de Declaration', the Commission took note of the European Parliament's 1989 and 1994 Resolutions, but underscored that as far as the harmonization of substantive private law was concerned, the former Community (now Union) was only given competence under the limits and conditions set out in the Treaties, which excluded the possibility of adopting such a code.[182] It further stressed that all EU action must abide by the principle of subsidiarity and respect the national identities of the Member States then enshrined in Articles B and F EU (now replaced in substance by Articles 5(3) and 4(2) TEU, respectively).[183] The Commission reiterated these remarks in a somewhat stronger tone in the

[175] 1994 Report, n 164, point 2.2. The work of the Lando Commission was cited alongside several international bodies as 'a very positive factor in the future short-term development of European private law': 1994 Report, n 164, point 3.

[176] 1994 Report, n 164, point 2.2.

[177] 1994 Report, n 164, point 2.2.

[178] 1994 Report, n 164, point 2.2.

[179] 1994 Report, n 164, point C.

[180] 1994 Report, n 164, point C.

[181] These two documents are part of the Commission's file on the 1994 Resolution and were attached to an Italian version of Part A of the Report on the harmonization of certain sectors of the private law of the Member States, A3-0329/94/Pt A, dated 27 April 1994 (on file with author). They are not dated, but the dates of facsimile at the bottom of each page indicate 29 April 1994.

[182] 'Project de Declaration—Harmonisation de certains secteurs du droit privé—Rapport Bru Puron', n 181 (author's translation). The original French version stated: 'La Commission prend note des souhaits du Parlement, elle tient toutefois à rappeller que les actions d'harmonisation des dispositions nationales du droit privé matériel ne sont adoptées que dans les domaines, dans les conditions et dans les limites prévus dans les traités. Ceci exclut la possibilité d'adopter un Code européen commun de droit privé.'

[183] 'Project de Declaration', n 182 (author's translation). The original French version stated: 'Enfin, il convient de rappeler qu'en tout état de cause les objectifs de l'Union européenne sont atteints

'Note d'information', stating that the Parliament's requests exceeded the Community's competences and that the Treaties excluded in principle the '*l'uniformisation totale*' of the substantive private law of the Member States and hence the adoption of a common European code of private law.[184] In the heading of both documents, reference was made to the 1994 Resolution and the accompanying Report of Mr Bru Puron. Yet, there was no mention in either document of the Explanatory Statement, which evidenced the Parliament's intent to scale down its approach in this regard.[185]

Not long thereafter, the Commission was given another chance to opine about the future course of private law, particularly contract law. By way of a written question dated 29 March 1995, a Belgian MEP, Marianne Thyssen, asked the Commission: 'What progress has it made with its work on the harmonization of contract law?'[186] About a month later, Commissioner Emma Bonino responded on behalf of the Commission, stating in relevant part: '*The Commission does not intend to present general proposals designed to harmonise the law of contract.* Certain specific initiatives at Community [now Union] level do however contribute to approximating certain aspects of national contract law', thereby citing the Unfair Contract Terms Directive and the proposal for the Consumer Sales Directive.[187] In hindsight, Commissioner Bonino's answer was tinged with a bit of irony when viewed in the light of the present state of the European contract law project. It garnered some attention, but did not halt the Parliament's activities.

4.3.4 The 1999 Working Paper

In the years following the 1994 Resolution, at the request of the Parliamentary Committee on Legal Affairs and the Internal Market,[188] the Directorate General for Research of the European Parliament commissioned a Working Paper titled 'The Private Law Systems in the EU: Discrimination on Grounds of Nationality and the Need for a European Civil Code' (1999 Working Paper).[189] It was completed in June 1999 by eleven pre-eminent European scholars in consultation with the Study Group.[190]

conformément aux dispositions de traités dans le respect du principe de subsidiarité et de l'identité nationale des Etats membres (articles B et F du Traité sur l'Union européenne).'

184 'Note d'information—Harmonisation de certains secteurs du droit privé—Rapport Bru Puron', n 181, point 4 (author's translation). In the original French version, this provision stated: 'Il est suggère que, devant le Parlement, la Commission fasse valoir le fait que les demandes du Parlement outrepassent les compétences de la Communauté. En principe la Communauté ou l'Union ne peuvent arrêter que les mesures d'harmonisation du droit privé matériel prévues dans les Traités et cela dans les domaines, les conditions et les limites fixés par ceux-ci: les traités excluent en principe l'uniformisation totale du droit privé matériel des Etats membres et en conséquence l'adoption d'un Code européen commun de droit privé.'

185 It is unknown whether Part B of the Report comprising the Rapporteur's Explanatory Statement was read by the Commission before these statements were written.

186 Written Question E-892/95 by M Thyssen, 'Harmonization of Member States' laws—procedural law and contract law', [1995] OJ C190/31.

187 Answer given by Mrs Bonino on behalf of the Commission, [1995] OJ C190/31, point 2 (emphasis added).

188 The Committee on Legal Affairs and Citizens' Rights, which was in charge of the 1989 and 1994 Resolutions, changed its name to the Committee on Legal Affairs and Internal Market in the 1999–2004 term. Since the 2004–2009 term, there are separate Committees on Legal Affairs and on Internal Market and Consumer Protection.

189 1999 Working Paper, n 43. There is no indication therein of the date on which it was commissioned or when work began.

190 1999 Working Paper, n 43, page following title page. The eleven authors are Professors Christian von Bar (head of team), Maurits Barendrecht, Jürgen Basedow, Ulrich Drobnig, Walter

The work was headed by Professor Christian von Bar, the chairman of the Study Group, and several of the Working Paper's authors were members of the Lando Commission and/or the Study Group.[191]

The 1999 Working Paper had a twofold aim: first, to examine, on the basis of a comparative study of legal provisions, the scope and need for the creation of a European civil code and the EU's competence to adopt such a code; and secondly, to investigate any forms of discrimination on grounds of nationality that may still be permissible under the private and procedural law of the Member States.[192] It was a hefty document totalling a little over 200 pages. As illustrated by its title, the Working Paper concerned various fields of national private law. It devoted specific sections to general contract law, specific types of contract law (service contracts and insurance contracts), the law of extra-contractual obligations (tort, unjust enrichment, and *negotiorum gestio*), the law governing credit security, and the law of civil procedure.[193] It specifically excluded family law and the law of succession,[194] but went somewhat further than the scope of European patrimonial law, given its inclusion of civil procedure. It was divided into four chapters, the fourth of which concerned the Community's (now Union's) competence to adopt a European civil code, also framed as a uniform European law of obligations and property.[195]

Chapter Four was co-authored by Professors Walter van Gerven and Winfried Tilmann, the two scholars who had taken up the morning session of the 1997 Scheveningen conference, 'Towards a European civil code', with the discussion of the existence, or not, of a possible legal basis for such a code.[196] Much of the chapter tracked their previous positions at this conference at which Professor Tilmann submitted that former Article 95 EC (now Article 114 TFEU) could serve as a viable legal basis and Professor van Gerven argued the opposite. The chapter presented two 'alternative' opinions: the first concerned the potential legal bases to support the adoption of a uniform European law of obligations and property law;[197] and the second concerned the use of an intergovernmental treaty concluded by all Member States.[198]

In the first opinion, former Articles 65, 94, 95, and 308 EC (now Articles 81, 115, 114, and 352 TFEU, respectively) were examined as potential legal bases for a European civil code,[199] with predominant focus placed on Article 95 EC.[200] Article 65 EC was dismissed as an inadequate legal basis, although it was surmised that it supported the case for Article 95 EC.[201] Articles 94 and 95 EC were deemed mutually exclusive,

van Gerven, Ewoud Hondius, Konstantinos Kerameus, Stelios Koussoulis, Ole Lando, Marco Loos, and Winfried Tilmann.

191 1999 Working Paper, n 43, page following title page.

192 1999 Working Paper, n 43, iii.

193 See generally 1999 Working Paper, n 43, chs I-II.

194 1999 Working Paper, n 43, iii.

195 See 1999 Working Paper, n 43, 181–182. As for the others, ch I summarized the main differences and common features among the various fields of private law and civil procedural law in the EU; ch II examined the extent of discrimination on grounds of nationality in relation to such fields; and ch III concerned the scope and need for the creation of a European civil code.

196 Compare W van Gerven, 'Coherence of Community and national laws. Is there a legal basis for a European Civil Code?' (1997) 5 *ERPL* 465, with W Tilmann, 'The legal basis for a European Civil Code' (1997) 5 *ERPL* 47.

197 1999 Working Paper, n 43, point 35.

198 1999 Working Paper, n 43, point 49.

199 1999 Working Paper, n 43, point 37. Former Art 293 EC was disposed of straight away: 1999 Working Paper, n 43, point 36.

200 1999 Working Paper, n 43, points 41–77. There was also brief discussion of the relationship between former Art 95 EC (now Art 114 TFEU) and the principle of subsidiarity; the principle of proportionality was presented alongside subsidiarity as regards the choice of legal instruments: see points 78–81.

201 1999 Working Paper, n 43, points 39–40, 76–77. See further Chapter 10, § 10.3.2.

with Article 95 EC taking precedence.[202] Article 308 EC was considered subsidiary to Article 95 EC such that it could not apply to matters within the scope of Article 95 EC, although it was considered relevant for the creation of optional instruments falling outside the scope of approximation.[203] As for Article 95 EC, the opinion indicated that this provision could in principle serve as the proper legal basis for the unification of the fields of private law concerned, including contract law. Admittedly, much of the discussion was phrased in malleable language, and there was no explicit affirmative statement about Article 95 EC in this regard.[204] Nevertheless, there were strong statements affirming that as far as Article 95 EC's contribution to the 'functioning' of the internal market was concerned, '[i]f the divergence or territorially limited effect of national provisions impedes cross-border activities between economic players, remedial action can be taken on the basis of Article 95, even if the activity is not classifiable as the exercise of a specific fundamental freedom'.[205] Specifically, if divergent laws of the Member States relate to the free movement of goods or freedom to provide services or if they burden businesses with divergent restrictions or charges which distort competition, then Article 95 EC comes into play.[206]

The second opinion advocated recourse to an international treaty among the Member States and was premised on the 'political assumption' that Article 95 EC would be inapplicable.[207] It submitted that 'on legal, political or tactical grounds, it is inadvisable to create any other legal instrument for the creation of a uniform European law of obligations and property than a treaty that would be concluded by all Member States'.[208] This opinion envisaged an intergovernmental convention negotiated by the Member States in accordance with the general rules of public international law.[209] As regards the choice between the two opinions, there was no stated preference. Instead, the authors recommended that 'the work on the formulation of standard legal texts for those areas where standardisation is needed be expedited by legal scholars and, when this work is nearing completion, that a decision be made in the light of prevailing political and legal circumstances as to which instrument should be used for the implementation of the code'.[210] As such, while the opinions differed as to the matter of competence, at least there seemed to be agreement that work should be undertaken to bring about a European civil code in the first place.

4.3.5 The 2000 Resolution

On 16 March 2000, the European Parliament reminded the Commission of its previous calls for Community (now Union) action in private law in its Resolution on the Commission's annual legislative programme for the year 2000 (2000 Resolution).[211]

[202] 1999 Working Paper, n 43, points 41–43.

[203] 1999 Working Paper, n 43, points 44, 50–58.

[204] It was also premised with a remark on the timeframe of the project: 'First of all, legal scholars and practitioners should draw up a model code. As this work nears completion, a decision should be take[n] in the light of the prevailing political and legal conditions as to which of the available legal bases should be used.' 1999 Working Paper, n 43, point 3. This opinion was issued in June 1999 while the *Tobacco Advertising I* case was pending before the Court of Justice, which may have been a contributing factor. For further discussion of this case, see Chapter 8, § 8.3.2.1.

[205] 1999 Working Paper, n 43, point 73.

[206] 1999 Working Paper, n 43, point 75.

[207] 1999 Working Paper, n 43, point 83.

[208] 1999 Working Paper, n 43, point 82.

[209] 1999 Working Paper, n 43, point 86.

[210] 1999 Working Paper, n 43, point 88.

[211] European Parliament Resolution of 16 March 2000 on the Commission's annual legislative programme for 2000, [2000] OJ C377/323 (2000 Resolution).

Originally, there had been three separate motions for a resolution on this subject,[212] one of which included a provision explicitly stating that 'greater harmonisation of civil law has become essential in the internal market, as it is becoming increasingly evident in respect of *a general law of obligations, contracts, consumer affairs and the family*', and therefore, the Commission was requested 'to draw up a study in this area, with the involvement of interested academic groups'.[213] Less than a week later, when the various motions were consolidated, this paragraph was changed. The references to specific fields of private law including contract law were gone. What remained was the following: 'The European Parliament. . . [c]onsiders that greater harmonisation of civil law has become essential in the internal market and calls on the Commission to draw up a study in this area'.[214] These changes were kept verbatim in the final text of the Resolution adopted by the Parliament a few days later.[215] Nevertheless, the Parliament's encouragement of the harmonization of civil law for the purposes of the internal market remained, although there was no specification of the relevant fields or any mention of the constitutionality of such endeavours.

On 9 June 2000, the Commission issued a response to the 2000 Resolution.[216] As regards the Parliament's request concerning the harmonization of civil law, the Commission stated its intention to issue a communication to the institutions and the general public 'with the aim of launching a detailed and wide-ranging discussion' on the matter.[217]

[212] Motion for a resolution by Mr Swoboda on behalf of the PSE Group on the Commission Annual Work Programme 2000 (B5-0228/2000), dated 9 March 2000; Motion for a resolution by Mrs Hautala, Mr Lannoye, and Mrs Maes on behalf of the Verts/ALE Group on the Commission's work programme for 2000 (B5-0229/2000), dated 9 March 2000; Motion for a resolution by the following Members: Poettering, Grossetê, Elles, Fiori, Suominen, and Van Velzen on behalf of the PPE-DE Group on the Commission's annual legislative programme for 2000 (B5-0230/2000), dated 9 March 2000.

[213] Motion for a resolution (B5-0230/2000), n 212, point 29 (emphasis added). This para was the first listed under the heading 'On the internal market'.

[214] Joint Motion for a resolution by the following Members: Poettering, on behalf of the PPE-DE Group, Swoboda on behalf of the PSE Group, and Lannoye on behalf of the Verts/ALE Group, replacing the motions by the following groups: PSE (B5-0228/2000), Verts/ALE (B5-0229/2000), PPE-DE (B5-0230/2000) on the Commission's annual legislative programme for 2000 (RC-B5-0228/2000), dated 14 March 2000, para 24. This language appeared in the first para of the section now titled 'Single market, information society and tax'.

[215] 2000 Resolution, n 211, point 28.

[216] Reply of the Commission to the European Parliament Resolution of 16 March 2000 on the Commission's annual legislative programme for 2000, SP (2000) 2019/3 (annule et remplace SP(2000) 2019/2), dated 9 June 2000 (2000 Commission Response). According to the minutes of the Heads of Cabinet meeting of 9 June 2000, this document was adopted on 9 June 2000, and then Commission President Romano Prodi and Commission Vice President Loyola de Palacio were instructed to send this reply to the Parliament. See SEC (2000) 1483, dated 9 June 2000. While the Commission later referred to the date of 25 July 2000 in its 2001 Communication on European Contract Law (COM (2001) 398 final, 11.7.2001, point 3), this seems to refer to the date of transmission of the reply or the date that the Commission's reply was registered with the Parliament.

[217] 2000 Commission Response, n 216, point 28 (author's translation). In doing so, the Commission took account of the Parliament's previous resolutions and the European Council's Tampere Conclusions, discussed below. In the original French version, this point read:

> La demande du Parlement Européen s'inscrit dans le context de ses deux résolutions de 1989 et 1994 ainsi que la demande correspondante du Conseil Européen de Tampere. Comme la Commission a déjà eu l'occasion d'indiquer dans son 'tableau du bord pour l'évaluation des progrès réalisés dans la création d'un espace de liberté, sécurité et Justice', elle soumettra une communication aux autres institutions communautaires et au public avec l'object d'une discussion approfondie et aussi large que possible en respectant la date de 2001 donné par le Conseil Européen. En tenant compte de son importance pour

In essence, the Commission was referring to what would be the 2001 Communication on European Contract Law.[218]

4.4 The European Council Meeting at Tampere

Alongside the European Parliament's early resolutions mentioned above, the European Council's 1999 meeting in Tampere has been viewed as an equally important catalyst for jump-starting the debate about European contract law at the European level. To understand its significance for the constitutional dimensions of European contract law, a brief overview of the events leading to Tampere, including the Vienna Action Plan, is offered before proceeding to the European Council's Tampere Conclusions.

4.4.1 Events leading to Tampere and the Vienna Action Plan

By way of background, one of the major breakthroughs of the Amsterdam Treaty was the creation of the Area of Freedom, Security and Justice (AFSJ). The AFSJ had its origins in the former third pillar, originally titled Justice and Home Affairs in the Maastricht Treaty. With the entry into force of the Amsterdam Treaty, several, but not all, of those fields were transferred to the then Community pillar and placed within former Title IV of the former EC Treaty concerning visas, asylum, immigration, and other policies related to free movement of persons. What was not transferred to Title IV remained in the so-called third pillar of the former EU Treaty, renamed Police and Judicial Cooperation in Criminal Matters (PJCCM). Together, Title IV of the EC Treaty and Title VI of the EU Treaty comprised the AFSJ until the entry into force of the Lisbon Treaty, whereby these provisions have been consolidated in Title V of the TFEU devoted to the AFSJ.

One of the fields within the AFSJ is judicial cooperation in civil matters, enshrined in former Article 65 EC, now Article 81 TFEU. Although this provision will be discussed at length in a coming chapter,[219] it must be pointed out here that among the various types of measures that were envisaged to be taken on the basis of former Article 65 EC were those 'eliminating obstacles to the good functioning of civil proceedings, if necessary by promoting the compatibility of the rules on civil procedure applicable in the Member States' pursuant to Article 65(c) EC. With the entry into force of the Lisbon Treaty, this provision appears in substantially similar form in Article 81(2)(f) TFEU, which provides for the adoption of measures aimed at ensuring 'the elimination of obstacles to the proper functioning of civil proceedings, if necessary by promoting the compatibility of the rules of civil procedure applicable in the Member States'. This language of former Article 65(c) EC, now Article 81(2)(f) TFEU, bears directly on the relationship between the European Council's Tampere Conclusions and European contract law.

The creation of the AFSJ received a major impetus from the European Council's meeting in Vienna, which served as the prelude to what would be decided in Tampere.

le développement du marché intérieur et des tendances commerciales et technologiques futures, cette communication analysera l'acquis—en vigeur our en préparation—au niveau communautaire dans les domains pertinents de droit civil afin d'identifier et d'evaluer les lacunes ainsi que les travaux académiques accomplis ou en cours.

[218] 2001 Communication, n 216.

[219] See Chapter 10.

To explain, at its meeting in Cardiff on 14–15 June 1998, the European Council requested the Council and the Commission to submit an action plan on the creation of the AFSJ for examination at its forthcoming meeting in Vienna on 11–12 December 1998.[220] This resulted in the Council and Commission Action Plan of 2 December 1998 on How Best to Implement the Provisions of the Treaty of Amsterdam on an Area of Freedom, Security and Justice, which is commonly referred to as the Vienna Action Plan.[221] It was organized into two main parts: first, an introductory section elaborated each of the elements of 'freedom', 'security', and 'justice' and their importance to the EU; and secondly, a list of priorities and measures were outlined for the areas falling within former Title IV of the EC Treaty and Title VI of the EU Treaty. Generally, the area of 'freedom' was linked to the free movement of persons and visa, asylum, and immigration policies,[222] and the area of 'security' denoted the Union's fight against crime, terrorism, trafficking in persons and offences against children, drug and arms trafficking, corruption, and fraud.[223] The area of 'justice' proved to be the embryo for what would become the European contract law project and thus deserves detailed scrutiny.

In the introductory part, the Vienna Action Plan explained that the aim of the area of 'justice' was to give citizens 'a common sense of justice throughout the Union'.[224] This would be achieved 'while respecting the reality that, for reasons deeply imbedded in history and tradition, judicial systems differ substantially between Member States'.[225] It delineated four areas comprising the area of 'justice': judicial cooperation in civil matters, judicial cooperation in criminal matters, procedures, and cross-border litigation. In particular, judicial cooperation in civil matters was deemed a fundamental stage in the creation of a European judicial area that would benefit all Union citizens as proclaimed by the following passage:

> Law-abiding citizens have a right to look to the Union to simplify and facilitate the judicial environment in which they live in the European Union context. Here principles such as legal certainty and equal access to justice should be a main objective, implying identification of the competent jurisdiction, clear designation of the applicable law, availability of speedy and fair proceedings and effective enforcement proceedings.[226]

These points found their way into the second part of the Vienna Action Plan listing the various priorities and measures for the field of judicial cooperation in civil matters.[227] Point 39 of the Vienna Action Plan declared:

> The aim is to make life simpler for European citizens by improving and simplifying the rules and procedures on cooperation and communication between authorities and on enforcing decisions, by promoting the compatibility of conflict of law rules and on jurisdiction and *by eliminating obstacles to the good functioning of civil proceedings in a European judicial area*.[228]

[220] Presidency Conclusions, Cardiff European Council, 14–15 June 1998, point 48; Presidency Conclusions, Vienna European Council, 11–12 Dec 1998.

[221] Action Plan of the Council and the Commission on How Best to Implement the Provisions of the Treaty of Amsterdam on an Area of Freedom, Security and Justice—Text adopted by the Justice and Home Affairs Council of 3 Dec 1998, [1999] OJ C19/1 (Vienna Action Plan). Although the Amsterdam Treaty was signed on 2 Oct 1997, it did not enter into force until 1 May 1999, which explains the timeframe of the Vienna Action Plan.

[222] Vienna Action Plan, n 221, points 6–8.

[223] Vienna Action Plan, n 221, points 9–14.

[224] Vienna Action Plan, n 221, point 15.

[225] Vienna Action Plan, n 221, point 15.

[226] Vienna Action Plan, n 221, point 16.

[227] Vienna Action Plan, n 221, pt II.B.II, at 10.

[228] Vienna Action Plan, n 221, point 39 (emphasis added).

There was no further elaboration of what was meant by 'eliminating obstacles to the good functioning of civil proceedings', nor was there any mention made of the fact that this phrase was identical to relevant language set forth in what was then Article 65(c) EC.[229]

Immediately following point 39 of the Vienna Action Plan came various measures to be taken in this field within two and five years after the entry into force of the Amsterdam Treaty. As for the two-year term, this pertained to EU private international law instruments.[230] As for the five-year term, this generally concerned additional EU private international law and procedural measures,[231] but two categories stood out because they were the only two explicitly referring to the approximation of the Member States' laws in this context. The first category listed measures 'identifying the rules on civil procedure having cross-border implications which are urgent to approximate for the purpose of facilitating access to justice for the citizens of Europe and examin[ing] the elaboration of additional measures accordingly to improve compatibility of civil procedures'.[232] This could include, for example, rules on deposition of security for litigation costs, the granting of legal aid, and 'other possible obstacles of an economic nature'.[233] The second category concerned measures that should 'examine *the possibility of approximating certain areas of civil law, such as creating uniform private international law applicable to the acquisition in good faith of corporal movables*'.[234] Together, these two categories concentrated on the approximation of private international law and procedural matters; there were no measures envisaged for the approximation of substantive civil law.

This was further underscored in the European Parliament's Resolution on the draft version of the Vienna Action Plan adopted a few months earlier on 13 April 1999.[235] The Parliament devoted several paragraphs to the measures envisaged for judicial cooperation in civil matters, stressing that 'there is an urgent and vital need to promote the compatibility of the rules applicable in the Member States concerning civil procedure, the conflict of laws and of jurisdiction'.[236] The Parliament also called on the Commission 'to take full advantage of the fresh possibilities offered by Article 73m (future Article 65) of the EC Treaty in order to draw up its own body of rules in the area of civil law and to promote the compatibility of civil procedures'.[237] What was meant by 'its own body of rules in the area of civil law' was not explained, but reference to Article 65 EC and 'the compatibility of civil procedures' seemed to imply a focus on private international law and procedural aspects of national laws. Again, there was no explicit discussion of substantive civil law.

[229] See text following n 219.

[230] Vienna Action Plan, n 221, point 40 (also mentioning the European judicial network).

[231] Vienna Action Plan, n 221, point 41.

[232] Vienna Action Plan, n 221, point 41(d).

[233] Vienna Action Plan, n 221, point 41(d).

[234] Vienna Action Plan, n 221, point 41(f) (emphasis added).

[235] European Parliament Resolution of 13 April 1999 on the draft action plan of the Council and Commission on how best to implement the provisions of the Treaty of Amsterdam on an area of freedom, security and justice, [1999] OJ C219/61 (1999 Vienna Action Plan Resolution).

[236] 1999 Vienna Action Plan Resolution, n 235, para 21. This statement initially read: 'there is an urgent and vital need *to harmonise* the basic provisions of procedural law and of European international private law': Report on the action plan of the Council and Commission on how best to implement the provisions of the Treaty of Amsterdam on an area of freedom, security and justice, A4-0133/99/Pt A, dated 18 March 1999, point III.I.2, at 9 (emphasis added). Thereafter, however, this was changed.

[237] 1999 Vienna Action Plan Resolution, n 235, point 23.

4.4.2 The Tampere Conclusions

Subsequently, however, the issue of the approximation of substantive and procedural civil law was placed squarely on the agenda of the European Council at its meeting held on 15–16 October 1999 in Tampere, Finland.[238] This meeting was convened specifically to discuss the creation of the AFSJ.[239] The importance of the meeting in Tampere was signalled by the first few lines of the Presidency Conclusions, in which the European Council stated its intention to send 'a strong political message to reaffirm the importance of this objective' and that it had agreed 'on a number of policy orientations and priorities which will speedily make this area a reality'.[240] To this end, the European Council set down the 'Tampere Milestones', which represented the political guidelines and concrete objectives for each of the fields falling within the AFSJ over the next five years. At the forefront was the creation of a genuine area of 'justice', in which 'people can approach courts and authorities in any Member State as easily as their own' and '[b]etter compatibility and more convergence between the legal systems of Member States should be achieved'.[241]

This was followed by a specific part of the Tampere Conclusions dedicated to 'justice', with the objective that, '[i]n a genuine European Area of Justice individuals and businesses should not be prevented or discouraged from exercising their rights by the incompatibility or complexity of legal and administrative systems in the Member States'.[242] Within this part, there were three sections: 'Better access to justice in Europe', 'Mutual recognition of judicial decisions', and 'Greater convergence in civil law', within which specific action to achieve each of these objectives was presented. Better access to justice included measures on legal aid and protection of victims of crime.[243] Mutual recognition of judicial decisions was heralded as the cornerstone of judicial cooperation in civil and criminal matters, and action to be taken in both areas was set down.[244] In the section concerning greater convergence in civil law, there were two points, points 38 and 39. In point 38, the European Council invited the Council and the Commission to prepare 'new procedural legislation in cross-border cases in particular on those elements which are instrumental to smooth judicial co-operation and to enhanced access to law', listing provisional measures, the taking of evidence, orders for money payment, and time limits as examples.[245] Then came point 39: 'As regards *substantive law*, an overall study is requested on the need to approximate Member States' legislation in civil matters in order to *eliminate obstacles to the good functioning of civil proceedings*. The Council should report back by 2001'.[246] Noticeably, the latter part of the first sentence—'to eliminate obstacles to the good functioning of civil proceedings'—resembled the identically numbered point of the Vienna Action Plan[247] and as such what was then Article 65(c) EC (now Article 81(2)(f) TFEU).[248] Yet, no mention was made of this lineage, and there was no elaboration as to what was meant by this passage.

238 Presidency Conclusions, Tampere European Council, 15–16 Oct 1999 (Tampere Conclusions).

239 Tampere Conclusions, n 238, first para.

240 Tampere Conclusions, n 238, second para.

241 Tampere Conclusions, n 238, point 5.

242 Tampere Conclusions, n 238, point 28.

243 Tampere Conclusions, n 238, points 29–32.

244 Tampere Conclusions, n 238, point 33. For civil matters, this included, eg, measures aimed at the recognition and enforcement of judgments and minimum standards on specific aspects of civil procedural law: see point 34. For criminal matters, rules regarding extradition, evidence, and the securing of assets were mentioned: see points 35–36.

245 Tampere Conclusions, n 238, point 38.

246 Tampere Conclusions, n 238, point 39 (emphasis added).

247 See n 228 and accompanying text.

248 See text following n 219.

Accordingly, it remained unclear to what extent point 39 of the Tampere Conclusions was aimed at the approximation of the substantive civil law of the Member States and/or somehow linked to procedural and private international law matters along the lines of point 39 of the Vienna Action Plan. A comparison of different language versions did not appear to be of much help in this regard.[249] The reference to 'greater convergence in civil law', as opposed to, say, approximation or harmonization, was also not explained, which injected further questions as to the aim of point 39.[250] These ambiguities were certainly not helped by the rephrasing of point 39 of the Tampere Conclusions in subsequent documents prepared by the Commission. For example, in its 2000 Implementation Report on the Unfair Contract Terms Directive, the Commission described point 39 in the following terms: 'The Council and the Commission were invited to strive towards greater convergence of private law and in particular to prepare a general study on the need to approximate the legislation of the Member States in civil matters with a view to eliminating barriers to the smooth functioning of *civil procedures*'.[251] On a similar note, certain documents issued by the Union institutions in the aftermath of Tampere seemed to keep the question regarding the confusing interplay between substantive and procedural law alive in relation to point 39.[252]

Despite these ambiguities, certain documents prepared by the Council leading up to Tampere appeared to confirm that substantive private law—and particularly contract law—had been intended. In a note prepared by the incoming Finnish Presidency on 23 June 1999[253] concerning the establishment of the European Area of Justice for the purposes of Tampere, express attention was given to 'harmonisation or minimum standards in the field of substantive and procedural legislation'.[254] Here, the need to

[249] Eg, in the French, Italian, and Spanish versions, the relevant part of point 39 of Tampere ('d'éliminer les obstacles au bon déroulement des procédures civiles'; 'eliminare gli ostacoli al corretto svolgimento dei procedimenti civili'; and 'eliminar los obstáculos al buen functionamiento de los procedimientos civiles', respectively) was substantially similar to former Art 65(c) EC ('éliminer les obstacles au bon déroulement des procédures civiles'; 'l'eliminazione degli ostacoli al corretto svolgimento dei procedimenti civili'; and 'eliminar obstáculos al buen funcionamiento de los procedimientos civiles', respectively). Other language versions framed point 39 of Tampere and former Art 65(c) EC differently. Eg, in the Dutch version, point 39 of Tampere read: 'onderling aan te passen teneinde belemmeringen voor een goede rechtsgang in burgerrechtelijke zaken weg te nemen', whereas former Art 65(c) EC provided for 'de afschaffing van hinderpalen voor de goede werking van burgerrechtelijke procedures'; in the German version, point 39 of Tampere read: 'die zivilrechtlichen Vorschriften der Mitgliedstaaten angeglichen werden müssen', whereas former Art 65(c) read:'Beseitigung der Hindernisse für eine reibungslose Abwicklung von Zivilverfahren'; and in the Portuguese version, point 39 of Tampere read: 'eliminar os entraves ao bom funcionamento dos processos civis', whereas Article 65(c) read: 'Eliminar os obstáculos à boa tramitação das acções cíveis'.

[250] In the debate preceding the Parliament's 2001 Resolution on the 2001 Communication (see Chapter 5, § 5.3.1.1), the choice of 'convergence' in the Tampere Conclusions was noted: see Remarks of Diana Wallis, European Parliament Debates, 13 Nov 2001–Strasbourg. As regards this term, see further Chapter 1, § 1.2.3.6.

[251] Commission Report on the implementation of Council Dir 93/13/EEC, COM (2000) 248 final, 27.4.2000, 31 fn 71 (emphasis added). This also seemed to be the case in the Commission Communication on the Consumer Policy Strategy 2002–2006, COM (2002) 208 final, 7.5.2002, point 3.2.3.3.

[252] See, eg, Council Reg (EC) No 743/2002 of 25 April 2002 establishing a general Community framework of activities to facilitate the implementation of judicial cooperation in civil matters, [2002] OJ L115/1, Art 2(1)(d); European Parliament Resolution of 12 Feb 2004 on the prospects for approximating civil procedural law in the European Union, [2004] OJ C97E/643, fifth indent. See also Dec No 1149/2007/EC of the European Parliament and of the Council of 25 Sept 2007 establishing for the period 2007–2013 the Specific Programme 'Civil Justice' as part of the General Programme 'Fundamental Rights and Justice', [2007] OJ L257/16: compare Arts 2(1)(b), 3(a)(iii).

[253] Finland held the Council Presidency from July to Dec 1999.

[254] DOC 9576/99, dated 23 June 1999, point 4, at 8; see also point 3, at 5.

define concrete areas of national law where harmonization efforts or the setting of minimum standards should be pursued was deemed a priority in the next few years and in the long run.[255] This should be focused on procedural law, as well as some areas of 'substantive civil law'.[256] As for procedural law, this included, for example, service of documents, taking of evidence, provisional measures, legal aid, and enforcement of judgments.[257] As for substantive civil law, '*the law of contracts, perhaps specific fields of it such as sales of goods, "new" types of contracts (franchise, lease), or bona fide acquisitions*' were listed as examples.[258] There was no further discussion as to the connection of the abovementioned areas to the AFSJ or to the EU's competences, however.

Nevertheless, the import of the European Council's proclamations at Tampere did not escape the attention of EU officials or scholars. For example, Dirk Staudenmayer, a member of the Commission's Working Group responsible for the drafting of the Commission's Communications on European contract law, repeatedly spotlighted Tampere as one of the crucial developments on the road towards the European contract law project.[259] Other prominent Commission members continue to do the same.[260] Indeed, references to Tampere are a constant fixture in many documents circulated by the Union institutions concerning European contract law through the present day.[261] In essence, point 39 of the Tampere Conclusions served as an important 'launching pad' for the debate about European contract law (and European private law generally), despite the fact that its underlying ambiguities went unaddressed.[262]

Instead, following Tampere, European contract law became cemented to the AFSJ. As requested by the European Council, the Commission drew up a 'Scoreboard' to review progress on the creation of the AFSJ every six months,[263] and in the Scoreboard issued in the first half of 2001, under the heading marked 'Greater convergence in civil law', the Commission indicated that it would be preparing 'a Green Paper on European Private Law with a view to launching a broad debate on the need for, possibilities and methods of harmonisation in certain areas of private law'.[264] Notwithstanding the

255 DOC 9576/99, n 254, point 4, at 8.

256 DOC 9576/99, n254, point 4, at 8.

257 DOC 9576/99, n 254, point 4, at 8.

258 DOC 9576/99, n 254, point 4, at 8 (emphasis added).

259 See, eg, Staudenmayer, 'Future Prospects', n 7, 683; Staudenmayer, 'What Future for European Contract Law?', n 7, 252. Dirk Staudenmayer is currently the Head of the Contract Law Unit at DG Justice and thus continues to be involved with the European contract law project.

260 See, eg, Speech of Robert Madelin, then Director General for Health and Consumer Protection at the Commission, 'A Common Frame of Reference for a more coherent European Contract Law', Joint European Parliament/Commission Conference on European Contract Law, held on 28 April 2004, available at <http://ec.europa.eu/consumers/archive/cons_int/safe_shop/fair_bus_pract/cont_law/speeches/madelins_opening_address.pdf>, 1.

261 The European Council's Tampere Conclusions is presently listed as a 'key date' in the European contract law project, as indicated by the Commission's website devoted to this topic within the rubric of DG Justice, <http://ec.europa.eu/justice/contract/dates/index_en.htm>.

262 That said, certain scholars have raised questions in relation to Tampere. See, eg, J-J Kuipers, 'The Legal Basis for a European Optional Instrument' (2011) 19 *ERPL* 545, 553–554; Twigg-Flesner, *The Europeanisation of Contract Law*, n 72, 168; W van Gerven, 'Comparative Law in a Regionally Integrated Europe' in A Harding and E Örücü (eds), *Comparative Law in the 21st Century—W.G. Hart Legal Workshop Series* (Kluwer, 2002) 155, 172 fn 68. Already with point 39 of the Vienna Action Plan, see, eg, J Basedow, 'EC Regulations in European Private Law' in J Basedow et al (eds), *Private Law in the International Arena: From National Conflict Rules Towards Harmonization and Unification—Liber Amicorum Kurt Siehr* (TMC Asser Press, 2000) 17, 21.

263 See Tampere Conclusions, n 238, Annex, third para.

264 Commission Communication, Biannual Update of the Scoreboard to Review Progress on the Creation of an Area of 'Freedom, Security and Justice' in the EU (First Half of 2001), COM (2001) 278 final, 23.5.2001, point 3.3. The two previous Scoreboards only mentioned that the Commission was preparing 'a communication'. See Commission Communication, COM (2000) 167 final/2,

reference to 'European Private Law', this implied its forthcoming 2001 Communication on European Contract Law.[265] The Commission's activities concerning the European contract law project continued to be listed under the section marked 'Greater convergence in civil law' for the entire duration of the Tampere Programme.[266] As a result, Tampere spearheaded the debate about European contract law at the same time that it raised questions concerning its linkage with the AFSJ and the EU's competence under what is now Article 81 TFEU.

4.5 Conclusions

By virtue of the work of several academic projects, the early European Parliament resolutions, and the European Council meeting at Tampere, three significant themes run through the beginnings of the debate about European contract law, which bear directly on the constitutional assessment of European contract law. First, the beginnings of this debate were to a large extent the product of the activities of the Union institutions themselves, namely the European Parliament, which represents the citizens of the Union, and the European Council, which constitutes a pre-eminent body comprising the Heads of State or Government of the Member States and certain Commission officials.[267] At the same time, this involved the unique blending of the work of European scholars and several European academic projects within such institutional activities, which would continue as the debate went on. References to the Lando Commission and the Study Group, among others, were sprinkled throughout many of the institutional documents discussed above, and as illustrated by the 1999 Working Paper, the participation of certain members of these projects and other prominent scholars was incorporated into the constitutional discourse on this debate at the European level.

Secondly, the impetus of this debate was largely framed from the wider perspective of European private law within which contract law was often singled out as a special field. This introduced the incestuous relationship between European contract law and European private law, which would stimulate tensions as regards the push-pull between contract law and the related fields of private law, for instance, whether contract law would be the forerunner of further approximation or the extent to which

13.4.2000, point 3.3; Commission Communication (Second Half of 2000), COM (2000) 782 final, 30.11.2000, point 3.3.

265 In later Scoreboards, the Commission continued to frame the matter in broader terms, citing its issuance of a communication on 'European contract law, with a view to launching a broad debate on the need for, possibilities and methods of harmonisation in certain areas of *substantive private law*'. Commission Communication (Second Half of 2001), COM (2001) 628 final, 30.10.2001, point 3.3 (emphasis added); Commission Communication (First Half of 2002), COM (2002) 261 final, 30.5.2002, point 3.3 (emphasis added) ; Commission Communication (Second Half of 2002), COM (2002) 738 final, 16.12.2002, point 3.3 (emphasis added); Commission Communication (First Half of 2003), COM (2003) 291 final, 22.5.2003, point 3.3 (emphasis added); Commission Communication (Second Half of 2003), COM (2003) 812 final, 30.12.2003, point 3.3 (emphasis added).

266 The Commission's Scoreboards on the Tampere Programme were issued in the first and second halves of the years 2000–2003. On 2 June 2004, the Commission issued a final six-month report on the achievements of the Tampere Programme, which also mentioned the European contract law project. See Commission Communication, Area of Freedom, Security and Justice: Assessment of the Tampere programme and future orientations, COM (2004) 401 final, 2.6.2004, point 2.7. See further Chapter 5, § 5.4.3.1.

267 With the entry into force of the Lisbon Treaty, the European Council is recognized as a Union institution: see Art 13(1), second para, TEU. See further Lenaerts and Van Nuffel, n 2, § 13-025–§ 13-037.

contract law could be segregated from other fields of private law, and continues to affect the discussion of the Union's competence in this setting.

Finally, as illustrated by the foregoing analysis, the discussion of constitutionality made its way into the debate from the very beginning, although this generally occurred behind the scenes and left various issues unaddressed. The European Parliament's early resolutions supported far-reaching action in areas of private law, including contract law, on the basis of the EU's competences related to the internal market, ie what are now Articles 114, 115, and 352 TFEU, though they raised questions concerning the role played by the principle of subsidiarity and the possible recourse to novel instruments, such as a hybrid regulation-convention, which would not be revisited in later resolutions. Likewise, what is now Article 114 TFEU was at the forefront of the 1999 Working Paper, but the very fact that the discussion was split between two alternative opinions signified the controversy underlying the EU's competence in this setting, and regrettably, constitutional issues relating to proceeding outside, as opposed to inside, the Treaty framework by way of an intergovernmental treaty were not dealt with. Furthermore, as a result of the European Council meeting at Tampere, the debate became fixed within the establishment of the AFSJ and the EU's objectives concerning the field of judicial cooperation in civil matters. Point 39 of the Tampere Conclusions implicitly brought what is now Article 81 TFEU into the debate, although the linkage between the two was not explained. As such, the scene was set for the Commission's three Communications on European contract law, which would invite additional constitutional complexities into the mix.

5

The Debate Solidifies

5.1 Introduction

In view of the momentum produced by the work of several academic projects, the European Parliament's early resolutions, and the European Council's meeting at Tampere discussed in the preceding chapter, the Commission disseminated three successive Communications concerning European contract law: the 2001 Communication on European Contract Law,[1] the 2003 Communication on a more coherent European Contract Law—An Action Plan,[2] and the 2004 Communication on European Contract Law and the revision of the *acquis*: the way forward.[3] These Communications constituted a fundamental stage in the evolution of the debate about European contract law. They identified the problems underlying the EU contract law *acquis* and advanced potential solutions to such problems at the European level, thereby solidifying the framework for the debate and the ensuing activities within the European contract law project through the present day. At the same time, these Communications and the responses they elicited from the Union institutions and bodies, Member States, and various stakeholders brought the constitutional dimensions of European contract law to the forefront. Therefore, this chapter is divided into three main parts in order to examine each Communication and the responses related thereto, with a view to highlighting the implications for the constitutional assessment of European contract law.

5.2 The 2001 Communication

On 11 July 2001, the Commission issued the Communication on European Contract Law (2001 Communication).[4] It was the first consultation document issued by the Commission that 'envisaged a more fundamental discussion about the way in which problems resulting from divergences between contract laws in the EU should be dealt with at European level'.[5] Its purpose was to encourage contributions from all interested parties on the need for 'farther-reaching EC action in the area of contract law'.[6] As indicated by the reference to European contract law in its title, the 2001 Communication was primarily focused on general rules of contract law and specific types of contracts, such as sales and services contracts, but also took account of rules on credit securities regarding movable goods, the law of unjust enrichment, and aspects of tort law.[7] As such, it placed the issue of the possible

[1] Commission Communication on European Contract Law, COM (2001) 398 final, 11.7.2001 (2001 Communication).

[2] Commission Communication, A more coherent European Contract Law—An Action Plan, COM (2003) 68 final, 12.2.2003 (2003 Action Plan).

[3] Commission Communication, European Contract Law and the revision of the *acquis*: the way forward, COM (2004) 651 final, 11.10.2004 (2004 Communication).

[4] 2001 Communication, n 1.

[5] 2003 Action Plan, n 2, point 1.

[6] 2001 Communication, n 1, points 10–11. Respondents were given about three months to submit their contributions (11 July to 15 Oct 2001): 2001 Communication, n 1, para below point 73.

[7] 2001 Communication, n 1, point 13. The inclusion of other fields of private law was also apparent in the Annexes of the 2001 Communication: see n 11. Yet, the Commission drew the line at the fields

approximation of contract law and other fields of private law firmly on the agenda of the Union institutions. Not surprisingly, it opened up 'a Pandora's box of controversy'[8] in the EU, as illustrated by the mountain of commentary that it generated.[9]

The body of the 2001 Communication was split into two parts concerning, first, the possible problems resulting from divergences among national contract laws, and secondly, the options for future EU initiatives in contract law.[10] In the first part, the Commission took note of relevant international instruments in the field of contract law, namely the 1980 Rome Convention on the law applicable to contractual obligations and the 1980 United Nations Convention on Contracts for the International Sale of Goods (CISG), as well as the relevant EU *acquis* in contract law and other fields of private law.[11] This led the Commission to raise the question of problems stemming from the *acquis* and existing divergences among national contract laws for the uniform application of EU law, on the one hand, and for the internal market, on the other. As regards the uniform application of EU law, the Commission requested information on practical problems resulting from the way in which Union rules were applied and implemented in the Member States, calling attention to inconsistencies in various directives and the use of abstract terms that were interpreted differently in the national legal orders, much of which related to the 'hard core' of the EU contract law *acquis*.[12] As far as the internal market was concerned, the Commission wanted to find out whether the co-existence of national contract laws hindered the functioning of the internal market and if so, to what extent.[13] It put forward a list of potential problems relating to the conclusion of contracts in cross-border trade, such as the use of standard form contracts and conflicting national rules on mandatory terms, higher transaction costs particularly for consumers and small and medium-sized enterprises (SMEs), and competitive disadvantages for businesses.[14]

In the second part of the 2001 Communication, the Commission set forth four possible options for future EU initiatives in contract law, stressing that these four options were neither exhaustive nor mutually exclusive.[15] It noted that another possible option

of employment and family law, which were deemed to 'give rise to particular issues' and thus were excluded: 2001 Communication, n 1, point 14.

[8] M Kenny, 'Globalization, Interlegality and Europeanized Contract Law' (2003) 21 *Penn St IL Rev* 569, 587.

[9] For a brief selection, see, eg, S Grundmann and J Stuyck (eds), *An Academic Green Paper on European Contract Law* (Kluwer, 2002); 'Editorial Comments: On the way to a European Contract Code?' (2002) 39 *CML Rev* 219; D Staudenmayer, 'The Commission Communication on European Contract Law and the Future Prospects' (2002) 51 *ICLQ* 673; D Staudenmayer, 'The Commission Communication on European Contract Law: What Future for European Contract Law?' (2002) 10 *ERPL* 249; W van Gerven, 'Communication on European Contract Law—Codifying European Private Law' in H Schulte-Nölke and R Schulze (eds), *European Contract Law in Community Law* (Bundesanzeiger, 2002) 241; S Weatherill, 'The European Commission's Green Paper on European Contract Law: Context, Content and Constitutionality' (2001) 24 *JCP* 339.

[10] 2001 Communication, n 1, point 15.

[11] 2001 Communication, n 1, points 17–22. This was fleshed out further in the accompanying annexes: Annex I ('Important Community *Acquis* in the Area of Private Law'); Annex II ('List of International Instruments Relating to Substantial Contract Law Issues'); and Annex III ('Structure of the *Acquis* and Relevant Binding Instruments').

[12] 2001 Communication, n 1, points 35–40 fns 18, 20 (referring to, inter alia, the Doorstep Selling, Timeshare, Commercial Agents, and Package Travel Directives). In doing so, the Commission called attention to the problems illustrated by *Travel Vac* (point 35 fn 17) and the then pending *Leitner* case (point 38 fn 19): see further Chapter 2.

[13] 2001 Communication, n 1, point 23. [14] 2001 Communication, n 1, points 26–33.

[15] 2001 Communication, n 1, points 41, 46–47. The Commission devised a separate section titled 'Any other option' to emphasize this: see point 70.

could be the Member States' negotiation of an international treaty in the area of contract law, but did not delve further into this matter, explaining that it went 'beyond the level of a European initiative'.[16] This option would not be raised again in the Commission's subsequent Communications on European contract law issued thus far. The four options were presented as follows:

(1) *Option I: No EC [now Union] action*;
(2) *Option II: Promote the development of common contract principles leading to more convergence of national laws*;
(3) *Option III: Improve the quality of legislation already in place*; and
(4) *Option IV: Adopt new comprehensive legislation at EC [now Union] level*.[17]

At first glance, the first three options seemed tame, some commentators even calling them 'non-options': *Option I* represented the status quo; *Option II* was already taking place in academic and business circles; and *Option III* was something that the Union institutions were supposed to do anyway.[18] Thus, it was really *Option IV* that represented a definitive advance in the EU's involvement with contract law, since it heralded a comprehensive European instrument in contract law.[19] On second thought, however, there was more than met the eye. Together, these four options served an important role in outlining the frame of the future path of the European contract law project. *Options II* and *III* contained the embryo for the Common Frame of Reference (CFR), and each option by itself embodied provocative arguments that coloured the constitutional assessment of European contract law.

As regards *Option I* (*no action*), this signified leaving the solution of any identified problems to the market.[20] This meant that it would be for the policymakers of one Member State to look for solutions to problems relating to contracts involving parties in other Member States.[21] The Commission surmised that various incentives offered by Member States and trade associations could act to channel the market in a specific direction, which could 'compensate for economic and psychological risks of cross-border trade activity, whether these risks are perceived or real'.[22] In essence, although dressed up in market mechanisms and never stated explicitly, *Option I* signified situating the resolution of problems caused by differences between national contract laws at the Member State, as opposed to the European, level.

Option II (common contract principles) encompassed two elements: first, devising a body of common contract law principles; and secondly, promoting EU-wide standard contract terms. For the first element, the Commission envisaged 'a kind of partnership' in which the institutions, namely the Commission, would promote comparative law research and cooperation among scholars and legal practitioners (including judges and experts) with the aim to delineate common principles in relevant areas of national contract law.[23] Such principles could then be used on a voluntary basis by various

[16] 2001 Communication, n 1, point 48.
[17] 2001 Communication, n 1, point 46.
[18] See, eg, M Kenny, 'The 2003 action plan on European contract law: is the Commission running wild?' (2003) 28 *ELR* 538, 542; N Reich, 'Some critical comments on the Commission Communication of 11.7.2001, Com (2001) 398 final "On European Contract Law"', available at <http://ec.europa.eu/consumers/cons_int/safe_shop/fair_bus_pract/cont_law/comments/5.14.pdf>, 6.
[19] 2001 Communication, n 1, point 41.
[20] 2001 Communication, n 1, point 49.
[21] 2001 Communication, n 1, point 51.
[22] 2001 Communication, n 1, point 50.
[23] 2001 Communication, n 1, point 52. This was not strictly limited to principles, but could also include guidelines or specific codes of conduct for specific contracts, and for cross-border contracts, 'some common solutions, principles or even sets of rules could be defined'. 2001 Communication, n 1, points 52–53.

entities at the Member State level—eg, contractual parties in drafting or executing contracts, national courts and arbitrators in deciding cases, or national legislatures in preparing legislative measures—and at the European level in the context of adopting or revising legislation on contract law.[24] These principles would be non-binding, the idea being that if used by a large number of national and EU entities, this would bring about greater convergence in contract law.[25] The non-binding character of this option and the potential involvement of scholars, judges, and practitioners may explain why this option became known as the 'Restatement' option in reference to the American Restatements in the US.[26] As for the second element concerning the promotion of EU-wide standard contract terms, the Commission explained that such contracts had an important role to play in economic transactions, but there were problems resulting from the use of different types of standard contracts in the Member States.[27] Such problems could be solved if the Commission were to promote the development of standard contracts for use throughout the EU.[28]

As regards *Option III (improving the acquis)*, the scope of the *acquis* was not defined and remained somewhat ambiguous when placed alongside the Annexes to the 2001 Communication, which took account of various fields of private law beyond contract law.[29] That said, the discussion was primarily aimed at the EU contract law *acquis*, especially that of the 'hard core',[30] with the idea to make it 'more coherent or to adapt it to cover situations not foreseen at the time of adoption'.[31] As such, this option was targeted at modernizing, simplifying, and adapting the *acquis* in response to the criticism regarding its inconsistencies and lack of coherence.[32] It was not altogether clear how far this would go. Tellingly, lodged in a footnote, the Commission quoted from the European Parliament's 1999 Working Paper so as to indicate the aim of fitting the *acquis* 'into the "overall picture" of a codified system'.[33] What was not mentioned, however, was that this quotation was taken from a section of the text pressing for a European civil code.[34]

Option IV (new comprehensive legislation) was the most far-reaching of the four options, denoting 'an overall text comprising provisions on general questions of contract law as well as specific contracts'.[35] The Commission did not elaborate further on the substantive content of such an instrument, but instead focused on the type of legal instrument and its binding nature. As far as legal instruments were concerned, the Commission presented three choices, and while not voiced outright, its preferences were not hard to pick out: first, a directive would give the Member States a certain

[24] 2001 Communication, n 1, point 53. [25] 2001 Communication, n 1, point 55.

[26] See, eg, Staudenmayer, 'Future Prospects', n 9, 679. This was subject to disagreement, as some scholars pointed out that adopting a Restatement of contract law was not an option available to the EU. See, eg, Reich, n 18, 6. For the Parliament's earlier discussion of this point, see Chapter 4, § 4.3.

[27] 2001 Communication, n 1, point 56.

[28] 2001 Communication, n 1. [29] See n 11.

[30] See 2001 Communication, n 1, point 60 fn 35 (citing the Doorstep Selling, Distance Selling, Timeshare, and Late Payment Directives); Annex III, n 11.

[31] 2001 Communication, n 1, Executive Summary, para 4.

[32] 2001 Communication, n 1, points 58–60. As regards the need for simplification, the Commission linked this objective to EU 'better lawmaking' programmes: see 2001 Communication, n 1, point 59 fns 32–33.

[33] 2001 Communication, n 1, point 60 fn 34 (quoting from 1999 Working Paper, n 34). See further Chapter 4, § 4.3.4.

[34] See European Parliament DG for Research Working Paper, *The Private Law Systems in the EU: Discrimination on Grounds of Nationality and the Need for a European Civil Code* (Legal Affairs Series, JURI-103 EN), available at <http://www.europarl.europa.eu/> (1999 Working Paper), 147.

[35] 2001 Communication, n 1, point 61.

degree of flexibility, but 'may allow differences in implementation which could constitute *obstacles to the functioning of the internal market*';[36] secondly, a regulation would give the Member States less flexibility but 'would ensure more *transparent and uniform conditions for economic operators in the internal market*';[37] and thirdly, a recommendation could *only* be used if a purely optional model would be chosen.[38] This issue corresponded to the binding nature of such an instrument for which there were also three choices presented: first, a purely optional model that would co-exist with national law ('opt-in'); secondly, a set of rules that would apply unless excluded under the contract and would either co-exist with national law or replace it ('opt-out'); and thirdly, a set of rules that would replace existing national law.[39] Given the attention put on these aspects and, in particular, the express linkage between the choice of legal instruments and the implications for the internal market, the lack of any discussion as to the Union's competence to undertake these options stood out.

On the whole, the issue of the *existence* of the EU's competence, namely the relevant legal basis, was an implicit, though not exactly explicit, theme running through the 2001 Communication. As repeatedly underscored by the Commission, one of the main objectives of the Communication was for the Commission to gather concrete proof as to 'whether the proper functioning of the Internal Market may be hindered by problems in relation to the conclusion, interpretation and application of cross-border contracts' and 'whether different national contract laws discourage or increase the costs of cross-border transactions'.[40] It was in this context that the Commission stated that the Treaties have given the institutions 'powers to facilitate the establishment and functioning of the internal market'.[41] Although no Treaty provisions were expressly mentioned, the Commission's statement strongly alluded to the EU's competence under former Article 95 EC (now Article 114 TFEU).[42] As such, the Commission's pointed questions were interpreted by many scholars as tacit compliance with the Court of Justice's *Tobacco Advertising I* judgment,[43] so as to lay the groundwork for adopting future measures on this provision.[44] This was so even though this judgment (or any

[36] 2001 Communication, n 1, point 63 (emphasis added).

[37] 2001 Communication, n 1, point 64 (emphasis added).

[38] 2001 Communication, n 1, point 65 (emphasis added).

[39] 2001 Communication, n 1, points 66–67. The Commission surmised that the second and third approaches could be combined in areas such as consumer protection where in addition to a general set of fall-back provisions, some mandatory provisions that could not be waived by the parties would apply: 2001 Communication, n 1, point 69.

[40] 2001 Communication, n 1, Executive Summary, third para. See also 2001 Communication, n 1, point 72.

[41] 2001 Communication, n 1, point 24. This was reinforced in other Commission documents, such as the Communication on E-commerce and Financial Services, issued a few months before the 2001 Communication (and referred to therein: see 2001 Communication, n 1, point 5). There, the 2001 Communication was described as 'launching a debate on the possible harmonisation of contract law in *order to improve the functioning of the internal market*'. Commission Communication, E-Commerce and Financial Services, COM (2001) 66, 7.2.2001, point 3, third para, at 10 (emphasis added).

[42] Yet, this did not discount the potential viability of former Art 308 EC (now Art 352 TFEU). Eg, as regards the proposal for a comprehensive instrument of contract law, the Commission posited the idea of an optional instrument, referring to the Council Reg on the Statute for a European Company adopted under this provision. See 2001 Communication, n 1, point 66 fn 37.

[43] Case C-378/96 *Germany v European Parliament and Council* ('*Tobacco Advertising I*') [2000] ECR I-8419.

[44] See, eg, 'Editorial Comments', n 9, 220; van Gerven, n 9, 241–242; Weatherill, n 9, 370–371. See also S Grundmann and J Stuyck, 'An Academic Green Paper on European Contract Law—Scope, Common Ground and Debated Issues' in *An Academic Green Paper on European Contract* Law, n 9, 3, 9 fn 25.

other case law concerning the EU's competence) was not cited anywhere in the 2001 Communication.[45]

The Commission's choice to deal with the issue of legal basis implicitly was jarring, however, when placed alongside its explicit discussion of the *exercise* of the EU's competence through the operation of the principles of subsidiarity and proportionality. In the context of addressing the proposed options for future EU initiatives in contract law, the Commission stated:

> Responses to this document may show that there are impediments to the functioning of the internal market for cross border transactions. If these problems cannot be solved satisfactorily through a case-by-case approach, a horizontal measure providing for comprehensive harmonisation of contract law rules could be envisaged at [Union] level. However, there are of course limits on the power of the Commission and the other [Union] institutions to intervene in this area. Any measure must be in accordance with the principles of subsidiarity and proportionality.[46]

Without pause, the Commission proceeded directly to these principles, devoting four paragraphs to their relevance in the discussion.[47]

The Commission's statements about these principles were generally geared at clarifying their operational role in this setting. As regards subsidiarity, the Commission stressed that this principle 'does *not* rule out the legitimate exercise of the EU's competencies' and where the intention is to have an impact throughout the EU, Union-level action 'is *undoubtedly the best way* of ensuring homogeneous treatment within national systems and stimulating effective co-operation between the Member States'.[48] As regards proportionality, the Commission stated that it was duty-bound to propose whatever measures were necessary to supplement the Member States' efforts to achieve Treaty objectives and such legislation should be 'effective and should not impose any excessive constraints on national, regional or local authorities, or on the private sector, including civil society'.[49] This led it to emphasize the preparation of communications and other types of consultative documents as an important way of involving civil society and business 'with a view to producing legislative instruments geared to users' real needs'.[50] It also underlined that the 2001 Communication and future documents on European contract law were intended to determine if Union action was needed at all and if so, to what extent.[51]

As a result, the Commission's differing treatment of legal basis, on the one hand, and the principles of subsidiarity and proportionality, on the other, was criticized largely because it was said to ignore a basic tenet of EU law, which predicates that the existence of the Union's competence must be verified *before* the matter of its exercise can be dealt with.[52] This is undoubtedly correct, but it may be wondered whether this underestimates the Commission's approach in some respects. By its acknowledgment in the 2001 Communication that subsidiarity pertained to how the EU's competences are to be exercised at the European level,[53] it is fair to say that the Commission was well aware of the distinction between the existence and the exercise of Union competence. On the

[45] See, eg, N Reich, 'Critical Comments on the Commission Communication "On European Contract Law"' in *An Academic Green Paper on European Contract Law*, n 9, 283, 285–286; Weatherill, n 9, 366–367.

[46] 2001 Communication, n 1, points 41–42.

[47] 2001 Communication, n 1, points 42–45.

[48] 2001 Communication, n 1, points 42–43 (emphasis added).

[49] 2001 Communication, n 1, point 44.

[50] 2001 Communication, n 1, point 45.

[51] 2001 Communication, n 1, point 45.

[52] See, eg, Weatherill, n 9, 371.

[53] 2001 Communication, n 1, point 43.

one hand, the Commission's repeated inferences to the EU's competence relating to the internal market suggests that it may have considered the choice of the relevant legal bases (whether former Article 95 EC (now Article 114 TFEU) and/or another Treaty provision[54]) more or less settled, thereby justifying its proceeding to the principles of subsidiarity and proportionality. On the other hand, in line with the emphasis on the consultative nature of the Communication as indicated above, the Commission did not necessarily need to deal with subsidiarity and proportionality at all at this stage. Thus, its emphasis on these principles may very well have been an indicator of the Commission's conception as to where the important issues may lie in the debate about European contract law, or at least may be read as a defensive manoeuvre to make clear that these principles did not stand in the way of the requisite Union action to be taken in this setting, depending upon the outcome of the consultation. The bottom line was that the 2001 Communication pinned Union action in European contract law to the Union's objectives related to the internal market. Yet, the Commission's lack of full engagement with constitutionality begged questions that the institutions, Member States, and various stakeholders attempted to confront in their responses to this Communication as documented as part of the 2003 Action Plan below.

5.3 The 2003 Action Plan

On 12 February 2003, the Commission disseminated the Communication on a more coherent European Contract Law—An Action Plan (2003 Action Plan).[55] This was about one year and seven months after the 2001 Communication, and truth be told, there were certain documents issued in the meantime that already hinted at the outlines of the Commission's plans elaborated in this document.[56] Nevertheless, the 2003 Action Plan constituted the next formidable step 'in the ongoing process of discussion on the developments in European contract law'.[57] Specifically, its purpose was to receive another round of feedback from the Union institutions and other interested parties as regards the set of solutions proposed by the Commission to the problems identified.[58] The 2003 Action Plan was intriguing as much for its substantive content as for the responses to the 2001 Communication submitted by the Union institutions, Member States, and stakeholders contained therein,[59] since both components spoke, explicitly and implicitly, to the constitutional dimensions of European contract law. Therefore, the discussion of the 2003 Action Plan is divided into two parts in order to

[54] See n 42. [55] 2003 Action Plan, n 2.

[56] See, eg, Green Paper on EU Consumer Protection, COM (2001) 531 final, 2.10.2001, point 3.4, first para; Commission Communication, Consumer Policy Strategy 2002–2006, COM (2002) 208 final, 7.5.2002, points 3.1.2.2–3.1.2.3; Commission Follow-up Communication to the Green Paper on EU Consumer Protection, COM (2002) 289 final, 11.6.2002, point 27.

[57] 2003 Action Plan, n 2, point 3. For a brief selection, see, eg, M Meli and MR Maugeri (eds), *L'Armonizzazione del Diritto Privato Europeo—Il Piano D'Azione 2003* (Giuffrè Editore, 2004); A Gambaro, 'The Plan d'Action of the European Commission—A Comment' (2003) 11 *ERPL* 768; J Karsten and AR Sinai, 'The Action Plan on European Contract Law: Perspectives for the Future of European Contract Law and EC Consumer Law' (2003) 26 *JCP* 159; Kenny, n 18; J Smits, 'Editorial: The Action Plan on a More Coherent European Contract Law' (2003) 10 *MJ* 111; D Staudenmayer, 'The Commission Action Plan on European Contract Law' (2003) 11 *ERPL* 113.

[58] 2003 Action Plan, n 2, point 98. Like the 2001 Communication, respondents were given about three months to submit their contributions (12 Feb to 16 May 2003): 2003 Action Plan, n 2, point 99.

[59] 2003 Action Plan, n 2, Annex ('Reactions to the Communication on European Contract Law').

analyse, first, the responses to the 2001 Communication; and secondly, the content of the 2003 Action Plan itself.

5.3.1 Responses to the 2001 Communication

A little over half of the 2003 Action Plan was taken up with the responses to the 2001 Communication. In addition to the Commission's introductory remarks,[60] the Action Plan contained an Annex summarizing the 181 responses that it received from the Union institutions and other interested parties.[61] Even so, the full extent of the contributors' engagement with constitutionality could only be gleaned by looking at the actual documents submitted by them.[62] Therefore, the responses of the European Parliament, the Council, the European Economic and Social Committee, and the stakeholder groups comprising the Member State Governments, businesses, consumer organizations, legal practitioners, and academics are discussed, respectively, in the next four sections.

5.3.1.1 The European Parliament's 2001 Resolution

On 15 November 2001, the European Parliament adopted a Resolution on the approximation of the civil and commercial law of the Member States (2001 Resolution).[63] The Resolution contained the Parliament's response to the 2001 Communication, as well as a broader outlook on the approximation of substantive civil law and private international law.[64] The chronology underlying the 2001 Resolution is important for understanding its content. About a month after the Parliament's 2000 Resolution,[65] and hence well before the publication of the 2001 Communication, the President of the European Parliament announced that the Committee on Legal Affairs and the Internal Market was authorized to draw up a report on the approximation of the civil

[60] 2003 Action Plan, n 2, points 4–11.

[61] 2003 Action Plan, n 2, point 4. See Annex. There were two Apps (somewhat confusingly also called Annexes) listing the names of the contributors and a statistical analysis of the contributions received per Member State.

[62] With regard to the European Council, there was no specific response to the 2001 Communication as had been anticipated. See Press release, 'European contract law: Commission sets the stage for a broad debate', IP/01/996, 13 July 2001 ('The European Council in Laeken is expected to take a decision as to the follow-up of the Communication'). This may have been because the Laeken European Council meeting in Dec 2001 was taken up with pressing political matters: see Chapter 7, § 7.3. Yet, the 2001 Communication and the Council's response (§ 5.3.1.2) were mentioned in certain documents submitted to the European Council at this meeting. See Presidency Conclusions, Laeken European Council, 14–15 Dec 2001, Annex IV, fifth–sixth indents.

[63] European Parliament Resolution of 15 November 2001 on the approximation of the civil and commercial law of the Member States, [2002] OJ C140 E/538 (2001 Resolution).

[64] The title of this Resolution (n 63) distinguished between civil and commercial law, with no explanation as to the reason for such a distinction. Given the Parliament's discussion of the need for approximating private international law rules and the former EC's (now Union's) competence under Art 65 EC (now Art 81 TFEU), this may have been intended to parallel the language of that Treaty provision (ie ex Art 65(a), third indent, EC) and measures associated therewith. See 2001 Resolution, n 63, recital D; point 17. In any event, as with its early resolutions, the Parliament seemingly used the terms civil law and private law interchangeably. See 2001 Resolution, n 63, recital C; point 1.

[65] European Parliament Resolution of 16 March 2000 on the Commission's annual legislative programme for 2000, [2000] OJ C377/323 (2000 Resolution). See further Chapter 4, § 4.3.5.

and commercial law of the Member States.[66] Klaus-Heiner Lehne, a German MEP, was appointed Rapporteur.[67]

Thereafter, the abovementioned Committee held a hearing on this subject, which was organized around three themes: the present state of Community [now Union] policy, initiatives aiming at codification at European level and what has been done so far, and what still needs to be done.[68] Several prominent European scholars participated, including the respective chairmen of the Commission on European Contract Law (CECL), the Study Group on a European Civil Code (Study Group), and the Gandolfi Group.[69] In preparation for this hearing, Mr Lehne drafted a Working Document, which dealt with the issue of legal basis for a European civil code.[70] He took account of former Article 95 EC (now Article 114 TFEU), which had served as the legal basis for a number of directives in areas of civil law,[71] but in accordance with the *Tobacco Advertising I* judgment, he found that it was 'not possible to base all measures' on this provision.[72] He concluded:

> In view of the jurisdiction situation adumbrated above, it would probably be difficult to adopt a complete EU civil law code on the model of those in the national states. However, it does appear feasible to identify certain areas of civil law which have a bearing on the internal market and to take action in these areas *on the legal basis of Article 95* [now Article 114 TFEU]. If the existing directives were consolidated in a single text and the outstanding civil law matters relating to the internal market were added, this would provide the nucleus and crystallisation point for a European Civil Law Code. Under present conditions this seems to be the most realistic approach.[73]

On that basis, he framed the possible contents of such a Code around two cornerstones. The first cornerstone would be the codification of the law of the existing Community [now Union] directives.[74] The second cornerstone would be 'further areas of civil law relevant to the internal market', and based on 'a study commissioned by the European Parliament', which can be assumed to denote the 1999 Working Paper,[75] the 'first priorities' should be service contracts, insurance contract law, non-contractual debt relations particularly liability law, credit security law, and discrimination on grounds of nationality in the abovementioned areas.[76] His remarks filtered into the text of the Parliament's 2001 Resolution, which was rooted in the Union's

[66] Report on the approximation of the civil and commercial law of the Member States, A5-0384/2001, dated 6 Nov 2001 (2001 Report), 4. This was done at the sitting of 14 April 2000; the 2000 Resolution was issued on 16 March 2000.

[67] 2001 Report, n 66, 4.

[68] See Agenda for the Hearing on Approximation of Member States' Civil and Commercial Law of 21 Nov 2000 (PE 294.924/ref), available at <http://www.europarl.europa.eu/>.

[69] Aside from Professors Ole Lando, Christian von Bar, and Giuseppe Gandolfi, other scholars included Professors Guido Alpa, Christoph Schmidt, and Ludovic Bernardeau. Members of certain employer and consumer organizations also attended.

[70] Working Document on the approximation of civil and commercial law in the Member States, PE 294.922, dated 6 Nov 2000.

[71] Working Document, n 70, point 2 (listing eight directives, all of which fell within the 'hard core' of the EU contract law *acquis*, save for the Product Liability and E-commerce Directives).

[72] Working Document, n 70, point 4. He also cited former Art 65 EC (now Art 81 TFEU), but merely noted that it allowed for EU legislation on, inter alia, conflict of laws and civil procedure. Working Document, n 70, point 4.

[73] Working Document, n 70, point 4 (emphasis added).

[74] Working Document, n 70, point 5(a) (drawing particular attention to the Doorstep Selling, Product Liability, Unfair Contract Terms, Timeshare, Distance Selling, and Consumer Sales Directives, as well as the future Directive on the provision of financial services by distance contracts).

[75] See Chapter 4, § 4.3.4.

[76] Working Document, n 70, point 5(b).

internal market objectives and contained express reference to former Article 95 EC (now Article 114 TFEU).

The tenor of the 2001 Resolution emerged from the beginning recitals, which placed emphasis on the gaps in the completion of the internal market emanating from problems with cross-border contractual transactions.[77] The Parliament also acknowledged at the outset that 'the discussion of large-scale harmonisation of Member States' core civil law is a politically charged and sensitive issue',[78] but was one in which 'the similarities between the legal traditions of the peoples of Europe ultimately outweigh the differences between them'.[79] This paved the way to the three substantive parts of the 2001 Resolution. In the first part, the Parliament called attention to the 'current situation' concerning various Community (now Union) measures in the areas of private law and private international law, which gave rise to problems related to their implementation in conjunction with the national civil codes in the Member States and ensuring the uniform application of EU law.[80] In the second part, the Parliament provided an 'assessment of future developments', underlining that the advent of electronic commerce and the euro stimulated 'the need to pursue the harmonisation of contract law with the aim of facilitating cross-border transactions in the internal market.[81] On this basis, it advocated 'a body of law which is close to citizens, accessible, respects established traditions and at the same time takes into account the requirements of the internal market'.[82] This led to the third part regarding the 2001 Communication.

The Parliament's response to the 2001 Communication centred on three key points concerning the scope, timeframe, and legal basis of the Commission's endeavours. First, as to scope, the Parliament regretted that the Commission had limited the 2001 Communication to the field of contract law,[83] reasoning that the current problems concerning the conclusion, performance, and termination of contracts in the EU could not be solved 'unless issues relating to general formal provisions, non-contractual liability, the law of restitution and property law' were also addressed.[84] Nevertheless, the Parliament prioritized the law of contract, underlining the need to pursue 'targeted' harmonization of contract law where mutual recognition of national rules cannot be applied and where divergences among these rules lead to obstacles to the functioning

[77] 2001 Resolution, n 63, recitals E–I.

[78] 2001 Resolution, n 63, recital C.

[79] 2001 Resolution, n 63, recital A.

[80] 2001 Resolution, n 63, points 1–4. The Parliament also mentioned the 1980 Rome Convention on the law applicable to contractual obligations in point 1, which it previously signalled was, along with the CISG, insufficient to solve the problem of cross-border legal relationships: 2001 Resolution, n 63, recital J. In the accompanying Report, there was a memorable passage describing the insufficiencies of EU law and private international law:

> What economic players find when they seek to engage in cross-border activities is the great ocean of international private law containing the 20 or 30 greater or smaller islands of European Community [now Union] law. As soon as users leave these safe harbours they risk running aground on shallows consisting of either unresolved conflicts of individual private law regulations or the absence of coordination between European law and international private law. In some places there is risk of the ocean drying up altogether, because the law of EU directives which is purely geared to individual conflict situations is in the long term upsetting the inner equilibrium of the national civil codes.

2001 Report, n 66, 11.

[81] 2001 Resolution, n 63, point 6.

[82] 2001 Resolution, n 63, point 8. It was not clear from the Resolution whether this 'body of law' should be viewed along the lines of the Parliament's previous requests for a European code of private law. Compare Remarks of Klaus-Heiner Lehne with Remarks of Joachim Wuermeling, Parliamentary Debates of 13 Nov 2001-Strasbourg.

[83] 2001 Resolution, n 63, point 9.

[84] 2001 Resolution, n 63, point 13.

of the internal market as defined in the case law.[85] In line with the types of contracts arising in cross-border trade, it therefore considered it appropriate that a European instrument in the form of a regulation should be drawn up for use on an optional basis for legal relationships concerning, for example, sales contracts, the law on security, and financial services.[86] It also urged the Commission to present proposals to revise the existing consumer protection directives relating to contract law in order to remove the minimum harmonization clauses, which prevented the establishment of uniform law at the European level to the detriment of the protection of consumers and the smooth functioning of the internal market.[87]

Secondly, as for the timeframe, the Parliament set forth an elaborate 'action plan' for the Commission's 'next step towards achieving the approximation of the civil and commercial law of the Member States'.[88] This action plan—the 'core' of the 2001 Resolution in the Commission's words[89]—was a five-step timetable for specific measures to be achieved between the years 2004 and 2010.[90] By the end of 2004, the Commission was to promote comparative law research with a view to finding common legal concepts, solutions, and terminology that could be applied on a voluntary basis along the lines of *Option II (common contract principles)* in several fields of private law including contract law, which largely corresponded to the areas of European patrimonial law covered by the Study Group.[91] In that regard, the Parliament urged the Commission to seek legal advice from various academic bodies 'whilst ensuring a balanced view from both civil law and common law traditions', thereby expressly naming the Study Group, the CECL, the Gandolfi Group, the European University Institute in Florence, the ERA, and national professional organizations of lawyers and reform bodies in the Member States.[92] Also by the end of 2004, the Commission was requested to put forward legislative proposals aimed at the 'consolidation' of the Community (now Union) *acquis*, which tracked *Option III (improving the acquis)* of the 2001 Communication.[93] In 2005, the common legal principles and uniform terminology would be disseminated among European academic and legal circles and used by the EU institutions in the decision-making process.[94] In 2006, they would be used in EU legislation concerning cross-border or domestic contractual relations,[95] and after a period of reflection on their utility in 2008, would ultimately lead to the adoption of a body of rules on contract law for the EU in 2010.[96] While the Parliament did not explicitly state whether this 'body

[85] 2001 Resolution, n 63, point 10 fn 4 (including a reference to *Tobacco Advertising I*).

[86] 2001 Resolution, n 63, point 11.

[87] 2001 Resolution, n 63, point 12. Although the Parliament did not name these directives explicitly in this point, it referred earlier on to various directives, including most falling within the 'hard core' of the EU contract law *acquis* (the Doorstep Selling, Consumer Credit, Package Travel, Unfair Contract Terms, Timeshare, Distance Selling, Consumer Sales, and Late Payment Directives): see 2001 Resolution, n 63, point 1.

[88] 2001 Resolution, n 63, point 14.

[89] 2003 Action Plan, n 2, Annex, point 2.2, fifth para.

[90] 2001 Resolution, n 63, point 14.

[91] 2001 Resolution, n 63, point 14(a).

[92] 2001 Resolution, n 63, point 16. The Parliament encouraged the Commission to establish by the end of 2002 a European Legal Institute in which legal policymakers, administrative authorities, judges, and bodies responsible for applying the law could cooperate on a scientific basis in relation to the activities elaborated in its action plan: 2001 Resolution, n 63, para 15. It is not clear whether the Parliament was aware of the Council's Report issued on 26 July 2001, rejecting the creation of a European Legal Institute and a European Legal Academy: see DOC 11317/01, dated 11 Sept 2001. This was in response to a previous Report issued by the Council Presidency raising this possibility: see DOC 9747/01, dated 20 June 2001. Ultimately, however, the Parliament's wish came true, with the establishment of the European Law Institute in 2011: see Introduction.

[93] 2001 Resolution, n 63, point 14(c).

[94] 2001 Resolution, n 63, points 14(e)–(g).

[95] 2001 Resolution, n 63, point 14(h)

[96] 2001 Resolution, n 63, point 14(i)–(j).

of uniform rules on contract law' represented *Option IV (new comprehensive legislation)*, the timeline essentially represented the steady progression towards the adoption of a European contract law instrument on the basis of the abovementioned options elaborated in the 2001 Communication.[97]

Finally, the Parliament expressly confronted the matter of legal basis, calling on the Commission 'to have recourse to the legal basis provided by Article 95 of the EC Treaty (now Article 114 TFEU) (internal market) for the further consolidation and development of the harmonisation of civil law'.[98] This statement strongly evidenced the Parliament's opinion that this provision could serve as the legal basis for the approximation of contract law and other fields of private law.[99] It paralleled the Parliament's repeated emphasis on the need for such approximation for sustaining the operation of the internal market,[100] and it tracked Mr Lehne's Working Document, taking a similar position. Yet, given the words 'further consolidation and development', questions remained as to whether the Parliament envisioned Article 95 EC (now Article 114 TFEU) for something less far-reaching, especially when placed alongside the Parliament's call for the 'consolidation' of the existing *acquis* and its subsequent statements espousing the use of regulations, as opposed to directives, and the importance of the co-decision procedure when adopting further measures in the field of civil law.[101] Nonetheless, this was one of the rare times in which the Parliament, much less any of the Union institutions, expressly cited a suitable legal basis in the text of the relevant institutional document itself and thus affirmed the Parliament's support for the use of the Union's competence under what is now Article 114 TFEU in this setting.

Notably, former Article 95 EC (now Article 114 TFEU) was not the only Treaty provision cited in the 2001 Resolution. Former Article 65 EC (now Article 81 TFEU) appeared quite early on in the recitals of the Resolution,[102] and although not named as a legal basis for any specific measures, it dovetailed with the Parliament's urgent request that 'owing to the topical nature of the problem, progress should be made first and foremost on the work on the harmonisation of the civil procedure of international law (jurisdiction and enforcement), the recognition of judgments and mutual assistance'.[103] It also brought to light various procedural issues related to the harmonization of contract law, such as determining the competent court in a given case, procedural costs, and the effectiveness of legal protection.[104] Still, former Article 65 EC, or what is now Article 81 TFEU, was divorced from the Parliament's discussion of the approximation of substantive civil law, including contract law.

[97] The relationship between such an instrument and the Parliament's advocacy of optional instruments in specific fields of contract law was not explained: see n 86 and accompanying text.

[98] 2001 Resolution, n 63, point 18.

[99] This may have been how the Commission interpreted the Parliament's statement, since it was mentioned as the very last sentence of its description of the 2001 Resolution, following the Parliament's ultimate aspiration for the establishment of a uniform body of contract law rules in the EU. See 2003 Action Plan, n 2, Annex, point 2.2, eighth para. Still, it was not explicitly stated whether the Commission took this to mean that former Art 95 EC (now Art 114 TFEU) was, in the Parliament's view, the proper legal basis for this endeavour or instead whether the Commission merely placed the reference to this Treaty provision at the end of the summary in the chronological order in which it was mentioned.

[100] 2001 Resolution, n 63, points 6, 8, 10. For further emphasis on the internal market and cross-border transactions generally, see also 2001 Resolution, n 63, recitals E–J.

[101] 2001 Resolution, n 63, points 20–21.

[102] 2001 Resolution, n 63, recital D.

[103] 2001 Resolution, n 63, point 17.

[104] 2001 Resolution, n 63, point 6.

5.3.1.2 *The Council's 2001 Report*

On 16 November 2001, the Council adopted a Report on the need to approximate Member States' legislation in civil matters, which contained its response to the 2001 Communication (2001 Council Report).[105] The Report was drawn up by the Justice and Home Affairs (JHA) configuration of the Council.[106] This had a noticeable impact on its content because the linkage between Union action in the context of the Area of Freedom, Security and Justice (AFSJ) and the European contract law project was apparent in most of the five sections of the Report. In fact, its title echoed point 39 of the Tampere Conclusions.[107] Similar to the Parliament's 2001 Resolution, the 2001 Council Report contained salient remarks concerning the scope of the 2001 Communication, the EU's competence in contract law, and specific recommendations for the Commission's future activities. In all, the Report manifested a clear intention to go beyond the Commission's focus on contract law, while at the same time underpinning the central role of this field to the internal market.

The first section of the Report, the Introduction, was concerned with the 'Tampere mandate'. The Council lost no time in making explicit reference to point 39 of the Tampere Conclusions to which it observed: 'On first reading, this objective seems extremely ambitious. A priori it could encompass all private law, including law of obligations, property law, family law, law of succession, etc.'[108] It noted that to date, most discussions had concentrated on the field of contract law and that the 2001 Communication signified 'the pioneering role of contract law in a possible Community (now Union) legislative policy in the field of private law'.[109] It then singled out contract law and other fields of private law as relevant to the internal market:

> [A]cademic studies, aimed primarily at giving guidelines on the law of obligations, have put forward an economic argument for convergence in European law of obligations. Law of obligations (and *contract law in particular*) constitutes the backbone of economic activity. It is argued that differences between national laws may therefore have a negative impact on cross-border transactions and on the functioning of the internal market.[110]

[105] 2385th Council meeting—Justice, Home Affairs and Civil Protection—Brussels, 16 Nov 2001, DOC 13758/01. Apart from an initial exchange of views concerning the 2001 Communication and the options presented therein (see DOC 11317/01, dated 11 Sept 2001), there were four draft reports issued by the Council that are publicly available: (1) DOC 11621/01, dated 7 Sept 2001; (2) DOC 11621/01REV1, dated 2 Oct 2001; (3) DOC 12735/01, dated 18 Oct 2001; and (4) DOC 13017/01, dated 29 Oct 2001. The last report of 29 Oct 2001 was adopted at the 16 Nov 2001 Council meeting without debate (albeit with slight amendments in certain non-English versions): see DOC 14104/01, dated 10 Jan 2002, point 2. Since the proceedings of that Council meeting contain a summary, the Council's Draft Report on the need to approximate Member States' legislation in civil matters, DOC 13017/01, dated 29 Oct 2001 (2001 Council Report) is cited for the purposes of this discussion.

[106] The Commission stated that the 2001 Communication had been presented to the Internal Market and Consumer Affairs configuration of the Council on 27 Sept 2001 (see 2003 Action Plan, n 2, Annex, point 2); however, it was not explained why the JHA configuration was charged with issuing the Council's response.

[107] To recall, point 39 read in relevant part: 'As regards substantive law, an overall study is requested on *the need to approximate Member States' legislation in civil matters* in order to eliminate obstacles to the good functioning of civil proceedings.' Presidency Conclusions, Tampere European Council, 15–16 Oct 1999 (emphasis added).

[108] 2001 Council Report, n 105, point 1, fourth para.

[109] 2001 Council Report, n 105, point 2, second indent.

[110] 2001 Council Report, n 105, point 2, third indent (emphasis added). Initially, this paragraph was phrased in slightly stronger terms: see Draft Report of 7 Sept 2001, n 105, point 2, third indent ('Differences between national laws can therefore have a negative impact on cross-border transactions and thereby hamper the potential effects of the internal market'). In the second draft, however, this

By comparison, '[t]hese economic considerations *cannot* be applied in the same terms to other areas of private law (family law, marriage law, and the law of succession)', although the free movement of persons and the creation of the AFSJ could provide 'an alternative justification' for adopting measures in these areas.[111] In the Council's view, these latter areas were 'very heavily influenced by the culture and traditions of national (or even regional) legal systems', which presented difficulties in the context of harmonization.[112] Still, if harmonization measures should prove necessary, 'the adequacy of the institutional framework should be looked into', with particular regard to the provisions of former Title IV of the EC Treaty on visas, asylum, immigration, and other policies related to free movement of persons, 'while bearing in mind the principles of subsidiarity and proportionality'.[113] Together, these statements appeared to situate the approximation of contract law and the law of obligations generally within the EU's internal market competences, as compared to these latter fields linked to its competences relating to the AFSJ. This was underscored in subsequent sections of the Report.

In the second section, 'How do we ensure better compatibility between legal systems', the Council noted the inadequacies of private international law instruments, which were an 'effective, albeit partial, means of providing greater legal certainty for operators within the internal market'.[114] This called for legislative improvements in this area.[115] The third section concerned the '*acquis communautaire* in matters relating to property rights', thereby implying examination of fields of law beyond contract. Here, the Council devoted ample space to the various problems resulting from Community (now Union) measures in private law, especially contract law,[116] concluding that 'the fragmented nature of European harmonisation seems to be behind the wish of some to go one step further and hammer out a common law of obligations'.[117] On that basis, it should be considered whether harmonization, not just coordination and simplification, of the Community (now Union) *acquis* would be beneficial,[118] and if so, the Council preferred 'a more "horizontal" approach aiming at the creation of a European "common core" of private law'.[119] Moreover, since the *acquis* was 'less significant' in the areas of non-contractual liability and property law, the Council found it wise to examine whether the differences between national laws in these two areas constituted barriers to the proper functioning of the internal market in practice.[120]

The fourth section concerned family law. The Commission neglected to summarize this part of the Report in the Annex to the 2003 Action Plan, presumably since family law was outside the scope of the 2001 Communication.[121] Given that this was the JHA Council, the inclusion of this field was not altogether surprising, considering the increasing attention given to family law measures within the AFSJ as cited in the Introduction to the Report. By calling attention to activities of the EU institutions on

language was scaled back to how it appeared in the final version: see Draft Report of 2 Oct 2001, n 105, point 2, third indent.

111 2001 Council Report, n 105, point 3 (emphasis added).

112 2001 Council Report, n 105, point 3.

113 2001 Council Report, n 105, point 4, first para.

114 2001 Council Report, n 105, point 6, first para.

115 See 2001 Council Report, n 105, point 6, fourth para; point 8.

116 2001 Council Report, n 105, point 9.

117 2001 Council Report, n 105, point 10. Reference to a European civil code had been previously tacked on to the end of this phrase: see Draft Report of 7 Sept 2001, n 105, para 26; Draft Report of 2 Oct 2001, n 105, para 26. Yet, this was dropped: see Draft Report of 18 Oct 2001, n 105, para 9a.

118 2001 Council Report, n 105, point 12.

119 2001 Council Report, n 105, point 11.

120 2001 Council Report, n 105, point 13.

121 2003 Action Plan, n 2, Annex, point 2.1, seventh para.

various subjects within family law,[122] the Council highlighted the importance of this field to the free movement of persons to which further study should be devoted.[123]

In the final section, the Council concluded by giving the Commission a clear mandate to communicate the results of the 2001 Communication in due time[124] and listing several recommendations including, among other things, 'the identification of areas in which the diversity of national legislation in the field of contract law may undermine the proper functioning of the internal market and the uniform application of [EU] law'.[125] It also reiterated its previous requests for the Commission to undertake the studies in the areas of family law, on the one hand, and on non-contractual and property law, on the other.[126] In response to the latter request, on 30 July 2002, the Commission published a contract notice for a 'Study on property law and non-contractual liability law as they relate to contract law'.[127] Technically speaking, the Council's Report had focused on the impact of divergences among national laws concerning non-contractual liability and property law without making the link to contract law.[128] Nonetheless, the Commission placed emphasis on this aspect of the study,[129] which left open the possibility that the approximation of contract law would not proceed alone.[130] On 21 January 2003, the Commission announced that the contract had been awarded to two members of the Study Group: its chairman, Professor Christian von Bar, and Professor Ulrich Drobnig.[131] The final report of this study was completed and submitted to the Commission on 23 February 2004[132] and published in book form in the same year.[133] As will be seen, it filtered into the Commission's plans elaborated in the 2004 Communication.[134]

5.3.1.3 The EESC's 2002 Opinion

In the meantime, on 17 July 2002, the European Economic and Social Committee (EESC) adopted an Opinion on the 2001 Communication (2002 Opinion).[135] Similar

122 2001 Council Report, n 105, points 14–17. This was not missed by jurists involved with European family law: see further G De Baere and K Gutman, 'The Impact of the EU and the ECJ on European Family Law' in JM Scherpe (ed), *Research Handbook on European Family Law* (Edward Elgar, forthcoming 2015).

123 2001 Council Report, n 105, points 18–19.

124 2001 Council Report, n 105, point 21(c), third indent (specifying 'no later than 31 December 2002'). Hence the 2003 Action Plan came a little late, as it was published on 12 Feb 2003.

125 2001 Council Report, n 105, point 21(c), second para, second indent.

126 2001 Council Report, n 105, points 21(d), (f).

127 Commission Contract Notice 2002/S 154-122573, SANCO 30.7.2002/B5(02)D/250202, available at the Tenders Electronic Daily (TED) website, <http://ted.europa.eu/>.

128 See n 120 and accompanying text.

129 Commission Contract Notice, n 127, point 2.6.

130 See, eg, C von Bar and S Swann, 'Response to the Action Plan on European Contract Law: A More Coherent European Contract Law (COM (2003) 63)' (2003) 11 *ERPL* 595, 601.

131 Commission Contract Award Notice 2003/S 23-018434, SANCO 21.1.2003/B4(02) D/240401, available at the TED website, n 127.

132 C von Bar and U Drobnig, *Study on Property Law and Non-contractual Liability Law as they relate to Contract Law*, submitted to the European Commission—Health and Consumer Protection DG—SANCO B5-1000/02/000574, available at <http://ec.europa.eu/consumers/archive/cons_int/safe_shop/fair_bus_pract/cont_law/study.pdf>. There is no date on the document itself, but 23 Feb 2004 is specified on the Study Group's website: <http://www.sgecc.net/pages/en/home/134.property_law_and_non_contractual_liability_law_study_prepared_for_sanco.htm>.

133 C von Bar and U Drobnig, *The Interaction of Contract Law and Tort and Property Law in Europe: A Comparative Study* (Sellier, 2004).

134 See ns 337–338 and accompanying text.

135 EESC Opinion on the 2001 Communication, [2002] OJ C241/1 (2002 EESC Opinion).

to the responses of the European Parliament and the Council, the EESC criticized the limited scope of the 2001 Communication and the insufficiencies of the EU contract law *acquis* and the relevant international instruments. It also linked the Commission's plans for European contract law to the EU's internal market competences. First, as regards the scope of the 2001 Communication, the EESC considered that, '[w]ith a single currency in the majority of its member countries and its Single Market, the [EU] economic area would indeed be well suited to the creation of a uniform contract law'.[136] Yet, a European initiative in this area 'may have to be enlarged, to ensure that it remains consistent, to encompass *a European law on contractual obligations* (with possible civil and criminal liability aspects, in addition to contractual liability in certain instances of poor execution or failure to execute the contract, or clauses incompatible with public policy)'.[137] In any event, the Commission should be encouraged to create 'a unitary law applicable to all types', and a European contract law instrument would be entirely justified for cross-border contracts.[138]

The Opinion also devoted attention to the insufficiencies of the relevant international instruments and the EU *acquis* in the field of contract law.[139] As illustrated by the beginning pages, it was globally minded as regards the situation of international commercial transactions.[140] In particular, it addressed the limits of the CISG not only in terms of breadth—its exclusion of the pre-contractual phase of the contract, consumer contracts, and services contracts[141]—but also in terms of its public international law character, which depended on ratification by the contracting parties and allowed such parties to opt out of specific sections.[142] Indeed, 'given the low levels of ratification of the international conventions relating to substantive contract law issues' as listed in Annex II of the 2001 Communication, '[a] code of international trade, universally applied and transcending legal systems and cultures, still remains a myth'.[143]

Finally, the EESC confronted the issue of legal basis in its Opinion. It acknowledged that there could be doubts as to whether the EU was competent to adopt a European contract law instrument understood in a wide sense (ie 'consumer law, the law on commercial contracts and contract and tort law and the liability arising therefrom').[144] Nevertheless, the EU's '*obligations concerning the protection of consumer rights and its powers with regard to completion of the Single Market certainly give it a solid basis for proposing initiatives pertaining to cross-border contracts*'.[145] On that basis, it recommended a European contract law instrument, adopted by way of a regulation, covering rules on general contract law and specific or more detailed provisions for certain contracts or consumer protection.[146] It also envisaged the steady progression from an opt-in to an opt-out instrument.[147] In its view, such an instrument would

[136] 2002 EESC Opinion, n 135, point 2.1.3. The EESC called attention to the US and UK legal systems, which seemed to be used to distinguish the EU setting: see 2002 EESC Opinion, n 135, point 2.1.2.

[137] 2002 EESC Opinion, n 135, point 2.1.3 (emphasis added).

[138] 2002 EESC Opinion, n 135, point 2.1.4.

[139] 2002 EESC Opinion, n 135, points 2.3–2.5.

[140] See 2002 EESC Opinion, n 135, point 1('Towards a globalisation law?').

[141] 2002 EESC Opinion, n 135, points 1.7–1.10.

[142] 2002 EESC Opinion, n 135, points 1.7–1.8.

[143] 2002 EESC Opinion, n 135, point 1.12.

[144] 2002 EESC Opinion, n 135, point 2.2.1.1.

[145] 2002 EESC Opinion, n 135, point 2.2.1.1 (emphasis added).

[146] 2002 EESC Opinion, n 135, points 3.5, 3.7–3.8.

[147] 2002 EESC Opinion, n 135, point 3.6.

reduce transaction costs and increase legal certainty, particularly in the case of small businesses and consumers.[148]

5.3.1.4 Stakeholder responses to the 2001 Communication

The Commission received contributions from several Member State Governments, as well as a host of businesses, consumer organizations, legal practitioners, and academics, most but not all from within the EU.[149] Of the then fifteen Member States, there were five Member States that did not submit a response.[150] The business category comprised the manufacturing industry, retail, financial services, media, and other business sectors.[151] Legal practitioners encompassed individuals and group organizations in various legal capacities, such as law firms and bar associations. The academic category comprised individual professors, institutes, and scholarly groups from various universities; certain academic projects involved with European contract and private law also submitted collective responses on behalf of their membership, including the Gandolfi Group,[152] the Insurance Group,[153] and the Joint Response of the CECL and the Study Group.[154] Although the Annex to the 2003 Action Plan provided a general summary of the responses,[155] there were three subjects that generated considerable controversy among the stakeholders: the scope of the 2001 Communication (ie the inclusion, or not, of fields of private law beyond contract law), the potential impact of divergences among national contract laws on the internal market, and the options set forth in the 2001 Communication, particularly *Option IV (new comprehensive legislation)*.

First, opinions were split as regards the focus on contract law vis-à-vis other fields of private law. As for the Member States, reactions centred on the inclusion, or not, of such fields. For example, France and the German Länder opposed the inclusion of property law (and tort law in the case of France), whereas Austria raised the possibility of including tort law.[156] Several European businesses underlined that contract law cannot be looked at in isolation from property law and posited the inclusion of areas such as tax and company law.[157] The academic responses indicated broad support for the inclusion of several fields beyond contract law, such as rules on property law (eg, intellectual

[148] 2002 EESC Opinion, n 135, points 3–7, 3.10–3.11.

[149] See App 2 ('Statistical Analysis of Contributions') annexed to the 2003 Action Plan, n 2. The stakeholders' individual responses are presently available at the Commission's website, <http://ec.europa.eu/justice/contract/> (through the link to the 'CESL Background').

[150] The five Member States were Greece, Ireland, Luxembourg, the Netherlands, and Spain. For the remaining ten Member States (Austria, Belgium, Demark, Finland, France, Germany, Italy, Portugal, Sweden, and the UK), some contributed more than one response or an amalgam of responses from various entities. See App 2, n 149.

[151] See App 1 ('List of All Contributing Stakeholders') annexed to the 2003 Action Plan, n 2.

[152] App 1, n 151, point 5.1.

[153] App 1, n 151, point 5.25.

[154] App 1, n 151, point 5.41 (published as C von Bar et al, 'Communication on European Contract Law: Joint Response of the Commission on European Contract Law and the Study Group on a European Civil Code' (2002) 10 *ERPL* 183).

[155] Yet, the Commission underlined that it was 'the Commission services' understanding of the contributions' and 'may not reflect everything that has been said in these contributions': 2003 Action Plan, n 2, Annex, point 1, fifth para.

[156] 2003 Action Plan, n 2, Annex, point 4.5.1, second para. Although family, succession, and immovable property law seemed to lie outside the scope of the 2001 Communication, the Austrian Government, the Belgian Ministry of Finance, and the German Länder still opposed the inclusion of these fields. 2003 Action Plan, n 2, Annex, point 4.5.1, second para.

[157] 2003 Action Plan, n 2, Annex, point 4.5.2.

property and intangible property, security rights in movables, and trusts) and even 'the entire law of obligations'.[158]

Secondly, there was anything but agreement among the stakeholders that there were significant problems caused by divergences among national contract laws that hindered the internal market. As regards the Member States, the Commission was forced to conclude that the submissions 'affirm that there are problems, or at least there may be',[159] although there were a few responses claiming that there were obstacles to cross-border transactions in this regard.[160] Although not discussed in the Annex, the responses of certain Member States attempted to ground their arguments in the American setting, stating that despite the variance in state private law, this did not hinder the single market in the US.[161] Legal practitioners echoed this sentiment, with certain contributions stressing that the lack of harmonization of contract law was not an obstacle to the development of an integrated market, referring to the US and the UK where no unified system of private law existed.[162] Among scholars, some responses also mentioned the US to illustrate that 'legal diversity cannot be a decisive barrier',[163] but many asserted that differences between national laws did give rise to problems, providing examples from several areas of patrimonial law.[164] Other stakeholders focused on specific types of contracts, such as consumer contracts and services contracts, as well as problems stemming from fields of law other than contract, namely tort and property law.[165] In all, the lukewarm responses to this issue dovetailed with arguments opposing far-reaching Union action in contract law, which leads to the next point.

Finally, as regards the proposed options, *Option I (no action)* generally merited opposition from all stakeholder groups.[166] The responses also exhibited a strong linkage between the remaining three options, some drawing on American techniques. For example, as for *Option II (common contract law principles)*, many responses considered this solution as the gateway towards *Option IV (new comprehensive legislation)* or the further approximation of national laws at the European level.[167] From the perspective of legal practitioners and academics, certain contributions suggested that *Option II* could lead to the adoption of a 'model law' following American practice,[168] and several academic contributions considered this option tantamount to a 'Restatement', although it was not stated whether this was meant to parallel the Restatements in the US.[169] In any event, peppered through some of the individual responses were allusions

[158] 2003 Action Plan, n 2, Annex, point 4.5.4, third, fifth paras.

[159] 2003 Action Plan, n 2, Annex, point 3.1.1, first para.

[160] Eg, the Portuguese Government and the German Länder: see 2003 Action Plan, n 2, Annex, point 3.1.1, second para. Compare the responses of the Danish and UK Governments, which could not confirm that differences between national contract laws hindered the internal market: 2003 Action Plan, n 2, Annex, point 3.1.1, third para.

[161] See, eg, Response of the Danish Government, point 3, fourth para; Response of the UK Government, point 14.

[162] 2003 Action Plan, n 2, Annex, point 3.1.4, third para.

[163] 2003 Action Plan, n 2, Annex, point 3.1.5, fifth para.

[164] 2003 Action Plan, n 2, Annex, point 3.1.5, first, second, fourth paras.

[165] 2003 Action Plan, n 2, Annex, point 3.1.1, second, third, fifth paras; point 3.1.2, first–third paras; point 3.1.3.

[166] 2003 Action Plan, n 2, Annex, point 4.1.1, first para; point 4.1.2; point 4.1.3; point 4.1.4; point 4.1.5, first para.

[167] 2003 Action Plan, n 2, Annex, point 4.2.1, first para; point 4.2.2, third para; point 4.2.3; point 4.2.5.

[168] 2003 Action Plan, n 2, Annex, point 4.2.4, first para; point 4.2.4, third para. Presumably, this meant a 'uniform law' in the sense of the uniform law process in the American setting, particularly if one compares the similar reference to the UCC as a 'model' code: 2003 Action Plan, n 2, Annex, point 3.1.4. On this distinction, see Chapter 3, § 3.3.1.2.

[169] 2003 Action Plan, n 2, Annex, point 4.2.5, first para.

to the creation of European bodies akin to the American Law Institute (ALI) and the elaboration of something similar to the Uniform Commercial Code (UCC).[170] This linkage between options was also evident for *Option III (improving the acquis)*, which evoked virtually unanimous support from all stakeholder groups.[171] A few Member States viewed this option as 'a potential step towards option IV',[172] and several academic contributions advocated 'the development of a European Consumer Code, covering all existing directives, and possibly other codes for public procurement law and intellectual property licensing law'.[173]

Option IV (new comprehensive legislation) provoked the most striking feedback as regards the EU's competence to adopt such legislation. The Member States were divided on this solution, with several challenging it on constitutional grounds.[174] For instance, the German Länder and the Polish Government stated that although this option may be appropriate in the medium or long term, at present a proper legal basis did not exist in the Treaties.[175] Austria, too, stressed the need to examine the question of competence,[176] whereas the UK raised potential conflict with the principles of subsidiarity and proportionality.[177] The business sector was also split on this option, with some emphasizing that the need for EU legislation should be tested on the basis of, inter alia, the principle of proportionality,[178] and others favouring comprehensive legislation only as an opt-out solution, as exemplified by the CISG and the American UCC.[179] Among consumer organizations, some stated that there was a lack of sufficient evidence to justify EU action,[180] and as for practitioners, English practitioners considered it would be disproportionate to impose a mandatory European contract law instrument on the Member States.[181] Other practitioners, however, approved of a European civil code, though preferring an opt-in system.[182] As for academics, several argued that the EU did not have sufficient competence for the general approximation

170 See, eg, Response of Professor CU Schmid, 4, 13–15 (dovetailing with CU Schmid, 'Legitimacy Conditions for a European Civil Code' (2001) 8 *MJ* 277); Response of the International Chamber of Commerce, 4.

171 2003 Action Plan, n 2, Annex, point 4.3.1, first para; point 4.3.2 (albeit diversity in the opinions of the media sector); point 4.3.3; point 4.3.4; point 4.3.5, first para.

172 2003 Action Plan, n 2, Annex, point 4.3.1, first para (citing the Italian, Portuguese, and Polish Governments).

173 2003 Action Plan, n 2, Annex, point 4.3.5, fourth para.

174 Perhaps explaining the Commission's comment: 'Governmental opinion on option IV is not as homogenous as governmental opinion on the other options.' 2003 Action Plan, n 2, Annex, point 4.4.1, first para.

175 2003 Action Plan, n 2, Annex, point 4.4.1, second para (though referring to the forthcoming 2004 Intergovernmental Conference).

176 2003 Action Plan, n 2, Annex, point 4.4.1, second para.

177 2003 Action Plan, n 2, Annex, point 4.4.1, fourth para.

178 2003 Action Plan, n 2, Annex, point 4.4.2, first para.

179 2003 Action Plan, n 2, Annex, point 4.4.2, second para.

180 2003 Action Plan, n 2, Annex, point 4.4.3. In particular, see Response of the European Consumer Law Group (ECLG), points 13–14 (finding insufficient competence for a European code of contract law, but sufficient competence under former Arts 95 and 153 EC (now Arts 114 and 169 TFEU) for EU action in consumer law).

181 2003 Action Plan, n 2, Annex, point 4.4.4, first para. Interestingly, the General Bar Council of England and Wales' contribution, aside from making the point that the comprehensive approximation of contract law was *ultra vires* and violated the principle of subsidiarity, stressed that the political climate in which the European Parliament issued its early resolutions was quite different than that existing at present because issues such as those relating to subsidiarity were not as entrenched. See Response of the General Bar Council of England and Wales, point 2.

182 2003 Action Plan, n 2, Annex, point 4.4.4, second para.

of contract law,[183] whereas others were in favour of ultimately replacing national law with a uniform European contract law or a European civil code, though a considerable number preferred an optional (opt-in or opt-out) solution.[184] In particular, there was a strong preference among scholars for a directly binding instrument, such as a regulation or an ad hoc treaty, rather than a directive or recommendation,[185] but no mention of the constitutionality of any of these instruments was raised in this regard. Standing above the fray, the discussion of constitutionality, whether positive or negative, was a seminal point running through the responses that stimulated the need to confront this matter at the European level, something which did not occur in the 2003 Action Plan.

5.3.2 Content of the 2003 Action Plan

The content of the 2003 Action Plan dealt with two main topics: first, the problems stemming from the EU contract law *acquis* and divergences among national contract laws in relation to the internal market, and secondly, the Commission's proposed solutions as to how to solve these problems. As regards the first topic, the Commission set forth 'a brief typology of the problems' in relation to the uniform application of EU law and the implications for the internal market so as to 'give the reader a general idea of the challenges that are to be faced and to stimulate debate' on the matter.[186] The section on the uniform application of EU law underlined several categories of inconsistencies in EU legislation in the field of contract law and their impact on the Member States, eg diverging requirements prescribed in directives and the lack of common definitions for abstract terms that led to fragmentation in the national regimes in the process of transposition, with particular regard to several directives within the 'hard core' of the EU contract law *acquis*.[187] The section on the internal market was framed carefully by the Commission as concerning '*obstacles and disincentives to cross-border transactions deriving directly or indirectly from divergent national contract laws or from the legal complexity of these divergences, which are liable to prohibit, impede or otherwise render less advantageous such transactions*'.[188] The Commission tackled the matter in five parts, dealing first with the general problem of the distinction between mandatory rules and non-mandatory (or default) contract law rules,[189] and then with four specific problems having to do with fundamental contract law rules,[190] standard contract terms,[191] contractual liability terms,[192] and special sectors inside and outside contract law, including rules on the transfer of property and securities concerning movable goods, insurance contracts, financial services contracts, transport contracts, and consumer contracts.[193] Importantly, this section

[183] See, eg, Response of Professor Norbert Reich, 2; Response of Professor Walter van Gerven, 4–5, 13.

[184] 2003 Action Plan, n 2, Annex, point 4.4.5, third para.

[185] 2003 Action Plan, n 2, Annex, point 4.4.5, fourth para. The proposal for an ad hoc treaty, as well as the use of 'model laws', was reiterated in the section concerning other options: see 2003 Action Plan, n 2, Annex, point 4.5.4, first para.

[186] 2003 Action Plan, n 2, point 15.

[187] 2003 Action Plan, n 2, points 16–24 (referring to, inter alia, the Doorstep Selling, Timeshare, Distance Selling, Package Travel, Commercial Agents, and Unfair Contract Terms Directives). In doing so, the 'old favourites' were brought home to roost, and the well-known cases of *Travel Vac* and *Leitner* were (again) used as examples: see 2003 Action Plan, n 2, points 17, 21, respectively; n 12. See further Chapter 2.

[188] 2003 Action Plan, n 2, point 25 (emphasis added).

[189] 2003 Action Plan, n 2, points 26–33.

[190] 2003 Action Plan, n 2, points 34–35.

[191] 2003 Action Plan, n 2, points 36–38.

[192] 2003 Action Plan, n 2, points 39–40.

[193] 2003 Action Plan, n 2, points 41–50.

of the 2003 Action Plan confirmed the existence of manifold problems caused by divergences among national contract laws for the internal market and stood as one of the most elaborate discussions of such problems in institutional documents concerning European contract law to date.

The Commission's discussion of the distinction between mandatory and default rules essentially amounted to arguments explaining why EU private international law rules were not a panacea for cross-border contracts. As it noted, the choice of applicable law did not help as regards mandatory rules that varied among the Member States but nonetheless applied even if not chosen by the parties.[194] Added to this was the fact that the distinction between mandatory and non-mandatory rules was not altogether clear in practice.[195] The Commission further noted that the choice of applicable law was not 'always commercially realistic or desirable' under circumstances where a party did not have sufficient bargaining power to impose its choice of law and where legal advice on foreign law involved considerable legal costs and commercial risks, as in the case of consumers and SMEs.[196] As regards the four specific problem areas, the 2003 Action Plan was replete with various ways in which divergences among contract laws created obstacles to the conclusion of cross-border contracts and higher transaction costs for businesses and consumers. For general contract law, this included, for example, different rules on the formation of contracts,[197] the admissibility of standard contract terms,[198] and clauses limiting the parties' contractual liability.[199] This was also the case for specific types of contracts. For instance, as regards consumer contracts, obstacles to cross-border transactions were attributed to minimum harmonization,[200] and for insurance contracts, the wording of a single policy marketed on the same terms in different Member States was deemed impossible in practice.[201] Beyond contract law, the Commission indicated that differing rules in movable property law meant, for example, that the security foreseen in the contract vanished when the goods were transferred across borders.[202]

The second part of the 2003 Action Plan set forth several proposed solutions. The Commission began by suggesting that 'a mix of non-regulatory and regulatory measures' be used to tackle some of these problems.[203] 'Regulatory measures' implied the standard legal instruments of regulations, directives, and recommendations mentioned in the 2001 Communication, whereas 'non-regulatory measures' denoted, in its view, 'other tools available which, in specific circumstances, can be used to achieve the objectives of the Treat[ies] while simplifying lawmaking activities and legislation itself (co-regulation, self-regulation, voluntary sectoral agreements, open method of coordination, financial interventions, information campaign)'.[204] This signalled that the Commission was thinking 'outside the box', so to speak, in terms of entertaining recourse to so-called 'new modes of governance', such as the Open Method of Coordination, which would gain prominence in some of the literature on European contract law in the years to come.[205] With that backdrop, the Commission proposed the following three measures as solutions to the problems identified:

194 2003 Action Plan, n 2, point 27.

195 2003 Action Plan, n 2, point 32.

196 2003 Action Plan, n 2, points 28–30. Similar remarks were made for specific types of contracts: see 2003 Action Plan, n 2, points 47–48.

197 2003 Action Plan, n 2, point 35.

198 2003 Action Plan, n 2, points 37–38.

199 2003 Action Plan, n 2, points 39–40.

200 2003 Action Plan, n 2, point 50.

201 2003 Action Plan, n 2, point 48. Similar remarks were made for financial services (2003 Action Plan, n 2, point 47) and cross-border transport contracts (2003 Action Plan, n 2, point 49).

202 2003 Action Plan, n 2, points 43–46.

203 2003 Action Plan, n 2, point 52.

204 2003 Action Plan, n 2, point 52.

205 See Chapter 11, § 11.4.1.

(1) *Measure I: Improve the quality of the Community [now Union] acquis in the area of contract law, which encompassed the creation of a Common Frame of Reference (CFR) in the area of European contract law*;
(2) *Measure II: Promote the elaboration of EU-wide standard contract terms*; and
(3) *Measure III: Further reflection on the opportuneness of non-sector specific measures such as an optional instrument in the area of European contract law.*[206]

Most of these solutions found their origins in the options previously presented in the 2001 Communication. Noticeably, however, *Option I (no action)* was dropped. As explained by the Commission, this was due to the responses it received from stakeholders, in which 'only a small minority' was in favour of it.[207] Yet, to recall, this option had essentially amounted to the EU taking a 'hands off' approach to further intervention in contract law. With the steady calls for leaving contract law to the Member States—many of which have been voiced in the name of subsidiarity—it is quite striking that the one option that would have allowed this to occur was deleted, signifying that action by the Member States alone was not enough to resolve the problems spotlighted in the debate about European contract law.

Measure I concerned measures to improve the quality of the Community (now Union) *acquis*. This was to some extent a reshaping of *Option III (improving the acquis)*. As with the 2001 Communication, the objective here, too, was to achieve utmost consistency and high quality in the EU contract law *acquis*,[208] eg, eliminating inconsistencies between provisions of directives, clarifying existing legislation, and adapting existing legislation to 'economic, commercial and other developments which were not foreseen at the time of adoption'.[209] Much of the Commission's remarks were framed in terms of fitting this solution within the EU's 'better regulation' agenda.[210] The Commission also stressed that this solution fell within its objectives to review the EU consumer contract law *acquis* to remove inconsistencies, fill gaps, and simplify legislation.[211] This solution was targeted at existing and future measures, but the Commission gave its assurance that it would only 'deal with areas already, at least partially, covered by Community [now Union] legislation'.[212]

As part of *Measure I*, the Commission introduced the CFR. The CFR greatly resembled *Option II (common contract principles)* set forth in the 2001 Communication, since the CFR was envisaged to carry out its aims in terms of establishing common principles and terminology in European contract law.[213] Technically, however, the CFR was reshuffled in the 2003 Action Plan under the first solution, rather than constituting a separate solution in its own right, since it was considered an important step towards the improvement of the EU contract law *acquis*.[214] The framing of the CFR as part of the Commission's plan for improving the *acquis* was significant, since this was the way that it would be 'packaged' to the Union institutions and stakeholders in the consultation process.

The CFR had three main objectives. First, the Commission could use the CFR in the context of reviewing the present *acquis* and proposing future measures because it would 'provide for best solutions in terms of common terminology and rules, i.e., the definition of fundamental concepts and abstract terms such as "contract" or "damage"

[206] 2003 Action Plan, n 2, points 4.1–4.3.
[207] 2003 Action Plan, n 2, point 7.
[208] 2003 Action Plan, n 2, points 56–58.
[209] 2003 Action Plan, n 2, point 76.
[210] See 2003 Action Plan, n 2, points 69–72, 77, 80.
[211] 2003 Action Plan, n 2, point 73.
[212] 2003 Action Plan, n 2, point 78.
[213] 2003 Action Plan, n 2, point 59.
[214] 2003 Action Plan, n 2, points 53–54, 59.

and of the rules which apply, for example, in the case of the non-performance of contracts'.[215] The intention was to obtain 'as far as possible, a coherent *acquis* in the area of European contract law based on common basic rules and terminology'.[216] Secondly, the CFR could become an instrument for achieving 'a higher degree of convergence' between the contract laws of the Member States and possibly certain third countries.[217] Thirdly, the Commission would use the CFR as the basis for its reflections on the need for *Measure III*, that is to say, non-sector specific measures such as an optional instrument in European contract law.[218]

As far as the scope of the CFR was concerned, the Commission carved out a box in the Action Plan to underscore the 'content areas' of the CFR and its 'basic sources'. The 'content areas' of the CFR would be decided on the basis of research and input from economic operators, but it would be expected to 'deal essentially with contract law, above all the relevant cross-border types of contract such as sale contracts and service contracts'.[219] However, in the very next line, the Commission invited inquiry into related fields: 'General rules on the conclusion, validity and interpretation of contracts as well as performance, non-performance and remedies should be covered as well as rules on credit securities on movable goods and the law of unjust enrichment'.[220] There were three 'basic sources' of the CFR that emanated from the national, EU, and international levels. Particular emphasis was placed on the national level, which involved national contract law rules, case law of the national courts, and established contractual practices.[221] The existing *acquis* and relevant binding international instruments such as the CISG were also cited.[222] Following this, the Commission explained that it did not intend 'to "reinvent the wheel" in terms of research activities' for the CFR, finding that 'it is remarkable that never before in the area of European contract law has there been such a concentration of ongoing research activities'.[223] What was more, these activities were not limited to contract law: 'the abovementioned areas to be covered do not preclude ongoing research projects from going beyond these areas, as they might have necessary links with other areas like property law or tort law.'[224] As a result, the scope of the CFR as regards the relationship between contract law and other fields of private law remained unclear. In turn, this injected further anxieties in the discussion of *Measure III* concerning 'non-sector specific measures' such as an optional instrument for which the CFR would lay the groundwork.

Before proceeding to that proposed solution, however, there was another solution that also emanated from *Option II (common contract principles)* of the 2001 Communication and was now reframed in the 2003 Action Plan as *Measure II* concerning the promotion of EU-wide standard contract terms. The subject of standard contract terms was carved out as a solution in its own right, which could ease the need for EU-wide unification of contract law.[225] Yet, it was relatively muted compared to the other measures proposed in the 2003 Action Plan. It centred on two strategies. First, the Commission would

[215] 2003 Action Plan, n 2, point 62. See also point 80 (considering use by the other EU institutions).
[216] 2003 Action Plan, n 2, point 62.
[217] 2003 Action Plan, n 2, point 62. No third countries were named, however.
[218] 2003 Action Plan, n 2, point 62.
[219] 2003 Action Plan, n 2, box below point 63, first indent.
[220] 2003 Action Plan, n 2, box below point 63, second indent.
[221] 2003 Action Plan, n 2, box above point 64, first–second indents.
[222] 2003 Action Plan, n 2, box above point 64, third indent.
[223] 2003 Action Plan, n 2, point 66. The Commission did not expressly refer to any academic projects, however.
[224] 2003 Action Plan, n 2, point 67.
[225] 2003 Action Plan, n 2, points 82–85.

facilitate the exchange of information regarding standard contracts, eg, setting up a website about existing initiatives at the national and European levels, although it made clear that the information posted would be the sole responsibility of the participants, not the Commission.[226] Secondly, the Commission would offer guidelines on the use of standard contract terms to ensure compliance with the relevant rules of EU law, but it underlined that this should not be interpreted as 'blanket approval'.[227] As a result, the Commission's approach to this solution largely amounted to 'an "external hands-off" involvement' not going beyond the level of information exchange.[228] Indeed, the promotion of standard contract terms paled when seen in the light of the major evolution heralded by the CFR and *Measure III* involving the optional instrument.

By the evasive, even tortuous, language used to describe it, *Measure III* concerning 'further reflection on the opportuneness of non-sector specific measures such as an optional instrument in the area of European contract law' embodied both caution and ambiguity. This solution was a reconfiguration of *Option IV (new comprehensive legislation)* of the 2001 Communication. The phrase 'non-sector specific measures' could be interpreted as comprehensive measures, only this time the words 'such as an optional instrument' placed attention on an instrument of optional character, though still giving the Commission some room for manoeuvre. Despite the commitment to engage in 'further reflection on the opportuneness' of such measures, the Commission seemed to direct the discussion towards an instrument of an 'optional' character.[229] As for the possible form, it opined that 'one could think of EU wide contract law rules in the form of a regulation or a recommendation, which would exist in parallel with, rather than instead of, national contract laws'.[230] Moreover, it repeatedly espoused the benefits of an opt-in instrument as giving the parties a greater degree of contractual freedom, which was 'one of the guiding principles of such a contract law instrument'.[231] The parties would only choose the new instrument if it suited their economic or legal needs better than the national law that was otherwise applicable.[232]

There was an important link drawn between the optional instrument and the CFR in the 2003 Action Plan. As noted above, the Commission posited that the CFR would serve as the basis for further reflection on non-sector specific measures in European contract law as a general matter.[233] This was so even though the Commission repeatedly considered the CFR as a basis for the development of the optional instrument in contract law specifically.[234] While it is unclear how far the Commission intentionally used the words 'non-sector specific measures' and 'optional instrument' interchangeably,[235] the relationship to the CFR created further ambiguities. Given that the CFR was envisaged to go beyond contract law, the scope of such an optional instrument was unclear. The Commission merely acknowledged: 'Whether the new instrument would cover the whole scope of the [CFR] or only parts thereof, or whether it would cover only general contract law rules or also specific contracts, is at present left open'.[236] At the very least,

[226] 2003 Action Plan, n 2, points 86–87, particularly point 87 fn 60.

[227] 2003 Action Plan, n 2, point 88.

[228] Karsten and Sinai, n 57, 168. See also Smits, n 57, 113–114.

[229] This was evidenced by the Commission's broaching the discussion with positive remarks about the utility of the optional instrument for the internal market: see 2003 Action Plan, n 2, points 90–91.

[230] 2003 Action Plan, n 2, point 92.

[231] 2003 Action Plan, n 2, point 93.

[232] 2003 Action Plan, n 2, point 92. But see point 94 (noting that further reflection would be needed as regards whether the optional instrument (if binding) could exclude the application of conflicting mandatory national provisions in the applicable area).

[233] 2003 Action Plan, n 2, point 62.

[234] 2003 Action Plan, n 2, points 64, 95, 98.

[235] 2003 Action Plan, n 2, points 54, 98.

[236] 2003 Action Plan, n 2, point 95.

the Commission's statements seemed to prefer an optional instrument falling alongside, rather than replacing, the national contract laws and potentially other related fields of private law, thereby raising crucial questions about the EU's competence to enact such an instrument.

As with the 2001 Communication, the Commission did not discuss the legal basis for the three proposed solutions in the 2003 Action Plan. In fact, it stated its intention to launch specific reflection on the legal basis, opportuneness, possible form, and contents of non-sector specific measures such as an optional instrument under *Measure III*.[237] Notably, it did not make the same mistake twice of mentioning the principles of subsidiarity and proportionality while ignoring legal basis. Yet, this is not to say that there were no implicit references to Community (now Union) competence in the 2003 Action Plan. With the Commission's documentation of the various problems caused by divergences among national contract laws for the internal market, this was again seen by commentators as signifying the Commission's implicit engagement with the potential use of former Article 95 EC (now Article 114 TFEU).[238] Added to this was the Commission's statement immediately following the description of such problems: 'In some cases, the Community Treaty [now Treaties] may already provide the legal base to solve the problems identified, although the present action plan does not take a position on the compatibility of the barriers identified' with EU law.[239] In the next line, the Commission explained that for other cases, 'non-regulatory as well as regulatory solutions may be required'.[240] In this way, the 2003 Action Plan continued the linkage between European contract law and the EU's internal market objectives, but given the questions raised in the responses of the Union institutions and stakeholders about the EU's competence in this setting, this made the Commission's failure to confront the constitutional dimensions of European contract law more apparent, a practice that continued with the 2004 Communication.

5.4 The 2004 Communication

On 11 October 2004, the Commission adopted its third Communication on European Contract Law and the revision of the *acquis*: the way forward (2004 Communication).[241] Looking back in hindsight, the title's equation of the European contract law project with the revision of the *acquis* was telling in terms of the Commission's focus in this next crucial step in the debate. The 2004 Communication concretized the Commission's proposed solutions based on the responses it received from the Union

[237] 2003 Action Plan, n 2, point 92.

[238] See, eg, S Weatherill, 'Constitutional Issues–How Much is Best Left Unsaid?' in S Vogenauer and S Weatherill (eds), *The Harmonisation of European Contract Law: Implications for European Private Laws, Business and Legal Practice* (Hart, 2006) 89, 96–97. But see Staudenmayer, n 57, 126 (citing former Arts 95 and 308 EC (now Arts 114 and 352 TFEU) as the most relevant legal bases in relation to the Commission's proposed solutions).

[239] 2003 Action Plan, n 2, point 52.

[240] 2003 Action Plan, n 2, point 52.

[241] 2004 Communication, n 3. Generally, much of the literature on this Communication is entangled with the general discourse on European contract law. But see, eg, 'Editorial Comments: European Contract Law: Quo Vadis?' (2005) 42 *CML Rev* 1; J Karsten and G Petri, 'Towards a Handbook on European Contract Law and Beyond: The Commission's 2004 Communication "European Contract Law and the Revision of the *Acquis*: The Way Forward"' (2005) 28 *JCP* 31; M Kenny, 'The 2004 Communication on European Contract Law: those magnificent men in their unifying machines' (2005) 30 *ELR* 724; D Staudenmayer, 'The Way Forward in European Contract Law' (2004) 13 *ERPL* 95.

institutions and bodies and various stakeholders to the 2003 Action Plan. In turn, the 2004 Communication fed into subsequent institutional activities, especially the European Council's Hague Programme on the AFSJ and the EESC's Opinion on European insurance contract law. Thus, the discussion of the 2004 Communication is subdivided into three sections so as to examine the responses to the 2003 Action Plan, the content of the 2004 Communication, and its aftermath.

5.4.1 Responses to the 2003 Action Plan

This time, the Commission prepared a separate summary of the responses to the 2003 Action Plan, rather than including it as an Annex to the 2004 Communication itself as had been done previously.[242] This summary contained a description of the responses of the Union institutions,[243] namely the European Parliament, the Council, and the European Central Bank, and other interested parties, as well as a list of the names of the contributors and an analysis of the source of the various contributions per Member State.[244] As before, the contributions raised salient points bearing on the constitutional assessment of European contract law. The responses of the European Parliament, the Council, the European Central Bank, and various stakeholders are analysed in turn.

5.4.1.1 The European Parliament's 2003 Resolution

On 2 September 2003, the European Parliament adopted a Resolution on the 2003 Action Plan (2003 Resolution).[245] As a harbinger for what was to come, the Parliament commenced the Resolution by declaring that 'the diversity of rules between the Member States hampers the proper operation of the internal market' and 'only concrete measures organised in accordance with a detailed timetable, with consistent use of a common terminology, can lead to a coherent system of European contract law'.[246] From there, it launched into a critique of the 2003 Action Plan. While praising the Commission's plans for the CFR, most of its comments were filled with disappointment at the Commission's failure, inter alia, to:

- consider the CFR a priority, thereby asking it to complete it by the end of 2006 and then start to introduce it;[247]
- consult adequately with all stakeholders, finding the contributions were not representative of all Member States and that the Commission had not taken notice of the 'users of law' such as judges, lawyers, notaries, undertakings, and consumers in the elaboration of the CFR;[248] and

[242] Reaction to the Action Plan—A More Coherent European Contract Law (Summary). As well as the Summary, the stakeholders' individual responses are also presently available at the Commission's website, n 149.

[243] As regards the EESC, apparently it did not issue an opinion in response to the 2003 Action Plan.

[244] Summary, n 242, App I ('List of all contributions'). The last page of the Summary set out a statistical analysis of the contributions received per Member State and as such resembled the layout of App 2 of the 2003 Action Plan: see Summary, n 242, 28.

[245] European Parliament Resolution of 2 Sept 2003 on the 2003 Action Plan, [2004] OJ C76E/95 (2003 Resolution).

[246] 2003 Resolution, n 245, recitals A–B.

[247] 2003 Resolution, n 245, point 12.

[248] 2003 Resolution, n 245, points 8–9.

- take early action to produce optional instruments in certain sectors, such as consumer transactions and insurance.[249]

Accordingly, 'as a matter of priority', the Parliament considered that the Commission should produce an optional instrument in the areas of consumer contracts and insurance contracts.[250] It also called for the elaboration of a body of rules based on the CFR that should initially be offered to the parties on an 'opt-in' basis, but later could become binding and be used on an 'opt-out' basis.[251] In doing so, it stressed the practical application of the CFR in conciliation proceedings among parties.[252] Finally, it reiterated the need to be kept regularly informed of the Commission's progress and called for a dialogue between the Union institutions under each successive Council presidency.[253] Noticeably absent was the Parliament's explicit discussion of the constitutionality of the Commission's proposed options, though its reference to problems caused by divergences between national laws in the internal market at least implicitly linked its envisaged instruments to the EU's competence related to the internal market.

5.4.1.2 *The Council's 2003 Resolution*

On 22 September 2003, the Council adopted a Resolution on the 2003 Action Plan (2003 Council Resolution).[254] In contrast to the 2001 Communication, the Competitiveness configuration of the Council dealing with the internal market, industry, and research, rather than that concerning JHA, issued the Council's response to the 2003 Action Plan.[255] While exhibiting a somewhat cautious approach, this Resolution generally supported the Commission's plans outlined in the 2003 Action Plan,[256] and references to the internal market were apparent throughout. As regards the CFR, the 2003 Resolution was peppered with statements affirming that it would not be a legally binding instrument[257] and would take account of 'all the different legal traditions of the Member States',[258] as well as 'the principle of subsidiarity, the practical needs of economic operators and consumers and the established structures and legal cultures in Member States'.[259] More generally, the Council emphasized that 'it would be useful

[249] 2003 Resolution, n 245, point 11. The criticism lodged against the 2003 Action Plan was echoed in stronger terms in the accompanying Report, where it was characterized as 'plenty of plan, too little action': see Report on the 2003 Action Plan, A5-0256/2003, dated 9 July 2003 (2003 Report), 8–10.

[250] 2003 Resolution, n 245, point 14.

[251] 2003 Resolution, n 245, point 15.

[252] 2003 Resolution, n 245, point 16. While the Parliament did not explain what was meant by 'conciliation proceedings', this request seems to make most sense when read against the accompanying Report, emphasizing the applicability of the CFR in arbitration proceedings, which would enable it to be tested in practice. See 2003 Report, n 249, point c, at 9.

[253] 2003 Resolution, n 245, points 4, 6.

[254] Council Resolution of 22 Sept 2003 on 'A More Coherent European Contract Law', [2003] OJ C246/1 (2003 Council Resolution).

[255] While this may not have been evident in the text of the Resolution published in the *Official Journal*, the Resolution was adopted at the 2525th Council meeting of the Competitiveness (Internal market, Industry, Research) configuration, held on 22 Sept 2003: DOC 12773/03, dated 21 Oct 2003, point 8. Nonetheless, the Council Committee on Civil Law Matters reviewed the 2003 Action Plan and requested that the JHA Council be involved in future work regarding European contract law, particularly as the envisaged initiatives embodied 'un caractère de droit civil general': DOC 12609/03, dated 16 Sept 2003, point f.

[256] 2003 Council Resolution, n 254, point III.1.

[257] 2003 Council Resolution, n 254, point II.1.

[258] 2003 Council Resolution, n 254, point III.2.

[259] 2003 Council Resolution, n 254, point V.

to take appropriate and proportionate measures' for ensuring that all economic operators and consumers could make full use of the internal market, and that any measure including the CFR should therefore correspond to the realities of the internal market and the needs of such operators and consumers.[260]

As regards the other proposed solutions in the 2003 Action Plan, the Council approved of the Commission's plans to improve, consolidate, and codify the EU contract law *acquis*.[261] It found the Commission's plans for promoting EU-wide standard contract terms 'useful', but stressed that such terms should be made by the parties themselves and that publication on the envisaged website should not be interpreted as approval for such initiatives.[262] As for non-sector specific measures such as the optional instrument, the Council emphasized that further reflection was needed and should be pursued in close collaboration with the Member States with due account for the principle of contractual freedom.[263] Like the European Parliament's 2003 Resolution, no explicit mention was made in the Council's 2003 Resolution to the EU's competence to adopt such measures, aside from the references to subsidiarity and proportionality indicated above. In a previous document, however, the Council noted that because of the scepticism of the Member States regarding the proposal for an optional instrument, the Commission had given its assurance that any concerns with respect to the issue of legal basis for such a proposal would be dealt with after 2007/2008 in the light of future institutional arrangements in the EU.[264]

5.4.1.3 The European Central Bank's 2003 Letter

By letter dated 21 July 2003, the Directorate General Legal Services submitted the response of the European Central Bank (ECB) to the 2003 Action Plan (2003 ECB Letter).[265] This letter was a noteworthy event, since it was the first time (and only time to date) that the ECB submitted a formal response to one of the Commission's Communications on European contract law. In this letter, the ECB wholeheartedly supported the Action Plan,[266] stating that 'the aim of harmonising substantive contract law in Europe is to be praised'.[267] In its view, possible distortions stemming from the existence of sometimes widely different national contract laws was a 'key concern', especially in view of the singleness of the monetary policy of the euro zone and the level playing field that must be achieved,[268] and that the choice of applicable law was not always an appropriate solution.[269] In fact, one of the most interesting parts of this letter concerned the ECB's discussion of the ways in which it attempted to overcome the existing divergences among national contract laws[270] and of the extent to which the approximation of certain issues and concepts of contract law would be of special interest to the ECB.[271]

[260] 2003 Council Resolution, n 254, point II.2.
[261] 2003 Council Resolution, n 254, point IV.1.
[262] 2003 Council Resolution, n 254, point IV.2.
[263] 2003 Council Resolution, n 254, point IV.3.
[264] DOC 9479/03, dated 23 May 2003, point 7. This seemingly referred to the institutional developments surrounding the Draft Constitutional Treaty, which would be signed by the Member States a few months later in July 2003. See further Chapter 7, § 7.3.
[265] Letter submitted by Antonio Sáinz de Vicuña, General Council, on behalf of the ECB, 'The Commission's Action Plan on European Contract Law', dated 21 July 2003 (2003 ECB Letter).
[266] 2003 ECB Letter, n 265, point 9.
[267] 2003 ECB Letter, n 265, point 4.
[268] 2003 ECB Letter, n 265, point 2.
[269] 2003 ECB Letter, n 265, point 4.
[270] See 2003 ECB Letter, n 265, points 2–3.
[271] See 2003 ECB Letter, n 265, points 5–8.

The ECB favoured all three proposed measures in the 2003 Action Plan. First, the improvement of the *acquis* would enhance the uniform application of EU law and facilitate the smooth functioning of cross-border transactions.[272] In particular, it considered that the CFR would be an important step towards the completion of the internal market and of particular assistance to the legal framework of the Eurosystem by ensuring the consistent interpretation and application of abstract terms found in Community (now Union) and Eurosystem measures.[273] Secondly, the ECB found the promotion of standard contract terms to be an 'interesting alternative' for use in monetary policy operations, although it stressed that such terms should not compromise the freedom to contract, eg, by imposing principles that were too stringent on market actors.[274] Thirdly, as regards non-sector specific measures such as an optional instrument, the ECB stated that having an optional body of European contract law that parties could freely use to facilitate cross-border contracts would help to reduce transaction costs and improve the competitiveness of the EU market in the international context, as parties investing in Europe would take advantage of a common set of contract rules.[275] It premised its findings on the fact that this type of instrument would not replace national contract laws, but would exist in parallel thereto, thereby adding an optional tool for market participants and upholding the parties' contractual freedom.[276] The ECB concluded the letter by recognizing that the Commission's plans were ambitious, but 'the potential benefits both for the Community [now Union] and the players in the Single Market would be considerable'.[277]

5.4.1.4 Stakeholder responses to the 2003 Action Plan

As a general matter, the 122 responses to the 2003 Action Plan that the Commission received from Member State Governments, businesses, consumer organizations, legal practitioners, and academics were a little sparse as compared to the 181 responses to the 2001 Communication. Only seven out of the then fifteen Member States submitted contributions,[278] although a few (soon-to-become) new Member States took part.[279] Thus, whereas the responses of five Member States were absent in the case of the 2001 Communication, here the number climbed to eight. The number of contributions from consumer organizations and legal practitioners was comparable, but the decrease in those coming from businesses and academics was markedly apparent.[280]

[272] 2003 ECB Letter, n 265, point 9.

[273] 2003 ECB Letter, n 265, point 9. See further points 5–7.

[274] 2003 ECB Letter, n 265, points 5–7.

[275] 2003 ECB Letter, n 265, point 10.

[276] 2003 ECB Letter, n 265, point 10.

[277] 2003 ECB Letter, n 265, point 11.

[278] The seven Member States were Austria, Denmark, France, Germany, Portugal, Sweden, and the UK. See Summary, n 242, App I. Accordingly, eight Member States (Belgium, Finland, Greece, Ireland, Italy, Luxembourg, the Netherlands, and Spain) did not submit any contribution. In fact, for Greece and Luxembourg, there were no responses from any stakeholder groups. See Summary, n 242, 28.

[279] The 2004 Communication was published on 11 Oct 2004, which was after the May 2004 accession of ten new Member States. Yet, much of the time for responding to the 2003 Action Plan had taken place before this date and certainly before the accession of Bulgaria and Romania in Jan 2007. Still, Hungary, Bulgaria, and Romania submitted responses: see Summary, n 242, App I, points 1.2, 1.8, 1.11.

[280] The 181 responses to the 2001 Communication were generally divided as follows: businesses (forty-nine); consumer organizations (five); legal practitioners (twenty-seven); and academics (eighty-six). See 2003 Action Plan, n 2, App 1. By comparison, the 122 responses to the 2003 Action Plan were broken down as follows: businesses (thirty); consumer organizations (four); legal practitioners (twenty); and academics (fifty-eight). See Summary, n 242, App I.

Nonetheless, there were responses submitted by several academic projects, such as the Acquis Group,[281] the *Association Henri Capitant*,[282] and the Ius Commune Casebook Project,[283] among others,[284] in addition to the contributions of individual scholars.

The Commission's summary of the contributions focused on the three proposed measures in the 2003 Action Plan.[285] As for *Measure I*, there was widespread approval among all stakeholder groups for measures to improve the *acquis*,[286] but the prospect of the CFR stimulated questions and concerns. Several Member States, businesses, legal practitioners, and academics raised a host of issues concerning the form and scope of the CFR,[287] many of which opined that it should go beyond the confines of contract law.[288] Contributions from these stakeholder groups also emphasized that the work on the CFR should not forestall measures to reform the *acquis*[289] and that its preparation should involve a wider spectrum of stakeholder participation including the Member States, businesses, and legal practitioners.[290] Only a few contributions raised the issue of the constitutionality of the CFR, with one finding the EU's competence questionable in this regard and another stressing that the principles of subsidiarity and proportionality must be considered in devising the CFR.[291] *Measure II* concerning the promotion of standard contract terms generally evoked mixed, if not sceptical, reactions from all stakeholder groups.[292] This was so although a few Member States and consumer organizations exhibited some willingness to support this solution if certain conditions were satisfied.[293] For the most part, the responses from academics apparently indicated disinterest in the matter.[294]

Of the three proposed measures, *Measure III* concerning the prospect of non-sector specific measures such as an optional instrument took up most of the discussion in the Commission's summary. Despite the diverse reactions, three distinct themes emerged across the stakeholder groups. First, several contributions, save for those from scholars,

[281] See Summary, n 242, App I, points 5.1, 5.51, 5.52.

[282] See Summary, n 242, App I, point 5.5.

[283] Summary, n 242, App I, points 5.15, 5.56, 5.57.

[284] The Gandolfi Group (Summary, n 242, App I, points 5.19–5.20: one was submitted by Professor Giuseppe Gandolfi and another by Professors Giuseppe Gandolfi and José Luis de los Mozos); the European University Institute (Summary, n 242, App I, point 5.13) and ERA (Summary, n 242, App I, point 5.18) also submitted contributions. The CECL and the Study Group did not submit a joint response, as they had done with the 2001 Communication (n 154), although the chairmen of both groups submitted individual responses: see Summary, n 242, App I, points 5.6–5.7, 5.32.

[285] As noted by the Commission, although several contributors addressed issues relating to the barriers preventing the uniform application of EU law or the smooth functioning of the internal market, its Summary did not delve into these topics. Summary, n 242, point 3.

[286] Summary, n 242, point 3.1.1, first para; point 3.1.2, first para (though some stressed the limited nature of the endeavour of not straying beyond the elimination of inconsistencies within the 'exact parameters' of the *acquis*); point 3.1.3, first para; point 3.1.4, first para; point 3.1.5, first para.

[287] Summary, n 242, point 3.1.1, third para; point 3.1.2, second para; point 3.1.4, third para; point 3.1.5, sixth para.

[288] Summary, n 242, point 3.1.1, fourth para; point 3.1.4, third para; point 3.1.5, ninth para.

[289] Summary, n 242, point 3.1.1, sixth para; point 3.1.2, first para; point 3.1.4, first para; point 3.1.5, second para.

[290] Summary, n 242, point 3.1.1, second para; point 3.1.2, third para; point 3.1.4, sixth para; point 3.1.5, seventh para.

[291] Summary, n 242, point 3.1.4, fifth para. Legal practitioners and businesses stressed the need for a cost-benefit analysis: see Summary, n 242, point 3.1.4, fifth para; point 3.1.2, third para.

[292] Summary, n 242, point 3.2.1, first para; point 3.2.2, first para; point 3.2.3, first para; point 3.2.4, first para; point 3.2.5, second–third paras.

[293] Summary, n 242, point 3.2.1, second para; point 3.2.3, second para.

[294] Summary, n 242, point 3.2.5, first para.

took a cautious approach as to the need for an optional instrument,[295] with many questioning its constitutionality[296] or at least contemplating the issue.[297] In contrast, many reactions from scholars went even further in advocating a European contract or civil code.[298] Secondly, there was a wide range of opinions on the scope, form, and application (ie opt-in, opt-out, or a combination of the two) of an optional instrument.[299] In particular, while not as apparent in the Commission's summary, various individual responses raised the question of the interplay between the optional instrument and the other measures proposed in the Action Plan. For example, some contributions highlighted that the prospect of the CFR took away the need for an optional instrument to some extent.[300] Thirdly, concerns about the operation of the optional instrument in relation to EU private international law rules and international conventions were strongly voiced.[301] Noticeably, in comparison to the 2001 Communication, there was not as much discussion of American techniques in the 2003 Action Plan, although there were a few references to the ALI and the UCC.[302] Altogether, these contributions from the stakeholder groups raised further questions about the CFR and the constitutional dimensions of the envisaged activities for European contract law. Although they fed into the Commission's next steps planned for the European contract law as outlined in the body of the 2004 Communication, these questions largely went unaddressed.

5.4.2 Content of the 2004 Communication

The 2004 Communication constituted the Commission's follow-up to the three measures set out in the 2003 Action Plan. Unlike the two previous Communications, however, this Communication did not seek further responses from the Union institutions and other interested parties. Its purpose was to outline the Commission's plans for future action in connection with each measure. As illustrated by the number of pages devoted to each measure and the two respective annexes, the 2004 Communication was mainly preoccupied with the CFR, and to a somewhat lesser extent, the optional instrument.[303] By comparison, as far as *Measure II (EU-wide standard contract terms)* was concerned, the Commission gave it short shrift. It quickly summarized the responses that it had received and announced that it would host a website to promote their use[304] and organize a survey to identify the existence

[295] Summary, n 242, point 3.3.1, first–fourth paras; point 3.3.2, first–second paras; point 3.3.3, first para; point 3.3.4, first para; point 3.3.5, first–second paras.

[296] Summary, n 242, point 3.3.4, second para; point 3.3.5, twelfth para. Constitutional concerns were also evident in certain individual responses: see, eg, Response of the Council of Bars and Law Societies of Europe (CCBE), 3.

[297] Summary, n 247, point 3.3.1, second para; point 3.3.5, twelfth–thirteenth paras. See also individual responses, eg, Response of the Hungarian Government, point 10, third para; Response of the Law Society of England and Wales, point 32(iii), at 11; Response of the European Consumers' Organization (BEUC), 4.

[298] Summary, n 242, point 3.3.5, first, fourteenth–fifteenth paras.

[299] Summary, n 242, point 3.3.1, fifth–ninth paras; point 3.3.2, fourth–sixth paras; point 3.3.4, third–fourth, sixth paras; point 3.3.5, fourth–eleventh, thirteenth paras.

[300] See, eg, Response of the Law Society of England and Wales, point 19.

[301] Summary, n 242, point 3.3.1, tenth–eleventh paras; point 3.3.2, second–third paras; point 3.3.3, second para; point 3.3.4, fifth para; point 3.3.5, sixteenth–eighteenth paras.

[302] See, eg, Response of the Hungarian Government, points 13–14.

[303] Discussion of the CFR constituted more than half of the total twenty-two pages of the 2004 Communication: see 2004 Communication, n 3, point 2.1, points 3.1–3.2; Annex I ('Possible structure of the CFR'). For the optional instrument, see 2004 Communication, point 2.3; Annex II ('Parameters concerning the optional instrument—For further discussion on the opportuneness of this instrument').

[304] 2004 Communication, n 3, points 2.2.2–2.2.3.

of any legislative obstacles to the use of EU-wide standard terms in the Member States, with a view to eliminating them where needed and appropriate.[305] Yet, it did not intend to publish guidelines on the relationship between standard terms and the relevant EU law rules[306] or to define itself a set of 'best practices'.[307] On the whole, the viability of this measure faded from view.

As regards *Measure I (improving the acquis in contract law)*,[308] the CFR was the centre of attention. The Commission declared that in light of the significant support of the stakeholders, it would pursue the elaboration of the CFR.[309] The Commission identified four main problems plaguing the *acquis* as brought to light by the 2003 Action Plan: (1) the use of abstract legal terms in directives that are not defined or defined too broadly; (2) areas where the application of directives do not solve the problems in practice; (3) differences between the national implementing laws stemming from the use of minimum harmonization clauses in consumer protection directives; and (4) inconsistencies in Community (now Union) contract law legislation.[310] It then underlined that the 'main role' of the CFR would be to remedy these problems,[311] coining the famous nickname for the CFR as a 'toolbox' for the Commission when presenting proposals to improve the quality and coherence of the existing and future *acquis* in the area of contract law.[312]

In a special box carved out from the rest of the 2004 Communication, the Commission highlighted an 'example' of the role that the CFR could play in connection with its plans for the review of the consumer *acquis*.[313] The Commission explained that it was going to review eight consumer directives to determine whether they met the Commission's goals of enhancing consumer and business confidence in the internal market through a high level of consumer protection and the elimination of internal market barriers.[314] Curiously, the Commission did not mention the CFR in much detail, save for the very last line in which it stated that any subsequent proposal would take into account the work on the draft CFR as appropriate.[315] Instead, this one and a half page box segregated from the rest of the Communication asked pointed questions, such as 'Is the level of consumer protection required by the directives high enough to ensure consumer confidence?' and 'Does consumer contract law need to be further harmonised?'.[316] The Commission then set down a number of actions planned for this

[305] 2004 Communication, n 3, point 2.2.3.3.

[306] 2004 Communication, n 3, point 2.2.3.2.

[307] 2004 Communication, n 3, point 2.2.3.1, second para.

[308] While the reference to future measures had merely appeared in the description, not the title, of this proposed solution in the 2003 Action Plan (see 2003 Action Plan, n 2, heading of 4.1, point 78), this was now elevated to the heading of this measure: 2004 Communication, n 3, point 2.1.

[309] 2004 Communication, n 3, point 2.1.

[310] 2004 Communication, n 3, point 2.1.1, first para. The Commission did not explicitly state whether it was referring to the *acquis* on contract law or private law more generally, but the discussion centred on contract law.

[311] 2004 Communication, n 3, heading of point 2.1.1.

[312] 2004 Communication, n 3, point 2.1.1, second para.

[313] 2004 Communication, n 3, box below point 2.1.1. This had already been stated in the Communication on the Consumer Policy Strategy 2002–2006, n 56, but at that point, the Commission had not picked out the eight directives specified here.

[314] 2004 Communication, n 3, box below point 2.1.1, first para. Six of the eight directives fell within the 'hard core' of the EU contract law *acquis*: the Doorstep Selling, Package Travel, Unfair Contract Terms, Timeshare, Distance Selling, and Consumer Sales Directives; the other two were the Injunctions and Price Indication Directives.

[315] 2004 Communication, n 3, box below point 2.1.1, sixth para.

[316] 2004 Communication, n 3, box below point 2.1.1, third para, first bullet point; fourth para, third bullet point.

area, including the development of a public database of the *acquis*, the establishment of a group of Member State experts, and the issuance of implementation reports on some of these directives.[317]

Following this, the Commission launched back into contemplating five additional roles to be played by the CFR, making clear that it was not to be used by the Commission alone.[318] First, at the European level, the European Parliament and the Council could use the CFR when tabling amendments to the Commission's proposals for improving the *acquis*, which would further promote simplicity, clarity, and consistency of EU legislation.[319] Secondly, the CFR could 'inspire' the Court of Justice when interpreting the EU contract law *acquis*.[320] Thirdly, at the national level, the CFR could be used by national legislators when transposing directives or enacting other contract law legislation and by arbitrators as had been suggested by the European Parliament.[321] Fourthly, the Commission stated that it was considering integrating the CFR into the contracts concluded with its contractors and would encourage other institutions and bodies to do the same.[322] Fifthly, it reiterated that the CFR would be used to develop other measures identified in the Action Plan, such as the optional instrument,[323] albeit without providing further insight on the interplay between these two measures as mentioned in the stakeholder responses. Furthermore, given the fact that just below this, the Commission declared that, at least at this stage of the consultation process, the CFR would be a non-binding instrument,[324] it was not clear how all of these possible roles of the CFR would be achieved in practice.

There was a specific section of the 2004 Communication devoted to the preparation of the CFR, which may be viewed to some extent as an attempt by the Commission to counter the criticisms lodged by the European Parliament as regards the adequate involvement of all relevant stakeholders and the establishment of stringent timelines. The Commission posited that by 2007, academic researchers would produce a draft CFR, ie a first academic version of the CFR.[325] Then, the draft CFR would undergo a period of review,[326] which would result in a Commission CFR, ie the final version of the CFR, being submitted to the Union institutions, Member States, and stakeholders for their consultation.[327] It was foreseen that the Commission would adopt this final CFR in 2009, at which point mechanisms for updating the CFR would be identified, and it would be widely published and reviewed as needed.[328] In short, there would be

[317] 2004 Communication, n 3, box below point 2.1.1, fifth para.

[318] 2004 Communication, n 3, point 2.1.2.

[319] 2004 Communication, n 3, point 2.1.1, third para.

[320] 2004 Communication, n 3, point 2.1.2, fifth para.

[321] 2004 Communication, n 3, point 2.1.2, first–second paras.

[322] 2004 Communication, n 3, point 2.1.2, fourth para.

[323] 2004 Communication, n 3, point 2.1.2, third para.

[324] 2004 Communication, n 3, point 2.1.3, second para. The Commission reserved the right to revisit the issue of the binding nature of the CFR, however. 2004 Communication, n 3, point 2.1.3, second para.

[325] 2004 Communication, n 3, point 3.1.1, second para. To ensure that the CFR was of 'high quality', the Commission stated its intention to finance three years of research under the FP6. 2004 Communication, n 3, point 3.1.1, first para. This would become the Co-PECL Network of Excellence discussed in Chapter 4, § 4.2.3.

[326] 2004 Communication, n 3, point 3.2.2. The Commission stated that it was not bound by the draft CFR and would amend it where necessary to achieve the 2003 Action Plan's objectives. 2004 Communication, n 3, point 3.2.1.

[327] 2004 Communication, n 3, point 3.2.3.

[328] 2004 Communication, n 3, point 3.2.4.

two versions of the CFR: an academic or draft CFR, and a political or final CFR.[329] As part of this process, the Commission elaborated an extensive framework for stakeholder participation.[330] There would be two 'strands' of input for the CFR. First, the technical input strand included the appointment of a network of stakeholder experts to make ongoing contributions to the researchers' work. This also involved holding regular workshops on research subjects and setting up an internet website for the posting of drafts and stakeholder comments.[331] Secondly, the political consideration and review strand concerned means for involving the Union institutions and the Member States, eg, providing regular updates to the European Parliament and the Council and establishing a group of Member State experts in order to keep the Member States informed about progress and to receive feedback.[332] These two strands could be brought together periodically by way of a discussion forum, to allow discussion in a broader context.[333]

As regards the researchers' formulation of the CFR, the Commission stated that the CFR would contain common fundamental principles of contract law, definitions of key concepts, and model rules.[334] Two specific types of contracts, consumer and insurance contracts, were singled out, since the Commission expected the CFR to 'pay specific attention to these areas'.[335] Yet, it surmised that the CFR could cover other areas, such as sale contracts, services contacts, and clauses relating to the retention of title and the transfer of title to goods.[336] In this regard, the Commission referred to the conclusions of the Study on the relationship between contract law and the fields of tort and property law which had been requested by the Council's 2001 Report[337] and concluded:

> [T]here are no appreciable problems arising from differences in the interaction between contract law and tort law in the different Member States. More significant problems appear to arise from the different transactions between contract and property law in Member States. The preparation of the CFR will need to consider how to resolve these problems, as far as necessary for improving the present and future *acquis*.[338]

The Commission's conclusion was surprising, at least for those scholars who had prepared the Study, since their conclusions had called attention to the crucial linkages between tort and contract law and discussed various problems associated with taking action in contract law without consideration of tort law.[339] In addition, glancing through the accompanying Annex setting forth the possible structure of the CFR in outline form, there were several topics that went beyond the confines of contract law

[329] Although the name 'Commission CFR' was used in the 2004 Communication, subsequent emphasis on the involvement of the other Union institutions (namely, the European Parliament and the Council) in its preparation, as discussed in Chapter 6, may explain why the reference to the political or final CFR has become more prominent.

[330] 2004 Communication, n 3, point 3.1.2.

[331] 2004 Communication, n 3, point 3.1.2, fourth para.

[332] 2004 Communication, n 3, point 3.1.2, fifth para.

[333] 2004 Communication, n 3, point 3.1.2, sixth para.

[334] 2004 Communication, n 3, point 3.1.3, second para.

[335] 2004 Communication, n 3, point 3.1.3, fourth para.

[336] 2004 Communication, n 3, point 3.1.3, fourth para.

[337] See n 120 and accompanying text.

[338] 2004 Communication, n 3, point 3.1.3, fifth para.

[339] See ns 132–133 and accompanying text. It should be noted that the Study was considered to deal more predominantly with issues of tort law. As a result, there was a subsequent book authored by certain scholars including one of the authors of the Study, Professor Ulrich Drobnig, in order to flesh out in more detail issues related to the approximation of property law and its relationship to contract law. See U Drobnig et al (eds), *Divergences of Property Law, an Obstacle to the Internal Market?* (Sellier, 2006), particularly U Drobnig et al, 'Divergences of Property Law, an Obstacle to the Internal Market?', 4, 4–5.

strictly speaking, such as rules concerning the plurality of parties, assignment of claims, and prescription periods.[340] The Commission attempted to provide some explanation as to the scope of the CFR by stating that the primary criterion for determining which areas would be covered should be 'the usefulness in terms of increasing the coherence of the *acquis*'; however, it was not clear whether this statement was limited to contract or other fields of private law.[341]

Ambiguities were also evident as regards *Measure III* on non-sector specific measures such as an optional instrument. The Commission prefaced its remarks with the statement that this solution was still subject to further reflection, particularly in light of the development of the CFR.[342] At this point, the Commission focused on the prospect of an optional instrument, as opposed to other conceivable types of non-sector specific measures. The Commission lost no time in attempting to defuse constitutional tensions underlying the optional instrument by explicitly affirming that it was not tantamount to a European civil code:

> Although it is premature to speculate about the possible outcome of the reflection, it is important to explain that it is neither the Commission's intention to propose a 'European civil code' which would harmonise contract laws of Member States, nor should the reflections be seen in any way calling into question the current approaches to promoting free circulation on the basis of flexible and efficient solutions.[343]

This passage became one of the most cited points of the 2004 Communication. It did not completely silence the controversy, however. In particular, scholars were quick to point out that the express disavowal of a European civil code came within the context of the optional instrument, not the CFR, which was considered by many just as likely to 'sow the seeds of a code'.[344]

Following this statement, the Commission explored several parameters for further reflection on the optional instrument on the basis of the stakeholder contributions and its own considerations.[345] While some aspects were hinted at in the body of the 2004 Communication,[346] the Commission preferred to place its discussion of the main points of the optional instrument—its binding nature, content, legal form, scope, and legal basis—at the very end of the Communication in an accompanying Annex.[347] There, the Commission stressed upfront that before any decision would be taken on the adoption of an optional instrument, an extended impact assessment would be conducted to address a number of questions, including how the principles of subsidiarity

[340] 2004 Communication, n 3, Annex I, 14. It was the inclusion of these areas that beckoned analogy between the CFR and the PECL, whose third volume greatly resembled the Commission's outline for the CFR. See Chapter 4, § 4.2.1.

[341] 2004 Communication, n 3, point 3.1.3, third para.

[342] 2004 Communication, n 3, point 2.3, second para.

[343] 2004 Communication, n 3, point 2.3, third para. On this basis, the Commission later reiterated that it had no intention of promoting a European civil code: see, eg, the Commission's response to Written Question E-4389/07 by G Papastamkos, 'European private law', available at <http://www.europarl.europa.eu/>. See further Chapter 6.

[344] S Vogenauer and S Weatherill, 'The European Community's Competence to Pursue the Harmonisation of Contract Law—an Empirical Contribution to the Debate' in *The Harmonisation of European Contract Law*, n 238, 105, 112. The conjunction of the CFR and a European contract, or even civil, code was also apparent in some of the contributions to the 2003 Action Plan: see, eg, Summary, n 242, point 3.1.1, fourth para; Response of Clifford Chance, 1; Response of Professor Martijn W Hesselink, 9 (see also MW Hesselink, 'The European Commission's Action Plan: Towards a More Coherent European Contract Law?' (2004) 12 *ERPL* 397).

[345] 2004 Communication, n 3, point 2.3, fourth para.

[346] 2004 Communication, n 3, point 2.3, fourth–fifth paras.

[347] 2004 Communication, n 3, Annex II.

and proportionality would be taken into account.[348] The Commission did not completely ignore the issue of legal basis, even if the discussion was quite slim and relegated to the very last point of the Annex.[349] It claimed that very few stakeholders had expressed their view on the matter, with one Member State proposing Article 308 EC (now Article 352 TFEU) for an 'opt-in' instrument and Article 95 EC (now Article 114 TFEU) for an 'opt-out' instrument, and a group of scholars preferring Article 65 EC (now Article 81 TFEU).[350] It then disposed of the matter by explaining that since the question of legal basis was linked to the legal form, content, and scope of the optional instrument, further discussion would be needed within the larger debate about the parameters of such instrument.[351]

At the same time, however, the Commission's discussion of the other four points concerning the optional instrument seemed at least implicitly to turn the constitutional attention to legal bases related to the internal market. First, as to *content*, the Commission declared that the optional instrument 'should only contain those areas of contract law, whether general or specific to certain contracts, which clearly contribute to addressing identified problems, such as barriers to the smooth functioning of the internal market'.[352] Secondly, as for *scope*, in response to the question whether the optional instrument should cover solely B2B contracts or also B2C contracts, the Commission answered that 'it is important to remember the main goal of the optional instrument, namely the smoother functioning of the internal market'.[353] It found that the inclusion of both types of contracts would ensure that goal, and as for consumer contracts, national mandatory rules concerning consumer protection can increase transaction costs and constitute obstacles to cross-border contracts.[354] As such, the inclusion of mandatory provisions in the optional instrument would provide parties with greater legal certainty in cross-border transactions and allow providers of goods and services to engage in transactions throughout the EU on the basis of a single contract.[355]

Thirdly, as regards the *binding nature* of the optional instrument, the Commission stressed that most stakeholders preferred an 'opt-in' model of contract rules chosen by the parties through a choice of law clause.[356] The Commission appeared to share this sentiment by virtue of its emphasis on the parties' contractual freedom and the fact that the use of an 'opt-out' instrument in relation to the application of the CISG would prove problematic in the case of B2B international sale of goods transactions.[357] Finally, as for *legal form*, the choice of a regulation was considered most appropriate for the 'opt-in' and 'opt-out' models.[358] In this way, the 2004 Communication signified a large step in the path towards the CFR and generated substantial commentary

[348] 2004 Communication, n 3, Annex II, point 1, second para, fifth indent. Although not referring specifically to subsidiarity, see also 2004 Communication, n 3, point 2.3, fourth para.

[349] 2004 Communication, n 3, Annex II, point 6.

[350] 2004 Communication, n 3, Annex II, point 6, first para. The Commission did not identify the particular Member State or academic group concerned.

[351] 2004 Communication, n 3, Annex II, point 6, second para.

[352] 2004 Communication, n 3, Annex II, point 4, third para.

[353] 2004 Communication, n 3, Annex II, point 5, third para.

[354] 2004 Communication, n 3, Annex II, point 5, third–fourth paras.

[355] 2004 Communication, n 3, Annex II, point 4, fourth para.

[356] 2004 Communication, n 3, Annex II, point 2, second para.

[357] 2004 Communication, n 3, Annex II, point 5, third, sixth paras. The Commission also advanced three viable approaches for the application of the optional instrument vis-à-vis the successor to the Rome Convention (the 'Rome I' Regulation, which had not yet been adopted). See 2004 Communication, n 3, Annex II, point 2, fifth para.

[358] 2004 Communication, n 3, Annex II, point 3, second–third paras.

regarding each of the proposed solutions. Yet, with its further elaboration of the shape of the CFR and the optional instrument, it made the question of competence in connection with these activities loom even larger in the debate.

5.4.3 Aftermath of the 2004 Communication

To recall, the nature of the 2004 Communication was such that the Commission did not request further feedback from the Union institutions and stakeholders, though it did eventually attract responses from the European Parliament and the Council in combination with the Commission's First Progress Report on European Contract Law,[359] as discussed in the next chapter. In the meantime, the 2004 Communication, as well as the Commission's previous Communications, filtered into institutional developments concerning the European Council's Hague Programme on the AFSJ and the EESC's Opinion on a European insurance contract instrument, both of which added to the constitutional fervor surrounding European contract law.

5.4.3.1 The Hague Programme

With the Tampere Programme coming to a close in 2004, the Commission issued its last six-month progress report in the form of a Communication regarding the assessment of the Tampere Programme and future orientations.[360] Under the heading 'Establish a judicial area in civil and commercial matters to facilitate cooperation and access to justice', the Commission turned to the matter of European contract law.[361] It explained that it was 'already engaged in drafting a Common Reference Framework to ensure greater consistency in the *acquis communautaire* and improve its quality in the field of contract law'.[362] In an accompanying footnote, the Commission added that the 'Common Reference Framework' (ie CFR) could serve as the basis for an optional instrument in the long term, which the parties could freely choose as the law applicable to their contract, thereby enhancing certainty as to the law in cross-border transactions.[363] Yet, the linkage between European contract law and the building of a 'European area of justice' went unaddressed.

Thereafter, then German Chancellor Gerhard Schröder published a statement in the *Wall Street Journal* concerning his intention to submit at the forthcoming November 2004 European Council meeting a programme called 'Seven Chances for the Internal Market'.[364] Situated within the context of the Lisbon Strategy,[365] this programme

[359] First Annual Progress Report on European Contract Law and the Acquis Review, COM (2005) 456 final, 23.9.2005.

[360] Commission Communication, Area of Freedom, Security and Justice: Assessment of the Tampere programme and future orientations, COM (2004) 401 final, 2.6.2004.

[361] Communication, n 360, heading of point 2.7.

[362] Communication, n 360, point 2.7, fourth para.

[363] Communication, n 360, point 2.7, fourth para, at 11 fn 10.

[364] Gerhard Schröder, 'Seven-Up for Europe', *Wall Street Journal*, 26 Oct 2004, A24.

[365] The Lisbon Strategy (also known as the Lisbon Agenda or Lisbon Process) was set out by the European Council at a special meeting in Lisbon with the aim to have the EU become 'the most dynamic and competitive knowledge-based economy in the world capable of sustainable economic growth with more and better jobs and greater social cohesion'. Presidency Conclusions, Lisbon European Council, 23–24 March 2000, point 5. It has since been superseded by the Europe 2020 Strategy, adopted by the European Council in 2010. See generally <http://ec.europa.eu/europe2020/index_en.htm>.

focused on measures to be taken in certain sectors to improve the internal market, one of which concerned the European contract law project. Chancellor Schröder explained: '[W]e need a European contract law. Companies who operate Europe-wide currently have to deal with 25 different legal systems. To make the internal market more efficient, the German [G]overnment supports the European Commission's action for "a coherent European Contract Law"'.[366] His support for 'a European contract law' instrument was not missed by those involved with the European contract law project.[367] Later, on 4–5 November 2004, the European Council held its meeting in Brussels,[368] where it discussed the Lisbon Strategy, but without specific mention of Chancellor Schröder's programme.[369] The European Council did, however, mention European contract law.

This meeting is probably best remembered for the European Council's declaration of the Hague Programme.[370] As the successor to the Tampere Programme, the Hague Programme constituted the second multiannual programme establishing the priorities for the AFSJ over the next five years.[371] European contract law was cited in this Programme as part of measures to ensure a European area of 'justice' in the context of judicial cooperation in civil matters. Under the heading 'Ensuring coherence and upgrading the quality of EU legislation', the European Council stated: '*In matters of contract law*, the quality of existing and future Community [now Union] law should be improved by measures of consolidation, codification and rationalisation of legal instruments in force and by developing a *common frame of reference*'.[372] It also requested that a framework be set up to explore the possibility of developing EU-wide standard contract terms that could be used by companies and trade associations.[373] These statements indicated the European Council's support, in quite a high-level political document, for two of the proposed measures identified in the 2003 Action Plan and elaborated further in the 2004 Communication: the CFR and the promotion of standard contract terms. The optional instrument was not mentioned, possibly because the prospect of such an instrument may have been too controversial or too indefinite at that stage of the consultation process as compared to the abovementioned initiatives.

Nevertheless, the heading and description of these two measures were telling. The CFR was linked to the improvement of the *acquis*. It sat alongside the European Council's other suggestion for ensuring that the Council was able to scrutinize the quality and coherence of EU instruments relating to judicial cooperation in civil matters.[374] Thus, it seemed to be viewed largely through the lens of 'better lawmaking' policy, although the promotion of standard contract terms alluded to the relevance of the European contract law project to economic operators in the EU. Additionally, by virtue of the introductory clause ('In matters of contract law'), the CFR was situated within European contract law, with no mention of other fields of private law. No reference was made to the lineage of the European contract law project in point 39 of the Tampere Conclusions, much less

[366] Schröder, n 364, sixth indent.

[367] See, eg, Remarks of Robert Madelin, then Director General for Health and Consumer Protection at the Commission, 'European Contract Law: the way forward', First workshop of the network of Member States experts in European Contract Law, held on 3 Dec 2004, 5–6.

[368] Presidency Conclusions, Brussels European Council, 4–5 Nov 2004.

[369] Presidency Conclusions, n 368, point I.

[370] Presidency Conclusions, n 368, Annex I ('The Hague Programme: Strengthening Freedom, Security and Justice in the European Union'), [2005] OJ C53/1 (Hague Programme).

[371] See Hague Programme, n 370, pt I.

[372] Hague Programme, n 370, point 3.4.4, first para (emphasis added).

[373] Hague Programme, n 370, point 3.4.4, first para.

[374] Hague Programme, n 370, point 3.4.4, second para.

why European contract law was mentioned here in the context of judicial cooperation in civil matters.

Similar sentiments ran through documents implementing the Hague Programme. For example, in the Commission's Action Plan outlining the priorities for the Hague Programme,[375] it framed the CFR as follows: 'Regarding the EU substantive contract law, a Common Frame of Reference (CFR), to be used as a toolbox to improve coherence and quality of EU legislation, will be adopted in 2009 at the latest'.[376] When this Action Plan was approved by the Council, the CFR was placed under the measures for 'ensuring consistency' within the field of judicial cooperation in civil matters.[377] Again, the CFR was conjoined with the improvement of the *acquis* and delimited to contract law.[378] There was no explanation as to the relationship between European contract law and the EU's objectives related to judicial cooperation in civil matters and the AFSJ.

5.4.3.2 The EESC's Opinion on European insurance contract law

On 15 December 2004, the EESC adopted an Opinion on 'The European Insurance Contract'.[379] The purpose of this Opinion was to alert national and EU authorities to the problems for consumers and the internal market caused by the diversity of national laws concerning insurance contracts and to propose possible solutions to secure more suitable legislation at the European level on this subject.[380] As the title implied, the EESC advocated the promulgation of a European insurance contract law instrument, which built on the Commission's previous Communications on European contract law.[381] The Opinion's conflation of approximation and optional instruments placed further attention on the constitutional dimensions of European contract law within which insurance contract law was situated.

After an extensive presentation of the reasons prompting the Opinion, which included documentation of the various problems caused by differences between national insurance contract laws for the internal market[382] and the role played by

[375] Commission Communication, The Hague Programme: Ten priorities for the next five years—The Partnership for European renewal in the field of Freedom, Security and Justice, COM (2005) 184 final, 10.5.2005.

[376] Communication, n 375, point 2.3, para 9. See also point 2.3, fourth para ('Improve the EU substantive contract law'); Annex, point 4, indents 17–18.

[377] The Action Plan was approved at the 2664th meeting of the JHA configuration of the Council on 2–3 June 2005, DOC 9778/2/05REV2, dated 10 June 2005; DOC 9682/05, dated 11 July 2005. It was then published in the *Official Journal*: see Council and Commission Action Plan implementing the Hague Programme on strengthening freedom, security and justice in the European Union, [2005] OJ C198/1 (Action Plan).

[378] By comparison, under the heading 'mutual recognition of decisions and elimination of obstacles to the proper functioning of proceedings', the Action Plan listed several measures which primarily concerned private international law and procedural matters, not substantive (private) law. Action Plan, n 377, point 4.3.

[379] EESC Opinion on 'The European Insurance Contract', [2005] OJ C157/1 (2004 EESC Opinion). Mr Pegado Liz, the Rapporteur, was a member of the Insurance Group which had an impact on this Opinion: see n 383.

[380] 2004 EESC Opinion, n 379, point 1.3.

[381] The EESC referred to the 2001 Communication and the 2003 Action Plan, along with the Parliament's request for the adoption of an optional instrument on insurance contract law in its resolution in response to the 2001 Communication. See 2004 EESC Opinion, n 379, points 2.3–2.4. The EESC did not, however, refer to the 2004 Communication, which may have been because it was published too close in time to the finalization of the Opinion. In any event, the EESC's discussion of the 2003 Action Plan covered the measures addressed in the 2004 Communication.

[382] See 2004 EESC Opinion, n 379, point 4, particularly point 4.2.

comparative research in this field,[383] the EESC evaluated whether the harmonization of insurance contract law warranted the harmonization of general contract law.[384] It concluded that while proceeding with both in tandem would be 'easier', it was not necessary and the harmonization of insurance contract law could proceed on its own.[385] The EESC also analogized the Commission's proposal for EU-wide standard contract terms to the insurance sphere, finding that the elaboration of EU-wide general terms of insurance was not helpful because, among other things, they disadvantaged mobile Union citizens and had adverse effects on competition.[386]

The EESC then weighed the advantages and disadvantages of harmonization versus the use of an optional instrument running parallel to the national legal orders along the lines of the Commission's proposed solution,[387] finding that either one was preferable to the status quo and the choice between them was 'ultimately a matter of policy not of principle'.[388] It considered that a degree of harmonization of the mandatory rules of the general part of insurance contract law could contribute decisively to removing obstacles and difficulties facing undertakings and consumers in carrying out cross-border insurance transactions.[389] It recommended that a gradual approach to harmonization should be taken, 'aiming initially at the possible adoption of an optional model insurance contract act all of whose terms and components would be mandatory'.[390] Specifically, a regulation should be used, and former Article 95 EC (now Article 114 TFEU) should be the legal basis.[391]

Given the EESC's recognition of the distinction between harmonization and optional instruments above, the juxtaposition of an optional instrument and Article 114 TFEU called into play crucial issues plaguing the constitutionality of European contract law generally, namely the scope of 'measures for the approximation' of national laws under Article 114 TFEU and the relationship between Articles 114 and 352 TFEU. Moreover, the Opinion tied EU-level action in insurance contract law to the functioning of the internal market and thus called attention to the interplay between general and specific fields of contract law in the wake of the Commission's Communications.

5.5 Conclusions

No matter how much time passes or where the endpoint of the European contract law project will eventually rest, the Commission's three Communications on European contract law will never lose their place as fundamental components in the debate about European contract law and European private law generally. They are cornerstones of the evolution, scope, and constitutionality of the European contract law project through to the present day. They also reopened themes concerning the EU's involvement with European contract law and European private law generally, which had been apparent since the beginnings of the debate.

383 2004 EESC Opinion, n 379, point 6.1. In particular, it highlighted the role played by the Insurance Group whose chairman, Professor Fritz Reichert-Facilides, had been appointed as an expert and submitted an initial position paper before his death: see 2004 EESC Opinion, n 379, point 1.4. For further discussion of this Group, see Chapter 4, § 4.2.3.

384 2004 EESC Opinion, n 379, point 6.4.

385 2004 EESC Opinion, n 379, point 6.4.4.

386 2004 EESC Opinion, n 379, point 6.6.

387 2004 EESC Opinion, n 379, point 6.5.

388 2004 EESC Opinion, n 379, point 6.5.2.1; see also point 6.5.2.6.

389 2004 EESC Opinion, n 379, point 8.4. As for what comprised the 'general part', this was elaborated in a multi-step plan: see 2004 EESC Opinion, n 379, points 7.4–7.5.

390 2004 EESC Opinion, n 379, point 8.6.

391 2004 EESC Opinion, n 379, point 8.8.

First, each Communication had a considerable impact in steering the evolution of the European contract law project. Looking back over the course of the three years and three months in which they were issued, these three Communications heralded a process by which to identify the extent of the problems underlying EU contract law and to put forth a targeted set of solutions to remedy these problems and the framework in which to put them into action orchestrated from the European level. In other words, by virtue of these Communications, the Commission instigated a *sui generis* process that had never before occurred in the EU, and in doing so, transfixed this process within the EU institutional framework.

Secondly, the scope of the European contract law project vis-à-vis related fields of private law was an incessant theme underpinning the Communications and responses of the Union institutions and bodies, Member States, and other stakeholders. On the whole, the Communications primarily concerned contract law, but other fields of private law were not left out. The failure to clarify the relationship between European contract law and European private law generally enlivened tensions about the breadth of the EU's involvement in European contract law, which gradually crept into ongoing discussion of the CFR and the optional instrument and hence the Union's competence to undertake such initiatives, which leads to the final point.

Thirdly, despite the fact that none of the Communications undertook detailed assessment of the constitutionality of the envisaged initiatives, all three Communications and the responses of the other Union institutions and bodies along the way strengthened, implicitly or explicitly, the linkage between the European contract law project and the Union's objectives related to the internal market, bringing provisions such as Article 114 TFEU to the fore. At the same time, each Communication and the solutions proposed raised questions bearing on the extent of the Union's competence in this setting. Starting with the 2001 Communication, issues concerning the existence, or not, of a sufficient legal basis under the Treaties for the adoption of a comprehensive contract law instrument, the roles played by the principles of subsidiarity and proportionality, and the possible recourse to other forms of action, such as an intergovernmental treaty, the Open Method of Coordination, and American techniques, came into view. With the 2003 Action Plan, the emergence of the CFR and the optional instrument stimulated discussion as regards the Union's competence to adopt such measures. Finally, with the 2004 Communication, the envisaged usage of the CFR in the context of the revision of the consumer *acquis* and the place of the European contract law project within the field of judicial cooperation in civil matters beckoned clarification as regards the linkage between European contract law and the Union's objectives related to consumer protection and the AFSJ, respectively. In this way, the three Communications augmented the need to confront the constitutionality of European contract law head-on. This would escalate further in the present path of European contract law as examined in the next chapter.

6

The Debate Continues

6.1 Introduction

As set in motion by the Commission's three Communications on European contract law, the debate currently embodies three main sets of activities or components. The first concerns the Common Frame of Reference (CFR). The second implicates the Commission's plans for the review of the consumer *acquis* and the adoption of the Consumer Rights Directive. The third revolves around the possible enactment of one or more optional instruments of contract law and the promotion of EU model contract terms, which has reached a critical juncture with the proposal for a Regulation on a Common European Sales Law (proposed CESL). Together, these components constitute an important turning point in the debate about European contract law, and each enlivens issues concerning the EU's competences related to the internal market, consumer protection, and judicial cooperation in civil matters in this setting.

The aim of this chapter is therefore to examine these three components and their bearing on the constitutionality of European contract law. It is divided into three main parts, which follow the ordering of these components set forth above. Notably, these components are largely intertwined in the various institutional documents, which make it virtually impossible to draw a clear dividing line between them, much less to avoid some overlap in the timeframe. This situation stems from the debate itself starting with the Commission's 2003 and 2004 Communications, which envisaged the CFR as a fulcrum for the improvement of *acquis* and an optional instrument of contract law. Admittedly, for the reader, this makes for a somewhat cumbersome presentation in which the discussion twists and turns through a dizzying array of documents that intersect with each other to varying degrees and seem to defy a clear organization or chronology. Nevertheless, the chapter's three-part structure is deliberate, so as to highlight the extent to which the discussion of the EU's competence, explicitly and implicitly, has figured into the ongoing course of events taking place in European contract law.

6.2 The Path to the CFR

6.2.1 The 2005 Progress Report

On 23 September 2005, the Commission issued the First Annual Progress Report on European Contract Law and the Acquis Review (2005 Progress Report).[1] Its purpose was to summarize the progress of the 'European Contract Law (ECL) Initiative' since the 2004 Communication and to outline the main policy issues.[2] While framed in terms of a 'progress report', this document went beyond a mere update and reconfigured the course of the activities envisaged for European contract law, bringing the CFR

[1] First Annual Progress Report on European Contract Law and the Acquis Review, COM (2005) 456 final, 23.9.2005 (2005 Progress Report).

[2] 2005 Progress Report, n 1, point 1.

and the revision of the consumer *acquis* to the forefront. Yet, it was devoid of any discussion of the constitutionality of these initiatives.

The first part of the 2005 Progress Report was devoted to the preparation of the CFR.[3] Building on the framework for stakeholder participation set forth in the 2004 Communication, the Commission set forth the three main groups involved in the work on the CFR: (1) the *Research Network*, composed of a group of academic researchers engaged in the drafting of the CFR;[4] (2) the *CFR-Net*, a network of stakeholder experts representing business, the legal professions, and consumer organizations, which would provide input to the academic researchers;[5] and (3) the *Member States Experts Network*, composed of persons nominated by their respective Member State to contribute to the consultation process on the CFR.[6] It then outlined certain issues arising in the first phase of the preparation of the CFR.[7] While this was mainly segregated between so-called 'procedural issues' and 'horizontal substantive issues',[8] two common themes were apparent: the interplay between the CFR and improving the *acquis*, on the one hand, and participatory issues related to the CFR drafting process, on the other. As regards the former theme, the Commission declared its intention to 'prioritise issues that are relevant to the consumer contract law *acquis* and other contract law related *acquis*'.[9] It insisted that appropriate differentiation between business-to-business (B2B) and business-to-consumer (B2C) contracts was paramount and advocated a case-by-case approach identifying where specific consumer rules were necessary and suggesting deviations from the general rules.[10] The interdependence between general and specific contract law also needed to be clarified.[11] As regards the latter theme, the Commission executed a number of changes designed to improve the participative nature of the CFR process. For example, it extended the time that the CFR-Net members were given to examine the researchers' drafts[12] and invited the Research Network to provide comprehensive outlines of the key features of each draft in advance of the workshops.[13]

In the second part of the 2005 Progress Report, the Commission set forth its detailed plans for the review of the eight directives within the EU consumer *acquis* following from the 2004 Communication, underlining that this process draws on the example of the consumer *acquis* because of its relevance to contract law.[14] The discussion centred on three points, each of which contained the embryo for the activities to come. First, the Commission explained that a comprehensive comparative analysis of these directives was currently being undertaken by a network of academics and legal practitioners on behalf of the Commission so as to examine the application of the directives in the

[3] 2005 Progress Report, n 1, point 2.

[4] 2005 Progress Report, n 1, point 2.1. In other words, this was the Network of Excellence: see Chapter 4, § 4.2.3.

[5] 2005 Progress Report, n 1, point 2.2.2; Annex ('CFR-net members: overview'). This was essentially a fancy name for the network of stakeholder experts within the 'technical input strand' elaborated in the 2004 Communication: see Chapter 5, § 5.4.2.

[6] 2005 Progress Report, n 1, point 2.3.

[7] 2005 Progress Report, n 1, point 2.6.

[8] Compare 2005 Progress Report, n 1, point 2.6.2, with point 2.6.3, respectively.

[9] 2005 Progress Report, n 1, point 2.6.1. See also point 2.6.2, second para, first bullet point.

[10] 2005 Progress Report, n 1, point 2.6.3, first para, sixth bullet point.

[11] 2005 Progress Report, n 1, point 2.6.3, first para, third bullet point.

[12] 2005 Progress Report, n 1, point 2.6.2, first para.

[13] 2005 Progress Report, n 1, point 2.6.2, second para, fifth bullet point. For further discussion of the various workshops, see, eg, H Beale, 'The European Commission's Common Frame of Reference Project' (2006) 2 *ERCL* 303.

[14] 2005 Progress Report, n 1, point 3.

Member States.[15] This would later be known as the EC Consumer Law Compendium. Secondly, the Commission made clear its intention to disseminate a communication on the review of the consumer *acquis* in the following year.[16] While published a bit later than initially foreseen, this would be the 2007 Green Paper. Thirdly, the Commission presented its preliminary findings on the review of four consumer directives so far,[17] surmising that there were two possible options if there was evidence that the *acquis* needed to be revised (which was pretty much a foregone conclusion at this point): a *vertical approach* consisting of the individual revision of the existing directives, or a *horizontal approach* denoting the adoption of one or more framework instruments providing common definitions and regulating the main consumer contractual rights and remedies.[18] As an example of this horizontal approach, the Commission opined that there could be a directive on B2C contract rules for the sale of goods, which were currently scattered across the Consumer Sales, Unfair Contract Terms, Distance Selling, and Doorstep Selling Directives.[19] Although presented in a somewhat understated fashion, this laid the seeds for the Consumer Rights Directive.

Finally, the third part of the 2005 Progress Report comprised brief, albeit important, discussion of the other two measures identified in the 2003 Action Plan and solidified in the 2004 Communication. First, as regards the promotion of EU-wide standard contract terms, the Commission decided for various reasons that it was not appropriate to host a website through which market participants could exchange information about the use of such terms.[20] As most of the other activities had been cancelled in the 2004 Communication,[21] this option seemed to be pretty much off the table for the time being.[22] Secondly, as regards further reflection on non-sector specific measures such as an optional instrument, the Commission focused on the optional instrument. It referred to such an instrument as a '26th regime' alongside the national contract law regimes as an additional option to contracting parties, thereby leaving the then twenty-five Member States' contract laws untouched.[23] Noticeably, the Commission concentrated on the use of such an instrument in specific fields concerning financial services, insurance, and mortgage credit.[24] This suggested that more than one optional instrument could be foreseen, but matters were left unclear.[25] With the emphasis placed on the CFR and the review of the consumer *acquis*, however, the prospect of an optional instrument seemed to fade from the Commission's short-term view.

[15] 2005 Progress Report, n 1, point 3.1, second para.

[16] 2005 Progress Report, n 1, point 3.1, third para.

[17] These were the Price Indication, Injunctions, Timeshare, and Distance Selling Directives: see 2005 Progress Report, n 1, points 3.2.1–3.2.4.

[18] 2005 Progress Report, n 1, point 3.3, first para.

[19] 2005 Progress Report, n 1, point 3.3, second para.

[20] 2005 Progress Report, n 1, point 4.1, second para.

[21] See Chapter 5, § 5.4.2.

[22] But not for long: see § 6.4. For further discussion, see, eg, S Whittaker, 'On the Development of European Standard Contract Terms' in H Collins (ed), *Standard Contract Terms in Europe: A Basis for and a Challenge to European Contract Law* (Kluwer, 2008) 141.

[23] 2005 Progress Report, n 1, point 4.2. Technically, it should have been a '28th regime' to account for the fact that the UK encompasses more than one legal system. Yet, this implied an additional regime alongside the regimes of the then twenty-five Member States. With the accession of Bulgaria, Romania, and Croatia, this would increase by three, but the reference to a '28th regime' is still used.

[24] 2005 Progress Report, n 1, point 4.2.

[25] Incidentally, a few months later, the possibility of an optional contract law instrument was considered in the context of the proposal for the 'Rome I' Regulation on the law applicable to contractual obligations: see COM (2005) 650 final, 15.12.2005, 5, 9.

6.2.1.1 The Council's 2005 Conclusions

On 28–29 November 2005, the Council adopted its conclusions on the 2005 Progress Report and the 2004 Communication (2005 Conclusions).[26] The fact that it was the Competitiveness (Internal Market, Industry, and Research) configuration of the Council should not be overlooked, since the Council situated its remarks largely within the EU's internal market objectives. On the whole, it praised the Commission's ongoing work on the review of the consumer *acquis* and welcomed its prioritization, such that the parts of the CFR directly relevant to this review would be treated at an earlier stage than previously envisioned.[27] In particular, it emphasized the need for the consumer *acquis* to be 'fit for purpose', meaning that it was able 'to protect the legal and economic interests and rights of consumers, to enhance the confidence of the EU's citizens in the Internal Market, and to promote the cross-border provision of goods and services, thus guaranteeing a high level of consumer protection'.[28] It also favoured the Commission's efforts concerning the CFR consultation process[29] and underlined the need to distinguish between B2C and B2B contracts so as to deliver 'real benefits' for consumers and businesses.[30] At the same time, however, it drew attention to the Commission's 'repeated reassurance' that it did not intend to propose a European civil code and that the Member States' differing legal traditions will be fully taken into account'.[31]

6.2.1.2 The European Parliament's 2006 Resolutions

In response to the 2004 Communication and the 2005 Progress Report, the European Parliament adopted not one, but two Resolutions. In contrast to the subtlety of the Council's 2005 Conclusions, these Resolutions went further in explicitly situating the activities of the European contract law project within the EU's internal market and consumer protection objectives.

On 23 March 2006, the European Parliament adopted a Resolution on European contract law and revision of the *acquis*: the way forward (first 2006 Resolution).[32] Its title was drawn from that of the 2004 Communication, but this Resolution also included comments on the 2005 Progress Report. In essence, what then Commissioner Markos Kyprianou had termed mere 'teething problems' at the start of a big project[33] were considered of greater concern in the Parliament's view. Starting with the Preamble, the Parliament declared that while it 'seems' as though the European contract law project should be seen as an exercise in better lawmaking at the European level, 'it is by no means clear what it will lead to in terms of practical outcomes or on what *legal basis* any binding instrument or instruments will be adopted'.[34] It continued: 'even though the Commission denies that this is its objective, it is clear that many of the researchers

[26] 2694th Council meeting, Competitiveness (Internal Market, Industry, Research), Brussels, 28–29 Nov 2005, DOC 15322/05, dated 2 Dec 2005 (2005 Conclusions).
[27] 2005 Conclusions, n 26, points 7, 8, 11, 14, 17.
[28] 2005 Conclusions, n 26, point 14.
[29] 2005 Conclusions, n 26, points 9, 12, 18.
[30] 2005 Conclusions, n 26, point 13.
[31] 2005 Conclusions, n 26, point 10.
[32] European Parliament Resolution of 23 March 2006 on European contract law and revision of the *acquis*: the way forward, [2006] OJ C292E/109 (first 2006 Resolution).
[33] Opening Address of Markos Kyprianou, then Commissioner for Health and Consumer Protection, Conference on 'European Contract Law: Better Lawmaking to the Common Frame of Reference', hosted by the UK Council Presidency and the European Commission, held on 26 Sept 2005, 4. He served in this position from Nov 2004 to Jan 2007; from Jan 2007 to March 2008, he served as the Commissioner for Health.
[34] First 2006 Resolution, n 32, recital A (emphasis added).

and stakeholders working on the project believe that *the ultimate long-term outcome will be a European code of obligations or even a full-blown European Civil Code*, and that in any event the project is by far the most important initiative under way in the civil law field.'[35] This led the Parliament to stress the importance of the oversight of the Union institutions, whether in relation to the adoption of such a Code or the final product of any initiative within the European contract law project.[36] It also underlined that this project went beyond merely the consumer *acquis* to encompass 'contract law as a whole', but that this should not lead to a diminution of the values lying at the heart of the *acquis*.[37] Taken together, these introductory comments embodied the main themes permeating this Resolution, which the Parliament conveniently organized under three headings concerning the underlying principles and objectives, substantive law issues, and procedural issues related to the European contract law project.

First, the Parliament essentially sought to 'return to its roots' enshrined in its early resolutions. Citing its 1989, 1994, 2001, and 2003 Resolutions, it reiterated that 'a uniform internal market cannot be fully functional without further steps towards the harmonisation of civil law'.[38] It requested the Commission to 'exploit straightaway' the results of the work of academic researchers and the CFR-Net towards the revision of the *acquis* in the field of civil law and eventually the development of 'a system of Community [now Union] civil law'.[39] It was not clear whether this denoted a code of European private law.[40] Suffice it to say, the Parliament continued its longstanding advocacy of far-reaching EU action beyond contract law grounded in the functioning of the internal market.[41]

Secondly, the Parliament highlighted a number of substantive law issues relating to the preparation of the CFR, as well as other measures to be taken in the field of contract (and civil) law.[42] In particular, there had not yet been a systematic distinction between rules applicable to B2B and B2C transactions,[43] and it was important to take into account the European social model when harmonizing contract law and to respect different legal systems and traditions.[44] The Parliament also requested the Commission to define precisely how its future proposals would interact with EU private international law and the national legal systems.[45]

Finally, the Parliament devoted attention to procedural (ie participatory) issues relating to the European contract law project. It called for the Commission 'as a whole' to manage the work on the project under the responsibility of the Directorate General (DG) for what was then called Justice, Freedom and Security (now Justice), rather than

[35] First 2006 Resolution, n 32, recital B (emphasis added).

[36] First 2006 Resolution, n 32, recitals C–D, F.

[37] First 2006 Resolution, n 32, recital G.

[38] First 2006 Resolution, n 32, point 1.

[39] First 2006 Resolution, n 32, point 2.

[40] The phrase 'a system of Community [now Union] civil law' was the subject of some interesting amendments. Initially, it read 'a Community civil law': Draft Report on European contract law and the revision of the *acquis*: the way forward, PE 359.934v01-00, dated 1 June 2005, point 2; Draft Report on European contract law and the revision of the *acquis*: the way forward, PE 359.934v02-00, dated 28 July 2005, point 2. In the Final Report preceding the Resolution, 'a common civil law' was used: Report on European contract law and the revision of the *acquis*: the way forward, A6-0055/2006, dated 2 March 2006 (2006 Final Report), point 2. It was subsequently altered to its present form. See also Remarks of Klaus-Heiner Lehne, Parliamentary Debates of 22 March 2006-Brussels.

[41] See, eg, Remarks of Klaus-Heiner Lehne; Remarks of Diana Wallis; Remarks of Giuseppe Gargani; Remarks of Manuel Medina Ortega, Parliamentary Debates of 22 March 2006–Brussels.

[42] First 2006 Resolution, n 32, points 3–11; compare point 12 (referring to 'all legislative measures concerning civil law').

[43] First 2006 Resolution, n 32, points 4–6.

[44] First 2006 Resolution, n 32, points 8–9.

[45] First 2006 Resolution, n 32, point 10.

that for Health and Consumer Protection, which had assumed the position thus far.[46] It also set forth a number of requests in connection with the preparation of the CFR.[47] It asked the Commission to keep it informed of progress on the CFR by way of quarterly reports[48] and to provide it with a diagram of the various groups, indicating their respective roles and positions.[49] It also made clear that it should be consulted not only on the final version of the CFR, but also on its draft structure and on each title or section as it is finalized,[50] underscoring that the academic researchers' work must follow clear guidelines adopted by the Union legislature and that the CFR could only be adopted following the political approval of the Parliament and the Council.[51]

On its face, the first 2006 Resolution contained no discussion of the legal form of the CFR or its legal basis. What is not commonly known, however, is that both of these issues had initially been mentioned, but ultimately excluded, from the final text. In the accompanying Report, one of the most prominent criticisms related to the Commission's failure to set out a clear legislative plan as to what legal form the CFR should take.[52] This Report was prepared by the Committee on Legal Affairs, but included the Opinion of the Committee on the Internal Market and Consumer Protection.[53] This Opinion was an important component because most of its provisions found their way into the final version of the Resolution. Yet, there was one paragraph of this Opinion concerning the CFR that was left out. This paragraph called on the Commission to submit 'a formal plan for the incremental consultation of Parliament as the work progresses, and for the ultimate implementation of the results of the work of the researchers and CFR-Net to be adopted *in the form of a binding legal instrument (or instruments) on the basis of Articles 95 and/or 153 of the Treaty* [now Articles 114 and/or 169 TFEU]'.[54] The use of 'and/or' suggested that the EU's competences concerning the internal market and consumer protection, respectively, may be used together or alone in the adoption of the envisaged instrument, thereby raising questions concerning the relationship between these two provisions. It was also not spelled out whether such an instrument was envisioned primarily for contract law or other fields of private law.[55] Regrettably, the reference to these Treaty provisions was not elaborated further in the Parliament's second 2006 Resolution, although the EU's internal market objectives remained an implicit theme.

On 7 September 2006, the European Parliament adopted another Resolution on European contract law (second 2006 Resolution).[56] The impetus for this Resolution came from an oral question submitted by MEP Giuseppe Gargani in June 2006.[57]

[46] First 2006 Resolution, n 32, point 14. This request has been carried out: see further Written Question E-0360/2010 by JO Kurski, 'Consumer rights in the new European Commission', available at <http://www.europarl.europa.eu/>. To date, many materials concerning the European contract law project are found on the Commission's website on DG Justice through the link to 'Contract law', <http://ec.europa.eu/justice/contract/index_en.htm>. Many materials relating to the review of the consumer *acquis* are found through the link to 'Consumer and marketing law', <http://ec.europa.eu/justice/consumer-marketing/index_en.htm>.

[47] First 2006 Resolution, n 32, points 15–28.

[48] First 2006 Resolution, n 32, points 21–22.

[49] First 2006 Resolution, n 32, point 19.

[50] First 2006 Resolution, n 32, point 23.

[51] First 2006 Resolution, n 32, points 18, 20.

[52] 2006 Final Report, n 40, 7–8.

[53] 2006 Final Report, n 40, 10.

[54] Opinion of the Committee on the Internal Market and Consumer Protection, dated 25 Jan 2006, in the 2006 Final Report, n 40, point 5 (emphasis added).

[55] Compare 2006 Final Report, n 40, recitals A–C, with 2006 Resolution, n 32, recitals A–C.

[56] European Parliament Resolution of 7 Sept 2006 on European contract law, [2006] OJ C305E/247 (second 2006 Resolution).

[57] Oral Question With Debate by Giuseppe Gargani on behalf of the Committee on Legal Affairs to the Commission, 'European contract law', O-0074/06 (B6-0326/2006), dated 27 June 2006.

On the basis of the 2004 Communication, 2005 Progress Report, and first 2006 Resolution,[58] he addressed five questions to the Commission concerning ambiguities surrounding the scope, legal form, and purpose of the CFR.[59] Much of the substance of these questions was then incorporated into a motion for a resolution.[60] As explained by MEP Klaus-Heiner Lehne, who spoke in place of Mr Gargani in the parliamentary debates on this Resolution, the reason why the Parliament deliberately put this oral question and the corresponding resolution on the agenda was 'to emphasise clearly once more the strength of the Parliament's support for this project' and to provide guidelines to the Commission in its future work on the CFR.[61] Accordingly, the second 2006 Resolution sought to build on certain points elaborated in the first 2006 Resolution. The Parliament restated its position that 'a uniform internal market cannot be fully functional without further steps towards the harmonisation of civil law' and that the European contract law initiative was 'the most important initiative under way in the field of civil law'.[62] It also advocated a 'wider CFR' on general contract law issues going beyond the consumer field and that such work should proceed in parallel with that on the revision of the consumer *acquis*.[63] Finally, it underlined that even though the purpose and legal form of the CFR were still unclear, the final outcome could be a binding legal instrument and hence all possible options should be kept open.[64]

6.2.1.3 *The Commission's 2006 Note to the Council*

While one cannot be sure of the impact of the European Parliament's and the Council's responses to the 2004 Communication and 2005 Progress Report, not long afterwards the Commission submitted a Note to the Council on 1 December 2006 in view of the forthcoming meeting of the Competitiveness Council on 4–5 December 2006.[65] Though directed at the Council, it addressed comments made by the Parliament in its 2006 Resolutions as well. In particular, the Commission declared that the CFR 'was not conceived to be a legislative instrument applicable to legal transactions and is *not* a European civil code'.[66] It also indicated that it will decide 'whether to continue the CFR project beyond consumer contract law so as to include other areas of the EU contract law *acquis* and directly relevant issues of general contract law'.[67] It concluded by stating that it would follow up on these matters in several ways, including its Second Progress Report on the CFR.[68]

[58] Oral Question, n 57, first–fifth indents.

[59] Oral Question, n 57, below fifth indent.

[60] Motion for a resolution further to Question for Oral Answer B6-0326/06 by Giuseppe Gargani on behalf of the Committee on Legal Affairs on European contract law, B6-0464/06, dated 4 Sept 2006.

[61] Remarks of Klaus-Heiner Lehne, Parliamentary Debates of 5 Sept 2006-Strasbourg.

[62] Second 2006 Resolution, n 56, points 1–2.

[63] Second 2006 Resolution, n 56, points 3-4.

[64] Second 2006 Resolution, n 56, point 5. See also recital A.

[65] Council Secretariat, Competitive Council (Internal Market, Industry and Research) meeting on 4–5 Dec 2006, Common Frame of Reference–Information from the Commission, DOC 16086/06, dated 1 Dec 2006, Annex ('Written Information from the Commission to the Competitiveness Council 4–5 December 2006').

[66] DOC 16086/06, n 65, Annex, first heading ('The CFR') (emphasis added).

[67] DOC 16086/06, n 65, Annex, second heading ('State of Play'), fourth para.

[68] DOC 16086/06, n 65, Annex, second heading ('State of Play'), third, fifth paras.

6.2.2 The 2007 Progress Report

On 25 July 2007, the Commission issued the Second Progress Report on the Common Frame of Reference (2007 Progress Report).[69] Its objective was to summarize the progress on the CFR since the first 2005 Progress Report.[70] As indicated by its title, it was focused on the CFR. Even so, it contained no discussion of its constitutionality. Aside from certain references to the review of the consumer *acquis*, there was no discussion of other proposed solutions, such as the optional instrument.

First, the Second Progress Report drove home measures taken to ensure the prioritization of consumer contract law issues in the CFR.[71] It indicated that the researchers agreed to divide their work into three distinct categories so as to ensure that matters relating to the EU consumer *acquis* were discussed as a priority at the CFR workshops.[72] Topics concerning general contract law that were directly relevant to the consumer *acquis* were only discussed if there was time, and topics of general contract law providing essential background for the *acquis* were mainly informative.[73] Secondly, the Commission discussed certain substantive law issues arising from the CFR workshops, devoting most of its attention to those on EU consumer contract law, as opposed to those on non-consumer contract law matters and general contract law.[74] Yet, it stated that it would take the issues concerning general contract law into consideration during the process of elaborating the CFR.[75] This begged the omnipresent question about the structure of the CFR, which the Commission dealt with next.

In two short paragraphs, the Commission summarized the results of two workshops, one with the stakeholder experts (CFR-Net) and the other with the Member State experts, on the subject of the structure of the CFR.[76] Despite some differences in the preferences of these two groups, there seemed to be agreement that the CFR should go beyond consumer contract law and encompass at least some issues of general contract law.[77] In other words, there seemed to be consensus for a 'wider CFR', as depicted in the Parliament's second 2006 Resolution. The Commission then highlighted the input in the preparation of the CFR from stakeholders and the Union institutions. Among other things, it briefly described the responses from the Council and the European Parliament, albeit without mention of the Parliament's critical remarks especially in its first 2006 Resolution.[78] It also responded to the Parliament's request for a diagram of the CFR process by attaching a flow chart identifying the various actors involved.[79]

[69] Second Progress Report on the Common Frame of Reference, COM (2007) 447 final, 25.7.2007 (2007 Progress Report).

[70] 2007 Progress Report, n 69, point 1.

[71] See further Answer given by Mr Kyprianou on behalf of the Commission, dated 25 Aug 2006, to Written Question P-3512/2006 by D Wallis, 'European contract law', available at n 46.

[72] 2007 Progress Report, n 69, point 2, fifth, eighth paras.

[73] 2007 Progress Report, n 69, point 2, sixth–eighth paras.

[74] Compare 2007 Progress Report, n 69, point 3.1, with points 3.2–3.3.

[75] 2007 Progress Report, n 69, point 3.3, first para.

[76] 2007 Progress Report, n 69, point 4, first para.

[77] Compare 2007 Progress Report, n 69, point 4, first para, with point 4, second para. See also point 6, fourth para.

[78] 2007 Progress Report, n 69, point 5.2, particularly point 5.2.2.

[79] 2007 Progress Report, n 69, point 5.2.2, fourth para. This flow chart was the last page of the 2007 Progress Report. It may be wondered whether it adequately responded to the Parliament's demand, given its elementary descriptions of the general roles of the Union institutions, academic researchers, CFR-Net, and Member State experts, without any specific information as to the names or positions of the persons involved for each component. Later, this invited Written Question P-5266/2007 by D Wallis, 'Further information on the "network of Member States Experts" detailed in the Second Progress Report on the Common Frame of Reference', dated 19 Oct 2007, available at n 46.

In its conclusions, the Commission stated that as far as EU consumer contract law was concerned, the relevant CFR findings would be incorporated, where appropriate, into the review of the consumer *acquis*.[80] As regards the scope of the CFR generally, the Commission noted that this issue still needed to be decided in order to steer the future work.[81] For now, it reiterated once again that its scope was '*not* a large scale harmonisation of private law or a European civil code'.[82] It also sought the position of the Parliament and the Council on this matter, and while the Parliament had already done so by virtue of its 2006 Resolutions, it awaited the Council's remarks on the remainder of the work to be done on the CFR.[83]

6.2.3 The publication of the Draft Common Frame of Reference

A few months later, on 28 December 2007, the Study Group on a European Civil Code (Study Group) and the Acquis Group submitted to the Commission an initial version of the Draft Common Frame of Reference (DCFR).[84] Formally titled 'Principles, Definitions and Model Rules of European Private Law—Draft Common Frame of Reference', the DCFR was published initially in 2008 in the form of an interim outline edition, meaning that certain substantive parts still needed to be added and there was not yet any comments or notes accompanying the model rules.[85] In early 2009, the full outline edition of the DCFR was published, though still without comments and notes.[86] The full edition of the DCFR was published in six volumes in late 2009 (in paperback), and again in 2010 (in hardback).[87] The full edition is basically identical to the outline edition, except for the inclusion of comments and comparative notes for most of the model rules and certain minor editorial corrections.[88] Three key points concerning the DCFR's purpose, scope, and content stand out because they have a direct bearing on the debate about European contract law and its constitutional dimensions.[89]

First, as envisaged by its drafters, the DCFR has a threefold purpose as: (1) a possible model for the final or political CFR; (2) an independent text for European legal science, research, and education; and (3) a source of inspiration for national authorities, thereby contributing to 'a harmonious and informal Europeanisation of private law'.[90] As emphasized therein, the academic DCFR and the political CFR are separate; the DCFR constitutes the product of the academic researchers and is not that of any political decision-making body at the national or European level.[91] In fact, the DCFR

[80] 2007 Progress Report, n 69, point 6, first para.

[81] 2007 Progress Report, n 69, point 6, third para.

[82] 2007 Progress Report, n 69, point 6, sixth para (emphasis added).

[83] 2007 Progress Report, n 69, point 6, seventh para.

[84] See the Joint Network on European Private Law (Co-PECL)'s website, <http://www.copecl.org/>. Additional materials were submitted by other groups in this network: see Chapter 4, § 4.2.3.

[85] C von Bar et al (eds), *Principles, Definitions and Model Rules of European Private Law—Draft Common Frame of Reference (DCFR)*, Interim outline edn (Sellier, 2008), point 2. One of the purposes of publishing an interim outline edition was to receive feedback from the legal community: point 3.

[86] C von Bar et al (eds), *Principles, Definitions and Model Rules of European Private Law—Draft Common Frame of Reference (DCFR)*, Outline edn (Sellier, 2009).

[87] C von Bar and E Clive (eds), *Principles, Definitions and Model Rules of European Private Law—Draft Common Frame of Reference (DCFR)*, Full edn (Sellier, 2009/Oxford Univ Press, 2010).

[88] *DCFR*, n 87, Vol 1, point 3.

[89] For a view on the DCFR drafting process, much of which related to these three aspects, see, eg, H Beale, 'European contract law: the Common Frame of Reference of Reference and Beyond' in C Twigg-Flesner (ed), *The Cambridge Companion to European Private Law* (Cambridge Univ Press, 2010) 116.

[90] *DCFR*, n 87, Vol 1, points 6–8.

[91] *DCFR*, n 87, Vol 1, point 5.

contains substantial discussion as to how it may be used as preparatory work for the CFR, with particular regard to the improvement of the *acquis*.[92] Moreover, although it remains unclear whether the CFR, or parts of it, may be used as the basis for an optional instrument, in the drafters' view, 'such an optional instrument would open attractive perspectives, not least for consumer transactions'.[93] As such, the DCFR has prompted an onslaught of scholarly literature on its content, as well as its relationship to what will become the final CFR.[94] This leads to the next point.

Secondly, as signified by the reference to 'European private law' in the title, the scope of the DCFR goes well beyond contract law and covers various fields of patrimonial law that largely parallel the work of the Study Group, one of its principal drafters.[95] Specifically, the six volumes of the DCFR are made up of ten Books, which encompass, apart from a general section, contract law, several types of specific contracts,[96] benevolent intervention in another's affairs (*negotiorum gestio*), non-contractual liability, unjust enrichment, acquisition and loss of ownership of goods, proprietary security rights in movable assets, and trusts.[97] As explained by the drafters, the wide scope of the DCFR is due to the link between contract law and these other areas, which justified treating the whole of the law of obligations as 'an organic entity or unit'.[98] Consequently, its structure, seen by many to resemble national codifications, and its content, enveloping various fields of private law, invigorated discussion concerning the use that will be made of it in the process of compiling the final CFR and the extent to which the DCFR may lead to far-reaching EU action in private law harking back to the early days of the debate.[99]

Thirdly, as also indicated by its title, the DCFR is comprised of 'principles, definitions and model rules'. The bulk of the DCFR consists of model or 'soft law' rules, which have no normative force and are accompanied by comments and notes.[100]

92 *DCFR*, n 87, Vol 1, points 49–61.

93 *DCFR*, n 87, Vol 1, point 62.

94 For a brief selection, see, eg, R Schulze (ed), *Common Frame of Reference and Existing EC Contract Law*, 2nd rev edn (Sellier, 2009); A Somma (ed), *The Politics of the Draft Common Frame of Reference* (Kluwer, 2009); A Vaquer (ed), *European Private Law Beyond the Common Frame of Reference: Essays in Honour of Reinhard Zimmermann* (Europa, 2008); (2007) 3 *ERCL* No 3; (2008) 4 *ERCL* No 3; (2008) 44 *RTDE* No 4; 'Special Issue on European Contract Law' (2008) 9 *ERA Forum*; (2009) 17 *ERPL* No 4. On a more critical bent, see also, eg, H-W Micklitz and F Cafaggi (eds), *European Private Law after the Common Frame of Reference* (Edward Elgar, 2010); H Eidenmüller et al, 'The Common Frame of Reference for European Private Law–Policy Choices and Codification Problems' (2008) 28 *OJLS* 658; R Schulze and T Wilhelmsson, 'From the Draft Common Frame of Reference towards European Contract Law Rules' (2008) 4 *ERCL* 154; J Smits, 'Editorial: The Draft-Common Frame of Reference for a European Private Law: Fit For Purpose?' (2008) 15 *MJ* 145.

95 *DCFR*, n 87, Vol 1, points 25–31.

96 See *DCFR*, n 87, Vols 2–3, Bk IV (sales; lease of goods; services; mandate; commercial agency, franchise, and distribution; loan; personal security; and donation contracts).

97 *DCFR*, n 87, Vol 1, point 34. For a summary, see, eg, B Akkermans et al, Book review (2012) 19 MJ 83.

98 *DCFR*, n 87, Vol 1, point 31. See also, eg, C von Bar, 'Is the Draft Frame of Reference compatible with the Position of the Council?' in J Kleineman (ed), *A Common Frame of Reference for European Contract Law* (Stockholm Centre for Commercial Law, 2011) 17, 23–24; C von Bar, 'The Draft Common Frame of Reference: scope and purpose' in V Sagaert et al (eds), *The Draft Common Frame of Reference: national and comparative perspectives* (Intersentia, 2012) 3.

99 Academic commentary is replete with references equating the DCFR with a code, especially a European civil code: see, eg, M Hesselink, 'The Common Frame of Reference as a Source of European Private Law (2009) 83 *Tul L Rev* 919, 923; N Jansen and R Zimmerman, '"A European Civil Code in All But Name": Discussing the Nature and Purposes of the Draft Common Frame of Reference' (2010) 69 *CLJ* 98. Compare, eg, C von Bar, 'A Common Frame of Reference for European Private Law—Academic Efforts and Political Realities' (2008) 23 *Tul Eur & Civ LF* 37, 39–40.

100 *DCFR*, n 87, Vol 1, point 24.

The function of the comments is to provide illustrations of the application of the rule concerned and to indicate the policy issues at stake, whereas the function of the notes is to indicate the present legal position of the particular rule in the Member States, as well as in EU and international instruments where relevant.[101] As for the content of the rules themselves, the drafters devoted an explicit section to the relationship between the DCFR, the Principles of European Contract Law (PECL), the Study Group's Principles of European Law, and the Acquis Principles, explaining that while many model rules are based on these previous works, deviations and improvements have been made.[102] As for definitions, these were developed in tandem with the model rules and seek to establish a uniform European terminology for concepts of private law.[103] They do not appear in the body of the text, but are placed in an Annex so as to keep the first chapter short and allow the list of definitions to be extended or updated without much editorial effort.[104]

The principles category generated significant discussion among the groups involved in the preparation of the DCFR, since it was not clear from the Commission's Communications whether it was meant as a synonym for rules without the force of law, rules of a more general nature such as those on freedom of contract or good faith, or 'fundamental' principles in the sense of abstract basic values underlying the model rules.[105] In the end, the drafters proposed two categories of principles in the DCFR, noting that it will be for others to decide how, if at all, to deal with fundamental principles in the final CFR.[106]

The first category of 'underlying principles' furnish grounds for arguments about the merits of a particular model rule and thus are placed under the specific headings of freedom, security, justice, and efficiency as defined in a special section preceding the model rules.[107] The second category of 'overriding principles' are deemed to be of a high political nature, such as the protection of fundamental rights, promotion of solidarity and social responsibility, and promotion of the internal market.[108] It also includes the underlying principles of freedom, security, justice, and efficiency, which are considered to have a 'double role' to play as part of both categories.[109] As regards the internal market, it is explained that the 'most obvious way in which the welfare of citizens and businesses of Europe can be promoted by the DCFR is by the promotion of the smooth functioning of the internal market', though whether this is just by way of improving the present and future EU legislation or developing one or more optional instruments are political decisions.[110] Likewise, as regards the role played by freedom, security, and justice as overriding principles, 'reference may also be made to the EU specific aims of establishing an area of freedom, security and justice and promoting the free movement of goods, persons, services and capital between the Member States', to which the DCFR may contribute if the political will is there.[111] Albeit not dealing directly with constitutionality, the reference to the EU's objectives related to the internal market and the AFSJ in this context may be considered to augment the linkage between these objectives and the activities taking place within the European contract law project.

[101] *DCFR*, n 87, Vol 1, point 4.

[102] *DCFR*, n 87, Vol 1, points 40–48. For further discussion of the relationship between the Acquis Principles and the DCFR, see, eg, *Common Frame of Reference and Existing EC Contract Law*, n 94.

[103] *DCFR*, n 87, Vol 1, point 23.

[104] *DCFR*, n 87, Vol 1, point 23.

[105] *DCFR*, n 87, Vol 1, points 10–14. This was a salient issue on which feedback was sought: *DCFR*, n 87, Vol 1, point 12.

[106] *DCFR*, n 87, Vol 1, point 14.

[107] *DCFR*, n 87, Vol 1, point 15.

[108] *DCFR*, n 87, Vol 1, point 16.

[109] *DCFR*, n 87, Vol 1, point 16.

[110] *DCFR*, n 87, Vol 1, point 21.

[111] *DCFR*, n 87, Vol 1, point 22.

6.2.4 Ongoing reflection about the CFR by the Union institutions

6.2.4.1 The European Parliament's 2007 Resolution

With the expected publication of the initial version of the DCFR, on 12 December 2007, the European Parliament adopted a Resolution on European contract law (2007 Resolution),[112] which was focused on the CFR. By way of background, on 4 September 2007, the Parliament adopted a Resolution on the use of 'soft law' instruments.[113] In that latter Resolution, it criticized the use of 'soft law', and in doing so, placed emphasis on its application in the European contract law project.[114] This was because there was concern that the use of 'soft law' in connection with the CFR would bypass the normal decision-making process and hence the participation of the Parliament.[115] As such, it considered that 'in areas such as the [European] contract-law project, a point must come where the Commission decides whether or not to use its right of initiative and *on what legal basis*'.[116]

On 21 November 2007, this Resolution on 'soft law' filtered into an oral question concerning the CFR submitted by MEP Giuseppe Gargani.[117] He explained that while the CFR was presently not intended to have any binding legal effects and thus remain 'soft law', it would nonetheless have 'indirect legal and practical effects' and determine future legislative measures to be taken in contract law.[118] He also stressed that the decisions on which parts of the DCFR would be incorporated into the final CFR were highly political in nature and that it was essential to ensure that the parts of the DCFR selected for the final CFR were coherent with each other, with the Commission's plans concerning the review of the consumer *acquis*, and with other EU legislation on contract law.[119] This led to five pointed questions addressed to the Commission on the selection process and the scope of the CFR, as well as the involvement of the Parliament and the various Commission DGs in the CFR project generally.[120] A few weeks later, these comments and questions were incorporated into a motion for a resolution on European contract law, which culminated in the 2007 Resolution.[121]

In the 2007 Resolution, the Parliament reiterated much of what was said above in Mr Gargani's oral question[122] and in its previous Resolution on 'soft law'.[123] It added that although the CFR was intended to be a 'better regulation' instrument for ensuring the consistency and quality of EU legislation in contract law, the aim of better regulation was '*not* to limit the room for manoeuvre of the European Union co-legislators'.[124] On that note, it repeated its support for a 'wider CFR', including both general and

[112] European Parliament Resolution of 12 Dec 2007 on European contract law (P6_TA(2007)0615) (2007 Resolution).

[113] European Parliament Resolution of 4 Sept 2007 on institutional and legal implications of the use of 'soft law' instruments (PA_TA(2007)0366) (2007 Resolution on soft law).

[114] 2007 Resolution on soft law, n 113, recital W.

[115] See Remarks of Diana Wallis, Parliamentary Debates, 3 Sept 2007-Strasbourg.

[116] 2007 Resolution on soft law, n 113, point 13 (emphasis added).

[117] Oral Question With Debate by Giuseppe Gargani on behalf of the Committee on Legal Affairs to the Commission, 'Common frame of reference for European contract law', O-0073/07 (B6-0386/2007), dated 21 Nov 2007, first indent.

[118] Oral Question, n 117, third–fourth indents.

[119] Oral Question, n 117, fifth–sixth indents.

[120] Oral Question, n 117, below sixth indent.

[121] Motion for a resolution further to Question for Oral Answer B6-0387/2007 by Giuseppe Gargani on behalf of the Committee on Legal Affairs on European contract law, B6-0513/2007, dated 6 Dec 2007.

[122] 2007 Resolution, n 112, recitals A–D; points 2–7.

[123] 2007 Resolution, n 112, recital F.

[124] 2007 Resolution, n 112, recital E.

consumer contract law,[125] and requested the Commission to keep all options open as regards the purpose and legal form of a future CFR instrument, which included an optional instrument.[126] While matters of Union competence were not mentioned in the Resolution itself, several MEPs stressed during the Parliamentary debate the need for the approximation of private law and the use of an optional instrument for solving practical problems faced by Union citizens in the internal market,[127] with one MEP even advocating the model of the American Uniform Commercial Code (UCC).[128] Then Commissioner Meglena Kuneva responded by stating once again that the CFR 'will not be a large-scale harmonisation of private law or a European civil code'.[129] She also indicated that the Commission intended to take a decision on the scope, content, and form of the CFR sometime in 2008.[130]

6.2.4.2 The European Parliament's 2008 Resolution

On 3 September 2008, the European Parliament adopted a Resolution on the common frame of reference for European contract law (2008 Resolution).[131] As the DCFR had since been submitted to the Commission, the Parliament began by welcoming the DCFR and noting that the Commission had launched an internal selection process with the aim of identifying which parts of the DCFR will be integrated into a forthcoming Commission document (eg, a White Paper) on the CFR.[132] As the selection process was a 'highly political exercise', it requested the Commission to present a 'precise and transparent plan' as to how this selection process will be coordinated, with particular regard to the involvement of all relevant DGs,[133] underlining that it should be fully consulted throughout.[134]

It also observed that this Commission document would be the basis for the decision on the purpose, content, and legal effects of the CFR, which could range from a non-binding legislative tool to an optional instrument in European contract law.[135] Heeding the Council's 2008 Report, discussed below, the Parliament stated that if the CFR should be a set of non-binding guidelines for lawmakers at the European level, it should be as wide-ranging as possible and there may be no need to exclude any content or materials at this stage.[136] In such a case, the relevant parts of the CFR could be appended to any future legislative proposals or communications made by the Commission touching on contract law, so as to ensure that they were considered by the Union legislature.[137] However, if the CFR results in an optional instrument, it should be confined to those areas where the Union legislature has been active, is likely to be

[125] 2007 Resolution, n 112, points 7–8. [126] 2007 Resolution, n 112, point 9.

[127] See Parliamentary Debates, 10 Dec 2007-Strasbourg, particularly Remarks of Rainer Wieland and of Klaus-Heiner Lehne.

[128] Remarks of Manuel Medina Ortega, Parliamentary Debates, 10 Dec 2007-Strasbourg.

[129] First Set of Remarks of Meglena Kuneva, Member of the Commission, Parliamentary Debates, 10 Dec 2007-Strasbourg. She served as the Commissioner for Consumer Protection from Jan 2007 to Feb 2010.

[130] Second Set of Remarks of Meglena Kuneva, Member of the Commission, Parliamentary Debates, 10 Dec 2007-Strasbourg.

[131] European Parliament Resolution of 3 Sept 2008 on the common frame of reference for European contract law, [2009] OJ C295E/31 (2008 Resolution). Despite the emphasis on the CFR, the Parliament paid homage to its previous resolutions going back to 1989: see first–fourth indents.

[132] 2008 Resolution, n 131, recitals A, C; point 1.

[133] 2008 Resolution, n 131, points 2, 4. [134] 2008 Resolution, n 131, point 13.

[135] 2008 Resolution, n 131, point 5. [136] 2008 Resolution, n 131, point 8.

[137] 2008 Resolution, n 131, point 10.

active in the near future, or which are closely linked to contract law.[138] Since any optional instrument should be based on the DCFR, care should be taken to ensure that the instrument's overall coherence is not jeopardized by the selection process.[139] While this was not evident in the text, the need for an optional instrument for the purposes of the internal market was again expressed, as well as the eventual need to confront its legal basis, in the Parliamentary debate on this Resolution.[140]

6.2.4.3 The Council's 2008 Report on four fundamental aspects of the CFR

On 18 April 2008, at the 2863rd meeting of the Justice and Home Affairs (JHA) configuration, the Council adopted a Report containing its position on four fundamental aspects of the CFR: its purpose, scope, content, and legal effects (2008 Report).[141] The 2008 Report was the culmination of several months, indeed years, of consultation with the Member State delegations and of various documents disseminated by successive Council Presidencies.[142]

Starting on 20 December 2006, the incoming German Council Presidency circulated a document in expectation of the Commission's 2007 Progress Report.[143] In this document, it noted that in contrast to the Parliament which had continually dealt with the matter of European contract law, so far the Council had done so only sporadically.[144] Thus, the Council was urged to develop its own position, and to that end, several questions concerning the CFR were presented for further discussion.[145] To flesh out matters in more detail, in February 2007, the German Council Presidency circulated a document to the Member State delegations identifying four key aspects to be examined in relation to the Council's forthcoming position on the CFR.[146] These aspects concerned the purpose, content, scope, and binding effect of the CFR, and for each, the Presidency made certain observations.[147] This document was then revised in line with comments submitted by Member State delegations.[148] Before long, the proposed approach set forth in the final text of this document was confirmed at the 2794th JHA meeting on 19–20 April 2007, at which the Council agreed to define its position on these four fundamental aspects of the CFR and instructed the Committee on Civil Law Matters to examine this topic on the basis of a forthcoming document of the Council Presidency.[149]

Accordingly, on 7 June 2007, the German Council Presidency circulated a discussion paper on the CFR.[150] In its preliminary remarks, it proposed that a European civil

[138] 2008 Resolution, n 131, points 11-12.

[139] 2008 Resolution, n 131, point 12.

[140] See, eg, Remarks of Hans-Peter Mayer and of Diana Wallis, Parliamentary Debates, 1 Sept 2008-Brussels.

[141] 2863rd Council meeting, JHA, Luxembourg, 18 April 2008, DOC 8622/08, dated 12 June 2008, point 12. The Council approved the 2008 Report, DOC 8286/08, dated 11 April 2008 (2008 Report).

[142] Certain documents issued by the Council and Member State delegations in connection with this Report, as well as other Council documents relating to the CFR and the European contract law project generally, have not been disclosed to the public, despite requests submitted by the present author. Thus, the discussion proceeds from the relevant documents that have been made publicly available at the time of writing.

[143] DOC 16605/06, dated 20 Dec 2006, point 1.

[144] DOC 16605/06, n 143, point 2.

[145] DOC 16605/06, n 143, point 3.

[146] DOC 6057/07, dated 13 Feb 2007.

[147] DOC 6057/07, n 146, points 5–10.

[148] See DOC 7784/07, dated 26 March 2007; DOC 8403/07, dated 13 April 2007; DOC 8548/07, dated 17 April 2007.

[149] Press Release, 2794th Council meeting, JHA, Luxembourg, 19–20 April 2007, DOC 8364/07 (Presse 77) 21.

[150] DOC 10235/07, dated 7 June 2007 (2007 Discussion Paper).

code should not be envisaged as a possible solution, since this was not a 'working option' for many Member State delegations.[151] It also indicated that this exercise should be carried out in the context of 'civil law', but that it should exclude all aspects relating to judicial cooperation in civil matters.[152] Therefore, any envisaged instrument in this context should not be based on what was then Article 65 EC (now Article 81 TFEU).[153] Even though the German Presidency framed this as something it wished to 'recall', this was one of the rare instances, at least by way of Council documents available to the public,[154] that this provision was explicitly cited, much less excluded, by the Council in connection with European contract law.

The core of the discussion paper concerned these four aspects of the CFR, providing three possible options for each.[155] Truth be told, the paper resembled the English children's story, 'Goldilocks and the three bears', in the sense that of the three options presented, it was often the case that one was too small, the other too big, and the remaining one just right. First, as regards the *purpose* of the CFR, of the three options presented—rejection of the CFR altogether, a 'toolbox' for the Union legislature, and a complete set of rules harmonizing contract law to be used by parties on an optional basis—the second would serve the purpose of 'better lawmaking' in the EU and make it possible to give a more coherent shape to EU legislation and achieve greater harmony with the national legal systems, whereas the first would conflict with the Council's previous resolutions and guidelines set out in the Hague Programme, and the third would mean that its purpose of 'better lawmaking' would become secondary.[156] Secondly, the *scope* of the CFR implicated the relationship between consumer contract law and general contract law, and of the three options proposed—consumer contract law only, general contract law only with consumer contract law regulated separately, or both—the third option would ensure that solutions to problems arising under consumer contract law would not be solved in isolation from the national contract law regimes, whereas the second option would be difficult given the nature of most EU contract law measures as governing specific situations (eg, distance selling or doorstep selling).[157] Interestingly, it was surmised that the first option, restricting the CFR to consumer contract law and thus excluding general contract law, may be on account of the EU's lack of competence to adopt more extensive rules in contract law, but was not elaborated further.[158]

Thirdly, the *content* of the CFR could be a systematic collection and compilation of national legal principles and legislation, of the EU contract law developed so far, or both: the first option would take due account of the national legal traditions, whereas the second may not, even though it would contribute to the goal of 'better regulation',[159] thus appearing to leave open the third option of taking the two together. Finally, as for the CFR's *binding effect*, the three options consisted of: first, the entire CFR would be non-binding, as in the form of a recommendation addressed to the Union legislature, which would use the CFR merely as a 'guide' for adopting new measures or amending existing ones;[160] secondly, only some parts of the CFR would be binding (eg, its principles and definitions), which would mean that the Union legislature would have to take those aspects into account when drafting new legislation, but the other elements (such

151 2007 Discussion Paper, n 150, point 5.
152 2007 Discussion Paper, n 150, point 6.
153 2007 Discussion Paper, n 150, point 6.
154 See n 142.
155 2007 Discussion Paper, n 150, point 2.
156 2007 Discussion Paper, n 150, points 9–16.
157 2007 Discussion Paper, n 150, points 19, 22–26, 29.
158 2007 Discussion Paper, n 150, point 20.
159 2007 Discussion Paper, n 150, points 30, 32–37.
160 2007 Discussion Paper, n 150, points 39–40.

as the model rules) would be non-binding;[161] and thirdly, the entire CFR would be binding, taking the form of a legal instrument or an interinstitutional agreement from which the Union legislature would not be able to derogate, or at the very least, reasons would have to be given in the case of any such derogation.[162]

This discussion paper was subject to deliberation by the Committee on Civil Law Matters pursuant to the Council Presidency's invitation.[163] Reactions to the discussion paper were collected by the Portuguese Council Presidency in a summary document distributed to the Member State delegations at the end of November 2007.[164] Several delegations also issued separate written remarks. From the documents available, it appeared that many Member States rejected the possibility of a contract law instrument, let alone the whole-scale approximation of private law, at the European level,[165] but at least one Member State stressed the importance of an optional instrument for the internal market.[166] There was also support for a CFR of a more limited nature, namely as a 'toolbox', rather than a binding instrument.[167] However, as far as its content and scope were concerned, the Member States' views were more divided.[168] Still, there seemed to be general agreement that the CFR should include both consumer and general contract law and that it should constitute a systematic compilation of both national and EU legislation.[169] As highlighted by the French delegation's comments, although there was some ambiguity in the relationship between the CFR and the review of the consumer *acquis*,[170] the two were separate projects, with different goals, different legal bases, and different applications of the principles of subsidiarity and proportionality.[171]

Thereafter, on 28 January 2008, the Slovenian Council Presidency disseminated a draft report of the Council's position on the CFR, which summarized the preferences for each of the four aspects of the CFR in line with the foregoing discussions.[172] This draft report then went through another round of revision as a result of further discussions among the delegations. In these discussions, some Member States sought to make the purported lack of Union competence in contract law explicit in the text. In particular, the French delegation sought to insert language in the section on the CFR's legal effects to acknowledge that the rejection of the options making the CFR a binding instrument was based on 'the lack of legal basis of any binding instrument in the field of contract law'.[173] The Portuguese delegation sought to insert similar language in the section on the CFR's purpose to make clear that using the CFR to harmonize the national contract laws was rejected on account of 'the absence of legal basis for a binding instrument containing substantive provisions in the field of contract law'.[174] The Portuguese delegation also proposed replacing the references to 'civil law' with 'contract law'.[175]

[161] 2007 Discussion Paper, n 150, point 41.
[162] 2007 Discussion Paper, n 150, point 42.
[163] 2007 Discussion Paper, n 150, points 43–44.
[164] DOC 13145/07, dated 22 Nov 2007 (2007 Summary Document).
[165] 2007 Summary Document, n 164, point 5. See, eg, German Delegation, DOC 15124/07, dated 15 Nov 2007, 2, 4; UK Delegation, DOC 15124/07 ADD 1, dated 15 Nov 2007, 2; Czech Delegation, DOC 15124/07 ADD 2, dated 21 Nov 2007, para 2.
[166] See Estonian Delegation, DOC 15124/07 ADD 3, dated 19 Nov 2007, 1–2.
[167] 2007 Summary Document, n 164, point 7.
[168] 2007 Summary Document, n 164, point 8.
[169] 2007 Summary Document, n 164, point 8.
[170] French Delegation, DOC 15124/07 ADD 4, dated 21 Nov 2007, 2.
[171] French Delegation, n 170, 3.
[172] DOC 5665/08, dated 28 Jan 2008.
[173] French Delegation, DOC 6718/08 ADD 1, dated 3 March 2008, 5.
[174] Portuguese Delegation, DOC 6718/08 ADD 2, dated 4 March 2008, 2, 4.
[175] Portuguese Delegation, n 174, 3, 5.

This was seconded by the Irish and UK delegations,[176] which along with the Belgian and Czech delegations, wanted to ensure the purely voluntary, non-binding character of the CFR.[177]

On 17 March 2008, the Slovenian Council Presidency distributed a revised version of the draft report on the CFR.[178] Among the noticeable changes, the references to 'civil law' were replaced by 'contract law' in relation to the content and scope of the CFR.[179] The section on the legal effects of the CFR was amended to make explicit that the CFR would be used on a 'voluntary basis' by the Union lawmakers.[180] As for the matter of legal basis, no provisions were added concerning Union competence as suggested by the French and Portuguese delegations, but a new provision was inserted at the very end of the draft report, which stated that the Council's position did not 'in any way prejudge a discussion on the need or the possibility of a legal basis' for the CFR.[181] Initially, this provision indicated that the issue of legal basis could be considered once a draft was submitted,[182] but this language was subsequently deleted.[183] The rest of the changes were maintained as the draft report proceeded to its final form.[184]

The final version of the draft report was presented to the Council at its 2863rd JHA meeting in Luxembourg on 18 April 2008, at which time the Council endorsed the report and summarized its position as follows:

(a) **Purpose of the Common Frame of Reference**: a tool for better lawmaking targeted at Community [now Union] lawmakers
(b) **Content of the Common Frame of Reference**: a set of definitions, general principles and model rules in the area of contract law to be derived from a variety of sources
(c) **Scope of the Common Frame of Reference**: general contract law including consumer contract law
(d) **Legal effect of the Common Frame of Reference**: a set of non-binding guidelines to be used by the lawmakers at Community [now Union] level on a voluntary basis as a common source of inspiration or reference in the lawmaking process.[185]

Noticeably, neither the German Presidency's remarks about former Article 65 EC (now Article 81 TFEU) nor the French and Portuguese delegations' proposed amendments concerning the lack of Union competence to adopt a contract law instrument made it into the final text and thus remained in the shadows. The Council essentially bypassed this matter, with even its futile attempt to put a definitive timeline on consideration of the legal basis for the CFR deleted. The constitutionality of the CFR and related activities of the European contract law project remained simmering below the surface.

[176] Irish and UK Delegations, DOC 6718/08 ADD 3, dated 4 March 2008, 5.
[177] Irish and UK Delegations, n 176, 5; Belgian Delegation, DOC 6718/08 ADD 4, dated 4 March 2008, 1–2; Czech Delegation, DOC 6718/08, dated 20 Feb 2008, 3.
[178] DOC 5665/1/08REV1, dated 17 March 2008.
[179] DOC 5665/1/08REV1, n 178, points 9, 11, 14(b).
[180] DOC 5665/1/08REV1, n 178, points 13, 14(d).
[181] DOC 5665/1/08REV1, n 178, point 15.
[182] DOC 5665/1/08REV1, n 178. Presumably, this meant once a draft of the final version of the CFR was submitted.
[183] DOC 8092/08, dated 4 April 2008.
[184] 2008 Report, n 141.
[185] 2008 Report, n 141, point 14.

6.2.4.4 *The Council's 2008 and 2009 Reports on further aspects of the CFR*

In the aftermath of the 2008 Report, the Council adopted two additional reports in 2008 and 2009 on further aspects of the CFR.[186] Events began with a working document submitted by the French Council Presidency on 28 July 2008,[187] which focused on four points concerning: (1) the CFR's three-part structure and the relationship between principles, model rules, and definitions;[188] (2) its scope as regards whether it should include not only general and consumer contract law, but also rules on specific types of contracts;[189] (3) its ordering in terms of the advisability of presenting the CFR's components from the formation of contracts to performance or non-performance;[190] and (4) its 'respect for diversity' in the sense that, in addition to the materials produced by the researchers and stakeholders, account should be taken of other important work with particular regard to the analysis of the Member States' laws and legal traditions.[191] The Presidency sought written remarks from the Member States from which it would draw up conclusions to be submitted for approval at the JHA Council meeting in November 2008.[192]

On the basis of further discussions and a set of draft conclusions,[193] the Council adopted a Report at its meeting on 27–28 November 2008, which set out some basic guidelines for future work on the CFR concerning its structure, scope, respect for diversity, and the involvement of the Union institutions (second 2008 Report).[194] First, as for *structure*, the Council concluded that the three parts of the CFR (definitions, principles, and model rules) should be seen as an 'indissoluble whole', since no part can be fully understood except in relation to the others, and in any event, the CFR should be clear, concise, and easy to understand.[195] Secondly, as for its *scope*, it decided that the CFR should envelop the general law of contracts (ie rules common to all contracts) and consumer contract law, but not other specific types of contracts, although this issue could be revisited at a later stage.[196] Thirdly, it emphasized that 'respect for diversity' meant that all legal traditions of the Member States should be fully respected in setting up the CFR such that all relevant work, academic and practical, should be taken into account, along with comparative analysis of national laws and the EU *acquis*, and that alternative solutions on certain subjects could be provided.[197] Fourthly, it considered that in order to ensure optimum use of the CFR, the European Parliament, the Council, and the Commission must be involved in setting it up, since if the CFR were to be adopted by only one of them, its significance would be reduced.[198]

Building on these guidelines in the second 2008 Report, the Czech Republic Presidency circulated a questionnaire on the setting up of the CFR to Member State delegations in January 2009 and invited them to reply in writing.[199] The questionnaire

[186] See DOC 14745/09, dated 21 Oct 2009 (comprising the Council's conclusions on the CFR adopted in April 2008, Nov 2008, and June 2009).

[187] DOC 11880/08, dated 28 July 2008.

[188] DOC 11880/08, n 187, points 2–5.

[189] DOC 11880/08, n 187, points 6–9.

[190] DOC 11880/08, n 187, points 10–12.

[191] DOC 11880/08, n 187, points 13–16.

[192] DOC 11880/08, n 187, point 18.

[193] DOC 14787/08, dated 28 Oct 2008.

[194] 2908th Council meeting, JHA, Brussels, 27–28 Nov 2008, DOC 16395/08, dated 29 Jan 2009. The Council approved the Draft Report on the setting up of a Common Frame of Reference for European contract law, DOC 15306/08, dated 7 Nov 2008; *corrigendum*, DOC 15306/08 COR 1, dated 16 Dec 2008 (second 2008 Report). For a consolidated version of the Council's conclusions on the CFR up to that point, see also DOC 5784/09, dated 27 Jan 2009.

[195] Second 2008 Report, n 194, point 9.

[196] Second 2008 Report, n 194, point 12.

[197] Second 2008 Report, n 194, point 15.

[198] Second 2008 Report, n 194, point 17.

[199] DOC 5116/09, dated 15 Jan 2009.

comprised six questions, three of which concerned the CFR's content (ie the inclusion of general principles and definitions, as well as aspects relating to the drafting of the model rules so as to ensure that the CFR is clear, concise, and easy to understand).[200] The fourth question concerned the relationship between the CFR and the then proposal for a Consumer Rights Directive issued a few months before.[201] The fifth question posited whether it was appropriate, at that stage, to initiate discussion on what kind of legal instrument the CFR should be, and if so, to specify which instrument(s) were acceptable.[202] The sixth question asked for comments on other aspects of the CFR that should be discussed at that stage.[203]

Based on the responses of the Member State delegations[204] and several prior drafts,[205] on 15 May 2009, the Committee on Civil Law issued a Report setting forth the Council's position on certain aspects of the CFR, which was subsequently adopted at the 2946th meeting of the JHA Council on 4–5 June 2009 (2009 Report).[206] This Report is divided into five points, presenting the Council's conclusions on the fundamental principles, definitions, and model rules of the CFR, its relationship with the proposed Consumer Rights Directive, and its form. First, it was advisable to lay down now certain *fundamental principles* to appear in the CFR, which should reflect values underpinning the CFR and apply to all stages of the contractual relationship.[207] Secondly, it was considered too early to determine precisely what *definitions* the CFR should include, but at any rate, they should relate directly to general contract law and to the scope and priorities of the CFR as described in previous Council conclusions, with due attention given to the definitions in the area of consumer contracts, since it was an important part of the EU contract law *acquis*.[208] Thirdly, it was underlined, among other things, that *model rules* should be drafted in broad terms so that they can apply to all contracts and be easily adaptable to all contractual situations, and that the CFR could, under certain conditions, offer alternative solutions for situations where a substitute model rule may prove useful.[209] Fourthly, while there should be consistency between the CFR and the *proposed Consumer Rights Directive*, the

[200] DOC 5116/09, n 199, questions (1)–(3); point 1.

[201] DOC 5116/09, n 199, question (4); point 2.

[202] DOC 5116/09, n 199, question (5); point 3.

[203] DOC 5116/09, n 199, question (6).

[204] There appears to have been responses from nineteen Member State delegations: (1) Austrian Delegation, DOC 5821/09 ADD 18, dated 25 Feb 2009; (2) Belgian Delegation, DOC 5821/09 ADD 10, dated 3 Feb 2009; (3) Bulgarian Delegation, DOC 5821/09 ADD 16, dated 11 Feb 2009; (4) Estonian Delegation, DOC 5821/09 ADD 11, dated 3 Feb 2009; (5) Finnish Delegation, DOC 5821/09, dated 29 Jan 2009; (6) French Delegation, DOC 5821/09 ADD 5, dated 29 Jan 2009; (7) German Delegation, DOC 5821/09 ADD 1, dated 29 Jan 2009; (8) Greek Delegation, DOC 5821/09 ADD 7, dated 29 Jan 2009; (9) Hungarian Delegation, DOC 5821/09 ADD 3, dated 29 Jan 2009; (10) Italian Delegation, DOC 5821/09 ADD 14, dated 11 Feb 2009; (11) Luxembourg Delegation, DOC 5821/09 ADD 15, dated 11 Feb 2009; (12) Maltese Delegation, DOC 5821/09 ADD 17, dated 13 Feb 2009; (13) The Netherlands Delegation, DOC 5821/09 ADD 2, dated 29 Jan 2009; (14) Polish Delegation, DOC 5821/09 ADD 12, 9 Feb 2009; (15) Slovak Delegation, DOC 5821/09 ADD 6, dated 29 Jan 2009; (16) Slovenian Delegation, DOC 5821/09 ADD 8, dated 29 Jan 2009; (17) Spanish Delegation, DOC 5821/09 ADD 4, dated 29 Jan 2009; (18) Swedish Delegation, DOC 5821/09 ADD 9, dated 2 Feb 2009; and (19) UK Delegation, DOC 5821/09 ADD 13, dated 11 Feb 2009.

[205] See DOC 6094/09, dated 10 Feb 2009; DOC 6094/1/09REV1, dated 24 April 2009.

[206] 2946th Council meeting, JHA, Luxembourg, 4–5 June 2009, DOC 10654/09, dated 16 July 2009. The Council approved the Draft Report on the setting up of a common frame of reference for European contract law, DOC 9741/09, dated 15 May 2009; *corrigendum*, DOC 9741/09 COR 2, dated 12 June 2009 (2009 Report).

[207] 2009 Report, n 206, points 8–10.

[208] 2009 Report, n 206, points 13–14.

[209] 2009 Report, n 206, points 16–17.

two projects were separate and intended to pursue objectives that may not always coincide.[210] Finally, it was deemed too early to decide on the *form* of the CFR, but nonetheless, it must be such as to allow a non-binding instrument to be drawn up, comprising a set of guidelines that the Union legislators would use at the level of the Council, the European Parliament, and the Commission 'as a common source of inspiration or reference in the legislative process'.[211] In other words, a binding instrument appeared to be off the table.

6.3 The Review of the Consumer *Acquis* and the Path to the Consumer Rights Directive

6.3.1 The EC Consumer Law Compendium

As stated in the 2005 Progress Report, the comparative analysis of the Member States' implementation of eight consumer (mostly contract) law directives was an important part of the Commission's plans for the review of the consumer *acquis*.[212] This comparative analysis in fact comprised two aspects. First, the EC Consumer Law Compendium contained an extensive comparative study of the transposition of those eight directives in the Member States and the problems resulting therefrom.[213] Secondly, the EU Consumer Law Acquis Database linked the eight directives under review to a database comprising the national implementing measures and related legislation, relevant case law of the Court of Justice and the national courts, and bibliographical information on each directive.[214] The work on the Compendium and Database was awarded to the University of Bielefeld and carried out by an international research group coordinated by Professor Hans Schulte-Nölke, the Acquis Group's coordinator.[215] The Compendium was edited by him in cooperation with Professor Christian Twigg-Flesner and Professor Martin Ebers, also both members of the Acquis Group.[216] The first edition of the Compendium was submitted to the Commission in December 2006.[217] It then underwent a series of revisions.[218]

210 2009 Report, n 206, point 19.

211 2009 Report, n 206, point 20.

212 See 2005 Progress Report, n 1. These eight directives are the Doorstep Selling, Package Travel, Unfair Contract Terms, Timeshare Directive, Distance Selling, Consumer Sales, Injunctions, and Price Indication Directives. See further Chapter 1, § 1.3.

213 H Schulte-Nölke et al (eds), *EC Consumer Law Compendium—Comparative Analysis* (Version of Feb 2008), available at <http://ec.europa.eu/consumers/rights/docs/consumer_law_compendium_comparative_analysis_en_final.pdf> (Consumer Law Compendium). It was completed in the context of the former Treaty framework, thus explaining the reference to 'EC' in its title.

214 Available at <http://www.eu-consumer-law.org/>. As indicated on this website, there was a follow-up project to keep the Database up to date; with the final update completed, the Database contains information on the transposition of the directives concerned in the then twenty-seven Member States as of March 2012.

215 Consumer Law Compendium, n 213, 30–31, 33.

216 Consumer Law Compendium, n 213, 33. For the list of contributors, see Consumer Law Compendium, n 213, 37–43. Professor Jules Stuyck of the University of Leuven served as the independent evaluator of the study: Consumer Law Compendium, n 213, 43.

217 H Schulte-Nölke et al (eds), *EC Consumer Law Compendium—Comparative Analysis* (Version of 12 Dec 2006) (on file with author).

218 H Schulte-Nölke et al (eds), *EC Consumer Law Compendium—Comparative Analysis* (Version of April 2007), available at <http://ec.europa.eu/consumers/cons_int/safe_shop/acquis/comp-analysis_en.pdf>. This version included the then twenty-five Member States, excluding Bulgaria and Romania, which acceded to the EU a few months before on 1 Jan 2007. It was subsequently published as H Schulte-Nölke et al (eds), *EC Consumer Law Compendium: The Consumer Acquis and its transposition in the Member States* (Sellier, 2008): see point 4, at 2.

At the time of writing, the most recent version of the Compendium was completed in February 2008 and took into account the accession of Bulgaria and Romania in 2007, thereby covering the then twenty-seven Member States.[219]

The Compendium is a hefty document, totalling about 845 pages. Apart from its introductory sections and three annexes, it was divided into four main parts. Part One provided an overview of the Member States' legislative techniques or 'transposition culture'[220] in relation to the eight directives concerned. Part Two examined the Member States' transposition of these directives. Part Three highlighted the commonalities among these directives concerning the notions of 'consumer' and 'business', the right of withdrawal, and information duties. Part Four presented the researchers' final conclusions and recommendations to solve some of the problems highlighted in the study. While matters of space preclude a detailed account of each part,[221] three important findings of this study can be singled out, which concern the discussion of potential or existing barriers to the functioning of the internal market caused by divergences among national consumer (contract) laws, the shift from minimum to maximum harmonization, and the adoption of one or more horizontal instruments of consumer contract law. Indeed, it was these points that reverberated strongly in the Commission's subsequent activities in this setting.

First, a notable component of the Compendium was the study of possible barriers to trade or distortions of competition resulting from the differences among the national measures transposing the directives.[222] In Part Two, there was a specific section devoted to this point for each directive. The extent of the barriers and distortions was not the same for all directives: for several, there were various examples that were deemed likely, in varying degrees, to result in barriers to trade,[223] whereas for others, 'obvious' barriers were found.[224] Nevertheless, the study confirmed the impact of such differences on the internal market, and in their recommendations, the authors advanced certain proposals to overcome the barriers to trade caused by divergences between the national laws concerned,[225] which leads to the next two points.

Secondly, the authors supported a selective shift from minimum to maximum harmonization for certain areas covered by the directives.[226] The Member States' use of minimum harmonization clauses was envisaged by the Commission as an important part of the Compendium,[227] and it both began and ended with statements to the effect that the various divergences between the national laws were caused by, among other things, minimum harmonization clauses in the various directives.[228] Accordingly, among their recommendations, the authors advocated a selective shift to maximum

[219] Consumer Law Compendium, n 213. It did not cover Croatia, which acceded to the EU on 1 July 2013.

[220] Consumer Law Compendium, n 213, 33.

[221] See, eg, 'Special Issue: The Consumer Law Compendium Conference (Leuven, 21 Sept 2007)' (2009) 20 *EBLR* No 3.

[222] This had been called for by the Commission in its tender notice for the study. See Commission Contract Notice 2004/S 80-068070, s II.1.6 ('Comparative analysis of the different national regulations including the barriers to trade or distortions of competition resulting from them'). See further Consumer Law Compendium, n 213, 30 fn1.

[223] See Consumer Law Compendium, n 213, 173 (Doorstep Selling Directive); 214 (Package Travel Directive); 441 (Timeshare Directive); 582 (Price Indication Directive); 612 (Injunctions Directive); 650 (Consumer Sales Directive).

[224] See Consumer Law Compendium, n 213, 348 (Unfair Contract Terms Directive); 504 (Distance Selling Directive).

[225] Consumer Law Compendium, n 213, 789.

[226] Consumer Law Compendium, n 213, 796.

[227] See Commission Contract Notice, n 222, point 11.2.1(c).

[228] Consumer Law Compendium, n 213, 30, 789.

harmonization for those areas in which the use of minimum harmonization clauses by the Member States 'clearly' caused barriers to trade in the internal market without substantially strengthening consumer protection.[229] It was foreseen, however, that this shift would be 'controversial' in cases where it would force the Member States to reduce the established level of consumer protection.[230] This was somewhat of an understatement. As documented in the Compendium, for all but one of the directives, the Member States had made extensive use of the minimum harmonization clause.[231] The exception was the Price Indication Directive, whereby the Member States had made 'practically no use' of such a clause.[232] Thus, as a possible solution, the authors contemplated the introduction of a special 'safeguard procedure' allowing the Member States to adopt urgent, short-term consumer protection measures as long as the EU had not acted, with the provisions of former Article 95 EC (now Article 114 TFEU) serving as a useful model. [233]

Thirdly, one of the most noteworthy outcomes of the Compendium was support for the adoption of one or more horizontal instruments of consumer contract law. One of the authors' recommendations was a proposal for restructuring the consumer *acquis* through a horizontal measure comprising a set of uniform definitions and key general rules applicable to all B2C contracts, generally comprising information duties, withdrawal rights, and unfair terms, which were mainly found in the Unfair Contract Terms, Doorstep Selling, and Distance Selling Directives.[234] Moreover, the authors considered the possibility of adopting an EU measure dealing with cross-border consumer transactions across the board.[235] In their view, this would 'give a boost' to consumers' use of the internal market, particularly once the CFR had been finalized, but a number of questions would have to be addressed if this option was pursued, such as its mandatory character, the possibility for consumers to opt-out, and the interplay with national consumer law.[236] On the whole, these three points emanating from the Compendium provided an important platform for the Commission's 2007 Green Paper on the review of the consumer *acquis*.

6.3.2 The 2007 Green Paper

On 8 February 2007, the Commission published the Green Paper on the Review of the Consumer Acquis (2007 Green Paper).[237] It summarized the Commission's initial findings and sought contributions from the Union institutions, the Member States, and other interested parties on possible policy options.[238] Quite memorably, the Commission summed up the idea behind the 2007 Green Paper by stating that at the end of this exercise, 'it should, ideally, be possible to say to EU consumers "wherever you are in the EU or wherever you buy from it makes no difference: your essential

[229] Consumer Law Compendium, n 213, 797 (citing rules on information duties and withdrawal rights).

[230] Consumer Law Compendium, n 213, 796.

[231] See Consumer Law Compendium, n 213, 171 (Doorstep Selling Directive); 211 (Package Travel Directive); 343 (Unfair Contract Terms Directive); 439 (Timeshare Directive); 502 (Distance Selling Directive); 610 (Injunctions Directive); 648 (Consumer Sales Directive).

[232] See Consumer Law Compendium, n 213, 582.

[233] Consumer Law Compendium, n 213, 796.

[234] Consumer Law Compendium, n 213, 790–793.

[235] Consumer Law Compendium, n 213, 798.

[236] Consumer Law Compendium, n 213, 798.

[237] Green Paper on the Review of the Consumer Acquis, COM (2006) 744 final, 8.2.2007 (2007 Green Paper).

[238] 2007 Green Paper, n 237, point 1.

rights are the same"'.[239] This may explain why its mention of a horizontal instrument of consumer contract law started to be called a 'consumer rights directive' before the Commission's formal proposal to that effect.[240]

The Commission underlined that the overarching aim of this review was 'to achieve a real consumer internal market striking the right balance between a high level of consumer protection and the competitiveness of enterprises, while ensuring the strict respect of the principle of subsidiarity'.[241] That said, the 2007 Green Paper was devoid of any substantive discussion of the principle of subsidiarity, not to mention other principles guiding the exercise of the Union's competence and possible legal bases in relation to the envisaged initiatives. It generally comprised three aspects: (1) the problems plaguing the consumer *acquis*;[242] (2) the general policy options to be taken to resolve these problems;[243] and (3) issues for further consultation.[244]

First, the Commission took up the main problems with the consumer *acquis*. In particular, it pointed to the fragmentation caused by minimum harmonization clauses and inconsistencies and gaps in the directives themselves.[245] In its view, this fragmentation triggered extra compliance costs for businesses, such as having to acquire the relevant legal advice, and was one of the reasons why businesses purportedly chose not to conduct cross-border transactions in the internal market.[246] It also cited further problems in the internal market stemming from the lack of consumer confidence.[247] Specifically, it reasoned that on account of differing rules resulting from the minimum harmonization clauses in the directives, consumers were reluctant to engage in cross-border transactions because they could not be sure that the level of consumer protection in their Member State applied cross-border.[248]

Secondly, the Commission focused on the general policy options for future work. This implicated the general legislative approach to be taken, the scope of a horizontal instrument if it was chosen, and the degree of harmonization involved, the latter of which dovetailed with the problems relating to minimum harmonization mentioned above. As far as the general legislative approach was concerned, the Commission presented three options: a vertical approach, whereby the directives would be amended separately,[249] a horizontal approach, also termed the 'mixed approach', involving the combination of a horizontal instrument with the necessary vertical measures,[250] and no legislative action, although this would mean that the existing fragmentation would remain, or even increase,[251] which essentially took it out of the running. Despite the Green Paper's consultative nature, it was not difficult to recognize which approach the Commission preferred. It highlighted that there were a number of disadvantages to the vertical approach, eg, it would take longer, not be able to achieve the

[239] 2007 Green Paper, n 237, point 2.1, second para.

[240] See, eg, European Parliament Resolution of 6 Sept 2007 on the 2007 Green Paper, [2008] OJ C187E/231)(Resolution on the 2007 Green Paper), point 10; Response of the UK Government to the 2007 Green Paper (see n 287), point 4.

[241] 2007 Green Paper, n 237, point 2.1, second para.

[242] 2007 Green Paper, n 237, point 3 ('The Main Issues').

[243] 2007 Green Paper, n 237, point 4 ('Possible Options for the Future').

[244] 2007 Green Paper, n 237, Annex I ('Issues for Consultation'). The Commission also provided a chart summarizing the subject matter of each question: see 2007 Green Paper, n 237, point 4.6. For detailed discussion, see, eg, B Heiderhoff and M Kenny, 'The Commission's 2007 Green Paper on the consumer *acquis*: deliberate deliberation?' (2007) 32 *ELR* 740.

[245] 2007 Green Paper, n 237, point 3.2.

[246] 2007 Green Paper, n 237, point 3.2.

[247] 2007 Green Paper, n 237, point 3.3.

[248] 2007 Green Paper, n 237, point 3.3.

[249] 2007 Green Paper, n 237, point 4.1.

[250] 2007 Green Paper, n 237, point 4.2.

[251] 2007 Green Paper, n 237, point 4.3.

'simplifying effect' of the horizontal approach, and give rise to a fragmented regulatory environment.[252] In contrast, the adoption of a horizontal instrument consisting of two parts—a general part covering a number of issues applicable to all consumer contracts[253] and a specific part regulating the sales contract—would greatly simplify the *acquis* and reduce its volume by repealing the existing directives, either in full or in part.[254]

If the horizontal approach was taken up, the Commission set forth three possible options as regards the scope of the horizontal instrument, which again implicitly conveyed the Commission's preferences.[255] As the first option, the horizontal instrument could apply to domestic and cross-border transactions, which would simplify the regulatory environment considerably for both consumers and businesses.[256] As the second option, the horizontal instrument could apply only to cross-border transactions, but this would require delineating the notion of cross-border contract and invariably increase legal fragmentation, since consumers and businesses would be subject to different rules depending upon whether the transaction was deemed cross-border or domestic.[257] As the third option, the horizontal instrument could apply only to distance shopping transactions, whether cross-border or domestic, but again, this would result in legal fragmentation on account of the fact that different conditions would apply to distance, as opposed to face-to-face, transactions.[258]

Whatever approach was chosen, the last policy option surveyed by the Commission concerned the degree of harmonization, which was essentially the 'hot button' issue of the 2007 Green Paper. The Commission started off by explaining that the directives concerned were all based on minimum harmonization, which had the effect of deterring consumers and businesses from engaging in cross-border transactions.[259] On that basis, it floated three options to remedy this. The first was full harmonization combined with the use of mutual recognition on a case-by-case basis for certain aspects where it would be difficult to achieve full harmonization.[260] The second was minimum harmonization in conjunction with a mutual recognition clause, with the result that a Member State would retain the possibility of imposing stricter consumer protection rules in its national law, but would be generally precluded from imposing such rules on businesses established in other Member States.[261] The third was minimum harmonization and a country of origin approach, which would allow a Member State to retain the possibility of imposing stricter consumer protection rules in its national law, but undertakings established in other Member States would only have to comply with the rules applicable in their home country.[262] As regards the latter two options, the Commission stressed their disadvantages, eg, they would neither remedy the regulatory fragmentation and negative effects on consumers' confidence in the internal market nor provide for a solution ensuring a high common level of consumer protection as required by the Treaties.[263] This implicitly left the first option, that of full harmonization with limited mutual recognition, remaining.

[252] 2007 Green Paper, n 237, points 4.1–4.2.
[253] 2007 Green Paper, n 237, point 4.2.
[254] 2007 Green Paper, n 237, point 4.2.
[255] 2007 Green Paper, n 237, point 4.4.
[256] 2007 Green Paper, n 237, point 4.4, first para.
[257] 2007 Green Paper, n 237, point 4.4, second para.
[258] 2007 Green Paper, n 237, point 4.4, third para.
[259] 2007 Green Paper, n 237, point 4.5, second–third paras.
[260] 2007 Green Paper, n 237, point 4.5, fourth, sixth paras.
[261] 2007 Green Paper, n 237, point 4.5, seventh para.
[262] 2007 Green Paper, n 237, point 4.5, eighth para.
[263] 2007 Green Paper, n 237, point 4.5, ninth–tenth paras.

Finally, more than half of the 2007 Green Paper was devoted to the list of specific questions, numbering thirty in all, put to the various stakeholders. Apart from the three questions concerning general policy issues discussed above and a catch-all question for additional remarks,[264] the other twenty-six questions were grouped into two categories: those dealing with horizontal issues common to the whole of the *acquis* or to more than one directive, on the one hand, and those dealing specifically with the sales contract, on the other.[265] Many of these questions were premised on the assumption that a horizontal instrument would be adopted.[266] Several questions also went beyond the scope of the directives concerned. For example, in the 'horizontal issues' category, there were questions as to whether the horizontal instrument should include an overarching obligation on professionals to act in accordance with the principles of good faith and fair dealing that exceeded what was presently found in the Unfair Contract Terms Directive.[267] As regards specific rules on sales contracts, several questions pertained to matters lying at the heart of black-letter contract law, in this case for consumer contracts, such as how delivery should be defined,[268] how the passing of the risk should be regulated,[269] and who should bear the burden of proof that defects existed at the time of delivery.[270] In short, the Green Paper was subtly aimed at a far-reaching horizontal instrument regulating consumer contract transactions and contained quite pointed questions asking the stakeholders to decide major, and often controversial, issues of consumer contract law, which implicated the relationship between the review of the consumer *acquis* and other activities taking place in the European contract law project.

6.3.2.1 *Responses to the 2007 Green Paper*

The 2007 Green Paper was addressed to the Council, the European Parliament, and the European Economic and Social Committee (EESC), but only the latter two replied. Although it took note of the 2007 Green Paper,[271] the Council did not issue a formal response.[272] The 2007 Green Paper also prompted an extensive collection of responses from various stakeholders. Each is briefly evaluated in turn.

6.3.2.2 *The EESC's 2007 Opinion*

On 12 July 2007, the EESC adopted an Opinion on the 2007 Green Paper.[273] On the whole, this Opinion was finely balanced. On the one hand, the EESC approved

[264] 2007 Green Paper, n 237, Annex I, points 1–3, 6.

[265] 2007 Green Paper, n 237, point 4.6, third para. The sales contract was stressed elsewhere: see 2007 Green Paper, n 237, point 4.2, third para.

[266] See, eg, 2007 Green Paper, n 237, Annex I, point 4.3 (question C); point 4.5 (question D2); point 4.9 (question G1); point 4.10 (question G2). This was criticized by scholars: see, eg, JW Rutgers and R Sefton-Green, 'Revising the Consumer *Acquis*: (Half) Opening the Doors of the Trojan Horse' (2008) 16 *ERPL* 427.

[267] 2007 Green Paper, n 237, Annex I, point 4.3 (question C).

[268] 2007 Green Paper, n 237, Annex I, point 5.3 (question I1).

[269] 2007 Green Paper, n 237, Annex I, point 5.4 (question I2).

[270] 2007 Green Paper, n 237, Annex I, point 5.6 (question J4).

[271] See 2784th Council meeting, Competitiveness (Internal Market, Industry, and Research), Brussels, 19 Feb 2007, DOC 6044/07 (Presse 19) 12.

[272] This was so even though the Commission had sent the Council an informational note on the 2007 Green Paper ahead of time. See DOC 16077/06, dated 1 Dec 2006, Annex ('Written Information from the Commission to the Competitiveness Council 4–5 December 2006').

[273] EESC Opinion on the 2007 Green Paper, [2007] OJ C256/27.

of the Commission's plans to provide a common framework for consumer rights to eliminate barriers to the internal market while maintaining a high level of consumer protection, albeit requesting the Commission to extend its review to a broader array of consumer directives.[274] On the other hand, the EESC acknowledged the difficulties associated with the Commission's approach, foreseeing that the shift from minimum to maximum harmonization—in its view, the 'pivotal issue' of the Green Paper—would encounter resistance in the Member States, but considered that for cases where the completion of the internal market was the primary concern, there was reason to have recourse to maximum harmonization.[275]

6.3.2.3 The European Parliament's 2007 Resolution

On 6 September 2007, the European Parliament adopted a Resolution on the 2007 Green Paper.[276] It welcomed the 2007 Green Paper as crucial for facilitating cross-border trade in the internal market and strengthening consumer confidence.[277] In particular, it cited several surveys indicating that retailers considered that cross-border sales would increase if the laws concerning consumer transactions were the same throughout the EU and that the majority of consumers were wary of engaging in cross-border transactions.[278] It also stressed that minimum harmonization did not achieve the aim of harmonization and that the past twenty years of consumer law had not created a truly integrated internal market.[279] It was therefore determined to complete the internal market by removing 'the remaining restrictions on competition in contract and commercial law' and enhancing legal certainty and citizens' confidence in the market.[280]

As for the key issues concerning the general approach and degree of harmonization, the Parliament's opinion generally coincided with the Commission's veiled preferences. It supported the 'mixed approach', involving a horizontal instrument containing cross-cutting issues common to all the directives applicable to all consumer contracts, both domestic and cross-border, based on maximum harmonization.[281] However, the Parliament called attention to the relationship between the 2007 Green Paper and the European contract law project, urging that the review of the consumer *acquis* should be coherently integrated with the work on contract law in general within the CFR project.[282] It also called attention to the overlap between several questions raised in the 2007 Green Paper and the ongoing work on the CFR,[283] thereby voicing its disapproval for including matters outside the ambit of consumer contract law. For example, it opposed the inclusion of a general clause on good faith and fair dealing and the introduction of general remedies in the horizontal instrument.[284] Initially, there had been explicit language in the text explaining that such concepts instead fell within the broader context of European contract law.[285] Although such language was later

[274] EESC Opinion, n 273, points 1.7, 4.4.
[275] EESC Opinion, n 273, point 5.3.
[276] Resolution on the 2007 Green Paper, n 240.
[277] Resolution on the 2007 Green Paper, n 240, point 1.
[278] Resolution on the 2007 Green Paper, n 240, recitals A–B.
[279] Resolution on the 2007 Green Paper, n 240, recital E.
[280] Resolution on the 2007 Green Paper, n 240, recitals G–H.
[281] Resolution on the 2007 Green Paper, n 240, points 5, 8, 10, 15.
[282] Resolution on the 2007 Green Paper, n 240, point 41.
[283] Resolution on the 2007 Green Paper, n 240, point 14.
[284] Resolution on the 2007 Green Paper, n 240, points 19, 29.
[285] See Draft Report on the Green Paper on the Review of the Consumer Acquis, PE 388.688v01-00, dated 15 May 2007, points 11, 19.

deleted, it was still recognized that these matters related to general contract law and went beyond the confines of consumer contract law.[286]

6.3.2.4 Stakeholder responses to the 2007 Green Paper

The Commission received responses from various stakeholders, including the Member States, national public authorities, businesses, consumer organizations, legal practitioners, and academics.[287] In an effort to collate these responses, an independent analytical report was issued by the Consumer Policy Evaluation Consortium, an external group of consulting companies, on behalf of the Commission on 6 November 2007, which set forth a detailed analysis of the 307 stakeholder responses received.[288] Taking this analytical report into account, the Commission published its own Staff Working Paper,[289] which identified, 'as objectively as possible', the main trends, viewpoints, and concerns of the stakeholders in response to the questions posed by the 2007 Green Paper.[290]

While space precludes detailed inquiry into the responses for each question, there appeared to be general consensus on the key issues concerning the legislative approach, scope of the horizontal instrument, and degree of harmonization involved, although certain sensitivities concerning the constitutionality of the horizontal instrument and its relationship to the CFR were evident. As noted by the Commission, the 'great majority' of stakeholders favoured the adoption of a horizontal instrument, flanked by the necessary vertical measures, applicable to domestic and cross-border transactions.[291] Yet, constitutional concerns relating to the legal basis of the horizontal instrument and compliance with the principles of subsidiarity and proportionality were prevalent.[292] In fact, a common issue among the responses of all stakeholder groups was the need for more evidence to underpin the Commission's proposals.[293] Still, there was a 'strong message' in support of further EU action, as opposed to maintaining the status quo.[294] Likewise, as regards the degree of harmonization, the Commission reported that a majority of the stakeholders favoured a horizontal instrument based on maximum (or full targeted) harmonization, as opposed to minimum harmonization.[295] That said,

[286] See Report on the Green Paper on the Review of the Consumer Acquis, A6-0281/2007, dated 16 July 2007, 11.

[287] The Commission's website used to provide the stakeholders' responses; however, it appears that this is no longer the case and now only provides summaries of the responses: see n 46. The individual responses cited herein are on file with the author.

[288] GHC Civic Consulting, 'Preparatory Work for the Impact Assessment on the Review of the Consumer Acquis', DG Health and Consumer Protection, Analytical Report on the Green Paper on the Review of the Consumer Acquis submitted by the Consumer Policy Evaluation Consortium, dated 6 Nov 2007 (Analytical Report), point 2.1. For discussion of the representativeness of the responses, see point 1.1.

[289] Commission Staff Working Paper, Report on the outcome of the public consultation on the Green Paper on the Review of the Consumer Acquis, not dated, available at <http://ec.europa.eu/consumers/cons_int/safe_shop/acquis/acquis_working_doc.pdf> (Working Paper).

[290] Working Paper, n 289, point 1, fourth, seventh paras.

[291] Working Paper, n 289, points 3, 4.1–4.2. The general legislative approach and scope of the horizontal instrument were considered among those issues meriting an 'obvious, overall consensus': Analytical Report, n 288, point 1.2.

[292] See Analytical Report, n 288, point 5.2.1, at 41, 42, 44.

[293] Analytical Report, n 288, point 4.2, ninth para.

[294] Analytical Report, n 288, point 1.2, fifth para.

[295] Working Paper, n 289, point 3, first indent; point 4.3.1. The contributions distinguished between full harmonization and full targeted harmonization. See Working Paper, n 289, point 4.3.1, third para; Analytical Report, n 288, point 5.2.3, at 48.

issues concerning a proper legal basis and compliance with the principles of subsidiarity and proportionality were used as arguments opposing the shift from minimum to maximum harmonization.[296]

Finally, various stakeholders highlighted the ambiguous relationship between the review of the consumer *acquis* and the activities taking place within the European contract law project. Another issue common to the responses of all stakeholder groups related to the need for clarification about the interplay between the review of the consumer *acquis* and the CFR.[297] This was particularly apparent in the responses to certain questions that touched on more general matters of contract law, which echoed the Parliament's 2007 Resolution. For instance, as regards the introduction of a general concept of good faith and fair dealing, scholars noted that comprehensive answers to this question could only be formulated on the basis of the CFR.[298] Similarly, as for the inclusion of a set of general contract remedies in the horizontal instrument, national authorities and businesses considered this subject to be reserved to the Member States, and some scholars pointed out that it was preferable to deal with this issue within the framework of the CFR.[299] Together, the issues raised in the stakeholder responses animated matters concerning not only the relationship between consumer contract law and general contract law already plaguing the CFR, but also the scope of the EU's competence in this setting.

6.3.3 The Consumer Rights Directive

In the aftermath of the Commission's 2007 Green Paper, the Commission announced its forthcoming plans to take a legislative initiative.[300] On 8 October 2008, the Commission submitted a proposal for a Directive on consumer rights.[301] Under this proposal, four of the eight directives under review—the Doorstep Selling, Distance Selling, Unfair Contract Terms, and Consumer Sales Directives—would be merged into a horizontal instrument that aimed to regulate their common aspects in a systematic fashion, to simplify and update the existing rules, and to eliminate inconsistencies and gaps.[302] The proposed Directive was divided into six chapters, which established a set of common rules according to the types of contracts and contractual situations concerned.[303] It was based on what is now Article 114 TFEU (ex Article 95 EC). Linked to the use of this Treaty provision was the proposed shift from minimum to maximum (or so-called 'full targeted'[304])

[296] See, eg, Analytical Report, n 288, point 5.2.3, at 51; Response of the French Government, 3; Joint Response of Professors Hans-W Micklitz and Nobert Reich, 12–13; Response of the European Consumers' Organization (BEUC), 10–11.

[297] Working Paper, n 289, point 4.2.8, second para; Analytical Report, n 288, point 4.2, seventh para.

[298] Analytical Report, n 288, point 5.2.4, at 62.

[299] Analytical Report, n 288, point 5.2.4, at 86.

[300] See Commission Communication, Commission Legislative and Work Programme for 2008, COM (2007) 640 final, 23.10.2007, Annex I ('List of strategic and priority initiatives') 28; Annex II ('List of simplification initiatives') 36.

[301] Proposal for a Directive of the European Parliament and of the Council on consumer rights, COM (2008) 614 final, 8.10.2008 (Proposal). It was accompanied by three Commission Staff Working Documents: (1) Impact Assessment Report, SEC (2008) 2544, 8.10.2008; (2) Summary of the Impact Assessment Report, SEC (2008) 2545, 8.10.2008; and (3) Annexes, SEC (2008) 2547, 8.10.2008.

[302] See Proposal, n 301, Explanatory Memorandum, point 1, at 3.

[303] See Proposal, n 301, Explanatory Memorandum, point 5, at 9–10. There were also five Annexes: see Proposal, n 301, 38–51.

[304] Proposal, n 301, Explanatory Memorandum, point 2, at 4 (ie 'targeted at the issues raising substantial barriers to trade for business and/or deterring consumers from buying cross-border'). See further Chapter 1, § 1.2.3.2.

harmonization.[305] This shift was one of the main sources of criticism of this proposal in academic circles.[306] It also proved to be one of its biggest hurdles in the decision-making process,[307] despite the Commission's attempts to stress the proposal's impact for the internal market and its contribution to a high level of consumer protection in the EU.[308] Ultimately, this resulted in the adoption of a less ambitious text, excluding for the most part two of the four Directives (the Unfair Contract Terms and Consumer Sales Directives).[309]

Directive 2011/83/EU on consumer rights (Consumer Rights Directive)[310] establishes a set of harmonized Union rules for certain aspects of consumer contracts, mainly concerning off-premises (eg, 'doorstep selling' situations[311]) and distance contracts, thereby repealing the Doorstep Selling and Distance Selling Directives.[312] Specifically, it lays down rules on information to be provided for distance, off-premises, and

[305] Proposal, n 301, fifth, eighth recitals; Art 4. In the Explanatory Memorandum, there was a specific section devoted to the Commission's consultation with interested parties and the impact assessment conducted in order to support recourse to maximum harmonization: see Proposal, n 301, Explanatory Memorandum, point 2. It acknowledged that this shift 'marks a new departure in the area of consumer contractual rights': Proposal, n 301, Explanatory Memorandum, point 3, at 7.

[306] The majority of literature on the proposal was negative: see, eg, H Eidenmüller et al, 'Towards a Revision of the Consumer Acquis' (2011) 48 *CML Rev* 1077, 1079; S Weatherill, 'The Consumer Rights Directive: How and Why a Quest for "Coherence" Has (Largely) Failed' (2012) 49 *CML Rev* 1279, 1288. For a brief selection of literature on the proposal, see, eg, G Howells and R Schulze (eds), *Modernising and Harmonising Consumer Contract Law* (Sellier, 2009); H Schulte-Nölke and L Tichý (eds), *Perspectives for European Consumer Law—Towards a Directive on Consumer Rights and Beyond* (Sellier, 2010); (2010) 18 *ERPL* 1; G. Howells, 'The Future of the Proposed Consumer Rights Directive' (2009) *REDC* 805; H-W Micklitz and N Reich, 'Crónica de una muerte anunciada: The Commission proposal for a "Directive on consumer rights"' (2009) 46 *CML Rev* 471; P Rott and E Terryn, 'The Proposal for a Directive on Consumer Rights: No Single Set of Rules' (2009) *Z Eu P* 456; S Whittaker, 'Unfair Contract Terms and Consumer Guarantees: the Proposal for a Directive on Consumer Rights and the Significance of "Full Harmonisation"' (2009) 5 *ERCL* 223.

[307] See, eg, Report on the Proposal, n 301, A7-0038/2011, dated 22 Feb 2011 (European Parliament Report) 115,119–120; DOC 16928/10, dated 29 Nov 2010; DOC 7650/11, dated 30 March 2011, 2–3. See also Opinions of the Committee of the Regions (CoR), [2009] OJ C200/76, and of the EESC, [2009] OJ C317/54, on the Proposal, n 301. It attracted the criticism of certain national parliaments for non-compliance with subsidiarity, but was not subject to the *ex ante* procedure put in place by the Lisbon Treaty: see Weatherill, n 306, 1310 fn 104.

[308] See Commission document, 'The Proposal for a Directive on Consumer Rights: Scope, Relationship with National General Contract Law and Relationship with other Community Legislation', Brussels, 9 Oct 2009 (2009 Working Document), point 3, at 4; and Commission document, 'The Proposal for a Directive on Consumer Rights: Impact on Level of National Consumer Protection—Comparative Table', Brussels, 9 Oct 2009, available at <http://ec.europa.eu/consumers/rights/cons_acquis_en.htm>. The first was referred to as the Commission's 'non-paper' on the proposed Directive: see, eg, MBM Loos, 'Full harmonisation as a regulatory concept and its consequences for the national legal orders. The example of the Consumer rights directive', CSECL Working Paper Series No 2010/03, 13 fn 83.

[309] See, eg, C Cauffman, 'The Consumer Rights Directive—Adopted' (2012) 19 *MJ* 1, 1–2; E Hondius, 'Editorial, The Proposal for a Directive on Consumer Rights: The Emperor's New Clothes?' (2011) 19 *ERPL* 163.

[310] Dir 2011/83/EU of the European Parliament and of the Council of 25 Oct 2011 on consumer rights, amending Council Dir 93/13/EEC and Dir 1999/44/EC of the European Parliament and of the Council and repealing Council Dir 85/577/EEC and Dir 97/7/EC of the European Parliament and of the Council, [2011] OJ L304/64 (Consumer Rights Directive). The deadline for transposition was 13 Dec 2013, and it applies to contracts concluded after 13 June 2014: see Art 28.

[311] See Consumer Rights Directive, n 310, twenty-first recital; Art 2(8).

[312] See Consumer Rights Directive, n 310, second recital; Art 31. There is a correlation table in Annex II.

other consumer contracts, as well as rules on the right of withdrawal for distance and off-premises contracts and some 'other consumer rights', such as that concerning delivery and passing of risk.[313] Its amendment of the Unfair Contract Terms and Consumer Sales Directives basically amounts to reporting requirements for the Member States, obliging them to inform the Commission of their adoption of more stringent provisions under the minimum harmonization clauses provided therein.[314] Full harmonization is retained,[315] but its application is scaled back in light of the Directive's reduced scope, and there are various provisions making clear that the Member States are allowed to maintain or adopt national rules in relation to certain aspects covered by the Directive or to issues that are not specifically regulated by it.[316] Although it certainly makes improvements to the legislative framework,[317] by and large, it signified something of a letdown, especially as far as the aims envisaged by the review of the consumer *acquis* were concerned.[318]

As could be expected, the Consumer Rights Directive has amassed a voluminous literature, offering detailed analysis of its provisions.[319] For this discussion, three points are singled out, since they hark back to the perennial themes underlying the 'hard core' of the EU contract law *acquis*.[320] First, as regards the matter of competence, the Directive is based on Article 114 TFEU and espouses the dual aim to contribute to the proper functioning of the internal market and to achieve a high common level of consumer protection by approximating certain aspects of the consumer contract laws of the Member States.[321] As with previous directives within the EU contract law *acquis*, including the two that it repeals, it applies to cross-border and domestic transactions.[322] Still, its implications for cross-border transactions are emphasized. For instance, the Directive states: 'Certain disparities create significant internal market barriers affecting traders and consumers. Those disparities increase compliance costs to traders wishing to engage in the cross-border sale of goods or provision of services. Disproportionate fragmentation also undermines consumer confidence in the internal market.'[323] Thus,

[313] Consumer Rights Directive, n 310, ninth recital. This corresponds to chs II–IV of the Directive; see also Annex I ('Information concerning the exercise of the right of withdrawal'). Ch I deals with the subject matter, definitions, and scope; chs V and VI set forth the general and final provisions, respectively.

[314] Consumer Rights Directive, n 310, sixty-third recital; Arts 32–33. These provisions are singled out as part of the Commission's review of the Directive in 2016: see sixty-second recital; Art 30.

[315] Consumer Rights Directive, n 310, seventh recital; Art 4.

[316] See, eg, Consumer Rights Directive, n 310, second, thirteenth–sixteenth, twenty-eighth recitals; Art 3(4); Art 5(3)–(4); Art 6(7)–(8); Art 7(4); Art 8(6); Art 9(3); Art 18(4). Some of the foregoing Articles entail reporting requirements for the Member States: see Art 29.

[317] See, eg, Cauffman, n 309; P Rott, 'More coherence? A higher level of consumer protection?—A review of the new Consumer Rights Directive 2011/83/EU' (2012) *REDC* 371.

[318] See, eg, K Tonner and K Fangerow, 'Directive 2011/83/EU on consumer rights: a new approach to European consumer law?' (2012) 1 *EUVR* 67; Weatherill, n 306. As such, some commentators stress that that there is still need for a critical review and revision of the *acquis*: see, eg, Eidenmüller et al, n 306, 1079; R Zimmerman, 'The Present State of European Private Law' (2009) 57 *AJCL* 479, 511.

[319] See, eg, Special Issue, (2012) *RAE* 521; E Hall et al, 'The Consumer Rights Directive—An Assessment of its Contribution to the Development of European Consumer Contract Law' (2012) 8 *ERCL* 139; see also citations in ns 306, 309.

[320] See Chapter 1, § 1.4.

[321] Consumer Rights Directive, n 310, Art 1. Not to be confused, Art 169 TFEU is cited in the third recital (as had been done in the proposal) to underscore the Union's contribution to the attainment of a high level of consumer protection through measures based on Art 114 TFEU.

[322] See Proposal, n 301, Explanatory Memorandum, point 3, at 8.

[323] Consumer Rights Directive, n 310, sixth recital. As regards specific aspects covered, see also fifth, fortieth, forty-fourth recitals.

it expressly refers to the so-called 'consumer confidence' rationale, but similar to other measures in the EU contract law *acquis*, such a rationale appears to stand alongside, not in place of, arguments concerning existing and potential barriers to trade.[324] Moreover, interwoven with the justification for the use of Article 114 TFEU is the shift from minimum to maximum harmonization. Although the Directive has a more limited scope than the proposal, criticism of the proposal's shift from minimum to maximum harmonization already helped to place attention on the potential viability of Article 169 TFEU to preserve the Member States' recourse to minimum harmonization and prevent a diminution in the level of consumer protection in the national legal orders.[325]

Secondly, the shift from minimum to maximum harmonization dovetails with issues concerning the Directive's coverage. As already mentioned, it regulates only 'certain aspects' of consumer contract law,[326] and does not interfere with general contract law rules on, for instance, the conclusion or validity of a contract or general contractual remedies.[327] To paraphrase the remarks of then Commissioner Meglena Kuneva at a conference concerning the proposal, the measure may be viewed as a well-conceived island in the sea of national consumer contract law.[328] Thus, it perpetuates issues concerning the 'fit' of the special set of EU consumer contract law rules within the national contract law regimes, which is heightened by the shift to maximum harmonization and the Commission's purported failure to make much use of the DCFR in the formulation of the proposal.[329]

Finally, by its very name, the Consumer Rights Directive concerns consumer contract law, meaning B2C, not B2B, transactions. It underpins the familiar interplay between consumer and general contract law in the debate. It also does not address the problems emanating from divergences among general contract law rules that place further attention on the prospect of a comprehensive contract law instrument for B2B transactions in the internal market. Consequently, the Consumer Rights Directive constitutes a solution in the debate about European contract law in its own right, at the same time that it enlivens, rather than silences, questions concerning the Union's competence in European contract law and the need for a comprehensive contract law instrument covering B2C and B2B transactions. By virtue of its somewhat sparse justification on internal market grounds and its emphasis on the 'consumer confidence' rationale, the Directive provokes questions concerning the scope of the Union's competence under Article 114 TFEU in relation to the adoption of a horizontal consumer contract law instrument such as the Directive itself,[330] as well as its commercial law counterpart. By virtue of its shift to maximum harmonization, it raises issues concerning the potential recourse to Article 169 TFEU in place of Article 114 TFEU and hence the relationship between the two provisions.

[324] Compare Proposal, n 301, sixth–seventh recitals, which illustrate this point more clearly. Also as compared to the sixth recital of the Proposal, there is no mention of appreciable distortions of competition in the Directive as adopted.

[325] See, eg, CoR Opinion, n 307, points 7–9; EESC Opinion, n 307, points 4.4–4.5.

[326] See, eg, Consumer Rights Directive, n 310, fourth, seventh, eighth recitals; Art 1.

[327] See, eg, Consumer Rights Directive, n 310, fourteenth recital; Art 5; Art 18(4). As regards the proposal, see also 2009 Working Document, n 308, point 3, at 4–6.

[328] 'Modernising and Harmonising Consumer Contract Law', Conference held at the University of Leuven, 7 April 2009 (on file with author).

[329] See MW Hesselink, 'The Consumer Rights Directive and the CFR: two worlds apart?' (2006) 5 *ERCL* 290. That said, some amendments put forward in the decision-making process appear to have been inspired by the DCFR: see, eg, European Parliament Report, n 307, 120.

[330] See, eg, Weatherill, n 306, 1306–1309.

6.4 The Path to the Proposed CESL and Beyond

6.4.1 The Stockholm Programme

Although considerable attention had been placed on the CFR and the review of the consumer *acquis*, it was not long before the other proposed solutions emanating from the Commission's Communications on European contract law, namely one or more optional instruments of contract law and the promotion of EU-wide standard contract terms, came back into the spotlight. This largely began with institutional developments laying the groundwork for the Stockholm Programme, the third multiannual programme on the AFSJ, for the next five years. This is not to exclude the fact that Presidency Conclusions of European Council meetings continued to be peppered with references to the CFR and its linkage to the improvement of the *acquis*.[331] Still, certain Commission documents issued in the follow-up to the Hague Programme began to invigorate the discussion of the viability of these solutions in the further development of the European contract law project.

On 10 June 2009, as part of its final assessment of the Hague Programme,[332] the Commission issued a Communication setting forth the list of the priorities for the forthcoming Stockholm Programme.[333] One of these priorities was 'Making life easier—a Europe of justice', which meant that as far as 'contracts and commerce are concerned, this should give those involved in economic life the tools they need to take full advantage of the opportunities offered by the single market'.[334] This included consideration of the use of EU standard contracts and an optional instrument of contract law.[335] This Communication was welcomed by the European Parliament[336] and the EESC,[337] both of which supported these solutions under specific headings that appeared to link these measures to the EU's internal market objectives.[338]

The Commission's references to these solutions did not make it into the Stockholm Programme—An open and secure Europe serving and protecting citizens,[339] adopted by the European Council at its meeting on 10–11 December 2009.[340] Yet, the European Council did not neglect European contract law completely in this Programme. Within the section on '[t]he benefits for citizens of a European judicial area',[341] there is a

[331] See, eg, Presidency Conclusions, Brussels European Council, 21–22 June 2007, point 39; Presidency Conclusions, Brussels European Council, 19–20 June 2008, point 20.

[332] There was another Commission Communication published on the same day (Justice, Freedom and Security in Europe since 2005: An Evaluation of the Hague Programme and Action Plan, COM (2009) 263 final, 10.6.2009), but it did not mention the European contract law project.

[333] Commission Communication, An area of freedom, security and justice serving the citizen, COM (2009) 262 final, 10.6.2009, point 1, at 4–5.

[334] Communication, n 333, point 1, subpoint 2, at 5.

[335] Communication, n 333, point 3.4.2, at 13–14.

[336] European Parliament Resolution of 25 Nov 2009 on the Commission Communication, An area of freedom, security and justice serving the citizen—Stockholm Programme (PA_TA(2009)0090)), points 99–101 (under the heading 'Reaping the full benefits of the single market through European contract law').

[337] EESC Opinion on the Communication, n 333, [2010] OJ C128/80, point 4.2.4.1 (under the heading 'The role of the legal professions in supporting economic activity').

[338] Opinions of the CoR ([2010] OJ C79/37) and European Data Protection Supervisor ([2009] OJ C276/8) on this Communication did not cite the European contract law project.

[339] The Stockholm Programme—An open and secure Europe serving and protecting citizens, [2010] OJ C115/1 (Stockholm Programme).

[340] Presidency Conclusions, Brussels European Council, 10–11 Dec 2009.

[341] Stockholm Programme, n 339, point 3.4.

specific heading titled 'Supporting economic activity',[342] under which it is envisaged that the European judicial area should 'support economic activity in the single market'.[343] In this context, the European Council reaffirmed that the CFR for European contract law should be 'a non-binding set of fundamental principles, definitions and model rules to be used by the law-makers at Union level to ensure greater coherence and quality in the law-making process' and invited the Commission to submit a proposal on the CFR.[344] It then highlighted the need to study further measures regarding business law and to create a clear regulatory environment allowing small and medium-sized enterprises (SMEs) in particular to take full advantage of the internal market, noting that '[t]he issue of contractual law also needs to be examined further'.[345] It invited the Commission to evaluate whether measures were needed in 'these areas' and to put forward proposals where appropriate.[346] Accordingly, similar to the Hague Programme, the Stockholm Programme depicted the CFR as a 'better lawmaking' tool in contract law. Yet, this time, the European Council's framing of the CFR and the 'issue of contractual law' as part of 'supporting economic activity' drew an explicit link between the European contract law project and the EU's internal market objectives, even though it left in place ambiguities regarding the relationship between this project and the EU's objectives relating to the AFSJ.

These points carried through to the Commission's Action Plan for the implementation of the Stockholm Programme.[347] Within the context of 'strengthening confidence' in the European judicial area, the Commission considered: 'Cross-border transactions can be made easier by increasing the coherence of European contract law. Businesses are not taking sufficient advantage of the internet's potential to boost sales: Union law can help by increasing businesses' need for legal certainty and at the same time guaranteeing the highest level of consumer protection'.[348] In the Annex providing a timetable of the actions to be taken, the Commission listed a forthcoming Communication and legislative proposal on the CFR.[349] In hindsight, these actions alluded to what would become the Commission's 2010 Green Paper and the proposed CESL, which brought an optional instrument of contract law centre stage.[350]

6.4.2 The 2010 Green Paper

On 1 July 2010, the Commission issued the Green Paper on policy options for progress towards a European Contract Law for consumers and businesses (2010 Green Paper).[351]

[342] Stockholm Programme, n 339, point 3.4.2.

[343] Stockholm Programme, n 339, point 3.4.2, first para.

[344] Stockholm Programme, n 339, point 3.4.2, fourth para.

[345] Stockholm Programme, n 339, point 3.4.2, fifth para.

[346] Stockholm Programme, n 339, point 3.4.2, sixth para.

[347] Commission Communication, Delivering an area of freedom, security and justice for Europe's citizens—Action Plan Implementing the Stockholm Programme, COM (2010) 171 final, 20.4.2010.

[348] Communication, n 347, point 4, sixth para.

[349] Communication, n 347, Annex, 24–25.

[350] The press release on this Communication drew an analogy to the UCC in its reference to an optional instrument: see Press Release, MEMO/10/139, Brussels, 20 April 2010, point 6 ('The Commission is preparing an additional and optional contract law instrument—something similar to the US Uniform Commercial Code'). The optional instrument was also emphasized in the European Parliament Resolution of 23 Nov 2010 on civil law, commercial law, family law and private international law aspects of the Action Plan Implementing the Stockholm Programme, [2012] OJ C99E/19, recital G; point 16.

[351] Green Paper on policy options for progress towards a European Contract Law for consumers and businesses, COM (2010) 348 final, 1.7.2010 (2010 Green Paper). For detailed discussion, see, eg, (2011) 7 *ERCL* 115.

Its purpose was to set out the options on how to strengthen the internal market by making progress in the area of European contract law and to launch a public consultation on them.[352] In advancing a set of options that started to give shape to a future European contract law instrument, the 2010 Green Paper marked a new stage in the debate about European contract law, and in doing so, tightened the linkage between such an instrument and the internal market.

In fact, the discussion of the impact of divergences between national contract laws on the internal market was a predominant theme running through all four sections of the 2010 Green Paper. In the first introductory section, the Commission opened with a summary of the problems that may be caused by such divergences for the internal market.[353] In the second section on the background to the 2010 Green Paper, it considered that a European contract law instrument could help the EU to meet its economic goals, citing the Stockholm Programme and certain Communications issued in the preceding months, which referred to an optional instrument and the promotion of EU model contract clauses.[354]

The third section was devoted to 'challenges for the internal market', and began with the Commission's affirmative statement that divergences between national contract laws feature among the barriers to the completion of the internal market, as had emerged from various studies.[355] The Commission then delineated the specific problems associated with B2C and B2B contracts for the internal market. As regards B2C contracts, it explained that as a result of EU private international law instruments (namely the 'Rome I' Regulation[356]), businesses faced high legal costs because such contracts are subject to the relevant rules where the consumer is resident and that they may even refuse to conclude contracts due to such costs, which meant that cross-border commerce remains unfulfilled to the detriment of both businesses and consumers.[357] It also acknowledged that the then proposal for a Consumer Rights Directive only addressed some of the problems, since it did not render the national contract laws fully compatible in the non-harmonized areas, and even in the harmonized areas, there would be a need to apply them in conjunction with other national provisions of general contract law.[358] As regards B2B contracts,

[352] 2010 Green Paper, n 351, point 1, third para. See also point 5, first para. Respondents had about six months (1 July 2010 to 31 Jan 2011), as compared to three months in the case of the 2001 Communication and the 2003 Action Plan, to submit their contributions: 2010 Green Paper, n 351, point 5, second para. See V Reding, 'The Next Steps Towards a European Contract Law for Businesses and Consumers' in R Schulze and J Stuyck (eds), *Towards a European Contract Law* (Sellier, 2011) 9, 14.

[353] 2010 Green Paper, n 351, point 1.

[354] 2010 Green Paper, n 351, point 2, fourth para. In these Communications, the Commission already referred to its intention to offer an optional instrument of contract law: see Commission Communication, EUROPE 2020—A strategy for smart, sustainable and inclusive growth, COM (2010) 2020 final, 3.3.2010, point 3.1, seventh para, fourth indent, at 21; Commission Communication, A Digital Agenda for Europe, COM (2010) 245 final/2, 26.8.2010, point 2.1.3, at 13 (although it was published after the 2010 Green Paper, it replaced the previous Communication on this subject, COM (2010) 245 final, 19.5.2010, containing identical language on an optional instrument).

[355] 2010 Green Paper, n 351, section 3, first para (citing the consultation launched by the 2001 Communication, two Eurobarometer surveys, and the Clifford Chance survey). See further Chapter 8, § 8.3.2.2.

[356] Reg (EC) No 593/2008 of the European Parliament and of the Council of 17 June 2008 on the law applicable to contractual obligations (Rome I), [2008] OJ L177/6.

[357] 2010 Green Paper, n 351, section 3.1, first–third paras.

[358] 2010 Green Paper, n 351, section 3.1, fourth para.

the Commission posited that notwithstanding the parties' freedom to choose the applicable law, large companies with strong bargaining power can ensure that their contracts are subject to a particular law, which may be more difficult for SMEs and thus raise obstacles to pursuing a uniform commercial policy across the EU.[359] In addition, ensuring compliance with different contract laws or obtaining information about the applicable law in another Member State might increase legal costs[360] and thus, businesses may benefit from a European contract law instrument that could come to be seen as a neutral regime and an alternative to the national contract laws.[361]

This paved the way to the fourth section on 'choosing the best instrument for European contract law', which should respond to the foregoing problems caused by diverging contract laws for the internal market.[362] The inquiry was divided into three parts concerning the legal nature, scope of application, and material scope of a future European contract law instrument. In what is probably the most cited portion of the 2010 Green Paper, the Commission floated seven options for the legal nature of such an instrument. Given the drawbacks associated with all but an optional instrument, it was not difficult to pick out which option the Commission implicitly preferred.[363]

The first three options largely concerned non-binding instruments. *Option 1* entailed the publication of the results of the Expert Group, established by the Commission to study the feasibility of a European contract law instrument a few months before,[364] which could be used by European and national legislators, contractual parties, or for the purposes of higher education and professional training, thereby contributing to the 'voluntary convergence' of national contracts laws.[365] However, it would not address divergences in contract law and hence the internal market barriers.[366] *Option 2* constituted the adoption of an official 'toolbox' for the Union legislator by way of either: (a) a Commission act (eg, communication or decision); or (b) an interinstitutional agreement between the Commission, the European Parliament, and the Council.[367] Yet, the disadvantage of any 'toolbox' is that it would not provide 'immediate, tangible internal market benefits' because it did not remove divergences in law and could not ensure a convergent application and interpretation of EU contract law by the courts.[368]

Option 3 envisaged the attachment of a European contract law instrument to a Commission recommendation encouraging the Member States either: (a) to replace national law with the recommended instrument, or (b) to incorporate such an instrument into national law as an optional regime which would stand beside other alternative

[359] 2010 Green Paper, n 351, section 3.2, first–second paras.

[360] 2010 Green Paper, n 351, section 3.2, second para.

[361] 2010 Green Paper, n 351, section 3.2, third para.

[362] 2010 Green Paper, n 351, point 4.

[363] In fact, several respondents drew attention to the fact that the Commission already appeared to favour an optional instrument (*Option 4*) before the consultation period had ended: see, eg, Response of the Republic of Austria; Response of the UK Government; Response of the European Consumer Consultative Group (ECCG). See also Written Question P-9461/2010 by A Fox, 'Green Paper on policy options for progress towards a European Contract Law for consumers and businesses', available at n 46.

[364] 2010 Green Paper, n 351, point 2, sixth para. See further § 6.4.3.

[365] 2010 Green Paper, n 351, point 4.1 (Option 1), first para.

[366] 2010 Green Paper, n 351, point 4.1 (Option 1), second para.

[367] 2010 Green Paper, n 351, point 4.1 (Option 2). For (b) the Parliament and the Council would be required to take its recommendations into consideration when preparing and adopting new legislative instruments, whereas this would not be the case for (a): 2010 Green Paper, n 351, point 4.1 (Option 2), first–second paras.

[368] 2010 Green Paper, n 351, point 4.1 (Option 2), third para.

instruments to be chosen as the applicable law.[369] Within the context of Option 3(a), the Commission referred by analogy to the UCC and mentioned, in an accompanying footnote, uniform laws and the 'influential scholarly work to clarify, modernise and improve the law' produced by the American Law Institute, thereby alluding to the Restatements,[370] which was the first time that these American techniques explicitly appeared in the text of one of its Communications on European contract law.[371] The Commission's critique of this option echoed some of the problems associated with these techniques in the US.[372] It pointed out that it would have no binding effects on the Member States and bears the risk of an incoherent and incomplete approach, since they may enact the recommendation differently and at different times or not at all.[373]

The other four options concerned binding instruments. *Option 4* envisaged a Regulation setting up an optional instrument of contract law, which would constitute a '2nd Regime' in each Member State, thus giving parties an option between two regimes of domestic contract law.[374] It would be a 'comprehensive and, as much as possible, self-standing set of contract law rules', which would form part of each Member State's national law for the purposes of private international law, thereby referring in accompanying footnotes to some additional documents espousing the benefits of optional instruments.[375] It could bring about important internal market benefits without necessitating further inroads into national law, since 'in line with the principle of subsidiarity, an optional instrument could constitute an alternative to full harmonisation of national laws by offering a proportionate solution to internal market barriers stemming from diverging national contract laws'.[376] *Option 5* denoted a Directive harmonizing the national contract laws on the basis of minimum common standards, prompting the Commission to note the drawbacks of minimum harmonization.[377] *Option 6* involved a Regulation replacing the national contract laws with a uniform set of rules.[378] It would remove legal fragmentation in contract law, but 'could raise sensitive issues of subsidiarity and proportionality', since replacing national contract laws, especially if domestic contracts were covered, with a single set of rules may not be a proportionate measure to deal with the obstacles to trade in the internal market.[379] Finally, *Option 7* denoted a Regulation establishing a 'European civil code'. This proposed solution went one step further than *Option 6* in the sense that it would cover contract law and other types of obligations.[380] In the Commission's view, although impediments to the smooth functioning of the internal market existed in areas of law other than contract law, it was yet to be established to what extent such an extensive instrument could be justified on grounds of subsidiarity.[381]

[369] 2010 Green Paper, n 351, point 4.1 (Option 3).
[370] 2010 Green Paper, n 351, point 4.1 (Option 3(a)), at 8–9 fn 23.
[371] K Gutman, 'The Commission's 2010 Green Paper on European Contract Law: Reflections on Union Competence in Light of the Proposed Options' (2011) 7 *ERCL* 151, 171.
[372] See further Chapter 11, § 11.4.2.
[373] 2010 Green Paper, n 351, point 4.1 (Option 3), first, third paras.
[374] 2010 Green Paper, n 351, point 4.1 (Option 4), first para.
[375] 2010 Green Paper, n 351, point 4.1 (Option 4), first–second paras, at 9 fns 24–26.
[376] 2010 Green Paper, n 351, point 4.1 (Option 4), sixth para.
[377] 2010 Green Paper, n 351, point 4.1 (Option 5). The Commission did not explicitly mention why this option was limited to minimum harmonization, but implicitly, this may be explained by its recognition of the 'limits of the full harmonization approach' in connection with the then proposed Consumer Rights Directive: see 2010 Green Paper, n 351, point 3.1, fourth para.
[378] 2010 Green Paper, n 351, point 4.1 (Option 6), first para.
[379] 2010 Green Paper, n 351, point 4.1 (Option 6), second–third paras.
[380] 2010 Green Paper, n 351, point 4.1 (Option 7).
[381] 2010 Green Paper, n 351, point 4.1 (Option 7).

Following this list of seven options, the Commission surveyed the possibilities regarding the scope of application and material scope of the future instrument, each of which invited inquiry into three related aspects, with the Commission offering some 'pros' and 'cons' along the way. As regards the instrument's scope of application, this implicated questions concerning: first, whether it should cover both B2C and B2B contracts or instead there should be separate instruments for each;[382] secondly, whether it should cover cross-border and domestic contracts or just cross-border contracts;[383] and thirdly, the possibility of developing an instrument focused on contracts concluded in the online environment.[384] Likewise, the material scope of the instrument implicated three questions concerning: first, whether it should be interpreted in a narrow or broad manner,[385] namely whether it should be primarily limited to matters of contract law,[386] or include related topics;[387] secondly, whether it should contain rules on specific types of contracts;[388] and thirdly, its scope if it were to take the form of a European civil code, since it would need to cover not only contract law and specific types of contracts, but also tort law, unjustified enrichment, and benevolent intervention in another's affairs.[389]

Similar to the 2001 Communication, the 2010 Green Paper did not engage in discussion of the limits of Union competence, ie the potential legal bases to support the proposed options, as compared to the exercise of Union competence. As seen above, the principles of subsidiarity and proportionality were cited several times, positively in relation to an optional instrument (*Option 4*), and in more negative terms as regards a Regulation unifying the national contract laws (*Option 6*) and a Regulation establishing a European civil code (*Option 7*). Despite the Commission's reticence to discuss legal basis explicitly, the linkage between a European contract law instrument and the EU's competences related to the internal market was implicitly apparent. Yet, its choice not to provide at least some initial reflection on this topic left crucial issues concerning the scope of Union competence in connection with these options unaddressed, especially with regard to the optional instrument. No doubt, sensitivities related to Union competence in this setting were not soothed by the Commission's inclusion of a European civil code as one of the options, in light of its prior repeated admonitions to the contrary. Its failure to address matters of Union competence would come back to haunt it in the stakeholders' responses.

6.4.2.1 Responses to the 2010 Green Paper

The Commission received about 320 responses to the 2010 Green Paper from a wide range of stakeholders.[390] The European Parliament and the EESC issued formal responses; although the Council did not, discussions were held on the subject.[391] Each is taken in turn.

[382] 2010 Green Paper, n 351, point 4.2.1.

[383] 2010 Green Paper, n 351, point 4.2.2, first–second paras.

[384] 2010 Green Paper, n 351, point 4.2.2, third para.

[385] The Commission noted that in any case, it should cover mandatory consumer contract law rules taking the Union *acquis* as a starting point: 2010 Green Paper, n 351, point 4.3.

[386] 2010 Green Paper, n 351, point 4.3.1.

[387] 2010 Green Paper, n 351, point 4.3.2.

[388] 2010 Green Paper, n 351, point 4.3.3.

[389] 2010 Green Paper, n 351, point 4.3.4.

[390] Commission Staff Working Paper, Impact Assessment accompanying the Proposal for a Regulation of the European Parliament and of the Council on a Common European Sales Law, SEC (2011) 1165 final, 11.10.2011 (CESL Impact Assessment), Annex I ('Procedural Issues and Consultation of Interested Parties'), point 1.3.1, at 59.

[391] See DOC 16577/10, dated 19 Nov 2010.

6.4.2.2 *The EESC's 2011 Opinion*

On 19 January 2011, the EESC adopted an Opinion on the 2010 Green Paper (2011 Opinion).[392] Generally, it concurred with the Commission's view on the need to complete the internal market in respect of European contract law and recognized the importance of the academic work on the CFR, which ought to be put to practical use.[393] It favoured a 'hybrid option', comprising a 'toolbox' serving as a CFR available to parties in drawing up cross-border contracts, accompanied by an optional instrument (or an 'optional advanced new regime', as it was called), which could be used by the parties for cross-border contracts as an alternative to the relevant national law.[394] This should be done incrementally, starting with cross-border B2B sales contracts for goods, as a useful means of putting the co-existence of the regimes to the test, before extending the instruments to other kinds of contracts.[395] It also suggested the promotion of EU-wide standard contract terms as part of the combination of legislative and non-legislative measures to be availed of.[396] There was no discussion of Union competence in connection with its preferred solutions, but in the context of the problems posed by diverging contract laws for the internal market, it stated that the Commission should 'go beyond measures for judicial cooperation in civil-law matters, which, while necessary, are not sufficient to ensure the proper functioning of the internal market'.[397] This alluded to Article 81 TFEU and its relationship with Treaty provisions concerning the Union's internal market competences, such as Article 114 TFEU, but matters were left unclear.

6.4.2.3 *The European Parliament's 2011 Resolution*

On 8 June 2011, the European Parliament adopted a Resolution on the 2010 Green Paper (2011 Resolution).[398] Overall, it supported action to address the range of barriers faced by those who wish to engage in cross-border transactions in the internal market and considered that along with other measures, the European contract law project could be useful for realizing the full potential of the internal market,[399] especially for SMEs.[400] Yet, in almost schizophrenic fashion, the Resolution began by recognizing the various problems, such as transaction costs and legal complexity, posed by diverging contract laws and the resulting contribution of a future European contract law instrument to the internal market,[401] while at the same time, calling for further study and evidence of such problems[402] and highlighting that there were other types of problems besides divergences among national contract laws in this regard.[403]

In the first two sections, the Parliament set forth its responses to the specific questions raised in the 2010 Green Paper.[404] It favoured *Option 4* setting up an optional

392 EESC Opinion on the 2010 Green Paper, [2011] OJ C84/1 (2011 Opinion).

393 2011 Opinion, n 392, point 1.1.

394 2011 Opinion, n 392, point 1.2.

395 2011 Opinion, n 392, points 1.3, 1.6, 1.8, 4.10.

396 2011 Opinion, n 392, point 4.12.

397 2011 Opinion, n 392, point 4.5.

398 European Parliament Resolution of 8 June 2011 on the 2010 Green Paper, [2012] OJ C380E/59 (2011 Resolution).

399 2011 Resolution, n 398, point 1. See also Parliamentary Debates, 6 June 2011-Strasbourg, particularly Remarks of Diana Wallis.

400 See 2011 Resolution, n 398, point 3.

401 See 2011 Resolution, n 398, recitals A, B, E, H, J, L, M, Q.

402 See 2011 Resolution, n 398, recitals D, I, K, O, P. But see Report on the 2010 Green Paper, A7-0164/2011, dated 18 April 2011, Explanatory Statement, 13–15.

403 See 2011 Resolution, n 398, recitals G, N.

404 Report, n 402, Explanatory Statement, 15.

instrument, 'after an impact assessment and clarification of the legal basis', complemented by a 'toolbox' that could eventually be endorsed as an interinstitutional agreement.[405] An optional instrument would improve the internal market 'without affecting Member States' national systems of contract law', and it welcomed the fact that it takes account of the principle of subsidiarity and is without prejudice to the legislative powers of the Member States in the area of contract and civil law.[406] Yet, it called on the Commission to clarify various aspects, such as its relationship with the 'Rome I' Regulation and international conventions, such as the United Nations Convention on Contracts for the International Sale of Goods (CISG).[407] As regards its scope of application, the Parliament considered that both B2C and B2B transactions should be covered[408] and that it should be available on an opt-in basis for cross-border situations in the first instance.[409] Moreover, although the material scope of the 'toolbox' could be quite broad, that of the optional instrument should be limited to the 'core contractual issues', which should be clarified, and contain provisions on certain specific types of contracts, in particular those for the sale of goods, provision of services, and insurance contracts.[410] However, it urged the Commission to take a cautious approach to financial services contracts and to set up an expert group for future work on this subject.[411] It also urged further study of other kinds of contracts, including those related to digital rights.[412]

The third and fourth sections of the Resolution addressed some additional issues that were considered of 'specific importance' concerning the application of a European contract law in practice and matters relating to stakeholder involvement and the impact assessment.[413] As regards the former, the Parliament considered that notwithstanding the optional instrument, there was still a need to provide EU-wide standard contract terms,[414] as well as certain 'flanking' measures, such as further work on cross-border alternative dispute resolution (ADR) and redress systems.[415] As regards the latter, it stressed, among other things, that it should be fully involved 'in the framework of the ordinary legislative procedure' with regard to any future optional instrument.[416] Although it did not explicitly discuss the legal basis for such an instrument, its reference to the 'ordinary legislative procedure' coupled with the linkage between the optional instrument and the internal market implied the use of a Treaty provision requiring such a procedure in relation to the Union's internal market competence, namely Article 114 TFEU. In the accompanying Report, there had been a suggestion to include a specific provision that 'it needs to be further considered if Articles 114 and 169 or 352 of the Treaty on the Functioning of the European Union would constitute the appropriate legal basis for an instrument regulating business-to-business (B2B) and business-to-consumer (B2C) contracts',[417] but this was not taken up.

405 2011 Resolution, n 398, point 5. It envisaged that the 'toolbox' could be put into practice step by step, starting as a Commission tool and being converted into a tool for the Union legislature: 2011 Resolution, n 398, point 9.

406 2011 Resolution, n 398, points 7–8, 19.

407 2011 Resolution, n 398, points 11, 13. See also more generally point 28.

408 2011 Resolution, n 398, point 14.

409 2011 Resolution, n 398, point 20.

410 2011 Resolution, n 398, points 23–25.

411 2011 Resolution, n 398, point 25.

412 2011 Resolution, n 398, point 26. See also points 21–22 regarding e-commerce and distance-selling contracts.

413 Report, n 402, Explanatory Statement,15.

414 2011 Resolution, n 398, point 30.

415 See 2011 Resolution, n 398, points 31–36.

416 2011 Resolution, n 398, point 41. See also recital T.

417 Opinion of the Committee on the Internal Market and Consumer Protection, dated 22 March 2011, in the Report, n 402, 17, 19 (point 9).

6.4.2.4 *Stakeholder responses to the 2010 Green Paper*

The Commission did not issue a specific document on the stakeholder responses to the 2010 Green Paper, but eventually included a brief summary in the 2011 Feasibility Study[418] and the Impact Assessment accompanying the proposed CESL,[419] which are discussed further below. Responses were submitted by most Member States, and business organizations constituted the largest percentage, as compared to legal practitioners, consumer organizations, and academics.[420] This included responses from several academic projects, such as the *Association Henri Capitant*, Gandolfi Group, and Insurance Group.[421]

According to the Commission's summary, there was support for *Option 1* (*publication of the Expert Group results*) and *Option 2* (*toolbox*), but not so much for *Option 3* (*Commission Recommendation*), *Option 5* (*minimum harmonization Directive*), and *Option 7* (*European civil code*). For *Option 4* (*optional instrument*), the responses were 'more varied': several Member States and a considerable number of other stakeholders supported an optional instrument provided that it fulfilled certain conditions (eg, it had a high level of consumer protection and a clear and user-friendly nature), whereas a large number of Member States and business organizations did not want to take a position because they did not know the details of this option and the work of the Expert Group; still other stakeholders expressed a preference for *Option 6* (*Regulation*). As regards the scope of the instrument, most respondents only expressed opinions on *Option 2* (*toolbox*), the majority of which wanted it to be as comprehensive as possible (ie it should not be restricted to certain types of contracts and should have a broad scope) and *Option 4* (*optional instrument*), the majority of which appeared to favour an instrument focused on B2C contracts. [422]

Missing from this summary, however, was mention of the stakeholders' remarks on Union competence in relation to the proposed options.[423] Taking a look at the stakeholders' individual responses, two common themes stood out. First, there was considerable discussion across the stakeholder groups of the Commission's assertions concerning the impact of diverging national contract laws on the internal market.[424] Many respondents questioned the contribution to be made by a future European

[418] Commission, 'A European contract law for consumers and businesses: Publication of the results of the feasibility study carried out by the Expert Group on European contract law for stakeholders' and legal practitioners' feedback', not dated, available at n 46 (2011 Feasibility Study) 2–3. See further § 6.4.3.

[419] CESL Impact Assessment, n 390, point 1.3.1, at 5–6; Annex I, point 1.3.1, at 59–60. These two summaries are largely the same.

[420] See CESL Impact Assessment, n 390, Annex I, point 1.3.1, at 59; see also 2011 Feasibility Study, n 418, Annex II (providing figures on consultation by type of stakeholder and by origin).

[421] The stakeholders' responses are currently available at the Commission's website, n 46.

[422] CESL Impact Assessment, n 390, point 1.3.1, at 5; Annex I, point 1.3.1, at 59.

[423] There were other interesting aspects of the responses that did not make it into the Commission's summary, such as the advocacy of an option not mentioned in the 2010 Green Paper relating to a European instrument on, or EU-wide promotion of, standard contract terms (see, eg, Response of the *Association Henri Capitant*; Response of the Law Society of England and Wales) and the assertion that the US could not serve as an example given various differences with the EU (see, eg, Response of the Republic of Cyprus; Response of the Max Planck Institute for Comparative and International Private Law (published in (2011) 75 *RabelsZ* 371, 386)).

[424] In the time between the issuance of the 2010 Green Paper and the deadline for the responses, the Commission carried out some additional surveys: the SME Panel Survey on the Impacts of European Contract Law (Oct–Dec 2010) and the European Business Test Panel (EBTP) Survey (26 Nov 2010–23 Dec 2010), available at n 46. Both indicated that contract law-related obstacles were an important barrier to cross-border trade. In particular, the EBTP survey was discussed in certain responses to the 2010 Green Paper, with some scepticism about the methodology used.

contract law instrument for furthering cross-border trade, especially as far as B2B transactions and the utility of an optional instrument were concerned,[425] whereas some took the opposite view.[426] Secondly, as a related point, emphasis was put on the need to consider the question of legal basis and compliance with the principles of subsidiarity and proportionality in connection with a future European contract law instrument,[427] especially the optional instrument.[428] In this regard, several contributions doubted whether the optional instrument could be based on Article 114 TFEU, since it did not 'approximate' national contract laws within the meaning of the Court's case law.[429] Both themes carried over to subsequent events concerning the 2011 Feasibility Study.

6.4.3 The Expert Group and the 2011 Feasibility Study

On 26 April 2010, the Commission adopted a Decision setting up an Expert Group on a Common Frame of Reference in the area of European contract law.[430] According to this Decision, the Expert Group was to assist the Commission in preparing a proposal for a CFR in the area of European contract law, using the DCFR as a starting point and taking into account other research conducted in this area and the Union *acquis*, and in particular, to help the Commission select those parts of the DCFR that were of direct or indirect relevance for contract law and to restructure, revise, and supplement the selected contents.[431] In other words, the Group's main task was to conduct a 'feasibility study' on a future European contract law instrument.[432] It was viewed as a 'feasibility

[425] As regards the Member States, see, eg, Response of the Belgian Delegation; Response of the Republic of Cyprus; Response of the French Delegation; Response of the German Federal Government (in respect of the optional instrument); Response of Ireland; Response of the Swedish Government; Response of the UK Government. As regards practitioners, see, eg, Response of the Law Society of England and Wales; Response of the Law Society of Ireland; Response of Allen & Overy; Response of Clifford Chance; Response of Linklaters. As regards consumer organizations, see, eg, Response of the BEUC; Response of the European Consumer Consultative Group (ECCG). As regards business organizations, see, eg, Response of the American Chamber of Commerce to the EU; Response of the Federation of Small Businesses.

[426] See, eg, Response of the Finland Chamber of Commerce (which discussed additional surveys supporting these assertions); Response of Luxembourg; Response of the Scottish Law Commission (which discussed evidence gathered by its Business Advisory Group); Response of the European Small Business Alliance; Response of e-Bay.

[427] As regards the Member States, see, eg, Response of the Republic of Cyprus; Response of the Czech Republic; Response of the German Federal Government; Response of the Netherlands. As regards academics, see, eg, Response of the Working Group on European Private Law of the University of Luxembourg. As regards business organizations, see, eg, Response of the Financial Markets Law Committee.

[428] As regards the Member States, see, eg, Response of the French Delegation; Response of Ireland, point 21; Response of the UK Government, points 22–25. As regards practitioners, see, eg, Response of the Law Society of England and Wales; Response of Allen & Overy; Response of Clifford Chance.

[429] See, eg, Response of the French Delegation; Response of the Max Planck Institute for Comparative and International Private Law; Response of the Bar Council of England and Wales; Response of the Law Society of England and Wales; Response of the BEUC; Response of the Financial Markets Law Committee.

[430] Commission Dec 2010/233/EU of 26 April 2010 setting up the Expert Group on a Common Frame of Reference in the area of European contract law, [2010] OJ L105/109.

[431] Dec 2010/233/EU, n 430, eighth recital; Art 2. Under Art 5(2), sub-groups could be created to examine specific questions under the terms of reference established by the Expert Group. This was taken up, with sub-groups devoted to, eg, scope-related issues, consumer protection rules, and services contracts. See Commission Synthesis of the fifth meeting, 30 Sept–1 Oct 2010, first–third paras, at 2; Commission Synthesis of the eighth meeting, 20–21 Dec 2010, point VI, at 4.

[432] 2011 Feasibility Study, n 418, 5. See also Commission Synthesis of the first meeting, 21 May 2010, second para, at 1.

exercise' since it did not prejudge the decision on the need and/or legal form of such an instrument to be taken by the Commission following the public consultation on the 2010 Green Paper,[433] and therefore, the Expert Group was to work on an 'as if' basis with a view to drafting a study that could be used in different scenarios.[434] This was so although the Expert Group was asked to work exclusively on the assumption of an optional instrument.[435]

According to the Commission's Decision, the Expert Group was to be composed of up to twenty members, with outstanding competence in civil law, with special regard to contract law, drawn from the categories of academia, legal practitioners, and civil society.[436] As it turned out, it comprised seventeen experts, the majority of which were academics.[437] This may in part explain the reason for the establishment in July 2010 of the Key Stakeholder Experts Group or the so-called 'Sounding Board', composed of representatives of consumer organizations, businesses (including SMEs), and the legal profession, which met on a monthly basis to provide input on the Expert Group's work.[438]

The Expert Group held monthly meetings, chaired by the Commission, from May 2010 to mid-April 2011.[439] At the end of April 2011, the Expert Group delivered its feasibility study to the Commission.[440]

On 3 May 2011, the Commission published this study as an annex to a document providing further background on the Expert Group's work and asking for feedback from interested parties (2011 Feasibility Study).[441] In doing so, the Commission

[433] 2011 Feasibility Study, n 418, 1. Yet, difficulties associated with drafting rules without knowing the nature or form of the legal instrument were alluded to at certain meetings: see, eg, Commission Synthesis of the second meeting, 24 June 2010, 2; Commission Synthesis of the third meeting, 22–23 July 2010, point 7.

[434] 2011 Feasibility Study, n 418, 5. But see Commission Synthesis of the fourth meeting, 1–2 Sept 2010, first para, at 1.

[435] Commission Synthesis of the fourth meeting, 1–2 Sept 2010, first para, at 1. This point was not mentioned in the Commission's discussion of the mandate of the Expert Group in its document on the results of the feasibility study: see 2011 Feasibility Study, n 418.

[436] Dec 2010/233/EU, n 430, seventh, ninth recitals; Art 4(1)–(4).

[437] See Commission document, 'The composition of the Expert Group on European contract law', available at n 46; it was also published as Annex I of the 2011 Feasibility Study, n 418. Professors Bénédicte Fauvarque-Cosson and Christian von Bar (chairman of the Study Group) were appointed as special advisers to Commissioner Viviane Reding to give advice on the conclusions of the Expert Group's work: see Press Release for the Expert Group's first meeting, Brussels, 21 May 2010, IP/10/595, p 3 (this was indicated in prior versions of the above Commission document, but was later removed). Of the seventeen members, twelve (or thirteen) were mainly professors from various universities in the EU: (1) Hugh Beale; (2) Eric Clive; (3) Fernando Gomez; (4) Luc Grynbaum; (5) Martijn Hesselink; (6) Miklos Kiraly; (7) Irene Kull; (8) Paulo Mota Pinto; (9) Jerzy Pisulinski; (10) Hans Schulte-Nölke; (11) Jules Stuyck; and (12) Anna Veneziano (initially, Professor Simon Whittaker had been a member, but subsequently withdrew), several of which were members of academic projects involved with European contract or private law, such as the Study Group (eg, Professors Beale, Clive, Hesselink, Kull, and Veneziano) or the Acquis Group (eg, Professors Grynbaum, Mota Pinto, Pisulinski, and Schulte-Nölke). Of the remaining 5 members, 3 could be considered to fall into the practitioner category: (1) Torgny Håstad (Judge of the Swedish Supreme Court until Dec 2010 and Professor at a Swedish university); (2) Pierre Levêque (lawyer at the Paris Bar); and (3) Ioana Lambrina Vidican (notary in Bucharest), and 2 from civil society: (1) Suzanne Czech (trade association); and (2) Bob Schmitz (consumer organization).

[438] 2011 Feasibility Study, n 418, 3. A list of the organizations comprising this Group and summaries of nine meetings held from 7 Sept 2010 to 12 April 2011 are available at n 46. The list of members and a brief summary of the subjects of each meeting were included as Annex III to the 2011 Feasibility Study, n 418.

[439] See Dec 2010/233/EU, n 430, Art 5(1). Summaries of twelve monthly meetings held from 21 May 2010 to 13–15 April 2011 are available at n 46.

[440] See n 46.

[441] 2011 Feasibility Study, n 418. It was divided into five main parts: (1) the context for the study; (2) the practical relevance of differences in national contract laws; (3) the mandate of the Expert

underlined the linkage between the European contract law project and the internal market. For instance, it devoted a specific section to offering examples of how differences between national contract laws could lead in practice to additional transaction costs and increased legal uncertainty for businesses and consumers' lack of confidence when they shop across borders.[442] In any event, the bulk of this document constituted the Expert Group's feasibility study, which strived 'to constitute a complete set of contract law rules covering those issues which, at a practical level, are relevant in a contractual relationship in the internal market'.[443] It was divided into eight parts, composed of one or more chapters or a total of 189 Articles, concerning: (1) introductory provisions; (2) making a binding contract; (3) assessing what is in the contract; (4) obligations and remedies of the parties to a sales contract; (5) obligations and remedies of the parties to a related services contract; (6) damages, stipulated payments for non-performance, and interest; (7) restitution; and (8) prescription.[444] This text would serve as a 'toolbox' for the Commission in preparing a possible future initiative on European contract law.[445]

The Commission provided for a period of about two months for interested parties to submit feedback on the study and in particular on seven questions concerning certain Articles and general issues of approach.[446] It received 120 responses.[447] Although it did not issue a specific document on these contributions, it offered a brief summary in subsequent documents concerning the proposed CESL, noting that the majority of comments were broadly grouped around three main issues: its user-friendliness, the balance between business and consumer interests, and legal certainty.[448] It also indicated that the majority of respondents replied positively to the question whether digital content should be included.[449] Although space precludes detailed inquiry of each contribution,[450] some respondents reiterated issues raised in connection with the 2010 Green Paper concerning the need for sufficient evidence to support the Commission's assertions of problems caused by divergences between national contract laws in the internal market and the lack of discussion of the legal basis to support Union action in this area.[451]

Group; (4) the text of the feasibility study; and (5) the next steps. There were also four annexes concerning: (1) the composition of the Expert Group; (2) statistical analysis of the responses to the 2010 Green Paper; (3) the composition and meetings of the Stakeholder Expert Group; and (4) the text of the feasibility study prepared by the Expert Group (which contained two annexes (a) and (b), providing information on the exercise of the right of withdrawal and a standard withdrawal form).

[442] 2011 Feasibility Study, n 418, 3. [443] 2011 Feasibility Study, n 418, 8.

[444] 2011 Feasibility Study, n 418, Annex II; see also 7–8 (providing a summary of each part, albeit inadvertently labelling the last three parts on damages, restitution, and prescription as Pt VI). For detailed discussion, see, eg, *Towards a European Contract Law*, n 352.

[445] 2011 Feasibility Study, n 418, 8. This led to the production of several Commission 'working drafts' that modified the Expert Group's text, but apparently without it being consulted: see E Hondius, 'Towards an Optional Common European Sales Law' (2011) 19 *ERPL* 709, 711. The first working draft was referred to as the '8 July 2011 draft', but was not publicly available. The second working draft was titled 'Contract Law, Work in Progress, Version of 19 August 2011' and is currently available at n 46.

[446] See 2011 Feasibility Study, n 418, 8–9 (from 3 May to 1 July 2011).

[447] Commission Communication, A Common European Sales Law to Facilitate Cross-Border Transactions in the Single Market, COM (2011) 636 final, 11.10.2011 (CESL Communication) point 1.2, at 6. The Commission's website (n 46) currently indicates that it received 106 contributions, which are available in spreadsheet form. This discrepancy may be an inadvertent error or due to the fact that some contributions were not made publicly available.

[448] CESL Communication, n 447, point 1.2, at 6. See also CESL Impact Assessment, n 390, point 1.3.1, at 6. [449] CESL Communication, n 447, point 1.2, at 6.

[450] For further discussion, see, eg, W Bull, 'Expert Group Feasibility Study on European contract law' (2011) 18 *MJ* 392.

[451] See, eg, Response of the Permanent Representation of France to the EU; Response of the UK Government; Response of the Bar Council of England and Wales; Response of Allen & Overy;

6.4.4 The Proposal for a Regulation on a Common European Sales Law

On 11 October 2011, the Commission issued the proposal for a Regulation on a Common European Sales Law (proposed CESL),[452] which is accompanied by a Communication[453] and an extensive Impact Assessment.[454] The proposed CESL represents an optional instrument comprising a comprehensive set of contract rules for consumer and commercial transactions based on the 'toolbox' developed by the Expert Group and the 'Sounding Board' and further input received from stakeholders and experts.[455] It is spread across the sixteen Articles of the Regulation, which set forth the definitions and certain general and final provisions (eg, on its aim, scope, and use) and an Annex, which contains the text of the instrument, composed of 186 Articles that are organized into eight parts (with two appendices) resembling the 2011 Feasibility Study.[456] In short, it is the first legislative initiative for a European contract law instrument and constitutes a crucial culmination stage in the debate.

The proposed CESL has several key features.[457] As indicated by its name, it would establish a 'common European' contract law regime in all Member States focused on 'sales' contracts (including those for the supply of digital content and for related services). It would be optional, meaning that the choice to use the proposed CESL would be voluntary for traders and consumers under an opt-in system. As far as its scope of application is concerned, it would cover B2C and B2B contracts where at least one party is an SME (with an option for Member States to extend its application to B2B contracts where neither trader is an SME), be limited to cross-border transactions (with an option for the Member States to extend its application to domestic transactions), and encompass issues of contract law deemed to be of practical relevance during the life cycle of a cross-border contract, with residual aspects of contract law and non-contractual matters governed by the applicable national rules.[458] It would also have an international dimension, since in order to be applicable, it would be sufficient that only one party is established in a Member State and hence it could be used in contracts involving parties established outside the EU. In order to ensure its effective application and uniform interpretation, several 'flanking' measures are envisioned: the development of European model contract terms for specialist areas of trade or sectors of activity, a publicly accessible database of European and national judicial decisions, and training sessions for practitioners.[459] As such, the proposal embodies two proposed solutions stemming from the Commission's previous Communications on European contract

Response of Clifford Chance. Certain respondents considered the term 'feasibility study' to be a misnomer, since it contained a draft code of contract law without any evidence or discussion as to whether it would work in practice: see, eg, Response of the Bar Council of England and Wales; Response of the City of London Law Society.

[452] Proposal for a Regulation of the European Parliament and of the Council on a Common European Sales Law, COM (2011) 635 final, 11.10.2011 (CESL Proposal).

[453] CESL Communication, n 447.

[454] CESL Impact Assessment, n 390. See also Commission Staff Working Paper, Executive Summary of the Impact Assessment, SEC (2011) 1166 final, 11.10.2011.

[455] CESL Communication, n 447, point 2.1, at 7.

[456] For a summary, see CESL Proposal, n 452, Explanatory Memorandum, point 5.

[457] CESL Communication, n 447, point 2.1.

[458] See in the latter regard CESL Proposal, n 452, twenty-sixth–twenty-eighth recitals; Explanatory Memorandum, point 1, at 6. The proposed CESL envisages a review of its operation after five years, which would take account of, inter alia, the need to extend its application in relation to B2B contracts: see thirty-fifth recital; Art 15(2).

[459] CESL Communication, n 447, point 2.4.

law, that of an optional instrument of contract law and the promotion of EU-wide standard contract terms.

Not surprisingly, the proposed CESL has attracted an immense literature on various aspects and from various perspectives.[460] For this discussion, three related points stand out in respect of its constitutionality. First, its legal basis is Article 114 TFEU, with the overall objective to improve the establishment and functioning of the internal market by making available to parties a uniform set of contract law rules, thereby facilitating the expansion of cross-border trade for businesses and consumers, while at the same time ensuring a high level of consumer protection.[461] The Commission presents several arguments to justify the proposed CESL under this provision, which are generally focused on alleged obstacles to trade on account of divergences between national contract laws; there is no mention of 'appreciable' distortions of competition in this regard.[462]

In the Explanatory Memorandum, the Commission affirms that differences between national contract laws hinder traders and consumers who want to engage in cross-border trade and that contract law-related obstacles are among the top barriers to such trade based on certain surveys.[463] The need for traders to adapt to the different national contract laws that may apply in cross-border dealings makes cross-border trade more complex and costly compared to domestic trade in respect of B2C and B2B transactions.[464] Additional transaction costs for traders in cross-border situations include difficulties in finding out about the applicable foreign contract law, obtaining legal advice, negotiating the applicable law in B2B transactions, and adapting contracts to the requirements of the consumer's law in B2C transactions.[465] These costs and the complexity caused by differences in contract law dissuade traders, particularly SMEs, from expanding into markets of other Member States, amounting to tens of billions of euros of lost trade between Member States each year.[466] The missed opportunities for cross-border trade also have a negative impact on European consumers, since less cross-border trade results in fewer imports, and less competitiveness between traders results in more limited products at higher prices.[467] Moreover, one of the most important reasons why the majority of consumers shop domestically is on account of uncertainty about their rights in cross-border situations.[468] With the proposed CESL, traders would save on the additional transaction costs and take better advantage of the internal market. For B2C transactions, there would be no need to identify the mandatory consumer protection provisions in the consumer's law, since the proposed CESL would contain fully harmonized consumer

[460] For a brief selection, see, eg, G Alpa et al (eds), *The Proposed Common European Sales Law—the Lawyer's View* (Sellier, 2013); U Magnus (ed), *CISG vs. Regional Sales Law Unification—With a Focus on the New Common European Sales Law* (Sellier, 2012); R Schulze (ed), *Common European Sales Law (CESL) Commentary* (CH Beck/Hart/Nomos, 2012); for citations to further commentary, including special issues of several journals, see also E Hondius, 'Common European Sales Law: If It Does Not Help, It Won't Harm Either(?)' (2013) 21 *ERPL* 1.

[461] CESL Proposal, n 452, Explanatory Memorandum, point 1, at 4; point 3, at 8–9.

[462] This is not to say that the word 'appreciable' is not used: see CESL Proposal, n 452, seventh recital.

[463] CESL Proposal, n 452, Explanatory Memorandum, point 1 fn 1, at 2 (citing Eurobarometers 320 and 321).

[464] CESL Proposal, n 452, Explanatory Memorandum, point 1, at 2.

[465] CESL Proposal, n 452, Explanatory Memorandum, point 1, at 2–3.

[466] CESL Proposal, n 452, Explanatory Memorandum, point 1, at 3.

[467] CESL Proposal, n 452, Explanatory Memorandum, point 1, at 3.

[468] CESL Proposal, n 452, Explanatory Memorandum, point 1, at 3–4.

protection rules, providing consumers with greater certainty about their rights when shopping cross-border. Statements to this effect are found in the Preamble and the very first Article of the proposed CESL.[469] They are further elaborated in the accompanying Communication, which discusses additional surveys conducted on the matter.[470] They are also backed up by the Impact Assessment, which contains detailed sections on the contract law-related barriers for businesses and consumers in the internal market based on the various surveys.[471]

Secondly, the Commission takes a novel approach by basing the proposed CESL on Article 114 TFEU as a measure that approximates national law notwithstanding its optional character. In its view, the proposed CESL 'harmonises the national contract laws of the Member States not by requiring amendments to the pre-existing national contract law, but by creating within each Member State's national law a second contract law regime for contracts covered by its scope that is identical throughout the European Union and will exist alongside the pre-existing rules of national contract law'.[472] The nature of the proposed CESL as a '2nd', as opposed to what was then a '28th', regime of contract law has important implications for its relationship with the 'Rome I' Regulation as far as B2C contracts are concerned.[473] As stressed by the Commission, the agreement to use the proposed CESL is a choice between two different sets of contract law within the same national law; as a result, the limitations placed on the choice of law for consumer contracts under Article 6 of the 'Rome I' Regulation have no practical relevance in this regard, although under Art 114(3) TFEU, the proposed CESL would provide for a high level of consumer protection by establishing its own set of mandatory rules.[474] This is one of the most discussed aspects of the proposal so far,[475] and certain scholars

[469] CESL Proposal, n 452, first–eighth recitals; Art 1. As with previous measures in the EU contract law *acquis* (see Chapter 1, § 1.4.1), the claim that the proposed CESL would enhance 'consumer confidence' is presented alongside arguments concerning its aptitude for eradicating contract law-related obstacles to trade.

[470] See CESL Communication, n 447, point 1 fns 2–7, at 3. In doing so, the Commission compares the situation in the US with that in the EU, finding that for US traders, the economic area of the fifty states is 'much more of an internal market in contract law terms' than the then twenty-seven (now twenty-eight) Member States are for EU traders: CESL Communication, n 447, point 1 fn 1, at 2.

[471] See CESL Impact Assessment, n 390, points 2.3–2.4, at 10–22; Annex III ('Calculation of Opportunity and Transaction Costs'); Annex IX ('Ranking of Barriers to Trade'). It has been mentioned as part of various parliamentary questions on the CESL and the Commission's responses thereto: see, eg, Written Question E-000098/2012 by M Flašiková Beňová, 'Common sales law', available at n 46; Written Questions E-008066/2012 and E-008067/2012 by A Fox, 'Common European Sales Law', available at n 46.

[472] CESL Proposal, n 452, Explanatory Memorandum, point 3, at 8. This is reiterated in the text of the CESL Proposal, n 452, ninth recital.

[473] As defined in the discourse, under a so-called '28th regime', an optional instrument is an additional contract law outside the national legal system that parties may choose in accordance with private international law rules as with any other national contract law, whereas under a '2nd regime', an optional instrument is an additional contract law inside the national legal system, with the result that the private international law rules indicating the applicable law come first. See, eg, R Schulze (ed), *Common European Sales Law (CESL) Commentary* (CH Beck/Hart, 2012) 30–34; G Rühl, 'The Common European Sales Law: 28th Regime, 2nd Regime or 1st Regime' (2012) 19 *MJ* 148. Presumably, this would now be a '29th regime': see n 23.

[474] CESL Proposal, n 452, Explanatory Memorandum, point 1, at 6; point 3, at 9. This is stated in the text of the CESL Proposal, n 452, tenth–twelfth recitals.

[475] See, eg, C Bisping, 'The Common European Sales Law, Consumer Protection and Overriding Mandatory Provisions in Private International Law' (2013) 62 *ICLQ* 463; H Eidenmüller et al, 'The proposal for a Regulation on a common European sales law: deficits of the most recent textual layer of European contract law' (2012) 16 *Edin L Rev* 301, 312–322; M Kenny et al, 'The EU Optional Instrument: Absorbing the Private International Law Implications of a Common European Sales Law' (2011) 13 *YPIL* 315; S Whittaker, 'The Proposed "Common European Sales Law": Legal

have surmised that the Commission's choice to frame the proposed CESL as a second regime is the result of its preference for the use of Article 114 TFEU as the legal basis.[476] Yet, there is no detailed discussion in the documents on the proposed CESL as to how this squares with the Court's case law or that addresses doubts in previous stakeholder responses that this provision is the proper legal basis for an optional instrument.

Nevertheless, as the final point, the novel approach embodied by the proposed CESL is linked to its compliance with the principles of subsidiarity and proportionality.[477] As regards the principle of subsidiarity, its objective—to contribute to the proper functioning of the internal market by making available a voluntary uniform set of contract law rules—has a 'clear cross-border dimension' and cannot be sufficiently achieved by the Member States in the framework of their national systems, whereas the Union is best placed to address the problems of legal fragmentation by a measure taken in the field of contract law that approximates the rules applicable to cross-border transactions.[478] As regards the principle of proportionality, the scope of the proposed CESL is confined to the aspects that pose real problems in cross-border transactions and does not extend to aspects that are best addressed by national law.[479] Its material scope is limited to provisions regulating the rights and obligations of parties during the lifecycle of the contract; its territorial scope is limited to cross-border contracts; and its personal scope is limited to transactions where the internal market problems are mainly found, ie B2C contracts and B2B contracts where at least one of the parties is an SME, as opposed to B2B contracts across the board.[480] It is also deemed to be a proportionate action on account of its voluntary and optional nature: its application is dependent on the agreement of the parties, and it is an optional regime in addition to the pre-existing contract laws without replacing them, which means that it can lower barriers to cross-border trade 'without interfering with deeply embedded national legal systems and traditions'.[481] In this way, the proposed CESL represents both 'a concrete solution for a tangible problem for businesses and consumers' in the internal market and an 'innovative approach' by preserving the Member States' laws,[482] as compared to the more intrusive and politically sensitive means of replacing the national contract laws.

The Commission stated that it would work closely with the European Parliament, Council, and national parliaments to ensure its swift agreement in time for the 20th anniversary of the single market in 2012.[483] At the time of writing, however, it is undergoing discussion by the other Union institutions and bodies, and many national parliaments have already given their feedback. Each is discussed further below.

Framework and the Agreement of the Parties' (2012) 75 *MLR* 578, 587–595. The level of consumer protection in the proposed CESL is also controversial (see, eg, n 497), and has attracted parliamentary questions (see, eg, Written Question E-003803/2012 by E Regner and J Weidenholzer, 'Greater consumer protection through a regulation on a Common European Sales Law?', available at n 46; Written Question E-008067/2012, n 471).

[476] See, eg, 'Editorial Comments: A Common European Sales Law (CESL) ahead?' (2012) 49 *CML Rev.* 1267, 1275–1276; Eidenmüller et al, n 475, 317–318.

[477] See also CESL Proposal, n 452, Explanatory Memorandum, point 5, at 11 ('simplification' of the legal environment).

[478] CESL Proposal, n 452, Explanatory Memorandum, point 3, at 9; see also CESL Impact Assessment, n 390, point 2.5, at 22.

[479] CESL Proposal, n 452, Explanatory Memorandum, point 3, at 10.

[480] CESL Proposal, n 452, Explanatory Memorandum, point 3, at 10.

[481] CESL Proposal, n 452, Explanatory Memorandum, point 3, at 10. See also CESL Communication, n 447, point 2.2, at 9.

[482] CESL Communication, n 447, point 3, first para.

[483] CESL Communication, n 447, point 3, second para.

6.4.4.1 *Opinions of the national parliaments*

In line with the procedure introduced by the Lisbon Treaty,[484] the national parliaments scrutinized the proposed CESL for its compliance with the principle of subsidiarity. The national parliaments of twenty Member States submitted opinions,[485] and of those, reasoned opinions were issued by national parliaments from Austria, Belgium, Germany, and the UK on account of its purported non-compliance with this principle.[486] Although this did not rise to the requisite threshold for review of the proposal under the so-called 'yellow card' procedure set forth in the Treaties,[487] these reasoned opinions likely carried some weight in the political dialogue on the proposal and drew attention to key issues concerning its constitutionality. In particular, several reasoned opinions challenged the Commission's assertions that differences between national contract laws pose real obstacles impeding cross-border transactions in the internal market,[488] and most of them doubted whether Article 114 TFEU is a proper legal basis because the envisaged instrument does not 'approximate' national laws in light of the Court's judgment in the *European Cooperative Society* case[489] and thus contemplated the use of Article 352 TFEU instead.[490] Several national parliaments that issued critical responses, albeit not formal objections, to the proposed CESL also put forward similar views, asserting that it is not an approximation measure and could not be based on Article 114 TFEU.[491]

[484] See further Chapter 7, § 7.4.3.3.

[485] They are available at the IPEX website, <http://www.ipex.eu/>. The deadline for scrutiny of the proposed CESL was 12 Dec 2011, but certain national parliaments issued opinions after that date. The national parliaments of the then seven remaining Member States (Cyprus, Denmark, Estonia, Greece, Hungary, Latvia, and Slovenia) and Croatia, which acceded to the EU in 2013, are listed as not having submitted an opinion.

[486] Apparently, there were five, as opposed to four, reasoned opinions, since in the case of Belgium, they were issued by the Senate and Chamber of Representatives. See Commission Report on Subsidiarity and Proportionality (19th Report on Better Lawmaking covering the year 2011), COM (2012) 373 final, 10.7.2012, Annex, point 4. This is so although the IPEX website, n 485, does not indicate that the Belgian Chamber of Representatives issued a reasoned opinion on the proposed CESL within the requisite timeframe. The proposed CESL figured among the proposals attracting the highest number of reasoned opinions in 2011. See Commission Annual Report 2011 on relations between the European Commission and National Parliaments, COM (2012) 375 final, 17.7.2012, point 3, at 5; Annex 2.

[487] See Protocol (No 2) on the application of the principles of subsidiarity and proportionality, annexed to the TEU and the TFEU, [2012] OJ C326/206, Art 7(2)–(3).

[488] See Reasoned Opinion of the Austrian Federal Council (Bundesrat) (English version), third and sixth paras, at 2–3; Reasoned Opinion of the Belgian Chamber of Representatives, p III, at 9. Reasoned Opinion of the German Bundestag (English version), point 3, at 6; Reasoned Opinion of the UK House of Commons, points 19–26, at 7–9. Compare Reasoned Opinion of the Belgian Senate, points 5.2–5.3, at 6–7.

[489] Case C-436/03 *European Parliament v Council* ('*European Cooperative Society*') [2006] ECR I-3733. See further Chapter 8, § 8.4.3.1.

[490] See Reasoned Opinion of the Austrian Federal Council (Bundesrat) (English version), fourth–fifth paras, at 2; Reasoned Opinion of the Belgian Chamber of Representatives, pt III, at 9; Reasoned Opinion of the Belgian Senate, point 5.1, at 5; Reasoned Opinion of the German Bundestag (English version), point 2, at 4. This point was not addressed in the text of the Reasoned Opinion of the UK House of Commons, but was highlighted in related documents: see House of Commons European Scrutiny Committee, Twenty-fifth Report of Session 2012–2013, point 7.5, at 53; point 7.10, at 55; point 7.15, at 56; see also n 491.

[491] See, eg, Opinion of the Senate of the Parliament of the Czech Republic (English version of the 493rd Resolution of the Senate of the Parliament of the Czech Republic, delivered on the 16th meeting held on 25 Jan 2012), pt II, point 1; Opinion of the French National Assembly, 35–37; Opinion of the UK House of Lords comprising letters between Chairman and Government dated 24 Nov 2011, 8 Dec 2011, 12 Jan 2012, and 19 Dec 2012, particularly Annex to the Letter from Government to

In its responses to some of these reasoned opinions, the Commission defended the proposed CESL, contending on the basis of the findings in relevant surveys and the Impact Assessment that differences between national contract laws amount to obstacles to cross-border trade that substantiate the need for Union action.[492] It was convinced that Article 114 TFEU is a proper legal basis, since it would reduce these obstacles, and according to the Court's case law, the Union legislature has a margin of discretion to consider the most appropriate approximation technique to achieve the intended result, thereby allowing it to adopt a measure under Article 114(1) TFEU even if that measure does not modify the pre-existing national laws. It reiterated that it brings about the approximation of national laws by introducing a second regime of contract law; once the parties to a cross-border contract have chosen the application of this second regime, the national legal orders cannot prevent this choice from producing its effects in the national legal system concerned. It referred to the Opinion of the Council Legal Service,[493] affirming that Article 114 TFEU is a proper legal basis for the proposed CESL, and hence Article 352 TFEU, a residual legal basis, need not be resorted to.[494] Furthermore, it considered that the *European Cooperative Society* case was not applicable, since the proposed CESL does not establish a new supranational legal entity superimposed on the national systems, that is to say, the parties to a cross-border contract do not choose or create a new 'European sales contract' that differs conceptually from a national sales contract and that is comparable to a new legal entity or a new intellectual property right invocable against a third party.[495]

6.4.4.2 Responses of the Union institutions and bodies

On 29 March 2012, the EESC adopted its Opinion on the proposed CESL.[496] It welcomed the Commission's intentions to facilitate the expansion of cross-border trade for businesses (especially SMEs) and encourage cross-border purchases by consumers in the internal market, but in line with its Opinion on the 2010 Green Paper, it considered that these objectives should be achieved incrementally, thereby again urging the Commission to divide up the proposed CESL with the rules on B2B and B2C contracts to be set out in two separate documents with clear timeframes for each.[497] It also underlined the need for European model contracts, which should be made available simultaneously with the publication of the Regulation.[498] Still, it was pleased that its previous proposals concerning the form (regulation) and option chosen (an

Chairman, dated 8 Dec 2011, Q9, at 13. Compare, eg, Opinion of the Portuguese Assembly, pt III, point 3, at 6.

[492] See, eg, Commission Reply to the Reasoned Opinion of the UK House of Commons, dated 27 Sept 2012, point 2(a), at 6–9, available at the House of Commons European Scrutiny Committee's website, <http://www.parliament.uk/business/committees/committees-a-z/commons-select/european-scrutiny-committee/>.

[493] Doc 7139/12, dated 16 March 2012, which is not publicly available.

[494] See, eg, Commission Reply to the Reasoned Opinion of the Belgian Senate, dated 27 Sept 2012, third–fifth paras, at 1–2.

[495] See Commission Reply to the Opinion of the Belgian Chamber of Representatives, dated 18 Oct 2012, 7 (Dutch version); 4 (French version).

[496] EESC Opinion on the CESL Proposal and Communication, [2012] OJ C181/75.

[497] EESC Opinion, n 496, points 1.1–1.2, 1.5, 4.5. There were several points that did not make it into the EESC's Opinion, which stressed the exclusion of consumer transactions in the proposed CESL for the time being: see App, points I(c)–(d). Also, the EESC pointed to the current dissatisfaction with the content of the proposed CESL by consumer organizations and SMEs: see points 1.10–1.11, 4.6–4.7, 5.1–5.2.

[498] EESC Opinion, n 496, point 1.7, third indent; point 5.3. See also App, points I(b)–(f).

optional second regime) had been taken on board, and attached great importance to the optional nature of the proposed CESL.[499] It did not delve into its constitutionality, save for pointing out that it must comply fully with the principles of subsidiarity and proportionality[500] and that it poses problems in terms of 'establishing the appropriate legal basis'.[501]

The European Parliament recently adopted its position at first reading on the proposed CESL.[502] In particular, it sets forth various amendments to limit the scope primarily to distance contracts, including online contracts, and to improve the text, eg, merging the Regulation and Annex into one consolidated instrument, clarifying the relationship with the 'Rome I' Regulation, and anchoring the development of European model contract terms and other flanking measures in the operative part.[503] So far, there is no detailed discussion of the Union's competence to adopt the proposed CESL, but the amendments appear to coincide with the Commission's views on the use of Article 114 TFEU as the legal basis.[504]

Discussion of the proposed CESL in the Council is ongoing. This includes the issue of its legal basis, but no final assessment has yet been made. At its meeting held on 27–28 October 2011, the Council held a first exchange of views on the proposed CESL, and the main points raised in the discussion included the legal basis, level of consumer protection, and complexity of embedding it into the national legal systems.[505] Thereafter, in its Report on the state of play of the proposal, the Polish Council Presidency suggested dealing with the legal basis when at least some of the content-specific issues had been settled and its economic impact had been evaluated.[506] This Report was taken into account at the Council's meeting held on 13–14 December 2011,[507] at which time several Member States requested having a general policy debate before entering into a detailed, technical debate on the proposal.[508] This prompted the issuance of a discussion paper,[509] identifying a number of general issues relating to the type of instrument (binding, non-binding, or a combination of both), its nature (optional or otherwise), and its scope (material, personal, and territorial).[510]

As mentioned above, in 2012, the Council Legal Service issued its Opinion on the legal basis of the proposed CESL,[511] concluding that Article 114 TFEU is the correct legal basis.[512] Yet, in an exchange of views on this Opinion, some Member States questioned the Commission's assertions that the differences between national contract laws have a deterrent effect on the internal market, and others expressed

499 EESC Opinion, n 496, points 1.2, 1.6, 4.3, 4.8.

500 EESC Opinion, n 496, points 1.3, 4.2.

501 EESC Opinion, n 496, point 5.4.1.

502 European Parliament Legislative Resolution of 26 Feb 2014 on the proposed CESL (P7_TA(2014)0159).

503 See Report on the proposed CESL, A7-0301/2013, dated 24 Sept 2013, Explanatory Statement, 128–132.

504 See Legislative Resolution, n 502, particularly amendments 1–2, 4, 7, 26–27.

505 Press Release, 3121st Council meeting, JHA, Luxembourg, 27–28 Oct 2011, DOC 16042/11. The proposed CESL's nature as a '2nd regime' was also cited as one of the issues for consideration by the Member State delegations the following month: see DOC 17097/11, dated 17 Nov 2011, point 4(a), at 3.

506 DOC 18353/11, dated 8 Dec 2011, point 10, at 4.

507 Press Release, 3135th Council meeting, JHA, Brussels, 13–14 Dec 2011, DOC 18498/11, 25.

508 DOC 10611/12, dated 1 June 2012, point 4.

509 DOC 7102/12, dated 12 March 2012, which is largely redacted.

510 DOC 10611/12, n 508, point 5.

511 DOC 7139/12, n 493.This document is confidential, and most of its content is redacted. The Council Legal Service issued an Opinion on the relationship between the proposed CESL and the 'Rome I' Regulation, which is publicly available: see DOC 14997/12, dated 26 Oct 2012.

512 DOC 10611/11, n 508, point 3.

doubts as to whether the proposed CESL is an approximation measure on the grounds that the creation of a new regime for sales, be it a '2nd' or a '28th' regime, constitutes an optional instrument and the diverging national laws would remain in place, unchanged.[513] Consequently, in addition to the issues covered in the discussion paper, several delegations requested that discussions be opened on the legal basis of the proposed CESL and the actual need for such an instrument, whereas others preferred to start examining the Annex first.[514]

In June 2012, the Danish Council Presidency circulated an orientation paper, summarizing the views on these specific matters,[515] as well as more general issues.[516] It then invited the Council to express its views on the way forward, including the question as to whether there was agreement among the ministers that the determination of the legal basis could await further clarification on the content and shape of the instrument.[517] A few days later, at its meeting held on 7–8 June 2012, the Council agreed that work should begin on the examination of the content of the proposal and that even though a final position on the legal basis can only be taken once the structure and scope of the proposal are clear, the Member States' diverging views on this issue should not be an obstacle to starting work on the examination of the Annex.[518] Study of the various provisions of the Annex has proceeded accordingly.

6.4.5 Ongoing reflection about specific types of contracts

In the meantime, work within the European contract law project has extended to additional areas of contract law. To date, such work concerns two specific types of contracts, insurance and cloud computing contracts. Similar to the proposed CESL, each is tied to the EU's internal market objectives and involves the establishment of an Expert Group to help the Commission formulate possible future initiatives in the area concerned.

On 17 January 2013, the Commission adopted a Decision on setting up the Expert Group on European insurance contract law.[519] Based on responses to the 2010 Green Paper, the Commission considered that the insurance sector merited in-depth analysis.[520] The Expert Group's main task is to examine whether differences between national contract laws pose an obstacle to cross-border trade in insurance products, and if so, in which specific insurance areas, and to issue a report based on its findings.[521] Thus, it remains to be seen whether its work may lead to the adoption of future measures at the European level, such as an optional instrument, modelled on the work conducted by the Insurance Group as part of the DCFR.

[513] DOC 9538/12, dated 6 June 2012, point 2, third–fourth paras.

[514] DOC 10611/12, n 508, points 5–6. See also DOC 9538/12, n 513, point 3(A), second para, at 2; DOC 9622/12, dated 6 June 2012, point 4.

[515] DOC 10611/12, n 508, pt II (points 8–18).

[516] DOC 10611/12, n 508, pt III (points 19–22).

[517] DOC 10611/12, n 508, point 24(b).

[518] Press Release, 3172nd Council meeting, JHA, Brussels, 7–8 June 2012, DOC 10760/12, 20. See also DOC 14077/12, dated 25 Sept 2012, point 1, first para.

[519] Commission Dec of 17 Jan 2013 on setting up the Commission Expert Group on a European Insurance Contract Law (2013/C 16/03), [2013] OJ C16/6. In the English language version, among others, the title may imply some sort of European initiative by virtue of the reference to 'a European Insurance Contract Law', but the name of the Expert Group is framed more generally in Art 1 as the 'Commission Expert Group on European Insurance Contract Law'.

[520] Commission Dec, n 519, fifth recital. This had been foreseen in a previous White Paper: see fourth recital.

[521] Commission Dec, n 519, seventh recital; Art 2. For recent activities, see the Commission's website, n 46.

On 18 June 2013, the Commission adopted a Decision on setting up the Expert Group on cloud computing contracts.[522] Cloud computing generally denotes the storing, processing, and use of data on remotely located computers accessed over the internet.[523] The Expert Group is tasked to help the Commission carry out complementary work on safe and fair contract terms for consumers and small firms for cloud-related issues falling outside the proposed CESL.[524] In a previous Communication, the Commission indicated that this work would ensure that other contractual questions relevant for cloud computing services can be addressed by 'a similar optional instrument approach'.[525] Along these lines, the Expert Group's work may lead to the development of EU model contract terms and an optional instrument in this area.

6.5 Conclusions

In view of the foregoing discussion, the debate about European contract law, very much like a meandering stream, continues to ebb and flow through the Union's activities traversing the internal market, consumer protection, and the AFSJ. While the Commission's 2005 and 2007 Progress Reports and its plans for the review of the consumer *acquis* may have narrowed the focus to the CFR project and the Consumer Rights Directive, more recent institutional documents, such as those culminating in the proposed CESL, indicate that one or more optional instruments and the promotion of EU model contract terms may become a reality in the near future. In short, 'all bets are off' as to the endpoint of the debate on European contract law, but at least for now, these documents attest to certain themes concerning the evolution, scope, and constitutional dimensions of European contract law.

First, the debate continues to evolve within the EU institutional framework. Despite the different positions on certain initiatives, the ongoing activities taking place within the European contract law project, such as the CFR, the Consumer Rights Directive, the proposed CESL, and future work in other areas of contract law, are orchestrated from the European level in which various actors, such as the Union institutions, Member States, and stakeholder groups, take part. As such, the need for some sort of Union action and the failure of the Member States to 'go it alone' continues to be confirmed.

Secondly, the scope of the European contract law project remains ambiguous to some extent. As far as the interplay between contract law and other fields of private law is concerned, this is aptly illustrated by the discussion of the content of the final CFR in light of the DCFR's coverage of European private law, as well as the Commission's inclusion of a 'European civil code' as a potential option for a future European contract law instrument in the 2010 Green Paper. Moreover, the Consumer Rights Directive and the proposed CESL provoke further questions concerning Union action in relation to general contract law vis-à-vis special fields, such as consumer contract law. In this

[522] Commission Dec of 18 June 2013 on setting up the Commission expert group on cloud computing contracts (2013/C 174/04), [2013] OJ C174/6.

[523] Commission Communication, Unleashing the Potential of Cloud Computing in Europe, COM (2012) 529 final, 27.9.2012, point 1, first para. See also Commission Staff Working Document, SWD (2012) 271 final, 27.9.2012, point 2, at 2–5.

[524] Commission Dec, n 522, sixth recital; Art 2. For recent activities, see the Commission's website, n 46.

[525] Communication, n 523, point 3.4.

way, while European contract law remains the focus, questions concerning its breadth and depth remain.

Finally, the constitutional dimensions of European contract law have largely remained on the sidelines in the activities taking place at the European level, particularly as regards the CFR and the proposed CESL. The Commission's 2005 and 2007 Progress Reports and its 2007 and 2010 Green Papers failed to confront constitutionality head-on, and the documentation accompanying the proposed CESL failed to provide detailed discussion as to how to reconcile the recourse to Article 114 TFEU with the Court's case law. Additionally, the occasions on which the other Union institutions have expressly addressed this subject—eg, the European Parliament's reference to Articles 114 and/or 169 TFEU in the context of its first 2006 Resolution or the exclusion of Article 81 TFEU, not to mention the rejection of the Union's competence altogether, underlying the Council's 2008 Report on the CFR—add impetus to the need for a thorough constitutional assessment. Yet, as before, whether implicitly or explicitly, the progressive array of institutional documents discussed throughout this chapter illustrate the extent to which issues concerning the EU's competence lay beneath the scenes and the Union's objectives related to the internal market, consumer protection, and judicial cooperation in civil matters became further ingrained in the debate. This sets the stage for delving into the extent of the EU's competence in these three policy fields for the purposes of European contract law in Part Three.

PART THREE

CONSTITUTIONALITY

7

The Constitutional Parameters of European Contract Law

7.1 Introduction

As illustrated in Part Two, the discussion of the EU's competence in contract law (and other fields of private law) has steadily made its way into the institutional record of the debate on European contract law. Yet, for the most part, this has occurred on an ad hoc basis, with no cohesive approach or detailed engagement with this topic so far at the European level. It is therefore the aim of this chapter to examine why this is so and to provide a clear understanding of the constitutional parameters of European contract law to lay the basis for the forthcoming chapters. This will be done in three parts concerning: first, reasons for the neglect of constitutionality at the European level; secondly, the overarching Treaty framework underpinning the constitutional assessment of European contract law; and thirdly, the constitutional parameters governing the existence and exercise of the EU's competence in European contract law, with focus placed on illuminating the roles played by the principles of conferral, subsidiarity, proportionality, and sincere cooperation in the debate and the interaction between them.

7.2 Reasons for the Neglect of Constitutionality at the European Level

Over the years, various reasons have been offered in the commentary to explain why the discussion of the EU's competence in contract law has generally remained on the sidelines of the debate at the European level. So far, such reasons largely emanate from four main arguments, which are evaluated in turn.

First, the *'political will' argument* generally posits that if there is the requisite political will on the part of the Member States for Union action in contract law (or other fields of private law), a legal basis will be found.[1] For the most part, this argument was voiced as the debate about European private law was starting up, but more recently has been used in conjunction with assumptions made about constitutionality in the sense that the political will of the Member States can make up for the purported lack of Union competence in this setting.[2] It is undoubtedly correct that the political will of the Member States is a key component in the debate and that the Member States' advocacy of a particular course of action would have a great impact in propelling the momentum of certain initiatives envisaged for European contract law forward.[3] Yet, this argument has the potential to downgrade

[1] See, eg, C Hertel, 'Preventive Consumer Protection in an Optional Instrument—A Practitioner's View' (2003) 4 *ERA Forum* 70, 73.

[2] See, eg, WH van Boom, 'European Tort Law: An Integrated or Compartmentalized Approach?' in A Vaquer (ed), *European Private Law Beyond the Common Frame of Reference: Essays in Honour of Reinhard Zimmermann* (Europa, 2008) 131, 135 fn 11.

[3] See, eg, RC van Caenegem, *European Law in the Past and the Future: Unity and Diversity over Two Millennia* (Cambridge Univ Press, 2002) 36–37.

the importance of a solid constitutional grounding for the eventual success of whatever course of action is undertaken.[4] In fact, it seems to assume that the political will of the Member States is something divorced from constitutionality when instead the two are directly related, ie the political will of the Member States can be changed in view of discussions concerning the constitutionality of Union action. Thus, this argument may to some extent provide further support for the constitutional assessment of European contract law, instead of detracting from it.

Secondly, the *'too early' argument* has been used to mean that only when a definitive proposal is on the table can the constitutional inquiry be undertaken, since doing so before such a time would be premature. This arose in certain past publications concerning a European civil code,[5] but may have relevance in the context of current activities, such as the Common Frame of Reference (CFR) and the prospect of one or more optional instruments of contract law. As regards the CFR, the Commission so far seems to have postponed delving into constitutional questions until after the process of going from the academic or draft CFR (DCFR) to the final or political CFR has been completed. Similarly, given the fact that the CFR is envisaged to lay the basis for an optional instrument of contract law, this may explain why the legal basis of such an instrument was not discussed in the Commission's 2004 Communication and had to await the elaboration of a definitive proposal, which is now on the table in the form of the proposal for a Regulation on a Common European Sales Law (proposed CESL). This argument has merit, particularly as the debate about European contract law is ongoing. Yet, again, this does not mean that the constitutionality of such initiatives cannot be aired along the way given its impact on shaping the course of the activities envisaged. Moreover, as demonstrated in Chapter 6, this argument fails to speak to the fact that key questions concerning the use of Article 114 TFEU as the legal basis of the proposed CESL have not yet been fully addressed at the European level notwithstanding the issuance of the proposal.

Thirdly, the *'no need' argument* is a more recent argument largely connected to the CFR project. It has been considered by some that if the CFR remains a 'soft', non-binding instrument, especially one that would be used by the Union institutions, then there may be less impetus to delve into issues of constitutionality.[6] Conversely, others have surmised that the Commission's plans for a non-binding CFR have been prompted in part by the alleged lack of Union competence in the field.[7] These arguments threaten to misdirect or short-change the activities of the European contract law project. They may also discount the distinction between the CFR as a non-binding instrument for lawmaking and as the basis for an optional instrument of contract law, each of which merit different constitutional inquiries.[8]

Finally, as regards the Commission's Communications, there have been specific reasons advanced by scholars[9] and at least one Commission official involved with

[4] See J Basedow, 'Codification of Private Law in the European Union: the making of a Hybrid' (2001) 9 *ERPL* 35, 43.

[5] See, eg, C von Bar, 'From Principles to Codification: Prospects for European Private Law' (2002) 8 *CJEL* 379, 387–388.

[6] See D Wallis, 'Expectations for the Final Common Frame of Reference' (2008) 9 *ERA Forum* S7, S10.

[7] See, eg, B Fauvarque-Cosson, 'The Contribution of European Jurists in the Field of Contract Law' in M Andenas et al (eds), *Liber Amicorum Guido Alpa—Private Law Beyond the National Systems* (BIICL, 2007) 363, 372; W van Gerven, 'Bringing (Private) Laws Closer at the European Level' in F Cafaggi (ed), *The Institutional Framework of European Private Law* (Oxford Univ Press, 2006) 37, 75.

[8] See further Chapter 11, § 11.4.3.

[9] See, eg, S Weatherill, 'Constitutional Issues—How Much is Best Left Unsaid?' in S Vogenauer and S Weatherill (eds), *The Harmonisation of European Contract Law: Implications for European Private Laws, Business and Legal Practice* (Hart, 2006) 89, 97–103.

the European contract law project (albeit in his private capacity)[10] to explain the Commission's reticence to confront the constitutional dimensions of European contract law. These reasons generally concern the consultative nature of the Communications, the complexity of the issues involved, and the prospect of Treaty revision. First, as regards the *consultative nature of the Communications*, the idea seems to be that since it was the Commission's intention to receive feedback from the Union institutions and other interested parties on the issues raised in the Communications, the Commission held back its own preferences.[11] With respect to the 2001 Communication and even the 2003 Action Plan, this argument has considerable weight, given the fact that much was open-ended and fluid at the time. Yet, with respect to the Commission's 2004 Communication, the 2005 and 2007 Progress Reports, and the 2010 Green Paper in which the outlines of some of the proposed solutions became more definitive, namely the preparation of the CFR and an optional instrument of contract law, the argument for holding back for the purposes of consultation gives way. Indeed, the Commission's failure to entertain or at least broach the subject of the constitutionality of these solutions in the foregoing documents served to exacerbate tensions relating to the scope of the intended action.

Secondly, as regards the *complexity* of the constitutional inquiry, the idea seems to be that given the complex issues at stake, especially as regards the EU's competence under Treaty provisions such as Article 114 TFEU, the Commission preferred to leave constitutionality aside. In truth, this is one of the most underestimated arguments of all. As will be seen in the forthcoming chapters, it is striking how many issues arise as part of the constitutional assessment of European contract law that are not clarified by the Treaties and not yet settled by the Court of Justice. Be that as it may, as one scholar surmised, this has certainly not stopped the Commission from relying on such provisions in its proposals,[12] as illustrated by the proposed CESL.

Thirdly, there was the likelihood of *Treaty revision*, making the constitutional assessment of the envisaged initiatives subject to change. This was relevant in relation to the Commission's 2001 Communication and 2003 Action Plan, which were issued while institutional developments leading to the Draft Constitutional Treaty were underway. As documented in Chapter 10, such developments could have changed matters drastically, since there were a few proposals advocating the introduction of a specific legal basis providing for the approximation of contract law (and other fields of private law) during the European Convention, but they did not succeed.[13] At present, however, given the near decade that it has taken for the completion of the institutional reforms culminating with the Lisbon Treaty, there does not seem to be much impetus for amending the Treaties further in this regard, at least for the foreseeable future.[14]

In sum, while most of the reasons used to explain the neglect of constitutionality of European contract law at the European level may have been credible early on, they have lost much of their salience at this stage of the debate and underline the importance of not putting this matter off any longer. The common theme underlying these arguments is that they minimize the role that constitutionality can play, and has played, in shaping the debate about European contract law and affecting the decisions taken by the

[10] See, eg, D Staudenmayer, 'The Commission Action Plan on European Contract Law' (2003) 11 *ERPL* 113, 116–117.

[11] This also dovetails with the 'too early' argument discussed above.

[12] See W van Gerven, 'Codifying European private law? Yes, if...!' (2002) 27 *ELR* 156, 168 fn 61.

[13] See Chapter 10, § 10.2.1.

[14] But this is not necessarily ruled out. See the third para of Declaration (No 18) in relation to the delimitation of competences, annexed to the Lisbon Treaty, [2012] OJ C326/346.

Union institutions and the opinions of the Member States and the various stakeholders as part of the process. It is somewhat remarkable that in the present constitutional climate of greater sensitivity to Union competence by building boundaries and categories to 'fence' it in, initially under the Draft Constitutional Treaty and ultimately under the Lisbon Treaty, perhaps one of the greatest issues to provoke such sensitivity in the relationship between the EU and the Member States is left unaddressed. This in turn warrants inquiry into the institutional developments surrounding the failed Draft Constitutional Treaty and the entry into force of the Lisbon Treaty for the constitutional assessment of European contract law.

7.3 The Overarching Treaty Framework

The Treaties establish the overarching framework for the constitutional assessment of European contract law. As already mentioned in the Introduction, the past Treaty framework comprising the former EU and EC Treaties was replaced by the present Treaty framework composed of the amended TEU and the TFEU brought about by the entry into force of the Lisbon Treaty.[15] In between, there lies a complex set of activities involving the European Convention and the failed Draft Constitutional Treaty, which do not as a formal matter constitute primary Union law, but have nonetheless left an indelible constitutional imprint on the debate about European contract law. This merits brief explanation.

As prompted by the Nice Treaty,[16] on 15 December 2001, the European Council adopted the Declaration on the Future of the European Union at its meeting in Laeken (Laeken Declaration),[17] which posed several questions centred around four main themes: (1) a better definition and division of competence in the EU; (2) the simplification of legal instruments; (3) more democracy, transparency, and efficiency in the EU; and (4) moving towards a Constitution for European citizens.[18] It foresaw that a Convention would be convened to examine these questions with a view to the drafting of a Constitution for Europe.[19] As a result, the Laeken Declaration heralded the Convention on the Future of Europe, also referred to as the European Convention, with a view to preparing a Treaty on a Constitution for Europe.[20] The European Convention was comprised of representatives of the Union institutions and bodies, the Member State Governments, and the national parliaments of the then fifteen Member States, as well as several candidate countries slated for eventual accession to the EU.[21] The work of the European Convention started on 28 February 2002, the date of its first inaugural meeting, and concluded on 10 July 2003, after reaching agreement on a proposed Draft

[15] See Introduction.

[16] Declaration (No 23) on the future of the Union, annexed to the Nice Treaty, [2001] OJ C80/85.

[17] Presidency Conclusions, Laeken European Council, 14–15 Dec 2001, Annex I: Laeken Declaration on the Future of the European Union, [2001] 12 EU Bulletin, point I.27 (Laeken Declaration).

[18] Laeken Declaration, n 17, Pt II. [19] Laeken Declaration, n 17, Pt III.

[20] See further K Lenaerts and P Van Nuffel (N Cambien and R Bray (eds)), *European Union Law*, 3rd edn (Sweet & Maxwell, 2011) § 4-001–§ 4-002. For an 'inside' account, see A Lamassoure, *Histoire secrète de la Convention européenne* (Albin Michel, 2004).

[21] Of the candidate countries, this included the twelve Member States that acceded to the EU in 2004 and 2007, as well as Turkey. This used to be indicated on the European Convention's official website, but at the time of writing, it appears to have been taken down; all Convention documents cited in this book are on file with the author.

Treaty establishing a Constitution for Europe (Draft Constitutional Treaty).[22] It was submitted to the President of the European Council in Rome on 18 July 2003, thus constituting the 2003 version of the Draft Constitutional Treaty.[23] It underwent further revision and was subsequently approved at the 2004 Intergovernmental Conference (IGC), resulting in the 2004 version of the Draft Constitutional Treaty.[24] It was then submitted for ratification by the Member States. As is now well-known, in 2005, France and the Netherlands rejected the Draft Constitutional Treaty, which led other Member States to postpone ratification of this Treaty, ultimately resulting in its demise.[25] A few years later, in 2007, the European Council agreed to the convening of another IGC and put forth a detailed mandate on the revision of the Treaty framework,[26] which led to the Draft Reform Treaty.[27] Final agreement on this Treaty was reached at the informal European Council meeting convened by the Portuguese Presidency in October 2007, and on 13 December 2007, the EU Heads of State of the then twenty-seven Member States signed the Lisbon Treaty.[28] The Lisbon Treaty was eventually ratified by all Member States and entered into force on 1 December 2009.[29]

In light of this chronology, there are four key components that are relevant to the constitutional assessment of European contract law. First, there is the past Treaty framework comprised of the former EU and EC Treaties. Secondly, there are the documents emanating from the European Convention, especially the various Working Groups appointed to examine certain subjects in greater detail.[30] Surprisingly, given the Laeken Declaration's emphasis on the need for a better definition and division of competence, there was no Working Group specifically devoted to this subject. Instead, there was a Working Group on 'complementary competencies', whose title was somewhat misleading in the sense that its focus was on this specific type of competence, but it

[22] This was several months after the 2003 Action Plan, issued on 12 Feb 2003. See Chapter 5, § 5.3.

[23] Draft Treaty establishing a Constitution for Europe (DCT), CONV 850/03, dated 18 July 2003 (2003 DCT). For a brief selection, see, eg, M Andenas and JA Usher (eds), *The Treaty of Nice and Beyond: Enlargement and Constitutional Reform* (Hart, 2003) pt I; O De Schutter and P Nihoul (eds), *Une Constitution pour l'Europe: Réflexions sur les transformations du droit de l'Union européenne* (Larcier, 2004); B de Witte (ed), *Ten Reflections on the Constitutional Treaty* (European University Institute, 2003); I Pernice and M Poiares Maduro (eds), *A Constitution for the European Union: First Comments on the 2003-Draft of the European Convention* (Nomos, 2004).

[24] Draft Treaty establishing a Constitution for Europe, [2004] OJ C310/1 (2004 DCT). For a brief selection, see, eg, G Amato et al (eds), *Genesis and Destiny of the European Constitution* (Bruylant, 2007); J-C Piris, *The Constitution for Europe: A Legal Analysis* (Cambridge Univ Press, 2006); DN Triantafyllou, *La Constitution de l'Union européenne selon le Traité de Rome de 2004*, 2nd edn (Bruylant, 2005).

[25] See further *Genesis and Destiny of the European Constitution*, n 24, pt II; Piris, n 24, 5–37.

[26] IGC 2007 Mandate, CONV 11218/07, dated 26 June 2007.

[27] Draft Treaty amending the Treaty on European Union and the Treaty establishing the European Community, CIG 4/07, dated 24 July 2007 (Draft Reform Treaty).

[28] Treaty of Lisbon amending the Treaty on European Union and the Treaty establishing the European Community, [2007] OJ C306/1; consolidated versions of the Treaty on European Union (TEU), [2012] OJ C326/13, and the Treaty on the Functioning of the European Union (TFEU), [2012] OJ C326/47. See Presidency Conclusions, Brussels European Council, 14 Dec 2007, DOC 16616/1/07REV1, dated 14 Feb 2008, point 3.

[29] For detailed discussion, see, eg, J-C Piris, *The Lisbon Treaty—A Legal and Political Analysis* (Cambridge Univ Press, 2010) ch 1.

[30] The list of Working Groups is as follows: Working Group I Subsidiarity, Working Group II Charter/ECHR, Working Group III Legal Personality, Working Group IV National Parliaments, Working Group V Complementary Competencies, Working Group VI Economic Governance, Working Group VII External Action, Working Group VIII Defence, Working Group XI Simplification, Working Group X Freedom, Security and Justice, and Working Group XI Social Europe.

delved into other provisions, such as what are now Articles 114 and 352 TFEU, beyond this limited category. Likewise, there was a Working Group devoted to 'subsidiarity', although to some extent the principle of proportionality came into play. The Area of Freedom, Security and Justice (AFSJ) had its own Working Group, which constituted the funnel for discussion and proposed amendment of what is now Article 81 TFEU. The documents from these three Working Groups are the source of much of the discussion concerning the various Treaty provisions relevant to the constitutionality of European contract law.[31]

Thirdly, there are the texts of the 2003 and 2004 versions of the Draft Constitutional Treaty. The recommendations of the various Working Groups filtered into the 2003 version of the Draft Constitutional Treaty, which was then further amended by the 2004 version of the Draft Constitutional Treaty. In large part, the substance of the two versions is the same, but there are differences between them, as highlighted in the analysis of some of the Treaty provisions under discussion. Finally, there is the present Treaty framework comprising the TEU and the TFEU, representing the changes brought about by the Lisbon Treaty. The Lisbon Treaty took up much, though not all, of the proposed changes advanced by the Draft Constitutional Treaty.[32] The amendments introduced by the Lisbon Treaty to the relevant Treaty provisions and the overarching principles governing Union competence are of crucial importance for the constitutional assessment of European contract law. Accordingly, all four components are taken into account in the discussion where relevant, although emphasis is placed on the present Treaty framework. This is so even though the components other than the TEU and the TFEU do not, or no longer, constitute primary Union law. The former EU and EC Treaties provide the basis on which to understand the changes brought about by the Lisbon Treaty. The European Convention and the failed Draft Constitutional Treaty shed light on the perceptions of the Treaty framers and various institutional actors as regards the interpretation of the Treaty provisions and principles under discussion, which paved the way to the Lisbon Treaty.

7.4 The Principles of Conferral, Subsidiarity, Proportionality, and Sincere Cooperation

7.4.1 General overview

To recall, in Chapter 1, the term 'constitutionality' and related terms with the 'constitutional' designation were generally defined as denoting inquiry into the existence and exercise of the Union's competence in contract law, thereby encompassing the principles of conferral, subsidiarity, proportionality, and sincere cooperation, with the caveat that these principles would be explored in greater detail in this chapter since they raised complex questions concerning their relationship, as well as differences with the American constitutional framework, which were more appropriate to be dealt with together here.[33] Therefore, the constitutional parameters of European contract law centre on the roles played by these four principles.

[31] This is so although the work of other Working Groups is taken into account on occasion, eg, with respect to Open Method of Coordination in Chapter 11, § 11.4.1.

[32] For a brief selection, see, eg, D Ashiagbor et al (eds), *The European Union After the Treaty of Lisbon* (Cambridge Univ Press, 2012); A Biondi et al (eds), *EU Law After Lisbon* (Oxford Univ Press, 2012); P Craig, *The Lisbon Treaty—Law, Politics and Treaty Reform* (Oxford Univ Press, 2010); Piris, n 29.

[33] See Chapter 1, § 1.2.1.

As demonstrated by the debate, there are certain secondary elements that feed into the constitutional parameters of European contract law. As a general matter, they comprise the following six elements: (1) the potential *forms of Union and/or Member State action* inside and outside the Treaty framework, ranging from approximation and optional instruments pursuant to a particular provision of the Treaty to voluntary harmonization *à la américaine* (eg, uniform laws) and intergovernmental cooperation among the Member States (eg, an intergovernmental treaty entered into by the Member States); (2) the *legal instrument(s)* used, which include those falling inside or outside the Treaty framework (eg, a regulation or an intergovernmental treaty); (3) the *method of application* denoting the compulsory and/or optional (opt-in and/or opt-out) character of the instrument(s) or other form of action envisaged; (4) the *material scope of application* of the particular instrument, denoting the fields or sub-fields of contract law covered (and though outside the scope of this discussion, other fields of private law related to contract law as part of the debate); (5) the *territorial scope of application* of the particular instrument in terms of covering cross-border and/or domestic transactions among the Member States, as well as transactions involving States outside the EU, as in the case of the proposed CESL; and (6) the *personal scope of application* of the particular instrument in terms of the specific kinds of private and/or public parties involved, as illustrated by the proposed CESL's application to business-to-consumer (B2C) contracts and business-to-business (B2B) contracts where at least one of the parties is a Small and Medium-sized Enterprise (SME); this could likewise include the Union institutions in their contractual dealings, and with the ongoing discussion of the CFR as an instrument for lawmaking purposes, this could predicate that instrument's application to certain Union institutions alone. While additional elements could certainly be postulated, it is mainly these six elements that provide the contours for potential action contemplated on the part of the EU and/or the Member States thus far in the debate about European contract law.

These secondary elements are emphasized here because they amplify the application of the principles of conferral, subsidiarity, proportionality, and sincere cooperation in various ways. For example, this is illustrated by the interplay between the principle of conferral (ie the legal basis requirement) and the scope of application of a European contract law instrument to cross-border and domestic transactions, or that between the principles of subsidiarity and proportionality and the choice of legal instruments resorted to. Overall, the constitutional parameters of European contract law can be said to encompass the inquiry into these various elements, and thus, they will be incorporated within the discussion concerning the scope of the Union's competence pursuant to the particular Treaty provisions and certain alternative or complementary forms of Member State action in the forthcoming chapters.

Nevertheless, these secondary elements are highlighted at the outset for two reasons. The first reason is that they show that the constitutional assessment of European contract law takes place on several levels simultaneously, in which the constitutional parameters and these secondary elements are interrelated and interdependent. This has the result that decisions taken for one component implicate, even dictate, the choices made for the others. A classic example concerns the use of Article 114 TFEU for the adoption of a European contract law instrument: recourse to this Treaty provision, among other things, excludes the adoption of an optional instrument to the extent that it falls outside the ambit of approximation as discussed in Chapter 8. The second reason is that these elements make apparent the entangled relationship among these four principles. The majority of these elements implicate issues that bear as much on the existence of Union competence as its exercise. For instance, the choice concerning the legal instrument to be used (regulation, directive, etc), the method of application (opt-in, opt-out, and/or compulsory), the material scope of application (what fields of contract law or other fields of private law for that matter should be covered), and the territorial scope (cross-border and/or domestic contract transactions) speak to the legal basis requirement and to the principles of subsidiarity and proportionality. As such, these elements demonstrate the difficulties in parsing out these principles governing the Union's competence and hence identifying the roles to be played by each in this setting.

Altogether, the principles of conferral, subsidiarity, proportionality, and sincere cooperation share a somewhat different lineage, but either originally[34] or eventually[35] came to be explicitly set forth in Title I of the TEU housing several principles underpinning the Union legal order.[36] The first three principles are presented in 'cascading' form in successive paragraphs of Article 5 TEU, the idea being that the principle of conferral regulates the existence of Union competence; subsidiarity regulates whether the competence so conferred should be exercised by the Union or left to the Member States; and proportionality regulates how the competence so conferred should be exercised by the Union in terms of the intensity of the action.[37] Then, depending upon the choices made as regards whether the Member States or the Union should take the action envisaged pursuant to the conferral-subsidiarity-proportionality calculus, this is followed up by the principle of sincere cooperation set forth in Article 4(3) TFEU, which among other things makes clear that the Member States are under an obligation to cooperate among themselves and with the Union in achieving the objectives of the particular action.

When it comes to European contract law, however, the relationship between these principles becomes far less fixed. Depending upon the way they are viewed, conferral starts to bleed into subsidiarity and proportionality; subsidiarity and proportionality become very difficult to distinguish; and the principle of sincere cooperation transcends its role as a mere 'follow-up' provision. Certainly, this may arise in other settings as well, but the constitutional dimensions of European contract law uniquely bear this out. On the negative side, this makes pinning down the meaning and operation of these principles particularly challenging. Yet, on the positive side, exploring how these principles operate in relation to European contract law exposes several provocative issues

[34] The principle of sincere (or loyal) cooperation was an original fixture of the EEC Treaty inscribed in ex Art 5 EEC, later Art 10 EC (now Art 4(3) TEU).

[35] The principles of conferral, subsidiarity, and proportionality as 'fundamental' (see, eg, Lenaerts and Van Nuffel, n 20, § 7-008) or 'constitutional' principles governing the division of competences between the EU and the Member States were first introduced in the Maastricht Treaty under ex Art 3b EC, later Art 5 EC (now Art 5 TEU). As regards subsidiarity's earlier appearance in the Single European Act (SEA), see n 144.

[36] As noted in the literature, some of these so-called 'principles' are different in nature. See, eg, U Bernitz and J Nergelius (eds), *General Principles of European Community Law* (Kluwer, 2000); particularly G de Búrca, 'Proportionality and Subsidiarity as General Principles of Law', 95; and B de Witte, 'Institutional Principles: A Special Category of General Principles of EC Law', 143; D Edward, 'Subsidiarity as a Legal Concept' in P Cardonnel et al (eds), *Constitutionalising the EU Judicial System: Essays in Honour of Pernilla Lindh* (Hart, 2012) 93; T Schilling, 'A New Dimension of Subsidiarity: Subsidiarity as a Rule and a Principle' (1994) 14 *YEL* 203. While that may be, the use of 'principles' parallels the language of the past and present Treaty frameworks; see also A von Bogdandy, 'Founding Principles' in A von Bogdandy and J Bast (eds), *Principles of European Constitutional Law*, 2nd rev edn (Hart/Verlag CH Beck, 2010) 11, 21–23.

[37] This was vividly captured in the Presidency Conclusions, Edinburgh European Council, 11–12 Dec 1992, Annex 1 to Pt A ('Overall Approach to the Application by the Council of the Subsidiarity Principle and Article 3b of the Treaty on European Union') (Edinburgh Conclusions), point I(1)–(2), at 14–15. As regards their significance, see n 183.

that have lain dormant for some time and may to some extent release the principles of subsidiarity and proportionality from being over or underestimated in the debate.

To be clear, taken by themselves, these four principles have generated a wealth of literature that rivals or even surpasses that concerning European contract law (and European private law generally), and it is not the object here to replicate such work or to set forth an exhaustive study. Instead, as presented in the next four sections, the aim is to pinpoint the definitions of these principles, their linkages, and notable changes brought about by the Lisbon Treaty. Certain 'comparative leaps' to the US are made along the way so as to illuminate salient differences in approach. In this way, this chapter seeks to highlight issues that have not been mentioned much, if at all, in the discourse so far in order to be of functional value in assessing the application of these principles in the context of European contract law.

7.4.2 The principle of conferral

7.4.2.1 The definition of the principle of conferral

Under the principle of conferral set forth in Article 5(2) TEU, 'the Union shall act only within the limits of the competences conferred upon it by the Member States in the Treaties to attain the objectives set out therein'.[38] Over the years, the principle of conferral has been called a variety of names, such as the principle of attribution or the principle of conferred or attributed competences or powers.[39] They are all meant to denote the same thing: that the Union can only act pursuant to the competences conferred or attributed to it, either explicitly or implicitly, under the Treaties. Union action taken outside of these confines is *ultra vires*, that is to say, it exceeds the competences conferred upon it under the Treaties and may be declared unconstitutional by the Union courts.

In practical terms, there is a bit of a 'slant' when it comes to the principle of conferral. In theory, it can be used in a purely neutral way as regards the relationship between the Union and the Member States or even on the side of the Union in the sense of protecting the Union's competences from repatriation on the part of the Member States, which, as they are the framers of the Treaties, is not a completely far-flung idea.[40] Yet, the principle of conferral has more often been equated with guarding the competences of the Member States against potential encroachment on the part of the Union.[41] As such, the principle of conferral may said to be the 'first line of defence' in the division of competences between the EU and the Member States in terms of safeguarding the

[38] As regards the Union institutions, see also Art 13(2) TEU.

[39] See, eg, E Sharpston and G De Baere, 'The Court of Justice as a Constitutional Adjudicator' in A Arnull et al (eds), *A Constitutional Order of States? Essays in EU Law in Honour of Alan Dashwood* (Hart, 2011) 123, 125 fn 11; see also A von Bogdandy and J Bast, 'The Federal Order of Competences' in *Principles of European Constitutional Law*, n 36, 275, 280 (referring to the principle of positive legality).

[40] See the third para of Declaration (No 18), n 14. See further LS Rossi, 'Does the Lisbon Treaty Provide a Clearer Separation of Competences between EU and Member States?' in *EU Law After Lisbon*, n 32, 85, 94.

[41] See, eg, JT Lang, 'What Powers Should the European Community Have?' (1995) 1 *EPL* 97, 99 (referring to it as a 'safeguard' for curbing excessive Community (now Union) action); A von Bogdandy, 'Constitutional Principles' in A von Bogdandy and J Bast (eds), *Principles of European Constitutional Law* (Hart, 2006) 3, 43–44 (considering it within the category of 'principles protecting diversity'); this was deleted in the subsequent edition, though recognition of this aspect remains: see von Bogdandy, n 36, 36. This in turn explains the emphasis placed on this principle, among others, in the Lisbon Treaty: see citations in n 87.

regulatory autonomy of the Member States from such encroachment by the Union.[42] Framed another way, the principle of conferral stands for the fact that the bulk of regulatory competence lies with the Member States, with the Union given only those competences that have been conferred upon it under the Treaties.[43]

In line with the principle of conferral, the Union's competences are conferred upon it in a *functional* manner, meaning that the principle of conferral links the competence of the Union to the achievement of a range of objectives set forth in Article 2 TEU, which are carried out via the relevant legal basis or bases.[44] Union competence is therefore not merely divided up according to subject matter in a list of enumerated fields, but instead is functionally limited to what is required by the objectives set out in the Treaties.[45] Consequently, the principle of conferral in the EU cannot be strictly equated with the principle of enumerated powers associated with the US, whereby the particular powers accorded to the federal level are listed or 'enumerated' in the US Constitution, since this may be seen as implying some sort of catalogue that is in fact missing in the Treaties.[46] In effect, the principle of conferral in the EU necessitates a functional inquiry different from that in the US, since in evaluating the extent of Union competence, the relevant legal basis is always tied to and informed by the objectives set out for the Union in Article 2 TEU, even though such objectives do not themselves serve as the actual legal basis for the Union measure concerned.

Nevertheless, similar to the American constitutional framework, tensions underpin the principle of conferral on account of the fact it has been perceived, especially in past years, as framing the scope of Union competence through a so-called 'dualist' lens of strict boundary lines between areas of Union and Member State competence, which in practice have been eroded to a great extent.[47] In the US, this is exemplified by relevant jurisprudence concerning the Tenth Amendment of the US Constitution,[48] which represents the failed attempts to shield off certain domains of the constituent states from

[42] In the German Federal Constitutional Court's decision on the Lisbon Treaty, it was framed as a 'protection mechanism' to preserve Member States' responsibility: see Bundesverfassungsgericht, judgment of 30 June 2009, 2 BvE 2/08, available at <http://www.bverfg.de/entscheidungen/es20090630_2bve000208en.html>, point 301 (English transl).

[43] See, eg, K Lenaerts, 'The Principle of Subsidiarity and the Environment in the European Union: Keeping the Balance of Federalism' (1994) 17 *Fordham ILJ* 846, 848–849. See also Edinburgh Conclusions, n 37, point 2(i), at 14.

[44] Lenaerts and Van Nuffel, n 20, § 7-002.

[45] Lenaerts and Van Nuffel, n 20, § 7-002.

[46] See Von Bogdandy and Bast, n 39, 280 fn 37. This is not to imply that there is a list or 'catalogue' of competences in the US that strictly carves out the competences attributed to the federal level as opposed to that of the states. Similar to the EU, much of the breadth of federal power (or at least where much of the tensions emanate) is grounded not so much in the subjects that are explicitly elaborated in the text of the US Constitution, but rather from the purported link or relationship to such subjects. See GA Bermann, 'The Role of Law in the Functioning of Federal Systems' in K Nicolaidis and R Howse (eds), *The Federal Vision: Legitimacy and Levels of Governance in the United States and the European Union* (Oxford Univ Press, 2001) 191, 199.

[47] See, in particular, JHH Weiler, *The Division of Competences in the European Union*, External study commissioned by the European Parliament DG for Research, POLI W-26 (1997) (on file with author). This is not to discount the claimed transition of the EU from a so-called 'dual' to 'cooperative federalism' model (see R Schütze, *From Dual to Cooperative Federalism—The Changing Structure of European Law* (Oxford Univ Press, 2009)) or that there are several factors to explain the gradual aggregation of Union competence through successive Treaty amendments (see P Craig, 'Competence and Member State Autonomy: Causality, Consequence and Legitimacy' in H-W Micklitz and B de Witte (eds), *The European Court of Justice and the Autonomy of the Member States* (Intersentia, 2012) 11).

[48] The Tenth Amendment provides: 'The powers not delegated to the United States by the Constitution, nor prohibited by it to the States, are reserved to the States respectively, or to the people.'

action taken at the federal level.[49] Likewise, in the EU, as remarked by a well-known jurist, '[t]here is simply no nucleus of sovereignty that the Member States can invoke, as such, against the Community', now Union.[50]

Thus, while perhaps all well and good in theory, on account of the functional approach, the principle of conferral has given way to tensions under circumstances where the Union is perceived to trespass into areas that have *not* (yet) been explicitly or implicitly conferred upon the Union within the context of achieving the objectives that have been set down in the Treaties pursuant to the competences that *have* been conferred upon the Union.[51] In other words, the limits placed on the Union's competence under the Treaties are feared to be transgressed by virtue of the Union's indirect reach into areas that in principle remain within the competences of the Member States. This has become increasingly apparent in various areas touched by EU law, but is particularly borne out by European contract law.

To date, there has not been any explicit competence set down in the Treaties concerning matters of contract law per se.[52] There is no title in the Treaties, for example, labelled 'contract law' (or any other field of private law). Rather, as far as contract law is concerned, Union action has generally proceeded via indirect routes to achieve the objectives set down in the Treaties, whether for the purposes of the internal market, competition policy, public procurement, transport policy, etc. This is illustrated by the EU contract law *acquis*, which has been centred on the Union's objectives related to the internal market and consumer protection. Thus, for those claiming that the Union has no explicit competence over contract law (or other fields of private law), this is by all means true. Yet, it does not answer the question as to the scope of the Union's competences related to the achievement of the various objectives listed in the Treaties, which encompass action to be taken in the field of contract law corresponding to the legal basis concerned.

7.4.2.2 The legal basis requirement

It follows from the above that the principle of conferral is equated with the requirement of a legal basis. This is because, in principle, for the adoption of a particular Union measure, there must be a legal basis in the Treaties providing the Union with the requisite competence to take such action. The legal basis constitutes the particular provision (or provisions as discussed below) of the Treaties that sets forth the Union's sphere of action in the area concerned and includes the relevant legal instruments and decision-making procedure to be followed.[53] This may seem rudimentary, but in the context of European contract law, legal basis often gets confused with the objectives and values that exist or should be considered or developed within the framework of the European contract law project. For example, given the infusion of consumer protection in the EU contract law *acquis*, it is sometimes surmised that what is now Article 169 TFEU (ex

[49] See, eg, LH Tribe, 1 *American Constitutional Law*, 3rd edn (Foundation Press, 2000) § 5-11–§ 5-12.

[50] K Lenaerts, 'Constitutionalism and the Many Faces of Federalism' (1990) 38 *AJCL* 205, 220.

[51] This was already mentioned with specific regard to the Court of Justice's lawmaking role and European 'federal common law': see Chapter 2, § 2.3.1.

[52] There were no changes brought about by the Lisbon Treaty in this regard, despite certain proposals submitted during the European Convention: see Chapter 10, § 10.2.1.

[53] The legal basis requirement is related to the obligation to state reasons under Art 296 TFEU, and in principle the legal basis is explicitly specified in the measure concerned. See, eg, Case C-370/07 *Commission v Council* [2009] ECR I-8917.

Article 153 EC) constitutes a legal basis for some of the measures comprising the 'hard core' of this *acquis*, when as already discussed, it is primarily what is now Article 114 TFEU and to some extent Article 115 TFEU (ex Articles 95 and 94 EC) that constituted the legal basis for these measures.[54] This is certainly not to say that Article 169 TFEU could not serve as the legal basis for Union action in European contract law, which is further explored in Chapter 9. It is only to make clear the difference between the legal basis upon which Union competence to adopt a particular measure rests and particular objectives underpinning the Union measure concerned.

It may also seem rudimentary to emphasize that the legal basis requirement does not necessarily implicate only one Treaty provision by itself, but given recent case law, this begs a much more nuanced inquiry. Under vested case law of the Court of Justice emanating from the *Titanium Dioxide* judgment,[55] the legal basis of a Union measure can be based on one or more Treaty provisions depending upon the principal objectives of the measure concerned, except where such provisions are incompatible with one another as regards differences in the decision-making procedures to be followed.[56] However, this has not been viewed as precluding a practical approach taken by the Union institutions in certain instances, whereby two seemingly incompatible legal bases are combined and essentially 'levelled up' by way of choosing the procedure that affords the greatest involvement to the Union institutions concerned, in particular the European Parliament.[57]

For instance, in *Commission v European Parliament and Council*,[58] the Court of Justice annulled the Regulation implementing the Rotterdam Convention on the grounds that it should have been adopted on the dual legal basis of what were then Articles 133 and 175 EC (now Articles 207 and 192 TFEU), and not just Article 175 EC alone. Former Article 133 EC concerned Community action in the Common Commercial Policy and stipulated qualified majority voting in the Council with at most optional consultation of the European Parliament.[59] Former Article 175 EC concerned Community action in the field of environmental protection and required qualified majority voting in the Council and the co-decision procedure involving the

[54] As noted in Chapter 1, sometimes, reference to what is now Art 169 TFEU (ex Art 153 EC) is made in recitals of particular Union consumer contract law measures, but again, this is not the same thing as serving as the legal basis of the Union measure concerned.

[55] Case C-300/89 *Commission v Council* ('*Titanium Dioxide*') [1991] ECR I-2867.

[56] See, eg, Case C-155/07 *European Parliament v Council* [2008] ECR I-8103, paras 34–37; Case C-130/10 (Judgment of 19 July 2012) *European Parliament v Council* ('*Legal Basis for Restrictive Measures*'), not reported, paras 42–45. It has been specifically stated that this is where the use of two or more legal bases is liable to undermine the rights of the Parliament: see, eg, Case C-178/03 *Commission v European Parliament and Council* [2006] ECR I-107, para 57.

[57] But see Opinion of AG Poiares Maduro in Case C-411/06 *Commission v European Parliament and Council* [2009] ECR I-7585, point 6 fn 5. This should not be taken to mean that the legal basis (or bases) of the measure concerned is chosen according to which affords the greatest participation of the Parliament; the legal basis of the measure dictates which procedure to be followed, not the other way around: Case C-130/10 (Judgment of 19 July 2012) *European Parliament v Council*, not reported, paras 79–82.

[58] Case C-178/03 *Commission v European Parliament and Council* [2006] ECR I-107, paras 56–60. There was a companion case concerning the legal basis of the Rotterdam Convention, in which the Court made similar findings: see Case C-94/03 *Commission v Council* [2006] ECR I-1, paras 51–56. For detailed discussion, see, eg, N de Sadeleer, 'Environmental Governance and the Legal Basis Conundrum' (2012) 31 *YEL* 373, 286–292; M Klamert, 'Conflicts of legal basis: no legality and no basis but a bright future under the Lisbon Treaty?' (2010) 35 *ELR* 497; P Koutrakos, 'Legal Basis and Delimitation of Competence in EU External Relations' in M Cremona and B de Witte (eds), *EU Foreign Relations Law: Constitutional Fundamentals* (Hart, 2008) 171.

[59] Ex Art 133(4) EC (now Art 207 TFEU).

Council and the European Parliament as co-legislators.[60] Notwithstanding Advocate General Kokott's Opinion concluding that the two legal bases were incompatible and could not be combined,[61] the Court found that they were in fact compatible because the Council votes in both cases by qualified majority, and the Parliament would be involved by way of co-decision, thereby not undermining its rights.[62] This position has been affirmed in more recent jurisprudence concerning these provisions and others.[63]

European Parliament v Council ('*International Fund for Ireland*')[64] presented a more challenging case.[65] This dispute concerned the legal basis of a Regulation concerning what was then the Community's financial contributions to the International Fund for Ireland, which had been adopted under former Article 308 EC (now Article 352 TFEU).[66] The European Parliament argued that it should have been adopted under the third paragraph of former Article 159 EC (now Article 175 TFEU) on economic and social cohesion, which required qualified majority voting in the Council and the co-decision procedure, as opposed to former Article 308 EC, then requiring unanimous voting in the Council and consultation of the European Parliament.[67] In his Opinion, Advocate General Bot concluded that the Regulation should have been adopted solely under Article 159 EC.[68] The Court disagreed and found that the third paragraph of Article 159 EC did not by itself confer on the Community the necessary competence to adopt the measure concerned.[69] Instead, the Community legislature should have had recourse to both the third paragraph of Article 159 EC and Article 308 EC, 'while complying with the legislative procedures laid down therein, that is to say, both the "co-decision" procedure referred to in Article 251 EC and the requirement that the Council act unanimously'.[70] While not saying as much, the Court essentially combined the co-decision procedure of Article 159 EC, affording the Parliament the greatest involvement in the legislative procedure, with the unanimous voting requirement of Article 308 EC, thereby knocking out the qualified majority voting and consultation requirements that had been stipulated for each provision, respectively.

[60] Ex Art 175(1) EC (now Art 192(1) TFEU), also providing for consultation of the European Economic and Social Committee (EESC) and the Committee of the Regions (CoR).

[61] See Opinion of AG Kokott in Case C-178/03 *Commission v European Parliament and Council*, points 56–65.

[62] Case C-178/03 *Commission v European Parliament and Council*, paras 57–59.

[63] See, eg, Case C-155/07 *European Parliament v Council* [2008] ECR I-8103, paras 75–83; Case C-411/06 *Commission v European Parliament and Council* [2009] ECR I-7585, paras 73–76 (distinguishing it from the present proceedings). See also Opinion of AG Kokott in Case C-370/07 *Commission v Council* [2009] ECR I-8917, point 79 fn 36 and citations therein.

[64] Case C-166/07 *European Parliament v Council* ('*International Fund for Ireland*') [2009] ECR I-7135.

[65] Notably, this issue had been percolating below the surface of the *Kadi* and *Yusuf* cases involving a measure based on the combination of former Arts 60, 301, and 308 EC, the first two provisions requiring qualified majority voting in the Council and the third requiring unanimous voting in the Council and consultation of the Parliament. Although the legal basis of the measure was challenged, the Court did not delve into the matter of the compatibility of these three legal bases used together, presumably because it was not a plea raised by the parties. Joined Cases C-402/05 P and C-415/05 P *Kadi and Al Barakaat International Foundation v Council and Commission* [2008] ECR I-6351. For further discussion of this case, see Chapter 8, § 8.4.2.

[66] Council Reg (EC) No 1968/2006 of 21 Dec 2006 concerning Community financial contributions to the International Fund for Ireland (2007 to 2010), [2006] OJ L409/86.

[67] Case C-166/07 *International Fund for Ireland*, paras 21–22. The third para of former Art 159 EC (now Article 175 TFEU) also stipulated consultation of the EESC and CoR.

[68] Opinion of AG Bot in Case C-166/07 *International Fund for Ireland*, points 83–98.

[69] Case C-166/07 *International Fund for Ireland*, para 65.

[70] Case C-166/07 *International Fund for Ireland*, para 69.

At first glance, *International Fund for Ireland* appears to constitute a reversal of the Court's position taken in *Titanium Dioxide*, in which the Court had considered former Article 130s EEC (now Article 192 TFEU), then stipulating unanimous voting in the Council and consultation of the Parliament, to be incompatible with former Article 100a EEC (now Article 114 TFEU), then specifying qualified majority voting in the Council and the cooperation procedure involving the Parliament.[71] With a closer look, however, there may be a way to reconcile the two judgments to some extent, even if the full outline of the Court's approach is not yet clear.

The Court's ruling in *International Fund for Ireland* may be attributed to a preference for ensuring due respect for the vertical division of competences between the EU and the Member States under the Treaties, albeit at the expense of the horizontal division of competences among the Union institutions laid down in the legal bases concerned. It signified that the Union's competence under what was then Article 308 EC (now Article 352 TFEU) is needed when the particular Union measure contains even minor elements that fall outside the more specific legal basis at issue, with the result that the choice is either to split the measure concerned or to combine the relevant Treaty provisions serving as the legal basis, whatever be the practical effects on decision-making.[72] In this case, the Court tacked on Article 308 EC for those elements of the measure that fell outside the more specific legal basis of the third paragraph of Article 159 EC, thus ensuring that the latter was not unduly stretched to encompass elements that exceeded the Community's competence under that provision. The Court's designation of the co-decision procedure and unanimous voting in the Council was not exactly a standard combination of decision-making procedures, but it was not altogether novel under the past Treaty framework.[73]

That being said, there are several issues that are left unresolved by the Court's judgment in *International Fund for Ireland* and warrant clarification in the case law,[74] such as its application to the present (post-Lisbon) Treaty framework[75] and whether it represents a specific approach in connection with Article 352 TFEU as compared to other Treaty provisions.[76] This is particularly the case in view of the Court's subsequent

[71] Case C-300/89 *Titanium Dioxide* [1991] ECR I-2867. Since the case was decided, former Arts 130s and 100a EEC were amended, and what are now Arts 192(1) and 114(1) TFEU (ex Arts 175(1) and 95(1) EC) provide for qualified majority voting in the Council and the co-decision procedure. Art 192(1) TFEU also provides for consultation of the EESC and the CoR, whereas Art 114(1) TFEU specifies consultation of the EESC.

[72] Or, as framed extrajudicially by a member of the Court, the case sought to preserve both the horizontal and vertical 'checks and balances' put in place by the Treaty framers at the expense of the decision-making procedures involved, thereby distinguishing such procedures from the role of the particular Union institutions (namely the European Parliament) in the EU decision-making process: see K Lenaerts, 'EU Federalism in 3-D' in E Cloots et al (eds), *Federalism in the European Union* (Hart, 2012) 13, 30–31.

[73] See ex Arts 42, 47(2), and 151(5) EC. With the changes brought about by the Lisbon Treaty, however, these provisions no longer provide for this combination: see Arts 48, 53, and 167(5) TFEU, respectively.

[74] See, eg, T Corthaut, Case note (2011) 48 *CML Rev* 1271; Sharpston and De Baere, n 39, 136–150.

[75] See, eg, K St Clair Bradley, 'Powers and Procedures in the EU Constitution: Legal Bases and the Court' in P Craig and G de Búrca (eds), *The Evolution of EU Law*, 2nd edn (Oxford Univ Press, 2011) 85, 92–93.

[76] See Lenaerts and Van Nuffel, n 20, § 7-019. The present author agreed with this approach in a previous publication (see K Gutman, 'The Commission's 2010 Green Paper on European Contract Law: Reflections on Union Competence in Light of the Proposed Options' (2011) 7 *ERCL* 151, 162); however, as rightly posed by commentators, further clarification of this issue is warranted, if that is indeed the underlying rationale.

judgment in *European Parliament v Council* (*'Legal Basis for Restrictive Measures'*),[77] in which it underscored the viability of the *Titanium Dioxide* case law following the entry into force of the Lisbon Treaty in connection with the ordinary legislative procedure, implicitly calling to mind the exact combination at issue in *International Fund for Ireland*.[78]

Still, as far as the debate about European contract law is concerned, the Court's judgment in *International Fund for Ireland* is of great importance. It signals the combination of Article 352 TFEU with a Treaty provision stipulating qualified majority voting and co-decision, which is characteristic of several Treaty provisions implicated in the debate (ie Articles 114, 169, and 81 TFEU).[79] This is so even though as a formal matter, the Court has not (yet) confronted the combination of these sets of provisions, especially Article 114 TFEU.[80] In the discourse on European contract law so far, the approach has usually been to assess the scope of the relevant Treaty provisions individually, and if anything, to discount their potential combination in light of the *Titanium Dioxide* case law. As a result of this judgment, however, the potential combination of some of these provisions must be looked into, even if for the time being, certain issues must await further jurisprudence of the Court of Justice.

7.4.2.3 The Lisbon Treaty

On the whole, the Lisbon Treaty did not alter the meaning of the principle of conferral laid down in what is now Article 5(2) TEU, but made certain points more explicit, as compared to the first paragraph of Article 5 EC, which set out the principle of conferral without referring to it by name.[81] Accompanying the definition of the principle of conferral, Article 5(2) TEU contains an additional sentence stating: 'Competences not conferred upon the Union in the Treaties remain with the Member States'.[82] While this sentence is not altogether novel, its explicit inclusion in the Treaties may be considered to ingrain even further the limited nature of competences conferred on the Union, as well as casting an implicit glance at the language of the Tenth Amendment enshrined in the US Constitution.[83] Moreover, the previous list of 'objectives' and 'activities' set out in former Articles 2 and 3 EC is reconfigured in the Lisbon Treaty.[84] Former Article 2 EC was replaced in substance by Article 3 TEU,[85] which streamlines, and to

[77] Case C-130/10 (Judgment of 19 July 2012) *European Parliament v Council* (*'Legal Basis for Restrictive Measures'*), not reported. For detailed discussion, see G De Baere, 'From "Don't Mention the *Titanium Dioxide* Judgment" to "I Mentioned it Once, But I Think I Got Away with it All Right"—Reflections on the Choice of Legal Basis in EU External Relations after the *Legal Basis for Restrictive Measures* Judgment' (2013–2014) 15 *CYELS* 537.

[78] Case C-130/10 *Legal Basis for Restrictive Measures*, paras 45–46. On this basis, the Court held incompatible the combination of Arts 75 and 215(2) TFEU (paras 47–49) and upheld the Council's adoption of the measure concerned under Art 215(2) TFEU, as opposed to Art 75 TFEU, as the Parliament had argued (para 85).

[79] The exception is Art 115 TFEU (ex Art 94 EC), which stipulates unanimous voting in the Council and consultation of the Parliament (as well as consultation of the EESC), thereby resembling the decision-making procedures set down in former Art 308 EC, as compared with what is now Art 352 TFEU, requiring unanimous voting in the Council and the consent of the Parliament.

[80] See further Chapter 8, § 8.4.2.

[81] Ex Art 5, first para, EC stated: 'The Community shall act within the limits of the powers conferred upon it by this Treaty and of the objectives assigned to it therein'.

[82] See also Art 4(1) TEU; Declaration (No 18), n 14, first para.

[83] See n 48.

[84] For detailed discussion, see, eg, Lenaerts and Van Nuffel, n 20, § 7-003–§ 7-007.

[85] Table of equivalences, [2012] OJ C326/363.

some extent augments, the objectives to be achieved by the Union, with the caveat that the Union will pursue its objectives 'by appropriate measures commensurate with the competences which are conferred upon it in the Treaties'.[86] The long list of 'activities' in former Article 3 EC was taken over by a set of new provisions (Articles 3–6 TFEU), which along with Article 2 TFEU elaborate and organize the distribution of competence between the Union and the Member States by carving out certain categories and areas of Union competence within which the various activities are placed.

Generally, there are three main categories of Union competence, that of exclusive, shared, and complementary competence, which are flanked by specific policy fields deserving special consideration.[87] As defined in the Treaties, an exclusive competence is one in which 'only the Union may legislate and adopt legally binding acts, the Member States being able to do so themselves only if so empowered by the Union or for the implementation of Union acts'.[88] In contrast, a shared competence is one in which both the Union and the Member States can legislate and adopt legally binding acts in a specific area; the caveat is that the Member States are only able to 'exercise their competence to the extent that the Union has not exercised its competence', but they are able to exercise their competence in the particular area again 'to the extent that the Union decided to cease exercising its competence'.[89] The shared competence category pertains to most policy fields in the Treaties and thus embodies somewhat of a 'catch-all' category.[90] Finally, the complementary competence category denotes those areas in which 'the Union shall have competence to carry out actions to support, coordinate or supplement the actions of the Member States, without thereby superseding their competence in these areas'.[91] Harmonization of national laws is explicitly excluded in the areas falling within this category,[92] which are expressly listed seriatim in the Treaties.[93]

As regards European contract law, most of the Union's competences relevant for European contract law—ie those relating to the Union's objectives in the internal market, consumer protection, and the AFSJ—are explicitly labelled as falling within the category of shared competence, which to some extent filters into the examination of the corresponding Treaty provisions examined in the forthcoming chapters.[94] Despite this classification, however, many issues were left unaddressed by the Lisbon Treaty in this regard. In particular, the categorization of competences does not by itself indicate the scope of Union competence in the particular area, as in the case of the internal market, consumer protection, the AFSJ, and so on.[95] One is still required to look to the relevant Treaty provision to determine the exact ambit of the Union's action allowed in the relevant field.[96] Likewise, the Lisbon Treaty did not provide

[86] Art 3(6) TEU.

[87] This had previously been the case with the DCT. For detailed discussion, see, eg, Craig, n 32, ch 5; B Guastaferro, 'The European Union as a *Staatenverbund*? The endorsement of the principle of conferral in the Treaty of Lisbon' in M Trybus and L Rubini (eds), *The Treaty of Lisbon and the Future of European Law and Policy* (Edward Elgar, 2012) 117; R Schütze, 'Lisbon and The Federal Order of Competences: A Prospective Analysis' (2008) 33 *ELR* 709; T Tridimas, 'Competence after Lisbon: The elusive search for bright lines' in *The European Union After the Treaty of Lisbon*, n 32, 47.

[88] Art 2(1) TFEU. These are listed in Art 3 TFEU.

[89] Art 2(2) TFEU. See also Protocol (No 25) on the exercise of shared competence, annexed to the TEU and the TFEU, [2012] OJ C326/307.

[90] See Art 4(1) TFEU.

[91] Art 2(5), first para, TFEU.

[92] Art 2(5), second para, TFEU.

[93] See Art 6 TFEU.

[94] See Art 4(2)(a), (f), (j) TFEU. There is no specific listing for judicial cooperation in civil matters.

[95] This resonates with the impetus for the Commission's proposed 'intensity scheme' for Union action in the European Convention: see § 7.4.4.3.

[96] See Arts 1(1) and 2(6) TFEU.

any typology of the kinds of Treaty provisions housed within each category of competence, especially as regards the mainstay of most Union action in the shared competence category. Accordingly, it left out a crucial distinction between the Union's 'functional competences in a particular policy field', also referred to as specific or sectoral competences, and its 'functional competences of a cross-sectoral character', also referred to as horizontal or general competences, among other things,[97] which comes into play in European contract law.

The Union's functional competences in a particular policy field are those that outline the extent of the Union's competence within a particular subject matter *ratione materiae*. As far as the debate about European contract law is concerned, Article 169 TFEU is a good example, since this Treaty provision delineates the scope of Union action that may be taken within a particular policy field, that of consumer protection. Some scholars also include what is now Article 81 TFEU in this category.[98] Admittedly, this provision has a somewhat chameleonic character, since it cuts across various areas of national law relating to, for example, civil procedure, private international law, and litigation matters, and at least pre-Lisbon, it did not exhaustively delimit the kinds of Union measures that may be taken on the basis of this provision. Yet, its substantive scope is nonetheless limited to measures falling within the field of 'judicial cooperation in civil matters' under the Treaties.[99]

By comparison, the Union's functional or horizontal competences of a cross-sectoral character cut across various areas or policy fields in order to achieve certain 'pre-set' objectives as prescribed in the Treaties.[100] The most well-known provisions are undoubtedly Articles 114, 115, and 352 TFEU, among others.[101] Articles 114 and 115 TFEU are linked to the Union's objective to ensure the establishment and functioning of the internal market, and thus, rather than being encased within a single subject matter, cover a wide expanse traversing various domains of the Member States in relation to the pursuit of this objective. Article 352 TFEU goes one step further, since it bestows 'supplementary competence' on the Union to take action that although not as yet foreseen in the Treaties is nonetheless deemed necessary for the achievement of the Union's objectives set down therein.[102] While these three provisions are subject to detailed discussion in Chapter 8, suffice it to say that given their potential reach, it is not coincidental that they stand at the forefront of the controversy concerning the constitutionality of European contract law. While not found in the Lisbon Treaty, the distinction between these types of competences is directly linked to the operation of the principle of subsidiarity in the context of European contract law, as seen below.

[97] Von Bogdandy and Bast, n 39, 288. For other labels, see, eg, Lenaerts and Van Nuffel, n 20, § 7-014; K St Clair Bradley, n 75, 86; Opinion of AG Fennelly in Case C-376/98 *Germany v European Parliament and Council* ('*Tobacco Advertising I*') [2000] ECR I-8419 and Case C-74/99 *Imperial Tobacco and Others* [2000] ECR I-8599, point 63.

[98] See I Pernice, 'Rethinking the Methods of Dividing and Controlling the Competencies of the Union' in *The Treaty of Nice and Beyond*, n 23, 121, 125.

[99] As compared to ex Art 65 EC, Art 81 TFEU is generally considered to be exhaustive: see Chapter 10, § 10.2.2.

[100] See Note from the European Commission on 'Delimitation of powers: a matter of scale of intervention', Working Group V Complementary Competencies, Working Document 4, dated 10 July 2002, 3 fn 1.

[101] See Von Bogdandy and Bast, n 39, 288.

[102] See, eg, Lenaerts and Van Nuffel, n 20, § 7-018.

7.4.3 The principle of subsidiarity

7.4.3.1 The definition(s) of the principle of subsidiarity

The principle of subsidiarity is notoriously elusive. Despite the fact that it has been considered to have been part of the Treaties since the early days of European integration,[103] there is no single, universal definition of subsidiarity in the EU. Rather, the principle of subsidiarity embodies an assortment of values[104] and may be viewed in a multitude of ways,[105] all of which serve to illuminate the varying and nuanced roles it plays in the EU and on a broader scale. As one scholar put it, 'there is a general agreement that there is no agreement on the definition of this concept'.[106] This is evidenced by the standard 'mantra' of many publications on subsidiarity, which begin with a few lines espousing the difficulties of defining this term and the lack of agreement as to its meaning. Be that as it may, in the context of European contract law, subsidiarity largely assumes two main forms as identified in the literature: first, as a supra-constitutional principle overseeing the division of competence in the EU; and secondly, in its more well-known form as a constitutional principle governing the exercise of Union competence.[107] As illustrated below, both forms of subsidiarity impact the scope of Union competence under the Treaty provisions at issue in the debate.

First, *subsidiarity as a supra-constitutional principle* denotes the conception of subsidiarity as guiding the way in which the competences are organized in the Treaties and divided between the EU and the Member States.[108] In this form, subsidiarity oversees the choices as to what competences are given to the Union, to what extent, and how they are framed. There are no explicit legal requirements attached to this form of subsidiarity, and the Court of Justice does not play any role in enforcing it. As such, subsidiarity is not an operational principle in this sense, but instead, it hovers above the Treaties, feeding into and informing the constitutional fabric of the EU itself. To be clear, although it concerns the division, as opposed to the exercise, of competence, this conception of subsidiarity is not the same thing as the principle of conferral. Rather, supra-constitutional subsidiarity precedes it. It filters into the way in which competences of the EU are formulated in the Treaties, which then gives way to the principle of conferral and the various legal bases found in the Treaties.

[103] See, eg, M Wilke and H Wallace, *Subsidiarity: Approaches to Power-Sharing in the European Community*, RIIA Discussion Paper No 27 (The Royal Institute of International Affairs, 1990) 1; 'Editorial Comments: Subsidiarity: Backing the right horse?' (1993) 30 *CML Rev* 241, 241–242.

[104] See, eg, GA Bermann, 'Taking Subsidiarity Seriously: Federalism in the European Community and the United States' (1994) 94 *Col L Rev* 332, 340–343.

[105] For a brief selection, see, eg, E Albertí et al, *The principle of subsidiarity in the European Union* (Parlament de Catalunya, 2005) 135; *Subsidiarity: The Challenge of Change—Proceedings of the Jacques Delors Colloquium* (EIPA, 1991); M Verdussen (ed), *L'Europe de la subsidiarité* (Bruylant, 2000); Wilke and Wallace, n 103, 11–18.

[106] N Emiliou, 'Subsidiarity: An Effective Barrier Against "The Enterprises of Ambition"?' (1992) 17 *ELR* 383, 383. See also 'Editorial Comments', n 103, 241.

[107] See, eg, A Dashwood et al, *Wyatt and Dashwood's European Union Law*, 6th edn (Hart, 2011) 114–115; Lenaerts and Van Nuffel, n 20, § 7-027; K Lenaerts and P van Ypersele, 'Le principe du subsidiarité et son contexte: étude de l'article 3B du traité CE [now Art 5(3) TEU]' (1994) *CDE* 3, 8; M Wathelet, 'La subsidiarité au sein de l'Union européenne: le processus décisionnel' in *L'Europe de la subsidiaritié*, n 105, 131, 132–133. Compare V Constantinesco, 'Le principe de subsidiarité: un passage obligé vers l'Union européenne?' in *L'Europe et le droit: Mélanges en hommage à Jean Boulouis* (Dalloz, 1991) 35, 39–42.

[108] Lenaerts and van Ypersele, n 107, 8–10.

This form of subsidiarity is rarely mentioned, if at all, in the commentary concerning European contract law, but in fact, is readily borne out in the framing of certain Treaty provisions relevant to the debate. Article 169 TFEU is perhaps the most apt example by virtue of the inscription of the Union's 'supporting' role in the field of consumer protection and the stipulation of minimum harmonization in its text.[109] Article 81 TFEU concerning judicial cooperation in civil matters also bears the imprint of supra-constitutional subsidiarity, for example, in the way its text is grounded in 'promoting the compatibility' of Member State laws in certain areas generally associated with matters of private international law, civil procedural law, and transnational litigation (with no explicit mention of substantive civil law) and the limitations placed on Union action having 'cross-border implications'.[110] And although perhaps not obvious at first sight, aspects of supra-constitutional subsidiarity may be considered to infuse some of the Union's functional competences. In particular, what is now Article 115 TFEU has been deemed 'an implicit illustration of subsidiarity', since in principle the Member States' competences continue to operate in full in the relevant areas, and the Union only steps in when their exercise hinders the internal market.[111] Presumably, a similar logic can be applied to Article 114 TFEU. In this way, Union action in these areas can be seen to play a somewhat 'subsidiary' role, and even if the debate about European contract law questions that assumption, it is the way in which these provisions have been depicted in the Treaties that evidences the handiwork of subsidiarity in its supra-constitutional form.

Subsidiarity as a supra-constitutional principle has been viewed by scholars as neutral in relation to the division of competences between the EU and the Member States, since while it affects issues relative to the EU-Member State relationship via the framing and organization of the Treaties, it does not seek to protect the Member States' competences against potential encroachment by the EU, as compared to the constitutional form of subsidiarity described below.[112] Supra-constitutional subsidiarity still carries the potential to impact the assessment of the Treaty provisions relevant to the debate about European contract law in various ways. With respect to Article 169 TFEU, as will be seen, the considerable restraint on the part of the Union in adopting consumer protection measures has been attributed at least in part to supra-constitutional subsidiarity, which influences the consideration of the scope of the Union's competence under this provision.[113] Moreover, supra-constitutional subsidiarity may even go so far as influencing the operation of the more traditional subsidiarity calculus in certain instances. For instance, as regards Article 81 TFEU, the fact that its field of application has already been framed as having 'cross-border implications' by and large predicates Union measures that by their very nature are unlikely to be achieved by the Member States, thereby making it easier to satisfy the requirements of constitutional subsidiarity.[114] This sets the scene for delving into subsidiarity's other meaning.

Secondly, *subsidiarity as a constitutional principle* governs the exercise of Union competence as provided in the first paragraph of Article 5(3) TEU: 'Under the principle of subsidiarity, in areas which do not fall within its exclusive competence, the Union shall act only if and in so far as the objectives of the proposed action cannot be sufficiently achieved by the Member States, either at central level or at regional and local level, but can rather, by reason of the scale or effects of the proposed action, be better achieved at

[109] See further Chapter 9.

[110] This requirement and that relating to the internal market were framed differently in former Art 65 EC and led to heated controversy in recent years: see Chapter 10, § 10.3.1.

[111] See V Constantinesco, 'Who's Afraid of Subsidiarity?' (1991) 11 *YEL* 33, 44–45.

[112] See Lenaerts and van Ypersele, n 107, 9 fn 16.

[113] See Chapter 9, particularly § 9.3.2.

[114] See Chapter 10, § 10.3.1, § 10.3.3.

Union level.'[115] This meaning of subsidiarity is the predominant one in the discourse, as evidenced by its references as its 'legal hard core'[116] or subsidiarity in its 'strict sense'.[117] It is generally termed a constitutional or legal principle because it is this meaning of subsidiarity that sets limits on the exercise of Union competence pursuant to the Treaties.[118]

Formally speaking, the requirements laid down in the Treaties, the so-called subsidiarity calculus, determine whether the competence conferred on the Union should be exercised by it. The basic idea is that if the Member States can 'sufficiently' achieve the objectives of the action concerned, such action should be left there at the lower level of the constituent entities and should not be undertaken at the central Union level. As noted above, this conception of subsidiarity is often considered to carry a bias or presumption in favour of the Member States, since as dictated by Article 5(3) TEU, it is only under circumstances where the Member States are unable to 'do the job', so to speak, that the Union steps in.[119] Subsidiarity can therefore be viewed as the 'second line of defence' in the division of competences between the EU and the Member States by setting (along with proportionality) limits, *intra vires*, on the exercise of Union competence.[120] Viewed in this light, subsidiarity is a quite unique and extraordinary feature of the EU, as compared to the US. Neither the principle of subsidiarity nor the principles of proportionality and sincere cooperation for that matter are inscribed as explicit requirements in the text of the US Constitution, although as a practical matter, it has been noted that there are various ways in which subsidiarity could be said to infuse the American constitutional framework.[121] Yet, as emphasized by Professor George Bermann in his definitive publication on the subject: 'In a seasoned federalism like that of the United States, accustomed to taking [a] variety of considerations into account, the notion of subsidiarity may, in the end, have a somewhat hollow, even foolish, ring to it.'[122] Indeed, as demonstrated by the discussion of the American contract law framework, it remains unknown to what degree the numerous attempts to federalize areas of state commercial and contract law failed on account of Congress' deference to the states in matters of private law that may run along the lines of subsidiarity, as opposed to or in conjunction with other considerations.[123]

As far as European contract law is concerned, the principle of subsidiarity casts a long shadow over the debate. To a great extent, subsidiarity (sometimes accompanied by proportionality) appears as an argument for preserving the bulk of regulatory action in contract law (and other fields of private law) with the Member States and hence as a defensive argument opposing far-reaching Union action in this setting.[124] To be

115 Art 5(3), first para, TEU.

116 G de Búrca, 'Reappraising Subsidiarity's Significance After Amsterdam' (2000) Harvard Jean Monnet Working Paper No 7/99, 15.

117 Edinburgh Conclusions, n 37, point 2(iii).

118 Now made clear by virtue of the changes introduced by the Lisbon Treaty: see n 165.

119 See, eg, T Hartley, *The Foundations of European Law: An Introduction to the Constitutional and Administrative Law of the European Union*, 7th edn (Oxford Univ Press, 2010) 122.

120 See, eg, Lenaerts, n 43, 849.

121 See, eg, Bermann, n 104, 403–448; GA Bermann, 'Subsidiarity as a Principle of U.S. Constitutional Law' (1994) 42 *AJCL* Supp 555; D Halberstam, 'Federalism: Theory, Policy, Law' in M Rosenfeld and A Sajó (eds), *The Oxford Handbook of Comparative Constitutional Law* (Oxford Univ Press, 2012) 576; D Halberstam, 'Federal Powers and the Principle of Subsidiarity' in VD Amar and MV Tushnet (eds), *Global Perspectives on Constitutional Law* (Oxford Univ Press, 2009) 34; A Mills, 'Federalism in the European Union and the United States: Subsidiarity, Private Law, and the Conflict of Laws' (2010) 32 *U Pa JIL* 369.

122 Bermann, n 104, 452. See also Bermann, n 121, 561.

123 See Chapter 3.

124 See, eg, H Collins, 'European Private Law and the Cultural Identity of States' (1995) 3 *ERPL* 353, 355; R Van den Bergh, 'Subsidiarity as an Economic Demarcation Principle and the Emergence

clear, since subsidiarity (in its constitutional form) is concerned with the exercise, not the existence, of Union competence, it cannot be applied abstractly, but rather in relation to the previous identification and confirmation of sufficient Union competence in the first place. In other words, those attempting to use subsidiarity by itself as an argument precluding Union action in contract law may inadvertently imply the assumption that the existence of Union competence (ie the principle of conferral) has been fulfilled. This explains why the Commission's discussion of subsidiarity and proportionality, and not legal basis, caused such a stir in the 2001 Communication,[125] and more recently in the 2010 Green Paper.[126] Moreover, as a related point, there seems to be a paradox underlying the principle of subsidiarity in relation to European contract law. On the one hand, as just mentioned, subsidiarity is commonly touted as a barrier to far-reaching Union action in contract law (and private law generally) by way of the adoption of a European contract law instrument. On the other hand, however, there is growing recognition of the ineffectiveness of the principle of subsidiarity in relation to Union action taken on the basis of the Treaty provisions relevant to the debate, particularly Article 114 TFEU.[127] This brings into play the distinction between material and procedural subsidiarity, which illuminates the roles that the principle of subsidiarity plays in the debate about European contract law and may help to lessen some of the tensions associated with the operation of subsidiarity in this context.

7.4.3.2 The distinction between material and procedural subsidiarity

As a constitutional principle guiding the exercise of Union competence under the Treaties, subsidiarity can be divided into two categories or subsets, which are referred to in the literature by the labels 'material' and 'procedural' subsidiarity.[128] *Material subsidiarity* is equated with the requirements set down in the first paragraph of Article 5(3) TEU cited above and fleshed out further in the Protocol on the application of the principles of subsidiarity and proportionality annexed to the Treaties by the Lisbon Treaty (Lisbon Protocol),[129] compliance with which is subject to enforcement before the Union courts. *Procedural subsidiarity* is equated with the more political and institutional processes that allow material subsidiarity to function, meaning the ways in which the Union institutions ensure compliance with material subsidiarity as part of the EU lawmaking process. It does not appear as such in the Treaties, but tenets are found in the Lisbon Protocol. Notably, the Lisbon Protocol eliminates much of the language concerning both material and procedural subsidiarity found in the former Protocol on the application of the principles of subsidiarity and proportionality annexed to the EC Treaty by the Amsterdam Treaty (Amsterdam Protocol),[130] but

of European Private Law' (1998) 5 *MJ* 129. See also E Hondius, 'Towards a European Civil Code' in AS Hartkamp et al (eds), *Towards a European Civil Code*, 4th rev and expanded edn (Kluwer/Ars Aequi Libri, 2011) 3, 4.

125 See Chapter 5, § 5.2.

126 See Chapter 6, § 6.4.2.

127 See, eg, G Davies, 'Subsidiarity: The Wrong Idea, In The Wrong Place, At The Wrong Time' (2006) 43 *CML Rev* 63.

128 See, eg, A Estella, *The EU Principle of Subsidiarity and Its Critique* (Oxford Univ Press, 2002) 105; H Bribosia, 'De la subsidiarité à la coopération renforcée' in Y Lejeune (ed), *Le traité Amsterdam: espoirs et déceptions* (Bruylant, 1998) 23.

129 Protocol (No 2) on the application of the principles of subsidiarity and proportionality, annexed to the TEU and the TFEU, [2012] OJ C326/206 (Lisbon Protocol). See also Art 5(3), second para, TEU; Art 5(4), second para, TEU.

130 Ex Protocol (No 30) on the application of the principles of subsidiarity and proportionality annexed to the EC Treaty, [1997] OJ C340/105; consolidated version, [2006] OJ C321E/308

vestiges do remain. In addition, although the Amsterdam Protocol has been repealed by the Lisbon Protocol,[131] as a practical matter, its language has not been completely erased from the EU legal and political landscape,[132] which explains why it is included in the discussion.

Admittedly, the terms 'material' and 'procedural' subsidiarity are not perfect. For example, by using the word 'procedural', this may serve to stress the procedural context surrounding the reasoned justification for subsidiarity at the risk of neglecting the more 'substantive' elements of the subsidiarity assessment at the input stage that feeds into the proposed initiative and the lawmaking process itself, eg, by virtue of the consultation and information disseminated and gathered by the Commission. The terms 'legal' and 'political' subsidiarity could be surmised to be ready substitutes, but they may invite even more terminological problems given the mixture of legal and political components on both sides of the material and procedural line. This may explain the reason why one scholar has resorted to the distinction between '*subsidiarity from within*' to lay claim to various ways in which notions of subsidiarity infuse the institutional and organizational processes, as opposed to subsidiarity's standard conception regulating the exercise of Union competence under the Treaties denoted by '*subsidiarity from without*'.[133] This is extremely useful for demonstrating the role of subsidiarity 'inside' the EU lawmaking process, as opposed to 'outside' this process once the particular measure has been adopted. As such, it will be used here in tandem with the notions of 'material' and 'procedural' subsidiarity. In any event, the classification of subsidiarity in these two categories should not be taken to mean that they are mutually exclusive. As one scholar put it, the terms are merely heuristic devices for parsing out the requirements within each category, so that the various aspects of subsidiarity can be fully grasped.[134]

Starting with the *requirements for procedural subsidiarity*, these are elaborated in the Lisbon Protocol in connection with the 'constant respect' given to this principle on the part of each Union institution.[135] They largely implicate the Commission's duties of consultation and the relevant institution's obligation to provide reasoned justification for compliance with subsidiarity (and proportionality) in respect of draft legislative acts.[136] Albeit blurring somewhat with the principle of proportionality,[137] the Amsterdam Protocol had further specified that the form of what was then Community action should be 'as simple as possible' in line with the fact that the Community should legislate only to the extent necessary.[138] This explains at least in part why subsidiarity

(Amsterdam Protocol). See further T von den Brink, 'The substance of subsidiarity: the interpretation and meaning of the principle after Lisbon' in *The Treaty of Lisbon*, n 87, 160, 161–163.

[131] Protocol (No 1) amending the Protocols annexed to the EU Treaty, to the EC Treaty and/or to the EAEC Treaty, annexed to the Lisbon Treaty, [2007] OJ C306/165, point 9(g).

[132] Eg, aspects of the Amsterdam Protocol are incorporated into the Commission's Impact Assessment Guidelines in relation to the assessment of subsidiarity and proportionality: see SEC (2009) 92, particularly points 5.2, 7.2. They may also be taken into account as part of the national parliaments' scrutiny of legislative proposals: eg, in the reasoned opinion of the UK House of Commons on the proposed CESL (see Chapter 6, § 6.4.4.1), the Amsterdam Protocol was considered relevant.

[133] H-W Micklitz, 'The Maastricht Treaty, the Principle of Subsidiarity and the Theory of Integration' (1993) *Lakimies 4/1993* 508.

[134] Estella, n 128, 105–106.

[135] Lisbon Protocol, n 129, Art 1; see also Art 5(3), second para, TEU. This includes, but is not necessarily limited to, 'legislative' action: see Case C-539/09 *Commission v Germany* [2011] ECR I-11235, para 84; Opinion of AG Trstenjak, points 79–86.

[136] See Lisbon Protocol, n 129, Arts 2–5. These requirements are linked to the enhanced role played by the national parliaments: see § 7.4.3.3.

[137] See § 7.4.4.2.

[138] Amsterdam Protocol, n 130, points 6–7. Notwithstanding the linkage to proportionality, these points have been considered by the Union courts as part of the subsidiarity assessment: see,

has become infused with notions of 'better lawmaking' in the EU, as illustrated by the conflation of the two in the Commission's reports on the principles of subsidiarity and proportionality as stipulated by the relevant Protocol,[139] which in turn is linked to the framework set up for assessing subsidiarity (as well as proportionality) in the various stages of policy development through, for example, impact assessments and added-value reports.[140] In this way, procedural subsidiarity focuses on the ways in which the EU system of governance is responsive to the citizens and the way in which subsidiarity informs the choices made by the Union institutions within the EU decision-making process.

When viewed in this sense, procedural subsidiarity and European contract law go hand-in-hand. This is illustrated in several ways as the debate has progressed at the European level, for instance, in the way in which the European contract law project and the related work on the revision of the EU consumer contract law *acquis* are part of the simplification and improvement of EU lawmaking[141] and the depiction of the CFR as a 'better lawmaking' device in documents issued by various Union institutions and bodies. This is also shown by the extent to which the Commission 'consults widely' with the Union institutions, the Member States, and various stakeholders by way of its numerous Communications and Progress Reports on European contract law in order to gauge the choices as to the type of action to be taken at the European level in contract law, which have so far directed the process away from full-scale approximation and towards the CFR and optional instruments such as the proposed CESL, mechanisms that are depicted as having a 'softer touch' on the national legal orders. The CFR is presently envisaged as a lawmaking tool to help ensure a 'smooth fit' between Union measures in contract law and the national contract law regimes, and the proposed CESL is framed as an optional regime that exists alongside the pre-existing national contact laws without replacing them. Additionally, as a legislative proposal, the proposed CESL is accompanied by an extensive Impact Assessment containing various data to support the proposed action. Consequently, it can be said that procedural subsidiarity is ingrained in the debate about European contract law itself. Of course, this is not to dismiss the ongoing sensitivities in this regard, for example, as regards claims concerning the lack of clarity surrounding the aims and scope of the CFR project, the sufficiency of the evidence to substantiate the proposed CESL, or the fact that there is not always a complete 'track record' of the various choices that have been weighed by the Union institutions in the solutions proposed. Nonetheless, it is particularly by virtue of the consultation process in relation to European contract law that important

eg, Case C-58/08 *Vodafone and Others* [2010] ECR I-4999, para 73; Case C-176/09 *Luxembourg v European Parliament and Council* [2011] ECR I-3727, para 77.

[139] Lisbon Protocol, n 129, Art 9; Amsterdam Protocol, n 130, point 9, fourth indent. Eg, Commission Report on Subsidiarity and Proportionality (19th Report on Better Lawmaking covering the year 2011), COM (2012) 373 final, 10.7.2012.

[140] See, eg, D Chalmers et al, *European Union Law: Cases and Materials*, 2nd edn (Cambridge Univ Press, 2010) 372–373; Craig, n 32, 190–192; and recently, Commission Annual Report 2012 on Subsidiarity and Proportionality, COM (2013) 566 final, 30.7.2013, points 2.1, 2.3.

[141] See, eg, Commission Communication on European Contract Law, COM (2001) 398 final, 11.7.2001 (2001 Communication), points 58–59; Commission Communication, A more coherent European Contract Law—An Action Plan, COM (2003) 68 final, 12.2.2003 (2003 Action Plan), points 52, 70–71; Commission Communication, European Contract Law and the revision of the *acquis*: the way forward, COM (2004) 651 final, 11.10.2004 (2004 Communication), point 2.1.1. Outside the debate, see, eg, Commission Communication, Updating and simplifying the Community acquis, COM (2003) 71 final, 11.2.2003, 9, 27.

decisions regarding the action to be taken, or not, by the Union have been identified and progressively streamlined to target areas where the Member States fall short.

Moving to the *requirements for material subsidiarity*, as already mentioned, these denote the requirements set forth in Article 5(3) TEU that must be satisfied in order to justify the exercise of Union competence under the Treaties. Frankly speaking, this provision is not a model of absolute clarity notwithstanding the changes introduced by the Lisbon Treaty, and its past lineage in the EC Treaty bears the imprint of considerable political negotiation that merged different tests for subsidiarity into one provision.[142] Still, the requirements prescribed by Article 5(3) TEU are vital for applying the principle of subsidiarity in its material form. Scholars tally them in various ways, but the subsidiarity test or calculus boils down to three main requirements:

(1) whether the proposed action falls within an exclusive competence of the Union (ie 'areas which do not fall within its exclusive competence');
(2) whether the objectives of the proposed action cannot be 'sufficiently achieved' by the Member States (either at the central level or at regional and local level), but can rather be 'better achieved' at Union level; and
(3) whether the proposed action complies with a specific application of the principle of proportionality (ie 'only if and in so far as' the objectives of the proposed action cannot be sufficiently achieved by the Member States, but can rather be better achieved at Union level).[143]

By and large, the heart of the subsidiarity calculus centres on the second requirement, but the other two necessitate some explanation, especially on account of their interplay with the principles of conferral and proportionality.

The first requirement generated much debate when the principle of subsidiarity first emerged as a general constitutional principle in the former EC Treaty by way of the Maastricht Treaty.[144] This was because the notion of exclusive competence was not defined in the former Treaty framework, which harked back to the principle of conferral in terms of the types of competence wielded by what was then the Community (or by the Union outside the Community pillar). Thus, some scholars, no doubt helped along by the Commission's thoughts on the matter,[145] initially surmised that various competences related to the internal market, particularly former Articles 94 and 95 EC, were exclusive competences, thereby removing action taken pursuant to these provisions from the purview of the subsidiarity test under the EC Treaty.[146] Yet, as clarified by the case law on former Article 95 EC (now Article 114 TFEU), subsidiarity must be complied with in this context.[147] This was made explicit as part of the categorization of competences introduced by the Lisbon Treaty.[148] In any event, it was not so much

[142] See, eg, Chalmers et al, n 140, 363–364; Emiliou, n 106, 401. For further discussion, see, eg, J Cloos et al, *Le traité de Maastricht: genèse, analyse, commentaires* (Bruylant, 1994) 141–151; R Corbett, *The Treaty of Maastricht—From Conception to Ratification: A Comprehensive Reference Guide* (Longman, 1993) 53.

[143] Art 5(3), first para, TEU.

[144] The principle of subsidiarity was given expression in former Art 130r(4) EEC by virtue of the SEA in the field of environmental policy, but its terms were different from the subsidiarity calculus of what is now Art 5(3), first para, TEU. See further Lenaerts, n 43, 858–865.

[145] See Commission Communication, The principle of subsidiarity, SEC(92) 1990 final, 27.10.1992, Annex ('The Subsidiarity Principle'), pt II.

[146] See, eg, AG Toth, 'A Legal Analysis of Subsidiarity' in D O'Keeffe and PM Twomey (eds), *Legal Issues of the Maastricht Treaty* (Wiley Chancery Law, 1994) 37.

[147] See Chapter 8, § 8.3.3.1.

[148] See § 7.4.2.3.

the application in theory that mattered, but the way in which the subsidiarity calculus came out in practice, which leads to the second requirement.

The second requirement predicates that the Union exercises the relevant competence only if the proposed action 'cannot be sufficiently achieved by the Member States, either at central level or at regional and local level, but can rather, by reason of the scale or effects of the proposed action, be better achieved at Union level'.[149] In effect, there are two requirements that must be satisfied: the first concerns the capabilities of the Member States, which may be referred to as the so-called 'effectiveness' requirement, and the second concerns the capabilities of the Union, or the so-called 'efficiency' requirement.[150] However, the two requirements must be read together and do not stand on equal ground. The first requirement, that of the Member States, takes precedence; it is only when it is determined that the Member States are not able to do the job 'sufficiently' that the Union's capabilities then come into play.[151] Framed another way, just because the Union can do it 'better' is not enough; the Member States must first be found not able to do the job themselves. There are some interesting trade-offs here. First, this text may be read to incorporate a bias in favour of the Member States. In other words, the Union and the Member States do not come to the table equally, but the Member States get the 'upper hand' at least in principle, in the sense that it is only if they cannot do the job 'sufficiently' that the Union steps in. There are of course ways in which to counteract cases under circumstances where the Union's action would yield much more efficient results by reassessing the objectives of the proposed action within the EU decision-making process.[152]

Even so, this somewhat restrictive framing of subsidiarity from the perspective of the Union is (or used to be) curtailed to some extent by virtue of the guidelines set forth in the Amsterdam Protocol that were to be used in determining whether these two requirements were fulfilled in connection with the action pursued:

(1) the issue under consideration has *transnational aspects* which cannot be satisfactorily regulated by action by Member States;

(2) *actions by Member States alone or lack of Community* [*now Union*] *action would conflict with the requirements of the Treaty* (such as the need to correct distortions of competition or avoid disguised restrictions on trade or strengthen economic and social cohesion) or would otherwise significantly damage Member States' interests;

[149] Art 5(3), first para, TEU. With respect to the Lisbon Treaty's introduction of language referring to the regional and local levels, see § 7.4.3.3. As highlighted in the commentary (see, eg, Lenaerts and Van Nuffel, n 20, § 7-028), in contrast to point 5, first para, of the Amsterdam Protocol, the Lisbon Protocol does not expressly stipulate that for Union action to be justified with regard to subsidiarity, both requirements must be satisfied; however, Art 5 of the Lisbon Protocol states that draft legislative acts must be justified with respect to subsidiarity (and proportionality) and requires, inter alia, the 'reasons for concluding that a Union objective can be better achieved at Union level' to be 'substantiated by qualitative and, wherever possible, quantitative indicators'.

[150] Different labels may be used. See, eg, the Commission's reference to the 'necessity' and 'added value' tests in its Impact Assessment Guidelines, n 132, point 5.2; Lenaerts and Van Nuffel, n 20, § 7-028 (referring to the 'decentralisation' and 'efficiency' criteria). The Commission's reference to 'comparative efficiency' also caught on: see Communication, n 145, 2; and more recently, eg, P Craig and G de Búrca, *EU Law: Text, Cases, and Materials*, 5th edn (Oxford Univ Press, 2011) 94, 97; M Gennart, *Le contrôle parlementaire du principe de subsidiarité* (Larcier, 2013) 175.

[151] See Lenaerts, n 43, 876.

[152] Lenaerts, n 43, 877.

(3) action at Community [now Union] level would produce *clear benefits* by reason of its scale or effects compared with action at the level of the Member States.[153]

Much has been made of the repetitive and potentially even conflicting nature of these guidelines. Nonetheless, the common theme running through them is that they veered on the side of the Community (now Union) in the sense of elaborating circumstances, such as 'transnational aspects', 'distortions of competition', and 'clear benefits', in which action at the European level was called for. Conceivably, there could have been (and may be in the future) guidelines delineating instances that would have ruled out such action, but these were not framed as such. Rather, they emphasized circumstances where the balance fell on the side of the EU. This is particularly evident in circumstances implicating the then Community's objectives relating to the internal market.[154] By the explicit emphasis on the transnational aspects of the action concerned, the need to correct distortions of competition, and restrictions on trade, the guidelines were essentially a siren call to former Article 95 EC, among other provisions, suggesting the outcome of the subsidiarity calculus in its favour. To the extent that such guidelines or similar formulations are taken into account in the context of the exercise of the Union's competence under the present Treaty framework, the same remarks hold, with particular regard to Article 114 TFEU.[155]

This is where the distinction between procedural and material subsidiarity comes into play. In the literature, certain scholars have contended that there is a distinction in the application of subsidiarity depending upon whether the Union's competence concerns a particular subject matter *ratione materiae* or is of a horizontal or cross-sectoral nature: for the former, subsidiarity operates in the 'material' sense of regulating the exercise of Union competence in line with the subsidiarity calculus set down in the Treaties, whereas for the latter, subsidiarity operates at an earlier stage, in the 'procedural' sense, of influencing the way in which the action proposed for the Union is defined.[156] As illustrated by the chapters to come, however, this distinction can be taken one step further. While the foregoing remarks are readily borne out in relation to functional competences such as Articles 114 and 352 TFEU, it seems that the Union's competences in certain policy fields *ratione materiae*, such as Article 81 TFEU, may also have the potential to manifest the similar operation of subsidiarity in terms of subsidiarity's role 'inside' as well as 'outside' the EU decision-making process, as illustrated by the adoption of optional instruments under this provision.[157] The bottom line is that the infusion of procedural subsidiarity may help to offset some of the tensions stemming from material subsidiarity, since it can accommodate a broader range of power-sharing between the Union and the Member States, as opposed to an 'either/or' choice presented by material subsidiarity that often plays out in favour of the Union in relation to prominent provisions at issue in the debate.

It also bears emphasis that the second guideline of the Amsterdam Protocol referred to the Member States acting 'alone'.[158] Going back to the text of Article 5(3) TEU,

[153] Amsterdam Protocol, n 130, point 5, second para (emphasis added). In the Edinburgh Conclusions, n 37, 'and/or' was placed after the second guideline (see point II(ii), at 19), but this was left out in the Amsterdam Protocol.

[154] On the linkage between the legal basis and subsidiarity requirements, with special regard to former Art 95 EC (now Art 114 TFEU), see J Timmermans, 'La justiciabilité de la subsidiarité' in *Festskrift til Claus Gulmann* (Forlaget Thomsen, 2006) 449, 456–458.

[155] See, eg, the Commission's Impact Assessment Guidelines, n 132, point 5.2, at 23.

[156] N Bernard, 'The Future of European Economic Law in the Light of the Principle of Subsidiarity' (1996) 33 *CML Rev* 633. See also, eg, Bermann, n 104, 383–384.

[157] See further Chapter 10, § 10.3.3.

[158] See text accompanying n 153. This was stated verbatim in the Edinburgh Conclusions, n 37, point II(ii), second indent, at 19.

it is aimed at the assessment of the capabilities of the Member States to achieve the proposed action, since if they can do so, this removes the basis for such action to be exercised at Union level. For a long time, this begged the question whether this assessment was limited to action taken by each Member State individually or whether action taken by the Member States together, in all or in part, could also be included in the subsidiarity calculus. There is no explicit answer to this question in the text of the Treaties.[159] Yet, as discussed in Chapter 8, the Court of Justice has given an answer to this question in the context of its case law on what is now Article 114 TFEU (ex Article 95 EC) by way of its express reference to the Member States acting individually and its negation of the potential for an international treaty involving the Member States outside the Treaty framework to preclude approximation in the area concerned.[160] Furthermore, in the literature, there seems to be some agreement that the subsidiarity test can include either individual action on the part of each Member State or cooperation between a certain number of Member States concerned, but cannot include all Member States acting together, since the prospect of intergovernmental cooperation would make the subsidiarity test illogical and forestall, even jeopardize, the Union (formerly Community) method and the objectives to be achieved.[161] As such, action via an intergovernmental treaty involving all the Member States may be an alternative solution contemplated in the debate about European contract law, but it does not automatically offset Union action pursuant to the subsidiarity calculus under the Treaties.[162]

Finally, the third requirement envelops the principle of proportionality. To recall, it requires that action can be taken by the Union 'only if and in so far as the objectives of the proposed action cannot be sufficiently achieved by the Member States, but can rather be better achieved at Union level'.[163] The reference to 'in so far as' has been deemed to embody a specific application of the principle of proportionality apart from the principle of proportionality now enshrined in Article 5(4) TEU.[164] Thus, the two applications of the principle of proportionality are saved for treatment together below. For now, it should be clear that by virtue of the Treaties, proportionality is inscribed in subsidiarity itself, making it difficult to separate the two.

7.4.3.3 The Lisbon Treaty

The Lisbon Treaty did not change the meaning of the principle of subsidiarity (in its constitutional form), but sought to make certain aspects more explicit. It clarified that while the principle of conferral governs the 'limits' of Union competences, the principle

[159] Apparently, there had been previous drafts of former Art 5, second para, EC, which specified the Member States acting in isolation. See Lenaerts and van Ypersele, n 107, 46 fn 98. In the European Parliament's 1984 Draft Treaty on European Union, Art 12 on the principle of subsidiarity specified the Member States 'acting separately'. For commentary on this provision, see R Bieber et al, *An ever closer Union: A critical analysis of the Draft Treaty establishing the European Union* (European Commission, 1985); F Capotorti et al, *The European Union Treaty: Commentary on the draft adopted by the European Parliament on 14 February 1984* (Clarendon Press, 1986); Constantinesco, n 111, 46–47.

[160] See Chapter 8, § 8.3.2.1.

[161] See, eg, Gennart, n 150, 177; P Kiiver, 'The conduct of subsidiarity checks of EU legislative proposals by national parliaments: analysis, observations and practical recommendations' (2012) 12 *ERA Forum* 535, 546; T Koopmans, 'The Quest for Subsidiarity' in D Curtin and T Heukels (eds), *II Institutional Dynamics of European Integration: Essays in Honour of Henry G. Schermers* (Martinus Nijhoff, 1994) 43, 44; Lenaerts and Van Nuffel, n 20, § 7-028; Lenaerts and van Ypersele, n 107, 46–47.

[162] See further Chapter 11, § 11.3.2.2.

[163] See text accompanying n 143.

[164] See § 7.4.4.2.

of subsidiarity, as well as the principle of proportionality, govern the 'use' of such competences.[165] Moreover, as regards the subsidiarity test laid down in the first paragraph of Article 5(3) TEU, the requirements generally remain the same as compared to the second paragraph of former Article 5 EC,[166] save for additional language providing that the Union can act only if and in so far as the objectives of the proposed action cannot be sufficiently achieved by the Member States, 'either at central level or at regional and local level'.[167] While certainly emboldening the Union's respect for the varying levels of governance within a Member State for the purposes of assessing its capabilities, in the end, what matters is the determination as to whether the Member States can, at whatever level, achieve the proposed objectives sufficiently for the purposes of the assessment.[168]

Most of the attention regarding the changes brought about by the Lisbon Treaty in connection with the principle of subsidiarity focuses on the enforcement mechanisms to ensure compliance with this principle. Following from the Draft Constitutional Treaty, the Lisbon Treaty introduces an *ex ante* procedure allowing for the national parliaments' scrutiny of draft legislative acts for compliance with subsidiarity as part of the lawmaking process.[169] It also introduces certain changes in an effort to strengthen the *ex post* enforcement of subsidiarity before the Union courts.[170] While the full implications of these new additions[171] and their relationship[172] remain to be seen, they

[165] Art 5(1) EU. It may have been more accurate to use the words 'existence' and 'exercise', respectively, in the English version; for other language versions, however, this was done. See, eg, Dutch version ('De *afbakening* van de bevoegdheden van de Unie wordt beheerst door het beginsel van bevoegdheidstoedeling. De *uitoefening* van die bevoegdheden wordt beheerst door de beginselen van subsidiariteit en evenredigheid.'); French version ('Le principe d'attribution régit la *délimitation* des compétences de l'Union. Les principes de subsidiarité et de proportionnalité régissent *l'exercice* de ces compétences.'); German version ('Für die *Abgrenzung* der Zuständigkeiten der Union gilt der Grundsatz der begrenzten Einzelermächtigung. Für die *Ausübung* der Zuständigkeiten der Union gelten die Grundsätze der Subsidiarität und der Verhältnismäßigkeit.'); Italian version ('La *delimitazione* delle competenze dell'Unione si fonda sul principio di attribuzione. *L'esercizio* delle competenze dell'Unione si fonda sui principi di sussidiarietà e proporzionalità.'); Spanish version ('La *delimitación* de las competencias de la Unión se rige por el principio de atribución. El *ejercicio* de las competencias de la Unión se rige por los principios de subsidiariedad y proporcionalidad.') (emphasis added).

[166] Ex Art 5, second para, EC provided: 'In areas which do not fall within its exclusive competence, the Community shall take action, in accordance with the principle of subsidiarity, only if and in so far as the objectives of the proposed action cannot be sufficiently achieved by the Member States and can therefore, by reason of the scale or effects of the proposed action, be better achieved by the Community'. Art 5(3), first para, TEU uses the words 'but rather', as opposed to 'and can therefore', which has been deemed to make clear that a two-part test is required: see von Bogdandy and Bast, n 39, 302–303.

[167] See text accompanying n 115. See also Lisbon Protocol, n 129, Art 2 (in connection with the Commission's duties of consultation).

[168] See, eg, Lenaerts and Van Nuffel, n 20, § 7-028.

[169] See Art 5(3), second para, TEU; Lisbon Protocol, n 129, Arts 6–7. This procedure is also mentioned in other Treaty provisions concerning the national parliaments: see, eg, Art 12(b) TEU. For its usage in respect of the proposed CESL, see Chapter 6, § 6.4.4.1.

[170] Lisbon Protocol, n 129, Art 8.

[171] In particular, concerns emanate from singling out subsidiarity from other provisions and principles, such as proportionality, and the functioning of the procedure in practice. For a brief selection, see, eg, P Kiiver, *The Early Warning System for the Principle of Subsidiarity: Constitutional theory and empirical reality* (Routledge, 2012); I Cooper, 'The Watchdogs of Subsidiarity: National Parliaments and the Logic of Arguing in the EU' (2006) 44 *JCMS* 281; A Cygan, '"Collective" subsidiarity monitoring by national parliaments after Lisbon: the operation of the early warning mechanism' in *The Treaty of Lisbon*, n 87, 55; S Weatherill, 'Better competence monitoring' (2005) 30 *ELR* 23; see also citations in n 172.

[172] Commentators have increasingly noted the relationship between the two mechanisms, ie the 'procedural' record including the opinions of the national parliaments through the *ex ante* procedure

essentially embody elements of procedural and material subsidiarity, in terms of placing renewed emphasis on subsidiarity 'inside' the EU lawmaking process by virtue of the introduction of this new *ex ante* procedure involving the national parliaments, as well as bolstering to some extent subsidiarity 'outside' the lawmaking process in terms of ensuring compliance with the subsidiarity test under the Treaties.

7.4.4 The principle of proportionality

7.4.4.1 The definition(s) of the principle of proportionality

Alongside subsidiarity, the principle of proportionality also governs the exercise of Union competence as set forth in Article 5(4) TEU: 'Under the principle of proportionality, the content and form of Union action shall not exceed what is necessary to achieve the objectives of the Treaties'.[173] This definition of proportionality as a constitutional principle governing the exercise of Union competence sets it apart from its other roles as a general principle of Union law, which come into play in the assessment of the legality of Union measures, on the one hand, and the compatibility of national measures with Union law, on the other. While there is certainly overlap, proportionality as a constitutional principle is primarily concerned with the establishment of limits on the exercise of Union competence so as to ensure that it does not 'go too far' and exert a 'disproportionate' impact on Member State competence, as opposed to the regulation of public power, whether at the Union or national level, vis-à-vis individuals.[174]

One of the major challenges presented by proportionality is distinguishing it from subsidiarity. Indeed, scholars have commonly noted their blurring,[175] and in many instances, proportionality is treated as a part of subsidiarity or vice versa.[176] In principle, proportionality and subsidiarity are generally presented as answering distinct, albeit related, questions regarding the exercise of Union competence: proportionality regulates the nature and intensity of the exercise of Union competence,[177] whereas subsidiarity determines whether there is a need for the exercise of Union competence in the first place. This suggests that proportionality essentially takes up where subsidiarity leaves off. Yet, in practice, it is not so simple to separate the two principles, and in fact, they are entangled by virtue of the incorporation of proportionality as part of the

is viewed as a means by which to facilitate the Union courts' *ex post* review of a Union measure's compliance with subsidiarity. See, eg, A Biondi, 'Subsidiarity in the Courtroom' in *EU Law After Lisbon*, n 32, 213; P Craig, 'The ECJ and Ultra Vires Action: A Conceptual Analysis' (2011) 48 *CML Rev* 395, 425–427; T Konstadinides, *Division of Powers in European Union Law* (Kluwer, 2009) ch 4; D Wyatt, 'Could a "Yellow Card" for National Parliaments Strengthen Judicial as well as Political Policing of Subsidiarity?' (2006) 2 *Croatian YELP* 1. But compare, eg, S Weatherill, 'The Limits of Legislative Harmonisation Ten Years after *Tobacco Advertising*: How the Court's Case Law has become a "Drafting Guide"' (2011) 12 *GLJ* 827, 859–860.

173 Art 5(4), first para, TEU.

174 See T Tridimas, *The General Principles of EU Law*, 2nd edn (Oxford Univ Press, 2006) 175–176.

175 See, eg, G de Búrca, 'Legal Principles as an Instrument of Differentiation? The Principles of Proportionality and Subsidiarity' in B de Witte et al (eds), *The Many Faces of Differentiation in EU Law* (Intersentia, 2001) 135–138.

176 See, eg, M Kumm, 'Constitutionalising Subsidiarity in Integrated Markets: The Case of Tobacco Regulation in the European Union' (2006) 12 *ELJ* 503; R Schütze, 'Subsidiarity after Lisbon: reinforcing the safeguards of federalism?' (2009) 68 *CLJ* 525. As far as institutional documents are concerned, see, eg, Communication, n 145, Annex, pt IV.

177 See, eg, Edinburgh Conclusions, n 37, point 2(iii), at 14 (referring to 'the principle of proportionality or intensity').

subsidiarity test enshrined in Article 5(3) TEU and the requirements for the principle of proportionality standing alone under Article 5(4) TEU.

7.4.4.2 Proportionality inside and outside subsidiarity

As regards the requirements set forth in Article 5(4) TEU, in contrast to the arduous language of subsidiarity set forth in the Treaties, the principle of proportionality amounts to only one sentence, albeit a powerful one. It ensures that both 'the content and form of Union action' taken pursuant to the Union's competences under the Treaties do 'not exceed what is necessary to achieve the objectives of the Treaties'.[178] The general reference to 'Union action' means that proportionality, unlike subsidiarity, must be complied with, regardless as to whether the Union is acting within the scope of its exclusive or non-exclusive competence.[179] Under the case law, the principle of proportionality generally mandates compliance with the following requirements: first, that Union action is 'appropriate' for attaining the legitimate objectives pursued by the measure in question (also referred to as the suitability test); secondly, that such action is 'necessary' (or 'indispensable'), meaning that it does not go beyond what is necessary to achieve those objectives and where there is a choice between several appropriate measures, recourse must be had to the least onerous; and thirdly, depending upon the case concerned, such Union action may be subject to showing that the disadvantages caused by such action are not disproportionate to the aims pursued, meaning that it must not have an excessive effect on the applicant's interests (also referred to as the proportionality *sensu stricto* test).[180] In light of these requirements, the principle of proportionality is essentially concerned with gauging the intensity of Union action to ensure that it is properly attuned to achieve the objectives proposed. As such, aspects hinging on the content and form of Union action are the bastion of proportionality, as made explicit in the text of Article 5(4) TEU and complemented by the Lisbon Protocol.[181]At the same time, however, such matters seem to invite aspects of subsidiarity, and thus, it becomes difficult to draw the line between the two.

[178] Art 5(4), first para, TEU.

[179] This had already been the case with regard to former Art 5, third para, EC, which referred to 'any action' on the part of the Community. See, eg, N Emiliou, *The Principle of Proportionality in European Law: A Comparative Study* (Kluwer, 1996) 140.

[180] See Lenaerts and Van Nuffel, n 20, § 7-035–§ 7-037. At present, the case law is not entirely consistent when it comes to the formulation of the proportionality requirements as far as Union measures are concerned. In some cases, only the first two requirements are mentioned in the standard 'formula' elaborated by the Union courts (see, eg, Case C-380/03 *Germany v European Parliament and Council* ('*Tobacco Advertising II*') [2006] ECR I-11573, para 41), whereas in others, all three requirements are expressly mentioned together (see, eg, Joined Cases C-581/10 and C-629/10 (Judgment of 23 Oct 2012) *Nelson and Others*, not reported, para 71; Case T-370/11 (Judgment of 7 March 2013) *Poland v Commission*, not reported, para 64) or in separate paragraphs (see, eg, Case C-58/08 *Vodafone and Others* [2010] ECR I-4999, paras 51, 53; Case C-176/09 *Luxembourg v European Parliament and Council* [2011] ECR I-3727, paras 61, 63). The Union courts' recitation of two versus three requirements may be explained by a number of factors, eg, they may not distinguish between the second and third requirements or may assess the third requirement, despite not including it as part of the standard 'formula', depending upon the arguments put forward by the applicant. See further P Craig, *EU Administrative Law*, 2nd edn (Oxford Univ Press, 2012) 591–592, 601–604; HCH Hofmann, 'Which Limits? Control of Powers in an Integrated System' in C Barnard and O Odudu (eds), *The Outer Limits of European Union Law* (Hart, 2009) 45, 54 fn 34; T von Danwitz, 'Thoughts on Proportionality and Coherence in the Jurisprudence of the Court of Justice' in *Constitutionalising the EU Judicial System*, n 36, 367, 372–373.

[181] See Lisbon Protocol, n 129, Art 5.

This was aptly demonstrated by several articles of the Amsterdam Protocol, which no longer appear in the Lisbon Protocol as such, but have filtered into more recent institutional documents.[182] In particular, points 6 and 7 of the Amsterdam Protocol were sometimes deemed as falling within the rubric of proportionality, even though there was no heading to indicate this, as was the case with the previous 1992 Edinburgh Conclusions,[183] but nonetheless, served to interweave components of subsidiarity into the equation. Point 6 devoted attention to the matter of legal instruments, making clear that: 'Other things being equal, directives should be preferred to regulations and framework decisions to detailed measures.'[184] In doing so, it reiterated the salient features of directives as defined in what is now Article 288 TFEU (ex Article 249 EC) in terms of leaving the choice of form and methods of the result to be achieved to the Member States, which explain their association with the principle of subsidiarity.[185] This point indicated that the form and choice of instrument bore upon the intensity of the action and the way in which such action is formulated, thereby laying claim to proportionality and subsidiarity. Point 7 continued with the discussion of the nature and the extent of what was then Community (now Union) action as follows:

> Community measures should leave as much scope for national decision as possible, consistent with securing the aim of the measure and observing the requirements of the Treaty. While respecting Community law, care should be taken to respect well established national arrangements and the organisation and working of Member States' legal systems. Where appropriate and subject to the need for proper enforcement, Community measures should provide Member States with alternative ways to achieve the objectives of the measures.[186]

These various aspects—respecting national regimes, providing the Member States with alternative means of action, and leaving as much scope for Member State action as possible—touched just as much on the proportionality inquiry in terms of how far the EU should go as on the subsidiarity inquiry in terms of the extent to which the EU should act.

Incidentally, many 'juicy tidbits' regarding proportionality in the 1992 Edinburgh Conclusions were dropped in the Amsterdam Protocol, eg, the references to non-binding or 'soft law' measures, such as recommendations and voluntary codes of conduct;[187] choosing the type of Community (now Union) action with a view to 'encouraging cooperation between Member States, coordinating national action or to complementing, supplementing or supporting such action';[188] and where it was necessary to set standards at the European level, 'consideration should be given to setting minimum standards, with freedom for Member States to set higher national standards' in all areas where appropriate, not just where mandated by the former EC Treaty.[189] Such matters equally called attention to subsidiarity.

[182] See the Commission's Impact Assessment Guidelines, n 132, point 7.2, at 29–30.

[183] See Edinburgh Conclusions, n 37, 20. The Edinburgh Conclusions were deemed to have continuing significance in guiding the action of the institutions and the development of the application of the principle of subsidiarity in the Amsterdam Protocol: see Amsterdam Protocol, n 130, fourth recital.

[184] Amsterdam Protocol, n 130, point 6. See, in this regard, Case T-526/10 (Judgment of 25 April 2013) *Inuit Tapiriit Kanatami and Others v Commission*, not reported, paras 99–100 (appeal pending in Case C-398/13 P).

[185] Amsterdam Protocol, n 130, point 6.

[186] Amsterdam Protocol, n 130, point 7.

[187] Edinburgh Conclusions, n 37, point v, at 21.

[188] Edinburgh Conclusions, n 37, point vi, at 21.

[189] Edinburgh Conclusions, n 37, point iv, at 20.

The linkage between proportionality and subsidiarity is further apparent when it comes to the specific application of the proportionality test as part of the requirements for subsidiarity set down in Article 5(3) TEU. Here, proportionality is incorporated as part of the subsidiarity test itself.[190] The idea is that this allows the principle of subsidiarity, infused with proportionality, to temper or gauge the scope of Union action to only that part of the proposed action where the Member States fall short and thus seeks to preserve the action of the Member States for that part of the proposed action which they are capable of achieving.[191] In short, proportionality under Article 5(2) TEU is an ingenious element of the subsidiarity test that ensures that Union action only 'fills the gaps' and does not intrude into areas where the Member States are capable of taking action themselves.

So far, the interplay between the principle of proportionality set down in Article 5(3) TEU as compared to that in Article 5(4) TEU does not appear to have garnered much detailed attention in the literature, and in fact, this is a subject into which further research is warranted. Formally, proportionality under Article 5(4) TEU comes into play in all instances of Union action, not just under circumstances relating to non-exclusive Union competence under Article 5(2) TEU. Yet, practically speaking, it is often difficult to distinguish the impact of proportionality in Article 5(2) TEU, as opposed to Article 5(3) TEU. The bottom line for this discussion is that subsidiarity and proportionality are inextricably intertwined. While the requirements of the proportionality test under Article 5(4) TEU are formally distinct from those set down in Article 5(3) TEU, both pay tribute to the intimate connection between proportionality and subsidiarity. This means that for the purposes of the constitutional assessment of European contract law, very often a distinct line between the two cannot be drawn, and thus, the two must be referred to together. This also means that for those seeking to find refuge in the principle of proportionality to offset subsidiarity's apparent ineffectiveness in relation to provisions such as Article 114 TFEU,[192] questions remain open in this regard given the bond between the two. At the same time, however, the combination of subsidiarity and proportionality make for a powerful pair in terms of amplifying the roles that can be played by these principles 'inside' as well as 'outside' the EU lawmaking process when it comes to European contract law. While the principle of subsidiarity has been criticized for its inability to express the nuances of the relationship between the powers wielded by the Union and the Member States,[193] it is submitted here that this viewpoint discounts the viable role that it can play alongside proportionality in relation to provisions at issue in European contract law. Specifically, in line with the distinction between material and procedural subsidiarity elaborated above, proportionality can further contribute to the more nuanced role that subsidiarity can play inside the lawmaking process vis-à-vis provisions such as Articles 114 and 352 TFEU relevant to the debate.

7.4.4.3 The Lisbon Treaty

As with the principles of conferral and subsidiarity, the Lisbon Treaty did not fundamentally change the meaning and operation of the principle of proportionality (in its constitutional form), but made certain aspects more explicit. There is additional

[190] See, eg, Tridimas, n 87, 52.
[191] Lenaerts and Van Nuffel, n 20, § 7-039.
[192] See Davies, n 127, 81–84; citations in n 176. Compare P Craig, 'Subsidiarity: A Political and Legal Analysis' (2012) 50 *JCMS* 72, 82–84.
[193] See, eg, Estella, n 128, 134–136.

language set forth in the second paragraph of Article 5(4) TEU, stipulating that the Union institutions must apply the principle of proportionality as laid down in the Lisbon Protocol. Moreover, as compared to the former third paragraph of Article 5 EC,[194] the first paragraph of Article 5(4) TEU refers to the 'content and form' of Union action as part of the proportionality assessment. As seen above, that was already made clear in the Amsterdam Protocol, but not so much in the third paragraph of Article 5 EC itself. This may to some extent compensate for the fact that the Lisbon Protocol eliminates much of the language in the Amsterdam Protocol concerning proportionality's application, including points 6 and 7, discussed above. Nonetheless, by leaving intact the definition of subsidiarity, the Lisbon Treaty retains the specific form of proportionality incorporated as part of the subsidiarity calculus, and by laying claim to both the 'content' and the 'form' of Union action, it would seem to draw proportionality and subsidiarity closer together. Yet, unlike the principle of subsidiarity, the principle of proportionality is not subject to the *ex ante* procedure involving the national parliaments. Given the relationship between the two, difficulties in checking compliance with subsidiarity, and not proportionality, have been spotlighted in the commentary.[195]

Perhaps one of the most provocative points about proportionality is that which never made it into the Lisbon Treaty. This concerns the Commission's unsuccessful proposal to put forward a scheme concerning the classification of Union powers based on the scale of intensity of Union action in the context of the European Convention.[196] The impetus of this proposal stemmed from the Commission's view that categorizing Union competences (based on the distinction between exclusive, shared, and complementary competences) would not sufficiently clarify the division of competences between the Union and the Member States, since in most areas, both the Union and the Member States could in principle take action and the nature and arrangements for their interaction were extremely variable.[197] As such, the Commission advocated another approach based on a typology of Union action, classified on a sliding scale of the intensity of Union action in the legislative and non-legislative spheres.[198] For the legislative sphere, this category was composed of four types of action, proceeding from uniform regulation, harmonization, minimum harmonization, and finally, mutual recognition and 'interconnection' of the Member State' legal systems.[199] For the non-legislative sphere, this ranged from joint action, compulsory coordination of national policies, financial support programmes, and non-binding coordination of national policies.[200] The Commission's proposal was ultimately passed over in favour of the categorization of competences inserted initially in the Draft Constitutional Treaty and ultimately in the Lisbon Treaty as elaborated above.[201] As a formal matter, the Commission's proposal was framed within the context of the division of competences between the EU and the Member States, as opposed to the principle of proportionality as such. Nonetheless, it had potential to breathe new life into the principle of proportionality in the sense of expressly matching up forms of Union action based on their intensity in relation to the national legal orders. That said, from the vantage point of European

[194] Ex Art 5, third para, EC provided: 'Any action by the Community shall not go beyond what is necessary to achieve the objectives of the Treaty'.

[195] See citations in n 171. [196] Note, n 100. [197] Note, n 100, 5–7.

[198] Note, n 100, 7–8. [199] Note, n 100, 9–10. [200] Note, n 100, 10–11.

[201] The proposal was mentioned in the Final Report of Working Group V on Complementary Competencies, although it was not formulated as an explicit recommendation: see CONV 375/1/02REV1 WGV14, dated 4 Nov 2002, 12–14.

contract law, certain viable forms of Union action contemplated in the debate, such as optional instruments, were not mentioned.

7.4.5 The principle of sincere cooperation

7.4.5.1 The definition of the principle of sincere cooperation

The principle of sincere cooperation has garnered several labels, such as the principle of loyal cooperation or the principle of loyalty,[202] but they generally point to the requirements now enshrined in Article 4(3) TEU.[203] This provision contains three key paragraphs. The first is concerned with the relationship between the Union and the Member States and provides: 'Pursuant to the principle of sincere cooperation, the Union and the Member States shall, in full mutual respect, assist each other in carrying out tasks which flow from the Treaties'.[204] The second is concerned with the 'positive' obligations placed on the Member States, stipulating that: 'Member States shall take any appropriate measures, general or particular, to ensure fulfillment of the obligations arising out of the Treaties or resulting from acts of the institutions of the Union'.[205] The third is largely concerned with 'negative' obligations on the Member States, placing them under the duty 'to facilitate the achievement of the Union's tasks and refrain from any measure which could jeopardise the attainment of the Union's objectives'.[206] Compared to the principles of conferral, subsidiarity, and proportionality, the principle of sincere cooperation transcends matters of Union competence and is concerned with the relationship between the Union and the Member States on a much wider scale.[207] Nonetheless, it has an important role to play in the debate about European contract law, despite its low profile so far. Indeed, it is somewhat underestimated in the debate, as has been said in relation to the EU institutional framework generally.[208]

7.4.5.2 The role(s) of the principle of sincere cooperation in European contract law

As far as matters of Union competence are concerned, the operation of the principle of sincere cooperation generally depends on the previous assessment of the principles of conferral, subsidiarity, and proportionality. By and large, it is a 'follow-up' provision,

[202] Although ex Art 10 EC contained no heading, the principle of loyal cooperation has been cited in the case law. See, eg, Case C-105/03 *Pupino* [2005] ECR I-5285, para 42.

[203] See also Art 13(2) TEU, second sent.

[204] Art 4(3), first para, TEU.

[205] Art 4(3), second para, TEU.

[206] Art 4(3), third para, TEU.

[207] See, eg, LW Gormley, 'The Development of General Principles of Law within Article 10 (ex Article 5) EC [now Art 4(3) TEU]' in *General Principles of European Community Law*, n 36, 113; LW Gormley, 'Some Further Reflections on the Development of General Principles of Law within Article 10 EC [now Article 4(3) TEU]' in U Bernitz et al (eds), *General Principles of EC Law in a Process of Development* (Kluwer, 2008) 303; JT Lang, 'Article 10 EC [now Article 4(3) TEU]—The Most Important 'General Principle' of Community Law' in *General Principles of EC Law in a Process of Development*, 75; von Bogdandy, n 36, 41–42; R Widdershoven, 'The Principle of Loyal Cooperation: Lawmaking by the European Court of Justice and the Dutch Courts' in F Stroink et al (eds), *Judicial Lawmaking and Administrative Law* (Intersentia, 2005) 3. In particular, it has a key role in EU external relations. See, eg, G De Baere, *Constitutional Principles of EU External Relations* (Oxford Univ Press, 2008) 250–264 and citations therein.

[208] See, eg, JT Lang, 'Community Constitutional Law: Article 5 EEC Treaty [now Art 4(3) TEU]' (1990) 27 *CML Rev* 645, 647. See also S Weatherill, 'Beyond Preemption? Shared Competence and Constitutional Change in the European Community' in *Legal Issues of the Maastricht Treaty*, n 146, 13, 31.

which comes after the decision has been made as to what level and to what extent the proposed action should be exercised by the Union or by the Member States. But importantly, it is triggered in either case. As expressly recognized in the Amsterdam Protocol, though no longer in the Lisbon Protocol, '[w]here the application of the principle of subsidiarity leads to no action being taken by the Community [now Union], Member States are required in their action to comply with the general rules laid down in Article [10] of the Treaty [now Article 4(3) TEU]', that is to say with the positive and negative obligations cited above.[209] Likewise, where the application of subsidiarity leads to action being taken by the Union, the principle of sincere cooperation places the Member States under various duties related to ensuring that the objectives of the Union measure concerned is fully achieved, eg, that it is properly and timely implemented and that it receives its full effectiveness in the national legal orders. The Union institutions, too, are under various duties, such as cooperating with the Member States and with each other within the context of ensuring the objectives of the particular measure are achieved. It is often overlooked, however, that the principle of sincere cooperation has another role to play in the constitutional assessment of European contract law. As will be seen, this is in connection with the recourse to an intergovernmental treaty among the Member States outside the Treaty framework as a potential alternative route to far-reaching Union action in contract law.[210]

7.4.5.3 The Lisbon Treaty

Generally speaking, the Lisbon Treaty further ingrained the overriding importance of the principle of sincere cooperation and made certain aspects more explicit. As compared to the former EC Treaty, the principle of sincere cooperation is placed upfront before the principles of conferral, subsidiarity, and proportionality in the TEU. Furthermore, former Article 10 EC contained only two paragraphs dealing with the 'positive' and 'negative' obligations of the Member States; however, it was not limited as such, and over the years had been interpreted as covering the duties owed by the Member States to the Union institutions and to each other, as well as those owed by the Union institutions to the Member States and to each other.[211] Consequently, additional language was inserted by the Lisbon Treaty in Article 4(3) TEU and Article 13(2) TEU to confirm this.[212] In short, the role played by the principle of sincere cooperation in connection with European contract law is not substantially altered by the Lisbon Treaty.

7.5 Conclusions

In summary, this chapter sought to illustrate three main points. First, while most of the reasons used to explain the neglect of the constitutionality of European contract law at the European level were viable as the debate was gearing up, they have lost much of their salience as far as the activities contemplated within the European contract law project are concerned and make the need to confront the constitutional dimensions of European contract law more apparent. Secondly, with the changes introduced by

[209] Amsterdam Protocol, n 130, point 8.
[210] See Chapter 11, § 11.3; see also § 11.2.2.3.
[211] See Lenaerts and Van Nuffel, n 20, § 7–043.
[212] See ns 203–204.

the Lisbon Treaty, which were preceded by the European Convention and the Draft Constitutional Treaty, the constitutional climate surrounding the division of competences between the EU and the Member States adds to this momentum, and as will be seen, has great significance in connection with the interpretation of the Treaty provisions and other forms of Member State action contemplated in the debate.

Finally, the complexities underlying the constitutional parameters of European contract law should not be underestimated. While in principle, the meanings of the principles of conferral, subsidiarity, proportionality, and sincere cooperation may be clear cut, in practice, these principles do not operate in a single, standardized way, which makes it challenging to parse out the roles that each plays in this setting. As regards the principle of conferral, the type of legal basis in terms of distinction between cross-sectoral competences and those in a particular policy field impacts the operation of subsidiarity and proportionality, and the combination of legal bases in light of current case law directs attention to the possible use of more than one Treaty provision to support Union action in contract law. As regards the principles of subsidiarity and proportionality, it is difficult to find the boundary line between them, but their combination may be considered to contribute to a more multi-dimensional inquiry as regards their potential role 'inside' as well as 'outside' the EU decision-making process, despite the fact that either alone or together, there are tensions associated with their perceived ineffectiveness in relation to functional provisions, such as Article 114 TFEU. As regards the principle of sincere cooperation, it plays a role not only as a 'follow-up' to conferral, subsidiarity, and proportionality, but also in connection with the potential recourse to forms of intergovernmental cooperation among the Member States contemplated as part of the debate. The foregoing examination of these principles sets the scene for examining the scope of the Union's competence to take action in contract law under specific Treaty provisions at issue in the debate, starting with those related to the internal market in the next chapter.

8

European Contract Law and the Internal Market

8.1 Introduction

As illustrated in Part Two, the Union's objectives rooted in the internal market have stood at the forefront of the debate about European contract law, either implicitly or explicitly, starting from the European Parliament's 1989 Resolution through to the Commission's three Communications on European contract law, and the recent proposal for a Regulation on a Common European Sales Law (proposed CESL). This brings Articles 114, 115, and 352 TFEU into play. Article 114 TFEU has attracted much, if not most, of the attention and controversy in the debate as regards its scope, interaction with the free movement rules, and interplay with the principles of subsidiarity and proportionality. Articles 115 and 352 TFEU have also made their way into the discussion, each attracting diverse opinions as to the extent to which they may play a residual or complementary role vis-à-vis Article 114 TFEU to support Union action in contract law, with particular regard to the possible use of Article 352 TFEU for the adoption of an optional instrument of contract law, as illustrated by the proposed CESL.

The aim of this chapter is therefore to examine the extent of the Union's competence to adopt a European contract law instrument on the basis of Articles 114, 115, and/or 352 TFEU. It is divided into three main parts in line with the key issues surrounding the use of these provisions in the debate: first, the relationship between Articles 114 and 115 TFEU; secondly, the scope of Article 114 TFEU; and thirdly, the relationship between Articles 114 and 352 TFEU. As will be seen, the relationship between Articles 114 and 115 TFEU not only determines the potential role to be played, or not, by Article 115 TFEU, but also exposes aspects concerning Article 114 TFEU, which sets the stage for the analysis of that provision, and in turn, for delving into the relationship between Articles 114 and 352 TFEU, especially as far as an optional instrument such as the proposed CESL is concerned. In effect, the case law on Article 114 TFEU serves as the template or 'springboard' for evaluating the breadth of this provision and its relationship to Articles 115 and 352 TFEU in this setting (as well as other Treaty provisions and alternative solutions put forward in the debate as detailed in forthcoming chapters), much like the hub of a wheel and its radiating spokes.

8.2 The Relationship between Articles 114 and 115 TFEU

8.2.1 Overview of approximation in the Treaties and the three-level hierarchy

To understand why focus is placed on Articles 114 and 115 TFEU, as opposed to other provisions conferring competence on the Union to approximate national laws, the discussion begins with a brief overview of approximation in the Treaties and the three-level hierarchy within which the various provisions allowing for the approximation of national laws are situated. As stressed time and time again inside and outside the debate about European contract law, the approximation of national laws is not an objective in and of itself in the system of the Treaties. Rather, in line with the principal of conferral, approximation constitutes a tool, alongside others, to help the Union achieve various objectives set forth in the Treaties. Still, there is good reason why approximation is intimately associated with the internal market, since it is particularly in that context that approximation plays a crucial role.

From the founding of what was then the European (Economic) Community, the objective to establish a common market had been inscribed upfront in former Article 2 EC, which at the same time framed the common market as an instrument to achieve larger goals in the European integration process. This was augmented by former Article 3 EC, which listed among the Community's various activities: 'an internal market characterised by the abolition, as between Member States, of obstacles to the free movement of persons, services and capital',[1] 'a system ensuring that competition in the internal market is not distorted',[2] and 'the approximation of the laws of Member States to the extent required for the proper functioning of the common market'.[3] These provisions were complemented by former Article 14 EC, which defined the internal market as 'an area without internal frontiers in which the free movement of goods, persons, services and capital is ensured in accordance with the provisions of this Treaty'[4] and expressly referred to several Treaty provisions to accomplish this objective.[5] Leaving aside the discussion of the internal/common market for the moment,[6] what is important to grasp is that in line with former Articles 2 and 3 EC, the Community was given the task to create an integrated market among the Member States, which would be carried out via various provisions of the EC Treaty.

The same can be said for the present Treaty framework, even though as a result of the changes brought about by the Lisbon Treaty, some of the salient language cited above was removed.[7] As discussed in the previous chapter,[8] former Article 2 EC was replaced in substance by Article 3 TEU, which includes, in more sparse terms, the establishment of the internal market as one of the Union's objectives.[9] Former Article 3 EC was replaced in substance by Articles 3–6 TFEU, which reconfigure the extensive list of activities within the frame of the categorization of Union competences. Yet, Article 26 TFEU, corresponding to former Article 14 EC, retains the definition of the internal market and envisages the adoption of measures to achieve the Union's internal market objectives 'in accordance with the relevant provisions of the Treaties' without naming them as such.[10] Consequently, under the present (as well as the past) Treaty framework, there is (or was) not just one 'go to' provision governing the Union's (or former Community's) competence to approximate national laws for the purposes of the internal (or what was then called the common) market.

[1] Ex Art 3(1)(c) EC. [2] Ex Art 3(1)(g) EC. [3] Ex Art 3(1) (h) EC.

[4] Ex Art 14(2) EC.

[5] Ex Art 14(1) EC listed former Arts 15, 26, 47(2), 49, 80, 93, and 95 EC 'without prejudice to the other provisions of this Treaty'. [6] See § 8.2.3.1.

[7] See, eg, K Lenaerts and P Van Nuffel (R Bray and N Cambien (eds)), *European Union Law*, 3rd edn (Sweet & Maxwell, 2011) § 9-002.

[8] See Chapter 7, § 7.4.2. [9] Art 3(3) TEU.

[10] Art 26(1)–(2) TFEU. See Joined Cases C-274/11 and C-295/11 (Judgment of 16 April 2013) *Spain and Italy v Council*, not reported, para 21.

Following from this, there is a hierarchy in the system of the Treaties with respect to the recourse to the various approximation provisions, which generally comprises three levels: first, specific approximation provisions; secondly, general approximation provisions including Articles 114 and 115 TFEU; and finally, the 'catch-all' provision of Article 352 TFEU. This hierarchy is not explicitly elaborated in the Treaties as such (past or present), but emerged on account of the text of certain Treaty provisions as interpreted by the Court of Justice. Specifically, in view of the clause, 'save where otherwise provided in the Treaties', in Article 114(1) TFEU, this predicates that if there is a provision setting out a more specific approximation competence in the area concerned, that provision takes priority over the general approximation provisions found on the second level, namely Articles 114 and 115 TFEU.[11] This is essentially an expression of the relationship between general and specific legal bases in the Treaties within the context of the principle of conferral, in the sense that if the Treaties contain a more specific legal basis that is applicable to achieve the objectives of the measure concerned, it takes precedence over the more general legal basis (*lex specialis derogat legi generali*).[12] This hierarchy demonstrates that there is no 'cherry picking' between the various provisions; rather, there are rules laid down in the Treaties as regards the choice between certain provisions. In other words, as far as European contract law is concerned, there is no free choice as between Articles 114 and 115 TFEU, or even Article 352 TFEU, depending on subjective preferences concerning the relevant decision-making procedures, legal instruments, etc. This hierarchy is therefore beneficial for singling out Articles 114 and 115 TFEU, as opposed to others in the internal market setting, with Article 352 TFEU playing a 'backup' role.

The first level concerns specific approximation provisions that confer competence on the Union to approximate national laws in particular policy fields *ratione materiae*. As already noted in Chapter 7, at present, there are no specific approximation provisions concerning contract law. Thus, as far as the Union's internal market objectives are concerned, specific approximation provisions do not play a key role in the discussion of the potential legal bases to support the adoption of a European contract law instrument.[13]

The second level concerns general approximation provisions, which denote the Union's functional competences of a cross-sectoral character.[14] So far, it has been primarily Articles 114 and 115 TFEU (ex Articles 95 and 94 EC) that lie at the crux of the debate about European contract law in the internal market setting, as opposed to other approximation provisions found within this level. For example, Articles 116 and 117 TFEU (ex Articles 96 and 97 EC) follow Articles 114 and 115 TFEU in the chapter of the TFEU on the 'Approximation of Laws'. Article 116 TFEU deals with situations involving existing distortions of competition in the internal market, whereas Article 117 TFEU is concerned with the risk of future distortions in this regard. As original fixtures of the EEC Treaty, they were intended to serve as a *lex specialis* in

[11] See, eg, Case C-84/94 *UK v Council* ('*Working Time*') [1996] ECR I-5755, para 12; Case C-271/94 *European Parliament v Council* [1996] ECR I-1689, para 33; Case C-338/01 *Commission v Council* [2004] ECR I-4829, para 59; Case C-533/03 *Commission v Council* [2006] ECR I-1025, para 44.

[12] See, eg, Case C-338/01 *Commission v Council* [2004] ECR I-4829, para 60; Case C-533/03 *Commission v Council* [2006] ECR I-1025, para 45; Case C-155/07 *European Parliament v Council* [2008] ECR I-8103, para 34.

[13] Such provisions may still have relevance, eg, in the case of Art 118 TFEU for the relationship between Arts 114 and 352 TFEU in connection with an optional instrument of contract law: see § 8.4.3.

[14] See Chapter 7, § 7.4.2.3.

relation to what is now Article 115 TFEU because they were aimed at remedying specific cases of distortions of competition in what was then the common market involving one or more Member States.[15] Thus, they are not commonly viewed as having much relevance as far as the adoption of a European contract law instrument is concerned.[16] Furthermore, Articles 53 and 62 TFEU (ex Articles 47 and 55 EC) have been considered, like Article 114 TFEU, to be horizontal competences, albeit with a more limited reach, since they pertain specifically to the right of establishment and the free movement of services, respectively.[17] One might have expected them to merit some attention in the debate, but so far, this has not generally been the case. It may very well be that these provisions would at most be used in conjunction with Article 114 TFEU, and therefore they are not considered the sole or main peg upon which to hang the adoption of a European contract law instrument. In any case, as made clear by *Tobacco Advertising I*,[18] the Court interprets the scope of these provisions akin to that of Article 114 TFEU. Consequently, their viability may increase, likely in combination with Article 114 TFEU, and as such, the examination of Article 114 TFEU has relevance for the potential recourse to these provisions.

Finally, the third level concerns the 'catch-all' provision of Article 352 TFEU. It comes into play under circumstances where Union action proves necessary 'to attain one of the objectives of the Treaties, and the Treaties have not provided the necessary powers'.[19] In other words, Article 352 TFEU may only be used under circumstances where a more specific legal basis cannot be found in the Treaties that confers the requisite competence on the Union to adopt the measure concerned, whether in relation to the achievement of the Union's internal market objectives or otherwise. Accordingly, Article 352 TFEU's potential to serve as the legal basis for a European contract law instrument follows from the determination of the Union's competence under Articles 114 and 115 TFEU.

8.2.2 Text of Articles 114 and 115 TFEU compared and the order of preference

Articles 114 and 115 TFEU sit side by side in the specific chapter of the TFEU devoted to the 'Approximation of Laws'.[20] It is quite remarkable that the Treaties provide for not one, but two distinct provisions that embody startlingly similar language.[21] This is no coincidence. It is the product of the chronological development of the Treaties. By virtue of the Single European Act (SEA), former Article 95 EC (originally Article 100a EEC, now Article 114 TFEU) was inserted into the former EC Treaty amidst

[15] See R Barents, 'The Competition Policy of the EC' in PJG Kapteyn et al (eds), *The Law of the European Union and the European Communities*, 4th rev edn (Kluwer, 2008) 785, 872–874. See also Opinion of AG Geelhoed in Case C-308/01 *GIL Insurance and Others* [2004] ECR I-4777, points 58–67.

[16] See, eg, J Ziller, 'The Legitimacy of the Codification of Contract Law in View of the Allocation of Competences between the European Union and its Member States' in MW Hesselink (ed), *The Politics of a European Civil Code* (Kluwer, 2006) 89, 97–98.

[17] See Opinion of AG Fennelly in Case C-376/98 *Germany v European Parliament and Council* ('*Tobacco Advertising I*') [2000] ECR I-8419 and Case C-74/99 *Imperial Tobacco and Others* [2000] ECR I-8599, point 63.

[18] Case C-376/98 *Tobacco Advertising I*. See § 8.3.2.1.

[19] Art 352(1) TFEU.

[20] Ch 3 ('Approximation of Laws') of Title VII of the TFEU ('Common Rules on Competition, Taxation and Approximation of Laws').

[21] This was highlighted by the European Convention, in which there were proposals to merge the two into one provision, but were not taken up.

institutional activities that placed renewed stimulus on the creation of the internal market while attempting to overcome the limitations of former Article 94 EC (originally Article 100 EEC, now Article 115 TFEU).[22] Former Article 94 EC comprised the following single sentence: 'The Council shall, acting *unanimously* on a proposal from the Commission and after consulting the European Parliament and the Economic and Social Committee, issue *directives* for the approximation of such laws, regulations or administrative provisions of the Member States as *directly affect* the establishment *or* functioning of the *common market*'.[23] In contrast, former Article 95(1) EC provided:

> *By way of derogation from Article 94* and *save where otherwise provided in this Treaty*, the following provisions shall apply for the achievement of the objectives set out in Article 14. The Council shall, acting in accordance with the *procedure referred to in Article 251* and after consulting the Economic and Social Committee, adopt the *measures* for the approximation of the provisions laid down by law, regulation or administrative action in Member States which have as their *object* the establishment *and* functioning of the *internal market*.[24]

This was immediately followed by Article 95(2) EC, which laid down the proviso that Article 95(1) EC could not be used for the adoption of measures relating to fiscal provisions, the free movement of persons, and the rights and interests of employed persons.

As indicated by the italicized language, there were several differences between former Articles 94 and 95 EC in terms of their decision-making procedures, legal instruments, and substantive scope, which embodied trade-offs between the two. With respect to decision-making procedures, Article 94 EC provided for unanimous voting in the Council and consultation of the European Parliament (and the European Economic and Social Committee (EESC)), whereas Article 95 EC provided for qualified majority voting in the Council and (eventually) the co-decision procedure allowing for greater involvement of the European Parliament (also with consultation of the EESC).[25] As for the choice of legal instruments, Article 94 EC was limited to the use of directives, whereas Article 95 EC stipulated 'measures', including but not limited to directives. As is well-known, the use of directives under Article 95 EC was encouraged by a special Declaration attached to the SEA.[26] Nonetheless, it was, and continues to be, a crucial point in the debate that this provision allows for a broader array of legal instruments, such as regulations, which has been contemplated in discussions concerning an optional instrument, as exemplified by the proposed CESL. As regards substantive scope, there were three glaring differences in the wording of Articles 94 and 95 EC, which concerned the respective references to directives or measures that (1) 'directly affect' versus have as their 'object' the (2) establishment 'or' versus 'and' functioning of the (3) 'common market' versus 'internal market'. Some of these differences led commentators to contemplate the merits of both provisions in connection with European

[22] The rich discourse on this course of events transcends this discussion. See, eg, JHH Weiler, 'The Transformation of Europe' (1991) 100 *YLJ* 2403 (reprinted in JHH Weiler, *The Constitution of Europe—'Do the New Clothes Have an Emperor?' and Other Essays on European Integration* (Cambridge Univ Press, 1999) 10).

[23] Ex Art 94 EC (emphasis added).

[24] Ex Art 95(1) EC (emphasis added).

[25] Originally, ex Art 100a EEC required the cooperation procedure.

[26] The Declaration on Article 100a EEC, [1987] OJ L169/24, provides: 'In its proposals pursuant to Article 100a(1) the Commission shall give precedence to the use of the instrument of a directive if harmonization involves the amendment of legislative provisions in one or more Member States.' It was not formally repealed by the Lisbon Treaty, unlike the Amsterdam Protocol on the application of the principles of subsidiarity and proportionality, which also indicated a preference in point 6 for directives over regulations '[o]ther things being equal' (see Chapter 7, § 7.4.4.2): Max Planck Institute for Comparative and International Private Law, 'Policy Options for Progress Towards a European Contract Law' (2011) 75 *RabelsZ* 371, 393.

contract law. Yet, there was, and still is, a specific order of preference between the two provisions prescribed by the past and present Treaty frameworks prioritizing the use of former Article 95 EC, now Article 114 TFEU.

By virtue of the first sentence of former Article 95(1) EC—'By way of derogation from Article 94 and save where otherwise provided in this Treaty, the following provisions shall apply for the achievement of the objectives set out in Article 14'—Article 95 EC was considered to be a *lex specialis* in relation to Article 94 EC as far as the achievement of the objectives relating to the internal market were concerned.[27] The language of Article 95 EC ('By way of derogation from Article 94') was considered somewhat deceptive, since it stated that Article 95 EC was merely a 'derogating' provision from Article 94 EC, when in fact the breadth of the objectives related to the internal market indicated a wide expanse for the scope of Article 95 EC, with the result that Article 95 EC effectively overtook Article 94 EC as the primary source of what was then the Community's approximation competence.[28] Thus, already under the past Treaty framework, recourse had to be made to Article 95 EC first,[29] and Article 94 EC came to occupy a residual role vis-à-vis Article 95 EC for the three fields fenced off from that latter provision to the extent that more specific approximation provisions were not applicable.[30]

The primary role assumed by Article 95 EC in the former Treaty framework is enhanced in the present Treaty framework by virtue of the Lisbon Treaty's reconfiguration of Articles 94 and 95 EC as Articles 115 and 114 TFEU, respectively. These two provisions remain side by side, and their substantive content has been left virtually untouched. Article 114(1) TFEU provides in relevant part: 'The European Parliament and Council shall, acting in accordance with the *ordinary legislative procedure* and after consulting the European Economic and Social Committee, adopt the *measures* for the approximation of the provisions laid down by law, regulation or administrative action in Member States which have as their *object* the establishment *and* functioning of the *internal market*.'[31] Article 114(2) TFEU lays down the exclusion of the same three areas from the scope of Article 114(1) TFEU. By comparison, Article 115 TFEU still comprises a single sentence, stipulating that: 'the Council shall, acting *unanimously* in accordance with a special legislative procedure and after *consulting* the European Parliament and the Economic and Social Committee, issue *directives* for the approximation of such laws, regulations or administrative provisions of the Member States as *directly affect* the establishment *or* functioning of the internal market'.[32] Apart from the change in wording from common market to internal market in Article 115 TFEU, discussed below,[33] the differences between Articles 114 and 115 TFEU as regards the respective decision-making procedures,[34] legal instruments, and substantive scope are the same as former Articles 94 and 95 EC.

[27] See citations in n 35. [28] Weiler, *YLJ*, n 22, 2459.

[29] See, eg, CD Ehlermann, 'The Internal Market Following the Single European Act' (1987) 24 *CML Rev* 361, 382.

[30] A classic example concerns the first category of fiscal provisions: see, eg, Case C-338/01 *Commission v Council* [2004] ECR I-4829; Case C-533/03 *Commission v Council* [2006] ECR I-1025.

[31] Art 114(1) TFEU (emphasis added). [32] Art 115 TFEU (emphasis added).

[33] See § 8.2.3.1.

[34] Under Art 114 TFEU, the ordinary legislative procedure denotes qualified majority voting in the Council and the co-decision procedure involving the Council and Parliament, whereas for Art 115 TFEU, the special legislative procedure means that the Council acts alone via unanimous voting with consultation of the Parliament.

However, the order between them is now reversed, and Article 114 TFEU comes before Article 115 TFEU as the first provision of the chapter on the 'Approximation of Laws'. This explains the alterations to the first sentence of each provision. Article 114(1) TFEU states in relevant part: 'Save where otherwise provided by the Treaties, the following provisions shall apply for the achievement of the objectives set out in Article 26.' The introductory clause in former Article 95(1) EC—'By way of derogation from Article 94'—was removed, and Article 115 TFEU now begins, 'Without prejudice to Article 114'. As a result, the Treaties expressly recognize Article 114 TFEU as the pre-eminent approximation provision of the two, with Article 115 TFEU literally taking a 'backseat' role, as had come to be considered under the former EC Treaty.[35]

8.2.3 Lingering ambiguities concerning Articles 114 and 115 TFEU

Despite the order of preference between Articles 114 and 115 TFEU dictated by the Treaties, ambiguities concerning their relationship still exist. The substantive differences between these two provisions mentioned above, especially the respective 'object' versus 'directly affect' language, has provoked controversy in the literature over the years as regards whether the scope of what is now Article 114 TFEU extends further than that of Article 115 TFEU or vice versa and hence whether there is a residual role for Article 115 TFEU under circumstances where Article 114 TFEU would be deemed an insufficient legal basis to support Union action in contract law (or other fields of private law as the case may be).[36]

Save for that concerning the common/internal market, these are issues to which neither the Treaties (in their past or present form) nor the case law of the Union courts (yet) provide explicit answers. There were a few cases that had the potential to place such issues before the Court of Justice, but they generally amounted to missed opportunities. For example, in *Spain v Council*,[37] Spain argued that former Articles 94 or 308 EC (then Articles 100 or 235 EEC, now Articles 115 or 352 TFEU) should have been used instead of former Article 95 EC (then Article 100a EEC, now Article 114 TFEU) as the legal basis for a Regulation creating a supplementary certificate for medicinal

[35] See, eg, C Barnard, *The Substantive Law of the EU—The Four Freedoms*, 3rd edn (Oxford Univ Press, 2010) 604 fn 5; Lenaerts and Van Nuffel, n 7, § 9-113–§ 9-114; PJ Oliver (S Enchelmaier et al (contributing eds)), *Oliver on Free Movement of Goods in the European Union*, 5th edn (Hart, 2010) § 13-07, § 13-10–§ 13-11.

[36] For arguments that Art 115 TFEU (ex Art 94 EC)'s 'directly affect' language is more restrictive than Art 114 TFEU (ex Art 95 EC)'s 'object' language, see, eg, R Barents, 'The Internal Market Unlimited: Some Observations on the Legal Basis of Community Legislation' (1993) 30 *CML Rev* 85, 105; X Debroux, 'Le choix de la base juridique dans l'action environnementale de l'Union européenne' (1995) 31 *CDE* 383, 386 fn 8; B de Witte et al, 'Legal Instruments, Decision-Making and EU Finances' in *The Law of the European Union and the European Communities*, n 15, 273, 309; Ehlermann, n 29, 370; KD Kerameus, 'Procedural Harmonization in Europe' (1995) 43 *AJCL* 401, 409–410; W Sauter, 'The Economic Constitution of the European Union' (1998) 4 *CJEL* 27, 52 fn 93; D Vignes, 'The Harmonisation of National Legislation and the EEC' (1990) 15 *ELR* 358, 360. For arguments that Art 114 TFEU (ex Art 95 EC)'s 'object' language is more restrictive than Art 115 TFEU (ex Art 94 EC)'s 'directly affect' language, see, eg, P Nebbia, 'Internal Market and the Harmonisation of European Contract Law' in T Tridimas and P Nebbia (eds), 2 *European Union Law for the Twenty-First Century: Rethinking the new legal order* (Hart, 2004) 89, 91; AAM Schrauwen, *Marché interieur: recherches sur une notion* (Academisch Proefschrift, Universiteit van Amsterdam, 1997) 148; W van Gerven, 'Coherence of Community and national laws. Is there a legal basis for a European civil code?' (1997) 5 *ERPL* 465, 467 fn 16; Ziller, n 16, 98.

[37] Case C-350/92 *Spain v Council* [1995] ECR I-1985.

products,[38] since those two provisions required unanimity in the Council and thus did not 'trespass on national sovereignty' as compared to Article 95 EC.[39] Not surprisingly, this argument did not find sympathy with the Court for the purposes of challenging the legal basis of a Community (now Union) measure. The Court ultimately upheld the use of Article 95 EC and dismissed Spain's action in full. As far as Article 94 EC was concerned, the Court merely stated that Spain had not put forward any valid argument that this provision constituted the proper legal basis for the Regulation.[40] Curiously, though, in the process of substantiating the use of Article 95 EC, the Court relied on the sixth recital of the Regulation, which espoused the aim 'to prevent the heterogeneous development of national laws leading to further disparities which would be likely to create obstacles to the free movement of medicinal products within the Community and thus *directly affect* the establishment and functioning of the internal market'.[41] However, no mention was made of the use of Article 94 EC's language in a measure based on Article 95 EC. Furthermore, the Court ruled that since the Regulation was validly adopted under Article 95 EC, it did not have to be adopted on the basis of Articles 94 or 308 EC.[42] This seemed to imply, on the basis of the current framework, that if Article 114 TFEU was insufficient, then Article 115 TFEU or Article 352 TFEU could be used, but this was left unclear.

Although the Court has not yet dealt with this matter explicitly, the case law on Article 114 TFEU and relevant changes introduced by the Lisbon Treaty can nevertheless be read to have, explicitly or implicitly, moved in the direction of merging the three salient differences in substantive scope between Articles 114 and 115 TFEU, thereby doing much to silence arguments that Article 115 TFEU has a residual position vis-à-vis Article 114 TFEU in European contract law. While this case law is analysed in the next section, certain cases are briefly mentioned here to flesh out the Court's approach in this regard.

8.2.3.1 The 'internal market' versus the 'common market'

The debate regarding the concepts of, and relationship between, the internal market and the common market is largely moot with the entry into force of the Lisbon Treaty, which replaced the references to the common market with those to the internal market in the Treaties.[43] These changes essentially codified what had already largely occurred under the former Treaty framework.

As regards the former EC Treaty, there appeared to be agreement among most scholars that in theory the notion of the common market may have been broader than that of the internal market, but in practice, such a distinction had not been recognized in the Court's case law.[44] By virtue of the definition of internal market introduced by the SEA and set forth in former Article 14 EC (originally Article 8a EEC, now Article 26 TFEU), this could be taken to mean that the internal market was limited to

[38] Council Reg (EEC) No 1768/92 of 18 June 1992 concerning the creation of a supplementary protection certificate for medicinal products, [1992] OJ L182/1.

[39] Case C-350/92 *Spain v Council*, para 25.

[40] Case C-350/92 *Spain v Council*, para 28.

[41] Case C-350/92 *Spain v Council*, para 35 (emphasis added).

[42] Case C-350/92 *Spain v Counci*, para 40.

[43] Lisbon Treaty, Horizontal Amendments to the EC Treaty, [2007] OJ C306/42, point 2(g).

[44] See, eg, LW Gormley, 'The internal market: history and evolution' in NN Shuibhne (ed), *Regulating the Internal Market (*Edward Elgar, 2006) 14, 14; M. Radeideh, *Fair Trading in EC Law: Information and Consumer Choice in the Internal Market* (Europa, 2005) 78.

the elimination of obstacles to the fundamental freedoms.[45] In contrast, although the notion of common market was never defined in the original EEC Treaty, it was viewed as having a much broader expanse in line with the Community's objectives in former Articles 2 and 3 E(E)C, thereby traversing the rules on free movement to encompass various other policies (eg, trade, agriculture, and transport) and the elimination of distortions of competition.[46]

While perhaps economically speaking, the scope of the internal market could be deemed narrower than that of the common market, politically speaking, the converse seemed to be true. In light of its definition espousing an 'area without internal frontiers', the internal market was perceived as embodying a holistic view of wider political and social objectives going beyond the economic objectives generally associated with the common market.[47] The term single market, which rose in prominence around the same time, was viewed in similar fashion, which helps to explain why the two started to be used interchangeably.[48] Thus, the aura around the internal market (and single market) emanates a richer conception in depth, even if not matching the breadth of the common market. Viewed in this way, the common market seemed to stand largely as a relic linked to the early days of European economic integration, whereas the internal market and single market came to represent a broader embodiment of European integration. Indeed, as a matter of common usage, references to the internal market and single market became the rule and those to the common market the more archaic exception largely where citation to the former Treaty was involved.[49]

In any event, both before and after the SEA, the Court's case law treated the common market and internal market the same way. In the 1982 *Schul* case,[50] for example, the Court conflated the three terms—common market, internal market, and single market—all in one sentence: 'The concept of a *common market* as defined by the Court in a consistent line of decisions involves the elimination of all obstacles to intra-Community trade in order to merge the national markets into a *single market* bringing about conditions as close as possible to those of a genuine *internal market*.'[51] Yet, it was the *Titanium Dioxide* case[52] which strongly cemented the two. This was the first case to come before the Court concerning former Article 95 EC (then Article 100a EEC, now Article 114 TFEU).[53] On the basis of the definition of internal market laid down in

[45] See ns 4, 10 and accompanying text. But this was not unanimous. Compare, eg, P Pescatore, 'Some Critical Remarks on the "Single European Act"' (1987) 24 *CML Rev* 9, 11, with Ehlermann, n 29, 369–370.

[46] See, eg, A Dashwood, 'Article 308 EC as the Outer Limit of Expressly Conferred Community Competence' in C Barnard and O Odudu (eds), *The Outer Limits of European Union Law* (Hart, 2009) 35, 36–37; LW Gormley, 'Competition and Free Movement: Is the Internal Market the Same as a Common Market?' (2002) 13 *EBLR* 517.

[47] See, eg, Lenaerts and Van Nuffel, n 7, § 9-011; Opinion of AG Léger in Case C-293/02 *Jersey Produce Marketing Organisation* [2005] ECR I-9543, point 135. For a broader perspective, see, eg, JM Broekman, *A Philosophy of European Union Law* (Peeters, 1999) 355–368.

[48] See, eg, KA Armstrong, 'Governance and the Single European Market' in P Craig and G de Búrca (eds), *The Evolution of EU Law* (Oxford Univ Press, 1999) 745, 747–748; Barnard, n 35, 12; K Mortelmans, 'The Common Market, the Internal Market and the Single Market, What's in a Market?' (1998) 35 *CML Rev* 101, 107–108.

[49] See, eg, M Monti, 'A New Strategy for the Single Market', Report to the President of the European Commission José Manuel Barroso, dated 9 May 2010, 13 fn 1 (preferring single market).

[50] Case 15/81 *Gaston Schul Douane Expediteur* [1982] ECR 1409.

[51] Case 15/81 *Gaston Schul Douane Expediteur*, para 33 (emphasis added). In some past cases, the Court referred less often to internal market than to common market and single market. See, eg, Case 270/80 *Polydor and Others* [1982] ECR 329, para 16. Given the linkage between the notions of single market and internal market, this would not appear to alter the discussion here.

[52] Case C-300/89 *Commission v Council* ('*Titanium Dioxide*') [1991] ECR I-2867.

[53] Opinion of AG Tesauro in Case C-300/89 *Titanium Dioxide*, point 1 fn 1.

former Article 14 EC as well as former Articles 2 and 3 E(E)C, the Court held that 'a pre-condition' for the internal market was the existence of conditions of competition which were not distorted.[54] It then affirmed that former Article 95 EC encompassed measures that could be used to eliminate distortions of competition in the internal market, as was the case for the measure at issue.[55] The Court did not confront the terminological distinction between the common market and internal market directly in relation to former Articles 94 and 95 EC, but Advocate General Tesauro dealt with the issue head-on:

> [N]o difference—from the present standpoint, needless to say—can exist between the concept of 'common market' and that of 'internal market'; the two concepts differ in breadth, in that the 'common market' extends to areas which are not part of the 'internal market', but not in depth, in that both concepts relate to the same level of integration. . . . [T]o conclude that the harmonization of conditions of competition falls outside Article [95], even though it is common ground that such harmonization previously fell within the scope of Article [94], would be equivalent to concluding that the concept of 'internal market' in Article [95] involved a *less advanced* level of integration than that of 'common market' within the meaning of Article [94]. And that, in the absence of textual confirmation in the Single [European] Act, seems to me to be quite unacceptable . . .[56]

While the Advocate General's rationale did not figure expressly in the Court's findings, its judgment in *Titanium Dioxide* at least implicitly strengthened the reading of the two terms together.

In this way, the Court's approach under the past Treaty framework was taken over in the changes brought about by the Lisbon Treaty in this respect. As already mentioned, all references to the common market have been replaced with those to the internal market, including that found in former Article 94 EC, now Article 115 TFEU. This has the effect of bringing the text of Article 115 TFEU in line with current practice regarding the conflation of common market and internal market for the purposes of interpreting this provision vis-à-vis Article 114 TFEU.

8.2.3.2 'Object' versus 'directly affect'

Long before the SEA, there had already been extensive discussion as to what was meant by 'directly affect' inscribed in former Article 94 EC.[57] With the introduction of former Article 95 EC, the matter took on renewed importance, and as noted above, there continues to be debate as to whether the use of 'object' as opposed to 'directly affect' is meant to embody a less or more restrictive scope for Article 114 TFEU vis-à-vis Article 115 TFEU.[58] From the text of the two provisions, it is impossible to get a clear sense of their relative meanings. As far as can be seen, there is no explanation in the *travaux préparatoires* as to what the Treaty framers had in mind in relation to the juxtaposition of the two.[59] There had been several legal basis disputes concerning

[54] Case C-300/89 *Titanium Dioxide*, para 14.

[55] Case C-300/89 *Titanium Dioxide*, paras 15, 23.

[56] Opinion of AG Tesauro in Case C-300/89 *Titanium Dioxide*, point 10, at I-2888–2889.

[57] See particularly House of Lords Select Committee on the European Communities, 'Approximation of Laws under Article 100 of the EEC Treaty', 22nd Report, Session 1977–78, including App 3(b) (CD Ehlermann, Director General, Legal Service of the European Commission, 'Community Policy with regard to the Approximation of Laws').

[58] See n 36. Others have downplayed the importance of this issue: see, eg, Oliver, n 35, § 13-10.

[59] As regards the SEA, see, eg, J De Ruyt, *L'acte unique européen* (Editions de l'Université de Bruxelles, 1987); Ehlermann, n 29 (though noting on p 381 that there had been support to amend then Art 100 EEC, as opposed to inserting then Art 100a EEC into the Treaty).

what is now Article 114 TFEU, in which the Court declared that this provision could not be used for measures with merely an 'incidental effect' on the internal market.[60] While approaching the 'directly affect' language of Article 115 TFEU in the sense of ensuring that Article 114 TFEU must be used for measures that veered on the side of a more direct, as opposed to tangential, link to the internal market, this did not truly settle the matter.

In recent years, however, the incorporation of Article 115 TFEU's 'directly affect' language into the interpretation of Article 114 TFEU was introduced by the Court itself in the companion cases of *Swedish Match*[61] and *Arnold André*.[62] In seemingly rehearsing the requirements for former Article 95 EC (now Article 114 TFEU), the Court 'recalled that, while a mere finding of disparities between national rules is not sufficient to justify having recourse to Article 95 EC, it is otherwise where there are differences between the laws, regulations or administrative provisions of the Member States which are such as to obstruct the fundamental freedoms and thus have a *direct effect* on the functioning of the internal market'.[63] Lest one think this was a mere slip of the pen or translation error, the same phrasing was used in the French version, which as the Court's working language referred to '*une incidence directe*', thereby paralleling the exact language found in what was then Article 94 EC, now Article 115 TFEU.[64] No attention was drawn to this linkage between Articles 114 and 115 TFEU by the Court, and it does not seem to have been noticed so far in most of the commentary.[65]Nonetheless, such language has been repeated by the Court (and the General Court) in the jurisprudence on Article 114 TFEU.[66] While it is not entirely clear that this was the Court's intention, it has minimized the differences between 'object' and 'directly affect' in Articles 114 and 115 TFEU.

8.2.3.3 Establishment 'and' versus 'or' functioning

There has not been much attention paid to Article 114 TFEU's coverage of approximation measures that have as their object the establishment 'and' functioning of the internal market, as compared to Article 115 TFEU's reference to the establishment 'or' functioning of the internal market.[67] Read literally, this could possibly indicate that measures based on Article 115 TFEU may be targeted at either the establishment or the functioning of the internal market, whereas those based on Article 114 TFEU must be targeted at both. Yet, in practice, the Court's case law on what is now Article 114 TFEU has not made a distinction as regards measures gauged at the establishment as opposed

[60] See, eg, Case C-209/97 *Commission v Council* ('*CIS*') [1999] ECR I-8067, paras 35–37.

[61] Case C-210/03 *Swedish Match* [2004] ECR I-11893.

[62] Case C-434/02 *Arnold André* [2004] ECR I-11825.

[63] Case C-210/03 *Swedish Match*, para 29 (citations omitted) (emphasis added); Case C-434/02 *Arnold André*, para 30 (citations omitted) (emphasis added).

[64] Case C-210/03 *Swedish Match*, para 29 (French version) (emphasis added); Case C-434/02 *Arnold André*, para 30 (French version) (emphasis added).

[65] But see, eg, R Schütze, *From Dual to Cooperative Federalism—The Changing Structure of European Law* (Oxford Univ Press, 2009) 148 fn 77.

[66] See, eg, Joined Cases C-154/04 and C-155/04 *Alliance for Natural Health and Others* [2005] ECR I-6451, para 28; Case C-380/03 *Germany v European Parliament and Council* ('*Tobacco Advertising II*') [2006] ECR I-11573, para 37; Case C-301/06 *Ireland v European Parliament and Council* [2009] ECR I-593, para 63; Case C-58/08 *Vodafone and Others* [2010] ECR I-4999, para 32; Case T-18/10 R (Order of the President of 30 April 2010) *Inuit Tapiriit Kanatami and Others v European Parliament and Council* [2010] ECR II-75*, Summ pub, para 74; Case T-526/10 (Judgment of 25 April 2013) *Inuit Tapiriit Kanatami and Others v Commission*, not reported, para 28 (appeal pending in Case C-398/13 P).

[67] But see, eg, Schrauwen, n 36, 148.

to the functioning of the internal market,[68] nor it seems has the Union legislature.[69] As far as the Union's competence is concerned, what counts is that a particular Union measure is at least aimed at one or the other. This is borne out by the Lisbon Treaty. In its replacement of former Article 14 EC with Article 26 TFEU, the first paragraph was changed so as to provide in relevant part: 'The Union shall adopt measures with the aim of establishing *or* ensuring the functioning of the internal market.'[70] At any rate, the differences between 'and' and 'or' in the text of Articles 114 and 115 TFEU have not played a role in differentiating the scope of these provisions in current case law, and at most could be read as drawing the two provisions closer together.

At the end of the day, attempts to discern the relative meanings of these so-called 'Byzantine' differences between Articles 114 and 115 TFEU do not seem productive.[71] They appear to manifest their own balancing with respect to the scope of the relevant provision at the time that each was formulated. Presumably, controversy will continue so long as the matter of the scope of Article 114 TFEU vis-à-vis Article 115 TFEU has not been definitively addressed by the Court of Justice. Yet, the foregoing case law indicates that the Court is mindful not to create artificial distinctions between the substantive scope of the two provisions, which could undercut the means at the Union's disposal to achieve its internal market objectives. Therefore, although the Court has not yet pronounced on the matter explicitly, there is strong evidence from the case law so far that, aside from the matters fenced off from Article 114 TFEU under the Treaties, if a measure falls outside the substantive scope of Article 114 TFEU, most likely it will not be able to fall within that of Article 115 TFEU on the basis of the differences discussed above. Consequently, by virtue of the order of preference between these two provisions in the Treaties and the Court's case law, it is Article 114 TFEU, not Article 115 TFEU, on which the Union's approximation competence hinges in the debate about European contract law.

8.3 The Scope of Article 114 TFEU

8.3.1 The 'object' and 'approximation' prongs of the case law

As a general matter, Article 114 TFEU encompasses an increasing body of case law and commentary, which could be a book in itself.[72] This analysis draws upon the most salient aspects of the case law for the purposes of assessing the Union's competence to adopt a European contract law instrument and does not claim to be comprehensive or exhaustive. Still, it is the case law on Article 114 TFEU that serves as the centrepiece guiding the discussion. It can be divided into two subsets or prongs, both of which follow from the text of Article 114 TFEU. The 'object' prong emanates primarily (though not solely[73]) from the first *Tobacco Advertising* case and its progeny, which established

[68] See, eg, text accompanying n 63.

[69] See Opinion of AG Geelhoed in Case C-491/01 *British American Tobacco (Investments) and Imperial Tobacco* ('*BAT*') [2002] ECR I-11453, point 147 fn 73.

[70] Art 26(1) TFEU (emphasis added). Ex Art 14 EC stated in relevant part: 'The Community shall adopt measures with the aim of progressively establishing the internal market'. In the provision corresponding to Art 114 TFEU in the Draft Constitutional Treaty (DCT), language versions differed on this issue, eg, the French and German versions of 2004 DCT, Art III-172 referred to establishment 'or' functioning, whereas the English version referred to establishment 'and' functioning.

[71] G Dellis, 'Le rapprochement des législation' in P Léger (ed), *Commentaire article par article des traités UE et CE* (Bruylant, 2000) 896, 908.

[72] See, eg, M Ludwigs, *Rechtsangleichung nach Art. 94, 95 EG-Vertrag* (Nomos, 2004).

[73] See, eg, § 8.3.2.3.

and refined the threshold conditions placed on the use of Article 114 TFEU for the adoption of measures 'which have as their object the establishment and functioning of the internal market' as set forth in Article 114(1) TFEU. It pertains to the requirements for recourse to Article 114 TFEU radiating from the *Tobacco Advertising I* case law as regards the elimination of obstacles to trade and appreciable distortions of competition in the internal market. By comparison, the 'approximation' prong emanates from a more recent set of cases heralded by *Smoke Flavourings*[74] and *ENISA*,[75] which are concerned with the scope of 'measures for the approximation' of national laws under Article 114(1) TFEU. It pertains to the permissible methods or techniques that may be used by the Union legislature to bring about the approximation of national laws under Article 114 TFEU. Admittedly, the Court has not (yet) categorized the case law in this way, although it has taken pains to distinguish the relevant requirements set down in the two sets of cases to ensure that each is fulfilled.[76]

To be clear, both prongs have equal bearing on discerning the limits and exercise of Union competence under Article 114 TFEU. The 'object' prong delineates not only the requirements for measures based on Article 114 TFEU, but also the Court's approach for assessing the compliance of such measures with the principles of subsidiarity and proportionality. Although the 'approximation' prong is not formally concerned with these principles, they nonetheless crept into the cases as a practical matter. Thus, it could be thought preferable to treat all of the relevant case law on Article 114 TFEU together in chronological order. Yet, dividing the case law into two prongs has considerable functional utility because it allows the various issues brewing below the surface of Article 114 TFEU in connection with European contract law to be parsed out in the three sections that follow. First, honing in on the 'object' prong allows for evaluation of the obstacles to trade and appreciable distortions of competition requirements, which is a complex and controversial undertaking in itself. Secondly, while it is not disputed that the 'approximation' prong places further limits on measures adopted under Article 114 TFEU, the interplay between the two prongs helps to illuminate the roles played by subsidiarity and proportionality in guiding the exercise of Union competence under this provision inside, as well as outside, the EU lawmaking process. Thirdly, the discussion of the limits and exercise of Union competence under Article 114 TFEU prompts a 'comparative leap' to the US in connection with the approximation of contract law in the European and American settings.

8.3.2 The limits of Union competence under Article 114 TFEU

Much of the discussion of Article 114 TFEU in the debate about European contract law has been focused on the key requirements stemming from the first *Tobacco Advertising* judgment as regards the elimination of obstacles to trade and appreciable distortions of competition in the internal market. This judgment led many to take the view that the adoption of a comprehensive instrument of contract law (as well as other fields of

[74] Case C-66/04 *UK v European Parliament and Council* ('*Smoke Flavourings*') [2005] ECR I-10553.

[75] Case C-217/04 *UK v European Parliament and Council* ('*ENISA*') [2006] ECR I-3771. The *European Cooperative Society* case is equally intertwined with the limits of approximation and the use of optional instruments, which explains why it is discussed in § 8.4.3.1.

[76] See, eg, Case C-66/04 *Smoke Flavourings*, paras 41–44; C-217/04 *ENISA*, para 42; Case C-380/03 *Tobacco Advertising II* [2006] ECR I-11573, para 42; Case C-58/08 *Vodafone and Others* [2010] ECR I-4999, para 35.

private law) exceeded the Union's competence under what is now Article 114 TFEU. While perhaps understandable at the time that this judgment was delivered, arguably, this may have overshot the mark a bit when placed alongside the steady stream of subsequent cases in which the Court further developed its approach to these requirements. At the same time, both inside and outside the debate, there have been varying opinions regarding the extent to which the obstacles to trade requirement under Article 114 TFEU is restricted, or not, by the 'negative' prohibitions of the free movement rules, namely the provisions concerning the free movement of goods under Articles 34–36 TFEU. Therefore, the assessment of the limits of Union competence under Article 114 TFEU in relation to European contract law entails: (1) delineating the path of the 'object' prong of the case law that has been considerably 'refined' since the first *Tobacco Advertising* judgment; (2) confronting the relationship between Article 114 TFEU and the free movement rules as part of evaluating the parameters of the obstacles to trade requirement; and (3) evaluating Article 114 TFEU's use in relation to eliminating existing and possibly future appreciable distortions of competition. Each of these aspects is evaluated in turn.

Before proceeding further, however, certain caveats must be placed on this analysis. To begin with, there is considerable controversy permeating the debate as to whether, or to what extent, divergences among national contract laws constitute obstacles to trade and/or appreciable distortions of competition in the internal market, for which the lack of sufficient evidence has been repeatedly noted.[77] That said, a complete array of data that would satisfy all participants in the debate may be difficult, if not impossible, to come by, and the absence of it has certainly not foreclosed the discussion.[78] Thus, this analysis is based on the institutional record produced this far in the debate, with particular regard to the Commission's Communications on European contract law and documentation accompanying the proposed CESL, as well as the relevant academic commentary. The extent of the divergences between national contract laws itself is also somewhat ambiguous.[79] Indeed, it may be wondered whether certain activities taking place in the European contract law project, such as the promulgation of the Draft Common Frame of Reference (DCFR), will have an impact on closing certain gaps in this regard. Nonetheless, institutional documents, including those just mentioned, evidence that such divergences exist in respect of rules concerning business-to-consumer

[77] See, eg, House of Lords EU Committee, 'European Contract Law: the Draft Common Frame of Reference', 12th Report of Session 2008–09, point 83; J Smits, 'European Private Law: A Plea for a Spontaneous Legal Order' in *European Integration and Law: Four Contributions on the Interplay between European Integration and European and National Law to Celebrate the 25th Anniversary of Maastricht University's Faculty of Law* (Intersentia, 2006) 55, 71; R Van den Bergh, 'Private law in a globalizing world: economic criteria for choosing the optional regulatory level in a multi-level government system' in M Faure and A van der Walt (eds), *Globalization and Private Law—The Way Forward* (Edward Elgar, 2010) 57, 68; T Wilhelmsson, 'The Design of an Optional (Re)statement of European Contract Law—Real Life Instead of Dead Concepts' in S Grundmann and J Stuyck (eds), *An Academic Green Paper on European Contract Law* (Kluwer, 2002) 353, 355–356. See also Chapter 6, § 6.4.2.4, § 6.4.3.

[78] See, eg, J Smits (ed), *The Need for a European Contract Law: Empirical and Legal Perspectives* (Europa, 2005); F Chirico, 'The Function of European Contract Law: An Economic Analysis' in P Larouche and F Chirico (eds), *Economic Analysis of the DCFR* (Sellier, 2010) 9, 29; E McKendrick 'Harmonisation of European Contract Law: The State We Are In' in S Vogenauer and S Weatherill (eds), *The Harmonisation of European Contract Law: Implications for European Private Laws, Business and Legal Practice* (Hart, 2006) 5, 14–15; G Wagner, 'The Economics of Harmonization: The Case of Contract Law' (2002) 39 *CML Rev* 995. In particular, economic analysis of the proposed CESL is gaining ground: see, eg, (2012) 33 *EJL & Econ* 473; (2013) 50 *CML Rev* 1.

[79] See Chapter 1, § 1.2.2.1.

(B2C) and business-to-business (B2B) contracts, which also constitute the basis for the analysis. Finally, there is an overlap when it comes to the requirements concerning obstacles to trade and appreciable distortions of competition. As one scholar noted, 'any obstacle to trade is also likely to distort competition' for the purposes of Article 114 TFEU.[80] As illustrated by the debate and the EU contract law *acquis*, the dividing line between them is difficult to draw in many respects, and often, they blur together. Even so, separate assessment of these requirements is undertaken here because each highlights a distinct set of issues in relation to European contract law.

8.3.2.1 The 'object' prong: Tobacco Advertising I *and its evolving 'refinement'*

The Court of Justice's seminal judgment in *Germany v European Parliament and Council* (*'Tobacco Advertising I'*)[81] was not the first to address the scope of what is now Article 114 TFEU, since cases such as *Titanium Dioxide*[82] and *Spain v Council*[83] paved the way in this regard. Yet, it will forever remain a landmark in the jurisprudence on Article 114 TFEU because it constituted the first time that the Court annulled a Union measure in its entirety on the grounds that the Union legislature acted *ultra vires*.[84] This was not a complete surprise, since there was substantial commentary to that effect prior to the judgment.[85] Still, the case was praised as establishing clear 'outer limits' for the scope of Article 114 TFEU.[86]

[80] Barnard, n 35, 610.

[81] Case C-376/98 *Germany v European Parliament and Council* (*'Tobacco Advertising I'*) [2000] ECR I-8419.

[82] Case C-300/89 *Commission v Council* (*'Titanium Dioxide'*) [1991] ECR I-2867.

[83] Case C-350/92 *Spain v Council* [1995] ECR I-1985.

[84] This is in contrast to previous case law concerning the choice between former Art 95 EC (now Art 114 TFEU) and another legal basis or the annulment of only portions of a Community (now Union) measure. See G de Búrca, 'The Tobacco Advertising Saga: Political Aspirations and Constitutional Restraints' (2001) Univ of Cambridge CELS Occasional Paper No 5, 5, 7–8. While the judgment is not clear on this point, it has been considered that no other provision, especially former Arts 94 or 308 EC (now Arts 115 or 352 TFEU), would have been a viable backup to adopt the measure concerned. See, eg, de Búrca, 9; H-P Schneider, 'Ultra Vires. The EU-Directive on Tobacco Advertising under the Searchlight of Legal Opinions' in H-P Schneider and T Stein (eds), *The European Ban on Tobacco Advertising* (Nomos, 1999) 11, 19–20 (see also Opinion of the Council Legal Service in App 5, 365); G Tridimas and T Tridimas, 'The European Court of Justice and the Annulment of the Tobacco Advertising Directive: Friend of National Sovereignty or Foe of Public Health?' (2002) 14 *EJL & Econ* 171, 175. But compare, eg, K St Clair Bradley, 'Powers and Procedures in the EU Constitution: Legal Bases and the Court' in P Craig and G de Búrca (eds), *The Evolution of EU Law*, 2nd edn (Oxford Univ Press, 2011) 85, 108.

[85] See, eg, *The European Ban on Tobacco Advertising*, n 84; A Dashwood, 'The Limits of European Community Powers' (1996) 21 *ELR* 113, 121–122; JHH Weiler, *The Division of Competences in the European Union*, External study commissioned by the European Parliament DG for Research, POLI W-26 (1997) (on file with author). See also Written Question No 1379/93 by Lord Inglewood, 'Tobacco advertising', [1993] OJ C264/66.

[86] A Knook, 'Guns and Tobacco. The Effect of Interstate Trade Case Law on the Vertical Division of Powers' (2004) 11 *MJ* 347, 358. For further discussion, see, eg, JA Usher, Case note (2001) 38 *CML Rev* 1519; de Búrca, n 84; R Gosalbo Bono, Case note (2001) *RTDE* 790; EI Obergfell, 'On Division of Competence in the EU: The Tobacco Advertising Prohibition Directive Test Case' (2000/1) 3 *ELF* 153; DA Wyatt, 'Constitutional Significance of the Tobacco Advertising Judgment of the European Court of Justice' (2001) Univ of Cambridge CELS Occasional Paper No 5, 19.

As is well-known, Germany brought an action to annul Directive 98/43/EC[87] relating to the advertising and sponsorship of tobacco products.[88] It was adopted under what are now Articles 53(2), 62, and 114 TFEU (ex Articles 47(2), 55, and 95 EC and originally Articles 57(2), 66, and 100a EC). It aimed to ban virtually all forms of tobacco advertising and sponsorship within the EU.[89] Ironically, this had not been the original plan. In the early proposals, the Commission advocated a measure of more limited scope, seeking to regulate, not ban, only tobacco advertising in the press and by means of bills and posters, based solely on Article 114 TFEU.[90] Had such a measure been adopted, it may be wondered whether this momentous case would have come before the Court. Yet, prompted by the European Parliament and certain Member States in the Council, the Commission put forward a more comprehensive proposal constituting a near complete ban of the advertising of tobacco products, still relying solely on Article 114 TFEU.[91] Ultimately, the measure also came to include the ban on tobacco sponsorship, and Articles 53(2) and 62 TFEU were added as legal bases.[92] Nevertheless, the key issue in the case was Germany's claim that Article 114 TFEU did not constitute a proper legal basis for the Directive.[93] This was primarily on the grounds that the Directive lacked the requisite link to the internal market and was essentially a measure concerning the protection of public health for which harmonization was expressly precluded under what is now Article 168 TFEU (ex Article 152 EC).[94]

In its judgment, delivered in 2000, the Court addressed both points. It began by dealing with the argument concerning the use of Article 114 TFEU for measures based on public health. Despite the express exclusion of harmonization under Article 168 TFEU, this did not mean that harmonization measures adopted on the basis of other

[87] Dir 98/43/EC of the European Parliament and of the Council of 6 July 1998 on the approximation of the laws, regulations and administrative provisions of the Member States relating to the advertising and sponsorship of tobacco products, [1998] OJ L213/9.

[88] Around the same time, an action to annul the Directive was also brought before what is now the General Court by several private parties, but was dismissed as inadmissible. See Joined Cases T-172/98 and T-175 to T-177/98 *Salamander and Others v European Parliament and Council* [2000] ECR II-2487 (appeals withdrawn, Case C-281/00 P (Order of 23 Oct 2001), not reported; Case C-313/00 P (Order of 23 Oct 2001), not reported). A few months after Germany lodged its action, the Court received a request for a preliminary ruling on the validity of the Directive: Case C-74/99 *Imperial Tobacco and Others* [2000] ECR I-8599. While the two cases were combined in AG Fennelly's Opinion, the Court disposed of this latter case by ruling that on the basis of *Tobacco Advertising I*, there was no need to answer the questions submitted.

[89] See Opinion of AG Fennelly in Case C-376/98 *Tobacco Advertising I* and Case C-74/99 *Imperial Tobacco*, points 109–110.

[90] As evidenced by the initial proposal's title: see Proposal for a Council Directive on the advertising of tobacco products in the press and by means of bills and posters, COM (89) 163 final/2, 7.4.1989, reiterated in the amended proposal, COM (90) 147 final, 19.4.1990.

[91] See Opinion of AG Fennelly in Case C-376/98 *Tobacco Advertising I* and Case C-74/99 *Imperial Tobacco*, points 14–19.

[92] See Opinion of AG Fennelly in Case C-376/98 *Tobacco Advertising I* and Case C-74/99 *Imperial Tobacco*, points 5–6, 19, 63.

[93] See Case C-376/98 *Tobacco Advertising I*, para 9. The parties agreed that their arguments concerning what is now Art 114 TFEU also applied to what are now Arts 53(2) and 62 TFEU: Case C-376/98 *Tobacco Advertising I*, paras 10–11.

[94] See Case C-376/98 *Tobacco Advertising I*, paras 12–35. Ex Art 152(4)(c) EC (then Art 129(4)) EC) provided in relevant part: 'The Council . . . shall contribute to the achievement of the objectives referred to in this Article through adopting . . . incentive measures designed to protect and improve human health, excluding any harmonisation of the laws and regulations of the Member States.' This provision was reframed by the Lisbon Treaty as Art 168(5) TFEU, which provides that the European Parliament and the Council may adopt, inter alia, 'measures which have as their direct objective the protection of public health regarding tobacco and the abuse of alcohol, excluding any harmonisation of the laws and regulations of the Member States'.

Treaty provisions could not have any impact on the protection of public health, though these other provisions could not be used to circumvent that exclusion.[95] Thus, so long as the conditions for recourse to Article 114 TFEU were satisfied, the Union legislature could rely on this provision, even though public health protection was 'a decisive factor' in the choices made with respect to the measure concerned.[96] The Court then proceeded to elaborate these conditions.

Distilled from the judgment, the Court established four key conditions for recourse to Article 114 TFEU.[97] *First*, in one of the most celebrated passages of the judgment, the Court declared:

> [A] measure adopted on the basis of Article [114 TFEU] must genuinely have as its object the improvement of the conditions for the establishment and functioning of the internal market. If a mere finding of disparities between national rules and of the abstract risk of obstacles to the exercise of the fundamental freedoms or of distortions of competition liable to result therefrom were sufficient to justify the choice of Article [114 TFEU] as a legal basis, judicial review of compliance with the proper legal basis might be rendered nugatory.[98]

This meant that the measure must actually contribute to the elimination of obstacles to the exercise of the fundamental freedoms or to the elimination of distortions of competition in the internal market.[99] In short, Article 114 TFEU did not confer 'a general power to regulate the internal market' on the Union legislature.[100] *Secondly*, a measure can be adopted under former Article 114 TFEU if its 'aim is to prevent the emergence of future obstacles to trade resulting from the multifarious development of national laws', provided that 'the emergence of such obstacles must be likely and the measure in question must be designed to prevent them'.[101] *Thirdly*, a measure adopted under Article 114 TFEU can include provisions that do not contribute to the elimination of obstacles to trade, provided that such provisions are 'necessary to ensure that certain prohibitions imposed in pursuit of that purpose are not circumvented'.[102] *Fourthly*, Article 114 TFEU can be used to eliminate distortions of competition only if they are 'appreciable'.[103] Otherwise, the Union's competence under Article 114 TFEU would be 'practically unlimited' and hence allowing the elimination of 'the smallest distortions of competition' would be incompatible with the principle of conferral.[104] In light of these conditions, the Court concluded that the Directive could not be adopted under

[95] Case C-376/98 *Tobacco Advertising I*, paras 78–79.

[96] Case C-376/98 *Tobacco Advertising I*, para 88.

[97] These requirements have been summarized by AGs in later cases. See, eg, Opinion of AG Geelhoed in Case C-491/01 *BAT* [2002] ECR I-11453, point 18; Opinion of AG Léger in Case C-380/03 *Tobacco Advertising II* [2006] ECR I-11573, point 90.

[98] Case C-376/98 *Tobacco Advertising I*, para 84.

[99] Case C-376/98 *Tobacco Advertising I*, paras 95, 108.

[100] Case C-376/98 *Tobacco Advertising I*, para 83.

[101] Case C-376/98 *Tobacco Advertising I*, para 86 (citing Case C-350/92 *Spain v Council*, para 35). This built upon *Spain v Council*, but the twofold requirements that such obstacles be likely and the measure be designed to prevent them were new.

[102] Case C-376/98 *Tobacco Advertising I*, para 100.

[103] Case C-376/98 *Tobacco Advertising I*, para 106 (citing Case C-300/89 *Titanium Dioxide*, para 23). Although the Court relied on *Titanium Dioxide* in this regard, it did not tack on the condition of 'appreciable' distortions of competition until *Tobacco Advertising I*. See, eg, Opinion of AG Léger in Case C-380/03 *Tobacco Advertising II*, point 80. Also, the 'appreciable' standard was not applied by the Court to obstacles to trade, despite Germany's arguments to the contrary. See Case C-376/98 *Tobacco Advertising I*, paras 29, 31. The use of the adjective 'appreciable' in connection with distortions of competition had already appeared in early case law on Art 115 TFEU. See Case 91/79 *Commission v Italy* [1980] ECR 1099, para 8; Case 92/79 *Commission v Italy* [1980] ECR 1115, para 8.

[104] Case C-376/98 *Tobacco Advertising I*, para 107.

Article 114 TFEU because it did not, as a whole, actually contribute to the elimination of either obstacles to trade or appreciable distortions of competition and must be annulled in its entirety.[105] A directive prohibiting only certain forms of tobacco advertising and sponsorship could have been adopted under Article 114 TFEU, but due to the prohibition's general nature, it could not annul the Directive only partially.[106]

On the whole, *Tobacco Advertising I* was a delicately balanced, indeed ingenious, judgment. On the one hand, it was truly a constitutional case par excellence because it signified the Court's willingness to protect the competences of the Member States from the legislature's overreaching under Article 114 TFEU.[107] On the other hand, the Court went to some lengths to ensure that Article 114 TFEU was not unduly constricted. In particular, it allowed this provision to be used for measures whose main aim was rooted in public health protection, provided that the threshold requirements were crossed. It also allowed it to be used for measures involving the elimination of potential future obstacles to trade, which in one Advocate General's view was 'less exacting' than the standard for appreciable distortions of competition.[108] And, rather uniquely, it gave the legislature a 'gentle nudge' in terms of signaling the types of measures concerning tobacco advertising and sponsorship that could be based on Article 114 TFEU.[109] As such, while *Tobacco Advertising I* was considered to lay the groundwork for tightening the scope of Article 114 TFEU,[110] much depended on how the various requirements would play out in later cases.

In 2001, the Court of Justice decided *Netherlands v European Parliament and Council* ('*Biotechnology*'),[111] which came fast on the heels of *Tobacco Advertising I*.[112] At issue was the legality of Directive 98/44/EC on the legal protection of biotechnological inventions,[113] based on what is now Article 114 TFEU (ex Article 95 EC and originally Article 100a EC). The purpose of the Directive was to require the Member States to provide protection for biotechnological inventions under their national patent laws, without prejudice to their obligations relating to the international conventions in the field.[114] The Netherlands asserted, among other things,[115] that Article 114 TFEU was not a proper legal basis because differences between the national laws either did not exist or had not been shown to result in barriers to trade in the internal market.[116] It also argued that even assuming such problems were found to exist, they should have been removed by renegotiation of the relevant international convention, not the Directive.[117]

105 Case C-376/98 *Tobacco Advertising I*, paras 116, 118.

106 Case C-376/98 *Tobacco Advertising I*, paras 98, 111, 117.

107 See, eg, N Fennelly, 'The Tobacco Judgment', Documentation for ERA Conference, The Tobacco Regulation in the European Community, Luxembourg, 18–19 May 2001; Tridimas and Tridimas, n 84, 180.

108 Opinion of AG Jacobs in Case C-377/98 *Netherlands v European Parliament and Council* ('*Biotechnology*') [2001] ECR I-7079, point 47.

109 See Tridimas and Tridimas, n 84, 179.

110 See, eg, 'Editorial Comments: Taking (the limits of) competences seriously' (2000) 37 *CML Rev* 1301, 1304.

111 Case C-377/98 *Netherlands v European Parliament and Council* ('*Biotechnology*') [2001] ECR I-7079.

112 This is meant literally. The case was lodged on the same day as *Tobacco Advertising I* (19 Oct 1998), assigned the very next case number, and the numbering of the Directive at issue (Dir 98/44/EC) followed the annulled Directive (Dir 98/43/EC) in direct succession.

113 Dir 98/44/EC of the European Parliament and of the Council of 6 July 1998 on the legal protection of biotechnological inventions, [1998] OJ L213/13.

114 Case C-377/98 *Biotechnology*, para 2.

115 See Case C-377/98 *Biotechnology*, para 12.

116 Case C-377/98 *Biotechnology*, para 14.

117 Case C-377/98 *Biotechnology*, para 19.

In its judgment, the Court rejected these contentions and upheld Article 114 TFEU as the legal basis for the Directive.[118] Relying on the relevant passages of *Tobacco Advertising I*, allowing recourse to this provision to prevent the emergence of future obstacles to trade provided that such obstacles were likely and the measure was designed to prevent them, the Court found both conditions satisfied.[119] First, there were differing national interpretations of the relevant international convention as regards the patentability of biotechnological inventions, which were 'liable to give rise to divergences of practice and case-law prejudicial to the proper operation of the internal market'.[120] Moreover, 'marked differences with significant consequences were already apparent between certain national laws' at the time the Directive was adopted.[121] Secondly, by requiring the Member States to protect such inventions in their national patent law, the Directive 'in fact aims to prevent damage to the unity of the internal market which might result from the Member States' deciding unilaterally to grant or refuse such protection'.[122] As regards the attempted reliance on the international route, the Court ruled that there was nothing to prevent the Union legislature from having recourse to harmonization by means of a directive in preference to the more indirect and unpredictable approach of seeking to amend the wording of the international convention concerned.[123] It declared that the purpose of harmonization was '*to reduce obstacles, whatever their origin, to the operation of the internal market which differences between the situations in the Member States represent*'.[124] Thus, 'if divergences are the result of an interpretation which is contrary, or may prove contrary, to the terms of international legal instruments to which the Member States are parties, there is nothing in principle to prevent recourse to adoption of a Directive as a means of ensuring a uniform interpretation of such terms by the Member States'.[125]

In 2002, in *British American Tobacco* ('*BAT*'),[126] the Court issued a preliminary ruling in response to a reference from an English court on the validity of another tobacco directive, Directive 2001/37/EC approximating national laws concerning the manufacture, presentation, and sale of tobacco products.[127] The Directive included an export ban, prohibiting the manufacture of tobacco products within the EU for export to third countries that did not comply with its requirements.[128] This explains why it was enacted under what is now Article 114 TFEU (ex Article 95 EC) as well as Article 207 TFEU (ex Article 133 EC) concerning the Common Commercial Policy.[129] As framed by Advocate General Geelhoed, the case represented 'the opportunity to examine in general the powers of the [Union] legislature under Article [114 TFEU]'.[130] While perhaps not equivalent to the firestorm set off by the annulled Tobacco Advertising

[118] Case C-377/98 *Biotechnology*, para 29. The Court ultimately dismissed the action: paras 88, 90.

[119] Case C-377/98 *Biotechnology*, para 15.

[120] Case C-377/98 *Biotechnology*, para 16.

[121] Case C-377/98 *Biotechnology*, para 17.

[122] Case C-377/98 *Biotechnology*, para 17.

[123] Case C-377/98 *Biotechnology*, para 22.

[124] Case C-377/98 *Biotechnology*, para 20 (emphasis added).

[125] Case C-377/98 *Biotechnology*, para 20. See also Opinion of AG Jacobs, points 52–53.

[126] Case C-491/01 *BAT* [2002] ECR I-11453.

[127] Dir 2001/37/EC of the European Parliament and of the Council of 5 June 2001 on the approximation of the laws, regulations and administrative provisions of the Member States concerning the manufacture, presentation and sale of tobacco products, [2001] OJ L194/26.

[128] See Opinion of AG Geelhoed in Case C-491/01 *BAT*, point 2.

[129] See Opinion of AG Geelhoed in Case C-491/01 *BAT*, points 85–86.

[130] Opinion of AG Geelhoed in Case C-491/01 *BAT*, point 6. The referring court submitted two questions, which challenged the Directive's validity on several grounds: see Case C-491/01 *BAT*, para 25.

Directive, this Directive had triggered criticism that the legislature exceeded the limits of its competence under Article 114 TFEU.[131]

The Court examined the Directive in light of the requirements set down in *Tobacco Advertising I*[132] and held that it was properly adopted under Article 114 TFEU.[133] It began by emphasizing that the market for tobacco products, especially cigarettes, constituted a large portion of cross-border trade and that national rules laying down requirements for such products were in themselves liable, in the absence of approximation at the European level, to constitute obstacles to the free movement of goods.[134] From there, the Court found that differences among national laws on the manufacture, presentation, and sale of tobacco products created obstacles to trade, which had 'already emerged, or were likely to emerge, by the time the Directive was adopted'.[135] It was therefore likely that obstacles to the free movement of tobacco products would arise as the result of the Member States' adoption or contemplation of more restrictive legislation.[136] Also, unlike the annulled Directive in *Tobacco Advertising I*, the Directive contained a free movement clause, which guaranteed the free movement of tobacco products that complied with its requirements throughout the Member States.[137] As regards the export ban, it did not undermine the use of Article 114 TFEU, since it ensured, in line with *Tobacco Advertising I*, that the Directive's provisions were not circumvented by unlawful reimports of products that did not meet the Directive's requirements.[138] While the Court did not deny that the amount of unlawful trade could not be quantified and was motivated by factors unrelated to circumventing the Directive, the risk of unlawful trade must be assessed by taking into account not only the situation before it was adopted, but also the foreseeable effects on the nature and volume of unlawful trade that were liable to increase.[139]

In 2004, the companion cases of *Swedish Match*[140] and *Arnold André*[141] revisited the use of what is now Article 114 TFEU (ex Article 95 EC) as the legal basis of Directive 2001/37/EC, the same Directive at issue in *BAT*.[142] By way of references for preliminary rulings from English and German courts, these cases concerned the validity of Article 8,[143] prohibiting the Member States from placing on the market tobacco products for oral use including the product known as 'snus',[144] save for an exception carved out for the sale of 'snus' in Sweden in its Act of Accession.[145] These cases turned on the

[131] See S Crosby, 'The New Tobacco Control Directive: An Illiberal and Illegal Disdain for the Law' (2002) 27 *ELR* 177. This case could have been the sequel to *Tobacco Advertising I* as the second time Germany would have brought an action against the Parliament and Council based upon the alleged insufficiency of what is now Article 114 TFEU but for the fact that Germany's application was lodged one day too late and thus dismissed by the Court. See Case C-406/01 (Order of 17 May 2002) *Germany v European Parliament and Council* [2002] ECR I-4561.

[132] See Case C-491/01 *BAT*, paras 60–62, 82.

[133] Case C-491/01 *BAT*, paras 91, 193. As regards Art 207 TFEU (ex Art 133 EC), see paras 97–99.

[134] Case C-491/01 *BAT*, para 64 (citing Joined Cases C-267/91 and C-268/91 *Keck and Mithouard* [1993] ECR I-6097, para 15).

[135] Case C-491/01 *BAT*, para 65.

[136] Case C-491/01 *BAT*, paras 67–73.

[137] Case C-491/01 *BAT*, paras 74–75.

[138] Case C-491/01 *BAT*, paras 84–85.

[139] Case C-491/01 *BAT*, paras 86–90.

[140] Case C-210/03 *Swedish Match* [2004] ECR I-11893.

[141] Case C-434/02 *Arnold André* [2004] ECR I-11825. Since the Court's judgments are similar, reference is made to *Swedish Match*.

[142] See Opinion of AG Geelhoed in Case C-434/02 *Arnold André* and Case C-210/03 *Swedish Match*, point 3. *BAT* did not definitively pronounce on the validity of Art 8: see points 24–29.

[143] Case C-210/03 *Swedish Match*, paras 20–21.

[144] Snus is a kind of oral tobacco product. See further Opinion of AG Geelhoed, points 35–54; E Karlsson, '"Snus" and the Swedish Integration into the EU' in M Johansson et al (eds), *Liber Amicorum in Honour of Sven Norberg—A European for all seasons* (Bruylant, 2006) 301.

[145] Case C-210/03 *Swedish Match*, paras 10–11.

issue whether a ban on the marketing of certain products in the EU could be based on Article 114 TFEU.[146] The Court answered in the affirmative, proclaiming:

> [W]here there are obstacles to trade or it is likely that such obstacles will emerge in the future because the Member States have taken or are about to take divergent measures with respect to a product or a class of products such as to ensure different levels of protection and thereby prevent the product or products concerned from moving freely within the [Union], Article [114 TFEU] authorises the [Union] legislature to intervene by adopting appropriate measures, in compliance with Article [114(3) TFEU] and with the legal principles mentioned in the Treat[ies] or identified in the case-law, in particular the principle of proportionality. Depending on the circumstances, those appropriate measures may consist in requiring all the Member States to authorise the marketing of the product or products concerned, subjecting such an obligation of authorisation to certain conditions, *or even provisionally or definitively prohibiting the marketing of a product or products*.[147]

On that basis, the Court found that the conditions for recourse to Article 114 TFEU were satisfied in relation to Article 8.[148] At the time the Directive was adopted, differences existed among national laws concerning the marketing of tobacco products for oral use which contributed to the heterogeneous development of that market and thus constituted obstacles to the free movement of goods.[149] It was also likely that further obstacles would arise in view of the Member States' adoption of new rules to combat the consumption of tobacco products.[150] Action on the basis of Article 114 TFEU was therefore justified, and the Court upheld the Directive in full.[151]

In 2005, *Alliance for Natural Health*[152] confronted the Court with another reference for a preliminary ruling from an English court, this time concerning the validity of three provisions of Directive 2002/46/EC approximating national laws relating to food supplements,[153] adopted under what is now Article 114 TFEU (ex Article 95 EC). Under Article 3, only food supplements in conformity with the Directive could be marketed within the EU. This meant, pursuant to Article 4(1), only the vitamins and minerals appearing in the positive lists annexed to the Directive. Under Article 15(b), as from a specified date, trade in products that did not comply with the Directive was prohibited. Several parties involved with the marketing of food supplements brought an action before the national court, alleging among other things that Article 114 TFEU was not a proper legal basis for these provisions because they did not improve the conditions for the establishment and functioning of the internal market, and on the assumption that the prohibition was intended to protect public health, this contravened the explicit exclusion of harmonization under what is now Article 168 TFEU (ex Article 152 EC).[154] In essence, the case served to rehash familiar issues from the previous case law.

[146] See Opinion of AG Geelhoed, point 6. See already Usher, n 86, 1538–1539.
[147] Case C-210/03 *Swedish Match*, paras 33–34 (citations omitted) (emphasis added).
[148] Case C-210/03 *Swedish Match*, para 35.
[149] Case C-210/03 *Swedish Match*, paras 37–38.
[150] Case C-210/03 *Swedish Match*, para 40.
[151] Case C-210/03 *Swedish Match*, paras 41–42. AG Geelhoed came to the same conclusion, taking care to distinguish this case from *Tobacco Advertising I*: see Opinion of AG Geelhoed, points 79–83.
[152] Joined Cases C-154/04 and C-155/04 *Alliance for Natural Health and Others* [2005] ECR I-6451.
[153] Dir 2002/46/EC of the European Parliament and of the Council of 10 June 2002 on the approximation of the laws of the Member States relating to food supplements, [2002] OJ L183/51.
[154] Joined Cases C-154/04 and C-155/04 *Alliance for Natural Health*, para 25. As regards former Art 152(4)(c) EC, corresponding to what is now Art 168(5) TFEU, see n 94.

The Court lost no time in upholding Article 114 TFEU as the legal basis of the Directive. According to the second recital, food supplements were regulated by differing national rules that were liable to impede their free movement and therefore have a direct impact on the functioning of the internal market.[155] As noted in the Parliament's and Council's submissions, this was borne out by the fact that prior to the Directive's adoption, there had been several cases brought before the Court relating to situations in which traders encountered obstacles when attempting to market food supplements in Member States other than their own.[156] Additionally, the Explanatory Memorandum of the proposal indicated that the Commission had received several complaints from economic operators on account of differences between the national rules that the principle of mutual recognition had failed to overcome.[157] As a result, the legislature was justified in taking action in this area, and Article 114 TFEU was 'the only appropriate legal basis' for the provisions of the Directive.[158]

In 2006, the Court delivered its much-anticipated judgment in *Germany v European Parliament and Council* (*'Tobacco Advertising II'*).[159] The case concerned the legality of Directive 2003/33/EC on the approximation of national laws relating to the advertising and sponsorship of tobacco products,[160] based on what are now Articles 53(2), 66, and 114 TFEU (ex Articles 47(2), 55, and 95 EC), the same provisions used for the previously annulled Directive. In truth, the Directive at issue had *Tobacco Advertising I* written all over it, as illustrated by various provisions paying heed to its more limited scope and the inclusion of a free movement clause.[161] Still, Germany brought an action to annul Articles 3 and 4 of the Directive primarily on the grounds that Article 114 TFEU was not a proper legal basis.[162] Article 3 set forth a general prohibition on tobacco advertising in the press, and Article 4 did the same in relation to radio advertising and sponsorship of tobacco products.

This time, the Court upheld Articles 3 and 4 of the Directive as properly based on Article 114 TFEU and dismissed Germany's action in full.[163] This outcome had been predicted by commentators,[164] and was in line with Advocate General Léger's Opinion.[165] In principle, the judgment heeded *Tobacco Advertising I*. The Court began by reciting the requirements set down in the previous cases,[166] and as Advocate General

[155] Joined Cases C-154/04 and C-155/04 *Alliance for Natural Health*, para 35.

[156] Joined Cases C-154/04 and C-155/04 *Alliance for Natural Health*, para 36.

[157] Joined Cases C-154/04 and C-155/04 *Alliance for Natural Health*, para 37.

[158] Joined Cases C-154/04 and C-155/04 *Alliance for Natural Health*, paras 38, 42. See also Opinion of AG Geelhoed, point 32.

[159] Case C-380/03 *Germany v European Parliament and Council* (*'Tobacco Advertising II'*) [2006] ECR I-11573.

[160] Dir 2003/33/EC of the European Parliament and of the Council of 26 May 2003 on the approximation of the laws, regulations and administrative provisions of the Member States relating to the advertising and sponsorship of tobacco products, [2003] OJ L152/16.

[161] See Opinion of AG Léger in Case C-380/03 *Tobacco Advertising II*, points 140–143, 157–162.

[162] See Case C-380/03 *Tobacco Advertising II*, para 16.

[163] Case C-380/03 *Tobacco Advertising II*, paras 88, 160.

[164] See, eg, M Alegre, 'We've Come A Long Way Baby (Or Have We?): Banning Tobacco Advertising and Sponsorship in the European Union' (2003) 26 *BCICL Rev* 157; TK Hervey, 'Up in Smoke? Community (Anti-) Tobacco Law and Policy' (2001) 26 *ELR* 101; G Howells, 'Federalism in USA and EC—The Scope for Harmonised Legislative Activity Compared' (2002) 10 *ERPL* 601, 621. Incidentally, this is not to say that all issues concerning EU tobacco-related legislation have been settled. See, eg, A Alemanno, 'Out of Sight, Out of Mind—Towards a New EU Tobacco Products Directive' (2012) 19 *CJEL* 197; F Nicola and F Marchetti, 'Constitutionalizing Tobacco: The Ambivalence of European Federalism' (2005) 46 *Harv ILJ* 507.

[165] Opinion of AG Léger in Case C-380/03 *Tobacco Advertising II*, point 173.

[166] Case C-380/03 *Tobacco Advertising II*, paras 36–44.

Léger had done, divided its analysis into three parts to verify: (1) the existence of disparities in national laws; (2) the effect of those disparities in presenting obstacles to trade and/or appreciable distortions of competition; and (3) the actual contribution of Articles 3 and 4 to eliminating the identified obstacles and/or distortions.[167] Yet, it was the Court's rationale that stood out. As regards the first point, the Court considered the context surrounding the annulled Directive and the text of the Directive concerned, which indicated that there were differences among national laws on advertising and sponsorship that justified intervention by the legislature.[168] In doing so, it stressed that the prospect of an international convention did not change this finding, since it did not enter into force until after the Directive was adopted, not all Member States had yet ratified it, and it would not rule out the risk of divergences among national laws.[169]

As for the second point, the Court started with tobacco advertising in the press, finding that the disparities in national laws were liable to impede the free movement of goods and services on several grounds.[170] In particular, national measures prohibiting or restricting the advertising of tobacco products were liable to impede access to the market by products from other Member States more than domestic products.[171] Such measures also restricted the ability of undertakings to offer advertising space in their publications to advertisers established in other Member States, which affected the cross-border supply of services.[172] Furthermore, while in reality certain publications were not sold in other Member States, divergent laws of the Member States still create, or are likely to create, legal obstacles to trade in respect of press products, which also 'exist for publications placed essentially on a local, regional or national market that are sold in other Member States, *even if only by way of exception or in small quantities*'.[173] For radio advertising and sponsorship of tobacco products, the Court drew similar conclusions, finding that it was likely that new barriers would emerge on account of the Member States' adoption or contemplation of more restrictive legislation, eg, radio broadcasters in Member States prohibiting sponsorship would be denied the benefit of sponsorship from tobacco companies established in other Member States where such prohibitions did not exist.[174] This led the Court to surmise: 'As pointed out in the first and fifth recitals in the preamble to the Directive, those differences also meant that there was an appreciable risk of distortions of competition'.[175] Yet, it declined to delve further into the matter, declaring that as already held in *BAT*, 'when the existence of obstacles to trade has been established, it is not necessary also to prove distortions of competition in order to justify recourse to Article [114 TFEU]'.[176]

As for the final point, the Court confirmed that Articles 3 and 4 were designed to eliminate or prevent obstacles to trade and thus had as their object the improvement of the conditions for the functioning of the internal market.[177] It underlined that its

[167] Case C-380/03 *Tobacco Advertising II*, paras 45, 52, 69. Compare Opinion of AG Léger, points 90, 95.

[168] Case C-380/03 *Tobacco Advertising II*, paras 46–51.

[169] Case C-380/03 *Tobacco Advertising II*, paras 48–50.

[170] Case C-380/03 *Tobacco Advertising II*, para 55.

[171] Case C-380/03 *Tobacco Advertising II*, para 56.

[172] Case C-380/03 *Tobacco Advertising II*, para 57 (citing Case C-405/98 *Gourmet International Products* [2001] ECR I-1795, paras 38–39). The Court cited the relevant passages of that case on the free movement of services and did not mention its relevance to the *Keck* case law on the free movement of goods. Compare Opinion of AG Léger, points 115–120.

[173] Case C-380/03 *Tobacco Advertising II*, para 58 (emphasis added).

[174] Case C-380/03 *Tobacco Advertising II*, paras 61–65.

[175] Case C-380/03 *Tobacco Advertising II*, para 66.

[176] Case C-380/03 *Tobacco Advertising II*, para 67 (citing Case C-491/01 *BAT*, para 60).

[177] Case C-380/03 *Tobacco Advertising II*, paras 69–78.

findings were not called into question by Germany's argument that those Articles only concerned advertising media of a local nature and thus lacked cross-border effects.[178] Relying on its previous rulings in *Österreichischer Rundfunk*[179] and *Lindqvist*,[180] it declared that recourse to Article 114 TFEU did not presuppose the existence of an actual link with free movement in every situation covered by the measure; what mattered was that the measure must actually be intended to improve the conditions for the establishment and functioning of the internal market as Articles 3 and 4 had been shown to do.[181]

In 2010, the Court issued its ruling in *Vodafone*.[182] By way of a request for a preliminary ruling from an English court, the case involved a challenge to the validity of the so-called 'Roaming Regulation'[183] on certain grounds, including the alleged inadequacy of what is now Article 114 TFEU (ex Article 95 EC) as the legal basis.[184] As explained in the Preamble, there was a series of measures comprising the regulatory framework for electronic communications, but the mechanism allowing for *ex ante* regulatory intervention by national authorities had not proven sufficient as regards the regulation of EU-wide roaming charges for mobile phones.[185] This called for amending the framework through this Regulation, which departed from the rules that were otherwise applicable (ie that prices for service offerings should be determined by commercial agreement involving private actors) and established a common approach to the regulation of roaming charges to ensure that mobile phone users were not charged excessive prices when travelling within the EU.[186] This was done by setting a maximum average per minute charge at the wholesale level and limiting charges at the retail level through the introduction of a Eurotariff.[187]

In its judgment, the Court upheld the validity of the Regulation under Article 114 TFEU. On the basis of Article 1 of the Regulation and certain recitals in its Preamble, the Court considered that by introducing a common approach so that mobile phone users do not pay excessive prices for roaming services and mobile operators could operate within a single coherent framework, the Regulation aimed to contribute to the smooth functioning of the internal market in order to achieve a high level of consumer protection and maintain competition among operators of mobile telephone networks.[188] As indicated in several recitals, the high level of retail charges, resulting both from wholesale charges imposed by foreign operators and from high retail mark-ups charged by home providers, was a persistent problem that could not be solved under the existing framework.[189] In view of the Member States' residual competence to adopt consumer protection rules and pressure on the Member States to take action, the legislature was faced with a situation in which it was likely that the Member States would adopt measures to address the persisting problem of the high level of retail-wide

[178] Case C-380/03 *Tobacco Advertising II*, paras 79–81.

[179] Joined Cases C-465/00, C-138/01, and C-139/01 *Österreichischer Rundfunk and Others* [2003] ECR I-4989. For further discussion, see, eg, C-D Classen, Case note (2004) 41 *CML Rev* 1377.

[180] Case C-101/01 *Linqvist* [2003] ECR I-12971. For further discussion, see, eg, L Coudray, Case note (2004) 41 *CML Rev* 1361.

[181] Case C-380/03 *Tobacco Advertising II*, paras 80–81.

[182] Case C-58/08 *Vodafone and Others* [2010] ECR I-4999.

[183] Reg (EC) No 717/2007 of the European Parliament and of the Council of 27 June 2007 on roaming on public mobile telephone networks within the Community and amending Dir 2002/21/EC, [2007] OJ L171/32.

[184] Case C-58/08 *Vodafone*, para 31.

[185] Reg No 717/2007, n 183, fourth–tenth recitals.

[186] Reg No 717/2007, n 183, twelfth, sixteenth recitals.

[187] Reg No 717/2007, n 183, seventeenth–eighteenth recitals.

[188] Case C-58/08 *Vodafone*, para 38.

[189] Case C-58/08 *Vodafone*, paras 39–42.

roaming charges that would have led to a divergent development of national laws.[190] Given the interdependence between retail and wholesale charges for roaming services, a divergent development of national laws seeking to lower retail charges only, without affecting the level of costs for wholesale provision of EU-wide roaming services, would have been liable to cause 'significant'[191] distortions of competition and disrupt the orderly functioning of the EU-wide roaming market, thereby justifying the action taken.[192] The Court concluded that the object of the Regulation was indeed to improve the conditions for the functioning of the internal market and that it could be adopted on the basis of Article 114 TFEU.[193]

To summarize, in the battery of cases decided since *Tobacco Advertising I*, the Court has not yet again struck down a measure as exceeding the scope of the Union's competence under what is now Article 114 TFEU. The evolution of the case law so far indicates that the limits placed on this provision reach further than may have been initially apparent in that judgment.[194] For example, in *Biotechnology*, the Court accepted that differing national interpretations of an international convention were liable to give rise to divergences 'prejudicial to the internal market', without engaging in the detailed analysis of the types of obstacles to trade as had been posited in *Tobacco Advertising I*. The fact that the Court allowed Article 114 TFEU to be used merely to foreclose different national interpretations of the relevant convention led one scholar to conclude that as far as a European contract law instrument was concerned, *Biotechnology* only strengthened the case for this provision.[195] *BAT* was also viewed as a retreat from *Tobacco Advertising I* because its reasoning relied heavily on the content of the Directive concerned and hence constituted a less-rigorous check to determine whether the conditions for Article 114 TFEU were satisfied.[196] And then there was *Tobacco Advertising II*, which was perceived by some scholars as evidencing such a low standard for measures seeking to combat future obstacles to trade that it

[190] Case C-58/08 *Vodafone*, paras 43–45.

[191] The Court used the word 'significant', as opposed to 'appreciable', distortions of competition: see Case C-58/08 *Vodafone*, paras 32, 47. It is not clear whether this was intentional, since in para 36, the Court cited in support the relevant paragraph of *Tobacco Advertising 1*, in which the term 'appreciable' was established. In the French version (the Court's working language), the same term '*distorsions de concurrence sensibles*' appears in the relevant paragraphs of this judgment and in related case law, including *Tobacco Advertising I* and *Leitner* (see n 256), but this is not the case for other language versions.

[192] Case C-58/08 *Vodafone*, para 47.

[193] Case C-58/08 *Vodafone*, para 48.

[194] See, eg, Barnard, n 35, 612–613; P Craig and G de Búrca, *EU Law: Text, Cases, and Materials*, 5th edn (Oxford Univ Press, 2011) 92–93; D Wyatt, 'Community Competence to Regulate the Internal Market' in M Dougan and S Currie (eds), *50 Years of the European Treaties: Looking Back and Thinking Forward* (Hart, 2009) 93 (reiterated in, eg, D Wyatt, 'Is the European Union an Organisation of Limited Powers?' in A Arnull et al (eds), *A Constitutional Order of States? Essays in EU Law in Honour of Alan Dashwood* (Hart, 2011) 3, 11–15). This is not to say that the breadth of Art 114 TFEU is entirely of the Court's making: see further, eg, S Weatherill, 'The Limits of Legislative Harmonization Ten Years after *Tobacco Advertising*: How the Court's Case Law has become a "Drafting Guide"' (2011) 12 *GLJ* 827; S Weatherill, 'The Court's Case Law on the Internal Market: "A Circumloquacious Statement of the Result, Rather than a Reason for Arriving at It"?' in M Adams et al (eds), *Judging Europe's Judges* (Hart, 2013) 87; compare, eg, B de Witte, 'A competence to protect: The pursuit of non-market aims through internal market legislation' in P Syrpis (ed), *The Judiciary, the Legislature and the EU Internal Market* (Cambridge Univ Press, 2012) 25, 45–46.

[195] J Basedow, 'The Case for a European Contract Act' in *An Academic Green Paper on European Contract Law*, n 77, 147, 156–157.

[196] See, eg, RSJ Mumford, Case note (2003) 11 *TFL Rev* 578, 580–581; D Slater, 'The scope of EC harmonising powers revisited?' (2003) 4 *GLJ* 137, 146; Wyatt, 'Community Competence', n 194, 122–127.

prompted concern that the Court was coming frightfully close to being satisfied with a mere showing of disparities among national laws in contrast to *Tobacco Advertising I*.[197] For tobacco advertising in the press, the Court was satisfied that divergences among national laws created, or were liable to create, obstacles to trade even for publications in domestic markets 'if only by way of exception or in small quantities'.[198] For radio sponsorship, the Court was likewise content that disparities in national laws were liable to impede the free movement of services on the grounds that radio broadcasters would be denied the benefit of sponsorship.[199] The Court also affirmed that Article 114 TFEU could be used for measures that covered domestic situations bearing no direct relationship to cross-border trade in the internal market. In *Vodafone*, the Court once again paid tribute to the threshold conditions established in the case law, but nonetheless edged away from *Tobacco Advertising I* in terms of the scrutiny of the measure concerned.[200]

It remains to be seen whether the Union courts may 'clip the wings' of Article 114 TFEU or again strike down a measure based on this Treaty provision in future case law.[201] Arguably, however, *Tobacco Advertising I* alongside its progeny have already mapped out a wider ambit for measures based on Article 114 TFEU than may have been evident on the face of that judgment alone, which cannot be totally undone. This sets the scene for the analysis of the parameters of obstacles to trade and appreciable distortions of competition.

8.3.2.2 *Parameters of obstacles to trade: Distinguishing obstacles* sensu lato *and obstacles* sensu stricto

As illustrated by the foregoing case law, the Court of Justice has generally framed the requirements for Article 114 TFEU (ex Article 95 EC) in two-dimensional terms: the measure concerned must contribute to the elimination of obstacles to trade and/or appreciable distortions of competition in the internal market. In other words, it has not as yet considered a measure's potential for improving the conditions for the establishment and functioning of the internal market for the purposes of Article 114 TFEU apart from these two routes. In the literature, there has been ongoing discussion as to what extent this provision leaves open an additional route for the adoption of measures that are not gauged at eliminating obstacles to the fundamental freedoms in the strict sense or appreciable distortions of competition, but nonetheless seek to encourage cross-border activities by remedying uncertainties or other risks resulting from differences in national laws that somehow deter economic actors from engaging in cross-border trade in the internal market.[202]

[197] See, eg, M Ludwigs, Case note (2007) 44 *CML Rev* 1159, 1167–1169, 1176; 'Editorial Comments: The Court of Justice in the limelight—again' (2008) 45 *CML Rev* 1571, 1574.

[198] See n 173 and accompanying text.

[199] See n 174 and accompanying text.

[200] See, eg, M Brenncke, Case note (2010) 47 *CML Rev* 1793, 1801–1802; I Maletic, 'The Story of the EU and the Happily Roaming Consumers' (2011) 38 *LIEI* 199, 200; S Weatherill, 'Free Movement of Goods' (2012) 61 *ICLQ* 541, 547–548.

[201] See, eg, Case T-526/10 (Judgment of 25 April 2013) *Inuit Tapiriit Kanatami and Others v Commission*, not reported (appeal pending in Case C-398/13 P).

[202] Compare, eg, J Basedow, 'A Common Contract Law for the Common Market' (1996) 33 *CML Rev* 1169 (reiterated in, eg, J Basedow, 'The Court of Justice and Private Law: Vacillations, General Principles and the Architecture of the European Judiciary' (2010) 18 *ERPL* 443, 452); Max Planck, n 26, 390–391; P-C Müller-Graff, 'Closer Cooperation in European Community Contract Law' in K Boele-Woelki and W Grosheide (eds), *The Future of European Contract Law—Essays in honour of Ewoud Hondius* (Kluwer, 2007) 91, 100; D Wyatt, 'Community Competence to Regulate the

While not said in so many words, this alludes to the discussion, and terminological problems associated therewith, of delineating the dimensions of obstacles to trade under Article 114 TFEU and its relationship to the free movement rules. To some extent, it appears that it is not so much an additional route that is at issue, but rather unearthing the breadth of the parameters of obstacles to trade within Article 114 TFEU itself. This highlights the importance of distinguishing between obstacles *sensu stricto* and obstacles *sensu lato* in connection with Article 114 TFEU. On the one hand, Article 114 TFEU encompasses obstacles to trade resulting from a national rule of a Member State taken by itself that falls foul of the free movement rules, which can be called obstacles *sensu stricto*. On the other hand, Article 114 TFEU also encompasses obstacles to trade that result from the fact that there are differences among the national laws of the several Member States that must be approximated so as to achieve the Union's objectives to ensure the smooth functioning of the internal market, which can be called obstacles *sensu lato*. This is not to say that approximation under Article 114 TFEU can be justified merely on the basis of a finding of differences among the national laws, as prohibited by *Tobacco Advertising I*. This is only to make clear that Article 114 TFEU covers obstacles to trade that result not from the effect of a particular national rule taken on its own, but rather from the impact on cross-border trade by virtue of the parallel differences among the laws of the Member States that renders such laws subject to approximation under Article 114 TFEU.

The relationship between Article 114 TFEU and the free movement rules, especially those concerning the free movement of goods under Articles 34–36 TFEU, is one of the most controversial topics in EU law. It has attracted differing views among scholars, with some arguing that approximation under Article 114 TFEU is limited by the reach of these provisions,[203] others taking the converse view,[204] and still others who have not yet taken a firm position but do not preclude the possibility that Article 114 TFEU may be broader.[205] To date, the Court has not yet squarely addressed the parameters of obstacles to trade under Article 114 TFEU vis-à-vis the free movement rules. The fact that the matter has not been decided expressly by the Court thus far is not altogether surprising, considering that the majority of cases—*Tobacco Advertising I, BAT,*

Internal Market', Univ of Oxford Faculty of Law Legal Studies Research Paper Series Working Paper No 9/2007, 41–46.

[203] See, eg, Barnard, n 35, 148; G Howells, 'Introduction' in G Howells et al, *European Fair Trading Law: The Unfair Commercial Practices Directive* (Ashgate, 2006) 1, 10; K Mortelmans, 'The Relationship between the Treaty Rules and Community Measures for the Establishment and Functioning of the Internal Market—Towards a Concordance Rule' (2002) 39 *CML Rev* 1303, 1326; JW Rutgers, 'European Competence and a European Civil Code, a Common Frame of Reference or an Optional Instrument' in AS Hartkamp et al (eds), *Towards a European Civil Code*, 4th rev and expanded edn (Kluwer/Ars Aequi Libri, 2011) 311, 318–320; A von Bogdandy and J Bast, 'The Federal Order of Competences' in A von Bogdandy and J Bast (eds), *Principles of European Constitutional Law*, 2nd edn (Hart/Verlag CH Beck, 2010) 275, 293.

[204] See, eg, T Ackermann, 'Buying Legitimacy? The Commission's Proposal on Consumer Rights' (2010) 21 *EBLR* 587, 594–595; G Davies, 'Can selling arrangements be harmonised?' (2005) 30 *ELR* 370; Radeideh, n 44, 280–281; J Stuyck, 'Patterns of Justice in the European Constitutional Charter: Minimum Harmonisation in the Field of Consumer Law' in *Law and Diffuse Interests in the European Legal Order—Liber amicorum Norbert Reich* (Nomos, 1997) 279, 286, 288; S Weatherill, 'Justifying Limits to Party Autonomy in the Internal Market—EC Legislation in the Field of Consumer Protection' in S Grundmann et al (eds), *Party Autonomy and the Role of Information in the Internal Market* (Walter de Gruyter, 2001) 173, 193–194 (but compare, eg, S Weatherill, 'European Private Law and the Constitutional Dimension' in F Cafaggi (ed), *The Institutional Framework of European Private Law* (Oxford Univ Press, 2006) 79, 105).

[205] See, eg, C Twigg-Flesner, *The Europeanisation of Contract Law* (Routledge-Cavendish, 2008) 30.

Swedish Match, *Arnold André*, *Alliance for Natural Health*, and *Tobacco Advertising II*—concerned measures laying down rules on the circulation of products and services in the EU, with the result that the Court could be expected to interweave its free movement case law on obstacles presented by the relevant national rules, such as the citation to *Keck* in *BAT*[206] and to *Gourmet International Products* in *Tobacco Advertising II*,[207] with its findings regarding the existence of existing or potential obstacles to trade resulting from disparities among the national laws concerned. Importantly, however, in those cases, the Court did not merge its consideration of a particular national rule's compliance with the free movement rules with its inquiry into obstacles to trade for the purposes of what is now Article 114 TFEU. Moreover, the key point in most of those cases was whether a prohibition placed on particular goods and/or services in the internal market could be adopted on the basis of a Treaty provision that is supposed to make the market work, not eliminate the relevant market in those products and/or services. As such, these cases did not concern measures that sought to promote or facilitate cross-border transactions in the internal market in a 'positive' way.

By comparison, in cases outside these confines, the Court has taken a wide view of obstacles to trade without being tied to the free movement rules. This is illustrated by *Biotechnology*, in which the Court ruled that approximation under what is now Article 114 TFEU is directed at reducing 'obstacles, whatever their origin, to the operation of the internal market which differences between the situations in the Member States represent'.[208] While not mentioned by the Court, this statement echoed early case law on what is now Article 115 TFEU, distinguishing the scope of approximation under that provision from the more limited scope of the rules on the free movement of goods, ie Article 34 TFEU (ex Article 28 EC).[209] Likewise, in *Tobacco Advertising II*, Article 114 TFEU was found applicable to obstacles to trade that could not in principle fall within the ambit of the free movement rules, considering that, in the case of prohibition of tobacco advertising in the press, the obstacles to trade existed in relation to publications which, by the Court's admission, were placed on essentially local markets with tenuous links to cross-border trade. This case also confirmed that Article 114 TFEU could extend to purely domestic situations with no link to cross-border trade, thereby going beyond the ambit of the free movement rules. At least implicitly, the case law evinces the notion that obstacles to trade for the purposes of the free movement rules are encompassed within the inquiry into Article 114 TFEU, but do not constitute by themselves the outer limit to the scope of Article 114 TFEU.

Unfortunately, the Court did not clarify matters in *Vodafone*. To recall, this case concerned a measure approximating rules on tariff setting for mobile phone roaming charges that had previously been set by commercial undertakings, as opposed to State bodies. In his Opinion, Advocate General Poiares Maduro drew attention to the relationship between the free movement rules and what is now Article 114 TFEU in relation to the actions of private parties and advocated the extension of the Court's case law on the horizontal application of the free movement rules to the analysis of Article 114 TFEU.[210] The Court did not take up this issue in its judgment, which may be explained by the controversial and quite expansive approach advocated by the Advocate General.[211] Consequently, it is hoped that future cases may present the Court

[206] See n 134 and accompanying text. [207] See n 172 and accompanying text.
[208] See n 124 and accompanying text.
[209] See Case 193/80 *Commission v Italy* [1981] ECR 3019, para 17.
[210] Opinion of AG Poiares Maduro in Case C-58/08 *Vodafone*, points 21–23.
[211] See, eg, Brenncke, n 200, 1807–1809.

with the opportunity to delineate the relationship between Article 114 TFEU and the free movement rules. In the meantime, admittedly, the Court's case law on Article 114 TFEU has not been very forthcoming in fleshing out the relationship between this provision and the free movement rules, given the nature of most cases so far. Nevertheless, from the tenor of judgments such as *Biotechnology* and *Tobacco Advertising II*, there are indications that Article 114 TFEU encompasses obstacles to trade that go beyond those presented by the free movement rules.

As far as the debate about European contract law is concerned, the distinction between obstacles *sensu lato* and obstacles *sensu stricto* is pivotal. As far as obstacles *sensu stricto* are concerned, there seems to be an assumption that the case law deeming contract law rules as falling outside the scope of the free movement rules forecloses the Union's competence under Article 114 TFEU. Specifically, it is often argued on the basis of certain cases on the free movement of goods concerning Articles 34 and 35 TFEU (ex Articles 28 and 29 EC), such as *CMC Motorradcenter*[212] and *Alsthom Atlantique*,[213] respectively, that national contract law rules cannot be considered obstacles to trade, at least to the extent that parties can deviate from them by virtue of choice of law rules.[214] Certainly, other scholars have cautioned not to generalize too much from these cases,[215] and there continues to be differing opinion as to the extent to which national contract law rules may be classified as 'selling arrangements' within the meaning of the *Keck* case law or deemed to impede 'market access'.[216] Yet, these cases should be read against the Court's more recent jurisprudence that places emphasis on the practical effects of particular national rules on free movement, whether in terms of acknowledging that a trader's uncertainty causing him to abstain from cross-border trade may be caught by Article 35 TFEU on exports[217] or making access to the market more difficult for the purposes of Article 34 TFEU on imports.[218] As a result, there is much debate to be had as regards the extent to which a particular national contract law rule can under certain circumstances constitute an obstacle *sensu stricto*, and the assumption of a general exclusion of non-mandatory contract law rules from the Treaty

[212] Case C-93/92 *CMC Motorradcenter* [1993] ECR I-5009.

[213] Case C-339/89 *Alsthom Atlantique* [1991] ECR I-107.

[214] See, eg, MW Hesselink et al, 'The legal basis for an optional instrument on European contract law', CSECL Working Paper Series No 2007/04, 53 and citations therein; S Leible, 'Fundamental Freedoms and European Contract Law' in S Grundmann (ed), *Constitutional Values and European Contract Law (*Kluwer, 2008) 63, 68; JW Rutgers, 'The Rule of Reason and Private Law or the Limits of Harmonization' in A Schrauwen (ed), *Rule of Reason: Rethinking Another Classic of European Legal Doctrine* (Europa, 2005) 144.

[215] See, eg, M Fallon and J Meeusen, 'Private International Law in the European Union and the Exception of Mutual Recognition' (2002) 4 *YPIL* 37, 48–49; A Hartkamp, *European Law and National Private Law* (Kluwer, 2012) § 34–§ 38.

[216] See, eg, M Schillig, 'The Interpretation of European Private Law in the Light of Market Freedoms and EU Fundamental Rights' (2008) 15 *MJ* 285, 289–291. Compare Nebbia, n 36, 92–101.

[217] See, eg, Case C-205/07 *Gysbrechts and Saturel Inter* [2008] ECR I-9947, paras 40–44. Compare Opinion of AG Trstenjak, points 48–89. For detailed discussion, see, eg, W-H Roth, Case note (2010) 47 *CML Rev* 509; M Szydło, 'Export Restrictions within the Structure of the Free Movement of Goods. Reconsideration of an Old Paradigm' (2010) 47 *CML Rev* 753; see also citations in n 218.

[218] See, eg, Case C-110/05 *Commission v Italy* [2009] ECR I-519. Compare Opinion of AG Bot, points 107–136. For a brief selection, see, eg, Special Issue, 'What Standard After *Keck*?' (2012) *REDC* 199; G Davies, 'Understanding Market Access: Exploring the Economic Rationality of Different Conceptions of Free Movement Law' (2011) 11 *GLJ* 671; S Enchelmaier, '*Moped Trailers, Mickelsson & Roos, Gysbrechts*: The ECJ's Case Law on Goods Keeps on Moving' (2010) 29 *YEL* 190; P Oliver, 'Of Trailers and Jet Skis: Is the Case Law on Article 34 TFEU Hurtling in a New Direction?' (2010) 33 *Fordham ILJ* 1423; J Snell, 'The Notion of Market Access: A Concept or a Slogan?' (2010) 47 *CML Rev* 437.

provisions concerning free movement on the basis of earlier case law does not necessarily hold. Importantly, however, the inquiry into the extent to which a particular national contract law rule constitutes a hindrance to cross-border trade in either the same or other Member States (obstacles *sensu stricto*) must be distinguished from the inquiry as regards the extent to which differences among the various national contract law rules result in obstacles hindering cross-border trade in the internal market (obstacles *sensu lato*).

In this regard, European contract law is perhaps the quintessential example of the use of Article 114 TFEU to reach obstacles to trade in this wider sense. The fact that there exist parallel national contract law regimes in the Member States, each of which embodies different contract rules, may be deemed to preclude parties from taking advantage of the internal market, even though a particular national contract law rule by itself does not fall foul of the free movement rules. As ventilated in the institutional documents and scholarly literature, the majority of the attention centres on three interrelated problems relating to the insufficiency of choice of law rules, higher transaction costs, and so-called 'psychological barriers', all of which underpin the justification for the proposed CESL.

First, one of the key problems presented in the debate relates to the *insufficiency of choice of law rules*. As already noted, several commentators have opined that obstacles to trade can be found as regards mandatory rules of contract law, as in the case of consumer contract law, which the parties are not free to contract out of and thus require traders to comply with now twenty-eight different legal regimes as predicated by the 'Rome I' Regulation, as opposed to non-mandatory rules of contract law in which the parties are free to do so.[219] Yet, as documented in the Commission's 2003 Action Plan and 2010 Green Paper, problems arise in connection with both consumer and commercial transactions by virtue of the fact that the line between mandatory and non-mandatory contract law is unclear due to different approaches in the Member States and that the choice of law is not always viable for consumers and businesses, particularly small and medium-sized enterprises (SMEs).[220] In fact, one scholar found that various non-mandatory rules are in fact mandatory, with the result that there is no reason to exclude non-mandatory rules as a category from unification efforts in relation to contract law.[221] In the proposed CESL, the problems for traders on account of the 'Rome I' Regulation for B2C contracts, especially in the online environment, as well as those experienced by traders, with particular regard to SMEs, in negotiating and applying a foreign contract law in B2B contracts are considered part of the obstacles to cross-border trade stemming from divergences between national contract laws.[222]

Secondly, as further underscored in the Commission's Communications starting with the 2003 Action Plan, differences between national contract laws present obstacles in the form of *higher transaction costs* for obtaining information on foreign law, engaging legal advice for consumers and businesses, and having to undertake certain formalities that place financial burdens on such parties or otherwise dissuade them from engaging in cross-border transactions.[223] While there had been divergent opinion in the commentary over the years as to the extent to which such costs rise to the level of obstacles to trade,[224] proof of problems resulting from such costs was given a particular

[219] See n 214 and accompanying text.

[220] As regards the 2003 Action Plan, see Chapter 5, § 5.3.2; as regards the 2010 Green Paper, see Chapter 6, § 6.4.2.

[221] MW Hesselink, 'Non-Mandatory Rules in European Contract Law' (2005) 1 *ERCL* 44.

[222] See Chapter 6, § 6.4.4. [223] See Chapter 5, § 5.3.2.

[224] Compare, eg, H Collins, *The European Civil Code: The Way Forward* (Cambridge Univ Press, 2008) 65–72; J Smits, 'Diversity of Contract Law and the European Internal Market' in *The Need for a European Contract Law*, n 78, 154, 166–169; Wagner, n 78, 1013–1017.

boost by the 2005 study conducted by Clifford Chance whose findings—comprising the responses of about 175 businesses, large and small, from eight representative Member States—were presented at an academic conference on European contract law held at Oxford University.[225] One of the most striking results of this study was that roughly two-thirds of companies experienced obstacles to cross-border trade as the result of certain factors including variations among national contract laws and costs of obtaining foreign legal advice.[226] This study prompted certain scholars to conclude that a case could be made for the adoption of a European contract law instrument on the basis of what is now Article 114 TFEU.[227] Since then, there have been some additional studies conducted on the matter at the European level,[228] which as noted in Chapter 6 were taken into account in the 2010 Green Paper and documentation accompanying the proposed CESL, so as to support the assertions that these additional transaction costs and related complexities imposed on traders, particularly SMEs, with having to deal with different contract laws constitute obstacles to trade in connection with B2C and B2B transactions.[229]

Thirdly, there are various arguments that may be classified under the heading of so-called '*psychological barriers*'. The general idea underlying this category seems to be that as a result of divergences among national contract laws, consumers and businesses are deterred from engaging in cross-border transactions on account of the perception of legal risks and/or legal uncertainties involving the use of non-domestic contract law, which have a detrimental impact on the free flow of goods and services in the internal market. Frankly speaking, the conjunction of the word 'psychological' with 'barriers' may inadvertently impart a degree of fuzziness based on parties' perceptions, which may result in sensitivities regarding the use and abuse of Article 114 TFEU. Yet, removing 'psychological' from the equation, such arguments highlight serious problems hindering consumers and traders from engaging in cross-border transactions. In the 2003 Action Plan, this was emphasized in the case of contractual liability rules and the interaction between disparities in contract law and movable property law since they presented commercial risks for operators that impeded the conclusion of cross-border transactions.[230] More generally, the fact that consumers and businesses must rely on foreign contract law has been depicted as a 'jump in the dark', which makes such parties wary of taking part in such transactions and thus stunting the growth of the internal market.[231] The 'psychological barrier' argument was bolstered by a famous article by Professor Jürgen Basedow, in which he posited that what is now Article 114 TFEU encompassed measures that helped to break down barriers on account of uncertainties and risks caused by differences in contract law.[232] Likewise, while some have

[225] S Vogenauer and S Weatherill, 'The European Community's Competence to Pursue the Harmonisation of Contract Law—an Empirical Contribution to the Debate' in *The Harmonisation of European Contract Law*, n 78, 105. The book went beyond this empirical analysis. See J Stuyck, Book review (2007) 44 *CML Rev* 528.

[226] Vogenauer and Weatherill, n 225, 125–127, 136.

[227] Vogenauer and Weatherill, n 225, 136. See also S Weatherill, 'Competence and European private law' in C Twigg-Flesner (ed), *The Cambridge Companion to European Union Private Law* (Cambridge Univ Press, 2010) 58, 68–69.

[228] For discussion of other studies, see, eg, G Rühl, 'Regulatory Competition in Contract Law: Empirical Evidence and Normative Implications' (2013) 9 *ERCL* 61, 68–70.

[229] Discussion of the relevant studies filtered into the 2010 Green Paper (§ 6.4.2), stakeholder responses thereto (§ 6.4.2.4), and documentation related to the proposed CESL (§ 6.4.4).

[230] See Chapter 5, § 5.3.2.

[231] See, eg, O Lando, 'Optional or Mandatory Europeanisation of Contract Law' (2000) 8 *ERPL* 59.

[232] Basedow, *CML Rev*, n 202, 1182–1184.

questioned the sufficiency of uncertainties rising to the level of obstacles to trade,[233] others have taken a middle ground in the sense of either finding that legal uncertainties can be regarded as a non-tariff barrier to trade, but dispute the method to go about remedying it,[234] or acknowledging that while not an obstacle to trade per se, such legal uncertainties do act as a deterrent to the expansion of the internal market.[235] This set of arguments figures into the justification for the proposed CESL, on account of the way in which differences between national contract laws dissuade traders, particularly SMEs, from expanding into the markets of other Member States and discourage consumers from shopping cross-border because they are often uncertain about their rights in cross-border situations.[236]

Consequently, despite differing views in the commentary, the record of institutional documents and accompanying studies produced in the debate provides a basis for arguing that the sheer parallel differences between national contract law rules—the lack of familiarity with foreign law and the additional costs, complexities, and risks that are imposed—can act as obstacles to trade hindering or precluding consumers and businesses from making the most of the internal market. As such, the adoption of a European contract law instrument as exemplified by the proposed CESL, establishing a common set of contract law rules by which to further cross-border transactions among parties from different Member States and thus surmounting the obstacles that exist, would make a definitive contribution to the establishment and functioning of the internal market in line with the requirements for Article 114 TFEU. Moreover, while it is readily admitted that there are some rules of contract law that may not present obstacles to trade in the internal market and relate purely to domestic as opposed to cross-border transactions, this is not fatal to the use of Article 114 TFEU. Following from *Tobacco Advertising II*, provided that the threshold requirements concerning obstacles to trade and/or appreciable distortions of competition have been crossed, recourse to Article 114 TFEU 'does not presuppose the existence of an actual link with free movement between the Member States in every situation' covered by the measure concerned, as long as the measure is actually intended to improve the conditions for the establishment and functioning of the internal market.[237] This provides grounds for arguing that certain national contract law rules that may not be considered to present obstacles to trade by themselves may nonetheless be included in a European contract law instrument adopted under Article 114 TFEU so as to ensure that the objectives of such an instrument relating to the elimination of obstacles to trade in the internal market can be achieved. Although at present the scope of the proposed CESL is limited in various ways in order to target the problems posed by divergences among contract laws for cross-border transactions in the internal market, these findings may help to strengthen the case for the use of Article 114 TFEU as the legal basis for the proposed CESL to the extent that such issues may arise.

[233] See, eg, H Collins, 'Transaction Costs and Subsidiarity in European Contract Law' in *An Academic Green Paper on European Contract Law*, n 77, 269, 272–275.

[234] See H Wagner, 'Economic Analysis of Cross-Border Legal Uncertainty' in *The Need for a European Contract Law*, n 78, 25, particularly 44; Smits, n 224, 179.

[235] Collins, n 224, 72.

[236] See Chapter 6, § 6.4.4.

[237] Case C-380/03 *Tobacco Advertising II*, para 80.

8.3.2.3 *Parameters of existing (and future?) appreciable distortions of competition*

As further illustrated by the foregoing case law, the Court of Justice has yet to define the concept of 'appreciable distortions of competition' for the purposes of Article 114 TFEU, but instead has pointed to certain situations to show what does, or does not, rise to the level of 'appreciable' or constitute a 'distortion of competition' in the first place. *Tobacco Advertising I* is the landmark case (and only case so far) in which the Court has engaged in ample discussion of this subject. It highlighted four situations, two that did not meet the threshold requirements for appreciable distortions of competition and two that did. *In the context of advertising agencies and producers of advertising media*, the Court found that (1) undertakings in Member States that imposed less restrictions on tobacco advertising received advantages in terms of economies of scale and an increase in profits, but this was too 'remote and indirect' to rise to the level of 'appreciable', as compared to (2) distortions caused by differences in production costs relating to environmental protection standards illustrated by the Directive at issue in *Titanium Dioxide*.[238] Yet, (3) the Court singled out certain forms of tobacco sponsorship where their prohibition would give rise to the relocation of sports events, since this 'gives rise to considerable repercussions on the conditions of competition for undertakings associated with such events' and could be based on Article 114 TFEU.[239] *In the context of the market of tobacco products*, this type of distortion was not mentioned in the Directive itself.[240] Thus, the Court seemed intent on pointing out that (4) the fact that producers and sellers of tobacco products were required to resort to price competition to influence their market share in Member States with more restrictive legislation on tobacco advertising was not a distortion of competition, but rather a restriction on the form of competition that applied equally to all economic operators in those Member States.[241] Together with the emphasis on ensuring that Article 114 TFEU could not be used to combat the 'smallest distortions of competition', the Court's approach manifested the intention to ensure that the limits of this provision were not exceeded. However, the Court's anecdotal examples invited some flexibility into the assessment, and much depended upon how the 'appreciable' formula would be applied in later cases.[242]

In the aftermath of *Tobacco Advertising I*, the Court has been reluctant to elaborate the standard for appreciable distortions of competition. This is demonstrated by a comparison between the Court's judgment and the Opinions of the Advocates General in *Biotechnology*[243] and even more so in *BAT*,[244] the latter of which contained extensive discussion of this issue in connection with the export ban. This was also evident in *Tobacco Advertising II*, in which the Court declared that there was no need to delve into the issue under circumstances where the requisite showing of obstacles to trade had been fulfilled. Certainly, this may have been intentional in order to confirm that what is now Article 114 TFEU did not require a showing of both the obstacles to trade and appreciable distortions of competition requirements, which the Court's prior ruling in *BAT* had presented in understated fashion. Yet, the Court relied on the first and fifth

[238] Case C-376/98 *Tobacco Advertising I*, para 109.
[239] Case C-376/98 *Tobacco Advertising I*, paras 110–111.
[240] Case C-376/98 *Tobacco Advertising I*, para 112.
[241] Case C-376/98 *Tobacco Advertising I*, para 113.
[242] See S Weatherill, 'The Commission's Options for Developing EC Consumer Protection and Contract Law: Assessing the Constitutional Basis' (2002) 13 *EBLR* 497, 506; Wyatt, n 202, 111–112.
[243] See Opinion of AG Jacobs in Case C-377/98 *Biotechnology*, point 48.
[244] See Opinion of AG Geelhoed in Case C-491/01 *BAT*, points 137–166.

recitals of the Directive to confirm that disparities in national laws relating to radio sponsorship gave rise to an '*appreciable risk of distortions of competition*' in the internal market.[245] This language seemed to indicate that a measure based on Article 114 TFEU could be used to combat the mere risk of future appreciable distortions, as opposed to existing ones.

This issue had been lying dormant since *Titanium Dioxide*.[246] In that case, the Court proclaimed that what is now Article 114 TFEU could be used where disparities in national laws were 'liable to create or maintain distorted competition'.[247] This language was then incorporated into *Spain v Council*,[248] in which the Court ruled that what is now Article 114 TFEU could be used to deal with disparities in national laws that were not only 'liable to create or maintain distortions of competition', but also 'liable to hinder' the free movement of goods in the EU.[249] In turn, the Court's ruling in *Spain v Council* found its way into *Tobacco Advertising I* as regards the use of Article 114 TFEU for preventing the emergence of future obstacles to trade,[250] but its counterpart in *Titanium Dioxide* did not. The Court only cited *Titanium Dioxide* in support of establishing the standard for 'appreciable' distortions.[251] It made no mention of its relevance in connection with the use of Article 114 TFEU for preventing future appreciable distortions from arising. Thus, it remained unclear whether the Court was shutting the door on this possibility.

Subsequent case law enlivened the issue further. In 2002, two years after *Tobacco Advertising I*, the Court delivered its judgment in *Leitner*.[252] As discussed in Chapter 2,[253] this case concerned a reference for a preliminary ruling on the interpretation of the Package Travel Directive as regards whether the notion of 'damage' included non-material damage. To recall, the likelihood of distortions of competition was part of what prompted the Austrian court to make a reference, since differences between certain Member States as regards the extent of liability for tour operators were contemplated as incompatible with the objectives of the Directive to eliminate distortions of competition and provide for a uniform level of consumer protection in the internal market.[254] In its judgment, the Court found that it was clear, on the basis of the second and third recitals of the Directive, that its aim was to eliminate disparities between national laws in the area of package holidays which were '*liable to give rise to distortions of competition*' between operators established in different Member States.[255] Following this, the Court declared: 'It is not in dispute that, in the field of package holidays, the existence in some Member States but not in others of an obligation to provide compensation for non-material damage *would cause significant distortions of competition*, given that, as the Commission has pointed out, non-material damage is a frequent occurrence in that field'.[256]

The use of what is now Article 114 TFEU as the legal basis for the Package Travel Directive was not in dispute in *Leitner*, and therefore, the 'appreciable' standard for

[245] See n 175 and accompanying text (emphasis added).
[246] Case C-300/89 *Titanium Dioxide* [1991] ECR I-2867.
[247] Case C-300/89 *Titanium Dioxide*, para 15.
[248] Case C-350/92 *Spain v Council* [1995] ECR I-1985.
[249] Case C-350/92 *Spain v Council*, paras 32–33. [250] See n 101. [251] See n 103.
[252] Case C-168/00 *Leitner* [2002] ECR I-2631. [253] See Chapter 2, § 2.3.2.
[254] Case C-168/00 *Leitner*, para 12; Opinion of AG Tizzano, point 16.
[255] Case C-168/00 *Leitner*, para 20 (emphasis added).
[256] Case C-168/00 *Leitner*, para 21 (emphasis added). Similar to *Vodafone*, the Court referred to 'significant', as opposed to 'appreciable', distortions of competition. Again, it is not clear whether this was intentional: see n 191.

distortions of competition in relation to this Directive was not directly before the Court to decide. Still, the Court's judgment manifested a less restrained approach to the 'appreciable' requirement in relation to problems stemming from divergences among national (consumer) contract laws. As emphasized by one scholar, the Court's approach in *Leitner* suggested that if the sole disparity between national laws is the possibility of securing certain kinds of damages in some Member States but not in others, that aspect of contract law could be subject to approximation under what is now Article 114 TFEU (ex Article 95 EC), which was a 'far cry' from the threshold of 'appreciable' distortions elaborated in *Tobacco Advertising I*.[257] Also, by basing its rationale on the recitals of the Directive concerned, the Court's judgment imparted that Article 114 TFEU could be used to combat potential future appreciable distortions that were liable to arise as a result of the disparities in the national laws concerned.

In *Tobacco Advertising II*, the Court reopened the matter with its substantiation, on the basis of the first and fifth recitals of the Directive at issue, that the differences between national laws regarding the advertising and sponsorship of tobacco products in the press and radio meant that there was an 'appreciable risk of distortions of competition'.[258] Yet, in doing so, it left many questions open. On the one hand, the Court was quoting from the fifth recital of the Directive[259] so the reference to an 'appreciable risk of distortions' was not entirely of the Court's own making. Indeed, the Directive's Preamble seemed to have gone overboard in attempting to demonstrate the measure's compliance with *Tobacco Advertising I*, mentioning not only an 'appreciable risk of distortions of competition', but also an 'appreciable risk of obstacles' to free movement in the fourth recital,[260] which was also cited by the Court in its judgment.[261] Thus, it is not clear whether the use of 'appreciable' as an adjective for 'risk', as opposed to 'distortion', was intentional on the legislature's part in transposing the requirements of *Tobacco Advertising I* into the Directive, which then inadvertently filtered into the Court's judgment in *Tobacco Advertising II*.[262] On the other hand, in referring to two recitals—the first and the fifth—of the Directive, the Court could have just as easily cited the first recital, which mentioned existing, as opposed to a risk of, appreciable distortions of competition.[263] This lends support for the view that the Court knew what it was doing when it chose to rest its finding on the wording of the fifth recital and hence to inject the possibility of recourse to Article 114 TFEU on grounds of 'appreciable risks of distortions'.

While further case law on this issue is needed, the jurisprudence so far, especially taking *Leitner* and *Tobacco Advertising II* into account, seems to indicate the possibility

257 See Wyatt, n 202, 129–130 (calling the Court's approach 'impressionistic').

258 Case C-380/03 *Tobacco Advertising II*, para 66.

259 The fifth recital states in relevant part: 'The laws, regulations and administrative provisions of the Member States relating to certain types of sponsorship for the benefit of tobacco products with cross-border effects give rise to an appreciable risk of distortion of the conditions of competition for this activity within the Internal Market'.

260 The fourth recital states in relevant part: 'The circulation in the Internal Market of publications such as periodicals, newspapers and magazines is subject to an appreciable risk of obstacles to free movement as a result of Member States' laws, regulations and administrative provisions which prohibit or regulate tobacco advertising in those media'.

261 See Case C-380/00 *Tobacco Advertising II*, paras 85, 111; see also para 47 ('appreciable risk of disparities increasing').

262 Reference to an 'appreciable risk of obstacles' seems to be intentional in view of the Parliament's and Council's arguments: see Case C-380/00 *Tobacco Advertising II*, para 27.

263 The last sentence of the first recital states: 'In the case of sponsorship, distortions of the conditions of competition are likely to increase and have already been noted as regards the organisation of certain major sporting and cultural events'.

that Article 114 TFEU may be used to approximate national laws in order to eliminate existing appreciable distortions of competition resulting from differences between such laws and to prevent potential future appreciable distortions from arising.[264] At the very least, as demonstrated by these two cases, the Court takes a more pragmatic or flexible approach to the standard for appreciable distortions of competition than may have been initially indicated in *Tobacco Advertising I*. Under *Leitner*, differences in liability rules among national consumer contract laws were viewed by the Court as presenting 'significant' distortions justifying the use of Article 114 TFEU on the basis of the text of the measure concerned. *Tobacco Advertising II* appears to have stepped further than *Tobacco Advertising I* in the sense of carving out leeway for finding a risk of appreciable distortions even in the case of radio sponsorship without delving into the exact nature of what such distortions would be. This has implications for the debate about European contract law.

Generally speaking, although the extent to which disparities among national contract laws may be deemed to constitute appreciable distortions of competition in the internal market remains controversial, it is perhaps one of the rare points of agreement in the commentary so far that this basis cannot be used to justify a European contract law instrument on its own. It is difficult to make a definitive judgment whether rules concerning consumer and commercial contracts would be considered to constitute appreciable distortions of competition, since by and large, the problems presented by disparities in national contract laws for the purposes of identifying appreciable distortions of competition in many ways mirror or are intertwined with the problems identified above in connection with obstacles to trade. In addition, the 2010 Green Paper and documentation concerning the proposed CESL are grounded in apparent obstacles to trade resulting from divergences between national contract laws and do not rely expressly on arguments concerning appreciable distortions of competition for the purposes of Article 114 TFEU.[265] Nevertheless, on the basis of certain institutional documents and scholarly literature in the debate, the discussion has largely centred on two key sets of problems, which may to some extent provide further 'cushioning' for Union action in certain areas of contract law depending on the future course of the European contract law project.

First, there seems to be a general set of problems concerning the competitive advantages or disadvantages placed on consumers and businesses in cross-border transactions in the form of information asymmetries and costs placed on businesses and consumers resulting from disparities among national contract laws. For example, one scholar singled out three situations: (1) information between competitors regarding the contract law rules is distributed unequally in the sense that some competitors are more familiar with such laws than others whether by their size or accessibility to legal expertise; (2) the situation between domestic and foreign firms is different in the sense that foreign, as opposed to domestic, firms have the advantage of being able to escape from domestic laws, but in cases where domestic law is more favourable, the domestic firm is placed at a competitive advantage by being more familiar with such law; and (3) information is distributed differently between the parties, as in the case of consumer contracts in

[264] Given the lineage of *Titanium Dioxide* and *Spain v Council*, it may be wondered whether the Court will do for distortions of competition what it did for obstacles to trade in the sense of fixing certain conditions (eg, that such distortions must be likely and that the measure concerned must be designed to prevent them) for the Union legislature's reliance on such grounds.

[265] See Chapter 6, § 6.4.2, § 6.4.4.

which consumers do not conclude contracts on a daily basis compared with traders.[266] Disparities in contract law are also posited to distort competition by virtue of the different bargaining positions of parties, even under circumstances where such rules are only dispositive, since such bargaining is conducted 'in the shadow of the law' and the knowledge of contract law by one party as opposed to another presents a decisive competitive advantage in its favour.[267]

In large part, these arguments seem to depend upon the 'playing field' taken into consideration. The fact that foreign and domestic companies occupy different positions when it comes to the negotiation and knowledge of contract law seems to fall on the line of applying equally to all foreign and domestic operators depending upon the setting and hence it remains uncertain whether this could be deemed to rise to the level of an appreciable distortion of competition. The fact that parties are precluded from using standard form contracts throughout the EU, which would provide them with advantages in economies of scale and greater profits, would also seem to find analogy with the Court's rationale in *Tobacco Advertising I* in the sense of being too tenuous to rise to the level of 'appreciable'. Yet, in comparison to the factual circumstances upon which the Court's ruling was predicated in that case—ie that prohibitions on tobacco advertising would have a marginal impact on advertising agencies—the fact that some companies as opposed to others are precluded from utilizing competitive devices relating to standard form contracts and other marketing techniques could be considered to have a more serious impact in terms of creating an unlevel playing field. At the very least, it could be posited that such arguments could fall within the ambit of presenting an 'appreciable risk' of distortions of competition in line with what was said above.

Secondly, there are particular types of contract rules that are associated with the likelihood of appreciable distortions of competition. Liability rules in contract law and the interface between contract law and movable property law are often mentioned in this regard. As emphasized in the 2003 Action Plan, for example, divergences between national liability rules expose traders to differing costs and insurance fees and the fact that certain types of credit instruments are favoured in some Member States but greatly restricted or non-existent in other Member States may lead to distortions of competition among traders with respect to having recourse to such instruments for cross-border transactions.[268] Such arguments appear to present a strong case for the use of Article 114 TFEU. As confirmed by the Court in *Leitner*, differences in liability rules in B2C contracts give rise to 'significant' distortions of competition in the sense of imposing on some traders, as opposed to others, the obligation to provide compensation to consumers on account of the non-performance of such contracts. Along these lines, similar arguments could be made for B2B contracts, since the impact of liability rules on companies, as opposed to consumers, could, arguably, be as significant in terms of effects. This could also presumably fall within the category of 'appreciable risks' of distortions of competition, which a European contract law instrument would eliminate by providing a uniform set of contract rules applicable to all traders. Likewise, as regards contract rules relating to movable property law, this constitutes one of the most convincing cases. Akin to *Tobacco Advertising I* and *II*, the differences in treatment,

[266] J Drexl, 'Continuing Contract Law Harmonisation under the White Paper of 1985?—Between Minimum Harmonisation, Mutual Recognition, Conflict of Laws, and Uniform Law' in *An Academic Green Paper on European Contract Law*, n 77, 103, 114–115.

[267] Basedow, *CML Rev*, n 202, 1174–1177.

[268] Commission Communication, A more coherent European Contract Law—An Action Plan, COM (2003) 68 final, 12.2.2003 (2003 Action Plan), points 46, 49.

or lack thereof, of various types of credit instruments among the Member States place undertakings at a competitive disadvantage depending upon the extent to which such instruments are recognized in a particular Member State, which a European contract law instrument would eliminate by providing a uniform set of rules allowing actors to engage in transactions across the EU without the potential for such arrangements to be jeopardized once the internal border of one Member State or another was crossed.

Taking all of the foregoing into account, many questions remain open as regards the obstacles to trade and appreciable distortions of competition requirements of Article 114 TFEU. Still, on the basis of the case law so far, it is submitted that a case can be made that the adoption of a European contract law instrument, as presented by the proposed CESL, goes beyond 'a mere finding of disparities among national rules and of the abstract risks of obstacles to the exercise of the fundamental freedoms or of distortions of competition'[269] and falls within the scope of the Union's competence under Article 114 TFEU. This is based upon: (1) the course of development of the *Tobacco Advertising I* case law, taking account of that judgment alongside its progeny; (2) Article 114 TFEU's coverage of obstacles *sensu lato* as opposed to merely obstacles *sensu stricto*; and (3) Article 114 TFEU's potential for combating existing as well as future appreciable distortions of competition. This finding may invigorate arguments concerning the roles played by the principles of subsidiarity and proportionality, which leads to the next section.

8.3.3 The exercise of Union competence under Article 114 TFEU

8.3.3.1 The 'object' prong

The 'object' prong has been the source of much of the Court's jurisprudence on the principles of subsidiarity and proportionality. This is because in addition to arguments contesting the use of what is now Article 114 TFEU as a proper legal basis, several cases involved challenges to the measure's compliance with one or both of these principles. Over the years, this case law has been noted for the Court's lack of rigorous examination of the principles of subsidiarity and proportionality.[270] The Court's approach to the principle of subsidiarity has proven to be 'a particularly sensitive issue', in the words of one scholar,[271] due to growing tensions about its ineffectiveness in relation to measures based on Article 114 TFEU.

Starting with *Tobacco Advertising I*, although the Court did not pronounce on the matter,[272] Advocate General Fennelly contended that Article 114 TFEU (ex Article 95 EC) was an exclusive competence, rendering the principle of subsidiarity inapplicable.[273] In his view, the character of approximation was such that the Member States simply could not approximate each other's laws in fields falling within the Treaties: 'Individual action is excluded as a matter of logic and collective action by the [then] 15 Member States (for example, by way of a treaty concluded under public international law) is excluded, in my view, as a matter of law, having regard, in particular, to the terms of

[269] Case C-376/98 *Tobacco Advertising I*, para 84.

[270] See, eg, Barnard, n 35, 618–620; D Chalmers et al, *European Union Law: Cases and Materials*, 2nd edn (Cambridge Univ Press, 2010) 364, 369; T Tridimas, *The General Principles of EU Law*, 2nd edn (Oxford Univ Press, 2006) 177–180, 183–188. But compare, eg, Craig and de Búrca, n 194, 99–100.

[271] Barnard, n 35, 618.

[272] Case C-376/98 *Tobacco Advertising I*, para 118.

[273] Opinion of AG Fennelly in Case C-376/98 *Tobacco Advertising I* and Case C-74/99 *Imperial Tobacco*, points 142–144.

[Article 4(3) TEU] concerning the principle of sincere cooperation'.[274] In *Biotechnology*, the Court confronted this issue. There, the Netherlands fell back on the points it made in relation to legal basis, ie since national patent laws were almost entirely harmonized by the relevant international convention, any disparities arising thereunder should have been addressed by renegotiation of that convention, which the Member States were perfectly able to achieve on their own.[275] In its judgment, the Court went through the subsidiarity calculus to find that the Directive complied with the principle of subsidiarity:

> The objective pursued by the Directive, to ensure smooth operation of the internal market by preventing or eliminating differences between the legislation and practice of the various Member States in the area of the protection of biotechnological inventions, could not be achieved by action taken by the *Member States alone*. As the scope of that protection has immediate effects on trade, and, accordingly, on intra-[EU] trade, it is clear that, given the scale and effects of the proposed action, the objective in question could be better achieved by the [Union].[276]

While not saying so explicitly, the Court implicitly rejected that subsidiarity was inapplicable to Article 114 TFEU and that collective action by the Member States could be used as a counterweight to Union action; the focus was placed on the Member States acting 'alone'.

Thereafter, in *BAT*, the Court expressly declared that what is now the Union's competence under Article 114 TFEU (ex Article 95 EC) was not exclusive and hence the principle of subsidiarity was applicable.[277] Yet, it concluded that the Directive did not violate this principle, since the objective of approximating national laws could not be 'sufficiently achieved' by the Member States individually and called for action at the European level.[278] As such, the Court did not do much to contradict the assertions of the Netherlands and the Commission that where the conditions for the use of Article 114 TFEU have been satisfied, those concerning the principle of subsidiarity are too.[279] Advocate General Geelhoed's treatment of subsidiarity in this case was even shorter, amounting to one paragraph: 'As I have concluded that action by the [Union] legislature under Article [114 TFEU] was necessary, no further significance attaches to the appraisal of subsidiarity.'[280]

Although the issue of subsidiarity did not arise in *Swedish Match* and *Arnold André*, the Court's judgment in *Alliance for Natural Health* substantiated this remark. Again, Advocate General Geelhoed recognized that he could be 'very short on this point', boiling down the analysis to the main question whether the objective of the Directive could be better achieved by the Union, which he found was fulfilled.[281] The Court proceeded by way of similar analysis, finding the objective pursued by the contested provisions could be best achieved at the European level.[282] Likewise, in *Vodafone*, the Court

[274] Opinion of AG Fennelly in Case C-376/98 *Tobacco Advertising I* and Case C-74/99 *Imperial Tobacco*, point 136.

[275] See Opinion of AG Jacobs in Case C-377/98 *Biotechnology*, point 79.

[276] Case C-377/98 *Biotechnology*, para 32 (emphasis added). Compare Opinion of AG Jacobs, point 81.

[277] Case C-491/01 *BAT*, para 179.

[278] Case C-491/01 *BAT*, paras 180–185. In its subsidiarity inquiry, the Court examined the intensity of the measure concerned, which led scholars to find that the Court's subsidiarity and proportionality tests had become blurred. See Barnard, n 35, 619; Mumford, n 196, 585. Yet, this may be explained by the infusion of proportionality within the subsidiarity calculus: see Chapter 7, § 7.4.4.2.

[279] Case C-491/01 *BAT*, para 176.

[280] Opinion of AG Geelhoed in Case C-491/01 *BAT*, point 285.

[281] Opinion of AG Geelhoed in Joined Cases C-154/04 and C-155/04 *Alliance for Natural Health*, points 92–95.

[282] Joined Cases C-154/04 and C-155/04 *Alliance for Natural Health*, paras 104–107.

summarily found that by virtue of the common approach laid down by the Regulation, the objective pursued by that Regulation could best be achieved at the European level and held that the relevant provisions did not infringe the principle of subsidiarity.[283] In his Opinion, Advocate General Poiares Maduro paid utmost vigilance to ensuring the legislature's compliance with this principle,[284] but considered that the cross-border or transnational nature of the economic activity in question (here roaming) put the Union in a better position than the national authorities to regulate that activity.[285] Consequently, the commentary has increasingly acknowledged that the subsidiarity inquiry in practice has become largely moot in relation to Article 114 TFEU.[286] Given that no Member State can carry out approximation for the purposes of ensuring the smooth functioning of the internal market on its own, the Union automatically seems better suited to the task.

Along similar lines, the principle of proportionality has been given a 'light touch' by the Court in several cases within the 'object' prong. In *BAT*, the Court declared that the legislature must be given 'broad discretion', and therefore the legality of the measure would be affected only if it was 'manifestly inappropriate having regard to the objective which the competent institution is seeking to pursue', which was not the case as regards the measure at issue.[287] Advocate General Geelhoed reached the same conclusion, emphasizing that on the whole the Union courts exercise a limited appraisal of this issue.[288] The Court continued its approach in *Swedish Match* and *Arnold André*.[289] Thereafter, in *Alliance for Natural Health*, despite Advocate General Geelhoed's contention that the Directive infringed the principle of proportionality and should be annulled on such grounds,[290] the Court swiftly concluded that it fully complied with this principle.[291] In *Tobacco Advertising II*, the Court, echoing the conclusions of Advocate General Léger,[292] ruled that Articles 3 and 4 of the Directive did not violate the principle of proportionality.[293] With regard to Article 3's prohibition on tobacco advertising in the press, the Court considered that it was not possible to adopt as a less restrictive measure exempting publications intended for local markets, since this would have made the Directive's field of application uncertain.[294] And as for Article 4's prohibition on radio sponsorship, it was not apparent from the Preamble of the Directive, particularly the fifth recital, that the legislature exceeded the limits of its discretion by not limiting the measure to activities or events with cross-border effects.[295]

Recently, the Court's judgment in *Vodafone* suggests a subtle change of approach. In this case, the Court began its assessment of the principle of proportionality by

[283] Case C-58/08 *Vodafone*, paras 78–79. See, in this regard, A Biondi, 'Subsidiarity in the Courtroom' in A Biondi et al (eds), *EU Law After Lisbon* (Oxford Univ Press, 2012) 213, 218–219.

[284] Opinion of AG Poiares Maduro in Case C-58/08 *Vodafone*, point 30.

[285] Opinion of AG Poiares Maduro in Case C-58/08 *Vodafone*, points 33–34.

[286] See, eg, G Davies, 'Subsidiarity: The Wrong Idea, In The Wrong Place, At The Wrong Time' (2006) 43 *CML Rev* 63; F Sander, 'Subsidiarity Infringements Before the European Court of Justice: Futile Interference With Politics or a Substantial Step Towards EU Federalism?' (2006) 12 *CJEL* 517; Weatherill, n 227, 64; Wyatt, 'Limited Powers?', n 194, 19.

[287] Case C-491/01 *BAT*, paras 124–141.

[288] Opinion of AG Geelhoed in Case C-491/01 *BAT*, points 224–225, 230.

[289] Case C-210/03 *Swedish Match*, paras 47–58.

[290] Opinion of AG Geelhoed in Joined Cases C-154/04 and C-155/04 *Alliance for Natural Health*, points 68–89, 111.

[291] Joined Cases C-154/04 and C-155/04 *Alliance for Natural Health*, paras 109–112.

[292] See Opinion of AG Léger in Case C-380/03 *Tobacco Advertising II*, points 218–227.

[293] Case C-380/03 *Tobacco Advertising II*, paras 146–152.

[294] Case C-380/03 *Tobacco Advertising II*, para 149 (citing Case C-101/01 *Lindqvist*, para 41).

[295] Case C-380/03 *Tobacco Advertising II*, para 152.

reiterating that the criterion for judicial review of this principle is not whether the measure concerned is the only or best possible measure, but rather whether it is manifestly inappropriate, having regard to the objective which the competent institution is seeking to pursue.[296] However, it underlined that notwithstanding its broad discretion, the legislature must base its choice on objective criteria and, in assessing the burdens associated with various possible measures, must examine whether the objectives pursued by the measure chosen are such as to justify even substantial negative economic consequences for certain operators.[297] On this basis, it devoted attention to ensuring that each requirement of the proportionality calculus was satisfied, looking to the text of the Regulation and accompanying documentation, including the Explanatory Memorandum of the proposal and Impact Assessment, to verify that the provisions of the Regulation were appropriate, necessary, and proportionate to the aim pursued.[298] It concluded that they did not infringe the principle of proportionality.[299] Noticeably, the Court did not take up Advocate General Poiares Maduro's view that the impact on Member State autonomy must be considered as part of the proportionality assessment,[300] although he also concluded that the legislature's approach was a reasonable and proportionate response to the problem at hand.[301] As a result, although the Court's ruling in this case did not eradicate the high standard of 'manifest' inappropriateness that must be met, it has been considered to herald more stringent 'procedural' review of proportionality in terms of verifying compliance with this principle on the basis of the documents issued by the Union institutions and thus placing emphasis on its operation inside the EU decision-making process.[302] This dovetails with the operation of both subsidiarity and proportionality under the 'approximation' prong of the case law.

8.3.3.2 *The 'approximation' prong*

The 'approximation' prong represents the other set of cases concerning the limits of 'measures for the approximation' of the laws of the Member States under Article 114 TFEU. While some previous case law touched on this issue,[303] *Smoke Flavourings* and *ENISA* definitively addressed this aspect of the scope of Article 114 TFEU for the first time.[304] *UK v European Parliament and Council* ('*Smoke Flavourings*')[305] concerned the issue whether 'multi-stage approximation' was permitted under Article 114 TFEU. It involved an action for annulment brought by the UK against a Regulation concerning smoke flavourings used or intended for use in foods,[306] adopted under what is now

[296] Case C-58/08 *Vodafone*, para 52. [297] Case C-58/08 *Vodafone*, para 53.

[298] Case C-58/08 *Vodafone*, paras 55–70.

[299] Case C-58/08 *Vodafone*, para 71. Recent case law of the EGC has taken a similar tack on the basis of *Vodafone*: see, eg, Case T-526/10 (Judgment of 25 April 2013) *Inuit Tapiriit Kanatami v Commission*, not reported, paras 88–103. As with its findings concerning subsidiarity (para 85), this portion of the General Court's ruling was not appealed to the Court in Case C-398/13 P, [2013] OJ C274/12.

[300] Opinion of AG Poiares Maduro in Case C-58/08 *Vodafone*, points 37, 44.

[301] Opinion of AG Poiares Maduro in Case C-58/08 *Vodafone*, points 38–43.

[302] See, eg, D Keyaerts, Case note (2010) 35 *ELR* 869; K Lenaerts, 'The European Court of Justice and Process-Oriented Review' (2012) 31 *YEL* 3, 7–9. Compare, eg, Weatherill, *GLJ*, n 194, 859–860.

[303] See, eg, Case C-359/92 *Germany v Council* ('*Product Safety*') [1994] ECR I-3681. See further L Gormley, Case note (1996) 21 *ELR* 59.

[304] See further K Gutman, Case note (2006) 13 *CJEL* 147.

[305] Case C-66/04 *UK v European Parliament and Council* ('*Smoke Flavourings*') [2005] ECR I-10553.

[306] Reg (EC) No 2065/2003 of the European Parliament and of the Council of 10 Nov 2003 on smoke flavourings used or intended for use in or on foods, [2003] OJ L309/1.

Article 114 TFEU (ex Article 95 EC). The Regulation provided for a procedure whereby the Commission would authorize the substances used for the production of smoke flavourings and then place such authorized substances on a positive list annexed to the Regulation.[307] Only smoke flavourings included on the list could be marketed in the EU.[308] Accordingly, the Regulation did not regulate directly which smoke flavourings could be authorized for use in the internal market; it was only with the Commission's adoption of implementing legislation in the form of the positive list that approximation was achieved. Or, as framed by Advocate General Kokott, the Regulation 'at most regulates an intermediate step on the way to an approximation of the laws of the Member States'.[309]

The UK's central argument was that this type of multi-stage approximation was not permitted under Article 114 TFEU, and thus, Article 352 TFEU (ex Article 308 EC) should have been used instead.[310] In its view, Article 114(1) TFEU was restricted to measures leading to a result that could have been achieved by the simultaneous enactment of identical legislation in each of the Member States, which was not the case here.[311] The UK submitted additional arguments during the proceedings, asserting the Regulation's lack of compliance with the principle of proportionality.[312]

In her Opinion, Advocate General Kokott considered that they were submitted too late and dealt with them in the alternative.[313] In any event, she boiled the matter of proportionality down to the issue of whether the aims of the Regulation could have been achieved by equally effective provisions leaving more responsibility to the Member States.[314] In her view, 'everything suggests that the solution chosen is, of the various conceivable regulatory models, the most appropriate', finding that alternatives, such as those relating to mutual recognition, a 'coordinating solution' among national laws, or the inclusion of the positive list in the basic (legislative) act were unworkable.[315] Her findings evoked some of the parties' arguments in the case. In particular, the European Parliament stressed that in light of the fact that it was not possible to take a common approach to evaluating the safety of smoke flavourings, the legislature was forced to provide for this type of procedure.[316] The Commission seconded this view, stressing that the two-stage process constituted 'a proportionate and scientifically founded approach', since it was necessary to draw up a list that was both detailed and open-ended given the circumstances involved.[317]

In line with Advocate General Kokott's Opinion,[318] the Court held that Article 114 TFEU could be used to adopt multi-stage approximation measures as in the case of the Regulation. By virtue of the term 'measures for the approximation' set down in Article 114(1) TFEU, the Treaty framers intended to confer on the legislature a discretion, depending on the general context and the specific circumstances of the matter to be harmonized, as regards the most appropriate harmonization technique for achieving

[307] Reg No 2065/2003, n 306, Art 1(2). This involved the participation of the European Food Safety Authority: see eleventh, fourteenth recitals; Art 8.

[308] Reg No 2065/2003, n 306, Art 4(2).

[309] Opinion of AG Kokott in Case C-66/04 *Smoke Flavourings*, point 25.

[310] Case C-66/04 *Smoke Flavourings*, paras 18, 26.

[311] Case C-66/04 *Smoke Flavourings*, para 20.

[312] Opinion of AG Kokott in Case C-66/04 *Smoke Flavourings*, point 16.

[313] Opinion of AG Kokott in Case C-66/04 *Smoke Flavourings*, points 42–43.

[314] Opinion of AG Kokott in Case C-66/04 *Smoke Flavourings*, points 44–45.

[315] Opinion of AG Kokott in Case C-66/04 *Smoke Flavourings*, point 47.

[316] Case C-66/04 *Smoke Flavourings*, para 31.

[317] Case C-66/04 *Smoke Flavourings*, para 39.

[318] Opinion of AG Kokott in Case C-66/04 *Smoke Flavourings*, points 35–40.

the desired result, with particular regard to fields characterized by complex technical features.[319] Such discretion should be used especially when the proposed approximation requires physical, chemical, or biological analyses to be made, and scientific developments in the field concerned must be taken into account.[320] The Court then attached two conditions for cases involving multi-stage approximation: the legislature must determine in the basic (legislative) act the 'essential elements' of the harmonization measure concerned, and the mechanism for implementing these elements must be designed in such a way that it leads to a harmonization (more aptly, approximation) within the meaning of Article 114 TFEU.[321] The Court applied these two conditions to the Regulation and found both to be fulfilled.[322] As such, it was properly based on Article 114 TFEU, and the action was dismissed.[323]

The following year, in *UK v European Parliament and Council* ('*ENISA*'),[324] the Court was faced with the issue of whether the establishment of a Union (then Community) body fell within the scope of 'measures for the approximation' of national laws under Article 114(1) TFEU. The case concerned another action for annulment brought by the UK, this time against the Regulation establishing the European Network and Information Security Agency (ENISA),[325] based on what is now Article 114 TFEU (ex Article 95 EC). As explained in the Preamble, '[t]he technical complexity of networks and information systems, the variety of products and services that are interconnected, and the huge number of private and public actors that bear their own responsibility risk undermining the smooth functioning of the [i]nternal [m]arket'.[326] Several directives had already been adopted in this area,[327] but they required different forms of technical and organizational applications by the Member States and the Commission, and their heterogeneous application could lead to inefficient solutions and create obstacles in the internal market.[328] This called for the creation of a centre of expertise at the European level to provide advice and assistance to the Union institutions and national authorities.[329] ENISA did not have the means of directly approximating the laws of the Member States, that is to say, it could not adopt approximating measures, and did not take part in procedures for the adoption of such measures.[330] It was intended to contribute to the approximation process indirectly by way of basic tasks, such as giving advice and facilitating cooperation between the Member States and Union institutions with a view to combating network and information security problems and ensuring the uniform application of the measures adopted in this field.[331]

[319] Case C-66/04 *Smoke Flavourings*, para 45.

[320] Case C-66/04 *Smoke Flavourings*, para 46.

[321] Case C-66/04 *Smoke Flavourings*, para 49.

[322] Case C-66/04 *Smoke Flavourings*, paras 54–63.

[323] Case C-66/04 *Smoke Flavourings*, para 64.

[324] Case C-217/04 *UK v European Parliament and Council* ('*ENISA*') [2006] ECR I-3771. For detailed discussion, see, eg, Gutman, n 304; V Randazzo, Case note (2007) 44 *CML Rev* 155; T Tridimas, 'Community Agencies, Competition Law, and ECSB Initiatives on Securities Clearing and Settlement' (2009) *YEL* 216, 237–240.

[325] Reg (EC) No 460/2004 of the European Parliament and of the Council of 10 March 2004 establishing the European Network and Information Security Agency, [2004] OJ L77/1.

[326] Reg No 460/2004, n 325, third recital.

[327] Reg No 460/2004, n 325, fourth–ninth recitals. All of the previous directives were adopted solely under what is now Article 114 TFEU (ex Art 95 EC), save for the last two listed in the fifth recital, which were also adopted under what are now Arts 53(2) and 62 TFEU (ex Arts 47(2) and 55 EC).

[328] Reg No 460/2004, n 325, tenth recital.

[329] Reg No 460/2004, n 325, tenth recital.

[330] Opinion of AG Kokott in Case C-217/04 *ENISA*, point 28.

[331] See Reg No 460/2004, n 325, tenth–eleventh recitals; Arts 1–3.

Similar to *Smoke Flavourings*, the UK argued that the creation of such a body exceeded the ambit of approximation under Article 114 TFEU, and the Regulation should have been based on Article 352 TFEU (ex Article 308 EC).[332] Compared to *Smoke Flavourings*, the UK did not rely on the principle of proportionality, or the principle of subsidiarity for that matter, to challenge the Regulation. Yet, these principles fed into the arguments of the defending institutions, particularly those of the European Parliament, which emphasized that the Treaties did not require that measures based on Article 114 TFEU 'approximate substantive rules of national legislation where a lesser degree of [Union] action would be more appropriate'.[333] In its view, while in theory the legislature could have adopted rules directly approximating the laws of the Member States, given the technical complexity of the area concerned and its rapidly evolving character, it drew up the Regulation embodying '*low intensity approximation*', thereby enabling the Member States to adopt homogeneous measures to implement the various measures in the field.[334]

In her Opinion, Advocate General Kokott concluded that the Regulation could not be based on Article 114 TFEU and should be annulled.[335] Despite ENISA's 'potential contributions' to approximation in various ways, such as rendering advice to the institutions and serving as a discussion forum to promote voluntary parallel action in the Member States, it was not predictable whether and in what form ENISA would concretely contribute to the approximation of laws.[336] Moreover, the Regulation was not actually tied to the implementation of the directives in the field.[337] As such, the Regulation was 'not so much an intermediate step on the way to the approximation of laws of the Member States as a step into the uncertain'.[338]

The Court disagreed and upheld the use of Article 114 TFEU as the legal basis for the Regulation. It reiterated on the basis of *Smoke Flavourings* that the term 'measures for the approximation' of national laws under Article 114(1) TFEU bestowed the legislature with a discretion, depending on the circumstances involved, as regards the most appropriate method of approximation for achieving the desired result, particularly in complex technical fields.[339] It then added:

> Nothing in the wording of Article [114 TFEU] implies that the addressees of the measures adopted by the [Union] legislature on the basis of that provision can only be the individual Member States. The legislature may deem it necessary to provide for the establishment of a [Union] body responsible for contributing to the implementation of a process of harmonisation in situations where, in order to facilitate the uniform implementation and application of acts based on that provision, the adoption of non-binding supporting and framework measures seems appropriate.[340]

In such cases, two conditions must be satisfied: the tasks and objectives of the Union body must be 'closely linked' to the subject matter of the approximation legislation in the field concerned,[341] and those objectives and tasks must be regarded as 'supporting and providing a framework' for the implementation of that legislation.[342] As regards

[332] See Case C-217/04 *ENISA*, paras 12–21. [333] Case C-217/04 *ENISA*, para 22.
[334] Case C-217/04 *ENISA*, para 25 (emphasis added).
[335] Opinion of AG Kokott in Case C-217/04 *ENISA*, point 53.
[336] Opinion of AG Kokott in Case C-217/04 *ENISA*, points 31–34.
[337] Opinion of AG Kokott in Case C-217/04 *ENISA*, point 35.
[338] Opinion of AG Kokott in Case C-217/04 *ENISA*, point 36.
[339] Case C-217/04 *ENISA*, paras 42–43. [340] Case C-217/04 *ENISA*, para 44.
[341] Case C-217/04 *ENISA*, paras 45, 47. [342] Case C-217/04 *ENISA*, para 47.

the Regulation in question, both conditions were fulfilled.[343] The Court upheld Article 114 TFEU as the legal basis for the Regulation and dismissed the action.[344]

8.3.3.3 *Implications for European contract law*

As glimpsed through the lens of the 'object' prong, even if in principle the Court has confirmed that action under what is now Article 114 TFEU must comply with the principles of subsidiarity and proportionality, in practice once the threshold requirements placed on the limits of Article 114 TFEU have been met, it is difficult to demonstrate lack of compliance with these principles. In other words, for those looking to subsidiarity and proportionality as a barrier to Union action under Article 114 TFEU in relation to European contract law, this case law disappoints. To take a practical example, arguably, the proposed CESL would be deemed to comply with these principles on the basis of the Court's approach in the foregoing cases. As far as the principle of subsidiarity is concerned, the Commission's assertions that by adopting uncoordinated measures at the national level, the Member States will not be able to remove the problems hindering the functioning of the internal market stemming from divergences among national contract laws and the Union is best placed to address this matter is likely to be sustained by the Union courts.[345] Moreover, as regards the principle of proportionality, not only is the scope of the proposed CESL limited in various ways to targeting problems relating to cross-border transactions without extending to aspects best addressed at the national level, but also there is an extensive record set out in the Explanatory Memorandum of the proposal and Impact Assessment, not to mention the consultation conducted through the 2010 Green Paper,[346] on which basis the Union courts, along the lines of *Vodafone*, would likely find that the proposed action is appropriate, necessary, and proportionate as compared to the other possible policy options put forward.

Taking account of the 'approximation' prong of the case law, however, has the potential to provide a more nuanced reading of the operation of the principles of subsidiarity and proportionality in relation to measures adopted under Article 114 TFEU. By allowing the use of approximation techniques that indirectly, not just directly, approximate the laws of the Member States, the Court's judgments in *Smoke Flavourings* and *ENISA* can be read to expand the reach of approximation under Article 114 TFEU. Yet, at the same time, by emphasizing the legislature's discretion to choose the most appropriate approximation technique depending upon the relevant circumstances, these judgments allow for recourse to techniques that may be less intrusive on the competences of the Member States and narrowly tailored to targeting areas where the Member States fall short in line with the tenets of subsidiarity and proportionality. Such techniques have the potential to provide for more 'cooperative' solutions between the Union and the Member States, and especially to the extent that such solutions are situated at the national level, this may in turn trigger a role for the principle of sincere cooperation to play. Given the Court's approach in underscoring the legislature's discretion to choose the most appropriate approximation technique under Article 114 TFEU, this makes it conceivable that other types of approximation

[343] See Case C-217/04 *ENISA*, paras 48–66. [344] Case C-217/04 *ENISA*, para 67.

[345] See Proposal for a Regulation of the European Parliament and of the Council on a Common European Sales Law, COM (2011) 635 final, 11.10.2011 (CESL Proposal), Explanatory Memorandum, point 3, at 9.

[346] CESL Proposal, n 345, Explanatory Memorandum, point 2, at 7–8; point 3, at 10.

techniques in addition to those at issue in *Smoke Flavourings* and *ENISA* could be contemplated in this regard. Consequently, the 'approximation' prong demonstrates that the expansion of the scope of Article 114 TFEU does not necessarily lead to the curtailment of the principles of subsidiarity and proportionality, but in fact, may contribute to their fulfilment. As the scope of approximation within Article 114 TFEU expands, this may be considered to allow greater space 'inside' the lawmaking process within which to give expression to tenets of subsidiarity and proportionality in guiding the legislature's exercise of its competence under Article 114 TFEU than may be apparent 'outside' the lawmaking process once the requirements for Article 114 TFEU have been met as illustrated by the 'object' prong. The interplay between the 'object' and 'approximation' prongs may help to lessen tensions regarding the perceived failure of the principles of subsidiarity and proportionality in relation to measures based on Article 114 TFEU as compared to considering the 'object' prong alone.

As far as European contract law is concerned, the interplay between the two prongs provides possibilities for the operation of subsidiarity and proportionality, depending upon the dimensions of a European contract law instrument and the approximation technique used. This is illustrated by the proposed CESL, which is touted as a measure that complies with these principles by virtue of the fact that the approximation technique chosen, that of an optional system within the national contract law regimes, preserves the pre-existing national contract laws and thus intrudes less on the national legal systems.[347] Certainly, as discussed in the next section, this implicates important issues relating to the relationship between Articles 114 and 352 TFEU in connection with the legal basis of an optional instrument comparable to the proposed CESL. Nevertheless, the 'approximation' prong shows that there is leeway for the legislature to devise approximation techniques that reconcile the need for EU rules in contract law and the accommodation of residual space for the Member States if Article 114 TFEU is resorted to.

8.3.4 Comparative reflection with the US

The foregoing analysis of Article 114 TFEU cannot help but prompt a 'comparative leap' to the US. This is because in the wake of *Tobacco Advertising I*, there was a flurry of literature[348] comparing this case to certain jurisprudence of the US Supreme Court decided around the same time period, particularly *United States v Lopez*[349] and *United States v Morrison*,[350] in which that Court struck down somewhat egregious federal statutes as beyond the scope of Congress' competence under the Interstate Commerce Clause and ushered in a new era of federalism in the American setting.[351] Putting the two sets of cases side by side illuminated similar roles of the Court of Justice and the US Supreme Court in guarding the competences of the (Member) States from potential encroachment by the Union or federal legislature. At the same time, however, these two sets of cases evidenced examples of both Courts

347 See Chapter 6, § 6.4.4.

348 See, eg, Fennelly, n 107; Howells, n 164; Knook, n 86; P-J Slot, 'A Contribution to the Constitutional Debate in the EU in the Light of the Tobacco Judgment—What can be learned from the USA?' (2002) 13 *EBLR* 3.

349 514 US 548 (1995).

350 529 US 598 (2000).

351 For a brief selection, see, eg, 'Symposium: Reflections on *United States v. Lopez*' (1995) 94 *Mich L Rev* 533; 'Symposium: The New Federalism After *United States v. Lopez*' (1996) 46 *Case WRL Rev* 635; see also citations in n 355.

being mindful not to unduly constrict the ambit for legislative action on the basis of those respective provisions. Akin to avenues afforded to the Union legislature under *Tobacco Advertising I*, discussed earlier, *Lopez* left untouched certain aspects of Congress' power under the Interstate Commerce Clause, which prompted remarks that its impact would depend upon later cases.[352]

Likewise, the further development of the Court of Justice's *Tobacco Advertising I* case law highlights some striking parallels with the US Supreme Court's more recent jurisprudence on the Interstate Commerce Clause.[353] For example, just as the second Tobacco Advertising Directive was upheld by the Court of Justice in *Tobacco Advertising II*, the statute struck down in *Lopez* was readopted by Congress with a revised jurisdictional 'hook' indicating a link between the measure concerned and interstate commerce, which passed muster in the American federal courts.[354] And just as the Court of Justice confirmed in *Tobacco Advertising II* that measures adopted under Article 114 TFEU could extend to purely intrastate transactions so as not to preclude the internal market objectives of the measure concerned, the US Supreme Court upheld the application of federal drug legislation to purely intrastate, non-commercial usage of medical marijuana on the basis of the cumulative effects of such local usage on interstate commerce in *Gonzales v Raich*.[355] Furthermore, although at face value there may not (yet) appear to be a ready counterpart in the Court of Justice's case law to the US Supreme Court's decision in *Sebelius*,[356] in which a majority of the Justices (albeit not in a single opinion) found that the individual mandate of the Affordable Care Act (so-called Obamacare),[357] requiring individuals to maintain minimum health insurance coverage, exceeded Congress' powers under the Interstate Commerce Clause,[358] that decision nevertheless substantiated the wide latitude given to Congress under this Clause on the basis of previous case law, including *Gonzalez v Raich*.[359] In this way, the recent line of cases attests to the importance of reading cases such as *Tobacco Advertising I* and *Lopez* alongside their progeny manifesting more room for manoeuvre at the central (Union or federal) level than may initially have been evident from the tenor of those cases alone.

Yet, there is a glaring difference in approach when it comes to the recourse to Article 114 TFEU and the Interstate Commerce Clause, respectively, in relation to the approximation of contract law in the EU and the US. From the American perspective, the discussion of the constitutionality of a European contract law instrument may seem bizarre. As illustrated in Chapter 3, it has been posited by commentators over the years that there is sufficient federal competence primarily on the basis of the Interstate

[352] See *Lopez*, 514 US at 614–615 (Souter, J, dissenting). See further LH Tribe, 1 *American Constitutional Law*, 3rd edn (Foundation Press, 2000) § 5-5.

[353] See, eg, C Barnard, 'What the *Keck*? Balancing the needs of the single market with state regulatory authority in the EU (and the US)' (2012) *REDC* 201, 209–212; Weatherill, *GLJ*, n 194, 860–863.

[354] See *United States v Danks*, 221 F3d 1037 (8th Cir 1999). See also *Alderman v United States*, 131 S Ct 700 (2011) (Thomas, J, dissenting).

[355] 545 US 1 (2005). For a general overview, see, eg, E Chemerinsky, *Constitutional Law: Principles and Policies*, 4th edn (Kluwer, 2011) § 3.3.5; RD Rotunda and JE Nowak, 1 *Treatise on Constitutional Law: Substance and Procedure*, 5th edn (West, 2012) § 4.9(d)(i); Symposium, 'Federalism after *Gonzales v. Raich*' (2005) 9 *Lewis & Clark L Rev* 743 and citations therein.

[356] *National Federation of Independent Business v Sebelius*, 132 S Ct 2566 (2012).

[357] The Patient Protection and Affordable Care Act, Pub L No 111-148, 124 Stat. 119 (2010) (codified in scattered sections of 25, 26, and 42 USC).

[358] Ultimately, a majority of the Court upheld the individual mandate as a proper exercise of Congress' taxing power. For detailed discussion, see, eg, 'The Supreme Court 2011 Term Comment' (2012) 126 *Harv L Rev* 72.

[359] See Barnard, n 353, 212.

Commerce Clause to approximate areas of contract law. Despite numerous attempts, however, this has not occurred. Instead, action continues to be situated largely at the state level apart from or outside the federal constitutional framework in the US. By comparison, in the EU, the ongoing activities concerning European contract law are ingrained inside, not outside, the constitutional framework. As a result, mechanisms inside this framework by which to guide the exercise of Union competence under Article 114 TFEU assume greater importance. This directs attention to the multi-directional force of the principles of subsidiarity and proportionality inside, as well as outside, the law-making process in relation to Union action under Article 114 TFEU by virtue of the 'object' and 'approximation' prongs of the case law. This also raises the prospect of other mechanisms embodying tenets of subsidiarity and proportionality, namely optional instruments, which generally have not been resorted to in the American contract law framework,[360] but figure prominently in the debate about European contract law, which leads to the final section.

8.4 The Relationship between Articles 114 and 352 TFEU

8.4.1 The roles played by Article 352 TFEU vis-à-vis Article 114 TFEU

Under the case law, Article 352 TFEU (ex Article 308 EC) is designed to fill the gap where no specific provisions of the Treaties confer on the Union institutions express or implied powers to act, if such powers appear nonetheless to be necessary to enable the Union to carry out its functions with a view to attaining one of the objectives laid down in the Treaties.[361] As far as the adoption of a European contract law instrument is concerned, this means that Article 352 TFEU has the potential to play two roles in order to achieve the Union's internal market objectives. First, in the context of an instrument approximating the contract laws of the Member States by modifying them to some degree, Article 352 TFEU may play a residual or complementary role in relation to Article 114 TFEU where Article 114 TFEU would be deemed an insufficient legal basis, in all or in part, for such an instrument. Secondly, in the context of an optional instrument setting forth an additional contract law regime without modifying the contract laws of the Member States as in the case of the proposed CESL, Article 352 TFEU may serve as the legal basis for such an instrument to the extent that it would be considered to fall outside the scope of approximation under Article 114 TFEU. Both roles squarely implicate the relationship between Articles 114 and 352 TFEU.[362] Admittedly, they may overlap to some extent on account of the interplay between approximation and optional instruments, as will be seen in the discussion of the proposed CESL. Nevertheless, they are discussed separately so as to spotlight the relevant issues associated with each.

[360] Yet, an optional instrument, at the state level, was aired as a possible solution in the American setting: see Chapter 3, § 3.3.2.

[361] See, eg, Joined Cases C-402/05 P and C-415/05 P *Kadi and Al Barakaat International Foundation v Council and Commission* [2008] ECR I-6351, para 211 and citations therein.

[362] Art 115 TFEU is not mentioned here because Art 114 TFEU takes precedence over Art 115 TFEU in this regard: see § 8.2.

8.4.2 A contract law instrument modifying national contract law

The relationship between Articles 114 and 352 TFEU presents two situations in the context of an instrument approximating the national contract laws by modifying them to some degree. The first situation posits that Article 114 TFEU is entirely insufficient to serve as a legal basis for a European contract law instrument, and therefore Article 352 TFEU serves as the 'fallback' position. The second situation posits that Article 352 TFEU could be used in combination with Article 114 TFEU under circumstances where particular aspects of a European contract law instrument would exceed the scope of Article 114 TFEU. In other words, in the first situation, Article 352 TFEU plays a residual role in relation to Article 114 TFEU, whereas in the second situation, Article 352 TFEU plays a complementary role alongside Article 114 TFEU.

As far as the first situation is concerned, the case law has not yet definitively addressed the extent to which approximation measures falling outside the scope of Article 114 TFEU may still be covered under Article 352 TFEU. To recall, in *Spain v Council*,[363] Spain sought to justify recourse to what is now Article 352 TFEU (as well as Article 115 TFEU), as opposed to Article 114 TFEU, for the legal basis of the measure concerned on the grounds that since it required unanimous voting in the Council, it did not trespass on the sovereignty of the Member States.[364] This argument was quickly rejected by the Court and did not provide a platform for detailed guidance on the relationship between Articles 114 and 352 TFEU. As far as Article 352 TFEU was concerned, the Court recalled previous case law in the intellectual property field substantiating that this provision could be used as the basis for creating new rights superimposed on national rights, which was not at issue in that case.[365] It concluded that since Article 114 TFEU was the proper legal basis for the measure at issue, it did not have to be adopted under Articles 115 or 352 TFEU.[366] This seemed to imply that if Article 114 TFEU was insufficient, then recourse could have been made to Article 352 TFEU, but it was not clear whether the Court's statement referred to Article 352 TFEU as a 'last resort' in the context of approximation or to its previous finding regarding its use for the creation of European legal forms. Thereafter, in *Tobacco Advertising I*,[367] the issue as to whether the annulled Tobacco Advertising Directive could have been adopted under another legal basis was not before the Court.[368] Given the far-reaching nature of that Directive, however, it was surmised by scholars, as well as the Council's Legal Service, that Article 352 TFEU (ex Article 308 EC) could not have been used.[369] Still, the relationship between Articles 114 and 352 TFEU as regards less extreme measures remained ambiguous.

While further case law is warranted, as far as European contract law is concerned, this issue may present somewhat of a theoretical problem. In principle, there are strong arguments that what is now Article 352 TFEU can serve as the legal basis for a

[363] Case C-350/92 *Spain v Council* [1995] ECR I-1985. [364] See § 8.2.3.
[365] Case C-350/92 *Spain v Council*, para 27.
[366] Case C-350/92 *Spain v Council*, para 40.
[367] Case C-376/98 *Tobacco Advertising I* [2000] ECR I-8419.
[368] That said, the Court's language in *Tobacco Advertising I*, cautioning that Treaty provisions could not be used to circumvent the express exclusion of harmonization under former Art 152 EC (see ns 94–95 and accompanying text), was deemed to be implicitly directed at former Art 308 EC. See, eg, de Búrca, n 84, 13. This has since been written into the text of Art 352(3) TFEU.
[369] See n 84.

European contract law instrument, whether under the former or present Treaty framework. Under the former EC Treaty, Article 308 EC read in full:

If action by the Community should prove necessary to attain, in the course of the operation of the common market, one of the objectives of the Community, and this Treaty has not provided the necessary powers, the Council shall, acting unanimously on a proposal from the Commission and after consulting the European Parliament, take the appropriate measures.

Taking apart this paragraph, the limits and exercise of Community competence under former Article 308 EC were generally framed around the following five requirements: (1) the necessity test ('action by the Community should prove necessary'); (2) linkage to what was then called the common market ('in the course of the operation of the common market'); (3) linkage to Community objectives ('one of the objectives of the Community'); (4) no other provision of the EC Treaty was sufficient ('this Treaty has not provided the necessary powers'); and (5) the adoption of 'appropriate measures'.[370] There was certainly much debate in the literature regarding these requirements, but in view of the Court's expansive interpretation of each,[371] they did not seem to present major hurdles for the purposes of European contract law. Indeed, a major complaint with former Article 308 EC over the years was its use precisely for measures that had nothing to do with 'the operation of the common market',[372] as illustrated by the case law involving Union measures for combating terrorism,[373] among other things.[374]

Moreover, one of the most well-known cases often mentioned in the debate about European contract law is *Opinion 2/94*,[375] in which the Court rejected the use of former Article 308 EC (then Article 235 EC) as the legal basis for the Community's accession to the European Convention for the Protection of Human Rights and Fundamental Freedoms (ECHR).[376] Famously, the Court declared:

Accession to the Convention would, however, entail a substantial change in the present Community system for the protection of human rights in that it would entail the entry of the Community into a distinct international institutional system as well as integration of all the provisions of the Convention into the Community legal order. Such a modification of the system for the protection of human rights in the Community, with equally fundamental institutional

[370] The necessity and appropriateness requirements have been tied to the principles of subsidiarity and proportionality in some respects. See further TC Hartley, *The Foundations of European Union Law: An Introduction to the Constitutional and Administrative Law of the European Union*, 7th edn (Oxford Univ Press, 2010) 114; R Schütze, 'Organized Change towards an "Ever Closer Union": Article 308 EC and the Limits of the Community's Legislative Competence' (2003) 22 *YEL* 79 (2003).

[371] See, eg, Craig and de Búrca, n 194, 90–91; Dashwood, n 46; Hartley, n 370, 112–114; Schütze, n 65, 133–143.

[372] See Dashwood, n 46, 36–38.

[373] Joined Cases C-402/05 P and C-415/05 P *Kadi and Al Barakaat International Foundation v Council and Commission* [2008] ECR I-6351, particularly paras 229–231. For detailed discussion, see, eg, A Gattini, Case note (2009) 46 *CML Rev* 213, 223–224; D Halberstam and E Stein, 'The United Nations, The European Union, and The King of Sweden: Economic Sanctions and Individual Rights in a Plural World Order' (2009) 46 *CML Rev* 13, 39–42; T Tridimas, 'Terrorism and the ECJ: Empowerment and Democracy in the EC Legal Order' (2009) 34 *ELR* 103, 107–109. The Court's judgment in '*Kadi II*' (Joined Cases C-584/10 P, C-593/10 P, and C-595/10 P (Judgment of 18 July 2013) *Commission and Others v Kadi*, not reported) did not deal with issues relating to Union competence under Art 352 TFEU.

[374] See T Konstadinides, 'Drawing the line between Circumvention and Gap-Filling: An Exploration of the Conceptual Limits of the Treaty's Flexibility Clause' (2012) 31 *YEL* 227, 243 and citations therein.

[375] Opinion 2/94 *Accession by the Communities to the Convention for the Protection of Human Rights and Fundamental Freedoms* [1996] ECR I-1759.

[376] For a brief selection, see, eg, 'The Human Rights Opinion of the ECJ and Its Constitutional Implications' (1996) Univ of Cambridge CELS Occasional Paper No 1; JH Bello et al, Case note (1996) 90 *AJIL* 664; G Gaja, Case note (1996) 33 *CML Rev* 973; see also citations in ns 370–374.

implications for the Community and for the Member States, would be of constitutional significance and would therefore be such as to go beyond the scope of Article [308]. It could be brought about only by way of Treaty amendment.[377]

Thereafter, this passage fed into the debate about the constitutionality of a European civil code on the grounds that the adoption of such a code could be deemed of 'constitutional significance' for the framework of the Community legal order and hence exceed the Community's competence under former Article 308 EC.[378] Yet, leaving aside a European civil code, which by virtue of the Commission's repeated admonitions and the negative response to the 2010 Green Paper appears to be out of the running at present, a European contract law instrument does not appear to raise such flags. In comparison to the former Community's accession to an international convention that would have subjected it to the jurisdiction of the European Court of Human Rights and had major implications for the EU institutional framework, a European contract law instrument was, and continues to be, situated within the EU legal framework, with a view to achieving the Union's objective to ensure the functioning of the internal market. In other words, the latitude for recourse to former Article 308 EC in the context of contract law does not seem to have been severely curtailed by this Opinion.

Much the same can be said as regards the Lisbon Treaty's reframing of former Article 308 EC as Article 352 TFEU. It is perhaps an understatement to say that this provision received its fair share of attention in the events paving the way for this Treaty. It was singled out alongside former Article 95 EC for specific mention in the Laeken Declaration and for elimination from the Treaty framework in the context of the European Convention.[379] It initially emerged in the Draft Constitutional Treaty as the 'flexibility clause',[380] whose text was largely taken over by the Lisbon Treaty.[381] Article 352(1) TFEU provides:

If action by the Union should prove necessary, within the framework of the policies defined by the Treaties, to attain one of the objectives set out in the Treaties, and the Treaties have not provided the necessary powers, the Council acting unanimously on a proposal from the Commission and after obtaining the consent of the European Parliament, shall adopt the appropriate measures.[382]

In contrast to former Article 308 EC, Article 352 TFEU eliminates the reference to 'in the course of the operation of the common market', albeit linking the objectives to be achieved explicitly to those set out in the Treaties, of which those relating to the internal market are included. There are also some changes as regards the decision-making procedure to be followed: unanimous voting in the Council is retained, but the European Parliament is afforded the right not merely to be consulted, but to give its consent to action taken under this provision. Additionally, the Commission is obliged to draw the national parliaments' attention to proposals based on this provision, using the

[377] Opinion 2/94, paras 34–35. This led to the insertion in the Treaties of an explicit legal basis for the Union's accession to the ECHR: see Art 6(2) TEU.

[378] See, eg, van Gerven, n 36, 468. This was certainly not the only potential objection in this regard. See V Constantinesco, 'La "codification" communautaire du droit privé à l'épreuve du titre de compétence de l'Union européenne' (2008) *RTDE* 707, 719–722.

[379] See S Weatherill, 'Competence Creep and Competence Control' (2004) 23 *YEL* 1.

[380] 2003 DCT, Art 17; 2004 DCT, Art I-18. See further P Craig, 'Competence: Clarity, Conferral, Containment and Consideration' (2004) 29 *ELR* 323; S Weatherill, 'Better competence monitoring' (2005) 30 *ELR* 23.

[381] A new paragraph relating to Union action in the CFSP was added: see Art 352(4) TFEU.

[382] Art 352(1) TFEU.

procedure for monitoring the principle of subsidiarity under Article 5(3) TEU.[383] As such, Article 352 TFEU is situated within a constitutional climate of greater vigilance with respect to proposals based on this provision.[384] While that may be, arguably, the extent of the Union's competence under Article 352 TFEU, as compared to former Article 308 EC, has not been substantially altered as far as the adoption of a European contract law instrument is concerned.

In practice, it is difficult to picture a European contract law instrument approximating the national contract laws as falling completely outside the scope of the Union's competence under Article 114 TFEU in line with the analysis of the previous section. In other words, given the scope of Article 114 TFEU under the case law so far, this serves to undercut arguments concerning Article 352 TFEU in this regard. Nonetheless, for those who consider that Article 114 TFEU cannot serve as a legal basis for a European contract law instrument *in toto*, the residual role of Article 352 TFEU as the legal basis for such an instrument cannot be foreclosed. Such a position also points to issues concerning the potential for Article 352 TFEU to play a complementary role alongside Article 114 TFEU.

As far as the second situation is concerned, it used to be presumed on the basis of the *Titanium Dioxide* case law[385] that the combination of what are now Articles 114 and 352 TFEU was not possible because the respective decision-making procedures were incompatible with each other: Article 114 TFEU stipulates qualified majority voting in the Council and the co-decision procedure, whereas Article 352 TFEU, as noted above, requires unanimous voting in the Council and the consent of the European Parliament. With recent case law, however, this is no longer certain. As discussed in Chapter 7, *European Parliament v Council ('International Fund for Ireland')*[386] confirmed the combination of former Articles 159 and 308 EC. Former Article 159 EC, or what is now Article 175 TFEU, stipulates the same decision-making procedures as former Article 95 EC or what is now Article 114 TFEU, that is to say, qualified majority voting in the Council and the co-decision procedure (the ordinary legislative procedure post-Lisbon). Accordingly, there are compelling arguments that the Court's rationale in that case may apply *mutatis mutandis* to Articles 114 and 352 TFEU, since it would ensure that the limits of the Union's more specific competence under Article 114 TFEU vis-à-vis Article 352 TFEU would not be transgressed, while still allowing for an optimal way by which to achieve the Union's internal market objectives, as opposed to splitting the particular measure as between the elements that would fall within Article 114 TFEU and those that would not, thereby requiring Article 352 TFEU, if another more specific legal basis was not available.

The combination of the co-decision procedure (from ex Article 159 EC) and unanimous voting in the Council (from ex Article 308 EC) in that case was made under the former Treaty framework. The Court has yet to pronounce on the treatment of a similar case following the entry into force of the Lisbon Treaty involving the changes to the decision-making procedures prescribed for Article 352 TFEU, requiring the consent, as opposed to the consultation, of the Parliament, in addition to unanimous voting in the Council. Arguably, however, the Court's approach would not dramatically change,

[383] Art 352(2) TFEU. See further Craig and de Búrca, n 194, 92.

[384] Certain Member States have enhanced requirements for parliamentary agreement to proposals based on Art 352 TFEU: see, eg, Konstandinides, n 374, 260–261 and citations therein. This makes the procedure under Art 352 TFEU 'heavier' for the purposes of basing legislation on this provision in the context of the debate about European contract law or otherwise.

[385] Case C-300/89 *Titanium Dioxide* [1991] ECR I-2867.

[386] Case C-166/07 *European Parliament v Council ('International Fund for Ireland')* [2009] ECR I-7135. See Chapter 7, § 7.4.2.2.

since, as a practical matter, aspects of the consent procedure could be read into the co-decision procedure (under Article 114 TFEU), in tandem with unanimous voting in the Council (under Article 352 TFEU), which would uphold the Parliament's rights of participation in the decision-making process. Admittedly, as already mentioned, several questions remain open concerning the implications to be drawn from that case. Nevertheless, as things stand now, *International Fund for Ireland* suggests that Articles 114 and 352 TFEU may be used together for the adoption of a European contract law instrument approximating the contract laws of the Member States. As a result, depending upon the dimensions of such an instrument, elements that would be considered to fall outside the scope of Article 114 TFEU, say in relation to aspects that were not deemed to be tied to eliminating obstacles to trade and/or appreciable distortions of competition, could conceivably be covered by Article 352 TFEU, thereby conferring on the Union the requisite competence to adopt it.

8.4.3 An optional instrument of contract law

8.4.3.1 The European Cooperative Society *case and related jurisprudence*

As the debate about European contract law developed, the progression towards one or more optional instruments of contract law instigated discussion of the relationship between Articles 114 and 352 TFEU and whether one or the other provision, or the two together, would be a suitable legal basis.[387] As highlighted in Chapter 6, this issue has become critical and contentious in respect of the proposed CESL, with much of the focus placed on the applicability, or not, of the *European Cooperative Society* case.[388]

By way of background, over the past years, there were several cases in the intellectual property field in which the Court of Justice was confronted with the relationship between these two provisions. Some of these cases intersected with its jurisprudence concerning Article 114 TFEU as part of arguments put forward to challenge the legal basis of the measure concerned. For example, as already noted, in *Spain v Council*,[389] the Court underscored previous rulings, namely *Opinion 1/94*,[390] that the Union (then Community) was competent in the intellectual property field to harmonize national laws under Articles 114 and 115 TFEU (ex Articles 95 and 94 EC), whereas Article 352 TFEU (ex Article 308 EC) may be used as the basis for creating new rights superimposed on national rights, which was not at issue in that case.[391] Later, in *Biotechnology*,[392] the Netherlands contested the use of Article 114 TFEU (ex Article 95 EC) on the grounds that, inter alia, the Directive in question went beyond approximation and created a new type of property right distinct from the rights covered by existing national patent law.[393] The Court dismissed this argument, again relying on *Opinion 1/94* to hold that the patents issued under that Directive were national patents governed by national law and that the Directive did not introduce a new right superimposed on national rights,

[387] See, eg, D Staudenmayer, 'Un instrument optionnel en droit européen des contrats?' (2003) 102 *RTDC* 629.

[388] See Chapter 6, § 6.4.2.4, § 6.4.4.1.

[389] Case C-350/92 *Spain v Council* [1995] ECR I-1985. See further § 8.2.3.

[390] Opinion 1/94 *Agreement establishing the World Trade Organization* [1994] ECR I-5267, para 59. See also Case C-9/93 *Ideal-Standard* [1994] ECR I-2789, paras 55–58.

[391] Case C-350/92 *Spain v Council*, paras 23, 27.

[392] Case C-377/98 *Biotechnology* [2001] ECR I-7079. See further § 8.3.2.

[393] Case C-377/98 *Biotechnology*, para 23.

which would have required recourse to Article 352 TFEU (ex Article 308 EC).[394] The Directive sought to have the Member States 'adjust' their national patent laws to a uniform standard, not to create any sort of European framework with respect to patents at the European level.[395] The fact that it extended patentability to cover matters not previously protected by national patent laws only served to reinforce the need for harmonization itself.[396] As such, the case hinted at the subtlety between approximation and the creation of new legal forms at the European level in the sense that this depended on the conception of a new 'right', which some commentators found present in relation to changes made to national law, as opposed to the creation of a European legal form, which was not.[397]

Yet, it was the *European Cooperative Society* case[398] which squarely confronted the Court with the line between approximation and new legal forms outside the confines of the intellectual property field for the first time.[399] It concerned a dispute between the European Parliament and the Council concerning the legal basis of the Regulation on the Statute for a European Cooperative Society, adopted under what is now Article 352 TFEU (ex Article 308 EC).[400] In the Parliament's view, Article 114 TFEU (ex Article 95 EC) should have been used instead, and thus, it brought an action to annul the Regulation on this ground.[401] The purpose of the Regulation was to introduce a European form of cooperative society, which would allow this type of business form to be established by persons or entities from different Member States.[402] As indicated in the Preamble, cross-border cooperation between cooperatives was hampered by legal and administrative difficulties presented by the various national legal regimes, and the previously adopted Regulations establishing other European business forms were not well suited to the specific features of cooperatives.[403] The legislature could have adopted a directive or regulation approximating the national laws in this area, but that was not the approach taken.[404] Instead, the Regulation established an optional European legal form for cooperatives, so as to enable them to operate outside their own national borders in all or part of the territory of the EU.[405]

In its judgment, the Court upheld the Regulation as properly based on what is now Article 352 TFEU. After recalling previous case law on Articles 114 and 352 TFEU, including that in the intellectual property field,[406] the Court found that it was

394 Case C-377/98 *Biotechnology*, paras 24–25.

395 See ER Gold and A Gallochat, 'The European Biotech Directive: Past as Prologue' (2001) 7 *ELJ* 331, 352–353 (2001).

396 See Case C-377/98 *Biotechnology*, para 25.

397 See, eg, A Scott, 'The Dutch Challenge to the Bio-Patenting Directive' (1999) 21 *EIPR* 212, 213; R Weekes, 'Challenging The Biotechnology Directive: A Letter from America' (2003) 14 *EBLR* 325, 346.

398 Case C-436/03 *European Parliament v Council* ('*European Cooperative Society*') [2006] ECR I-3733.

399 The interplay between approximation and European legal forms had been touched upon in the Opinion of AG Kokott in Case C-66/04 *Smoke Flavourings* [2005] ECR I-10553, points 29–31; and Opinion of AG Kokott in Case C-217/04 *ENISA* [2004] ECR I-3771, points 22–24. However, the matter was not before the Court.

400 Council Reg (EC) No 1435/2003 of 22 July 2003 on the Statute for a European Cooperative Society (SCE), [2003] OJ L207/1; *corrigendum*, [2007] OJ L49/35. The acronym SCE is derived from the French translation, 'société coopérative européenne'.

401 Case C-436/03 *European Cooperative Society*, para 18.

402 Reg No 1435/2003, n 400, thirteenth recital.

403 Reg No 1435/2003, n 400, third–fifth recitals.

404 See Opinion of AG Stix-Hackl in Case C-436/03 *European Cooperative Society*, points 51–52.

405 Reg No 1435/2003, n 400, twelfth, twentieth recitals.

406 Case C-436/03 *European Cooperative Society*, paras 36–39.

apparent from the content and purpose of the Regulation that it aimed to introduce a new legal form in addition to the national forms of cooperative societies, according to which the European cooperative society must be considered to be a 'European legal form for cooperative societies which has a specific [Union] character'.[407] First, the legal form of the European cooperative society was governed primarily by the Regulation.[408] Secondly, the conditions of formation of a European cooperative society and the transfer of its registered seat from one Member State to another, without that resulting in its winding-up or the creation of a new legal person, were specific to the European cooperative society.[409] Thirdly, as indicated by Article 9 of the Regulation, providing that a European cooperative society is to be treated in every Member State as if it were a cooperative formed in accordance with the law of the Member State in which it has its seat, the European cooperative society was a form that co-existed with cooperative societies under national law.[410] The Court then declared: 'In those circumstances, the contested regulation, which leaves unchanged the different national laws already in existence, cannot be regarded as aiming to approximate the laws of the Member States applicable to cooperative societies, but has as its purpose the creation of a new form of cooperative society in addition to the national forms.'[411] It stressed that this finding was not affected by the fact that the Regulation did not lay down exhaustively all of the rules applicable to European cooperative societies and referred to national law for certain matters, since that referral was of a subsidiary nature.[412] On those grounds, the Court held that Article 114 TFEU could not constitute a legal basis for the Regulation and that it was correctly adopted under Article 352 TFEU.[413]

In her Opinion, Advocate General Stix-Hackl reached the same conclusion, but delved into the ambiguities underlying the relationship between Articles 114 and 352 TFEU. She started with the framework established by the case law in the intellectual property field, which indicated that recourse was to be had to Article 352 TFEU (ex Article 308 EC) for the creation of legal institutions or legal forms governed by EU law.[414] Yet, she found that it was not possible to derive from that case law any clear distinction between harmonization in the sense of reducing disparities between national laws and the creation of new legal forms, as illustrated by the present case in which the new legal framework created by the Regulation also helped to reduce disparities by virtue of the fact that the Member States would adhere to those uniform Union rules.[415] She then surmised:

> Whilst the creation of new [Union] legal forms alongside national legal forms is not therefore covered by Article [114 TFEU], the legal position is not as clear in the case of legal forms that are not independent of national legislation or in the case of legal rights that are afforded protection independently of national law. It is not finally established, in particular, where the dividing line runs between genuine or completely new legal forms and those new legal forms to which national law also applies.[416]

[407] Case C-436/03 *European Cooperative Society*, para 40.
[408] Case C-436/03 *European Cooperative Society*, paras 40–41.
[409] Case C-436/03 *European Cooperative Society*, para 42.
[410] Case C-436/03 *European Cooperative Society*, para 43.
[411] Case C-436/03 *European Cooperative Society*, para 44.
[412] Case C-436/03 *European Cooperative Society*, para 45.
[413] Case C-436/03 *European Cooperative Society*, para 46.
[414] Opinion of AG Stix-Hackl in Case C-436/03 *European Cooperative Society*, points 65–67.
[415] Opinion of AG Stix-Hackl in Case C-436/03 *European Cooperative Society*, point 71.
[416] Opinion of AG Stix-Hackl in Case C-436/03 *European Cooperative Society*, point 73.

This led her to conclude that the question of the use of Article 114 TFEU vis-à-vis Article 352 TFEU must be examined on a case-by-case basis.[417] As regards the Regulation in question, it created a Union structure in parallel with national structures and thus, despite the occasional references to national law, was considered a genuinely new creation.[418] In her view, its essential feature was the creation of 'something new', which could only be achieved by Article 352 TFEU; the aim that it pursued in connection with the internal market was secondary.[419]

By and large, the Court's judgment in *European Cooperative Society* was not terribly surprising, since it was in line with prior case law in the intellectual property field mentioned above. Nevertheless, as highlighted in the Advocate General's Opinion, there had been disagreement among scholars on the use of Article 114 TFEU for creation of new legal forms,[420] and even the Parliament had attempted to argue that the intellectual property field should be considered a special case.[421] Therefore, it affirmed that Article 114 TFEU could not be used for the creation of supranational or European legal forms; recourse had to be made to Art 352 TFEU if there was not a more specific legal basis available.

Looked at from another vantage point, however, the *European Cooperative Society* case spoke as much to the limits as to the exercise of Union competence under Article 352 TFEU. Not coincidentally,[422] this case was decided on the same day as *ENISA*,[423] and took its place alongside that case and *Smoke Flavourings* in terms of delineating the scope of 'measures for the approximation' of national laws under Article 114(1) TFEU as part of the 'approximation' prong of the case law.[424] Under *Smoke Flavourings* and *ENISA*, multi-stage approximation and the creation of Union bodies, respectively, fall within the legislature's discretion to choose the most appropriate approximation technique (provided that the requisite conditions are satisfied) under what is now Article 114 TFEU. However, the *European Cooperative Society* case makes clear that Article 114 TFEU cannot be stretched to encompass the creation of European legal forms that are not aimed at the approximation of laws. In other words, these cases indicate that although the legislature's discretion under Article 114 TFEU may be wide, it does not extend so far as to exceed the bounds of 'approximation' under Article 114 TFEU altogether; it must be tied to techniques that are in some shape or form destined to contribute to the process of approximating national laws. At the same time, by virtue of its ruling in the *European Cooperative Society* case, the Court upheld the use of a complementary mechanism on the basis of what is now Article 352 TFEU, alongside the legislature's 'arsenal' of approximation techniques allowed under Article 114 TFEU, to achieve the Union's internal market objectives, which also evinces a 'softer touch' vis-à-vis the national legal orders.[425] Thus, although there was no explicit mention of subsidiarity or proportionality in the case, *European Cooperative Society* was nonetheless infused with these principles.

Since that case, the Court has not yet issued further rulings clarifying the relationship between Articles 114 and 352 TFEU as far as the boundary line between

[417] Opinion of AG Stix-Hackl in Case C-436/03 *European Cooperative Society*, point 74.
[418] Opinion of AG Stix-Hackl in Case C-436/03 *European Cooperative Society*, points 87, 89.
[419] Opinion of AG Stix-Hackl in Case C-436/03 *European Cooperative Society*, points 96, 98.
[420] See Opinion of AG Stix-Hackl in Case C-436/03 *European Cooperative Society*, points 68, 72.
[421] See Opinion of AG Stix-Hackl in Case C-436/03 *European Cooperative Society*, points 69–70.
[422] See Gutman, n 304, 175.
[423] Case C-217/04 *ENISA* [2004] ECR I-3771.
[424] See § 8.3.3.2.
[425] This is also apparent in the context of optional instruments adopted under what is now Art 81 TFEU: see Chapter 10, § 10.3.3.

approximation and the creation of optional legal forms is concerned. Moreover, its judgment in *European Cooperative Society* was delivered in 2006 and thus preceded the entry into force of the Lisbon Treaty, which brought about certain changes to the Treaty framework regarding the legislature's reliance on Article 352 TFEU, or what was then Article 308 EC, for European legal forms in the intellectual property field.[426] Inserted into the chapter of the Treaties on the 'Approximation of Laws', Article 118 TFEU provides that in the context of the establishment and functioning of the internal market, the European Parliament and Council may adopt 'measures for the creation of European intellectual property rights to provide uniform protection of intellectual property rights throughout the Union and for the setting up of centralized Union-wide authorization, coordination and supervision arrangements'.[427] Such measures are adopted by the Parliament and the Council pursuant to the ordinary legislative procedure, meaning co-decision along with qualified majority voting in the Council, subject to the exception involving language arrangements, which require a special legislative procedure, meaning unanimous voting in the Council and consultation of the Parliament.[428] Article 118 TFEU therefore constitutes a specific legal basis for the creation of unitary intellectual property rights in order to achieve the Union's internal market objectives and removes the need to rely on what is now Article 352 TFEU in this regard.[429]

The stringent decision-making procedures for language arrangements may forestall the adoption of Union measures in this field, as illustrated by the creation of unitary patent protection in the EU, which resulted in recourse to the enhanced cooperation mechanism on account of the failure to find unanimous agreement concerning such arrangements. While this mechanism will be discussed in further detail in Chapter 11, suffice it to say that in a recent case challenging its use in this context, the Court discussed Article 118 TFEU in order to substantiate the shared, as opposed to exclusive, nature of the Union's competence under this provision,[430] but did not elaborate on its ruling in *European Cooperative Society*.[431] Yet, the introduction of Article 118 TFEU into the Treaty framework bears on the relationship between Articles 114 and 352 TFEU in connection with the proposed CESL, which leads to the next section.

8.4.3.2 *Dimensions of a European optional instrument of contract law*

As the debate about European contract law has evolved, so have the dimensions of one or more potential optional instruments of contract law.[432] As evidenced by the parameters of an optional instrument outlined in Annex II of the Commission's 2004 Communication,[433] such an instrument was depicted as a so-called '28th regime'

[426] There had been a similar provision in the DCT: see 2004 DCT, Art III-176.

[427] Art 118, first para, TFEU. [428] Art 118, second para, TFEU.

[429] See, eg, PA de Miguel Asensio, 'Intellectual Property in European Private Law' in E Poillot and I Rueda (eds), *The Boundaries of European Private Law* (Larcier, 2012) 189; C Geiger, 'The construction of intellectual property in the European Union: searching for coherence' in C Geiger (ed), *Constructing European Intellectual Property* (Edward Elgar, 2013) 5.

[430] Joined Cases C-274/11 and C-295/11 (Judgment of 16 April 2013) *Spain and Italy v Council*, not reported, paras 16–26.

[431] AG Bot discussed this case for the purposes of distinguishing it from those proceedings: see Opinion of AG Bot in Joined Cases C-274/11 and C-295/11 *Spain and Italy v Council*, points 61–66.

[432] The prospect of more than one optional instrument has been noted. See, eg, D Staudenmayer, 'European Contract Law—What Does It Mean and What Does It Not Mean?' in *The Harmonisation of European Contract Law*, n 78, 235, 237. In the interests of consistency, reference is made to an optional instrument in the singular.

[433] See Chapter 5, § 5.4.2.

of contract law running alongside the national contract law regimes with a view to facilitating cross-border transactions in the internal market. Consequently, in line with *European Cooperative Society*, there appeared to be considerable agreement that what is now Article 352 TFEU, as opposed to Article 114 TFEU, would be the proper legal basis.[434] Still, some ambiguity remained in light of the chameleonic nature of such an instrument. In particular, it was presented as manifesting either an opt-in or opt-out regime, although in the 2004 Communication, the Commission indicated that there was a preference for an opt-in approach. Some of the commentary on the Commission's Communications also considered that the optional instrument could give way to combinations or alternatives including, but not limited to, opt-in/opt-out regimes. For example, such an instrument could provide for an opt-out regime for cross-border contracts and an opt-in regime for domestic contracts, or start out as either opt-in or opt-out, but eventually lead to a compulsory instrument replacing the national contract laws.[435]

Subsequent developments concretized certain aspects of an optional instrument and indicated a slight change of course. The Commission's 2010 Green Paper proposed as *Option 4* an optional instrument that would be conceived as a '2nd regime' of contract law, providing parties wishing to operate in the internal market with an alternative set of contract law rules within the law of each Member State.[436] This paved the way for the proposed CESL, representing a comprehensive set of uniform contract law rules that is also conceived as a '2nd regime' of contract law within the law of each Member State to be chosen by the parties concerned on an opt-in basis for primarily cross-border contracts.[437] Thus, as it is currently framed, the proposed CESL embodies a novel hybrid approach[438] because it combines approximating and optional elements. On the one hand, it constitutes a set of 'harmonized' (or approximated) contract law rules in terms of its substantive content and is envisaged to approximate national laws by inserting this set of rules into the legal system of each Member State. On the other hand, it is an optional, as opposed to compulsory, instrument establishing an additional, alternative contract law regime alongside the pre-existing national contract laws without modifying them.

Notably, the proposed CESL dovetails with the increasing attention given to optional instruments in documents of the Union institutions and bodies[439] and the scholarly literature[440] inside and outside the debate about European contract law.

[434] See, eg, K Gutman, 'The Commission's 2010 Green Paper on European Contract Law: Reflections on Union Competence in Light of the Proposed Options' (2011) 7 *ERCL* 151, 159–161; Hesselink et al, n 214, 71; G Howells, 'European Contract Law Reform and European Consumer Law—Two Related but Distinct Regimes' (2011) 7 *ERCL* 173, 190; Vogenauer and Weatherill, n 225, 113 fn 27.

[435] See, eg, C von Bar and S Swann, 'Response to the Action Plan on European Contract Law: A More Coherent European Contract Law (COM (2003) 63)' (2003) 11 *ERPL* 595.

[436] See Chapter 6, § 6.4.2. [437] See Chapter 6, § 6.4.4.

[438] See, eg, MW Hesselink, 'How to Opt into the Common European Sales Law? Brief Comments on the Commission's Proposal for a Regulation' (2012) 20 *ERPL* 195, 204.

[439] See, eg, European Parliament DG for Internal Policies Study, *Implementation of optional instruments within European civil law* (Legal Affairs Series, PE 462.425, 2012), available at <http://www.europarl.europa.eu/> (authored by Professors Bénédicte Fauvarque-Cosson and Martine Behar-Touchais) (EP Study); EESC Opinion on 'The 28th regime—an alternative allowing less lawmaking at Community level', [2011] OJ C21/26 (EESC Opinion); Monti, n 49. The latter two documents were cited in the 2010 Green Paper: see Chapter 6, § 6.4.2.

[440] See, eg, (2012) 76 *RabelsZ* 235; B Fauvarque-Cosson, 'European Contract Law Through and Beyond Pluralism: the Case of an Optional Instrument' in L Niglia (ed), *Pluralism and European*

Some of these documents offer confusing, even conflicting, arguments as regards the Union's competence to adopt such instruments, since in assimilating the proposed CESL to previous examples of optional instruments, including those in the company and intellectual property law fields, the reader is left wondering why not the similar reliance on Article 352 TFEU, as opposed to Article 114 TFEU, for the proposed CESL. This is illustrated by the extensive study commissioned by the European Parliament on optional instruments[441] and the EESC's Opinion on 'The 28th regime—an alternative allowing less lawmaking at Community [now Union] level',[442] in which it cautioned not to exclude the possibility of relying on Article 114 TFEU as the legal basis of an optional instrument of contract law,[443] but at the same time, cited as other examples of '2nd regimes' at the European level[444] the regulations establishing European business forms, including the European cooperative society and those in the intellectual property field,[445] without explaining how to reconcile this with the Court's case law.

Notwithstanding the present focus on the proposed CESL, it may be the case that additional optional instruments are proposed in other areas of contract law, depending on the future course of the debate.[446] The dimensions of such instruments and whether the approach used in respect of the proposed CESL may be taken up remain to be seen. Thus, following from Advocate General Stix-Hackl's reasoning in *European Cooperative Society*, the assessment of the legal basis of the particular instrument must proceed on a case-by-case basis depending on its aim and content.[447] This demonstrates that there are several aspects of a possible European optional instrument of contract law that must be evaluated as far as the relationship between Articles 114 and 352 TFEU is concerned. The discussion begins with the examination of an optional instrument akin to the proposed CESL, followed by mention of other aspects concerning the use of opt-out versus opt-in models and progressive methods involving optional and compulsory instruments, with the assumption that the other requirements relating to the use of Articles 114 and 352 TFEU have been fulfilled.

As already noted, at present, the issue whether Article 114 or 352 TFEU is the proper legal basis for the proposed CESL is controversial.[448] Scholars are divided over this issue and take a variety of positions. In line with the Commission'

Private Law (Hart, 2013) 95; H Schulte-Nölke, 'How to realize the "Blue Button"?—Reflections on an optional instrument in the area of contract law' in R Schulze and H Schulte-Nölke (eds), *European Private Law—Current Status and Perspectives* (Sellier, 2011) 89; J Smits, 'Editorial—Optional Law: A Plea for Multiple Choice in Private Law' (2010) 17 *MJ* 347.

441 EP Study, n 439, particularly 33.

442 EESC Opinion, n 439. See further J Pegado Liz, 'Developments at EESC Level' in H Heiss et al (eds), *Principles of European Insurance Contract Law: A Model Optional Instrument* (Sellier, 2011) 25. For other examples, see EESC Opinion on the proposals relating to matrimonial property regimes and the property consequences of registered partnerships, [2011] OJ C376/87, points 1.4, 2.1.2; EESC Opinion on 'The proactive law approach: a further step towards better regulation at EU level', [2009] OJ C175/26, point 6.1.2.7; EESC Opinion on the proposal for the 'Rome I' Regulation, [2006] OJ C318/56, point 3.2.3; see also Chapter 5, § 5.4.3.2.

443 EESC Opinion, n 439, points 3.3.1–3.3.4.

444 EESC Opinion, n 439, point 3.5.3.

445 EESC Opinion, n 439, point 3.6.3.

446 The Parliament discussed the use of an optional instrument in relation to specific contracts in several resolutions. See Chapter 5, § 5.3.1.1; Chapter 6, § 6.4.2.3. The work on insurance contract law as part of the DCFR (the Principles of European Insurance Contract Law (PEICL)) is also envisaged as an optional instrument: see Chapter 4, § 4.2.3. As regards further work on insurance and cloud computing contracts, see Chapter 6, § 6.4.5.

447 See n 417 and accompanying text.

448 See Chapter 6, § 6.4.4.1. See further citations in R Schulze (ed), *Common European Sales Law (CESL) Commentary* (CH Beck/Hart, 2012) 10 fn 1.

view,[449] some consider that Article 114 TFEU constitutes a proper legal basis and *European Cooperative Society* is not determinative, at least as far as the proposed CESL is concerned.[450] Others take the converse view that Article 352 TFEU is, or is more likely to be, the proper legal basis for the proposed CESL in line with *European Cooperative Society*,[451] with some pointing to Article 118 TFEU as an additional argument supporting this position on the grounds that the introduction of this Treaty provision would not have been necessary if Article 114 TFEU already equipped the Union with sufficient competence to adopt optional instruments.[452] There are also those who do not appear to take a firm stand one way or the other, attesting to the uncertainty regarding this issue.[453] Indeed, neither the text of the Treaties nor the Court's case law so far provide a definitive answer to the question whether Article 114 or 352 TFEU is a proper legal basis for an optional instrument comparable to the proposed CESL. Consequently, it is difficult to predict at this stage whether the Union courts, if faced with a challenge to the legality of such an instrument, would find that it is sufficiently tied to the process of approximating national contract laws, or whether its optional nature as an instrument co-existing with the national contract laws without modifying their content would preclude such a finding and thus warrant recourse to Article 352 TFEU. In short, there are plausible arguments to support both sides, and the proposed CESL represents a borderline case with a significant margin of appraisal that could go either way. It also bears emphasis that the proposed CESL may be reconfigured or altered as it makes its way through the decision-making process. Depending on the final outcome of this process, the text of the instrument as adopted may diverge significantly from that of the proposed CESL as it stands now. This means that only tentative conclusions on the legal basis of the proposed CESL can be drawn at this stage.

With those caveats in place, there are several arguments that have been put forward to support the use of Article 114 or 352 TFEU, which merit scrutiny. The first set of arguments concerns the relevance, or not, of *European Cooperative Society*. To recall, this case involved a Regulation establishing a supranational form of company law, the European cooperative society, which much like the other supranational company forms adopted so far is aimed at creating a new entity that is autonomous from

[449] As regards publications by Commission officials involved in the debate, see, eg, D Staudenmayer, 'The Common European Sales Law—Why do we Need it and how should it be Designed' in G Alpa et al (eds), *The Proposed Common European Sales Law—the Lawyers' View* (Sellier, 2013) 17, 21–22.

[450] See, eg, E Clive, 'A General Perspective on the European Commission's Proposal for a Regulation on a Common European Sales Law' (2012)19 *MJ* 120, 123–125; G Maier-Reimer, 'The Common European Sales Law—A German Perspective on the CESL' in *The Proposed Common European Sales Law*, n 449, 79, 83–87; H-W Micklitz and N Reich, 'The Commission's Proposal for a "Regulation on a Common European Sales Law (CESL)"—Too Broad or not Broad Enough?' in L Moccia (ed), *The Making of European Private Law: Why, How, What, Who* (Sellier, 2013) 21, 23–26. Some find the distinction between a '2nd' and a '28th' (now '29th') regime important in this regard: see, eg, G Conte, 'The Proposed Regulation on a Common European Sales Law—An Italian Perspective' in *The Proposed Common European Sales Law*, n 449, 61, 67; Hesselink, n 438, 199 fn 11.

[451] See, eg, 'Editorial Comments: A Common European Sales Law (CESL) ahead?' (2012) 49 *CML Rev* 1267, 1276–1277; H Eidenmüller et al, 'The proposal for a Regulation on a common European sales law: deficits of the most recent textual layer of European contract law' (2012) 16 *Edin L Rev* 301, 317–318; J-J Kuipers, 'The Legal Basis for a European Optional Instrument' (2011) 19 *ERPL* 545; Weatherill, n 227, 67.

[452] See, eg, Max Planck, n 26, 388–389.

[453] See, eg, G Low, '*Unitas Via Diversitas*. Can the Common European Sales Law Harmonize Through Diversity?' (2012) 19 *MJ* 132; L Miller, *The Emergence of EU Contract Law: Exploring Europeanization* (Oxford Univ Press, 2011) 147; JW Rutgers, 'An optional instrument on contract law: is there a competence to adopt one?' in *The Boundaries of European Private Law*, n 429, 37.

those national forms of company law in the Member States.[454] In that case, the Court was not faced with a measure that had as its aim to bring about the approximation of national laws; indeed, it was very much the opposite, as evidenced by the fact that in light of the difficulties involved with approximation in the area concerned, the Union legislature turned to the creation of a supranational or European optional regime of company law that was not formally tied to the approximation of national laws. This led the Court to hold that the purpose of the Regulation was the creation of a new form of cooperative society in addition to the national forms, not the approximation of national laws. Admittedly, the Court placed emphasis on the fact that the Regulation left the national laws unchanged in connection with its finding that it did not aim to carry out approximation; viewed through the lens of *ENISA*, however, this does not necessarily mean that a particular instrument does not carry out an approximation. Simply put, the *European Cooperative Society* case concerned an instrument that had nothing to do with the approximation of national laws. This seems to be what the various arguments asserted in the literature and in the Commission's responses to the reasoned opinions of certain national parliaments on the proposed CESL are getting at: in contrast to the Regulation in *European Cooperative Society*, the proposed CESL is not aimed at the creation of a European legal form that is autonomous from the national legal orders, but in fact is aimed at the approximation of laws by virtue of the establishment of a set of uniform contract law rules at the European level that is inserted inside the national legal orders so as to substantiate the use of Article 114 TFEU.

This should be distinguished from the formal and practical aspects of approximation in connection with the proposed CESL. Although in principle the proposed CESL is envisaged to provide an alternative contract law regime without modifying the national contract laws, in practice it may nevertheless instigate the Member States to change their contract laws and hence lead to approximation in practice.[455] This is not unique to the proposed CESL. There is ongoing discussion in other fields, including those concerning supranational company forms, as regards the extent to which the Member States may be led to adjust their own laws, or not, as a result of the Union measure concerned.[456] As such, this does not necessarily lend further support for the use of Article 114 TFEU as opposed to Article 352 TFEU in connection with the proposed CESL.

In any event, taking the converse position, there are still troubling aspects of the proposed CESL that are not easily solved. *ENISA* and *Smoke Flavourings* involved measures that were considered to be linked to an approximation process designed to bring national laws closer together. As a formal matter, it is difficult to understand how the proposed CESL may bring about an approximation of national contract laws on account of its optional elements, that is to say, how national contract laws will be brought closer together by virtue of an instrument co-existing with the national contract laws without modifying their content. Needless to say, this point was not elaborated in detail as part of the documentation accompanying the proposed CESL.

[454] For detailed discussion, see H Fleischer, 'Supranational Corporate Forms in the European Union: Prolegomena to a Theory on Supranational Forms of Association' (2010) 47 *CML Rev* 1671. See also Commission Report on the application of Council Reg (EC) No 1435/2003 of 22 July 2003 on the Statute for a European Cooperative Society (SCE), COM (2012) 72 final, 23.2.2012.

[455] See, eg, O Ben-Shahar, 'Introduction: A Law and Economics Approach to European Contract Law' (2013) 50 *CML Rev* 3, 6; C von Bar, 'Statements on Perspectives for European Private Law' in *European Private Law—Current Status and Perspectives*, n 440, 265, 266–267.

[456] See, eg, O Uziahu-Santcroos, 'The SPE: A Necessary Tool for SMEs?' in DFMM Zaman et al (eds), *The European Private Company (SPE)—A Critical Analysis of the EU Draft Statute* (Intersentia, 2009) 1, 7–9.

Thus, it is to be wondered whether this aspect of the proposed CESL will be fleshed out further through the course of the decision-making process.

Be that as it may, in the present author's view, there are convincing arguments that the proposed CESL can be readily distinguished from *European Cooperative Society* and falls within the scope of approximation under Article 114 TFEU. As indicated in the proposal and accompanying documentation, the proposed CESL aims to carry out the approximation of national laws by providing an alternative set of harmonized contract law rules that is inserted into the fabric of national law. This has the result that the legal system of each Member State contains two legal forms—the pre-existing national contract law of the Member State concerned and the set of harmonized contract law rules based on the laws of the Member States for the whole of the EU. The fact that the proposed CESL is optional and there is no binding legal obligation on the parties to use it does not change the fact that it sets forth a harmonized set of contract law rules that is integrated inside, as opposed to remaining outside, national law. Moreover, the proposed CESL interacts with, and has an impact on, the pre-existing national contract laws. Although it represents a comprehensive set of harmonized contract law rules for the purposes of facilitating cross-border transactions in the internal market, it is not entirely self-sufficient in the sense that there are various contractual (and non-contractual) matters that fall outside the scope of the proposed CESL and would be governed by the purely national contract law rules. Even though it is optional, the choice of the contracting parties to use the proposed CESL also has the effect of displacing the pre-existing national contract law rules that would have otherwise applied in the context of B2B and B2C transactions. Under these circumstances, it appears that a key criterion for Article 114 TFEU is not so much whether the instrument in question is an optional or a compulsory instrument, but rather, whether it seeks to approximate national laws and is integrated within such laws so as to interact with them and impact them to some degree. As compared to the instrument at issue in the *European Cooperative Society* case, these requirements are, arguably, satisfied in the case of the proposed CESL.

Secondly, as a related point, there are arguments concerning the possible relevance of Article 118 TFEU, which concerns the creation of EU intellectual property rights that pre-Lisbon had to be based on former Article 308 EC. The argument opposing Article 114 TFEU for the proposed CESL seems to be that if optional instruments could be based on Article 114 TFEU, then Article 118 TFEU would be superfluous. Yet, there are means to distinguish this provision in relation to an optional instrument comparable to the proposed CESL. Article 118 TFEU essentially codifies the Court's case law in the intellectual property field, discussed earlier, that Article 114 TFEU cannot serve as the legal basis for measures establishing EU intellectual property rights existing outside the national legal regimes and not seeking to approximate national laws. It does not pertain to the adoption of optional instruments that are tied to the approximation of national laws for the purposes of the Union's internal market objectives outside the intellectual property field, as in the case of the proposed CESL. On this basis, it can be argued that Article 118 TFEU is not determinative as far as the use of Article 114 TFEU for the legal basis of the proposed CESL is concerned.

Thirdly, there are certain 'policy arguments' related to the principles of subsidiarity and proportionality that have been put forward to bolster the case for Article 114 TFEU as the legal basis for the proposed CESL.[457] Importantly, however, there must

[457] See, eg, EESC Opinion, n 439, points 3.3.3, 4.1.1; A Fuchs, 'European contract law: the way forward' (2011) 12 *ERA Forum* 1, 4; A Wiewiórowska-Domagalska, 'An Optional Instrument in Contract Law and the Polish Presidency of the Council of the EU 2011' (2012) 3 *EUVR* 183, 187–188.

be caution in the way that such arguments are framed. On the one hand, just because a Union measure has a lesser impact on the national legal systems does not mean that the Union may exceed its competence under the relevant Treaty provision, *in casu* Article 114 TFEU.[458] On the other hand, as illustrated by the 'approximation' prong of the case law, the Court is not averse to widening the scope of the 'measures for the approximation' of national laws under Article 114(1) TFEU so as to allow approximation techniques that advance the operation of the principles of subsidiarity and proportionality, provided that the measure concerned is shown to contribute to bringing about an approximation of laws in some shape or form, as may be argued in the case of the proposed CESL in line with the remarks above. Accordingly, although the principles of subsidiarity and proportionality cannot be used to justify the proposed CESL under circumstances where it would be considered to fall outside the scope of approximation under Article 114 TFEU, these principles are nonetheless imbued in the proposed CESL in terms of embodying a novel approximation technique that is less intrusive on the national legal systems.

Fourthly, there is the question whether the constitutional assessment of the proposed CESL would change if it were to be depicted as a '28th', as opposed to a '2nd', regime. As highlighted in certain materials on optional instruments, both terms may be used to describe such instruments, but a '2nd regime' is considered more appropriate because it makes clear that the additional regime offered by the optional instrument is inserted inside the national legal systems, which apparently applies not only to the proposed CESL, but also to various other optional instruments adopted so far in the EU, such as those establishing supranational legal forms in the intellectual property and company law fields.[459] This is certainly true by virtue of the fact that a regulation is being used, since the optional instruments set down therein are binding and directly applicable in the Member States in accordance with the second paragraph of Article 288 TFEU. Yet, if all such optional instruments may be classified as '2nd regimes', including those establishing EU business and intellectual property forms, this appears to gloss over the particular features of the optional instrument at issue, namely an instrument establishing a truly supranational legal form that is not aimed at approximation as compared to an instrument like the proposed CESL, which is.

Consequently, the arguments opposing the use of Article 114 TFEU for a '28th regime' as opposed to a '2nd regime' may essentially correspond to the distinction between an optional instrument that is integrated inside each national legal system and deemed to impact the national contract laws, as opposed to an optional instrument existing autonomously from the national legal systems and not having any effect on the national contract laws. While it is difficult to conceive of the proposed CESL as a '28th regime' in theory, there are plausible arguments to support the use of either Article 114 or 352 TFEU,[460] depending on how it would be framed. On the one hand, for example, even as a '28th regime', the proposed CESL may still constitute a set of harmonized contract law rules and be considered to interact with the national contract laws as far as aspects not covered by the proposed CESL are concerned. On the other hand, however, it would not be integrated into the fabric of national law, but would constitute an autonomous regime outside the national legal systems and thus in principle not be expected to interact with the purely national contract laws. The bottom line is that this distinction directs attention to the key criterion elaborated above for

[458] See Opinion of AG Kokott in Case C-217/04 *ENISA*, point 39.
[459] See, eg, EP Study, n 439, 29; EESC Opinion, n 439, points 3.1, 3.5.3, 3.6.3.
[460] See, eg, Low, n 453, 145–146.

the purposes of determining whether a particular optional instrument falls within Article 114 TFEU.

As a last point, it may be wondered whether Articles 114 and 352 TFEU can be used together for the adoption of the proposed CESL. As noted earlier, on the basis of the case law so far, it is not foreclosed that these two provisions may be combined under circumstances where certain elements fall outside the scope of Article 114 TFEU and thus may be covered by Article 352 TFEU to the extent that there is no other provision available. It could be surmised that in view of the hybrid nature of the proposed CESL, Article 352 TFEU may be used in combination with Article 114 TFEU to the extent that certain elements, such as the optional elements embodied by the proposed CESL, fall outside the scope of approximation under Article 114 TFEU. Yet, in the case of the proposed CESL, the approximating and optional elements are inextricably intertwined in the sense that the proposed CESL seeks to bring about an approximation by virtue of its optional scheme. On that basis, arguably, the combination of Articles 114 and 352 TFEU would not be applicable in relation to the proposed CESL.

Finally, there have been a variety of other methods associated with the use of optional and compulsory instruments. As regards the recourse to an opt-out versus an opt-in model, both conceivably concern an optional instrument, but whereas an opt-in model provides parties with an instrument that they would be free to choose, or not, as the applicable law for their contract, an opt-out model makes the instrument the applicable law for the contract unless the parties choose to opt out of such an instrument. To recall, this is not the same thing as optional harmonization, where the parties are required to follow the rules set down in the harmonization measure for cross-border transactions, but are given the option to choose either the EU rules or the relevant national rules for domestic transactions.[461] That situation involves a body of Union rules that modifies national rules as far as certain (cross-border) transactions are concerned. In the case of an opt-out or opt-in model, the optional instrument would still constitute an additional regime next to the pre-existing national contract laws without modifying them; the parties would not be required to utilize such an instrument for cross-border transactions, but would merely do so under circumstances where they did not specify another applicable law. Accordingly, whether the optional instrument concerned may embody an opt-out as opposed to an opt-in regime, the legal basis for such an instrument, arguably, follows the discussion above, meaning that it would involve the determination, in light of its aim and content, to what extent the instrument aims to bring about an approximation of laws and is integrated within national law so as to fall within the scope of approximation under Article 114 TFEU.

Progressive methods have also been contemplated in the discourse on European contract law, for example, starting out with an optional instrument that would culminate in a compulsory instrument. Arguments relating to the practical necessity of using Article 114 TFEU for an optional instrument so as to avoid difficulties in converting it into a compulsory instrument later on are not determinative as far as the legal basis of the particular instrument is concerned. It may certainly be the case that the same legal basis may be used for the adoption of an optional and a compulsory instrument of contract law in line with the analysis offered here. Yet, depending on whether a particular optional instrument falls outside the scope of Article 114 TFEU, another legal basis, namely Article 352 TFEU, may have to be resorted to.

461 See Chapter 1, § 1.2.3.2.

8.5 Conclusions

With the growing emphasis put on optional, as opposed to compulsory, instruments of contract law, as concretized by the proposed CESL, in the debate, this has only served to reinforce the importance of the foregoing analysis. First, by addressing the relationship between Articles 114 and 115 TFEU, it helps to resolve longstanding controversy concerning the apparent differences in scope between the two provisions. Secondly, by examining the scope of Article 114 TFEU, it reveals that the limits of Article 114 TFEU cannot be restricted to myopic focus on *Tobacco Advertising I* or tied to the scope of the free movement rules (namely, Articles 34–36 TFEU on the free movement of goods), and that there is a nuanced relationship between Article 114 TFEU and the principles of subsidiarity and proportionality, which may go some way towards soothing tensions with respect to their role in guiding the exercise of Union competence in this context. Finally, by delving into the relationship between Articles 114 and 352 TFEU, it indicates that there are convincing arguments that Article 114 TFEU is the proper legal basis for an instrument approximating national contract laws by modifying them to some degree, but that Article 352 TFEU has the potential to play a 'backup' or complementary role vis-à-vis Article 114 TFEU in this regard. In the case of an optional instrument of contract law comparable to the proposed CESL, there are credible arguments to support the use of either Article 114 or 352 TFEU, but in the present author's view, such arguments weigh on the side of Article 114 TFEU as the proper legal basis for such an instrument. In sum, while questions remain open, the foregoing analysis indicates that there is a solid basis to find that the Union has been conferred sufficient competence to adopt a European contract law instrument, optional or otherwise, on the basis of Articles 114 and/or 352 TFEU, depending on the instrument in question.

Undoubtedly, this finding may not be welcomed by all audiences. Long before the debate about European contract law, Articles 114 and 352 TFEU had been depicted as notorious provisions responsible for the undue extension of Union (then Community) competence. By their very nature, these two provisions will probably forever generate tensions related to fears of the Union's encroachment on Member State domains, especially as regards contract law and other fields of private law. Yet, such tensions should not obscure the important role played by these provisions to help the Union to achieve its objective to ensure the establishment and functioning of the internal market, within which a European contract law instrument can play an important role. It remains to be seen whether the final text of the proposed CESL will be adopted under Article 114 TFEU (and if so, withstand challenge before the Union judicature if a case is brought before it) and whether Articles 114 and/or 352 TFEU will be put to use by the Union legislature for the adoption of other (optional) instruments of contract law as the debate proceeds. Yet, this analysis demonstrates that to the extent a European contract law instrument is needed, its constitutionality should not be considered to present an insurmountable barrier in this regard.

9

European Contract Law and Consumer Protection

9.1 Introduction

As illustrated in Part Two, what is now Article 169 TFEU (ex Article 153 EC), either by itself or alongside what is now Article 114 TFEU (ex Article 95 EC), steadily filtered into documents issued by the Union institutions and stakeholders as part of the debate about European contract law.[1] Article 169 TFEU also makes an appearance in much of the scholarly literature surrounding this debate. On the one hand, this is not all that surprising. Given that much of the 'hard core' of the EU contract law *acquis* concerns consumer contract law, the reference to Article 169 TFEU, equipping the Union with specific competence in the field of consumer protection, would seem to be expected.[2] Yet, on the occasions in which this provision has been contemplated in the literature, it is usually passed over without much detailed analysis, often due to perceptions of its limited scope and its aptitude for being overshadowed by Article 114 TFEU.[3] As a result, Article 169 TFEU seems to play more of a role akin to 'second runner up' at a beauty pageant—mentioned but never chosen in the end.

Upon closer examination, however, inquiry into Article 169 TFEU in the context of European contract law breaks open long-standing ambiguity and controversy regarding the scope of this provision and its linkage to Article 114 TFEU. The shift from minimum to maximum harmonization in the context of the Commission's review of the consumer *acquis* placed renewed focus on the potential recourse to Article 169 TFEU by virtue of its allowance—unlike Article 114 TFEU—for minimum harmonization as a matter of primary Union law.[4] Given the interplay between consumer contract law and general contract law in the debate, this begs provocative questions as regards the extent to which Article 169 TFEU may be used as a legal basis alongside others, such as Articles 114 or 352 TFEU, for the adoption of a European contract law instrument, optional or otherwise, encompassing consumer contract law. In fact, both inside and outside the confines of the debate, there have been instances in which what

[1] See Chapter 6, § 6.2.1.2.

[2] As regards terminology, there has been attention drawn to the distinction between 'consumer protection' and 'consumer policy' in the sense that the former may carry connotations of paternalism that the latter does not. See EESC Opinion on the 'Consumer policy action plan 1999–2001', [1999] OJ C209/1, point 2.4. Yet, for the most part, the two terms have been used interchangeably in the various institutional documents, and the term 'consumer protection' is used as the heading of the specific title of the TFEU encompassing Art 169 TFEU, as had been the case for the former EC Treaty.

[3] See, eg, V Constantinesco, 'La "codification" communautaire du droit privé à l'épreuve du titre de compétence de l'Union européenne' (2008) 44 *RTDE* 707, 716–717; SA de Vries, *Tensions within the Internal Market: The Functioning of the Internal Market and the Development of Horizontal and Flanking Policies* (Europa, 2006) 301–303; C Twigg-Flesner, *The Europeanisation of Contract Law* (Routledge-Cavendish, 2008) 33–34; S Weatherill, 'Competence and European private law' in C Twigg-Flesner (ed), *The Cambridge Companion to European Union Private Law* (Cambridge Univ Press, 2010) 58, 63.

[4] Art 169(4) TFEU.

is now Article 169 TFEU was advocated either by itself or in tandem with what is now Article 114 TFEU as a legal basis for a particular Union measure, but was not taken up.[5] This seems to indicate some uncertainty among the Union institutions themselves as regards the use of Article 169 TFEU and its interplay with Article 114 TFEU, among other Treaty provisions.[6]

The aim of this chapter is therefore to examine the extent of the Union's competence under Article 169 TFEU to adopt a European contract law instrument including or limited to consumer contract law and the linkage between this provision and Articles 114 and 352 TFEU in this regard, which will be done in three main parts. The first part sets forth the template for the analysis of Article 169 TFEU, which encompasses the chronological development of Article 169 TFEU in the past and present Treaty frameworks, relevant case law of the Court of Justice, and institutional practice concerning the use, or lack thereof, of Article 169 TFEU. The second part analyses the scope of the Union's competence under Article 169 TFEU in relation to the achievement of consumer protection objectives *sensu stricto* on the basis of Article 169(2)(b) TFEU. The third part evaluates the relationship between Articles 169, 114, and 352 TFEU as far as the adoption of a European contract law instrument encompassing consumer contract law, optional or otherwise, is concerned, drawing in relevant part on comparative reflection with the US.

The structure of this chapter is intentional. The three components comprising the template for the analysis of Article 169 TFEU—the Treaties, case law, and usage—are presented together in the first part because they lay the groundwork for the analysis of Article 169 TFEU and its linkage to Articles 114 and 352 TFEU in the parts that follow. Admittedly, this makes the chapter 'top heavy', and it could be thought preferable to incorporate these components within the inquiry of Article 169 TFEU itself. Yet, methodologically, there are good reasons to justify the approach taken here. In view of the considerable ambiguity surrounding Article 169 TFEU and divergent opinion among commentators regarding the potential role, or not, to be played by this provision in European contract law, it is only by examining these three components together that the ambit of Article 169 TFEU and its linkage to Article 114 TFEU comes into view. Moreover, each of these components is inextricably intertwined with both the scope of the Union's competence under Article 169 TFEU and the interplay between Articles 169 and 114 TFEU as far as EU consumer contract law is concerned, which makes separating out the elements associated with each extremely difficult. For that matter, these three components are themselves interlocking: one cannot assess the case law or institutional practice regarding Article 169 TFEU, for example, without first understanding its evolution in the Treaty framework.

This in turn alludes to certain challenges underlying this inquiry. First, Article 169 TFEU is deeply embedded in the emergence and development of EU consumer policy, which commands a quite extensive body of materials of its own. The purpose of this chapter is not to engage in comprehensive study of EU consumer policy, but it cannot be left out entirely because it not only permeates the text of Article 169

[5] See, eg, T Bourgoignie, 'European Community consumer law and policy: from Rome to Amsterdam' (1998) 16 *Cons LJ* 443, 447–448.

[6] Eg, with the growing attention given to the need to ensure adequate enforcement of consumer measures and means of redress for consumers, this implicates issues concerning the relationship between Articles 169, 81, and 114 TFEU, which exceed the scope of this book. For further discussion, see, eg, J Stuyck, 'Public and Private Enforcement in Consumer Protection: General Comparison EU-USA' in F Cafaggi and H-W Micklitz (eds), *New Frontiers of Consumer Protection: The Interplay Between Private and Public Enforcement* (Intersentia, 2009) 63, 65–69.

TFEU and institutional practice surrounding this provision, but also bears directly on the relationship between Articles 169 and 114 TFEU as far as the adoption of a European consumer contract law instrument is concerned. Secondly, Article 169 TFEU is presently one of the most underdeveloped, if not underestimated, provisions of the Treaties. It is couched in notoriously vague language, which has not yet received much clarification in the Court's case law, and is used only exceptionally by the Union institutions, despite the consistent avowal to do so. This no doubt explains one of the reasons why in much of the scholarly literature on Article 169 TFEU, commentators are loath to go into considerable detail as regards the extent of the Union's competence under this provision. In other words, there is simply not a plethora of materials on Article 169 TFEU to work with. That said, the field is by no means barren, and the relevant case law, commentary, and institutional documents that are available provide salient indications of the dimensions of Article 169 TFEU and its linkage to Article 114 TFEU, as well as Article 352 TFEU to some extent, in relation to the constitutionality of European contract law on the basis of the template presented below.

9.2 The Template for the Analysis of Article 169 TFEU

9.2.1 The Treaties: The emergence and development of Article 169 TFEU

Article 169 TFEU was a relative latecomer to the Treaty framework. Neither the EEC Treaty nor the Single European Act (SEA) contained any provision conferring specific competence on what was then the Community in the field of consumer protection. It was the Maastricht Treaty that first introduced such a competence under former Article 129a EC. With some adjustments in the Amsterdam Treaty, this became former Article 153 EC, whose substance remained unchanged in the former Treaty framework and continues to do so as Article 169 TFEU with the entry into force of the Lisbon Treaty.

By virtue of this heritage, what is now Article 169 TFEU possesses certain unique attributes. First, this provision was introduced into the Treaty framework long after the development of EU consumer policy was underway. Unlike other Treaty provisions that provided the basis upon which to spur Union (formerly Community) action, Article 169 TFEU was the product or outcome of the steady progression of EU consumer policy, which filtered into the framing of this provision. Furthermore, Article 169 TFEU was not inserted into the Treaty framework on an entirely clean slate. It was laid on the foundation of previous institutional practice in which consumer policy had long been considered within the context of other policy fields, particularly the internal market programme. This was augmented by explicit mention of consumer protection within the confines of what was originally Article 100a EC (later Article 95 EC, now Article 114 TFEU) in the SEA, which set the groundwork for the fusion between Articles 169 and 114 TFEU in the text of Article 169 TFEU itself. Finally, the fact that Article 169 TFEU was introduced by the Maastricht Treaty joined the analysis of this provision with the principle of subsidiarity and certain so-called 'flanking policies', such as education, public health, and culture, which were introduced into the Treaty framework at the same time and coloured the interpretation of Article 169 TFEU in subsequent years. In turn, these attributes of Article 169 TFEU filtered into discussion of this provision as part of the European Convention and the Draft Constitutional

Treaty, which paved the way for the Lisbon Treaty. As such, the chronological development of Article 169 TFEU in the Treaty framework provides the starting point for the assessment of the Union's competence under this provision and its linkage to Article 114 TFEU.

9.2.1.1 The former Treaty framework

Looking back at the former EC Treaty, Article 3 EC listed as one of the Community's activities 'a contribution to the strengthening of consumer protection'.[7] This corresponded to the specific title of that Treaty devoted to consumer protection, within which Article 153 EC was the sole provision.[8] Article 153 EC consisted of five paragraphs. The first paragraph set forth the Community's objectives 'to promote the interests of consumers and to ensure a high level of consumer protection' by contributing 'to protecting the health, safety and economic interests of consumers, as well as to promoting their right to information, education and to organise themselves in order to safeguard their interests'.[9] The second paragraph made explicit the 'horizontal' nature of consumer protection requirements, stating that such 'requirements shall be taken into account in defining and implementing other Community policies and activities'.[10] The third paragraph constituted the 'heart' of Article 153 EC as far as the scope of Community competence was concerned, providing that:

> The Community shall contribute to the attainment of the objectives referred to in paragraph 1 through:
> (a) measures adopted pursuant to Article 95 in the context of the completion of the internal market;
> (b) measures which support, supplement and monitor the policy pursued by the Member States.[11]

As regards the measures adopted under indent (b), the fourth paragraph stipulated the decision-making procedure to be followed, ie qualified majority voting in the Council and the co-decision procedure, with consultation of the European Economic and Social Committee (EESC).[12] This was followed by the fifth paragraph, the so-called 'minimum harmonization' provision, which stipulated that the measures adopted under paragraph 4 (meaning those concerning indent (b)) 'shall not prevent any Member State from maintaining or introducing more stringent protective measures', provided that such measures were compatible with the Treaty and the Commission was notified of them.[13]

As already alluded to, the text of former Article 153 EC did not spring magically out of thin air, but in fact drew greatly upon previous institutional developments concerning Community consumer policy starting in the 1970s.[14] To explain, in the early years of European integration, the need for a specific competence in the Treaty concerning consumer protection was not foremost on the minds of the

[7] Ex Art 3(1)(t) EC. [8] Ex Title XIV EC. [9] Ex Art 153(1) EC.
[10] Ex Art 153(2) EC. [11] Ex Art 153(3) EC. [12] Ex Art 153(4) EC.
[13] Ex Art 153(5) EC.
[14] See, eg, S Weatherill, *EU Consumer Law and Policy*, 2nd edn (Edward Elgar, 2005), ch 1; Bourgoignie, n 5; H-W Micklitz and S Weatherill, 'Consumer Policy in the European Community: Before and After Maastricht' (1993) 16 *JCP* 285; J Stuyck, 'European Consumer Law After the Treaty of Amsterdam: Consumer Policy In or Beyond the Internal Market?' (2000) 37 *CML Rev* 367.

framers. In the original EEC Treaty, consumers were mentioned only in the context of Community policies concerning the Common Agricultural Policy (CAP), competition law, and State aid.[15] Still, it was not long before consumer protection became the focus of attention by the EU institutions. This was evident early on with the 1969 European Parliament Resolution and accompanying 'Boersma Report', which were concerned with the strengthening of the position of the consumer in the common market and called for the increased recognition of consumer interests within the various Community policies in the Treaty.[16] Yet, most often in the literature, emphasis is placed on the 1972 Paris Summit and the subsequent 1975 Council Resolution laying out a preliminary programme on consumer protection, two foundational events credited for giving birth to Community consumer policy.

The proceedings of the 1972 Paris Summit,[17] comprising the meeting of the Heads of State of the then nine Member States,[18] were encapsulated in an ambitious Declaration concerned with the development of a multitude of different policy fields.[19] This included the category of 'social policy', which contained instructions for the institutions to draw up an action programme with a view to, among other things, 'strengthen and coordinate action for protecting the consumer'.[20] This Declaration proved to be the catalyst for Community action in this area[21] and stimulated the publication of the first consumer protection programme three years later.

In 1975, the Council adopted its landmark Resolution setting forth a Preliminary Programme of the EEC for a consumer protection and information policy.[22] The Resolution itself was quite short; the accompanying Preliminary Programme was considerably longer and essentially contained the 'meat' for the creation of a Community consumer policy.[23] Famously, it established the following five basic consumer rights:

(1) the right to protection of health and safety;
(2) the right to protection of economic interests;
(3) the right of redress;

[15] Weatherill, n 14, 3.

[16] Résolution sur le renforcement de la position du consommateur dans le marché commun, [1969] OJ C17/4; Rapport fait au nom de la commission économique sur la proposition de résolution présentée au nom du groupe socialiste par M Metzger (Doc 95/68) relative au renforcement de la position du consommateur dans le marché commun (referred to as the Boersma Report after the Rapporteur, Mr J Boersma), Doc 189/68, Parlement Européen Documents de Séance 1968–1969, dated 20 Jan 1969.

[17] Meetings of the Heads of State or Government, Paris, 19–20 Oct 1972, *Bulletin of the European Communities* No 10/1972 (1972 Paris Summit).

[18] This included the six original Member States (Belgium, France, Germany, Italy, Luxembourg, and the Netherlands), as well as Denmark, Ireland, and the UK. Norway was initially involved, but with the negative referendum, it did not attend the conference: see 1972 Paris Summit, n 17, 14 fn 1. Technically speaking, this was not considered a meeting of the 'European Council'; the creation of this distinct body (now Union institution) came later. See K Lenaerts and P Van Nuffel (R Bray and N Cambien (eds)), *European Union Law*, 3rd edn, (Sweet & Maxwell, 2011) § 2-005, § 13-025.

[19] 1972 Paris Summit, n 17, 14–23.

[20] 1972 Paris Summit, n 17, point 6, second para.

[21] See, eg, Commission Communication, A New Impetus for Consumer Protection Policy, COM (85) 314 final, 27.6.1985 (1985 Communication), point 2.

[22] Council Resolution of 14 April 1975 on a preliminary programme of the EEC for a consumer protection and information policy, [1975] OJ C92/1 (1975 Council Resolution).

[23] Preliminary Programme of the EEC for a consumer protection and information policy, [1975] OJ C92/2 (1975 Preliminary Programme).

(4) the right to information and education; and
(5) the right of representation (the right to be heard).[24]

According to the Council, these rights should be 'given greater substance' by action taken under specific Community policies and the approximation of laws, both of which fell within the context of the Community's objective to improve living conditions under then Article 2 EEC.[25] These five consumer rights informed the objectives, governing principles, and priority action to be taken in relation to the elaboration of a Community consumer policy detailed in the Programme.

Importantly, the section concerning the protection of the economic interests of consumers contained the embryo for several measures within the 'hard core' of the EU contract law *acquis*. Among the principles governing this type of protection, listed first was the protection of purchasers of goods and services from abuse of power by the seller, particularly against one-sided standard contracts, the unfair exclusion of essential rights in contracts, harsh conditions for credit, demands for payment for unsolicited goods, and high-pressure selling methods.[26] As regards the priority measures to be taken, the harmonization of consumer credit laws and the protection of consumers involving contract terms, conditions in guarantees for consumer goods, and door-to-door sales were listed.[27] In hindsight, this would pave the way for the Consumer Credit, Unfair Contract Terms, Consumer Sales, and Doorstep Selling Directives, respectively.

The Council's 1975 Preliminary Programme was followed by a successive string of further action programmes. In 1981, the Council adopted a Resolution on a Second Programme of the EEC for a consumer protection and information policy,[28] which reiterated the importance of consumers' five basic rights,[29] and akin to the first Programme, was to be carried out using the appropriate means laid down in the Treaty.[30] In 1985, in light of the tenth anniversary of the Council's 1975 Preliminary Programme, the Commission issued a Communication on 'A New Impetus for Consumer Protection Policy',[31] which coincided with the publication of Lord Cockfield's famous White Paper on the Internal Market and increased consciousness of addressing consumer concerns as part of preparations for the internal market.[32] One of the Commission's objectives was that consumers must be able to benefit from what was then called the common market, explaining that, 'If the common market is to be fully effective, it must be made easier for consumers to buy goods in other countries, to use them at home, to get them repaired

[24] 1975 Preliminary Programme, n 23, point 3. In this regard, a 'comparative leap' to the US has often been made in the literature by virtue of President John F Kennedy's 1962 Special Message to the Congress on Protecting the Consumer Interest, which espoused a similar, though not identical, list of consumer rights. See *Public Papers of the Presidents of the United States, John. F. Kennedy, Containing the Public Messages, Speeches, and Statements of the President, 1962* (GPO, 1963) 235, 236. It was considered to have had some influence on the Council's 1975 Preliminary Programme: see, eg, Stuyck, n 14, 377. For a recent outlook, see (2012) 1 *EUVR* 207.

[25] 1975 Preliminary Programme, n 23, point 4; 1975 Council Resolution, n 22, first–third recitals.

[26] 1975 Preliminary Programme, n 23, point 19(i).

[27] 1975 Preliminary Programme, n 23, point 24.

[28] Council Resolution of 19 May 1981 on a second programme of the EEC for a consumer protection and information policy, [1981] OJ C133/1.

[29] The language describing these rights was noticeably strengthened in this Programme, as demonstrated by the Council's reference to them as 'fundamental rights' (Council Resolution, n 28, point 6, first para).

[30] Council Resolution, n 28, points 8(1), 10.

[31] 1985 Communication, n 21.

[32] Commission Communication, Three-Year Action Plan of Consumer Policy in the EEC 1990–1992, COM (90) 98 final, 3.5.1990 (First Three-Year Action Plan) 2.

like domestically purchased products, and to see complaints handled effectively'.[33] The Commission outlined various measures that were necessary to protect the economic interests of consumers, including proposals on unfair contract terms, and consumer credit, guarantees and warranties for consumer goods, and package travel, among many others.[34] It underscored that the actions set out in the Communication complemented those within the larger programme for the completion of the internal market.[35] The Communication was welcomed by the Council, which adopted a Resolution endorsing the objectives of the programme, especially those concerned with the completion of the internal market.[36]

This linkage between consumer protection and the internal market programme soon became constitutionalized in the EC Treaty itself with the adoption of the SEA. In the newly minted Article 100a EEC (later Article 95 EC, now Article 114 TFEU), the third paragraph provided: 'The Commission, in its proposals envisaged in paragraph 1 concerning health, safety, environmental protection and *consumer protection*, will take as a base a high level of protection'.[37] Later reframed as former Article 95(3) EC, this language was not altered in subsequent revisions of the EC Treaty or by the renumbering of this provision as Article 114(3) TFEU with the entry into force of the Lisbon Treaty.[38] Article 100a(3) EEC was the first formal recognition of consumer protection as an autonomous policy objective in the Treaty, but noticeably, it was grounded in the Community's action to achieve its internal market objectives.[39] There was no explicit legal basis in the SEA conferring specific competence on the Community in the field of consumer protection.[40]

The Maastricht Treaty heralded a sea change in relation to the Community's competence in this field. It added consumer protection to the Community's activities in Article 3 EC[41] and inserted a new title of the Treaty concerning consumer protection, thereby introducing Article 129a EC, a relatively short provision comprised of three paragraphs. The first paragraph delineated the framework for the Community's competence in this field:

[33] 1985 Communication, n 21, point 18, second indent; point 29.

[34] 1985 Communication, n 21, points 29–31, 35, 37.

[35] 1985 Communication, n 21, 23.

[36] Council Resolution of 23 June 1986 concerning the future orientation of the policy of the EEC for the protection and promotion of consumer interests, [1986] OJ C167/1. This was reiterated in the Council Resolution of 15 Dec 1986 on the integration of consumer policy in the other common policies, [1987] OJ C3/1.

[37] Ex Art 100a(3) EEC (emphasis added).

[38] Starting with the Amsterdam Treaty, some additional language was added to former Art 95(3) EC, reading in full: 'The Commission, in its proposals envisaged in paragraph 1 concerning health, safety, environmental protection and consumer protection, will take as a base a high level of protection, taking account in particular of any new development based on scientific facts. Within their respective powers, the European Parliament and the Council will also seek to achieve this objective.' This was not changed by the Lisbon Treaty, and Art 114(3) TFEU provides the same.

[39] Stuyck, n 14, 378.

[40] For possible reasons why, see, eg, K Mortelmans and S Watson, 'The Notion of Consumer in Community Law: A Lottery?' in J Lonbay (ed), *Enhancing the Legal Position of the European Consumer* (BIICL, 1996) 36, 39. There had been a specific provision concerning consumer policy in the European Parliament's 1984 Draft Treaty on European Union, but it did not make its way into the SEA. Art 57 stated: 'The Union may lay down rules designed to protect the health and safety of consumers and their economic interests, particularly in the event of damage. The Union may encourage action to promote consumer education, information and consultation.' It was part of the framework setting out Union concurrent competence in relation to various fields under the rubric of 'policy for society' in Art 55. This Treaty is reprinted in R Bieber et al, *An ever closer Union: A critical analysis of the Draft Treaty establishing the European Union* (European Commission, 1985); see also F Capotorti et al, *The European Union Treaty: Commentary on the draft adopted by the European Parliament on 14 February 1984* (Clarendon Press, 1986).

[41] Ex Art 3(s) EC (later Art 3(1)(t) EC).

The Community shall contribute to the attainment of a high level of consumer protection through:

(a) measures adopted pursuant to Article 100a in the context of the completion of the internal market;

(b) specific action which supports and supplements the policy pursued by the Member States to protect the health, safety and economic interests of consumers and to provide adequate information to consumers.[42]

The second paragraph stipulated the decision-making procedures for the 'specific action' referred to in indent (b), which required qualified majority voting in the Council and the co-decision procedure (with consultation of the EESC),[43] which were the same decision-making procedures prescribed for measures adopted under Article 100a EC via indent (a).[44] The third paragraph provided that '[a]ction adopted pursuant to paragraph 2 shall not prevent any Member State from maintaining or introducing more stringent protective measures', but such measures must be compatible with the Treaty and notified to the Commission.[45]

Looking closely at the text of Article 129a EC, it drew from the elaboration of the specific consumer rights enshrined in the previous programmes on Community consumer policy, even if inadvertently or not, three out of the five consumer rights relating to education, redress, and representation were left out.[46] More to the point, however, the Community's competence under Article 129a EC was saddled to Article 100a EC and linked to the principle of subsidiarity and several neighbouring policies introduced by the Maastricht Treaty at the same time, which left an indelible imprint on this provision.

As regards its relationship to Article 100a EC, Article 129a EC dictated a dual route by which Community action would proceed via measures adopted under Article 100a EC under indent (a) and 'specific action to support and supplement' national consumer policy under indent (b). Thus, rather than cutting the cord with the internal market, it strengthened it further by containing an express *renvoi* to Article 100a EC, something that was quite novel in the system of the Treaties.[47] In the negotiations surrounding the Maastricht Treaty, Article 129a EC was said to embody a crucial compromise between those who favoured Community action in the consumer field and those who found it impossible to sever the ties between internal market and consumer protection and hence preferred indirect action relating to consumer interests in the internal market programme.[48] This played out in the framing of Article 129a EC in the sense it was praised for establishing an autonomous Community competence in consumer protection for the first time, while at the same time, it was criticized for generating ambiguity as regards measures to be adopted under indent (a) as opposed to indent (b).[49]

Moreover, the text of Article 129a EC was conjoined with the principle of subsidiarity, which was also introduced by the Maastricht Treaty as a constitutional principle governing the exercise of Community competence. This was illustrated by the fact

[42] Ex Art 129a(1) EC. [43] Ex Art 129a(2) EC.

[44] Ex Art 100a EC. The Maastricht Treaty amended this provision so as to substitute the co-decision procedure for that of cooperation.

[45] Ex Art 129a(3) EC. [46] Bourgoignie, n 5, 448.

[47] See J Cloos et al, *Le traité de Maastricht: genèse, analyse, commentaires*, 2nd edn (Bruylant, 1994) 335.

[48] Cloos et al, n 47, 335. See also R Corbett, *The Treaty of Maastricht—From Conception to Ratification: A Comprehensive Reference Guide* (Longman, 1993) 52.

[49] See, eg, Bourgoignie, n 5, 447–448; Micklitz and Weatherill, n 14, 300; S Weatherill, 'The Evolution of European Consumer Law and Policy: From Well Informed Consumer to Confident Consumer?' in H-W Micklitz (ed), *Rechtseinheit oder Rechtsvielfalt in Europa?* (Nomos, 1996) 423, 448.

that the Community would 'contribute' to consumer policy by way of 'specific action' that 'supports and supplements the policy pursued by the Member States', exuding the notion that Member State action was primary and Community action merely played a secondary role.[50] Additionally, scholars espoused the merits of inscribing minimum harmonization in the text of this provision so as to preserve leeway for the Member States to provide for more stringent protection in areas covered by the 'specific action' taken under this provision.[51]

Along with subsidiarity, Article 129a EC entered the Treaty framework alongside other new, so-called 'flanking policies', which included education, culture, and public health. These three policy fields were listed right before Article 129a EC in the EC Treaty, and their nuances in language as compared to Article 129a EC stood out. As with consumer protection, they, too, were added to the list of activities in Article 3 EC, stipulating the Community's 'contribution' to the area concerned.[52] For each, a new title of the EC Treaty was created, and their provisions also began with mention that the Community would 'contribute' to the policy field concerned, but here, Community action was aimed at 'encouraging cooperation between Member States, and *if necessary*, by supporting and supplementing their action' in the case of education and culture[53] or by 'lending support to their action' in the case of public health.[54] In contrast, Article 129a EC did not prioritize Member State cooperation, but placed Community supporting and supplementing action at the forefront. Moreover, Community action in those three fields was expressly restricted to 'incentive measures, excluding any harmonization of laws' or to non-binding recommendations,[55] which was absent in the text of Article 129a EC. This drew comparison with some of the more heartier 'flanking policies', especially environmental policy and social policy that were inserted into the Treaty framework earlier on, but revised in the Maastricht Treaty.[56] These latter two policy fields expressly provided for harmonization measures, and both contained provisions allowing the Member States to take more stringent protective measures in the areas concerned, which were substantially identical to Article 129a(3) EC.[57] In this way, Article 129a EC seemed to sit somewhere in the middle, straddling the more limited provisions concerning education, public health, and culture and the more robust provisions concerning environmental policy and social policy. This continued in the Amsterdam Treaty.

The Amsterdam Treaty made certain changes to the text of Article 129a EC, but on the whole, did not resolve the ambiguities surrounding the demarcation between

[50] See, eg, G Close, 'The Consumer Protection Programme of the EC in the 1990's' in *Enhancing the Legal Position of the European Consumer*, n 40, 18, 23; G Howells and S Weatherill, *Consumer Protection Law*, 2nd edn (Ashgate, 2005) 128. The interplay between subsidiarity and EU consumer policy arose well before the Maastricht Treaty: see Weatherill, n 14, 19–20.

[51] See, eg, Bourgoignie, n 5, 447; Micklitz and Weatherill, n 14, 301–302.

[52] See ex Art 3(o) EC (later Art 3(1)(p) EC); ex Art 3(p) EC (later Art 3(1)(q) EC).

[53] See ex Art 126(1) EC (emphasis added); ex Art 128(1)–(2) EC (emphasis added).

[54] See ex Art 129(1) EC.

[55] See ex Art 126(4) EC; ex Art 128(5) EC; ex Art 129(4) EC.

[56] Provisions on social policy had been an original fixture of the EEC Treaty, whereas those concerning environmental policy were introduced by the SEA. Aside from changes to their substantive provisions, the Maastricht Treaty included them in former Art 3 EC, espousing a 'policy', as opposed to a 'contribution', in these fields: see ex Art 3(i) EC (later Art 3(1)(j) EC); ex Art 3(k) EC (later Art 3(1)(l) EC).

[57] For social policy, see ex Art 118a(3) EC. This had been inserted by the SEA; the Maastricht Treaty revised the decision-making procedures to be followed. For environmental policy, see ex Art 130t EC. This provision was augmented by the Maastricht Treaty so as to make clear that such measures must be compatible with the Treaty and notified to the Commission, verbatim to ex Art 129a(3) EC.

measures adopted under indent (b) of this provision as opposed to those enacted under former Article 95 EC via indent (a).[58] In fact, it is not clear to what extent these issues were addressed, since as noted by one jurist, little is known about the negotiations concerning the revision of this provision, save that it was 'a hardly debated compromise between Scandinavian proposals for broader Community powers and, in particular, German and British opposition'.[59] In any event, while not wholly insignificant, the changes brought about by the Amsterdam Treaty amounted to more tinkering than fundamental reworking of this provision on the competence front.

Under the Amsterdam Treaty, Article 129a EC, now renumbered Article 153 EC, was enlarged to five paragraphs. The first paragraph of Article 153 EC provided:

> In order to promote the interests of consumers and to ensure a high level of consumer protection, the Community shall contribute to protecting the health, safety and economic interests of consumers, as well as to promoting their right to information, education and to organise themselves in order to safeguard their interests.[60]

This language attempted to rectify the neglect of certain consumer rights in the previous Article 129a EC by tacking on the rights to education and representation, although the right to redress was still not explicitly mentioned.[61] Furthermore, by moving up the Community's objectives, Article 153(1) EC made clear that measures taken on the basis of Article 95 EC via indent (a) encompassed the abovementioned rights and interests including the protection of consumers' economic interests within which EU consumer contract law was situated, as compared to Article 129a(1) EC that had listed such rights and interests in relation to measures taken under indent (b).[62] The second paragraph finally made explicit the 'horizontal' nature of consumer protection requirements to be taken into account as part of other Community policies, which had been neglected in Article 129a EC.[63] The fourth and fifth paragraphs of Article 153 EC copied the relevant paragraphs of Article 129a EC as regards the decision-making procedures to be followed and the recourse to minimum harmonization, respectively.[64]

Notably, under the third paragraph of Article 153 EC, the dual track remained. The reference to measures adopted under Article 95 EC 'in the context of the completion of the internal market' in indent (a) stayed the same. It was indent (b) where certain changes had been made: 'specific action' was replaced by 'measures', and the word 'monitor' was added, now reading 'measures which support, supplement and monitor the policy pursued by the Member States'. No explanation was provided as regards what was meant by these revisions. Scholars came to surmise that 'measures' adopted under indent (b) could be of a legislative nature and that the word 'monitor' implied some sort of enforcement role at the European level.[65] Regrettably, any opportunity to clarify matters left open by the Amsterdam Treaty was foregone in the subsequent round of Treaty amendments, and the framing of Article 153 EC in the Amsterdam Treaty was untouched by the Nice Treaty.

[58] See Bourgoignie, n 5, 461. [59] Stuyck, n 14, 383. [60] Ex Art 153(1) EC.
[61] See Bourgoignie, n 5, 461. [62] Stuyck, n 14, 386.
[63] Ex Art 153(2) EC provided: 'Consumer protection requirements shall be taken into account in defining and implementing other Community policies and activities.' The lack of such a provision in ex Art 129a EC was criticized: see Bourgoignie, n 5, 448.
[64] Ex Art 153(4)–(5) EC.
[65] See N Reich, 'Economic Law, Consumer Interests and EU Integration' in H-W Micklitz et al (eds), *Understanding EU Consumer Law* (Intersentia, 2009) 1, 33–35; Stuyck, n 14, 387–388 and citations therein. See also n 184 and accompanying text.

9.2.1.2 *The present Treaty framework*

Needless to say, the lingering ambiguities underlying former Article 153 EC, especially as regards the boundary line between indents (a) and (b) of Article 153(3) EC, were not addressed by the Lisbon Treaty in the renumbering of this provision as Article 169 TFEU. Still, the progression from the European Convention and the Draft Constitutional Treaty shed some light on the extent of the Union's competence under this provision.

Starting with the European Convention, former Article 153 EC was discussed within Working Group V on 'Complementary Competencies'. Weaved through much of the discussion of this Working Group was the issue of which Community (now Union) competences could be classified under the category of complementary competence, which espoused a more limited role for the Union vis-à-vis the Member States than that of shared competence.[66] With respect to consumer protection, opinions became divided, since for some the reference to Article 95 EC in Article 153 EC made this a shared competence, whereas others thought that measures adopted under Article 95 EC in the framework of the internal market constituted a shared competence, whereas consumer protection remained a complementary competence.[67] In the Working Group's Final Report, this was settled in favour of shared, not complementary, competence, on the grounds that EU legislation in the form of regulations and/or directives was 'clearly' authorized under Article 153 EC, and even though most Community acts adopted in this field were based on other provisions, 'the fact that (minimum) directives could be adopted under Article 153 made it logical that consumer protection should be classified as shared competence'.[68]

During the European Convention, there were only a handful of proposals concerning the revision of Article 153 EC, and of those, most were not concerned with changing the language of Article 153(3) EC as regards the scope of the Community's competence under indent (b) vis-à-vis indent (a).[69] Of note, however, was the submission of certain Swedish Government and National Parliament representatives who suggested inserting an additional clause between indents (a) and (b), allowing for 'other measures including those which ensure the effective enforcement of the Union's measures adopted to achieve a high level of consumer protection'.[70] As explained therein, the reason for this change was that '[a] firm legal base, as a supplement to Article 95 EC, is required for common consumer legislation in areas which do not primarily relate to the functioning of the Internal Market'.[71] This submission also advocated the deletion of Article 153(5) EC, on the grounds that '[t]he appropriate level of harmonisation should

[66] See Mandate of the Working Group on Complementary Competencies, CONV 75/02, dated 31 May 2002, 2–3. Incidentally, the Working Group considered the term 'complementary competence' inadequate and misleading and recommended that it be replaced by another term, such as 'supporting measures', which better denoted the essence of the relationship between the Union and the Member States. Final Report of Working Group V on Complementary Competencies, CONV 375/1/02REV1 WGV14, dated 4 Nov 2002, point 2. This was not taken up in the Draft Constitutional Treaty (DCT), which paved the way for the Lisbon Treaty. See further Chapter 7, § 7.3.

[67] Summary of the meeting on 7 Oct 2002, CONV 347/02 WGV12, dated 16 Oct 2002, 2.

[68] Working Group V Final Report, n 66, point 6, at 9.

[69] See Proposed Amendments, Part III of the Constitution, Section 6-Consumer protection.

[70] Suggestion for amendment of Article III-127 (ex 153) by Mrs Lena Hjelm-Wallén and Mr Sven-Olof Petersson, government representatives, and Mr Sören Lekberg, Swedish national parliament representative.

[71] Suggestion for amendment of Article III-127, n 70, para 3 fn 2. This seemed to imply that measures under indent (b) were not considered as such, but in any event, the proposal was meant to bolster EU competence in the field of consumer protection apart from the internal market.

be assessed on a case-by-case basis' and '[t]he present minimum harmonisation rule is bound to diminish the impact of the article as a base for consumer legislation'.[72]

The Draft Constitutional Treaty did not take up this proposal and was conservative as to the changes made to Article 153 EC.[73] In the 2003 version, the corresponding provision of Article III-132 was slimmed to four paragraphs. The 'horizontal' clause of Article 153(2) EC was moved to the forefront of that Treaty with other clauses of general application.[74] For indent (b), 'measures' were to be enacted by European laws or framework laws, which made clear that legislative measures essentially in the form of regulations or directives, respectively, could be adopted under this provision.[75] In the 2004 version, the renumbered Article III-235 retained the aforementioned changes and made a slight adjustment to indent (a) in relation to measures adopted pursuant to Article 95 EC (corresponding to Article III-172) 'in the context of the establishment and functioning of the internal market', as opposed to the previous wording ('in the context of the completion of the internal market') of Article 153 EC, thereby attempting to align the two provisions.[76]

More interesting was the comparison in treatment between consumer protection and the other 'flanking policies' in the 2003 and 2004 versions of the Draft Constitutional Treaty. Consumer protection was classified alongside the internal market, environmental policy, social policy, and certain aspects of public health, among others, as shared competences,[77] whereas other aspects of public health, along with education and culture, were listed as complementary competences for which harmonization measures were expressly excluded.[78] Consequently, Article 153 EC's counterpart was placed right after the Treaty provisions concerning environmental policy in the specific chapter concerning Union policies in other (specific) areas,[79] as opposed to the provisions concerning education, culture, and public health, which were segregated to a wholly different chapter of that Treaty concerned with Union supporting, coordinating, or complementary action.[80]

The Lisbon Treaty followed along similar, albeit not identical, lines of the Draft Constitutional Treaty in the reframing of Article 153 EC as Article 169 TFEU. Gone were the revisions related to European laws and framework laws and the attempted symmetry with the text of former Article 95 EC, now Article 114 TFEU, in indent (a). Yet, like the Draft Constitutional Treaty, the same classification of shared and complementary competences was retained, with the result that consumer protection has been placed next to the internal market, environmental policy, social policy, and certain aspects of public health policy in the category of shared competence.[81] The only

[72] Suggestion for amendment of Article III-127, n 70, para 5 fn3.

[73] It should be emphasized that by its incorporation of the Charter of Fundamental Rights of the European Union, the DCT included Art II-38, stating: 'Union policies shall ensure a high level of consumer protection'. With the entry into force of the Lisbon Treaty, the text of the Charter is not included in the Treaties as such; it was re-enacted by the European Parliament, Council, and Commission and published separately in the *Official Journal*, [2007] OJ C303/1; consolidated version, [2012] OJ C326/391. Nevertheless, the Charter has legally binding force (see Art 6(1), first para, TEU; Declaration (No 1) concerning the Charter of Fundamental Rights of the European Union, [2012] OJ C326/339) and thus, Art 38 is hailed as an important attribute of the consumer protection framework. But see L Defalque, 'Vers une plus grande cohérence dans la protection du consommateur?' in A De Walsche and L Levi (eds), *Mélanges en hommage à Georges Vandersanden—Promenades au sein du droit européen* (Bruylant, 2008) 465–466.

[74] 2003 DCT, Art III-5.

[75] 2003 DCT, Art III-132(2)(b), (3); Art 32.

[76] 2004 DCT, Art III-235(2)(a).

[77] 2003 DCT, Art 13(2); 2004 DCT, Art I-14(2).

[78] 2003 DCT, Art 16; 2004 DCT, Art I-12(5), second para; Art I-17.

[79] 2003 DCT, Pt III, Title III, Ch III; 2004 DCT, Pt III, Title III, Ch III.

[80] 2003 DCT, Pt III, Title III, Ch V; 2004 DCT, Pt III, Title III, Ch V.

[81] Art 4(2) TFEU; compare Art 6 TFEU.

difference is that these various policy fields are not split into different chapters, but instead remain side by side in successive titles of Part Three of the TFEU. Likewise, the 'horizontal' (also called the 'integration') clause of Article 153(2) EC was moved up front to Part One of the TFEU concerning provisions having general application.[82] The remaining four paragraphs of Article 169 TFEU are virtually identical to former Article 153 EC, save for a few clerical alterations.[83] As a result, the assessment of the Union's competence under Article 169 TFEU follows that of former Article 153 EC.[84]

9.2.2 The case law: The indirect role of Article 169 TFEU

As already noted, there is not yet a substantial body of case law on Article 169 TFEU. As seen below, in the most well-known cases so far, the Court of Justice[85] has engaged in limited analysis of this provision, with the accompanying Opinions of the Advocates General containing the more detailed inquiry. Moreover, the vast majority of cases concern the indirect use of Article 169 TFEU as a 'defensive shield' or an 'interpretative device' vis-à-vis other Treaty provisions, as opposed to the direct use of Article 169 TFEU as the legal basis for a particular Union measure. Consequently, until cases challenging Article 169 TFEU in the latter sense arise, the Court of Justice (or the General Court, as the case may be) may not be given any opportunity to pronounce on the extent of the Union's competence under this provision. Admittedly, this is something of a 'vicious circle' in the sense that as long as Article 169 TFEU is not widely resorted to by the Union legislature, there is less likelihood of cases challenging its use before the Court; conversely, the more there is no case law, the less likely it may be that the legislature will be more attracted to its use. Nonetheless, the present case law helps to outline the scope of Article 169 TFEU and its relationship to Article 114 TFEU.

In 1996, *El Corte Inglés*[86] presented the first real occasion for assessment of Article 169 TFEU, then Article 129a EC in its Maastricht version.[87] The case concerned a reference for a preliminary ruling from a Spanish court on the interpretation of the (old) Consumer Credit Directive,[88] namely whether this Directive could be considered to have 'direct effect' in a dispute between two private parties. In its reference, the national court took account of previous jurisprudence precluding the direct effect of unimplemented directives in disputes between private parties (ie the so-called 'horizontal direct effect' of directives), but it wondered whether the introduction of Article 129a EC prompted any change

[82] Art 12 TFEU. For the implications of this provision, see, eg, S de Vries, 'Consumer protection and the EU Single Market rules—The search for the "paradigm consumer"' (2012) 1 *EUVR* 228, 236–237.

[83] Aside from the renumbering of ex Art 95 EC as Art 114 TFEU in Art 169(2)(a) TFEU, the 'ordinary legislative procedure' stipulated under Art 169(3) TFEU essentially denotes the same decision-making procedures as ex Art 153(4) EC, ie qualified majority voting in the Council and the co-decision procedure, along with the consultation of the EESC. Also, the former reference to 'this Treaty' was replaced by 'the Treaties' in Art 169(4) TFEU.

[84] The right of redress is still not mentioned explicitly in this provision: see, eg, Defalque, n 73, 465–466.

[85] The focus on the Court of Justice is not to discount the potential role played by the other Union courts in this regard, but stems from the fact that the case law to date concerns the Court's jurisdiction over preliminary rulings and infringement actions.

[86] Case C-192/94 *El Corte Inglés* [1996] ECR I-1281.

[87] For earlier cases that included mention of this provision but with minimal results, see n 116.

[88] Council Dir 87/102/EEC of 22 Dec 1986 for the approximation of the laws, regulations and administrative provisions of the Member States concerning consumer credit, [1987] OJ L42/48. It has been replaced by a new Directive: see Chapter 1, § 1.3.3.

in this regard.[89] Thus, this provision entered into play indirectly in the national proceedings as potentially relevant in relation to the Court's case law on the direct effect of directives. The case did not concern the use of former Article 129a EC (now Article 169 TFEU) as the legal basis for a particular measure; this Directive, one of the 'hard core' of the EU contract law *acquis*, was based on former Article 100 EC (now Article 115 TFEU).

In its judgment, the Court reiterated its previous case law precluding the direct effect of unimplemented directives vis-à-vis private parties.[90] It then declared that 'Article 129a of the Treaty cannot alter that case-law, even if only in relation to directives on consumer protection'.[91] It explained:

> Suffice to say *in this connection* that the scope of Article 129a is limited. On the one hand, it provides that the Community is under a duty to contribute to the attainment of a high level of consumer protection. On the other, it creates Community competence with a view to specific action relating to consumer protection policy *apart* from measures taken in connection with the internal market.[92]

As this provision 'merely assigns an objective to the Community and confers powers on it to that end without also laying down any obligation on Member States or individuals', it cannot justify the 'horizontal direct effect' of directives on consumer protection.[93] The Court did not elaborate further as regards the ambit of what could be considered 'specific action relating to consumer protection policy' under Article 129a EC.

By comparison, Advocate General Lenz's Opinion contained more ample discussion, delving into the function and significance of Article 129a EC. He found it 'conspicuous' that Article 129a(a)(1) EC provided that the Community was to 'contribute' in the sphere of consumer protection, with the result that 'it was evidently intended also to leave leeway for competence on the part of the Member States' and thus embodied a 'concurrent' (or shared) competence subject to compliance with the principle of subsidiarity.[94] As such, 'even if Article 129a contained something novel, it would be subject to Community action being necessary rather than action on the part of the Member States'.[95]

From there, he delved into the independent significance of Article 129a EC vis-à-vis Article 100a EC, emphasizing that although indent (b) of Article 129a(1) EC established Community competence to take 'specific action' in consumer protection policy outside the ambit of measures relating to the internal market, it authorized the Community only to support and supplement the policies of the Member States and hence to act on an ancillary basis.[96] The placement of Article 129a EC at the end of the part of the Treaty relating to Community policies and the use of 'specific action' as opposed to 'measures' suggested, in his view, that measures adopted under indent (b) were not binding.[97] Given that a large number of internal market measures contained references to consumer protection, 'Article 100a might have to be regarded as the more specific provision, compared with Article 129a, as regards consumer protection in the context of the internal market'.[98] Moreover, indent (a) of Article 129a(1) EC was intended to make use of the possibilities already available in the context of the completion of the

[89] Case C-192/94 *El Corte Inglés*, paras 11–13. For detailed discussion, see, eg, J Stuyck, Case note (1996) 33 *CML Rev* 1261.

[90] Case C-192/94 *El Corte Inglés*, paras 15–17.

[91] Case C-192/94 *El Corte Inglés*, para 18.

[92] Case C-192/94 *El Corte Inglés*, para 19 (emphasis added).

[93] Case C-192/94 *El Corte Inglés*, paras 20, 23.

[94] Opinion of AG Lenz in Case C-192/94 *El Corte Inglés*, point 27.

[95] Opinion of AG Lenz in Case C-192/94 *El Corte Inglés*, point 27.

[96] Opinion of AG Lenz in Case C-192/94 *El Corte Inglés*, point 32.

[97] Opinion of AG Lenz in Case C-192/94 *El Corte Inglés*, point 32.

[98] Opinion of AG Lenz in Case C-192/94 *El Corte Inglés*, point 31.

internal market pursuant to Article 100a EC and the only divergence between the two provisions was that the former committed the Community to achieving a 'high level of consumer protection', whereas the latter placed only the Commission under such a duty.[99] This led him to conclude that no competence on the part of the Community to adopt measures binding on private persons, upon which the 'horizontal direct effect' of directives would depend, could be inferred from Article 129a EC and the insertion of this provision did not change the Court's case law in this regard.[100]

In 1997, *Germany v European Parliament and Council* ('*Deposit Guarantees*')[101] constituted the second major opportunity for the Court to address Article 169 TFEU, still in its Maastricht Treaty version as former Article 129a EC. In this case, Germany sought the annulment of Directive 94/19/EC[102] on deposit-guarantee schemes on various grounds, including that former Article 57(2) EC (now Article 53(2) TFEU) could not serve as the sole legal basis.[103] Germany contended the Directive should have also been based on what was then Article 235 EC (now Article 352 TFEU), reasoning that neither Article 100a EC (now Article 114 TFEU) nor Article 129a EC were applicable: Article 57 EC was the more specific provision vis-à-vis Article 100a EC, and although Article 129a EC concerned the protection of consumers as in the case of depositors at issue here, it did not empower the Community legislature to adopt measures, apart from those under Article 100a EC, falling within the scope of the legal instruments set forth in Article 189 EC (now Article 288 TFEU).[104] In its view, by authorizing 'specific action', Article 129(1)(b) EC only allowed the use of non-binding action plans and programmes, and the condition that this provision be used to support and supplement the policy pursued by the Member States was lacking because two Member States had not previously introduced a deposit-guarantee scheme.[105]

In its judgment, the Court upheld the use of Article 57(2) EC as the legal basis for the Directive, but made no mention of Article 129a EC, even if only to clarify whether Germany's arguments regarding the scope of this provision were correct.[106] Yet, the Court was more forthcoming in the context of one of Germany's alternative claims to annul a particular provision of the Directive on the ground that it was incompatible with the objective of ensuring a high level of consumer protection under Articles 3 and 129a EC.[107] In that regard, the Court held that 'no provision of the Treaty obliges the Community legislature to adopt the highest level of protection which can be found in a particular Member State'.[108] Although there may be a reduction in the level of

[99] Opinion of AG Lenz in Case C-192/94 *El Corte Inglés*, point 28. This was changed with the later revision of former Art 95(3) EC (now Art 114(3) TFEU): see n 38.

[100] Opinion of AG Lenz in Case C-192/94 *El Corte Inglés*, points 33, 36.

[101] Case C-233/94 *Germany v European Parliament and Council* ('*Deposit Guarantees*') [1997] ECR I-2405.

[102] Dir 94/19/EC of the European Parliament and of the Council of 30 May 1994 on deposit-guarantee schemes, [1994] OJ L135/5. For recent activities concerning the revision of this Directive, see the Commission's website, <http://ec.europa.eu/internal_market/bank/guarantee/index_en.htm>.

[103] See Case C-233/94 *Deposit Guarantees*, paras 1, 9, 30. For detailed discussion, see, eg, W-H Roth, Case note (1998) 35 *CML Rev* 459.

[104] Case C-233/94 *Deposit Guarantees*, paras 10–11.

[105] Opinion of AG Léger in Case C-233/94 *Deposit Guarantees*, points 55–56.

[106] Case C-233/94 *Deposit Guarantees*, paras 12–21.

[107] See Case C-233/94 *Deposit Guarantees*, paras 30, 33, 46–47.

[108] Case C-233/94 *Deposit Guarantees*, para 48. The Court did not discuss the fact that Art 129a EC did not (yet) contain a 'horizontal' clause and that Art 57 EC did not refer to a 'high level of consumer protection' akin to Art 100a(3) EC. Yet, this was not viewed as problematic by commentators, especially in light of changes brought by the Amsterdam Treaty. See further Roth, n 103, 472–473.

protection in certain cases via the application of the provision concerned, this did not call into question the general result which the Directive sought to achieve, namely the considerable improvement in depositor protection within the Community.[109] Ultimately, the Court dismissed Germany's case in full.

Unlike the Court's judgment, Advocate General Léger's Opinion in *Deposit Guarantees* delved into the applicability of Article 129a EC as a legal basis for the Directive concerned, thereby disputing Germany's assertions about the limited scope of this provision. First, he found that nothing in the text of Article 129a EC implied that its field of application was limited, since when the Community legislature's powers were limited to actions of a non-binding nature or harmonization was excluded in relation to a particular provision, this was explicitly stated in the Treaty, as in the case of the provisions on education, culture, and public health.[110] In addition, there was no indication that Community action under Article 129a EC must be linked to the policy of *each* Member State in a given sphere, but instead should 'be understood as describing specific action which supports and supplements the policy pursued by the Member States as a whole', as in the present proceedings concerning the protection of the economic interests of consumers.[111] Thus, it mattered little that some Member States had not yet introduced a deposit-guarantee scheme; it was 'enough that internally there is an overall policy undertaken to protect the interests of consumers, a fact of which there is no doubt' in the case.[112] Indeed, Community action in this area was confirmed by the fact that, as indicated in the Directive, the objective of ensuring consumer protection in the field of bank deposit guarantees had not yet been fully attained by action taken by the Member States.[113] Finally, he attributed significance to the fact that the decision-making procedures provided in Articles 57(2), 100a, and 129a EC were the same, which demonstrated that the areas covered by those provisions were, from an institutional perspective, of equal importance.[114] On that basis, he concluded that Article 129(1)(b) EC did allow for the adoption of binding provisions, and should a second legal basis be necessary for the Directive concerned, it would have to be that provision.[115]

In the years following these cases, the Court's jurisprudence came to be even more confined to the indirect relevance of Article 169 TFEU vis-à-vis measures based on other Treaty provisions.[116] Notable examples were the three companion cases concerning

Accordingly, the judgment foresaw consumer protection as a 'horizontal' matter before the explicit reference to such in the Treaties.

[109] Case C-233/94 *Deposit Guarantees*, paras 48–49.

[110] Opinion of AG Léger in Case C-233/94 *Deposit Guarantees*, point 57.

[111] Opinion of AG Léger in Case C-233/94 *Deposit Guarantees*, points 58–59 (emphasis added).

[112] Opinion of AG Léger in Case C-233/94 *Deposit Guarantees*, point 60.

[113] Opinion of AG Léger in Case C-233/94 *Deposit Guarantees*, point 61.

[114] Opinion of AG Léger in Case C-233/94 *Deposit Guarantees*, point 62.

[115] Opinion of AG Léger in Case C-233/94 *Deposit Guarantees*, point 64. In his later discussion of Germany's alternative claim concerning the incompatibility of a provision of the Directive with the objective of attaining 'a high level of consumer protection' enshrined in Arts 3(s) and 129a EC, AG Léger may have inadvertently confused matters by stating in reference to Art 129a EC that he did not consider this provision to constitute the legal basis for the Directive. See Opinion of AG Léger in Case C-233/94 *Deposit Guarantees*, point 108. Yet, looking at the context of these statements, he seemed to be making clear that consumer protection was not the main objective pursued by the Directive, and thus, this statement appears to dovetail with his previous assertions that Art 129(1)(b) EC was merely a secondary, not sole, legal basis of the Directive in relation to the Community's consumer protection objectives.

[116] There have been other cases mentioning what is now Art 169 TFEU (ex Art 153 EC, originally Art 129a EC), but they have yielded minimal results. See, eg, Case C-85/94 *Piageme and Others* [1995] ECR I-2955, para 19; Case C-259/95 *European Parliament v Council* [1997] ECR I-5303, paras 5, 23, 26; Case C-236/01 *Monsanto Agricoltura Italia and Others* [2003] ECR I-8105, paras 115–121; Case

the Product Liability Directive[117]—*Commission v France*,[118] *Commission v Greece*,[119] and *González Sánchez*[120]—decided by the Court in 2002. The crucial issue in those cases was the degree of harmonization established by this Directive, namely whether it provided for minimum harmonization so as to preserve the particular French, Greek, and Spanish legislation that laid down more stringent protection than what had been set forth in the Directive.[121] The Directive had been adopted in 1985 on the basis of what was originally Article 100 EEC (later Article 94 EC, now Article 115 TFEU).[122] Certain Member States sought to rely on the subsequent introduction of former Article 153 EC (now Article 169 TFEU) and its stipulation for minimum harmonization in Article 153(5) EC (now Article 169(4) TFEU) as support for interpreting the Directive in favour of minimum harmonization.[123]

This argument did not go over well with the Court or Advocate General Geelhoed. In line with the Advocate General's Opinion, the Court held that the competence retained by the Member States pursuant to Article 153(5) EC only concerned those measures adopted under indent (b), not those adopted pursuant to indent (a) in the context of Article 95 EC with which measures adopted under Article 94 EC must be equated.[124] Referring to the Advocate General's Opinion, the Court declared that Article 153 EC was worded in the form of an instruction addressed to the Community concerning future policy and did not permit the Member States autonomously, in light of the direct risk that it would pose to the *acquis communautaire*, to adopt measures contrary to the Community law contained in directives already adopted.[125] The Court then underscored that the margin of discretion left to the Member States must be assessed on the basis of the Directive, looking to its wording, purpose, and

C-479/04 *Laserdisken* [2006] ECR I-8089, paras 71–81; Opinion of AG Saggio in Case C-140/97 *Rechberger and Others* [1999] ECR I-3499, point 17 fn 7. But see Opinion of AG Ruiz-Jarabo Colomer in Case C-269/95 *Benincasa* [1997] ECR I-3767, point 47. It may also be the case that what is now Art 169 TFEU (ex Art 153 EC) is cited by the national court in its order for reference, but the Court rules on other grounds, thus not warranting discussion of that provision: see, eg, Case C-227/08 *Martín Martín* [2009] ECR I-11939; Case C-102/10 (Order of 28 Oct 2010) *Bejan* [2010] ECR I-139*, Summ pub, paras 47–53; Case C-315/08 (Order of 29 Sept 2011) *Grisoli* [2011] ECR I-139*, Summ pub; Case C-30/12 (Order of the President of 4 Oct 2012) *Marcinová*, not reported.

[117] Council Dir 85/374/EEC on the approximation of the laws, regulations and administrative provisions of the Member States concerning liability for defective products, [1985] OJ L210/29 (Product Liability Directive).

[118] Case C-52/00 *Commission v France* [2002] ECR I-3827.

[119] Case C-154/00 *Commission v Greece* [2002] ECR I-3879.

[120] Case C-183/00 *González Sánchez* [2002] ECR I-3901.

[121] See Case C-52/00 *Commission v France*, paras 1, 10–12; Case C-154/00 *Commission v Greece*, paras 6–8; Case C-183/00 *González Sánchez*, paras 6–13. See also Opinion of AG Geelhoed in Case C-52/00 *Commission v France* and Case C-183/00 *González Sánchez*, points 1, 22; Opinion of AG Geelhoed in Case C-154/00 *Commission v Greece*, point 3.

[122] See n 117.

[123] Case C-52/00 *Commission v France*, para 13; Case C-154/00 *Commission v Greece*, para 9; Opinion of AG Geelhoed in Case C-52/00 *Commission v France* and Case C-183/00 *González Sánchez*, points 31, 41.

[124] Case C-52/00 *Commission v France*, para 15; Case C-154/00 *Commission v Greece*, para 11; Case C-183/00 *González Sánchez*, para 24.

[125] Case C-52/00 *Commission v France*, para 15; Case C-154/00 *Commission v Greece*, para 11; Case C-183/00 *González Sánchez*, para 24. Compare Opinion of AG Geelhoed in Case C-52/00 *Commission v France* and Case C-183/00 *González Sánchez*, points 42–43. In particular, the AG opined that under former Art 153 EC, 'the Community legislature would be entitled to undertake initiatives to shift, in favour of consumers, the current balance between the interests of producers and those of consumers which is laid down in the Directive'. Opinion of AG Geelhoed in Case C-52/00 *Commission v France* and Case C-183/00 *González Sánchez*, point 43. Although the Court took up much of the AG's reasoning, it did not refer to this point.

structure,[126] thereby noting in relevant part that unlike the Unfair Contract Terms Directive, the Directive in question did not contain a minimum harmonization clause.[127] Ultimately, the Court concluded that the Product Liability Directive provided for complete harmonization,[128] which effectively precluded the national measures concerned.[129] As such, it was readily assumed by the Court, the Advocate General, and the parties involved that Article 153 EC preserved recourse to minimum harmonization for measures adopted under indent (b); it was the alleged cross-application to measures adopted under Articles 94 and 95 EC that was the problem.

Gintec[130] presented a similar case in which discussion of former Article 153 EC (now Article 169 TFEU) arose in relation to the interpretation of Directive 2001/83/EC on the Community code relating to medicinal products for human use,[131] based on former Article 95 EC (now Article 114 TFEU). Again, the heart of the case turned on the degree of harmonization involved, so as to determine whether German rules providing for more stringent protection in relation to the advertising of medicinal products were precluded by the Directive.[132] The Court ruled that the Directive provided for complete harmonization, with the result that Member States, such as Germany, could not derogate from or go further than what was provided therein.[133] More provocative was Advocate General Ruiz-Jarabo Colomer's Opinion, which seemed to glean further support for this finding from the text of Article 153 EC:

Under that article consumer protection is to be attained through approximation measures based on Article 95 EC, as well as through other measures which support, supplement and monitor

[126] Case C-52/00 *Commission v France*, para 16; Case C-154/00 *Commission v Greece*, para 12; Case C-183/00 *González Sánchez*, para 25.

[127] Case C-52/00 *Commission v France*, para 18; Case C-154/00 *Commission v Greece*, para 14; Case C-183/00 *González Sánchez*, para 27.

[128] Case C-52/00 *Commission v France*, para 24; Case C-154/00 *Commission v Greece*, para 20; Case C-183/00 *González Sánchez*, para 30. The Court and the AG either explicitly or implicitly recognized that these cases concerned the degree of harmonization involved. See, eg, Case C-52/00 *Commission v France*, heading above para 13; Case C-154/00 *Commission v Greece*, heading above para 9; Case C-183/00 *González Sánchez*, paras 24, 33; Opinion of AG Geelhoed in Case C-52/00 *Commission v France* and Case C-183/00 *González Sánchez*, point 22; Opinion of AG Geelhoed in Case C-154/00 *Commission v Greece*, point 3. Aspects concerning the scope of the Directive were also in play. See, eg, Case C-154/00 *Commission v Greece*, points 22–24; Opinion of AG Geelhoed in Case C-52/00 *Commission v France* and Case C-183/00 *González Sánchez*, point 22. This may explain why neither the Court nor the AG employed the term 'maximum' harmonization. Instead, the Court preferred the term 'complete' harmonization. By comparison, the AG used the terms 'total', 'complete', and 'exhaustive' harmonization interchangeably: see Opinion of AG Geelhoed in Case C-52/00 *Commission v France* and Case C-183/00 *González Sánchez*, points 1, 22, 45, 47, 56, 63; Opinion of AG Geelhoed in Case C-154/00 *Commission v Greece*, points 3, 5. See further Chapter 1, § 1.2.3.2.

[129] Case C-52/00 *Commission v France*, para 49; Case C-154/00 *Commission v Greece*, para 34; Case C-183/00 *González Sánchez*, para 34. Procedurally, *Commission v France* and *Commission v Greece* were infringement actions, with the result that the Court found that the national legislation was incompatible with the Directive and that the Member States concerned failed to fulfil their obligations under the Treaties; as regards the former case, this led to a subsequent ruling under ex Art 228 EC (now Art 260 TFEU) ordering France to pay a penalty payment for its non-compliance with the Court's judgment: Case C-177/04 *Commission v France* [2006] ECR I-2461. *González Sánchez* concerned a preliminary ruling on the interpretation of the Directive, with the result that the Court's ruling, albeit indirectly, dictated whether the relevant Spanish provisions were compatible with the Directive.

[130] Case C-374/05 *Gintec International Import-Export* [2007] ECR I-9517.

[131] Dir 2001/83/EC of the European Parliament and of the Council of 6 Nov 2001 on the Community code relating to medicinal products for human use, [2001] OJ L311/67.

[132] Case C-374/05 *Gintec*, para 17.

[133] Case C-374/05 *Gintec*, paras 19–39. Technically, the Court referred to both 'complete' and 'exhaustive' harmonization: see paras 18, 20, 25, 27, 29, 34, 39, 63. The AG used the terms 'full', 'maximum', 'complete', and 'exhaustive' harmonization: see Opinion of AG Ruiz-Jarabo Colomer in Case C-374/05 *Gintec*, points 29, 31, 33, 47, 81; caption A. See further Chapter 1, § 1.2.3.2.

the policies of the Member States (Article 153(3)), adopted by the Council in accordance with Article 251 EC (Article 153(4)). Thus, national initiatives giving a higher level of protection are authorised *only* under the second limb, from which it can be concluded that the harmonisation under Article 95 EC is maximum harmonisation apart from the exceptions provided for by that provision.[134]

Read at face value, the Advocate General's statements were quite far-reaching, since he appeared to infer from the dual route provided by Article 153 EC that minimum harmonization was required only for measures adopted under indent (b), thereby predicating the use of maximum harmonization for measures adopted under indent (a) via Article 95 EC. He did not explain how to reconcile this position with the Court's case law mandating a case-by-case approach on the basis of the wording, purpose, and structure of the particular measure concerned, as highlighted by the previous judgments. Given the technical subject of the harmonized rules at issue (that of medicinal products for human use) and prior case law in the field,[135] however, it may be wondered whether the Advocate General's statements were meant to be confined to the context at hand. In any event, the Court did not take up the Advocate General's reasoning or cite Article 153 EC in its judgment.

Ironically, an important case bearing on the scope of Article 169 TFEU never mentioned Article 169 TFEU itself: *Tobacco Advertising I*.[136] To recall from Chapter 8, the Court ruled in *Tobacco Advertising I* and several cases thereafter that what is now Article 114 TFEU (ex Article 95 EC) is a proper legal basis for a Union measure even if public health protection is a 'decisive factor' in the choices to be made, provided that the requirements for recourse to that Treaty provision are satisfied.[137] The Court's rationale in that case was underpinned by Article 114(3) TFEU (ex Article 95(3) EC), stipulating a 'high level' of public health protection for measures based on Article 114 TFEU, and by the 'horizontal' provision set forth in Article 168 TFEU (ex Article 152 EC) ensuring that public health requirements are taken into account in relation to other Union policies. Admittedly, Article 169 TFEU was not at issue in this case and not explicitly referred to therein. Nevertheless, *Tobacco Advertising I* laid the basis for an analogous reading of Article 114 TFEU vis-à-vis Article 169 TFEU, as was done in relation to Article 168 TFEU. In fact, arguments supporting such a reading appeared even stronger in the case of Article 169 TFEU, given the reference to consumer protection in Article 114(3) TFEU and the 'horizontal' provision of Article 12 TFEU, as well as the express *renvoi* to Article 114 TFEU via indent (a) of Article 169(2) TFEU, without any such express preclusion of harmonization in its text.

Several years later, in *Vodafone*, the Court did just this, reasoning by analogy from *Tobacco Advertising I* and related case law that 'provided that the conditions for recourse to Article [114 TFEU] are fulfilled, the [Union] legislature cannot be prevented from relying on that legal basis on the ground that consumer protection is a decisive factor in the choices to be made'.[138] As such, the *Tobacco Advertising I* case law strongly argues for the use of Article 114 TFEU under circumstances where consumer protection

[134] Opinion of AG Ruiz-Jarabo Colomer in Case C-374/05 *Gintec*, point 29 (emphasis added).

[135] See Case C-374/05 *Gintec*, para 26.

[136] Case C-376/98 *Germany v European Parliament and Council* ('*Tobacco Advertising I*') [2000] ECR I-8419.

[137] Case C-376/98 *Tobacco Advertising I*, para 88. See further Chapter 8, § 8.3.2.1.

[138] Case C-58/08 *Vodafone and Others* [2010] ECR I-4999, para 36.

objectives are taken into account as part of the achievement of the Union's internal market objectives in a particular Union measure in line with Article 114(3) TFEU and Article 12 TFEU, leaving indent (b) of Article 169(2) TFEU for the adoption of Union measures that are rooted in the achievement of the Union's consumer protection objectives *sensu stricto* separate from those relating to the internal market.

Taking the foregoing case law into account, further jurisprudence on Article 169 TFEU is sorely needed. Notably, the two principal cases dealing with Article 169 TFEU so far—*El Corte Inglés* and *Deposit Guarantees*—were both decided over a decade ago and concerned the old version of Article 169 TFEU under the Maastricht Treaty before its substantial revision in the Amsterdam Treaty, which constituted the basis for the reframing of Article 153 EC as Article 169 TFEU in the Lisbon Treaty. Indeed, Advocate General Lenz's assertion in his Opinion in *El Corte Inglés* that what was then Article 129a EC was limited to non-binding measures has been superseded by later cases in which the use of what is now Article 169 TFEU to adopt minimum harmonization measures has been readily acknowledged. Moreover, it is commonly missed that the Court's consideration of former Article 129a EC as 'limited' in *El Corte Inglés* was tied to the specific context of that case in relation to its impact on previous jurisprudence on the 'horizontal direct effect' of directives; the Court's assessment of the Union's competence under Article 169 TFEU in and of itself remains to be seen.

In any event, a common theme running through the cases discussed above is the recognition of two routes enshrined in Article 169 TFEU concerning measures adopted under indent (b) of Article 169(2) TFEU relating to the achievement of the Union's consumer protection objectives, on the one hand, and measures adopted under Article 114 TFEU via indent (a) of Article 169(2) TFEU that incorporate the Union's consumer protection objectives within the internal market programme, on the other. This is strongly evidenced by the Court's express language (echoed by Advocate General Lenz) in *El Corte Inglés* that measures under indent (b) are taken 'apart' from those relating to the internal market under indent (a). Arguably, this also emanates, albeit implicitly, to some extent from the Court's *Tobacco Advertising I* case law. Furthermore, while the language of indent (a) in reference to measures adopted under Article 114 TFEU 'in the context of the completion of the internal market' is not identical to what is found in the text of Article 114(1) TFEU as regards measures having as 'their object the establishment and functioning of the internal market', this discrepancy does not seem to have bothered the Court of Justice or the Advocates General, and it seems to be generally assumed that the two refer to the same thing, regardless of the failed attempt to align them in the Draft Constitutional Treaty.[139] In other words, such measures are adopted under Article 114 TFEU and must satisfy the requirements set down in the case law as regards that provision. In fact, this is supported by the various language versions of indent (a) of Article 169(2) TFEU, which demonstrate that 'in the context of the completion of the internal market' is not meant to diverge from the text of Article 114(1), but instead to imply that such measures are situated within the overall context of the realization or the achievement of the internal market, thereby reconciling the two.[140]

[139] See n 76 and accompanying text.

[140] See, eg, Dutch version ('maatregelen die zij op grond van artikel 114 in *het kader van de totstandbrenging* van de interne markt neemt'); French version ('des mesures qu'elle adopte en application de l'article 114 dans le cadre de la *réalisation* du marché interieur'); German version ('Maßnahmen, die sie im Rahmen der *Verwirklichung* des Binnenmarkts nach Artikel 114 erlässt'); Italian version ('misure adottate a norma dell'articolo 114 nel quadro della *realizzazione* del mercato interno'); Spanish version ('medidas que adopte en virtud del artículo 114 en el marco de la *realización* del mercado interior') (emphasis added).

9.2.3 Usage: Theory versus practice and proposals for change

As things stand at present, there is a striking paradox underlying the use of Article 169 TFEU by the Union institutions: while there is a steady stream of institutional documents extolling the importance of Article 169 TFEU and encouraging greater recourse to this provision in theory, Article 169 TFEU is rarely resorted to in practice. To date, the number of measures based on Article 169 TFEU (or its predecessor in the former EC Treaty) is few, and after isolating those measures adopted pursuant to indent (b) of what is now Article 169(2) TFEU, as opposed to Article 169 TFEU more generally,[141] the number becomes even smaller. As a result, Article 169 TFEU has attracted more than its fair share of proposals to entice the institutions to its use. Each of these aspects—theory, practice, and proposals for change—are evaluated in turn.

9.2.3.1 Theory

Following the early programmes mentioned above, what was then Community (now Union) consumer policy continued to advance by virtue of a successive stream of action plans and communications disseminated by the Commission, which in turn led to documents issued by the other EU institutions and bodies. As examined below, many of these institutional documents contained fruitful discussion of what is now Article 169 TFEU, often in conjunction with the principle of subsidiarity, at the same time that they ingrained EU consumer contract law within the internal market programme.

In 1990, the Commission published the First Three-Year Action Plan of Consumer Policy for the years 1990 to 1992.[142] The Action Plan identified four main areas of focus concerning consumer representation, consumer information, consumer safety, and consumer transactions, in view of 'their importance in building the consumer confidence necessary to support the implementation of the internal market'.[143] In the section on consumer transactions, the Commission devoted attention to the field of consumer contract law, explaining that:

> The differences in conditions of sale in contracts across the twelve Member States are such as to inhibit consumers from purchasing significant items or services away from his or her place of residence. The risks involved in so doing, without hiring a lawyer to guide and advise on the purchase, will be formidable. Most prudent consumers will not take such risks. With each Member State having a different legal system, complicated additionally by nine Community languages, the inability of citizens to confidently cope with such complexities will inhibit purchasing across frontiers.[144]

[141] Recourse to Art 169 TFEU generally has been made for institutional matters relating to EU consumer policy. Eg, measures establishing the general framework and financing for Union (ex Community) action in consumer policy for a certain period of years starting in 1999 to the present have been based on Art 169 TFEU (ex Art 153 EC), of which the most recently adopted is Reg (EU) No 254/2014 of the European Parliament and of the Council of 26 Feb 2014 on a multiannual consumer programme for the years 2014–20 and repealing Dec No 1926/2006/EC, [2014] OJ L84/42. Art 169 TFEU has also been included alongside other legal bases in relation to the adoption of Union measures that are linked to or otherwise incorporate EU consumer policy in some way, eg, as regards measures relating to the conclusion of framework agreements with third States involving the application of Union programmes (see, eg, with respect to Moldova, Council Dec 2011/283/EU, [2011] OJ L131/1), or measures relating to the composition of certain committees involved in the EU decision-making process (see, eg, Commission Dec 2010/309/EU, [2010] OJ L138/24, based on Arts 168 and 169 TFEU).

[142] First Three-Year Action Plan, n 32.

[143] First Three-Year Action Plan, n 32, point B, second para, at 5.

[144] First Three-Year Action Plan, n 32, point 4(i), at 14.

On this basis, the Commission found it necessary to identify the elements in the contract laws of the Member States that were likely to inhibit consumer purchasing, as in the case of unbalanced and potentially damaging contract terms that were often not expected by consumers.[145] In addition, 'consideration must be given to whether, in the internal market, it might not be helpful to both producers and consumers alike to construct a model set of contract conditions (ie a sale of goods act) as part of the appraisal of civil law in the Community', which would include guarantees and warranties available on a uniform basis across the whole internal market.[146] The section ended with a list of actions to be taken in this field, which included proposals for directives concerning unfair contract terms and distance selling, and possible initiatives to simplify cross-frontier consumer contracts, guarantees, and after sales service.[147]

In the aftermath of this Action Plan, the European Parliament adopted a Resolution on the consumer protection and health requirements to be taken into account in the completion of the internal market.[148] The first recital called attention to the Maastricht Treaty's introduction of Article 129a EC, which created 'a separate, well-defined Community competence in the field of consumer protection legislation'.[149] In the accompanying Report, it was stressed that European consumer protection resembled a 'patchwork quilt' in part because the original 1957 Treaties of Rome contained no suitable legal basis for the legislation that rapidly became necessary, and thus, such a legal basis must be created for consumer protection in the forthcoming Treaty revision, which could give a boost to its importance.[150] A few months later, the Council adopted a Resolution on future priorities for the development of consumer protection policy,[151] which was prompted by the fact that the Commission's First Action Plan had not yet been fully realized.[152] It invited the Commission, among other things, to adopt measures as soon as possible to create consumer confidence in the single market, particularly in the context of the protection of consumers' economic interests, and to adopt another action plan to develop Community consumer policy in the coming years.[153]

In response, in 1993, the Commission published the Second Three-Year Action Plan on Consumer Policy for the years 1993 to 1995, which was titled 'Placing the single market at the service of European consumers'.[154] It was introduced as belonging in the context of the implementation of the Maastricht Treaty, since that Treaty 'raised consumer protection to the rank of a genuine Community policy', as illustrated by former Articles 3(s) and 129a EC, both of which were cited in full.[155] The Commission proclaimed: 'By conferring on the Community competences which are

[145] First Three-Year Action Plan, n 32, point 4(ii), at 15.

[146] First Three-Year Action Plan, n 32, point 4(iii), at 15.

[147] First Three-Year Action Plan, n 32, 16, 19.

[148] European Parliament Resolution of 11 March 1992 on the consumer protection and public health requirements to be taken into account in the completion of the internal market, [1992] OJ C94/217.

[149] European Parliament Resolution, n 148, recital A.

[150] Report on the consumer protection and public health requirements to be taken into account in the completion of the internal market, A3-0060/92, dated 6 Feb 1992, point III, at 12.

[151] Council Resolution of 13 July 1992 on future priorities for the development of consumer protection policy, [1992] OJ C186/1.

[152] Council Resolution, n 151, sixth indent.

[153] Council Resolution, n 151, points 1–2.

[154] Commission Communication, Second Three-Year Action Plan on Consumer Policy 1993–1995—Placing the single market at the service of European consumers, COM (93) 378 final, 28.7.1993 (Second Three-Year Action Plan).

[155] Second Three-Year Action Plan, n 154, point 10. As regards ex Art 3(s) EC (later Art 3(t) EC), see n 41 and accompanying text.

both wider and better defined in this area, the Maastricht Treaty opens up a new domain of Community action' and it 'intends to exploit the full potential of the new provisions'.[156] It added that this would be done with due account of the principle of subsidiarity 'interpreted in a positive manner, ie in such a way as to ensure that an optimum result is obtained by Community action'.[157]

This Action Plan focused on two basic approaches: first, consolidation of Community legislation; and secondly, selective priorities to raise the level of consumer protection and to make consumers more aware of their rights.[158] As for the former, the Commission reasoned that in order to place the internal market at the service of consumers and to prepare for the implementation of the Maastricht Treaty, the existing *acquis* must be consolidated by ensuring the implementation of the measures in force and the adoption of proposals on which the Council has not yet reached agreement and by preparing new proposals.[159] In this regard, the Commission cited several measures within the 'hard core' of the EU contract law *acquis*, including the Package Travel, Consumer Credit, Unfair Contract Terms, Distance Selling, and Timeshare Directives.[160]

In 1995, the Commission issued the Third Three-Year Consumer Policy Action Plan for the years 1996 to 1998, which was titled 'Priorities for Consumer Policy'.[161] The Commission explained that while it remained necessary to complete the work envisaged by the previous action plans, it was important at this stage 'to face up to other questions and problems which confront consumers, building on what has been achieved but which are not exclusively linked to the Internal Market'.[162] It then referred to former Article 129a EC:

> The insertion of Article 129A into the Treaty clearly requires the European Community to deal with a broad range of consumer issues, not just those related to the Internal Market project. This obligation implies careful consideration of subsidiarity at all stages so that appropriate solutions vis-à-vis Member States are adopted.[163]

This led the Commission to list ten priorities for action, some of which focused on the Community realm, such as improving consumer education, information, and representation, and others manifesting broader considerations, such as assisting the development of consumer policy in third countries.[164]

This Action Plan was well received by the other EU institutions and bodies.[165] Yet, the EESC emphasized that it would be useful to know the Commission's judgment on

[156] Second Three-Year Action Plan, n 154, point 10.

[157] Second Three-Year Action Plan, n 154, point 10.

[158] Second Three-Year Action Plan, n 154, point 11.

[159] Second Three-Year Action Plan, n 154, point 12. As regards the latter, the Commission focused on consumer information and representation and carved out two additional fields warranting particular attention: access to justice and financial services: see points 24–43.

[160] Second Three-Year Action Plan, n 154, point 14.

[161] Commission Communication, Priorities for Consumer Policy 1996–1998, COM (95) 519 final, 31.10.1995 (Third Three-Year Action Plan). While not explicitly called as such, this Communication effectively constituted the third three-year Community action programme on consumer policy.

[162] Third Three-Year Action Plan, n 161, 1–2.

[163] Third Three-Year Action Plan, n 161, 1–2; see also point 1, at 3 ('Questions raised are, since the introduction of Article 129a, broader than the Internal Market dimension').

[164] See Third Three-Year Action Plan, n 161, 4.

[165] The Council's conclusions on the Communication, which were made during the session which took place on 23 April 1996, are unavailable for access; however, thereafter, the Council mentioned the Communication in its Resolution of 19 Jan 1999 on the Consumer Dimension of the Information Society, [1999] OJ C23/1.

the functioning of Article 129a EC[166] and its choice of priorities to be taken from the point of view of subsidiarity, that is to say, where does the Commission aim at proposing harmonized solutions and where does it intend to leave Member States a framework, or other instruments, to help them find solutions?[167] Similarly, the Committee of the Regions (CoR) stressed that Article 129a EC should be strengthened and clarified, with a view to improving consumer rights and recognizing consumer policy as an independent policy area, but it agreed with the Commission's view that this provision required the Community to deal with other consumer issues beyond those affecting the internal market.[168] In its Resolution, the European Parliament paid particular attention to the role played by the principle of subsidiarity, stating that 'the priority objectives and measures of a European consumer policy, particularly in view of the consequences of the single market for the consumer, can be attained more successfully at Community level than at Member State level' and cautioning that this principle 'must not be abused to prevent action in the interest of Europe's consumers'.[169]

By the time of the Commission's Fourth Three-Year Consumer Policy Action Plan for the years 1999 to 2001[170], issued at the end of 1998, the Amsterdam Treaty was undergoing ratification in the Member States, which prompted even greater attention being placed on what was then Article 153 EC.[171] The Commission carved out discussion of Article 153 EC in a special box titled 'The Treaty of Amsterdam', stressing that this provision 'confirms that consumer policy is an area where the EU can really add value' and 'enhances the capacity of the EU to discharge its responsibilities in this area'.[172] It then evaluated each paragraph of Article 153 EC, although as regards the Community's competence under Article 153(3) EC, the Commission merely stated that this paragraph provided for 'legislative and other measures' to be adopted either in the context of the internal market, on the basis of Article 95 EC, or 'which support, supplement and monitor the policy pursued by the Member States' under Article 153(3)(b) EC.[173] After citing other provisions relevant to consumer policy,[174] it acknowledged that the EC Treaty did not spell out the priorities for action and the measures to be taken. On that basis, it opined: 'If the Treaty does not include a detailed road map, the main tasks for consumer policy set out in Article 153 are an effective compass'.[175]

Emphasis on former Article 153 EC also ran through the responses of the EU institutions and bodies to this Action Plan. In particular, the European Parliament

166 EESC Opinion on the Third Three-Year Action Plan, [1996] OJ C295/64, point 1.3.

167 EESC Opinion, n 166, point 1.6.

168 CoR Opinion on the Third Three-Year Action Plan, [1996] OJ C337/49, point 1.1.2.

169 European Parliament Resolution of 20 Feb 1997 on the Third Three-Year Action Plan, [1997] OJ C85/133, point 4. In the accompanying Report, it was further emphasized that Art 129a EC 'established a basis on which to build a consumer policy independent of that designed to complete the internal market' and given the fact that it has been used only twice, that it would be useful, particularly in the context of the IGC, to consider how it 'could be exploited to the full benefit of Europe's consumers'. Report on the Third Three-Year Action Plan, A4-0317/96, dated 11 Oct 1996, section ('The Need for Consolidation'), second para.

170 Commission Communication, Consumer Policy Action Plan 1999–2001, COM (1998) 696 final, 1.12.1998 (Fourth Three-Year Action Plan).

171 The Amsterdam Treaty was signed on 2 Oct 1997 and entered into force on 1 May 1999.

172 Fourth Three-Year Action Plan, n 170, point 2, at 6.

173 Fourth Three-Year Action Plan, n 170, point 2, at 6.

174 Fourth Three-Year Action Plan, n 170, point 2, at 6 (ie ex Arts 28, 65, and 152 EC (now Arts 34, 81, 168 TFEU)).

175 Fourth Three-Year Action Plan, n 170, point 2, at 6. These tasks were summed up as: (1) a more powerful voice for the consumer throughout the EU; (2) a high level of health and safety for EU consumers; and (3) full respect for the economic interests of EU consumers. They dictated the structure for the remaining body of the Action Plan.

called on the Commission to employ Article 153 EC more consistently as the legal basis in the development of EU consumer policy.[176] Likewise, the EESC stressed that the Amsterdam Treaty had expanded the scope for an effective consumer policy, and while the need for a high level of consumer protection continued to be the basic requirement, it was now stipulated in Article 153 EC that account had to be taken of consumer protection in other policy areas.[177] The Council was more cautious, noting that Community consumer policy must respect the principles of subsidiarity and proportionality and, without citing Article 153 EC explicitly, reiterated its 'supporting and supplementing' language and its stipulation of minimum harmonization.[178] Taking a similar tone, the CoR opined that under Article 153 EC, the EU is enjoined merely to 'contribute' to this objective[179] and Community action must be in accordance with the principles of subsidiarity and proportionality.[180] That said, it stressed the need to forge ahead with the approximation of European consumer protection law, albeit on the basis of minimum standards as predicated by the Treaty, and backed 'moves to standardise rights in the consumer protection directives', finding that it 'makes sense, for example, to harmonise the different withdrawal rights and deadlines, to have standard definitions of consumers and enterprises and to develop a standard form of words in an international private law clause'.[181]

Through the present decade, references to Article 169 TFEU (ex Article 153 EC) continue to filter through EU consumer policy documents right alongside Article 114 TFEU (ex Article 95 EC), leaving some pregnant pauses as regards the relationship between the two provisions. For example, in the 2001 Green Paper on EU Consumer Protection,[182] the Commission noted that former Article 153 EC enshrined a number of consumer rights but that the consumer protection directives 'usually' based on former Article 95 EC have fleshed out the detail of some of these rights.[183] It also aired its perceptions of the 'monitoring' language in former Article 153 EC, which was linked to the internal market programme:

> A fully functioning consumer internal market depends on enforcement that is more or less equally effective in all Member States. Article 153 of the EC Treaty was amended by the Treaty of Amsterdam to clarify the Commission's role as monitor of the effectiveness of national policies. At present there is no framework for the Commission to carry out this monitoring role and help to improve enforcement standards across the internal market. The need for the Commission to play this supportive role will increase with enlargement, and the accession of countries without a long history of consumer protection enforcement.[184]

The following year, in its 2002 Communication on the Consumer Policy Strategy for the years 2002 to 2006,[185] the Commission highlighted various principles underlying

[176] European Parliament Resolution of 4 May 1999 on the Fourth Three-Year Action Plan, [1999] OJ C279/84, point 10.

[177] EESC Opinion, n 2, point 2.2.

[178] Council Resolution of 28 June 1999 on Community consumer policy 1999 to 2001, [1999] OJ C206/1, point 6.

[179] CoR Opinion on the Fourth Three-Year Action Plan, [2000] OJ C57/74, point 3.4.

[180] CoR Opinion, n 179, point 3.6.

[181] CoR Opinion, n 179, points 5.3, 5.7.

[182] Green Paper on EU Consumer Protection, COM (2001) 531 final, 2.10.2001.

[183] Green Paper, n 182, point 2.1, second para.

[184] Green Paper, n 182, point 5.1, eighth bullet point, at 18. See further Commission Communication on the enforcement of the consumer acquis, COM (2009) 330 final, 2.7.2009, point 2.3; compare, in this regard, the EESC Opinion on this Communication, [2011] OJ C18/100, point 4.2; European Parliament Resolution of 9 March 2010 on consumer protection, [2010] OJ C349E/1, point 40.

[185] Commission Communication, Consumer Policy Strategy 2002–2006, COM (2002) 208 final, 7.5.2002.

Community consumer policy, namely those relating to consumer representation, consumer confidence in shopping across borders, and integration of consumer concerns in other Community policies, which were enshrined in former Articles 153 and 95 EC,[186] though without providing any clarification between the two. In its response, the European Parliament stressed that Article 153 EC had only been used once as a legal basis for consumer protection legislation and asked the Commission to reflect on ways of ensuring its greater use.[187] In doing so, the Parliament called for legislation to be drafted on the legal basis provided by Articles 95 and 153 EC.[188]

More recently, Article 169 TFEU came to the fore in the context of the Commission's 2007 Communication on the EU Consumer Policy Strategy for the years 2007 to 2013.[189] Previously, in 2005, the Commission had issued a Communication on a joint Public Health and Consumer Protection Strategy,[190] taking the view that in light of the synergy between these two policy fields, they should be joined together into one action programme.[191] This was much to the consternation of the other EU institutions and bodies.[192] In particular, the EESC and the CoR stressed that, in contrast to public health policy, EU consumer policy was largely subject to a 'common approach', with a view to promoting consumers' rights and protecting their interests, especially where this concerned the completion of the internal market.[193] In the CoR's view, bringing consumer protection policy into line with the strict complementarity and subsidiarity criteria of public health policy could have an adverse effect on the EU's consumer protection competence.[194] Ultimately, the Commission separated the two policy fields, which led to the abovementioned Communication.[195] Yet, in the accompanying Impact Assessment, Article 169 TFEU (ex Article 153 EC) was cited as part of the discussion concerning the need to enhance cross-border transactions in the internal market, thereby noticeably blurring with Article 114 TFEU (ex Article 95 EC).[196]

9.2.3.2 Practice

In 1993, in the wake of the introduction of Article 129a EC into the Maastricht Treaty, Professors Hans-W Micklitz and Stephen Weatherill opined: 'The practical test of the

[186] Communication, n 185, point 2.1.

[187] European Parliament Resolution of 13 March 2003 on the Communication, n 185, [2003] OJ C61E/401, point 16.

[188] European Parliament Resolution, n 187, point 15.

[189] Commission Communication, EU Consumer Policy Strategy 2007–2013—*Empowering consumers, enhancing their welfare, effectively protecting them*, COM (2007) 99 final, 13.3.2007. It has been superseded by the Commission Communication, A European Consumer Agenda—Boosting confidence and growth, COM (2012) 225 final, 22.5.2012, which does not cite Art 169 TFEU, but for its mention of the proposed CESL, see n 268. See also n 141.

[190] Commission Communication, Healthier, safer, more confident citizens: a Health and Consumer Protection Strategy/Proposal for a Decision of the European Parliament and of the Council establishing a Programme of Community action in the field of Health and Consumer Protection 2007–2013, COM (2005) 15 final, 6.4.2005.

[191] See Communication, n 190, point 1.2.

[192] See Amended proposal for a Decision of the European Parliament and of the Council establishing a Programme of Community action in the field of consumer policy (2007–2013), COM (2006) 235 final, 24.5.2006, point 1.

[193] CoR Opinion on the Communication and Proposal, n 190, [2006] OJ C192/8, point 1.10; EESC Opinion on the Proposal, n 190, [2006] OJ C88/1, point 3.1.1.

[194] CoR Opinion, n 193, point 1.10.

[195] See n 189.

[196] Commission Staff Working Document, Summary of the Impact Assessment, SEC (2007) 322, 13.3.2007, 2.

impact of Article 129a as a basis for increasing the profile of formal Community action will be measurable only some years in the future by reference to the list of measures adopted under it'.[197] By that standard, the impact of Article 169 TFEU has been low, given the number of measures enacted pursuant to the Union's competence under Article 169(2)(b) TFEU (ex Article 153(3)(b) EC) via the decision-making procedures set down in Article 169(3) TFEU (ex Article 153(4) EC).

The most well-known measure to date is Directive 98/6/EC on consumer protection in the indication of the prices of products offered to consumers,[198] often referred to as the Unit Pricing or Price Indication Directive, which was included as part of the Commission's review of the consumer *acquis*. It was adopted under Article 129a(2) EC, the Maastricht version of former Article 153(4) EC, now Article 169(3) TFEU. While the reference to the internal market appears in certain recitals,[199] the Directive is rooted in the primary objective to ensure a high level of consumer protection by taking 'specific action' supporting and supplementing the policy of the Member States regarding precise, transparent, and unambiguous information for consumers on the prices of products offered to them.[200] No distinction is made as regards consumer products sold cross-border, meaning that it applies to cross-border and domestic situations. While the Directive does not state explicitly whether it harmonizes the laws of the Member States,[201] it seems to be readily considered to be a (minimum) harmonization measure.[202] It sets forth a set of common rules regarding the prices of products, albeit leaving certain options to the Member States.[203] It also contains an explicit minimum harmonization clause along the lines of Article 169(4) TFEU.[204] To the author's knowledge, it is the only directive based on the Union's competence under what is now Article 169 TFEU/Article 169(2)(b) TFEU, and as yet, there have been no regulations adopted pursuant to this provision.

There have been a few decisions, however. Decision No 3092/94/EC introducing a Community system of information on home and leisure accidents (referred to as EHLASS) was adopted under Article 129a(2) EC (later Article 153(4) EC, now

[197] Micklitz and Weatherill, n 14, 299.

[198] Dir 98/6/EC of the European Parliament and of the Council of 16 Feb 1998 on consumer protection in the indication of the prices of products offered to consumers, [1998] OJ L80/27 (Price Indication Directive).

[199] Price Indication Directive, n 198, first, twelfth recitals.

[200] Price Indication Directive, n 198, second recital; Art 1.

[201] The Directive states rather ambiguously that Community (now Union)-level rules can ensure homogeneous and transparent information that will benefit all consumers in the context of the internal market. See Price Indication Directive, n 198, twelfth recital.

[202] See, eg, H Schulte-Nölke et al (eds), *EC Consumer Law Compendium—Comparative Analysis* (Version of Feb 2008), available at <http://ec.europa.eu/consumers/rights/docs/consumer_law_compendium_comparative_analysis_en_final.pdf> (Consumer Law Compendium), 581; K Boele-Woelki and RH van Ooik, 'The Communitarization of Private International Law' (2002) 5 *YPIL* 1, 15–16. Compare M Radeideh, *Fair Trading in EC Law: Information and Consumer Choice in the Internal Market* (Europa, 2005) 122–123.

[203] For detailed discussion, see Consumer Law Compendium, n 202, 581–608.

[204] Price Indication Directive, n 198, Art 10. See, eg, Opinion of AG Trstenjak in Case C-540/08 *Mediaprint Zeitungs- und Zeitschriftenverlag* [2010] ECR I-10909, point 64 fn 44. This provision has hardly been used and prompted questions by the Commission as part of a public consultation on the Directive as to whether it should be retained or replaced with a 'fully harmonised regime'. Commission Communication on the implementation of Dir 1998/6/EC[sic], COM (2006) 325 final, 21.6.2006, 11, 13–14. The Commission's summary of the responses indicated support for retaining minimum harmonization. See Commission Working Document, Summary of Responses to the Consultation of the Price Indication Directive (COM (2006) 325 final), available at <http://ec.europa.eu/justice/consumer-marketing/unfair-trade/price/index_en.htm>, 7.

Article 169(3) TFEU).[205] As explained in the Preamble, in view of the increasing circulation of consumer products in the framework of the internal market, it was considered necessary for the Community to take 'specific action' concerning the identification of the products involved in home and leisure accidents, and this would provide national authorities with 'sufficiently homogeneous instruments' so that the information documented in one Member State could be used in other Member States and at the European level.[206] Therefore, for the period of 1994 to 1997, a Community system of information on home and leisure accidents was set up, with the objective to collect data with a view to promoting accident prevention, improving the safety of consumer products, and informing and educating consumers so that they could make better use of products at the national and European levels.[207] When the specified time period expired, the EHLASS system was extended by way of Decision No 372/1999/EC, which was adopted under former Article 129(4) EC concerning public health policy (corresponding to what is now Article 168(4) TFEU).[208]

Decision No 276/1999/EC establishing a multiannual Community action plan on promoting safer use of the Internet by combating illegal and harmful content on global networks was also adopted under former Article 129a(2) EC (later Article 153(4) EC, now Article 169(3) TFEU).[209] As the Preamble indicated, 'specific action' by the Community supporting and supplementing the policy pursued by the Member States was needed in order to provide information for consumers on the safer use of the Internet.[210] To carry this out, the Decision set forth various courses of action to be taken under the guidance of the Commission, for example, promoting industry self-regulation and monitoring schemes, encouraging industry to provide filtering tools and rating systems for children, and fostering cooperation and exchange of best practices at the European and international levels.[211] Incidentally, the use of Article 129a(2) EC as the legal basis for this Decision had not been envisaged in the Commission's proposal, but was later proposed by the European Parliament in the decision-making process.[212] The Decision initially covered a four-year

[205] Dec No 3092/94/EC of the European Parliament and of the Council of 7 Dec 1994 introducing a Community system of information on home and leisure accidents, [1994] OJ L331/1, amended by Council Dec No 95/184/EC, [1995] OJ L120/36 (the acronym EHLASS stands for European Home and Leisure Accident Surveillance System). It was the subject of an annulment action involving the constitutionality of the legal basis of certain implementing measures, not the legal basis of the Decision itself. See Case C-259/95 *European Parliament v Council* [1997] ECR I-5303. As indicated by the first and second recitals, its predecessors, establishing a system of information for previous years, were based on ex Art 235 EC (later ex Art 308 EC, now Art 352 TFEU).

[206] Dec No 3092/94/EC, n 205, third recital.

[207] Dec No 3092/94/EC, n 205, Art 1(1)–(2).

[208] Dec No 372/1999/EC of the European Parliament and of the Council of 8 Feb 1999 adopting a programme of Community action on injury prevention in the framework for action in the field of public health (1999 to 2003), [1999] OJ L46/1. It was repealed by Dec No 1786/2002/EC, [2002] OJ L271/1 (based on ex Art 152 EC), which in turn was replaced by Dec No 1350/2007/EC, [2007] OJ L301/3 (based on ex Art 152 EC), and now by Reg (EU) No 282/2014 of the European Parliament and of the Council of 11 March 2014 on the establishment of a third Programme for the Union's action in the field of health (2014–2020) and repealing Dec No 1350/2007/EC, [2014] OJ L86/1 (based on Art 168(5) TFEU).

[209] Dec No 276/1999/EC of the European Parliament and of the Council of 25 Jan 1999 adopting a multiannual Community action plan on promoting safer use of the Internet by combating illegal and harmful content on global networks, [1999] OJ L33/1.

[210] Dec No 276/1999/EC, n 209, fourth recital.

[211] Dec No 276/1999/EC, n 209, Art 3.

[212] Commission Communication, Action Plan on promoting safe use of the Internet/Proposal for a Council Decision adopting a multiannual Community action plan on promoting safe use of the Internet, COM (97) 582 final, 27.11.1997 (specifying ex Art 130(3) EC (later ex Art 157(3) EC, now Art 173(3) TFEU) concerning industry). See Legislative Resolution embodying Parliament's

period, from 1999 to 2002,[213] but it was extended and ultimately replaced by subsequent measures, which were based on the 'horizontal' provision that used to be inscribed in Article 153(2) EC (now Article 12 TFEU) or on Article 153 EC (now Article 169 TFEU) generally,[214] instead of Article 153(4)/153(3)(b) EC (now Article 169(3)/169(2)(b) TFEU).

In all, there is a paltry amount of measures based on what is now Article 169(2)(b) TFEU, and all three measures described above were based on the older version of this provision under the Maastricht Treaty. They are also mainly concerned with the consumer's right of information (ie information about prices, information about accidents, and information about safe use of the Internet), leaving the other consumer rights and interests listed in Article 169(1) TFEU on the sidelines. Of the group, the Price Indication Directive seems to represent a stronger example of Union (formerly Community) action in the sense of constituting minimum harmonization of national laws in the area concerned, whereas the EHLASS and Internet Decisions were tethered to lesser forms of Union (formerly Community) action along the lines of coordinating national laws and strengthening action taken at the national level. That being said, each of the foregoing measures represents the achievement of the Union's consumer protection objectives removed from the internal market programme. Noticeably, there is no mention of the particular measure's aptitude for eliminating obstacles to trade or distortions of competition, for example. Where relevant, they cover both cross-border and domestic transactions; in fact, by their subject matter, they seem to be predicated in large part on the domestic context. Still, the fact that there has only been one directive to date and 'backtracking' regarding the other two decisions signifies the timidity on the part of the legislature in relying on this provision. This explains the impetus for proposals to revise former Article 153 EC.

9.2.3.3 Proposals for change

In 1996, amidst the impending Intergovernmental Conference (IGC) leading to the Amsterdam Treaty, the Commission received two related written questions, inviting it to comment on the merits of former Article 129a EC. The two questions, submitted by an Italian MEP, Amedeo Amadeo, concerned 'the single market and consumer protection', and though worded somewhat differently, both asked the Commission to respond as to whether improvements to Article 129a EC were needed.[215] About a month later, then Commissioner Emma Bonino gave a joint answer to these questions,[216] in

Opinion on the Proposal, [1998] OJ C226/7; Amended proposal for a European Parliament and Council Decision adopting a multiannual Community action plan on promoting safer use of the Internet, [1998] OJ C324/6.

[213] Dec No 276/1999/EC, n 209, Art 1(2).

[214] Dec No 1151/2003/EC of the European Parliament and of the Council of 16 June 2003 amending Dec No 276/1999/EC adopting a multiannual Community action plan on promoting safer use of the Internet by combating illegal and harmful content on global networks, [2003] OJ L162/1 (based on ex Art 153(2) EC); Dec No 854/2005/EC of the European Parliament and of the Council of 11 May 2005 establishing a multiannual Community programme on promoting safer use of the Internet and new online technologies, [2005] OJ L149/1 (based on ex Art 153(2) EC); Dec No 1351/2008/EC of the European Parliament and of the Council of 16 Dec 2008 establishing a multiannual Community programme on protecting children using the Internet and other communication technologies, [2008] OJ L348/118 (based on ex Art 153 EC).

[215] Written Question No 1697/96 by A Amadeo, 'Single market and consumer protection', [1996] OJ C345/99, particularly point 2; Written Question No 1705/96 by A Amadeo, 'Single market and consumer protection', [1996] OJ C345/99, particularly point 1.

[216] Joint Answer to Written Questions E-1697/96 and E-1705/96 given by Emma Bonino on behalf of the Commission, [1996] OJ C345/99. Mrs Bonino was the Commissioner for Health and Consumer Protection during the Santer Commission (1995–1999).

which she declared: 'As things stand, Article 129a appears to be an adequate, appropriate legal basis for the development of consumer policy at Community level'.[217] In that regard, she underscored that Article 129a(1)(b) EC had already been used on two occasions as the legal basis for the EHLASS Decision and the proposal for the Price Indication Directive.[218] She added that although the IGC was not designed to increase Community powers, 'the Commission considers that the conference could provide a forum for looking into ways of achieving more effectively a high level of consumer protection under the different Community policies'.[219]

Notwithstanding Commissioner Bonino's statements, this provision has attracted an array of proposals on account of its weaknesses and underuse. Over the years, the literature has been sprinkled with calls for revising former Article 153 EC so as to break the tie with former Article 95 EC and to fortify Community action on the basis of this provision. A notable example was Professor Sandie Chillon's advocacy of the emancipation of then Article 129a EC from Article 100a EC by deleting indent (a) and the 'support and supplement' language of indent (b) so as to make Article 129a EC a more capable legal basis for consumer protection measures.[220] One of the most definitive proposals was submitted by Professors Hans-W Micklitz, Norbert Reich, and Stephen Weatherill in the wake of the 2004 version of the Draft Constitutional Treaty.[221] While cognizant of the political unacceptability of making major changes to either Articles 153 or 95 EC at that point, they nonetheless advocated a wholly revised version of Article 153 EC in order to augment and clarify the extent of Community action under both provisions.[222] In particular, they argued for the insertion of an additional indent as part of Article 153(3) EC denoting 'measures which contribute to the protection and promotion of the interests of consumers [within the framework of EU policy]', with a view to extending autonomous consumer protection competence at the European level.[223] They also advocated replacing the 'horizontal' clause of Article 153(2) EC with a new paragraph, stipulating that '[t]he interests of the consumer in participating actively and confidently in the internal market shall be fully taken into account in the development of the Union's activities'.[224] This change was aimed not so much at Article 153 EC, but to affect the interpretation of Article 95 EC so as to strengthen the argument that it could be used for consumer-friendly measures even if the *Tobacco Advertising I* case law was read in a narrow manner.[225] They further supported replacing the minimum harmonization clause laid down in Article 153(5) EC with a procedure modelled after Article 95(4)–(10) EC so as to align Articles 153 and 95 EC and thus allow for maximum harmonization in areas of consumer protection policy unrelated to the internal market.[226]

[217] Joint Answer, n 216, point 1, second para.

[218] Joint Answer, n 216, point 1, second para. Incidentally, she opined in reference to Art 129a(3) EC—which required the Member States to notify to the Commission consumer protection measures that were more stringent than those adopted pursuant to para 2 of the same provision—that no legislative measure had yet been adopted at Community level under the said para 2, and as such, there had been no call for implementation of the notification procedure set down in that para (point 3). It is not clear whether she intended to indicate that the two aforementioned Community measures were not legislative in nature or whether she had erred in understanding the cross-relationship between measures under indent (b) and para 2 of the provision.

[219] Joint Answer, n 216, point 1, second para; point 2.

[220] S Chillon, *Le droit communautaire de la consommation après les traités de Maastricht et d'Amsterdam* (CDC, 1999) 304, 547–549.

[221] H-W Micklitz et al, 'EU Treaty Revision and Consumer Protection' (2004) 27 *JCP* 367.

[222] See Micklitz et al, n 221, 377–380.

[223] Micklitz et al, n 221, 394–395.

[224] Micklitz et al, n 221, 395.

[225] Micklitz et al, n 221, 394–395.

[226] Micklitz et al, n 221, 393–396.

Proposals urging revision of former Article 153 EC have also emanated from the European level, particularly from the EESC, which has played a seminal role in calling for the strengthening of this provision, as well as its very creation, in several Opinions. In 1991, before the entry into force of the Maastricht Treaty, the EESC adopted an Opinion on 'Consumer Protection and Completion of the Internal Market', which evaluated the constraints of the reference to consumer protection as part of former Article 95 EC (then Article 100a EEC) and asserted the need for a specific provision in the Treaty on consumer protection policy.[227] In 1995, following the entry into force of the Maastricht Treaty, the EESC's Opinion on the 'Single Market and Consumer Protection: opportunities and obstacles' took issue with the lack of Community measures based on what was then Article 129a(1)(b) EC and cautioned that the principle of subsidiarity should not be interpreted too narrowly so as to preclude the adoption of measures under this legal basis, thereby advocating the revision of Article 129a EC to stipulate, among other things, that the measures adopted by the Community in this area fell within its own competence and not that of the Member States in line with the principle of subsidiarity.[228] This was echoed in the EESC's 2005 Opinion on 'Consumer policy post-enlargement', which highlighted that former Article 153 EC gave rise to 'dual subsidiarity': in addition to the subsidiarity test inscribed in the second paragraph of Article 5 EC (now Article 5(3) TEU), Article 153(3)(b) EC (now Article 169(2)(b) TFEU) was perceived as subjecting measures to an even more stringent test of secondary subsidiarity by virtue of the fact that Community measures must 'supplement' or 'support' Member States' initiatives in the areas concerned.[229] In the EESC's view, it was essential that the application of subsidiarity not hold up the adoption of much-needed consumer protection measures.[230]

In 2006, the EESC's Opinion on the 'Legal framework for consumer policy' contained ambitious reform of former Article 153 EC.[231] The EESC set the stage by discussing the chronological development of Article 153 EC in the Treaty framework, noting that with the Maastricht Treaty, Article 129a EC was an inadequate basis for developing a fully-fledged consumer policy and the changes brought about by the Amsterdam Treaty did not address these shortcomings.[232] In its view, the Commission's approach confirmed a 'worrying decline' in the promotion and protection of consumer interests, and the deficiencies in the text of Article 153 EC were at the root of why it was not used much as the legal basis for developing consumer policy in the EU.[233] It reiterated that 'dual subsidiarity' paralysed, at the European and national levels, any policy designed to enhance consumer protection and needed to be abandoned.[234] Accordingly, it proposed two new provisions, Articles 153 and 153a, to replace what was then Article 153 EC.[235] The proposed Article 153 outlined the general dimensions

[227] EESC Opinion on 'Consumer Protection and Completion of the Internal Market', [1991] OJ C339/16, point 1.2.2. See further EESC Opinion on 'The Consumer and the Internal Market', [1993] OJ C19/22, which, as noted in point 2.1, constituted a follow-up to the 1991 Opinion as regards the content of a Community consumer policy.

[228] EESC Opinion on the 'Single Market and Consumer Protection: opportunities and obstacles', [1996] OJ C39/55, points 1.1.1, 2.1.2.1–2.1.2.2, 6.1.2.1–6.1.2.2, 6.2.3.

[229] EESC Opinion on 'Consumer policy post-enlargement', [2005] OJ C221/153, points 6.3–6.4.

[230] EESC Opinion, n 229, point 6.4.

[231] EESC Opinion on the 'Legal framework for consumer policy', [2006] OJ C185/71. It was adopted by a bare majority: 45 votes to 26, with 2 abstentions. Certain members supported deletion of many points, including the proposal for new Arts 153 and 153a. See App, point 6.

[232] EESC Opinion, n 231, points 1.3–1.5.

[233] EESC Opinion, n 231, points 1.7, 2.1.1.

[234] EESC Opinion, n 231, point 4.6.5.

[235] EESC Opinion, n 231, point 6.

of Community consumer policy, setting forth an enlarged list of Community objectives to be achieved[236] and providing that it should aim at the 'highest' level of protection based upon a number of framing principles.[237] The proposed Article 153a EC outlined the scope of Community action in this field. Of particular note was the fact that the dual route of Article 153 EC was gone; the 'support, supplement and monitor' language was replaced by measures 'as are necessary to obtain the objectives' listed in Article 153;[238] and although the recourse to minimum harmonization was retained, the proposed Article 153a contained a special procedure for the Commission's review of more stringent national measures.[239]

Taken together, the proposals emanating from scholars and the EESC share the objective to embolden Union action under what is now Article 169 TFEU. Part and parcel of this, some sought to break the tie between Articles 169 and 114 TFEU inscribed in Article 169 TFEU. Yet, they were not generally concerned with severing the link between Article 114 TFEU and the protection of consumers' economic interests within which EU (consumer) contract law was, and continues to be, situated. If anything, as exemplified by the proposal of Professors Micklitz, Reich, and Weatherill, by making clear that consumer-related measures seeking to increase consumer confidence could be based on what is now Article 114 TFEU, this only seemed to tie the two more tightly together. By and large, it was the other consumer rights and interests that had lain fallow in the ongoing developments concerning EU consumer policy that were given a boost by many of the proposals. This was amplified by the various institutional documents espousing the merits of Article 169 TFEU above. What was stressed, particularly consistently by the Commission, was the encouragement of recourse to Article 169 TFEU in relation to other areas of Union action separate from that concerning the internal market. As such, the linkage between consumer protection and internal market policy, especially in connection with the protection of consumers' economic interests, has continued unimpeded, indeed strengthened, in the progression of EU consumer policy programmes to date.

9.3 The Scope of Article 169 TFEU

By virtue of the dual route inscribed in Article 169 TFEU, the scope of the Union's competence under this provision denotes the limits and exercise of such competence under indent (b) of Article 169(2) TFEU to take action to achieve the objectives relating to consumer protection as elaborated in Article 169(1) TFEU. This should be distinguished from indent (a) of Article 169(2) TFEU, which is targeted at the achievement

[236] EESC Opinion, n 231, point 6. The proposed Art 153(1) expanded former Art 153(1) EC, so as to include, inter alia, 'recognition of individual and collective rights' and 'promoting consumers' legal, economic, social and cultural interests'.

[237] EESC Opinion, n 231, point 6. See proposed Art 153(2). This was to respond to the lack of any criteria in former Art 153 EC as regards the meaning of a 'high' level of consumer protection: see point 4.6.4.

[238] EESC Opinion, n 231, point 6. See proposed Art 153a(1).

[239] EESC Opinion, n 231, point 6. See proposed Art 153a(2)–(3). There had been a proposal specifying that harmonization measures adopted under proposed Art 153a 'shall as a matter of priority, take the form of a regulation', but this was deleted. See App II. It should also be mentioned that there were bold new paras in the proposed Art 153a requiring the Member States to take certain steps to ensure the effective application of Community (now Union) consumer measures and widening the standing requirements of former Art 230 EC (now Art 263 TFEU) to ensure direct access for consumer associations in challenging measures based on this provision. See proposed Art 153a(4)–(5).

of such objectives within the context of internal market measures adopted under Article 114 TFEU. By parsing out the limits and exercise of Union competence under Article 169(2)(b) TFEU, Article 169 TFEU, arguably, has somewhat greater ambit than is commonly perceived.

9.3.1 The limits of Union competence under Article 169(2)(b) TFEU

The limits of the Union's competence under Article 169(2)(b) TFEU denotes the extent of Union action that can be taken in pursuit of the objectives elaborated in Article 169(1) EC, that is to say, the Union's contribution to 'protecting the health, safety and economic interests of consumers' and 'promoting their right to information, education and to organise themselves in order to safeguard their interests'. This invites inquiry into two interrelated aspects: the forms of Union action that may be taken on the basis of this provision to achieve these objectives, and what is meant by action 'to support, supplement and monitor' the policies of the Member States in that regard.

First, on the basis of the chronological development of Article 169 TFEU in the Treaties, case law, and institutional practice discussed in the preceding section, the stipulation of 'measures' under Article 169(2)(b) TFEU allows for binding legislative action on the basis of legal instruments, such as directives, regulations, and decisions. This coincides with the way the term 'measures' is used in other provisions of the Treaties, such as Articles 81, 114, and 352 TFEU, implicated in the debate. This is further evidenced by the acts adopted under this provision already and by the revision of this provision in the European Convention (referring to regulations and/or directives) and in the Draft Constitutional Treaty (citing European laws and European framework laws), which paved the way for the Lisbon Treaty. As a result, in principle, it is arguable that Article 169 TFEU has the potential to carry out not only the harmonization of national laws by way of directives, but also the unification of national laws by way of regulations, thereby encompassing approximation in the general sense.[240] This does not necessarily undercut the stipulation inscribed in Article 169(4) TFEU that Member States are allowed to maintain or introduce more stringent protection in relation to the measure concerned, since scholars have pointed out that regulations may be used to lay down minimum standards.[241] Moreover, given the prevalent use of regulations for optional instruments in institutional practice, there does not appear to be any grounds to preclude, at least by virtue of its wording, the use of Article 169(2)(b) TFEU for the adoption of optional instruments setting forth an alternative regime alongside the national consumer laws.[242] That being said, given the limited measures adopted under this provision to date and the prominence of the Price Indication Directive, harmonization is more commonly associated with Article 169 TFEU.

[240] See further Chapter 1, § 1.2.3.1.

[241] See R Schütze, 'The Morphology of Legislative Power in the European Community: Legal Instruments and the Federal Division of Powers' (2006) 25 *YEL* 92, 118. Perhaps on account of the lack of measures adopted under Art 169 TFEU so far, there does not appear to be discussion in the literature on this provision, as compared to the field of EU environmental policy, regarding the extent to which minimum harmonization prescribed in the Treaties allows for recourse to more intensive forms of harmonization as a matter of secondary Union law. See, eg, JH Jans and HHB Vedder, *European Environmental Law After Lisbon*, 4th edn (Europa, 2012) ch 3; R Schütze, *From Dual to Cooperative Federalism—The Changing Structure of European Law* (Oxford Univ Press, 2009) 270–279.

[242] See, eg, C Twigg-Flesner, *A Cross-Border-Only Regulation for Consumer Transactions in the EU: A Fresh Approach to EU Consumer Law* (Springer, 2012) 58.

Importantly, within this context, there appears to be controversy as regards Article 169 TFEU's allowance for harmonization, with several scholars disavowing the use of what is now Article 169(2)(b) TFEU for the adoption of measures harmonizing the laws of the Member States.[243] Looking more closely, however, this divergence of opinion may boil down to the objectives to be achieved by such harmonization as regards consumer protection 'inside' versus 'outside' the internal market or the degree of harmonization involved. As demonstrated above, it is widely recognized by the Union institutions (including the Court of Justice), scholars, and members of the European Convention that Article 169(4) TFEU (ex Article 153(5) EC) embodies a minimum harmonization clause.[244] It would therefore be illogical if this provision did not allow for harmonization in the first place, and as evidenced by the Price Indication Directive, this has been done. Furthermore, the express preclusion of harmonization in the fields of public health, education, and culture, which entered into the Treaty framework at the same time and have continued to sit alongside Article 169 TFEU through the subsequent course of Treaty revisions through to the Lisbon Treaty, indicates the intention of the Treaty framers not to restrict Article 169 TFEU in this way. While not always stated clearly, Article 169 TFEU (ex Article 153 EC)'s allowance for harmonization to achieve the Union's consumer protection objectives *sensu stricto* seems to be readily agreed.[245] Thus, it may be the potential recourse to Article 169 TFEU outside the confines of consumer protection to carry out harmonization in the context of the internal market that is rejected in the literature, or the fact that although minimum harmonization may be allowed, a more intensive degree of harmonization such as maximum harmonization may not be.[246] In any case, to the extent that such commentators submit that harmonization is precluded on the basis of indent (b) of Article 169(2) TFEU *in toto*, the position of the present author departs from that view.

As regards the scope of such harmonization (or potentially approximation), Article 169(2)(b) TFEU is silent on the issue of whether such measures must be limited to cross-border situations or can extend to domestic situations. Yet, at least as regards the Union measures adopted under this provision so far, no such limitation has been

[243] See, eg, T Ackermann, 'Buying Legitimacy? The Commission's Proposal on Consumer Rights' (2010) 21 *EBLR* 587, 590; Max Planck Institute for Comparative and International Private Law, 'Policy Options for Progress Towards a European Contract Law' (2011) 75 *RabelsZ* 371, 394; J Stuyck et al, 'Confidence through fairness? The new Directive on unfair business-to-consumer commercial practices in the internal market' (2006) 43 *CML Rev* 107, 113 fn 32 (but see n 246); S Weatherill, 'Justifying Limits to Party Autonomy in the Internal Market—EC Legislation in the Field of Consumer Protection' in S Grundmann et al (eds), *Party Autonomy and the Role of Information in the Internal Market* (Walter de Gruyter, 2001) 173, 188–190 (reiterated in, eg, S Weatherill, 'European Private Law and the Constitutional Dimension' in F Cafaggi (ed), *The Institutional Framework of European Private Law* (Oxford Univ Press, 2006) 79, 93; but compare Weatherill, n 3, 63).

[244] Art 169(4) TFEU provides that measures adopted under Art 169 TFEU 'shall not prevent any Member State from maintaining or introducing more stringent protective measures. Such measures must be compatible with the Treaties. The Commission shall be notified of them.'

[245] See, eg, Boele-Woelki and van Ooik, n 202, 15–16; de Vries, n 3, 305; KJ Mortelmans, 'Horizontal and Flanking Policies' in PJG Kapteyn et al (eds),*The Law of the European Union and the European Communities*, 4th rev edn (Kluwer, 2008) 1087, 1106; Stuyck, n 6, 68; J Ziller, 'The Legitimacy of the Codification of Contract Law in View of the Allocation of Competences between the European Union and its Member States' in MW Hesselink (ed), *The Politics of a European Civil Code* (Kluwer, 2006) 89, 100. See also, albeit on tentative grounds, W van Gerven, 'Codifying European private law? Yes, if. . .!' (2002) 27 *ELR* 156, 167.

[246] See, eg, J Stuyck, 'Enforcement and Compliance: An EU Law Perspective' in R Brownsword et al (eds), *The Foundations of European Private Law* (Hart, 2011) 513, 517. But compare, eg, Commission Communication on the Price Indication Directive, n 204, floating the possibility of proceeding to a 'fully harmonised regime'.

imposed. In fact, considering that Union action is predicated on 'the policy pursued by the Member States', the coverage of both cross-border and domestic situations in a measure based on this provision would presumably not be foreclosed, depending upon the objectives to be achieved by the measure concerned.

Secondly, the 'stickier' part of the inquiry concerns what is meant by measures 'which support, supplement and monitor the policy pursued by the Member States'. This is especially so on account of the 'baggage' of the Draft Constitutional Treaty and the Lisbon Treaty, whereby the words 'supporting' and 'supplementing' became conjoined with the category of complementary competence, which denotes more limited Union action vis-à-vis the Member States.[247] That said, the words 'support, supplement and monitor' have varying connotations that could in principle veer on the side of Union action or that of the Member States. Delving deeper into the text, the word 'supplement' in the English version assumes a somewhat stronger tenor in other language versions of Article 169(2)(b) TFEU in the sense of Union action 'completing' or 'complementing', even 'integrating',[248] national consumer policy.[249]

Although the Court of Justice has not yet addressed the matter, the 'supporting and supplementing' language was interpreted broadly by Advocate General Léger in *Deposit Guarantees*, underscoring that Community (now Union) action was not linked to the existence of a specific policy in each and every Member State; what mattered was the existence of an overall policy to protect consumers in the Member States as a whole.[250] This is also echoed by scholars, such as Professor Jules Stuyck who remarked that 'the actual subject-matter of the Community [now Union] measure may differ from anything already existing in the Member States, so long as it supplements existing goals of consumer policy in (some of) the Member States'.[251] Indeed, the text of Article 169 TFEU is framed in relation to the policy 'pursued' by the Member States, which seems to invite some flexibility in the assessment. As a practical matter, it is doubtful at this stage of European integration that the Member States would not have at least some sort of consumer policy, even if at different stages of development.[252] For that matter, while the 'monitoring' (as well as 'supporting and supplementing') language of Article 169 TFEU remains to be fleshed out in the case law, the Commission's musings discussed above appear to indicate, at least in its view, a palpable role in enforcing consumer protection standards across the EU.[253] By and large, the 'supporting, supplementing and monitoring' language of Article 169(2)(b) TFEU seems to invite a wider margin for Union action in pursuit of its objectives, without being tied to particular consumer policies of the Member States. And while measures so far have been mainly targeted at consumer information, the protection of the other consumer rights and interests set forth in Article 169(1) TFEU also provide the basis for Union action in this regard.

To summarize, in line with the objectives set forth in Article 169(1) TFEU, Union action under this provision can conceivably encompass both harmonization and unification of national laws, can potentially extend to both cross-border and domestic

[247] See Chapter 7, § 7.4.2.3.

[248] In relevant part, the Italian version of indent (b) reads: 'misure *di sostegno, di integrazione e di controllo* della politica svolta dagli Stati membri' (emphasis added).

[249] See, eg, Dutch version ('maatregelen om het beleid van de lidstaten *te ondersteunen, aan te vullen en te controleren*'); French version ('des mesures qui *appuient et complètent* la politique menée par le États membres, et *en assurent le* suivi'); German version ('Maßnahmen zur *Unterstützung, Ergänzung und Überwachung* der Politik der Mitgliedstaaten'); Spanish version ('medidas que *apoyen, complementen y supervisen* la política llevada a cabo por los Estados miembros') (emphasis added).

[250] See ns 111–112 and accompanying text.

[251] Stuyck, n 14, 387.

[252] See Reich, n 65, 33.

[253] See n 184 and accompanying text.

situations, and can diverge from the consumer policies of the Member States to varying degrees so long as the measures concerned 'support, supplement and monitor' national consumer policy as a whole. In fact, it is in large part the confluence of the 'support, supplement and monitor' language with the principle of subsidiarity that has been credited with holding Article 169 TFEU back, which leads to the next section.

9.3.2 The exercise of Union competence under Article 169(2)(b) TFEU

As captured in scholarly literature and some of the institutional documents described above, there is perceived to be a 'dual role' played by the principle of subsidiarity in relation to Article 169 TFEU.[254] The idea is that subsidiarity infiltrates Union action under Article 169 TFEU in two ways: first, in the framing of the provision itself, in the sense that Union action must only 'support, supplement and monitor' Member State action under Article 169(2)(b) TFEU and that the Member States are not precluded from setting more stringent protection standards by virtue of the minimum harmonization clause of Article 169(4) TFEU; and secondly, that Union action under Article 169 TFEU must satisfy the subsidiarity test outlined in Article 5(3) TEU, ie that such action cannot be sufficiently achieved by the Member States, but can rather be better achieved by the Union. Both applications embody the perspective that action taken at the Member State level in the consumer sphere is prioritized, with Union action assuming a secondary, literally supporting, role. Yet, it is often overlooked that these two roles manifest different conceptions of subsidiarity. As discussed in Chapter 7,[255] the first embodies a 'supra-constitutional' conception of subsidiarity in the sense that tenets of subsidiarity infuse the way that Article 169 TFEU is framed in the Treaties, which then impact the principle of conferral in the sense of delineating the scope of Union competence under this provision. In other words, it informs the language of Article 169 TFEU, which necessitates inquiry into what it means to 'support, supplement or monitor' Member State action, the preservation of minimum harmonization, etc. The second constitutes the traditional 'constitutional' conception of subsidiarity relating to its potential to guide the exercise of Union competence in line with the subsidiarity calculus of Article 5(3) TEU.

Admittedly, on a practical level, it is difficult to differentiate the outcome of these different conceptions of subsidiarity. Whether on the basis of a limited interpretation of the text of Article 169 TFEU or on the basis of Article 5(3) TEU, the result could be just the same, that action at the Member State level concerning a certain matter of consumer policy is preferred. Even so, these two conceptions of subsidiarity must be distinguished because they have very different consequences for the analysis of the Union's competence under Article 169 TFEU. On the one hand, supra-constitutional subsidiarity seems to have had a considerable impact in restraining the course of Union action under this provision. Remarkably, in contrast to other provisions such as Article 114 TFEU where the principle of subsidiarity (as well as the principle of proportionality) underlie tensions as regards the need for protecting or preserving Member State competence in the face of Union action, in the case of Article 169 TFEU, the converse seems to be true. As illustrated by some of the literature and institutional documents on

[254] See, eg, R Dehousse, 'Integration v. Regulation? On the Dynamics of Regulation in the European Community' (1992) 30 *JCMS* 383, 388; EESC Opinions cited in § 9.2.3.3.
[255] See Chapter 7, § 7.4.3.1.

Article 169 TFEU, subsidiarity carries concerns that it has operated too far in the opposite direction, that is to say, that it has been abused or interpreted narrowly in favour of the Member States at the expense of unduly emasculating Union action in areas where it is needed.[256] As such, the predominant role of subsidiarity in relation to Article 169 TFEU may have obfuscated the scope of Union action in the sense of unduly painting the dimensions of Union competence under Article 169 TFEU in a very restrictive manner. On the other hand, as regards constitutional subsidiarity, Union action in this field is taken with a view to 'supporting, supplementing and monitoring' Member State action, meaning that it is intended to provide added value to the protection of consumers, which is not capable of being achieved by national consumer policies. Thus, assuming that such Union action falls within the boundaries of Article 169(2)(b) TFEU, the hurdle posed by the subsidiarity test of Article 5(3) TEU would not appear to be insurmountable. This may explain why scholars have found the impact of the principle of subsidiarity (in its constitutional form) to be low in relation to Union competence under Article 169 TFEU.[257]

Moreover, by separating these two conceptions of subsidiarity, this may place further attention on the roles played by the other constitutional principles alongside subsidiarity that guide the exercise of Union competence under Article169 TFEU, namely the principles of proportionality and sincere cooperation, which taken together may offset tensions relating to the perceived ineffectiveness of (constitutional) subsidiarity acting alone. Compared to the principle of subsidiarity, the principle of proportionality has not seemed to garner as much attention in the literature or institutional documents in connection with Article 169 TFEU so far. Nonetheless, at least one scholar emphasized the importance of this principle in the sense of guiding the intensity of Union action in the field of consumer policy by limiting the scope and type of action taken.[258] The role played by the principle of sincere cooperation has also been underlined by several scholars in the literature. In particular, Professor Sandie Chillon considered the operation of the principle of sincere cooperation as an 'antidote' for the subsidiarity barrier in the sense of enhancing the synergy between action taken in the field of consumer policy at the European and national levels.[259] Likewise, Professors Hans W-Micklitz and Stephen Weatherill highlighted the shared responsibility of the Union and the Member States for consumer policy on the basis of the relationship between Article 169 TFEU, the principle of subsidiarity, and the principle of sincere cooperation, with the result that action situated at the Union, national, and even regional levels can have a role to play within the EU framework concerning consumer policy.[260]

Certainly, the lack of Union measures based on Article 169 TFEU makes it difficult to assess the operation of the principles of subsidiarity, proportionality, and sincere cooperation, and therefore, the analysis may be rooted more in theory than practice at this point. Still, drawing from the foregoing observations, the interplay between

[256] See, eg, Chillon, n 220, 381–425; L Gibson, 'Subsidiarity: The Implications for Consumer Policy' (1993) 16 *JCP* 323.

[257] See, eg, Reich, n 65, 20; Stuyck, n 14, 382 (reiterated in, eg, J Stuyck, 'Class Actions in Europe? To Opt-In or to Opt-Out, that is the Question' (2009) 20 *EBLR* 483, 501–502).

[258] See Stuyck, n 14, 397 (albeit his discussion seems to be situated in relation to consumer measures taken within the field of internal market policy).

[259] See Chillon, n 220, 446.

[260] Micklitz and Weatherill, n 14, 303–304, 310–316. See also S Weatherill, 'Shaping Responsibilities in the Legal Order of the European Community' in H-W Micklitz et al (eds), *Federalism and Responsibility: A Study on Product Safety Law and Practice in the European Community* (Graham and Trotman, 1994) 153.

these three principles has the potential to contribute to a more balanced or cooperative relationship between the Union and the Member States in relation to the exercise of the Union's competence under Article 169 TFEU. Proportionality cum subsidiarity has the potential to eradicate fears of unduly precluding Union action by working to target the areas in which Union action is needed, and within those areas, to regulate the intensity of such action at the European level, whether as part of the subsidiarity calculus under Article 5(3) TEU or the proportionality assessment pursuant to Article 5(4) TEU.[261] Furthermore, under circumstances where the subsidiarity calculus indicates that the objectives of the proposed action can be sufficiently achieved by the Member States, the principle of sincere cooperation ensures that the Member States, whether at national, regional, or local level, must achieve such objectives so as to ensure that consumer protection does not 'fall between the cracks', so to speak, between the European and the national levels. In this way, distinguishing the different conceptions of subsidiarity may help to remedy misperceptions about the extent of Union competence under Article 169 TFEU emanating from its supra-constitutional form and to illuminate the role played by the principles of proportionality and sincere cooperation, alongside subsidiarity in its constitutional form, in relation to Article 169 TFEU.

9.4 The Relationship between Articles 169, 114, and 352 TFEU in European Contract Law

9.4.1 European consumer contract law and ties that bind: Consumer protection and the internal market

The prospect of a European contract law instrument including or limited to consumer contract law strikes at the heart of the relationship between Articles 169 and 114 TFEU. Noticeably, the Treaties are silent when it comes to answering questions about the linkage between the two provisions, namely how to determine the boundary line between them and whether a measure may be based jointly on the two together or instead on one alone. In the literature, there does not seem to be firm agreement on the matter. Certain scholars opine that Articles 169 and 114 TFEU are mutually exclusive and thus cannot be used together, since they have different scopes of application and manifest different effects on Member State competence,[262] whereas some, at least tentatively, have considered proposals for a European consumer contract law instrument on a combination of the two.[263] Added to this is the case law of the Court of Justice, which has not provided definitive answers so far. In *El Corte Inglés*, the Court's finding that Article 129a EC (now Article 169 TFEU) created limited EU competence in the consumer field 'apart' from measures taken in connection with the internal market strongly supports the separation of consumer measures into two categories: one related to the internal market and the other divorced from it. Yet, this ruling did not answer the question of the overlap between the two, and as yet, there has been no case that has confronted the Court with such an issue.

Basically, the inquiry revolves around the objectives to be achieved by the measure concerned, in terms of the distinction emanating from the case law and institutional

[261] See further Chapter 7, § 7.4.4.2.

[262] See, eg, S Weatherill, 'Legal bases for EC consumer policy: Paper prepared for ECLG' in *Legal bases for EC consumer policy* (2005) ECLG/036/05, 2–3.

[263] See, eg, van Gerven, n 245, 167.

practice as regards the extent to which a particular measure is rooted in consumer protection objectives *sensu stricto* under indent (b) of Article 169(2) TFEU, as opposed to the achievement of such objectives as part of the internal market programme, which merits recourse to Article 114 TFEU pursuant to indent (a) of Article 169(2) TFEU. Generally speaking, there are compelling arguments that in principle Articles 169 and 114 TFEU may be used together as the legal basis for a particular Union measure under circumstances where the measure is predicated equally and indissociably on the Union's objectives related to the internal market, on the one hand, and consumer protection, on the other. To some extent, this was alluded to in Advocate General Léger's Opinion in *Deposit Guarantees*, in which he posited that what is now Article 169 TFEU (then Article 129a EC) could potentially serve as a second legal basis alongside what is now Article 53 TFEU (then Article 57 EC) for the Directive at issue, although this did not squarely implicate Article 114 TFEU. As also highlighted in that Opinion, the decision-making procedures for what are now Articles 169 and 114 TFEU are compatible, indeed identical. Furthermore, such a combination is not expressly foreclosed by the Treaties. The dual route laid down in Article 169(2) TFEU has been separated by a semi-colon from its introduction in the Maastricht Treaty to its reframing in the Lisbon Treaty. Arguably, this can be viewed as an ingenious way on the part of the Treaty framers to leave open the possibility for the Union legislature to have recourse to both provisions under the relevant circumstances.

With regard to institutional practice, there has not yet been any measure adopted under both Articles 114 and 169 TFEU, at least that the present author is aware of. Yet, there has been recourse to the combination of Article 114 TFEU and Article 192 TFEU concerning environmental policy[264] and that of Article 114 TFEU and Article 168(4)(b) TFEU concerning public health protection,[265] which provide concrete examples of measures, or portions thereof, rooted in the Union's objectives in the internal market, on the one hand, and the Union's objectives specific to those policy fields, on the other. In fact, sometimes the provisions are separated in the measure itself according to each set of objectives, whereby different levels of harmonization are established.[266] This demonstrates that in situations where the chosen degree of harmonization may diverge,

[264] See, eg, Dir 2008/112/EC of the European Parliament and of the Council of 16 Dec 2008 amending Council Dirs 76/768/EEC, 88/378/EEC, 1999/13/EC and Dirs 2000/53/EC, 2002/96/EC and 2004/42/EC of the European Parliament and of the Council in order to adapt them to Reg (EC) No 1272/2008 on classification, labelling and packaging of substances and mixtures, [2008] OJ L345/68, based on Arts 114 and 192(1) TFEU (ex Arts 95 and 175(1) EC). As regards justification for this dual legal basis, see Proposal, COM (2007) 611 final, 16.10.2007, 5. There are also measures based on Art 114 TFEU (ex Art 95 EC) or Art 192(1) TFEU (ex Art 175(1) EC), but utilize the other respective provision in relation to particular Arts. See, eg, Reg (EC) No 842/2006 of the European Parliament and of the Council of 17 May 2006 on certain fluorinated greenhouse gases, [2006] OJ L161/1 (based on ex Art 175(1) EC, as well as ex Art 95 EC in relation to Arts 7–9); Dir 2009/28/EC of the European Parliament and of the Council of 23 April 2009 on the promotion of the use of energy from renewable sources and amending and subsequently repealing Dirs 2001/177/EC and 2003/30/EC, [2009] OJ L140/16 (based on ex Art 175(1) EC, as well as ex Art 95 EC in relation to Arts 17–19).

[265] See, eg, Dir 2004/28/EC of the European Parliament and of the Council of 31 March 2004 amending Dir 2001/82/EC on the Community code relating to veterinary medicinal products, [2004] OJ L136/58, based on Arts 114 and 168(4)(b) TFEU (ex Arts 95 and 152(4)(b) EC). As regards justification for this dual legal basis, see Proposal, COM (2001) 404 final, 26.11.2001, point D, at 12–13.

[266] See, eg, Dir 2006/66/EC of the European Parliament and of the Council of 6 Sept 2006 on batteries and accumulators and waste batteries and accumulators and repealing Dir 91/157/EEC, [2006] OJ L266/1; *corrigendum*, [2006] OJ L311/58. It is based on Art 192(1) TFEU (ex Art 175(1) EC), as well as Art 114(1) TFEU (ex Art 95(1) EC) in relation to Arts 4, 6, and 21. See further Proposal, COM (2003) 723 final, 21.11.2003, point 9, at 24–25.

for example, minimum versus maximum harmonization, this does not necessarily preclude the combination of Articles 114 and 169 TFEU, but may require the measure to be compartmentalized. Certainly, in accordance with vested case law, institutional practice is not determinative, and the matter will inevitably remain unsettled until the Court of Justice is given the opportunity to address it. Nevertheless, such examples find ready analogy to the situation involving Articles 114 and 169 TFEU, which indicate that such a possibility cannot be foreclosed.

That all being said, as far as the adoption of a European contract law instrument encompassing consumer contract law in all or in part is concerned, there are good arguments that a combination of Articles 114 and 169 TFEU is generally precluded and that action must be taken on the basis of Article 114 TFEU alone pursuant to indent (a) of Article 169(2) TFEU. This goes back to the objectives underlying the Union measures concerning consumer contract law adopted thus far. Interwoven through the constitutional fabric of EU consumer contract law is that the various measures espouse dual objectives related to ensuring the establishment and functioning of the internal market and attaining a high level of consumer protection.[267] In other words, consumer protection objectives are part of the Union's objectives to make the internal market function on the basis of the particular measure adopted. As demonstrated by the analysis above, since the very beginning of Union (formerly Community) consumer policy, EU consumer contract law continues to be situated within the context of the protection of consumers' economic interests as part of the internal market programme. This has become more apparent in the Commission's plans for the review of the consumer *acquis* and the Consumer Rights Directive, as well as the proposed CESL.[268] In short, EU consumer contract law measures are generally not concerned with consumer protection policy *sensu stricto* divorced from the internal market, but in fact are part of it.

Consequently, this makes proposals made by scholars to take the EU consumer contract law measures adopted under what are now Articles 114 and 115 TFEU and convert them into a comprehensive instrument based on Article 169 TFEU confusing. For instance, Professor Norbert Reich proposed the codification of EU consumer contract law under what is now Article 169(2)(b) TFEU, which seems to be motivated in large part by the 'double advantage' of preserving recourse to minimum harmonization and having recourse to a regulation, as opposed to a directive.[269] With the greatest respect to this prominent jurist, it is not clear how measures rooted in the Union's dual objectives related to the internal market and consumer protection can be adopted, at

[267] See Chapter 1, § 1.4.1. Also, in much of the case law concerning the 'hard core' of the EU contract law *acquis*, the dual objectives of consumer protection and the internal market have been underlined: see Chapter 2.

[268] See Chapter 6. As regards the proposed CESL, it has been cited in Commission documents on consumer policy that highlight the linkage between the EU's consumer protection and internal market objectives: see, eg, Communication on A European Consumer Agenda, n 189, points 2, 4.4.

[269] See N Reich, 'A European Contract Law, or an EU Contract Law Regulation for Consumers?' (2005) 28 *JCP* 383, 398 (reiterated in, eg, N Reich, 'Crisis or Future of European Consumer Law?' in D Parry et al (eds), *The Yearbook of Consumer Law 2009* (Ashgate, 2008) 3, 33). This position has been seconded by other scholars: see, eg, H-W Micklitz, 'The Targeted Full Harmonisation Approach: Looking Behind the Curtain' in G Howells and R Schulze (eds), *Modernising and Harmonising Consumer Contract Law* (Sellier, 2009) 47, 55. See also C Twigg-Flesner, 'Time to Do the Job Properly—The Case for a New Approach to EU Consumer Legislation' (2010) 33 *JCP* 355, 366, 370 (reiterated in, eg, Twigg-Flesner, n 242; C. Twigg-Flesner, 'Comment: the future of EU consumer law—the end of harmonisation?' in J Devenney and M Kenny (eds), *European Consumer Protection: Theory and Practice* (Cambridge Univ Press, 2012) 6).

least as they are framed now, under Article 169(2)(b) TFEU, since they do not embody consumer protection objectives separate from those relating to the internal market.

Understandably, this may stimulate sensitivities regarding the imbalance between the two provisions in the sense of preferring Union action under Article 114 TFEU at the expense of that taken under Article 169 TFEU. Yet, from another vantage point, this constitutes a well-devised trade-off dictated by the Treaties in terms of allowing for a more holistic and well-rounded conception of the internal market as encompassing 'social' interests such as those relating to consumer protection, environmental protection, and public health as dictated by Article 114(3) TFEU, as opposed to an internal market rooted only in the 'economic' side of the equation.[270] Looked at more closely, it is not so much tensions relating to the overuse of Article 114 TFEU, but those relating to the underuse of Article 169 TFEU that are at issue. In view of the emergence and development of EU consumer policy presented earlier, it has become commonplace to view consumer protection as part of the internal market programme and thus more difficult, in view of the arrested development of an autonomous EU consumer policy separate from the internal market, to envisage the kinds of measures that could be adopted under Article 169 TFEU.[271] This is at the crux of the various proposals and institutional activities seeking to bolster former Article 153 EC, and it remains to be seen whether they might stimulate Union action in future years, which may remedy, or at least lessen, the asymmetry in the relationship between Articles 114 and 169 TFEU in this regard.

Certainly, it can be wondered whether the assessment of the constitutionality of a European contract law instrument encompassing consumer contract law in all or in part would be different if the EU consumer contract law *acquis* were to be reconfigured to embody consumer protection objectives outside the confines of the Union's internal market programme. Yet, given the path of European consumer contract law as it stands now, there is a convincing case on the basis of the Treaties, case law, and institutional practice that Article 114 TFEU, not Article 169 TFEU, is a proper legal basis for the adoption of an instrument that is rooted in the Union's dual consumer protection and internal market objectives. As such, Article 169 TFEU plays an important role in the debate by placing further attention on the recourse to Article 114 TFEU in connection with the adoption of a European contract law instrument approximating the consumer contract laws of the Member States by displacing them to some degree.

Similar remarks can be made in relation to the relationship between Articles 169 and 114 in connection with the adoption of a European optional instrument comprising consumer contract law. As highlighted in Part Two, institutional documents in the debate have put emphasis on the prospect of one or more optional instruments concerned with specific types of contracts, including consumer contracts. In particular, the proposed CESL represents an optional instrument setting forth a comprehensive set of harmonized contract law rules pertaining to business-to-consumer (B2C) and business-to-business (B2B) transactions based on Article 114 TFEU, with a view to promoting the smooth functioning of the internal market. Consequently, as regards the adoption of an optional instrument comprising consumer contract law as illustrated by the proposed CESL, the arguments above in relation to the relationship between

[270] The 'holistic' vision of the internal market has been emphasized in recent institutional documents: see, eg, European Parliament Resolutions of 20 May 2010 on delivering a single market to consumers and citizens, [2011] OJ C161E/84, and of 6 April 2011 on a Single Market for Europeans, [2012] OJ C296E/59.

[271] See L Gormley, 'The Consumer *Acquis* and the Internal Market' (2009) 20 *EBLR* 409, 421–422; S Weatherill, 'Consumer Policy' in P Craig and G de Búrca (eds), *The Evolution of EU Law*, 2nd edn (Oxford Univ Press, 2011) 837, 845.

Articles 114 and 169 TFEU are applicable here, since the Union's internal market and consumer protection objectives are infused in such an instrument, thereby justifying the use of Article 114 TFEU as opposed to Article 169 TFEU.

Although there are convincing arguments, in the present author's view, that an optional instrument along the lines of the proposed CESL may be based on Article 114 TFEU, to the extent that such an instrument, or others that may be contemplated in the debate, would be considered to fall outside the scope of approximation under this provision,[272] this may conceivably bring the relationship between Articles 169 and 352 TFEU to the fore. In principle, there are grounds to argue on the basis of *International Fund for Ireland*[273] that a Union measure may be based on a combination of Articles 169 and 352 TFEU under circumstances corresponding to those implicated in that case, that is to say, where a measure based on the Union's specific competence of Article 169(2)(b) TFEU contains elements that exceed the scope of the Union's competence under that provision and thus Article 352 TFEU must be resorted to, provided that there are no other Treaty provisions that could be used. With respect to an optional instrument comprising consumer contract law, however, the arguments above concerning the relationship between Articles 114 and 169 TFEU have resonance here in the sense that the achievement of the Union's consumer protection objectives are part of, not separate from, its internal market objectives, which argues for the use of Article 352 TFEU, as opposed to a combination of Articles 169 and 352 TFEU. Therefore, to the extent that such an instrument would be based on Article 352 TFEU to achieve the Union's internal market objectives, the Union's consumer protection objectives can be taken into account by virtue of the 'horizontal' nature of consumer protection policy prescribed in Article 12 TFEU.

9.4.2 Comparative reflection with the US

The prominent role played by the Union's internal market competences in the consumer sphere cannot help but invite comparative reflection with the US. Noticeably, there is no provision in the US Constitution conferring specific competence on the Federal Government to take action in the field of consumer protection, as there is in the Treaties governing the EU under Article 169 TFEU. Yet, when it comes to consumer contract law, there are remarkable parallels in the approaches taken in the American and European settings. As discussed in Chapter 3, federal measures in the field of consumer protection bearing on consumer contract law were enacted in large part pursuant to the Interstate Commerce Clause of the US Constitution and embody the dual objectives of ensuring the free flow of interstate commerce and sufficient protection for consumers, and in fact, some notable case law confirming Congress' reach to intrastate transactions under the Interstate Commerce Clause emanated from such measures.[274] Moreover, akin to the European setting, the American approach to matters of consumer contract law demonstrates considerable respect for action situated at the (Member) State level, as illustrated by recourse to minimum harmonization and the limitations placed on the pre-emption of state laws in this area. In this way, despite the lack of any equivalent to Article 169 TFEU in the American constitutional framework, the US and the EU appear to be travelling down similar paths in the area of consumer contract law in terms

[272] See Chapter 8, § 8.4.3.2.

[273] Case C-166/07 *European Parliament v Council* ('*International Fund for Ireland*') [2009] ECR I-7135. See Chapter 7, § 7.4.2.2.

[274] See Chapter 3, § 3.5.3.3.

of situating measures within the internal market programme within which consumer protection objectives take part.

Going one step further, federal intervention in matters of consumer contract law in the US has resonance with the approach taken by the Union legislature underlying the debate about European contract law. Federal action in this setting has been largely piecemeal in response to particular problems without blanketing the field completely. This has given way to a complex array of federal and state sources in the consumer field, particularly when it comes to matters of consumer contract law. Consequently, it may be wondered to what extent this may find the US following in the footsteps of the EU in the sense of attempting to address problems caused by the ad hoc federal approach and the lack of coherency in the consumer sphere, which may in turn provide new avenues for comparative discourse in connection with the debate.[275]

9.5 Conclusions

On the basis of the foregoing analysis, there is a strong case that it is unlikely that Article 169 TFEU can serve as the legal basis for a European contract law instrument comprising consumer contract law. On the one hand, as demonstrated above, the scope of the Union's competence under Article 169 TFEU is wider than is commonly perceived once the limits of this provision and its relationship with the principle of subsidiarity are fully gleaned. On the other hand, given the entrenchment of EU consumer contract law within the context of the internal market programme, Article 169 TFEU plays an important role, albeit an indirect one, in the debate by placing further impetus on the use of the Union's internal market competence of Article 114 TFEU (and potentially Article 352 TFEU depending upon the instrument concerned) for the adoption of a European contract law instrument, optional or otherwise, which includes or is limited to consumer contract law in this setting. While this may generate tensions about the overshadowing of the Union's consumer protection competence of Article 169 TFEU by its internal market competence of Article 114 TFEU, this analysis demonstrates a readiness on the part of the Union institutions to take action under Article 169 TFEU in various areas of consumer protection outside the confines of the internal market, which may lead to a more balanced relationship between the two provisions in the foreseeable future.

[275] For further discussion in light of recent legislative developments, see, eg, K Gutman, 'The Development of Consumer Law in the US: Comparisons with the EU Experience' (2012) 1 *EUVR* 212 and citations therein.

10

European Contract Law and Judicial Cooperation in Civil Matters

10.1 Introduction

At first glance, there seems to be a paradox concerning the role played by Article 81 TFEU in the debate about European contract law. On the one hand, Article 81 TFEU (ex Article 65 EC), conferring competence on the Union to adopt measures in the field of judicial cooperation in civil matters, is generally perceived as relating to matters of procedural law, private international law, and transnational litigation, not substantive contract law (or substantive private law generally).[1] This explains why on the occasions in which this provision has been contemplated in the debate, it is often dismissed as being incapable of providing a legal basis for a European contract law instrument.[2] On the other hand, as discussed in Chapter 4, a major catalyst for the debate was point 39 of the European Council's Tampere Conclusions, which was grounded in the text of former Article 65 EC, or what is now Article 81 TFEU, itself.[3] This set into motion the infusion of European contract law within the institutional activities taking

[1] See, eg, J Basedow, 'The Communitarization of the Conflict of Laws under the Treaty of Amsterdam' (2000) 37 *CML Rev* 687, 702 (reiterated in, eg, J Basedow, 'The Communitarisation of Private International Law' (2009) 73 *Rabels Z* 455, 457; J Basedow, 'The Case for a European Insurance Contract Act' in AS Hartkamp et al (eds), *Towards a European Civil Code*, 4th rev and expanded edn (Kluwer/Ars Aequi Libri, 2011) 735, 749); G Betlem and E Hondius, 'European Private Law after the Treaty of Amsterdam' (2001) 9 *ERPL* 3, 4; S Peers, *EU Justice and Home Affairs Law*, 3rd edn (Oxford Univ Press, 2011) 615.

[2] As regards the Union institutions, see Chapter 6, § 6.2.4.3. As regards the scholarly literature, see, eg, MW Hesselink et al, 'The legal basis for an optional instrument on European contract law', CSECL Working Paper Series No 2007/04, 43; P-C Müller-Graff, 'Closer Cooperation in European Community Contract Law' in K Boele-Woelki and W Grosheide (eds), *The Future of European Contract Law—Essays in honour of Ewoud Hondius* (Kluwer, 2007) 91, 99–100; JW Rutgers, 'European Competence and a European Civil Code, a Common Frame of Reference or an Optional Instrument' in *Towards a European Civil Code*, n 1, 311, 315; J Ziller, 'The Legitimacy of the Codification of Contract Law in View of the Allocation of Competences between the European Union and its Member States' in MW Hesselink (ed), *The Politics of a European Civil Code* (Kluwer, 2006) 89, 101. But this is not always the case: compare, eg, J-J Kuipers, 'The Legal Basis for a European Optional Instrument' (2011) 19 *ERPL* 545. As regards the definition of a European contract law instrument, see Chapter 1, § 1.2.2.1.

[3] To recall, point 39 stated in relevant part: 'As regards substantive law, an overall study is requested on the need to approximate Member States' legislation in civil matters in order *to eliminate obstacles to the good functioning of civil proceedings*.' Presidency Conclusions, Tampere European Council, 15–16 Oct 1999 (Tampere Conclusions) (emphasis added). By comparison, former Art 65(c) EC referred to: '*eliminating obstacles to the good functioning of civil proceedings*, if necessary by promoting the compatibility of the rules on civil procedure applicable in the Member States' (emphasis added). Art 81(2)(f) TFEU refers to: '*the elimination of obstacles to the proper functioning of civil proceedings*, if necessary by promoting the compatibility of the rules on civil procedure applicable in the Member States' (emphasis added). This is not to say that questions had not arisen, even before Tampere, as regards whether the approximation of substantive private law could be considered to fall within the ambit of judicial cooperation in civil matters: see, eg, U Drobnig, 'European Private International Law After The Treaty of Amsterdam: Perspectives for the Next Decade' (2000) 11 *KCLJ* 190, 191–192.

place within the Area of Freedom, Security and Justice (AFSJ) through the foundations established by the European Council's Hague and Stockholm Programmes. As a consequence, it has become something of 'popular sport' to witness the increasing number of instances in the literature in which scholars routinely refer to the European contract law project amidst discussion of judicial cooperation in civil matters and the AFSJ without much critical analysis of why that is even so.[4]

Taking a closer look, however, this situation may not be so paradoxical after all, once Article 81 TFEU's role in European contract law is further examined. Article 81 TFEU underpins two key issues bearing directly on the constitutional assessment of European contract law, which demonstrate that it is a mistake to discount or dispose of Article 81 TFEU too quickly.[5] First, there is Article 81 TFEU's role as a potential legal basis for a European contract law instrument. Remarkably, although Article 81 TFEU has generally not been given much credence in the debate by commentators, it was mainly in relation to this provision, as opposed to others such as Article 114 TFEU (ex Article 95 EC), that proposals were submitted during the European Convention to introduce a specific legal basis in the Treaties for the approximation of contract law (as well as other fields of private law). The fact that such proposals were made begs questions concerning the Union's competence under this provision in relation to European contract law, and the fact that they failed necessitates inquiry as to whether this cuts against arguments supporting the Union's competence in this domain under the Treaty framework as it stands now with the entry into force of the Lisbon Treaty.

Secondly, there is Article 81 TFEU's linkage to Articles 114 and 352 TFEU (ex Articles 95 and 308 EC) as far as the adoption of a European contract law instrument is concerned. In the discourse, certain scholars have claimed that even though Article 81 TFEU cannot itself serve as a legal basis for such an instrument, it strengthens the case for recourse to Article 114 TFEU.[6] Moreover, the exercise of the Union's competence under Article 81 TFEU has relevance for the interplay between the principles of subsidiarity and proportionality and the use of optional instruments, which also directs attention to Article 114 TFEU, as well as Article 352 TFEU. As such, the extent to which Article 81 TFEU may bolster potential recourse to the Union's internal market competences of Articles 114 and 352 TFEU in relation to the adoption of a European contract law instrument, optional or otherwise, merits inquiry. Both issues are dealt with seriatim in the sections below.

[4] See, eg, PE Herzog, 'TEC, Article 65 on Judicial Cooperation in Civil Matters' in H Smit et al (eds), 2 *Smit and Herzog on The Law of the European Union* (Matthew Bender, 2007) 146-1, 146-85–146-86; 'Le rapprochement des législations pour réaliser l'espace de liberté, de sécurité et de justice' in C Blumann (ed), *Commentaire J. Mégret: Marché interieur*, 3rd edn (IEE, 2006) 271, 284–285; Peers, n 1, 644–646; 'Editorial Comments: The EU as an Area of Freedom, Security and Justice: Implementing the Stockholm Programme' (2010) 47 *CML Rev* 1307, 1314. Compare E Storskrubb, *Civil Procedure and EU Law: A Policy Area Uncovered* (Oxford Univ Press, 2008) 7 fn 10. In all fairness, the transfer of responsibility over the European contract law project to DG Justice as the debate proceeded has resulted in the listing of this topic on the Commission's website (<http://ec.europa.eu/justice/>), which may provide the basis for such references in more recent literature: see, eg, P Craig, *The Lisbon Treaty—Law, Politics and Treaty Reform* (Oxford Univ Press, 2010) 360; E Storskrubb, 'Civil Justice—A Newcomer and an Unstoppable Wave?' in P Craig and G de Búrca (eds), *The Evolution of EU Law*, 2nd edn (Oxford Univ Press, 2011) 299, 314–316.

[5] There are other issues related to the scope of Union competence under Art 81 TFEU that bear some relation to European contract law, eg, in connection with Union action concerning consumer enforcement and redress. See Chapter 9, § 9.1.

[6] See § 10.3.2.

10.2 Article 81 TFEU as a Potential Legal Basis in European Contract Law

10.2.1 The former Treaty framework

As a formal matter, Article 81 TFEU (ex Article 65 EC) was the creation of the Amsterdam Treaty. In the original EEC Treaty, there was no mention of 'judicial cooperation in civil matters', let alone any provision resembling what is now Article 81 TFEU. Yet, there were certain provisions that were concerned in one way or another with the topic of private international law, which was eventually covered by Article 81 TFEU. In particular, former Article 220 EEC (later Article 293 EC) provided:

> Member States shall, so far as is necessary, enter into negotiations with each other with a view to securing for the benefit of their nationals: . . . the simplification of formalities governing the reciprocal recognition and enforcement of judgments of courts or tribunals and of arbitration awards.[7]

Indeed, it was this provision on which the 1968 Brussels Convention on jurisdiction and the enforcement of judgments in civil and commercial matters was based, before its subsequent conversion into a Community instrument under former Article 65 EC.[8] Former Article 293 EC remained unchanged over the years, until it was repealed with the entry into force of the Lisbon Treaty.[9] Its authorization of the use of intergovernmental conventions in matters that would eventually come to be encompassed within Article 81 TFEU was echoed in Article 81 TFEU's predecessor in the Maastricht Treaty.

The Maastricht Treaty introduced the notion of 'judicial cooperation in civil matters' within the newly constructed third pillar of the EU, then called Justice and Home Affairs (JHA).[10] The third pillar essentially took intergovernmental cooperation in this area 'up a notch' by housing it within the Treaty framework itself. Under Article K.1 EU, as part of the EU's objectives in this field, there were nine areas regarded as 'matters of common interest' for the Member States, the sixth of which was labelled 'judicial cooperation in civil matters'.[11] There were no further provisions elaborating the meaning or scope of this concept, save for Article K.3 EU, which specified the types of measures that could be taken by the Council in this field, thereby including, 'without prejudice to Article 220 EC', recourse to conventions that would be recommended to the Member States for adoption in accordance with their respective constitutional requirements.[12]

In view of the minimalist approach of the Maastricht Treaty, the momentous changes brought about by the Amsterdam Treaty stand out in terms of fleshing out in greater detail the field of judicial cooperation in civil matters and transferring it, along with certain other fields, to the first or Community pillar under Title IV of the

[7] Ex Art 293, fourth indent EC (originally Art 220, fourth indent, E(E)C). For discussion as to why this field was chosen, see J Pipkorn, 'Les methodes de rapprochement des législations à l'intérieur de la C.E.E' in P Bourel et al, *The Influence of the European Communities upon Private International Law of the Member States* (Larcier, 1981) 13, 31. The other three fields singled out in this provision were: (1) the protection of persons and the enjoyment of rights under the same conditions as those accorded by each State to its own nationals; (2) the abolition of double taxation within the Community; and (3) the mutual recognition of companies, the retention of legal personality in the event of transfers of company seat from one Member State to another, and the possibility of mergers between companies governed by laws of different countries.

[8] See n 92.

[9] Table of equivalences, [2012] OJ C326/363.

[10] Maastricht Treaty, Title VI EU.

[11] Maastricht Treaty, Art K.1(6) EU.

[12] Maastricht Treaty, Art K.3(2)(c) EU.

EC Treaty concerning visas, asylum, immigration, and other policies related to free movement of persons. Title IV of the EC Treaty in conjunction with Title VI of the EU Treaty, the third pillar of the EU concerning 'Police and Judicial Cooperation in Criminal Matters' (PJCCM), comprised the AFSJ, which was introduced by the Amsterdam Treaty as a foremost objective of the EU.[13]

As far as former Article 65 EC was concerned, the Amsterdam Treaty gave with one hand what it took away with the other. It put flesh on the bones of judicial cooperation in civil matters and cemented it to the achievement of the AFSJ at the same time that it housed it in a special section of the EC Treaty, the so-called 'ghetto' of Title IV EC,[14] saddling it to sensitive policies concerning visas, asylum, immigration, and the free movement of persons, much to the chagrin of commentators who viewed this as stifling or marginalizing the viability of this provision.[15] The placement of Article 65 EC in Title IV of the EC Treaty had crucial implications for the institutional framework concerning Community action in judicial cooperation in civil matters, which diverged somewhat from mainstream Community practice, as illustrated by the prominent role of the Member States and the Council in the decision-making process,[16] the opt-outs for the UK, Ireland, and Denmark,[17] and the restrictions placed on the Court of Justice's jurisdiction.[18] It also filtered into the academic debate on the scope of Article 65 EC and the extent to which it would displace, or not, the Community's competence under other Treaty provisions, particularly as regards the approximation of private international law rules vis-à-vis former Article 95 EC (now Article 114 TFEU).[19] Thereafter, Article 65 EC was not modified by the Nice Treaty aside from arrangements concerning the requisite decision-making procedures.[20] Thus, the scope of the Community's competence under Article 65 EC was fixed by the Amsterdam Treaty, which sets the stage for this discussion.

At the forefront of the former EU Treaty, Article 2 EU had declared as one of the Union's objectives 'to maintain and develop the Union as an area of freedom, security and justice, in which the free movement of persons is assured in conjunction with appropriate measures with respect to external border controls, asylum, immigration and

[13] Amsterdam Treaty, Art B, fourth indent; Preamble of EU Treaty, tenth recital (later Art 2, fourth indent, EU; Preamble of EU Treaty, eleventh recital, now corresponding to Art 3(3) TEU; Preamble of TEU, twelfth recital).

[14] See, eg, E Guild and S Peers, 'Out of the Ghetto? The Personal Scope of EU Law' in S Peers and N Rogers (eds), *EU Immigration and Asylum Law* (Martinus Nijhoff, 2006) 81, 83.

[15] See, eg, Drobnig, n 3, 193; J Meeusen, 'Fifteen Theses on Brussels I, Rome I and the European Union's Institutional Framework' in J Meeusen et al (eds), *Enforcement of International Contracts in the European Union: Convergence and divergence between Brussels I and Rome I* (Intersentia, 2004) 43, 47–50; P-E Partsch, *Le droit international privé européen: De Rome à Nice* (Larcier, 2003) 295–298.

[16] See ex Art 67 EC.

[17] See generally Peers, n 1, 73–90.

[18] See ex Art 68 EC.

[19] Compare, eg, Basedow, n 1, 696–708; J. Israël, 'Conflicts of Law and the EC after Amsterdam: A Change for the Worse?' (2000) 7 *MJ* 81, 88–98; Partsch, n 15, 414–450; O Remien, 'European Private International Law, The European Community and Its Emerging Area of Freedom, Security and Justice' (2001) 38 *CML Rev* 53, 72–73. More recently, see, eg, M Fallon and S Francq, 'Vers un droit proprement communautaire des conflits de lois ou de juridiction' in O De Schutter and P Nihoul (eds), *Une Constitution pour l'Europe* (Larcier, 2004) 239, 259–260; Meeusen, n 15, 51–55; Peers, n 1, 613–615.

[20] Ex Art 67 EC had stipulated recourse to unanimous voting in the Council and consultation of the Parliament on proposals submitted by the Commission or a Member State for an initial period of five years from entry into force of the Amsterdam Treaty. As part of the revisions made by the Nice Treaty, this provision was changed so as to provide, inter alia, that 'the measures provided for in Article 65 EC with the exception of aspects relating to family law' would be adopted by the co-decision procedure of ex Art 251 EC with qualified majority voting in the Council. See ex Art 67(5), second indent, EC.

the prevention and combating of crime',[21] thereby leaving out judicial cooperation in civil matters, inadvertently or not. Nevertheless, as the first provision of Title IV of the EC Treaty, Article 61 EC stipulated that '[i]n order to establish progressively an area of freedom, security and justice, the Council shall adopt . . . measures in the field of judicial cooperation in civil matters as provided for in Article 65'.[22] Proceeding to Article 65 EC, this provision stated in full: 'Measures in the field of judicial cooperation in civil matters having *cross-border implications*, to be taken in accordance with Article 67[23] and *insofar as necessary for the proper functioning of the internal market*, shall *include*:

(a) improving and simplifying:
   - the system of cross-border service of judicial and extrajudicial documents;
   - cooperation in the taking of evidence;
   - the recognition and enforcement of decisions in civil and commercial cases, including decisions in extrajudicial cases;

(b) promoting the compatibility of the rules applicable in the Member States concerning the conflict of laws and of jurisdiction;

(c) eliminating obstacles to the good functioning of civil proceedings, if necessary by promoting the compatibility of the rules on civil procedure applicable in the Member States.[24]

As highlighted by the italicized language, the requirements relating to Article 65 EC's 'cross-border implications' and its linkage to the 'proper functioning of the internal market' resulted in substantial controversy concerning the Community's competence under Article 65 EC, as discussed in the next section. Moreover, the word 'include' was interpreted as meaning that the measures elaborated under Article 65 EC were not exhaustive.[25] These attributes, in combination with the particular language used for each of the three subsections, made Article 65 EC a difficult and complex provision, entailing scrutiny of its various components, none of which were fleshed out with much guidance. This was symptomatic of the political negotiations surrounding Article 65 EC, as well as Title IV of the EC Treaty generally.[26] There has been much in-depth study made of the genesis of Article 65 EC, which need not be rehearsed here.[27] Suffice it to say that the approximation of substantive private law does not seem to have figured in the discussion, with the Commission explicitly opining that the objective of Article 65 EC was not to establish a civil code or even a code of civil procedure.[28]

Given the text of former Article 65 EC, this explains why this provision was not generally considered by commentators to support the adoption of a European contract law instrument. For European contract law, aside from the fact that such an instrument continues to be rooted in the Union's internal market objectives, the major stumbling block centred on Article 65 EC's substantive scope of application in terms of the subject matter or areas covered by this provision. By virtue of the topics listed in its three subsections, Article 65 EC expressly excluded matters of substantive private

[21] Ex Art 2, fourth indent, EU. [22] Ex Art 61(c) EC. [23] See n 20.

[24] Ex Art 65 EC (emphasis added). [25] See ns 31–32 and accompanying text.

[26] See, eg, Herzog, n 4, 146–5; C Kohler, 'Interrogations sur les sources du droit international privé européen après le traité d'Amsterdam' (1999) 88 *RCDIP* 1, 13 fn 22.

[27] See Kohler, n 26, 9–14; H. Labayle, 'Un espace de liberté, de sécurité et de justice' (1997) 33 *RTDE* 105, 148–150; Partsch, n 15, 299–302.

[28] Kohler, n 26, 11–12 fn 16. Despite suggestions for mentioning 'access to justice' and 'approximation', among other things, explicitly in the text of Art 65 EC, this was not taken up (Kohler, n 26, 11–12 fn 16). As seen below, these matters would eventually make their way into the Draft Constitutional Treaty (DCT) and the Lisbon Treaty.

law, including substantive contract law, from its scope, thereby putting an immediate end to the discussion. Admittedly, there were certain ambiguities raised by Article 65 EC's non-exhaustive nature and terminological concepts related to the scope of this provision, but with closer examination, these points, arguably, did not alter the constitutional assessment of former Article 65 EC in relation to the adoption of a European instrument of substantive contract law.

First, as regards terminology, the terms used in Article 65 EC—eg, 'civil proceedings', 'civil procedure', 'conflicts of law', and even 'judicial cooperation in civil matters' itself—were left undefined.[29] As emphasized by scholars, the term 'judicial cooperation in civil matters' was particularly misleading: the matters listed in Article 65 EC were not solely 'judicial' by virtue of its coverage of 'conflicts of law' and 'extrajudicial cases'; the reference to 'cooperation' harked back to its intergovernmental lineage in the Maastricht Treaty, even though Article 65 EC had been used to approximate national laws; and 'civil matters' could be read to imply a narrow scope, but in fact, had been understood more broadly as pertaining to non-criminal or administrative matters.[30] Although each of Article 65 EC's components could have assumed different shapes if taken in isolation, it was their placement within the provision as a whole that was determinative for the substantive scope of Article 65 EC, which excluded action to approximate substantive private law, including contract law.

Furthermore, the fact that former Article 65 EC was considered to be non-exhaustive did not alter this situation. The English version, among other language versions, of Article 65 EC used the word 'include', which strongly suggested that the specific topics explicitly listed in the various subsections of Article 65 EC were not exhaustive.[31] The French version made this explicit, by stipulating '*entre autres*' (among others) in the text of Article 65 EC.[32] Nonetheless, taking into account the list of topics that were elaborated in Article 65 EC and both the purpose and context of this provision in relation to the Community's objectives to be achieved in the field of judicial cooperation in civil matters, it would have been a difficult stretch, arguably *ultra vires*, to extend what was the Community's competence under this provision to the adoption of a European substantive contract law instrument.[33] In any event, this issue has become moot with

[29] Ironically, while the term 'private international law' was readily associated with former Art 65 EC, it was not explicitly cited therein. From the European standpoint, the term may be viewed in broad or limited ways, ie it can be restricted to conflicts of law matters or extend to other matters such as jurisdiction, recognition, and enforcement of judgments. See Storskrubb, *Civil Procedure and EU Law*, n 4, 9–10 and citations therein; Green Paper on the conversion of the Rome Convention of 1980 on the law applicable to contractual obligations into a Community instrument and its modernisation, COM (2002) 654 final, 14.1.2003, point 1.2 fn 2. Under ex Art 65(b) EC, conflicts of law are distinguished from jurisdiction, although recognition and enforcement appeared one line up in ex Art 65(a) EC. Thus, despite the somewhat awkward division, the broad conception of 'private international law' was generally covered in former Art 65 EC. The same holds true with the Lisbon Treaty's reframing of this provision as Art 81 TFEU, which largely reproduces this language in Arts 81(2)(a) and (c) TFEU.

[30] See Meeusen, n 15, 48–49; Storskrubb, *Civil Procedure and EU Law*, n 4, 9–12. See also Opinion of AG Kokott in Case C-435/06 *C* [2007] ECR I-10141, point 52.

[31] See, eg, Dutch version ('omvatten'); German version ('schließen ein'); Spanish version ('incluirán'); Italian version ('includono'). See further Basedow, n 1, 700–701 (noting that the Dutch proposal for exhaustive wording rejected).

[32] French version ('entre autres').

[33] This was alluded to in relation to European private law as a whole in the chapter concerning the EU's competence to adopt a European civil code authored by Professors Wilfried Tilmann and Walter van Gerven in the 1999 Working Paper (Chapter 4, § 4.3.4): see European Parliament DG for Research Working Paper, *The Private Law Systems in The EU: Discrimination on Grounds of Nationality and the Need for a European Civil Code* (Legal Affairs Series, JURI-103 EN), available at <http://www.europarl.europa.eu/>, 192. See also, eg, A Staudinger and S Leible, 'Article 65 of the EC Treaty in the EC System of Competencies' (2000/01) *ELF* 225, 228.

the changes brought about by the Lisbon Treaty, whereby Article 81 TFEU is generally considered to be exhaustive, and while adding to the list of matters, still explicitly excludes mention of substantive private law, which leads to the next section.

10.2.2 The present Treaty framework

Paving the way for the Draft Constitutional Treaty and ultimately the Lisbon Treaty, the framework comprising the AFSJ, including former Article 65 EC, was the focal point of Working Group X on 'Freedom, Security and Justice' within the European Convention. To a great extent, the discussion of Article 65 EC was largely overshadowed by other policy fields, such as asylum, immigration, and criminal matters, or institutional topics, such as the regime of legal instruments and decision-making procedures, in this area.[34] However, Article 65 EC was not wholly neglected, and it stimulated proposals by various members of the Convention.[35] More to the point, it had the potential to change the course of the constitutional dimensions of European contract law by virtue of certain proposals that sought to amend Article 65 EC so as to provide for a specific legal basis explicitly conferring competence on the EU to approximate several fields of private law, including contract law.

This was not altogether unexpected in light of the contribution submitted by the Working Group's sole expert in judicial cooperation in civil matters, Professor Alegría Borrás.[36] In the very last point of her extensive discussion of Article 65 EC, she drew a link between the revision of this provision and European private law:

> En fin [sic], pour ne pas alourdir cette exposée sur des aspects systématiques, on ne peut pas ignorer qu'au sein de la Communauté a vu le jour une tendance en faveur de l'élaboration d'un *Droit privé européen*, même si les méthodes pour y arriver, l'étendue du processus d'unification et sa force, contraignante ou non, sont encore l'objet d'un débat assez complexe. Une fois encore, si cette tendance pourrait être accueillie dans le Traité, il conviendrait d'examiner ses rapports avec les mesures pouvant être adoptées sur la base d'un article 65 révisé.[37]

Article 65 EC was certainly not the only provision in which discussion of the Community's competence to approximate substantive private law, particularly contract law, was aired during the European Convention. The issue also filtered through a few contributions submitted in other contexts, particularly in connection with the

[34] See, eg, Mandate of Working Group X 'Freedom, Security and Justice', CONV 258/02 WGX3, dated 12 Sept 2002, point II; Summary of the meeting on 16 Sept 2002, CONV 274/02 WGX4, dated 17 Sept 2002, point 2; Note on the plenary meeting—Brussels, 6 and 7 June 2002, CONV 97/02, dated 19 June 2002, point II.10.

[35] See, eg, Summary of proposed amendments regarding the area of freedom, security and justice—Draft Article 31 (Part One) and draft Articles from Part Two, CONV 644/1/03REV1, dated 7 May 2003, 26–29 (Summary Document). There also used to be a list of proposed amendments available at the European Convention's official website, but as noted in Chapter 7, this website appears to have been taken down; all Convention documents cited in this book are on file with the author.

[36] Exposé de Mme Alegría Borrás, Professeur de Droit international privé de l'Université de Barcelone, lors de l'audition du 30 Oct 2002, WGX Working Document 08, dated 4 Nov 2002. For the list of experts invited by Working Group X, see Final Report of Working Group X 'Freedom, Security and Justice', CONV 426/02 WGX14, dated 2 Dec 2002, Annex.

[37] Exposé de Mme Alegría Borrás, n 36, point c, at 16 (emphasis added). To be complete, she went on to add: 'Et cela d'autant plus qu'un Droit privé européen, quelle que soit sa nature et son domaine, n'exclue pas les règles de conflit de lois et de juridictions incluses dans les Directives communautaires sectiorelles qui sont un *acquis* indéniable de Droit communautaire, et il n'exclue non plus des règles de Droit international privé pour les relations transfrontières adoptées sur la base d'un article 65 révisé.' Exposé de Mme Alegría Borrás, n 36, point c, at 16.

internal market and Article 95 EC.[38] Nonetheless, it was primarily in connection with Article 65 EC, as opposed to other Treaty provisions, that proposals were submitted in this regard.

In total, there appears to have been only two formal proposals for amendment of Article 65 EC relevant to European contract law, both of which emanated from representatives from Germany.[39] Of the two, the most high-profile proposal came from Joschka Fischer, Representative of the German Government,[40] who sought to introduce a new provision concerning 'substantive civil law' as part of Article 65 EC.[41] Translated from German, the proposal read in full:

> Notwithstanding Art. (95 EC Single Market), the European Parliament and the Council may, in accordance with the legislative procedure, adopt laws and framework laws for legislative approximation in the domain of civil law, which have the following fields as subject-matter:
> - *Out of the law of obligations, the general and special law of contracts, especially rights and obligations from a contract, fulfillment, default, prescription, and law of enrichment,*
> - Out of material family law, the right to a name, the European contractual matrimonial regime, the right of access and the cross-border right of custody of children,
> - Out of the law of succession, a European contractual regime in law of succession.[42]

[38] See, eg, Proposals by the CDU and CSU for a European Constitutional Treaty, CONV 616/03, dated 1 April 2003, Annex to the Annex, 'Internal Market', 10 ('examine the need for *new EU legal bases for the harmonisation of certain aspects of civil law (e.g., commercial and contract law)*, with a view to preventing the fragmentation of law caused by one-off EU regulation based hitherto on general internal market provisions, where necessary by allowing individuals and firms to choose which law to apply to EU regulation') (emphasis added); see also ns 46–48 and accompanying text.

[39] There were other proposals for amendment of Art 65 EC, which pertained to matters within the realm of private law, but without direct bearing on the approximation of substantive contract law or related fields. Eg, there was a proposal submitted by Joachim Wuermeling, an alternate representative of the European Parliament, which concerned the approximation of copyright law and the creation of the European company: see Summary Document, n 35, 29.

[40] At the time of the European Convention, he was the German Minister for Foreign Affairs.

[41] Suggestion for amendment of Article 14a(neu) by Mr Joschka Fischer ('Artikel: 14a neu (Materielles Zivilrecht)') (Fischer Proposal). To be distinguished, he had submitted a separate proposal regarding the amendment of Art 65 EC in connection with family matters: see Suggestion for amendment of Article 14 by Mr Joschka Fischer ('Artikel 14: [Justizielle Zusammenarbeit in Zivilsachen]'). At the time, Art 14 was the counterpart to Art 65 EC.

[42] Fischer Proposal, n 41 (author's translation; no official translation exists) (emphasis added). In the original German version, it read:

> Unbeschadet des Art. (95 EG Binnenmarkt) können das Europäische Parlament und der Rat nach dem Gesetzgebungsverfahren Gesetze und Rahmengesetze zur Rechtsangleichung auf dem Gebiet des Zivilrechts erlassen, die folgende Sachgebiete zum Gegenstand haben:
> - aus dem Recht der Schuldverhältnisse das allgemeine und besondere Vertragsrecht, insbesondere Rechte und Pflichten aus einem Vertrag, Erfüllung, Leistungsstörungen, Verjährung, und Bereicherungsrecht,
> - aus dem materiellen Familienrecht das Namensrecht, einen europäischen Wahlgüterstand, das Umgangsrecht und das grenzüberschreitende Sorgerecht
> - aus dem Erbrecht ein europäisches Wahlerbrecht.

Incidentally, as regards the translation of 'Rechtsangleichung', the English word 'approximation' is chosen to correspond to its usage in the Treaties, eg, in relation to Articles 114 and 115 TFEU and the heading of the chapter concerning 'Approximation of Laws' in the TFEU. But scholars have noted there is some discrepancy between the German language version and others in this regard. See, eg, EJ Lohse, 'The meaning of harmonisation in the context of European Union law—a process in need of definition' in M Andenas and CB Andersen (eds), *Theory and Practice of Harmonisation* (Edward Elgar, 2011) 282, 309.

In his explanation for this proposal, Mr Fischer stated:

> Until now, the legislative approximation in material civil law takes place on the basis of Article 95 EC competence within the Single Market. In the framework of the creation of the new title Area of Freedom, Security and Justice, an express competence for harmonization should be created in material civil law, like in material criminal law, also in order to remove any doubt on the scope of actual Article 95.[43]

In other words, it appeared that this proposal sought to ground the EU's competence for the approximation of contract law and other fields of private law listed above under Article 65 EC, not Article 95 EC.[44] Yet, the consequences for the EU's competence under Article 95 EC in the field of contract law were not further elaborated.

Incidentally, Professor Jürgen Meyer, a member of the European Convention representing the German National Parliament on behalf of the Bundestag,[45] submitted a contribution titled 'An area of freedom, security and justice'.[46] This contribution was not presented in the form of a formal amendment to the text of Article 65 EC.[47] Nonetheless, it was strikingly similar, though not exactly identical, to Mr Fischer's proposal. The section on 'Cooperation in civil matters' contained one paragraph, which stated:

> As far as substantive civil law is concerned, the provisions of Article 95 of the EC Treaty relating to the approximation of laws should be supplemented by means of a catalogue enumerating the areas of civil law in which approximation is required and eliminating any doubts as to the reliability of the present Article 95. This catalogue should comprise the following subject matter:
> - *the law of contracts, particularly with regard to rights and obligations from a contract;*
> - selected areas of substantive family law, particularly married couples' choice of surname, European rules permitting a choice of marital property regime, the right of access to children and cross-border custody rights;
> - certain matters relating to the law of succession, particularly European provisions on testamentary freedom.[48]

On its face, this paragraph concerned Article 95 EC, not Article 65 EC, thereby advocating that the text of Article 95 EC should be revised so as to encompass the above-listed catalogue of topics that included contract law.[49] Yet, its placement in a

[43] Fischer Proposal, n 41 (author's translation; no official translation exists). In the original German version, it read:

> Bisher erfolgt die Rechtsangleichumg [sic] im materiellen Zivilrecht aufgrund der Binnenmarktkompetenz des Art. 95 EG. Im Rahmen der Schaffung des neuen Titels Raum der Freiheit der Sicherheit und des Rechts sollte wie für das materielle Strafrecht eine ausdrückliche Harmonisierungskompetenz für das materielle Zivilrecht geschaffen werden, auch um Zweifel an der Tragfähigkeit des derzeitigen Art. 95 zu beseitigen.

[44] The summary of proposed amendments may have misstated or misrepresented the import of this proposal, since it was framed as primarily relating to family law. See Summary Document, n 35, 29.

[45] In brief, the German National Parliament is composed of two chambers, the Bundestag and the Bundesrat: the Bundestag is composed of representatives of the people, whereas the Bundesrat is composed of representatives of the federal States (Länder) at the federal level.

[46] Contribution by Professor Jürgen Meyer, member of the Convention—'An area of freedom, security and justice', CONV 447/02 CONTRIB 164, dated 12 Dec 2002 (Meyer Contribution).

[47] As such, it was not mentioned in the list of proposed amendments to Art 65 EC that used to be posted on the European Convention's official website: see n 35.

[48] Meyer Contribution, n 46, point B, at 4 (emphasis added).

[49] Eg, this is how other scholars read it: see, eg, Ziller, n 2, 110.

contribution concerning the AFSJ under the specific heading pertaining to the field of judicial cooperation in civil matters and its resemblance to Mr Fischer's proposal raised questions as to the extent to whether this suggestion was in some way related to Article 65 EC.

The second formal proposal came from Erwin Teufel, one of the representatives of the German National Parliament from the Bundesrat.[50] He also proposed inserting an additional paragraph within the confines of Article 65 EC so as to provide for an explicit legal basis for the approximation of contract law:

> The European Parliament and the Council, in accordance with the legislative procedure, shall adopt laws and framework laws for the *approximation of substantive civil law concerning contract law*, commercial law and law of associations as well as [C]ommunity-wide industrial property and copyright law. Beyond these areas of substantive civil law a resort to other legal bases or harmonization under Article 16, Part One,[51] for purposes of approximating national law is excluded.[52]

He explained the reason for his proposal as follows: 'Already at the current level of integration there is a need for approximation of substantive civil law in cross-border cases. The legal areas which are concerned have to be named explicitly and in detail. Beyond theses [sic] areas harmonization must be excluded.'[53]

This proposal did not provide further elaboration as to the ambit of the fields of national substantive law listed therein, namely what was meant by 'contract law' or even 'commercial law'. With the emphasis on cross-border cases, it was also unclear whether this proposal was meant to limit the measures to be adopted under this new provision from applying to domestic transactions. In that regard, it should be noted that Mr Teufel and Mr Wolfgang Senff, an alternate member of the Convention,[54] submitted a separate contribution to the Convention concerning the 'German Bundesrat Resolution Having Regard to the Themes of the Convention on the Future of the European Union'.[55] Among the recommendations for reform of Title IV of the EC Treaty, the Resolution stated: 'In the field of private law, harmonisation competences should be created for concrete sectors of law with a typically cross-border importance (contractual law, commercial and company law, Community-wide protection of industrial property, copyright).'[56] Assuming that Mr Teufel, as a member of the Bundesrat, sought to align his proposal with this Resolution, this seemed to

[50] Suggestion for amendment of Article 14bis (Part Two, JHA) by Mr Erwin Teufel (Teufel Proposal). There were both English and German versions provided. See n 45 as regards the German National Parliament structure.

[51] At the time, 'Article 16, Part One' concerned the areas of supporting, coordinating, or complementary action of the Union, which was generally denoted by the category of complementary competence. See further Chapter 7, § 7.4.2.3.

[52] Teufel Proposal, n 50 (emphasis added). Although Art 14 corresponded to Art 65 EC, with subsequent renumbering of the provisions, Art III-165 replaced references to Art 14. As such, Mr Teufel submitted a separate proposal concerning the amendment of Art III-165bis, which was substantially the same as that above. See Suggestion for amendment of Article 165bis (nouveau) by Mr Erwin Teufel.

[53] Teufel Proposal, n 50.

[54] Wolfgang Senff, a member of the Bundesrat, served as an alternative member of the German National Parliament at the European Convention, although he was replaced by Wolfgang Gerhards in March 2003.

[55] Contribution of Mr Erwin Teufel, member of the Convention, and Mr Wolfgang Senff, alternate member of the Convention: 'German Bundesrat Resolution Having Regard to the Themes of the Convention on the future of the European Union', dated 12 July 2002.

[56] Contribution of Mr Erwin Teufel and Mr Wolfgang Senff, n 55, 12 ('Title III-Free movement of persons, services and capital (Article 39 et seqq. EC Treaty), and Title IV: Visas, asylum, immigration and other policies relating to free movement of persons (Article 61 et seqq. EC Treaty)').

suggest that it was the character of contract law, that is to say, its cross-border dimension, which was why it was singled out along with the other areas specified in Mr Teufel's proposal.

Altogether, the abovementioned proposals and related contributions apparently did not attract much attention during the Convention proceedings.[57] At least there was no indication in Convention documents that they generated substantial debate among the participants, and they did not garner any mention in the Final Report of Working Group X on the AFSJ. None found their way into the text of the Draft Constitutional Treaty and ultimately the Lisbon Treaty. Instead, the Final Report of Working Group X concluded:

> The Group has had a discussion about the current drafting of Article 65 TEC, and in particular about the limitation of that article to action on 'civil matters having cross-border implications' and 'insofar as necessary for the proper functioning of the internal market'. While some Members have questioned these limitations, the majority of the Group, after careful examination, believes that they could be maintained, and that the wording of the current legal base is broadly appropriate. However, it takes the view that this legal basis on judicial co-operation in civil matters could, within the new overall structure of a single Constitutional Treaty, be dissociated from matters of asylum and immigration and visa policies. Furthermore, the principle of mutual recognition of judicial decisions as a cornerstone of this common policy should be enshrined in the Treaty.[58]

The Working Group's recommendations filtered into the substance of the revised text of Article 65 EC in the Draft Constitutional Treaty.

To recall, there were two versions of the Draft Constitutional Treaty: the 2003 version adopted by the European Convention (by consensus) and the 2004 version signed by representatives of the then twenty-five Member States at the subsequent Intergovernmental Conference (IGC).[59] They shared much in common as regards certain structural changes to the Treaty framework in connection with the AFSJ, such as the placement of the AFSJ as a foremost objective of the Union side by side with the internal market[60] and the consolidation of the various provisions on the AFSJ, including Article 65 EC, in a distinct chapter in Part Three of that Treaty.[61] Yet, as regards the text of Article 65 EC, they were not the same.

In the 2003 version of the Draft Constitutional Treaty, Article 65 EC was renumbered Article III-170 and contained three paragraphs. The first paragraph provided the overarching requirements:

> The Union shall develop judicial cooperation in civil matters *having cross-border implications*, based on the principle of mutual recognition of judgments and decisions in extrajudicial cases. Such cooperation may include the adoption of measures for the *approximation* of the laws and regulations of the Member States.[62]

Aside from explicit language concerning the principle of mutual recognition and approximation, the reference to the internal market was deleted, although the 'cross-border implications' requirement remained. Changes were also made as regards the various matters to be addressed within judicial cooperation in civil matters. Now expanded to eight topics, the second paragraph of Article III-170 provided: 'To this

[57] Ziller, n 2, 110–111.
[58] Working Group X Final Report, n 36, point 5.
[59] See further Chapter 7, § 7.3.
[60] See 2003 DCT, Art 3(2); 2004 DCT, Art I-3(2).
[61] See 2003 DCT, Pt III, Title III, Ch IV; 2004 DCT, Pt III, Title III, Ch IV.
[62] 2003 DCT, Art III-170(1) (emphasis added).

end, [European] laws or framework laws shall lay down measures aimed inter alia at ensuring:

(a) the mutual recognition and enforcement between Member States of judgments and decisions in extrajudicial cases;
(b) the cross-border service of judicial and extrajudicial documents;
(c) the compatibility of the rules applicable in the Member States concerning conflict of laws and of jurisdiction;
(d) cooperation in the taking of evidence;
(e) *a high level of access to justice*;
(f) the proper functioning of civil proceedings, if necessary by promoting the compatibility of the rules on civil procedure applicable in the Member States;
(g) *the development of alternative methods of dispute settlement*;
(h) *support for the training of the judiciary and judicial staff*.'[63]

As signalled by the italicized language, three new topics concerning access to justice, alternative dispute resolution, and judicial training were added to those already found in Article 65 EC, though noticeably the 'eliminating obstacles' language in Article 65(c) EC was deleted in subsection (f) above. The insertion of 'inter alia'—harking back to the French version of Article 65 EC—indicated that the list of various topics was not exhaustive. Finally, the third paragraph of Article III-170 dealt with measures concerning family law with cross-border implications.[64]

In the 2004 version of the Draft Constitutional Treaty, Article 65 EC's counterpart was renumbered Article III-269 and left the first and third paragraphs of the 2003 version of that Treaty cited above relatively untouched.[65] Yet, as regards the second paragraph, several changes were made: the internal market requirement of Article 65(1) EC was reintroduced in modified form; 'inter alia' was taken out; the 'eliminating obstacles' language of Article 65(c) EC was brought back in; and 'a high level of access to justice' was changed to 'effective access to justice'. Thus, Article III-269(2) read in full: 'For the purposes of paragraph 1, European laws or framework laws shall establish measures, *particularly when necessary for the proper functioning of the internal market*, aimed at ensuring:

(a) the mutual recognition and enforcement between Member States of judgments and decisions in extrajudicial cases;
(b) the cross-border service of judicial and extrajudicial documents;
(c) the compatibility of the rules applicable in the Member States concerning conflict of laws and of jurisdiction;
(d) cooperation in the taking of evidence;
(e) *effective access to justice*;
(f) *the elimination of obstacles to* the proper functioning of civil proceedings, if necessary by promoting the compatibility of the rules on civil procedure applicable in the Member States;

[63] 2003 DCT, Art III-170(2) (emphasis added). European laws and framework laws essentially referred to legislative measures akin to the present regulations and directives, respectively. See 2003 DCT, Art 32.
[64] 2003 DCT, Art III-170(3).
[65] 2004 DCT, Art III-269(1), (3).

(g) the development of alternative methods of dispute settlement;

(h) support for the training of the judiciary and judicial staff.'[66]

The 2004 Draft Constitutional Treaty's reframing of Article 65 EC made its way into the Lisbon Treaty, with some further changes.

Starting with the revisions to the EU Treaty, the Lisbon Treaty split up the AFSJ's placement on a par with the internal market, although the AFSJ is still enshrined—now one provision higher than the internal market—as a foremost objective of the Union.[67] In comparison to the sparse language of the Draft Constitutional Treaty—'The Union shall offer its citizens an area of freedom, security and justice without internal frontiers'[68]—Article 3(2) TEU states: 'The Union shall offer its citizens an area of freedom, security and justice without internal frontiers, in which the free movement of persons is ensured in conjunction with appropriate measures with respect to external border controls, asylum, immigration and the prevention and combating of crime.'[69] Save for the reference to 'without internal frontiers', this provision reiterates the old version of Article 2 EU, thereby failing to mention judicial cooperation in civil matters.

As regards the revisions made to the former EC Treaty, now TFEU, the Lisbon Treaty consolidates the various provisions of the former Community and third pillars into a special title devoted to the AFSJ.[70] In the chapter concerning judicial cooperation in civil matters, Article 65 EC is reframed as Article 81 TFEU, which is virtually identical to Article III-269 of the 2004 version of the Draft Constitutional Treaty, save for certain institutional adjustments. For example, the references to European laws and framework laws were replaced by 'measures', to be adopted under the ordinary legislative procedure (ie qualified majority voting in the Council and the co-decision procedure)[71]. Leaving the third paragraph concerning family law aside,[72] the first two paragraphs of Article 81 TFEU read in full:

1. The Union shall develop *judicial cooperation in civil matters having cross-border implications*, based on the *principle of mutual recognition* of judgments and of decisions in extrajudicial cases. Such cooperation may include the adoption of measures for the *approximation* of the laws and regulations of the Member States.
2. For the purposes of paragraph 1, the European Parliament and the Council, acting in accordance with the ordinary legislative procedure, shall adopt measures, *particularly when necessary for the proper functioning of the internal market, aimed at ensuring*:
   (a) the mutual recognition and enforcement between Member States of judgments and of decisions in extrajudicial cases;
   (b) the cross-border service of judicial and extrajudicial documents;
   (c) the compatibility of the rules applicable in the Member States concerning conflict of laws and of jurisdiction;

[66] 2004 DCT, Art III-269(2) (emphasis added). As with the 2003 DCT, the reference to European laws and framework laws in the 2004 DCT referred to legislative acts that were essentially akin to the present regulations and directives, respectively. See 2004 DCT, Art I-33.

[67] See Art 3(2)–(3) TEU. [68] See n 60.

[69] Art 3(2) TEU. See also Preamble of TEU, twelfth recital.

[70] TFEU, Pt Three, Title V. [71] Art 81(2) TFEU.

[72] See further, eg, G De Baere and K Gutman, 'The Impact of the EU and the ECJ on European Family Law' in JM Scherpe (ed), *Research Handbook on European Family Law* (Edward Elgar, forthcoming 2015) and citations therein.

(d) cooperation in the taking of evidence;
(e) *effective access to justice*;
(f) the elimination of obstacles to the proper functioning of civil proceedings, if necessary by promoting the compatibility of the rules on civil procedure applicable in the Member States;
(g) *the development of alternative methods of dispute settlement*;
(h) *support for the training of the judiciary and judicial staff.*[73]

With regard to these two paragraphs, the remodelling of Article 65 EC in Article 81 TFEU can be considered something of a *quid pro quo*. On the one hand, Article 81 TFEU broadens to some extent the ambit of the Union's competence in the field of judicial cooperation in civil matters. It provides for the adoption of measures 'particularly when'—as opposed to 'in so far as'—'necessary for the proper functioning of the internal market',[74] which implies less stringent linkage between measures adopted under Article 81 TFEU and the internal market, as compared to Article 65 EC.[75] Moreover, the 'cross-border implications' requirement of Article 65 EC is still there, only now it is housed in a separate provision apart from the internal market requirement. Under the first paragraph of Article 81 TFEU, it is stated more generally that the 'Union shall develop judicial cooperation in civil matters having cross-border implications'.[76] Although Article 65(1) EC was not exactly crystal clear as regards to whether it was 'matters' or 'measures' that the cross-border requirement modified ('Measures in the field of judicial cooperation in civil matters having cross-border implications'), Article 81 TFEU seems to indicate that it is the former, not the latter.[77]

On the other hand, Article 81 TFEU embodies a more circumscribed provision by virtue of the 'aimed at ensuring' language, which suggests that it is confined to an exhaustive list of topics still generally concerned with procedural, transnational litigation, and private international law matters.[78] The three new topics added to the list—'effective access to justice', 'development of alternative methods of dispute settlement', and 'support for the training of the judiciary and judicial staff'—are by no means novel. The legislature had already adopted, pursuant to its competence under former Article 65 EC, measures concerning access to justice,[79] alternative methods of dispute

[73] Art 81(1)–(2) TFEU (emphasis added). [74] Art 81(2) TFEU.

[75] This has not gone unnoticed in the case law. See, eg, Opinion of AG Sharpston in Case C-353/06 *Grunkin and Paul* [2008] ECR I-7639, point 5 fn 2. [76] Art 81(1) TFEU.

[77] Compare Art 81(3), first para, TFEU ('measures concerning family law with cross-border implications'); Art 81(3), second para, TFEU ('a decision determining those aspects of family law with cross-border implications').

[78] This seems to be more apparent in certain language versions than others. Compare, eg, Dutch version ('maatregelen vast die het volgende beogen'); German version ('Maßnahmen, die Folgendes sicherstellen sollen'); French version ('mesures visant à assurer'); Italian version ('misure volte a garantire'); Spanish version ('medidas para garantizar'). Noticeably, however, the various topics are separated by semi-colons, with no 'and' following subsection (g), which would have clarified matters. The exhaustive nature of Art 81 TFEU is recognized in the literature: see, eg, Max Planck Institute for Comparative and International Private Law, 'Policy Options for Progress Towards a European Contract Law' (2011) 75 *Rabels Z* 371, 387 ('probably'); Peers, n 1, 605, 608; J-C Piris, *The Lisbon Treaty—A Legal and Political Analysis* (Cambridge Univ Press, 2010) 179. But some disagree: see, eg, G Wagner, 'Harmonisation of Civil Procedure: Policy Perspectives' in *Civil Litigation in a Globalising World* (TMC Asser Press/Springer, 2012) 93, 97.

[79] See, eg, Council Dir 2003/8/EC of 27 Jan 2003 to improve *access to justice* in cross-border disputes by establishing minimum common rules relating to legal aid for such disputes, [2003] OJ L26/41; *corrigendum*, [2003] OJ L32/15 (Legal Aid Directive) (emphasis added).

settlement,[80] and the training of the judiciary,[81] some of which bear almost identical language used to describe these three fields in Article 81 TFEU. The approximation of national laws in the fields of procedure, transnational litigation, and private international law also had a well-established record under former Article 65 EC. Basically, nothing added to the text of Article 81 TFEU explicitly has anything to do with (the approximation of) substantive private law.

Consequently, the changes brought about by the Lisbon Treaty in connection with the text of Article 65 EC largely fall more on the side of explicit recognition of what was already going on, as opposed to heralding revolutionary change.[82] The additional fields, the explicit reference to approximation and the principle of mutual recognition, and the adjustments to the internal market and cross-border requirements—each of these modifications already bore some linkage to institutional activities taking place under the former Treaty framework pursuant to Article 65 EC. This is certainly not to downplay their insertion in the present Treaty framework and their bearing on the scope of Article 81 TFEU.[83] This is also not to discount the fact that certain ambiguities concerning the scope of the Union's competence under Article 81 TFEU which existed under the former Article 65 EC, remain, such as the extent to which this provision may extend to matters concerning substantive (private) law,[84] the meaning of the cross-border requirement,[85] and the concept of 'judicial cooperation in civil matters' generally.[86] Nevertheless, on the whole, the changes introduced by the Lisbon Treaty did not fundamentally alter the scope of Union competence under Article 81 TFEU as compared to former Article 65 EC.[87] Therefore, in the view of the present author, these changes further substantiate that the adoption of a European contract law instrument falls outside of the Union's competence in the field of judicial cooperation in civil matters, taking account of Article 81 TFEU's substantive scope of application

[80] See, eg, Dir 2008/52/EC of the European Parliament and of the Council of 21 May 2008 on certain aspects of mediation in civil and commercial matters, [2008] OJ C136/3 (Mediation Directive), which emanated from the Commission's Green Paper on *alternative dispute resolution* in civil and commercial law, COM (2002) 196 final, 19.4.2002 (emphasis added).

[81] See, eg, Dec No 568/2009/EC of the European Parliament and of the Council of 18 June 2009 amending Council Dec No 2001/470/EC establishing a European Judicial Network in civil and commercial matters, [2009] OJ L168/35.

[82] This is not to discount the changes to the institutional framework surrounding Art 81 TFEU and the AFSJ generally as a result of the Lisbon Treaty, eg, as regards decision-making, the opt-out regimes for the UK, Ireland, and Denmark, and the elimination of certain restrictions on the Union courts' jurisdiction in the areas covered by the former Title IV of the EC Treaty and the former third pillar. For detailed discussion, see, eg, Peers, n 1, ch 2; with regard to the Union courts' jurisdiction in the AFSJ, see also K Lenaerts, I Maselis, and K Gutman (JT Nowak (ed)), *EU Procedural Law* (Oxford Univ Press, 2014) ch 22.

[83] See, eg, R Baratta, 'Réflexions sur la coopération judiciaire civile suite au traité de Lisbonne' in G Venturini and S Bariatti (eds), *New instruments of private international law—Liber Fausto Pocar* (Giuffrè Editore, 2009) 3; Storskrubb, 'Civil Justice', n 4, 306–307.

[84] Indeed, it is often acknowledged that Art 81 TFEU's potential application to measures approximating substantive (private) law is unsettled. See, eg, Max Planck, n 78, 386–387; HW Micklitz and N Reich, 'The Commission Proposal for a "Regulation on a Common European Sales Law (CESL)"—Too Broad or not Broad Enough?' in L Moccia (ed), *The Making of European Private Law: Why, How, What, Who* (Sellier, 2013) 21, 27. This issue has generated particular controversy in relation to family law. See, eg, De Baere and Gutman, n 72, and citations therein.

[85] See, eg, A Fiorini, 'The Evolution of European Private International Law' (2008) 57 *ICLQ* 969, 977; see also n 155.

[86] See, eg, HE Hartnell, 'A Cinderella Story: "Judicial Cooperation in Civil Matters" Meets the Prince' (2010) 29 *YEL* 483, 485; B Hess, 'Procedural Harmonisation in a European Context' in *Civil Litigation in a Globalising World*, n 78, 159, 162–163; Storskrubb, 'Civil Justice', n 4, 309.

[87] See, eg, Fiorini, n 85, 976–977; Peers, n 1, 608; Piris, n 78, 179; Wagner, n 78, 96.

and the objectives to be achieved by such an instrument through the course of the debate. In sum, both under the past and present Treaty frameworks, there is a strong case that Article 81 TFEU (ex Article 65 EC) cannot serve as a potential legal basis for a European contract law instrument.

10.2.3 Missed opportunity for European contract law?

Given this finding, it may seem regrettable that the proposals submitted during the European Convention seeking to revise Article 65 EC so as to allow for the approximation of national contract laws were neglected in subsequent institutional developments culminating in the Lisbon Treaty. In fact, this was strongly lamented by one commentator amidst negotiations surrounding the Draft Constitutional Treaty:

> Given the long lasting debate on European contract law or even on a more general European civil law codification it would have seemed appropriate to provide at least a legal basis for a codification of contract law, company law and various other areas which have already received major attention during the development of the internal market, as has been suggested by members of the Convention. The draft Constitution has missed this timely opportunity.[88]

Taking a closer look, however, maybe not.

Taken seriously, these proposals had the potential to augment, not resolve, the current complexity and controversy concerning the Union's competence to approximate national contract law and to preclude the achievement of the Union's objectives underpinning the debate about European contract law as a whole. A common thread running through the aforementioned proposals was the intention to single out specific areas of private law, including contract law, and hence to 'fence them off' for Union action as compared to other areas, some of which have gained importance in the debate, such as extra-contractual obligations or movable property law. Moreover, to have abided by the preference for what is now Article 81 TFEU would have introduced considerable ambiguity with regard to Union action in the field of contract law under what is now Article 114 TFEU, and as for the proposal prohibiting further use of Article 114 TFEU in the realm of contract law, this sits uncomfortably with the ongoing activities of the European contract law project. To have revised the Treaties in such a manner could have put in jeopardy the possibility of adopting one or more European instruments going beyond the scope of contract law based on other Treaty provisions, thereby stunting Union action under Article 114 TFEU or Article 352 TFEU for the purposes of achieving the Union's internal market objectives. Ironically, then, the failure of such proposals may have done more for European contract law than their success.

Furthermore, for those eager to use these proposals to substantiate the lack of Union competence in contract law under the Treaty framework as it stands now, they are, arguably, of marginal value in this regard. It has been posited by at least one commentator that the fact that these proposals were made and failed demonstrates that amendments to the Treaties are needed to sustain the EU's competence to approximate substantive contract law.[89] Given that the proposals (and related contributions) emanated from one Member State (Germany) and did not attract much attention, it is difficult to assess how much importance, if any, to place on them. For example, it is not known whether the failure

[88] W Heusel, 'Editorial: The Emerging Constitution and the European Area of Justice' (2003) 4 *ERA Forum* 4, 7. See also W Heusel, 'European Contract Law—Towards a European Frame of Reference' (2006) 7 *ERA Forum* 4, 6–7.

[89] See, eg, Ziller, n 2, 111–112.

of these proposals was due more to neglect in favour of more important matters on the agenda concerning the AFSJ, as opposed to intentional rejection of Union action in contract law or even preference for such action to proceed under other Treaty provisions in line with the concerns expressed above. It should also be remembered that these proposals concerned what is now Article 81 TFEU, a provision customarily considered to exclude the approximation of substantive private law, and therefore, they did not speak to the extent of the Union's competences under other provisions, such as Articles 114 and 352 TFEU. If anything, these proposals highlighted the uncertainties surrounding the use of Article 81 TFEU for the approximation of substantive contract law and underscored the importance of leaving open potential recourse to Articles 114 and 352 TFEU.

The question remains why such proposals were advanced in connection with former Article 65 EC in the first place, since it was very much the intention of these Convention members to situate action in the field of contract law within the context of judicial cooperation in civil matters and the AFSJ, not the internal market programme. In other words, while they failed, these proposals still said something important about the linkage between European contract law and judicial cooperation in civil matters. As documented in Part Two, European contract law has steadily become interwoven within the ongoing activities concerning this field as part of the overarching frame of the AFSJ established by the European Council's Tampere, Hague, and Stockholm Programmes. Yet, so far, there has not been much detailed explanation provided by the European Council or the other Union institutions as to the connection between the two, with the result that the place of European contract law in this context remains ambiguous. Nevertheless, European contract law has consistently been viewed as making an important contribution to the building of a European area of 'justice', whereby judicial and legal barriers to the litigation and settlement of cross-border legal disputes are broken down in an effort to simplify the legal context for Union citizens. At the same time, activities in European contract law have been framed as part of the achievement of the Union's internal market objectives, as illustrated by the Stockholm Programme's reference to the developments concerning the Common Frame of Reference within the section concerning 'supporting economic activity' in the internal market. It remains to be seen whether the relationship between European contract law, the European area of 'justice', and the AFSJ may be fleshed out as the debate continues. As matters stand now, while European contract law may play a part in the building of a European area of 'justice', this does not necessarily mean that Article 81 TFEU is the legal basis upon which a European contract law instrument can be based.

10.3 The Relationship between Articles 81, 114, and 352 TFEU in European Contract Law

To date, there has been a growing volume of Union measures in the field of judicial cooperation in civil matters adopted by the Union legislature pursuant to what is now Article 81 TFEU (ex Article 65 EC).[90] Among the most well-known

[90] Incidentally, under the former Treaty framework, measures generally cited former Arts 61(c) and 67 EC in some shape or form, as opposed to former Art 65 EC, as the legal basis, with the result that it was not specified which subsection—(a), (b), or (c)—of former Art 65 EC was being resorted to, although it was often mentioned in the proposal and/or ultimately appeared in the preamble of the measure adopted. This situation was noticed by scholars. See, eg, K Boele-Woelki and RH van Ooik, 'The Communitarization of Private International Law' (2002) 5 *YPIL* 1, 12–13; 'Editorial

measures[91] are those relating to the jurisdiction, recognition, and enforcement of judgments (eg, the Insolvency Regulation, the 'Brussels I' and 'Brussels II *bis*' Regulations, and the European enforcement order for uncontested claims),[92] the choice of applicable law (eg, the 'Rome I' and 'Rome II' Regulations),[93] cross-border civil procedure (eg, service of documents and evidence),[94] alternative dispute resolution (eg, mediation),[95] and cooperation among judicial bodies (eg, the European judicial network).[96] In truth, there is no universal categorization, and the various measures may be organized in a number of ways that overlap and intersect with each other depending upon the labels used. The intention here is not to provide an exhaustive description of such measures, but instead to spotlight certain measures concerning legal aid, mediation, and European procedures for uncontested claims and small claims. Admittedly, these measures were based on former Article 65 EC, and thus incorporate the discussion of the internal market requirement, which has since been amended in Article 81 TFEU. Yet, as illustrated by the fact that they are commonly discussed in much of the literature

Comments: Sometimes it takes thirty years and even more . . .' (2007) 44 *CML Rev* 1567, 1574. It has not (yet) resulted in litigation, even though there were attempts during the decision-making process to modify the legal basis or preamble of a particular measure so as to specify the relevant subsection of former Art 65 EC. See, eg, European Parliament Legislative Resolution on the Proposal for the Legal Aid Directive, n 98, [2003] OJ C273E/184, 185 (Amendment 1). Moreover, this practice has not garnered much attention in the case law. See, eg, Case C-14/08 *Roda Golf and Beach Resort* [2009] ECR I-5439, para 53; Opinion of AG Kokott in Case C-435/06 *C* [2007] ECR I-10141, point 52; View of AG Jääskinen in Case C-400/10 PPU *McB.* [2010] ECR I-8965, point 40 fn 11. This situation has been remedied to some extent under the present Treaty framework. Measures adopted under Art 81 TFEU (apart from those concerning family law adopted under Art 81(3) TFEU) often specify upon which subsection(s) of Art 81(2) TFEU—(a) to (h)—they are based, which may or may not be accompanied by a reference to Art 67(4) TFEU. See, eg, the recast of the 'Brussels I' Regulation, n 92 (based on Art 67(4) TFEU and Art 81(2) (a), (c), and (e) TFEU). Yet, this is not always the case. Compare, eg, Reg (EU) No 650/2012 concerning matters of succession, [2012] OJ L201/107 (based on Art 81(2) TFEU).

[91] There are also numerous proposals at various stages of development in the EU decision-making process: see the Commission's website, n 4 (through the link to 'Civil Justice').

[92] Eg, Council Reg (EC) No 1346/2000 of 29 May 2000 on insolvency proceedings, [2000] OJ L160/1 (a proposal amending this Regulation is pending: COM (2012) 744 final, 12.2.2012); Council Reg (EC) No 44/2001 of 22 Dec 2000 on jurisdiction and the recognition and enforcement of judgments in civil and commercial matters ('Brussels I' Regulation), [2001] OJ L12/1; *corrigendum*, [2001] OJ L307/28, which was recast by Reg (EU) No 1215/2012 of the European Parliament and of the Council of 12 Dec 2012 on jurisdiction and the recognition and enforcement of judgments in civil and commercial matters, [2012] OJ L351/1 (a proposal to amend this Regulation is pending: COM (2013) 554 final, 26.7.2013); Council Reg (EC) No 2201/2003 of 27 Nov 2003 concerning jurisdiction and the recognition and enforcement of judgments in matrimonial matters and the matters of parental responsibility, repealing Reg (EC) No 1347/2000 ('Brussels II *bis*' Regulation), [2003] OJ L338/1; Reg (EC) No 805/2004 of the European Parliament and of the Council of 21 April 2004 creating a European Enforcement Order for uncontested claims, [2004] OJ L143/15; *corrigendum*, [2005] OJ L97/64.

[93] Eg, Reg (EC) No 593/2008 of the European Parliament and of the Council of 17 June 2008 on the law applicable to contractual obligations ('Rome I' Regulation), [2008] OJ L177/6; *corrigendum* [2009] OJ L309/87; Reg (EC) No 864/2007 of the European Parliament and of the Council of 11 July 2007 on the law applicable to non-contractual obligations ('Rome II' Regulation), [2007] OJ L199/40. The 'Rome III' Regulation, Council Reg (EU) No 1259/2010 of 20 Dec 2010 implementing enhanced cooperation in the area of the law applicable to divorce and legal separation, [2010] OJ L343/10, was the first time that the enhanced cooperation mechanism was used. See further Chapter 11, § 11.2.

[94] Eg, Council Reg (EC) No 1206/2001 of 28 May 2001 on cooperation between the courts of the Member States in the taking of evidence in civil or commercial matters, [2001] OJ L174/1; Reg (EC) No 1393/2007 of the European Parliament and of the Council of 13 Nov 2007 on the service in the Member States of judicial and extrajudicial documents in civil or commercial matters (service of documents), and repealing Council Reg (EC) No 1348/2000, [2007] OJ L324/79.

[95] Eg, Mediation Directive, n 80.

[96] Eg, Dec No 568/2009/EC, n 81.

concerning Article 81 TFEU, these measures remain relevant for highlighting the ongoing controversy surrounding the scope of the Union's competence under this provision and laying the groundwork for evaluating Article 81 TFEU's relationship to Articles 114 and 352 TFEU in the debate.

10.3.1 Union measures adopted under Article 81 TFEU (ex Article 65 EC)

Starting with *legal aid*, the Commission, prompted by the Tampere Programme, published a Green Paper on the subject, in which it stressed the problems of extra costs associated with cross-border litigation, eg, the necessity of hiring two lawyers, translation and interpretation costs, and miscellaneous factors, such as extra travel costs of litigants, witnesses, lawyers, etc.[97] This led to a proposal for a Directive to establish certain minimum standards for legal aid in cross-border disputes.[98] The Commission justified the use of former Article 61 EC viz Article 65 EC (now Article 81 TFEU) on the grounds that the establishment of minimum standards on legal aid would facilitate the free movement of persons and the smooth operation of the internal market.[99] As regards the principles of subsidiarity and proportionality, since the measure approximated national law by establishing certain minimum standards, these objectives could not be achieved by the Member States acting alone, and the proposal was limited to the minimum required to achieve the objectives pursued, respectively.[100] In response, the European Parliament deleted the restriction to cross-border disputes, so as to ensure that the proposed Directive facilitated access to justice whether in a cross-border or domestic context.[101] This was rejected by the Council, which reintroduced the cross-border requirement.[102] Ultimately, as adopted, Directive 2003/8/EC to improve access to justice in cross-border disputes by establishing minimum common rules relating to legal aid for such disputes[103] applies only to cross-border disputes,[104] as inscribed in its title.

Thereafter, legislation in the field of *mediation* added fuel to the fire. In line with the mandate set by the Tampere Programme, the Commission submitted a proposal for a Directive on certain aspects of mediation in civil and commercial matters.[105] The proposal devoted particular attention to the legal basis, subsidiarity, and proportionality requirements.[106] As part of the justification for former Article 65 EC (now Article 81 TFEU), the Commission explained that the proposal was 'necessary for the proper functioning of the internal market' in view of the need to ensure access to dispute resolution mechanisms for individuals and businesses exercising their rights of free movement and the freedom to provide and receive mediation services.[107] As regards the

[97] Green Paper, Legal aid in civil matters: The problems confronting the cross-border litigant, COM (2000) 51 final, 9.2.2000, 4, 12–13.

[98] Proposal for a Council Directive to improve access to justice in cross-border disputes by establishing minimum common rules relating to legal aid and other financial aspects of civil proceedings, COM (2002) 13 final, 18.1.2002.

[99] Proposal, n 98, Explanatory Memorandum, point 2.

[100] Proposal, n 98, Explanatory Memorandum, point 3.

[101] European Parliament Legislative Resolution, n 90, 186.

[102] 2455th Council meeting—Justice, Home Affairs and Civil Protection—Luxembourg, 14–15 Oct 2002, DOC 12894/02 (Presse 308), 8.

[103] Legal Aid Directive, n 79.

[104] Legal Aid Directive, n 79, ninth recital; Art 1.

[105] Proposal for a Directive of the European Parliament and of the Council on certain aspects of mediation in civil and commercial matters, COM (2004) 718 final, 22.10.2004.

[106] Proposal, n 105, Explanatory Memorandum, points 1.2–1.3.

[107] Proposal, n 105, Explanatory Memorandum, point 1.2.

requirement of 'cross-border implications', the Commission submitted that it would not be feasible to restrict the scope of the proposal to cross-border situations because this would carry the risk of creating arbitrary and discriminatory effects between parties, increase legal uncertainty, and substantially reduce the impact of the proposed Directive, and therefore, it should apply to domestic situations as well.[108] As for compliance with subsidiarity and proportionality, the Commission reasoned that in view of the need for legal certainty and predictability in situations involving mediation and to ensure the proper functioning of the internal market relating to mediation services, measures taken at the European level would be more effective than individual initiatives taken by each Member State.[109]

The Commission's position on the 'cross-border implications' requirement did not persuade the Council. The European Parliament noted in its first reading of the proposal that a majority of Member State delegations took the view that the proposed Directive should be limited to cross-border cases based on the text of former Article 65 EC (now Article 81 TFEU), which prompted it to propose a compromise, whereby the measure would apply only to cross-border cases, but additional language was inserted to encourage the Member States to apply its provisions to domestic cases.[110] As matters proceeded, the Council maintained a firm stance in limiting the proposed Directive to cross-border matters, though retaining the Parliament's suggestion.[111] The Commission responded that 'in a spirit of compromise', this limitation was accepted, provided that the definition of cross-border cases was as broad as possible.[112] Ultimately, with the adoption of Directive 2008/52/EC on certain aspects of mediation in civil and commercial matters, there is express recognition of its limitation to cross-border disputes (but allowing Member States to apply it to internal mediation processes) and a specific provision defining this concept.[113]

Matters intensified with measures establishing *European order for payment and small claims procedures*, which were conjoined in the Commission's Green Paper on these subjects.[114] The idea behind the European order for payment procedure was to establish in all Member States the same procedure for the rapid and effective recovery of uncontested claims, whereas the European small claims procedure was geared at simplifying the requirements of small claims litigation in order to speed up such proceedings and limit the costs associated with enforcing claims involving small sums of money.[115] As a harbinger of what was to come, the Commission posed two horizontal questions in the Green Paper concerning the applicability of a European instrument to cross-border cases only or also to domestic cases and the choice of the appropriate instrument to pursue the approximation of procedural law.[116] For the first point, the Commission advanced several arguments to support coverage of both cross-border and domestic situations.[117] In the second point, it referred to the use of an optional European procedure

[108] Proposal, n 105, Explanatory Memorandum, point 1.2.

[109] Proposal, n 105, Explanatory Memorandum, point 1.3.

[110] Report on the Proposal, n 105, A6-0074/2007, dated 22 March 2007, 6–7 (Amendment 4), 22.

[111] Common Position (EC) No 11/2008 adopted by the Council on 28 Feb 2008, [2008] OJ C122E/1, eighth recital.

[112] Commission Communication concerning the common position of the Council on the adoption of a Directive of the European Parliament and of the Council on certain aspects of mediation in civil and commercial matters, COM (2008) 131 final, 7.3.2008, 2.

[113] Mediation Directive, n 80, eighth recital; Arts 1–2.

[114] Green Paper on a European order for payment procedure and on measures to simplify and speed up small claims litigation, COM (2002) 746 final, 20.12.2002, point 1.

[115] See EESC Opinion on the Green Paper, n 114, [2003] OJ C220/5, point 2.

[116] Green Paper, n 114, points 1.1–1.2.

[117] Green Paper, n 114, point 1.1.

'happily co-existing' with the national mechanisms in the areas concerned.[118] The Commission's approach in the Green Paper filtered into two separate initiatives, which stand at the apex of the controversy surrounding Article 81 TFEU to date.

Starting with the earliest of the two proposals, in 2004, the Commission submitted a proposal for a Regulation creating a European order for payment procedure.[119] As regards the scope of the proposal, the Commission contended that it would be counterproductive to constrain this procedure to cross-border cases only.[120] In its view, such a restriction was not necessitated by the text of what was then Article 65 EC (now Article 81 TFEU);[121] it would cause undue complexity, thereby contravening the objective of the European order procedure to speed up and simplify the recovery of uncontested claims;[122] and it would jeopardize the functioning of the internal market on the grounds that access of economic operators to mechanisms of substantially differing performance levels entails a distortion of competition in the internal market, whether such operators were domiciled in different Member States or in the same Member State.[123] As it explained, enterprises from different Member States are not on an equal footing if only the one domiciled abroad can make use of an efficient European order for payment procedure, and an enterprise with a majority of clients abroad may enjoy a significant advantage over a competitor domiciled in the same Member State.[124] As regards the principle of subsidiarity, it 'goes without saying' that the creation of a uniform procedure could not be sufficiently accomplished by the Member States themselves because they cannot guarantee the equivalence of rules applicable throughout the EU.[125] Furthermore, as regards the principle of proportionality, the combination of the use of a regulation with the optional nature of the procedure as an additional tool lying alongside comparable mechanisms in the national legal orders meant that it 'encroaches much less' on national procedural systems than a harmonizing directive requiring adapting national legislation to the standards set down in that instrument.[126] Recourse to an optional European procedure allowed Member States with an even better functioning domestic system to retain it, thereby leaving it to the creditors to judge which procedure they considered superior or most convenient in terms of accessibility.[127] This was particularly relevant for creditors operating in several Member States, since they would be spared the need to make themselves familiar with the procedural law of each of the Member States involved by virtue of the availability of this procedure.[128]

The proposal beckoned responses from the other institutions that echoed previous practice. The European Parliament agreed with the Commission's internal market rationale, considering that with cross-border litigation: '[t]here is a risk that citizens may not be inclined to assert their rights because of the obstacles they could encounter in dealing with the legal systems in another Member State, in particular due to unfamiliar procedures and unknown costs. This is considered an obstacle to the proper

[118] Green Paper, n 114, point 1.2.
[119] Proposal for a Regulation of the European Parliament and of the Council creating a European order for payment procedure, COM (2004) 173 final/3, 25.5.2004.
[120] Proposal, n 119, Explanatory Memorandum, point 2.2.2.
[121] Proposal, n 119, Explanatory Memorandum, point 2.2.2.
[122] Proposal, n 119, Explanatory Memorandum, point 2.2.2.
[123] Proposal, n 119, Explanatory Memorandum, point 2.2.2.
[124] Proposal, n 119, Explanatory Memorandum, point 2.2.2.
[125] Proposal, n 119, Explanatory Memorandum, point 2.2.3.
[126] Proposal, n 119, Explanatory Memorandum, point 2.2.3.
[127] Proposal, n 119, Explanatory Memorandum, point 2.2.3.
[128] Proposal, n 119, Explanatory Memorandum, point 2.2.3.

functioning of the internal market and a potential disincentive to the development of cross-border business and trade'.[129] Yet, when it came to the cross-border requirement, given the Council's reluctance, the Parliament proposed a similar compromise, whereby the instrument would be limited to cross-border cases, but the Member States could voluntarily adopt the procedure for domestic cases.[130] As the proposal made its way through the decision-making process, the Council stood firm on limiting the procedure to cross-border cases only.[131] The Commission eventually agreed, but attached the following Declaration to the common position reached on the measure:

> The Commission declares that the definition of the term 'cross-border case' in the context of this Regulation is not an interpretation of the obligation foreseen in Article 65 of the Treaty [now Article 81 TFEU] to limit the action of the Community [now Union] to matters having cross-border implications, but only one among other possibilities to limit the scope of application of this Regulation in the context of Article 65 [now Article 81 TFEU]. It is not necessary to limit the scope of application by reference to a general definition of 'cross-border' in the instruments relating to private international law. The necessity or interest to resort to a general definition of 'cross-border' in other instruments which are not linked to private international law such as the proposed directive on mediation the character of which is different from this Regulation should be analysed carefully case by case, taking into account the objectives of each instrument.[132]

As adopted, Regulation (EC) No 1896/2006 creating a European order for payment procedure contains specific provisions making clear that it is applicable only to cross-border cases.[133] Still, certain recitals of the Preamble indicate that there were impediments to access to justice and distortions of competition in the internal market caused by imbalances in the functioning of procedural mechanisms afforded to creditors in the various Member States that necessitated legislation guaranteeing a level playing field for creditors and debtors throughout the EU.[134] It also indicates that this European procedure is 'an additional and optional means' available to creditors that neither replaces nor harmonizes the existing national mechanisms for the recovery of uncontested claims.[135]

Matters again came to a head with the Commission's proposal for a Regulation establishing a European small claims procedure.[136] As with the previous proposal, it contained extensive discussion of former Article 65 EC (now Article 81 TFEU).[137] Starting with the internal market requirement, the Commission declared that there was a margin of discretion for the legislature as to whether a measure is necessary for the proper functioning of the internal market,[138] and that it was fulfilled here:

[129] Report on the Proposal, n 119, A6-0240/2005, dated 18 July 2005, 17.

[130] Report, n 129, 5–8 (Amendments 1, 4), 17.

[131] See Commission Communication concerning the common position of the Council on the adoption of a Regulation of the European Parliament and of the Council creating a European order for payment procedure, COM (2006) 374 final, 4.7.2006, point 3.1.

[132] Communication, n 131, points 3.1, 5 (Declaration of the Commission).

[133] Reg (EC) No 1896/2006 of the European Parliament and of the Council of 12 Dec 2006 creating a European order for payment procedure, [2006] OJ L399/1; *corrigendum*, [2007] OJ L18/11, Arts 1, 2(1). There was no additional language inserted along the lines of the Parliament's suggested compromise above.

[134] Reg No 1896/2006, n 133, eighth recital.

[135] Reg No 1896/2006, n 133, tenth recital.

[136] Proposal for a Regulation of the European Parliament and of the Council establishing a European Small Claims Procedure, COM (2005) 87 final, 15.3.2005.

[137] Proposal, n 136, Explanatory Memorandum, point 2.2.

[138] Proposal, n 136, Explanatory Memorandum, point 2.2.1.

If some operators have access to efficient and effective procedures while others do not, there is no level playing field for operators competing in the internal market. The existing disparities in the laws of the Member States put obstacles to the proper functioning of the internal market. Consequently, a situation implying a marked disequilibrium with regard to the efficiency of the procedural means afforded to creditors under different national laws amounts to a distortion of competition within the internal market. A European Small Claims procedure would thus facilitate the proper functioning of the internal market.[139]

As for the cross-border requirement, the Commission surmised that it was sufficient that the 'matter' concerned had cross-border implications.[140] Small claims litigation was such a matter, since taking account of the development of the internal market, most economic operators and consumers would sooner or later be involved in such litigation abroad.[141] In its view, the internal market requirement of former Article 65 EC was a restriction on the cross-border requirement, not the other way around: a measure that is necessary for the proper functioning of the internal market has necessarily cross-border implications, whereas a measure having cross-border implications may not always also be necessary for the proper functioning of the internal market.[142] With respect to the European small claims procedure, it would be inappropriate and counterproductive to constrain the scope of application to cross-border cases. The creation of two different regimes for internal cases and for cases with cross-border aspects would be inconsistent with the objective of a single and coherent area of justice for all.[143] Additionally, speedy and inexpensive small claims procedures were not available to litigants in all Member States, and the lack of such procedures made judicial recourse economically questionable in many cases and often creditors abstained from taking legal action.[144] This limitation of effective access to justice caused economic costs that had significant negative macroeconomic effects on the proper functioning of the internal market.[145]

With respect to compliance with the principles of subsidiarity and proportionality, the Commission reiterated in this proposal its previous remarks with respect to the European order for payment procedure. As regards the principle of subsidiarity, the objective to simplify and speed up litigation concerning small claims by establishing a European procedure to that effect could not be sufficiently accomplished by the Member States, since they could not guarantee the equivalence of rules applicable throughout the EU.[146] As regards the principle of proportionality, the Commission stressed the combination of a regulation and the optional nature of the European small claims procedure: while ensuring uniformity and the direct applicability of the procedure, the proposed measure would only require the Member States to make the procedure available as an additional tool, with the result that it encroached much less on the national procedural systems and allowed the Member States with an even better functioning domestic mechanism to retain it.[147] It would be left to the creditors in the

[139] Proposal, n 136, Explanatory Memorandum, point 2.2.1.
[140] Proposal, n 136, Explanatory Memorandum, point 2.2.1.
[141] Proposal, n 136, Explanatory Memorandum, point 2.2.1.
[142] Proposal, n 136, Explanatory Memorandum, point 2.2.1.
[143] Proposal, n 136, Explanatory Memorandum, point 2.2.1. This language bore some resemblance to the Commission's remarks in its final progress report on the Tampere Programme: see Commission Communication, Area of Freedom, Security and Justice: Assessment of the Tampere programme and future orientations, COM (2004) 401 final, 2.6.2004, point 2.7 fn 11. See further Chapter 5, § 5.4.3.1.
[144] Proposal, n 136, Explanatory Memorandum, point 2.2.1.
[145] Proposal, n 136, Explanatory Memorandum, point 2.2.1.
[146] Proposal, n 136, Explanatory Memorandum, point 2.2.2.
[147] Proposal, n 136, Explanatory Memorandum, point 2.2.2.

various Member States to judge which procedure they considered as being superior in performance or more convenient in terms of accessibility.[148]

The Commission's remarks received mixed reactions from the other institutions and bodies. In its Opinion, the European Economic and Social Committee (EESC) endorsed the Commission's choice of legal basis, which went beyond a merely formal interpretation of the relevant legal concepts, and found that an initiative of this type and scope was only justified if it also applied, albeit optionally, to internal disputes in the Member States, since limiting it to cross-border disputes could cast doubt on its relevance or even on the need for it at all.[149] Yet, the Council and the European Parliament constricted the scope of the measure to cross-border cases.[150] As adopted, Regulation (EC) No 861/2007 establishing a European Small Claims Procedure[151] applies to cross-border cases only and is available to litigants as an optional procedure alongside national procedural mechanisms.[152] Still, semblances of the Commission's internal market rationale are apparent in the Preamble, with emphasis placed on the obstacles to obtaining fast, inexpensive judgments in cross-border cases and distortions of competition caused by imbalances with regard to procedural means afforded to creditors in different Member States, which justified the need for action at the European level to guarantee a level playing field for creditors and debtors throughout the EU.[153]

10.3.2 The limits of Union competence under Article 81 TFEU and the linkage to Article 114 TFEU

In light of the foregoing discussion, Article 81 TFEU's cross-border requirement has generated considerable debate concerning the limits of Union competence under this provision. So far, this issue (as well as the internal market requirement under former Article 65 EC) has not been addressed in the case law of the Union courts, since aside from marginal references to what is now Article 81 TFEU, there is not yet any definitive jurisprudence on this provision.[154] Noticeably, while there is a rising crescendo of discord among the Union institutions about the Commission's expansive approach taken

[148] Proposal, n 136, Explanatory Memorandum, point 2.2.2.

[149] EESC Opinion on the Proposal, n 136, [2006] OJ C88/1, point 4.4.

[150] See 2732nd Council meeting, JHA, Luxembourg, 1–2 June 2006, DOC 9409/06 (Presse 144), 15; Report on the Proposal, n 136, A6-0387/2006, dated 7 Nov 2006, 5 (Amendments 1, 7–8).

[151] Reg (EC) No 861/2007 of the European Parliament and of the Council of 11 July 2007 establishing a European Small Claims Procedure, [2007] OJ L199/1.

[152] Reg (EC) No 861/2007, n 151, seventh–eighth recitals; Arts 1–2.

[153] Reg (EC) No 861/2007, n 151, seventh recital.

[154] There is certainly a growing jurisprudence on the interpretation of the various measures adopted under what is now Art 81 TFEU (ex Art 65 EC). So far, however, no such measure has been challenged either directly (via an action for annulment) or indirectly (via a preliminary ruling on validity or an objection of illegality), and therefore, the case law of the Union courts elucidating the scope of Union competence under Art 81 TFEU is extremely limited. Eg, in *Opinion 1/03*, the Court of Justice requested the Member States and the EU institutions to submit observations on, inter alia, former Arts 61 and 65 EC, including the words 'necessary for the proper functioning of the internal market' in former Art 65 EC, but ultimately, this was deemed irrelevant for the determination of the issues at hand. See Opinion 1/03 *New Lugano Convention* [2006] ECR I-1145, paras 96–99, 131. References to former Art 65 EC (now Art 81 TFEU)'s cross-border requirement have made their way into AG Opinions in certain cases, but were not touched upon by the Court in its judgment. See, eg, Opinion of AG Léger in Case C-281/02 *Owusu* [2005] ECR I-1383, points 195–203 (making analogous reference to case law concerning former Art 95 EC (now Art 114 TFEU)); Opinion of AG Trstenjak in Case C-265/07 *Caffaro* [2008] ECR I-708, point 32.

to the cross-border requirement,[155] the Commission's approach to the internal market requirement as regards to the apparent obstacles to trade and distortions of competition caused by disparities in the national rules concerned did not appear to merit nearly as much dispute at the European level.

In view of the changes brought about by the Lisbon Treaty, discussion of the internal market requirement set forth in former Article 65 EC has become less relevant with respect to the scope of the Union's competence under Article 81 TFEU.[156] Yet, in the context of European contract law, this requirement was at the base of arguments concerning the potential linkage of former Article 65 EC to former Article 95 EC (now Article 114 TFEU). Famously, Professor Jürgen Basedow argued that even though Article 65 EC could not by itself serve as a legal basis for the approximation of contract law (and other fields of private law), it bolstered the case for Article 95 EC:

> Since [A]rticle 65 requires that Community measures taken under that provision are 'necessary for the proper functioning of the internal market', it presupposes that differences existing between the national legislations in the field of conflict of laws may effectively curtail the proper functioning of the internal market; if not the explicit reference to measures 'promoting the compatibility of the rules applicable in the [M]ember [S]tates concerning the conflict of laws' would be meaningless. Bearing in mind that conflict rules merely refer a case to a competent national legal system without providing for a substantive solution we must conclude that differences between the substantive private laws of the Member States are even more liable to impede the proper functioning of the internal market. If that is true in the context of [A]rticle 65, it cannot be denied when it comes to the application of [A]rticle 95. Thus, while [A]rticle 65 has a very limited bearing upon the harmonisation or unification of substantive private law for other reasons, it suggests a new reading of [A]rticle 95 which allows for the adoption of a comprehensive private law legislation on that basis.[157]

Other scholars voiced similar sentiments, as illustrated by the chapter authored by Professors Winfried Tilmann and Walter van Gerven in the 1999 Working Paper, which emphasized Article 65 EC's role for the assessment of Article 95 EC, even if Article 65 EC itself could not serve as a legal basis for a European civil code.[158] In their view, by virtue of Article 65 EC, differences between national provisions of private international law (via Article 65(b) EC) and civil procedural law (via Article 65(c) EC) were regarded as having an important bearing on the proper functioning of the internal market, which were relevant for the interpretation of Article 95 EC.[159]

[155] There also continues to be divergent opinion in the literature as to whether Art 81 TFEU (ex Art 65 EC) is limited to measures applicable to cross-border situations (see, eg, Kuipers, n 2, 554; Max Planck, n 78, 387), or may be interpreted more broadly so as to extend to domestic situations (see, eg, Peers, n 1, 609–613; M Storme, 'Closing Comments: Harmonisation or Globalisation of Civil Procedure?' in *Civil Litigation in a Globalising World,* n 78, 379, 382–383; R van Rhee, 'Civil procedure in a globalizing world' in M Faure and A van der Walt (eds), *Globalization and Private Law: The Way Forward* (Edward Elgar, 2010) 343, 355). See also House of Lords EU Committee, 'European Small Claims Procedure', 23rd Report of Session 2005–06, points 51–63 and the accompanying testimony of Dr Georg Haibach, DG Justice, Freedom, and Security, European Commission (Q5-Q23); F Frattini, 'European Area of Civil Justice—Has the Community Reached the Limits?' (2006) *Z Eu P* 225, 231–233. Franco Frattini was the Commissioner of Justice, Freedom, and Security from 2004–2008.

[156] Yet, it may still be relevant in the case of a challenge to the legality of a measure based on former Art 65 EC: Peers, n 1, 608.

[157] J Basedow, 'Codification of Private Law in the European Union: the making of a Hybrid' (2001) 9 *ERPL* 35, 46 (reiterated in, eg, J Basedow, 'Rapport de synthèse: Quel droit privé pour l'Europe?' in J-S Bergé and M-L Niboyet (eds), *La réception du droit communautaire en droit privé des États membres* (Bruylant, 2003) 234, 250).

[158] 1999 Working Paper, n 33, 192–193.

[159] 1999 Working Paper, n 33, 192–193.

Such arguments appeared enticing, and may continue to be even under the present Treaty framework, since the internal market requirement was not eliminated altogether from the text of Article 81 TFEU. Yet, with utmost respect to these prominent scholars, these arguments are open to question on several grounds. First, they seemed to be premised on a connection between former Article 65 EC's internal market requirement and the requirements that must be fulfilled for recourse to former Article 95 EC, even if the two provisions were not exactly the same. Although there was some disagreement in the literature as to what extent the requirements of former Articles 65 and 95 EC were aligned in this regard,[160] there were already compelling arguments that the internal market requirement of Article 65 EC could not be read in the same way as the standards set for Article 95 EC, which holds true as much under the former EC Treaty as it does post-Lisbon. As discussed in Chapter 8, former Article 95 EC or what is now Article 114 TFEU is one of the core provisions of the Treaties to carry out the Union's objectives concerning the internal market, and as dictated by the Treaties, measures adopted under this provision must 'have as their object the establishment and functioning of the internal market'.[161] In contrast, former Article 65 EC or what is now Article 81 TFEU is situated within the Union's objectives related to judicial cooperation in civil matters, which in turn gives indirect support for the internal market as enshrined in its text—'particularly when necessary for the proper functioning of the internal market' under Article 81(2) TFEU, and previously, 'in so far as necessary for the proper functioning of the internal market' under former Article 65 EC—but is not targeted at the establishment and functioning of the internal market as such. Consequently, while Article 81 TFEU (as with its predecessor) may allow for the approximation of national rules concerning private international law and civil procedural law, among other things, to achieve the Union's objectives in the field of judicial cooperation in civil matters, arguably, it is not determinative by itself as regards the extent to which Article 114 TFEU can serve as a proper legal basis for the approximation of substantive contract law. That inquiry depends upon whether the measure concerned satisfies the requirements set down in the *Tobacco Advertising I* case law, that is to say, whether differences between national contract laws result in obstacles to trade and/or appreciable distortions of competition for which the measure adopted under Article 114 TFEU must have as its object to eliminate.

Furthermore, such arguments seem to have lost much of their salience with the changes introduced by the Lisbon Treaty. To recall from the previous section, Article 81 TFEU considerably weakened the internal market requirement, so as to allow for the adoption of measures 'particularly when'—as opposed to 'in so far as' under former Article 65 EC—'necessary for the proper functioning of the internal market'.[162] Yet, Article 81 TFEU contains the same list of topics that had appeared in former Article 65 EC (supplemented by some additional ones), thereby indicating a looser connection to the internal market than its predecessor.[163] This further supports the view that the

[160] Compare, eg, A Dickinson, 'European Private International Law: Embracing New Horizons or Mourning the Past?' (2005) 1 *JPIL* 197, 214–218; 'Editorial Comments', n 90, 1574–1575; B Heß, 'The Integrating Effect of European Civil Procedural Law' (2002) 4 *EJLR* 3, 13. See also M Tenreiro and M Ekström, 'Unification of Private International Law in Family Law Matters within the European Union' in K Boele-Woelki (ed), *Perspectives for the Unification and Harmonisation of Family Law in Europe* (Intersentia, 2003) 185, 186–187.

[161] Art 114(1) TFEU (ex Art 95(1) EC).

[162] See ns 73–74 and accompanying text.

[163] See Meussen, n 15, 57 (referring to the DCT).

assessment of Articles 81 and 114 TFEU must be taken on their own terms as far as Union action in European contract law is concerned.

That being said, as illustrated by the measures discussed above, arguments justifying compliance with the internal market requirement set forth in former Article 65 EC (as well as that set forth in Article 81 TFEU to the extent that such arguments are still resorted to) have the potential, albeit implicitly, to provide further momentum for Union action in contract law on the basis of Article 114 TFEU. For example, as illustrated by the rationale for the measures establishing European order for payment and small claims procedures, disparities in national laws were deemed to cause distortions of competition in the internal market on account of the fact that undertakings were not given 'equal access to the weapons of law' and hence those undertakings that had recourse to certain national (procedural) rules had significant competitive advantages over others. It was also emphasized in relation to these measures, and to some extent the Directive on legal aid, that there were obstacles to trade in the internal market posed by the parties' lack of familiarity with foreign law and the costs associated with litigation and enforcement of cross-border disputes. Admittedly, the analogy between these measures and matters of substantive contract law is not exact. Nevertheless, the objectives underlying the foregoing measures to eradicate obstacles to trade and appreciable distortions of competition associated with cross-border disputes cannot help but cast an eye to similar issues simmering below the surface of substantive contract law in the context of the debate about European contract law, with the result that the discussion of the Union's competence under what is now Article 81 TFEU may to some extent be considered to exert 'gravitational pull' towards potential recourse to Article 114 TFEU, or at least give further credence to reliance on that provision.

10.3.3 The exercise of Union competence under Article 81 TFEU and the linkage to Articles 114 and 352 TFEU

As further illustrated by the measures described earlier, the roles played by the principles of subsidiarity and proportionality in guiding the exercise of Union competence under what is now Article 81 TFEU (ex Article 65 EC) bear some similarity to the exercise of Union competence under Article 114 TFEU in the context of European contract law. On the one hand, akin to Article 114 TFEU, once Union competence under Article 81 TFEU is verified, it seems to be the case that the principles of subsidiarity and proportionality are easily complied with. As reiterated time and time again, the objectives of the measures concerned transcend the capabilities of the Member States acting alone, thereby gliding over the subsidiarity hurdle of Article 5(3) TEU. Likewise, depending upon the objectives pursued by the particular measure, the principle of proportionality has also been readily justified. This may provoke concerns that the role played by the principles of subsidiarity and proportionality are ineffective to regulate the exercise of Union competence under Article 81 TFEU, although compared to the increasing controversy concerning Article 114 TFEU, this issue does not appear to have been discussed as much in the literature. On the other hand, inside the lawmaking process, the principles of subsidiarity and proportionality have played an important role, among other things, in guiding the choice towards the use of optional instruments in relation to Union action taken on the basis of what is now Article 81 TFEU (ex Article 65 EC). As evidenced by the measures concerning the European order for payment and small claims procedures, this has been framed within the context of the principle of proportionality, though in view of its role in guiding the intensity of Union action inside as well as outside the principle of subsidiarity, this conceivably has salience for the principle of subsidiarity as well. Noticeably, the potential use of optional instruments, that is to say, the creation of European procedures providing an alternative regime without displacing national laws, is not mentioned explicitly in the text of Article 81 TFEU. Yet, so far, this has not seemed to generate concerns on competence grounds at the European level.[164] Instead, as illustrated by the foregoing examples, the use of optional instruments have been accepted as a means by which to find a balance between achieving the Union's objectives in the field of judicial cooperation in civil matters and leaving sufficient leeway for the national legal regimes to flourish and thus, as repeatedly stated by the Commission, encroaching less on the legal systems of the Member States.

As far as European contract law is concerned, Article 81 TFEU therefore makes the fusion between the principles of subsidiarity and proportionality and the use of optional instruments more apparent. Until the Commission's 2010 Green Paper and proposal for a Regulation on a Common European Sales Law (proposed CESL),[165] this had not been explicitly highlighted in the institutional documents concerning the debate about European contract law in connection with the prospect of one or more optional instruments of contract law to achieve the Union's internal market objectives. Consequently, measures adopted under what is now Article 81 TFEU help to capture the ways in which the principles of subsidiarity and proportionality filter into the choice of resorting to an optional instrument of contract law, such as the proposed CESL, on the basis of Article 114 TFEU, or even Article 352 TFEU, to the extent that such an instrument may be considered to fall outside the scope of approximation under Article 114 TFEU.[166]

10.4 Conclusions

In sum, this analysis demonstrates that even if Article 81 TFEU may not have a direct role in serving as a legal basis for a European contract law instrument, this provision does have the potential to play an indirect role in placing further emphasis on the recourse to the Union's internal market competence of Article 114 TFEU, as well as Article 352 TFEU to some extent, depending upon the type of instrument concerned. First, whether under the past or present Treaty framework, there are strong arguments to find that Article 81 TFEU (ex Article 65 EC) cannot serve as a proper legal basis for the adoption of a European contract law instrument. While attempts were made to revise former Article 65 EC so as to provide for a specific legal basis for the approximation of contract law, paradoxically, the failure of these proposals may have done more to advance the long-term aims of the European contract law project than their success by not foreclosing action under Articles 114 and 352 TFEU to achieve the Union's internal market objectives in this area. Secondly, although arguments attempting to use the text of Article 81 TFEU (ex Article 65 EC) to strengthen the case for action under Article 114 TFEU (ex Article 95 EC) in European contract law are uncertain, especially in light of the changes brought

[164] This does not mean that there has not been criticism, eg, as regards the greater complexity and practical disadvantages resulting from optional instruments in this area. See, eg, House of Lords Report, n 155, points 73–78; Wagner, n 78, 99–101.

[165] See Chapter 6, § 6.4

[166] See further Chapter 8, § 8.4.3.2.

about by the Lisbon Treaty, Union measures based on what is now Article 81 TFEU (ex Article 65 EC) nevertheless reveal provocative analogies to arguments justifying resort to Article 114 TFEU and to the interplay between the principles of subsidiarity and proportionality and the use of optional instruments of contract law, which may be adopted under Article 114 TFEU or Article 352 TFEU depending upon the future course of the debate.

11

Alternative and Complementary Routes in European Contract Law

11.1 Introduction

Over the years, there have been various forms of Member State cooperation contemplated in the scholarly literature and institutional documents as alternative or complementary routes to the adoption of a European contract law (or private law) instrument. These have largely centred on the mechanism of enhanced cooperation, an intergovernmental treaty,[1] techniques drawn from the American setting (ie Restatements, uniform and model laws, and the Uniform Commercial Code), and the Open Method of Coordination (OMC). Moreover, the ongoing developments concerning the Common Frame of Reference (CFR) cannot be left out, since the involvement of various academic projects in its preparation and its envisaged status as a non-binding instrument for EU lawmaking embody linkage with 'softer' forms of Union action.

These alternative and complementary routes strike at the heart of the constitutionality of European contract law in three important ways, which explain why they are grouped together here. First, the extent to which they may be used to displace the need for far-reaching Union action in contract law warrants inquiry. Secondly, they have the potential to inject doubts about the constitutional assessment of European contract law altogether. By their very nature, several of these routes direct attention to the considerable overlap and interplay between Union and Member State action in the field of contract law and raise questions as to whether viewing the constitutionality of European contract law through the lens of the limits and exercise of Union competence is myopic or outmoded and hence whether a new frame is needed so as to better accommodate the interaction between the European, national, and even international levels in finding possible solutions in this setting. Finally, with particular regard to the American techniques, this is essentially where the 'fourteen carat gold' questions lie concerning the relevance of such techniques in the debate and the fruitful comparative reflection that can be gleaned through the approach taken to matters of contract law in the EU and the US.

Following from these remarks, the aim of this chapter is to explore the constitutionality and/or suitability of certain alternative and complementary routes to the adoption of a European contract law instrument contemplated in the debate. As the debate is ongoing, it cannot be ruled out that there may be additional solutions introduced in the coming years. Nevertheless, this chapter focuses on the following three categories that have gained a prominent place in the scholarly literature and institutional documents surrounding European contract law so far: enhanced cooperation, an

[1] For the purposes of this discussion, references to an international treaty, convention, or agreement are used synonymously. See B de Witte, 'Old-fashioned Flexibility: International Agreements between Member States of the European Union' in G de Búrca and J Scott (eds), *Constitutional Change in the EU: From Uniformity to Flexibility?* (Hart, 2000) 31, 32 fn 3.

intergovernmental treaty, and certain 'softer' models comprising the OMC, American techniques, and the CFR. This chapter is divided into three parts in order to examine each category in this order.

11.2 Enhanced Cooperation

11.2.1 The virtues and vices of enhanced cooperation

It may not be surprising that scholars have considered enhanced cooperation as a possible avenue in the debate about European contract law (and European private law generally).[2] This is because enhanced cooperation is a specific mechanism set down in the Treaties which, provided the requisite conditions are satisfied, allows a given number of Member States to accomplish certain objectives furthering the European integration process—as could be posed in the case of a European contract law instrument—while leaving recalcitrant Member States behind. It was formally introduced into the Treaty framework by the Amsterdam Treaty under the label of 'closer cooperation', but this was changed to 'enhanced cooperation' by the Nice Treaty. Still, both labels are equally apt for imparting the underlying idea that it is a subset or group of Member States engaging in cooperation among themselves in a particular matter covered by the Treaties, embodying a departure from the standard Union (formerly Community) method, which in principle involves the participation of all Member States in a given field. As such, the discussion of enhanced cooperation is largely situated within the broader discourse concerning 'flexibility' and 'differentiation' in the EU, terms which themselves embody a number of different conceptions and have given rise to a rich and multi-faceted debate in the literature.[3] Leaving that debate aside, suffice it to say that the association of enhanced cooperation with the terminology of 'flexibility' and 'differentiation' not only feeds into some of the reasons to explain why enhanced cooperation was inserted into the Treaty framework in the first place, but also is part and parcel of the virtues and vices associated with this mechanism, which sets the backdrop for its application to European contract law.

On the one hand, enhanced cooperation can be considered to embrace a positive outlook for furthering European integration, since it affords certain Member States means by which to reach objectives not shared by all Member States inside, as opposed to outside, the Treaty framework, which has been deemed particularly important with the progressive enlargement of the EU.[4] On the other hand, enhanced cooperation

[2] See, eg, P-C Müller-Graff, 'Closer Cooperation in European Community Contract Law' in K Boele-Woelki and W Grosheide (eds), *The Future of European Contract Law—Essays in honour of Ewoud Hondius* (Kluwer, 2007) 91; CU Schmid, 'Legitimacy Conditions for a European Civil Code' (2001) 8 *MJ* 277; M Storme, 'The Foundations of Private Law in a Multi-level Structure: Balancing, Distribution of Law-making Power and other Constitutional Issues' in R Brownsword et al (eds), *The Foundations of European Private Law* (Hart, 2011) 379, 389 (also published in (2012) 20 *ERPL* 237, 249).

[3] See generally *Constitutional Change in the EU: From Uniformity to Flexibility?*, n 1; B de Witte et al (eds), *The Many Faces of Differentiation in EU Law* (Intersentia, 2001); A Ott and E Vos (eds), *Fifty Years of European Integration: Foundations and Perspectives* (TMC Asser Press, 2009) pt II; F Tuytschaever, *Differentiation in European Union Law* (Hart, 1999). One scholar labelled enhanced cooperation the 'official' form of flexibility in the EU: see B de Witte, 'Future Paths of Flexibility: Enhanced Cooperation, Partial Agreements and Pioneer Groups' in JW de Zwaan et al (eds), *The European Union: An Ongoing Process of Integration—Liber Amicorum Alfred E. Kellermann* (TMC Asser Press, 2004) 141, 143.

[4] See, eg, S Weatherill, '"If I'd Wanted You to Understand I Would Have Explained it Better": What is the Purpose of the Provisions on Closer Co-operation Introduced by the Treaty of Amsterdam?' in

can be viewed in negative terms based on its aptitude for jeopardizing the uniform application of EU law and splintering the relationship of solidarity and trust among the Member States.[5] Enhanced cooperation therefore embodies both aspirations and tensions relating to the participation of less than all Member States, the lack of involvement of the Union institutions and bodies as would be the case under mainstream EU decision-making processes, and the need to constrict the proposed forms of enhanced cooperation so that it does not endanger the achievements of the Union *acquis*. This has important implications for its application to European contract law, which dictate the structure of the discussion.

First and foremost, enhanced cooperation is tightly controlled by the Treaties. The Treaty framework establishes a two-tier set of requirements that must be satisfied for the Member States concerned to avail themselves of this mechanism. Under the former Treaty framework, this involved a set of general requirements for enhanced cooperation established in a specific title of the EU Treaty,[6] as well as an additional set of specific requirements laid down in either the EC Treaty or the EU Treaty depending upon which pillar of the Union—the Community pillar, the second pillar concerning Common Foreign and Security Policy (CFSP), or the third pillar concerning Police and Judicial Cooperation in Criminal Matters (PJCCM)—was concerned.[7] With the entry into force of the Lisbon Treaty, this two-tier approach is retained, the difference being that with the elimination of the pillar structure, the various provisions on enhanced cooperation in each of the former pillars are consolidated into a specific title of the TFEU devoted to enhanced cooperation,[8] which sits alongside a specific title of the TEU on enhanced cooperation.[9] To be clear, while it is up to the particular Member States involved to decide whether they want to initiate, or join in, a form of enhanced cooperation, this mechanism is orchestrated from the European level by the Union institutions,[10] not by the Member States. As examined in the first part, these requirements highlight the linkage between enhanced cooperation and the Union's

D O'Keeffe and P Twomey (eds), *Legal Issues of the Amsterdam Treaty* (Hart, 1999) 21, 21–22. See also Opinion of AG Bot in Joined Cases C-274/11 and C-295/11 (Judgment of 16 April 2013) *Spain and Italy v Council*, not reported, point 82.

[5] See, eg, Weatherill, n 4, 22; J Weiler, 'Prologue: Amsterdam and the Quest for Constitutional Democracy' in *Legal Issues of the Amsterdam Treaty*, n 4, 1, 3.

[6] Ex Title VII EU (ex Arts 43–45 EU).

[7] As regards the former Community pillar, see ex Arts 11–11a EC; as regards CFSP, see ex Arts 27a–27e EU; and as regards PJCCM, see ex Arts 40–41 EU. With respect to the CFSP, enhanced cooperation was not allowed under the Amsterdam Treaty, but this was changed by the Nice Treaty, albeit with certain limitations. With the entry into force of the Lisbon Treaty, further changes were made in this regard, particularly in relation to allowing enhanced cooperation for military or defence matters. See Art 333(3) TFEU. There are also specific forms of enhanced cooperation set forth in the Treaties with respect to certain areas of PJCCM. See further S Peers, *EU Justice and Home Affairs Law*, 3rd edn (Oxford Univ Press, 2011) 64–71.

[8] Title III TFEU (Arts 326–334 TFEU).

[9] Title IV TEU (Art 20 TEU).

[10] This is so even if the participation of the Council, comprising Member State representatives, has a predominant role. Under the former Treaty framework, eg, the European Parliament was merely informed, consulted, or had to give its assent to the authorization of enhanced cooperation. Compare ex Art 11 EC; ex Art 27c EU; ex Art 40a EU. With the changes introduced by the Lisbon Treaty, the pillar structure has been eliminated, but there is still a distinction as regards the procedures to be followed for enhanced cooperation within the CFSP, as opposed to other areas (of non-exclusive Union competence) covered by the Treaties, with the result that the Parliament's role can vary. Compare Arts 329, 331, 333 TFEU. See further M Dougan, 'The Unfinished Business of Enhanced Cooperation: Some Institutional Questions and Their Constitutional Implications' in *Fifty Years of European Integration*, n 3, 157.

competence in European contract law and raise some questions as to whether enhanced cooperation may be authorized in this setting.

Secondly, until recently, enhanced cooperation had not been used in the formal sense. There had been a few occasions on which enhanced cooperation had been proposed, but this had not been followed through. [11] Moreover, the well-known instances that were often associated with enhanced cooperation—eg, Economic and Monetary Union (EMU), Schengen, and the Social Protocol—did not technically come about by way of the framework for enhanced cooperation established in the Treaties.[12] As such, for a long time, enhanced cooperation remained a hypothetical possibility, with no concrete evidence as to how it functioned in practice. This is no longer the case. In 2010, enhanced cooperation was used for the first time in connection with the 'Rome III' Regulation, laying down rules on the applicable law in divorce and legal separation in the field of judicial cooperation in civil matters pursuant to Article 81 TFEU.[13] The following year, enhanced cooperation was authorized for the second time with respect to the creation of unitary patent protection to achieve the Union's internal market objectives regarding the establishment of EU intellectual property rights under Article 118 TFEU.[14] In 2013, it was authorized for the third time in relation to the financial transaction tax (FTT), with a similar aim to achieve the Union's internal market objectives concerning the harmonization of indirect taxation under Article 113 TFEU.[15] It remains to be seen if, or more likely when, it will be used again. In the meantime, some of the foregoing measures have started to generate case law, which has helped to elucidate the various conditions for enhanced cooperation under the Treaties.[16] With

[11] See, eg, JM de Areilza, 'The Reform of Enhanced Cooperation Rules: Towards Less Flexibility?' in *The Many Faces of Differentiation in EU Law*, n 3, 27, 33–34; S Peers, 'Divorce, European Style: The First Authorization of Enhanced Cooperation' (2010) 6 *E Const L Rev* 339, 342; J Shaw, 'Enhancing Cooperation After Nice: Will the Treaty Do the Trick?' in M Andenas and J Usher (eds), *The Treaty of Nice and Beyond: Enlargement and Constitutional Reform* (Hart, 2003) 207, 217.

[12] See further K Lenaerts and P Van Nuffel (R Bray and N Cambien (eds)), *European Union Law*, 3rd edn (Sweet & Maxwell, 2011) § 12-013, § 19-005.

[13] Council Dec 2010/405/EU of 12 July 2010 authorising enhanced cooperation in the area of the law applicable to divorce and legal separation, [2010] OJ L189/12; Council Reg (EU) No 1259/2010 of 20 Dec 2010 implementing enhanced cooperation in the area of the law applicable to divorce and legal separation, [2010] OJ L343/10 ('Rome III' Regulation). See also Commission Dec 2012/714/EU of 21 Nov 2012 confirming the participation of Lithuania in enhanced cooperation in the area of the law applicable to divorce and legal separation, [2012] OJ L323/18. For detailed discussion, see, eg, K Boele-Woelki, 'For Better or For Worse: The Europeanization of International Divorce Law' (2010) 12 *YPIL* 1; A Fiorini, 'Harmonizing the law applicable to divorce and legal separation—enhanced cooperation as the way forward?' (2010) 59 *ICLQ* 1143; J-J Kuipers, 'The Law Applicable to Divorce as Test Ground for Enhanced Cooperation' (2012) 18 *ELJ* 201; Peers, n 11.

[14] Council Dec 2011/167/EU of 10 March 2011 authorising enhanced cooperation in the area of the creation of unitary patent protection, [2011] OJ L76/53; Reg (EU) No 1257/2012 of the European Parliament and of the Council of 17 Dec 2012 implementing enhanced cooperation in the area of the creation of unitary patent protection, [2012] OJ L361/1; Council Reg (EU) No 1260/2012 of 17 Dec 2012 implementing enhanced cooperation in the area of the creation of unitary patent protection with regard to the applicable translation arrangements, [2012] OJ L361/89. For detailed discussion (and the interplay with Opinion 1/09 *Draft Agreement on the European and Community Patents Court* [2011] ECR I-1137), see, eg, S Peers, 'The Constitutional Implications of the EU Patent' (2011) 7 *E Const L Rev* 229; H Ullrich, 'Enhanced cooperation in the area of unitary patent protection and European integration' (2013) 13 *ERA Forum* 589.

[15] Council Dec 2013/52/EU of 22 Jan 2013 authorising enhanced cooperation in the area of financial transaction tax, [2013] OJ L22/11. See also Proposal for a Council Directive implementing enhanced cooperation in the area of financial transaction tax, COM (2013) 71 final, 14.2.2013.

[16] As regards the unitary patent, a case challenging the legality of the Council's authorizing decision was dismissed by the Court of Justice in Joined Cases C-274/11 and C-295/11 (Judgment of 16 April 2013) *Spain and Italy v Council*, not reported. At the time of writing, litigation has also been brought against both measures implementing enhanced cooperation in this area (see pending Case

these recent institutional developments, it may be wondered whether initiatives in the debate will come to be considered viable candidates for enhanced cooperation. So far, however, there appears to be scarce attention given to the concrete application of enhanced cooperation in European contract law. As demonstrated in the second part, even assuming that the various conditions could be met, there are grave drawbacks associated with its use in this setting.

11.2.2 Can enhanced cooperation be authorized?

As just mentioned, there is a specific procedure set down by the Treaties to allow recourse to the mechanism of enhanced cooperation. The former Treaty framework is taken first, since it laid the basis for the changes brought about by the Lisbon Treaty. The former EU and EC Treaties established a two-level inquiry: first, the general provisions (former Articles 43–45 EU) of the EU Treaty had to be satisfied; and secondly, there were additional requirements, depending upon the relevant pillar. For the Community pillar,[17] this meant former Articles 11 and 11a EC, which were mainly concerned with the procedure to be followed by Member States seeking to establish enhanced cooperation and by those wishing to participate, respectively.[18] While important from a procedural or organizational standpoint, they did not have further bearing on the substantive conditions placed on the types of matters that could be subject to enhanced cooperation, which explains why focus is placed on the general provisions in the former EU Treaty for the purposes of this discussion.

Under former Article 43 EU, 'Member States which intend to establish enhanced cooperation may make use of the institutions, procedures and mechanisms laid down by this Treaty and by the Treaty establishing the European Community', provided that the proposed cooperation fulfilled ten specific conditions listed therein.[19] Of the ten conditions, some concerned structural components relative to the participating and non-participating Member States, namely that enhanced cooperation involved a minimum of eight Member States, was open to all Member States, and respected the competences, rights, and obligations of those Member States which did not participate.[20] Yet, the majority of these conditions related in one way or another to the competences conferred on the former Community or Union in relation to the action concerned. In particular, former Article 43 EU required that enhanced cooperation:

- 'is aimed at furthering the objectives of the Union and of the Community, at protecting and serving their interests and at reinforcing their process of integration';[21]
- 'respects the said Treaties and the single institutional framework of the Union';[22]

C-146/13 *Spain v European Parliament and Council*; and pending Case C-147/13 *Spain v Council*), as well as the Council's decision authorizing enhanced cooperation with respect to the FTT (see pending Case C-209/13 *UK v Council*).

[17] The provisions for the other two former pillars fall outside this discussion: see n 7.

[18] See ex Arts 11–11a EC.

[19] Ex Art 43 EU.

[20] Ex Art 43(g), (h), (j) EU. Although not relevant here, there was a further condition concerning the Schengen Protocol: see ex Art 43(i) EU.

[21] Ex Art 43(a) EU. Compare Amsterdam Treaty, ex Art 43(1)(a) EU ('is aimed at furthering the objectives of the Union and at protecting and serving its interests').

[22] Ex Art 43(b) EU. Compare Amsterdam Treaty, ex Art 43(1)(b) EU ('respects *the principles of* the said Treaties and the single institutional framework of the Union') (emphasis added).

- 'respects the *acquis communautaire* and the measures adopted under the other provisions of the said Treaties';[23]
- 'remains within the limits of the powers of the Union or of the Community and does not concern the areas which fall within the exclusive competence of the Community';[24]
- 'does not undermine the internal market as defined in Article 14(2) of the Treaty establishing the European Community, or the economic and social cohesion established in accordance with Title XVII of that Treaty';[25] and
- 'does not constitute a barrier to or discrimination in trade between the Member States and does not distort competition between them'.[26]

In addition, former Article 43a EU stipulated that enhanced cooperation 'may be undertaken *only as a last resort*, when it has been established within the Council that the objectives of such cooperation cannot be attained within a reasonable period by applying the relevant provisions of the Treaties'.[27] Former Article 44 EU provided that acts and decisions adopted under the rubric of enhanced cooperation did not form part of the Union *acquis* and were binding only on the participating Member States.[28] This provision also assumed that for the adoption of measures under enhanced cooperation, 'the relevant institutional provisions' of the former EU and EC Treaties applied.[29]

Of these various requirements, most, but not all, had appeared in somewhat similar form in the Amsterdam Treaty.[30] That Treaty laid down certain requirements—that enhanced cooperation did 'not affect Community policies, actions or programmes'[31] and did 'not concern the citizenship of the Union or discriminate between nationals of Member States'[32]—that were eliminated by the Nice Treaty. Yet, the condition precluding enhanced cooperation from undermining the internal market was a new provision added by the Nice Treaty. Given this evolution, it is difficult to determine exactly the extent to which the Nice Treaty loosened, as opposed to fortified, the substantive conditions for allowing enhanced cooperation as compared to the Amsterdam Treaty. Under the Amsterdam Treaty, it was considered a point of general agreement among scholars that the provisions were drafted so restrictively that it was difficult to envision many forms of enhanced cooperation that could in principle be capable of satisfying all of the requisite conditions.[33] With the Nice Treaty, the changes made to the substantive conditions were deemed to lower the hurdles to recourse to enhanced cooperation.[34] This is often exemplified by the Nice Treaty's elimination of certain requirements noted above or the modification from negative to positive language, such that enhanced cooperation 'respects' the *acquis communautaire*, as opposed to 'does not

[23] Ex Art 43(c) EU. Compare Amsterdam Treaty, ex Art 43(1)(d) EU ('*does not affect* the *acquis communautaire* and the measures adopted under the other provisions of the said Treaties') (emphasis added).

[24] Ex Art 43(d) EU. Compare Amsterdam Treaty, ex Art 11(1)(d) EC (remains within the limits of the powers *conferred upon the Community by this Treaty*') (emphasis added).

[25] Ex Art 43(e) EU. This was a new provision introduced by the Nice Treaty, which had no counterpart in the Amsterdam Treaty. See ns 36–37 and accompanying text.

[26] Ex Art 43(f) EU. Compare Amsterdam Treaty, ex Art 11(e) EC ('does not constitute a discrimination or a *restriction* of trade between Member States and does not distort *the conditions of* competition between the latter') (emphasis added).

[27] Ex Art 43a EU (emphasis added).

[28] Ex Art 44(1), second para, EU; ex Art 44(2) EU.

[29] Ex Art 44(1), first para, EU.

[30] See ns 21–24, 26.

[31] Amsterdam Treaty, ex Art 11(b) EC.

[32] Amsterdam Treaty, ex Art 11(c) EC.

[33] Shaw, n 11, 216.

[34] Shaw, n 11, 222.

affect' it, as had been the case under the Amsterdam Treaty.[35] Still, certain conditions, especially those relevant to this discussion, remained somewhat ambiguous. A salient example is the Nice Treaty's introduction of the explicit requirement that enhanced cooperation should not undermine the internal market as defined in what was then Art 14(2) EC (now Art 26(2) TFEU).[36] On the one hand, this may be viewed as signalling the intention to guard the sanctity of the EU's internal market policy from the potential disintegrating effects of enhanced cooperation. The fact that the Nice Treaty preserved the other conditions precluding barriers to trade and distortions of competition implies that this condition added something more; otherwise, it could have been subsumed under the conditions already in place under the Amsterdam Treaty. On the other hand, this condition may be read as making clear for the first time that enhanced cooperation could indeed apply to areas relating to the internal market, so long as it was not undermined.[37]

Needless to say, these ambiguities were not clarified by the Lisbon Treaty.[38] With the entry into force of that Treaty, there were certainly notable changes with respect to the structural or procedural aspects of enhanced cooperation, for instance, the minimum number of Member States that must be involved, the decision-making procedures to be followed, and the special rules concerning the CFSP, which may be considered to inject greater flexibility into the process and relax the conditions for enhanced cooperation even further.[39] However, the substantive conditions listed above for enhanced cooperation were not fundamentally altered, and the changes in this regard generally amounted more to reshuffling, with the result that these conditions are now scattered across the TEU and TFEU.[40]

As regards the specific title of the TEU on enhanced cooperation, the sole provision, Article 20 TEU, stipulates that Member States wishing to establish enhanced cooperation 'within the framework of the Union's non-exclusive competences' may make use of its institutions and exercise those competences 'by applying the relevant provisions of the Treaties', subject to the limits and detailed arrangements laid down in this Article

[35] See n 23. [36] See text accompanying n 25.

[37] See J Wouters, 'Constitutional Limits of Differentiation: The Principle of Equality' in *The Many Faces of Differentiation in EU Law*, n 3, 301, 339.

[38] For institutional questions left open, especially as regards a Member State's participation and withdrawal from enhanced cooperation, see, eg, 'Editorial Comments: Enhanced cooperation: A Union à taille réduite or à porte tournante?' (2011) 48 *CML Rev* 317.

[39] See, eg, P Craig, *The Lisbon Treaty—Law, Politics and Treaty Reform* (Oxford Univ Press, 2010) 440–442 (even finding certain substantive conditions to signify a subtle encouragement of enhanced cooperation); T Konstadinides, *Division of Powers in European Union Law* (Kluwer, 2009) 255–256. With regard to the 'last resort' condition, see also Opinion of AG Bot in Joined Cases C-274/11 and C-295/11 (Judgment of 16 April 2013) *Spain and Italy v Council*, not reported, point 111.

[40] See ns 8–9 and accompanying text. This had already been the case under the Draft Constitutional Treaty (DCT). See 2004 DCT, Art I-44; Arts III-416–423, which substantially resembled 2003 DCT, Art 43; Arts III-322–329. During the European Convention, the provisions on enhanced cooperation attracted a host of amendments and contributions, but were generally concerned with the specific application of enhanced cooperation in specific fields, such as the CFSP, or pertained to more structural or procedural matters, such as the minimum participation threshold, the qualified majority requirement, and clarification of the 'last resort' condition. See Proposed amendments concerning enhanced cooperation: draft Articles for Part One, CONV 779/03, dated 4 June 2003; and for Part Three, CONV 791/03, dated 6 June 2003 (there also used to be a list of proposed amendments available at the European Convention's official website, but as noted in Chapter 7, this website appears to have been taken down). In other words, such proposals were not primarily concerned with the substantive conditions discussed earlier, which are of relevance to European contract law. Yet, certain contributions submitted at the European Convention did revisit the tensions associated with enhanced cooperation and its questionable utility: see, eg, n 51.

and those Articles in the specific title of the TFEU concerning enhanced cooperation.[41] In addition, this provision requires that enhanced cooperation 'shall aim to further the objectives of the Union, protect its interests and reinforce the integration process' and can only be employed 'as a last resort'.[42] It also makes clear that the acts adopted in the framework of enhanced cooperation 'bind only participating Member States' and 'shall not be regarded as part of the *acquis* which has to be accepted by candidate States for accession to the Union'.[43]

Moving to the specific title of the TFEU on this topic, the very first provision, Article 326 TFEU, declares that enhanced cooperation 'shall not undermine the internal market or economic, social and territorial cohesion', 'not constitute a barrier to or discrimination in trade between Member States, nor shall it distort competition between them'.[44] The only glaring omission in comparison to the corresponding provisions of the former EU Treaty listed above is the deletion of the language stipulating that enhanced cooperation 'respects the *acquis communautaire* and the measures adopted under the other provisions of the said Treaties,[45] though presumably this is encompassed within Article 326 TFEU's stipulation that '[a]ny enhanced cooperation shall comply with the Treaties and Union law'.[46]

The bottom line is that under the present Treaty framework, as with the former Treaty framework, the substantive conditions that must be satisfied for enhanced cooperation are no 'walk in the park'. Save for the explicit addition of the condition concerning the internal market, the other requirements have remained firmly inscribed in the Treaty framework, even if in slightly modified form, from the beginning. These conditions have decisive bearing on the potential for enhanced cooperation to play a role in European contract law, and in the interests of clarity, their evaluation is divided into three subsets relating to the existence of Union competence, the internal market-related conditions, and the status of enhanced cooperation as a last resort.

11.2.2.1 *The existence of Union competence: A 'boomerang' to constitutionality*

As seen above, several conditions governing enhanced cooperation in the Treaties make clear or assume that enhanced cooperation is limited to activities for which there exists a proper legal basis. In other words, enhanced cooperation is permitted for areas in which the Union has been conferred the requisite competence under the principle of conferral; conversely, in areas where the Union does not have the requisite competence, enhanced cooperation cannot be resorted to.[47] Consequently, it is often missed that the application of enhanced cooperation to European contract law acts as a 'boomerang' to constitutionality because it predicates the inquiry as to whether the adoption of a European contract law instrument falls within the Union's competences and can be

[41] Art 20(1) TEU. [42] Art 20(1)–(2) TEU. [43] Art 20(4) TEU.

[44] Art 326, second para, TFEU. [45] See n 23 and accompanying text.

[46] Art 326, first para, TFEU. See, eg, Fiorini, n 13, 1152. This has been borne out in institutional practice: see, eg, Proposal for a Council Decision authorising enhanced cooperation in the area of the law applicable to divorce and legal separation, COM (2010) 104 final/2, 30.3.2010, paras 37–38; Proposal for a Council Decision authorising enhanced cooperation in the area of the creation of unitary patent protection, COM (2010) 790 final, 14.12.2010, point 4.4, first para; Proposal for a Council Decision authorising enhanced cooperation in the area of financial transaction tax, COM (2012) 631 final/2, 25.10.2012, point 4.4, first para.

[47] See, eg, A Dashwood, 'States in the European Union' (1998) 23 *ELR* 201, 210–211; Tuytschaever, n 3, 52. See also Case C-370/12 (Judgment of 27 Nov 2012) *Pringle*, not reported, paras 167–169.

considered to be aimed at furthering the Union's objectives. This explains why in the relevant literature contemplating enhanced cooperation in the context of European contract (or private) law, the conversation eventually ends up raising the matter of competence anyway. Thus, for those who take a negative position on the Union's competence to adopt a European contract law instrument, it is strange that enhanced cooperation is put forward as a mechanism to salvage the endeavour.[48] Importantly, then, in order to have recourse to enhanced cooperation, this requires the determination that the particular contract law instrument falls within the scope of the Union's competence. If not, one need not proceed any further, as enhanced cooperation is precluded.

Interestingly, in a past publication, Professor John Usher pondered whether enhanced cooperation could serve as a useful method of resolving controversies concerning different Member States' perceptions about the scope of Union (formerly Community) competence: those Member States that were of the view that a particular matter fell outside the scope of Union competence would simply not participate in it.[49] This presumably would leave the Member States that were of the opposite opinion to proceed with such action under enhanced cooperation. Although it is unclear how much Professor Usher himself was advocating such a position,[50] with all due respect to the late scholar, this may not be beneficial for European contract law, since it would leave the matter of competence unsettled and have the potential to exacerbate tensions among the Member States even further. Such a position would also seem to depend upon the area of competence concerned, since it may have more relevance to discrete areas divorced from the Union's core competences and objectives such as those concerning the internal market in which a European contract law instrument, optional or otherwise, has consistently been framed.[51]

As discussed in Chapter 8, a case can be made that Article 114 TFEU and/or Article 352 TFEU confer sufficient competence on the Union to adopt a European contract law instrument, optional or otherwise, for the achievement of its internal market objectives. Of course, there may continue to be differing opinions on the subject. The point here is that either way, the determination of competence has to be made; it is a precondition for enhanced cooperation, which adds further impetus to the constitutionality of European contract law. Moreover, in view of the linkage of a European contract law instrument to the Union's competences under Articles 114 and 352 TFEU, this beckons inquiry into the internal market-related conditions stipulated for enhanced cooperation.

[48] See, eg, J Ziller, 'The Legitimacy of the Codification of Contract Law in View of the Allocation of Competences between the European Union and its Member States' in MW Hesselink (ed), *The Politics of a European Civil Code* (Kluwer, 2006) 89, 113.

[49] See JA Usher, 'Enhanced Cooperation or Flexibility in the Post-Nice Era' in A Arnull and D Wincott (eds), *Accountability and Legitimacy in the European Union* (Oxford Univ Press, 2002) 97, 112.

[50] He framed the matter as being suggested by a recent doctoral thesis: Usher, n 49, 112 fn 48.

[51] This was strongly asserted in a contribution submitted by MEP Andrew Duff during the European Convention, which provided a well-versed summary of the various reasons why enhanced cooperation should not be used on a general basis. See Contribution by Mr Andrew Duff, member of the Convention: 'Do we really need enhanced cooperation?', CONV 759/03 CONTRIB 336, dated 22 May 2003. In particular, he stressed that while it was well suited for the security and defence dimension, it was 'a much less satisfactory way to manage disagreements over the core competences of the Union to which all [Me]mber [S]tates have in any case to subscribe, and where the integrity of the *acquis* is at stake'. Contribution by Mr Andrew Duff, 3.

11.2.2.2 *The internal market-related conditions: Linkage to Articles 114 and 352 TFEU*

Assuming a proper legal basis, some of the aforementioned substantive conditions, which can be grouped under the category of internal market-related conditions for convenience, may be considered to present further stumbling blocks to the allowance of enhanced cooperation in relation to European contract law. To recall, under the Treaties, enhanced cooperation must not, inter alia, 'undermine the internal market', 'constitute a barrier to or discrimination in trade between the Member States', or 'distort competition between them'.[52] Although there is not yet a great abundance of case law on the internal market-related conditions, the one judgment that has been delivered so far indicates some room for manoeuvre in the assessment of these conditions.

Spain and Italy v Council[53] constituted the first time that the Court of Justice ruled on the legality of a decision authorizing enhanced cooperation, here in the area of the creation of unitary patent protection.[54] One of the arguments put forward by the applicants was that the decision infringed the second paragraph of Article 326 TFEU because the enhanced cooperation in question would violate the internal market-related conditions (as well as that concerning economic, social, and territorial cohesion).[55] The Court swiftly rejected this argument, holding that 'it cannot validly be maintained that, by having it in view to create a unitary patent applicable in the participating Member States and not in the Union, the contested decision damages the internal market'.[56] In his Opinion, Advocate General Bot was more forthcoming, finding that far from undermining the internal market, the enhanced cooperation in question did precisely the opposite by helping to improve the functioning of the internal market, as well as to reduce barriers to trade and distortions of competition, through remedying the existing fragmentation in the internal market caused by disparities among national laws.[57]

Notwithstanding a flexible interpretation of these conditions inferred by this judgment, there are textual and structural arguments underlying enhanced cooperation in the Treaties, which may at least suggest that some caution should be taken when using it in the internal market setting. Textually, the conditions precluding barriers to trade and distortions of competition were perceived from the beginning as discouraging the use of enhanced cooperation in areas that could gravely affect the achievements made in the internal market, especially in fields involving EU harmonization measures.[58] Going back to the political negotiations surrounding enhanced cooperation in the Amsterdam Treaty, there had been attempts by several Member States to exclude enhanced cooperation explicitly from various fields, including the fundamental freedoms, the internal market, and the competition rules, among others.[59] The fact that an additional provision was added by the Nice Treaty protecting the internal market, even if implying that enhanced cooperation could indeed touch upon this area, may be taken to ingrain even further that the EU's activities revolving

[52] See n 44 and accompanying text.

[53] Joined Cases C-274/11 and C-295/11 (Judgment of 16 April 2013) *Spain and Italy v Council*, not reported.

[54] Opinion of AG Bot in Joined Cases C-274/11 and C-295/11 *Spain and Italy v Council*, point 26.

[55] See Joined Cases C-274/11 and C-295/11 *Spain and Italy v Council*, paras 70–73.

[56] Joined Cases C-274/11 and C-295/11 *Spain and Italy v Council*, para 75.

[57] See Opinion of AG Bot in Joined Cases C-274/11 and C-295/11 *Spain and Italy v Council*, points 142–152.

[58] H Kortenberg, 'Closer Cooperation in the Treaty of Amsterdam' (1998) 35 *CML Rev* 833, 849.

[59] See H Bribosia, 'De la subsidiarité à la coopération renforcée' in Y Lejeune (ed), *La traité d'Amsterdam: Espoirs et déceptions* (Bruylant, 1998) 23, 55 fn 118; Tuytschaever, n 3, 55–56.

around the internal market must not be endangered by enhanced cooperation. Thus, while enhanced cooperation is not excluded from areas within the internal market, those matters vital for its functioning may warrant the need for special vigilance so as to ensure that enhanced cooperation is not taken so far as to destroy the uniform application of Union measures in the field. This view helps to reconcile the reason for inserting a specific provision precluding the internal market from being undermined alongside conditions that already existed precluding barriers to trade and distortions of competition.

Structurally, much has been made of the apparent resemblance of the internal market-related conditions for enhanced cooperation to the requirements of what are now Articles 114 and 115 TFEU, even if situated in different contexts. For example, in the years following the *Tobacco Advertising I* judgment, one scholar considered that just as the Court of Justice had circumscribed the use of Article 114 TFEU (ex Article 95 EC) to eliminate only 'appreciable' distortions of competition, the differences in national legislation resulting from enhanced cooperation would only fall foul of the Treaties if they were deemed 'appreciable'.[60] This view seems to suggest that Article 114 TFEU and enhanced cooperation are in something of an inverse relationship: as the requirement for distortions of competition is interpreted narrowly under Article 114 TFEU, this serves to loosen up recourse to enhanced cooperation, or vice versa. Presumably, similar remarks could be made for barriers to trade in this regard. Yet, a crucial assumption appears to be that the concept of distortions of competition or barriers to trade for the purposes of Article 114 TFEU is interpreted in similar fashion to its usage in the Treaties as regards the conditions for enhanced cooperation.

So far, there is no case law of the Union courts that has addressed this issue. Nevertheless, the context and teleology of the two sets of provisions are, arguably, quite different. Generally speaking, Article 114 TFEU is used for the adoption of measures to achieve the Union's objective of ensuring the establishment and functioning of the internal market by eliminating obstacles to the exercise of the fundamental freedoms and/or appreciable distortions of competition. Much of the concern underlying the requirement of 'appreciable' distortions of competition in *Tobacco Advertising I* was to ensure that the legislature had recourse to Article 114 TFEU to combat distortions of competition, but that a limit must be placed on this condition so that it was not stretched too far. By comparison, enhanced cooperation is a departure from the Union method altogether, permitting further action in areas covered by the Treaties involving some, not all, Member States; thus, the limitations on recourse to enhanced cooperation stem from preservation of the functioning of the internal market from possible fragmentation by allowing a proposed form of enhanced cooperation to proceed. As such, the provisions on enhanced cooperation embody different aims than Article 114 TFEU. Ensuring that proposed enhanced cooperation does not distort competition, constitute barriers to trade, or otherwise undermine the internal market takes on a broader cast in light of protecting the achievements of the Union *acquis sensu lato* that is similar to, but is not necessarily directly transferable from, the case law on Article 114 TFEU.

That being said, the two sets of provisions do appear to be related to each other to some extent. Assuming that the legal basis of the action envisaged—as in the case of a

[60] Usher, n 49, 99. Before the *Tobacco Advertising I* judgment was delivered, Professor Stephen Weatherill noted that with the wide breadth given to distortions of competition under what is now Article 114 TFEU (ex Art 95 EC), this cut down on potential recourse to enhanced (then closer) cooperation. See Weatherill, n 4, 28–30; S Weatherill, 'Flexibility or Fragmentation: Trends in European Integration' in JA Usher (ed), *The State of the European Union* (Longman, 2000) 1, 10.

European contract law instrument—is Article 114 and/or Article 352 TFEU (depending upon the type of instrument) with the objective of eliminating barriers to trade and/or appreciable distortions of competition in the internal market, it could be surmised that this would present tensions with the resort to enhanced cooperation. As regards Article 114 TFEU, it is on the basis of the problems plaguing the internal market that action is envisaged to approximate the contract laws of the Member States under this provision. As such, resort to enhanced cooperation, which by its nature involves only a number of participating Member States, has the potential to preclude the objectives of approximation in the first place. Likewise, as regards an optional instrument that may be adopted under Article 114 TFEU or Article 352 TFEU depending upon the future course of the debate, it could be argued that such an instrument merely adds an additional regime to be availed of by parties of their own choosing and hence would not unduly disrupt the functioning of the internal market. Still, proceeding via enhanced cooperation could be considered to reintroduce problems for the internal market that the instrument concerned is intended to remedy. If such an instrument, whether optional or not, could be availed of by parties only in certain Member States, this carries the potential to preserve, even exacerbate, some of the apparent barriers or distortions of competition as between the Member States that do and do not participate or have the effect of partitioning the internal market into different stages of development depending upon the Member States in which the instrument would be adopted or not, thereby falling on the side of undermining the internal market. Consequently, for European contract law, this could be viewed as indicating a structural tension between the Union's internal market competences and the internal market-related conditions of enhanced cooperation: as the arguments for recourse to Articles 114 and/or 352 TFEU became more pressing, this could conceivably detract from the possible recourse to enhanced cooperation in this setting.

Importantly, however, these arguments may have to be revisited in light of recent institutional developments concerning the operation of enhanced cooperation in practice. So far, two of the three instances in which enhanced cooperation has been resorted to—the unitary patent and the FTT—have been linked to the achievement of the Union's internal market objectives.[61] Looking at the reasoning in the accompanying proposals regarding compliance with the internal market-related conditions, both take a similar approach based on the fact that the enhanced cooperation in question at least goes some way towards remedying the current problems hindering the functioning of the internal market in the area concerned.[62] This echoes to some extent the Court's assessment of these conditions and even more so Advocate General Bot's Opinion in *Spain and Italy v Council*, discussed earlier. As illustrated by these instances, when the problems in the internal market in the area concerned call for a solution, enhanced cooperation may essentially be considered 'better than nothing' in terms of making progress with addressing those problems, thereby getting it past the hurdle of the internal market-related conditions. In this way, the justification for use of the Union's internal market competences under Articles 114 and/or 352 TFEU may in fact help to bolster compliance with these conditions. Certainly,

[61] See ns 14–15 and accompanying text. As regards the 'Rome III' Regulation, its internal market rationale was more controversial, but the softening of the internal market requirement under Art 81 TFEU, as compared to former Art 65 EC, put a damper on the discussion: see, eg, Peers, n 11, 351. See further Chapter 10, § 10.2.2.

[62] See Proposal for a Council Decision authorising enhanced cooperation in the area of the creation of unitary patent protection, n 46, points 4.3.1, 4.5; Proposal for a Council Decision authorising enhanced cooperation in the area of financial transaction tax, n 46, points 4.3, 4.5.

each proposed form of enhanced cooperation is taken on a case-by-case basis. For European contract law, this may have the result that the arguments for recourse to Articles 114 and/or 352 TFEU may lend further support for enhanced cooperation in this setting.

11.2.2.3 Enhanced cooperation as a last resort: Linkage to the principle of sincere cooperation

To recall, former Article 43a EU stipulated that enhanced cooperation 'may be undertaken only as a last resort, where it has been established within the Council that the objectives of such cooperation cannot be attained within a reasonable period by applying the relevant provisions of the Treaty'. As highlighted in the discussion of this provision during the European Convention, it left certain questions open, such as when and how the Council can establish that the situation is deadlocked, which the changes introduced by the Draft Constitutional Treaty and ultimately the Lisbon Treaty attempted to resolve.[63] Article 20(2) TEU provides in relevant part: 'The decision authorising enhanced cooperation shall be adopted by the Council as a last resort, when it has established that the objectives of such cooperation cannot be attained within a reasonable period by the Union as a whole'.[64] In any event, whether under the past or present Treaty framework, an express condition for enhanced cooperation continues to be that it is a mechanism of 'last resort', meaning that it is only triggered under circumstances when action under the Union method has failed,[65] or in the Court's words, 'only in those situations in which it is impossible to adopt such legislation in the foreseeable future'.[66] In effect, the Treaties dictate that the Member States do not have 'free choice' to pick and choose between proceeding via the normal decision-making process or enhanced cooperation. The former comes first.

In this regard, the principle of sincere cooperation enshrined in Article 4(3) TEU may play a role here, even if it has not (yet) been mentioned by the Court in the assessment of this condition. On the basis of this provision, Member States are under the obligation to 'facilitate the achievement of the Union's tasks and refrain from any measure which could jeopardise the attainment of the Union's objectives'.[67] This provision suggests that the Member States have a duty to work with each other, and with the Union institutions concerned, to direct action under the decision-making process involving in principle all Member States as far as possible in the area concerned, which again focuses attention on constitutionality. For European contract law, this means that the Member States and the Union institutions must work as much as possible through the decision-making procedure stipulated under the legal basis concerned for the adoption of a European contract law instrument. Enhanced

[63] See Praesidium Document on enhanced cooperation, CONV 723/03, dated 14 May 2003, 4–5.

[64] The DCT contained an identical provision: see 2003 DCT, Art 43(2); 2004 DCT, Art I-44(2).

[65] Among the proposals for revising the 'last resort' condition during the European Convention, see Suggestion for amendment of Article 32b(2) (Enhanced cooperation) by Mr Michael Frendo, member of the Maltese National Parliament (considering this condition as a 'safety valve' in terms of serving as 'an exceptional measure of last resort, in extremis, when all else fails' and not a method of governance).

[66] Joined Cases C-274/11 and C-295/11 (Judgment of 16 April 2013) *Spain and Italy v Council*, not reported, para 50. The Court found that this condition was satisfied: paras 47–59. The AG reached the same conclusion, noting that this condition (as well as that concerning a reasonable period) had not been defined in the Treaties: see Opinion of AG Bot in Joined Cases C-274/11 and C-295/11 *Spain and Italy v Council*, points 108–126.

[67] Art 4(3), third para, TEU.

cooperation is therefore not an automatic solution that can be thrown out as a middle ground so as to allow those Member States most desiring of future progress in European contract law to go ahead, while appeasing the more sceptical Member States that prefer to stay behind, without first proceeding through the normal channels involving all Member States pursuant to the relevant legal basis. It is incumbent upon the Member States to attempt to cooperate among each other to reach agreement in the decision-making process before resorting to enhanced cooperation. As such, enhanced cooperation is at most a 'second rate' solution coming after Union action under the normal route has been tried.

11.2.3 Should enhanced cooperation be used?

Even if a proposed form of enhanced cooperation in connection with European contract law could be deemed to satisfy all of the requisite conditions, there are further practical arguments that strongly counsel against the use of enhanced cooperation in this setting. Two main arguments stand out.

First, as specified by the Treaties, measures adopted under the auspices of enhanced cooperation are only binding on the participating Member States and not regarded as part of the Union *acquis* that has to be accepted by candidate States for accession to the EU.[68] Accordingly, a European contract law instrument adopted via enhanced cooperation would not apply to non-participating Member States or to future Member States acceding to the EU, and would exist apart from the Union *acquis* in (consumer) contract law. As scholars have noted, this presents difficulties for any proposed enhanced cooperation since it is assumed that the proposed enhanced cooperation can be neatly segregated from the Union *acquis*, 'which is entirely at odds with the intertwining evolution of [EU] activity'.[69] This explains why new or discrete policy areas without extensive linkage to the Union *acquis* have been considered more suitable for enhanced cooperation,[70] which is in fact illustrated by the instances in which enhanced cooperation has been employed so far.[71]

For European contract law, this is especially burdensome because it is rooted in various Union measures concerning consumer and commercial contract law. The relationship between the European contract law project and the revision of the consumer *acquis* aptly bears this out. Even if, formally speaking, action taken under enhanced cooperation may be deemed to comply with the Treaties and Union law (including the relevant *acquis*),[72] practically speaking, there would be manifold complexities in terms of interplay between the proposed instrument and the surrounding body of Union measures. This is so, especially in connection with the CFR and related initiatives, such as the proposal for a Regulation on a Common European Sales Law (proposed CESL).[73] Unless the CFR is adopted under the auspices of enhanced cooperation—which as envisaged now as a tool for 'better lawmaking' by the Union institutions seems unlikely—action under enhanced cooperation for the adoption of an optional contract

[68] See n 43 and accompanying text.

[69] Weatherill, n 60, 11 (in reference to the conditions introduced by the Amsterdam Treaty). See also Craig, n 39, 449.

[70] Peers, n 11, 355.

[71] See, eg, Proposal for a Council Decision authorising enhanced cooperation in the area of the law applicable to divorce and legal separation, n 46, para 38; Proposal for a Council Decision authorising enhanced cooperation in the area of the creation of unitary patent protection, n 46, point 4.4, third–fourth paras; Proposal for a Council Decision authorising enhanced cooperation in the area of financial transaction tax, n 46, point 4.4, second para.

[72] See n 46 and accompanying text.

[73] See Chapter 6, § 6.4.4.

law instrument as in the case of the proposed CESL would create the situation that it would be based—as envisaged by the Commission—on the CFR, but would then be situated outside the institutional framework. Moreover, it may be the case that more than one optional instrument will eventually be adopted. As such, using enhanced cooperation in this context may involve a different set of Member States for one instrument or type of action versus another. Basically, it would be devastating, and not the least bit ironic, that enhanced cooperation would be used as part of a project that was built on the impetus of improving the coherence of the Union *acquis*.

Secondly, enhanced cooperation presents further drawbacks on account of problems stemming from the lack of involvement of all Member States, the Union institutions and bodies, and other relevant actors inside and outside the EU decision-making process. Starting with the Member States, at least one commentator has stressed that while enhanced (then closer) cooperation may have value for promoting specific projects with limited impact on the integration process, it is unlikely to 'serve as an appropriate vehicle to advance highly debated projects of major interest for all Member States'.[74] By the very nature of the European contract law project, there are important reasons why it should involve the participation of all Member States in principle, such as their input as part of the comparative nature of the project, as had already occurred with respect to the CFR, and leaving some Member States out may create tensions or present difficulties with those Member States joining later on. For example, non-participating Member States may likely be suspicious as to the framing of an instrument that may or may not adequately reflect their contract law regime and could very well present problems for the possibility of adopting such an instrument in those Member States in future years. This would be so, whether the proposed enhanced cooperation has to do with the framing of a binding contract law instrument or something akin to the CFR, in which the participation of all Member States is part of its value and utility. In short, the European contract law project represents a comparative project for the whole of the EU; splintering it into different factions of Member States could stunt its progress and eventual success.

Similar remarks can be made with respect to the participation of the Union institutions and bodies, as well as various stakeholder groups, involved in the debate. From the very beginning, European contract law has been a project in which the Union institutions and bodies have played important roles. In large part, the European Parliament and the European Council have served as motors and monitors of the project, and in their own way, the Council and the Commission have steered the discussion and approach to be undertaken. The European Economic and Social Committee and the Committee of the Regions have each done their part to express the views of their composite members. Likewise, the various stakeholders, including businesses, consumer organizations, legal practitioners, and academics, throughout the EU (and to some extent beyond) have played an indelible role in the development of the European contract law project, which has been carried through in the specific stakeholder and expert groups set up in connection with the various initiatives envisaged, such as the CFR and the Feasibility Study. Consequently, resort to enhanced cooperation could stymie the channels set up within the institutional framework concerning European contract law for ensuring the participation of these actors. Certainly, as dictated by the Treaty framework, the Union institutions would still claim involvement and the Member States concerned would make use of such institutions in proceeding with enhanced cooperation.

[74] D Hanf, 'Flexibility Clauses in the Founding Treaties, From Rome to Nice' in *The Many Faces of Differentiation in EU Law*, n 3, 3, 24.

Nevertheless, there is a perceptible danger that the roles played by the Union institutions and bodies, as well as the various stakeholder groups, could be changed and to some extent undercut by recourse to enhanced cooperation in this setting.

To sum up, while in principle there may be a case that a form of enhanced cooperation relating to European contract law could survive the hurdles of the requisite Treaty conditions, in practice the European contract law project seems particularly ill-suited to this mechanism. As demonstrated by the foregoing analysis, enhanced cooperation makes the need to address the constitutionality of European contract law more apparent, highlights the importance of involving all the Member States, the Union institutions and bodies, and the various stakeholders within the institutional framework established for the European contract law project so far, and carries the potential to weaken the achievements that can be attained by this project in various ways.

11.3 An Intergovernmental Treaty

11.3.1 Distinguishing levels and approaches

In the debate about European contract law, two key approaches to intergovernmental cooperation among the Member States have emerged so far: first, the possible recourse to an intergovernmental treaty adopted by the Member States under the auspices of public international law outside the EU institutional framework; and secondly, the proposal for an ad hoc convention among the Member States inside this framework. As regards the first category, this can be further subdivided according to the number of Member States involved. In the literature, this is often embodied by the distinction between 'parallel agreements' and 'partial agreements': parallel agreements involve all Member States, whereas partial agreements, as the name implies, involve only some Member States.[75] Yet, at least so far, partial agreements have not been contemplated much, if at all, as a distinct route in the debate.[76] In any case, partial agreements involve problems and drawbacks that to a large extent are already addressed in other sections of this chapter. In particular, the problems concerning the lack of participation of all Member States echo the discussion in the previous section concerning enhanced cooperation, and the drawbacks concerning the use of international conventions generally follow the discussion below.[77] Thus, an intergovernmental treaty involving in principle all Member States will be the focal point of this discussion.

[75] See, eg, B de Witte, 'Chameleonic Member States: Differentiation By Means of Partial and Parallel International Agreements' in *The Many Faces of Differentiation in EU Law*, n 3, 231. For a broader outlook, see, eg, A Rosas, 'The Status in EU Law of International Agreements Concluded by EU Member States' (2011) 34 *Fordham ILJ* 1304.

[76] Incidentally, as regards matters of substantive family law, France and Germany concluded a bilateral agreement setting forth an optional matrimonial property regime, which has been posited as a model in the context of European family law, as well as other fields of European private law. See, eg, K Boelke-Woelki, 'Cross-border family law relations in Europe: towards a common European matrimonial property law based upon cooperation between private international law and substantive law' in ALM Keirse and MBM Loos (eds), *Alternative Ways to Ius Commune: The Europeanisation of Private Law* (Intersentia, 2012) 33; A Fötschl, 'The Common Optional Matrimonial Property Regime of Germany and France—Epoch-Making in the Unification of Law' (2009) 11 *YPIL* 395, 403–404 (also published in (2010) 18 *ERPL* 881, 889) (considering its viability in connection with the CFR). So far, however, this kind of bilateral agreement has not been broached in the activities taking place in the European contract law project.

[77] Eg, as regards possible problems associated with the Franco-German bilateral agreement in n 76, see, eg, CG Beilfuss, 'The Franco-German Treaty Instituting a Common Matrimonial Regime

11.3.2 An intergovernmental treaty under public international law

11.3.2.1 Historical relic of days past in the debate about European private law?

In the 1990s, when the debate about European private law was getting underway, mention was frequently made in the literature to the possible recourse to an intergovernmental treaty adopted under the auspices of public international law as an alternative to the far-reaching approximation of national private law at the European level. Yet, as the debate evolved through to the present day, references to this route dropped off. This is illustrated by the successive editions of the comprehensive work, *Towards a European Civil Code*, encompassing the views of prominent scholars on various aspects of the debate about European private law through the course of its four editions published in 1994, 1998, 2004, and 2011. Originally, in the general introductory chapter authored by Professor Ewoud Hondius in the first edition, he surmised that 'a European Civil Code, although raising serious constitutional issues, is not constitutionally impossible (e.g., by way of a Treaty)'.[78] In subsequent editions of this work, however, the parenthetical reference to the use of a Treaty was gone, albeit the general statement remained.[79] Just as subtle was the transformation of Professor Peter-Christian Müller-Graff's chapter in the same work, which originally framed the discussion of various alternatives including the use of an intergovernmental treaty as 'Private Law Unification by Means other than of Codification',[80] but eventually gave way to a focus on 'Directives as a Means of Private Law Unification' in the three later editions,[81] even though his largely negative opinion on the prospect of resorting to such a treaty remained steady throughout.

The popularity of an intergovernmental treaty during this time period is not altogether surprising, since by and large these were the years when the use of an international convention was envisaged by the Treaties in relevant areas, eg, conventions in the former third pillar[82] and for particular matters under former Article 293 EC in the former Community pillar.[83] Yet, starting with the Amsterdam Treaty, the tide gradually turned away from the use of intergovernmental conventions within the EU institutional framework, particularly for policy fields falling within Community (now

of Participation in the Acquisitions: How Could Catalonia Opt In?' in A-L Verbeke et al (eds), *I Confronting the Frontiers of Family and Succession Law—Liber Amicorum Walter Pintens* (Intersentia, 2012) 623, 631; Commission Communication, Bringing legal clarity to property rights for international couples, COM (2011) 125 final, 16.3.2011, 5. For other limitations, see, eg, B de Witte, 'The Emergence of a European System of Public International Law: The EU and its Member States as Strange Subjects' in J Wouters et al (eds), *The Europeanisation of International Law* (TMC Asser Press, 2008) 39, 45–48.

[78] E Hondius, 'Towards a European Civil Code. General Introduction' in A Hartkamp et al (eds), *Towards a European Civil Code*, 1st edn (Martinus Nijhoff/Ars Aequi Libri, 1994) 1, 8.

[79] See E Hondius, 'Towards a European Civil Code' in A Hartkamp et al (eds), *Towards a European Civil Code*, 2nd rev and expanded edn (Kluwer/Ars Aequi Libri, 1998) 3, 14; E Hondius, 'Towards a European Civil Code' in A Hartkamp et al (eds), *Towards a European Civil Code*, 3rd rev and expanded edn (Kluwer/Ars Aequi Libri, 2004) 3, 9; E Hondius, 'Towards a European Civil Code' in A Hartkamp et al (eds), *Towards a European Civil Code*, 4th rev and expanded edn (Kluwer/Ars Aequi Libri, 2011) 3, 11.

[80] P-C Müller-Graff, 'Private Law Unification by Means other than of Codification' in *Towards a European Civil Code*, 1st edn, n 78, 19, 23–25.

[81] P-C Müller-Graff, 'EC Directives as a Means of Private Law Unification' in *Towards a European Civil Code*, 2nd edn, n 79, 71, 77–79; P-C Müller-Graff, 'EC Directives as a Means of Private Law Unification' in *Towards a European Civil Code*, 3rd edn, n 79, 77, 83–84; P-C Müller-Graff, 'EU Directives as a Means of Private Law Unification' in *Towards a European Civil Code*, 4th edn, n 79, 149, 157–158.

[82] See ex Art 34(2)(d) EU.

[83] See further Chapter 10, § 10.2.1.

Union) law.[84] The quintessential example is the field of judicial cooperation in civil matters under what was then Article 65 EC (now Article 81 TFEU), whereby various international conventions—including those that entered into force, such as Brussels and Rome Conventions, and others that had not yet obtained all the necessary ratifications, such as the Insolvency, Service, and Brussels II Conventions—were progressively converted into Community (now Union) instruments.[85] With the entry into force of the Lisbon Treaty, this has become even more apparent, with the elimination of Article 293 EC and the use of conventions in the former third pillar. Interestingly, in the European Convention, the Final Report of Working Group IX on 'Simplification' emphasized that there were a number of reasons why conventions in the third pillar should be abolished: they had rarely been used since the Amsterdam Treaty, and most never entered into force and were replaced by Community (now Union) measures in any event.[86]

As a result, while an intergovernmental treaty may understandably have been a 'tool of the trade' during the timeframe in which the debate about European private law was gearing up, matters have changed since then. In other words, the potential recourse to such a treaty can be viewed at least to some extent as a historical relic of days past in the debate about European private law, which has largely been superseded by more recent developments concerning the European contract law project, such as the revision of the consumer *acquis*, the CFR, and the proposed CESL, among other things. That being said, the alternative route of an intergovernmental treaty has not been entirely lost from view. Scholars still continue to refer to this possibility in the literature,[87] which leaves questions open as to the extent to which it may serve as a potential vehicle in the future course of European contract law.

Noticeably, the use of an intergovernmental treaty in this context hinges on the constitutional assessment of European contract law. To some extent, the suggestion for an intergovernmental treaty appears to have been motivated by scholars' assumptions about the lack of sufficient Union competence over the whole of contract law or private law generally.[88] Thus, part and parcel of this mechanism is the inquiry into the EU's competence in contract law or other fields of private law, since it is to be wondered

[84] That being said, there are significant issues, constitutional and otherwise, raised by recent developments in which some Member States have resorted to treaties outside the EU institutional framework and thus bypassed the mechanisms inside such framework, such as the revision procedures, which regrettably exceed the scope of this book. For detailed discussion (including the Court's judgment in Case C-370/12 (Judgment of 27 Nov 2012) *Pringle*, not reported), see, eg, P Craig, 'The Stability, Coordination and Governance Treaty: principle, politics and pragmatism' (2012) 37 *ELR* 231; S Peers, 'Towards a New Form of EU Law?: The Use of EU Institutions outside the EU Legal Framework' (2013) 9 *E Const L Rev* 37.

[85] This was a point of emphasis in the joint submission by Mr Michel Barnier and Mr António Vitorino, representatives of the European Commission at the European Convention, on the 'Community method', CONV 231/02 CONTRIB 80, dated 3 Sept 2002, 6–7.

[86] Final Report of Working Group IX on Simplification, CONV 424/02 WGIX13, dated 29 Nov 2002, 5.

[87] See, eg, M Heidemann, 'European Private Law at the Crossroads: The Proposed European Sales Law' (2012) 20 *ERPL* 1119, 1125; MBM Loos, 'The influence of European consumer law on general contract law and the need for spontaneous harmonisation', CSECL Working Paper Series No 2006/02, 7–8; Storme, n 2; W van Gerven, 'Bringing (Private) Laws Closer to Each Other at the European Level' in F Cafaggi (ed), *The Institutional Framework of European Private Law* (Oxford Univ Press, 2006) 37, 39, 64.

[88] See, eg, van Gerven, n 87; G Howells, 'The Role of the *Acquis Communautaire* in Consumer Law for a European Contract Law Code—A Comment' in S Grundmann and M Schauer (eds), *The Architecture of European Codes and Contract Law* (Kluwer, 2006) 271, 279. See also the 1999 Working Paper (n 90), discussed in Chapter 4, § 4.3.4.

whether if such competence can be found, this would remove much of the impetus for this mechanism in the first place. As a related point, the use of an intergovernmental treaty could presumably involve non-Member States. As such, it places emphasis on the objectives sought by the European contract law project in the sense of requiring verification as to whether it is the Union's objectives related to the functioning of the internal market at stake or other objectives that would be best served, or not, by the inclusion of third States and the proper placement of the project as a matter best suited for the European or international fora. Consequently, while perhaps the use of an intergovernmental treaty is more historical relic than present day reality, it draws further attention to matters bearing on the constitutionality of European contract law.

11.3.2.2 Problems associated with an intergovernmental treaty

Surprisingly, detailed inquiry is rarely given to the question of whether an intergovernmental treaty would be allowed under EU law, let alone suitable for the purposes of European contract law. On close inspection, there are, arguably, several problems raised by this alternative route. To begin with, it is often overlooked that for matters falling within the Treaties, there is not necessarily a 'free choice' as between the Member States proceeding outside the Treaty framework by way of an intergovernmental treaty and inside the Treaty framework pursuant to the relevant legal basis. As underscored by commentators, the allowance for all (as opposed to just some) Member States to proceed via an intergovernmental treaty would pose a direct threat to the achievements of the Union legal order and may even constitute a violation of the principle of sincere cooperation under what is now Article 4(3) TEU to the extent that the treaty concerned was not permitted by the Treaties themselves.[89] This would be particularly grave in relation to European contract law, since the envisaged solutions in the debate have been framed inside, not outside, the EU institutional framework with a view to resolving problems concerning the Union *acquis* and based on the Union's objectives set down in the Treaties.

Secondly, the use of an intergovernmental treaty heralds countless drawbacks that would constitute in many ways a 'backwards move' for the European contract law project. As witnessed by the debate, the path of European contract law is littered with various international conventions, most of which have not yet been ratified by all Member States, are plagued with Member State reservations and derogations, and lack uniform interpretation by an authoritative judicial body, namely the Court of Justice of the European Union.[90] Instruments at the heart of European contract law, such as the 1980 United Nations Convention on Contracts for the International Sale of Goods (CISG)[91] amply bear this out.[92] Taken seriously, an intergovernmental treaty would augment

[89] See, eg, de Witte, n 75, 232–233, 262–267; R. Schütze, 'EC Law and International Agreements of the Member States—An Ambivalent Relationship?' (2006–2007) 9 *CYELS* 386, 411–416.

[90] See, eg, Müller-Graff, n 81; C von Bar, 'A European Civil Code, international agreements and European directives' in European Parliament DG for Research Working Paper, *The Private Law Systems in the EU: Discrimination on Grounds of Nationality and the Need for a European Civil Code* (Legal Affairs Series, JURI-103 EN), available at <http://www.europarl.europa.eu/> (1999 Working Paper), 147, 147–148. For an earlier, though still valuable, account of the problems associated with international conventions, see IE Schwartz, 'Voies d'uniformisation du droit dans la Communauté européenne: règlements de la Communauté ou conventions entre les États membres?' (1978) *JDI* 751.

[91] 11 April 1980, 1489 UNTS 3. It is presently not in force in all Member States: see Chapter 1, § 1.2.2.1.

[92] Annex II ('List of International Instruments Relating to Substantial Contract Law Issues') of the 2001 Communication (Chapter 5, § 5.2) is a testimonial of this.

some of the very problems for European contract law in terms of precluding a single set of uniform rules for parties engaging in cross-border transactions throughout the EU, which prompted much of the debate in the first place. Accordingly, it would be likely to perpetuate problems concerning the coherency and the uniform application of Union law that the European contract law project seeks to remedy.

Finally, in the interests of completeness, there may be misconceptions that such a treaty can be taken into account in connection with the principle of subsidiarity. As discussed in Chapter 7, over the years, there was considerable ambiguity as regards the extent to which intergovernmental cooperation among all the Member States, as opposed to each Member State acting individually or merely some Member States, could act as a counterweight to Union action for the purposes of the principle of subsidiarity under what is now Article 5(3) TEU.[93] At present, however, there are strong indications in the case law on Article 114 TFEU that the Court of Justice takes a negative view to such a position. In *Biotechnology*, the Court ruled that it was the action of the Member States 'alone' that is taken into account in the subsidiarity calculus and that intergovernmental cooperation did not displace the need for Union action in the internal market under Article 114 TFEU (ex Article 95 EC).[94] This was further underscored in *Tobacco Advertising II*, in which the Court took note of the problems plaguing the relevant convention in the area concerned—for instance, that not all Member States had ratified it and that it would not rule out the risk of divergences between national laws—so as to find that it did not detract from intervention by the Union legislature via approximation under Article 114 TFEU (ex Article 95 EC).[95] As demonstrated by these cases, recourse to an intergovernmental treaty does not offset Union action in the internal market, but in fact has the tendency to bolster the need for such action under the relevant provisions of the Treaties.

11.3.3 An ad hoc convention method

Among the forms of intergovernmental cooperation inside the EU institutional framework contemplated as part of the debate about European private law generally,[96] one of the most well-known is the potential recourse to an ad hoc convention method proposed by Professor Walter van Gerven. As he explained:

> Under that procedure codification could be prepared by experts designated by the [M]ember [S]tates who, at an early stage, would take the advice from parliamentary commissions in the European Parliament and the national parliaments on the basis, for example, of a questionnaire

[93] See Chapter 7, § 7.4.3.2. This should be distinguished from the situation involving consideration of an instrument of secondary Union law or an international treaty concluded by the EU (either alone or with the Member States) with third States to achieve the objectives concerned. See, eg, B de Witte, 'International Law as a Tool for the European Union' (2009) 5 *E Const L Rev* 265, 280–281.

[94] See Chapter 8, § 8.3.3.1. As noted in that section, even earlier in *Tobacco Advertising I*, AG Jacobs had considered that collective action by all Member States was excluded by virtue of the principle of sincere cooperation, but the Court never got to the issue.

[95] See Chapter 8, § 8.3.2.1.

[96] To recall, as part of the European Parliament's 1989 Resolution, recourse to a 'convention-regulation' hybrid was advocated. Although associated with a convention, it may be seen as a novel attempt to harness the benefits of intergovernmental cooperation inside, as opposed to outside, the EU institutional framework. In the Rapporteur's view, this proposal was not an alternative route, but instead was considered to fall within the ambit of the Community's (now Union's) competence under former Art 100a EC (later Art 95 EC, now Art 114 TFEU). It was also assumed that all Member States would be concerned with the project and thus seemed to embody a progressive route to the achievement of a European private law code. See Chapter 4, § 4.3.1.

approved by the European Parliament concerning important value judgments to be made or policy decisions to be taken. Once answers would have been received from those parliamentary commissions, draft bills could be prepared, on any one subject, by committees of experts, and then made public to invite comments from all segments of society. After such broad consultation and ensuing amendments, the draft bills would be submitted to final deliberation in a 'Convention' (which may take the advice of any group or person it wants to hear) and finally adopted, in view of submission to approval by the [M]ember [S]tates, by the Council and the European Parliament. As was the case of the special body set up for the drafting of the European Charter of Fundamental Rights, the 'Convention' would be composed of representatives from the Community [now Union] institutions and the national parliaments. Obviously, the agreement should provide for a preliminary ruling procedure before a Community [now Union] court to maintain uniformity of interpretation. After it has been approved by all [M]ember [S]tates, the agreement would come into force, e.g., when half of them have ratified it, on those [M]ember [S]tates' territory.[97]

He attempted to counter criticism that the use of a convention would tend to 'bury' the project for a European civil code for several years by pointing out that it would encourage the Member States to cooperate and could even provide the impetus for the insertion of a solid legal basis into the Treaty framework for such an endeavour.[98]

In view of the foregoing, this proposal for an ad hoc convention seems to have been based on two key motivations. First, as alluded to by the foregoing statement, it was generally concerned with far-reaching EU action in national private law (that is to say, a 'European civil code', which was in vogue at the time) and outlined an alternative course of action on the grounds that the EU lacked sufficient competence under the Treaties.[99] Secondly, the proposal sought in large part to ensure the involvement of the European Parliament and national parliaments, as well as other interested parties, so as to instill the proposed initiative with democratic elements.[100] It was not clear whether, assuming that the EU could be considered to have sufficient competence in this regard, the impetus for such an ad hoc procedure would lessen, given the emphasis placed on these elements.[101]

In any event, the proposal brought the constitutionality of European contract law and other fields of private law to the fore. It also drew attention to the importance of ensuring the participation of various actors, which have played an increasing role in the activities concerning European contract law. Arguably, with the advances made since this proposal was aired, these latter aspects are capable of being dealt with and improved upon within the framework of the European contract law project itself. Indeed, with the ensuing progression of this project, the ad hoc convention method has lost much of its salience, and in later years, seems to have been replaced by other suggestions, such as an intergovernmental treaty under public international law[102] or the OMC.[103] In all fairness, it was made long before this project was underway, and thus presented a novel solution for European private law at the time. With a present day perspective, however, it seems to have been superseded by the framework of activities and groups within this project, with the prospect of a 'European civil code' taken off the political agenda

[97] W van Gerven, 'Communication on European Contract Law—Codifying European Private Law' in H Schulte-Nölke and R Schulze (eds), *European Contract Law in Community Law* (Bundesanzeiger, 2002) 241, 254–255 (reiterated in, eg, W van Gerven, 'Codifying European private law? Yes, if. . .!' (2002) 27 *ELR* 156, 173).

[98] van Gerven, 'Communication on European Contract Law', n 97, 254.

[99] van Gerven, 'Communication on European Contract Law', n 97, 253–254.

[100] van Gerven, 'Communication on European Contract Law', n 97, 253–254.

[101] See van Gerven, 'Codifying European private law?', n 97, 173–174.

[102] See n 87.

[103] See ns 110–113 and accompanying text.

(at least for now) as a result of the Commission's 2010 Green Paper. Furthermore, given the constitutional climate in the aftermath of the failed Draft Constitutional Treaty, the Lisbon Treaty has likely sapped much of the impetus for another 'convention' for the foreseeable future.

11.4 'Softer' Models: The OMC, American Techniques, and the CFR

This section examines the viability of three so-called 'softer' models implicated in the debate about European contract law: the OMC, certain American techniques (Restatements, uniform and model laws, and the Uniform Commercial Code (UCC)), and the CFR. They are referred to as 'softer' models on account of the fact that they carry the potential to exert a lesser impact on the national contract law regimes or afford latitude to the Member States in varying degrees as compared to the adoption of a European contract law instrument. To be clear, however, this should not be taken to mean that these models are strictly equated with 'soft' or non-binding law. In fact, each evidences a significant blurring of the traditional dichotomy between 'soft' and 'hard' or binding law. As regards the OMC, scholars have been adamant in much of the recent literature that it must not be associated purely with 'soft' law and does in fact involve 'hard' law in particular instances.[104] As regards the American techniques, uniform laws and the UCC start out 'soft', but are envisaged to end up as 'hard' law when adopted by the state legislatures, whereas the Restatements retain a 'soft' law quality, even though in principle they are considered to wield persuasive authority in the American courts.[105] And as for the CFR, it is presently envisaged as a non-binding instrument for EU lawmaking, as well as laying the groundwork for the potential adoption of binding optional instruments of contract law at the European level, such as the proposed CESL.[106] As such, these three mechanisms are not such unusual bedfellows as may first appear, and in particular, placing the American techniques side by side with the CFR and related initiatives yields fruitful comparative reflection on the European and American approaches to matters of contract law.

11.4.1 The OMC

At present, the Open Method of Coordination or the OMC is a hotly debated subject in European scholarship. As indicated by the rising volume of literature devoted to it, the OMC evades a short or easy description, since despite the label, it does not constitute a single mechanism that applies the same way in the relevant areas, but rather embodies a wide variety of processes and proceeds on a case-by-case basis in relation to the particular policy field concerned.[107] Still, it has been summarily defined as follows:

> It is a new form of coordination of national policies consisting of the Member States, at their own initiative or at the initiative of the Commission, defining collectively, within the respect

[104] See, eg, DM Trubek and LG Trubek, 'Hard and Soft Law in the Construction of Social Europe: the Role of the Open Method of Co-ordination' (2005) 11 *ELJ* 343.

[105] See Chapter 3. [106] See § 11.4.3.

[107] For a brief selection, see, eg, P Craig, *EU Administrative Law*, 2nd edn (Oxford Univ Press, 2012) ch 7; C Shaw, 'Classifying and mapping the OMC in different policy areas' in U Diedrichs et al (eds), *The Dynamics of Change in EU Governance* (Edward Elgar, 2011) 52.

of national and regional diversities, objectives and indicators in a specific area, and allowing those Member States, on the basis of national reports, to improve their knowledge, to develop exchanges of information, views, expertise and practices, and to promote, further to agreed objectives, innovative approaches which could possibly lead to guidelines or recommendations.[108]

By taking account of the standard 'laundry list' of general characteristics usually associated with it, such as general benchmarking, mutual learning, etc, the OMC is a method that essentially places the Member States in the driver's seat, so to speak, with respect to the action to be achieved.

As far as European contract law is concerned, discussion as to the potential relevance of the OMC is just beginning to flourish. The linkage between the OMC and European contract law is not altogether surprising, given that the Commission's 2003 Action Plan noted the possibilities offered by the OMC as part of the 'mixed approach' to be taken in this setting.[109] Since then, however, it has not been mentioned further by the Union institutions in the institutional documents disseminated in the debate thus far. In the scholarly literature, the OMC has been considered to have value for the European contract law project. For example, Professor Walter van Gerven is a well-known advocate of the role to be played by what he calls the 'Open Method of Convergence' in European contract law (and European private law generally).[110] Distilled from his various publications, his advocacy of this mechanism seems to rest on the following two-part rationale: first, this field is a sensitive area in which the Union has not been given sufficient competence to approximate the whole of contract law, let alone private law generally;[111] and secondly, it constitutes a beneficial mode by which to further the convergence of contract (or private) law and address the 'spill-over' effects resulting from the interaction between national law and EU law by various means, such as sharing best practices, enhancing mutual learning, and increasing familiarity with the national legal systems among national and European authorities.[112] Notably, he finds similarities between the function of the OMC and the CFR as promoting cross-border dialogue between the Member States on matters of private law, but envisages the specific application of the OMC in this setting as a complementary mechanism to the CFR project so as to bolster educational aspects and practical aspects involving judges and practitioners.[113] Similarly, other scholars have considered the potential role of the OMC in European contract (and private) law, and in doing so, some have stressed the competence factor, that is to say, finding it suitable in areas where the Union has limited or no competence.[114]

[108] Final Report of Working Group XI on Social Europe, CONV 516/1/03REV1 WGXI9, dated 4 Feb 2003, point 37.

[109] See Chapter 5, § 5.3.2.

[110] See, eg, van Gerven, n 87, 60–77; W van Gerven, 'About Rules and Principles, Codification and Legislation, Harmonization and Convergence, and Education in the Area of Contract Law' in A Arnull et al (eds), *Continuity and Change in EU Law: Essays in honour of Sir Francis Jacobs* (Oxford Univ Press, 2008) 400, 411–412; W van Gerven, 'The Open Method of Convergence' (2008) 14 *JI* 32; W van Gerven, 'Private Law in a Federal Perspective' in R Brownsword et al (eds), *The Foundations of European Private Law* (Hart, 2011) 337, 343–344.

[111] See van Gerven, n 87, 38–39, 62.

[112] This is generally presented in terms of judicial, regulatory, and educational components: see van Gerven, n 87, 65–74.

[113] See van Gerven, 'About Rules and Principles', n 110, 411–412.

[114] See, eg, F Cafaggi, 'The making of European private law: governance design' in F Cafaggi and H Muir-Watt (eds), *Making European Private Law: Governance Design* (Edward Elgar, 2008) 289, 343–345; N Reich, 'A Common Frame of Reference (CFR)—Ghost or host for integration?' (2006) *ZERP-Diskussionspapier 7/2006*, 43.

In this way, the potential application of the OMC to matters of European contract law (or European private law generally) enlivens questions about Union competence. This is so particularly since thus far it has been a common attribute of the OMC that it has largely taken place in areas where Union competence is limited or non-existent under the Treaties, as in the case of policy fields restricting the Union to taking merely 'supporting measures' and thus where approximation is excluded. Indeed, this aspect was emphasized by several Working Groups during the European Convention.[115] Moreover, it should be recognized that the OMC carries with it the 'baggage' associated with the so-called 'new modes of governance' in terms of both giving way to novel solutions in European policymaking and generating tensions resulting from its aptitude to bypass the mainstream decision-making process.[116] The OMC stands apart from the traditional Union (formerly Community) method and breathes fresh air into other, more flexible ways of policymaking involving a wide variety of actors in the EU.[117] By the same token, it breeds fears of evasion of this method involving the Union institutions and elitism in terms of the lack of involvement of various interested parties and groups.[118]

Consequently, as applied to European contract law, the potential role played by the OMC necessitates caution so as not to inject inadvertently even more controversy into the debate.[119] Much will depend upon its particular form and application in this setting, and it remains to be seen whether it will be 'picked up' by the Union institutions in the forthcoming years. In fact, this is a subject that warrants further research within the context of European contract law.[120] Nevertheless, at present, the OMC has generally not been posited as an alternative route standing on its own to displace the initiatives of the European contract law project, such as the CFR or the proposed CESL, but instead to play a complementary role largely tied to bolstering the institutional framework surrounding European contract law (or European private law generally) and activities taking place therein.[121] Thus, it is arguable that attributes or expressions of the OMC can be subsumed and even improved upon inside, as opposed to outside, the European contract law project.

[115] See Final Report of Working Group XI on Social Europe, n 108, point 43; Final Report of Working Group IX on Simplification, n 86, 7. Incidentally, while there had been attempts to insert a specific provision on the OMC in the DCT, this was not done; however, its specific applications to certain policy fields remained. See G de Búrca, 'The constitutional challenge of new governance in the European Union' (2003) 28 *ELR* 814.

[116] See citations in n 107.

[117] For a brief selection of literature on 'new modes of governance', see, eg, *The Dynamics of Change in EU Governance*, n 107; P Craig and G de Búrca, *EU Law: Text, Cases and Materials*, 5th edn (Oxford Univ Press, 2011) ch 6; and on a comparative note, G de Búrca and J Scott (eds), *Law and New Governance in the EU and the US* (Hart, 2006).

[118] See, in particular, V Hatzopoulos, 'Why the Open Method of Coordination Is Bad For You: A Letter to the EU' (2007) 13 *ELJ* 309.

[119] See, eg, CU Schmid, 'The "Three Lives" of European Private Law' in L Antoniolli and F Fiorentini (eds), *A Factual Assessment of the Draft Common Frame of Reference* (Sellier, 2011) 299, 303. For other limitations, see, eg, JM Smits, 'Plurality of Sources in European Private Law, or How to Live With Legal Diversity?' in *The Foundations of European Private Law*, n 2, 323, 332–333.

[120] See, eg, C Twigg-Flesner, *The Europeanisation of Contract Law* (Routledge-Cavendish, 2008) 172.

[121] See, eg, L Miller, *The Emergence of EU Contract Law: Exploring Europeanization* (Oxford Univ Press, 2011) 201–204.

11.4.2 American techniques

Techniques taken from the American contract law framework in the form of Restatements, uniform and model laws, and the UCC have a complex and ambiguous relationship to the debate about European contract law. As underscored in the Report accompanying the Parliament's 1994 Resolution, Restatements, uniform laws, and model laws are not formally recognized in the European setting, and there are certain legal instruments already at the disposal of the Union legislature that serve a similar role.[122] Nevertheless, references to such techniques have made their way into the debate[123] and therefore raise questions as to their potential viability in this setting.

First, as far as Restatements are concerned, this American technique seems to attract divergent views. On the one hand, as discussed in Chapter 4, the American Restatement is readily associated with the work of several academic projects involved with European contract (and private) law.[124] On the other hand, when the American Restatement is specifically contemplated for use in the European setting, its utility is more speculative on account of the fact that it was built on the foundations of the American common law tradition and as such was meant for a judicial context different from the European setting.[125] When examined more closely, however, this situation can be said to boil down to the distinction between the Restatement in its more 'functional', as opposed to 'pure', sense. By and large, the American Restatement project has played a much more prominent role in its 'functional' sense as a general comparative method by which to formulate common rules or principles concerning a particular field of private law, as compared to the transplantation of the American Restatement in its 'pure' sense associated with the origins and development of the American Law Institute (ALI). Importantly, unlike the American Restatements that were intentionally conceived as non-binding instruments divorced from the legislative setting, several European academic projects with which the American Restatements are affiliated espouse the aim to turn their 'comparative' product into binding law at the European level, which goes against the *modus operandi* of the Restatement in its American origins. In addition, the conception of the American Restatement in its 'functional' form has much in common with the CFR in terms of its envisaged comparative role for use by Union and national authorities. It thus may be wondered whether the discussion of the possible recourse to the American Restatement technique in the European contract law project has been transfigured

[122] See Chapter 4, § 4.3.3.

[123] See generally Part Two. As regards remarks of members of the Union institutions involved with the debate, see, eg, V Reding, 'The Next Steps Towards a European Contract Law for Businesses and Consumers' in R Schulze and J Stuyck (eds), *Towards a European Contract Law* (Sellier, 2011) 9, 20. As regards the scholarly literature, see, eg, G Howells, 'Consumer Protection and European Contract Law Harmonisation' (2006) 7 *ERA Forum* 45; R Hyland, 'The American Experience: Restatements, the UCC, Uniform Laws, and Transnational Coordination' in *Towards a European Civil Code*, 3rd edn, n 79, 59; R Hyland, 'American Private Legislatures and the Process Discussion' in *Towards a European Civil Code*, 4th edn, n 79, 71. For a critical view on the use of American techniques and aspects of the 'Americanization' of the debate generally, see U Mattei, *The European Codification Process: Cut and Paste* (Kluwer, 2003). Notably, early on, Professor Ole Lando advocated the adoption of a so-called 'European uniform commercial code' (as well as European 'Restatements' that would precede such a 'code'), but given the tenor of the discussion, it seems that he was advocating the adoption of an EU instrument approximating the law of obligations and property, as opposed to its meaning in the American setting. See O Lando, 'Unfair Contract Clauses and A European Uniform Commercial Code' in M Cappelletti (ed), *New Perspectives for A Common Law of Europe* (Bruylant, 1978) 269, 283–288.

[124] See Chapter 4, § 4.2.

[125] Müller-Graff, *Towards a European Civil Code*, 4th edn, n 81, 159–160.

by the current activities envisaged for the CFR or could even be viewed as already encompassed to some extent within the CFR project itself.

Secondly, the American technique of uniform and model laws, which includes the UCC as a comprehensive type of uniform law, has also permeated the debate. As a starting point, it is not always clear whether either or both of these terms are being used in the strictly American sense as linked to the uniform law process of the National Conference of Commissioners on Uniform State Laws (NCCUSL) or in conjunction with the ALI in the case of the UCC. As already explained in Chapter 3, there is an important distinction to be made in relation to the way in which uniform laws and model laws are viewed in the American setting: uniform laws are specifically envisaged for adoption by state legislatures in principle without the insertion of non-uniform amendments in areas where uniformity among the states is needed, whereas model laws constitute more of a guiding norm pertaining to areas where uniformity is not a priority or where a particular uniform law has not garnered general acceptance across the states and has essentially been demoted.[126] Thus, from the American perspective, talking about the possible use of uniform laws is a very different story than that concerning model laws, and in various instances it seems to be the case that it is really uniform laws, not model laws, that are being referred to in the commentary on European contract law. Nevertheless, both uniform and model laws seem equally ill-equipped and even superfluous in connection with European contract law.

For both uniform and model laws, there is no exact equivalent in the EU. Yet, there are already several legal instruments in the Treaties that can, arguably, 'do the job' better, particularly when it comes to matters of contract law. The recommendation has been considered comparable to uniform and model laws (as well as Restatements[127]) by scholars[128] and the Union institutions, as illustrated by the Commission's 2010 Green Paper.[129] This is because it allows the Union institutions to adopt a non-binding instrument at the European level that can 'recommend' suggested action to the Member States, but does not place them under a binding obligation to do so.[130] Additionally, the directive is somewhat similar to a uniform law, but with 'bite', since it is binding on the Member States as regards the result to be achieved, but allows the Member States leeway as to the form and methods. Thus, it evades one of the chief defects of a uniform law in the sense that a Member State cannot choose to forego transposition of a directive or do so with the inclusion of non-uniform amendments that preclude its effectiveness and hence the objectives to be achieved.

Moreover, it is not clear to what extent those who advocate the use of uniform and model laws are fully aware of their defects. Particularly in the case of uniform laws, despite their name, they embody a route that gives the states full room for manoeuvre when it comes to the adoption of a particular act and thus provide no guarantee that any such uniformity will be achieved. As illustrated in Chapter 3, this was as apparent with uniform laws covering a particular area of contract or commercial law, as it was with the UCC cutting across such areas. This may of course be why they were proposed, so as to lay the primary responsibility for European contract (or private) law in the hands of the Member States. The uniform law process could therefore be seen to represent a solution imbued in subsidiarity.[131] Yet, making this proposal a reality has great aptitude

[126] See Chapter 3, § 3.3.1.2. [127] See Chapter 4, § 4.3.3.

[128] See, eg, A von Bogdandy and J Bast, 'Legal Instruments in European Union Law and their Reform: A Systematic Approach on an Empirical Basis' (2004) 23 *YEL* 91, 113.

[129] See Chapter 6, § 6.4.2. [130] See Art 288, fifth para, TFEU.

[131] See, eg, FH Miller, 'The Uniform Law Process For The Development of Private State Law in the United States: A Model For Other Systems?' (2006) 60 *Cons Fin LQ Rep* 4, 8–9.

to do more harm than good in the context of the European contract law project. To the extent that a contract law instrument is needed in the European setting, it is highly questionable whether utilizing a method that leaves the Member States free to adopt it, or not, and to insert non-uniform amendments would be the answer. This was alluded to in the Commission's 2010 Green Paper in its discussion of the proposed option to use a Recommendation on European contract law, which it found comparable to the approach taken in the US with regard to the UCC, emphasizing that it bore the risk of an incoherent and incomplete approach between the Member States, as they may enact the Recommendation differently and at different moments in time or not at all.[132] In short, transplanting some variety of the uniform law process in the European contract law project carries the danger of injecting the very problems that this project is attempting to overcome.

Finally, with particular regard to the UCC, to recall from Chapter 3, it embodies a functional approach, encompassing rules in various areas of private law including, but not limited to, contract law, with a view to ensuring a systematic approach to commercial transactions among the states.[133] Thus, the UCC automatically carries with it the assumption that the scope of coverage goes well beyond contract law into other fields of private law. As discussed in Part Two, the extent to which rules on related fields of private law should be included in a European contract law instrument has been a controversial issue in the debate from the very beginning, and still remains in the background. Consequently, it should not be overlooked that, in addition to the problems associated with uniform laws generally, the contemplation of an American-type UCC in the European setting implies more comprehensive action, which has the potential to exacerbate tensions regarding the linkage of contract law to other areas of private law in the debate.

Taking the foregoing into account, there is a strong case to be made that, aside from the 'functional' form of the Restatement already resorted to in the context of European contract law, the American techniques of Restatements, uniform and model laws, and the UCC carry significant drawbacks in comparison to the instruments already available in the European setting, have the potential to hamper the objectives to be achieved by the European contract law project, and in the case of the UCC, may even inflame sensitivities regarding the scope of action that needs to be taken. Taking a step back, however, the American techniques illuminate striking parallels between the EU and the US in their respective approaches to matters of contract law. On the one hand, as demonstrated above, there are various arguments to support the position that techniques taken from the American contract law framework should not be readily grafted onto the debate about European contract law and that the EU has at its disposal a different array of legal instruments and techniques that are better suited to remedy the problems identified in the debate. On the other hand, even though the specific techniques used in the EU and the US may be different, both legal orders seem to be moving in similar directions. The American contract law framework as a whole embodies the use of *sui generis* instruments or hybrids—Restatements, uniform laws, model laws, and the UCC—that sit apart from the traditional federal and state statutes and constitute creative and novel solutions to address the problems associated with the diversity of state private law, including contract law, in the US. The EU appears to be travelling down a similar path in terms of creating its own *sui generis*, hybrid forms suitable

[132] See Chapter 6, § 6.4.2. See also Max Planck Institute for Comparative and International Private Law, 'Policy Options for Progress Towards a European Contract Law' (2011) 75 *Rabels Z* 371, 381–382.

[133] See Chapter 3, § 3.5.1.2.

for and adjusted to the European contract (or private) law context, as illustrated by the (D)CFR and the proposed CESL (as well as additional optional instruments of contract law as the case may be).

As a result, while the EU and the US have created mechanisms uniquely suited to each setting, both manifest similar approaches in attempting to find the balance between 'unity' and 'diversity' in terms of what is needed to remedy the problems associated with the diversity of national or state contract laws (and other fields of private law) and what can be done to preserve leeway for the (Member) States in this regard. Therefore, although American techniques, at least in the way in which they have been conceived of in the US, involve difficulties that affect their viability in the debate about European contract law, they still play an indirect role in directing attention towards the novel instruments that are being created or will be created at the European level and their importance for the relationship between the EU and the Member States in this setting. This leads to the discussion of the CFR.

11.4.3 The CFR

At the time of writing, the constitutionality of the CFR is unsettled. This is understandable in the sense that the CFR project is ongoing, such that the final decisions on this and other issues are still to come with the conversion of the academic version or DCFR, in all or in part, to the final, political version of the CFR to be adopted at the European level in some shape or form. This may explain why the Commission was loath to examine this subject in the 2004 Communication and subsequent 2005 and 2007 Progress Reports. Delving into the attributes of the CFR, however, reveals the importance of its place in the debate about European contract law and the need to confront its constitutional dimensions.

In light of the evolution of the CFR within the European contract law project, the CFR essentially can be viewed in two ways. As widely heralded by the Union institutions, the *first view* of the CFR is that of a 'better lawmaking' instrument for the Union institutions in the formulation of measures in contract law (and other fields of private law as the case may be). From this angle, it provides the background tools that feed into EU policymaking, with a view to improving the problems concerning the coherence and quality of Union measures and making the Union institutions aware of the background of national private law systems so as to ensure a 'better fit' between such measures and the national legal orders. As the UK delegation framed the matter in past discussions in the Council, the CFR allows the Union legislature to make an 'informed decision' as to how it should address a particular issue in the decision-making process.[134] As such, labels affixed to the CFR such as the 'toolbox' description or even its very name—'Common Frame of Reference'—aptly fit this view.[135] The *second view* of the CFR is linked to the prospect of an (or more than one) optional instrument of contract law, the idea being that the work on the CFR will constitute the basis for further discussion as to the need for such an instrument in European contract law. From this angle, it serves as a gateway to a European contract

[134] See UK Delegation, 'Common Frame of Reference for European Contract Law', DOC 13697/08ADD7, dated 16 Oct 2009, 5.

[135] See also House of Lords EU Committee, 'European Contract Law: the Draft Common Frame of Reference', 12th Report of Session 2008–09, point 70 (noting Lord Bach's description of the CFR as a '*vade mecum*' (Latin for 'constant companion')).

law instrument or at the very least helps to refine the future path to be taken, which has now come to fruition with the proposed CESL.

These two views are useful for distinguishing the overarching character of the CFR from the tensions associated with it. On the one hand, they demonstrate that the CFR stands as a novel, *sui generis* private law experiment taking place in the EU. From its envisaged progression from academic to political versions, the CFR constitutes the unique blending of the input of the Union institutions and several academic projects, and involves a wide range of actors at the European and national levels. Indeed, it is easy to miss that the CFR represents a project that is wholly unprecedented in the European setting. Each in their own way, the academic DCFR and the political CFR are destined to change the face of EU law, for instance, as regards the DCFR's implications for comparative private law research and scholarship[136] or in relation to the political CFR's implications for judicial and lawmaking processes and European 'governance' generally. On the other hand, the CFR beckons considerable sensitivity particularly from the standpoint of Union competence, which was greatly stimulated by the breadth of the academic DCFR to matters going well beyond contract law and its structure resembling aspects of a code familiar to many Member States. As the Commission has not yet been forthcoming with its plans for the form that the CFR will take and the legal basis upon which it will be adopted, concerns continue to percolate throughout the literature stemming from the fears that the CFR is a 'Trojan horse' for a full-blown European private law code or some form of far-reaching Union action in various fields of private law including contract law.[137]

As a result, it seems to be the case that a large part of the sensitivity surrounding the CFR is not so much a criticism of its nature as a novel instrument never before known in the EU as the 'Common Frame of Reference', but more on account of the lack of engagement as to where the CFR is going to lead and the form it will take, which then stimulates fears of its potential encroachment on the Member States' competence over private law. In other words, distinguishing the two views of the CFR makes for a very different 'constitutional' picture.[138] As a non-binding instrument for 'better lawmaking' in the EU so as to underpin the framing of Union legislation with a view to upgrading its quality and ensuring its coherence with the national legal orders, the CFR embodies tenets of the principles of subsidiarity and proportionality. Its flipside as a pathway for far-reaching Union action in contract law and other fields of private law evokes a very different response.

This argues for a start to be made in confronting the constitutional dimensions of the CFR. Even if it is a long-term project, the initiation of further dialogue among the Union institutions and other interested parties and possibly further documentation at the European level would at least allow the matter to be placed on the table, as opposed to remaining hidden underneath. While it is difficult at this juncture to provide a definitive constitutional assessment, it is nevertheless important that the constitutionality

[136] See Chapter 6, § 6.2.3.

[137] See, eg, H Collins, 'The "Common Frame of Reference" for EC Contract Law: A Common Lawyer's Perspective' in M Meli and MR Maugeri (eds), *L'Armonizzazione del Diritto Privato Europeo—Il Piano D'Azione 2003* (Giuffrè Editore, 2004) 107; B Lurger, 'The Common Frame of Reference/Optional Code and the Various Understandings of Social Justice in Europe' in T Wilhelmsson et al (eds), *Private Law and the Many Cultures of Europe* (Kluwer, 2007) 177. See further Chapter 6, § 6.2.3.

[138] This distinction is also important for other aspects: see, eg, H Beale, 'The Content of the political CFR—how to prioritise' in J Kleinman (ed), *A Common Frame of Reference for European Contract Law* (Stockholm Centre for Commercial Law and Jure Förlag, 2011) 27.

of the CFR as a non-binding instrument for Union lawmaking is distinguished from its pathway to an optional instrument. The objectives, form, binding nature, and hence legal basis and operation of the principles of subsidiarity and proportionality are different, even if the two views of the CFR are interrelated. As illustrated by the debate so far, an optional instrument of contract law, such as the proposed CESL, is rooted in the Union's objectives to improve the functioning of the internal market, and in line with the analysis presented in Chapter 8, there are convincing arguments that the Union has sufficient competence to adopt an instrument comparable to the proposed CESL under Article 114 TFEU, although recourse to Article 352 TFEU cannot be foreclosed depending upon the assessment whether it may be considered to fall within the scope of approximation under Article 114 TFEU.[139] By comparison, a non-binding instrument to provide guidelines for the Union institutions in preparing legislation in matters relating to contract law (and other fields of private law as the case may be) has not been framed in terms of its aptitude for achieving the Union's objectives related to the internal market and thus may likely claim a different legal basis and form, such as an interinstitutional agreement contemplated in the Commission's 2010 Green Paper[140] and other discourse.[141]

Importantly, however, as illustrated by the American setting, one does not replace the other. In the US, instruments establishing a set of uniform rules for facilitating transactions in the American 'internal market' embodied by uniform laws and the UCC stand alongside the Restatement project generally envisaged to provide greater coherence and simplification in areas of state private law, including contract law, on a non-binding basis. Likewise, in the EU, whatever may come of the final CFR, the extent of the problems generated by disparities among national contract laws that present obstacles to trade and/or appreciable distortions of competition in the internal market are likely to persist notwithstanding an instrument targeted at improving the coherence of contract law and EU lawmaking by the Union institutions. As such, while the final stages of the CFR project remain to be seen, the constitutionality of a European contract law instrument, as in the case of the proposed CESL, loses none of its salience.

11.5 Conclusions

As the debate about European contract law (and European private law generally) has progressed, it has become something of a 'buffet table' in which scholars often pick and choose among various alternative and complementary routes without detailed consideration as to whether such routes are allowed under EU law or would be better suited than mainstream forms of EU action under the Treaties. Leaving aside the CFR, this analysis shows that most of the commonly mentioned alternative routes in European contract law, namely enhanced cooperation, an intergovernmental treaty, and certain American techniques, entail drawbacks to varying degrees, which make them ill-equipped to provide a suitable working alternative to a European contract law instrument and have the potential to take the European contract law project 'backwards' by

[139] See Chapter 8, § 8.4.3.2. [140] See Chapter 6, § 6.4.2; see also § 6.2.4.3, § 6.4.2.3.
[141] See, eg, MW Hesselink et al, 'The legal basis for an optional instrument on European contract law', CSECL Working Paper Series No 2007/4, 66–69; House of Lords Report, n 135, points 72–73; H Schulte-Nölke, 'Contract Law or Law of Obligations—The Draft Common Frame of Reference as a Multifunction Tool' in R Schulze (ed), *Common Frame of Reference and Existing EC Contract Law*, 2nd rev edn (Seller, 2009) 47, 61.

reintroducing problems that this project is trying to solve and jeopardizing the progress already attained. With regard to the OMC, while its role in the European contract law project warrants further research, at present it constitutes a complementary route that in large part embodies methods that are capable of being subsumed within the activities taking place inside this project, as opposed to standing outside on its own.

Together, these alternative and complementary routes illuminate three common themes. First, they assume or raise questions concerning Union competence that stimulate the need for the constitutional assessment of European contract law, rather than demoting it as a passé topic. Secondly, they demonstrate the apparent tensions in proceeding outside, as opposed to inside, the confines of the EU institutional framework. Thirdly, the American techniques reveal striking parallels between the EU and the US in relation to the approach taken to matters of contract law. In this way, these various routes make the constitutionality of European contract law shine brighter than ever and call attention to the unique and *sui generis* path of European contract law in attempting to find a balance in the relationship between the Union and the Member States in this setting.

Conclusion

Looking back over the various chapters, the constitutional dimensions of European contract law are much more nuanced and complex than is commonly perceived. At first glance, it could be assumed that the evaluation of the EU's competence in contract law merely required parsing out the scope of certain prominent Treaty provisions cited in the debate—namely, Articles 114, 115, 169, 81, and 352 TFEU—on the basis of the relevant literature and case law. Yet, in undertaking this task, it became apparent that, for example, there were no universal definitions for most of the terms used in the debate, not much consideration had been given to the extent to which matters of Union competence had been discussed in the institutional documents, and all of the foregoing Treaty provisions, as well as certain alternative and complementary routes to a European contract law instrument, sat atop their own distinct set of institutional developments and controversies, all of which necessitated the construction of a semantic and legal framework from the 'ground up' to provide a cohesive assessment of this subject. Much the same may be said for comparative inquiry into the American contract law framework. Several American techniques that have made their way into the debate, such as uniform laws, Restatements, and the Uniform Commercial Code (UCC) in fact embodied a deeper story of numerous problems and repeated attempts to federalize areas of contract law. Altogether, this makes the constitutional assessment of European contract law a 'heavy' topic, both literally and figuratively. Nevertheless, by taking into account, first, the central findings of this book, and secondly, the implications of the three-part framework established therein for the future path of the debate, this may offer a workable basis to guide further discussion of this subject on both sides of the Atlantic.

The Constitutionality of European Contract Law *In Toto*

The central findings of this book may be summarized in the following five points. First, a case can be made that the Union has been conferred sufficient competence under Articles 114 and/or 352 TFEU to adopt a European contract law instrument in order to achieve its objectives to ensure the establishing and functioning of the internal market. On the basis of the analysis set forth in Chapter 8, there are sound arguments that Article 114 TFEU constitutes a proper legal basis for such an instrument based on: (1) the course of development of the *Tobacco Advertising I* case law, taking account of that judgment alongside its progeny; (2) Article 114 TFEU's coverage of obstacles *sensu lato* as opposed to merely obstacles *sensu stricto*; and (3) Article 114 TFEU's potential for combating existing as well as future appreciable distortions of competition. Yet, as far as a contract law instrument approximating the national contract laws by modifying them to some degree is concerned, it cannot be foreclosed that Article 352 TFEU may be used alone or in combination with Article 114 TFEU to the extent that such an instrument, in all or in part, may be deemed to fall outside the scope of Article 114 TFEU on those grounds. Moreover, although the final text of the Commission's proposal for a Regulation on a Common European Sales Law (proposed CESL) remains to be seen, there are convincing arguments that Article 114 TFEU constitutes a proper legal basis for an optional instrument of contract law such as the proposed CESL based on: (1) the situation presented by the proposed CESL can be distinguished from the *European Cooperative Society* case and Article 118 TFEU; and (2) it constitutes a harmonized set of contract law rules that is integrated into the fabric of national law and both interacts with and has an impact on the national contract laws, even though it represents an optional regime. However, given the novelties involved and the lack of case law on point, it cannot be foreclosed that Article 352 TFEU may be used as the legal basis for an optional instrument such as the proposed CESL to the extent that it may be found to exceed the scope of approximation under Article 114 TFEU.

Secondly, with respect to the other relevant Treaty provisions, Articles 115, 169, and 81 TFEU are unlikely to serve as a proper legal basis for a European contract law instrument. As discussed in Chapter 8, Article 115 TFEU is unlikely to constitute a proper legal basis for such an instrument on account of the order of preference set forth in the Treaties for recourse to Article 114 TFEU. Although in principle there could be said to be differences in the substantive scope of Articles 114 and 115 TFEU emanating from their wording, the Court's case law and institutional developments brought about by the Lisbon Treaty strongly suggest that apart from the particular fields 'fenced off' from Article 114 TFEU, Article 115 TEU does not have a residual role vis-à-vis Article 114 TFEU as regards the adoption of a European contract law instrument. With respect to Article 169 TFEU, the analysis in Chapter 9 indicates that although this provision has a broader ambit than is commonly perceived, it is not likely to serve as a viable legal basis for a European contract law instrument encompassing or limited to consumer contract law given the nature of the EU consumer contract law *acquis*, at least as it stands now, which is rooted in the Union's dual objectives relating to the internal market and consumer protection, as opposed to the achievement of consumer protection objectives divorced from the internal market. Likewise, as evaluated in Chapter 10, Article 81 TFEU is unlikely to constitute a proper legal basis for a European contract law instrument on the grounds that such an instrument would, arguably, exceed the substantive scope of the Union's competence under this provision, despite attempts made during the European Convention to revise this provision in order to set forth an explicit legal basis allowing for the approximation of contract law.

Thirdly, as regards the constitutionality and viability of several alternative and complementary routes examined in Chapter 11, the majority of these routes—enhanced cooperation, an intergovernmental treaty, and certain American techniques—entail drawbacks to varying degrees, which make them ill-equipped to provide a suitable working alternative to the adoption of a European contract law instrument and have the potential to detract from the objectives to be achieved by the European contract law project. The Open Method of Coordination (OMC) has been viewed as a complementary, as opposed to alternative, route that can, arguably, be taken into account inside the framework of the European contract law project. Although the outcome of the preparation of the final or political version of the Common Frame of Reference (CFR) remains to be seen, distinguishing its status as an instrument geared at 'better lawmaking' from its linkage to the adoption of one or more optional instruments of contract law is critical for assessing its constitutional dimensions as the debate progresses. In all, these various alternative and complementary routes make the need to confront the constitutionality of European contract law more apparent and highlight the importance of proceeding inside, as opposed to outside, the framework established for the European contract law project, which encompasses the participation and involvement of the Union institutions and bodies, Member States, and various stakeholder groups.

Fourthly, on the whole, this book demonstrates that it is important to look at the constitutionality of European contract law *in toto* since it is the linkages between and within the existence and exercise of Union competence under Articles 114, 115, 169, 81, and 352 TFEU that loom large in the debate about European contract law. Although Articles 115, 169, and 81 TFEU may not play a direct role in serving as a legal basis for a European contract law instrument, they still play an indirect role, to varying degrees, by drawing further attention to the viability of the Union's internal market competence under Article 114 TFEU and to a lesser extent Article 352 TFEU. Moreover, despite sensitivities underpinning the apparent weaknesses of the principles of subsidiarity and proportionality in conjunction with Article 114 TFEU, this book highlights that these principles have the potential to play an important role 'inside' as well as 'outside' the lawmaking process in guiding the exercise of Union competence under this provision and thus may help to lessen some of the tensions associated with the adoption of a European contract law instrument based on Articles 114 and/or 352 TFEU, depending upon the nature (optional or otherwise) of the contract law instrument concerned.

Fifthly, comparative reflection with the US provides striking parallels for the constitutional assessment of European contract law. The American contract law framework is imbued to a considerable degree with attempts to approximate areas of contract law at the federal level, as illustrated by the origins of American 'federal common law', the National Conference of Commissioners on Uniform State Laws, and the UCC. In addition, each strand of the American contract law framework— involving American 'federal common law', the uniform law process, the Restatement project, and the UCC—embodies its own distinctly American connotation and its own share of problems, which is not often recognized in the European setting. There are compelling arguments that the American techniques of uniform and model laws, Restatements, and the UCC carry significant drawbacks for potential use in the debate on European contract law and that the EU has an array of techniques at its disposal that are better suited to remedy the problems highlighted in this debate, such as the CFR and the proposed CESL. Yet, although the techniques used in the European and American settings may be different, the overall approach taken to matters of contract law in the EU and the US is similar in the sense that each legal order manifests its own particular form of *sui generis* or hybrid instruments that are aimed at improving the coherence of contract law and ensuring the smooth functioning of the internal market. As a result, although these American techniques, at least in the way in which they have been conceived of in the US, may not be utilized in the debate about European contract law, they still play an indirect role in directing attention to the novel instruments that are being created, or will be created, at the European level and their importance for the relationship between the Union and the Member States in this setting.

The Future Path of European Contract Law

The controversy brewing over the extent of the Union's competence to take far-reaching action in contract law is not likely to abate in the near future, and this book's substantiation that the Union has been conferred sufficient competence under the Treaties to adopt a European contract law instrument, optional or otherwise, may have the tendency to exacerbate tensions even further in this regard. Importantly, as repeated time and time again, just because the Union has sufficient competence to act does not necessarily mean that it must do so. The activities taking place in the European contract law project, such as the proposed CESL, indicate that such a need is present; this book merely aims to clarify matters concerning the Union's competence in this area so that the debate on such matters may proceed on a sound footing.

Irrespective of where the reader's opinion may fall, the three-part framework may still be of use in the future path of European contract law and its constitutional dimensions. The template in Part One provides the 'grounding' for the constitutional assessment of European contract law and comparative reflection with the US, taking into account the semantic framework for the prevalent terminology used in the debate, the perennial themes underlying the so-called 'hard core' of the EU contract law *acquis*, the role of the Court of Justice, and the detailed inquiry into the American contract law framework. The 'institutional record' of the debate in Part Two reveals the extent to which the constitutionality of European contract law (and European private law generally) was discussed, either implicitly or explicitly, at the European level. The legal framework underpinning the constitutional assessment of European contract law in Part Three lays the basis for examining the roles played by the principles of conferral, subsidiarity, proportionality, and sincere cooperation in this setting, analysing the scope of the Union's competence under Articles 114, 115, 169, 81, and 352 TFEU, and evaluating certain alternative and complementary routes to a European contract law instrument. In this way, while there may never be unanimous agreement on the scope of the Union's competence in relation to European contract law (or European private law for that matter), these three parts establishing the constitutional foundations of European contract law may at least provide common ground on which to frame the relevant arguments concerning the possible recourse to the abovementioned Treaty provisions and these alternative and complementary routes.

In closing, in view of the ongoing development of the debate about European contract law, it remains to be seen whether the final product of the proposed CESL will be adopted under Article 114 TFEU and to what extent the Union may utilize its competence under this provision and others to take further action in this area. But whatever happens, it is the modest hope of the present author that this book may facilitate a 'constitutional conversation' about European contract law and a fruitful 'comparative conversation' with the US and thus may help to identify the most appropriate solutions to the problems raised by the debate about European contract law in the years to come.

Index

academic projects 148–56
Commission 2003 Action Plan 196
Commission 2004 Communication 209
European Parliament Resolutions 157, 167
1999 Working Paper 169
see also Acquis Group; Gandolfi Group; Insurance Group; Ius Commune Casebook Project; Lando Commission; Network of Excellence; Study Group; Trento Common Core Project
Academy of European Law (ERA) 190
Academy of European Private Lawyers *see* Gandolfi Group
acquis communautaire 394, 455–7
Commission 2003 Action Plan 193
Commission 2004 Communication 216
Acquis Group 152, 154–5
Commission 2004 Communication 209
Draft Common Frame of Reference (DCFR) 229
Acquis Principles (Principles of the Existing EC Contract Law) 88, 91, 155, 231
Action Plan 2003 *see* Commission 2003 Action Plan
Ajani, G 154
alternative and complementary routes 4, 450–80
Common Frame of Reference (CFR) 477–9
Open Method of Coordination (OMC) 471–3
United States: Restatements, uniform and model laws, and the UCC 474–7
see also enhanced cooperation; intergovernmental treaty
Amadeo, A 406
American Bar Association (ABA) *see* United States
American contract law framework 24, 93–143
American 'federal common law' 4, 76–7, 93, 94–103, 142, 483
origins 95–101
Erie Railroad Co. v Tompkins 97–101
Swift v Tyson 95–7
overview 94
Restatement project 121
tensions underlying 101–3
Uniform Commercial Code (UCC) 483
uniform law process 483
American Law Institute (ALI) 9, 115–24, 133, 136, 138, 474–5
Commission 2003 Action Plan 198
Commission 2004 Communication 209
Commission 2010 Green Paper 256
Committee on the Establishment of a Permanent Organization for the Improvement of the Law 119–20
Model Penal Code 116
origins 119–21
overview 115–16
'private legislatures' 10
see also Restatement project; Restatements; Uniform Commercial Code (UCC)
Amsterdam Protocol:
proportionality principle 307, 309
sincere cooperation principle 311
subsidiarity principle 297–8, 301–2
Amsterdam Treaty:
Article 81 (TFEU): judicial cooperation in civil matters 423–4
Article 169 (TFEU): consumer protection 380, 386–7, 397, 401–2, 406, 408
enhanced cooperation 451, 455–6, 459
intergovernmental treaty 466
Tampere European Council meeting 172, 174
Vienna Action Plan 172–4
approximation 13–14, 27–31
'approximation' prong 324–5, 353–7
Article 81 (TFEU): judicial cooperation in civil matters 424, 431
Article 114 and Article 352 (TFEU) 360–1, 366, 368–70, 373–6
Article 114 (TFEU): exercise of competence 350–8
Article 114 (TFEU): limits of competence 325–50
Article 169 (TFEU): limits of competence 410, 411
Commercial Agents Directive 45
constitutional framing 43, 56
low intensity 356
multi-stage 353–5, 368
see also approximation and related processes; approximation and three-level hierarchy

approximation and related processes 25–41
codification 37–9
convergence 40
coordination 36–7
Europeanization (and formerly Communitarization) 39–40
harmonization models 31–6
harmonization and unification 27–31
United States: comparative leaps 40–1
approximation and three-level hierarchy 313–16
catch-all provision 315–16
general approximation provisions 315
specific approximation provisions 315–16
Area of Freedom, Security and Justice (AFSJ) 172, 179, 220
Article 81 (TFEU): judicial cooperation in civil matters 424–5, 427, 429–31, 433, 437
Commission 2003 Action Plan 192, 193
Commission 2004 Communication 205, 217
conferral principle 292
Draft Common Frame of Reference (DCFR) 231
Hague Programme 217
judicial cooperation in civil matters 172, 422
Stockholm Programme 252–3
Tampere European Council meeting 172–3, 175, 177–8
Treaty framework 282
Vienna Action Plan 172–4
Article 81, Article 114, and Article 352 (TFEU), relationship between 437–48
exercise of competence under Article 81 and linkage to Articles 114 and 352 (TFEU) 447–8
limits of competence under Article 81 and linkage to Article 114 (TFEU) 444–7
Union measures adopted under Article 81 (TFEU) 439–44
Article 81 (TFEU) 423–37
former Treaty framework 423–7
present Treaty framework 427–36
see also Article 81, Article 114, and Article 352 (TFEU), relationship between
Article 114 and Article 115 (TFEU) 56–9, 313–24
ambiguities 319–24
establishment 'and' versus 'or' functioning 323–4
'internal market' versus 'common market' 320–2
'object' versus 'directly affect' language 319–20, 322–3
approximation and three-level hierarchy 313–16
comparison and order of preference 316–19
Article 114 and Article 352 (TFEU) 360–76, 459–62
contract law instrument modifying national contract law 361–5
European Cooperative Society case and related jurisprudence 365–9
optional instrument 369–76
roles 360
Article 114 (TFEU): scope 324–60
'approximation' prong 324–5, 353–7
exercise of Union competence 350–8
limits of Union competence 325–50
distortions of competition parameters 345–50
obstacles to trade parameters 338–44
'object' prong 324–5, 327–38, 350–3
United States: comparative reflection 358–60
see also Article 114 and Article 115 (TFEU); Article 114 and Article 352 (TFEU); Article 81, Article 114, and Article 352 (TFEU), relationship between; Article 169 (TFEU)
Article 115 (TFEU) *see* Article 114 and Article 115 (TFEU)
Article 169, Article 114, and Article 352 (TFEU), relationship between 415–19
United States: comparative reflection 419–20
Article 169 (TFEU) 380–409
case law 390–7
exercise of Union competence 413–15
limits of Union competence 410–13
scope 409–15
Treaties 380–90
former Treaty framework 381–7
present Treaty framework 388–90
usage 398–409
practice 403–6
proposals for change 406–9
theory 398–403
Article 352 (TFEU) *see* Article 81, Article 114, and Article 352 (TFEU), relationship between; Article 114 and 352 (TFEU); Article 169, Article 114, and Article 352 (TFEU), relationship between

Association of American Law Schools (AALS) *see* United States
Association Henri Capitant 147, 154
Commission 2004 Communication 209
Commission 2010 Green Paper 260
Austria:
Article 114 (TFEU): limits of competence 346
CESL, proposed (Common European Sales Law Regulation) 268
Commission 2003 Action Plan 196, 198

Bangemann, M 164–5, 166
Basedow, J 343, 445
Belgium: Council 2008 Report 237
Benelux Uniform Law on Trademarks 167
Berliner 65–9
Bermann, G 296
Bielefeld University 240
biotechnological inventions (legal protection) 330–1
Boersma Report 382
Bogert, G G 113
Bonino, E 168, 406–7
Borrás, A 427
Braucher, R 134
Bru Puron, C M 165–6, 168
Brussels Convention (1968) 164, 423
'Brussels I' Regulation 86–7
Bulgaria (accession) 223, 241
2003 Action Plan 208
EC Consumer Law Compendium 240–1
business-to-business (B2B) 283
academic projects 152
Article 114 and Article 352 (TFEU) 374
Article 114 (TFEU): limits of competence 327, 342, 349
Article 169, Article 114, and Article 352 (TFEU) 418
CESL, proposed (Common European Sales Law Regulation) 264, 265, 267, 269
Commission 2004 Communication 215
Commission 2005 Progress Report 222, 225
Commission 2010 Green Paper 254–5, 257, 258, 259
constitutional framing 59–60
business-to-consumer (B2C) 283
academic projects 152
Article 114 and Article 352 (TFEU) 374
Article 114 (TFEU) (limits of competence) 326–7, 342, 349
Article 169, Article 114, and Article 352 (TFEU) 418
CESL, proposed (Common European Sales Law Regulation) 264, 265–6, 267, 269
Commission 2004 Communication 215
Commission 2005 Progress Report 222, 223, 225
Commission 2010 Green Paper 254, 257, 259, 260, 261
constitutional framing 59–60
Consumer Rights Directive 251
EC Consumer Law Compendium 242

cancellation, right of 63–4, 82–3
CESL, proposed (Common European Sales Law Regulation) 1, 4, 7, 10, 264–73, 283, 481–4
American techniques 477
Article 81, Article 114, and Article 352 (TFEU): exercise of competence 448
Article 114 and Article 115 (TFEU): approximation 317
Article 114 and Article 352 (TFEU) 360, 365, 369, 370–7
Article 114 (TFEU): exercise of competence 357–8
Article 114 (TFEU): limits of competence 326, 342–4, 348, 350
Article 169, Article 114, and Article 352 (TFEU) 417–19
Common Frame of Reference (CFR) 478, 479
constitutional framing 14, 26, 35, 60
constitutional parameters of contract law 278, 279
enhanced cooperation 463–4
Expert Group and 2011 Feasibility Study 263
hybrid approach 370, 376
Impact Assessment 260, 266, 269, 299, 357
intergovernmental treaty 467
legal basis 371–7
national parliament opinions 268–9
Open Method of Coordination (OMC) 473
responses of Union institutions and bodies 269–71
Stockholm Programme 253
subsidiarity principle 299
see also European Cooperative Society case and related jurisprudence; '2nd regime'

CFR-Net 222, 225, 226, 228
Chandler, W 129, 130
Chillon, S 407, 414
CISG *see* United Nations Convention on Contracts for the International Sale of Goods
civil law 23
general principles 83
substantive 177
Clifford Chance study 343
cloud computing contracts 271–2
co-decision procedure:
Article 81 (TFEU): judicial cooperation in civil matters 433
Article 114 and Article 115 (TFEU): approximation 317
Article 114 and Article 352 (TFEU) 364–5, 369
Article 169 (TFEU): consumer protection 381, 385
conferral principle 288–91
Co-PECL *see* Joint Network on European Private Law
Cockfield White Paper on the Internal Market 383
codification 37–9, 123
Collier, W A 109–10
Commercial Agents Directive 45–6
Commission 2001 Communication 1, 178, 180–6, 279, 297
1999 Working Paper 183
Option I: no action 182, 197, 201
Option II: common contract principles 182–3, 190, 197, 201, 202
Option III: improving the *acquis* 182, 183, 190, 198, 201
Option IV: new comprehensive legislation 182, 183–4, 191, 196, 197–8, 203
responses to 2001 Communication *see* Commission 2003 Action Plan
Commission 2001 Green Paper on EU Consumer Protection 402
Commission 2002 Communication on the Consumer Policy Strategy 402–3
Commission 2003 Action Plan 186–204, 208, 217, 220
2001 Communication responses 187–99
Council 2001 Report 192–4
European Economic and Social Committee (EESC) 2002 Opinion 194–6
European Parliament 2001 Resolution 187–91
stakeholder responses to 2001 Communication 196–9
Article 114 (TFEU): limits of competence 342–3, 349
constitutional parameters of contract law 279
content 199–204
Measure I: quality of the Union *acquis* 201, 209, 211
Measure II: promotion of EU-wide standard contract terms 202, 209–11
Measure III: non-sector specific measures 202–4, 209–10, 214
Leitner 84
Open Method of Coordination (OMC) 472
responses to 2003 Action Plan *see* Commission 2004 Communication
Commission 2004 Communication 204–19, 220
2003 Action Plan responses 205–10
Council 2003 Resolution 206–7
European Central Bank (ECB) 2003 Letter 207–8
European Parliament 2003 Resolution 205–6
stakeholder responses to 2003 Action Plan 210
aftermath 216–19
Article 114 and Article 352 (TFEU) 369–70
Commission 2005 Progress Report 223, 227
Common Frame of Reference (CFR) 210–14, 477
Court of Justice 212
constitutional parameters of contract law 278, 279
content 210–16
optional instrument 214–16
Commission 2005 Progress Report 221–7, 272–3
CFR-Net 222, 225
Commission 2006 Note to the Council 227
Common Frame of Reference (CFR) 221–2, 477
constitutional parameters of contract law 279
Council 2005 Conclusions 224
EC Consumer Law Compendium 240
European Parliament 2006 Resolutions 224–7
Member States Experts Network 222

Research Network 222
review of the consumer *acquis* 222–3
Commission 2005 Public Health and Consumer Protection Strategy 403
Commission 2006 Note to the Council 227
Commission 2007 Communication on the EU Consumer Policy Strategy 403
Commission 2007 Green Paper 223, 242–8, 273
degree of harmonization 244
horizontal (mixed) approach 243–4, 245
responses 245–8
European Economic and Social Committee (EESC) 2007 Opinion 245–6
European Parliament 2007 Resolution 246–7
stakeholder responses to 2007 Green Paper 248
Commission 2007 Progress Report 227, 228–9, 272–3
CFR-Net 228
Common Frame of Reference (CFR) 477
constitutional parameters of contract law 279
Council 2008 Report 234
Member State Experts Network 228
Commission 2010 Green Paper 253–61, 272–3
American techniques 256, 475–6
Article 81, Article 114, and Article 352 (TFEU) and exercise of competence 448
Article 114 and Article 352 (TFEU) 363, 370
Article 114 (TFEU): exercise of competence 357
Article 114 (TFEU): limits of competence 342–3, 348
CESL, proposed (Common European Sales Law Regulation) 269
Common Frame of Reference (CFR) 479
constitutional parameters of contract law 279
contract types 271
Expert Group and 2011 Feasibility Study 262, 263
intergovernmental treaty 471
Option 1 (publication of Expert Group results) 255, 260
Option 2 (toolbox) 255, 260
Option 3 (Commission Recommendation) 255–6, 260
Option 4 (optional instrument) 256, 257, 258–9, 260, 370
Option 5 (minimum harmonization Directive) 260
Option 6 (Regulation) 257, 260
Option 7 (European civil code) 257
responses 257–61
European Economic and Social Committee (EESC) 2011 Opinion 258
European Parliament 2011 Resolution 258–9
stakeholder responses 260–1
subsidiarity principle 297
Commission Communication (for Stockholm Programme) 253
Commission on European Contract Law (CECL) *see* Lando Commission
Commission First Three-Year Consumer Policy Action Plan 398–9
Commission Fourth Three-Year Consumer Policy Action Plan 401
Commission Green Paper on payment procedure and small claims procedures 440–1
Commission 'Note d'information' 167–8
Commission 'Projet de Declaration' 167
Commission response to 'Problems of harmonizing civil law' 163–5
Commission Second Three-Year Consumer Policy Action Plan 399–400
Commission Third Three-Year Consumer Policy Action Plan 400–1
Committee on Civil Law: Council 2008 and 2009 Reports 234, 236, 239
Committee on the Establishment of a Permanent Organization for the Improvement of the Law *see* American Law Institute (ALI)
Committee (European Parliament) *see* Parliamentary Committees
Committee of the Regions (CoR) 401–3
Common Agricultural Policy (CAP) 382
Common Core Project *see* Trento Common Core Project
Common Foreign and Security Policy (CFSP) 452, 456
Common Frame of Reference (CFR) 4, 7, 220, 221–40, 272–3, 477–9
academic or draft 213, 478
academic projects 153

Common Frame of Reference (CFR) (*cont.*):
alternative and complementary routes 450–1
American techniques 474–5
Article 81 (TFEU): judicial cooperation in civil matters 437
basic sources 202
Commission 2001 Communication 182
Commission 2003 Action Plan 201–2, 203
Commission 2004 Communication 205–7, 208, 209–14, 215–16, 217–18
Commission 2005 Progress Report 221–7
Commission 2007 Progress Report 228–9
Commission 2010 Green Paper 258
constitutional framing 60
constitutional parameters of contract law 278, 279, 283
constitutionality 482–3
content areas 202
Council 2008 and 2009 Reports 234–7, 238–40
Court of Justice 91–2
enhanced cooperation 463–4
European Parliament 2007 Resolution 232–3
European Parliament 2008 Resolution 233–4
Expert Group and 2011 Feasibility Study 261
intergovernmental treaty 467
Open Method of Coordination (OMC) 472–3
political or final 213
Stockholm Programme 252–3
subsidiarity principle 299
see also Draft Common Frame of Reference (DCFR)
common market *see* internal market
'Common Principles of European Contract Law' 154
Communications on European contract law *see* Commission Communication
comparative law/materials 19, 22, 89–91, 92
competence 4–5, 7–9, 10, 179, 313–77
'boomerang' to constitutionality 457–8
Commission 2001 Communication 184–6
Commission 2003 Action Plan 198
complementary 282, 292, 388–9
conferral principle 286
constitutional framing 14–16, 56–9
Consumer Rights Directive 250
exclusive 292
exercise of 2
existence of 2
functional 293
horizontal division 17, 290
limits of 2, 410–13
scope of 57
shared 292, 293, 388–9
supplementary 293
vertical division 17
see also Article 81 (TFEU); Article 114 (TFEU); Article 114 and Article 115 (TFEU); Article 114 and Article 352 (TFEU); Article 169 (TFEU); conferral
competition law 43, 382
compulsory instruments 371, 374, 376
conferral, principle of 15, 282–4, 285–93, 484
Article 114 and Article 115 (TFEU): approximation 314–15
definition 285–7
legal basis requirement 287–91
Lisbon Treaty 291–3, 303
constitutional framing 13–61
comparative materials 19
European conventions 19
future view 18, 20–1, 22–3
international conventions 18
lex mercatoria 19–20, 22
narrow view 18, 20, 22
national laws 19
perennial themes 56–61
primary and secondary Union law 18
terminology 13–41
approximation and related processes 25–41
constitutionality and the 'constitutional' designation 14–17
contract law's relationship to private law 17–24
United States: comparative leaps 24
wide view 18, 22
see also scope of contract law and its 'hard core'
constitutional parameters of contract law 277–312
complexity of constitutional inquiry 279
consultative nature of communications 279
forms of Union and/or Member State action 283
legal instruments 283, 284
material scope of application 283, 284
method of application 283, 284
neglect of constitutionality at European level 277–80
'no need' argument 278

personal scope of application 283
'political will' argument 277–8
territorial scope of application 283, 284
'too early' argument 278
Treaty framework 280–2
see also conferral; proportionality; sincere cooperation; subsidiarity
constitutionalism 16
constitutionality 4, 13, 17, 179
constitutionalization 16
consumer confidence 43, 47, 54, 58–9, 251, 266
Consumer Credit Directive 67–9
repealed by new Consumer Credit Directive 46–8
Consumer Credit Protection Act (United States) 139, 140
consumer law and general contract law, relationship between 59–60
Consumer Policy Evaluation Consortium 247
consumer protection 2, 5, 226, 378–420
conferral principle 292
constitutional framing 56–7, 59
and internal market 415–19
sensu stricto objectives 379, 411, 416
Uniform Commercial Code (UCC) 138–41
vs consumer policy 378
see also Article 169 (TFEU); Article 169, Article 114, and Article 352 (TFEU), relationship between
consumer rights *see* Council 1975 Preliminary Programme
Consumer Rights Directive 1, 4, 7, 248–51
Consumer Sales Directive 54, 85
contract law's relationship to private law 17–24
definitions of European contract law 17–21
definitions of European private law and similar variants 21–4
Convention on the Future of Europe *see* European Convention
conventions 159–60
international 18
convergence 25, 40, 255
Tampere Conclusions 176
see also Open Method of Convergence
coordination 14, 36–7
mandatory or binding 36
softer forms of 36–7
see also Open Method of Coordination (OMC)
Council 1975 Preliminary Programme 382–3
Council 1975 Resolution 382
Council 1981 Second Programme of the EEC 383
Council 2001 Report 192–4, 213
Council 2003 Resolution 206–7
Council 2005 Conclusions 224
Council 2008 Report 234–7, 273
Council 2008 and 2009 Reports 238–40, 273
Council Legal Service 270, 361
Opinion on legal basis of CESL, proposed (Common European Sales Law Regulation) 269
country of origin principle 26, 244
Court of Justice 4, 62–92, 484
Article 81 (TFEU): judicial cooperation in civil matters 424
Article 169, Article 114, and Article 352 (TFEU) 417
Article 169 (TFEU): consumer protection 390
Article 169 (TFEU): limits of competence 412
Common Frame of Reference (CFR): 2004 Communication 212
comparative contract law materials, recourse to by Advocates General 84–91
illustrations: *Quelle*, *Ilsinger*, and *Messner* 85–9
constitutional framing 29, 31, 39, 44, 58, 61
consumer protection 379, 390
intergovernmental treaty 468, 469
interpretative role 62–76, 77, 92
directives, relationship between 63–9
national contract law regimes and EU contract law, relationship between 69–76
lawmaking role 63, 76–84, 92
European 'federal common law' and 'hard core': definitions 77–8
European 'federal common law' illustrations 78–84
Crawford, J 112
Croatia (accession) 223, 268
EC Consumer Law Compendium 241
culture, policy 380, 386–7, 389, 393, 411
Czech Republic: Council 2008 and 2009 Reports 237, 238–9

damage 78–80, 84
material 78–9
non-material 78–9
Database Group (*Institut Charles Dumoulin*) 154

decision-making procedure:
Article 81 (TFEU): judicial cooperation in civil matters 427
Article 114 and Article 115 (TFEU): approximation 317–18
Article 114 and Article 352 (TFEU) 364–5
Article 169 (TFEU): consumer protection 381, 385–6
see also co-decision procedure
definitions of European contract law 17–21
definitions of European private law and similar variants 21–4
Denmark:
Article 81 (TFEU): judicial cooperation in civil matters 424
CESL, proposed (Common European Sales Law Regulation) 271
Dietzinger 65–9
differentiation 3, 451
direct effect, horizontal 390–2, 397
directives:
Article 114 and Article 115 (TFEU): approximation 317
Article 169 (TFEU): consumer protection 389
Article 169 (TFEU): limits of competence 410
European Parliament Resolutions 159
and harmonization link 29
Directorate General (DG) 225
Directorate General (DG) for Research of the European Parliament 168
Distance Selling Directive 88
repealed by Consumer Rights Directive 53–4
distortions of competition 345–50, 481
appreciable: parameters 345–50
Article 81 (TFEU): limits of competence 446–7
Article 114 (TFEU): limits of competence 329–338
Common Frame of Reference (CFR) 479
EC Consumer Law Compendium 241
enhanced cooperation 459–61
subsidiarity, principle of 301–2
Door to Door Sales Rule (United States) 141
Doorstep Selling Directive 63–7, 69, 82
repealed by Consumer Rights Directive 44–5
Draft Common Frame of Reference (DCFR) 1, 7, 229–31, 272–3, 478
academic projects 149, 153–6
American techniques 477
Article 114 (TFEU): limits of competence 326
Books 230
comments and notes 230–1
constitutional parameters of contract law 278
Consumer Rights Directive 251
contract types 271
Court of Justice 85–7, 88, 91
definitions 230, 231
European Parliament 2007 Resolution 232
European Parliament 2008 Resolution 233, 234
Expert Group and 2011 Feasibility Study 261
model rules 230–1
principles 229–31
Draft Constitutional Treaty (DCT) 7, 280–2, 312, 407
Article 81 (TFEU): judicial cooperation in civil matters 427, 431–3, 436
Article 114 and Article 352 (TFEU) 363
Article 169 (TFEU): consumer protection 380–1, 388–9, 397
Article 169 (TFEU): limits of competence 410, 412
constitutional framing 16
constitutional parameters of contract law 279–81
enhanced cooperation 462
intergovernmental treaty 471
proportionality principle 309
subsidiarity principle 304
Drobnig, U 194

Ebers, M 240
EC Consumer Law Compendium 223, 240–2
see also EU Consumer Law Acquis Database
Economic Impact Group (Tilburg Law and Economics Center (TILEC)) 154
economic interests, protection of (consumers) 382–4, 387, 410, 417
Edinburgh Conclusions (1992) 307
education, policy 380, 386, 389, 393, 411
education, right to (consumers) 383, 385, 387, 410
effectiveness principle 70
'effectiveness' requirement 301
'efficiency' requirement 301
enhanced cooperation 2, 3, 5, 451–65, 479, 482
advantages and disadvantages 451–4
alternative and complementary routes 450

arguments against 463–5
Article 118 (TFEU) 369
authorization 454–63
competence: 'boomerang' to constitutionality 457–8
internal market-related conditions: linkage to Article 114 and Article 352 (TFEU) 459–62
linkage to sincere cooperation principle 462–3
environmental policy/protection 384, 386, 389, 410, 416, 418
equivalence principle 70
Erie Railroad Co. v Tompkins 97–101
establishment 'and' versus 'or' functioning 323–4
EU Consumer Law Acquis Database 240
European Central Bank 2003 Letter *see* Commission 2004 Communication
European civil code 8, 23, 38, 169, 256
European Code of Private Law 161, 164–5
European Commission *see* Commission
European contract law initiative 21, 221
European contract law instrument 21, 38
European contract law project 21
European Convention 7, 312, 482
Article 81 (TFEU): judicial cooperation in civil matters 279, 287, 427–31, 436
Article 114 and Article 352 (TFEU) 316, 363
Article 169 (TFEU): consumer protection 380, 388
Article 169 (TFEU): limits of competence 410, 411
Article 352 (TFEU) 363
Commission 'intensity scheme' 292, 309
enhanced cooperation 456, 458, 462
intergovernmental treaty 467
Open Method of Coordination (OMC) 473
Treaty framework 280–2
Working Group 281, 282, 427, 473
Final Report 309, 388, 427, 431, 467, 472–3
European Convention for the Protection of Human Rights and Fundamental Freedoms (ECHR) 39, 362–3
***European Cooperative Society* case and related jurisprudence** 365–9
European Council Meeting at Tampere 1, 4, 172–8
Article 81 (TFEU): judicial cooperation in civil matters 437
events leading to Tampere and Vienna Action Plan 172–4
Tampere Conclusions 175–8
Tampere Conclusions: point 39 175–6, 177, 179, 192, 217, 421
Union measures 439
European Court of Human Rights 363
European Economic and Social Committee (EESC) 187, 269, 381, 400–3, 409
2002 Opinion 194–6
2004 Opinion 205, 216, 218–19
2005 Opinion 408
2006 Opinion 408
2007 Opinion 245–6
2011 Opinion 258
2012 Opinion 269–71
Opinions on consumer policy/protection 408–9
Opinion on 'The European Insurance Contract' 205, 218–19
Opinion on 'The 28th regime' 371
European Home and Leisure Accidents Surveillance System (EHLASS) 404–7
European Law Institute (ELI) 9, 190
European Parliament 1969 Resolution 382
European Parliament 1989 Resolution 156–63, 165, 167, 225
European Parliament 1990 Resolution 162–3
European Parliament 1994 Resolution 163, 165–8, 225, 474
European Parliament 1999 Resolution 174
European Parliament 2000 Resolution 170–2
European Parliament 2001 Resolution 187–91, 225
European Parliament 2003 Resolution 205–6, 225
European Parliament 2006 Resolutions 224–7, 229
first 2006 Resolution 224–6, 227–9, 273
second 2006 Resolution 226–7, 228
European Parliament 2007 Resolution 232–3, 246–7, 248
European Parliament 2008 Resolution 233–4
European Parliament 2011 Resolution 258–9
European Parliament Resolutions 1, 4, 156–72
Commission response to 'Problems of harmonizing civil law' 163–5
1999 Working Paper 168–70
European Research Group on Existing EC Private Law *see* Acquis Group
European Tort Law Principles 85
European University Institute (Florence) 190

Europeanization (and formerly Communitarization) 39–40
Expert Group on cloud computing contracts 272
Expert Group on a Common Frame of Reference in the area of European contract law 255, 261–3, 264
see also Feasibility Study 2011
Expert Group on European insurance contract law 271

fair dealing 245, 246, 248
Fauvarque-Cosson, B 262
Feasibility Study 2011 260, 261–3, 464
responses 263
see also Expert Group on a Common Frame of Reference in the area of European contract law
Federal Bills of Exchange Act 108–9
Federal Sales Act 127–33
federalization 41
and Uniform Commercial Code (UCC) 136–8
financial transaction tax (FTT) 453, 461
Fischer, J 428–30
flanking policies 380, 386, 389
flexibility 3, 363, 451
France:
Article 169 (TFEU): consumer protection 394
Commission 2003 Action Plan 196
Council 2008 and 2009 Reports 236, 237, 238
free movement of goods, persons, services, and capital:
Article 81 (TFEU): judicial cooperation in civil matters 433, 439
Article 114 and Article 115 (TFEU): approximation 314
Article 114 (TFEU): limits of competence 326, 338–42, 377
constitutional framing 33, 37
Draft Common Frame of Reference (DCFR) 231
Freiburger 71–3, 75–6
full/full targeted harmonization *see* maximum harmonization

Gandolfi Group (Academy of European Private Lawyers) 148
Commission 2003 Action Plan 188, 190, 196
Commission 2010 Green Paper 260
Gargani, G 226, 232
Gazis, N 156–60
General Court (EGC) 62, 390
Germany:
Article 81 (TFEU): judicial cooperation in civil matters 428, 429–30, 436
Article 114 (TFEU): limits of competence 327–8, 332, 334
Article 169 (TFEU): consumer protection 387, 392–3, 395
CESL, proposed (Common European Sales Law Regulation) 268
Commission 2003 Action Plan 196, 198
Council 2008 Report 234–5, 237
Giscard d'Estaing, V 163
good faith:
Court of Justice 70, 74–5, 89
Draft Common Frame of Reference (DCFR) 231
EU contract law *acquis* 46, 50, 53
2007 Green Paper 245–6, 248
Uniform Commercial Code (UCC) 126
'Greater convergence in civil law' 175, 177–8
Greece:
Article 169 (TFEU): consumer protection 394
European Parliament Resolutions 157
'Problems of harmonizing civil law' 164

Hague Programme 205, 216–18, 252–3, 422, 437
Hamilton 81–4
'hard core':
EU contract law *acquis see* scope of contract law and its 'hard core'
European 'federal common law' *see* Court of Justice
harmonization 14, 27–31
alternative 34
Article 114 and Article 352 (TFEU) 366–7, 370, 376
Article 114 (TFEU): limits of competence 328, 331
Article 169, Article 114, and Article 352 (TFEU) 416–17
Article 169 (TFEU): consumer protection 383, 388–9, 396, 410–11, 412
Article 169 (TFEU): limits of competence 410–11, 412
Commission 2003 Action Plan 193
Commission 2004 Communication 219

Commission 2007 Green Paper 247
complete (exhaustive) 32, 395
constitutional framing 26, 39, 40, 41, 61
and coordination, blurring of 37
Court of Justice 75
European Parliament 1989 Resolution 159, 161
European Parliament 1994 Resolution 165–6
of indirect taxation 453
level or degree of 33–4
models 31–6
optional 34–5
partial 32–3, 34
scope 33–4
see also approximation and related processes; maximum harmonization; minimum harmonization
health and safety protection 384
right to (consumers) 382, 410
see also public health
Heininger 81–2
Heiss, H 156
Hondius, E 466
hybrid:
CESL, proposed (Common European Sales Law Regulation) 370, 376
European Parliament 1989 Resolution 469
option: European Economic and Social Committee (EESC) 2011 Opinion 258

Ilsinger 85–9
Impact Assessment: CESL, proposed (Common European Sales Law Regulation) 260, 266, 269, 299, 357
Implementation Report on the Unfair Contract Terms Directive 176
information, right to (consumers) 383, 410
institutional framework 9–10
institutional practice: Article 114 and Article 169 (TFEU) 416–17
insurance contracts 271
Insurance Group 154–6, 271
Commission 2003 Action Plan 196
Commission 2010 Green Paper 260
see also European Economic and Social Committee (EESC) Opinion on 'The European Insurance Contract'
intellectual property rights 365–9, 371, 374–5, 453
Intergovernmental Conference (IGC) 281, 406–7, 431
intergovernmental treaty 2, 5, 220, 465–71, 479, 482
ad hoc convention method 469–71
alternative and complementary routes 451
levels and approaches, distinction of 465
problems associated with 468–9
under public international law 466–9
internal market:
Article 169 (TFEU): consumer protection 385, 387, 389
conferral principle 292
definition 314, 320, 324
Draft Common Frame of Reference (DCFR) 231
single market 321
vs common market 320–2
internal market-related conditions: enhanced cooperation 459–62
Interstate Commerce Clause (US Constitution) 9, 100, 108, 128, 131, 133, 136–8, 140
Article 114 (TFEU) 358–60
consumer protection 419
Ireland:
Article 81 (TFEU): judicial cooperation in civil matters 424
Council 2008 Report 237
Italy:
European Parliament Resolutions 157
'Problems of harmonizing civil law' 164
'ius commune' 39
Ius Commune Casebook Project 85, 148, 209

Joint Network on European Private Law (Co-PECL) *see* Network of Excellence
Joint Response of the CECL and the Study Group 196
judicial cooperation in civil matters 2, 5, 173, 220, 421–49
Commission 2004 Communication 217–18
conferral principle 293
Council 2008 Report 235
enhanced cooperation 453
missed opportunity 436–7
subsidiarity principle 295
Tampere European Council meeting 172, 174
see also Article 81 (TFEU)

judicial cooperation in criminal matters 173
Justice and Home Affairs (JHA) 192
Article 81 (TFEU): judicial cooperation in civil matters 423
Council 2008 and 2009 Reports 193, 234, 238, 239
see also Area of Freedom, Security and Justice (AFSJ)

Kuneva, M 233, 251
Kyprianou, M 224

Laeken Declaration 6, 280, 363
Lando Commission (Commission on European Contract Law) (CECL) 148, 149–52, 156, 157, 178
Commission 2003 Action Plan 188, 190, 196
European Parliament 1994 Resolution 165–7
1999 Working Paper 169
Lando, O 149–50
Late Payment Directive, repealed by new Late Payment Directive 55–6
legal aid 439, 447
legal basis requirement 191, 264, 287–91
legal certainty 263, 440
legal instruments 283, 284, 317–18, 427
legitimacy 15–16
Lehne, K-H 188–9, 191, 227
Leitner 78–81, 83–4
Lewis, W D 117, 123
lex mercatoria 19–20, 22, 97
liability rules 63, 349
Liebman, L 122
Lisbon Protocol 297–8, 306, 309
Lisbon Strategy 216–17
Lisbon Treaty 3, 7, 285, 312, 482
Article 81 (TFEU): judicial cooperation in civil matters 423, 427, 433, 435, 436
Article 81 (TFEU): limits of competence 445, 446
Article 114 and Article 115 (TFEU): approximation 314, 318, 320, 322
Article 114 and Article 352 (TFEU) 363, 369
Article 169, Article 114, and Article 352 (TFEU) 416
Article 169 (TFEU): consumer protection 380–1, 384, 388–9, 397
Article 169 (TFEU): limits of competence 410, 411, 412
CESL, proposed (Common European Sales Law Regulation) 268
conferral, principle of 291–3
constitutional framing 39
constitutional parameters of contract law 279–80
enhanced cooperation 452, 454, 456, 462
intergovernmental treaty 467, 471
judicial cooperation in civil matters 422, 449
proportionality, principle of 308–10
sincere cooperation, principle of 311
subsidiarity, principle of 300, 303–5
Tampere European Council meeting 172
Treaty framework 281, 282
Llewellyn, K 113, 127, 130–2, 133

Maastricht Treaty:
Article 81 (TFEU): judicial cooperation in civil matters 423, 426
Article 169, Article 114, and Article 352 (TFEU) 416
Article 169 (TFEU): consumer protection 380, 384, 385–6, 390, 392, 397, 399–400, 403–4, 406, 408
subsidiarity principle 300
Tampere European Council meeting 172
Magnuson-Moss Warranty Act (United States) 141
mandatory rules/law 199–200, 342
Mavros, G 156–7
maximum harmonization 31, 32, 33–4
Article 169, Article 114, and Article 352 (TFEU) 417
Article 169 (TFEU): consumer protection 396, 407
Article 169 (TFEU): limits of competence 411
Commission 2007 Green Paper 244, 246–8
Commission 2010 Green Paper 256
constitutional framing 58–9
consumer protection 378, 396, 407
Consumer Rights Directive 48–51
EC Consumer Law Compendium 241–2
full 32
vs full targeted 33–4, 247–9
new Consumer Credit Directive 47
new Timeshare Directive 52
mediation 439–40
Member States Experts Network 222, 228
Mentschikoff, S 133
Mercer, G A 109
Merchants' Association Federal Sales Act 130–1, 132
Messner 85–9

method of application 283, 284
Meyer, J 429
Michigan Law Review 136–7
Micklitz, H-W 403–4, 407, 409, 414
minimum harmonization 31, 34, 35–6
Article 169, Article 114, and Article 352 (TFEU) 417
Article 169 (TFEU): consumer protection 381, 386, 387, 389, 394, 395–7, 402, 404, 409
Article 169 (TFEU): exercise of competence 413
Article 169 (TFEU): limits of competence 411
Commission 2007 Green Paper 243, 244, 246
Commission 2010 Green Paper 256
constitutional framing 58–9
Consumer Credit Directive 46–7
Consumer Rights Directive 250–1
Consumer Sales Directive 54
Court of Justice 79
Distance Selling Directive (repealed by Consumer Rights Directive) 53
Doorstep Selling Directive (repealed by the Consumer Rights Directive) 45
EC Consumer Law Compendium 241–2
Late Payment Directive 55
Package Travel Directive 48–9
Timeshare Directive 51
Unfair Contract Terms Directive 50
model laws 3, 4, 5, 166–7, 197, 450, 479
and uniform laws, distinction between 105–6
Model Penal Code *see* American Law Institute (ALI)
movable property law 24, 349–50
Müller-Graff, P-C 466
mutual recognition 26, 175, 244, 431–3

National Conference of Commissioners on Uniform State Laws (NCCUSL) 10, 93, 103–15, 116, 118, 120–1, 124, 131–2, 141, 475
and federal system 106–7
name Uniform Law Commission (ULC) 103
origins 107–14
overview 103–4
'private legislatures' 10
Uniform Commercial Code (UCC) 124, 133
consumer protection 138
interstate/intrastate uniformity 136
origins 127, 131–2
Uniform Consumer Credit Code 139–40
see also uniform law process; uniform laws; Uniform Commercial Code (UCC)
'national procedural autonomy' 70
'Necessity for Uniformity in the Laws Governing Commercial Paper, The' (Tompkins) 109–10
Netherlands:
Article 114 and Article 352 (TFEU) 365
Article 114 (TFEU): limits of competence 330
Treaty framework 281
Network of Excellence 149, 153–6
new legal forms *see European Cooperative Society* case and related jurisprudence
new modes of governance 3, 473
New York Law Revision Commission 135
Nice Treaty 280
Article 81 (TFEU): judicial cooperation in civil matters 424
Article 169 (TFEU): consumer protection 387
enhanced cooperation 451, 455–6, 459
non-mandatory (default) rules/law 199–200, 342
non-regulatory measures 200

Obamacare 359
'object' prong 324–5
Article 114 (TFEU): exercise of competence 350–3, 357–8, 360
Article 114 (TFEU): limits of competence 327–38
'object' versus 'directly affect' 319–20, 322–3
obstacles to trade, parameters of (Article 114 TFEU) 338–44
barriers to trade: EC Consumer Law Compendium 241–2
distortions of competition 327
enhanced cooperation 459–62
Océano Grupo 70–3
Open Method of Convergence 472
Open Method of Coordination (OMC) 2, 3, 5, 220, 471–3, 480, 482
alternative and complementary routes 450, 451
Commission 2003 Action Plan 200
constitutional framing 37
intergovernmental treaty 470

Opinions of the Advocates General 29, 63
see also Court of Justice
opt-in/opt-out models 184, 283–4
Article 81 (TFEU): judicial cooperation in civil matters 424
Article 114 and Article 352 (TFEU) 370–1, 376
Commission 2003 Action Plan 195, 199, 203
Commission 2004 Communication 206, 215
optional instruments:
American techniques 112, 477
Article 114 and Article 352 (TFEU) 369–77
Articles 81, 114, and 352 (TFEU): exercise of competence 447–8
Commission 2003 Action Plan 201, 202, 203–4
Commission 2004 Communication 210, 214–16
Commission 2010 Green Paper 256
Common Frame of Reference (CFR) 479
constitutional framing 14, 26
enhanced cooperation 461
insurance contracts 156, 218–19
judicial cooperation in civil matters 422, 449
vs optional harmonization 35, 376
see also CESL, proposed (Common European Sales Law Regulation); Commission 2003 Action Plan; Commission 2010 Green Paper
ordinary legislative procedure 259

Package Travel Directive 48–9, 78–9
parallel agreements 465
Paris Summit (1972) 382
Parliamentary Committees 157–8, 163, 165, 168, 187–8, 226
partial agreements 465
patent protection 365–8, 369, 453, 459, 461
Patient Protection and Affordable Care Act (United States) 359
patrimonial law 23–4, 152–3, 230
payment procedure and small claims procedures 440–4, 447
Pearson, H 130
Permanent Editorial Board (PEB) 136
Piatt, W H H 128–9
piecemeal approach of legislature (Union) 60–1
Pierros, F 163–5
Poland:
CESL, proposed (Common European Sales Law Regulation) 270
Commission 2003 Action Plan 198
Police and Judicial Cooperation in Criminal Matters (PJCCM) 172, 424, 452
Portugal:
Council 2008 Report 236, 237
Treaty framework 281
preliminary ruling procedure 63–4
Principles of European Contract Law (PECL) 19, 148, 149–52, 154
Court of Justice 85–7, 91
Draft Common Frame of Reference (DCFR) 231
Principles of European Insurance Contract Law (PEICL) 155
Principles of European Law (PEL) series 85, 152, 231
Principles of the Existing EC Contract Law *see* Acquis Principles
private law 9, 23, 24
'Problem of Uniform Legislation in the United States, The' (Snyder) 112
'Problems of harmonizing civil law' 163–5
Product Liability Directive 42, 80, 394–5
Progress Report *see* Commission 2005 Progress Report; Commission 2007 Progress Report
Project Group on a Restatement of European Insurance Contract Law *see* Insurance Group
proportionality, principle of 2, 4, 10, 282–5, 305–10, 483, 484
Article 81, Article 114, and Article 352 (TFEU): exercise of competence 447–8
Article 81 (TFEU): judicial cooperation in civil matters 439–40, 441, 443
Article 114 and Article 352 (TFEU) 368, 374–5, 377
Article 114 (TFEU): exercise of competence 350, 352–3, 354, 357–8, 360
Article 114 (TFEU): limits of competence 333, 350
Article 114 (TFEU): 'object' and 'approximation' prongs 325
Article 169 (TFEU): consumer protection 402
Article 169 (TFEU): exercise of competence 413–15
CESL, proposed (Common European Sales Law Regulation) 267
Commission 2001 Communication 185–6
Commission 2003 Action Plan 193, 198, 204
Commission 2004 Communication 207, 209–10, 215

Commission 2007 Green Paper 247–8
Commission 2010 Green Paper 256–7, 261
Common Frame of Reference (CFR) 478–9
constitutional framing 15
constitutional parameters of contract law 282–5, 297, 300, 303, 305–10, 312
Council 2008 Report 236
definition 305–6
European Parliament 1989 Resolution 225
inside and outside subsidiarity 306–8
judicial cooperation in civil matters 422, 449
Lisbon Treaty 304, 308–10
sensu stricto test 306
suitability test 306
'psychological barriers' 342–4
public health policy/protection 380, 386, 389, 393, 416, 418
Article 114 (TFEU): limits of competence 328–30
Article 169 (TFEU): consumer protection 393, 396, 403
Article 169 (TFEU): limits of competence 411

qualified majority voting:
Article 81 (TFEU): judicial cooperation in civil matters 433
Article 114 and Article 115 (TFEU): approximation 317
Article 114 and Article 352 (TFEU) 364, 369
Article 169 (TFEU): consumer protection 381, 385
conferral principle 289–91
Quelle 85–9

Reding, V 38, 262
redress, right of (consumers) 379, 382, 385, 387, 390, 409
regulations:
Article 114 and Article 115 (TFEU): approximation 317
Article 169 (TFEU): consumer protection 389
Article 169 (TFEU): limits of competence 410
European Parliament Resolutions 159–60
and unification link 29
regulatory measures 200
Reich, N 407, 409, 417
Reichert-Facilides, F 156
representation, right to (consumers) 383, 385, 387
Research Group on the Economic Assessment of Contract Law Rules (Tilburg Law and Economics Center (TILEC)) 154
Research Network 222
Resolutions *see* Council; European Parliament Resolutions
Restatement project (American Law Institute (ALI)) 93, 115–24
academic projects 149, 151, 153, 156
codification 123
impact 123–4
origins of 119–21
overview 115–19
restating the law 'as it is' versus 'as it ought to be' 122
tensions underlying 121–4
see also American Law Institute (ALI); Restatements
Restatements 3, 4, 5, 117–19, 142, 474–7, 479–82
academic projects 155
alternative and complementary routes 450
authoritativeness 117, 120
Black-letter rule 117–18
chapters 117
Comment 117–18
Commission 2001 Communication 183
Commission 2003 Action Plan 197
Commission 2010 Green Paper 256
definition/meaning 117–19
descriptive approach 120, 142
European Parliament 1989 Resolution 157
European Parliament 1994 Resolution 166–7
form 117
functional form 474
Illustrations 117–18
normative aspirations 120, 142
prescriptive approach 120
purpose 120
Reporter's Note 118
representativeness 121
Restatement (First) of Contracts 117, 122
Restatement (Fourth) series 117
Restatement (Second) of Contracts 117, 122
Restatement (Third) series 117
uniform and model laws 476
see also American Law Institute (ALI); Restatement project
'Roaming Regulation' 336–7
Romania (accession) 223, 241
Commission 2004 Communication 208
EC Consumer Law Compendium 240–1

Rome Convention (1980) 164, 181
'Rome I' Regulation 18
Article 114 (TFEU): limits of competence 342
CESL, proposed (Common European Sales Law Regulation) 266, 270
Commission 2010 Green Paper 254, 259
'Rome III' Regulation 453

'safeguard procedure' 242
Scheveningen conference 1, 169
Schnader, W A 127, 131–2, 134, 136–7
Schröder, G 216–17
Schulte-Nölke, H 154, 240
scope:
of application 255, 257, 259
material 25, 255, 257, 267, 283, 284
substantive 317–18
territorial 267, 283, 284
see also scope of contract law and its 'hard core'
scope of contract law and its 'hard core' 41–56
Commercial Agents Directive 45–6
Consumer Credit Directive, repealed by new Consumer Credit Directive 46–8
Consumer Sales Directive 54
Distance Selling Directive, repealed by Consumer Rights Directive 53–4
Doorstep Selling Directive, repealed by Consumer Rights Directive 44–5
Late Payment Directive, repealed by new Late Payment Directive 55–6
Package Travel Directive 48–9
Timeshare Directive, repealed by new Timeshare Directive 51–2
Unfair Contract Terms Directive 49–50
see also Court of Justice
'2nd regime' 256, 266–7, 271, 370–2, 375
vs '28th/29th regime' 223, 266, 369–72, 375
see also CESL, proposed (Common European Sales Law Regulation); '28th regime'; '29th regime'
Senff, W 430
***sensu lato* obstacles** 338–44, 484
***sensu stricto* obstacles** 338–44, 484
'Seven Chances for the Internal Market' (Schröder) 216
sincere cooperation, principle of 2, 4, 282–4, 310–11, 312, 484
Article 114 (TFEU): exercise of competence 351, 357
Article 169 (TFEU): exercise of competence 414–15
constitutional framing 15
definition 310
and enhanced cooperation 462–3
Lisbon Treaty 311
role(s) 310–11
single market *see* internal market
Sixth Framework Programme for Research and Technological Development (FP6) 153
Slovenia:
Council 2008 Report 236, 237
Snyder, W L 112
social justice 8, 16
social policy 382, 386, 389
'Sounding Board' (Key Stakeholder Experts Group) 262, 264
Spain:
Article 114 and Article 352 (TFEU) 361
Article 169 (TFEU): consumer protection 390, 394
special legislative procedure 369
specific action: Article 169 (TFEU) 385, 386–7, 391, 404–5
Staff Working Paper: Commission 2007 Green Paper 247
stakeholder responses:
Commission 2001 Communication 196–9
Commission 2003 Action Plan 208–10
Commission 2007 Green Paper 247–8
Commission 2010 Green Paper 260–1
State aid 382
Staudenmayer, D 177
Stockholm Programme 252, 254, 422, 437
Study Group 149, 152–3, 154, 178
academic projects 156
Commission 2003 Action Plan 188, 190, 196
Court of Justice 85, 91
Draft Common Frame of Reference (DCFR) 229–30
1999 Working Paper 168–9
Principles of European Law (PEL) series 85, 152, 231
Study Group on a European Civil Code *see* Study Group
'Study on property law and non-contractual liability law as they relate to contract law' 194
Stuyck, J 412
subsidiarity, principle of 2, 4, 10, 179, 282–4, 294–305, 483, 484
American techniques 475
Article 81, Article 114, and Article 352 (TFEU): exercise of competence 447–8

Article 81 (TFEU): judicial cooperation in civil matters 439–40, 441, 443
Article 114 and Article 352 (TFEU) 364, 368, 374–5, 377
Article 114 (TFEU): exercise of competence 350–3, 357–8
Article 114 (TFEU): 'object' and 'approximation' prongs 324–5, 360
Article 169 (TFEU): consumer protection 380, 385–6, 391, 400, 401–2, 408
Article 169 (TFEU): exercise of competence 415
CESL, proposed (Common European Sales Law Regulation) 267
Commission 2001 Communication 185–6
Commission 2003 Action Plan 193, 198, 201, 204
Commission 2004 Communication 206–7, 209–10, 214
Commission 2007 Green Paper 243, 247–8
Commission 2010 Green Paper 256–7, 259, 261
Common Frame of Reference (CFR) 478–9
constitutional framing 15
constitutional parameters of contract law 283–5, 294–305, 310, 311, 312
constitutional principle 294, 295–6, 413–15
Council 2008 Report 236
definition 294–7
dual 408, 413
effectiveness requirement 301
efficiency requirement 301
European Parliament Resolutions 162
inside and outside the decision-making process 302, 305, 360
intergovernmental treaty 469
judicial cooperation in civil matters 422, 449
Lisbon Treaty 303–5, 309
material subsidiarity 297–303, 305
national parliaments 304
  CESL, proposed (Common European Sales Law Regulation) 268–9
procedural subsidiarity 298–300, 302, 305
proportionality principle 306–8
secondary subsidiarity 408
subsidiarity calculus 296, 300–3
subsidiarity from within/without 298
supra-constitutional principle 294–5, 413–15
Treaty framework 282

'support, supplement and monitor' language: Article 169 (TFEU) 412–13
supranational company forms 372–3, 375
  see also European Cooperative Society case and related jurisprudence
supranational legal forms 373, 375
  see also European Cooperative Society case and related jurisprudence
Sweden:
  Article 114 (TFEU): limits of competence 332
  Article 169 (TFEU): consumer protection 388
Swift v Tyson 95–7

Tampere *see* European Council Meeting at Tampere
Teufel, E 430–1
Thomas, H 130–1, 133
Thyssen, M 168
Tilmann, W 169, 445
Timeshare Directive 64–5
  repealed by new Timeshare Directive 51–2
Tobacco Advertising I **and its evolving 'refinement'** 327–38
Tompkins, H C 109–10
'toolbox': Common Frame of Reference (CFR) 211, 477
  Commission 2010 Green Paper 255, 258, 259, 260
  Council 2008 Report 235–6
  Hague Programme 218
Towards a European Civil Code 466
transaction costs 342–3
Travel Vac 64–5
Treaty framework 280–2
Trento Common Core Project 148, 154
'26th regime' 223
'28th regime' 223, 266–7, 271, 369–72, 375
  vs '2nd regime' 266, 369–72, 375
'29th regime' 223, 266
Twigg-Flesner, C 240

unanimous voting 289–90, 317, 364–5, 369
Unfair Contract Terms Directive 49–50, 69
UNIDROIT Principles of International Commercial Contracts 85
unification 26, 27–31, 39, 41, 166
  see also approximation and related processes
Uniform Bills of Lading Act 113–15

Uniform Chattel Mortgage Act 113
Uniform Commercial Code (**UCC**) 3–5, 10, 93, 116, 124–42, 475–6, 479, 481, 483
alternative and complementary routes 450
American techniques 476
Articles 125, 126
co-sponsored by NCCUSL and ALI 124
Commission 2003 Action Plan 198
Commission 2004 Communication 209
Commission 2010 Green Paper 256
constitutional framing 24, 40
consumer protection 138–41
definition 125–7
European Parliament 2007 Resolution 233
European Parliament Resolutions 157
and Federal Sales Act 127–9, 131–3
federal and state versions 133–5
federalization 136–8
functional approach 125, 476
interstate/intrastate uniformity 135–6
meaning 125–7
Merchants' Association Federal Sales Act 130–1
New York Law Revision Commission 135
official comments 125
open-textured nature 126
origins 127–35
overview 124–7
parts 125
Permanent Editorial Board (PEB) 136
sections 125
structure 125
tensions underlying 135–41
Uniform Sales Act 127–9
Uniform Conditional Sales Act 113–14
Uniform Consumer Credit Code 139–40
Uniform Law Commission (**ULC**) *see* National Conference of Commissioners on Uniform State Laws (NCCUSL)
uniform law process (National Conference of Commissioners on Uniform State Laws (NCCUSL)) 103–15
definition of uniform laws 104–5
model laws and uniform laws, distinction between 105–6
overview 103–7
revision, necessity for 115
state variation 114
state-by-state enactment 114
tensions underlying 114–15
see also National Conference of Commissioners on Uniform State Laws (NCCUSL); uniform laws
uniform laws 3, 4, 5, 120–1, 142, 450, 475, 479–82
Commission 2010 Green Paper 256
European Parliament 1994 Resolution 166–7
see also National Conference of Commissioners on Uniform State Laws (NCCUSL); uniform law process
Uniform Negotiable Instruments Act 112–14
Uniform Sales Act 113–15, 127–32
Uniform Stock Transfer Act 113
Uniform Trust Receipts Act 113–14
Uniform Warehouse Receipts Act 113–15
'uniformity' 30
United Kingdom:
Article 81 (TFEU): judicial cooperation in civil matters 424
Article 114 (TFEU): exercise of competence 354–6
Article 114 (TFEU): limits of competence 331, 332, 333
Article 169 (TFEU): consumer protection 387
CESL, proposed (Common European Sales Law Regulation) 268
Commission 2003 Action Plan 197, 198
Common Frame of Reference (CFR) 477
Council 2008 Report 237
United Nations Convention on Contracts for the International Sale of Goods (CISG) 151, 181, 468
Commission 2003 Action Plan 195, 198, 202
Commission 2010 Green Paper 259
United States 4, 9–10, 93–143, 220, 285, 379, 419–20, 484
American Bar Association (ABA) 107–10, 111–12, 129, 130
Commercial Law Committee 128
Committee on Uniform State Laws 109, 110–11
American contract law framework 24, 93–143
approximation and related processes 40–1
Association of American Law Schools (AALS) 115, 130, 133
Commission 2003 Action Plan 197
Commission 2004 Communication 209
Constitution 9, 14, 94, 98, 100, 111, 128, 138, 139, 142, 296
Supremacy Clause 100–1
Tenth Amendment 286–7, 291
see also Interstate Commerce Clause

constitutional framing 14, 24, 61
Consumer Credit Protection Act 139, 140
diversity jurisdiction 95, 98
Door to Door Sales Rule 141
Federal Bills of Exchange Act 108
Federal Sales Act 127–33
Federal Trade Commission (FTC) 141
federalism 17
federalization 141
Magnuson-Moss Warranty Act 141
Patient Protection and Affordable Care Act 359
Rules of Decision Act 95–6
Supreme Court 94–101, 113, 358–9
see also American 'federal common law'; American Law Institute (ALI); National Conference of Commissioners on Uniform State Laws (NCCUSL); Restatements; Restatement project; Uniform Commercial Code (UCC); uniform law process; uniform laws
Usher, J 458
van Gerven, W 169, 445, 469–70, 472
Vienna Action Plan 172–4
Virginia Law Review 130–1
visas, asylum, immigration and other policies related to free movement of persons 172, 193, 424, 427, 433
von Bar, C 152–3, 162, 169, 194, 262
voting *see* qualified majority voting; unanimous voting

Wall Street Journal 216
Weatherill, S 403–4, 407, 409, 414
Wechsler, H 122
Williston, S 113, 127–8, 130–1
Williston-ABA Federal Sales Act 127–9, 131–3
Working Group *see* European Convention
Working Paper 1999 168–70, 178, 179, 188, 445

'yellow card' procedure 268